ON THE ROAD

YOUR COMPLETE DESTINATION GUIDE
In-depth reviews, detailed listings
and insider tips

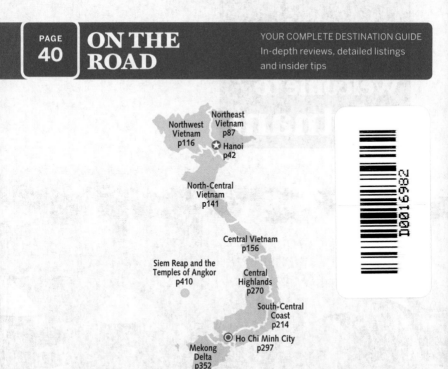

SURVIVAL GUIDE

VITAL PRACTICAL INFORMATION TO
HELP YOU HAVE A SMOOTH TRIP

THIS EDITION WRITTEN AND RESEARCHED BY

Iain Stewart,

Brett Atkinson, Peter Dragicevich, Nick Ray

welcome to
Vietnam

The Vietnamese Experience

Vietnam is a nation going places. Fast. Its people are energetic, direct, sharp in commerce and resilient by nature. This is an outrageously fun country to explore, the locals love a laugh (and a drink) and you'll have plenty of opportunities to socialise with them and hear their tales. The American War is over, and yet its impact endures – you'll find reminders of that cataclysmic conflict everywhere you travel. That said, the country was never broken and emerged with its pride intact. Poor in parts but never squalid, Vietnam is developing at an astonishing pace. For travellers, there are issues to consider (including minor scams), but little real danger – on the whole it's a safe, wonderfully rewarding and incredibly varied country to explore.

A Cultural Smorgasbord

This is a country of myriad influences and reference points. In the south, Indian and Hindu culture had a lasting influence in the Cham temples and spicy regional cuisine, spiked with chilli and tempered with coconut. Head north and Chinese connections are far more apparent. Between these two competing cultures, you'll find a quintessential Vietnam in the central provinces: the graceful historic old port of Hoi An, and the royal tombs, pagodas and imperial cuisine of Hue. Oh, and there's

Blessed with a ravishing coastline, emerald-green mountains, breathtaking national parks, dynamic cities, outstanding cultural interest and one of the world's best cuisines, Vietnam has it all.

(left) Women sitting by the beach near moored fishing boats, Mui Ne
(below) Woman burning incense at Thien Hau Pagoda, Ho Chi Minh City

more, far more. Factor in an enduring French colonial legacy, which is evident in Hanoi's graceful boulevards, in Ho Chi Minh City's stately museums and in the crispy baguettes and coffee culture you'll find on every street corner. Add the American interlude, more than 50 hill tribes, and of course the proud (battle-tested and victorious) ruling Communist Party ideology and you've got Vietnam: heady, intoxicating and unique.

Big Nature, Booming Cities

If you want visual dramatics, Vietnam delivers. Cruise an azure ocean pierced by surreal-looking limestone islands in Halong Bay, slalom through the majestic inland karst mountains of Cao Bang. Hike mountain tracks and explore tribal villages near Sapa and Bac Ha. Then witness the spectacular sandy bays of the central coastline and explore the reefs and coves of the Cham and Con Dao Islands. Highway 1 is near-relentlessly urban, so get off it at regular intervals to see the astonishing cave systems of Phong Nha, national parks like Cat Tien, and the bewitching backwaters of the Mekong Delta. Finally, no visit would be complete without experiencing the energy of big-city life in Vietnam's capital Hanoi, the grand old lady of the Orient, and Ho Chi Minh City, the engine room of the economy and the nation.

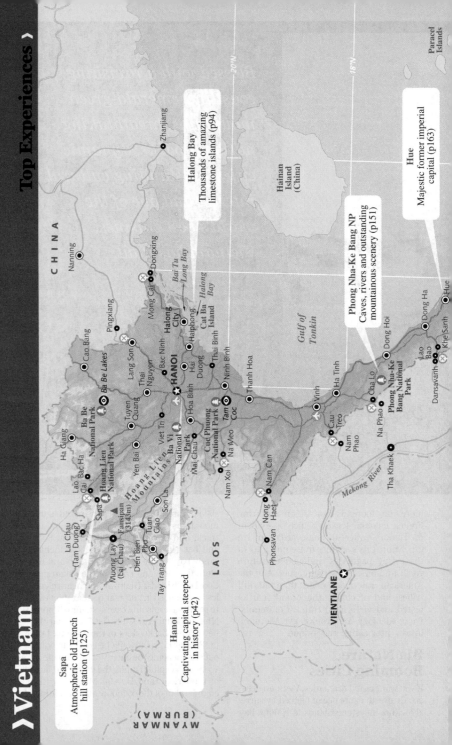

»Vietnam

Sapa
Atmospheric old French
hill station (p125)

Hanoi
Captivating capital steeped
in history (p42)

Halong Bay
Thousands of amazing
limestone islands (p94)

Phong Nha-Ke Bang NP
Caves, rivers and outstanding
mountainous scenery (p151)

Hue
Majestic former imperial
capital (p163)

MYANMAR
(BURMA)

CHINA

Nanning

Zhanjiang

Lai Chau
(Tam Duong)

Muong Lay
(Lai Chau)

Ha Giang

Lao
Cai
Bac Ha

Sapa

Fansipan
(3143m)

Dien Bien

Pho
Tuan

Giao

Son La

Tay Trang

Cao Bang

Pingxiang

Lang Son

Tuyen
Quang

Yen Bai

Viet Tri

Hoang Lien
National Park

Hoang Lien
Mountains

Ba Vi
National
Park

Mai Chau

Cuc Phuong
National Park

Na Meo

Nam Xoi

Dongxing

Mong Cai

Bai Tu
Long Bay

Halong
City

Haiphong

Cat Ba
Island

Thai Binh

Halong
Bay

Ba Be Lakes

Ba Be
National Park

Thai
Nguyen

Bac Ninh

HANOI

Hai
Duong

Hoa Binh

Tam
Coc

Ninh Binh

Thanh Hoa

Nam Can

Nong
Haet

Phonsavan

LAOS

Cau
Treo

Nam
Phao

Tha Khaek

Mekong River

VIENTIANE

Vinh

Ha Tinh

Cha Lo

Na Phao

Dansavanh

Lao
Bao

Phong Nha
Bang National
Park

Dong Hoi

Dong Ha

Khe Sanh

Hue

Gulf of
Tonkin

Hainan
Island
(China)

Paracel
Islands

20°N

18°N

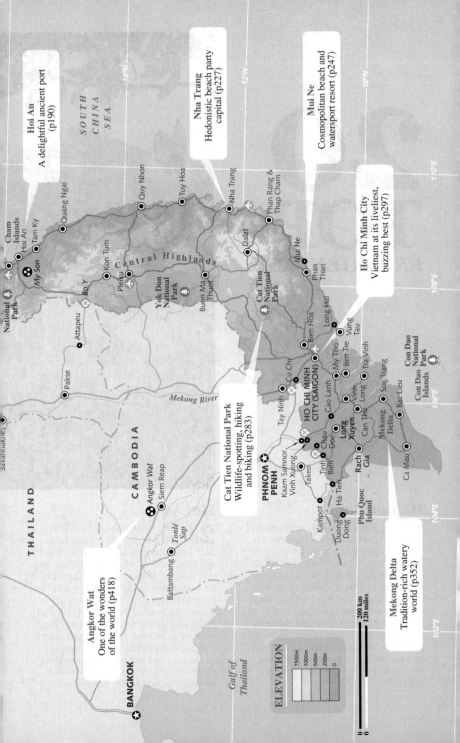

20 TOP EXPERIENCES

Halong Bay

1 Halong Bay's stunning combination of karst limestone peaks and sheltered, shimmering seas is one of Vietnam's top tourist draws, but with more than 2000 different islands there's plenty of superb scenery to go around. Definitely book an overnight cruise and make time for your own special moments on this World Heritage wonder – rising early for an ethereal misty dawn, or piloting a sleek kayak into grottoes and lagoons. If you're hankering for more karst action, move on to the less touristed but equally spectacular Lan Ha Bay (p100).

Hoi An

2 Medieval-looking Hoi An (p190) was once Vietnam's most cosmopolitan port. Today the good times have returned and this beautiful, ancient town is bursting with gourmet Vietnamese restaurants, hip bars and cafes, quirky boutiques and expert tailors. Immerse yourself in history in the warren-like lanes of the Old Town, shop till you drop, tour the temples and pagodas, dine like an emperor on a peasant's budget (then learn how to cook like the locals), hit glorious An Bang Beach, explore the riverside and back roads – Hoi An has it all. Riverfront restaurants along Bach Dang Street, Hoi An, right

Phong Nha-Ke Bang National Park

3 Just opening up to tourism, Phong Nha (p151) won't be a secret for long, such is its allure and beauty. Picture jungle-crowned limestone hills, rainforest, turquoise streams and traditional villages. Then throw in some of the globe's most impressive cave systems – the river-created Phong Nha Cave, the aircraft hanger-like space and ethereal beauty of aptly named Paradise Cave – and you can see why Phong Nha's star is on the rise. Accommodation options are fast improving and the national park is perfect for exploring on two wheels.
Rock formations in Phong Nha Cave, below

Food

4 Perhaps Asia's greatest culinary secret, Vietnamese food is on the radar but hardly a global phenomenon. Essentially it's all about the freshness of the ingredients – chefs shop twice-daily to source just-picked herbs from the market. The result? Incomparable texture and flavour combinations. For the Vietnamese, a meal should balance sour and sweet, crunchy and silky, fried and steamed, soup and salad. Wherever you are, you'll find exquisite local specialities (p477) – the 'white rose' of Hoi An, the *canh chua* of the Mekong Delta or good ol' *pho* of the north. A dish of steamed crab with herbs, below

ANDERS BLOMQVIST / LONELY PLANET IMAGES ©

Hanoi Old Quarter

5 Don't worry, it happens to everyone when they first get to Hanoi. Get agreeably lost in the city's centuries-old Old Quarter (p43), a frantic commercial labyrinth where echoes of the past are filtered and framed by a thoroughly 21st-century energy. Discover Vietnam's culinary flavours and aromas at street level, perched on a tiny chair eating iconic Hanoi dishes like *pho bo*, *bun cha* and *banh cuon*. Later at night, join the socialising throngs enjoying refreshingly crisp *bia hoi* at makeshift street corner bars.

Ho Chi Minh City

6 Increasingly international but still unmistakably Vietnamese, the former Saigon's visceral energy will delight big-city devotees. HCMC doesn't inspire neutrality; either you'll be drawn into its thrilling vortex, hypnotised by the perpetual whir of its orbiting motorbikes, or you'll find the whole experience overwhelming. Dive in and you'll be rewarded with a wealth of history, delicious food and a vibrant nightlife that sets the standard for Vietnam. The heat is always on in Saigon; loosen your collar and enjoy. Spirals of incense in Quan Am Pagoda, Ho Chi Minh City, above

PETER STUCKINGS / LONELY PLANET IMAGES ©

Con Dao Islands

7 Once hell on earth for a generation of political prisoners, Con Dao (p263) is now a heavenly destination known for its remote beaches, pristine dive sites and diverse nature. Life is extraordinarily slow paced here compared with the frenetic mainland and it's a wonderful place to explore by bike. The remote islands also provide a refuge for the rare green sea turtle and it is possible to visit nesting sites from May to November, and camp on a remote and isolated beach.

Sapa & the Tonkinese Alps

8 Dubbed the Tonkinese Alps by the French, the spectacular Hoang Lien Mountains soar skywards along the rugged, uncompromising edges of northwest Vietnam towards the Chinese border. Shape-shifting banks of cloud and mist ebb and flow in this mountainous area, parting teasingly to reveal a glimpse of Fanispan (p126), Vietnam's highest peak. From the sinuous and spidery ridges, rice terraces cascade down into river valleys, home for several centuries to ethnic minority villages of H'mong, Red Dzao and Giay peoples. Red Dzao girls in Sapa, left

Hue

9 The capital of the nation for 150 years in the 19th and early 20th centuries, Hue is perhaps the easiest Vietnamese city to love and spend time in. Its situation on the banks of the Perfume River is sublime, its complex cuisine is justifiably famous and its streets are relatively traffic free. And that's without the majesty of the Hue Citadel (p164), its royal residences and elegant temples, formidable walled defences and gateways. On the city's fringes are some of Vietnam's most impressive pagodas and royal tombs, many in wonderful natural settings. Ngo Mon Gate at Hue Citadel, above

Cat Tien National Park

10 One of the most accessible and impressive protected areas in Vietnam, Cat Tien lies conveniently midway between Ho Chi Minh City and Dalat. Set on a bend in the Dong Nai River, there is something vaguely *Apocalypse Now* about arriving here. Popular activities include trekking, cycling and wildlife-spotting. The park is home to the Dao Tien Endangered Primate Species Centre (p284) where gibbons and langurs are coaxed back into their natural environment. The Wild Gibbon Trek is a must, one of the wildlife highlights of Vietnam.

Mui Ne

11 One of Vietnam's most popular beach destinations, Mui Ne has more than 20km of beachfront that stretches invitingly along the shores of the South China Sea. From guesthouses to boutique resorts, family-run seafood shacks to designer bars, Mui Ne has a broad appeal. If you tire of spa treatments and sundowner cocktails, there are plenty of high-adrenaline activities on offer (p248): Mui Ne is the kitesurfing capital of Vietnam when the waves come crashing in during the second half of the year. For those who prefer dry land, sandboarding is a popular pastime.

10

CHRISTER FREDRIKSSON / LONELY PLANET IMAGES ©

JOHN BORTHWICK / LONELY PLANET IMAGES ©

JOHN ELK III / LONELY PLANET IMAGES ©

Biking the Northwest Loop

12 Saddle up for the ride of a lifetime into the mountains of Vietnam's deep north. Bicycle or motorbike? The choice is yours, but the roads are absolute roller coasters, the scenery simply stunning and the population an ethnic mosaic. The journey starts in Sapa and switchbacks up endless hairpins to the 1900m Tram Ton Pass (p127), then follows idyllic river valleys past minority villages. Stop to take in the battlefields and war museums of Dien Bien Phu before looping back to Hanoi via the White Thai homestays of Mai Chau.

Nha Trang

13 Welcome to Vietnam's beach-party capital. Subtle Nha Trang is not, but it is a whole lot of fun. Boasting the best municipal beach in the country, sun seekers flock here to bask on the sand, trip around the bay islands by boat and crawl the many bars and pubs. Other activities on tap include surfing the breaks of nearby Cam Ranh Bay (p243) and getting deep down and dirty in the local mud baths. Throw in some ancient Cham towers (p228) and Nha Trang has something for everyone. Po Nagar Cham Towers, Nha Trang, above

Bia Hoi

14 One of the great pleasures of travelling in Vietnam, *bia hoi* (fresh beer) is brewed daily, without additives or preservatives, to be drunk that day. Incredibly cheap and widely available, *bia hoi* places offer a very local experience. Park (or attempt to park) your rear on one of the tiny plastic stools and get stuck in. Bites to eat are often sold too. Said to have been introduced to Hanoi by Czech brewers, every town in the nation now has a *bia hoi* place, often with a street terrace.

Mekong Delta

15 Where Saigon sizzles, its rural southern neighbours saunter, floating through life in a watery world of canals and broad river branches. The food bowl of Vietnam, the Mekong Delta is an overwhelmingly green expanse but surprisingly heavily populated all the same. Those longing for a taste of local life far from fellow travellers will find it in many of the small, isolated cities in the Mekong's forgotten (by tourism at least) corners. Down here, it's less about the sights and more about the experience. Floating market in the Mekong Delta, right

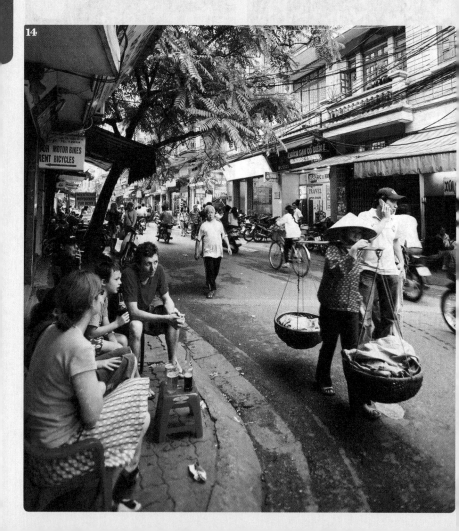

Ba Be Lakes

16 Detour off the regular Vietnam tourist trail in Ba Be National Park (p89), an essential destination for active and intrepid travellers with towering limestone mountains, plunging valleys and evergreen forests. Waterfalls, caves and lakes combine in a landscape that sustains over 550 different plants and hundreds of different bird and animal species. Explore Ba Be's natural spectacle by boat or on trekking and mountain biking excursions, before relaxing and recharging in the rustic homestays and village guesthouses of the local Tay ethnic minority.

PETER STUCKINGS / LONELY PLANET IMAGES ©

Mai Chau

17 Mai Chau is the perfect relaxing antidote to the incessant energy and bustle of Hanoi. Just a few hours from the close shaves with Old Quarter motorcycle traffic, this sleepy valley is surrounded by paddy fields and lush countryside. Spend a few nights chilling out in traditional Thai stilt houses in the friendly villages (p119), and fill your days with gentle bursts of trekking, mountain biking and kayaking. For even more laid-back travellers, there's the opportunity to visit local village markets or learn to cook Vietnamese food. Woman tending rice paddies, Mai Chau, above

Dalat

18 Perched at a lofty 1475m, Dalat (p272) is the queen of the central highlands and has been popular with international tourists since the days of the French colonialists. Grand French villas are dotted amid pine groves and Vietnamese tourists flock here in their thousands for a summer escape from the heat. Natural attractions include waterfalls and roller-coaster roads for mountain biking. An up-and-coming activity centre, it is also possible to try abseiling, canyoning and rafting. New coastal roads to Mui Ne and Nha Trang are paradise for motorcyclists. Central Market, Dalat, above

Angkor Wat

19 One of world's most magnificent sights, the temples of Angkor (p418) are so much better than the superlatives. Choose from Angkor Wat, the world's largest religious building; Bayon, the world's weirdest, with its immense stone faces; or Ta Prohm, where nature runs amok. Siem Reap is the base for exploring Angkor and is a buzzing destination with a superb selection of restaurants and bars. Beyond the temples lie floating villages on the Tonle Sap Lake, adrenaline-filled activities like quad biking and microlighting, and cultured pursuits like cooking classes and bird-watching.

19

Phu Quoc Island

20 At some stage of every Southeast Asian odyssey it's necessary to stop and rest, with a cocktail in hand on the white sands of a tropical beach, and catch your breath. Phu Quoc Island (p381), in the extreme south of Vietnam, provides just such an opportunity. When you've had enough of lazing around, hire a motorbike or bicycle and gad about the island until your hair is full of red dust and the warm waters of the Gulf of Thailand once again beckon.

20

need to know

Currency
» Dong (d)

Language
» Vietnamese

When to Go

■ Warm to hot summers, mild winters
■ Tropical climate, wet & dry seasons

Sapa
GO Mar-May & Sep-Nov

Hanoi
GO Mar-May & Sep-Nov

Danang
GO Mar-Sep

Ho Chi Minh City
GO Nov-Feb

High Season
(Jul–Aug)

» Prices increase by up to 50% by the coast; book hotels well in advance.

» All Vietnam, except the far north, is hot and humid, with the summer monsoon bringing downpours.

Shoulder
(Dec–Mar)

» During the Tet festival, the whole country is on the move and prices rise.

» North of Nha Trang can get cool weather. Expect cold conditions in the far north.

» In the south, clear skies and sunshine are the rule.

Low Season
(Apr–Jun, Sep–Nov)

» Perhaps the best time to tour the whole nation.

» Typhoons can lash the central and northern coastline until November.

Set Your Budget

Budget less than
US$40

» Cheap hotel: US$10–15 a night, dorms less

» Eat at local, not Western-style places

» Get a taste for *bia hoi*

» Can survive on as little as US$15 a day

Midrange
US$40–100

» Comfortable double room: US$20–50

» Eat and drink almost anywhere

» Indulge in the odd spa treatment

» Travel by taxi when necessary

Top End over
US$100

» Luxury hotel room: from US$70

» Shop in smart boutiques

» Hit Vietnam's gourmet restaurants

Money

» ATMs widely available except well off the beaten track. Credit cards accepted in upmarket hotels but rarely in restaurants.

Visas

» Most nationalities need a visa, which must be arranged in advance.

Mobile Phones

» Local SIM cards can be used in most European, Asian and Australian (and many North American) phones.

Transport

» Buses, trains and planes between regions. Motorbikes are widely available for hire.

Websites

» **Living in Vietnam** (www.livinginvietnam .com) Expat website.

» **Lonely Planet** (www .lonelyplanet.com /vietnam) Destination information, hotel bookings, traveller forum and more.

» **Thanh Nien News** (www.thanhniennews .com) Government-approved news.

» **Things Asian** (www .thingsasian.com) Culture and arts.

» **Vietnam Adventures Online** (www. vietnamadventures .com) Travel info.

» **Vietnam Online** (www.vietnamonline .com) Good all-rounder.

Exchange Rates

Australia	A$1	22,269d
Canada	C$1	21,711d
Euro	€1	29,547d
Japan	¥100	26,285d
New Zealand	NZ$1	17,783d
UK	£1	33,500d
US	US$1	20,570d

For current exchange rates see www.xe.com.

Important Numbers

To call Vietnam from outside, drop the initial 0 from the area code. Mobile numbers begin with ☏09.

Country Code	☏84
International Access Code	☏00
Directory Assistance	☏116
Police	☏113
General Information Service	☏1080

Arriving in Vietnam

» **Ho Chi Minh City Airport (P341)**
Taxi to central districts – 100,000d; around 30 minutes.
Air-conditioned bus (Route 152) to centre – 4000d; every 15 minutes, 6am–6pm; around 40 minutes.

» **Hanoi Airport (p82)**
Taxi to the centre – 300,000d; around one hour.
Vietnam Airlines mini-bus to centre – US$3; every 30 minutes.
Route 17 public bus from airport to Long Bien bus station (walking distance from Old Quarter) – 5000d.

Internet

Getting online in Vietnam is remarkably easy, with most guesthouses and hotels having free wi-fi and complimentary computer terminals for their guests' use. Cafes and restaurants are increasingly wired too. Internet connection speeds are generally moderate in urban areas and pedestrian in the countryside.

For Skype calls and tech stuff it's usually best to head to a cybercafe, which are very widespread. Here you'll usually share an environment with hardcore Viet gamers.

Be aware that the Vietnamese government regularly blocks access to social networking sites, so don't plan to keep in touch, upload and update friends via Facebook – it's sometimes down for months. Proxy servers, including www.hidemyass.com, are one possible way around this issue, but don't count on it.

what's new

For this new edition of Vietnam our authors have hunted down the fresh, the transformed, the hot and the happening. These are some of our favourites. For up-to-the-minute recommendations, see lonelyplanet.com/vietnam.

Paradise Cave

1 This extraordinary cave system, only discovered in 2005, is now open to the public. It's been professionally developed and has staggeringly beautiful rock formations to marvel at (p152).

Gibbon Trek

2 Experience gibbons in the wild on a new trek inside Cat Tien National Park, then take in the Dao Tien Primate Centre (p285).

The Ride of Your Life

3 Vietnam is densely populated. Get off the truck-plagued highways and onto one of Hoi An Motorbike Adventures' classic Minsk bikes to experience rural Vietnam at its best (p208).

Beachside Chic

4 The scene looks set to explode at glorious An Bang beach, just west of Hoi An, where a strip of wonderful new restaurants like Soul Kitchen are opening (p209).

High Rise in Ho Chi Minh City

5 The extraordinary 68-storey, 262m Bitexco Financial Tower is Saigon's newest iconic structure. Take a lift to the Skydeck on the 48th floor for an unrivalled city panorama (p303).

Loop the Loop

6 Improved transport connections in the country's northwest have opened up Vietnam's most spectacular mountain pass. Minibuses now link Ha Giang with Meo Vac and Cao Bang (p136).

Mind the Minorities

7 H'mong-owned-and-operated trekking agencies Sapa O'Chau and Sapa Sisters mean that you can directly help minority villagers (p126).

Home on the Range

8 Explore astonishing caves, wonderful countryside, forest trails and remote swimming holes around the Phong Nha Farmstay, a fabulous new guesthouse that offers excellent tours (p153).

Danang Riverside Takes Off

9 Busy reinventing itself as one of the nation's most progressive cities, Danang has a modish new riverside that includes the excellent Waterfront bar-restaurant (p184).

Big Buddha

10 Near Ninh Binh, the huge new Buddhist complex of Chua Bai Dinh is the largest in Vietnam and boasts a pagoda skyscraper (p146).

Great Wall

11 Its existence was only announced in 2011, but this ancient, 127km defence wall is considered the longest monument in Southeast Asia (p216).

Bridging the Delta

12 A bunch of new bridges in the Mekong Delta, including links between My Tho and Ben Tre, and from Ben Tre towards Tra Vinh, have made travel much easier (p354).

if you like...

Fabulous Food

Eating out in Vietnam is nothing short of exceptional. From street food served by hawkers to Hue imperial-style banquets, it's rarely less than wonderful. But in many ways there is no national cuisine, as each region has a unique culinary tradition.

Hoi An Head here to taste Central Vietnamese herb-rich dishes and unique creations like *banh bao* and *banh xeo* then take a cooking course and do it yourself (p199).

Hanoi Dive into Hanoi's endlessly tasty street food scene at one of the stalls famous for *bun cha*, sticky rice creations, fried eel or crab noodle soup (p65).

Ho Chi Minh City A cornucopia of roadside stalls, gourmet Vietnamese restaurants and an ever-expanding selection of international cuisines (p325).

Markets

To get a flavour of any Vietnamese town, head to the central market, the heart of the community. Even touristy destinations like Sapa and Hoi An boast excellent markets, full of unfamiliar spices and herbs, and fascinating food stalls. The photo opportunities are unrivalled too.

Bac Ha One of the most colourful markets in Southeast Asia, at Bac Ha you'll have the chance to see the unique costumes of the Flower H'mong (p134).

Mekong Delta's floating markets Get up early and experience the Delta's famous floating markets, selling everything from durian to dog meat (p372).

Sinho Experience an authentic minority market in this isolated highland town, which now has a good new hotel (p125).

Ben Thanh Market A symbol of Ho Chi Minh City since 1914 and still as frenetic as ever (p336).

Tombs & Temples

Vietnam boasts an eclectic collection of monuments. Many of the Cham culture's towers and temples have fallen victim to wartime bombs and neglect, but you'll still find impressive remains. Outside Hue there's an outstanding number of imperial tombs and monuments, while all the big cities have striking temples.

Hue Vietnamese emperors constructed dazzling monuments to their rule around the city of Hue. Perhaps the highlights are the extraordinarily grandiose tombs of Tu Duc and Minh Mang (p174).

My Son Unquestionably the most impressive Cham site, and the forested hilltop location is very special too (p211).

Hanoi Come face-to-face with history in Ho Chi Minh's austere mausoleum (p51).

Cao Dai Great Temple The home-grown religion's Holy See is an exuberant explosion of styles and colour (p346).

If you like...Vietnamese food
Hoi An has terrific cooking courses (p199)

If you like...caves
Phong Nha-Ke Bang National Park is a world-class experience (p151)

Colonial Architecture

Architecturally, the French left their mark throughout the nation – all the cities have a number of stately structures that date from colonial times. Hanoi, and to a lesser extent Hoi An, even boast French quarters.

Ho Chi Minh City Saigon is still administered from the chateau-style People's Committee Building, once the colonists' Hôtel de Ville. Also check out the Municipal Theatre, a sumptuous survivor from France's belle époque (p300).

Hanoi Dine in style or enjoy a night at the opera in the colonial villas and grandiose public buildings of the French Quarter (p74).

Dalat There are 2500 French villas dotted about the city; some have been turned into gourmet restaurants and boutique accommodation like Ana Mandara Villas (p278).

Haiphong Stroll around Haiphong's sleepy boulevards to uncover French-era gems like the city's Opera House (p91).

Spectacular Treks

The mountains of northwest Vietnam offer perhaps the nation's most dramatic hiking, but you'll also find excellent trails in other regions and inside most national parks.

Sapa Join chatty H'mong guides to explore the ethnic minority villages around Sapa, framed by cascades of verdant rice terraces. (p126).

Bac Ha Much less hyped than Sapa, Bac Ha offers mountain scenery and minority culture, waterfalls and crowd-free trails (p135).

Hang Son Doong Hike pristine mountain and valley trails to the entrance of the world's largest cave (p154).

Mai Chau Escape the incessant energy of Hanoi with a take-it-easy trekking, kayaking and mountain biking sojourn around sleepy Mai Chau (p118).

Cuc Phuong You'll find outstanding hikes through wildlife-rich forests and up to tribal villages in the Cuc Phuong National Park (p147).

Beautiful Beaches

Spectacular ocean-washed stretches of sand define Vietnam's coastline. Some of the very best are on the south-central coast, while all the offshore islands boast delightful coves.

Mui Ne Squeaky sands along the shore, towering sand dunes nearby and expanses of empty beaches up the coast (p248).

Nha Trang Flop on the inviting sands, then explore the bay's islands by boat (p227).

Con Dao Islands We suggest a self-imposed exile of at least three nights (p263).

Phu Quoc Stretching for many kilometres, Long Beach offers white sand in profusion while Sao Beach is a quieter stretch of sand (p383).

Lan Ha Bay Kayak to hidden sandy coves amid the karst labyrinths of spectacular Lan Ha Bay (p100).

Bai Tu Long Bay Find your own slice of sandy perfection around the remote islands of Bai Tu Long Bay (p108).

month by month

Major religious festivals in Vietnam have lunar dates; check against any Vietnamese calendar for the Gregorian dates. If you know when Tet kicks off, simply count from there. Special prayers are held at Vietnamese and Chinese pagodas when the moon is full or a thin sliver. Many Buddhists eat only vegetarian food on these days, which according to the Chinese lunar calendar, fall on the 14th and 15th days of the month and from the last day of the month to the first day of the next month.

January

Winter temperatures can be bitterly cold in the far north, with snow possible. The further south you go the milder the weather. Watch out for Tet celebrations towards the end of the month (or in February).

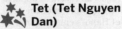 Dalat Flower Festival

Held early in the month, this is always a wonderful occasion, with huge elaborate displays and the whole town involved. Increasingly it's become an international event, with music and fashion shows and a wine festival.

February

North of Danang, chilly 'Chinese winds' usually mean grey, overcast conditions. Conversely, sunny hot days are the norm in the southern provinces.

Tet (Tet Nguyen Dan)

The Big One! Falling in late January or early February, Vietnamese Lunar New Year (see p451) is like Christmas, New Year and birthdays all rolled into one. Travel is difficult at this time, as transport is booked up and many businesses close.

March

Grey skies and cool temperatures can affect anywhere north of Hoi An, but towards the end of the month the thermometer starts to rise. Down south, the dry season is ending.

Buon Ma Thuot Coffee Festival

Caffeine cravers should make for the Central Highlands during March, as Buon Ma Thuot plays host to an annual coffee festival. Growers, grinders, blenders and addicts rub shoulders in the city's main park and local entertainment is provided.

Saigon Cyclo Race

On your marks...get peddling. Ho Chi Minh City's fastest rickshaw drivers battle it out in their three-wheeled chariots to raise funds for charity. The event takes place in mid-March every year and is a lot of fun.

April

Generally an excellent time to cover the nation, as the winter monsoon rains should have subsided and there are some excellent festivals. Flights are usually moderately priced (unless Easter falls in this month).

Holiday of the Dead (Thanh Minh)

It's time to honour the ancestors with a visit to graves of deceased relatives to tidy up and sweep tombstones. Offerings of flowers, food and paper are presented. It's held on the first three days of the third moon.

Hue Festival (biennial)

Vietnam's biggest cultural event (www.huefestival .com) is held every two years, with events in 2012, 2014 and 2016. Most of the art, theatre, music, circus and dance performances, including many international acts, are held inside Hue's Citadel.

Danang Firework Festival

Danang's riverside explodes with sound, light and colour during this spectacular event, which features competing pyrotechnic teams from China, Europe and Vietnam, and accompanying musical performances. Held in the last week of the month.

May

A fine time to tour the centre and north, with a good chance of clear skies and warm days. Sea temperatures are warming up nicely and it's a pretty quiet month for tourism.

Buddha's Birth, Enlightenment and Death (Phong Sinh)

A big celebration at Buddhist temples with lively street processions and lanterns used to decorate pagodas. Complexes including Chua Bai Dinh (p146) near Ninh Binh and HCMC's Jade Emperor Pagoda (p304) host lavish celebrations. Fifteenth day of the fourth lunar month.

Nha Trang Sea Festival

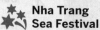

Officially it's the Nha Trang–Khanh Hoa Vietnam Civilisation and Friendliness, but we can't see that catching on. It falls at the end of May (and the beginning of June) and includes a street festival, photography exhibitions, embroidery displays and kite-flying competitions.

CAMA Festival, Hanoi

Run by an energetic bunch of music-mad expats, Hanoi's Club for Art and Music (www.cama vietnam.org) promote this annual one-day festival (p59), an excellent opportunity to experience the best of Hanoi's emerging music scene.

June

A great time to tour Vietnam as it's just before the peak domestic season. Humidity can be punishing at this time of year, so plan to spend some time by the coast.

Summer Solstice Day (Tet Doan Ngo)

Keep the epidemics at bay with offerings to the spirits, ghosts and the God of Death on the fifth day of the fifth moon. Sticky rice wine (*ruou nep*) is consumed in industrial quantities.

August

This is the peak month for tourism with domestic and international tourists flocking to the coast and main sights. Book flights and accommodation well ahead. Weather-wise it's hot, hot, hot.

Wandering Souls Day (Trung Nguyen)

Second in the pecking order to Tet is this ancient Vietnamese tradition. Huge spreads of food are left out for lost spirits who, it's believed, wander the earth on this day. Held on the 15th day of the seventh moon.

Children's (or Mid-Autumn) Festival, Hoi An

This is a big event in Hoi An, when citizens celebrate the full moon, eat moon cakes and beat drums. The lion, unicorn and dragon dance processions are enacted and children are fully involved in the celebrations.

October

A good time to visit the far north, with a strong chance of clear skies and mild temperatures. Winter winds and rain begin to affect the centre, but down south it's often dry.

Mid-Autumn Festival (Trung Thu)

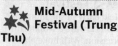

A fine time for foodies with moon cakes of sticky rice filled with lotus seeds,

watermelon seeds, peanuts, the yolks of duck eggs, raisins and other treats. It's celebrated across the nation on the 15th day of the eighth moon and can fall in September or October.

Cham New Year (Kate)

This is celebrated at Po Klong Garai Cham Towers in Thap Cham (p244) on the seventh month of the Cham calendar. The festival commemorates ancestors, Cham national heroes and deities, such as the farmers' goddess Po Ino Nagar.

Khmer Oc Bom Boc Festival

The Mekong Delta's Khmer community celebrate on the 15th day of the 10th moon of the lunar calendar (late October or November) with colourful boat races at Ba Dong Beach (p363) in Tra Vinh Province and on the Soc Trang River.

December

The month begins quietly, but from mid-December the popular tourist resorts get increasingly busy and you should book well ahead to secure a room over the Christmas break. It's still steamy in the south but can get chilly up north.

Christmas Day (Giang Sinh)

This is not a national holiday, but it is celebrated throughout Vietnam, particularly by the sizeable Catholic population. It's a special time to be in places like Phat Diem (p149) and HCMC where thousands attend midnight mass.

(Above) Modelling the costumes of Asia during the biennial Hue Festival
(Below) Cham elders attend Kate festivities (Cham New Year) at Po Klong Garai Cham Tower

itineraries

Whether you've got six days or 60, these itineraries provide a starting point for the trip of a lifetime. Want more inspiration? Head online to lonelyplanet.com /thorntree to chat with other travellers.

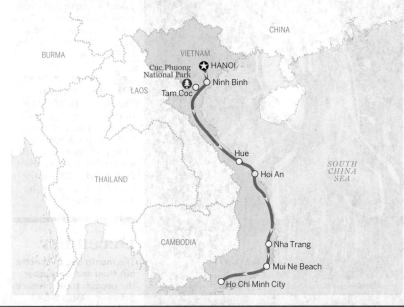

Two Weeks
The Great Ocean Road

Acclimatise in the capital, **Hanoi**; see the sights, wine and dine, take in a temple or two and experience the Old Quarter's street life. Then head to nearby **Ninh Binh** for a couple of days. It's the gateway to the striking scenery of **Tam Coc** and the primates and trails of **Cuc Phuong National Park**. Next it's a long train or bus journey south to experience **Hue**, imperial and irresistible capital of old. Then head up and over (or under) the mighty Hai Van Pass before hitting charming **Hoi An**, the perfect place for some time out – sightseeing, shopping and sunning yourself on the beach. Enter **Nha Trang**, the biggest and brashest beach resort in Vietnam, and try a hedonistic boat trip to nearby islands. If that's all too much, carry on south to **Mui Ne Beach**, a tropical idyll with smart resorts, blissed-out budget options, towering dunes and crazy kitesurfing. Finish up in **Ho Chi Minh City**, where you can indulge in sophisticated shopping, delectable dining and the liveliest nightlife in the country.

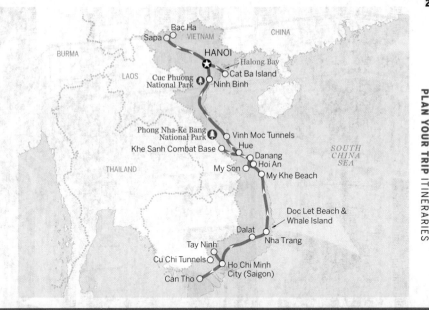

One Month
The Works

Run this one in reverse, and start out in the cauldron of commerce that is **Ho Chi Minh City**. Spend three days hitting the markets, browsing museums and eating some of the globe's best cuisine. Take a day trip to discover wartime history at the **Cu Chi Tunnels** and then carry on to **Tay Ninh**, headquarters of the Cao Dai religion, and its fairy-tale temple. Dip into the Mekong Delta for a day or two. Stay at **Can Tho**, the social and commercial heart of the region, and take to the water to cruise through the floating markets. Head up into the central highlands to the romantic hill station of **Dalat** to tour its quirky sights. Back down on the coast, the beach resort of **Nha Trang** has some serious partying, boat trips, scuba diving and snorkelling. Ease you way up the stunning central coastline stopping at beaches like **Doc Let** or **My Khe** when you fancy, visiting **Whale Island** and taking in Cham ruins including **My Son**. Cultured charmer and culinary mecca **Hoi An** is the next essential stop, before a quick look at booming **Danang** and on to the old imperial capital of **Hue** and its citadel, tombs and pagodas. Take a day trip to the former Demilitarised Zone (DMZ) where you'll find famous sites from the American War, including **Khe Sanh Combat Base** and the **Vinh Moc Tunnels**. Then head into the hills to the **Phong Nha-Ke Bang National Park**, a World Heritage site where the world's largest cave has been discovered. From here, follow the stunning Ho Chi Minh Highway to the capital, stopping to see **Cuc Phuong National Park** and the surreal landscapes around **Ninh Binh**. To the east lies **Halong Bay**, with more than 2000 limestone outcrops dotting the scenic bay. Stop for a couple of days on rugged **Cat Ba Island**, an important adventure-sports centre, before looping back to the capital. Arrive in time to catch the night train to **Sapa**, unofficial capital of the northwest hill-tribe region and a beautiful base for hiking and biking. Be sure to take a side trip to **Bac Ha** to catch its famous markets and tribal villages before the return journey to Vietnam's intoxicating capital, **Hanoi**, and its evocative Old Quarter.

» (above) Street vendors selling vegetables, Hanoi
» (left) Tourist junks glide past a floating village near Cat Ba Island, Halong Bay

PETER UNGER / LONELY PLANET IMAGES ©

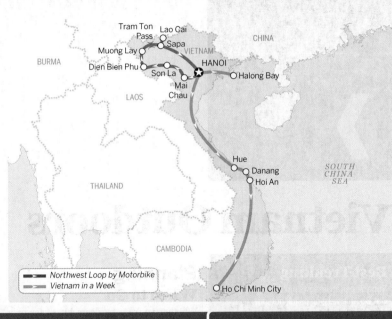

Northwest Loop by Motorbike
Vietnam in a Week

Seven Days
Vietnam in a Week

Vietnam is a large, densely-populated developing country where journeys are slow. To get an overview of the nation in a week you're going to have to take a couple of internal flights (or overnight train journeys). Begin in **Hanoi**, basing yourself in the Old Quarter, for a full-on introduction. Hit the ground running, spend a day touring the capital's sights and a night munching street food and sampling *bia hoi*. Then take a day-trip to **Halong Bay** for magnificent scenery and revitalising sea air. Day three takes in a morning flight to **Hue** and an afternoon exploring the imperial citadel (with a good guide to make the most of your time).

On day four bus, train or automobile down to **Hoi An**, making sure you have dinner at one of the town's sublime Vietnamese restaurants. The following morning, soak up Hoi An's unique atmosphere and explore its pagodas and temples on foot. If the sun's out, hit nearby An Bang Beach for a swim later on. On day six it's up to **Danang** airport and a flight to **Ho Chi Minh City**, for a brief taste of Vietnam's most dynamic city: its fabled restaurants, nightlife and sights.

10 Days
Northwest Loop by Bike

Northern Vietnam is a world unto itself, a land of brooding mountains, a mosaic of ethnic minorities, a region of overwhelming beauty. It's ideal terrain to cover on two wheels with light traffic, breathtaking views and pretty decent paved roads. Leaving **Hanoi**, head west to **Mai Chau**, home to the White Thai people, for your first two nights; it's a perfect introduction to the life of the minorities. Northwest of here, where the road begins to climb into the Tonkinese Alps, a logical stop is **Son La**. **Dien Bien Phu** is a name that resonates with history; it was here that the French colonial story ended with defeat. Plan on two nights here. Tour the military sights then revel in the stunning alpine scenery to the north, breaking the journey with a night in **Muong Lay**. On day seven, climb over the mighty **Tram Ton Pass** to **Sapa**. This is the premier destination in the northwest, thanks to the infinite views (on a clear day!), an amazing array of minority peoples and some of the region's most colourful markets. On your last day, head down to **Lao Cai**, then let the train take the strain – load your bike on a goods carriage while you slumber on a sleeper berth back to Hanoi.

Vietnam Outdoors

Best Trekking

Sapa Superlative views but can be crowded.
Cat Ba An emerging hiking hotspot.
Mai Chau Sublime landscapes and tribal villages.
Bac Ha Explore fascinating hill-tribe terrain.
Cuc Phuong National Park A network of well-established trails.

Best Surfing & Kitesurfing

China Beach When it rolls, it rolls.
Mui Ne Southeast Asia's kitesurfing capital.
Vung Tau Post-storm it can kick-off.

Best Diving & Snorkelling

Con Dao Islands Remote, but the best.
Nha Trang Professional scuba schools and many dive sites.
Hoi An Macro life is fascinating.

Planning

When to Go

Whether you're a hardcore kitesurfer or a genteel walker, some careful planning is essential – Vietnam's climate is extremely variable and monsoon-dependent.

Best

Surfers should be aware that the wave action peaks in winter (November to April). Kitesurfing also excels at this time of year. Divers take note that water visibility is best in the calm months of June, July and August.

Avoid

It would be foolish to attempt an ascent of Fanispan in the height of the rainy season, from May to September. Snorkelling and diving is virtually impossible between November and April when the winter winds blow and visibility drops.

Activities

If you're looking for outdoor action, Vietnam can increasingly deliver. Okay you have to get off your sunlounger and make an effort, but the rewards are amazing.

Cycling and hiking are taking off. Offshore there's surfing, sailing, kayaking and kitesurfing above the water, and diving and snorkelling beneath.

Or, if this all sounds like far too much hard work, stroll around a golf course or jump on a motorbike and let the engine take the strain.

Trekking

Vietnam offers excellent trekking and less-strenuous walks. The scenery is often remarkable – think plunging highland valleys, tiers of rice paddies and soaring limestone mountains. Anything is possible, from half-day hikes to assaults on Fansipan, Vietnam's highest mountain. Even if you're somewhere like An Bang Beach near Hoi An, you can stroll along the sands for an hour or two and experience a near-pristine coastal environment.

Where To Hike

Generally northern Vietnam is your best bet: its dramatic mountain paths and fascinating minority culture are a huge draw. Elsewhere, national parks and nature reserves have established trails (and usually guides available to keep you on them).

Northern Vietnam

The region north of Hanoi is truly spectacular. **Sapa** (p125) is Vietnam's trekking hub, full of hiking operators and hire stores (renting out sleeping bags, boots and waterproof gear). Maps detailing trails are available, as are guides. The scenery is remarkable, with majestic mountains, impossibly green rice paddies and some fascinating tribal villages. But prepare yourself – the main trails are incredibly popular and some villagers see hiking groups on an hourly basis. To trek remote paths you'll have to find an expert local guide.

Bac Ha (p135) is at a lower elevation, less rainy and the trails are not heavily trampled. Though it's very picturesque, it lacks Sapa's jaw-dropping mountain scenery – but you will find great hikes to waterfalls and to Flower H'mong and Nung villages.

Other key destinations include **Ba Be** (p89), with its network of beautiful trails amid spectacular karst scenery, and **Cat Ba** (p101), which has a popular 18km hike as well as shorter alternatives.

Central Vietnam

You'll find excellent trails inside **Cuc Phuong National Park** (p147) through superb forest and past ancient trees and caves to a minority village. **Phong Nha-Ke Bang National Park** (p151) is just opening up to tourism but hiking trails here between the limestone hills include a trek to the world's largest cave, Hang Son Doong.

Close to Danang, **Bach Ma National Park** (p178) has some good trails (though there's road construction ongoing here) while the **Ba Na Hill Station** (p180) has short trails and awesome views. Adventure tours operators in **Hoi An** (p208) also offer some intriguing treks in the tribal areas west of town.

Southern Vietnam

With a bit of luck you might glimpse one of the dozens of mammals present in **Yok Don** (p288) near Buon Ma Thuot. You'll need to hire a guide to see the best of **Cat Tien National Park** (p283), where crocodiles can be seen and night hikes are possible. The Wild Gibbon Trek here is proving a big hit. Over in **Dalat** (p272), several adventure tour operators offer short hiking trips.

Further south there's little for hikers to get excited about – the climate is perennially hot and humid and landscape largely flat. **Con Son** (p263) is one curious exception, an island with cooling sea breezes and hikes through rainforest and mangroves.

Safety Guidelines for Hikers

» Don't stray from established paths – Vietnam is full of unexploded ordnance.

» Guides are usually worth hiring; they're inexpensive, speak the language and understand indigenous culture.

» Dogs can be aggressive; a stout stick can come in handy.

» Boots with ankle support are a great investment.

Hiking Tour Operators

Agencies are recommended in the relevant destination chapters. Rangers inside national parks can also help craft trekking itineraries. It may be necessary to arrange special permits, especially if you plan to spend the night in remote mountain villages.

Cycling

Cycling is an excellent way to experience Vietnam as bikes are a popular mode of transport. Basic bicycles can be rented for US$1–3 per day, and good-quality mountain bikes for US$7–12. For cycling tour operators see p519.

The flatlands of the Mekong Delta region are ideal for long-distance rides down backroads. The entire coastal route along Hwy 1

CYCLING HIGHLIGHTS

LOCATION	DETAILS	PAGE
Dalat	Lots of dirt trails and base camp for the dramatic two-day descent to Mui Ne	p277
Hoi An	Flat terrain to explore craft villages and cut across rice paddies using paths and country lanes	p208
Mekong Delta	Backroads beside waterways under the shade of coconut palms	p361
Hue	Temples, pagodas and the Perfume river	p174

has allure, but the insane traffic makes it tough going and dangerous. Consider the inland Ho Chi Minh Highway (Hwys 14, 15 and 8), which offers stunning scenery and little traffic. Hoi An is an excellent base for village tours.

North of the old Demilitarised Zone (DMZ), cycling is a bad idea in the winter months thanks to northerly monsoon winds. There are some incredible, and incredibly challenging, rides through the Tonkinese Alps (Hoang Lien Mountains).

For the lowdown on cycling in Vietnam, visit the website www.mrpumpy.net.

Motorbiking

Motorbiking through Vietnam is an unforgettable way to experience the nation. It's the mode of transport for most Vietnamese, so you'll find repair shops everywhere. It puts you closer to the countryside – its smells, people and scenery – compared with getting around by car or bus. For those seeking true adventure there is no better way to go.

If you're not confident riding a motorbike, it's comparatively cheap to hire someone to drive one for you. Easy Riders (p282) is one such scheme.

Unless you relish getting high on exhaust fumes and barged by trucks, avoid Hwy 1 if you can. Many bikers are now choosing to follow the Ho Chi Minh Highway (p291) running the spine of the country from north to south instead of Hwy 1.

For more on what to take and expect see the boxed text on p139. And for more information about motorbiking tours see p520 and for rentals see p517.

Surfing

There's surf most times of year in Vietnam, though it isn't an acclaimed destination – the wave scene in *Apocalypse Now* was shot in the Philippines. Dedicated surf shops are rare, though the odd guesthouse and adventure sport tour operator have boards for hire.

When to Surf

Surf's up between November and April when the winter monsoon blows from the north. Several typhoons form in the South China Sea each year, and these produce the biggest wind swells, though the action is usually short lived.

Surf Safety

Anyone searching for fresh waves in remote locations should be extremely wary of unexploded ordnance, which litters the countryside, particularly near the DMZ. Garbage, stormwater run-off and industrial pollution are other hazards, particularly near cities. Rip tides can be powerful, so use a leash on your board.

Kitesurfing & Windsurfing

Windsurfing and kitesurfing have only recently arrived on the scene, but these are quickly catching on. Mui Ne Beach (p247) is fast becoming a windchasers' hotspot in Asia with competitions and a real buzz about the place. Nha Trang and Vung Tau are other possibilities.

If you've never kitesurfed, have a taster lesson (from US$75) first before enrolling on a lengthy course – a three-day course costs around US$250. It's tough to get your head around all the basics (and also tough on your body).

The best conditions in Mui Ne are in the dry season from November to April. Mornings are ideal for beginners, while in the afternoon wind speeds regularly reach 35 knots. Nha Trang and Vung Tau are also best at this time of year.

» (above) Kitesurfers in action, Mui Ne
» (left) Traveller trying to repair a broken down Minsk bike, northwest Vietnam

Diving & Snorkelling

Vietnam is not a world-class dive destination but it does have some fascinating dive sites. If you've experienced reefs in Indonesia or Australia, prepare yourself for less sea life and reduced visibility however. The most popular scuba-diving and snorkelling is around Nha Trang (p234) where there are several reputable dive operators with equipment and training up to international standards. Hoi An's two dive schools head to the lovely Cham Islands (p198) where macro life can be impressive. Phu Quoc Island (p386) is another popular spot.

The Con Dao Islands (p266) offer unquestionably the best diving and snorkelling in Vietnam, with bountiful marine life, fine reefs and even a wreck dive. Two professional dive schools are based here but expect to pay more than you would elsewhere in Vietnam.

It is also possible to hire snorkelling gear and scuba equipment at several beach resorts along the coast, including Cua Dai Beach (p208), Ca Na (p247) and China Beach (p189).

Dive & Snorkelling Costs

» **Discover Scuba** US$60–80

» **2 Fun Dives** US$70–80 (US$140 in Con Dao Islands)

» **Padi Open Water** US$350–500

» **Snorkelling Day Trip** US$30–40

Kayaking & Sailing

Kayaking has exploded in popularity around Halong Bay in the past few years.

Many standard Halong Bay tours now include an hour or so of kayaking through the karsts, or you can choose a kayaking specialist and paddle around majestic limestone pinnacles, before overnighting on a remote bay.

The rest of the nation is catching up and other kayaking destinations now include Cat Ba Island, Phong Nha, Dalat and rivers in the Hoi An region. You can also rent sea kayaks on beaches including Nha Trang.

Sailing trips, lessons and courses are available; Nha Trang is a excellent base.

Operators include:

» **Blue Swimmer** (p103) Guided kayak tours around the glorious islets of Lan Ha Bay. Also rents kayaks and organises sailing trips.

» **Cat Ba Ventures** (p103) Kayak trips around Halong Bay, Lan Ha Bay and Cat Ba Island.

» **Marco Polo Travel** (p79) Kayak Ba Be Lakes, Bai Tu Long bay or Halong Bay.

» **Waves Watersports** (p235) Sail a fast catamaran or kayak around Nha Trang's beaches and islands.

White-Water Rafting

Rafting is in its infancy in Vietnam. One company offering trips is Dalat-based Phat Tire (p285) which runs a day trip down the Langbian River with Class 2, 3 or 4 rapids, depending on the season. Prices start at US$57. Companies based in Nha Trang, including Whitewater Rafting (p235), also offer trips.

MOTORBIKING HIGHLIGHTS

LOCATION	DETAILS	PAGE
Ho Chi Minh Highway: Duc Tho–Phong Nha	Wonderful karst scenery, forests, little traffic and an excellent paved road	p151
Hai Van Pass	Reach for the stars, this coastal pass features hairpin after hairpin and outstanding ocean views	p180
Sapa–Dien Bien Phu	Glorious mountain scenery, river valleys and tribal villages	p139
Ha Giang–Dong Van–Bao Lac	The ultimate. Superlative vistas, stupendous mountain roads. Feels like the end of the earth	p138
Nha Trang–Dalat	This spectacular new road cuts through forests and takes in a 1700m pass	p282

RIDE THAT WAVE: VIETNAM'S BEST SURF SPOTS

LOCATION	DETAILS	SURF SHOPS
China Beach	The original GI Joe break on a 30km stretch of sand. Can produce clean peaks of over 2m, though watch out for pollution after heavy rains. Nice left and rights over the sand bank offshore from Hoa's Place.	**Tam's Pub & Surf Shop** (p185) **Da Boys Surf** (p189) **Hoa's Place** (p190)
Nha Trang area	In season, head to Bai Dai beach, 27km south of Nha Trang, where's there's a good left-hand break up to 2m during stormy conditions. Powerful body surfing on Nha Trang's main beach.	**Shack Vietnam** (p243) **Waves Watersports** (p236)
Mui Ne	Ideal for beginners. Multiple breaks around the bay including short right and left-handers. Occasionally barrels. Several places rent boards.	**Surf Point** (p249)
Vung Tau	Inconsistent, but when conditions are right some of Vietnam's best waves.	**Surf Station** (p261)

Rock Climbing

It's early days, but with the sheer range of limestone karsts found up and down the country, it is only a matter of time before Vietnam becomes a climbing mecca. The pioneers, and acknowledged specialists, are Asia Outdoors, a highly professional outfit based in Cat Ba Town that has instruction for beginners and dedicated trips for rock addicts. For a taste of what's on offer check out p104. In Dalat there are a couple of good adventure tour operators offering climbing and canyoning too (p277).

Golf

Most Vietnamese golf clubs will allow you to pay a guest fee. The best golf courses in Vietnam include those around Dalat (p277), Mui Ne and Phan Thiet (p248), but there are also plenty of courses in and around Hanoi and HCMC.

Golfing package deals are offered by **Luxury Travel** (www.luxurytravelvietnam .com) and UK-based **Vietnam Golf** (www .vietnamgolf.co.uk).

regions at a glance

Occupying a slender slice of the east Asian landmass, Vietnam combines jagged alpine peaks in the north, a pancake-flat river delta in the south, cave-riddled limestone hills in its central provinces and dense rainforest along its western border with some of the world's most productive rice-growing terrain. And that's just the countryside.

Climatically the northern half of the nation experiences a much cooler winter, and the cuisine, lifestyle and character of the people reflect this. As you head south, the country has more of a tropical feel, with coconut trees outnumbering bamboo plants and fish sauce replacing soy sauce on the menu. The southern provinces are always humid, hot and sticky, their food sweet, spicy, aromatic and complex.

Hanoi

Food ✓✓✓
History ✓✓
Culture ✓✓

Food
Discover – meal by tasty meal – that Hanoi is one of the planet's great food cities. Dine in restored colonial villas or contemporary cafes, or pull up a stool and chow down on street food classics like *pho bo* (beef noodle soup) or *bun cha* (barbecued pork and rice vermicelli).

History
Explore the centuries-old commercial labyrinth of the Old Quarter, before moving on to understand the tumultuous events of the 20th century, recounted in fascinating detail at Hanoi's excellent museums.

Culture
There's a lot more to Hanoi's cultural scene than bootleg DVDs and karaoke. Experience the ancient art of water puppetry, before graduating to the more challenging cultural spectacle of *hat tuong* (Vietnamese opera).

p42

Northeast Vietnam

Landscapes ✓✓✓
Beaches ✓✓
Adventure ✓✓

Landscapes
You'll probably be sharing the majesty of Halong Bay with a few nearby tour boats, but don't worry, there's plenty of stunning scenery to go around – especially when breakfast comes with ethereal, misty morning views.

Beaches
Invest in leisurely off-the-beaten-path travel by catching a slow boat to the laid-back islands of Bai Tu Long Bay. Expect scenery very similar to Halong Bay, but this time with the addition of glorious beaches.

Adventure
Challenge yourself on one of Asia's best rock climbing destinations around Cat Ba, where you can also trek through lush forest and negotiate a kayak to hidden coves and sandy beaches.

p87

Northwest Vietnam

Trekking ✓✓✓
Culture ✓✓✓
History ✓

Trekking
Trek along centuries-old paths to hill-tribe villages or set the bar higher with an ascent of Fansipan, Vietnam's highest peak. For a truly rustic trekking experience, continue further west to the wild landscapes of Ha Giang.

Culture
Experience the diversity of northern Vietnam's ethnic minorities from the Black H'mong around Sapa to the Flower H'mong people of the Bac Ha region. Time your travels to visit the northwest's fascinating and incredibly colourful weekly markets.

History
Understand Vietnam's robust and singular determination to remain independent in the museums, war cemeteries and battlefields around the isolated town of Dien Bien Phu. They commemorate Vietnam's defeat of the colonial French in 1954.

p116

North-Central Vietnam

Wildlife ✓✓
Landscapes ✓✓✓
Adventure ✓✓

Wildlife
Cuc Phuong National Park's wildlife, including clouded leopards and brown bears, is normally elusive but monkeys (including gibbons and langurs) and turtles are impossible to miss at the twin rehabilitation centres here. Van Long Nature Reserve is a paradise for bird-watchers.

Landscapes
The area around Ninh Binh is typified by stunning limestone mountains known as karst hills. Further south, the Phong Nha-Ke Bang National Park offers more of the same, with the addition of several immense cave systems to explore.

Adventure
Riding the Ho Chi Minh Highway through the Truong Son mountains south of Vinh is an unforgettable experience. There's also terrific hiking and tribal villages to investigate in the Pu Luong Nature Reserve.

p141

Central Vietnam

Architecture ✓✓✓
Food ✓✓✓
Beaches ✓✓

Architecture
At Hue's citadel, despite wartime bombing, you'll still see a unique collection of palaces, temples, gateways and towers. Then take in the majestic royal tombs and soaring pagodas that line the Perfume River. Hoi An's Old Town represents a perfectly preserved trading port. Down the road, Danang riverfront is looking impressive these days, with several sleek new modernist structures.

Food
Hoi An is one of the foodie capitals of the nation, replete with outstanding Vietnamese and Western restaurants, excellent cafes and delicious local dishes. While you're in Hue, be sure to sample its incredibly intricate imperial cuisine.

Beaches
An Bang Beach is one of Vietnam's most enjoyable places to lounge by the waves, or you could head to the Cham Islands and search for a secret cove beach.

p156

South-Central Coast

Beaches ✓✓✓
Ancient Temples ✓
Food ✓✓

Beaches
This is Vietnam's coastline at its most voluptuous. Mui Ne and Nha Trang are the big hitters, but there are hundreds of kilometres of empty beaches to discover, including the invitingly empty shores of the Con Dao Islands.

Ancient Temples
The Kingdom of Champa once held sway over much of this region and the legacy is still visible in a host of ancient brick temples dotting the coastal region, including the Po Nagar towers of Nha Trang and the Po Klong Garai towers of Thap Cham.

Food
Vietnamese cuisine is always a delight, but in this region fresh seafood stands out. Choose from succulent prawns, soft squid or juicy crabs, grilled on a barbecue at your table.

p214

Central Highlands

Adventure ✓✓
Wildlife ✓✓
Culture ✓

Adventure
Get off the trail with a motorbike trip into the hinterlands. Self-drive like the *Top Gear* boys on a Minsk, Vespa or Honda Cub. Or hook up with the Easy Riders to explore a Vietnam less travelled on the backroads between Dalat and Hoi An.

Wildlife
Explore some of Vietnam's leading national parks where the wild things are. Cat Tien is home to endangered primates and the innovative Gibbon Trek. Yok Don is where the elephants roam and is easily accessible from Buon Ma Thuot.

Culture
Leave the lowlanders behind on the busy coast and meet some of the minority people who inhabit the high ground. Get to know them with a traditional village homestay around Kon Tum.

p270

Ho Chi Minh City

War History ✓✓✓
Nightlife ✓✓
Food ✓✓✓

War History
The fall of Saigon (or liberation, depending on your perspective) was one of the most dramatic events of the latter part of the 20th century. Military and history buffs will find plenty to interest them here, including the War Remnants Museum, Reunification Palace and the fascinating Cu Chi Tunnels.

Nightlife
Saigon's nightlife was legendary during the American War and Ho Chi Minh City's is hardly less-so now, with burgeoning hip cocktail bars, boozy pubs and old faithfuls such as Apocalypse Now.

Food
There's so much variety on offer, it's difficult to know where to start. Even if you stick to Vietnamese cuisine, there is a baffling array on offer – from the finest street food to innovative linen-tablecloth dining.

p297

Mekong Delta

Beaches ✓
Boat Trips ✓✓✓
Pagodas ✓

Beaches
The white sands and warm waters of Phu Quoc Island and Mui Nai offer plenty of sedentary allure for beach lovers. These Gulf of Thailand resorts are a world away from the muddy shores of the Mekong Delta.

Boat Trips
This is a region where life is lived on the water and women still paddle their boats to floating markets to stock up on fruit and vegetables for their families. Travellers can get a taste of the life aquatic in journeys ranging from paddle-powered explorations of the canal network to luxurious overnight cruises heading into Cambodia.

Pagodas
As well as numerous Vietnamese Buddhist sites, including the holy Sam Mountain, the Delta region offers a wealth of Khmer pagodas to explore, populated by young shaven-headed monks in saffron robes.

p352

Every listing is recommended by our authors, and their favourite places are listed first

Look out for these icons:

TOP CHOICE Our author's top recommendation

A green or sustainable option

FREE No payment required

On the Road

Hanoi

📍 04 / POP 6.5 MILLION

Best Places to Eat

» Hanoi's street food kitchens (p65)
» La Badiane (p68)
» Highway 4 (p64)
» Ly Club (p66)
» Quan An Ngon (p68)

Best Places to Stay

» Sofitel Metropole Hotel (p62)
» Daluva Home (p70)
» Art Hotel (p59)
» Hanoi Elite Hotel (p59)
» 6 on Sixteen (p62)

Why Go?

Showcasing sweeping boulevards, tree-fringed lakes and ancient pagodas, Hanoi is perhaps Asia's most graceful, atmospheric and exotic capital city. It's an energetic city on the move, and it often seems Hanoi's ambitious citizens are determined to make up for lost time.

As motorbikes and pedestrians ebb and flow through the Old Quarter's centuries-old commercial chaos, hawkers in conical hats ply their wares while other locals sip drip-coffee and *bia hoi* (beer). At dawn on the shores of Hoan Kiem Lake, synchronised t'ai chi sessions take place beside goateed grandfathers contemplating their next chess moves.

In Lenin Park, Communist Party youth practise military drills, while nearby, Hanoi's bright young things celebrate contrasting values in cosmopolitan restaurants and bars.

Real estate development and traffic chaos increasingly threaten to subsume Hanoi's compelling blend of Parisian grace and Asian pace, but a beguiling coexistence of the medieval and the modern still enthrals.

When to Go
Hanoi

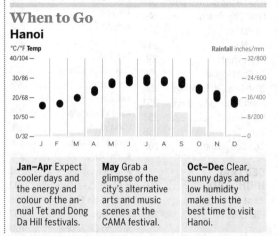

°C/°F Temp — Rainfall inches/mm
40/104 — — 32/800
30/86 — — 24/600
20/68 — — 16/400
10/50 — — 8/200
0/32 — J F M A M J J A S O N D — 0

Jan–Apr Expect cooler days and the energy and colour of the annual Tet and Dong Da Hill festivals.

May Grab a glimpse of the city's alternative arts and music scenes at the CAMA festival.

Oct–Dec Clear, sunny days and low humidity make this the best time to visit Hanoi.

History

The site where Hanoi stands today has been inhabited since the neolithic period. Emperor Ly Thai To moved his capital here in AD 1010, naming it Thang Long (City of the Soaring Dragon). Spectacular celebrations were held in honour of the city's 1000th birthday in 2010.

The decision by Emperor Gia Long, founder of the Nguyen dynasty in 1802, to rule from Hue relegated Hanoi to the status of a regional capital for a century. The city was named Hanoi (The City in a Bend of the River) by Emperor Tu Duc in 1831. From 1902 to 1953, Hanoi served as the capital of French Indochina.

Hanoi was proclaimed the capital of Vietnam after the August Revolution of 1945, but it was not until the Geneva Accords of 1954 that the Viet Minh, driven from the city by the French in 1946, were able to return.

During the American War, US bombing destroyed parts of Hanoi and killed hundreds of civilians. One of the prime targets was the 1682m-long Long Bien Bridge. US aircraft repeatedly bombed this strategic point, yet after each attack the Vietnamese managed to improvise replacement spans and return road and rail services. It is said that the US military ended the attacks when US POWs were put to work repairing the structure. Today the bridge is renowned as a symbol of the tenacity and strength of the people of Hanoi. An essential Hanoi experience is to ride by *xe om* (motorcycle taxi) across this iconic structure.

As recently as the early 1990s, motorised transport was rare; most people got around on bicycles and the only modern structures were designed by Soviet architects. Today Hanoi's conservationists fight to save historic structures, and the city struggles to cope with a booming population, soaring pollution levels and an inefficient public transport system.

⊙ Sights

Note that some museums are closed on Mondays and take a two-hour lunch break on other days of the week. Check the following opening hours carefully before setting off.

OLD QUARTER

This is the Asia dreamed of from afar. Steeped in history, pulsating with life, bubbling with commerce, buzzing with motorbikes and rich in exotic scents, the Old Quarter is Hanoi's historic heart. The streets

---

HANOI IN...

One Day

Rise early for a morning walk around misty **Hoan Kiem Lake** before a classic Hanoi breakfast of *pho bo* (beef noodle soup) at **Pho Gia Truyen**. Pay your respects at the **Ho Chi Minh Mausoleum**, before checking out the surreal **museum** and **stilt house**. Wander down P Dien Bien Phu to the interesting **Vietnam Military History Museum**. Have lunch at the nearby **Matchbox Winebar & Restaurant** before taking in the cultural treasures at the adjacent **Fine Arts Museum**. After lunch, walk five minutes to the peaceful **Temple of Literature**, before catching a cab back to jettison your new-found serenity amid the irresistible chaos of the **Old Quarter**. Browse the ancient neighbourhood's buildings, shops and galleries, stopping for a well-earned and refreshing glass of *bia hoi* (draught beer). Catch a performance of the **water puppets** before heading to the sprawling **Quan An Ngon** for dinner. Good luck in choosing from the diverse menu, which spans all of Vietnam's regional cuisines.

Two Days

Hanoi has some terrific sights away from the central zone, so head into the suburbs to the excellent **Vietnam Museum of Ethnology** to discover the ethnic mosaic that makes up Vietnam today. Have a local lunch in **Nha Hang Lan Chin**, tucked away next to the **Museum of Vietnamese Revolution** and hop across the road to the **National Museum of Vietnamese History**. The building is stunning and the contents a fine introduction to 2000 years of highs and lows. After this focus on what's gone before, detour north by taxi to the emerging restaurant and bar scene on trendy **P Xuan Dieu** near Tay Ho (West Lake). Dinner and cocktails at the **House of Son Tinh** is recommended as a glimpse into the Hanoi of tomorrow.

Hanoi Highlights

1 Experience Asia at its raw, pulsating best in the labyrinthine streets of the **Old Quarter** (p43)

2 Step into history, and a spiritual retreat from the busy streets, at the **Temple of Literature** (p49)

3 Get an authentic taste of the city while exploring Hanoi's intoxicating **street food** scene (p65)

4 Awake at dawn to ease peacefully into another Hanoi day with the t'ai chi buffs along **Hoan Kiem Lake** (p47)

5 Piece together the country's ethnic mosaic at the wonderful **Vietnam Museum of Ethnology** (p53)

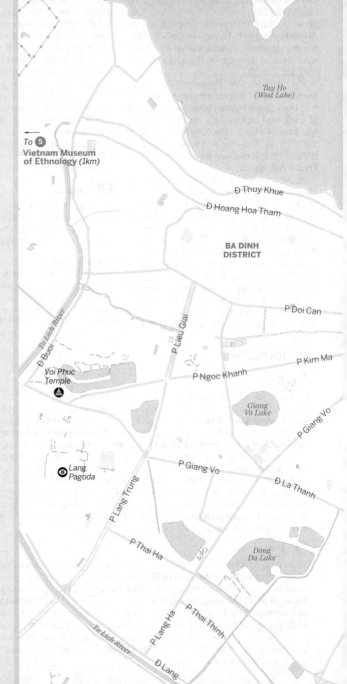

To **5**
Vietnam Museum
of Ethnology (1km)

*Tay Ho
(West Lake)*

Đ Thuy Khue

Đ Hoang Hoa Tham

**BA DINH
DISTRICT**

P Doi Can

P Lieu Giai

P Kim Ma

To Lich River

Đ Buoi

Voi Phuc
Temple

P Ngoc Khanh

*Giang
Vo Lake*

P Giang Vo

Lang
Pagoda

P Giang Vo

Đ La Thanh

P Lang Trung

P Thai Ha

*Dong
Da Lake*

To Lich River

P Lang Ha

P Thai Thinh

Đ Lang

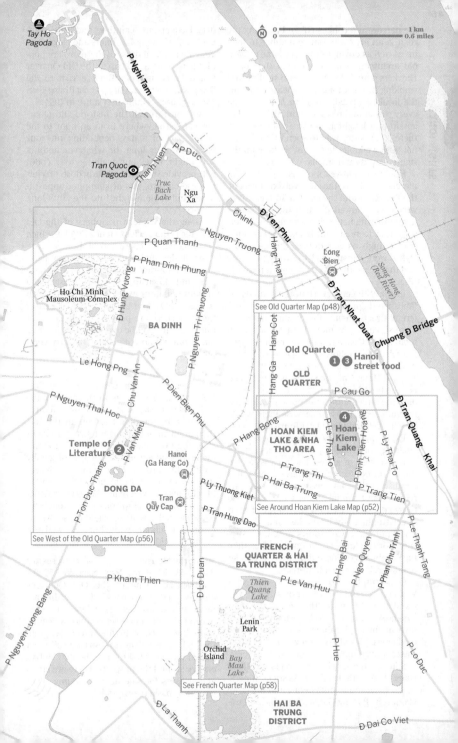

are narrow and congested, and crossing the road is an art form, but remember to look up as well as down, as there is some elegant old architecture in and among the chaos. Hawkers pound the streets with sizzling and smoking baskets that hide cheap meals for the locals. *Pho* stalls and *bia hoi* dens hug every corner and resonate with the sound of gossip and laughter. Modern yet medieval, there is no better way to spend time in Hanoi than walking the streets, soaking up the sights, sounds and smells.

Home to 1000 years of history, the commercial quarter of the city evolved alongside the Red River and the smaller To Lich River, which once flowed through the city centre in an intricate network of canals and waterways that teemed with boats. Waters could rise as high as 8m during the monsoon. Dykes were constructed to protect the city and these can still be seen along Tran Quang Khai.

In the 13th century, Hanoi's 36 guilds established themselves here, each taking a different street – hence the original name '36 Streets'. There are more than 50 streets in today's Old Quarter, typically named *Hang* (merchandise) followed by the word for the product traditionally sold in that street. Thus, P Hang Gai translates as 'Silk Street'. See the boxed text on p76 for the rest. These days the street name may not indicate what businesses are there; otherwise there would be lots of P Hang Du Lich (Tourism Streets).

Exploring the maze of backstreets is fascinating: some open up while others narrow into a warren of alleys. The area is known for its tunnel (or tube) houses – so called because of their narrow frontages and long rooms. These tunnel houses were developed to avoid taxes based on the width of their street frontage. By feudal law, houses were also limited to two storeys and, out of respect for the king, could not be taller than the royal palace. These days there are taller buildings, but no real high-rises.

Opportunities to dispense with your Vietnamese dong are endless. As you wander, you'll find clothes, cosmetics, fake sunglasses, luxury food, T-shirts, musical instruments, plumbing supplies, herbal medicines, jewellery, religious offerings, spices, woven mats and much, much more.

Some of the specialised streets include P Hang Quat, with its red candlesticks, funeral boxes, flags and temple items; and the more glamorous P Hang Gai, with its silk, embroidery, lacquerware, paintings and water puppets – silk sleeping-bag liners and elegant *ao dai* (the national dress of Vietnam) are popular here. Finally, no trip to the Old Quarter would be complete without a visit to the **Dong Xuan Market** (Map p48; cnr P Hang Khoai & P Dong Xuan), rebuilt after a fire in 1994.

A stroll through the historic Old Quarter can last anywhere from an hour to the better part of a day, depending on your pace. However long, or whatever detours you might take, our walking tour (p60) will provide you with a heady dose of Vietnamese culture, lots of shopping opportunities and some insight into the city's long history.

Along the western periphery of the Old Quarter is the ancient Hanoi Citadel, which was originally constructed by Emperor Gia Long. Today the citadel is a military base, home to high-ranking officers and their families, and closed to the public. Most of the ancient buildings were destroyed by French troops in 1894, and US bombers took care of the rest. There are persistent rumours that this area will soon be opened up to development, but for now it's still a military compound.

Bach Ma Temple   TEMPLE
(Map p48; cnr P Hang Buom & P Hang Giay; ☺8-11am & 2-5pm Tue-Sun) In the heart of the Old Quarter, the small Bach Ma Temple is said to be the oldest temple in the city, though much of the current structure dates from the 18th century and a shrine to Confucius was added in 1839. It was originally built by Emperor Ly Thai To in the 11th century to honour a white horse that guided him to this site, where he chose to construct his city walls. Pass through the wonderful old wooden doors of the pagoda to see a statue of the legendary white horse, as well as a beautiful red-lacquered funeral palanquin.

Memorial House   HISTORICAL BUILDING
(Map p48; 87 P Ma May; admission 5000d; ☺8.30am-5pm) One of the Old Quarter's best-restored properties, this traditional merchants' house is sparsely but beautifully decorated, with rooms set around two courtyards and filled with fine furniture. Note the high steps between rooms, a traditional design incorporated to stop the flow of bad energy around the property. There are crafts and trinkets for sale here, including silver jewellery, basketwork and Vietnamese tea-

sets, and there's usually a calligrapher or another craftsperson at work too.

AROUND HOAN KIEM LAKE

Hoan Kiem Lake   LAKE

(Map p52) The epicentre of old Hanoi, Hoan Kiem Lake is an enchanting body of water. Legend has it that, in the mid-15th century, Heaven sent Emperor Le Thai To (Le Loi) a magical sword, which he used to drive the Chinese out of Vietnam. One day after the war he happened upon a giant golden turtle swimming on the surface of the lake; the creature grabbed the sword and disappeared into the depths. Since that time, the lake has been known as Ho Hoan Kiem (Lake of the Restored Sword) because the turtle restored the sword to its divine owners.

Ngoc Son Temple sits on an island in Hoan Kiem Lake. The ramshackle **Thap Rua** (Turtle Tower), on an islet near the southern end, is topped with a red star and is often used as an emblem of Hanoi. Every morning at around 6am local residents practise traditional t'ai chi on the shore.

Ngoc Son Temple   TEMPLE

(Jade Mountain Temple; Map p52; admission 10,000d; ⊗7.30am-5pm) Perhaps the most visited temple in Hanoi, Ngoc Son Temple sits pretty on a delightful little island in the northern part of Hoan Kiem Lake. An elegant scarlet bridge, Huc (Rising Sun) Bridge, constructed in classical Vietnamese style and lined with flags, connects the island to the lake shore. Surrounded by water and shaded by trees, the small temple is dedicated to General Tran Hung Dao (who defeated the Mongols in the 13th century), La To (patron saint of physicians), and the scholar Van Xuong. Inside you'll find some fine ceramics, a gong or two, some ancient bells and a glass case containing a stuffed lake turtle, which is said to have weighed a hefty 250kg during its life.

The nearby **Martyrs' Monument** was erected as a memorial to those who died fighting for Vietnam's independence.

TOP CHOICE **National Museum of Vietnamese History**   MUSEUM

(Map p52; www.nmvnh.org.vn; 1 P Trang Tien; adult/student 20,000/10,000d; ⊗8am-4.30pm) A must for both the architecture and the collection, the history museum was formerly home to the École Française d'Extrême Orient in Vietnam. It is an elegant, ochre-coloured structure built between 1925 and

---

ⓘ UP CLOSE & PERSONAL WITH CU RUA

We were there! On a misty day in April 2011, our latest Vietnam research trip was put on hold as we joined thousands of curious locals and tourists around the northern end of Hoan Kiem Lake. The singular attraction was to see Cu Rua ('Great Grandfather'), the lake's legendary turtle, being captured so it could receive medical treatment for lesions caused by pollution. Cu Rua is the last of the lake's turtles – others were killed by fishermen in the 1960s – and he's definitely not your common garden-variety turtle. On display in the lake's Ngoc Son Temple is a specimen from 1968 weighing in at 250kg and 2.1m long, and Cu Rua is a hefty 200kg and 2m long.

Many Hanoians believe Cu Rua to be magical and sacred, potentially over 600 years old, or at the very least, a direct descendant of the same turtle that reclaimed the lake's magic sword used by Emperor Ly Thai To in the 15th century to defeat China's Ming dynasty.

Scientists consider Cu Rua to be around 100 years old, but this urban centenarian is still very special. It's reckoned there are only three other freshwater turtles of the genus *Rafetus swinhoei* living today – one in a lake outside Hanoi and two others in China. Little wonder Cu Rua was the biggest news in town for a few days.

Search YouTube for 'Hanoi' and 'turtle' to see how a crack team including Vietnamese Special Forces gently captured the city's most revered reptile.

1932. French architect Ernest Hebrard was among the first in Vietnam to incorporate a blend of Chinese and French design elements.

Highlights include some excellent bronzes from the Dong Son culture (3rd century BC to 3rd century AD), striking Hindu statuary from the Khmer and Champa kingdoms, and beautiful jewellery and accoutrements from imperial Vietnam. More recent history includes the struggle against the French and the story of the Communist Party.

Everything is comprehensively labelled in English and French.

Old Quarter

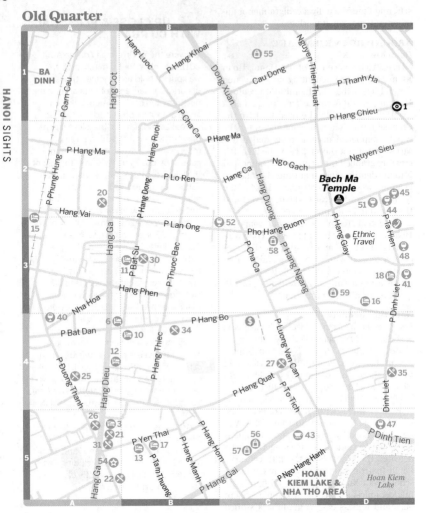

Hoa Lo Prison Museum

TOP CHOICE

HISTORIC BUILDING

(Map p52; cnr P Hoa Lo & P Hai Ba Trung; admission 10,000d; ⊗8am-5pm) This thought-provoking site is all that remains of the former Hoa Lo Prison, ironically nicknamed the 'Hanoi Hilton' by US POWs during the American War.

The vast prison complex was built by the French in 1896. Originally intended to house around 450 inmates, records indicate that by the 1930s there were close to 2000 prisoners. Hoa Lo was never a very successful prison, and hundreds escaped its walls over the years – many squeezing out through sewer grates.

The bulk of the exhibits here relate to the prison's use up to the mid-1950s, focusing on the Vietnamese struggle for independence from France. A notable gruesome relic in its dark chambers is the ominous French guillotine, used to behead Vietnamese revolutionaries.

Recently installed are several displays focusing on the American pilots who were incarcerated at Hoa Lo, including Pete Peterson (the first US Ambassador to a unified Vietnam in 1995), and Senator John

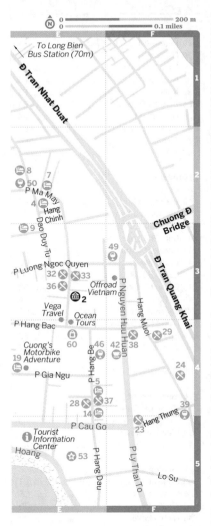

Tue-Sun) One of Hanoi's most overlooked museums is also one of its best. Recently reopened after a four-year renovation, the collection showcases women's role in Vietnamese society and culture. Superbly laid out and labelled in English and French, it's the memories of the wartime contribution by individual heroic women that are most poignant. There is a stunning collection of propaganda posters, as well as costumes, tribal basketware and fabric motifs from Vietnam's ethnic minority groups. Regular special exhibitions are held on topics as diverse as human trafficking, street vendors and traditional medicine. Check the website for what's on.

St Joseph Cathedral CHURCH

(Map p52; P Nha Tho; ⏱main gate 5am-noon & 2-7.30pm) The striking neo-Gothic St Joseph Cathedral was inaugurated in 1886, and boasts a soaring facade that faces a little plaza. Its most noteworthy features are its twin bell towers, elaborate altar and fine stained-glass windows.

The main gate to St Joseph Cathedral is open when Mass is held. Guests are welcome at other times of the day, but must enter via the compound of the Diocese of Hanoi, the entrance to which is a block away at 40 P Nha Chung. Walking through the main gate, go straight and then turn right. When you reach the side door to the cathedral, ring the small bell high up to the right-hand side of the door.

On Sunday for the evening Mass (usually at 6pm), the congregation spills out on the streets, hymns are beamed out, and the devout sit on motorbikes listening intently to the sermon. Other Mass times are listed on a sign on the gates to the left of the cathedral.

Museum of The Vietnamese Revolution MUSEUM

(Map p52; 216 Đ Tran Quang Khai; admission 15,000d; ⏱8-11.30am & 1.30-4.15pm) A must for all budding revolutionaries, the history of the Vietnamese Revolution is enthusiastically presented in this museum. It's diagonally across the road from the History Museum.

WEST OF THE OLD QUARTER

TOP
CHOICE **Temple of Literature** TEMPLE

(Map p56; P Quoc Tu Giam; adult/student 10,000/5,000d; ⏱8am-5pm) About 2km west of Hoan Kiem Lake, the Temple of Literature is a rare example of well-preserved traditional Vietnamese architecture.

McCain (the Republican nominee for the US presidency in 2008). McCain's flight suit is displayed, along with a photograph of Hanoi locals rescuing him from Truc Bach Lake after being shot down in 1967.

Use your discretion when visiting this part of the prison as the photographs of seemingly content American POWs playing basketball and decorating Christmas trees are at odds with John McCain's memories of being tortured during his time here.

Vietnamese Women's Museum MUSEUM

(off Map p52; www.baotangphunu.org.vn; 36 P Ly Thuong Kiet; admission 30,000d; ⏱8am-4.30pm

Old Quarter

Founded in 1070 by Emperor Ly Thanh Tong, the temple is dedicated to Confucius (Khong Tu) and honours Vietnam's finest scholars and men of literary accomplishment. Vietnam's first university was established here in 1076, though at this time entrance was only granted to those of noble birth. After 1442, a more egalitarian approach was adopted and gifted students from all over the nation headed to Hanoi to study the principles of Confucianism, literature and poetry.

In 1484 Emperor Le Thanh Tong ordered that stelae be erected to record the names, places of birth and achievements of exceptional scholars: 82 stelae remain standing. The imposing tiered gateway (on P Quoc Tu Giam) which forms the main entrance is preceded by a curious plaque, whose inscription requests that visitors dismount their horses before entering. Make sure you do.

Paths then lead through formal gardens to the Khue Van pavilion, constructed in 1802, beyond which is a large square pond known as the Well of Heavenly Clarity.

The northern side of this courtyard is marked by a low-slung pagoda housing an extraordinary statue of a majestic-looking Confucius, depicted with a goatee and bearing scarlet robes, flanked by four of his disciples.

Ho Chi Minh Mausoleum
Complex   HISTORICAL SITE

(Map p56; entrance cnr P Ngoc Ha & P Doi Can) This is the holiest of the holies for many Vietnamese. To the west of the Old Quarter, the Ho Chi Minh Mausoleum Complex is an important place of pilgrimage. A traffic-free area of **botanical gardens**, monuments, memorials and pagodas, it's usually crowded with groups of all ages, from all over the nation, who have come to pay their respects.

Ho Chi Minh's Mausoleum

(admission free; ⊘8-11am Tue-Thu, Sat & Sun Dec-Sep, last entry 10.15am) In the tradition of Lenin and Stalin before him – and Mao afterwards – Ho Chi Minh's Mausoleum is a monumental marble edifice. Contrary to his desire for a simple cremation, the mausoleum was constructed from materials gathered from all over Vietnam between 1973 and 1975. The roof and peristyle are said to evoke either a traditional communal house or a lotus flower, though to many tourists it looks like a concrete cubicle with columns. Set deep in the bowels of the building in a glass sarcophagus is the frail, pale body of Ho Chi Minh. The mausoleum is closed for about two months each year while the embalmed body goes to Russia for maintenance.

The queue, which moves quite quickly, usually snakes for several hundred metres to the mausoleum entrance itself. Inside, adopt a slow but steady pace as you file past Ho's body. Guards, regaled in snowy-white military uniforms, are posted at intervals of five paces, giving an eerily authoritarian aspect to the slightly macabre spectacle of the body with its wispy white hair.

The following rules are strictly applied to all visitors to the mausoleum:

» People wearing shorts, tank tops and so on will not be admitted.

» Nothing (including day packs, cameras and mobiles) can be taken inside.

» Maintain a respectful demeanour at all times: no talking or sniggering.

» Photography is absolutely prohibited inside the mausoleum.

» It is forbidden to put your hands in your pockets.

» Hats must be taken off inside the mausoleum building.

Most of the visitors are Vietnamese and it's interesting to watch their reactions. Most show deep respect for Ho Chi Minh, who is honoured for his role as the liberator of the Vietnamese people from colonialism, as much as for his communist ideology. This view is reinforced by Vietnam's educational system, which emphasises Ho's deeds and accomplishments.

If you're lucky, you'll catch the changing of the guard outside Ho's mausoleum – the pomp and ceremony displayed here rivals the British equivalent at Buckingham Palace. Photography is permitted outside the building but not inside and visitors will be asked to leave bags and mobile phones at a counter just inside the entrance.

Ho Chi Minh's Stilt House &
the Presidential Palace

(admission 15,000d; ⊘summer 7.30-11am & 2-4pm, winter 8-11am & 1.30-4pm, closed Mon, closed Fri afternoon) Behind Ho Chi Minh's Mausoleum is a humble stilt house, where Ho lived intermittently from 1958 to 1969. The house is an interpretation of a traditional rural dwelling, and has been preserved just as Ho left it. It's set in a well-tended garden next to a carp-filled pond. Just how much time he actually spent here is questionable – the house would have been a tempting target for US bombers had it been suspected that Ho was hanging out here. In an adjacent building a sign proclaims, 'Ho Chi Minh's Used Cars' – in reality, automobiles he used during his life.

In stark contrast to the understated stilt house is the imposing Presidential Palace, a beautifully restored colonial building constructed in 1906 as the Palace of the Governor General of Indochina. It is now used for official receptions and isn't open to the public. There is a combined entrance gate to the stilt house and Presidential Palace grounds on P Ong Ich Kiem, inside the mausoleum complex; when the main mausoleum entrance is closed, enter from Đ Hung Vuong near the palace building.

Ho Chi Minh Museum

(www.baotanghochiminh.vn; admission 15,000d; ⊘8-11.30am daily & 2-4.30pm Tue-Thu, Sat & Sun) Adjacent to Ho's Mausoleum, the huge

Around Hoan Kiem Lake

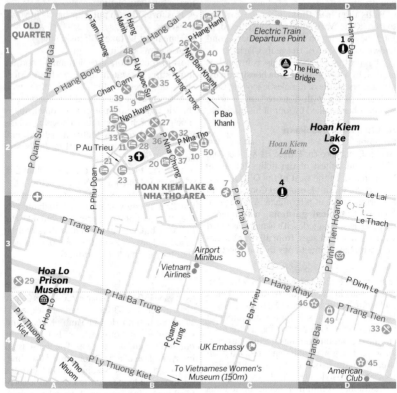

concrete Soviet-style Ho Chi Minh Museum is a triumphalist monument dedicated to the life of the founder of modern Vietnam and to the onward march of revolutionary socialism. Mementos of Ho's life are showcased, and there are some fascinating photos and dusty official documents relating the overthrow of the French and the rise of communism.

Photography is forbidden and you may be asked to check your bag at reception. An English-speaking guide costs around 100,000d, and given the quite surreal nature of the exhibition it's a worthwhile investment.

One Pillar Pagoda

(P Ong Ich Kiem) A Hanoi landmark, the One Pillar Pagoda was originally built by the Emperor Ly Thai Tong, who ruled from 1028 to 1054. According to the annals, the heirless emperor dreamed that he had met Quan The Am Bo Tat, the Goddess of Mercy, who while seated on a lotus flower, handed him a male child. Ly Thai Tong then married a young peasant girl and had a son and heir by her. As a way of expressing his gratitude for this event, he constructed a pagoda here in 1049. The delicate One Pillar Pagoda, built of wood on a single stone pillar, is designed to resemble a lotus blossom, the symbol of purity, rising out of a sea of sorrow. One of the last acts of the French before quitting Hanoi in 1954 was to destroy the original One Pillar Pagoda; the structure was rebuilt by the new government.

Vietnam Military History Museum MUSEUM
(Map p56; www.btlsqsvn.org.vn; P Dien Bien Phu; admission 20,000d, camera 20,000d; ⊘8-11.30am & 1-4.30pm, closed Mon & Fri) Easy to spot thanks to a large collection of weaponry out front, the Military Museum displays Soviet and Chinese equipment alongside French- and US-made weapons captured during years of warfare. The centrepiece is a Soviet-built MiG-21 jet fighter, triumphant amid the wreckage of French aircraft downed at Dien

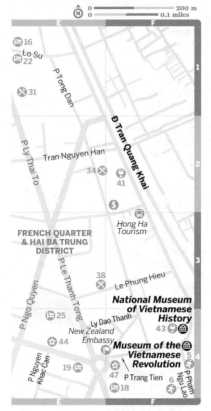

armed) goddess of compassion. Look out too for the remarkable lacquered-wood statues of robed Buddhist monks, complete with drooping earlobes and fabulously expressive faces, from the Tay Son dynasty. There's also a large collection of contemporary art.

There are a couple of galleries with contemporary art and folk-naive paintings. Reproductions of antiques are available, but ask for a certificate to clear these goods through customs when you leave Vietnam.

Ambassadors' Pagoda
PAGODA

(Map p56; 73 P Quan Su) The official centre of Buddhism in Hanoi, the Ambassadors' Pagoda attracts quite a crowd on holidays. During the 17th century there was a guest-house here for the ambassadors of Buddhist countries. Today there are about a dozen monks and nuns based at the Ambassadors' Pagoda. Next to the pagoda is a shop selling Buddhist ritual objects. The Ambassadors' Pagoda is located between P Ly Thuong Kiet and P Tran Hung Dao.

Quan Thanh Temple
TEMPLE

(Map p56; P Quan Thanh) Shaded by huge trees, Quan Thanh Temple was established during the Ly dynasty (1010–1225) and was dedicated to Tran Vo (God of the North), whose symbols of power were the tortoise and the snake. A bronze statue and bell date from 1677. The temple is on the shores of Truc Bach Lake, near the intersection of Đ Thanh Nien and P Quan Thanh.

FRENCH QUARTER

Hai Ba Trung Temple
TEMPLE

(Map p58; P Tho Lao) Two kilometres south of Hoan Kiem Lake, this temple was founded in 1142. A statue shows the two Trung sisters (who lived in the 1st century AD) kneeling with their arms raised in the air, as if they are addressing a crowd. Some say the statue shows the sisters, who had been proclaimed the queens of the Vietnamese, about to dive into a river. They are said to have drowned themselves rather than surrender in the wake of their defeat at the hands of the Chinese.

GREATER HANOI

TOP
CHOICE / Vietnam Museum of
Ethnology
MUSEUM

(off Map p44; www.vme.org.vn; Đ Nguyen Van Huyen; admission 25,000d, guide 50,000d, camera fee 50,000d; ⊙8.30am-5.30pm Tue-Sun) The outstanding Vietnam Museum of Ethnology is one of the country's premier museums. Occupying a fine modern structure, the

Bien Phu, and a US F-111. Adjacent is the hexagonal **Flag Tower**, one of the symbols of Hanoi. Access is possible to a terrace overlooking a rusting collection of war matériel. Opposite the museum is a small park with a commanding **statue of Lenin**.

Fine Arts Museum
MUSEUM

(Map p56; 66 P Nguyen Thai Hoc; admission 20,000d; ⊙9.15am-5pm Tue-Sun) Hanoi's excellent Fine Arts Museum is housed in two buildings that were once the French Ministry of Information.

There's some outstanding art here, with a collection of superb textiles, furniture and ceramics in the first building, which also showcases some terrific temporary exhibitions. But over in the magnificent main building things get even more impressive as room after room reveals artistic treasures from Vietnam including ancient Champa stone carvings and some astonishing effigies of Guan Yin (the thousand-eyed, thousand-

Around Hoan Kiem Lake

terrific collection features well-presented tribal art, artefacts and everyday objects gathered from across the nation. Displays are well labelled in Vietnamese, French and English. For anyone with an interest in Vietnam's minorities, it's an essential visit – though it is located way out in the suburbs.

In the grounds are examples of traditional village houses – a Tay stilt house, an impressive Bahnar communal structure and a Yao home. Don't miss the soaring, thatched-roofed Giarai tomb, complete with risqué wooden statues.

A fair-trade craft shop sells books, beautiful postcards, and arts and crafts from ethnic communities.

The museum is in the Cau Giay district, about 7km from the city centre and around 120,000d each way in a taxi. Local bus 14 (3000d) departs from P Dinh Tien Hoang on the east side of Hoan Kiem Lake and passes within a couple of blocks of the museum – get off at the Nghia Tan bus stop and head to Đ Nguyen Van Huyen.

Tay Ho (West Lake) LAKE

(Map p44) The city's largest lake, Tay Ho is around 13km in circumference and ringed by upmarket suburbs. On the south side of the lake, along Đ Thuy Khue, is a string of popular seafood restaurants, and to the east, the Xuan Dieu strip is lined with restaurants, cafes, boutiques and luxury hotels. You'll also find two temples on its shores; the Tay Ho and Tran Quoc pagodas.

A newly installed pathway now circles the lake, making for a great bicycle ride. To rent a bike ask at lakeside restaurant Don's A Chef Bistro (p70).

Two legends explain the origins of Tay Ho, which is also known as the Lake of Mist and the Big Lake. According to one legend, Tay Ho was created when the Dragon King drowned an evil nine-tailed fox in his lair, in a forest on this site. Another legend relates that in the 11th century a Vietnamese Buddhist monk, Khong Lo, rendered a great service to the emperor of China, who rewarded him with a vast quantity of bronze. The monk cast the bronze into a huge bell, the sound of which could be heard all the way to China, where the Golden Buffalo Calf, mistaking the ringing for its mother's call, ran southward, trampling on the site and turning it into a lake.

The geological explanation is that it was created when Song Hong (Red River) overflowed its banks. The flood problem has been partially controlled by building dykes – the highway along the eastern side of Tay Ho is built upon one.

Tay Ho Pagoda PAGODA

(Map p44; P Tay Ho) Jutting into West Lake, beautiful Tay Ho Pagoda is perhaps the most popular place of worship in Hanoi. Throngs of people come here on the first and 15th day of each lunar month in the hope of receiving good fortune from the Mother Goddess, to whom the temple is dedicated.

Tran Quoc Pagoda PAGODA

(Map p44) One of the oldest pagodas in Vietnam, Tran Quoc Pagoda is on the eastern shore of Tay Ho, just off Đ Thanh Nien, which divides this lake from Truc Bach Lake. A stela here, dating from 1639, tells the history of this site. The pagoda was rebuilt in the 15th century and again in 1842.

Truc Bach Lake LAKE

(Map p44) Separated from Tay Ho only by Đ Thanh Nien, this lake is lined with flame trees. During the 18th century the Trinh lords built a palace on the lakeside; it was later transformed into a reformatory for wayward royal concubines, who were condemned to spend their days weaving pure white silk.

Activities

Sports & Swimming

Daewoo Hotel Fitness Centre FITNESS CLUB

(3835 1000; www.hanoi-daewoohotel.com; 360 Đ Kim Ma;) Situated 5km west of Hoan Kiem Lake along Đ Kim Ma, the Daewoo Hotel Fitness Centre has a day-use fee of US$25 for all facilities including the pool. There's also a good spa.

Hash House Harriers RUNNING

(www.hanoih3.com; 100,000d incl beer; from 1.30pm Sat) For the uninitiated, these are drinkers with a running problem. The 'hash' meets at the American Club (p57).

Army Hotel SWIMMING

(Map p52; 33C P Pham Ngu Lao;) In central Hanoi, the Army Hotel charges US$4 for day use of its pool, which is big enough for laps and open all year. It gets very busy with children in the afternoon.

Hanoi Water Park SWIMMING

(9am-9pm Wed-Mon Apr-Nov) Hanoi Water Park is around 5km north of the city centre and has pools, slides and a lazy river. Entry costs 50,000d for those over 110cm tall, and 30,000d for shorter people, translating roughly to adults and children. Again, it gets extremely busy here on hot summer afternoons. It's a 15-minute taxi ride from central Hanoi on the northern edge of Tay Ho.

King's Island GOLF

(3772 3160; www.kingsislandgolf.com; from US$70) King's Island, 45km west of Hanoi, close to the base of Ba Vi Mountain, is north Vietnam's first 36-hole golf course. The course offers lakeside or mountain-view play. There is also a popular course at Tam Dao Hill Station; see p86.

Zenith Yoga YOGA

(904 356 561; www.zenithyoga.posterous.com; 111 P Xuan Dieu; per class 250,000d) Zenith Yoga has daily Asthanga, Iyengar and Hatha yoga sessions in a smart studio. It's in the expat area near Tay Ho, around 5km north of central Hanoi. Phone ahead for the schedule of classes.

Massage & Spa

Hanoi has an expanding choice of spas and massage centres. Rates are less than in the West, or richer Asian countries, so it's a great place for a little indulgence.

West of the Old Quarter

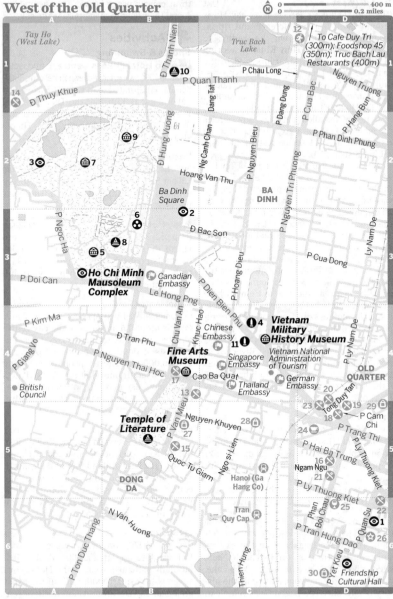

0 — 400 m
0 — 0.2 miles

La Siesta Spa SPA

(Map p52; ☎3935 1632; www.hanoielegancehotel
.com/spa; 32 P Lo Su) Escape from the incessant
energy of the Old Quarter with spa, massage
and beauty treatments across two floors of the
Hanoi Elegance Diamond Hotel (p63).

QT Anam Spa SPA

(Map p52; ☎3928 6116; www.qtanamspa.com;
26-28 Le Thai To) Excellent spa, massage and
beauty treatments.

West of the Old Quarter

Cultural Centres

All of the following have newspapers and magazines to browse. Bring your passport to gain access.

American Club   CULTURAL CENTRE
(Map p52; ☑3824 1850; amclub@fpt.vn; 19-21 P Hai Ba Trung) Also has a huge DVD library and is the venue for the annual CAMA Festival (p59)

British Council   CULTURAL CENTRE
(☑3728 1922; www.britishcouncil.org/vietnam; 20 Thuy Khue, Tay Ho) Located in the Tay Ho area, it hosts cultural events, exhibitions, workshops and fashion shows.

Centre Culturel Français de Hanoi   CULTURAL CENTRE
(Map p52; ☑3936 2164; www.ifhanoi-lespace.com; 24 P Trang Tien) In the L'Espace building near the Opera House.

🍴 Courses

Hanoi Cooking Centre   COOKING
(Map p56; ☑3715 0088; www.hanoicookingcentre. com; 44 Chau Long; per class US$50) Excellent interactive classes including market visits and a special Kids Club – handy if your children are aspiring chefs. The Hanoi Cooking Centre also runs a highly recommended walking tour exploring Hanoi's street food scene, and cookery classes conclude with a shared lunch in its elegant restaurant.

Hidden Hanoi   COOKING
(☑091 225 4045; www.hiddenhanoi.com.vn; 137 P Nghi Tam, Tay Ho; per class with market tour US$50) Offers cooking classes from its kitchen near the eastern side of Tay Ho. Options include seafood and village food menus. Walking tours exploring Hanoi street food also available. Hidden Hanoi also offers a language study program (per person from $US200) including two field trips.

Highway 4   COOKING
(Map p48; ☑3715 0577; www.highway4.com; 3 Hang Tre; per class US$50) Classes begin at their Old Quarter eatery (p64), incorporate a *cyclo* ride and market tour, and continue on to Highway 4's Tay Ho restaurant, the House of Son Tinh (p70). And yes, you can learn how to make their signature catfish spring rolls. Also on offer are cocktail-making classes (US$29 per person) using Highway 4's traditional Son Tinh liquors (p73).

French Quarter

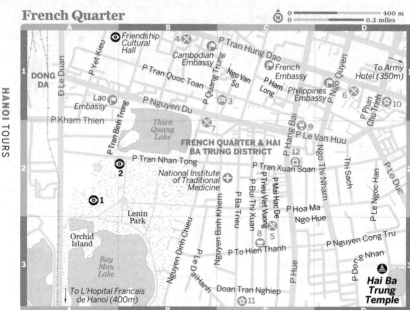

French Quarter

◎ Top Sights
Hai Ba Trung Temple D3

◎ Sights
1 Lenin Park A2
2 Lenin Park Main Gate B2

▣ Sleeping
3 Drift.. C1

✕ Eating
Cay Cau ....(see 10)
4 Chay Nang Tam B1
5 Izakaya Yancha....................................C3
6 Nha Hang Ngon D1
7 Wild Lotus B2

☕ Drinking
8 Cong Caphe C3
9 Quan Ly C2

✪ Entertainment
10 Cay Cau D1
11 Megastar Complex C3

🛍 Shopping
12 Hom Market C2

Hanoi Foreign Language College LANGUAGE
(Map p52; ☎3826 2468; 1 P Pham Ngu Lao)
Housed in the History Museum compound
this is a branch of Hanoi National University
where foreigners can study Vietnamese for
about US$10 per lesson.

Hanoi Language Tours LANGUAGE
(☎090 1352 2605; www.hanoilanguagetours.com;
per person from US$150) Courses from two to
10 days focusing on language and cultural
essentials for travellers, expats and businesspeople.

🇨 Tours

Most people prefer to explore Hanoi at their
own pace, but Hidden Hanoi and the Hanoi
Cooking Centre both offer interesting tours
with a foodie slant (see p57).

Also recommended is **Hanoi Kids** (www
.hanoikids.org), a student-run volunteer organisation that partners visitors with Hanoi
teens and young adults wishing to improve
their English-language skills. Tours are customised to the needs of visitors and can
include Hanoi sights like the Temple of Literature and Hoa Lo Prison Museum, or restaurant and market visits. It's best to arrange
tours online before you arrive in Hanoi.

Another worthwhile tour is with **Bloom
Microventures** (www.bloom-microventures.org

/vietnam), taking in the village of Soc Son 40km north of Hanoi. It's a good opportunity to see how micro-loans are funding rural entrepreneurs, and is an excellent insight into Vietnamese rural life.

✯✯ Festivals & Events

Tet   VIETNAMESE NEW YEAR
(Tet Nguyen Dan/Vietnamese Lunar New Year; late Jan or early Feb) During the week preceding Tet, there is a flower market on P Hang Luoc. There's also a colourful, two-week flower exhibition and competition, beginning on the first day of the new year, that takes place in Lenin Park near Bay Mau Lake. For more on Tet, see the boxed text on p451.

Quang Trung Festival   CULTURE
(Feb/Mar) Wrestling competitions, lion dances and human chess take place on the 15th day of the first lunar month at Dong Da Mound, site of the uprising against the Chinese led by Emperor Quang Trung (Nguyen Hué) in 1788.

CAMA Festival   MUSIC
(www.camavietnam.org; late May) Hanoi's Club for Art and Music Appreciation brings an eclectic bunch of performers to the city for an annual one-day music festival held in the grounds of the American Club (p57). Electronica, punky Japanese garage rock, and Polynesian hip hop – anything goes. It's also a good chance to see local bands and DJs.

Vietnam's National Day   FESTIVAL
(2 September) Celebrated with a rally and fireworks at Ba Dinh Sq, in front of Ho Chi Minh's Mausoleum. There are also boat races on Hoan Kiem Lake.

🛏 Sleeping

Much of Hanoi's cheap accommodation is in or around the Old Quarter. We receive numerous complaints about budget-hotel owners pressuring guests to book tours with them. Some travellers have even been turfed out into the street for not complying, while others have found mysterious taxes added to their bills. In addition, Old Quarter traffic is oppressive, particularly around Hang Be, Hang Bac and Ma May.

Emerging areas for good value accommodation include around St Joseph Cathedral, and on and around P Hang Dieu on the western edge of the Old Quarter.

Expect to pay US$20 to US$25 for a decent budget room. For around US$30 to US$45, rooms are loaded with gadgets and facilities including air-con, satellite TV, wi-

---

ⓘ HANOI FOR CHILDREN

Hanoi is a fun city for children thanks to the all-action Old Quarter and the city's many parks and lakes. Wandering the Old Quarter can be tiring for young ones, and you'll have to maintain a watchful eye for motorbikes, but there are enough diversions to keep them entertained, and plenty of ice-cream shops and fruit markets for those little treats along the way. If they like to cook their own food, book them in for a special Kid's Club session at the Hanoi Cooking Centre (p57).

Boating is a fun family activity and there is the choice of bigger boats on Tay Ho or pedal-powered boats in Lenin Park (Map p58). Hanoi Water Park (p55) is a great place to take children to cool off, but it is only open half the year. Come evening, there is only one place for any self-respecting child to be in Hanoi and that is at a water-puppet show (p74) – a Punch and Judy pantomime on water.

---

fi, a computer and minibar. There's been a mini-boom in efficiently run hostels, and dorm beds range from US$6 to US$9.

Contemporary boutique hotels are also emerging with tariffs around US$40 to US$80 a night. Above US$100, you're looking at luxury hotels with pools, fitness centres and restaurants.

Most budget and midrange hotels include free internet access, while top-end hotels levy a charge. Always check whether tax and service is included.

OLD QUARTER

TOP CHOICE ⟩ **Hanoi Elite**   BOUTIQUE HOTEL $$
(Map p48; ☎3828 1711; www.hanoielitehotel.com; 10/5032 Dao Duy Tu; r US$45-55; ❄@☎) It's surprising what you can find in the most narrow and hidden-away of lanes in the Old Quarter. Hanoi Elite features cool and classy décor, top-notch staff, and the kind of touches – rainforest shower-heads, breakfasts cooked to order and in-room computers – you'd expect only from more expensive accommodation.

Art Hotel   HOTEL $$
(Map p48; ☎3923 3868; www.hanoiarthotel.com; 65 P Hang Dieu; s/d from US$38/44; ❄@☎) The

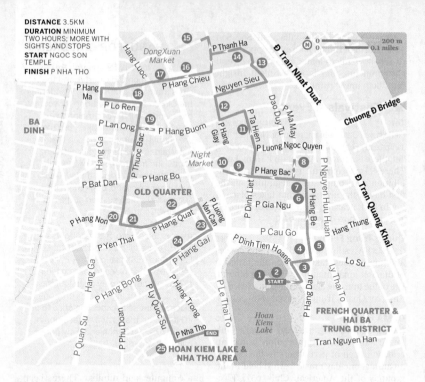

DISTANCE 3.5KM
DURATION MINIMUM TWO HOURS; MORE WITH SIGHTS AND STOPS
START NGOC SON TEMPLE
FINISH P NHA THO

Walking Tour
Old Quarter

❯ Start at the **1** **Ngoc Son Temple** on Hoan Kiem Lake. Return over the red **2** **Huc Bridge**, to the **3** **Martyrs' Monument**. Follow P Dinh Tien Hoang to the **4** **Water Puppet Theatre**. Head north on P Hang Dau to Hanoi's **5** **shoe shops**. Cross P Cau Go to P Hang Be, and the local **6** **market** on P Gia Ngu.

Back on P Hang Be, continue north to P Hang Bac. Look out for the artisans hand-carving intricate **7** **gravestones**. Next head up P Ma May to the beautifully restored **8** **Memorial House** at No 87.

Return to P Hang Bac, passing **9** **jewellery shops**, to **10** **house 102**, which includes a fully functioning temple. Retrace your steps slightly and head up narrow **11** **P Ta Hien**, popular for after-dark bars. Turn left on P Hang Buom to the **12** **Bach Ma Temple**, and continue to **13** **Cua O Quan Chuong**, the well-preserved Old East Gate.

Continue north on P Thanh Ha to a **14** **street market**. Veer left to **15** **Dong Xuan Market**.

Backtrack south on Nguyen Thien Thuat and turn right on to P Hang Chieu, past **16** **shops** selling straw mats and rope. This becomes **17** **P Hang Ma** where imitation 'ghost money' is sold for burning in Buddhist ceremonies. Follow your ears to the **18** **blacksmiths** near the corner of P Lo Ren and P Thuoc Bac. Adjoining P Thuoc Bac and P Lan Ong, the Thanh Binh store sells traditional rice wine. Continue along Lan Ong to the pungent fragrances of **19** **herb merchants**.

Double back to P Thuoc Bac and head south past the **20** **tin-box makers**, opposite the **21** **mirror shops** on P Hang Thiec. Continue left towards shops selling **22** **Buddhist altars and statues** along P Hang Quat.

Head south past P Luong Van Can's **23** **toy shops**, and continue along P Hang Gai for elegant **24** **silk shops**. Head south on P Ly Quoc Su to **25** **St Joseph Cathedral**, and the cafes on P Nha Tho.

young, friendly and very welcoming crew at the Art Hotel make this new opening really stand out. Rooms are spacious with spotless bathrooms and wooden floors, and within a 30-metre radius you'll find some of Hanoi's best opportunities for partaking in the city's great street food.

Tirant Hotel   HOTEL $$
(Map p48; ☑6269 8899; www.tiranthotel.com; 38 Gia Ngu; s/d from US$55/65; ✴@☎) Negotiate a good discount at this newly opened hotel and you'll be getting top-end digs for a mid-range price. Trendy decor, switched-on staff who speak excellent English and spacious bedrooms all conspire to make this one of Hanoi's best new hotels. The buffet breakfast is definitely worth lingering for and the huge Grand Suite (US$145) is undoubtedly the Old Quarter's best room.

Vega Hotel   HOTEL $$
(Map p48; ☑3923 3366; www.vegahotel.vn; 75 P Hang Dieu; US$50-55; ✴@☎) On the western edge of the Old Quarter, P Hang Dieu is emerging as a hub for great value midrange hotels. The Vega exemplifies what any new place in this part of town needs to offer; spacious bedrooms, balcony views and spotless modern bathrooms.

Hanoi Rendezvous Hotel   HOTEL $$
(Map p48; ☑3828 5777; www.hanoirendezvoushotel.com; 31 P Hang Dieu; dm/s/d/tr US$7.50/25/30/35; ✴@☎) Just one of the new Aussie-run accommodation options popping up in Hanoi. Deliciously close to several brilliant street food places, Hanoi Rendezvous features spacious rooms, friendly staff and well-run tours to Halong Bay, Cat Ba Island and Sapa. Don't miss the reproductions of classic Vietnam-themed movies in the downstairs breakfast bar.

Serenity Hotel   HOTEL $
(Map p48; ☑3923 3549; www.hanoiserenityhotel.com; 1B Cua Dong; s/d from US$18/20; ✴@☎) Spacious rooms, a friendly vibe at reception and a quieter location outside of Hanoi's backpacker hub all add up to one of the city's best budget sleeps. If you need more convincing, there's a terrific *bun cha* stall right on your doorstep. There's no lift, so be prepared to tackle up to six flights of stairs.

Hanoi Backpackers 2   HOSTEL $$
(Map p48; ☑3935 1890; www.hanoibackpackershostel.com; 9 Ma May; dm US$6-9, tw & d US$40; ✴@☎) It's same, same but different at this sprawling Hanoi Backpackers offshoot in the middle of Ma May's tourist throng. Room options range from spotless dorms to designer doubles, and there's a nicely social restaurant and bar downstairs. The relaxed Aussie-Kiwi team on reception books guests onto a range of well-run tours including to Halong Bay and Sapa.

Hanoi Guesthouse   GUESTHOUSE $
(Map p48; ☑3824 5732; www.hanoiguesthouse.com; 14 Bat Su; r $20-22; @☎) Tucked away on quiet Bat Su, the Hanoi Guesthouse is a bustling little spot with an eager young English-speaking crew on reception. A heritage Asian decor flows from reception through to the simple but spotless rooms. Hanoi's weekend night market is just a couple of blocks away.

Camel City Hotel   GUESTHOUSE $
(Map p48; ☑3935 2024; www.camelcityhotel.com; 8/50 Dao Duy Tu; s/d from US$20/25; ✴@☎) A family-owned operation in a quiet lane

---

DO THE HUSTLE

Hanoi is not only the political capital of Vietnam. It is also the capital of hotel hustles. Copycat and fly-by-night hotels abound. These will rent a building, appropriate the name of another hotel, and then work with touts to bring unwitting tourists to their 'chosen' accommodation. Visitors who question the alternative location are told the hotel has moved and it is not until they check the next day that they realise they have been had. These hotels overcharge on anything they can, often giving a price for the room on check-in and a price per person on check out. The best way to avoid this is to prebook a room by phone or email. This way, you know the hotel is still open, still in the same location and not full.

Airport taxis and minibuses often work in partnership with these copycat hotels, as they give the biggest commissions and there have even been reports of desperate Westerners working in tandem with these hotels, steering backpackers their way. For more on scams and how to avoid them, see p77 and the boxed text on p82.

just a short walk from the after dark attractions on P Ta Hien. Rooms are trimmed with Asian design touches and the service ethic is outstanding; yet more proof of good value budget sleeps in the heart of the Old Quarter.

Hanoi Gecko 3   HOSTEL $
(Map p48; ✆3923 3898; www.hanoigecko3hostel.com; 27 Bat Dan; dm US$6; ❄@🖳) Less social than Hanoi's larger hostels, the compact Hanoi Gecko 3 features simple bunk dorms, and is in a more local section of the Old Quarter. There's a pretty good restaurant downstairs and a 1st floor chill-out space with funky scatter cushions.

Classic Street Hotel   HOTEL $$
(Map p48; ✆3825 2421; www.classicstreet-phocohotel.com; 41 P Hang Be; r US$30-35; ❄🖳) This place on ever-busy Hang Be has cosy rooms with large beds and satellite TV. Plenty of paintings and ceramics brighten up the communal spaces and corridors.

Hanoi Boutique 2   HOTEL $$
(Map p48; ✆3929 0366; www.hanoiboutiquehotel.vn; 32 Dao Duy Tu; d US$40-50, f US$100; ❄@🖳) Smart mini-hotel with attentive staff, a bar and restaurant.

Rising Dragon Hotel   HOTEL $
(Map p48; ✆3926 3494; www.risingdragonhotel.com; 61 P Hang Be; s/d/tr from US$20/22/30; ❄@🖳) The attentive, helpful staff and spacious rooms make this place, though those at the rear only have a tiny (or no) window and there's no lift.

Thuy Nga Guesthouse   GUESTHOUSE $
(Map p48; ✆3826 6053; thuyngahotel@hotmail.com; 10D P Dinh Liet; r US$14; ❄@🖳) This homely little place is run by an accommodating family and has six rooms with natural light, a TV and fridge. Pop outside for lots of good bars.

Duc Thai Hotel   HOTEL $$
(Map p48; ✆3828 2897; www.ducthaihotel.com; 95B Hang Ga; r US$28-38; ❄🖳) Offering a convenient location near Hoan Kiem Lake, this recently renovated hotel has 15 well-appointed rooms with wi-fi and colonial features, including shuttered windows. It's run by a friendly, English-speaking team.

Sports Hotel   HOTEL $
(Map p48; ✆3926 0154; www.hanoisportshotel.com; 96 P Hang Bac; s/d/tr/q US$22/25/36/40; ❄@🖳) Located on busy Hang Bac, this

place has a long narrow lobby with several computer terminals and smart, well-presented (and equipped) rooms.

Thu Giang Guesthouse   GUESTHOUSE $
(Map p48; ✆3828 5734; www.thugianggh.com; 5A P Tam Thuong; dm US$5, r US$7-15; ❄@🖳) Hidden at the end of a narrow alley, this modest place is owned and run by a hospitable family who understand travellers' needs. There's a second branch for overspills at 35A P Hang Dieu.

Manh Dung Guesthouse   GUESTHOUSE $
(Map p48; ✆3826 7201; lethomhalong@yahoo.com; 2 P Tam Thuong; r US$12-18; ❄@🖳) Opposite the Thu Giang, this is a step up in quality and has a lift, though most rooms are on the small side.

AROUND HOAN KIEM LAKE

TOP CHOICE ▶ **6 on Sixteen**   BOUTIQUE HOTEL $$
(Map p52; ✆6673 6729; www.sixonsixteen.com; 16 Bao Kanh; r US$50-88; ❄@🖳) Decked out with designer textiles, ethnic art and interesting locally made furniture, 6 on Sixteen has a warm and welcoming ambience. There's just six concisely decorated rooms, but lots of shared areas to encourage guests to mingle and share travel tips. Breakfast includes freshly baked pastries and robust Italian coffee, and the hotel is aligned with Sapa Rooms and the Hmong Mountain Retreat in Sapa. Try to book a balcony room as those at the back have tiny windows.

Sofitel Metropole Hotel   HOTEL $$$
(Map p52; ✆3826 6919; www.sofitel.com; 15 P Ngo Quyen; r from US$210; ❄@🖳▨) A historic hotel and a supremely refined place to stay, the Metropole boasts an immaculately restored colonial facade, mahogany-panelled reception rooms and two well-regarded restaurants. Rooms in the old wing offer unmatched colonial style, while the modern Opera Wing has sumptuous levels of comfort but doesn't have quite the same heritage character. Even if you're not staying here, it's worth popping in for a drink at the Bamboo Bar.

Hotel L'Opera   HOTEL $$$
(Map p52; ✆6282 5555; www.mgallery.com; 29 P Trang Tien; r from US$150; ❄@🖳) Hanoi's newest luxury hotel – opened December 2010 – effortlessly combines French colonial style with a sophisticated design aesthetic. Rooms are trimmed in silk and Asian textiles, and splurge-worthy features include a

spa and the hip late-night vibe of the La Fée Verte (Green Fairy) bar. If you're wondering, it's a reference to absinthe, the infamous green alcoholic beverage.

Cinnamon Hotel
BOUTIQUE HOTEL **$$**

(Map p52; ☑3938 0430; www.cinnamonhotel .net; 26 P Au Trieu; r US$70-80; ☻❀@�) A hip hotel overlooking St Joseph Cathedral in the smartest enclave of the Old Quarter. The design is outstanding, combining the historic features of the building – wrought-iron and window shutters – with Japanese-influenced interiors and modern gadgetry. Of the six rooms, all with balcony and tropical names, 'Lime' has a commanding perspective of the cathedral. There's also a small bar-restaurant.

Golden Lotus Hotel
HOTEL **$$**

(Map p52; ☑3938 0901; www.goldenlotushotel .com.vn; 32 P Hang Trong; s/d from US$52/62; ❀@�) An elegant, polished lobby sets the tone at this atmospheric little hotel, which blends Eastern flavours and Western chic. All rooms have wooden floors, silk trim, art aplenty and broadband internet connections, though most rooms at the rear do not enjoy any natural light. Breakfast is included.

Madame Moon Guesthouse
GUESTHOUSE **$**

(Map p52; ☑3938 1255; www.madammoonguest house.com; 17 Hang Hanh; r US$22-25; ❀@�) Keeping it simple just one block from Hoan Kiem Lake, Madame Moon has surprisingly chic rooms and a (relatively) traffic-free location in a street filled with local cafes. If you're planning a bigger night out, pop around to Ngo Bao Khanh for a few good bars.

Hilton Hanoi Opera
HOTEL **$$$**

(off Map p52; ☑3933 0500; www.hanoi.hilton.com; 1 P Le Thanh Tong; r from US$160; ❀@�☀) Built in 1998, this impressive neoclassical edifice blends in well with its surroundings, especially the adjacent Opera House. Rooms are spacious and plush, and both business and leisure facilities – including a gym and a pool – are impressive.

Joseph's Hotel
HOTEL **$$**

(Map p52; ☑3939 1048; www.josephshotel.com; 5 P Au Trieu; r US$50-55; ❀@�) Tucked away in a quiet lane behind St Joseph Cathedral, this compact 10-room hotel features pastel tones, Mod-Asian decor and breakfasts cooked to order. Try to secure a room with

MAKE THAT COMPLAINT COUNT...

We get a lot of letters complaining about hotels, guesthouses, travel companies and more. It's great to give us feedback about all these things, as it helps to work out which businesses care about their customers and which don't. As well as telling us, make sure you tell the **Vietnam National Administration of Tourism** (Map p56; ☑3356 0789; www.hanoitourism.gov. vn; 3 Tran Phu); its Hanoi office is reasonably helpful and needs to know about the problems before it can do anything about them. Make a complaint here and in time it might well pressure the cowboys into cleaning up their acts.

views of the church's nearby towers. It's a laid-back location if the speed and scale of Hanoi's traffic doesn't appeal.

Hanoi Elegance Diamond Hotel
HOTEL **$$**

(Map p52; ☑3935 1632; www.hanoielegancehotel .com; 32 P Lo Su; s/d from US$55/65; ❀@�) With large rooms, each kitted out with a computer, wooden floors, modern furniture and cable TV, this is a solid choice. La Siesta Spa (p56) is on site and four other Elegance hotels are close by.

Church Hotel
BOUTIQUE HOTEL **$$**

(Map p52; ☑3928 8118; www.churchhotel.com .vn; 9 P Nha Tho; r US$50-88; ❀@�) Classy mini-hotel with real boutique appeal. Some rooms are smallish, but all have stylish furnishings and there's an elegant dining room for your complimentary breakfast. Location-wise this is as good as it gets, on Nha Tho's epicentre of Old Quarter chic.

Hanoi Backpackers Hostel
HOSTEL **$**

(Map p52; ☑3828 5372; www.hanoibackpackers hostel.com; 48 P Ngo Huyen; dm US$6, r US$25-36; ❀@�) An efficient, perennially popular hostel now occupying two buildings on a quiet lane. It's impressively organised, with custom-built bunk beds and lockers, and the dorms all have en-suite bathrooms. You'll also find a rooftop terrace for barbecues and a bar downstairs. A recent Hanoi Backpackers offshoot on P Ma May is even more impressive.

Central Backpackers Hanoi
HOSTEL **$**

(Map p52; ☑3938 1849; www.centralbackpackers hostel.com; 16 P Ly Quoc Su; dm US$5; @�)

Enjoying a prime spot on busy Ly Quoc Su, this well-run hostel is in close proximity to good cafes, street eats and the faded grandeur of St Joseph Cathedral. It's a pretty social spot, possibly due to the 'free beer' (very) happy hour every night from 8pm to 9pm.

Jasmine Hotel
HOTEL $$

(Map p52; ☎3926 4420; www.thejasminehotel.com; 57 Lo Su; s/d US$40/55; ✳@☎) Caution: must like carved dark wood. The Jasmine's decor is slightly ostentatious, but this hotel is handily near Hoan Kiem Lake and good restaurants. Standard rooms are a touch dark, and there's some road noise from the front rooms with balconies, but it's still good value for such a central location.

Especen Hotel
HOTEL $

(Map p52; ☎3824 4401; www.especen.vn; 28 P Tho Xuong & 41 P Ngo Huyen; s/d US$17/20; ✳@☎) Trying harder than most budget places, this hotel has two great locations near St Joseph Cathedral. The spacious and light rooms are well kept, and the location is almost tranquil (by Old Quarter standards anyway). The branches are a few doors apart and have near-identical facilities.

Hotel Thien Trang
GUESTHOUSE $

(Map p52; ☎3826 9823; thientranghotel24@hotmail.com; 24 P Nha Chung; r US$12-22; ✳@☎) This place enjoys a quiet location in the stylish Nha Tho area. Its spacious rooms retain a degree of period character alongside somewhat less pleasing modern additions.

Impressive Hotel
BOUTIQUE HOTEL $$

(Map p52; ☎3938 1590; www.impressivehotel.com; 54-56 P Au Trieu; s/d/tr from US$40/50/60; ✳@) Impressive in name and impressive in nature, with clean and cosy rooms and a top-notch location.

Heart Hotel
HOTEL $$

(Map p52; ☎3928 6682; www.heart-hotel.com; 11B P Hang Hanh; r US$40-50; ✳@) Popular little hotel with 10 neat rooms, some with lake views.

FRENCH QUARTER

Drift
HOSTEL $

(Map p58; ☎3944 8415; www.thedriftbackpackershostel.com; 42 Truong Han Sieu; dm US$6, r US$20-25; ✳@☎) You can always trust an Aussie-run hostel to know what travellers really need and want. In this case it's a social ambience, free breakfast and a dedicated movie room with a huge plasma screen. The attached cafe specialises in Western-style comfort food including fajitas, burgers and toasted sandwiches. The Old Quarter is a 20-minute walk away.

✖ Eating

Hanoi is an international city, and whatever your budget (or your tastes) it's available here. If you've just flown in, get stuck into the local cuisine, which is wonderfully tasty, fragrantly spiced and inexpensive. Don't miss the essential experience of dining on Hanoi's street food.

If you've been up in the hills of northern Vietnam subsisting on noodles and rice, the capital's cosmopolitan dining, including Japanese, French, Italian and Indian, will be a welcome change.

OLD QUARTER

TOP CHOICE Highway 4
VIETNAMESE $$

(Map p48; ☎3926 0639; www.highway4.com; 3 P Hang Tre & 25 Bat Su; meals 100,000-200,000d) Providing a memorable dining experience, this is the original location (inside a tottering old house) of an expanding family of restaurants that specialise in Vietnamese cuisine from the northern mountains. There's an astounding array of dishes from bite-sized snacks like superb *nem ca xa lo* (catfish spring rolls) through to meaty dishes like *lin luec mam tep* (pork fillet with shrimp sauce). Wash it all down with a bottle or two of delicious Son Tinh liquor made from sticky rice (p73). There is another, newer branch in the Old Quarter on Bat Su, and it owns the flash House of Son Tinh (p70) complex incorporating a restaurant and cocktail bar on the trendy Xuan Dieu strip near Tay Ho.

Cha Ca Thang Long
VIETNAMESE $$

(Map p48; 21 P Duong Thanh; cha ca fish 150,000d; ◷10am-3pm & 5-10pm) Bring along your DIY cooking skills here and grill your own succulent fish with a little shrimp paste and plenty of herbs. *Cha ca* is an iconic Hanoi dish, and while another nearby more famous *cha ca* eatery gets all the tour-bus traffic, the food here is equally good.

Quan Bia Minh
VIETNAMESE $

(Map p48; 7a Dien Liet; mains 80,000-120,000d) This *bia hoi* joint has evolved into an Old Quarter favourite with well-priced Vietnamese food and excellent service led by the eponymous Mrs Minh. Grab an outdoor table and a cold beer and watch the beautiful chaos unfold below.

TOP 10 STREET FOOD EXPERIENCES

Deciphering Hanoi's Old Quarter street food scene can be bewildering, but it's worth persevering and diving in. The city's best food definitely comes from the scores of vendors crowding the city's pavements with smoking charcoal burners, tiny blue plastic stools and expectant queues of canny locals. Many of the stalls have been operating for decades, and often they offer just one dish. After that long perfecting their recipes, it's little wonder the food can be sensational. Note that opening hours may be somewhat flexible.

Bun Cha Visiting Hanoi and not eating *bun cha* should be classed as a capital offence. Try the combination of grilled pork patties, crab spring rolls, vermicelli noodles and mountains of fresh herbs at **Bun Cha Nem Cua Be Dac Kim** (Map p48; 67 Duong Thanh; ⏰11am-3pm).

Banh Cuon (Map p48; 14 P Hang Ga; ⏰8am-4pm) Don't even bother ordering here; just squeeze onto a table, and a plate of gossamer-light *banh cuon* (steamed rice crepes filled with minced pork, mushrooms and ground shrimp) will be placed in front of you.

Pho Bo Service at the iconic **Pho Gia Truyen** (Map p48; 49 P Bat Dan; ⏰7-10am) can be a tad surly, but the hearty broth-laden combo of noodles and tender beef is truly a breakfast of champions. Get there when it opens at 7am and be prepared to queue.

Banh Ghoi (Map p52; 52 P Ly Quoc Su; ⏰10am-7pm) Nestled under a banyan tree near St Joseph Cathedral, this humble stall turns out *banh ghoi,* moreish deep-fried pastries crammed with pork, vermicelli, and mushrooms.

Bun Oc Saigon (Map p48; cnr P Nguyen Huu Huan & P Hang Thung; ⏰11am-11pm) Look closely in the plastic buckets and you'll see more than a few unfamiliar shellfish species. Try the *bun oc* (snail noodle soup) with a hearty dash of tart tamarind, or the steamed *so huyet xao toi* (blood cockles fried with garlic).

Bun Bo Nam Bo (Map p48; 67 P Hang Dieu; ⏰11am-10pm) *Bun bo nam bo* (dry noodles with beef) is a dish from southern Vietnam, but it's certainly travelled well this far north. Mix in bean sprouts, garlic, lemongrass and green mango for a zingy, filling treat.

Xoi Yen (Map p48; cnr P Nguyen Huu Huan & P Hang Mam; ⏰7am-11pm) Equally good for breakfast or as a hangover cure, Xoi Yen specialises in sticky rice topped with goodies, including sweet Asian sausage, gooey fried egg and slow-cooked pork.

Mien Xao Luon (Map p48; 87 P Hang Dieu; ⏰7am-2pm) OK, starting to feel more adventurous? Head to this humble stall trimmed with mini-mountains of crunchy fried eels for three different ways of eating the crisp little morsels. Try them stir-fried in vermicelli with egg, bean sprouts and fried shallots.

Bun Rieu Cua (Map p48; 40 P Hang Tre; ⏰7-9am) You'll need to get to this incredibly simple and incredibly popular spot early, as its sole dish of *bun rieu cua* (crab noodle soup) is only served for a couple of hours from 7am. Look forward to what is just maybe Hanoi's best breakfast, a hearty combo of noodles and broth made from tiny rice-paddy crabs. Laced with fried shallots and garlic, and topped with shrimp paste and chilli, it's a Hanoi classic.

Che (Map p48; 76 P Hang Dieu; ⏰7am-3pm) Always leave room for dessert, and in Hanoi that means leaving room for the many tasty variations of *che* (sweet mung beans). In winter try *che banh troi tau,* laced with sesame and ginger, or in summer the refreshing *che thap nam* with up to 10 colourful ingredients including coconut milk, crushed peanuts, lotus seeds and dried apples.

New Day VIETNAMESE **$**
(Map p48; 72 P Ma May; mains 30,000-60,000d) Despite being in the most touristy part of Hanoi, New Day continues to attract a mix of locals, expats and hungry travellers. The keen-as-mustard staff always find space for new diners, so look forward to sharing a table with some like-minded fans of Vietnamese food.

The Spot
INTERNATIONAL **$$**

(Map p48; 47 P Hang Be; mains 100,000-200,000d) Decorated with propaganda posters and with a soundtrack of great music, this er...Spot is good for a Western-style breakfast if you're fed up with *pho*. Healthy menu options include salads, grilled tuna, and a Greek-style salmon sandwich, and there's a good range of wines by the glass. Occasional DJs kick in later at night to energise the easygoing ambience.

Nola
CAFE **$**

(Map p48; 89 P Ma May; snacks 30,000-60,000d) Retro furniture is mixed and matched in this bohemian labyrinth tucked away from Ma May's tourist bustle. Pop in for coffee and cake, or return after dark for one of Hanoi's best little bars. Occasional exhibitions showcase local artists, and it's a good place to meet Hanoi's hip young things. Service can be a little slow, so just go with the flow.

Green Mango
MEDITERRANEAN **$$**

(Map p48; 3928 9917; www.greenmango.vn; 18 P Hang Quat; meals 180,000-250,000d) This hip restaurant-cum-lounge has a real vibe as well as great cooking. The stunning dining rooms, complete with rich silk drapes, evoke the feel of an opium den while the huge rear courtyard comes into its own on summer nights. Menu-wise there's everything from pizza and pasta to mod-Asian fusion creations. Pop in for a cocktail even if you're planning on dining somewhere else.

Green Tangerine
FUSION **$$**

(Map p48; 3825 1286; www.greentangerinehanoi.com; 48 P Hang Be; mains US$10-20; ☻) Experience the mood and flavour of 1950s Indochine at this elegant restaurant located in a beautifully restored colonial house with a cobbled courtyard. The fusion French-Vietnamese cuisine is not always entirely successful, but it's still worth popping in for coffee or a drink. Two-course lunches (198,000d) are good value.

Tamarind Cafe
VEGETARIAN **$$**

(Map p48; www.tamarind-cafe.com; 80 P Ma May; meals US$4-7; ☜☝) A relaxed cafe-restaurant with lounge-around cushioned seating and plenty of space. Offers an eclectic menu but is best for tabouli, eggplant claypot and salads. Drinks include heavenly lassis, zesty juices and wine by the glass.

AROUND HOAN KIEM LAKE

TOP CHOICE **Ly Club**
VIETNAMESE **$$$**

(Map p52; 3936 3069; www.lyclub.vn; 4 Le Phung Hieu; meals US$10-15) Set in an elegant French colonial mansion, this restaurant's impressive dining room is a great location for a gourmet meal. For Asian and Vietnamese flavours, try the soft-shell crab or sautéed clam with lemongrass and chilli. Standouts on the international menu include salmon baked in a banana leaf and chargrilled Australian Wagyu beef. When someone asks, 'So where did you go for your last night in Hanoi?', this is the correct answer.

Madame Hien
VIETNAMESE **$$$**

(Map p52; 3938 1588; www.verticale-hanoi.com; 15 P Chan Cam; mains US$10-15) Housed in a restored 19th-century villa, Madame Hien is a tribute to French chef Didier Corlu's Vietnamese grandmother. Look forward to more elegant versions of traditional Hanoi street food, with the '36 Streets' fixed menu (435,000d) a good place to kick off your culinary knowledge of the city. A good-value lunch (200,000d) is also available.

La
INTERNATIONAL **$$**

(Map p52; 3928 8933; 49 P Ly Quoc Su; mains US$13-18) An intimate, modest-looking and yet atmospheric bistro with a creative menu that includes roast pork loin with mango, coriander and garlic. Regular seasonal specials include Dalat strawberries, and La also offers wines by the glass.

Khazaana
INDIAN **$$**

(Map p52; www.khazaana.vn; 1C P Tong Dan, meals 100,000-270,000d) Very pukka, upmarket Indian restaurant with delicious cooking from the north and south of the subcontinent. There's plenty of vegetarian choice and the filling thalis offer great value.

La Salsa
MEDITERRANEAN **$$**

(Map p52; 3828 9052; www.lasalsa-hanoi.com; 25 P Nha Tho; meals 150,000-200,000d; ☻8am-11pm) Informal place on two floors that's good for tapas, or for something more substantial off the menu, which has both Spanish (try the paella) and French dishes (such as cassoulet).

Mediterraneo
ITALIAN **$$**

(Map p52; 3826 6288; www.mediterraneo-hanoi.com; 23 P Nha Tho; mains US$10-15) Popular, authentic little Italian restaurant that serves up great homemade pasta: try the gorgonzola ravioli or gnocchi, which go down perfectly with a crisp salad. The wood-fired pizzas are Hanoi's best and there's a cute upstairs terrace that looks out onto St Joseph

HANOI'S COFFEE CULTURE

Western-style cafes and coffee shops are becoming increasingly common in Vietnamese cities, but most of them pale in comparison to the traditional cafes dotted around central Hanoi. Here's where to go and what to order for an authentic local experience. Most cafes are open from around 7am to 7pm, but hours sometimes vary.

Café Duy Tri (off Map p56; 43a P Yen Phu) In the same location since 1936, this caffeine-infused labyrinth is a Hanoi classic. You'll feel like Gulliver as you negotiate the tiny ladders and stairways to reach the 3rd floor balcony. Order the delicious *caphe sua chua* (iced coffee with yoghurt), and you may have discovered your new favourite summertime drink. You'll find P Yen Phu a couple of blocks east of Truc Bach Lake.

Kinh Do Café (Map p56; 252 P Hang Bong) Fans of Catherine Deneuve will want to make a pilgrimage here, as this was the setting for her morning cuppa during the making of the film *Indochine*. It serves healthy yoghurt, plus tasty French pastries and feisty coffee. The toasted ham and cheese sandwiches are also very good.

Cafe Pho Co (Map p48; 11 P Hang Gai) One of Hanoi's best-kept secrets, this place has plum views over Hoan Kiem Lake. Enter through the silk shop, and continue through the antique-bedecked courtyard up to the top floor for the mother of all vistas. You'll need to order coffee and snacks before tackling the final winding staircase. For something deliciously different try the *caphe trung da*, coffee with a silkily smooth beaten egg white.

Cafe Lam (Map p48; 11 P Nguyen Huu Huan) Another classic cafe that's been around for yonks – long enough to build up a compact gallery of paintings left behind by talented patrons who couldn't afford to pay their tabs during the American War. These days, you're just as likely to spy Converse-wearing and Vespa-riding bright young things refuelling on wickedly strong *caphe den* (black coffee).

Cong Caphe (Map p58; 152 P Trieu Viet Vuong) As essential pilgrimage for coffee-fiends is P Trieu Viet Vuong, around 1km south of Hoan Kiem Lake. This street is lined with scores of cafes – some modern spots with iPad-toting teens and others more old school. Settle into the eclectic beats and kitsch Communist memorabilia at Cong Caphe with a *caphe sua da* (iced coffee with condensed milk).

Cathedral. We just wish the place wasn't quite so smoky.

Cart CAFE **$**
(Map p52; www.thecartfood.com; 18 P Au Trieu; baguettes 40,000d; ⊙7.30am-5pm; 🖋) Superlative pies, excellent juices and interesting baguette sandwiches feature at this little haven of Western comfort food tucked away near St Joseph Cathedral. Have a baguette crammed with roasted eggplant and coriander pesto, and a cleansing apple, carrot and ginger juice if you're recovering after a particularly social *bia hoi* session.

Apple Tart BAKERY **$**
(Map p52; 11 Ngo Bao Khanh; snacks 30,000-50,000d) Tiny hole-in-the-wall spot serving superlative eat-on-the-run French baked goods like *créme caramel* and apple *tartine*. Eat alfresco on the edge of nearby Hoan Kiem Lake, or pop next door and combine

your still-warm baked goodies with a robust espresso.

Hanoi House CAFE **$**
(Map p52; P 48A Ly Quoc Su; snacks 30,000-50,000d; 🖤) A chic and bohemian cafe with superb upstairs views of St Joseph Cathedral. Chill out in the lounge, which is decked out with rustic crafts from Sapa, or nab a spot on the impossibly slim balcony. Excellent juices and the best ginger tea in all of Hanoi.

Cine Café CAFE **$**
(Map p52; 22A P Hai Ba Trung; snacks US$2-4, drinks US$1-3) The Cinematheque's (p73) cafe-bar offers a quiet retreat from the fury of Hanoi's streets where you can enjoy a fresh juice, espresso or a snack in the courtyard. It's a bit difficult to find; from Hai Ba Trung walk down the lane beside the DVD shop for around 20m and then turn right.

La Place
CAFE $

(Map p52; 4 P Au Trieu; meals from 65,000d; 🛜) This stylish, popular little cafe adjacent to St Joseph Cathedral has walls covered in propaganda art and an East-West menu. Plenty of wine by the glass is on offer and the coffee has a real kick. Pop upstairs for great cathedral views and a cool collection of vintage propaganda posters.

Fanny Ice Cream
ICE CREAM $

(Map p52; 48 P Le Thai To; ice creams from 15,000d) The place for French-style ice creams and sorbets in Hanoi. During the right season try the *com*, a delightful local flavour extracted from young sticky rice; other innovative options include ginger and green tea.

Kem Dac Diet Trang Tien
ICE CREAM $

(Map p52; 35 P Trang Tien; ice creams from 5000d) It's barely possible to walk down the road to get to this parlour on hot summer nights, such is its popularity.

Fivimart
SELF CATERING

(Map p52; 27A P Ly Thai Tho) One of the best-stocked supermarkets in the centre of town.

Citimart
SELF-CATERING

(Map p52; Hanoi Towers, 49 Hai Ba Trung) Supermarket that has a good range of deli-style treats.

WEST OF THE OLD QUARTER

TOP CHOICE Quan An Ngon
VIETNAMESE $

(Map p56; 15 P Phan Boi Chau; dishes 35,000-80,000d; ⏱11am-11pm) Fancy that street-food experience, but afraid to take the plunge? Head to this incredibly busy, popular place that's crammed with locals and a smattering of expats. Mini-kitchens turn out terrific food, including specialities from all over the nation like squid with lemongrass and chilli or *chao tom* (grilled sugar cane rolled in spiced shrimp paste). Be prepared to wait for a table, or try to visit outside of the busy lunch and dinner periods.

TOP CHOICE La Badiane
INTERNATIONAL $$$

(Map p56; ☎3942 4509; www.labadiane.hanoi .sitew.com; 10 Nam Ngu; mains US$15) This stylish bistro is set in a restored whitewashed French villa arrayed around a breezy central courtyard. French cuisine underpins the menu – La Badiane translates to 'star anise' – but Asian and Mediterranean flavours also feature. Menu highlights include sea bass tagliatelle with smoked paprika, and prawn bisque with wasabi tomato bruschetta.

Three-course lunches for 255,000d are excellent value.

Southgate
FUSION $$

(Map p56; ☎3938 1979; www.southgatehanoi.com; 28 Tong Duy Tan; tapas 90,000-120,000d, mains 130,000-250,000d) Tempting fusion tapas – try the double-cooked pork belly – and superb desserts, including thyme, honey and yoghurt panna cotta, feature at this stylish restaurant and bar in a wonderfully restored colonial villa. Excellent cocktails hint at a hip vibe transplanted from New York or Sydney.

KOTO
CAFE $$

(Map p56; ☎3747 0338; www.koto.com.au; 59 P Van Mieu; meals 40,000-140,000d; ⏱closed dinner Mon; 😊🈺) Stunning four-storey modernist cafe-bar-restaurant overlooking the Temple of Literature, where the interior design has been taken very seriously, from the stylish seating to the fresh flowers by the till. Daily specials are chalked up on a blackboard and the short menu has everything from excellent Vietnamese food to yummy pita wraps and beer-battered fish 'n' chips. The bar also has a fine cocktail list. KOTO is an extraordinarily successful not-for-profit project that provides career training and guidance to disadvantaged kids.

San Ho Restaurant
SEAFOOD $$$

(Map p56; ☎3934 9184; 58 P Ly Thuong Kiet; meals around 300,000d) Set in an attractive French-era villa, San Ho is considered one of the best seafood restaurants in Hanoi. Crustaceans and molluscs come in every shape and size, bathed in delicious sauces. Most prices are by the kilogram.

Matchbox Winebar & Restaurant
MEDITERRANEAN $$

(Map p56; ☎3734 308; 40 Cao Ba Quat; mains 100,000-290,000d) Relocated to an elegant courtyard space beside the Fine Arts Museum, Matchbox delivers on its promise of well-priced food with a Mediterranean spin. Pop in for an informal plate of pasta and a glass of wine, or linger longer over dinner options including excellent steaks and Australian red wine.

Puku
CAFE $

(Map p56; 18 Tong Duy Tan; mains 60,000-110,000d; ⏱24hr; 😊🛜) A little slice of Kiwi cafe culture – Puku means 'stomach' in New Zealand's indigenous Maori language – with great burgers, Mexican wraps and all-day eggy

WORTH A TRIP

SPECIALITY FOOD STREETS

To combine eating with exploration, head to these locations crammed with interesting restaurants and food stalls.

» **Pho Cam Chi** This narrow lane (Map p56) is packed with local eateries turning out cheap, tasty food for a few dollars. Cam Chi translates as 'Forbidden to Point' and dates from centuries ago. It is said that the street was named as a reminder for the local residents to keep their curious fingers in their pockets when the king and his entourage went through the neighbourhood. Cam Chi is about 500m northeast of Hanoi train station. Adjoining Tong Duy Tan is an up-and-coming area for hip cafes and restaurants.

» **Đuong Thuy Khue** On the southern bank of Tay Ho, Đuong Thuy Khue (Map p56) features dozens of outdoor seafood restaurants with a lakeside setting. The level of competition is evident by the daredevil touts who literally throw themselves in front of oncoming traffic to steer people towards their tables. You can eat well here for about 150,000d per person.

» **Truc Bach** A quieter waterfront scene is around the northeast edge of Truc Bach Lake (off Map p56). Many *lau* (hotpot) restaurants are huddled together in an almost continuous strip for a few hundred metres. Grab a few friends and settle in at one of the dinky lakeside tables for a DIY session of fresh seafood, chicken or beef. Make a beeline for the busiest spots. It's perfect on a cool Hanoi night.

» **Pho Nghi Tam** About 10km north of central Hanoi, P Nghi Tam has a 1km-long stretch of about 60 dog-meat restaurants: keep an eye out for the words *thit cho*. Hanoians believe that eating dog meat in the first half of the month brings bad luck, so the restaurants are deserted. If you happen to drive past on the last day of the lunar month however, you'll see them packed with locals.

breakfasts. The coffee is terrific and it's a five-minute walk from the Hanoi railway station, ideal for a restorative brunch after the overnight train back from Sapa. Puku is also open 24 hours if you come down with the late-night/early-morning munchies.

Foodshop 45   INDIAN $
(off Map p56; ☎3716 2959; 59 Truc Bach; mains 70,000-100,000d) Hanoi's best Indian flavours feature at this cosy lakeside spot sandwiched between the *lau* (hotpot) restaurants on Truc Bach Lake. The ambience is more authentic at the rustic downstairs tables, and menu standouts include a superb *kadhai* chicken that will definitely have you ordering a second beer.

Net Hue   VIETNAMESE $
(Map p56; cnr P Hang Bong & P Cam Chi; mains 30,000-60,000d) Spread across three floors, this compact spot provides exceptional versions of food from the central Vietnamese city of Hue. Run by a friendly family, it's exceedingly well priced for such comfortable surroundings. Head to the top floor for the nicest ambience and enjoy Hue dishes including *bun bo Hue* (Hue-style noodles),

and *banh nam* (steamed rice pancake with minced shrimp).

Café Smile   CAFE $
(Map p56; 5 P Van Mieu; meals 70,000-120,000d; @) This relaxed cafe-restaurant is renowned for its cakes and pastries, but also serves delicious Vietnamese (try the *pho*) and Western dishes.

FRENCH QUARTER

Nha Hang Ngon   VIETNAMESE $$
(Map p58; 26A Tran Hung Dao; mains 80,000-130,000d; ⊙11am-11pm) If you find the food-court ambience of Quan An Ngon a little frenetic, consider detouring to this sister establishment. There's the same focus on authentic street food flavours from around Vietnam, but the courtyard ambience in a restored French villa is more romantic.

Izakaya Yancha   JAPANESE $$
(Map p58; ☎3974 8437; 121 Trieu Viet Vuong; meals 100,000-200,000d) Surrounded by local cafes on 'Coffee St', Izakaya Yancha serves *izakaya* – think Japanese tapas – in a buzzy and friendly atmosphere. Secure a spot near the open kitchen and work your way through lots of Osaka-style goodies

WORTH A TRIP

TAY HO – HANOI'S EMERGING HOTSPOT

Around 6km northwest of the Old Quarter, the Tay Ho (West Lake) area makes a fine alternative base out of the motorcycle-fuelled hubbub of central Hanoi. There are a few excellent accommodation options, and because it's a popular neighbourhood with expats, it's also an emerging area for restaurants, bars and nightlife. A taxi from the Old Quarter should be around 80,000-90,000d. Count on 30,000-40,000d for the hang-on-tight, after-dark thrills of a *xe om*.

Daluva Home
APARTMENT $$$

(☑3718 5831; www.daluva.com; 33 To Ngoc Van, Tay Ho; apt US$94; ✆❄❔) In a quiet residential neighbourhood above a tapas and cocktail bar (p71), Daluva Home features a spacious one-bedroom apartment trimmed in chic, designer decor. A king-sized bed, self-contained kitchen and super-comfortable lounge make it the kind of place you'd love to live in if you moved to Hanoi. It also makes perfect sense for a cosy holiday stay for couples. You can even stroll to a nearby farmers market every Sunday morning.

InterContinental Westlake Hanoi
LUXURY HOTEL $$$

(☑6270 8888; www.intercontinental.com/hanoi; 1A Nghi Tam, Tay Ho; d from US$120; ❄@❔❔) The most luxurious address in the north of the city, this hotel features a contemporary Asian-design theme, and the whole complex juts out into the lake. Many of the stunning rooms (all with balconies) are set on stilts above the water. The hotel's signature Sunset Bar celebrates some of the city's best cocktails (from 190,000d) and, sitting on its own man-made island, it's quite probably the most romantic spot in town. It's certainly expensive for Hanoi, but more classy and intimate than *bia hoi* junction.

House of Son Tinh
VIETNAMESE $$

(☑3715 0577; www.highway4.com; 31 P Xuan Dieu, Tay Ho; meals 100,000-200,000d) This showcase for the Highway 4 empire (p64) features the Son Tinh Lounge Bar, an intimate, downstairs cocktail bar specialising in delicious concoctions made from Son Tinh liquor (p73). Upstairs is the elegant Highway 4 restaurant with Vietnamese food inspired by the rustic flavours of the country's north.

including excellent tuna sashimi and chicken, and miso with udon noodles.

Wild Lotus
VIETNAMESE $$$

(Map p58; ☑3943 9342; www.wildlotus.com.vn; 55A P Nguyen Du; mains 180,000-250,000d) This seriously upmarket restaurant in a converted colonial mansion has a stately dining room full of dramatic artwork. The menu includes three spice journeys: set menus that guide you through the highlights of the Vietnamese table.

Chay Nang Tam
VEGETARIAN $$

(Map p58; 79A P Tran Hung Dao; meals from 80,000d; ⊘11am-11pm; ❔) Dishes of vegetables that look like meat, reflecting an ancient Buddhist tradition designed to make carnivore guests feel at home.

GREATER HANOI

Quan Hai San Ngon
SEAFOOD $$

(☑3719 3169; 198 Nghi Tam, Tay Ho; mains 150,000-200,000d) Just maybe Hanoi's most atmospheric dining space – arrayed elegantly around giant alfresco reflecting pools – Quan Hai San Ngon showcases excellent Vietnamese seafood. It's in the Tay Ho area, a 10-minute taxi ride north from central Hanoi, but dishes like sea bass with mango and chilli, and briny Halong Bay oysters topped with wasabi make the short hop worthwhile.

Oasis
SELF-CATERING

(24 P Xuan Dieu) Italian-owned deli with excellent bread, cheese and salami as well as homemade pasta and sauces. It's north of central Hanoi in the Tay Ho restaurant strip on P Xuan Dieu.

Don's A Chef's Bistro
INTERNATIONAL $$$

(☑3718 5988; www.donviet.vn; Lane 16, 27 P Xuan Dieu; mains US$14-25, pizza US$10-22; ⊘8.30am-midnight Mon-Fri, from 7.30am Sat & Sun) This multilevel lakeside spot is definitely worth the journey north to Tay Ho. It's really three restaurants in one with an innovative bistro (try the sashimi or crab cakes), an oyster bar, and excellent wood-fired pizzas. Check the website for what's happening with the live music schedule. From Xuan Dieu, turn left along the lake's edge and look for the 'Oyster Bar' neon sign. Don's is also a good spot to hire bicycles to negotiate the 13km-long lakeside pathway around Tay Ho. You could combine it with one of Don's legendary weekend brunches (11am to 5pm).

Daluva TAPAS $$
(☑3718 5831; www.daluva.com; 33 To Ngoc Van, Tay Ho; tapas 70,000-140,000d; mains 160,000-320,000d; ⊘8am-late) Tapas, gourmet burgers and pizzas all feature at this chic Tay Ho cocktail bar with cool beats and a great wine list. Try the bacon-wrapped prawns or the fried calamari with aioli, or come back for a lazy Sunday brunch of eggs Benedict with salmon.

Kitchen CAFE $$
(7A/40 P Xuan Dieu, Tay Ho; snacks & meals 80,000-130,000d; ⊘8am-9pm; ☏) This terrace cafe in Tay Ho ticks all the right boxes with a mellow buzz and a creative, healthy menu of delicious sandwiches and salads sourced from 'virtually' organic ingredients. Also great for breakfast, a juice (try the ginger and watermelon tonic), or just a quick espresso.

🍷 Drinking

Hanoi has a lively drinking scene, with an eclectic selection of places: grungy dive bars, a Western-style pub or two, sleek lounge bars, cafes and hundreds of *bia hoi* joints.

However, as the no-fun police supervise a strict curfew, and regularly show up to enforce the closure of places that flout this law, there's minimal action after midnight. Lock-in action after midnight does occur here and there though; ask around in Hanoi's hostels to find out which bars are currently staying open beyond the witching hour.

The best places for a bar crawl include P Ta Hien with its strip of traveller-friendly places, and Ngo Bao Khanh near the northwest edge of Hoan Kiem Lake. An alternative scene, popular with expats, is in the Tay Ho Lake area on P Xuan Dieu.

Le Pub PUB
(Map p48; 25 P Hang Be; ⊘7am-late) Sociable and enjoyable, Le Pub is a great place to hook up with others, as there's always a good mix of travellers and foreign residents here. There's a cosy, tavern-like interior (with big screens for sports fans), a street-facing terrace and a rear courtyard. Bar snacks are

---

DON'T MISS

BIA AHOY!

'Tram phan tram!' Remember these words, as all over Vietnam, glasses of *bia hoi* are raised and emptied, and cries of *tram phan tram* ('100%' or 'bottoms up') echo around the table.

Bia hoi (beer) is Vietnam's very own draught beer or microbrew. This refreshing, light-bodied pilsener was first introduced to Vietnam by the Czechs in a display of Communist solidarity. Brewed without preservatives, it is meant to be enjoyed immediately, and costs as little as 4000d a glass

Hanoi is the *bia hoi* capital of Vietnam and there are microbars on many Old Quarter street corners. A wildly popular place is **'bia hoi junction'** (Map p48) in the heart of the Old Quarter where P Ta Hien meets P Luong Ngoc Quyen. It's now packed with backpackers and travellers though, and has really lost most of its local charm. Did you really come all this way to drink Heineken and talk to boozed neighbours from Jersey City or Johnsonville?

An alternative, more local *bia hoi* junction is where P Nha Hoa meets P Duong Thanh on the western edge of the Old Quarter. For something to go with the beer, **Bia Hoi Ha Noi** (Map p48; 2 P Duong Thanh) also does the best spare ribs in town. You'll also have a great night at **Bia Hoi Hang Tre** at 22 P Hang Tre (Map p48) on the corner of P Hang Tre and P Hang Thung. Order the roast duck (*vit quay*). One of the most popular local lunch spots in town, **Nha Hang Lan Chin** (Map p52; 2 P Trang Tien) is also a great spot for *bia hoi*.

For another hoppy spin on the Cold War Czechoslovakia–Vietnam camaraderie that led to the development of *bia hoi*, visit **Gambrinus** (Map p52; 198 P Tran Quang Khai), a sprawling Prague-style brewhouse with shiny vats of freshly brewed Czech pilsener. The food – both Czech and Vietnamese – is pretty good and it's very popular with locals.

served, the service is slick and the music usually includes tunes you can sing along to. There's another more spacious **branch** (9 P Xuan Dieu) in the Tay Ho (West Lake) area.

Cheeky Quarter
BAR

(Map p48; 1 P Ta Hien) Quirky and sociable bar that comes complete with patterned wallpaper and intriguing framed portraits (that look vaguely like they're depicting some eccentric titled family). Table footy (foosball) is taken very seriously here and the tunes are contemporary: drum 'n' bass or house music. It's at the top end of the Ta Hien strip.

TOP CHOICE Quan Ly
BAR

(Map p58; 82 Le Van Huu) You're not at *bia hoi* corner now. Owner Pham Xuan Ly has lived on this block since 1950, and now runs one of Hanoi's most traditional *ruou* (Vietnamese liquor) bars. Kick off with the ginseng one, and work your way up to the snake or gecko variations. An English-language menu makes it easy to choose, and there's also cheap-as-chips *bia hoi* and good Vietnamese food on offer. Quan Ly is a classic slice of old Hanoi and yes, that is the owner meeting Ho Chi Minh in the photograph on the wall. If you're keen to take some *ruou* back to your drinking buddies at home, visit **Thanh Binh** (Map p48; 62 P Lan Ong). This rice-wine store has bottles marinated with all kinds of exotica.

21N Club
BAR

(49 Lang Yen Phu, Tay Ho) Here's something really different for Hanoi. A Tay Ho lakeside location spills out onto waterfront seating, there's regular live music and the added attraction of their own 'Sailor' microbrewed beer. Beer and cocktails are exceptionally well priced, and pretty good burgers and fries taste even better as the night goes on. Check the bar's listing on www.newhanoian.xemzi.com to see what events are planned.

Mao's Red Lounge
BAR

(Map p48; 5 P Ta Hien) Probably the most popular bar on Ta Hien, this place is crammed with a sociable crowd on weekend nights. It's a classic dive bar with dim lighting and air thick with tobacco smoke. Drinks are well priced and the music's usually good. If you don't like what's playing, just ask if you can hook your own iPod up to the sound system.

Funky Buddha
BAR

(Map p48; 2 P Ta Hien) Crowd around the L-shaped bar and enjoy some of Hanoi's better cocktails. Once the techno and house beats kick in, it's more of a nightclub than a bar. Cheap drinks make it a favourite for travellers from nearby backpacker hostels.

Factory
BAR

(Map p52; www.factory.org.vn; 11a P Bao Khanh) Raising the bar along slightly grungy P Bao Khanh, Factory combines a spacious roof terrace with a dramatic interior featuring interesting socialist paintings. Keep exploring the multiple floors and you'll also uncover funky artwork by local artist Le Quang Ha and a sheesha (water pipe) lounge. The bar is incredibly well stocked, good value Vietnamese snacks are available and there's usually a regular program of music and arts events. Check the website for listings.

Legends Beer
BREWERY

(Map p48; 109 P Nguyen Tuan; ☺11am-late) Yes, it's extremely touristy, but as every micro-brewed beer comes with fine balcony views of Hoan Kiem Lake it's still worth dropping by for a cold one. Bring your camera to capture essential video views of the incessant ebb and flow of Hanoi traffic around one of the city's busiest roundabouts.

Temple Bar
BAR

(Map p48; 8 P Hang Buom) Formerly called Egypt and celebrating a vaguely Middle Eastern theme, this vaguely-Irish themed place now channels punters through a narrow bar to a spacious dance floor. Regular DJs definitely make it more about drum 'n' bass than downing pints of Guinness. Expect a raucous and sweaty mix of Vietnamese locals and backpackers.

Green Mango
BAR

(Map p48; 18 P Hang Quat) This hotel-restaurant also has a great lounge bar, with stylish seating, a tempting cocktail list and plenty of beautiful people enjoying the relaxed vibe. It's an essential haven from the Old Quarter mayhem just outside.

Roots
BAR

(Map p48; 2 P Luong Ngoc Quyen) Primarily a reggae bar, this is the place for some serious bassline pressure, although other musical genres like salsa and Afrobeat are also played. It can be a riot on the right night with plenty of dance-floor skanking, and post-midnight lock-ins have been known.

Angelina
BAR

(Map p52; Sofitel Metropole Hotel, 15 P Ngo Quyen; ☺noon-2am) Flash hotel bar with glitzy decor and a late licence. DJs spin funky house and chill-out tunes here on weekend nights. Also in the Sofitel Metropole is the poolside **Bamboo Bar**, dripping in chic, heritage cool.

Dragonfly
BAR

(Map p48; 15 P Hang Buom) Bar-club with a handy Old Quarter location, it draws a (very) young crowd and the music is pretty mainstream.

Rooftop Bar
BAR

(Map p56; 19th fl, Pacific Place, 83B Ly Thuong Kiet) The place to come for 19th-floor views of the city – pop in for a beer and enjoy the vista.

Tet
BAR

(Map p48; 2A P Ta Hien) This compact bar has dim lighting and a great little mezzanine table for an intimate drink. It's at its best very late, when the music is turned up and it morphs into one of Hanoi's smallest clubs.

GC Pub
PUB

(Map p52; 7 P Bao Khanh) Looks pretty run down from the street but it gets very lively on weekend nights. Popular with gay Hanoians and has pool tables.

☆ Entertainment

Cinemas

Centre Culturel Français de Hanoi
CINEMA

(Map p52; www.ifhanoi-lespace.com, in French; 24 P Trang Tien) Set in the sublime L'Espace building near the Opera House, it offers a regular program of French flicks. Musical events are also staged on a regular basis; check the website for what's on.

Cinematheque
CINEMA

(Map p52; 22A Hai Ba Trung) A hub for arthouse film lovers, this is a Hanoi institution. There's a great little cafe-bar (p67) here too. It's nominally 'Members Only', but a 50,000d one-off membership usually secures visitors an always-interesting themed double bill.

Megastar Cineplex
CINEMA

(Map p58; www.megastar.vn; 6th fl, Vincom Tower, 191 Ba Trieu) Multiplex cinema with quality screen and audio and comfy seats. Here's your chance to see blockbuster movies a few days before they're on sale as cheap DVDs in the Old Quarter.

Nightclubs

Hanoi is definitely not a clubbers' paradise, and the often-enforced midnight curfew means dancing is pretty much confined to bar-clubs (p71) in and around the Old Quarter, and a couple of other options.

Face Club
NIGHTCLUB

(Map p52; 6 P Hang Bai) Formerly know as Loop, the narrow-as-anything Face Club dishes up lots of lasers, music from hip hop

---

LOCAL KNOWLEDGE

MARKUS MADEJA – SON TINH LIQUOR

Most *ruou* (Vietnamese rice liquor) made in rural areas has impurities and gives you a bad hangover. Our **Son Tinh** (www.sontinh.com) product is produced from quality sticky rice, processed with traditional ingredients and methods, and then left to mature for three to five years.

Recommended Food Matches

Try the **Tao Meo** (rose apple) flavour with smoked or charcoal grilled meat. Tao Meo comes from an increasingly rare fruit growing wild in Vietnam's northern mountains. If you like fish and seafood, try **Bach Sam** (white ginseng) *ruou*. It's got an earthy and slightly sweet taste, and is really good with the catfish spring rolls at **Highway 4** (p64). For chicken, the **Minh Mang** flavour is a good match. It's made from 19 different herbal ingredients and named after the 19th-century emperor Minh Mang who apparently fathered more than 140 children.

Taking Ruou into the Future

Our next project is to produce fruit schnapps from local Vietnamese fruit. Despite the abundance of tropical and sub-tropical fruits, there's no product like this in Vietnam. We're also using Vietnamese liquor in cocktails at the **Son Tinh Lounge Bar** (p70).

Going Local

Quan Ly (p72) is a great local spot that's also good for trying traditional Vietnamese liquor.

ℹ️ GAY & LESBIAN HANOI

There are very few gay venues in Hanoi, but plenty of places that are gay-friendly. However official attitudes are still fairly conservative and Hanoi is home to these official attitudes. Police raids in the name of 'social reform' aren't unknown and that tends to ensure the gay and lesbian community keeps a low profile.

The **GC Pub** is one of the more-established gay bars in Hanoi, and it's a good place to find out about the most happening new places in town. Accommodation-wise, the teams at the **Art Hotel** (p59) and **Daluva Home** (p70) are also gay-friendly.

The website www.utopia-asia.com has up-to-date information about gay Hanoi. See also the Vietnam information section on www.cambodiaout.com. See p77 for possible scams in the area around Hoan Kiem Lake.

to techno, and a booming sound system. Its popularity with well-off Hanoians – look for the BMWs and Audis outside – means it can be pretty kitsch.

Tunnel   NIGHTCLUB
(Map p52; 11b P Bao Khanh) Regular happy-hour promotions, DJ nights and parties make this a popular, if overly cosy, multi-floor spot on buzzy P Bao Khanh. There's a pretty good chance it will be open after midnight on Friday and Saturday nights.

Music

Traditional music is usually performed daily at the Temple of Literature (p49). Upmarket Vietnamese restaurants in central Hanoi are also good places to catch traditional Vietnamese music. Try **Cay Cau** (Map p58; 17A P Tran Hung Dao; ☺7.30-9.30pm) in the De Syloia Hotel.

Hanoi Opera House   OPERA
(Map p52; 1 P Trang Tien) This wonderfully elaborate French colonial 900-seat venue was built in 1911. On 16 August 1945 the Viet Minh–run Citizens' Committee announced that it had taken over the city from a balcony on this building. Performances of classical music and opera are periodically held here in the evenings. Most weekends you'll see Hanoi wedding couples getting photographed on the elegant front steps. Check

the website www.ticketvn.com for forthcoming performances.

Vietnam National Tuong Theatre   OPERA
(Map p48; www.vietnamtuongtheatre.com; 51 P Duong Thanh; admission 100,000d; ☺6.30pm Thu-Sun) *Hat tuong* is a uniquely Vietnamese variation of Chinese opera that enjoyed its greatest popularity under the Nguyen dynasty in the 19th century. Until 2007, performances at this theatre – originally a colonial French cinema – were by invitation only. Now performances are open to both locals and visitors, and a night watching *hat tuong* is an interesting traditional alternative to Hanoi's wildly popular water puppets. Expect highly-stylised acting, wonderfully elaborate costumes and comedy and tragedy with characters from Vietnamese folklore.

Hanoi Rock City   LIVE MUSIC
(www.hanoirockcity.com; 27/52 To Ngoc Van, Tay Ho) Hanoi finally has a great venue for live music, hip hop, and more innovative DJs. Hanoi Rock City is tucked away down a residential lane about 7km north of the city near Tay Ho, but it's a journey well worth taking for an eclectic mix including reggae, Hanoi punk and regular electronica nights. A few international acts also occasionally swing by, so check the website or www.newhanoian .xemzi.com for listings.

Jazz Club By Quyen Van Minh   LIVE MUSIC
(Map p56; www.minhjazzvietnam.com; 65 Quan Su; ☺performances 9-11.30pm) This atmospheric venue is the place in Hanoi to catch some live jazz. There's a full bar, food menu, and high-quality gigs featuring father-and-son team Minh and Dac, plus other local and international jazz acts. Check the website for listings.

Water Puppets

This fascinating art form (see the boxed text) originated in northern Vietnam, and Hanoi is the best place to catch a show. Performances are held at the **Municipal Water Puppet Theatre** (Map p48; 57B P Dinh Tien Hoang; admission 60,000-100,000d, camera fee 15,000d, video fee 60,000d; ☺performances 2.15pm, 3.30pm, 5pm, 6.30pm, 8pm & 9.15pm). Multilingual programs allow the audience to read up on each vignette as it's performed. Try to book well ahead.

🔒 Shopping

The area around St Joseph Cathedral has good-quality furnishing stores and clothing boutiques. Both P Nha Tho and P Au Trieu are filled with interesting shops, and there are also several good cafes in the neighbourhood. For Vietnamese handicrafts, including textiles and lacquerware, head to the stores along P Hang Gai, P To Tich, P Hang Khai and P Cau Go.

For upmarket art galleries stroll along P Trang Tien, between Hoan Kiem Lake and the Opera House. It's also worth dropping by the Fine Arts Museum (p53) which has a couple of interesting galleries.

P Hang Gai and its continuation, P Hang Bong, are good places to look for embroidered tablecloths, T-shirts and wall hangings. P Hang Gai is also a fine place to buy silk and have clothes custom-made.

Bookworm BOOKSTORE
(Map p56; www.bookwormhanoi.com; 44 Chau Long) Stocks over 10,000 new and used English-language books. There's plenty of fiction and it's good on South Asian history and politics.

Thang Long BOOKSTORE
(Map p52; 53-55 P Trang Tien) One of the biggest bookshops in town with English and French titles, international newspapers and magazines, and a good selection of titles on the history of Hanoi.

Dome FURNISHINGS
(Map p56; www.dome.com.vn; 71 P Yen The Trong) An elegant emporium with stylish furniture, gorgeous curtains and cushions made from

DON'T MISS

PUNCH & JUDY IN A POOL

The ancient art of water puppetry (roi nuoc) was virtually unknown outside of northern Vietnam until the 1960s. It originated with rice farmers who worked the flooded fields of the Red River Delta. Some say they saw the potential of the water as a dynamic stage, others say they adapted conventional puppetry during a massive flood. Whatever the real story, the art form is at least 1000 years old.

The farmers carved the puppets from water-resistant fig-tree timber (sung) in forms modelled on the villagers themselves, on animals from their daily lives and on fanciful mythical creatures such as the dragon, phoenix and unicorn. Performances were usually staged in ponds, lakes or flooded paddy fields.

Contemporary performances use a square tank of waist-deep water for the 'stage'; the water is murky to conceal the mechanisms that operate the puppets. The wooden puppets, up to 50cm long and weighing as much as 15kg, are decorated with glossy vegetable-based paints. Each lasts only about three to four months if used continually, so puppet production provides several villages outside Hanoi with a full-time livelihood.

Eleven puppeteers, each trained for a minimum of three years, are involved in the performance. The puppeteers stand in the water behind a bamboo screen and have traditionally suffered from a host of water-borne diseases – these days they wear waders to avoid this nasty occupational hazard.

Some puppets are simply attached to a long pole, while others are set on a floating base, in turn attached to a pole. Most have articulated limbs and heads, some also have rudders to help guide them. In the darkened auditorium, it looks as if they are literally walking on water.

The considerable skills required to operate the puppets were traditionally kept secret and passed only from father to son; never to daughters through fear that they would marry outside the village and take the secrets with them.

The music, which is provided by a band, is as important as the action on stage. The band includes wooden flutes (sao), gongs (cong), cylindrical drums (trong com), bamboo xylophones and the fascinating single-stringed zither (dan bau).

The performance consists of a number of vignettes depicting pastoral scenes and legends. One memorable scene tells of the battle between a fisherman and his prey, which is so electric it appears as if a live fish is being used. There are also fire-breathing dragons (complete with fireworks) and a flute-playing boy riding a buffalo.

The performance is a lot of fun. The water puppets are both amusing and graceful, and the water greatly enhances the drama by allowing the puppets to appear and disappear as if by magic. Spectators in the front-row seats can expect a bit of a splash.

Vietnamese fabrics. Also has very high quality basketry, lacquerware and gifts.

Khai Silk   CLOTHING
(Map p48; 96 P Hang Gai) Upmarket, nationwide store offering stylish, fashionable silk clothing, as well as more classical creations.

Hadong Silk   CLOTHING
(Map p48; 102 P Hang Gai) One of the biggest silk shops on (appropriately enough) 'silk street', with a terrific choice of designs.

Things of Substance   CLOTHING
(Map p52; 5 P Nha Tho) Tailored fashions and some off-the-rack items at moderate prices. The staff are professional and speak decent English.

Three Trees   ACCESSORIES
(Map p52; 15 P Nha Tho) Stunning, very unusual designer jewellery, including many delicate necklaces, which make special gifts.

Mai Gallery   ARTWORK
(Map p56; www.maigallery-vietnam.com; 183 P Hang Bong) Run by resident artist Mai, this is a good place to learn more about Vietnamese art before making a purchase.

Viet Art Centre   ARTWORK
(Map p56; www.vietartcentre.vn; 42 P Yet Kieu) A fine place to browse contemporary Vietnamese art including paintings, photography and sculpture.

OLD QUARTER STREET NAMES

STREET NAME	DESCRIPTION	STREET NAME	DESCRIPTION
Bat Dan	wooden bowls	Hang Giay	paper or shoes
Bat Su	china bowls	Hang Hanh	onions
Cha Ca	roasted fish	Hang Hom	cases
Chan Cam	string instruments	Hang Huong	incense
Cho Gao	rice market	Hang Khay	trays
Gia Ngu	fishermen	Hang Khoai	sweet potatoes
Hai Tuong	sandals	Hang Luoc	combs
Hang Bac	silversmiths	Hang Ma	votive papers
Hang Be	rafts	Hang Mam	pickled fish
Hang Bo	baskets	Hang Manh	bamboo screens
Hang Bong	cotton	Hang Muoi	salt
Hang Buom	sails	Hang Ngang	transversal street
Hang But	brushes	Hang Non	hats
Hang Ca	fish	Hang Phen	alum
Hang Can	scales	Hang Quat	fans
Hang Chai	bottles	Hang Ruoi	clam worms
Hang Chi	threads	Hang Than	charcoal
Hang Chieu	mats	Hang Thiec	tin
Hang Chinh	jars	Hang Thung	barrels
Hang Cot	bamboo lattices	Hang Tre	bamboo
Hang Da	leather	Hang Trong	drums
Hang Dao	(silk) dyers	Hang Vai	cloth
Hang Dau	beans or oils	Lo Ren	blacksmiths
Hang Dieu	pipes	Lo Su	coffins
Hang Dong	copper	Ma May	rattan
Hang Duong	sugar	Ngo Gach	bricks
Hang Ga	chicken	Thuoc Bac	herbal medicines
Hang Gai	silk		

Vietnam Quilts
HANDICRAFTS

(Map p48; www.vietnam-quilts.org; 13 P Hang Bac)
Beautiful quilts handcrafted by rural women working in a not-for-profit community development program.

Craft Link
HANDICRAFTS

(Map p56; www.craftlink.com.vn; 43 P Van Mieu) A not-for-profit organisation near the Temple of Literature that sells quality tribal handicrafts and weavings at fair-trade prices.

Mosaique
FURNISHINGS

(Map p52; www.mosaiquedecoration.com; 6 P Ly Quoc Su) Modern and chic updates of traditional lacquerware and silk. The ideal spot to pick up stylish cushion covers, linen and accessories.

Indigenous
HANDICRAFTS

(Map p52; 36 P Au Trieu) A top spot for quirky ethnic-style gifts and excellent fair-trade coffee. There's a great little cafe too, so you can choose your favourite Vietnamese java before you buy.

Old Propaganda Posters
ARTWORK

(Map p48; 122 P Hang Bac) For communist-propaganda art posters. Most are excellent reproductions, but a few pricier original examples are available. Keep an eye out for other similar stores throughout the Old Quarter.

Markets

Buoi Market
MARKET

Located near the southwest edge of Tay Ho at the intersection of Duong Buoi and Lac Long Quan, this market sells live animals like chickens, ducks and pigs, but also features ornamental plants.

Dong Xuan Market
MARKET

(Map p48) A large, nontouristy market located in the Old Quarter of Hanoi, 900m north of Hoan Kiem Lake. There are hundreds of stalls here, and it's a fascinating place to explore if you want to catch a flavour of Hanoian street life.

Hom Market
MARKET

(Map p58) On the northeast corner of P Hué and P Tran Xuan Soan, this is a good general-purpose market and excellent for local fabric, if you plan to have clothes made.

Night Market
MARKET

(Map p48; ⊙7pm-midnight Fri-Sun) This market runs north to south through the Old Quarter, from P Hang Giay to P Hang Dao.

Content-wise it's something of a spillover for the area's shops, but at least the streets are closed to traffic. Watch out for pickpockets.

ℹ️ Information

Emergency

The emergency services should be able to transfer you to an English speaker.

Ambulance (📞115)

Fire (📞114)

Police (📞113)

Dangers & Annoyances

First the good news: Hanoi is generally a very safe city to explore, and crimes against tourists are extremely rare. Most visitors are thoroughly seduced by the city and leave captivated by its charm. Don't let your guard down completely, however it's usually perfectly safe to walk around the streets of the Old Quarter at night, though it is best to avoid the darker lanes after 10pm or so. It's also sensible for solo women to take a metered taxi or *xe om* when travelling across the city at night. Do watch out for pickpockets around market areas and unwanted baggage 'helpers' in crowded transport terminals – particularly when boarding night trains.

Hanoi has more than its fair share of scam merchants and swindlers so be sure to keep your antennae up. Most problems involve budget hotels and tours (p79). Very occasionally things can get quite nasty and we've received reports of verbal aggression and threats of physical violence towards tourists who've decided against a hotel room or a tour. Stay calm and back away slowly or things could quickly flare up.

Traffic and pollution are other irritants. The city's traffic is so dense and unrelenting that simply crossing the street can be a real headache, and weaving a path through a tide of motorbikes (two million and counting) can be a hairy experience. Our advice is to walk slowly and at a constant pace, allowing motorcyclists sufficient time to judge your position and avoid you. Don't try to move quickly, as you'll just confuse them. Keep your wits about you as you explore the Old Quarter, as motorbikes come at you from all directions and pavements are obstructed by cooking stalls and yet more parked motorbikes. Pollution levels are punishing and air quality is poor, with levels of some contaminants higher than in Bangkok.

SCAMS Whilst there's no need to be paranoid, Hanoi is riddled with scams, many of them inextricably linked. The taxi and minibus mafia at the airport shuttle unwitting tourists to the wrong hotel. Invariably, the hotel has copied the name of another popular property and will then attempt to appropriate as much of your money as possible. Taxi swindles are also becoming increasingly common. Try to avoid the taxis loitering at Hanoi's bus stations; many have super-fast meters. For more on scams and how to avoid them, see the boxed texts on p61 and p82.

Some shoeshine boys and *cyclo* drivers attempt to add a zero or two to an agreed price for their services; stick to your guns and give them the amount you originally agreed.

Watch out for friendly, smooth-talking strangers approaching you around the Hoan Kiem Lake. There are many variations, but sometimes these con-artists pose as students and suggest a drink or a meal. Gay men are also targeted in this way. Your new friend may then suggest a visit to a karaoke bar, snake-meat restaurant or some other venue and before you know it you're presented with a bill for hundreds of dollars. Be careful and follow your instincts, as these crooks can seem quite charming.

We've also heard reports of male travellers being approached by women late at night in the Old Quarter, and then being forced at gunpoint by the women's male accomplices to visit multiple ATMs and empty their accounts. Keep your wits about you, and try to stay in a group if you're returning from a bar late at night.

Internet Access

Most budget and midrange hotels offer free internet access as standard: at fancier places in the rooms, at cheaper places in the lobby.

Internet cafes are ubiquitous in central Hanoi, particularly around P Hang Bac and P Hang Be in the Old Quarter. Many do not display prices, so make sure you check before you notch up a couple of hours online. Rates start as low as 5000d per hour.

Wi-fi is becoming widespread in many of the city's tourist-geared hotels, cafes and bars.

Internet Resources

There are several good websites to help get the most out of Hanoi.

Hanoi Grapevine (www.hanoigrapevine.com) Information about concerts, art exhibitions and cinema.

Infoshare (www.infosharehanoi.com) Geared towards expats but has plenty of useful content for visitors.

New Hanoian (www.newhanoian.com) This is the premier online resource for visitors and expats; well worth checking out for its up-to-date restaurant, bar and accommodation reviews.

Sticky Rice (www.stickyrice.typepad.com) Foodie website, with the lowdown on everything from gourmet Vietnamese to Hanoi street kitchens, plus some bar reviews.

The Word (www.wordhanoi.com) Online version of the excellent, free monthly magazine *The Word*.

Medical Services

Hanoi Family Medical Practice (☎3843 0748; www.vietnammedicalpractice.com; Van Phuc Diplomatic Compound, 298 P Kim Ma) Located a few hundred metres west of the Ho Chi Minh Mausoleum Complex, this practice includes a team of well-respected international physicians and dentists and has 24-hour emergency cover. Prices are high, so check that your medical travel insurance is in order.

L'Hopital Français de Hanoi (☎3577 1100, emergency 3574 1111; www.hfh.com.vn; 1 Phuong Mai; ☺24hr) Long-established, international-standard hospital with accident and emergency, intensive care, dental clinic and consulting services. It's around 3km southwest of Hoan Kiem Lake.

SOS International Clinic (☎3826 4545; www.internationalsos.com; 51 Xuan Dieu; ☺24hr) English, French, German and Japanese are spoken and there is a dental clinic. It's 5km north of central Hanoi near Tay Ho Lake.

Viet Duc Hospital (Benh Vien Viet Duc; Map p52; ☎3825 3531; 40 P Trang Thi; ☺24hr) Old Quarter unit for emergency surgery; the doctors here speak English, French and German.

TRADITIONAL MEDICINE **Institute of Acupuncture** (☎3853 3881; 49 P Thai Thinh) offers effective holistic medicine, located around 4km southwest of Hoan Kiem Lake. For Vietnamese-style medical solutions, visit **National Institute of Traditional Medicine** (Map p58; ☎3826 3616; www.yhcotruyentw.org.vn; 29 P Nguyen Binh Khiem).

Money

Hanoi has many ATMs, and on the main roads around Hoan Kiem Lake are international banks where you can change money and get cash advances on credit cards. There is no black market in Hanoi, and if someone offers to change money on the street, they're looking to rip you off. Note that some ATMs limit the amount you can withdraw to only 3,000,000d. ANZ and HSBC ATMs are usually more generous.

Post

Domestic post office (Buu Dien Trung Vong; Map p52; 75 P Dinh Tien Hoang; ☺7am-9pm) For internal postal services in Vietnam, and sells philatelic items.

International postal office (Map p52; cnr P Dinh Tien Hoang & P Dinh Le; ☺7am-8pm) With an entrance to the right of the domestic office. Courier companies:

DHL (☎3733 2086; www.dhl.com.vn)

Federal Express (☎3824 9054; www.fedex.com/vn)

Telephone

Guesthouses and internet cafes are convenient for local calls within Hanoi. For international

NEGOTIATING HANOI'S TRAVEL AGENCY MAZE

Hanoi has hundreds of travel agencies, most of a pretty dubious quality, while a few are downright dodgy. Many of the sketchy agencies operate with pushy, ill-informed staff out of Old Quarter budget hotels. It's these fly-by-night operations we receive the most complaints about. Some cheap hotels have been known to kick out travellers who book tours elsewhere. When you book accommodation, check to make sure there are no strings attached and that it's not mandatory to book tours at the same business also.

Look out for clones of the popular agencies, as it's common for a rival business to set up shop close to a respected agency and attempt to cream off a slice of their business. Often these impostors are staffed by ill-informed workers adopting a very hard sell. Visit online forums like Thorn Tree (www.lonelyplanet.com/thorntree) to check the latest travellers' buzz.

Some agencies have professional, knowledgeable staff and coordinate well-organised trips. These companies are inevitably more expensive, but offer a far greater degree of satisfaction. Look for companies that run small groups, use their own vehicles and guides, and offer trips away from the main tourist trail. The following are recommended.

Ethnic Travel (Map p48; ☎3926 1951; www.ethnictravel.com.vn; 35 P Hang Giay) Off-the-beaten-track trips across the north in small groups. Some trips are low-impact using public transport and homestays, others are activity based (including hiking, cycling and cooking). Offers Bai Tu Long Bay tours and also has an office in Sapa.

Free Wheelin' Tours (☎3926 2743; www.freewheelin-tours.com; 9 P Hang Vai) Located above Tet bar (p73) in the Old Quarter, this place offers motorbike and 4WD tours around the north, including an eight-day trip to the northeast on Minsk bikes.

Handspan Adventure Travel (☎3926 2828; www.handspan.com; 78 P Ma May) A wide range of tours including sea-kayaking trips in Halong Bay, its own island-based eco-camp in Lan Ha Bay, and jeep tours, mountain biking and trekking. New initiatives include community-based tourism projects in northern Vietnam and the Treasure Junk, the only true sailing craft cruising Halong Bay. Handspan is located inside the Tamarind Cafe (p66) and also has offices in Sapa and HCMC.

I Travel (Map p48; ☎3926 3678; www.itravel-online.com; 25 P Hang Be) Offering culturally and environmentally sensitive trips across Vietnam, I Travel is located at the same address as Le Pub (p71).

Marco Polo Travel (☎0913 571 687; www.kayakingvietnam.com) Runs kayaking trips around Halong Bay and Ba Be Lakes.

Ocean Tours (Map p48; ☎3926 0463; www.oceantours.com.vn; 22 P Hang Bac) Professional, well-organised tour operator with Halong Bay and Ba Be National Park options, and 4WD road trips around the northeast.

Vega Travel (Map p48; ☎3926 2092; www.vegatravel.vn; cnr P Ma May & 24A P Hang Bac) Family-owned and operated company offering well-run tours around the north and throughout Vietnam. Excellent guides and drivers, and the company also financially supports minority kindergartens and schools around Sapa and Bac Ha. Good value tours of Halong Bay.

For nationwide operators offering tours of Hanoi and northern Vietnam, see p519. For motorbike tours of the north, see p520.

services, internet cafes using Skype offer the cheapest rates.

International Call Service (Map p48; 3 P Ta Hien; ⏰7am-10pm) 1500d to 2000d per minute to most countries.

Tourist Information

Tourist Information Center (Map p48; P Dinh Tien Hoang; ⏰8.30am-9pm) City maps and brochures, but privately run with an emphasis on selling tours. Pick up a free copy of the handy pocket-sized *Hanoi City Pass* book. In the cafes and bars of the Old Quarter, also look for the excellent local magazine *The Word*.

MAPS Hanoi city maps come in every size and scale. Some are freebies subsidised by advertising and others are precise works of cartography.

Leading maps include detailed ones at a scale of 1:10,000 or 1:17,500. Covit produces a couple of hand-drawn 3D maps of Hanoi, including a detailed Old Town map, which make nice souvenirs. These are available at leading bookshops in Hanoi.

There is also an excellent bus map available: *Xe Buyt Ha Noi* (5000d).

❶ Getting There & Away

Air

Hanoi has fewer direct international flights than Ho Chi Minh City, but with excellent connections through Singapore, Hong Kong or Bangkok you can get almost anywhere. For further information about international flights, see p511.

Vietnam Airlines (Map p52; ☑1900 545 486; www.vietnamair.com.vn; 25 P Trang Thi; ⊙8am-5pm Mon-Fri) Links Hanoi to destinations throughout Vietnam. Popular routes include Hanoi to Dalat, Danang, Dien Bien Phu, HCMC, Hue and Nha Trang, all served daily.

Jetstar Airways (☑1900 1550; www.jetstar .com) Operates low-cost flights to Danang, HCMC and Nha Trang.

Bus & Minibus

Hanoi has three main long-distance bus stations of interest to travellers. They are fairly well organised, with ticket offices, fixed prices and schedules. Consider buying tickets the day before you plan to travel on the longer distance routes to ensure a seat. It's often easier to book through a travel agent, but you'll obviously be charged a commission.

Tourist-style minibuses can be booked through most hotels and travel agents. Popular destinations include Halong Bay and Sapa. Prices are usually about 30% to 40% higher than the regular public bus, but include a hotel pick-up.

Many open-ticket tours through Vietnam start or finish in Hanoi – for more details see p516.

Gia Lam bus station (Đ Ngoc Lam) Has buses to the northeast of Hanoi. It's located 3km northeast of the centre across the Song Hong (Red River).

Luong Yen bus station (Tran Quang Khai & Nguyen Khoai) Located 3km southeast of the Old Quarter, it operates services to the south and the east, including sleeper buses to HCMC, Hue, Dalat and Nha Trang. Transport to Cat Ba Island is best organised here (see p107). Note that the taxis at Luong Yen are notorious for dodgy meters. Walk a couple of blocks and hail one off the street.

My Dinh bus station (Đ Pham Hung) This station 7km west of the city provides services to the west and the north, including sleeper buses to Dien Bien Phu for onward travel to Laos.

Car

Car hire is best arranged via a travel agency or hotel. Rates almost always include a driver, a necessity as many roads and turnings are not signposted. The roads in the north are in OK shape, but narrow lanes, potholes and blind corners equate to an average speed of 35 to 40km per hour. During the rainy season, expect serious delays as landslides are cleared and bridges repaired. You'll definitely need a 4WD.

Rates start at about US$110 a day (including a driver and petrol). Make sure the driver's expenses are covered in the rate you're quoted.

Motorbike

Hanoi has several good operators with well-maintained bikes. See p520 for additional information.

Offroad Vietnam (Map p48; ☑913 047 509; www.offroadvietnam.com; 36 P Nguyen Huu Huan) For reliable Honda trail bikes (from US$25 daily) and road bikes (US$20). The number of rental bikes is limited, so booking ahead is recommended. Offroad's main business is running excellent guided tours, mainly dealing with travellers from English-speaking countries.

Cuong's Motorbike Adventure (Map p48; ☑913 518 772; www.cuongs-motorbike -adventure.com; 46 Gia Ngu) Also recommended, with bike rentals from US$30 per day.

Train

SOUTHBOUND TRAINS TO HUE, DANANG, NHA TRANG, HCMC Trains to southern destinations go from the main **Hanoi train station** (Ga Hang Co; Map p56; 120 Đ Le Duan; ⊙ticket office 7.30am-12.30pm & 1.30-7.30pm) at the

---

❶ THE SLOW BUS TO CHINA

Two daily services (at 7.30am and 9.30am) to Nanning, China (450,000d, eight hours) leave from the private terminal of **Hong Ha Tourism** (Map p52; ☑3824 7339; Hong Ha Hotel, 204 Tran Quang Khai). Tickets should be purchased in advance, though little English is spoken. You may be asked to show your Chinese visa.

The bus runs to the border at Dong Dang, where you pass through Chinese immigration. You then change to a Chinese bus, which continues to the Lang Dong bus station in Nanning. Reports from Nanning-bound travellers indicate that this route is less hassle and quicker than travelling by train.

BUSES FROM HANOI

GIA LAM BUS STATION

DESTINATION	DURATION	COST	FREQUENCY
(Bai Chay) Halong City	3½hr	100,000d	Every 30 min
Haiphong	2hr	70,000d	Every 20 min
Lang Son	4hr	110,000d	Every 45 min
Mong Cai	8hr	240,000d	Approx hourly
Lao Cai	9hr	250,000d	1pm & 7pm
Ha Giang	7hr	170,000d	Approx hourly
Cao Bang	8hr	180,000d	5 daily

LUONG YEN BUS STATION

DESTINATION	DURATION	COST	FREQUENCY
HCMC	36hr	650,000d	11am, 3pm & 6pm
Dalat	24hr	440,000d	11am & 6pm
Lang Son	3½hr	75,000d	Hourly
Hue	12hr	220,000d	Hourly, 2-6pm
Danang	13hr	240,000d	Hourly, 2-6pm
Ninh Binh	2½hr	55,000d	Every 20 min, 6am-6pm
Nha Trang	7hr	170,000d	10am & 6pm
Cao Bang	8hr	140,000d	5 daily
Mong Cai	10hr	180,000d	5 daily

MY DINH BUS STATION

DESTINATION	DURATION	COST	FREQUENCY
Cao Bang	10hr	135,000d	Every 45 min
Dien Bien Phu	24hr	440,000d	11am & 6pm
Mai Chau	2½hr	65,000d	6.30am & 2.30pm
Son La	7½hr	150,000d	7-8am
Ha Giang	7hr	140,000d	4-6am

western end of P Tran Hung Dao. Foreigners can buy tickets for southbound trains at counter 2, where the staff speak English. We recommend buying your tickets at least one day before departure to ensure a seat or sleeper. Tickets can be purchased from travel agencies, but will include a commission for booking.

Approximate journey times from Hanoi are as follows, but check when you book, as some trains are quicker than others: Hue (11 hours), Danang (13½ hours), Nha Trang (24½ hours), HCMC (31 hours). Approximate costs from Hanoi are shown in the Southbound Trains table, but note that different departures have different fare structures and available classes.

NORTHBOUND TRAINS TO LAO CAI (FOR SAPA) AND CHINA To the right of the main

entrance of the train station is a separate ticket office for northbound trains to Lao Cai (for Sapa) and China.

Tickets to China must be bought at a different counter. Note that all northbound trains leave from a separate station (just behind) called **Tran Quy Cap station** (B Station; P Tran Qui Cap). Tickets can be bought at the main station until about two hours before departure. Of course any travel agency (and many tour operators) can book train tickets for you for a commission. See p133 for details of trains to Lao Cai.

Once you're in China the train to Beijing is a comfortable, air-conditioned service with four-bed sleeper compartments and a restaurant. Note that you cannot board international Nanning-bound trains in Lang Son or Dong Dang.

SOUTHBOUND TRAINS

DESTINATION	HARD SEAT	SOFT SEAT	HARD SLEEPER	SOFT SLEEPER
Hue	From 216,000d	From 255,000d	From 540,000d	From 738,000d
Danang	From 270,000d	From 390,000d	From 554,000d	From 760,000d
Nha Trang	n/a	From 640,000d	From 847,000d	From 1,314,000d
HCMC	n/a	From 763,000d	From 920,000d	From 1,444,000d

EASTBOUND TRAINS TO HAIPHONG Eastbound (Haiphong) trains depart from **Gia Lam train station** on the eastern side of the Song Hong (Red River), or **Long Bien** (off Map p48) on the western (city) side of the river. Be sure to check which station.

See www.seat61.com for the latest information on all trains in Vietnam.

Getting Around

To/From the Airport

Hanoi's Noi Bai International Airport is about 35km north of the city. The trip here takes 45 minutes to an hour, along a fast modern highway.

MIND THE MAFIA

It happens all over the world and Hanoi is no exception. Many of the drivers who hang out at Noi Bai airport are working in cahoots with hotels and travel agencies in Hanoi. They know every trick in the book and usually carry the cards of all the popular budget hotels. 'It's full today' is popular, as is 'they have a new place, much nicer, number two'. Usually it's a bunch of lies. The best defence is to insist you already have a reservation. Even if the place does turn out to be full, you can plot your own course from there. When it comes to the Vietnam Airlines minibus, the best bet is to bail out at the Vietnam Airlines office, usually the first stop in the centre. Otherwise you will be dragged around endless commission-paying hotels in the Old Quarter. Another option to avoid the nonsense is to book a room in advance and arrange an airport pick-up. Someone will be waiting with a name board and you can wave to the taxi touts as you exit the airport.

BUS Public bus 17 runs to/from **Long Bien bus station** (off Map p48; 5000d; ☺5am-9pm) Allow around 90 minutes' travelling time.

TAXI Airport Taxi (☑3873 3333) charges US$15 for a taxi ride door-to-door to or from Noi Bai airport. From the terminal, look out for the official taxi drivers who wear bright yellow jackets. They do not require that you pay the toll for the bridge you cross en route. Some other taxi drivers do require that you pay the toll, so ask first. There are numerous airport scams involving taxi drivers and dodgy hotels (see p82). Don't use freelance taxi drivers touting for business – the chances of a rip-off are too high. If you've already confirmed accommodation, book a taxi through your hotel.

VIETNAM AIRLINES MINIBUS Links Hanoi and Noi Bai (US$3) every half hour to/from the Vietnam Airlines office (Map p52) on P Trang Thi. It's best – though not essential – to book the day before.

Bicycle

Many Old Quarter guesthouses and cafes rent bikes for about US$2 per day. Good luck with that traffic.

Bus

Hanoi has an extensive public bus system, though few tourists take advantage of the rock-bottom fares (3000d). If you're game, pick up the *Xe Buyt Hanoi* (Hanoi bus map; 5000d) from the Thang Long Bookshop (p75).

Car & Motorbike

Getting around Hanoi by motorbike means relentless traffic, non-existent road manners and inadequate street lighting. Factor in possible theft, parking hassles and bribe-happy police, and it's not for the timid. Intrepid types can arrange mopeds for around US$5 per day in the Old Quarter.

Cyclo

A few *cyclo* drivers still frequent the Old Quarter, and if you're only going a short distance, it's a great way to experience the city (despite the fumes). Settle on a price first and watch out for overcharging – a common ploy when carrying two passengers is to agree on a price, and then *double* it upon arrival, gesturing 'no, no, no...that was per person'.

Aim to pay around 25,000d for a shortish journey; night rides are more. Few *cyclo* drivers speak English so take a map with you.

Electric Train

Hanoi's recently launched eco-friendly **electric train** (per person 15,000d; ☺8.30am-10.30pm) is actually a pretty good way to get your bearings in the city. It traverses a network of 14 stops in the Old Quarter and around Hoan Kiem Lake, parting the flow of motorbikes and pedestrians like a slow-moving white dragon. Nothing really beats haphazardly discovering the nooks and crannies of the Old Quarter by foot, but if you're feeling a tad lazy, the train is worth considering. The main departure point is the northern end of Hoan Kiem Lake (p47). A full journey around the Old Quarter takes around 40 minutes.

Taxi

Several reliable companies offer metered taxis. All charge fairly similar rates. Flag fall is around 15,000d, which takes you 1km to 2km; every kilometre thereafter costs around 10,000d. Some dodgy operators have high-speed meters, so use the following more reliable companies.
Thanh Nga Taxi (☎3821 5215)
Van Xuan (☎3822 2888)

AROUND HANOI

The rich alluvial soils of the Red River Delta nurture a rich rice crop and many of the communities surrounding Hanoi are still engaged in agriculture. The contrast between modern Hanoi and the rural villages is stark. Many tour operators in Hanoi offer cycling tours to villages near Hanoi – a great way to discover a different world. **Lotussia** (☎2249 4668; www.vietnamcycling.com) specialises in cycling tours from Hanoi, some taking in the Thay and Tay Phuong pagodas and nearby handicraft villages. These tours also avoid having to struggle through Hanoi's ferocious traffic, as a minibus takes the strain through the suburbs.

Ho Chi Minh Trail Museum

The **Ho Chi Minh Trail Museum** (Hwy 6; admission 20,000d; ☺7.30-11.30am & 1.30-2.30pm Mon-Sat) is dedicated to the famous supply route from the communist north to the occupied south of Vietnam. The displays, including an abundance of American ammunition and weaponry as well as some powerful photography, document all too clearly the extreme effort and organisation needed to keep the show on the road – and the death and destruction involved. Quite simply, defeat was not an option for the VC, whatever the odds. There's a model of the trail, which shows the nightmarish terrain through which it passed. It's located about 13km southwest of Hanoi and can be combined with a visit to Van Phuc handicraft village or visited on the way to the Perfume Pagoda.

EASTBOUND & NORTHBOUND TRAINS

TO HAIPHONG

DEPARTURE	STATION	DURATION	HARD SEAT	SOFT SEAT
6.15am	Gia Lam	2hr	38,000d	50,000d
9.30am	Long Bien	2¾hr	38,000d	50,000d
3.35pm	Long Bien	3hr	38,000d	50,000d
6.10pm	Long Bien	2½hr	38,000d	50,000d

TO BEIJING

DEPARTURE	STATION	DURATION	HARD SLEEPER	SOFT SLEEPER
6.30pm Tue & Fri	Tran Qui Cap	18hr	US$258	US$378

TO NANNING

DEPARTURE	STATION	DURATION	HARD SLEEPER	SOFT SLEEPER
9.40pm	Gia Lam	12hr	US$66	US$96

Perfume Pagoda

North Vietnam's very own Marble Mountains, the **Perfume Pagoda** (Chua Huong; admission incl return boat trip 55,000d) is a striking complex of pagodas and Buddhist shrines built into the karst cliffs of Huong Tich Mountain (Mountain of the Fragrant Traces). Among the better-known sites here are Thien Chu (Pagoda Leading to Heaven); Giai Oan Chu (Purgatorial Pagoda), where the faithful believe deities purify souls, cure sufferings and grant offspring to childless families; and Huong Tich Chu (Pagoda of the Perfumed Vestige). This is a domestic drawcard and it's an interesting experience just to see the Vietnamese domestic tourists at play.

The entertaining boat trip along the scenic waterways between limestone cliffs takes about two hours return, and allow a couple more hours to climb to the top and return. The path to the summit is steep in places and if it's raining the ground can get *very* slippery. However, the good news is that there is now a cable car to the summit (one-way/return 60,000/100,000d). A smart combination is to use the cable car up and then walk down.

Great numbers of Buddhist pilgrims come here during a festival that begins in the middle of the second lunar month and lasts until the last week of the third lunar month (usually corresponding to March and April). It's very busy during this period, especially on the even dates of the lunar month; you'll have a much easier time if you establish the lunar date and plan to visit on an odd date. Weekends tend to draw crowds year-round, with pilgrims and other visitors spending their time boating, hiking and exploring the caves. Litter and hawkers are part and parcel of the visit, and some hawkers are persistent enough to hassle visitors all the way to the top; you have been warned!

The Perfume Pagoda is about 60km southwest of Hanoi by road. Getting there requires a journey first by road, then by river, then on foot or by cable car.

First, travel from Hanoi by car for two hours to the township of My Duc. Vehicles usually drop you about a 15-minute walk from the boat ramp, or you can hop on a *xe om*. Then take a small boat, usually rowed by women, for one hour to the foot of the mountain. The main pagoda area is a steep 3km hike from the boat dock. Allow yourself at least two hours to make the return trip, longer if it's been raining and is slippery.

Most tour operators and some traveller cafes in Hanoi offer inexpensive tours to the pagoda for around US$15 (inclusive of transport, guide and lunch). Small-group tours cost around US$25–30. This is one of those places where it is easier to take a tour, as it's a pain by public transport.

Handicraft Villages

Numerous villages surrounding Hanoi specialise in cottage industries. Visiting these settlements can make a rewarding day trip, though having a good guide helps make the journey really worthwhile.

Bat Trang is known as the 'ceramic village'. Here, artisans mass-produce ceramic vases and other pieces in their kilns. It's hot, sweaty work, but the results are superb and very reasonably priced compared with the boutiques in town. There are masses of ceramic shops, but poke around down the lanes and behind the shops to find the kilns. Bat Trang is 13km southeast of Hanoi. Public bus 47 runs here from Long Bien bus station (off Map p48).

Van Phuc specialises in silk. Silk cloth is produced here on looms and lots of visitors like to buy or order tailor-made clothes. Many of the fine silk items you see on sale in Hanoi's P Hang Gai are made in Van Phuc. There's a small daily fruit-and-vegetable market in the mornings, and a pretty village pagoda with a lily pond. Van Phuc is 8km southwest of Hanoi; take city bus 1 from Long Bien bus station.

Dong Ky was known as the 'firecracker village' until 1995, when the Vietnamese government banned firecrackers. With that industry now extinguished, the village survives by producing beautiful traditional furniture inlaid with mother-of-pearl. You can have handcrafted beds, chairs and tables, and wardrobes custom-made here and exported directly to your door. Dong Ky is 15km northeast of Hanoi.

Thay & Tay Phuong Pagodas

Stunning limestone outcrops loom up from the emerald-green paddy fields and clinging to the cliffs are these two pagodas, about 20 minutes apart from each other by road.

Thay Pagoda (Master's Pagoda; admission 5000d), also known as Thien Phuc (Heavenly Blessing), is dedicated to Thich Ca Buddha

(Sakyamuni, the historical Buddha). To the left of the main altar is a statue of the 12th-century monk Tu Dao Hanh, the master in whose honour the pagoda is named. To the right is a statue of King Ly Nhan Tong, who is believed to have been a reincarnation of Tu Dao Hanh.

In front of the pagoda is a small stage built on stilts in the middle of a pond where water-puppet shows are staged during festivals. Follow the path around the outside of the main pagoda building and take a steep 10-minute climb up to a beautiful smaller pagoda perched high on the rock. Thay Pagoda is a big and confusing complex for non-Buddhists – consider hiring a guide to get the most from your visit.

The pagoda's **annual festival** is held from the fifth to the seventh days of the third lunar month (approximately March). Pilgrims and other visitors enjoy watching water-puppet shows, hiking and exploring caves in the area.

Tay Phuong Pagoda (Pagoda of the West; admission 5000d), also known as Sung Phuc Pagoda, consists of three single-level structures built in descending order on a hillock that is said to resemble a buffalo. Figures representing 'the conditions of man' are the pagoda's most celebrated feature – carved from jackfruit wood, many date from the 18th century. The earliest construction here dates from the 8th century. Take the steep steps up to the main pagoda building, then find a path at the back that loops down past the other two pagodas and wander through the hillside village surrounding the complex.

The pagodas are about 30km west of Hanoi in Ha Tay province. Hanoi travel agents and tour operators offer day trips that take in both pagodas, from US$40 per person. Alternatively, hire a car and driver for about US$80 and plot a rewarding day trip that combines the pagodas and Ba Vi National Park.

Ba Vi National Park

034

Formerly a French hill station, the triple-peaked Ba Vi Mountain (Nui Ba Vi) has been attracting visitors for decades and remains a popular weekend escape for Hanoians. The limestone mountain is now part of the **Ba Vi National Park** (388 1205; per person/motorbike 10,000/5000d) which has several rare and endangered plants in its protected forest, as well as mammals including two species of rare 'flying' squirrel and bountiful bird life.

There's an orchid garden and a bird garden, and hiking opportunities through the forested slopes. A **temple** dedicated to Ho Chi Minh sits at the mountain's summit (1276m) – it's a difficult but beautiful 30-minute climb up 1229 steps through the trees. Fog often shrouds the peak, but despite the damp and mist it's eerily atmospheric – visit between April and December for the best chance of clear views down to the Red River valley and Hanoi in the distance.

🛏 Sleeping & Eating

Ba Vi Guesthouse   GUESTHOUSE $
(388 1197; r weekdays 180,000-240,000d, weekends 220,000-300,000d) Spreads over several blocks in the heart of the park and has a big swimming pool and a moderately priced restaurant (meals 60,000d). Go for one of the less noisy guesthouses away from the pool and restaurant area if you're here on a weekend. You'll need your passport to check in.

ℹ Getting There & Away

Ba Vi National Park is about 65km west of Hanoi, and the only practical option for visiting is by hired vehicle from Hanoi. Travelling by motorbike, it is possible to visit Ba Vi before taking a beautiful riverside road down to Hoa Binh and onwards into the northwest.

There has been some confusion between attractions near Ba Vi town – which is well away from the park boundaries – and Ba Vi National Park. Make sure your driver knows you want the national park.

Co Loa Citadel

Dating from the 3rd century BC, **Co Loa Citadel** (Co Loa Thanh; admission per person/car 3000/20,000d; 8am-5pm) was the first fortified citadel in Vietnamese history and became the national capital during the reign of Ngo Quyen (AD 939–44). Only vestiges of the ancient ramparts, which enclosed an area of about 5 sq km, remain.

In the centre of the citadel are temples dedicated to the rule of King An Duong Vuong (257-208 BC), who founded the legendary Thuc dynasty, and his daughter My Nuong (Mi Chau). Legend tells that My Nuong showed her father's magic crossbow trigger (which made him invincible in battle) to her husband, the son of a Chinese general. He stole it and gave it to his father. With this not-so-secret weapon, the Chinese defeated An Duong Vuong, beginning 1000 years of Chinese occupation.

Co Loa Citadel is 16km north of central Hanoi in Dong Anh district, and can be visited as a short detour while on the way to or from Tam Dao Hill Station. Public bus 46 runs here every 15 minutes from My Dinh bus station (p80) in Hanoi.

Tam Dao Hill Station

📞 0211 / ELEV 930M

Nestling below soaring forest-clad peaks, Tam Dao is a former French hill station in a spectacular setting northwest of Hanoi. Today it's a popular summer resort – a favoured weekend escape for Hanoians, who come here to revel in the temperate climate and make merry in the extensive selection of restaurants and bars. Founded in 1907 by the French, most of its colonial villas were destroyed during the Franco–Viet Minh War, only to be replaced with brutalist concrete architecture. Tam Dao is a useful base for hiking, but the town itself is an unattractive sprawl of hotel blocks.

Tam Dao National Park was designated in 1996 and covers much of the area around the town. Tam Dao means 'Three Islands', and the three summits of Tam Dao Mountain, all about 1400m in height, are sometimes visible to the northeast of the hill station, floating like islands in the mist. There are at least 64 mammal species (including langurs) and 239 bird species in the park, but you'll need a good local guide and be prepared to do some hiking to find them. Illegal hunting remains a big problem.

Hikes vary from half an hour return to the waterfall, to day treks taking in bamboo forest and primary tropical forest. A guide is essential for the longer hikes and can be hired from 300,000d; ask at the Mela Hotel. A 20,000d national park entrance fee is also payable.

Remember that it is cool up in Tam Dao, and this part of Vietnam has a distinct winter. Don't be caught unprepared.

The best time to visit is between late April and mid-October, when the mist sometimes lifts and the weather can be fine. As with other popular sites in Vietnam, weekends can be packed but weekdays are far less busy.

Tam Dao Golf and Resort (📞04-3736 6457; www.tamdaogolf.com) is set against the beautiful backdrop of the 'Three Islands'. A round of golf here costs US$45 during the week and US$90 on weekends.

🛏 Sleeping & Eating

There's a host of hotels and guesthouses in Tam Dao. The town is easy to navigate, so look around and negotiate. There are also plenty of hotel restaurants and good *com pho* (rice-noodle soup) places. Try to avoid eating the local wildlife; you'll frequently see civet, squirrel, porcupine, fox and pheasant advertised, but most of these are endangered species.

Huong Lien Hotel HOTEL $
(📞382 4282; r weekday/weekend 250,000/ 300,000d; 🛜) Offering decent value for the price, most of the rooms here have balconies to make the most of those misty mountain views. There's a little restaurant as well (mains 120,000d to 200,000d).

Mela Hotel HOTEL $$
(📞382 4321; melatamdao@yahoo.com; r from US$55; 🛜❄✖) A modern, attractive, European-managed hotel with 20 spacious, comfortable rooms (some include fireplaces) and most with balconies and wonderful valley views. The in-house Bamboo restaurant (meals US$4 to US$12) has an eclectic menu which features everything from French cuisine to the ubiquitous Vietnamese spring rolls. Rack rates are a little silly, so come midweek and start negotiating.

Nha Khach Ngan Hang GUESTHOUSE $
(📞0989 152 969; per person 120,000d; 🛜) In the centre of town opposite the Phuong Nam Quan restaurant is this simple, family-owned guesthouse. Rooms are spotless, there is unlimited hot water and the whole operation sits on the edge of a sprawling plot of *xu xu*, the local green vegetable. Try it in the restaurant with huge slivers of garlic when you ask about accommodation.

ℹ Getting There & Away

Tam Dao is 85km northwest of Hanoi in Vinh Phuc province. Buses run from Gia Lam bus station (p80) in Hanoi to Vinh Yen (10,000d, one hour). From there you can hire a motorbike (about 120,000d one-way), or a taxi (around 250,000d), to travel the 24km single-lane road that leads to the national park.

On a motorbike from Hanoi, the journey time is a little over two hours, and the last part of the ride into the park is beautiful.

Northeast Vietnam

Includes »

Best Places to Eat

» Big Man Restaurant (p93)

» BKK (p93)

» Bamboo Café (p105)

» Vien Duong (p106)

Best Places to Stay

» Monaco Hotel (p92)

» Nam Cat Island Resort (p105)

» Whisper of Nature (p105)

» Suoi Goi Cat Ba Resort (p105)

Why Go?

Northeast Vietnam's top ticket is Halong Bay, and while visiting the World Heritage site is an essential experience, the region also showcases craggy limestone peaks, tropical forests, caves, waterfalls and historic sights.

To the south of Halong Bay is Cat Ba, a verdant island renowned for its hiking, biking, sailing and world-class rock climbing. To the east, Bai Tu Long Bay continues nature's spectacular show all the way to the Chinese border, and Quan Lan Island is emerging as a destination for pioneering travellers.

Looming above the coast, the karst connection continues into Cao Bang province, and the brooding mountains are one of Vietnam's most idiosyncratic landscapes. With Sapa and northwest Vietnam firmly on the tourist map, head northeast instead to explore remote backroads and the sublime lakes of Ba Be National Park.

China-bound travellers can access two important border crossings at Mong Cai and Dong Dang.

When to Go
Halong City

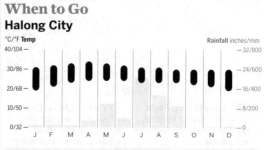

Feb–Apr The weather is often cool and drizzly, with fog making Halong Bay visibility low.

Jun & Jul Peak season for Vietnamese tourists; busy on Cat Ba Island, especially on weekends.

May–Sep The region is impacted by tropical storms, which may disrupt Halong Bay tours.

History

Dominated by the Red River basin and the sea, the fertile northeast is the cradle of Vietnamese civilisation. Until very recently, Vietnam has had challenging relations with the neighbouring Chinese. China occupied the country in the 2nd century BC, and were not vanquished until the 10th century.

Any time the Chinese wanted to advance upon Vietnam's affairs, they could do so through the northeast. The most recent occurrence was in a 1979 attempt to punish the Vietnamese for their occupation of Cambodia (p112). Thousands of ethnic Chinese also fled from this region in the 1970s and '80s.

More than three decades on, border trade is surging ahead and Chinese tourists flock to the region during summer.

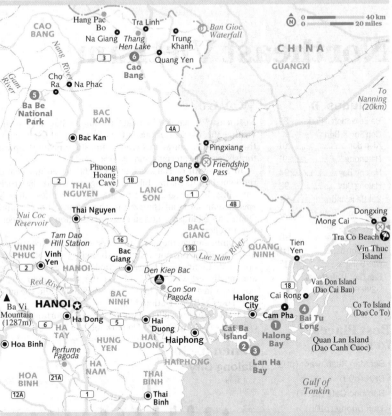

Northeast Highlights

1 Escape **Halong Bay's** (p94) tourist buzz by gently kayaking into hidden lagoons and grottoes

2 Hike, bike and climb your way around the great outdoors in **Cat Ba Island's** (p101) fascinating national park

3 Explore **Lan Ha Bay** (p100), an emerging area of gorgeous islands and beaches with superb rock climbing and sailing

4 Pioneer your own route around the off-the-beaten-path islands of **Bai Tu Long Bay** (p108)

5 Board a boat to glide through lakes and rivers, and spend the night with a local Tay family in **Ba Be National Park** (p89)

6 Check out the crazy karst scenery of **Cao Bang** (p112), and the province's waterfalls, caves, lakes and historic sights

National Parks

Northeast Vietnam's stunning national parks all involve water-based activities. Cat Ba National Park (p101), near Halong Bay, is a rugged island liberally shrouded in lush jungle. This park also includes the 300 or so limestone islands of Lan Ha Bay.

Further northeast, Halong Bay becomes Bai Tu Long National Park (p108), a procession of karst landscapes easily equal to its more famous neighbour. Bai Tu Long's isolation offers hidden beaches with a relative lack of tourists. Better boat services to Quan Lan Island is now making the Bai Tu Long region more accessible.

Ba Be National Park features emerald lakes, surrounded by soaring mountains and lush forest. Visit for hiking, biking and boat trips to caves and waterfalls, and staying in Ba Be's village homestays.

🛈 **Getting There & Away**

Hanoi is the gateway to the northeast.

BUS Buses are fast and frequent in the lowlands, but slow and creaking in the highlands.

CAR Road connections to Haiphong, Halong City and Lang Son are fast, but as the terrain gets more mountainous, things slow down considerably.

TRAIN There are also slow rail links to Haiphong and Lang Son.

Ba Be National Park

☑0281

Often referred to as the Ba Be Lakes, **Ba Be National Park** (admission per person 20,000d) was established in 1992 as Vietnam's eighth national park. The scenery here is breathtaking, with towering limestone mountains

peaking at 1554m, plunging valleys, dense evergreen forests, waterfalls, caves and, of course, the lakes themselves.

There are 13 tribal villages in the Ba Be region, with most belonging to the Tay minority, who live in stilt homes, plus smaller numbers of Dzao and H'mong. A village homestay program is now well established, allowing travellers to experience life in a tribal village.

Ba Be Center Tourism (☑389 4721; www .babecentertourism.com; Bolu village) is Tay-owned and can arrange homestays, boat trips and multi-day tours of Ba Be National Park including trekking and kayaking.

The park is a rainforest area with more than 550 named plant species, and the government subsidises the villagers not to cut down the trees. The hundreds of wildlife species here include 65 (mostly rarely seen) mammals, 353 butterflies, 106 species of fish, four kinds of turtle, the highly endangered Vietnamese salamander and even the Burmese python. Ba Be birdlife is equally prolific, with 233 species recorded, including the spectacular crested serpent eagle and the oriental honey buzzard. Hunting is forbidden, but villagers are permitted to fish.

Ba Be (meaning Three Bays) is in fact three linked lakes, which have a total length of 8km and a width of about 400m. More than a hundred species of freshwater fish inhabit the lake. Two of the lakes are separated by a 100m-wide strip of water called Be Kam, sandwiched between high walls of chalk rock.

Park staff can organise **tours**. Costs depend on the number of people, starting at about US$30 per day for solo travellers

PLAYING FOR HIGH STAKES

One of Vietnam's greatest heroes, the military general Tran Hung Dao (1228–1300) defeated the Mongol warriors of the Chinese army three times as they invaded Vietnam.

His most famous victory, at the Bach Dang River in northeast Vietnam in 1288, secured the country's sovereignty. He borrowed the military strategy of Ngo Quyen who had regained Vietnam's independence in 939 following 1000 years of Chinese rule. After dark, sharpened bamboo poles – of a length designed to remain hidden underwater at high tide – were set vertically in the river, in the shallows near the bank. At high tide, Tran Hung Dao sent small boats out – passing easily between the posts – to goad Chinese warships to approach. As the tide receded, the impaled Chinese boats were left high and dry, and flaming arrows destroyed the fleet. In Halong Bay, Hang Dau Go (Cave of Wooden Stakes; p96), is where Tran Hung Dao's forces are said to have prepared and stored the bamboo poles.

In memory of the victory, you'll find Tran Hung Dao streets in every Vietnamese town, and every street parallel to a river is called Bach Dang

and less if there's a group of you. The most popular excursion is a **boat trip** (around 550,000d) along the Nang River and around the lake - keep an eye out for kingfishers and raptors. The boats can accommodate up to 12 people and the tour usually takes in the tunnel-like **Hang Puong** (Puong Cave), which is about 40m high and 300m long, and completely passes through a mountain. As many as 7000 bats (belonging to 18 species) are said to live in this cave. Further stops can be made at the pretty Tay village of Cam Ha (where every timber house has a satellite dish) and to the startling circular, jungle-rimmed lagoon of Ao Tien before finishing at **An Ma Pagoda**, situated on a little island in the middle of the lake.

The **Thac Dau Dang** (Dau Dang or Ta Ken Waterfall), consisting of a series of spectacular cascades between sheer walls of rock, is another possible destination. Just 200m below the rapids is a small Tay village called Hua Tang.

Other options include dugout-canoe tours or combination cycling, boating and walking possibilities. Longer treks can also be arranged.

The park entrance fee is payable at a checkpoint on the road into the park, about 15km before the park headquarters, just beyond the town of Cho Ra.

🛏 Sleeping & Eating

The only hotel rooms inside the park are in a **government-owned complex** (☎389 4026; r from 220,000d, cabin 220,000d, bungalow 350,000d) next to the park headquarters. The best rooms here are in attractive semi-detached bungalows, each with two double beds, while the cabins are small and fairly basic. A few rooms are available too. The complex has two **restaurants** (meals from 50,000d), though you should place your order an hour or so before you want to eat. For a less formal setting, you'll find a line of cook-shacks by the chalets that sell cheap meals and snacks and are run by local villagers.

It's also possible to stay in Pac Ngoi village, where a successful **homestay** (per person 60,000d) program has been established so visitors can stay in a stilt house. The park office usually organises this, but you can just show up and check in too. The very well kept **Hoa Son Guesthouse** (☎389 4065) is one of the best, with a huge balcony and lake views, but there at least a dozen other options, all of which have hot-water bathrooms. Meals (40,000d to 60,000d) are available, and can include fresh fish from the lake.

Another option is to use the nearby town of Cho Ra as a base. The **Thuy Dung Guesthouse** (☎387 6354; 5 Tieu Khu; r 300,000d; ⊙) is a friendly family-run spot with balconies, wooden shutters and views of the nearby rice paddies. There's a good restaurant onsite, and the staff can arrange onward transport by boat (320,000d) from Cho Ra into the heart of the national park. The journey takes you past waterfalls and minority villages.

ℹ Information

Only cash is accepted and the nearest ATM and internet access is in Cho Ra.

THE LEGEND OF WIDOW'S ISLAND

A tiny islet in the middle of the Ba Be Lakes is the source of a local legend. The Tay people believe that what is a lake today was once farmland, and in the middle was a village called Nam Mau.

One day, Nam Mau residents found a buffalo wandering in the nearby forest. They caught it, butchered it and shared the meat. However, they didn't share any with a certain lonely widow.

Unfortunately for the villagers, this wasn't just any old buffalo. It belonged to the river ghost. When the buffalo failed to return home, the ghost went to the village disguised as a beggar. He asked the villagers for something to eat, but they refused to share their buffalo buffet and ran the poor beggar off. Only the widow was kind to him and gave him some food and a place to stay for the night.

That night the beggar told the widow to take some rice husks and sprinkle them on the ground around her house. Later in the evening, it started to rain and then a flood came. The villagers all drowned, and the flood washed away their homes and farms, thus creating the Ba Be Lakes. Only the widow's house remained: it's now Po Gia Mai (Widow's Island).

ⓘ Getting There & Away

Ba Be National Park is 240km from Hanoi, 61km from Bac Kan and 18km from Cho Ra.

Most people visit Ba Be as part of a tour, or by chartered vehicle from Hanoi (a 4WD is not necessary). The one-way journey from Hanoi takes about six hours. See p79 for recommended tour companies.

BUS & BOAT By public transport, the most direct route is on a daily bus at noon from the Gia Lam bus station in Hanoi to Cho Ra (150,000d, six hours). This allows travellers to overnight in Cho Ra before continuing on to Ba Be by boat the following morning.

BUS & MOTORBIKE Take a bus from Hanoi to Phu Thong (110,000d, five hours) via Thai Nguyen and/or Bac Kan, and from there take another bus to Cho Ra (30,000d, one hour). In Cho Ra arrange a motorbike (about 70,000d) to cover the last 18km.

If you're heading northeast from Ba Be, it's best to get a local bus from Cho Ra to Na Phac and get a connection there to Cao Bang.

Con Son & Den Kiep Bac

Most appealing to domestic travellers, Con Son and Den Kiep Bac are potential diversions en route to Haiphong or Halong City.

Con Son was home to Nguyen Trai (1380–1442), the famed Vietnamese poet, writer and general. Nguyen Trai assisted Emperor Le Loi in his successful battle against the Chinese Ming dynasty in the 15th century. **Con Son Pagoda** (Map p88; admission per person/ vehicle 5000/15000d) has a temple honouring Nguyen Trai. It's a strenuous 600-step climb. Alternatively, loop past a spring through pine forests, and return down the steps.

Nearby, **Kiep Bac temple** (Den Kiep Bac; Map p88; admission per person/vehicle 5000/15,000d) is dedicated to Tran Hung Dao (1228–1300). Founded in 1300, the temple sits where Tran Hung Dao is said to have died. Within the complex there's an exhibition on his exploits, but you'll need someone to translate. The annual **Tran Hung Dao Festival** is held from the 18th to the 20th day of the eighth lunar month, usually in October.

Den Kiep Bac and Con Son are in Hai Duong province, about 80km east of Hanoi. With your own wheels, it's easy to detour en route to Haiphong or Halong Bay.

Haiphong

🖉 031 / POP 1,884,600

With graceful tree-lined boulevards, an impressive array of colonial-era buildings and an unhurried air, Haiphong is a very approachable city. It's an important seaport and industrial centre, but few visitors linger. If you do pass through, you'll find minimal hassles compared to Vietnam's main tourism centres, with barely a tout to be found. Cafe culture is very strong here and many central places have street tables – perfect for people-watching.

Haiphong is a major transport hub, and well connected to Cat Ba Island and Hanoi by bus, boat and train.

History

The French took possession of Haiphong in 1874 and the city developed rapidly, becoming a major port. Heavy industry evolved through the proximity to coal supplies.

The French bombardment of Haiphong in 1946 killed thousands and was a catalyst for the ensuing Franco–Viet Minh War. Between 1965 and 1972 Haiphong came under air and naval attack from the US, and the city's harbour was mined to disrupt Soviet military supplies. In the late 1970s and the 1980s Haiphong experienced a mass exodus that included many ethnic Chinese refugees, who left taking much of the city's fishing fleet with them.

Today Haiphong is a fast-growing city, attracting investment from multinational corporations lured by its port facilities and transport links.

⊙ Sights & Activities

FREE **Haiphong Museum**   MUSEUM
(66 P Dien Bien Phu; ⊙8am-12.30pm & 2-4pm Mon-Fri, 7.30-9.30pm Wed & Sun) In a splendid colonial building, the Haiphong Museum concentrates on the city's history. Some displays have English translations and the museum's garden harbours a ragtag collection of war detritus.

FREE **Queen of the Rosary Cathedral**   CATHEDRAL
(P Hoang Van Thu) Haiphong's elegant Roman Catholic cathedral was built in the 19th century and comprehensively restored in 2010. The building's grey towers are a local landmark, and the inner courtyard is spacious and relaxing – until friendly children from the adjacent primary school are let loose after classes.

Opera House   HISTORIC BUILDING
(P Quang Trung) With a facade embellished with white columns, Haiphong's neoclassical Opera House dates from 1904.

Haiphong

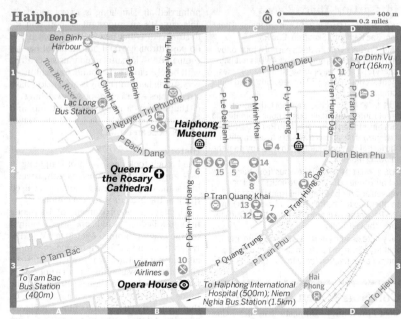

Du Hang Pagoda
PAGODA

(121 P Chua Hang) Du Hang Pagoda was founded three centuries ago. It's been rebuilt several times, but remains a fine example of traditional Vietnamese architecture and sculpture. P Chua Hang is a narrow thoroughfare, bustling with Haiphong street life. The pagoda is around 1.5km southwest of Haiphong's main street, Dien Bien Phu.

FREE Navy Museum
MUSEUM

(P Dien Bien Phu; ⊙8-11am Tue, Thu & Sat) A short walk from the Haiphong Museum, the Navy Museum is interesting for visiting sailors and US Vietnam veterans.

🛏 Sleeping

Monaco Hotel
HOTEL $$

(⌨374 6468; monacohotel@vnn.vn; 103 P Dien Bien Phu; r US$25, ste US$35-50; ❄🖅) This modern and central hotel has a real polish about it, including the smart lobby where the helpful reception staff speak some English. The spacious, spotless rooms come with two double beds, attractive bathrooms are well presented, and breakfast is included.

Bao Anh Hotel
HOTEL $$

(⌨382 3406; www.baoanhhotel.com; 22 P Minh Khai; r 600,000-800,000d; ❄@🖅) Recently refurbished in trendy minimalist style, the Bao Anh features a great location in a leafy street framed by plane tress and buzzy cafes. Just outside, there's also the excellent BKK Thai restaurant.

Harbour View Hotel
HOTEL $$$

(⌨382 7827; www.harbourviewvietnam.com; 4 P Tran Phu; s/d US$118/132; ❄❄@🖅🏊) Built in replica-colonial style in 1998, this stately hotel has comfortable rooms and excellent facilities, including a gym, spa and restaurant. Breakfast is included, and the super-friendly team on reception can arrange tours around Haiphong in a vintage Citroën car. Be sure to try for a substantial discount off rack rates.

Kim Thanh Hotel
HOTEL $

(⌨374 5264; kimthanhhotel@vnn.vn; 67 P Dien Bien Phu; r 320,000-500,000d; ❄🖅) Nothing fancy, but a good bet for a reasonably priced hotel in Haiphong. The rooms are old fashioned but kept clean, and have a TV and minibar. Breakfast is included. Ask for a room at the back to minimise road noise.

Hoa Viet Hotel
HOTEL $

(⌨384 2409; www.hoaviethotel.vn; 50 P Dien Bien Phu; r 250,000-400,000d; ❄🖅) Excellent value in central Haiphong, with simply furnished rooms arranged around a courtyard in a restored colonial building. Rates include breakfast served in the hotel's adjacent restaurant.

Haiphong

◉ Top Sights
Haiphong Museum	B2
Opera House	B3
Queen of the Rosary Cathedral	B2

◎ Sights
1	Navy Museum	C2

⊟ Sleeping
	Bao Anh Hotel	(see 8)
2	Duyen Hai Hotel	B1
3	Harbour View Hotel	D1
4	Hoa Viet Hotel	C2
5	Kim Thanh Hotel	C2
6	Monaco Hotel	B2

⊗ Eating
7	Big Man Restaurant	C2
8	BKK	C2
9	Com Vietnam	B2
10	Seafood Restaurants	B3
11	Van Tue	D1

⊙ Drinking
12	Caffe Tra Cuc	C2
13	Julie's Bar	C2
14	Maxims	C2
15	Phone Box	C2
16	Vuon Dua	D2

Duyen Hai Hotel HOTEL $
(☏384 2134; 6 Đ Nguyen Tri Phuong; r 250,000-400,000d; ❄️🛜) Offers fair value and is worth a try if other places are full.

✖ Eating

Haiphong is noted for its fresh seafood. Visit P Quang Trung for **seafood restaurants** with point-and-cook tanks as well as *bia hoi* (beer) joints. For more stylish cafes and restaurants, take a wander along P Minh Khai. Beer fans can rejoice that the city has two places serving decent microbrewed beer.

TOP CHOICE Big Man Restaurant BREWERY $$
(7 P Tran Hung Dao; mains from 80,000d; ⏲11am-11pm) This sprawling restaurant has an outdoor terrace and an extensive menu with brilliant seafood and excellent Vietnamese salads. It also doubles as a microbrewery, with light and dark lager. Don't be surprised if you return here for a second night.

BKK THAI $$
(22 P Minh Khai; mains 70,000-150,000d; ⏲11.30am-10pm) This meticulously restored old townhouse is the perfect setting for a memorable meal. Authentic Thai dishes are beautifully prepared and presented – try the *lab moo* (pork salad) or pepper squid; there's good vegetarian options too. Leave room for dessert, which includes delicious coconut ice cream.

Van Tue SEAFOOD $$
(1 P Hoang Dieu; mains 40,000-200,000d; ⏲11am-11pm) This elegant French colonial villa is renowned for seafood, including an amazing selection of crab dishes. Don't miss the two

varieties of Czech-style beer – light and dark – brewed on the premises.

Com Vietnam VIETNAMESE $
(4A P Hoang Van Thu; mains 30,000-65,000d) Diminutive, unpretentious restaurant with a small patio, this place hits the spot for its affordable local seafood and Vietnamese specialities. The kids at the school next door get pretty boisterous.

🍷 Drinking & Entertainment

P Minh Hieu is the heart of Haiphong's caffeine action. Virtually all of these cafes have street terraces, serve beer (try local brew Bia Haiphong), and have a snack menu.

Phone Box BAR
(79 P Dien Bien Phu; ⏲noon-11.30pm) This compact bar is run by a musician and is a great place for a relaxed drink. There's live music (usually an acoustic guitarist or jazz artist) on Mondays and Fridays, and you can expect good tunes at other times from the owner's extensive vinyl collection.

Vuon Dua BIA HOI
(5 P Tran Hung Dao) Boisterous beer garden with lots of cheap brews, and squid, chicken and pork prepared in lots of different ways. It's packed with locals every night enjoying a few (not so) quiet beers after work.

Maxims CAFE
(51B P Dien Bien Phu) A vague relation to the famous Maxims in Saigon, it has live music from classical to jazz most nights. Just pop in for a drink, because the food is pretty mediocre.

Julie's Bar
BAR

(22C P Minh Khai) Cosy expat hangout that's the ideal spot to get the lowdown on the latest Haiphong gossip. There's pretty good steaks and burgers available if you're hankering for comfort food.

Caffe Tra Cuc
CAFE

(46C P Minh Khai; ☎) The coffee, done loads of ways, and the free wi-fi is lapped up by grizzled regulars and Haiphong trendies alike.

ⓘ Information

Internet Access

Internet cafes along P Dien Bien Phu charge around 5000d per hour. Cafes on P Minh Khai have free wi-fi.

Medical Services

Haiphong International Hospital (☎395 5888; 124 Nguyen Duc Canh) Newly built and modern, with some English-speaking doctors.

Money

ATMs dot the city centre.

ⓘ Getting There & Away

AIR Haiphong's Cat Bi airport is 6km southeast of central Haiphong. A taxi should be around 120,000d.

Jetstar Pacific Airways (☎04-3955 0550; www.jetstar.com) Links Haiphong and Ho Chi Minh City.

Vietnam Airlines (☎381 0890; www.vietnamair .com.vn; 30 P Hoang Van Thu) Links Haiphong to HCMC and Danang.

BOAT Boats depart from **Ben Binh Harbour**, a short walk from the Lac Long bus station. See p107 for details of boats to Cat Ba Island.

BUS Haiphong has three long-distance bus stations.

Tam Bac bus station (P Tam Bac) Buses to Hanoi (70,000d, two hours, every 10 minutes).

Niem Nghia bus station (Đ Tran Nguyen Han) Buses south of Haiphong, such as to Ninh Binh (90,000d, 3½ hours, every 30 minutes).

Lac Long bus station (P Cu Chinh Lan) Buses to Halong City (Bai Chay; 50,000d, 1½ hours, every 30 minutes), and regular connections to Mong Cai (100,000d, four hours, approximately every two hours) near the Chinese border. Lac Long also has buses to and from Hanoi (70,000d, two hours, every 10 minutes) convenient for those connecting with the Cat Ba boats at nearby Ben Binh Harbour.

CAR & MOTORBIKE Haiphong is 103km from Hanoi on the expressway, Hwy 5.

TRAIN A slow spur line service travels daily to Hanoi's Long Bien station (48,000d; 2½ hours; 6.10am, 8.55am, 3.10pm & 6.40pm).

ⓘ Getting Around

Try **Haiphong Taxi** (☎383 8383) or **Taxi Mai Linh** (☎383 3833). A xe om (motorbike taxi) from the bus stations to the hotels should be around 20,000d.

HALONG BAY

☑033

Imagine 2000 or more islands rising from the emerald waters of the Gulf of Tonkin and you have a vision of breathtaking beauty. *Halong* translates as 'where the dragon descends into the sea', and legend claims the islands of Halong Bay were created by a great dragon from the mountains. As it charged towards the coast, its flailing tail gouged out valleys and crevasses. When it finally plunged into the sea, the area filled with water, leaving only the pinnacles visible.

Designated a World Heritage site in 1994, this mystical landscape of limestone islets is often compared to Guilin in China or Krabi in southern Thailand. In reality, Halong Bay is more spectacular. The bay's immense number of islands are dotted with wind- and wave-eroded grottoes, and their sparsely forested slopes ring with birdsong.

Beyond a boat cruise, visitors to Halong also come to explore the caves. There are few real beaches in Halong Bay, but Lan Ha Bay has idyllic sandy coves a short boat hop from Cat Ba Town.

HALONG BAY'S VERY OWN LOCH NESS MONSTER

The dragon that gave birth to Halong Bay may be legend, but sailors have often reported sightings of a mysterious marine creature of gargantuan proportions known as the *tarasque*. The more paranoid elements of the military suspect it's an imperialist spy submarine, while eccentric travellers believe they have discovered Vietnam's version of the Loch Ness monster. Meanwhile, the monster – or whatever it is – continues to haunt Halong Bay, unfettered by the marine police, Vietnam Tourism and the immigration authorities. Enterprising Vietnamese boat owners have made a cottage industry out of the creature, offering cash-laden tourists the chance to rent a junk and pursue the *tarasque* before it gets bored and swims away.

Halong Bay & Bai Tu Long Bay

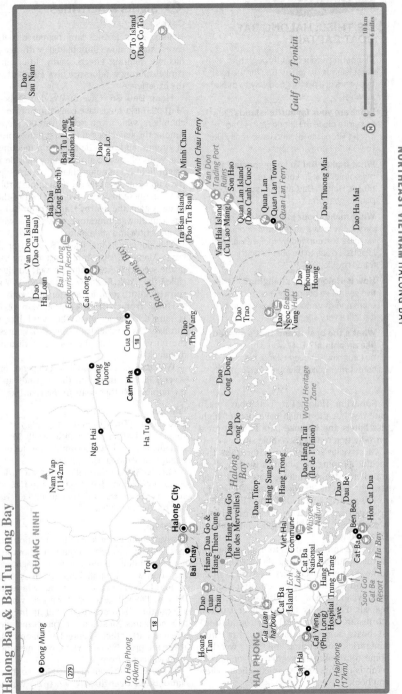

QUANG NINH

HAI PHONG

Gulf of Tonkin

Co To Island (Dao Co To)

Dao Sau Nam

Dao Cao Lo

Minh Chau

Minh Chau Ferry

Van Don Trading Port Ruins

Son Hao

Quan Lan Island (Dao Canh Cuoc)

Quan Lan

Quan Lan Town

Quan Lan Ferry

Van Hai Island (Cu Lao Mang)

Tra Ban Island (Dao Tra Ban)

Dao Thuong Mai

Dao Ha Mai

Bai Dai (Long Beach)

Bai Tu Long National Park

Van Don Island (Dao Cai Bau)

Dao Ha Loan

Bai Tu Long Ecotourism Resort

Cai Rong

Bai Tu Long Bay

Cua Ong

18

Mong Duong

Cam Pha

Dao The Vang

Dao Trao

Dao Phoung Hoang

Dao Ngoc Beach Vung Huts

World Heritage Zone

Nam Vap (1142m)

Nga Hai

Ha Tu

Dao Cong Dong

Dao Cong Do

Halong City

Bai Chay

Hang Dau Go & Hang Thien Cung

Dao Hang Dau Go (Ile des Merveilles)

Halong Bay

Dao Titop

Hang Sung Sot

Hang Trong

Dao Hang Trai (Ile de l'Union)

Dao Dau Be

Viet Hai Commune

Whisper of Nature

Ben Beo

Hon Cat Dua

Cat Ba National Park

Hang Trung Trang Cave

Dao Tuan Chau

Troi

18

Hoang Tan

Gia Luan harbour

Cat Ba Island Ech Lake

Cat Vieng (Phu Long) Hospital

Suoi Goi Cat Ba Resort

Cat Ba

Lan Ha Bay

Cat Hai

Dong Mung

229

To Hai Phong (40km)

To Haiphong (17km)

10 km
6 miles

N

LOCAL KNOWLEDGE

MR THIEU: HALONG BAY BOAT CAPTAIN

Skippering a tour boat through the karst islands of Halong Bay for the past five years is a pretty good way to make a living.

What are your favourite islands? My favourite place in Halong Bay is Dao Titop (Titop Island), and I also really like the Bai Tu Long area to the east.

What makes Bai Tu Long special? In my opinion Bai Tu Long is just as beautiful as Halong Bay, and not so many people go there.

What makes your job special? I'm very lucky to live on the boat and always be surrounded by these amazing islands. I'd like to be able to do this job for all my life.

How is Halong Bay changing? In the five years I've been on Halong Bay, I see more and more tourists every year, but it's still a very special place.

What's the best island that's shaped like an animal? That would have to be Laughing Chicken Island. It's also sometimes called Fighting Cock Island.

Sprawling Halong City is the bay's main gateway, but the raffish collection of high-rise hotels and karaoke bars is not a great introduction to this incredible site.

Most visitors sensibly opt for tours that include sleeping on a boat in the bay. Some travellers dodge Halong City and head straight for Cat Ba Town, from where trips to less-visited, equally alluring Lan Ha Bay are easily set up. Cat Ba Island can also be a good base for visiting the landscapes of Halong Bay itself.

As the number-one tourist attraction in the northeast, Halong Bay attracts visitors year-round. February to April is often cool and drizzly, and the ensuing fog can make visibility low, but also adds an ethereal air. From May to September tropical storms are frequent, and year round, tourist boats sometimes need to alter their itineraries, depending on the weather. Some tour companies offer full or partial refunds if tours are cancelled; check when you book.

⊙ Sights & Activities

Caves

Halong Bay's islands are peppered with caves, many now illuminated with technicolour lighting effects. Sadly, litter and trinket-touting vendors are now also part of the experience.

Hang Dau Go (Cave of Wooden Stakes; Map p95) is a huge cave consisting of three chambers which you reach via 90 steps. Among the stalactites of the first hall, scores of gnomes appear to be holding a meeting. The walls of the second chamber sparkle if bright light is shone on them. The cave derives its name from its third chamber's role in Vietnamese history – see p89. Part of the same system, the nearby **Hang Thien Cung** has 'cauliflower' limestone growths as well as stalactites and stalagmites.

The popular **Hang Sung Sot** (Surprise Cave; Map p95) has three vast chambers; in the second there's a pink-lit rock phallus, called the 'Cock Rock' by some guides. Not surprisingly it's regarded as a fertility symbol.

Hang Trong (Drum Grotto; Map p95) is named because when the wind blows through its stalactites and stalagmites, the effect resembles the sound of distant drumbeats.

Which of the caves you'll visit depends on several factors, including the weather and the number of other boats in the vicinity.

Islands

Dao Titop (Titop Island, Map p95) is a small island with a scruffy little beach. Make straight for the island's summit for superb panoramic views of Halong Bay.

Cat Ba Island (Map p95) is the most developed of Halong Bay's islands and Cat Ba Town is very close to the gorgeous Lan Ha Bay region (Map p95).

Kayaking

A kayak among the karsts is an option on most Halong Bay tours. Count on about an hour's paddling, often including negotiating your way through karst grottoes and around lagoons, or to a floating village in the bay. The villagers here farm fish, which are caught offshore and fattened up in netted enclosures. Most tour operators include a visit as part of their Halong Bay itineraries. These are probably also where your evening meal will come from.

If you're really keen on kayaking, contact **Handspan Adventure Travel** (p79) which runs professionally organised trips, has qualified guides, and operates beach camps. Trips are operated from less-touristed Lan Ha Bay (p100).

ⓘ Information

All visitors must purchase entry tickets to the national park. One-day tickets are 40,000d, including one cave or one beach. Entry for two days and one night is 60,000d. Additional caves and beaches are 10,000d each, and fishing-village visits are 20,000d. Most admission fees are included with organised tours, but check when you book.

The official **Halong Bay Tourist Information Centre** (off Map p98; ☎384 7481; www .halong.org.vn; ⊗7am-4pm) is at Bai Chay dock in Halong City. Here you'll find English-speaking staff, internet and excellent maps (20,000d). Another good operation is **Halong Tourism** (Map p98; ☎362 8862; www.halongtourism .com.vn; ⊗8am-noon & 1.30-4.30pm Mon-Fri), also in Bai Chay.

ⓘ Getting There & Away

Taking a tour (p97) is certainly convenient, and many are very cheap.

It's also possible to head here independently. The regular run is by bus from Hanoi to Bai Chay (Halong City), and then by *xe om* or taxi to Bai Chay harbour. At bustling Bai Chay, you can book a tour.

There are also tour boats running from Bai Chay via Halong Bay to Cat Ba Island (see p107). Alternatively, head directly to Cat Ba Island from Hanoi and arrange a boat trip from there to explore Lan Ha Bay.

ⓘ Getting Around

Most boat tours leave from Bai Chay tourist dock in Halong City. Prices are officially regulated and depend upon the route, length of trip and class of boat. This dock is pretty chaotic, with hundreds of people embarking and disembarking from dozens of boats.

To hire a one-star boat for a four-hour cruise costs around 1,000,000d, or it's around

---

DON'T MISS

CRUISING THE KARSTS: TOURS TO HALONG BAY

There are many ways to experience the ethereal beauty of Halong Bay. Unless you have a private yacht (or you're an Olympic kayaker), you'll have to take a tour of some kind.

For a serious splurge, cruising the karsts aboard a luxury Chinese-style junk is hard to beat. There's also a very luxurious paddle ship, based on a French craft from the early 20th century. But be aware that nearly all of these luxury trips operate on a fixed itinerary, taking in the well-known caves and islands, and simply do not have the time to stray far from Halong City. Many 'two-day' tours actually involve less than 24 hours on a boat (and cost hundreds of dollars per person).

At the other end of the scale, budget tours sold out of Hanoi start from a rock-bottom US$35 per person for a dodgy day trip, and rise to around US$150 for two nights on the bay with kayaking. For around US$80 to US$90, you should get a worthwhile overnight cruise.

We get many complaints about poor service, bad food and rats running around boats, but these tend to be on the ultrabudget tours. Spend a little more and enjoy the experience a whole lot more. It can be false economy signing up for one of the budget tours, and it's also potentially a matter of safety.

In February 2011, a budget boat tour sank near Dao Titop with the loss of 11 international tourists from eight countries and one Vietnamese tour guide. In May 2011, the provincial government of the area around Halong Bay enacted new regulations on working conditions and boat safety. Boat owners protested that the new regulations would make some tours unprofitable, so potentially budget tour operators will be looking to cut corners in other ways.

Most tours include transport and meals, and sometimes include island hikes. Drinks are extra. Most of these trips follow a strict itinerary, with planned stops at illuminated caves often at the same time as many of the other boats operating out of Bai Chay.

If you have more time and want to experience Halong Bay without the crowds, consider Cat Ba Island. Here you'll find operators who concentrate on Lan Ha Bay, which is less frequented, relatively untouched and has sublime sandy beaches (see p103).

Because of weather, boat tours are sometimes cancelled and you'll probably be offered a full or partial refund. Ascertain in advance what that will be.

For a list of reliable Hanoi-based tour operators operating in Halong Bay see p79.

1,500,000d for a six-hour cruise. You can rent out a whole two-star boat for the day for 2,500,000d. On weekends, prices rise by around 20%. Costs are usually divided between the total number of people on board.

Halong City

📞033 / POP 193,700

Halong City is the main gateway to Halong Bay. Though the city enjoys a stunning position on the cusp of Halong Bay, developers have not been kind to it, and high-rise hotels dot the shoreline. However, the majority of food, accommodation and other Halong Bay services are found here.

Most travellers don't stay in town, preferring to spend a night out in Halong Bay itself. Increased competition for a dwindling clientele means budget hotel rates are some of the cheapest in Vietnam. Chinese and Korean visitors are now more prevalent, preferring to enjoy the terra firma attractions of casinos and karaoke after a day exploring Halong Bay.

🛏 Sleeping

Most people stay on a boat in the bay but there are hundreds of hotels around Bai Chay, and prices are very reasonable outside the peak season (June to August) or during the Tet festival.

Virtually all budget accommodation is on the hotel alley of Đ Vuon Dao, home to around 50 near-identical mini-hotels. Comfortable doubles are around US$12. Midrange and top-end hotels are scattered along Đ Halong, many commanding great views.

Novotel   HOTEL $$$
(Map p98; 📞384 8108; www.novotelhalongbay .com; Đ Halong; r from US$115; ☞🌀@🛜🏊) This hip hotel fuses Asian and Japanese influences with contemporary details. The rooms are simply stunning, with teak floors, marble bathrooms and sliding screens to divide living areas. Facilities include an oval infinity pool, an espresso bar and a great restaurant. Check online for rates around US$80.

BMC Thang Long Hotel   HOTEL $$
(off Map p98; 📞384 6458; www.bmcthanglong hotel.com; Đ Halong; r US$25-75; 🌀@🛜) This popular lunch stop for Halong Bay tour groups also features spacious and recently redecorated rooms, some with ocean views. Despite the hotel's sprawling size, the staff are warm and personal, and the Bai Chay tourist docks are handily just across the road.

Tung Lam Hotel   HOTEL $
(Map p98; 📞364 0743; 29 Đ Vuon Dao; r US$10-12; 🌀🛜) This mini-hotel is making a little more effort than most on this strip. The rooms all have two beds, a TV, a minibar and en-suite bathrooms, and those at the front are spacious and include a balcony.

Thanh Hue Hotel   HOTEL $
(Map p98; 📞384 7612; Đ Vuon Dao; r US$12-15; 🌀@🛜) Continue uphill from the Tung Lam to this great-value hotel – look for the powder-blue paint job. Most rooms have cracking views of the bay from their balconies. It's a bit of a walk after a seafood meal and a few beers, but well worth it.

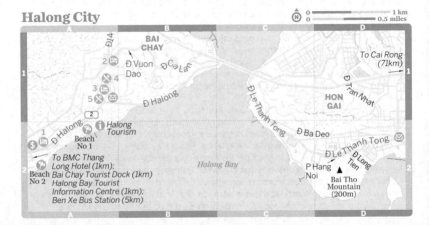

Halong City

✕ Eating

For cheap, filling food, there are modest places at the bottom of Đ Vuon Dao with English menus. Seafood lovers should gravitate to the harbour-front Đ Halong, where there's a cluster of good places.

Toan Huong   VIETNAMESE $
(Map p98; 1 Đ Vuon Dao; mains from 35,000đ) A simple place with friendly staff, a street terrace and an extensive menu (in English) with a bit of everything: Western breakfasts, salads, fresh seafood and imported wine.

Asia Restaurant   VIETNAMESE $
(Map p98; 24 Đ Vuon Dao; mains 40,000-80,000đ) A clean, attractive place that's geared to travellers' tastes, with good Vietnamese food and a smattering of Western favourites.

ℹ Information

Main post office (Đ Halong) At the bottom of Vuon Dao.
Vietcombank (Đ Halong) Exchanges cash and has an ATM.

ℹ Getting There & Away

BOAT For boat trips throughout Halong Bay, see p99 and p97. See p107 for boat travel from Halong Bay to Cat Ba Island.

In the past, hydrofoils ran from Bai Chay to Mong Cai (p110) for onward travel to China, but this route has been replaced by improved bus services.

BUS All buses leave **Ben Xe bus station**, 6km south of central Bai Chay, just off Hwy 18. Note that many long-distance buses will be marked 'Bai Chay' rather than 'Halong City'.

For Cai Rong Pier (Cai Rong Pha) on the island of Van Don – where you can catch onward ferries to the islands of Bai Tu Long – either catch a direct bus to Van Don, or get off at the junction town of Cua Ong on any Mong Cai or Lang Son bus. Then catch a xe om or taxi to the pier. Not all Van Don buses continue to Cai Rong Pier, so check at the Bai Chay bus station.

SOMETHING DIFFERENT

A selection of the more interesting cruises.

Emeraude Classic Cruise (☑04-3934 0888; www.emeraude-cruises.com; d US$255-490) A 56m replica paddle steamer with 38 air-conditioned cabins, all with elegant wooden furniture and smart hot-water showers. Lavish buffet-style meals are served. It is pricey for a cruise that's less than 24 hours.

Handspan (☑04-3926 2828; www.handspan.com) Launched in late 2011, Handspan's Treasure Junk is the only true sailing ship operating on the bay. That means you get to meander peacefully through the karsts without the constant hum of a diesel engine. Crack open a cold Bia Hanoi and you'll be in heaven.

Indochina Sails (☑04-3984 2362; www.indochinasails.com; s/d from US$310/358) Cruise Halong on a traditional junk kitted out to a three-star standard. Indochina operates two 42m junks and one smaller craft; all have attractive wooden cabins and great viewing decks.

CAR & MOTORBIKE Halong City is 160km from Hanoi and 55km from Haiphong. The one-way trip from Hanoi to Halong City takes about three hours by private vehicle.

ℹ Getting Around

Bai Chay is quite spread out; **Mai Linh** (☑382 2226) is a reliable taxi option. Taxis also wait by the bus station and post office.

Cat Ba Island
☑031 / POP 13,500

Rugged, craggy and jungle-clad Cat Ba, the largest island in Halong Bay, is emerging as Vietnam's adventure sport and ecotourism hub. There's an energetic roll-call of activities, including sailing, bird-watching, cycling, hiking and rock climbing.

Except for a few fertile pockets, Cat Ba's terrain is too rocky for serious agriculture. Most residents earn their living from the sea, while others work in tourism.

In recent years, Cat Ba Town has experienced a hotel boom, and a chain of ugly concrete hotels now frames a once-lovely

NORTHEAST VIETNAM HALONG CITY

Halong City

🛏 Sleeping
1 Novotel	....	A2
2 Thanh Hue Hotel	....	A1
3 Tung Lam Hotel	....	A1

✕ Eating
4 Asia Restaurant	....	A1
5 Toan Huong	....	A1

BAI CHAY BUS CONNECTIONS

DESTINATION	COST	DURATION	FREQUENCY
Hanoi	90,000d	3hr	Every 15 min
Haiphong	50,000d	1½hr	Every 20 min
Mong Cai	90,000d	4hr	Every 30 min
Van Don	55,000d	1½hr	Approx hourly
Lang Son	120,000d	5½hr	12.30pm

bay. But the rest of the island is largely untouched, and with idyllic Lan Ha Bay just offshore you'll soon overlook Cat Ba Town's overdevelopment.

Most of the year Cat Ba Town is a laidback place, and an excellent base for activities around the island, or sailing and kayaking around Lan Ha Bay. On summer weekends Cat Ba turns into a roaring resort, filling up with vacationing Vietnamese. Hotel prices double or treble and there's an excess of karaoke joints and hubbub. Cars are banned from the promenade, which is taken over by a sea of strolling holidaymakers. Weekdays are saner, but still busy between June and August.

Ho Chi Minh paid a visit to Cat Ba Island on April 1 1951 and there is an annual festival to commemorate the event. During this time, expect lots of waterfront karaoke and techno beats from 8am to midnight.

Almost half of Cat Ba Island (with a total area of 354 sq km) and 90 sq km of the adjacent waters were declared a national park in 1986 to protect the island's diverse ecosystems: subtropical evergreen forests on the hills, freshwater swamp forests at the base of the hills, coastal mangrove forests, small freshwater lakes and coral reefs. Most of the coastline consists of rocky cliffs, but there are some sandy beaches and tiny fishing villages hidden away in small coves.

Lakes, waterfalls and grottoes dot the spectacular limestone hills, the highest rising 331m above sea level. The island's largest body of water is Ech Lake, (3 hectares). Almost all of the surface streams are seasonal. Most of the island's rainwater flows into caves and follows underground streams to the sea, creating a shortage of fresh water during the dry season.

Lan Ha Bay, encompassing the southern seas off Cat Ba, is dotted with hundreds of jungle-topped limestone islands with many deserted beaches.

Cat Ba's best weather is from late September to November, when air and water temperatures are mild and the skies are mostly clear. December to February is cooler but pleasant. From February to April is still good, but you can expect some rain. Summer (June to August) is hot and humid with occasional thunderstorms. This is also peak season and the island is packed with Vietnamese tourists.

◉ Sights

First impressions of Cat Ba Town are not great, but the mediocre vision of a low-rent mini-Manhattan only extends for a street or two behind the promenade. A **monument** to Ho Chi Minh stands up on Mountain No 1, the hillock opposite the pier in Cat Ba Town. The **market** at the northern end of the harbour is a great local affair with twitching crabs, jumbo shrimps and pyramids of fresh fruit. Head out of the town for the island's best sights.

Lan Ha Bay   ISLANDS

(Map p95; admission 20,000d) The 300 or so karst islands of Lan Ha Bay are directly south and east of Cat Ba Town. Geologically they are very much an extension of Halong Bay, but geographically these islands lie in a different province of Vietnam. They share the same emerald sea, and the limestone pinnacles and scenery are every bit as beautiful as Halong Bay, but these islands have the additional attraction of numerous white sand beaches. Lan Ha Bay is a fair way from Halong City, so not so many tourist boats venture to this side of the bay. In short, Lan Ha Bay has a more isolated, off-the-beaten-track appeal (and far fewer visitors). There is a 20,000d admission fee to the bay, but this is often incorporated into the cost of tours.

Around 200 species of fish, 500 species of mollusc, 400 species of arthropod and numerous hard and soft coral live in Lan Ha Bay. Larger marine animals in the area include seals and three species of dolphin.

Sailing and kayak trips here are best organised in Cat Ba Town. With hundreds of beaches to choose from, it's easy to find your own private patch of sand for the day. Camping is permitted on gorgeous **Hai Pai beach** (also known as Tiger beach), which is used as a base camp by the Cat Ba adventure tour operators and also hosts occasional full-moon parties. Lan Ha Bay also offers superb rock climbing and is the main destination for trips run by Asia Outdoors (p107).

Cat Ba National Park
NATURE RESERVE

(Map p95; admission 30,000d; ☼ sunrise to sunset) This accessible national park is home to 32 types of mammal – langurs and macaques, wild boar, deer, civets, several species of squirrel including the giant black squirrel – and more than 70 species of bird, including hawks, hornbills and cuckoos. The golden-headed langur is officially the world's most endangered primate with around 65 remaining, most in this park. Cat Ba lies on a major migration route for waterfowl, which feed and roost on the beaches in the mangrove forests. Over a thousand species of plants have been recorded here, including 118 trees and 160 plants with medicinal value. The park is also home to the Cay Kim Gao tree. In ancient days, kings and nobles would eat only with chopsticks made from this timber, as anything poisonous it touches is reputed to turn the light-coloured wood to black.

A guide is not mandatory but is definitely recommended to help you make sense of the verdant canopy of trees. The multi-chambered **Hang Trung Trang** (Trung Trang Cave) is easily accessible, but you will need to contact a ranger to make sure it is open. Bring a torch (flashlight).

There's a challenging 18km hike through the park and up to one of the mountain summits. Arrange a guide for this six-hour hike and organise a bus or boat transport to the trailhead and a boat to get back to town. This can be arranged with the rangers at the national park headquarters, or at Asia Outdoors or Cat Ba Ventures in Cat Ba Town.

Many hikes end at **Viet Hai**, a remote minority village just outside the park boundary, from which boats shuttle back to Cat Ba Town (about 300,000d per boat). There is also accommodation here at Whisper of Nature (p105). Take proper hiking shoes, a raincoat and a generous supply of water for this hike. Independent hikers can buy basic snacks at the kiosks in Viet Hai, which is where many hiking groups stop for lunch. This is not an easy walk, and is much harder and more slippery after rain. There are shorter hiking options that are less hardcore.

To reach the national park headquarters at Trung Trang, take a green QH public bus from the hydrofoil docks at Cat Ba Town (15,000d, 20 minutes). Buses leave at 5am, 8.10am, 11.10am and 4pm. Another option is to hire *a xe om* for around 60,000d one-way, or hire your own motorbike for the day.

Cat Co Cove
BEACHES

(off Map p102) A 15-minute walk southeast from Cat Ba Town, the three beautiful Cat Co Cove beaches boast white sand and good swimming. Cat Co 2, backed by limestone cliffs, is the beach to head for. Here you'll find a lovely sheltered sandy bay, a snack bar and some simple thatched beach huts. However, as developers have been eyeing up this beach for some time, check first to see if it remains a haven of tranquillity.

DON'T MISS

FORT CANNON

For one of the best views in all of Vietnam – no, we're not kidding – head to **Fort Cannon** (off Map p102; admission 20,000d; ☼ sunrise to sunset). The underground tunnels and gun emplacements were first installed by the Japanese in WWII, but were also utilised by the French and Vietnamese during subsequent conflicts.

Well-labelled paths guide visitors past two well-preserved gun emplacements, one 'manned' by life-size Viet Minh mannequins, and the astounding vistas include the colourful tangle of fishing boats in Cat Ba harbour, and the perfect little coves of Cat Co 1 and Cat Co 2. The views out to a karst-punctuated sea are quite sublime, and there's even a terrific cafe and juice bar adjacent to the Fort's old helicopter landing pad. The entrance gate is a steep 10-minute walk or a 10,000d *xe om* ride from Cat Ba Town. From the gate, a **tourist train** (40,000d) trundles the last uphill journey, or it's another stiff 20-minute walk.

Cat Ba Town

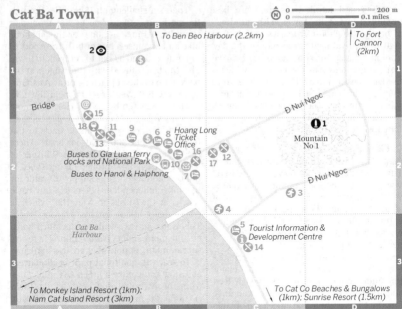

Cat Co 1 and 3 were once equally attractive, but both have now been developed as resorts. On weekends in summer they get packed with Vietnamese tourists and litter is a real blight.

Other beaches on the island include Cai Vieng, Hong Xoai Be and Hong Xoai Lon.

Hospital Cave   HISTORICAL SITE

(Map p95; admission 15,000d; ⊗7am-4.30pm) Oozing historical significance, Hospital Cave served both as a secret, bomb-proof hospital during the American War and as a safe house for VC leaders. Built between 1963 and 1965 (with assistance from China), this incredibly well-constructed three-storey feat of engineering was in constant use until 1975. A guide (most know a few words of English) will show you around the 17 rooms, point out the old operating theatre and take you to the huge natural cavern that as used as a cinema (and even had its own small swimming pool). The cave is about 10km north of Cat Ba Town on the road to the national park entrance.

Activities

Cat Ba is a superb base for adventure sports – on the island and in, on and over the water.

Mountain Biking

Hotels can arrange Chinese mountain bikes (around US$4 per day), and Blue Swimmer Adventures rents better quality mountain bikes for US$12 per day.

One possible route traverses the heart of the island, past Hospital Cave (p102) down to the west coast's mangroves and crab farms, and then in a loop back to Cat Ba Town past tidal mud flats and deserted beaches. Blue Swimmer and Asia Outdoors both arrange guided mountain-bike rides.

Rock Climbing

Cat Ba Island and Lan Ha Bay's spectacular limestone cliffs make for world-class rock climbing. See the boxed text, Climbing the Karsts (p104).

Based on Cat Ba, **Asia Outdoors** (p107) pioneered climbing in Vietnam and use fully licensed and certified instructors. Advanced climbers can hire gear here, talk shop, and pick up a copy of *Vietnam: A Climber's Guide* by Asia Outdoors' Erik Ferjentsik, which describes climbs and has some great tips about Cat Ba too. **Full-day climbing trips**, including instruction, transport, lunch and gear, start at US$52 per person for Cat Ba Island, or US$75 if you head for Lan Ha Bay. These longer trips by boat in-

Cat Ba Town

corporate kayaking, beach stops and exploring the amazing karst landscape. Other less-qualified Cat Ba operators also offer climbing trips, but Asia Outdoors are the authorities on the island.

Sailing & Kayaking
Don't miss exploring the spectacular islands and beaches of Lan Ha Bay (p100). **Blue Swimmer** (p103) offers **sailing excursions** to the myriad islands around Cat Ba. Overnight sailing trips through Lan Ha Bay to Nam Cat beach, including a night sleeping in a bamboo hut, cost US$39 per person. Also available are private boat charters with a skipper, and full-day trips on a Chinese junk to Long Chau lighthouse, built by the French in the 1920s, and still bearing bomb scars from the American War.

Plenty of hotels in Cat Ba Town rent **kayaks** (half-day around $8) and Blue Swimmer has good-quality kayaks (single/double per day US$12/20), ideal for exploring the Cat Ba coast independently. Guided overnight kayak tours from Blue Swimmer (per person $108) include Lan Ha Bay, sea caves, and camping on a deserted beach.

Trekking
Most of Cat Ba Island consists of protected tropical forest. For details of trekking routes in Cat Ba National Park see p101. Asia Outdoors and Blue Swimmer both offer a great hike around Cat Ba Island that takes in Butterfly Valley.

☞ Tours
Tours of the island and boat trips around Halong Bay are offered by nearly every hotel

in Cat Ba Town. Typical prices are around US$20 for day trips including kayaking and US$70 for two-day, one-night tours. We receive unfavourable feedback – cramped conditions and dodgy food – about some of these trips, but the following offer good prices and service.

Cat Ba Ventures BOAT TRIPS & KAYAKING
(Map p102; ☑368 8237; www.catbaventures.com; 223 Đ 14, Cat Ba Town) Locally owned and operated company offering boat trips to Halong Bay, kayaking, and hiking. Excellent service from Mr Tung is reinforced by multiple reader recommendations.

If you're looking for a different experience, the following adventure tour operators understand travellers' needs and will steer you away from the tourist trail to really special areas of Cat Ba, Lan Ha Bay, and beyond.

Asia Outdoors ROCK CLIMBING
(Map p102; ☑368 8450; www.slopony.com; Đ 1-4, Cat Ba Town) Formerly known as Slo Pony Adventures, this highly professional company is run by two uberpassionate climbers and explorers: Onslow Carrington and Erik Ferjentsik. Climbing instruction is Asia Outdoors' real expertise, but it also offers excellent well-structured sailing, biking and hiking trips. Rock up to its office in Noble House (at 6pm every night) to see what's planned.

Blue Swimmer SAILING & ADVENTURE
(Map p102; ☑369 6079; www.blueswimmersailing.com; 265 Đ Nui Ngoc) A very well-organised, environmentally conscious outfit established by Vinh, one of the founders of respected tour operator Handspan. Superb sailing and kayak trips, trekking and mountain biking

CLIMBING THE KARSTS

If you've ever considered it, or been tempted to climb, Halong Bay is a superb place to go for it – the karst cliffs here offer exceptional climbing amid stunning scenery. Most climbers in Cat Ba are complete novices, but as the instruction is excellent, many leave Cat Ba completely bitten by the bug.

You don't need great upper-body strength to climb, as you actually use your legs far more. The karst limestone of Halong Bay is not too sharp and quite friendly on the hands, and as many of the routes are sheltered by natural overhangs that prevent the climbable portion of the rock from getting wet, climbing is almost always possible, rain or shine.

A few inexperienced locals may offer climbing excursions to new arrivals on Cat Ba, but beginners should sign up with the experienced crew at Asia Outdoors (p107).

Climbing opportunities for beginners are located on walls inland on Cat Ba Island or out on beautiful Lan Ha Bay. You'll be kitted up with a harness and climbing shoes, given instruction and taught the fundamentals of the climbing and belaying techniques, then given a demonstration. Then it's over to you (with your climbing instructor talking you through each move and anchoring you, of course!). Most people are able to complete a couple of climbs at Hai Pai and Moody's Beach, which are both ideal for beginners.

The vertical cliffs of Halong and Lan Ha Bays are also perfect for deep-water soloing, which is basically climbing alone, without ropes or a harness, and using the ocean as a water bed in case you fall. This is obviously only for experienced climbers, and it's essential to know the depth of water and tidal patterns. We've heard reports of some climbers being injured falling into shallow waters, so it's vital to attempt deep-water soloing only with an experienced crew like Asia Outdoors. It's customary to finish a solo climb with a controlled freefall (or 'tombstone') into the sea and a swim back to the shore, or your boat.

excursions are offered. At the time of writing, Blue Swimmer had also just finalised the lease on its new Blue Swimmer Adventure Hotel. Check the website for details.

🛏 Sleeping

Most basic hotels are situated on (or just off) the waterfront in Cat Ba Town, but the area's accommodation scene is quickly evolving. More interesting options have opened in other parts of Cat Ba, and there are some wonderfully isolated spots on other islands in La Ha Bay.

Room rates fluctuate greatly. In the high-season summer months (June to August) you can expect to pay a minimum of US$15 per room; rates sink to below US$10 for a decent room outside this time. The rates given here are for low season. Peak season rates are impossible to determine as hotel owners tend to pick a number out of their heads depending on demand.

CAT BA TOWN

If the seafront hotels in Cat Ba Town are full, make a quick detour to Đ Nui Ngoc, which is lined with good-value accommodation.

Duc Tuan Hotel   HOTEL $
(Map p102; ☑388 8783; www.catbatravelservice.com; 210 Đ 1-4, Cat Ba Town; r US$8-15; ❊🛜)

Simple, but colourfully furnished rooms feature at this main-drag, family-owned spot. The rooms at the back are quieter, but lack windows. At less than 10 bucks a night, who's complaining? Downstairs is a good restaurant offering seafood *lau* (hotpot) meals, and the friendly owners can arrange all manner of Cat Ba excursions.

Cat Ba Dream   HOTEL $
(Map p102; ☑388 8274; www.catbadream.com.vn; 226 Đ 1-4, Cat Ba Town; r US$10-15; ❊@🛜) Slightly more expensive than Cat Ba's ultra cheapies, Cat Ba Dream is a recent addition to the town's seafront cavalcade of accommodation. Service is a tad perfunctory, but if you can angle for a seafront room, you'll have a cinematic scroll of Cat Ba action right in front of you.

Vien Dong   HOTEL $
(Map p102; ☑388 8555; www.viendong-hotel.com.vn, in Vietnamese; 225 Đ Nui Ngoc, Cat Ba Town; r US$12-15; ❊@🛜) Also known as the Far Eastern, the Vien Dong has sterling views of the bay, well-kept and spacious rooms, and a good grasp of English at reception. Yet more proof that Cat Ba offers some of Vietnam's best accommodation bargains.

Phong Lan Hotel   HOTEL $
(Map p102; ☑388 8605; Đ 1-4, Cat Ba Town; r US$8-12; ❊🛜) It is worth requesting a room at the

front of this hotel, located right in the middle of the seafront strip, to take advantage of balconies overlooking the harbour. The English-speaking owner is helpful and there's a travel agency here too.

Thu Ha
HOTEL $

(Map p102; ☑388 8343; Đ 1-4, Cat Ba Town; r US$8-12; ❄✉) With air-con, wi-fi, and a super-central seafront location, the recently refurbished Thu Ha offers great value in Cat Ba Town. Negotiate hard for a front room with a balcony, and wake up to sea views.

Noble House
GUESTHOUSE $

(Map p102; ☑388 8363; thenoblehousevn@yahoo.com; Đ 1-4, Cat Ba Town; r US$8-20; ❄✉) Simple rooms above the popular Good Bar; bring your earplugs or look forward to joining in.

CAT BA BEACHES & ISLANDS

TOP CHOICE Suoi Goi Cat Ba Resort
ECOLODGE $

(Map p95; ☑368 8966; www.suoigoicatbaresort.vn; Cat Ba Island; d from US$45; ❄✉) This new eco-resort celebrates a wonderfully quiet village location 12km from Cat Ba Town. Spacious wooden stilt houses sit around a breezy bar and restaurant, and activities include trekking, and riding bicycles to a beach 2km away. Most nights there is a seafood barbecue (US$10). Free pickups can be arranged from the ferry or Cat Ba Town.

Nam Cat Island Resort
RESORT $$

(off Map p102; ☑0989 555 773; namcatisland@gmail.com; Nam Cat Island; d US$25-60; ❄) Stop right now if you're looking for the secluded and isolated cove of your dreams. Nam Cat's prescription for relaxation includes simple bungalows plus flasher villas with private facilities; all located under looming indigo limestone cliffs. Spend your days swimming and kayaking, and kick back with seafood barbecues and beach bonfires after dark. Nam Cat is included on some itineraries arranged by Cat Ba Ventures (p103).

Whisper of Nature
GUESTHOUSE $

(Map p95; ☑265 7678; www.vietbungalow.com; Viet Hai Village; dm US$12, d US$22-28) Located in the hamlet of Viet Hai, Whisper of Nature's simple concrete-and-thatch bungalows are arrayed around a quietly-flowing stream on the edge of the forest. Accommodation ranges from shared dorms to bungalows with private bathrooms. Getting there is an adventure in itself, with the final stage a bike ride through lush scenery. Ask about transport when you book, or hire a bamboo boat

from Cat Ba Town to the Viet Hai village jetty (200,000d), and then a *xe om* (30,000d) for the final 5km to the village.

Sunrise Resort
RESORT $$$

(off Map p102; ☑388 7360; www.catbasunriseresort.com; Cat Co 3; r from US$110; ❄@✉❄) This beachfront resort is tastefully planned, with low-rise tiled-roofed blocks sitting below green cliffs. Rooms are spacious and smart, all with sea-view balconies, and the facilities include a swimming pool and spa and kiddies' playground. Breakfast is included.

Monkey Island Resort
RESORT $$

(off Map p102; ☑04-3926-0572; www.monkeyislandresort.com; d US$40-60; ❄) There's a nicely social vibe going down at Monkey Island with a nightly seafood buffet, cool R&B beats, and a bar with a pool table. Accommodation is in comfortable private bungalows, and beach barbecues, kayaks and volleyball keep the holiday spirit alive. The resort provides free transfers from Cat Ba Town, and for the eponymous primates, you'll need to take a short trek to a nearby karst peak. Look online for good value packages combining Halong Bay and Lan Ha Bay.

Bungalows
CAMPGROUND $

(☑093 447 8156; d 400,000d) On the sandy beach at Cat Co 2 are these thatched wooden bungalows. Though tiny and representing nothing much more than a mattress, a fan and a roof over your head, they are well spaced around an attractive, leafy beachside plot. There's a shower block and cafe for meals (around 70,000d). At the time of writing, a flash new five-star resort was planned for Cat Co 2, so this may change.

🍴 Eating

There are a couple of good places dotted along the Cat Ba Town's seafront strip, and the floating restaurants offshore are also worth a visit (see p106). For a cheaper feed, head to the food stalls in front of the market.

TOP CHOICE Bamboo Café
VIETNAMESE $

(Map p102; Đ 1-4, Cat Ba Town; dishes 80,000-120,000d) The best option for a casual bite on the seafront, this enjoyable little place has a small harbour-facing terrace and an intimate bamboo-walled interior. The genial owner is a fluent English speaker and serves up generous portions of Vietnamese and international food. The beer is super cold and there's wine available by the glass.

FLOATING RESTAURANTS

There are numerous 'floating' seafood restaurants just offshore in Cat Ba harbour. We've heard reports of over-charging, so it's essential to confirm the price of the food in advance, as well as the cost of a boat to get you out there and back. Locals actually advise heading around the bay to the float-ing restaurants in Ben Beo Harbour. They're less touristy and less likely to rip you off, but still check on the price of food upfront. A boat ride there and back, including waiting time, should cost around 100,000d. Hold off paying your boatman until the return journey is completed as we've also had reports of diners being left stranded on the restaurants. Ask your hotel to recom-mend a boat or catch a *xe om* (around 20,000d) over the hill to the harbour.

A recommended place at Ben Beo Pier is **Xuan Hong**. Choose your din-ner from the floating pens and they'll be grilled, fried or steamed for your table in no time. Prices simply go by weight and type of seafood; you can eat your fill of a selection of fish for around 150,000d per person. Just make sure you establish the estimated price be-fore you eat.

Vien Duong
VIETNAMESE $$

(Map p102; 12 Đ Nui Ngoc, Cat Ba Town; meals from 100,000d) One of the most popular of the seafood spots lining Đ Nui Ngoc, and often heaving with Vietnamese tourists diving into local crab, squid and steaming seafood hotpots. Definitely not the place to come if you're looking for a quiet night.

Family Bakery
BAKERY $

(Map p102; 196 Đ 1-4, Cat Ba Town; dishes 80,000-120,000d; ⏱7am-4pm) Friendly spot that opens early for goodies like Turkish bread and almond pastries. Pop in for a coffee and croissant before tackling the bus-ferry-bus combo back to Hanoi. Don't miss Cat Ba's best crème caramel.

Green Mango
INTERNATIONAL $$

(Map p102; Đ 1-4, Cat Ba Town; mains 150,000-220,000d; ☏) A good place for a glass of wine, cocktail or Cat Ba's best espresso, but the huge menu covering everything from pizza, pasta and occasional Asian flavours can tend towards mediocrity. Service can also be a tad surly. C'mon guys, a few smiles wouldn't go amiss.

Thao May
VIETNAMESE $

(Map p102; Đ Nui Ngoc, Cat Ba Town; mains 80,000-120,000d; ⏱11am-2pm & 5-9pm) Friendly family-run spot that's recommended by in-the-know expat locals. Look forward to a real pride in the food and exceptionally well-priced beer. You'll probably see some of the crew from Asia Outdoors there.

Phuong Nung
VIETNAMESE $

(Map p102; 184 Đ 1-4, Cat Ba Town; meals 35,000d; ⏱7-10am) Bustling breakfast spot that's the most popular place in town for a hearty bowl of *pho bo* (beef noodle soup) – just the thing you need before a day of climbing or kayaking.

CT Mart
SELF CATERING $

(Map p102; 18 Đ Nui Ngoc, Cat Ba Town; ⏱8am-8pm) Handy supermarket to stock up before heading off trekking or on the boat trip back to the mainland.

🍷 Drinking

Cat Ba Town has a couple of good bars, or you can head to the drink stalls at the east-ern end of the harbour.

Flightless Bird Café
BAR

(Map p102; Đ 1-4, Cat Ba Town; ☏) Discover your inner Kiwi at this friendly bar decorated with New Zealand memorabilia including pictures of the mighty All Blacks rugby team and the beautiful Southern Alps. There's free wi-fi for customers, and even well-priced massage and manicure services on offer. Kiwi owner Graeme is always up for a good chat, but no, he doesn't take part in either massage or manicure.

Good Bar
BAR

(Map p102; Đ 1-4, Cat Ba Town) Party HQ for trav-ellers, this upper-floor bar has a real vibe, and the drinking, flirting and story-telling goes on until late most nights. It comes fully equipped with pool tables, plenty of space and terrific harbour views.

ℹ Information

Internet Access

Cat Ba Town has several internet places on the waterfront.

Money

Agribank has an ATM on the harbour, and a **branch** 1km north of town for changing dollars.

Vu Binh Jewellers changes US dollars and offers credit-card cash advances at 5%.

Tourist Information

The best impartial advice is at **Asia Outdoors** (p107) where the helpful crew can bring you up to speed on everything from transport connections to the best family-run restaurants. Maps of Cat Ba Biosphere Reserve (encompassing Cat Ba and surrounding islands) are available. Online, see www.slopony.com and www.catbaventures.com for local information.

Don't expect much help from the official **Tourism Information & Development Centre** (Map p102; ☎ 368 8215; www.catba.com.vn; Đ 1-4, Cat Ba Town) where staff seem more interested in peddling tours than information.

ℹ Getting There & Away

Cat Ba Island is 45km east of Haiphong and 50km south of Halong City. Various boat and bus combinations make the journey, starting in either Hanoi or Haiphong.

It is possible to travel by boat from Halong City to Cat Ba Island, but it is a journey often blighted by scams (see p107).

To/from Hanoi

Departing from the Luong Yen bus station in Hanoi, **Hoang Long** (☎ 031-268 8008) operate a bus to Haiphong, followed by a minibus to Dinh Vu port near Haiphong, followed by a 40-minute boat trip to Cai Vieng harbour (also known as Phu Long) on Cat Ba Island. From there, another minibus whisks passengers around the coast road into Cat Ba Town. The complete bus-bus-boat-bus combo takes around three hours (210,000d) and is very efficiently run. Buses depart Hanoi at 10am, 2pm and 4pm, and return from Cat Ba Town at 7.15am, 9.15am, 1.15pm and 3.15pm. If you're travelling from Hanoi, this is the most hassle-free way.

To/from Haiphong

A fast boat departs Haiphong's Ben Binh Harbour for Cat Ba's Cai Vieng harbour and from there, a bus takes passengers into Cat Ba Town. This boat-and-bus combo takes around 1½ hours (130,000d). Cat Ba-bound boats depart from Haiphong at 7am and 10am, and return buses depart from the waterfront in Cat Ba Town at 2pm and 4pm.

A second option to/from Haiphong is a bus from Ben Binh Harbour in Haiphong to Dinh Vu port. A fast boat then skips across to Cai Vieng

ℹ HALONG BAY TO CAT BA (WITHOUT THE HASSLE)

Based on the Map p95, it looks like an easy undertaking to travel by sea from Bai Chay in Halong City to Cat Ba Island. And while it's not very far in terms of distance, it can be a journey fraught with hassle for some travellers.

Tourist boats (US$8) depart from Bai Chay in Halong City from around 1pm heading to Gia Luan harbour in the north of Cat Ba Island. The journey takes four hours, usually stopping for swimming and to visit a cave, but once you land at Gia Luan, you're actually still 40km from Cat Ba Town. We've heard many reports of travellers then being hassled by the local taxi and xe om mafia who will demand up to US$50 for onward travel to Cat Ba Town. Despite their claims, there is a local bus (20,000d) – the QH Green Bus – that travels from Gia Luan to Cat Ba Town. Unfortunately the last bus of the day (5pm) usually departs Gia Luan before the boats arrive from Bai Chay. Funny that…

Some boat owners in Halong Bay are part of the scam, so if you do book a tour or boat transport from Bai Chay to Cat Ba Island, ask specifically if there will be onward transport provided to Cat Ba Town once the boat lands at Gia Luan. Onward bus transport is included by some recommended operators, including Cat Ba Ventures (p103).

An alternative, and potentially hassle-free, way of getting from Halong Bay to Cat Ba is on the **passenger and vehicle ferry** (40,000d, one hour, departing on the hour 5am-5pm May to September, and 8am, 11.10am & 3pm October to April) that travels from the resort island of Tuan Chau to Gia Luan. From Halong City across the causeway to Tuan Chau by taxi is around 130,000d and by xe om is around 35,000d. Once on Cat Ba Island, travellers can then catch the QH Green Bus for 20,000d into Cat Ba Town. Simply purchase your ticket from the driver. Note that these buses leave Gia Luan for Cat Ba Town at 6am, 9.30am, 1.10pm, 4pm & 5pm, and despite what the local xe om and taxi drivers will tell you, foreigners are definitely allowed to travel on these services.

To travel the other way – Cat Ba Island to Bai Chay in Halong City – on the above services, contact Cat Ba Ventures (www.catbaventures.com) in Cat Ba Town for the latest information.

ℹ️ WATCH THOSE VALUABLES!

Take real care with your valuables when cruising the waters of Halong Bay. Do not leave them unattended as they might grow legs and walk. Always try to ensure there is someone you know and trust watching your gear on a day cruise. When it comes to overnight cruises, most boats have lockable cabins.

on Cat Ba, and another bus then continues into Cat Ba Town. The journey takes around two hours (150,000d). Buses depart Haiphong at 6.40am, 8.15am, 9.45am, 1.40pm, 3.10pm and 4.35pm. Return buses from Cat Ba depart at 6.10am, 7.50am, 9.10am, 1.10pm, 2.50pm and 4.10pm.

ℹ️ Getting Around

BICYCLE & MOTORBIKE Bicycle and motorbike rentals are available from most Cat Ba hotels (both around US$4 to US$7 per day). If you're heading out to the beaches or national park, pay the parking fee for security. If you're looking for a decent mountain bike or a guided bike tour, contact one of the tour operators on p103.

A *xe om* from Cat Ba Town to Cat Co 2 beach or Ben Beo harbour is around 10,000d, and in summer a kitsch tourist train also runs from Cat Ba Town to Cat Co 2 beach (5000d per person).

BUS Cat Ba's public **QH Green bus** (20,000d) trundles between Cat Ba harbour and the Gia Luan harbour in the north of the island, passing the national park headquarters en route. See the boxed text p107 for possible problems you may have catching this bus when arriving from Halong Bay.

Bai Tu Long Bay
📞 033

There's way more to northeast Vietnam than Halong Bay. The sinking limestone plateau, which gave birth to the bay's spectacular islands, continues for some 100km to the Chinese border. The area immediately northeast of Halong Bay is part of **Bai Tu Long National Park**.

Bai Tu Long Bay is every bit as beautiful as its famous neighbour. In some ways it's actually more stunning, since it's only in its initial stages as a destination for travellers. Improved boat transport means it is quickly growing in popularity with domestic tourists, but the bay and its islands are still unpolluted and relatively undeveloped. For Western travellers, it's a laid-back alternative to the touristy bustle of Halong Bay.

Charter boats can be arranged to Bai Tu Long Bay from Halong Bay; rates start at around 300,000d per hour and the trip there takes about five hours. A cheaper, and more flexible alternative is to travel overland to Cai Rong and visit the outlying islands by boat from here. An increased frequency of ferry sailings definitely makes this a more viable alternative than in earlier years.

Hanoi travel agencies, including Ethnic Travel (p79), run trips into the Bai Tu Long area. Another Hanoi contact for Bai Tu Long is **Le Pont Travel** (📞 04-3935-1889; www.leponttravel.com; 102 Ma May, Old Quarter, Hanoi).

VAN DON ISLAND

Van Don is the largest (around 30 sq km), most populated and most developed island in the Bai Tu Long archipelago. Now linked to the mainland by a series of bridges, it has a few places to stay, but more importantly it's the jumping off point to other islands.

Van Don's main town is **Cai Rong** (pronounced Cai Zong; Map p95). Nearby, **Bai Dai** (Long Beach; Map p95) runs along much of the island's southern side and has hard-packed sand with some mangroves. Just offshore there are stunning limestone **rock formations**.

Cai Rong Pier (Cai Rong Pha), about 8km north of the bridge to the mainland, is the key port for boats to other Bai Tu Long islands. It's a bustling port, full of karaoke bars and motorbikes, but there are decent hotels if you're forced to overnight before catching a morning ferry.

Hung Toan Hotel (📞 387 4220; r 200,000d; ❄️) is good value, while **Viet Linh Hotel** (📞 379 3898; r 350,000d; ❄️) is fancier. Both are around 300m north of the pier. Just opposite the Viet Linh Hotel is a simple, unnamed restaurant that does great seafood and pork dishes – try the pork with ginger, chilli and lemongrass.

Down on Bai Dai, the **Bai Tu Long Ecotourism Resort** (📞 379 3156; bungalows 275,000-500,000d; ❄️) has beachside bungalows and more traditional rooms in stilt houses. It gets pretty noisy with karaoke and Vietnamese tourists on weekends, but the proximity to an OK beach makes for a relaxing weekday break. However, if you've got the time, a journey further afield to Quan Lan Island is highly recommended.

Frequent buses run between Bai Chay (Halong City) and Cai Rong on Van Don Island (55,000d, 1½ hours). Alternatively catch a Mong Cai or Lang Son bus to the Cua Ong turn-off, and then catch a *xe om* or taxi to Cai Rong Pier.

QUAN LAN ISLAND

The main attraction on Quan Lan is the beautiful, 1km-long crescent-moon sweep of **Minh Chau beach** (Map p95) on the island's northeastern coast. The water is clear blue and the waves are suitable for surfing. There are several other blissful beaches on the eastern seaboard, though water temperatures are a bit chilly between January and April. Note that most accommodation is only open from May to October, and that June and July are more expensive with the influx of Vietnamese domestic tourists.

The northeastern part of the island also has some battered **ruins** of the old Van Don Trading Port, and other island attractions include forest walks and a beautiful 200-year-old **pagoda** in Quan Lan Town. Apart from hanging out on the beaches, and cycling or motorcycling around this long, slender island, there's not really much to do. It's a very laid-back place and a terrific detour off the usual tourist trail. There's no ATM on Quan Lan Island, so come armed with cash.

Quan Lan Town, the main town on the island, features an improving array of accommodation, from simple guesthouses to new midrange hotels, and travellers' needs are answered with a few decent restaurants, internet access and places to rent bicycles (US$4 per day) and motorcycles (US$6 per day). Most of Quan Lan is pretty flat, but it's a surprisingly large island, so maybe sign up for something with an engine. Quan Lan's second-largest settlement is Minh Chau, just a short walk from gorgeous Minh Chau beach. It lacks the facilities of Quan Lan Town, but has a couple of good places to stay, both around 3km from the pier.

🛏 Sleeping & Eating

Ann Hotel   HOTEL
(Quan Lan Town; r US$25; ❄) The brand new Ann Hotel offers spacious rooms, gleaming bathrooms, and balconies with ocean views. It's located around 200m from the centre of town towards the old pagoda.

Ngan Ha Hotel   HOTEL
(✆387 7296; Quan Lan Town; r 300,000d; ❄) This corner-front establishment in the heart of town has recently redecorated rooms and a good restaurant downstairs.

Quan Lan Ecotourism Resort   RESORT
(✆387 7417; Quan Lan Town; bungalows 500,000d) Out of Quan Lan Town en route to the pier, this beachfront resort has overpriced accommodation, but does sit amid the dunes on a gorgeous stretch of sand. It's only open from May to August.

Le Pont Hotel   HOTEL
(www.leponttravel.com; Minh Chau; r US$25; ❄) This hotel has brand-new rooms, a downstairs restaurant and also rents out bikes and motorcycles. The owner is looking to renovate an old house also on the property as accommodation, and Minh Chau beach is a short, forested walk away.

Minh Chau Resort   RESORT
(Minh Chau; ✆0904 081 868; r US$80-120) Bai Tu Long's flashest accommodation, arrayed across two leafy locations and featuring a very good restaurant. Rates rise by around 15% on weekends.

Bien Ngoc Hotel   HOTEL
(✆09 1323 7985; Son Hao Village; r without/with air-con 500,000/800,000d; ❄) Gloriously isolated 9km from Quan Lan Town and 3km from Minh Chau, Bien Ngoc has simply furnished rooms just a stone's throw from a beautiful beach. It's only open from June to August and you'll need to rent two wheels to get there.

ℹ Getting There & Away

TO/FROM CAI RONG Boats from Cai Rong dock at two places: the Quan Lan pier, 3km from the main township on the island's southern tip, and near Minh Chau Beach, on the island's northeastern coast. Boats to Minh Chau (120,000d, one hour) depart Cai Rong at 7.30am and 1.30pm. Boats to Quan Lan pier (100,000d, 1½ hours) depart Cai Rong at 8am and 2pm.

TO/FROM HALONG CITY An alternative route to Quan Lan pier is from the Hon Gai ferry terminal across the suspension bridge from Halong City. A speedboat leaves at 1.30pm (120,000d, 1½ hours). The Hon Gai ferry terminal is adjacent to the Vinashin bus station. There's generally no need to book ahead.

TRA BAN & NGOC VUNG ISLANDS

One of Bai Tu Long's largest islands, Tra Ban (Map p95) offers some of the bay's most dramatic karsts. The southern part is blanketed in thick jungle and provides a habitat for many colourful butterflies. Boats leave from Van Don's Cai Rong Pier at 7am and 2pm (50,000d, one hour). There's no accommodation, so check on times for return boats.

Dao Ngoc Vung (Map p95) borders Halong Bay and has some dramatic limestone cliffs and a great beach on its southern shore with some basic **beach huts** (200,000d). Bring along your own food. Daily boats link Cai Rong (departing 7.45am) and Ngoc Vung (departing 1.50pm), costing 50,000d and taking 2½ hours.

It's also possible to reach Ngoc Vung from Quan Lan pier on Quan Lan Island, but sailings at 6am are sporadic and mainly confined to June to August.

CO TO ISLAND

In the northeast, Co To Island is the furthest inhabited island from the mainland. Its highest peak reaches a respectable 170m. There are numerous other hills, and a large lighthouse. The coastline is mostly cliffs and large rocks, but there's at least one sandy beach.

There are a couple of newly built hotels and guesthouses on Co To, including the **Coto Lodge Hotel** (www.coto.vn; d 500,000d; ✳@🛜). The attached **Jellyfish restaurant** is surprisingly chic, and the hotel can arrange **beach barbecues** and **island tours**. Rates include breakfast. The hotel also rents out camping gear including tents and portable stoves.

Slow ferries bound for Dao Co To depart Cai Rong Pier at 7am daily (70,000d, three hours). There are also slow ferries departing Cai Rong at 1pm on Wednesday, Friday and Saturday.

A faster speedboat departs Cai Rong daily at 1.30pm (125,000d, two hours). See www.coto.vn for current schedules.

MONG CAI & THE CHINESE BORDER

Huge industrial zones are being created around Mong Cai, with plots being snapped up by Chinese and foreign corporations.

ⓘ **BORDER CROSSING: MONG CAI–DONGXING**

Mong Cai is located on the Chinese border in the extreme northeastern corner of Vietnam. One of three official international overland border crossings with China, it's open from 7am to 7pm daily, and there's a 5000d exit fee leaving Vietnam. It's about 3km between the border and Mong Cai bus station; aim to pay around 15,000d on a *xe om* or 30,000d in a taxi.

Shopping malls dot the city centre. For the Vietnamese, the big draw is the chance to purchase low-priced (and low-quality) Chinese-made consumer goods. For the Chinese, the attraction is two huge casinos and new golf courses. Elsewhere in this border region, travellers' highlights include the stunning karst scenery around Cao Bang, historical caves, and the thundering Ban Gioc Waterfall.

Mong Cai

📞 033 / POP 76,700

A bustling border city, Mong Cai is an upwardly mobile place that thrives on trade with China. But other than as a border crossing, Mong Cai holds no interest for tourists.

🛏 Sleeping & Eating

Nha Nghi Thanh Tam GUESTHOUSE $
(📞388 1373; 71 Đ Trieu Duong; r 250,000d; ✳) A family-run place with simple, clean, comfortable rooms with hot-water bathrooms that (for those who have just arrived and can't sort their dong from their yuan) cost just US$10. There are similar options on this street. Đ Trieu Duong runs south from Đ Tran Phu, two blocks before Mong Cai's main market

Hotel Hai Chi GUESTHOUSE $
(📞388 7939; 52 P Tran Phu; r 200,000d; ✳) A clean, well-kept place on Đ Tran Phu, which runs northeast from the main roundabout in the centre of town. Most of the attractive rooms are triples, with wooden furniture and wood panelling. Perfectly fine for one night if you're transiting to or from China.

Nam Phong Hotel HOTEL $$
(📞388 7775; P Hung Vuong; r 300,000-400,000d; ✳@🛜) A more upmarket place featuring spacious, well-equipped rooms with satellite TV. There's a bar and restaurant serving good Chinese and Vietnamese dishes. The hotel's showing its age, but definitely open to negotiation. This hotel is on P Hung Vuong, running southeast from the main roundabout in the centre of town. A few new hotels on the same road, closer to the bridge, were nearing completion at the time of writing.

Saigon Quan Banh Xeo VIETNAMESE $
(P Hung Vuong; mains 30,000-40,000d) Popular with local students, this modern cafe-style eatery features Vietnamese favourites including *banh xeo* (savoury filled pancakes) and zingy salads. It's on the ground floor of

MONG CAI BUS CONNECTIONS

DESTINATION	COST	DURATION	FREQUENCY
Hanoi	200,000d	8hr	Frequent until 1pm
Halong City	90,000d	4hr	Every 30 min
Lang Son	100,000d	7hr	6.30am & 12.30pm

the new Mong Cai Plaza shopping centre on P Hung Vuong, just opposite the post office.

Lan Ly
CAFE $

(2 P Ho Xuan Houng; coffee from 15,000d) In need of a caffeine fix before you deal with the border? Rev up here at this friendly coffee bar, which has a street terrace with a view of Mong Cai's traffic action. It overlooks Mong Cai's main roundabout just across the bridge crossing the Ka Long River.

There are also plenty of **food stalls** on P Hung Vuong, including several good spots near the Nam Phong Hotel.

ℹ Information

Internet access is available near the **post office** on P Hung Vuong, just southeast of the main roundabout.

Vietcombank (P Van Don) Located on the main roundabout, changes cash and has an ATM.

ℹ Getting There & Away

In the past, hydrofoils linked Mong Cai to Halong City and Haiphong, but improved bus services have made these options unprofitable. Mong Cai is located 340km from Hanoi. The bus terminal is on Hwy 18, about 3km from the border.

Lang Son

📞025 / POP 79,200

Very close to the Chinese border, Lang Son is a booming city. Surrounded by karst peaks, it is in an area populated largely by Tho, Nung, Man and Dzao tribal people, though their influence is not that evident in the city.

The city was partially destroyed in February 1979 by Chinese forces (see p112), and the ruins of the town and the devastated frontier village of Dong Dang were shown to foreign journalists as evidence of Chinese aggression. Although the border is still heavily fortified, both towns have been rebuilt and Sino–Vietnamese trade is in full swing again.

Lang Son has a good night market, and there's a great local restaurant. Most trav-

ellers come to Lang Son when crossing between Vietnam and China; the border is 18km north, just outside Dong Dang.

◉ Sights & Activities

There are two large and beautiful caves around 1200m from central Lang Son. Both are illuminated and have Buddhist altars inside. **Tam Thanh Cave** (combined admission with Nhi Thanh 5000d; ☉6am-6pm) is vast and seductive. There's an internal pool and natural 'window' offering a sweeping view of the surrounding rice fields. A few hundred metres up a stone staircase are the ruins of the **Mac Dynasty Citadel**. It's a lovely, deserted spot, with stunning rural views.

The Ngoc Tuyen River flows through **Nhi Thanh Cave** (combined admission with Tam Thanh 5000d; ☉6am-6pm), 700m beyond Tam Thanh. The entrance has a series of carved poems written by the cave's 18th-century discoverer, a soldier called Ngo Thi San. There's also a carved stone plaque commemorating an early French resident of Lang Son, complete with his silhouette in European clothing.

Lang Son's huge **night market** (☉5-11pm) is a bargain basement delight – cheap electrical goods and clothes. The agglomeration of food stalls and simple cafes out the front is good for a pre- or post-negotiation beer.

🛏 Sleeping & Eating

Van Xuan Hotel
HOTEL $

(📞371 0440; lsvanxuanhotel@yahoo.com.vn; 147 P Tran Dang Ninh; r 320,000-500,000d; ❄@🛜) All the rooms here are really well kept, light and airy, but the family rooms (500,000d) are particularly enormous and extremely comfortable. If you can, book room 606, which has a balcony overlooking Phai Loan Lake and the surrounding karst hills. The hotel is on the lake's eastern edge, around 50m from the Lang Son market.

Hoa Binh Hotel
HOTEL $

(📞025 870 807; 127 Đ Thanh Tam; r 250,000d ❄🛜) A reliable cheapie close to the Lang Son market and Miss Lan's terrific eatery. Cane furniture, spacious rooms, and spotless bathrooms add up to the best deal in town.

TOP CHOICE **Thanh Lan Com Binh Dan** VIETNAMESE **$**
(Tran Quoc Tran; meals 40,000-50,000d; ⊙11am-10pm) In a quiet lane one block south of the Lang Son market, the delightful Miss Lan serves up around 20 different dishes for lunch and dinner every day. It's a point-and-pick affair – all seasonal and all local. Dive in, pull up a chair outside and look forward to Northeast Vietnam's coldest beer. Don't miss the *cha khaoi tay* (Vietnamese potato croquettes).

New Dynasty Restaurant VIETNAMESE **$$**
(Phai Loan Lake; hotpots 120,000d; ⊙noon-11pm) The most famous place in town, this bar-restaurant complex sits on a little peninsula jutting into the lake. Everyone is here for the hotpots, but there's also a draught-beer emporium – perfect after a bumpy and dusty bus ride in these parts.

ⓘ Information

Vietin Bank (51 Đ Le Loi) has an ATM and changes money and the **post office** (Đ Le Loi) is adjacent. Both are around 300m from the lake on the road heading east towards Mong Cai. For internet access, the Van Xuan Hotel has several terminals in its lobby.

ⓘ Getting There & Away

BUS All buses leave from the terminal on Đ Le Loi, around 500m east of the post office. See p115 for bus connections. Count on 20,000d for a *xe om* and 20,000d for a taxi to get there. From the Vietin Bank and post office turn right into P Tran Dang Ninh, continue for 200m for the market, hotels and restaurants.

TRAIN There are only very slow trains between Lang Son and Hanoi (80,000d, 5½ hours).

Cao Bang
🎵026 / POP 48,200

Mountainous Cao Bang province is one of the most beautiful regions in Vietnam. Cao Bang itself is way more prosaic, but it is a useful base to explore the surrounding countryside. The climate is mild here, and winter days can get chilly when a thick fog clings to the banks of the Bang Giang River.

NEIGHBOURING TENSIONS

Mong Cai is a free-trade zone with plenty of frenetic market activity, but from 1978 to 1990 the border was virtually sealed and former friends China and Vietnam were bitter enemies. China and North Vietnam were on good terms following the defeat of the French in 1954, but after reunification the Vietnamese government became closer to China's rival, the USSR.

In March 1978 the Vietnamese government launched a campaign in the south against 'commercial opportunists', seizing private property to complete the country's 'socialist transformation'. The campaign hit the ethnic Chinese particularly hard, and up to 500,000 of Vietnam's 1.8 million ethnic Chinese citizens fled the country. To leave, refugees typically had to pay up to US$5000 each in 'exit fees'. Chinese entrepreneurs in Ho Chi Minh City (HCMC) had that kind of money, but northern refugees were mostly dirt poor. In response, China cut aid to Vietnam and cancelled many development projects.

Vietnam's invasion of Cambodia in late 1978 was the final straw. China was a close ally of the Khmer Rouge, and when there was a build-up of Soviet military forces on the China–USSR border, Beijing believed a USSR–Vietnam alliance was trying to surround China with hostile forces. Ironically, Vietnam had the same concerns about a Chinese–Khmer Rouge alliance.

In February 1979 China invaded northern Vietnam along the border. China's forces were withdrawn after 17 days and the operation was declared successful, but many observers concurred that China's army of 200,000 troops had been badly mauled by the battle-hardened Vietnamese. China suffered around 20,000 casualties in 29 days of fighting, despite many of Vietnam's strongest troops being in Cambodia at the time. Around 15,000 Vietnamese militia and civilians were killed or wounded.

Officially, this conflict is considered ancient history, but while trade booms, political tensions over the Spratly Islands and oil-drilling rights in the South China Sea continue. In China, you'll be told the Chinese acted in self-defence because the Vietnamese were launching raids across the border. Most Western observers disagree.

Read *Brother Enemy* (1988) by Nayan Chanda, an excellent account of these Cold War power plays.

ℹ️ BORDER CROSSING: YOUYI GUAN–HUU NGHI QUAN

The Friendship Pass at Dong Dang–Pingxiang is the most popular border crossing in the far north. The border post itself is at Huu Nghi Quan (Friendship Pass), 3km north of Dong Dang town; a *xe om* (motorbike taxi) ride here from Dong Dang will cost around 30,000d. The border is open from 7am to 5.30pm daily, and there's a 500m walk between the Vietnamese and Chinese frontiers.

Entering Vietnam this way, there's an Agribank ATM at the border (and another in Dong Dang). Ignore touts offering bus tickets at the border and head straight to the Dong Dang minibus terminal, which has services to Hanoi (130,000d, 3¼ hours) leaving every 30 minutes until 6pm. Otherwise head straight to Lang Son bus station and get a connection there; local minibuses are very regular and cost 15,000d for the 18km journey.

Leaving Vietnam, a taxi from the Lang Son bus station is 120,000d and a *xe om* about 60,000d. On the Chinese side, it's a 20-minute drive from the border to Pingxiang by bus or shared taxi. Pingxiang is connected by train and bus to Nanning, the capital of China's Guangxi province.

Three trains also link Hanoi and Lang Son daily, but these are very slow, taking more than five hours – the bus is a much better option. Trains from Hanoi to Nanning and Beijing pass through this border, but it's not possible to jump aboard these services in Lang Son or Dong Dang. For the full picture about these cross-border trains see p80.

👁 Sights

While in Cao Bang town, climb the hill leading up to a **War Memorial** (Map p114). Head up the second lane off Đ Pac Bo, go under the entrance to a primary school, and you'll see the steps. There are great 360-degree views from the summit, and it's a very peaceful spot.

Minority Markets MARKETS

In the province of Cao Bang, Kinh (ethnic Vietnamese) are a distinct minority. The largest ethnic groups are the Tay (46%), Nung (32%), H'mong (8%), Dzao (7%) and Lolo (1%). Intermarriage and mass education are gradually eroding tribal and cultural distinctions. Check out Tim Doling's *Mountains and Ethnic Minorities: North East Vietnam* for detailed accounts of tribal people in the region. It's available from the Vietnam Museum of Ethnology (p53) and bookshops in Hanoi.

Most of Cao Bang's minorities remain blissfully unaware about the ways of the outside world. Cheating in the marketplace, for example, is virtually unknown and even tourists are charged the same price as locals without bargaining. Whether or not this innocence can withstand the onslaught of even limited tourism remains to be seen. The following big markets in Cao Bang province are held every five days, according to lunar calendar dates. The Na Giang market, which attracts Tay, Nung and H'mong people, is one of the best and busiest in the provinces.

Nuoc Hai 1st, 6th, 11th, 16th, 21st and 26th day of each lunar month

Na Giang 1st, 6th, 11th, 16th, 21st and 26th day of each lunar month

Tra Linh 4th, 9th, 14th, 19th, 24th and 29th day of each lunar month

Trung Khanh 5th, 10th, 15th, 20th, 25th and 30th day of each lunar month

🛏 Sleeping

Hoanh Anh Hotel HOTEL **$$**
(Map p114; ☑ 385 8969; 131 Đ Kim Dong; r 400,000d; ❄@🛜) This smart mini-hotel has a snazzy lobby and friendly staff who speak a little English. The rooms are attractive, with modern furnishings, quality mattresses, wi-fi, stylish shower rooms and chintz-free minimalist decor. Try to book the room ending in 'one' on each floor (for example 201, 301 to 701) for views over the Bang Giang River.

Thanh Loan Hotel HOTEL **$$**
(Map p114; ☑ 385 7026; thanh_loan_hotel@hn.vnn.vn; 159 P Vuon Cam; r 380,000d; ❄@🛜) On a quiet street with cafes, this efficient, spotless place features spacious rooms with high ceilings, dark wood furniture and bathrooms with tubs. There's even a bar area for a nightcap.

Nguyet Nga Hotel GUESTHOUSE **$**
(Map p114; ☑ 385 6445; r from 150,000d; ❄) If you're on a real economy drive, this guesthouse fits the bill. The rooms are a bit gloomy, but they do all have a TV and fridge, and it's handily near the bus station.

✗ Eating & Drinking

Men Quyen Restaurant   VIETNAMESE $
(Map p114; meals 35,000-60,000d) Tucked away
behind the market, this modest little place
has a buffet style set-up – just point to the
dishes you want. Be sure to try the delicious
cha la lot (cabbage rolls).

Coffee Pho   VIETNAMESE $
(Map p114; 140 P Vuon Cam) A stylish little place
with pavement tables that serves good Vietnamese coffee, cappuccino, juices and beer
plus a snack or two.

You'll find cheap food stalls near the **night
market** (meals from 15,000d) on P Vuon
Cam near the Thanh Loan Hotel, at the
Trung Tau Market (Map p114), and also
opposite the Hoanh Anh Hotel on Đ Kim
Dong.

ⓘ Information

ATMs are in the centre of town across the Bang
Giang Bridge, and internet cafes are on P Vuon
Cam, near the Thanh Loan Hotel.

ⓘ Getting There & Away

Cao Bang is 272km north of Hanoi, along Hwy
3. It's a fully sealed road, but a full day's drive
through mountainous terrain. Buses depart Cao
Bang for Hanoi (140,000d, nine hours, 12 daily)
and Lang Son (70,000d, four hours, four daily
before 2pm).

 If you're heading for the Ba Be Lakes, catch
a local bus to Na Phuc and then another to Cho
Ra, where you'll need to hire a *xe om* for the final
stretch into the national park.

 A direct minibus to Ban Gioc Waterfall departs
Cao Bang most mornings at 6.30am and 7.30am.

Hang Pac Bo (Water-Wheel Cave)

After 30 years of exile, Ho Chi Minh re-entered
Vietnam in January 1941 and took shelter in a
small cave in one of the most remote regions
of Vietnam, 3km from the Chinese border. The
cave itself, Hang Pac Bo (Water-Wheel Cave;
Map p88), and the surrounding area are sacred ground for Vietnamese revolutionaries –
this is the base from which Ho launched the
revolution he'd long been planning.

 Even if you have little interest in the history of Vietnamese communism, the cave is in
a beautiful location surrounded by evergreen
forests filled with butterflies and birdsong,
and overlooked by limestone mountains.

 Ho Chi Minh lived in the cave for a few
weeks in 1941, writing poetry and translating key texts by the fathers of socialism. He
stuck close to China so that he would be able
to flee across the border if French soldiers
discovered his hiding place. Ho named the
stream in front of his cave Lenin Creek and
the jungle-clad mountain that overlooks this
stream Karl Marx Peak.

 There's a modest Uncle Ho **museum** (admission 20,000d; ◷7.30-11.30am & 1.30-5pm Wed-
Sun) at the entrance to the Pac Bo area. About
2km beyond this is a parking area. The **cave**
is a 10-minute walk away along a shady stone
path that follows the riverbank. You can step
inside the mouth of the small cave, but not
enter inside. The path then loops past various other points of interest, including a rock
table that Ho is said to have used as a kind of
jungle office for his translations and writing.

 In a patch of forest about a 15-minute
walk in the opposite direction is a **jungle**

Cao Bang   Ⓝ ⟋ 0 ⟍ 200 m / 0 ⟍ 0.1 miles

Cao Bang

◎ Sights
1 War Memorial B2

🛏 Sleeping
2 Hoanh Anh Hotel A2
3 Nguyet Nga Hotel B1
4 Thanh Loan Hotel A1

✗ Eating
5 Men Quyen Restaurant A1
6 Night Market A1
7 Trung Tau Market...............................A1

◉ Drinking
8 Coffee Pho...A1

LANG SON BUS CONNECTIONS

DESTINATION	COST	DURATION	FREQUENCY
Hanoi	80,000d	3hr	Frequent until 6pm
Cao Bang	70,000d	4hr	6am, 8am, 10am and 2pm
Mong Cai	100,000d	7hr	5am

hut, another of Ho's hideouts. On the way to the hut is a rock outcrop used as a 'dead-letter box', where he would leave and pick up messages.

Hang Pac Bo is 58km northwest of Cao Bang. Allow three hours to make the return trip by road, plus an hour to look around. To do this as a return half-day trip by *xe om,* expect to pay around 200,000d. No permits are currently needed, despite the proximity to the Chinese border.

Ban Gioc Waterfall & Nguom Ngao Cave

Ban Gioc Waterfall (admission 15,000d; ☉7.30am-5pm) is one of Vietnam's best-known waterfalls, and its image adorns the lobby of many a cheap guesthouse. The falls, fed by the Quay Son River that marks the border with China, are an impressive sight and in a highly scenic location.

The waterfall is the largest in the country, though not the highest. Its vertical drop is only around 30m, but it has an impressive 300m span; one side of the falls is in China, the other is in Vietnam. Water volume varies considerably between the dry and rainy seasons, and the sight is most impressive from May to September.

Boatmen will punt you on **bamboo rafts** (trips 100,000d) close enough to the waterfall so you can feel the spray on your hair (bring shampoo!) and skin. Rafts on the Vietnamese side have green canopies, and on the Chinese side canopies are blue. You're allowed to swim in the large natural pool on the Vietnamese side, but not in the river or close to the main waterfall.

It's a picturesque 10-minute stroll through paddy fields to reach the base of the falls from the parking area. If you're here at harvest time in September or October, the farmers may encourage you to try out their pedal-powered threshing machines.

A police permit (200,000d for up to 10 people) is required to visit this region. The permit has to be organised in advance but any hotel in Cao Bang can sort it out for you. You'll need to show your passport.

About 4km from the waterfall, **Nguom Ngao Cave** (admission incl guide 30,000d; ☉7.30am-4.30pm) is one of the most spectacular cave systems in Vietnam. Created by an underground river, it extends for several kilometres underground and villagers sheltered here during the 1979 war with China. Visitors are permitted in one section, where a 1km-long concrete path and excellent lighting have been installed. A guide (speaking very few words of English) accompanies you on an hour-long tour of the cave network, past huge stalagmite and stalactite outcrops that resemble a waterfall and chandelier, and through a vast 100m chamber. The 10-minute walk from the parking lot to the cave is also very beautiful, threading through the limestone hills that characterise Cao Bang province, past fields of soya beans.

A second, even bigger branch of the cave system, is said to extend almost all the way to the waterfall, though there's currently no visitor access to this section.

There are snack and drink stalls by the cave and by the waterfall, but the nearest accommodation is in Cao Bang.

❶ Getting There & Away

The journey to the falls and the cave is absolutely stunning, the road following a beautiful river valley and weaving through soaring karst peaks for much of the trip. It's an 87km journey along a decent paved road, and takes about 2½ hours.

BUS & BIKE Buses (50,000d, two hours, 12 daily) connect Cao Bang with Trung Khanh, 27km short of the falls. Negotiate for a *xe om* in Trung Khanh to take you onward, which should come to around 200,000d including a two-hour wait.

CAR & MOTORBIKE Alternatively, hotels and guesthouses in Cao Bang can arrange a motorbike (self-drive) or vehicle (with driver), or there is a direct minibus to Ban Gioc, departing Cao Bang bus station at 6.30am and 7.30pm.

Northwest Vietnam

Includes »

Best Places to Eat

» Sapa Rooms (p130)
» Red Dao House (p130)
» Viet Emotion (p130)
» Ngan Nga Gia Huy (p135)
» Café Pho Co (p139)

Best Places to Stay

» Mai Chau Nature Place (p119)
» Hmong Mountain Retreat (p127)
» Truong Xuan Resort (p137)
» Pan Hou Village (p137)
» Rocky Plateau Hotel (p140)

Why Go?

A landscape of towering evergreen peaks, fertile river valleys and scattered hill-tribe villages, sparsely populated northwest Vietnam is the country's most dramatic and mountainous region.

This is also the heartland of hill-tribe culture, and the region's markets are enlivened by the scarlet headdresses of the Dzao women, the indigo fabrics of the sociable Black H'mong, and the Flower H'mong's beautiful brocaded aprons.

Sapa is a great base for superb hiking and stunning vistas of Fansipan, Vietnam's highest peak, and from this old French hill station the fabled northwest loop road crosses high mountain passes to Dien Bien Phu, before crossing lush lowland valleys south to Mai Chau.

To the northeast, Bac Ha is home to a fascinating Sunday market, and the incredibly scenic province of Ha Giang hugs the Chinese border.

Public bus services and road conditions are improving, but many travellers explore the region by motorbike or 4WD.

When to Go
Sapa

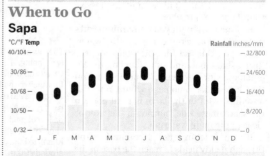

Jan–Feb The coldest (and foggiest) months with temperatures down as low as 0°C in Sapa.

Mar–Jun The weather is often excellent, but rains intensify from June onwards.

Sep–Dec Settled weather and a good time to be around Sapa.

History

The history of the northwest differs to low-land Vietnam. The Vietnamese traditionally avoided mountains, believing the terrain was not suitable for large-scale rice production. For many centuries the area remained inhabited by scatterings of minority people, joined in the 19th century by migrants from Yunnan, China and Tibet. This was the 'badlands', a buffer zone of bandits between China and Vietnam. During Ho Chi Minh's leadership, the North Vietnamese experimented with limited autonomy in 'special zones', but these were abolished after reunification.

Life for the minorities has always been difficult. Their most profitable crop was opium, but the authorities have clamped down and very little is now produced. Educational opportunities were limited, but new schools in remote areas now provide most children with education. Economic prospects remain limited, so many highlanders move to cities in search of work.

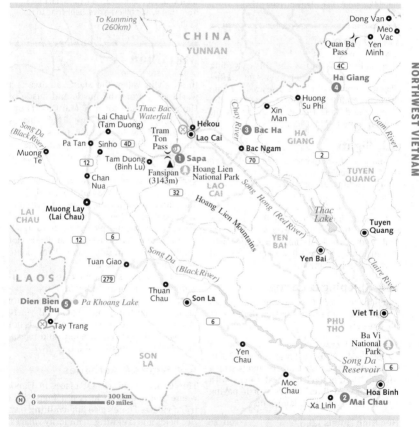

NORTHWEST VIETNAM

Northwest Vietnam Highlights

1 Walk misty mountain trails through sublime scenery and hill-tribe villages around **Sapa** (p125)

2 Escape from busy, busy Hanoi by trekking, kayaking and biking in the **Mai Chau** (p118) region

3 Make for the minority markets – a blaze of colour when the Flower H'mong are in town – around **Bac Ha** (p134)

4 Negotiate Vietnam's newest travellers' frontier, the improbably scenic

mountains and valleys of **Ha Giang** (p137) province

5 Explore the bunkers, museums and war memorials of **Dien Bien Phu** (p121), the end of the road for the French in Vietnam

ⓘ Getting There & Away

The main airport is at Dien Bien Phu, but most travellers take the train from Hanoi to Lao Cai, the gateway to Sapa. On a public bus, the mountain roads can be unforgiving. Consider renting a private 4WD and driver, or riding a motorbike.

To undertake the northwest loop, most travellers head for Mai Chau, then Son La and Dien Bien Phu. Continue north to Lai Chau, Sapa and back to Hanoi. Allow a week for this journey, and more time if using local buses.

Travellers are now crossing from Laos into Vietnam at the Tay Tran–Sop Hun border crossing, 34km from Dien Bien Phu (see p124).

Hoa Binh

ⓙ 0218 / POP 112,000

Hoa Binh means 'peace' and this easygoing nature town is a relief after the traffic-plagued suburbs of Hanoi. The area is home to many hill-tribe people, including the H'mong and Thai. Hoa Binh is a handy pit stop en route to Mai Chau.

◎ Sights

A small **museum** (admission free; ◷ 8-10.30am & 2-4.30pm Mon-Fri) showcases war memorabilia, including an old French amphibious vehicle. It's on Hwy 6, after the turnoff to Cu Chinh Lan.

Cross the bridge towards Phu Tho and you'll see the **dam wall** of a vast Russian-built hydroelectric station. Across the river is a memorial to the 161 workers who died during its construction.

🛏 Sleeping & Eating

You'll find *com pho* (rice-noodle soup) places lining Hwy 6, and both the Hoa Binh hotels have restaurants.

Thap Vang Hotel   HOTEL $
(ⓙ 385 2864; 213 Đ Cu Chinh Lan; r 150,000-200,000d; ❈ �) Set just off the main street, this smart minihotel has neat rooms with fridge and satellite TV. It's worth paying slightly more for the larger rooms.

Hoa Binh Hotels I & II   HOTEL $$
(ⓙ 385 2051; s/d US$30/35; ❈ �|) Heading west of the centre along Hwy 6, Hoa Binh Hotels I and II have comfortable accommodation in replica stilt houses. Rooms are showing some wear and tear, but the quiet, almost rural, location is a bonus.

ⓘ Information

There are ATMs along Hwy 6. Internet access is at the **main post office** (per hr 3000d).

Hoa Binh Tourism Company (ⓙ 385 4374; www.hoabinhtourism.com; Hoa Binh Hotels I & II) Has offices at both hotels; regional tours are offered.

ⓘ Getting There & Away

BUS Hoa Binh is 74km southwest of Hanoi and accessible by public bus (40,000d, two hours, every 30 minutes) from Hanoi's My Dinh bus station. For onward travel to Mai Chau, buses also leave Hoa Binh regularly to Tong Dau junction on Hwy 6 (40,000d, one hour).

CAR Visit Ba Vi National Park (p85) en route from Hanoi, and follow a riverbank road to Hoa Binh.

Mai Chau

ⓙ 0218 / POP 12,000

In an idyllic valley, the Mai Chau area is a world away from the hustle and bustle of Hanoi. The small town of Mai Chai is unappealing, but nearby are Thai villages surrounded by lush paddy fields. There's minimal traffic, and the rural soundtrack is defined by gurgling irrigation streams and birdsong.

The villagers are mostly White Thai, distantly related to tribes in Thailand, Laos and China. Most no longer wear traditional dress, but the Thai women are masterful weavers producing plenty of traditional-style clothing and souvenirs. Locals do not employ strong-arm sales tactics here: polite bargaining is the norm.

Mai Chau is a successful grassroots tourism project, though some find the experience too sanitised, and the villages are firmly on the tour-group agenda. If you're looking for hard-core exploration, this is not the place, but for biking, hiking and relaxation, Mai Chau fits the bill nicely.

◎ Sights & Activities

This is one of the closest places to Hanoi where you can sleep in a stilt house in a tribal village. There's also fine **walking** past rice fields and **trekking** to minority villages. A typical trek further afield covers 7km to 8km; a local guide can be hired for about US$10. Most homestays also rent bikes to explore the village at your own pace.

A popular 18km trek is from **Lac village** (Ban Lac) in Mai Chau to **Xa Linh village**, near a mountain pass (elevation 1000m) on Hwy 6. Lac village is home to White Thai, while the inhabitants of Xa Linh are H'mong. The trek is strenuous in one day, so most people spend a night in a village. Arrange a guide and a car to meet you at the mountain pass for the journey back to Mai Chau. Note there's a 600m climb in altitude, and the trail is slippery after rain.

Ask around in Mai Chau about longer treks of three to seven days. Other options include kayaking and mountain biking excursions; enquire at Mai Chau Lodge.

Many travel agencies in Hanoi run inexpensive trips to Mai Chau.

🛏 Sleeping & Eating

Most visitors stay in **Thai stilt houses** (per person incl breakfast around 150,000d) in the villages of Lac or Pom Coong, just a five-minute stroll apart.

Most people eat where they stay. Establish the price of meals first as some places charge up to 150,000d for dinner. Everything from fried eggs to French fries is available, but the local food is best.

Mai Chau Lodge   HOTEL **$$$**
(📞386 8959; www.maichaulodge.com; r US$90-160; 🌬@🛜🏊) This tour-group favourite has contemporary rooms with wooden floors and designer lighting, all trimmed with local textiles. Most rooms have balconies with rice-paddy views. The thatched-roof restaurant (meals US$10 to US$16) overlooks a small lake and the pool. Activities on offer include visits to nearby markets, caves and handicraft villages, cookery classes, and guided walking, kayaking and mountain biking excursions.

Mai Chau Nature Place   HOMESTAY **$**
(www.maichaunatureplace.com; dm $5, d $20) A step up from other Mai Chau homestays,

this friendly operation in Lac village also offers comfortable private rooms decked out with bamboo furniture and local textiles. Visitors are welcome to join the cooks in the kitchen.

ℹ️ Getting There & Away

Direct buses to Mai Chau leave Hanoi's My Dinh bus station regularly from 6am to 2pm (80,000d, 3¾ hours). Alternatively, catch a regular Son La or Dien Bien Phu bus to Tong Dau junction (80,000d, 3½ hours). From the junction it's another 5km by *xe om* (motorbike taxi) to Mai Chau (20,000d). There are also regular buses from Hoa Binh to Tong Dau (40,000d, one hour).

You may have to pay a 5000d entry fee to Mai Chau, but the toll booth is often not attended.

Son La
📞022 / POP 66,500

Son La has prospered as a logical transit point between Hanoi and Dien Bien Phu. It's not a must-see destination, but the surrounding scenery is impressive, and there are a few interesting diversions.

The region is one of Vietnam's most ethnically diverse and home to more than 30 different minorities including Black Thai, Meo, Muong and White Thai. Vietnamese influence was minimal until the 20th century, and from 1959 to 1980 the region was part of the Tay Bac Autonomous Region.

◎ Sights & Activities

Old French Prison & Museum   MUSEUM
(admission 15,000d; ⏰7.30-11am & 1.30-5pm) Son La's Old French Prison & Museum was a French penal colony where anticolonial

DON'T MISS

SLEEPING ON STILTS

If you are anticipating an exotic encounter – sharing a bowl of eyeball soup or entering a shamanic trance with the local medicine man – think again. Overnighting in Mai Chau's minority villages is a civilised experience. Electricity flows, there are Western-style toilets and hot showers, and roll-up mattresses and mosquito nets are provided. While this is eminently more comfortable, it probably won't fulfil your rustic hill-tribe trekking expectations.

Despite – or maybe because of – the modern amenities, it's still a memorable experience, and many people end up staying longer than planned. The surrounding area is beautifully lush, the Thai villages are attractive and tidy, and locals are exceedingly friendly. Even with a TV on and the hum of the refrigerator, it is a peaceful place, and you're still sleeping in a thatched-roof stilt house on split-bamboo floors.

Reservations are not necessary. Just show up, but try and arrive before dark so you can get your bearings.

CHOW DOWN IN MOC CHAU & YEN CHAU

Many travellers heading west enjoy the beautiful scenery around Mai Chau before kicking on to Laos via Dien Bien Phu, or heading north to Sapa. If you have a hankering for local flavours, especially if you've got a sweet tooth, it's worth stopping off at a couple of other towns along Hwy 6.

Around 200km west of Hanoi, Moc Chau boasts a pioneering dairy industry launched in the late 1970s with Australian and UN assistance. The dairy provides Hanoi with fresh milk, sweetened condensed milk and little tooth-rotting bars called *banh sua*, and the town is a good place to sample fresh milk and yoghurt. Moc Chau also produces some of Vietnam's best tea, and the surrounding area is home to ethnic minorities, including Green H'mong, Dzao, Thai and Muong.

A further 60km west, the agricultural Yen Chau district is known for its abundant fruit production. Apart from bananas, all fruits grown here are seasonal. Mangoes, plums and peaches are harvested from April to June, longans in July and August, and custard apples from August to September.

Yen Chau mangoes are renowned as Vietnam's tastiest, although travellers may initially find them disappointing, as they are small and green, rather than big, yellow and juicy like those of the tropical south. Most Vietnamese actually prefer the tart flavour of the green ones, especially dipped in *nuoc mam* (fish sauce) and sugar.

Both Moc Chau and Yen Chau can be reached on departures to either Son La or Dien Bien Phu from Hanoi's My Dinh bus station. Once on the road, travellers should find it relatively easy to flag down onward transport along Hwy 6 ranging from local minibuses to air-con coaches.

revolutionaries were incarcerated. It was destroyed by the 'off-loading' of unused ammunition by US warplanes after bombing raids, but is now partially restored. Rebuilt turrets stand guard over crumbling cells and a famous lone surviving peach tree. The tree, which blooms with traditional Tet flowers, was planted by To Hieu, a 1940s inmate.

Nearby the **People's Committee office** has a small museum, with local hill-tribe displays and good views of the prison.

Lookout Tower   LANDMARK

For an overview of Son La and the surrounding area, follow the stone steps to the left of the Trade Union Hotel. Look forward to a 20-minute walk to reach the lookout.

Craft Markets   MARKETS

Thuan Chau is about 35km northwest of Son La. Take a local bus or *xe om* here early in the morning, when its daily market is full of colourful hill-tribe women.

You'll also find woven shoulder bags, scarves, silver buttons and necklaces, and other hill-tribe crafts at Son La's market.

🛏 Sleeping & Eating

Hanoi Hotel   HOTEL $$

(☑375 3299; www.khachsanhanoi299.com; 228 Đ Truong Chinh; r $50; ❋@🛜) This gleaming main-drag edifice has spacious and modern rooms trimmed with colourful art, wooden furniture and surprisingly comfortable beds. Mod cons include a bar, restaurant and jacuzzi, and the massage chairs are definitely worth considering after a long bus journey. Bring along your negotiation A-game to get a good walk-in rate.

Viet Trinh   HOTEL $

(☑385 2263; 15 Đ 26/8; r 120,000d) Here's the best budget option for long-term Southeast Asian travellers, with simple but clean rooms in a small family-owned guesthouse. Maintain your thrifty travel habits with dinner and a beer at the small array of food stalls that sets up every night in the nearby park.

Trade Union Hotel   HOTEL $$

(☑385 2804; r US$25-40; ❋🛜) This large, rambling government-run place is showing its age, but the staff are very welcoming, and can arrange transport and tours. All the spacious rooms have desks, wardrobes, two beds and bathrooms with tubs. Rates include a hearty breakfast, and there's a decent on-site restaurant with exceptionally cold beer.

Long Phuong Restaurant   VIETNAMESE $

(P Thinh Doi; mains 30,000-70,000d) Located at one of the busier junctions in town, this restaurant features local minority dishes. Try sour *mang dang* (bamboo shoots) soup with sticky rice dipped in sesame-seed salt. Follow up with the local *ruou* (rice liquor), and you'll sleep very well.

Restaurant Com Pho   VIETNAMESE **$**
(8 Đ 26/8; dishes 25,000-40,000d) There's no English spoken at this humble but friendly place; just point to whatever takes your fancy.

ℹ Information

Agribank (8 Đ Chu Van Thinh) Has an ATM and changes dollars. The main post office is west of here.

ℹ Getting There & Away

Son La is 340km from Hanoi and 140km from Dien Bien Phu. The bus station is 5km southwest of town. See the table on p138 for details.

Tuan Giao

🖉 0230 / POP 28,000

This remote mountain town is at the junction of Hwy 279 to Dien Bien Phu (three hours, 80km) and Hwy 6 to Muong Lay (three hours, 98km). Few people overnight here unless they're behind schedule and can't make it to Dien Bien Phu, but it's an OK place to bed down. There's an Agribank (with ATM) 200m east of the main T-junction in town.

The **Tuan Giao Guest House** (🖉386 2316; Nguyen Trung Dao; r 160,000-200,000d; 🛜) has quiet rooms around a central courtyard. Ask for a room in building 'B' to get one of the newer, nicer rooms. The leafy courtyard is a good spot to plan your next move: south to Dien Bien Phu and Laos, or north to Sapa and China?

For simple rooms in the centre of town, try the **Hong Ky Hotel & Café** (🖉386 2355; r 220,000d; @🛜). A smidgen of English is (sometimes) spoken, and there's an on-site internet cafe and a simple restaurant.

About 500m west of the junction, towards Dien Bien Phu, **Hoang Quat Restaurant** (meals 100,000-120,000d) is a popular lunchtime stop for small tour groups. The beer is cold, and the Vietnamese food is plentiful, tasty and includes great grilled chicken with ginger and 'mountainous' rice.

Tuan Giao's bus station is just east of the junction; see the Northwest Bus Connections table on p138.

Pa Khoang Lake

Beautiful Pa Khoang Lake is 17km east of Dien Bien Phu on the road from Son La, and 4km off the highway. About a 15km drive around the lake's edge, or an hour's boat ride plus a 3km forest walk, is the restored **bunker of General Giap** (admission 5000d; ⊙7.30-11.30am & 1.30-4pm), the Vietnamese commander of the Dien Bien Phu campaign. The network of bunkers, tunnels, sentry boxes and huts is a fascinating diversion for those interested in Vietnam's legendary military tactician. There is also a remote **Thai village** across the lake. Hire a motor boat (200,000d return) to the bunker or villages.

Dien Bien Phu

🖉 0230 / POP 72,700

Around Dien Bien Phu on 7 May 1954, the French colonial forces were defeated by the Viet Minh in a decisive battle, and the days of their Indochina empire became numbered.

Dien Bien Phu (DBP) sits in the heart-shaped Muong Thanh Valley, surrounded by heavily forested hills. The scenery to or from DBP is stunning, with approach roads scything through thick forests and steep terrain. The city itself lies more prosaically on a broad dry plain. Thai, H'mong and Si La people live in the surrounding mountains, but the city and valley are mainly inhabited by ethnic Vietnamese.

Previously just a minor settlement, DBP only achieved town status in 1992. It became a city in 2003, and a year later was elevated to provincial capital. Expansive boulevards and civic buildings have been constructed and the airport now has daily flights from Hanoi. With the nearby Tay Trang–Sop Hun Laos–Vietnam border now open to foreigners, more travellers are passing through the city.

History is the city's main attraction, with colonial-era bunkers and museums.

⦿ Sights

Dien Bien Phu Museum   MUSEUM
(Đ 7-5; admission 5000d; ⊙7-11am & 1.30-5pm) Commemorating the 1954 battle, this well-laid-out museum features an eclectic collection. Alongside weaponry and guns, there's a bath tub that belonged to the French commander Colonel de Castries, a bicycle capable of carrying 330kg of ordnance, and

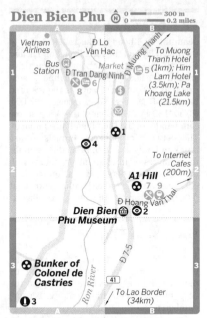

Dien Bien Phu Ⓝ ⟟ 0 ━━━━ 300 m
0 ━━━━ 0.2 miles

NORTHWEST VIETNAM DIEN BIEN PHU

plenty of photographs and documents, some with English translations.

Bunker of Colonel de Castries   WAR MEMORIAL
(admission 3000d; ◷7-11am & 1.30-5pm) Across the river the command bunker of Colonel Christian de Castries has been recreated. A few discarded tanks linger nearby, and you'll probably see Vietnamese tourists mounting the bunker and waving the Vietnamese flag, re-enacting an iconic photograph taken at the battle's conclusion.

A1 Hill   WAR MEMORIAL
(admission 5000d; ◷7-11am & 1.30-5pm) There are more tanks and a monument to Viet Minh casualties on this former French position, known to the French as Eliane and to the Vietnamese as A1 Hill. The elaborate trenches at the heart of the French defences have also been recreated.

Cemeteries   WAR MEMORIAL
A formal memorial to the 3000 French troops buried under the rice paddies was erected on the 30th anniversary of the 1954 battle. On the other bank of the Ron River, the immaculately maintained **Dien Bien Phu Cemetery** commemorates the Vietnamese dead, each gravestone bearing the gold star of the Vietnamese flag and a clutch of incense sticks.

Muong Thanh Bridge   BRIDGE
The old Muong Thanh Bridge is preserved and closed to four-wheeled traffic. Near the southern end of the bridge – though not much more than an overgrown crater – is the **bunker** where Chief Artillery Commander Pirot committed suicide.

🛏 Sleeping

Muong Thanh Hotel   HOTEL $$
(☏381 0043; www.muongthanhthanhnien.com; Đ Muong Thanh; r US$45-75; ✳️🛜♨️) Welcome to one of the northwest's comfortable hotels. A recent reconstruction has revealed modern rooms including satellite TV, elegant furniture and marble bathrooms. Added attractions include a wood-lined pub and a swimming pool watched over by a not-so-scary concrete dragon. A splurge-worthy introduction to Vietnam if you've been particularly thrifty in Laos.

Him Lam Hotel   RESORT HOTEL $$
(☏381 1999; www.himlamhotel.com.vn; Hwy 279; r US$30-45; ✳️@♨️) This resort-style hotel is one of Vietnam's best government-run places, with attractive wooden bungalows and modern rooms, and extensive grounds, tennis courts, pools, and a bar and restaurant. Consider taking your foot off the travel accelerator and staying a couple of nights in one of the private lakeside stilt houses. Just be mindful that weekends might see

your lakeside reverie interrupted by a local wedding.

Viet Hoang Hotel   GUESTHOUSE $
(☎373 5046; 67 Đ Tran Dang Ninh; s/d 100,000/120,000d; ✻@⊛) Right opposite the bus station, this friendly guesthouse is the ideal base if you're doing the early morning border run. Rooms are smallish but neat, and come with a splash of colour. Owner Mr Duc and his family are very hospitable and serve up free cups of tea for guests.

Binh Long Hotel   GUESTHOUSE $
(☎382 4345; 429 Đ Muong Thanh; d & tw US$10; ✻⊛) Another small, friendly, family-run place, but on a busy junction in the thick of things. The twin rooms aren't exactly huge, but they're neat and tidy, and the owners know about onward transport to Sapa and Laos. Breakfast is an additional $2.

✗ Eating & Drinking

Dining options are limited in DBP, though the Muong Thanh Hotel has a good restaurant. It's also worth considering eating at the Him Lam Hotel. A taxi from central DBP to Him Lam should be around 60,000d each way; count on 30,000d for a *xe om*.

For a cheaper pit stop, check out the inexpensive *pho* stalls and simple restaurants opposite the bus station; some serve delicious fresh sugar-cane juice.

The *bia hoi* (beer) gardens on Đ Hoang Van Thai are the best place to sink a local brew.

Lien Tuoi Restaurant   VIETNAMESE $
(Đ Hoang Van Thai; mains 60,000-90,000d) A long-running place famous for its filling Vietnamese and Chinese food, Lien Tuoi has a menu in English and French with some imaginative translations.

ℹ Information

There are internet cafes on Đ Hoang Van Thai.
Agribank (Đ 7-5) ATM and changes US$.
Main post office (Đ 7-5)

ℹ Getting There & Away

AIR Vietnam Airlines (☎382 4948; www.viet namairlines.com; Nguyen Huu Tho; ⊙7.30-11.30am & 1.30-4.30pm) Operates two flights daily between Dien Bien Phu and Hanoi. The office is near the airport, about 1.5km from the town centre, along the road to Muong Lay.
BUS DBP's bus station is on Hwy 12, at the corner of Đ Tran Dang Ninh. See p138 for details

---

THE SIEGE OF DIEN BIEN PHU

In early 1954 General Henri Navarre, commander of the French forces in Indochina, sent 12 battalions to occupy the Muong Thanh Valley in an attempt to prevent the Viet Minh from crossing into Laos and threatening the former Lao capital of Luang Prabang. The French units, of which 30% were ethnic Vietnamese, were soon surrounded by Viet Minh forces under General Vo Nguyen Giap. The Viet Minh outnumbered the French by five to one, and were equipped with artillery pieces and anti-aircraft guns, painstakingly carried by porters through jungles and across rivers. The guns were placed in carefully camouflaged concealed positions overlooking the French positions.

When the guns opened up, French Chief Artillery Commander Pirot committed suicide. He'd assumed there was no way the Viet Minh could get heavy artillery to the area. A failed Viet Minh human-wave assault against the French was followed by weeks of intense artillery bombardments. Six battalions of French paratroopers were parachuted into DBP as the situation worsened, but bad weather and the impervious Viet Minh artillery prevented sufficient French reinforcements from arriving. An elaborate system of trenches and tunnels allowed Viet Minh soldiers to reach French positions without coming under fire. The trenches and bunkers were overrun by the Viet Minh after the French decided against the use of US conventional bombers, and the Pentagon's proposal to use tactical atomic bombs. All 13,000 French soldiers were either killed or taken prisoner, and Viet Minh casualties were estimated at 25,000.

Just one day before the Geneva Conference on Indochina was set to begin in Switzerland, Viet Minh forces finally overran the beleaguered French garrison after a 57-day siege. This shattered French morale, and the French government abandoned all attempts to re-establish colonial control of Vietnam.

ℹ️ **BORDER CROSSING: TAY TRANG–SOP HUN**

The Lao border at Tay Trang, 34km from Dien Bien Phu, is open daily between 7am and 7pm. You'll need a pre-arranged visa to enter Vietnam here, but if you're crossing into Laos most nationalities can get a one-month visa on arrival. There are no banks on either side of the frontier, so have US dollars to pay for your Laos visa.

Buses from DBP (88,000d) leave daily at 5.30am. It's advisable to book your ticket the day prior to travelling. This bus takes you through the border crossing and drops you off in Muang Khua in Laos. The journey typically takes between seven and eight hours, but can be longer depending on the roads and border formalities.

It is possible to hire a *xe om* from DBP to the border for around 200,000d, but you'll probably then have to walk 5km to the nearest Lao village for transport to Muang May. Muang May has basic guesthouses and onward travel options to Muang Khua. You'll also need cash (US dollars or Lao kip) to do the trip this way, so it's really more straightforward to catch the daily 5.30am departure from DBP.

of bus connections with Hanoi among other destinations.

CAR & MOTORCYCLE The 480km drive from Hanoi to Dien Bien Phu on Hwys 6 and 279 takes around 11 hours.

Muong Lay

📞 0231 / POP 8800

Formerly known as Lai Chau, the small town of Muong Lay en route from Dien Bien Phu to Sapa has undergone a massive transformation in recent years. On our last research trip it was little more than a huge building site on the edge of a massive artificial lake.

The former town of Lai Chau was perched on the banks of the spectacular Da River valley, but has now been flooded to incorporate the Song Da Reservoir, part of a massive hydroelectricity scheme. The township's been moved up the riverbank, and an expansive new bridge crosses the newly formed lake. A couple of hotels are open high above the lake, but access was restricted to 4WD vehicles at the time of writing. It's envisaged that the new body of water will have a future as a tourist centre for boat trips and water sports.

🛏️ Sleeping & Eating

Lan Anh Hotel HOTEL **$$**

(📞385 2682; www.lananhhotel.com; r US$15-50; ❄️@) Relocated across the bridge onto a ridge overlooking the lake, the Lan Anh has rooms ranging from rustic stilt houses to VIP suites with flash marble bathrooms. The hotel's social hub is a terrific outdoor terrace and beer garden. Trekking to nearby minority villages can be arranged, and boat trips are planned as a future attraction. Pick ups can be arranged from Muong Lay's ad hoc bus station.

ℹ️ Getting There & Away

At the time of writing, Muong Lay had a makeshift bus station (see p138 for connections) on Hwy 12, a highway still undergoing a ton of construction work. If you can book ahead at Lan Anh Hotel, Muong Lay is worth a slightly surreal overnight stop, but given the town's current reinvention, a through bus from Dien Bien Phu to Lai Chau is the probably the best option.

Lai Chau

📞 0231 / POP 37,000

After passing through one of Vietnam's remotest regions, the new eight-lane boulevards and monumental government buildings of Lai Chau appear like some Vietnamese El Dorado. The reality is more prosaic.

Formerly known as Tam Duong, this remote town was renamed Lai Chau when a decision was made to flood 'old' Lai Chau (now called Muong Lay). 'New' Lai Chau is split between the old town, with its **market** full of hill-tribe people, and the concrete new town 3km to the southeast.

Despite it's grandiose streets and upgrade to provincial capital status, Lai Chau is still something of a one-horse town. Fortunately the surrounding scenery of verdant conical peaks is as beguiling as ever.

Most visitors stop for a lunch break between Dien Bien Phu, Muong Lay and Sapa. The drive from Lai Chau to Sapa along Hwy 4D, threading through the Fansipan Mountain Range near the Chinese border, is a beautiful stretch of road.

🛏️ Sleeping & Eating

Phuong Tanh HOTEL **$$**

(📞387 5235; Main Sapa Rd; US$23; ❄️📶) Part of a burgeoning mini-empire – the owners also run a nearby restaurant (mains 100,000d to 150,000d) – the Phuong Tanh overcomes a drab residential area with clean and well-lit rooms offering big bathrooms. On the 2nd floor, the Café Phan Xi Pan is a brightly coloured oasis with wi-fi, cold beer and tasty variations on rice and noodles.

Tay Bac Hotel   GUESTHOUSE $
(☏387 5879; 143 Trung Hang Dao; r 120,000-240,000d; ✴️🛜) This place has a bit of character, as some rooms in the three different buildings are in an attractive Thai-style wooden house with balconies. Other more comfortable rooms are also more prosaic.

Tuan Anh Restaurant   VIETNAMESE $
(meals 20,000-40,000d) This is a good option if you're Sapa-bound and on a lunch run. There are also plenty of *com pho* spots nearby.

ℹ️ Information

There's an Agribank and ATMs in the old town's main street.

ℹ️ Getting There & Away

The bus station is 1km out of town, on the road to Sapa. For Sapa, change in Lao Cai to a frequent minibus. See p138 for details.

Sapa

☏020 / POP 36,200 / ELEV 1650M

Established as a hill station by the French in 1922, Sapa is the one place in the northwest where tourism is booming. It's now firmly on the European and North American package tour circuit, and well-equipped trekkers toting lightweight walking sticks and wearing technical all-weather gear are a common sight around town.

The town is orientated to make the most of the spectacular views emerging on clear days. The town overlooks a plunging valley of cascading rice terraces, with mountains towering above on all sides. Views of this epic scenery are often subdued by thick mist rolling across the peaks, but even if it's cloudy, Sapa is still a fascinating destination, especially when local hill-tribe people fill the town with colour.

WORTH A TRIP

SINHO VILLAGE

Sinho is a scenic mountain village that is home to a large number of ethnic minorities. It should attract more tourists, but when you visit, there is a 'you ain't from around here' look on the faces of many locals.

However a new hotel and improved road access means it's an excellent detour if you're keen to see an authentic local market very different to the markets at Sapa and Bac Ha, which are now firmly on the tour bus route.

Sinho has markets on Saturday and Sunday, and the wildly colourful Sunday market is the more impressive of the two. Just don't expect trendy ethnic handicrafts; you're more likely to be confronted with a full-on mix of bovine moos and porcine squeals.

The best (only!) place in town that accepts foreign travellers is the welcoming **Thanh Binh Hotel** (☏0231-387 0366; Zone 5, Sinho; r US$25-27; @), a surprisingly comfortable spot comprising 17 spotless rooms with mountain and rice paddy views. Rates include breakfast, and lunch and dinner (100,000d) are on offer in cosy bamboo gazebos. Treks from 3km to 10km can be arranged to nearby White H'mong and Red Dzao villages.

Note there are no ATMs or banking services in Sinho, but there is internet access at the Thanh Binh Hotel.

A bus to Sinho leaves Dien Bien Phu daily (150,000d, six hours) at around 4.30am, transiting through Muong Lay around 7am. These times can be flexible, so check at the Dien Bien Phu bus station the day before you want to leave. From Sinho, a daily 1.15pm bus (40,000d, two hours) then trundles downhill to Lai Chau. If you're travelling between Dien Bien Phu, Muong Lay and Lai Chau, this detour is a nicely meandering alternative. Heading south from Lai Chau to Sinho, there are two buses per day at 6.30am and 1.30pm (35,000d, two hours).

It's definitely slow going by public transport, but certainly achievable with patience and a flexible attitude. If you're travelling on two wheels, the turn-off uphill to Sinho is 1km north of Chan Nua on the main road from Muong Lay to Lai Chau.

BUILDING A STRONGER H'MONG FUTURE

Traditionally, the H'mong have been employees of Vietnamese-owned trekking companies, restaurants and accommodation, but a new generation is now focused on securing a more independent and positive future for their people. Following are two prime examples.

Meaning 'thank you Sapa' in the H'mong language, **Sapa O'Chau** (☑0915 351 479; www.sapaochau.com) is a brilliant organisation helmed by the live wire Shu Tan. In her mid-20s, her background includes street peddling handicrafts to tourists as a child, but now her focus is on providing training and opportunities to a new generation of H'mong children.

It's not uncommon for H'mong children to be kept out of school to sell handicrafts or to be trekking guides, often walking up to 10km daily from their villages to Sapa to earn money. The Sapa O'Chau Learning Centre is a live-in school where up to 20 H'mong children can learn English and Vietnamese to equip them for a more positive future.

Sapa O'Chau is always interested to hear from travellers keen on volunteering as English-language teachers, and the organisation also runs excellent day walks, longer homestay treks and a challenging ascent of Fansipan. See the website for details and download an application form to become a volunteer.

Sapa Sisters (www.sapasisters.webs.com), a trekking company operated by four enterprising teenage H'mong girls, is getting great reviews from travellers. Email or text them to arrange day treks, two- to three-day village homestays or ascents of Fansipan. Excellent English is spoken, along with a smattering of French, Spanish and Japanese.

The town's French colonial villas fell into disrepair during successive wars with the French, Americans and Chinese, but following the advent of tourism, Sapa has experienced a renaissance. The downside is a hotel building boom, and because height restrictions are rarely enforced, the Sapa skyline is changing for the worse.

Inherent in this prosperity is cultural change for the hill-tribe people. The H'mong people are very canny traders, urging you to buy handicrafts and trinkets. Many have had little formal education, yet all the youngsters have a good command of English, French and a handful of other languages.

◉ Sights & Activities

Sapa Market   MARKET
Hill-tribe people from surrounding villages go to the Sapa market most days to sell handicrafts and ethnic-style clothing. Saturday is the most frantic, as tour groups from Hanoi visit for the evening 'love market', which sees hill-tribe teenagers trek into town to find a mate. It's still very coy, but has become commercial in recent years. These days there are more tourists than love-sick teenagers, as well as a few opportunistic prostitutes.

Chieu Suong   MASSAGE
(16 P Thach Son; massages from 150,000d) Hiking those mountain trails can be tough on your joints, so come to this humble spot for bona fide foot and body massages.

Victoria Spa   SPA
(☑387 1522; www.victoriahotels-asia.com; Victoria Sapa Resort & Spa) This upmarket spa complex has gorgeous massage and treatment rooms.

Local Villages   HIKING
For overnight stays in villages and longer treks into the mountains, it's important to hook up with someone who knows the terrain and culture and speaks the language. See p465 to brush up on your ethnic minority cultural etiquette before visiting. We recommend using minority guides, as this offers them a means of making a living. See the boxed text 'Building a Stronger H'mong Future' for more information.

Speak to travel agencies or guides – who'll probably approach you in the street – pick up a decent map and plot your course. The villages and the surrounding landscape are now part of Hoang Lien National Park.

The nearest village within walking distance is **Cat Cat** (admission 25,000d), 3km south of Sapa. It's a steep and beautiful hike down, and there are plenty of *xe om* for the return uphill journey.

Another popular hike is to **Ta Phin village** (admission 40,000d), home to Red Dzao and about 10km from Sapa. Most people take a *xe om* to a starting point about 8km from Sapa, and then make a 14km loop through the area, passing through Black H'mong and Red Dzao villages.

For spectacular valley views (if the mist and cloud gods relent), there's a beautiful hike along a high ridge east of Sapa through the Black H'mong settlements of **Sa Seng** and **Hang Da** down to the Ta Van River, where you can get transport back to Sapa.

There are also community-based tours to the nearby H'mong village of **Sin Chai**, with an overnight in the village to learn about textiles or music and dance. Other popular communities to visit include the Giay village of **Ta Van** and the H'mong village of **Mat-ra**. Note that admission charges (around 40,000d) also apply to these other villages.

Fansipan
CLIMBING

Surrounding Sapa are the Hoang Lien Mountains, dubbed the Tonkinese Alps by the French. These mountains include the often cloud-obscured Fansipan (3143m), Vietnam's highest peak. Fansipan is accessible year round to sensibly equipped travellers in good shape, but don't underestimate the challenge. It is very wet, and can be perilously slippery and generally cold. Don't attempt an ascent if Sapa's weather is poor, as limited visibility on Fansipan can be treacherous.

The summit of Fansipan is 19km from Sapa and can be reached only on foot. The terrain is rough and adverse weather is frequent. The round trip usually takes three days; some experienced hikers do it in two days, but you'll need to be fit. After walking through hill-tribe villages on the first morning, it's just forest, mountain vistas and occasional wildlife, including monkeys, mountain goats and birds.

No ropes or technical climbing skills are needed, just endurance. There are a few rudimentary shelters at a couple of base camps en route, but it's better to be self sufficient with sleeping bag, waterproof tent, food, stove, raincoat or poncho, compass and other miscellaneous survival gear. It's vital to carry out all your garbage, as some of the camps are now impacted by trash. Hiring a reputable guide is vital, and porters are also recommended.

Through local operators, count on an all-inclusive rate of around US$130 per person for a couple, US$100 per person for a group of four and US$80 per person for the sensible maximum group size of six.

Weather-wise the best time is from mid-October to mid-December, and in March, when wildflowers are in bloom.

Tram Ton Pass
CYCLING

The road between Sapa and Lai Chau crosses the Tram Ton Pass on the northern side of Fansipan, 15km from Sapa. At 1900m this is Vietnam's highest mountain pass, and acts as a dividing line between two weather fronts. Even if you're not touring the northwest, come up here to experience the often ferocious winds and the incredible views. Descending by mountain bike is a seriously spectacular ride – enquire at Sapa's travel agencies.

On the Sapa side, it's often cold and foggy, but drop a few hundred metres onto the Lai Chau side, and it can be sunny and warm. Surprisingly, Sapa is the coldest place in Vietnam, but Lai Chau can be one of the warmest.

Alongside the road, 12km from Sapa, is 100m-high **Thac Bac** (Silver Waterfall); the **loop track** (admission 3000d) is steep and scenic.

🐾 Courses

Sapa Rooms
COOKING

(☑650 5228; www.saparooms.com; Đ Phan Si; per person US$30) Pop into the Sapa Rooms cafe and ask about their cookery courses held at the Hmong Mountain Retreat. Classes kick off at 10am with a visit to Sapa market, just 10m from the cafe.

🛏 Sleeping

Sapa has accommodation ranging from bare-bones cheapies, through to boutique-style offerings, and a luxury hilltop resort. Most hotels listed have views, but Sapa's building boom can change that overnight; check when you book.

Prices are competitive, but often double on busy weekends around Saturday's love market. Note some midrange places also have excellent budget rooms.

Beware of hotels using old-style charcoal burners for heat, as the fumes can cause severe breathing problems if the room's not well ventilated. Most hotels have now switched over to electric heaters or open fireplaces for the winter.

🏡 Hmong Mountain Retreat
ECOLODGE **$$**

(☑650 5228; www.hmongmountainretreat.com; 6 Ban Ho Rd, Lao Chai; per person US$55; ☺Mar-Dec) Accommodation in bungalows is simple, but the real attraction here is sleeping above a verdant cascade of rice paddies several kilometres out of Sapa. Rates include all meals, taken in the retreat's restaurant crafted from an 80-year-old tribal house. Up to 95% of ingredients are sourced within a 2km radius, and the stunning grounds are dotted with the owner's artworks. The retreat is also the location for cookery classes offered by Sapa Rooms.

Boutique Sapa Hotel

BOUTIQUE HOTEL $$

(📞387 2727; www.boutiquesapahotel.com.vn; 41 Đ Phan Si; s/d from US$40/55; @🎅) This hotel features classy furniture, flat-screen TVs and superb vistas from the terrace cafe, while the downstairs dining room does great pizza (US$5 to US$8) and warming hotpots. Pay a little more for a room with valley views. Massage and cookery classes are both available.

Luong Thuy Family Guesthouse

GUESTHOUSE $

(📞387 2310; www.familysapa.com; 028 Đ Muong Hoa; s & d US$10-15; @🎅) Simple and spotless rooms feature at this friendly family owned guesthouse a short stroll from the hubbub of downtown Sapa. Motorcycles and bikes can be rented, trekking and transport arranged, and the misty valley view from the front balconies is quite superb.

Cat Cat View Hotel

HOTEL $$

(📞387 1946; www.catcathotel.com; 1 Đ Phan Si; s/d from US$25/30; @🎅) This excellent spot has 40 rooms over nine floors, many with great views. There's something for every budget, with homely, comfortable pine-trimmed accommodation, and even a seriously spacious two-bed apartment (US$180). The cheaper rooms are the best value: bargain hunters should check out the wing across the road for excellent budget rooms in the US$10 to US$15 range.

Sapa Rooms

BOUTIQUE HOTEL $$

(📞650 5228; www.saparooms.com; Đ Phan Si; r US$57-72; @🎅) Billing itself as a boutique hotel, this place is decorated in a highly quirky style and has an excellent lobby cafe. The rooms are more prosaic, but show some nice touches including fresh flowers. Prices include a good breakfast, and the Australian owner is helpful and friendly.

Victoria Sapa Resort & Spa

RESORT HOTEL $$$

(📞387 1522; www.victoriahotels-asia.com; r from US$175; ✳@🎅☒) This alpine-style hilltop hotel is a well-maintained establishment, right down to the manicured lawns. Rooms aren't large, but they do feature hand-carved

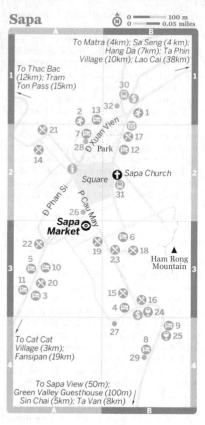

Sapa

To Matra (4km); Sa Seng (4 km); Hang Da (7km); Ta Phin Village (10km); Lao Cai (38km)

To Thac Bac (12km); Tram Ton Pass (15km)

Ham Rong Mountain

Sapa Market

Square — Sapa Church

Đ Phan Si

P Cau May

Đ Xuan Vien

Park

To Cat Cat Village (3km); Fansipan (19km)

To Sapa View (50m); Green Valley Guesthouse (100m); Sin Chai (5km); Ta Van (8km)

furniture and private balconies. Facilities include two bars, a heated swimming pool and a fitness centre. Get here in style from Hanoi on one of the resort's luxury *Victoria Express* train carriages.

Topas Eco Lodge

ECOLODGE $$$

(📞387 2404; www.topasecolodge.com; r US$99-129; @) Overlooking a plunging valley, this ecolodge has 25 lovely stone-and-thatch bungalows, each with front balconies to make the most of the magnificent views. The whole project is sustainable and environmentally friendly, with sunlight providing the power. The hotel staff and guides (for treks and mountain biking) are minority people. It's near Tan Kim village, about 18km from Sapa, and located at a much milder (and warmer) altitude. Unfortunately the construction of a nearby hydroelectricity project has damaged views from some bungalows; try and avoid the ones starting with '300'.

Sapa

Pinocchio Hotel   GUESTHOUSE $
(✆387 1876; www.pinocchiohotel.com; 15 Đ Muong Hoa; r US$15-20; @⑦) The young and friendly staff that run this excellent guesthouse really make the place. The rooms, all with simple but attractive decor, creep higher and higher up the hillside – those at the top enjoy a terrific valley aspect from their balconies. Topping it all is a rooftop restaurant.

Baguette & Chocolat   GUESTHOUSE $
(✆387 1766; www.hoasuaschool.com; Đ Thac Bac; r US$22; ⑦) Operated by Hoa Sua (a group helping disadvantaged youth), this place has charm and style, though, as there are just four rooms, it's essential to book ahead. The guesthouse is above an excellent French cafe, and rates include a great breakfast.

Sapa Hostel   GUESTHOUSE $
(✆387 3073; www. sapahostel.com; 9 & 33 Đ Phan Si; dm/s/d/tr US$5/12/15/18; @⑦) Located a few doors apart on Đ Phan Si, both of Sapa Hostel's locations feature spacious rooms and a laid-back travellers' vibe. Furniture is surprisingly chic, and the best of Sapa's restaurants are just a short stroll away. Rooms at Sapa Hostel 2 (33 Đ Phan Si) are cheaper by around three bucks, but the decor is not as modern.

Cha Pa Garden   BOUTIQUE HOTEL $$
(✆387 2907; www.chapagarden.com; 23B P Cau May; r US$65-85; ❄@⑦) Cha Pa occupies a sensitively restored colonial villa amid lush gardens in the heart of Sapa. There are just four rooms, all presented in contemporary style, with uncluttered lines and hip bathrooms. Aspects of the hotel are looking a little worn, so it's hoped new owners will once again improve standards.

Thai Binh Hotel   HOTEL $
(✆387 1449; 45 Đ Ham Rong; r US$22-25) Run by a couple of teachers, the Thai Binh enjoys a quiet location near Sapa's main square and church. Rooms are spotless and decked out with crisp pine furniture and cosy bedspreads. Rates include breakfast, and the owners are well equipped with information about onward travel to China.

Sapa Luxury Hotel   HOTEL $$
(✆387 2771; www.sapaluxuryhotel.com; 36 Đ Phan Si; s/d/tr from US$30/30/45; @⑦) One of the newest openings on Đ Phan Si features spacious rooms with wooden floors and trendy Asian decor last seen at your local furniture superstore. Good value in an up-and-coming part of town.

Sapa View   HOTEL **$$**
(☑387 2388; www.sapaview-hotel.com; 41 Đ Muong Hoa; s/d/ste from US$65/75/85; @☎) Expect no problems here with false advertising – look forward to excellent valley views, especially from the attached Tam Tam restaurant. The decor is a winning combination of local tribal art and lots of Scandinavian-style wood.

Fansipan View Hotel   HOTEL **$**
(☑387 3759; www.fansipanview.com; 45 Đ Xuan Vien; s/d from US$22/35; @☎) Here you'll find cosy rooms tucked away in a quiet lane en route to the Victoria Sapa Resort & Spa. Ask for a room at the front for views of the town. Downstairs is the good Sapa Cuisine restaurant.

Casablanca Sapa Hotel   HOTEL **$**
(☑387 2667; www.sapacasablanca.com; Đ Dong Loi; s/d/tr US$17/20/25; ☎) The once-trendy decor is now looking a tad weary, but this place is still OK value. Book a room at the rear for the cheapest rates. Mr Kien, the attentive owner, speaks fluent English.

Green Valley Hostel   GUESTHOUSE **$**
(☑387 1449; 45 Đ Muong Hoa; r US$15-20) This is the HI choice in town. While it could be a little better maintained, it still offers cheap rooms and unobstructed views. Motorbikes can be rented for $5 per day, and there's a cosy on-site bar with pool table.

✖ Eating

For Western and Vietnamese food in comfortable surroundings, head to the diverse scene along the main drag P Cau May. Most places in town open for breakfast, lunch and dinner.

Vietnamese-style hotpot (meat stew cooked with local vegetables, cabbage and mushroom) is a very popular local dish; try it at the hotpot stalls just south of the bus station.

For eating on a budget, humble Vietnamese restaurants huddle below the market on Đ Tue Tinh, and the night-market stalls south of the church can't be beaten for *bun cha* (barbecued pork).

Sapa Rooms   CAFE **$$**
(www.saparooms.com; Đ Phan Si; snacks 50,000d, meals around 90,000d) This flamboyantly decorated cafe looks like it should be in New York or London rather than the highlands of northern Vietnam. It's great for a snack (think corn fritters or a BLT baguette), meal (try the 'caramelised' pork fillet or fish 'n' chips) or just a pot of tea and a piece of cake.

Ask about the daily cookery classes it runs at the Hmong Mountain Retreat.

Red Dao House   VIETNAMESE **$$**
(4B Đ Thac Bac; meals from 100,000d) This smart restaurant in a mock hill-tribe house has a nice front terrace and staff who wear Dzao-style costume. There are set lunches and dinners, and plenty of Vietnamese seafood and chicken dishes. It's a short walk up behind the tourist information centre; look for the red Chinese lanterns.

Baguette & Chocolat   CAFE **$**
(Đ Thac Bac; cakes from 20,000d, snacks & meals 70,000-160,000d) Head to this elegant converted villa for a fine breakfast, open sandwich, baguette or yummy slab of gateau. There are also good salads, pastas and Asian and Vietnamese dishes, and the 'picnic kits' are a smart option for trekkers. On a misty and chilly Sapa day, a warming mug of ginger tea is impossible to beat.

Nature View   VIETNAMESE **$**
(Đ Phan Si; meals from 60,000d) Newish opening opposite the Cat Cat View Hotel offering a good mix of Vietnamese and Western flavours. Some of Sapa's best pizzas and terrific fruit smoothies effortlessly tick the box marked 'comfort food'. The set lunch of four courses (75,000d) is great value.

Viet Emotion   MEDITERRANEAN **$$**
(www.vietemotion.com; 27 P Cau May; meals 70,000-150,000d) This stylish and intimate bistro features a cosy fireplace and has bottles of wine hanging from the ceiling. Try the trekking omelette, homemade soup or something from the tapas menu, such as *gambas al ajillo* (garlic prawns). If the weather really sets in, there are books and magazines to browse, and games including chess.

Gecko   FRENCH **$$**
(Đ Ham Rong; mains US$7-10) This large, enjoyable French-owned place resembles an *auberge* (inn), with a rustic feel and a menu of flavoursome country cooking. Try the boeuf bourguignon or the 'gecko' soup (with potato, bacon and cheese). There's a bar area and a little park-facing front terrace.

Delta Restaurant   ITALIAN **$$**
(P Cau May; mains US$7-12) Another stylish and atmospheric place, Delta Restaurant is renowned for its pizzas, which are the most authentic in town, and the pasta is pretty decent too. Wash it all down with a drop of Aussie red.

Bombay   INDIAN **$$**
(36 P Cau May; mains US$7-10) Indian food in
Sapa? Certainly. Dhal, naan, and all your fa-
vourite curries and vegie dishes are present
and correct here, though the restaurant
lacks a little in terms of atmosphere.

Gerbera Restaurant   VIETNAMESE **$**
(P Cau May; mains from 40,000d) An old trav-
ellers' fave that's best for its filling, inex-
pensive Vietnamese food. Choose from the
looong menu.

Nature Bar & Grill   VIETNAMESE **$**
(P Cau May; meals 60,000-100,000d) Has a large
wood-panelled interior and a central fire-
place. The menu is a typical Sapa mix of Vi-
etnamese and Western dishes.

🍷 Drinking & Entertainment

A bar crawl in Sapa will take in a maximum
of three or four venues – this is not a party
town.

Mountain Bar & Pub   BAR
(2 Đ Muong Hoa) Dangerously strong cocktails,
cold beer and ultra-competitive games of
table football conspire to make this Sapa's
go-to place for a great night out. Even if
it's freezing outside, a *shisha* (water pipe)
beside the open fire will soon perk up the
chilliest of travellers. Try the warm apple
wine for some highland bliss.

Red Dragon Pub   PUB
(23 Đ Muong Hoa) Looking like something
transplanted from the Pembrokeshire coast,
this genteel place resembles a Welsh tea-
room, with plenty of knick-knacks on show.
It's good for a quiet drink, and serves filling
pub grub, including shepherd's pie.

🛍 Shopping

Scour the stores on P Cau May and Đ Phan
Si for clothing, accessories and jewellery
produced by the area's minority peoples.
Urban Vietnamese designers are also pro-
ducing clothes and household furnishings
inspired by tribal motifs.

Lots of the minority women and girls
have gone into the souvenir business; the
older women in particular are known for
their strong-armed selling tactics. When ne-
gotiating prices, hold your ground, but avoid
aggressive bargaining.

Note that on some cheaper clothing, the
dyes used are not set, which can turn any-
thing the material touches (including your
skin) a muddy blue-green colour. Wash the

fabric separately in cold salted water to
stop the dye from running, and wrap items
in plastic bags before packing it in your
luggage.

If you've arrived in town with insufficient
warm clothing, stores along P Cau May sell
lots of 'brand-name' walking shoes, parkas
and thermals. Some of it might even be
authentic.

ℹ Information

Internet Access

Internet access – including complimentary wi-fi
– is available at hotels, restaurants and cafes
around town.

Money

There are two ATMs in Sapa and many of the
hotels and businesses will change US dollars
and euros.
BIDV (Đ Ngu Chi Son) Has an ATM and will
exchange cash.

Post

Main post office (Đ Ham Rong)

Tourist Information

The *Sapa Tourist Map* is an excellent 1:75,000
scale map of the walking trails and attractions
around Sapa. The *Sapa Trekking Map* is a worth-
while hand-drawn map showing trekking routes
and the town.
Sapa Tourism (☑ 387 3239; www.sapa
-tourism.com; 103 Đ Xuan Vien; ◷ 7.30-
11.30am & 1.30-5pm) Helpful English-speaking
staff offering details about transport, trekking
and weather. Its website is also a mine of useful
information.

Travel Agencies

Note that trekking, homestays and climbing
Fansipan are also offered by two minority-owned
operations; see the boxed text on p126.
Duc Minh (☑ 387 1881; www.ducminhtravel
.vn; 10 P Cau May) Friendly English-speaking
operator organising transport, treks to hill-tribe
villages and assaults of Fansipan.
Handspan Travel (☑ 387 2110; www.handspan
.com; Chau Long Hotel, 24 Dong Loi) Offers
trekking and mountain-biking tours to villages
and markets.
Sapa Pathfinder Travel (☑ 387 3468; www
.sapapathfinder.com; 13 Đ Xuan Vien) Trek-
king, mountain biking, Fansipan and advice on
transport.
Topas Travel (☑ 387 1331; www.topastravel.vn;
24 Đ Muong Hoa) A Sapa-based operator that
has high-quality trekking, biking and village
encounters. Many options include a stay in
Topas Eco Lodge.

ⓘ Getting There & Away

The gateway to Sapa is Lao Cai, 38km away via a smooth, well-maintained highway.

BICYCLE & MOTORCYCLE Motorcycling from Hanoi to Sapa is feasible, but it's a long 380km trip. Put your bike on the train to Lao Cai and save yourself the hassle. The 38km between Lao Cai and Sapa is all uphill – hell on a bicycle.

BUS Sapa's bus station is in the north of town, but you can also check schedules at the tourist office or most travel agents. See p138 for a summary of bus connections.

MINIBUS Minibuses to/from Lao Cai are frequent between 5am and 5pm (40,000d, one hour), leaving from outside the church. Hotels and travel agents offer direct minibus services to Bac Ha (from US$15 return) for the Sunday market. It's cheaper, but slower, to go to Bac Ha by public minibus, changing buses in Lao Cai.

TRAIN There's no direct train line to Sapa, but regular services from Hanoi to Lao Cai. Book tickets back to Hanoi at the **Railway Booking Office** (⏱7.30-11am & 1.30-4pm), near the Sapa bus station.

ⓘ Getting Around

The best way to get around compact Sapa is to walk. A bicycle can be hired, but you'll spend half the time pushing it up steep hills.

For excursions further afield, motorbikes are available from about US$7 a day. If you've never ridden a motorbike before, this is not the place to learn. The weather can be wet and treacherous at any time of the year, and roads are steep and regularly damaged by floods and heavy rain. Consider hiring a bike with a local driver (about US$12 a day).

Cars, 4WDs and minibuses are also available for hire.

Lao Cai

☑020 / POP 46,700

Lao Cai is right on the Vietnam–China border. The town was razed in the Chinese invasion of 1979, so most of the buildings are new. The border crossing here slammed shut during the 1979 war and only reopened in 1993. Now it's a bustling spot fuelled by growing cross-border trade.

Today Lao Cai is also a destination for travellers journeying between Hanoi and Sapa, or further north to Kunming in China. With Sapa just an hour or so away, Lao Cai is no place to linger, but it offers everything China-bound travellers will need for an overnight stay.

ⓘ BORDER CROSSING: LAO CAI–HEKOU

The Lao Cai–Hekou crossing is a direct route between northern Vietnam and Yunnan in China. The border is open daily between 7am and 10pm. China is separated from Vietnam by a road bridge and a separate rail bridge over the Red River.

The border is about 3km from Lao Cai train station, a journey that is easily done on a xe om (20,000d). Note that travellers have reported Chinese officials confiscating Lonely Planet *China* guides at this border, so you may want to try masking the cover.

Trains no longer run from Hekou to Kunming, but there are several 'sleeper' buses (Y150). One bus leaves at 7pm and arrives in Kunming at around 7am, but there are also earlier departures. Reset your watch when you cross the border – the time in China is one hour later than in Vietnam. You'll need to have a pre-arranged visa for China.

🛏 Sleeping & Eating

Terminus Hotel & Restaurant　　HOTEL **$**
(☑383 5470; 342 P Nguyen Hue; r 200,000-300,000d; ❄🔊) Right across the square from the train station, this is a good spot for an early breakfast or a filling meal. The rooms are very clean and tidy, and have a few frilly decorative touches. Staff speak OK English.

Nga Nghi Tho Huong　　GUESTHOUSE **$**
(☑383 5111; 342a P Nguyen Hue; r 150,000-250,000d; ❄🔊) Just around the corner from the Terminus, this family-run spot is slightly kitsch – there's an overabundance of dolls and stuffed toys – but the rooms are clean and colourful, and there's a good tea house on the bottom floor.

Pineapple　　CAFE **$**
(Pha Dinh Phung; meals 60,000-100,000d; ❄@🔊) A stylish Sapa-esque cafe run by Bui Duc Thinh, a fluent English speaker and former guide. Try the full English breakfast or a salad, pizza or baguette. Shakes and juices are also available. Walk down the street in front of the train station for around 100m.

Viet Emotion　　CAFE **$**
(65 Pha Dinh Phung; meals 70,000-150,000d; ❄@🔊) Giving Pineapple a run for its money

is the adjacent Viet Emotion, an offshoot of the successful Sapa cafe, celebrating a handy spot midway between the train and bus stations. Good breakfasts, pizza and pasta are popular choices for transiting travellers to or from Hanoi.

ℹ Information

Be wary of being short-changed by black-market currency traders, especially on the Chinese side. If you do need to change money, just change a small amount.

There are two ATMs by the train station. **BIDV Bank** (Đ Thuy Hoa) on the west bank of the river changes cash.

ℹ Getting There & Away

BUS & MINIBUS Lao Cai is about 340km from Hanoi. Nine daily buses make the journey to Hanoi (155,000d, nine hours), leaving early in the morning from the **long-distance bus station** (P Nguyen Hue), but most travellers sensibly prefer taking the train.

Minibuses for Sapa (40,000d, one hour) wait by the station for trains that arrive from Hanoi, and also run regularly from the minibus terminal next to the Red River bridge. Minibuses to Bac Ha (50,000d, 2½ hours) also leave from here; there are five daily services at 6am, 7am, 10am, noon and 3pm.

TAXI A taxi to Sapa costs about US$20; it's around US$40 to Bac Ha.

TRAIN Virtually everyone travelling to and from Hanoi uses the train. There are several trains and also private rail carriages that hitch a ride on the main train. Hotels and travel agencies in Hanoi can book you tickets, or you can book at the station yourself. The journey takes around eight to nine hours.

Several companies operate special private carriages with comfortable sleepers, including affordable **ET Pumpkin** (www.et-pumpkin.com), midrange **Livitrans** (www.livitrantrain.com) and the luxurious and expensive **Victoria Express** (www.victoriahotels-asia.com), only available to guests at the Victoria Sapa Resort & Spa.

See www.seat61.com for the latest information on all trains between Hanoi and Lao Cai.

Bac Ha

⚑ 020 / POP 7400

An unhurried and friendly town, Bac Ha makes a relaxed base to explore the northern highlands and hill-tribe villages. The atmosphere is very different from Sapa, and you can walk the streets freely without being accosted by hawkers. To experience a small untouristy mountain town, Bac Ha is an excellent destination.

HANOI–LAO CAI TRAINS

From Hanoi

DEPARTURE	HARD SEAT (PRICES FROM)	SOFT SEAT (PRICES FROM)	HARD SLEEPER (PRICES FROM)	SOFT SLEEPER (PRICES FROM)
6.10am	110,000d	133,000d	n/a	n/a
7.40pm	125,000d	150,000d	195,000d	290,000d
8.35pm	125,000d	150,000d	195,000d	290,000d
9.10pm	125,000d	150,000d	195,000d	290,000d
9.50pm	125,000d	150,000d	195,000d	290,000d
10pm	120,000d	145,000d	190,000d	270,000d

From Lao Cai

DEPARTURE	HARD SEAT (PRICES FROM)	SOFT SEAT (PRICES FROM)	HARD SLEEPER (PRICES FROM)	SOFT SLEEPER (PRICES FROM)
6.55pm	110,000d	133,000d	n/a	n/a
7.30pm	125,000d	150,000d	195,000d	290,000d
8.05pm	125,000d	150,000d	195,000d	290,000d
8.45pm	125,000d	150,000d	195,000d	290,000d
9.20pm	120,000d	145,000d	190,000d	270,000d

The town has a certain charm, though its stock of traditional old adobe houses is dwindling and being replaced by concrete structures. Wood smoke fills the morning air and chickens and pigs poke around the back lanes. For six days a week, Bac Ha slumbers, but its lanes fill up to choking point each Sunday when tourists and Flower H'mong flood in for the weekly market.

This Sunday market is a riot of colour and commerce, and while the influx of day trippers from Sapa is changing things, it's still a worthwhile and relatively accessible place to visit. The other markets around Bac Ha are also gradually becoming more visited by tourists, so if you're after a truly authentic experience head to the mountain town of Sinho instead (p125).

Bac Ha is a good base to explore the surrounding highlands, as it has an improving choice of inexpensive hotels and the climate here is noticeably warmer than in Sapa. There are 10 hill-tribe groups that live around Bac Ha: the colourful Flower H'mong are the most visible, but other groups include Dzao, Giay (Nhang), Han (Hoa), Xa Fang, Lachi, Nung, Phula, Tay, Thai and Thulao.

One of Bac Ha's main industries is the manufacture of alcoholic home brews (rice wine, cassava wine and corn liquor). The *ruou* corn hooch produced by the Flower H'mong is so potent it can ignite; there's an entire area devoted to it at the Sunday market.

◎ Sights & Activities

There are several markets in and around Bac Ha. Organised trips to these can be booked in Bac Ha, and also at travel agencies in Sapa.

Bac Ha Market   MARKET
This Sunday market is Bac Ha's big draw. There is an increasing range of handicrafts for sale, but it's still pretty much a local affair. Bac Ha market is a magnet for the local hill-tribe people, above all the exotically attired Flower H'mong.

Flower H'mong women wear several layers of dazzling clothing. These include an elaborate collar-cum-shawl that's pinned at the neck and an apron-style garment; both are made of tightly woven strips of multicoloured fabric, often with a frilly edge. Highly ornate cuffs and ankle fabrics are also part of their costume, as is a checked headscarf (often electric pink or lime green).

If you can, stay overnight in Bac Ha on Saturday, and get here early before hundreds of day trippers from Sapa start arriving. Bac Ha market starts at sunrise and winds down by about 2pm.

Can Cau Market   MARKET
This open-air Saturday morning market, 20km north of Bac Ha and just 9km from the Chinese border, is attracting a growing number of outsiders. Some tour groups from Sapa now visit Can Cau on Saturday before moving onto Bac Ha for the Sunday market. A few Bac Ha stallholders also make the journey to Can Cau on Saturdays. It's still a mecca for the local tribal people though, including Flower H'mong and Blue H'mong (look out for the striking zigzag costume of the latter).

It spills down a hillside with basic food stalls on one level and livestock at the bottom of the valley, including plenty of dogs.

Bac Ha

0 ——————— 200 m
0 ——————— 0.1 miles

Bac Ha

◎ **Top Sights**
Bac Ha Market	B2
Vua Meo	B1

🛌 **Sleeping**
1	Congfu Hotel	A2
2	Hoang Vu Hotel	A2
3	Ngan Nga Gia Huy	A2
4	Sao Mai Hotel	A1
5	Toan Thang Hotel	A1

🍴 **Eating**
6	Duc Tuan Restaurant	B2
7	Hoang Yen Bar	A2

A ONE-MAN TOURISM DYNAMO

Spend any time at all in Bac Ha and the irrepressible **Mr Nghe** (☎0912 005 952; www .bachatourist.com) will no doubt find you – usually wearing his spiffy formal attire of a suit. Operating out of the Hoang Vu guesthouse and also involved with the Hoang Yen Bar, Mr Nghe is a one-man cheerleader for the considerable charms of the Bac Ha area.

His website is the best place to start; it outlines trekking and day trips to the best of the area's minority markets, longer two- to six-day adventures integrating village home-stays, and more physically challenging mountain hiking.

If you're keen to set out on your own, he also rents motorbikes (150,000d to 200,000d per day), and is hands down the best person in town to see to make sense of the intricacies of onward travel east to Ha Giang province.

Locals will implore you to drink the local *ruou* with them. Some trips from Bac Ha include the option of an afternoon trek (for those still standing after *ruou* shots) to the nearby village of Fu La.

Lung Phin
MARKET

Lung Phin market is between Can Cau market and Bac Ha, about 12km from the town. It's less busy than other markets, and is open on Sunday. It is a good place to move onto once the tour buses arrive in Bac Ha from Sapa, and has a really local feel.

Coc Ly
MARKET

The impressive Tuesday Coc Ly market attracts Dzao, Flower H'mong, Tay and Nung people from the surrounding hills. It's about 35km southwest of Bac Ha along reasonably good roads. Tour operators in Bac Ha can arrange day trips here, after which you can do a boat trip down the Chay River before heading back to Bac Ha.

Vua Meo
NOTABLE BUILDING

('Cat King' House; admission 5000d; ⊙7.30-11.30am & 1.30-5pm) Don't miss the outlandish Vua Meo, a palace constructed in a kind of bizarre 'oriental baroque' architectural style on the northern edge of town. It was built in 1921 by the French to keep the Flower H'mong chief Hoang A Tuong happy, and looks like a cross between an exotic church and a French chateau. A newly opened tourist information office and a shop selling ethnic minority crafts are also here.

Local Villages
HIKING

There's great hiking to remarkable hill-tribe villages around Bac Ha. The Flower H'mong village of **Ban Pho** is one of the nearest to town, from where you can walk to the Nung settlement of **Na Kheo**, then head back to Bac Ha. Other nearby villages include **Trieu**

Cai, an 8km return walk, and **Na Ang**, a 6km return walk; it's best to set up a trip with a local guide.

Until very recently most of the minority people in these hills had no formal education, but the government has opened several schools in the last few years. Most hill-tribe children now receive an education (in the Vietnamese language). Boarding schools are favoured because the communities are so spread out, so children spend the week away from their families and sleep in dormitories. Tour guides in Bac Ha can arrange **visits to rural schools** as part of a motorbike or trekking day trip.

Thai Giang Pho Waterfall
WATERFALL

There's a waterfall near Thai Giang Pho village, about 12km east of Bac Ha, which has a pool big enough for swimming.

🛏 Sleeping

Bac Ha offers simple guesthouses and a couple of more comfortable options. Room rates tend to increase by about 20% on weekends for the Sunday market; we've quoted the weekday rates here.

Hoang Vu Hotel
GUESTHOUSE **$**

(☎388 0264; www.bachatourist.com; 5 Tran Bac; r from US$8) It's nothing fancy, but the large spacious rooms do offer good value (all have TV and fan), and Bac Ha's best tour operator, Mr Nghe, is based here. He'll have plenty of ideas for exciting day trips to keep you staying longer than you planned. Hands down the best spot in town for budget travellers.

Ngan Nga Gia Huy
HOTEL **$$**

(☎388 0231; www.nganngabacha.com; 133 Ngoc Uyen; r US$25-35; ❄🐤) This friendly place is above a popular restaurant that does a roaring trade in tasty steamboats for travellers and the occasional tour group. A new

NORTHWEST VIETNAM BAC HA

upstairs wing out the back offers brand-new rooms; some are almost ridiculously roomy, and they're all spotless and quiet. Tours – including village homestays and hill-tribe market visits – can be arranged.

Congfu Hotel HOTEL $$
(☑388 0254; www.congfuhotel.com; 152 Ngoc Uyen; r US$30; ✳@🖰) This newish place has 21 attractive rooms demonstrating a notable absence of chintz. The bed linen is good quality, showers are modern and the restaurant (meals from 60,000d) is one of the best in town. Book rooms 205, 208, 305 or 308 for a floor-to-ceiling window overlooking Bac Ha market. Excursions to the Can Cau (US$30) and Coc Ly (US$50) markets can also be booked.

Sao Mai Hotel HOTEL $$
(☑388 0288; www.saomaitours.com; r US$15-35; ✳@🖰) The budget rooms are looking a tad weary – and the cheapest don't have windows – but more expensive rooms in a new wing are OK value. Worth considering if other places are full. Reception staff are usually keen to negotiate.

Toan Thang Hotel HOTEL $
(☑388 0444; r US$10-20) This hotel has two types of rooms: those in the old wooden block are OK for the tariff asked, with two beds, TV and fan, though they're a little dark. The newer rooms are somewhat overpriced.

🍴 Eating

Of Bac Ha's hotel restaurants, the Congfu has great views of the animal market area through huge plate-glass windows, while the Ngan Nga Gia Huy does great steamboats. Both get very busy for Sunday lunch on market day.

Note that tourists are often overcharged at the cafes near the market, so establish the cost of food and drink up front.

Hoang Yen Bar VIETNAMESE $
(mains 40,000-80,000d) Yes, the name does say 'bar', but it's more of a restaurant, with a well-priced menu of good breakfast options, tasty rice and noodle dishes, and robust pumpkin soup. Cheap beer and Dalat wine are both available. You'll find Hoang Yen opposite the Sao Mai Hotel, and Mr Nghe may well find you in Hoang Yen.

Duc Tuan Restaurant VIETNAMESE $$
(mains 40,000-50,000d) This place is handily near the market and has big portions of reliable Vietnamese food, plus it's usually largely free of tour groups.

ℹ Information

There's no ATM in Bac Ha but the Agribank will change cash dollars. Head to the Sao Mai Hotel to change euros and British, US and Chinese currency.

A newly opened **tourist information office** (⊙7.30-11.30am & 1.30-5pm) is in the Vua Meo,

---

THE MAN TO KNOW IN HA GIANG

As is the case with Mr Nghe in Bac Ha (see boxed text, p135), another travel impresario is at the forefront of the tourism scene in Ha Giang province. Mr Anh runs **Karst Plateau Travel** (☑0915 458 668; karstplateau@gmail.com; 50 P Hai Ba Trung, Ha Giang) and is currently the go-to person for information on exploring this emerging and amazing region.

As well as running the Rocky Plateau Hotel and Café Pho Co in Dong Van, he's behind a handy sightseeing minibus that runs to and from Ha Giang to Dong Van and Meo Vac, taking in key highlights including the **Quan Ba Pass**, the **Lung Cu Flag Tower** on the border of China, and the fascinating palace of the H'mong King in the village of **Sa Phin**. There's an English-speaking guide on board, and the precisely driven journey across the **Mai Pi Leng Pass** to Meo Vac is probably one of the most spectacular roads you'll ever cross.

Sightseeing minibuses depart at 8am from the **iLike Café** (☑386 0368; buses.ilike@ gmail.com; P Nguyen Trai; per person without/with lunch 150,000/200,000d) in Ha Giang, and take around seven hours to reach Dong Van via Meo Vac. Returning to Ha Giang, there's a minibus leaving Meo Vac at 8am, calling in at the Café Pho Co in Dong Van at 9am. We recommend making prior email contact with Mr Anh to confirm departure times, as the service only commenced in 2011.

Mr Anh can also arrange trekking to local H'mong villages in this stunning region, and can organise guided and unguided tours from Hanoi. He also maintains an **office in Hanoi** (63B Lane, Dao Tan 101, Hanoi). See www.karstplateau.com for more details.

and there's internet access next to the Hoang Vu Hotel.

ℹ️ Getting There & Away

BUS Buses run to/from Hanoi (400,000d, 11 hours, 8pm daily) and Lao Cai (60,000d, 2½ hours, 6am, 8am, noon, 1pm, 2pm).

If you're headed east to Ha Giang, you've got two options. Catch a *xe om* from Bac Ha 35km northeast to Xin Man (US$15), and then a public bus (400,000d, five hours, 6am and 11am) to Ha Giang. Option two is the public bus south from Bac Ha to Bac Ngam (40,000d, 45 minutes, 6am), followed by another bus from Bac Ngam to Ha Giang (350,000d, five hours, 7am). Note this is a very tight connection.

Tours to Bac Ha from Sapa cost from US$15 per person; on the way back you can bail out in Lao Cai and catch the night train back to Hanoi.

MOTORCYCLE & TAXI A motorbike/taxi to Lao Cai costs US$20/60, or to Sapa US$25/75.

Ha Giang Province

Ha Giang is the final frontier in northern Vietnam, a lunar landscape of limestone pinnacles and granite outcrops. The far north of the province has some of the most spectacular scenery in the country, and the trip between Dong Van and Meo Vac is quite mind-blowing. Ha Giang should be one of the most popular destinations in this region, but its proximity to the Chinese border still requires a travel permit, and the bureaucratic baloney keeps most at bay. However, roads are slowly improving, and the slight hassles of scoring a permit are effortlessly offset by some of Indochina's most jaw-dropping scenery.

HA GIANG
📞 0219 / POP 49,000

Ha Giang is somewhere to recharge the batteries on the long road north. This town, bisected by the broad river Lo, is a provincial capital with clean streets and an understated ambience. The main drag is P Nguyen Trai, which runs north–south paralleling the west bank of the Lo for 3km or so. You'll find hotels, banks and restaurants on this road.

Ha Giang is a mildly diverting town, but the spectacular limestone outcrops soaring skywards over the suburbs hint at the amazing scenery in the surrounding hinterland. Those heading further north to explore around Yen Minh, Dong Van and Meo Vac will need to arrange a travel permit here.

PAN HOU VILLAGE

(📞383 3565; www.panhou-village.com; s/d US$30/40; ❋📶) Tucked away in a hidden river valley in the High Song Chau mountains, Pan Hou's private bungalows are set in a riot of tropical gardens and rice paddies. This wonderfully isolated ecolodge is the base for trekking and ethnic-minority market visits. Rooms are smartly furnished with wooden furniture and tiled floors, and the restaurant pavilion (lunch US$10, dinner US$12) is spacious and social. Traditional spa treatments and baths are infused with medicinal healing herbs. From Tan Quang village south of Ha Giang, Pan Hou is 36km west up a winding mountain road.

🛏️ Sleeping & Eating

You'll find several cheap restaurants scattered along P Nguyen Trai.

Truong Xuan Resort   RESORT $
(📞381 1102; www.hagiangresort.com; Km 5, P Nguyen Van Linh; d US$15-20; ❋📶) An absolute riverside location and 13 spacious bungalows add up to the nicest place in town to overnight. There's a decent restaurant (mains 80,000d to 220,000d), and even kayaks for rent to explore the adjacent waterway. Red Dzao massages (60,000d) and herbal baths (60,000d) are on offer if you're feeling a bit saddle sore after too many days on two wheels. It's 5km out of town, so from the bus station count on 30,000d for a *xe om*, or 70,000d in a taxi.

Huy Hoan Hotel   HOTEL $
(📞386 1288; P Nguyen Trai; r 180,000-500,000d; 📶) This tall slim place offers large, clean, well-kept rooms with dark oriental furniture and (very) firm beds. New rooms are overly chintzy, and the cheapest rooms don't have windows. Your call, or ask the noisy bird in reception what he thinks. A string of good restaurants is just a short walk away.

Duc Giang Hotel   GUESTHOUSE $
(📞387 5648; 14 P Nguyen Trai; s/d/tr 140,000/150,000/200,000d; ❋) Centrally located, this family-run place has light and airy tiled rooms. Triples are also available if you're exploring Ha Giang with a few intrepid mates.

Bien Nho Thanh Thu Restaurant RESTAURANT
(17 P Duong Huu Nghi; meals from 100,000d) For something exotic, this place has crocodile, seafood, goose and traditional food from the ethnic minorities of Ha Giang.

A...Lo CAFE
(P Nguyen Trai; 🛜) This is a friendly but smoky place with wi-fi.

Trung Nguyen Café CAFE
(P Nguyen Trai; 🛜) Just opposite A...Lo, the wi-fi equipped Trung Nguyen Café is the nearest thing to a trendy hang-out for Ha Giang's bright young things.

🛈 Information

Travel permits (300,000d) are best organised through your accommodation or the **Ha Giang Police Immigration Office** (22 P Tran Quoc Toan; ⏰8am-noon & 2-5pm). There's also a small tourist information office next door, with an interesting model of the surrounding landscapes.

Agribank has a branch on P Nguyen Trai with an ATM; nearby are internet cafes.

🛈 Getting There & Away

Ha Giang's new bus station is on the northern edge of town near the 3 February Bridge. See table for bus connections and note that no buses run direct to Bac Ha from Ha Giang. The route is very beautiful, but you'll need to transit through Xin Man or Bac Ngam. See p137 for details.

An alternative option for getting to Dong Van and Meo Vac is the minibus service operated by Karst Plateau Travel (p136).

AROUND HA GIANG

It's all about the trip north to the districts of Dong Van and Meo Vac, nestled against the border with China. It's also now possible to complete a kind of 'extreme north' loop, continuing on from Bao Lac down towards Hwy 3 and Cao Bang. Public transport is infrequent and slow-going. Make sure you have your Ha Giang permit in order or you'll be

NORTHWEST BUS CONNECTIONS

CONNECTION	COST	DURATION	FREQUENCY
Dien Bien Phu–Hanoi	from 300,000d	11½hr	Frequently to noon
Dien Bien Phu–Lai Chau	130,000d	6hr	5am-2pm
Dien Bien Phu–Muong Lay	57,000d	2hr	5am-2pm
Dien Bien Phu–Son La	97,000d	4hr	Frequently to noon
Ha Giang–Dong Van	100,000d	5hr	10.30am
Ha Giang–Hanoi	from 170,000d	7hr	5am-9pm
Ha Giang–Meo Vac	100,000d	6hr	10.30am
Lai Chau–Dien Bien Phu	from 120,000d	6hr	5am-1.30pm
Lai Chau–Hanoi	from 280,000d	12hr	5am & frequently 4-8pm
Lai Chau–Lao Cai	65,000d	3½hr	5am-4pm
Lai Chau–Muong Lay	60,000d	3hr	5am-1.30pm
Lai Chau–Sinho	40,000d	2hr	6.30am & 1.30pm
Muong Lay–Dien Bien Phu	57,000d	2hr	5am-2pm
Muong Lay–Lai Chau	60,000d	3hr	5am-1.30pm
Muong Lay–Sinho	70,000d	2½hr	7am
Sapa–Dien Bien Phu	from 170,000d	8hr	7.30am
Sapa–Hanoi	from 210,000d	12hr	7.30am & 5.30pm
Sapa–Lai Chau	70,000d	3hr	6am-4pm
Son La–Dien Bien Phu	from 97,000d	4hr	Frequently, 5.30am-1.30pm
Son La–Hanoi	from 125,000d	8½hr	Every 30min, 5am-1pm
Son La–Ninh Binh	from 135,000d	9hr	5.30am
Tuan Giao–Dien Bien Phu	46,000d	2½hr	Frequently to 3.30pm
Tuan Giao–Hanoi	210,000d	11½hr	Frequently to 2pm
Tuan Giao–Son La	65,000d	3hr	Frequently to 3.30pm

THE HIGH ROADS ON TWO WHEELS

With spectacular scenery and relatively minimal traffic, more travellers are choosing to motorcycle around the northwest loop from Hanoi up to Lao Cai, over to Dien Bien Phu and back to the capital. For the really intrepid, the roads venturing north towards China into the spectacular provinces of Ha Giang and Cao Bang are the newest frontier for travel in Vietnam.

Hanoi is the place to start making arrangements. Consider joining a tour (p520) or hiring a guide, who will know the roads and can help with mechanical and linguistic difficulties. Be sure to get acquainted with your bike first and check current road conditions and routes.

Most motorbikes in Vietnam are small capacity (under 250cc). For years the sturdy Minsk, built in Belarus, was the bike of choice for travellers and it still has many devotees (see www.minskclubvietnam.com). Minsks are quirky bikes, not known for their reliability (though they deal with rutted rough roads well). They were common in northern Vietnam for years, and many mechanics know how to fix them. Today numbers have dwindled, as mopeds and Chinese road bikes have proliferated.

Honda road bikes (such as the Honda GL160) and trail bikes are other good choices. These bikes have a good reputation for reliability and have decent shock absorbers. Some folk bike it around Vietnam on mopeds (like the 100cc Honda Wave), which tend to be reliable and their automatic gears make things easier for inexperienced riders. However you'll find bumps tough on your butt.

Rental agencies will provide checklists, but essentials include a good helmet, local mobile phone for emergencies, rain gear, a spare parts and repair kit (including spark plugs, spanners, inner tube and tyre levers), air pump and decent maps. Knee and elbow pads and gloves are also a good idea.

Highways can be hell in Vietnam, so let the train take the strain on the long route north to Lao Cai. Load your bike into a goods carriage while you sleep in a berth. You'll have to (almost) drain it of petrol. Then in Lao Cai, pick it up, fill up and off you go.

Take it slowly, particularly in the rain: smooth paved roads can turn into muddy tracks in no time. Do not ride during or immediately after heavy rainstorms as this is when landslides might occur; many mountain roads are quite new and the cliff embankments can be unstable. Expect to average about 35km per hour. Only use safe hotel parking. Fill up from petrol stations where the petrol is less likely to have been watered down.

If running short on time or energy, remember that many bus companies will let you put your bike on the roof of a bus, but get permission first from your bike rental company.

Recommended specialists in Hanoi include Cuong's Motorbike Adventure (p80) and Offroad Vietnam (p80).

NORTHWEST VIETNAM HA GIANG PROVINCE

heavily fined by the officious police in Meo Vac and sent straight back to Ha Giang.

Leaving Ha Giang, the road climbs over the **Quan Ba Pass** (Heaven's Gate). Poetic licence is a national pastime in Vietnam, but this time the romantics have it right. The road winds over a saddle and opens up on to an awesome vista. It's dizzying to think of the forces of nature that carved out these incredible limestone towers.

At the top of Quan Ba Pass is a newly constructed information centre and lookout with amazing views down into Yen Minh. An English-language information board details the 2011 initiative to declare the **Dong Van Karst Plateau** part of the Unesco Global Network of National Geoparks. It's the first Unesco-recognised geopark in Vietnam and the second one in Southeast Asia, after Langkawi Geological Park in Malaysia. For more information see http://en.dongvangeo park.com.

Dropping into **Yen Minh** through pine forests, it is worth stopping for a drink before the final leg into the incredibly surreal scenery near China.

Dong Van is mainly a dusty outpost, but the town has a great Sunday market, and makes a good base for day treks around nearby minority villages. It also features an interesting old quarter, including a beautifully restored 100-year-old trader's house that's now the funky **Café Pho Co** (Old Market; ☺10am-11pm). The best accommodation in town – and the best source of information for travellers – is the **Rocky Plateau Hotel** (☑385 6868; rockyplateau@gmail.com; r 250,000d; @), a laid-back spot decorated with colourful artwork. Note the nearest ATM is in Ha Giang.

Beyond Dong Van the spectacular **Mai Pi Leng Pass** continues for 22km to **Meo Vac**. The road has been cut into the side of a cliff: far below are the distant waters of the Nho Que River, towering above, a mighty rock face.

Meo Vac is a district capital hemmed in by mountains and, like many towns in the northwest, it is steadily being settled by Vietnamese from elsewhere. Handily opposite the dusty bus station is the new **Hoa Cuong Hotel** (☑387 2888; r US$15-20; @✳️🛜), an impressive spot for such a one-horse town, with spacious rooms and flat-screen TVs. Next door is a compact supermarket offering instant noodles and snacks if Meo Vac's less-than-cosmopolitan food scene doesn't inspire you.

There are a couple of *com pho* places around town, plus the market has some food stalls. Don't be surprised to be offered a slug of a local speciality, 'bee wine'. We're still trying to work out if it is made from bees *and* honey, or just '100% bees'. Either way, it's a bracing drink on a chilly Meo Vac night.

Like Dong Van, Meo Vac has a good Sunday market, and it's easy enough to combine the two. A *xe om* between the two towns should be around 220,000d.

SOUTH TO CAO BANG

Foreigners are now permitted to travel from Meo Vac to Bao Lac in Cao Bang province. You must have your Ha Giang permit to do this spectacular trip. Most of the road is now paved, though it's best on trail bikes or 4WD. On public transport, one bus per day leaves Meo Vac at 9am (170,000d) to Cao Bang (p112).

Heading south from Meo Vac you'll pass through the town of Khau Vai after about 20km, which is famous for its annual **love market** where the tribal minorities swap wives and husbands. Though it's undoubtedly a fascinating tradition, around fifty busloads of Vietnamese tourists now gatecrash the dating scene, and this unique event has become something of a circus. It takes place on the 27th day of the 3rd lunar month in the Vietnamese calendar, usually from late April to mid-May.

After Khau Vai, a new bridge crosses the Nho Que River, and the road continues south to Bao Lac. From Bao Lac to Cao Bang is another seven hours on bumpy roads via Nguyen Binh.

It's not possible to do this trip in reverse from Cao Bang province, as you have to have a permit issued in Ha Giang town to enter this border region.

North-Central Vietnam

Best Places to Eat

» Thuong Hai (p150)

» Huong Mai Restaurant (p144)

» Visitor Centre, Cuc Phuong National Park (p148)

Best Places to Stay

» Phong Nha Farmstay (p153)

» Nam Long Hotel (p154)

» Thanh Thuy's Guest House & New Hotel (p143)

Why Go?

North-central Vietnam is never going to be Asia's next beach mecca or cultural hub – it's a poor, traditional region with a cool winter climate where cities like Vinh still bear the scars of the American War. And yet if you budget a little time here, you'll find some curious sights, outstanding scenery and wonderful excursions.

The one place that everyone's talking about is the extraordinary Phong Nha region, home to three gargantuan cave systems (including the world's largest cave) set in a stunning national park of towering limestone hills and pristine forests.

Ninh Binh, a region blessed with more karst-studded mountains, also has its charm, as well as the fecund beauty of Cuc Phuong on its doorstep. On the coast, port-resort Dong Hoi makes a pleasing base away from the tourist trail for a day or two.

When to Go
Ninh Binh

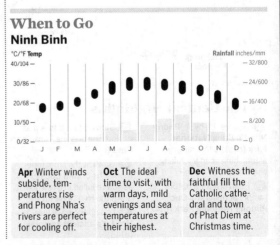

Apr Winter winds subside, temperatures rise and Phong Nha's rivers are perfect for cooling off.

Oct The ideal time to visit, with warm days, mild evenings and sea temperatures at their highest.

Dec Witness the faithful fill the Catholic cathedral and town of Phat Diem at Christmas time.

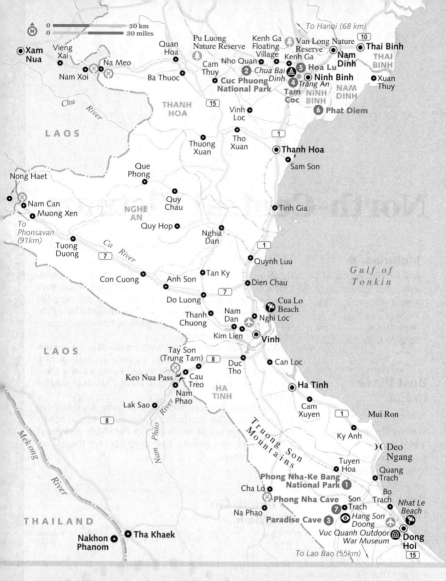

North-Central Highlights

1 Believe the hype, **Phong Nha-Ke Bang National Park** (p151) offers simply astonishing scenery, hiking and biking

2 Head out for a nature ramble at delightful **Cuc Phuong National Park** (p147)

3 Step up to the task and explore the pristine **Paradise Cave** (p152)

4 Gawk at the limestone monoliths of **Tam Coc** (p145) as you're lulled in a rowboat down the Ngo Dong River

5 Lap up the royal view at **Hoa Lu's ancient temples** (p145)

6 Confound your imagination with the East-meets-West architecture at **Phat Diem Cathedral** (p149)

7 Go with the flow into colossal **Phong Nha Cave** (p152)

History

Quiet though it is today, this region has seen its fair share of historical moments. After Vietnam shook off almost a millennium of Chinese rule in the 10th century, one of the earliest emperors established the capital at Hoa Lu, setting his citadel amid the protection of towering limestone cliffs. In the 13th and 14th centuries, the Tran dynasty introduced a peculiar administrative arrangement: the heirs to the throne partially succeeded their fathers as king, while the latter shared power in an unofficial capital in Tuc Mac, about 5km from Nam Dinh. This prevented succession disputes and made the Tran dynasty one of the most politically stable and prosperous in Vietnamese history.

During the American War, the region suffered tremendous damage from US bombing, with most towns reduced to rubble and the countryside littered with lethal ordnance. Today north-central Vietnam remains poor and under-developed, and many choose to emigrate to Vietnam's big cities in search of opportunity.

ⓘ Getting There & Away

The main north-south railway cuts directly through the region, as does Hwy 1. There are airports at Vinh and Dong Hoi, with flights to Ho Chi Minh City (HCMC) and Hanoi.

Ninh Binh Province

A short hop south of Hanoi, Ninh Binh Province is blessed with breathtaking natural beauty, intriguing cultural sights and the wonderful Cuc Phuong National Park. That said, Ninh Binh has become a massive domestic destination and many of its attractions are heavily commercialised. Expect plenty of hawkers and a degree of hassle at the main sights.

NINH BINH

⌕ 030 / POP 141,800

Ninh Binh is a resolutely provincial industrial city – not a destination in itself, but a good base for exploring some quintessentially Vietnamese limestone scenery. It's not a tranquil place (Hwy 1 thunders through the heart of town) but you'll find some attractive backstreets and traditional neighbourhoods. A steady trickle of Western tourists head here, but far larger numbers of holidaying Vietnamese flock to nearby sights that include the nation's biggest pagoda (p146) and the Trang An grottoes (p146).

So if you're weary of backpacker bars, Ninh Binh could make a congenial base for seeing some lovely rural landscapes by day, then unwinding at night like the locals do with grilled goat meat and *bia hoi* (draught beer) beside the local brewery.

☞ Tours

Tours of the sights around Ninh Binh Province can be set up in hotels including Thanh Thuy's, where guides **Truong** (☏091 566 6911; truong_tour@yahoo.com) and **Binh** (☏094 422 9166) are based. Reckon on US$10 per day for an escorted trip on a motorbike, using country backroads. Ask them about trekking in Pu Luong Nature Reserve, a fairly undisturbed area spread across two mountain ridges, where you can stay in Thai and H'mong homestays. Minsk bikes are also available for touring trips to minority markets and villages.

🛏 Sleeping

Ninh Binh offers some of the best-value accommodation in Vietnam. Most hotels can make tour arrangements, and staff and guides often speak good English.

⌖TOP CHOICE Thanh Thuy's Guest House & New Hotel   HOTEL $
(☏387 1811; www.hotelthanhthuy.com; 128 Đ Le Hong Phong; guesthouse r US$7-10, hotel r US$15-25; ❉@᎑) Probably the best place to meet and mingle with other travellers, this popular hotel is run by a friendly crew, including some very switched-on tour guides who really know the ins and outs of the area and offer some great trips. Rooms, all very clean and some with balcony, vary quite a bit – nearly all are set well back from the road. You'll feel at home here.

Thuy Anh Hotel   HOTEL $$
(☏387 1602; www.thuyanhhotel.com; 55A Đ Truong Han Sieu; s/d old wing US$20/25, s/d new wing US$30/45; ❉@᎑) This well-run hotel has been looking after travellers since 1993 and it's easy to understand why it remains so busy. The cheaper rooms in the old block are decent value, while the clean, modern rooms at the rear are spotless, very well equipped, tastefully furnished and comfortable. You'll also find a top-floor bar and a restaurant serving Western-style food (including hearty complimentary breakfasts).

Ninh Binh Legend Hotel   HOTEL $$$
(☏389 9880; www.ninhbinhlegendhotel.com; Tien Dong Zone; r/ste from US$77/126; ❉@᎑᎒)

Ninh Binh

To Ninh Binh Legend Hotel (2km)

Ninh Binh

Sleeping
1 Kinh Do Hotel A1
2 Thanh Binh Hotel A1
3 Thanh Thuy's Guesthouse &
   New Hotel A1
4 Thuy Anh Hotel A2

Eating
5 Huong Mai Restaurant A1
6 Snail Restaurants A1

Drinking
7 Bia hoi B1
8 Bia hoi A1

Landmark new four-star hotel about 2km northwest of the centre with 108 very well-appointed rooms in four price categories: all are light, spacious, well-equipped and boast hardwood floors and rice paddy views. There's a decent gym, spa, tennis courts and huge, though pricey, restaurant.

Thanh Binh Hotel   HOTEL $
(☑ 387 2439; www.thanhbinhhotelnb.com.vn; 31 Đ Luong Van Tuy; s US$10-25, d US$15-30; ✳@ 🗫) Just off the main highway, this popular hotel has a good selection of rooms, those on the upper floors are best (and include breakfast). The owner is friendly and the hotel is well set up for travellers, with a restaurant and inexpensive bicycle and motorbikes available.

Kinh Do Hotel   HOTEL $
(☑ 389 9152; http://kinhdohotel.vn; 18 Đ Phanh Dinh Phung; r 250,000d; ✳@) Little English is spoken on reception but the spacious, clean rooms with high ceilings here represent excellent value, even if the beds are on the firm side. There's a (basic) spa with steam room and massage too.

🍴 Eating & Drinking

The town doesn't have much in the way of restaurants so plan to eat early as there's

very little available after 9pm. The local speciality is *de* (goat meat), usually served with fresh herbs and rice paper to wrap it in – around 3km out of town, the road to the Trang An Grottoes is lined with dozens of **goat meat restaurants**.

Snails are another excellent local dish, the lanes north of Đ Luong Van Tuy, close to the stadium, have several **snail restaurants** serving delicious *oc luoc xa* (snails cooked with lemongrass and chilli); you'll also find a few casual bars in this area too.

Huong Mai Restaurant (12 Đ Tran Hung Dao; dishes 20,000-80,000d) has an English menu, though the staff don't speak the language. Rice cakes cooked in beef broth are delicious here, and you'll find good goat, seafood and exotica like eel cooked with banana too.

In the warmer months, **bia hoi** places become very tempting. Try the street-side set-ups directly opposite Thanh Thuy or the riverside places near the local brewery.

ℹ Information

BIDV (Đ Le Hong Phong) ATM and exchange service.
Hospital (Benh Vien Da Khoa Tinh; ☑ 387 1030; Đ Hai Thuong Lan)
Internet (Đ Luong Van Tuy; per hr 6,000d) There's a cluster of cybercafes here.
Main post office (Đ Tran Hung Dao)
Vietin Bank & ATM (Đ Tran Hung Dao)

ℹ Getting There & Away

BUS Ninh Binh's **bus station** (Đ Le Dai Hanh) is located near Lim Bridge, just below the overpass to Phat Diem. Public buses leave almost every 15 minutes until 7pm for the Giap Bat and Luong Yen bus stations in Hanoi (55,000d, 2½ hours, 93km). Ninh Binh is also a stop for open-tour buses between Hanoi (US$6, two hours) and Hue (US$13, 10 hours); hotel pick-up and drop-offs are offered.

TRAIN The **train station** (Ga Ninh Binh; 1 Đ Hoang Hoa Tham) is a scheduled stop on the main north–south line with destinations including Hanoi (55,000d, two to 2½ hours, four daily), Vinh (90,000d, six hours, three daily) and Hue (275,000d, 12½ to 13½ hours, four daily).

❶ Getting Around

Most hotels rent out bicycles (US$1 to US$2 per day) and motorbikes (US$5 to US$8 per day). Motorbike drivers charge around US$10 a day.

TAM COC

This is what most travellers come to Ninh Binh to see: limestone outcrops sweeping up from serene rice paddies, best appreciated on a languorous rowboat ride down the river, to the soundtrack of water lapping against the oars.

◉ Sights & Activities

Tam Coc Boat Trips   RIVER TRIP
(admission 30,000d, boat 60,000d) Yes Tam Coc (meaning 'three caves') covers a 2km stretch of the Ngo Dong River and boasts a landscape of surreal beauty, but it's also immensely popular – the river's often filled with a procession of boats, with all the accompanying babble and noise. To really enjoy the experience, come in the early morning or late afternoon.

Each rowboat carries two visitors. The route (around two hours) takes you through the three caves for which Tam Coc is named: Hang Ca (127m long), Hang Giua (70m long) and Hang Cuoi (45m long).

Remember to bring sunscreen and a hat or umbrella, as the boats aren't shaded. Rowers are adept at using their feet to propel the oars, which makes for a tourist-pleasing Kodak moment.

Van Lan   VILLAGE
The area behind the Tam Coc restaurants near the entrance is Van Lan village, famous for its embroidery. Local artisans make napkins, tablecloths, pillowcases and T-shirts, some of which you might encounter on the boat ride. Bargain hard if you're interested.

FREE **Bich Dong Pagoda**   TEMPLE
(Jade Grotto) This charming cluster of cave temples is a couple of kilometres north of Tam Coc. The Lower Pagoda is located at the foot of the outcrop, from which it's a climb of about 100 steps to the Middle Pagoda, then a shorter but still steep ascent to the Upper Pagoda. Inside each cave temple, looming statues and the smoke of burning incense create an otherworldly atmosphere. Outside, there are some incredible views of the countryside.

🛏 Sleeping & Eating

There are a few guesthouses in Van Lan including **Lang Khanh** (☑361 8073; langkhanhtc@yahoo.com.vn; r US$6-12; ❊), a family-run place with tidy, clean rooms and a simple restaurant (meals 35,000d to 60,000d).

❶ Getting There & Away

Tam Coc is 9km southwest of Ninh Binh. Ninh Binh hotels run tours, or make your own way by bicycle or motorbike. Hotel staff can advise you on some beautiful back roads.

Hanoi tour operators offer day-trips to Tam Coc and Hoa Lu for between US$20 and US$30.

MUA CAVE

Tucked away at the end of a road running between rice paddies, this **cave** (Cave of Dance; admission 20,000d) is not terribly impressive, but the main attraction is the panoramic view from the peak above. A stone staircase beside the cave entrance zigzags up the side of the karst (beware the goat droppings) and it's 450 steps to the top, where there's a simple altar to Quan Am (the Goddess of Mercy). Look west and you'll see Ngo Dong River winding through Tam Coc.

The climb is paved but steep in sections, so bring some water and allow an hour for the trip. Mua Cave is 5km from Ninh Binh and a popular stop on tours heading to Tam Coc.

HOA LU

Hoa Lu was the capital of Vietnam during the Dinh (AD 968–80) and early Le (AD 980–1009) dynasties. The Dinh chose the site to put some distance between them and China.

❶ THE TAM COC TANGO

Tam Coc's limestone scenery may be sublime, but less pleasing are the pushy drink vendors, handicraft hustlers and camera-touting hawkers eager to flog you a photo. It's not unusual to see boats returning from Tam Coc with frowning or exhausted-looking tourists. A polite but firm 'no' and adopting a complete lack of interest is the best way to combat the hassle.

Most of the ancient citadel is in ruins but Yen Ngua Mountain provides a scenic backdrop for two surviving **temples** (admission 12,000d). Dinh Tien Hoang is dedicated to the Dinh dynasty and has the stone pedestal of a royal throne. Inside are bronze bells and a statue of Emperor Dinh Tien Hoang with his three sons.

The second temple is dedicated to monarch Le Dai Hanh. It has the usual assortment of drums, gongs, incense burners, candle holders and weapons with a statue of the king in the middle, his queen on the right and their son on the left. A modest **museum** here features part of the excavations of a 10th-century city wall.

For a great perspective of the ruins, take the 20-minute hike up to the **tomb** of Emperor Dinh Tien Hoang. The access path is via the hill opposite the ticket office.

Hoa Lu is 12km northwest of Ninh Binh; turn left 6km north of town on Hwy 1. There is no public transport available.

CHUA BAI DINH

FREE Chua Bai Dinh (⊘7am-5.45pm) is a bombastic new sight northwest of Ninh Binh. The sheer scale of its Buddhist complex is astonishing, rising up the hillside of a rounded limestone mountain.

From the (small) entrance gateway, turn right and you'll pass through cloister-like walkways past 500 stone *arhats* (enlightened Buddhists) that line the route up to the main triple-roofed Phap Chu pagoda. This contains a 10m, 100-tonne bronze Buddha (surrounded by a gaudy collection of spinning lights and a pyramid or two for good measure), flanked by two more gilded Buddha figures.

Steps behind lead up to a viewpoint, a 13-storey pagoda (nearing completion at the time of research) and a giant Buddha. If you return via the central part of the compound you'll pass more temples, including one that harbours a 36-tonne bell – cast in Hue in 2006, it's the largest in Vietnam.

Chua Bai Dinh attracts thousands of Vietnamese visitors some days, including many day-trippers, so think twice if you're after a spiritual experience – the numbers here don't facilitate feelings of peace. That said, the complex does have its merits. Commendably, most of the structures have been constructed from natural materials, and some of the wood-detailing, lacquerwork and stone-carving is impressive.

Chua Bai Dinh is 11km northwest of Ninh Binh, you'll pass Trang An on the way as well as dozens of goat meat restaurants.

KENH GA

The village of Kenh Ga (Chicken Canal) gets its name, apparently, from the number of wild chickens that used to live here. Today it's the **riverine way of life** and stunning limestone formations that are its main draw.

The local people seem to spend most of their lives on or in the water: watching over their floating fish-breeding pens, harvesting river grass for fish feed or selling vegies boat-to-boat. Even the children commute to school by river. This used to be largely a floating village, but as fortunes have improved more and more houses have been built.

From the pier you can hire a motorboat (70,000d) for a 1½-hour ride along the river around the village.

Kenh Ga is 21km from Ninh Binh off the road to Cuc Phuong National Park. Follow Hwy 1 north for 11km, then it's a 10km drive west to the boat pier.

VAN LONG NATURE RESERVE

Set amid yet more glorious limestone pinnacles, this tranquil **reserve** (admission 15,000d, boat 90,000d) comprises a reedy wetland ideal for **bird-watching**. Rare black-faced spoonbill, cotton pygmy goose and white-browed crake have been seen here and the reserve is also one of the last refuges of the endangered Delacour's langur.

Row boat rides here (maximum two people per boat) are wonderfully relaxing.

Van Long is 2km east of Tran Me, a small town 23km from Ninh Binh along the road to Cuc Phuong.

TRANG AN GROTTOES

A huge new riverside development, **Trang An** (⊘7.30am-4pm) offers a similar experience to Tam Coc, though it's extremely commercial. The sheer number of boats, proximity to the highway, vast parking lots, weekend traffic jams and all-round hustle make it something approaching a tourist circus. Once you're actually on a row boat, bobbing along the Sao Khe River through a succession of **limestone caves**, obviously things improve considerably, but this is still an over-developed sight.

Boat trips (100,000d for up to four people) take two hours to tour the caves and tunnels. Bring a hat and sunscreen as the boats lack shade.

BORDER CROSSING BLUES 1

Those seeking a backwoods adventure can try crossing at **Nam Xoi–Na Meo** (Map p142; ☺7am-5pm), 175km northwest of Thanh Hoa (Vietnam) and 70km east of Sam Neua (Laos). Lao visas are now available at this border. If at all possible take a direct bus and avoid getting onward transport on the Vietnamese side of the border where foreigners are seriously ripped off.

From Sam Neua there's a daily direct bus at 7.30am that goes to Thanh Hoa (190,000 kip; 10 hours), where you can change buses for Hanoi, or south to Vinh. Otherwise it's possible to travel in stages, but you'll pay more and it'll take longer. *Songthaew* and minibuses (33,000 kip, four hours) leave Sam Neua for the border. Readers have reported no hassle from border officials, but they'll try to offer you bad rates for all currencies – you'll get a better deal in Na Meo hotels. Then the fun starts (unless you're on a direct bus). Vietnamese bus drivers outrageously overcharge foreigners on the route to Thanh Hoa, demanding up to US$50 for the journey (it should cost about US$7).

In the opposite direction, there's a daily 8am bus from Thanh Hoa's western bus station (*Ben Xe Mien Tay*) to Sam Neua (275,000d), but again expect overcharging. It's best not to get stuck on the Laos side of the border as transport is extremely irregular and there's no accommodation. Na Meo has several basic, serviceable guesthouses.

Trang An is 7km northwest of Ninh Binh. Follow the wide highway heading out of town.

CUC PHUONG NATIONAL PARK
♪030 / ELEV 150-656M

The primary forest in this gorgeous **national park** (Map p142; ☎384 8006; www.cucphuong tourism.com; adult/child 20,000/10,000d) is home to an amazing variety of animal and plant life, making it one of Vietnam's most important protected areas. Wildlife found here includes 307 bird species, 133 kinds of mammal, 122 species of reptile and more than 2000 different species of plant.

The national park covers an area spanning two limestone mountain ranges, across three provinces. Its highest peak is Dinh May Bac (Silver Cloud Peak) at 656m. No less than Ho Chi Minh took time off from the American War in 1962 to declare this Vietnam's first national park, saying: 'Forest is gold.'

Despite his exhortations, poaching and habitat destruction continue to plague the Cuc Phuong National Park. Improved roads have led to more illegal logging, and many native species – the Asiatic black bear, Siamese crocodile, wild dog and tiger – have vanished from the area as a result of human activity.

To learn more about the park's conservation efforts, visit the excellent Endangered Primate Rescue Center and Turtle Conservation Center (see the boxed text, p148) on the fringes of the park.

The park is also home to the minority Muong people, whom the government relocated from the park's central valley to its western edge in the late 1980s. This was ostensibly to encourage a shift from their slash-and-burn practices to sedentary farming, but the government's star project, the Ho Chi Minh Highway, subsequently cut across some of the former Muong parklands.

The best time of year to visit the park is in the dry months from November to February. From April to June it becomes increasingly hot, wet and muddy, and from July to October the rains arrive, bringing lots of leeches. Visitors in April and May might see some of the millions of butterflies that breed here. Weekends can be busy with Vietnamese families.

The visitor centre near the entrance has informative English-speaking staff, and guides and tours can be organised here.

◉ Sights & Activities

Cuc Phuong offers excellent hiking. Short walks include a large **botanic garden** with deer, civets, gibbons and langurs and, via a 220-step stairway, a trail up to the **Cave of Prehistoric Man**. Human graves and tools were found here that date back 7500 years, making it one of the oldest sites of human habitation in Vietnam.

Popular hikes include a 6km-return walk to the massive, 1000-year-old '**old tree**' (*Tetrameles nudiflora*) and a longer four-hour walk to **Silver Cloud Peak**. There's also a strenuous 15km (approximately five-hour) hike to **Kanh**, a Muong village. You can overnight here with local families and raft on the Buoi River (50,000d).

Park staff can provide you with basic maps, but a guide is recommended for day trips and mandatory for longer treks. For a group of up to five people, a night hike to spot nocturnal animals, or the Silver Cloud Peak hike both cost US$20. The Deep Jungle trek (US$50) gets into remote terrain where you might spot civets or flying squirrels.

Sleeping & Eating

There are three accommodation areas in the park.

At the **visitor centre** (r per person US$7, guesthouse US$23-27, bungalows US$30) beside the park entrance there are dark, basic rooms, en-suite guesthouse rooms and one bungalow. Perhaps the nicest accommodation are the bungalows overlooking **Mac Lake** (r $US25), 2km inside the park, which were being renovated at the time of research. Camping (per person US$2, with a tent US$4) is also available at the visitor centre or Mac Lake.

The **park centre** (stilt house per person US$7, q $US20, bungalows US$28) at Bong, 18km from the park entrance, is the best place to be for an early morning walk or bird-watching. Here you'll find simple rooms with no hot water in a pseudo-stilt house, a building with large four-bed rooms, and a few bungalows.

Kanh village homestays (per person US$5) with Muong families are available. The dwellings are predictably basic.

There are restaurants (meals 25,000–50,000d) at the park centre and visitor centre. Call ahead and place your order for each meal (except breakfast).

The park can get very busy at weekends and during school holidays, when you should make a reservation.

Getting There & Away

Cuc Phuong National Park is 45km from Ninh Binh. The turn-off from Hwy 1 is north of Ninh Binh and follows the road that runs to Kenh Ga and Van Long Nature Reserve.

Regular buses link Ninh Binh with Cuc Phuong (18,000d). A bus from Hanoi's Giap Bat bus station runs directly to Cuc Phuong (85,000d) at 9am, returning at 3pm. Alternatively, take a bus to Nho Quan (48,000d, 2½ to 3½ hours, six daily) and grab a motorbike (50,000d) to the park entrance.

SAVING MONKEYS & TURTLES

Cuc Phuong's **conservation centres** (admission free, with guide 10,000d) provide a glimpse of their work and the fascinating animals they're trying to help. The **Endangered Primate Rescue Center** (384 8002; www.primatecenter.org; 9.30-11.30am & 1.30-4.30pm) is home to around 150 monkeys: 12 kinds of langur, three species of gibbon and two loris. The langur is a long-tailed, tree-dwelling monkey; the gibbon is a long-armed, fruit-eating ape; and the loris is a smaller nocturnal primate with large eyes. Look out for Vinh, an incredibly agile though disabled gibbon (his arm was broken in a tussle with a hunter).

All the centre's animals were either bred here or rescued from illegal traders (in China monkeys can fetch large sums for their perceived 'medicinal worth').

The centre has bred more than 100 offspring in all, including the world's first captive-born Cat Ba langur and grey-shanked douc langur. But it's incredibly difficult to rehabilitate primates once they've lived in cages; it's only been possible to release 30 gibbons and langurs into semi-wild areas (one site adjacent to the centre, the other in Phong Nha-Ke Bang National Park) since the centre opened. Souvenirs including T-shirts are for sale here.

The **Turtle Conservation Center** (384 8090; www.asianturtlenetwork.org, see Project Profiles; 9-11.15am & 2-4.45pm) houses more than 1000 terrestrial, semi-aquatic and aquatic turtles representing 20 of Vietnam's 25 native species. Many animals here have been confiscated from smugglers. Again it's China (and Vietnam) generating the demand – eating turtle is thought to aid longevity. Professional hunters and opportunistic collectors have decimated wild populations of turtles throughout Vietnam and Southeast Asia, with as many as 10 million turtles traded per year through the 1990s.

You'll find excellent information displays, and there are incubation and hatchling viewing areas. The centre successfully breeds and releases turtles from 11 different species including six native turtles. Around 60 turtles are released back into the wild each year.

PHAT DIEM

Home of a celebrated **cathedral**, remarkable for its vast dimensions and unique Sino-Vietnamese cum European architecture, Phat Diem (Map p142) is an impressive sight.

During the colonial era Phat Diem's bishop ruled the area with his private army, Middle Ages–style, until French troops took over in 1951. The cathedral (1891) featured prominently in Graham Greene's novel *The Quiet American,* and it was from the bell tower that the author watched battles between the North Vietnamese Army (NVA) and the French.

At busy times you have to steer a path through aggressive sellers and beggars to earn your entrance, but inside it's peaceful in a sepulchre-like way. The cathedral's largely wooden interior boasts a vaulted ceiling supported by massive columns (almost 1m in diameter and 10m tall). Above the granite altar Vietnamese-looking cherubs with golden wings swarm, while Chinese-style clouds drift across the blue ceiling. Beneath them are icons of the martyrs slaughtered by Emperor Tu Duc during the anti-Catholic purges of the 1850s.

Opposite the cathedral's main doors is the free-standing bell tower, with stone columns carved to look like bamboo. At its base lie two enormous stone slabs. Their purpose was to provide a perch for mandarins to sit and observe the rituals of the Catholic mass.

Between the tower and the cathedral is the tomb of the Vietnamese founder, Father Six and a Lourdes-style grotto, with a somewhat spooky bust of Father Six beside it.

Hordes of Vietnamese tourists come to this place, few of them Catholic but many curious about churches and Christianity. Daily mass is celebrated at 5am and 5pm, when the massive bell is rung and the faithful stream into the cathedral, dressed in their finest.

Not far from this cathedral is a **covered bridge** dating from the late 19th century. **Dong Huong Pagoda** is the largest pagoda in the area, catering to the Buddhist community. Many of its congregation are from the minority Muong people. To find it, turn right at the canal as you're approaching town from the north and follow the small road alongside the water for 3km.

A Gothic counterpoint to Phat Diem is the cathedral at **Ton Dao**, along Route 10 about 5km from Phat Diem. It looks beatifically out over rice fields and, at the rear of the churchyard, a statue of the Virgin Mary keeps unexpected company with porcelain images of Quan Am.

🛈 **Getting There & Away**

Phat Diem, sometimes known by its former name Kim Son, is 121km south of Hanoi and 26km southeast of Ninh Binh. There are direct buses here from Ninh Binh (15,000d, one hour); *xe om* (motorbike) drivers charge about 140,000d (including waiting time) for a return trip.

Vinh

📞038 / POP 437,000

Practically obliterated during the American War, Vinh (Map p142) was hastily rebuilt with East German aid – hence the brutalist concrete architecture that dominates the downtown drag. Unlike other Vietnamese towns, it has wide boulevards and broad pavements.

Despite attempts to prettify the place with trees and parks, the city remains a resolutely bleak-looking industrial city, nicknamed 'grim Vinh' by some travellers. There are few reasons to stop here unless you are a Ho Chi Minh devotee (he was born in a nearby village) or heading to Laos.

History

Vinh came to prominence as the 'Phoenix Capital City' of the Tay Son Rebellion. A May Day demonstration in 1930 was suppressed by the police, who killed seven people. Nonetheless revolutionary fervour spread, with Vinh's Communist cells, trade unions and farmers' organisations earning it the appellation 'Red-Glorious City'.

In the early 1950s, the city was reduced to rubble by a three-punch whammy: French aerial bombing, the Viet Minh's scorched-earth policy and finally a huge fire. During the American War, the port of Vinh became a key supply point for the Ho Chi Minh Trail (see the boxed text, p291). Vinh was relentlessly pounded with bombs for eight years – until only two buildings were left standing. In 1972 its population was officially zero.

◉ **Sights**

There's not a lot left to see of Vinh's **citadel** (1831) apart from the sludgy green moat and three gates: **Left Gate** (Cua Ta; Đ Dao Tan), **Right Gate** (Cua Huu; Đ Dao Tan) and **Front Gate** (Cua Tien; Khoi 5 Đ Dang Thai Than). The walk between the Left and Right Gates provides a pleasant interlude and passes the little-visited **Xo Viet Nghe Tinh Museum** (Đ Dao Tan; free admission; ⊗7-11am & 1-5pm), which memorialises local heroes. Outside, in true socialist-art style, is a large stone **monument** to those who perished at the hands of the French.

🛏 Sleeping

Thanh An Hotel   HOTEL **$**
(✆384 3478; 156 Nguyen Thai Hoc; s/d 180,000 /200,000d; ✳🕏) Excellent new hotel with immaculately clean, modern, uncluttered rooms that all have minibar, good beds and attractive wooden furniture. Near-zero English is spoken on reception however. It's 300m south of the bus station and there's safe parking in the basement.

Saigon Kimlien Hotel   HOTEL **$$**
(✆383 8899; www.saigonkimlien.com.vn; 25 Đ Quang Trung; r US$38-50, ste US$100; ✳🕏@🏊) Something of a city landmark and institution, this large hotel offers three-star levels of comfort and service. You'll find it 1km south of the bus station. Rooms are well equipped, if slightly dated, and there's a restaurant, fancy lobby and small pool. Annoyingly, breakfast finishes at 9am sharp.

APEC Hotel   HOTEL **$**
(✆358 9466; apec_hotel_na@yahoo.com; Ngo 1 Đ Ho Tung Mau; r 190,000-240,000d; ✳🕏@) Tucked away in an alley behind Đ Ho Tung Mau (follow the signs from Đ Ho Tung Mau) this decent place offers comfortable, well-kept rooms that represent good value.

Asian Hotel   HOTEL **$**
(✆359 3333; 114 Tran Phu; r 240,000-300,000d; ✳@) This multi-storey hotel was modern a couple of decades ago. Rooms remain in fair condition and there's safe parking, a lift, a restaurant and massage/sauna facilities. It's about 300m southeast of the central city park.

🍴 Eating & Drinking

Dining selections are very thin on the ground in Vinh. Perhaps your best bet for tasty grub is the bustling **Thuong Hai** (144 Đ Nguyen Thai Hoc; meals 35,000-70,000d) whose speciality is delicious Shanghai-style chicken, though it also has good Vietnamese seafood and vegetarian dishes. Street food options include the Central Market, **pho bo food stalls** (beef noodle soup; Đ Phan Dinh Phung), **bun bo Hue food stalls** (Hue-style spicy beef noodle soup; off Đ Dinh Cong Trang); and **pho ga food stalls** (chicken noodle soup; Đ Ho Sy Doung).

You'll find a group of **bars** along Đ Quang Trung and **pool halls** on Đ Nguyen Thai Hoc.

ℹ Information

Cap Quang Internet (33 Đ Dinh Cong Trang) Located off Đ Quang Trung.
Main post office (Đ Nguyen Thi Minh Khai) Just northwest of the central city park.
Saigon Commercial Bank (25 Đ Quang Trang) ATM and exchange services on the main drag.
Vietcombank ATM (33 Đ Le Mao) West of the central city park.
Vinh City Hospital (Benh Vien Da Khoa Thanh Pho Vinh; ✆383 5279; 178 Đ Tran Phu) Just southwest of the central city park.

ℹ Getting There & Away

AIR Vietnam Airlines (✆359 5777; www.vietnamairlines.com; 2 Đ Le Hong Phong) flies from Vinh to Hanoi five times a week and HCMC daily.

BORDER CROSSING BLUES 2

The often mist-shrouded **Nong Haet–Nam Can** (⊙7am-5pm) border crossing is 119km east of Phonsavan in Laos and 250km northwest of Vinh.

Buses between Vinh and Phonsavan cross here, leaving Phonsavan daily (110,000 kip, 13 hours, 403km) and returning from Vinh on Wednesday, Friday, Saturday and Sunday (235,000d). Some buses from Phonsavan claim to continue to Hanoi or Danang, but unceremoniously discharge all their passengers in Vinh.

For a DIY journey, take a morning bus from Phonsavan to Nong Haet (30,000 kip, four hours, 119km), then hire a songthaew (30,000 kip, but travellers have been charged double or triple) for the 13km run to the border. On the Vietnam side, you'll haggle over a motorbike ride to the nearest town, Muong Xen. The route is breathtaking but only 25km downhill and should cost around US$5; drivers may ask for up to US$15. From Muong Xen there's a bus to Vinh (90,000d, eight hours, 250km).

For Laos-bound travellers, the bus leaves Vinh in the morning for Muong Xen. Get a motorbike to take you uphill to the border. Transport on the Laos side to Nong Haet is erratic, but once you get there you can pick up a bus to Phonsavan.

Jetstar Pacific (☑ 355 0550; 46 Đ Nguyen Thi Min Khai) has a daily link to HCMC. The airport is about 20km north of the city.

BUS Vinh **bus station** (Đ Le Loi) has a reasonably modern booking office (including departures board and price list) and is centrally located. Buses to Hanoi (110,000d to 145,000d, seven hours) leave every 30 minutes until 4.30pm, there are also 10 sleeper buses and you'll find services to all four Hanoi bus terminals. For Ninh Binh (70,000d) take a Hanoi-bound bus. Eight daily buses (including five sleepers) head for Danang (190,000d, 11 hours) stopping at Dong Hoi (60,000d, 4½ hours) and Dong Ha (95,000d, six hours) and Hue (145,000d, 7½ hours) en route. Open-tour buses pass through town between Hanoi and Hue, and while it's easy to ask to jump off here, it's harder to arrange a pick-up.

Buses to Vientiane in Laos (400,000d, 22 hours) travel on even-numbered days only, leaving at 6.30am. There are also daily buses to Phonsavan in Laos and Tay Son (also known as Trung Tam) on Hwy 8, near the Lao border. See the boxed text, p152) for more.

TRAIN Vinh **train station** (Ga Vinh; Đ Le Ninh) is on the northwestern edge of town. Destinations include Hanoi (175,000d, 5½ to eight hours, eight daily), Ninh Binh (114,000d, 3½ to 4½ hours, five daily), Dong Hoi (110,000d, 3½ to 6½ hours, eight daily) and Hue (196,000d, 6½ to 10½ hours, eight daily).

Around Vinh

CUA LO BEACH

Cua Lo is pleasant enough, with white sand, clean water and a shady grove of pine trees – but the concrete, karaoke, massage parlours and litter won't suit all travellers. Still, it's an option for a cooling dip and seafood lunch at one of the many beach restaurants.

Huge government hotels face the beach and behind them are uninspired **guesthouses** (r 200,000-250,000d). Most hotels offer 'massage' and karaoke; some with prostitutes. In summer, rooms can go for triple (or more) the usual price.

Cua Lo is 16km northeast of Vinh and can be reached easily by motorbike (100,000d including waiting time) or taxi (150,000d).

KIM LIEN

Ho Chi Minh's birthplace in Hoang Tru and the village of Kim Lien, where he spent some of his formative years, are 14km northwest of Vinh. For all that these are popular **pilgrimage spots** (free admission; ⊙7-11.30am & 2-5pm Mon-Fri, 7.30am-noon & 1.30-5pm Sat & Sun) for the party faithful, there's little to see other than recreated houses of bamboo and palm leaves, dressed (barely) with a few pieces of furniture.

Ho Chi Minh was born in Hoang Tru in 1890 and raised there till 1895, when the family moved to Hue. They returned in 1901, but it was to the house in Kim Lien, about 2km from Hoang Tru. Not far from this house is a shrine-like **museum**, and store packed with Ho memorabilia.

No English-language information is available at either site. From Vinh, *xe om* (motorbike) drivers charge 80,000d (including waiting time), taxis ask for around 140,000d.

Phong Nha-Ke Bang National Park

☑ 052

Designated a Unesco World Heritage site in 2003, the remarkable **Phong Nha-Ke Bang National Park** (admission free) contains the oldest karst mountains in Asia, formed approximately 400 million years ago. Riddled with hundreds of cave systems – many of extraordinary scale and length – and spectacular underground rivers, Phong Nha is a speleologists' heaven on earth.

Its collection of stunning dry caves, terraced caves, towering stalagmites and glistening crystal-edged stalactites represent nature on a very grand scale indeed, and are beginning to create a real buzz in Vietnam, as more and more riches are discovered.

Serious exploration only began in the 1990s, lead by the British Cave Research Association and Hanoi University. Cavers first penetrated deep into Phong Nha Cave, one of the world's longest systems. In 2005 Paradise Cave was discovered, and in 2009 a team found the world's largest cave – Son Doong (see p154).

Above the ground, most of the mountainous 885 sq km of Phong Nha-Ke Bang National Park is near-pristine tropical evergreen jungle, more than 90% of which is primary forest. It borders the biodiverse Hin Namno reserve in Laos to form an impressive, continuous slab of protected habitat. More than 100 types of mammal (including 10 species of primate, tigers, elephants, and the saola, a rare Asian antelope), 81 types of reptile and amphibian, and more than 300 varieties of bird have been logged in Phong Nha.

BORDER CROSSING BLUES 3

The border crossing at **Nam Phao–Cau Treo** (⊙7am-6pm) is 96km west of Vinh and about 30km east of Lak Sao in Laos.

This border has a dodgy reputation with travellers, who report chronic overcharging and hassle on local buses (such as bus drivers ejecting foreigners in the middle of nowhere unless they cough up extra bucks). Most transport to Phonsavan in Laos uses the Nam Can–Nong Haet border further north.

If you do decide to travel step-by-step, local buses leave Vinh to Tay Son (formerly Trung Tam) regularly from 6am (70,000d, three hours). From Tay Son, it's another 25km to the border. There are morning buses running from Tay Son to Lak Sao but these may not connect with services from Vinh (unless you get here by mid-morning). Otherwise motorbikes ask for up to 150,000d for the ride. On the Laos side, a jumbo or *songthaew* between the border and Lak Sao runs to about 45,000 kip (bargain hard).

Travelling in the opposite direction (from Laos), upon entering Vietnam expect bus drivers to quote up to US$40 for a ride to Vinh. A metered taxi costs about US$45, a motorbike about 270,000d. Some buses from Lak Sao claim to run to Danang or Hanoi, but in fact terminate in Vinh.

Until recently, access to the national park was very limited and strictly controlled by the Vietnamese military. Some sections remain off-limits, but things are gradually opening up and it's now possible to visit the astounding Paradise Cave, turquoise river, eco-trail of Nuoc Mooc and a war shrine known as Eight Lady cave, and hike up to the mouth of (but not enter) Hang Son Doong. More hiking trails and other sights will open in the future.

◎ Sights & Activities

Phong Nha Caves & Boat Trip   CAVE
This is the most popular excursion in the region and it's easy to understand why – it's a spectacular river trip. **Phong Nha Cave** (admission adult/child 40,000/20,000d, boat 220,000d; ⊙7am-4pm) is nearly 55km long, though only the first kilometre or so is open to visitors. Boats in Son Trach village cruise along the Son river past bathing buffalo, jagged limestone peaks and church steeples to the cave's gaping mouth – Phong Nha means 'Cave of Teeth', but the 'teeth' (stalagmites) by the entrance are long gone. Then the engine is cut and you're transported to another world, as you're paddled through cavern after cavern. It's a surreal experience, except for the garish lights that illuminate certain formations.

On the return leg you've the option to climb up to **Tien Son Cave** (admission adult/ child 40,000/20,000d; ⊙7am-4pm), a dry cave in the mountainside above Phong Nha Cave. It's a tough 330-step climb to the cave, where there are remains of Cham altars and

inscriptions that date back to the 9th century. The cave was used as a hospital and ammunition depot during the American War and consequently was heavily bombed.

The ticket office for both caves and the jetty for boat departures are in Son Trach village. Allow two hours to see Phong Nha, add an hour for Tien Son. In November and December seasonal floods may mean Phong Nha Cave is closed. Weekends are extremely popular with Vietnamese visitors, whose presence is magnified by the spectacular echoes and unventilated cigarette smoke.

Phong Nha Farmstay was planning to start night tours of Phong Nha Cave by kayak at the time of research.

Paradise Cave   CAVE
(Thien Dong; adult/child under 1.3m 120,000/ 60,000d; ⊙7.30am-4.30pm) Only open to the public since 2011, this remarkable cave system extends for 31km, though only a kilometre or so is accessible. It's said to be the longest dry cave in the world. Commendably, development has been incredibly sensitive: there's no litter and electric buggies whisk you from the ticket office to the 500-step staircase that leads to the (diminutive) cave mouth. Even the trees along the access tracks are labelled.

Once you're inside, the sheer scale of Paradise Cave is truly breathtaking, as wooden staircases descend into a cathedral-like space replete with colossal stalagmites and glimmering stalactites of white crystal that resemble glass pillars.

The whole experience is a lot less commercial than the Phong Nha Cave trip. Paradise

Cave is located deep in the national park, surrounded by dense forest and looming karst peaks. There's a good **restaurant** (meals 35,000-70,000d) next to the visitor centre and a cafe sells cold drinks near the cave entrance.

Paradise Cave is about 14km southwest of Son Trach.

FREE **Primate Reserve** NATURE RESERVE

Established around a small hill with support from Cologne Zoo, this small, semi-wild primate reserve has been set up as a breeding centre for critically-endangered Ha Tien langurs. The entire hillside is ringed by a fence, you can walk around the perimeter via a 1.8km trail (but not enter). Your chances of spotting a monkey are best in the early morning.

The centre is 3km from Son Trach, just off the national park entrance road.

Sleeping & Eating

There are a dozen or so guesthouses in Son Trach village, all charging the same rate (200,000d a double).

TOP CHOICE **Phong Nha Farmstay** GUESTHOUSE **$$**
(⏹367 5135; www.phong-nha-cave.com; Cu Nam village; dm US$8; r $US25-35; meals 30,000-90,000d; ✳@☎☀) Perhaps the best place to break the journey between Hanoi and Hue, this outstanding new guesthouse is owned by Ben and Bich, a welcoming and switched-on Australian–Vietnamese couple. Overlooking an ocean of rice paddies, the hotel is well set up for travellers, with a lounge-cum-bar with pool table, bikes and motorbikes for hire, tasty Asian and Western grub and a gregarious vibe. Rooms are smallish but neat, with high ceilings and shared balconies that make the most of the views. The 12-bed dorm building next door lacks aircon but enjoys the same vistas. Outstanding tours are offered, including kayaking, tubing, biking and hiking. It's in Cu Nam village, 13km southeast of Son Trach. Pick-ups can be arranged in Dong Hoi.

Song Son Phong Nha HOTEL **$$**
(⏹367 7241; Son Trach; r 200,000d; ✳@☎) This new hotel on the main drag represents excellent value. Its 27 rooms are immaculately clean and inviting, with TV and minibar, though beds are very firm; book rooms 214–217 for great countryside views. There's a restaurant with cold beer and good-value set meals.

You'll find several cheap dining options near Son Trach's marketplace, including **Thuy Thuyet** (meals 10,000-22,000d).

ℹ️ Information

Organised tours are an excellent way to explore the park – those run by **Phong Nha Farmstay** (p153) are highly recommended and cost 1,100,000d by motorbike or 900,000d by minibus. **Oxalis** (⏹090 337 6776, www.oxalis.com.vn) is a professional, locally-owned adventure tourism outfit based in Son Trach that offers treks and trips inside the national park.

ℹ️ Getting There & Around

Son Trach village is 50km northwest of Dong Hoi; from Dong Hoi head 20km north on Hwy 1 to Bo Trach, then turn west for another 30km.

Phong Nha-Ke Bang National Park abuts Son Trach village and spreads west to the Lao border. Information is very limited on the ground and some officials can still be less than helpful to independent travellers. At the time of research, travellers were entering freely via the Tro Mung ranger post on the Ho Chi Minh Highway but officials at the main park entrance gate on Hwy 20 were turning some back. Doubtless things will improve as organisation improves.

BUS Local buses (45,000d, two hours) offer irregular connections between Dong Hoi and Son Trach. There's also a daily minibus (200,000d) between Danang and Phong Nha Farmstay, stopping in Dong Ha and Hue en route.

TOURS Tours of Phong Nha can be set up in Dong Hoi, but as the region has so much to offer, try to base yourself locally if you can.

Dong Hoi & Around

⏹052 / POP 116,000

Pleasantly untouristed, Dong Hoi is a port and seaside town with no souvenir shops and

---

WORTH A TRIP

NUOC MOOC ECO-TRAIL

A beautiful riverside retreat inside the national park, the wooden walkways and paths of the **Nuoc Mooc Eco-Trail** (admission adult/child 6-16 30,000/50,000d; ☉7am-5pm) extend over a kilometre through woods to the confluence of two rivers. It's a gorgeous place for a swim, where you can wallow hippo-style in turquoise waters with a limestone-mountain backdrop. Bring a picnic. Nuoc Mooc is 12km southwest of Son Trach.

a lack of hassle. It enjoys an attractive location, clinging to the banks of the Nhat Le River and has beaches to the north and south.

As the main staging area for the NVA, Dong Hoi suffered more than most during the American War. The town has since recovered as a congenial provincial capital and a lot of development is ongoing at Nhat Le Beach.

◉ Sights

The Nhat Le River, which divides the city from a beautiful sandy spit, boasts a landscaped riverside promenade that includes the haunting, ruined facade of the **Tam Toa Church**, which was bombed in 1965.

All that remains of Dong Hoi Citadel (1825) are two restored **gates**, one close to the riverbank, the other on Đ Quang Trung.

Vuc Quanh Outdoor War Museum   MUSEUM
(Khu Du Lich Sinh Thai – Van Hoa Vuc Quanh; ☑224 0042; vucquanh@yahoo.com; Nghia Ninh; admission by appointment only 20,000d) This quirky outdoor museum, located 7km out of Dong Hoi, is a personal effort by one man – Mr Lien – to remember the civilian war experience in Quang Binh province. His approach: build a replica village for his personal collection of war relics and memorabilia.

The village consists of thatched huts scattered haphazardly along a maze of dirt paths and trenches. Each hut reproduces some aspect of village life: farmhouse, schoolroom, hospital or crèche. You can view poignant personal items as well as military relics, including American bomb casings and intrusion detectors and a reproduction of a letter from Ho Chi Minh, commending the province for shooting down more than 100 American warplanes.

To get to the museum, follow Đ Le Loi to the end, turn left and continue for just over 1km. At the signs for *chao sang bun be,* turn right and proceed for another kilometre. Alternatively, enquire at A2Z about tours here.

🛏 Sleeping & Eating

TOP CHOICE **Nam Long Hotel**   HOTEL **$**
(☑382 1851; sythang@yahoo.com; 22 Đ Ho Xuan Huong; r US$10-15; ✳@🛜) A terrific budget hotel, this is a welcoming and immaculately clean place run by Mrs Nga and her husband. The bright, airy rooms with enormous windows, high ceilings, minibars, cable TVs and modern decor are great value – book 301 for a river-view balcony or 201 for panoramic vistas. Breakfast and tour services are available.

Sun Spa Resort   RESORT HOTEL **$$$**
(☑384 2999; www.sunsparesortvietnam.com; My Canh; r US$122-165, ste from US$242; ✳@🛜♨) Huge five-star beachside resort in landscaped grounds complete with pool, tennis courts and commodious rooms. There's an impressive spa and complimentary yoga and tai chi.

Hotel Mau Hong   HOTEL **$**
(☑382 1804; Đ Truong Phap; r US$8-10; ✳) Ageing, basic but friendly place with large bare rooms, some of which have stupendous river views.

WORLD CLASS

Ho Khanh, a hunter from a jungle settlement close to the Vietnam–Laos border, would often take shelter in the caves that honeycomb his mountain homeland. He stumbled across gargantuan **Hang Son Doong** ('Mountain River Cave') in the early 1990s, but the sheer scale and majesty of the principal cavern (more than 5km long, 200m high and, in some places, 150m wide) was only confirmed as the world's biggest cave when British explorers returned with him in 2009.

The expedition team's biggest obstacle was to find a way over a vast overhanging barrier of muddy calcite they dubbed the 'Great Wall of Vietnam' that divided the cave. Once they did, its true scale was revealed – a cave big enough to accommodate a battleship. Sections of it are pierced by skylights that reveal formations of ethereal stalagmites that cavers have called the Cactus Garden. Colossal cave pearls have been discovered, measuring 10cm in diameter, formed by millennia of drips, as calcite crystals fused with grains of sand.

Hang Son Doong is one of the most spectacular sights in Southeast Asia, but as yet access is completely restricted to scientists and cavers. You can however, hike to the cave mouth with Son Trach-based Oxalis (p153) on a great two-day trek (three to four people, US$170 per person), allowing you a glimpse into the abyss along with pristine jungle on the way.

Dong Hoi

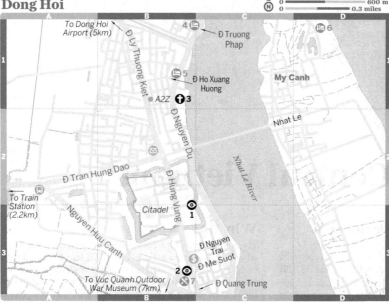

To Dong Hoi
Airport (5km)

Đ Ly Thuong Kiet

4 Đ Truong
Phap

5 Đ Ho Xuang
Huong

A2Z **3**

My Canh

Nhat Le

Đ Nguyen Du

Đ Tran Hung Dao

To Train
Station
(2.2km)

Nguyen Huu Canh

Citadel

Đ Hung Vung

Nhat Le River

1

Đ Nguyen
Trai
Đ Me Suot

To Vuc Quanh Outdoor
War Museum (7km)

2 **7**

Đ Quang Trung

6

0 / 600 m
0 / 0.3 miles

QB Teen INTERNATIONAL **$**
(3 Đ Le Loi; meals 26,000-80,000d) Small place
that's a good bet for Western fare, a cold
beer and conversation.

ℹ Information

A2Z (☑384 5868; info@atoz.com.vn; 29 Đ Ly
Thuong Kiet) Contact for tours to Phong Nha or
open-tour bus tickets.
Agribank (2 Đ Me Suot) Has an ATM and
exchange services.
Main post office (1 Đ Tran Hung Dao)

ℹ Getting There & Away

AIR The airport is 6km north of town. Vietnam
Airlines operates four flights per week to both
HCMC and Hanoi.

BUS From the **bus station** (Đ Tran Hung
Dao) you can catch services south to Danang (140,000d, five hours, six daily) via Hue
(105,000d, four hours) and Dong Ha (50,000d,
two hours), and north to Vinh (95,000d, four
hours, seven daily) and Hanoi (145,000d, seven
hours). It's easy to leave an open-tour bus in
Dong Hoi, but for a pick-up go through a travel
agency.

Buses leave for the Lao border at Lao Bao
(95,000d, four hours, five daily) and on to

Dong Hoi

⦿ Sights
1 Dong Hoi Citadel Gate.........................B3
2 Dong Hoi Citadel Gate.........................B3
3 Tam Toa Church..................................B1

🛏 Sleeping
4 Hotel Mau Hong..................................B1
5 Nam Long Hotel...................................B1
6 Sun Spa Resort....................................D1

🍴 Eating
7 QB Teen...B3

Muang Khammouan (230,000d, 11 hours) inside
Laos. The latter leaves Dong Hoi on Monday,
Wednesday and Friday, returning the next day.
It crosses at the quiet **Cha Lo–Na Phao border
crossing** (⊙7am-5pm); Lao visas are now avail-
able at this border.

TRAIN The **train station** (Ga Dong Hoi; Đ Thuan
Ly) is 3km west of the centre. Trains leave for
Hanoi (278,000d, nine to 12½ hours, seven
daily), Vinh (118,000d, 3½ to 6½ hours, seven
daily), Dong Ha (58,000d, two to three hours,
seven daily) and Hue (95,000d, 2½ to six hours,
nine daily), among other destinations.

Central Vietnam

Why Go?

The cultural hub of the nation, central Vietnam is fully loaded with historical sights and cultural interest, blessed with ravishing beaches and boasts nature reserves so unchartered that scientists are still discovering new creatures in them. Even long-ignored Danang is chipping in and emerging as one of the nation's most dynamic cities.

Marvel at Hue, the former imperial capital with its incredible Citadel and royal tombs. Wonder at the unique grace and sublime riverside setting of Hoi An. Explore rural back roads, through shimmering rice paddies to remote Cham ruins. Enrol in a course to learn to cook central Vietnamese cuisine, the nation's most complex. Then put it all into historical context by taking in the military sites of the Demilitarised Zone (DMZ). Enough? Invest in some well-deserved hammock time on the golden sands of An Bang beach or over on the idyllic Cham islands.

Best Places to Eat

» Morning Glory Street Food Restaurant (p202)

» Cargo Club (p202)

» Casa Verde (p203)

» Waterfront (p184)

Best Places to Stay

» Pilgrimage Village (p169)

» New Moon Hotel (p183)

» Ha An Hotel (p200)

» Violet Hotel (p162)

When to Go

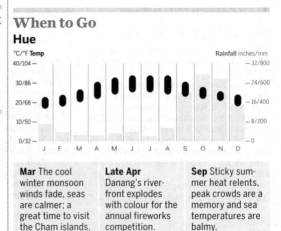

Hue

Mar The cool winter monsoon winds fade, seas are calmer; a great time to visit the Cham islands.

Late Apr Danang's riverfront explodes with colour for the annual fireworks competition.

Sep Sticky summer heat relents, peak crowds are a memory and sea temperatures are balmy.

History

This region's seen them all: kings and king-makers, warriors and occupiers, Vietnamese forces and many non-Vietnamese contenders. The ancient kingdom of Champa began here in the 2nd century and flourished for more than a thousand years. It left its mark in the myriad towers and temples dotting the landscape; the most renowned are at My Son.

The Vietnamese subdued Champa in the 15th century, while in subsequent centuries European, Japanese and Chinese traders established footholds in Hoi An.

In 1802 Vietnam's last royal dynasty, the Nguyens, set up court at Hue, which became the centre of political intrigue, intellectual excellence and spiritual guidance. Later emperors were subdued by expanding French ambitions in Vietnam, and by the

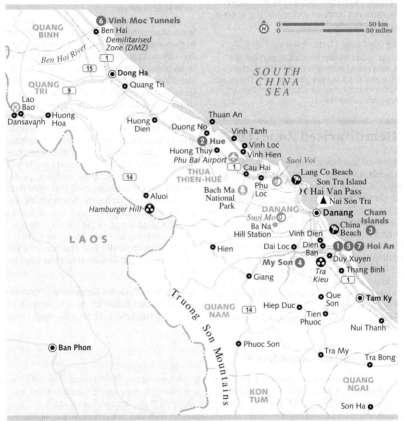

Central Vietnam Highlights

❶ Travel back in time in the historic houses and quaint streets of **Hoi An** (p190)

❷ Tread in the footsteps of emperors from the Forbidden Purple City to the imperial tombs of **Hue** (p163)

❸ Escape the mainland and search for that perfect beach in the pristine **Cham Islands** (p210)

❹ Wonder while you wander amid the enigmatic Cham ruins at **My Son** (p211)

❺ Test your two-wheel prowess on a **motorbike tour** (p208) around the idyllic back roads of central Vietnam

❻ Go underground at the **Vinh Moc Tunnels** (p158) in the Demilitarised Zone

❼ Learn a new culinary craft in a **Vietnamese cooking class** (p199)

time of independence the locus of national power had shifted back to Hanoi.

In 1954 Vietnam was fatefully partitioned into North and South, creating a DMZ that saw some of the heaviest fighting in the American War. Thousands of lives were lost in bloody battles. Even the former imperial capital of Hue was not spared during the Tet Offensive. Most towns in this region, with the magical exception of Hoi An, were almost completely rebuilt after the war. Today, central Vietnam's economy is buoyant with a burgeoning tourism sector and the booming city of Danang.

ⓘ Getting There & Away

Danang has an international airport (where a smart new terminal is under construction). Hue also has a busy regional airport. The major north–south rail route cuts straight through the region, as does Hwy 1.

Demilitarised Zone (DMZ)

📋 053

Most of the bases and bunkers have long vanished, but this 5km strip of land on either side of the Ben Hai River is still known by its American War moniker: the DMZ. From 1954 to 1975 it acted as a buffer between the North and the South. Ironically, the DMZ became one of the most militarised areas in the world, forming what *Time* magazine called 'a running sore'.

The area just south of the DMZ was the scene of some of the bloodiest battles in America's first TV war, turning Quang Tri, The Rockpile, Khe Sanh, Lang Vay and Hamburger Hill into household names.

Fast forward several decades and there's not much left to see. Most sites have been cleared, the land reforested or planted with rubber and coffee. Only Ben Hai, Vinh Moc and Khe Sanh have small museums. Unless you're an American veteran or military buff, you might find it a little hard to appreciate the place – which is all the more reason to hire a knowledgeable guide.

◉ Sights

Vinh Moc Tunnels   HISTORICAL SITE
A highly impressive complex of tunnels, **Vinh Moc** (admission 20,000d; ☉7am-4.30pm) is the remains of a coastal North Vietnamese village that literally went underground in response to unremitting American bombing. More than 90 families disappeared into three levels of tunnels running almost 2km in all, and continued to live and work while bombs rained down around them.

Most of the tunnels are open to visitors, and are kept in their original form (except for electric lights, a luxury the villagers certainly didn't have). An English-speaking guide will accompany you around the complex, pointing out the 12 entrances until you emerge at a glorious beach, facing the South China Sea. The **museum** has photos and relics of tunnel life, including a map of the tunnel network.

The turn-off to Vinh Moc from Hwy 1 is 6.5km north of the Ben Hai River in the village of Ho Xa. Follow this road east for 13km.

Truong Son National Cemetery   CEMETERY
An evocative memorial to the legions of North Vietnamese soldiers who died along

ⓘ WATCH YOUR STEP

Millions of tonnes of ordnance were dropped on Vietnam during the American War – it's estimated that a third did not explode. Death and injury still happen most days in the Demilitarised Zone (DMZ). At many of the places listed in this section there's still a chance of encountering live mortar rounds, artillery projectiles and mines. Watch where you step and don't leave the marked paths. Never touch any leftover ordnance – if the locals haven't carted it off for scrap it means that even they are afraid to disturb it.

It's not just the DMZ that's affected. It's estimated that as much as 20% of Vietnam remains uncleared, with more than 3.5 million mines and 350,000 to 800,000 tonnes of unexploded ordnance (UXO). Between 1975 and 2007 this resulted in 105,000 injuries and over 45,000 deaths. Every year on average around 1000 people die and 1700 are injured – a disproportionate number of them children or from the ethnic minority groups.

The People's Army is responsible for most ongoing mine clearance. It's joined by foreign NGOs such as the **Mines Advisory Group** (www.maginternational.org) and **Clear Path International** (www.clearpathinternational.org), whose efforts are well worth supporting.

Around the DMZ

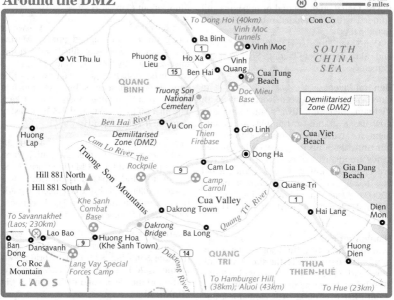

the Ho Chi Minh Trail, this cemetery is a sobering sight. More than 10,000 graves dot these hillsides, each marked by a simple white tombstone headed by the inscription *liet si* (martyr). Many graves lie empty, simply bearing names, representing a fraction of Vietnam's 300,000 soldiers missing in action.

Truong Son was used as a base by the May 1959 Army Corps from 1972 to 1975. The corps had the mission of constructing and maintaining the Ho Chi Minh Trail.

The cemetery is not on most tour itineraries, and its isolated location and simple design give it a powerful dimension. It's 27km northwest of Dong Ha; the turn-off from Hwy 1 is close to Doc Mieu.

Khe Sanh Combat Base   MILITARY SITE
The site of the most famous siege of the American War, the USA's Khe Sanh Combat Base was never overrun, but saw the bloodiest battle of the war (see the boxed text, p161). About 500 Americans, 10,000 North Vietnamese troops and uncounted civilian bystanders died around this remote highland base. It's eerily peaceful today, but in 1968 the hillsides trembled with the impact of 1000kg bombs, white phosphorus shells, napalm, mortars and endless artillery rounds, as desperate American forces

sought to repel the North Vietnamese Army, which they ultimately did.

Today the site is occupied by a small **museum** (admission 20,000d; ⊙7am-5pm), which contains some fascinating old photographs, plus a few reconstructed bunkers and American aircraft. Most of the area is now planted with coffee, and vendors offer high-grade local Arabica beans for sale at the entrance.

Khe Sanh is 3km north of Huong Hoa.

Huong Hoa (Khe Sanh Town)
The town has been officially renamed Huong Hoa, but the world remembers it as Khe Sanh. It's known for its coffee plantations, and many inhabitants are of the Bru tribe (the women wear sarong-like skirts). About the only reason for staying here is if you're planning to hit the road to Laos. **May Hong** (☎388 0189; Km 64, Khe Sanh; r US$12; ❄) has clean, functional rooms. The bus station is on Hwy 9. Buses to Dong Ha (33,000d, 1½ hours) and Lao Bao (22,000d, one hour) depart regularly. Change at Dong Ha for other destinations.

Con Thien Firebase   MILITARY SITE
Only one bunker remains of the US Marine Corps base that used to cover the three small hills here. In September 1967 Con Thien was besieged by the NVA, provoking a US

response of 4000 bombing sorties. Today the region (though cleared of mines) is still studded with unexploded ordnance – stick to the paths.

Con Thien Firebase is 15km west of Hwy 1 and 8km south of Truong Son National Cemetery.

Ben Hai River   RIVER

Once the border between North and South Vietnam, Ben Hai River's southern bank now has a grandiose reunification monument, its stylised palm leaves oddly resembling missiles. Cua Tung Beach's fine golden sands are just east of here. Ben Hai's northern bank is dominated by a reconstructed flag tower and small **museum** (admission 20,000d; ☺7am-5pm) full of war mementoes.

Ben Hai is 22km north of Dong Ha on Hwy 1.

Hamburger Hill   MILITARY SITE

Less than 2km from the Laos border, Hamburger Hill (Ap Bia) was the site of a tumultuous battle in May 1969 between US forces and the NVA over a 900m-high mountain – resulting in over 600 North Vietnamese and 72 American deaths. The infantry battle, and the loss of American life, caused outrage in the USA (and was the subject of the Hollywood movie). Today you need a special permit (obtained in the town of Aluoi) and a guide to get a glimpse of the remaining trenches and bunkers. A new war monument is currently under construction here.

Hamburger Hill is 8km northwest of Aluoi, about 6km off Hwy 14.

Camp Carroll   MILITARY SITE

Camp Carroll was named after a Marine Corps captain who was killed while trying to seize a nearby ridge. Its colossal cannons were used to shell targets as far away as Khe Sanh (though these days there isn't much to see except a Vietnamese memorial marker). The turn-off to Camp Carroll is 10km west of Cam Lo; it's 3km from Hwy 9.

The Rockpile   MILITARY SITE

Visible from Hwy 9, this 230m-high karst outcrop once had a US Marine Corps lookout on top and a base for American long-range artillery nearby. You'll need a guide to point out the hill to you. The Rockpile is 29km west of Dong Ha on Hwy 9.

Dakrong Bridge   BRIDGE

Crossing the Dakrong River 13km east of the Khe Sanh bus station, this bridge was rebuilt in 2001 and bears a marker hailing its importance as a conduit for the Ho Chi Minh Trail.

❶ Getting There & Around

Most visitors explore the DMZ on a tour. These are cheap (US$11 to US$15 for a day trip) and can be arranged by any hotel or cafe in Hue or Dong Ha. No matter where you sign up you'll probably wind up as part of a large group. A common complaint about DMZ tours is that more

GONE UNDERGROUND

In 1966 the USA began a massive aerial and artillery bombardment of North Vietnam. Just north of the Demilitarised Zone (DMZ), the villagers of Vinh Moc found themselves living in one of the most heavily bombed and shelled strips of land on the planet. Small family shelters could not withstand this onslaught and villagers either fled or began tunnelling by hand and with simple tools into the red-clay earth.

The Viet Cong (VC) found it useful to have a base here and encouraged the villagers to stay. After 18 months of tunnelling, an enormous complex was established, creating new homes on three levels from 12m to 23m below ground, plus meeting rooms and even a maternity unit (17 babies were born underground). Whole families lived here, their longest sojourn lasting 10 days and 10 nights. Later, the civilians and VC were joined by North Vietnamese soldiers, whose mission was to keep communication and supply lines to nearby Con Co Island open.

Other villages north of the DMZ also built tunnel systems, but none were as elaborate as Vinh Moc. The poorly constructed tunnels of Vinh Quang village (at the mouth of the Ben Hai River) collapsed after repeated bombing, killing everyone inside.

US warships stationed off the coast consistently bombarded the Vinh Moc tunnels (craters are still visible) and occasionally the tunnel mouths that faced the sea were struck by naval gunfire. The only ordnance that posed a real threat was the 'drilling bomb'. It scored a direct hit once but failed to explode, and no one was injured; the inhabitants adapted the bomb hole for use as an air shaft.

THE FIGHT FOR NOWHERE

Despite opposition from Marine Corps brass, the small US Army Special Forces (Green Beret) base at Khe Sanh was turned into a Marines' stronghold in late 1966. In April 1967 a series of 'hill fights' began between US forces and the well-dug-in North Vietnamese infantry, who held the hills 8km to the northwest. In only a few weeks, 155 Marines and thousands of North Vietnamese were killed.

In late 1967 American intelligence detected the movement of tens of thousands of North Vietnamese regulars, armed with mortars, rockets and artillery into the Khe Sanh region. General Westmoreland became convinced that the North Vietnamese were planning another Dien Bien Phu (see p123). This analogy was foolhardy, given American firepower and the proximity of Khe Sanh to supply lines and other US bases. President Johnson himself became obsessed by the spectre of 'Din Bin Foo', as he famously referred to it. He had a sand-table model of the Khe Sanh plateau constructed in the White House situation room and took the unprecedented step of requiring a written guarantee from the Joint Chiefs of Staff that Khe Sanh could be held.

Determined to avoid another Dien Bien Phu at all costs, Westmoreland assembled a force of 5000 planes and helicopters and increased the number of troops at Khe Sanh to 6000. According to the authors of *Nineteen Sixty-Eight (Vietnam Experience)*, he even ordered his staff to study the feasibility of using tactical nuclear weapons.

The 75-day siege of Khe Sanh began on 21 January 1968 with a small-scale assault on the base's perimeter. As the Marines and South Vietnamese Rangers braced for a full-scale ground attack, Khe Sanh became the focus of global media attention. It was the cover story for both *Newsweek* and *Life* magazines, and made the front pages of countless newspapers around the world. During the next two months the base was subjected to continuous ground attacks and artillery fire, and US aircraft dropped 100,000 tonnes of explosives in its vicinity. But the expected attempt to overrun the base never came. On 7 April 1968, after heavy fighting, US troops reopened Hwy 9 and linked up with the Marines, ending the siege.

It now seems clear that the siege was an enormous diversion to draw US attention away from the South Vietnamese population centres in preparation for the Tet Offensive, which began a week after the siege started. However, at the time, Westmoreland considered the entire Tet Offensive to be a 'diversionary effort' to distract attention from Khe Sanh.

After Westmoreland's tour of duty in Vietnam ended in July 1968, US forces in the area were redeployed. Holding Khe Sanh, for which so many men had died, was deemed unnecessary. After everything at Khe Sanh was buried, trucked out or blown up (leaving nothing recognisable that could be used in a North Vietnamese propaganda film), US forces upped and left under a curtain of secrecy. The American command had finally realised what Brigadier General Lowell English, assistant commander of the 3rd Marine Division, had expressed long before: 'When you're at Khe Sanh, you're not really anywhere. You could lose it and you really haven't lost a damn thing.'

time is spent driving than sightseeing due to the distances covered. Most tours take in The Rockpile, Khe Sanh, Vinh Moc and Doc Mieu and leave Hue at 7am, returning by about 5pm.

A more meaningful experience, particularly for American veterans, is to see the DMZ independently. Reckon on US$100 or so per day for a car and expert guide.

Dong Ha

☑053 / POP 85,200

Sitting at the intersection of Hwys 1 and 9, Dong Ha is an important transport hub. Its dusty, traffic-plagued main drag looks pretty dismal – this is because the town was completely flattened during the American War. However the town does have its attractive aspects, with a string of excellent riverside seafood restaurants. Accommodation options are fast improving too. Dong Ha makes a useful base for exploring the DMZ and is the gateway town to the Lao Bao border crossing.

FREE Bao Tang Quang Tri (8 Đ Nguyen Hue; ⊙7.30-11am & 1.30-5pm Tue, Thu, Sat & Sun) is a modest museum and the only real sight in town. It documents the history of Quang Tri province with a focus on ethnic minorities.

Tours

Several tour agencies offer tours of the DMZ and beyond. Tam, the genial owner of Tam's Cafe, can set you up with a motorbike and backpacker-geared tour of the DMZ and surrounding region.

Annam Tour   MILITARY
(☑0905 140 600; www.annamtour.com; 207B Đ Nguyen Du) Highly recommended tailor-made tours, guided by military historian Mr Vu (who speaks excellent English).

DMZ Tours   MILITARY, ADVENTURE
(☑356 4056; www.dmztours.net; 260 Đ Le Duan) Itineraries for American veterans, quality DMZ tours and adventure trips including boat trips to Can Co Island.

Sepon Travel   MILITARY, TRANSPORT
(☑385 5289; www.sepontour.com; 189 Đ Le Duan) DMZ tours and can book flights and buses to Savannakhet (Laos).

Sleeping

A new four-star hotel is under construction right where Hwy 1 crosses the river in the centre of Dong Ha.

TOP CHOICE / Violet Hotel   HOTEL $
(☑358 2959; Đ Ba Trieu; s 180,000d; tw 230,000-300,000d; ❄🅰) This modern minihotel represents outstanding value for money, offering immaculately clean rooms all with minibar, cable TV, fan, air-con and in-room wi-fi; some also have rice-paddy views and a balcony. It's a kilometre west of the main drag in a quiet location opposite a strip of great lake-facing restaurants. Staff speak almost no English, but will do their best to help out.

Huu Nghi Hotel   HOTEL $
(☑385 2361; www.huunghihotel.com.vn; 68 Đ Tran Hung Dao; s/d/tr 350,000/390,000/510,000d; ❄@🅰) At the time of research, this landmark five-storey hotel was the best address in town. Its renovated spacious rooms are excellent, all with smart furnishings including wardrobe, reading light, bed with comfortable mattress, and flat-screen TV – some have commanding river views. Breakfast is included.

Thuy Dien Guesthouse   HOTEL $
(☑385 7187; 9 Đ Le Van Huu; r 160,000d; ❄) Opposite the bus station, this place has clean, if bland rooms that are fair value for money.

Eating & Drinking

Dong Ha is famous for seafood. Head to the strip of riverside restaurants on Đ Hoang Dieu for wonderful *cua rang me* (crab in tamarind sauce), *vem nuong* (grilled clams) and steamed or roasted squid. There's another excellent crop of casual places by the Violet Hotel for Vietnamese meat and seafood.

TOP CHOICE / Tam's Cafe   CAFE $
(www.tamscafe.co.nr; 81 Đ Tran Hung Dao; meals US$2; 🅰) A great little place, with probably the only espresso machine in the province, Tam's offers excellent Vietnamese food and Western snacks like pizza, as well as smoothies and juices. It's run by the ever-helpful Tam, a switched-on, fluent English speaker who is working hard to put his home town on the map and show travellers around. The cafe employs and supports deaf people and has spot-on travel information.

Con Soi   VIETNAMESE $
(Đ Ba Trieu; meals 50,000d) The pick of the lakeside restaurants. All the local dishes here are wonderfully fresh and flavoursome. It's excellent for roast suckling pig, grilled fish and seafood.

Information

For impartial travel and tourist information, head to Tam's Cafe.

Post office (183 Đ Le Duan)
Vietcombank ATM (Đ Tran Hung Dao)
Vietin Bank ATM (Đ Hung Vuong)

Getting There & Away

BUS Dong Ha bus station (Ben Xe Khach Dong Ha; 68 Đ Le Duan) is near the intersection of Hwys 1 and 9. Vehicles to Dong Hoi (50,000d, two hours), Hue (42,000d, 1½ hours), Danang (65,000d, 3½ hours), Khe Sanh (28,000d, 1½ hours) and Lao Bao (45,000d, two hours) depart regularly.

It is sometimes necessary to change buses in Khe Sanh for Lao Bao. Buses are also advertised to Savannakhet in Laos, but the station won't book a ticket for foreigners; Sepon Travel (across the road) will.

There's also a daily minibus connection from Tam's Cafe to Phong Nha Farmstay (p153; 100,000d) at 3.30pm; on the return leg it heads south via Hue to Danang at 7.30am (100,000d).

You can check all transport schedules at Tam's Cafe.

CAR & MOTORCYCLE Motorbike tours to the DMZ start from US$15. A one-way car trip to

BORDER CROSSING: LAO BAO–DANSAVANH

Lao Bao, on the Sepon River (Song Xe Pon), is one of the most popular and least problematic **border crossings** (☉7am-6pm) between Laos and Vietnam. You can get a 30-day Lao visa on arrival, but Vietnamese visas need to be arranged in advance; drop in at the Vietnamese consulate in Savannakhet (Laos).

Buses to Savannakhet run from Hue via Dong Ha and Lao Bao. From Hue, there's a 7am air-con bus (280,000d, 9½ hours), on odd days only, that leaves from the Sinh Tourist office (p174). This travels via Dong Ha, where it makes a stop at the Sepon Travel office at around 8.30am to pick up more passengers (Dong Ha to Savannakhet costs 210,000d), before getting to Savannakhet at 4pm. The bus then returns from Savannakhet's Savanbanhao Hotel the next day.

It's also easy to cross the border on your own; Dong Ha is the gateway. Buses leave the town to Lao Bao bus station (50,000d, two hours, 85km) roughly every 15 minutes. From here *xe om* (motorbike taxis) charge about 12,000d to the border, or it's a 20-minute walk. Between the Vietnam and Laos border posts is a short walk of a few hundred metres.

There's a huge market on the Vietnamese side but no reason to linger. If you do stay the night, **Sepon Hotel** (☎377 7129; www.seponhotel.com.vn; Đ 82 Lao Bao; r US$20-27; ✳@) is a decent business hotel, while the ageing **Bao Son Hotel** (☎387 7848; r US$15-17; ✳) has cheap beds. Try not to change currency in Lao Bao: money changers offer terrible rates.

Once in Laos there is only one public bus a day direct to Savannakhet (60,000 kip, five hours, 250km), which leaves when full. *Songthaew* (pick-up trucks) head regularly to Sepon, from where you can get a bus or another *songthaew* to Savannakhet.

Coming the other way, buses from Savannakhet to Dansavanh run regularly during the day and there's an overnight bus that leaves at 10pm for Hue; be warned that the latter arrives at Dansavanh around 3am and is known to make passengers disembark and wait by the road till morning...

If you're taking a tourist bus, confirm (preferably in writing) that the same bus continues through the border. Travellers have reported being bundled off nice buses on the Vietnamese side onto overcrowded local buses in Laos. If the bus is likely to arrive at the border after it's closed, check if your ticket includes accommodation for the night, or be prepared to sleep on an overcrowded bus.

the Lao Bao border will set you back US$45. Motorbikes can be hired from Tam's Cafe from US$5 per day.

TRAIN Dong Ha's **train station** (Ga Dong Ha; 2 Đ Le Thanh Ton) has trains to destinations including Hanoi (sleeper from 480,000d, 12½ to 16 hours, five daily), Dong Hoi (from 58,000d, 1½ to three hours, seven daily) and Hue (from 44,000d, 1½ to 2½ hours, seven daily). Dong Ha train station is 2km south of the Hwy 1 bridge.

Remnants of the ancient moat, ramparts and gates of the **citadel** remain. It's off Đ Tran Hung Dao, 1.6km north of Hwy 1.

Outside Quang Tri, along Hwy 1 towards Hue, is the skeleton of **Long Hung Church**. It bears countless bullet holes and mortar damage from the 1972 bombardment.

The **bus station** (Đ Tran Hung Dao) is about 1km from Hwy 1, but buses can also be flagged down on the highway.

Quang Tri

☎053 / POP 28,600

Quang Tri once boasted an important citadel, but little of its old glory remains. In the Easter Offensive of 1972, North Vietnamese forces laid siege to and then captured the town. This provoked carpet bombing and artillery shelling by the USA and South Vietnamese forces, which all but destroyed Quang Tri.

Hue

☎054 / POP 358,000

Palaces and pagodas, tombs and temples, culture and cuisine, history and heartbreak – there's no shortage of poetic pairings to describe Hue (pronounced 'hway'). A Unesco World Heritage site, this deeply evocative capital of the Nguyen emperors still resonates with the glories of imperial Vietnam, even though many of its finest buildings were destroyed during the American War.

Hue owes its charm partly to its location on the Perfume River – picturesque on a clear day, atmospheric even in less flattering weather. There's always restoration work going on to recover Hue's royal splendour, but today the city is very much a blend of new and old: modern homes sit cheek by jowl with crumbling century-old Citadel walls, and sleek new hotels tower over stately colonial-era properties.

Tourism has brought an excess of touts (who can dog your every step), but, minor hassles aside, Hue remains a tranquil conservative city. There's no real bar scene and local tourism authorities have lamented the fact that locals go to bed before 10pm.

History

In 1802 Emperor Gia Long founded the Nguyen dynasty, moved the capital from Hanoi to Hue in an effort to unite northern and southern Vietnam, and commenced the building of the Citadel. The city prospered but its rulers struggled to counter the growing influence of France.

In 1885, French forces responded to a Vietnamese attack by storming the Citadel, burning the imperial library and removing every single object of value – from gold ornaments to toothpicks. The emperors continued to reside in Hue, but were very much sidelined from events of national importance.

It was only in 1968 that attention shifted to Hue again, during the Tet Offensive. While the Americans concentrated on holding Khe Sanh, North Vietnamese and Viet Cong (VC) forces seized Hue, an audacious assault that commanded headlines across the globe.

During the 3½ weeks that the North controlled the Citadel, more than 2500 people were summarily shot, clubbed to death or buried alive. The North called them – ARVN soldiers, wealthy merchants, government workers, monks, priests and intellectuals – 'lackeys who owed blood debts'. The USA and South Vietnamese responded by levelling whole neighbourhoods, battering the Citadel and even using napalm on the imperial palace. According to remarks attributed to an American soldier involved in the assault, they had to 'destroy the city in order to save it'. Approximately 10,000 people died in Hue, including thousands of VC troops, 400 South Vietnamese soldiers and 150 US Marines – but most of those killed were civilians.

◎ Sights

Citadel HISTORICAL SITE
Most of Hue's sights and a sizeable chunk of its population reside within the 2m-thick, 10km-long walls of its Citadel (Kinh Thanh) on the north bank of the river. Built between 1804 and 1833, its ramparts are encircled by a moat, 30m across and about 4m deep, and there are 10 fortified gates.

The Citadel has several distinct sections. The Imperial Enclosure and area beyond the Forbidden Purple City formed the epicentre of Vietnamese royal life. On the southwestern side were temple compounds. There were residences in the northwest, gardens in the northeast and in the north the **Mang Ca Fortress** still forms a military base.

Soaring over the entire complex, the 37m-high **Flag Tower** (Cot Co) is Vietnam's tallest. During the VC occupation in 1968, the National Liberation Front flag flew defiantly from the tower for 3½ weeks.

Located just inside the Citadel ramparts, near the gates to either side of the Flag Tower, are the **Nine Holy Cannons** (1804), symbolic protectors of the palace and kingdom. Commissioned by Emperor Gia Long, they were never intended to be fired. Each brass cannon is 5m long and weighs about 10 tonnes. The four cannons near **Ngan Gate** represent the four seasons, while the five cannons next to **Quang Duc Gate** represent the five elements: metal, wood, water, fire and earth.

Imperial Enclosure HISTORICAL SITE
(admission 55,000d; ◎6.30am-5.30pm summer, 7am-5pm winter) The Imperial Enclosure is a citadel-within-a-citadel, housing the emperor's residence and the main buildings of state within 6m-high, 2.5km-long walls. What's left today is only a fraction of the original – the enclosure was badly bombed

AN INSIDER'S TALE

Journalist Gavin Young's 1997 memoir *A Wavering Grace* is a moving account of his 30-year relationship with a family from Hue and with the city itself, during and beyond the American War. It makes a good literary companion for a stay in the city.

during the French and American wars, and only 20 of its 148 buildings survived. Restoration and reconstruction of damaged buildings is ongoing.

The Enclosure is divided into several walled sections, with the Forbidden Purple City at its centre. The formal state palaces are between this and the main gate. Around the perimeter is a collection of temples and residences, the better preserved of which are along the southwestern wall. In the southeast are the ruins of the **Thai To Mieu temple complex** (now a plant nursery) and behind it the **University of Arts**, housed in the former Royal Treasury. To the rear of this are gardens, a park and lake.

This is a fascinating site, worth exploring for the better part of a day. It's enjoyable as a leisurely stroll and some of the less-visited areas are highly atmospheric.

Ngo Mon Gate

The principal entrance to the Imperial Enclosure is Ngo Mon Gate (Noontime Gate; 1833), which faces the Flag Tower. The central passageway, with its yellow doors, was reserved for the use of the emperor, as was the bridge across the lotus pond.

On top of the gate is **Ngu Phung** (Belvedere of the Five Phoenixes); on its upper level is a huge drum and bell. The emperor appeared here on important occasions, most notably for the promulgation of the lunar calendar. On 30 August 1945, the Nguyen dynasty ended here when Emperor Bao Dai abdicated to a delegation sent by Ho Chi Minh.

Thai Hoa Palace

This palace (Palace of Supreme Harmony; 1803) is a spacious hall with an ornate timber roof supported by 80 carved and lacquered columns. It was used for the emperor's official receptions and important ceremonies. On state occasions the emperor sat on his elevated throne, facing visitors entering via the Ngo Mon Gate.

Be sure to take in the impressive audiovisual display here, which gives an excellent overview of the entire Citadel, its architecture and the historical context.

Halls of the Mandarins

Located immediately behind Thai Hoa Palace on either side of a courtyard, these halls were used by mandarins as offices and to prepare for court ceremonies.

The hall to the left has been set up for cheesy tourist photos where you can pose

---

CELEBRATING HUE

Having fallen into obscurity before, Hue seems determined not to let it happen again. The city hosts a huge biennial arts festival, the **Festival of Hue** (www.huefestival.com), in even-numbered years, featuring local and international artists and performers.

---

in imperial costume (20,000d to 100,000d) on a throne. The opposite hall showcases some fascinating old photographs (including boy-king Vua Duya Tan's coronation), gilded Buddha statues and assorted imperial curios.

Behind the courtyard are the ruins of the **Can Chanh Palace**, where two wonderful long **galleries**, painted in gleaming scarlet lacquer have recently been reconstructed.

Forbidden Purple City

Behind the palaces, in the very centre of the Imperial Enclosure, the Forbidden Purple City (Tu Cam Thanh) was a citadel-within-a-citadel-within-a-citadel. Almost entirely destroyed in the wars, it was once a walled compound solely for the personal use of the emperor. The only servants allowed were eunuchs who would pose no threat to the royal concubines.

Most of the area is now overgrown. Take care as you wander around the ruins as there are some gaping holes.

To the right the **Royal Theatre** (Duyen Thi Duong; ☎351 4989; www.nhanhac.com.vn; tickets 50,000d; ☺performances 9am, 10am, 2.30pm & 3.30pm), begun in 1826, has been rebuilt on its former foundations. Traditional dance and opera are performed here today by the Theatre of Hue Traditional and Royal Arts.

Behind this, the exquisite (though crumbling) little two-storey **Emperor's Reading Room** (Thai Binh Lau) was the only part of the Forbidden Purple City to escape damage during the French reoccupation of Hue in 1947. The structure is not open to visitors, but it's worth popping by to check out the Gaudi-esque roof mosaics.

To Mieu Temple Complex

Taking up the south corner of the Imperial Enclosure, this walled complex dedicated to the Nguyen emperors has been beautifully restored.

Hue

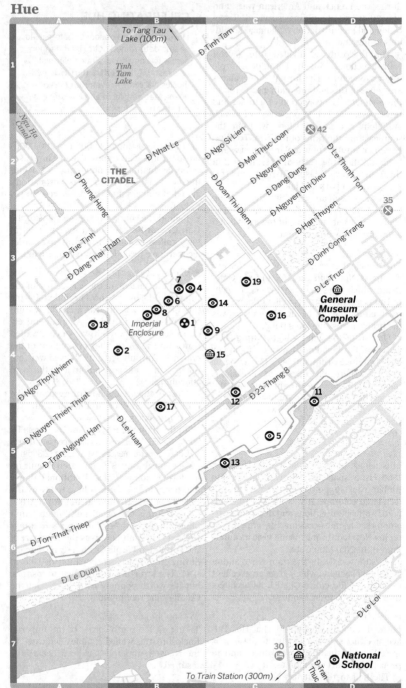

THE CITADEL

Tinh Tam Lake

To Tang Tau Lake (100m)

Imperial Enclosure

General Museum Complex

National School

To Train Station (300m)

Ngu Ha Canal

Đ Phung Hung
Đ Tue Tinh
Đ Dang Thai Than
Đ Ngo Thoi Nhiem
Đ Nguyen Thien Thuat
Đ Tran Nguyen Han
Đ Le Huan
Đ Ton That Thiep
Đ Le Duan
Đ Nhat Le
Đ Doan Thi Diem
Đ Ngo Si Lien
Đ Mai Thuc Loan
Đ Nguyen Dieu
Đ Dang Dung
Đ Nguyen Chi Dieu
Đ Han Thuyen
Đ Dinh Cong Trang
Đ Le Truc
Đ Le Thanh Ton
Đ Tinh Tam
Đ 23 Thang 8
Đ Tran Thuc
Đ Le Loi

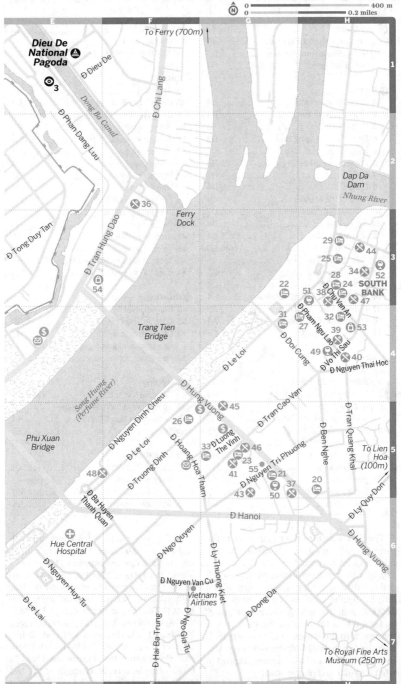

CENTRAL VIETNAM HUE

Dieu De National Pagoda

Đ Dieu De

Đ Chi Lang

Dong Ba Canal

Đ Phan Dang Luu

Đ Tong Duy Tan

Đ Tran Hung Dao

To Ferry (700m)

0   400 m
0   0.2 miles

Dap Da Dam

Nhung River

Ferry Dock

Trang Tien Bridge

Song Huong (Perfume River)

Phu Xuan Bridge

SOUTH BANK

Đ Chu Van An

Đ Pham Ngu Lao

Đ Doi Cung

Đ Vo Thi Sau

Đ Nguyen Thai Hoc

Đ Le Loi

Đ Hung Vuong

Đ Tran Cao Van

Đ Ben Nghe

Đ Tran Quang Khai

To Lien Hoa (100m)

Đ Nguyen Dinh Chieu

Đ Le Loi

Đ Truong Dinh

Đ Hoang Hoa Tham

Đ Luong The Vinh

Đ Nguyen Tri Phuong

Đ Ly Quy Don

Đ Ba Huyen Thanh Quan

Đ Hanoi

Đ Hung Vuong

Hue Central Hospital

Đ Nguyen Huy Tu

Đ Ngo Quyen

Đ Ly Thuong Kiet

Đ Dong Da

Đ Le Lai

Đ Hai Ba Trung

Đ Ngo Gia Tu

Đ Nguyen Van Cu

Vietnam Airlines

To Royal Fine Arts Museum (250m)

Hue

The first structure after you enter is the three-tiered **Hien Lam Pavilion**. On the other side of it stand **Nine Dynastic Urns** *(dinh),* cast between 1835 and 1836, each dedicated to one Nguyen sovereign. About 2m in height and weighing 1900kg to 2600kg each, the urns symbolise the power and stability of the Nguyen throne. The central urn, also the largest and most ornate, is dedicated to dynasty founder Gia Long. Also in the courtyard are two dragons, trapped in what look like red phone boxes.

On the other side of the courtyard is the solemn **To Mieu Temple**, housing shrines to each of the emperors, topped by their photos. Under the French, only the seven who met with colonial approval were honoured; Ham Nghi, Thanh Thai and Duy Tan were added in 1959. The temple gardens are a delight.

The temple is flanked by a small robing house and a shrine to a soil god. Behind each of these, a gate leads into the small walled enclosure that houses the **Hung To Mieu Temple**, a reconstruction of the 1804 original, built to honour Gia Long's parents.

Dien Tho Residence

Behind the two temples is this stunning, partially ruined residence (1804). This comprised the apartments and audience hall of the queen mothers of the Nguyen dynasty.

Just outside is an enchanting pleasure pavilion, a carved wooden building set above a lily pond. Sitting pretty to the left of the audience hall is Tinh Minh Building, which was used as a medical clinic and was also Bao Dai's private residence.

Truong San Residence

In 1844 Emperor Thieu Tri described this as one of the most beautiful spots in Hue, but it was utterly devastated by war. Check out the imposing entrance gate complete with prancing dragons and phoenixes. The interior has been partly restored, though remains empty except for its elaborate columns and tiles.

FREE **Dieu De National Pagoda**   PAGODA
(Quoc Tu Dieu De; 102 Đ Bach Dang) Overlooking Dong Ba Canal, this pagoda was built under Emperor Thieu Tri's rule (1841–47) and was once under the direct patronage of the emperor. It's famous for its four low towers, one to either side of the gate and two flanking the sanctuary.

Dieu De was a stronghold of Buddhist and student opposition to the South Vietnamese government and the American War and many arrests were made here when police stormed the building in 1966.

The pavilions on either side of the main sanctuary entrance contain the 18 La Ha, whose rank is just below that of Bodhisattva, and the eight Kim Cang, protectors of Buddha. In the back row of the main dais is Thich Ca Buddha, flanked by two assistants.

National School   NOTABLE BUILDING
(Truong Quoc Hoc; 10 Đ Le Loi; ⊙11.30am-1pm & from 5pm) One of the most famous secondary schools in Vietnam, the National School was founded in 1896. Many of its pupils later rose to prominence: General Vo Nguyen Giap, strategist of the Viet Minh victory at Dien Bien Phu; Pham Van Dong, former prime minister of North Vietnam; and Ho Chi Minh (who attended for a year in 1908).

The school admits students aged 16 to 18, but entrance examinations are notoriously difficult. You can visit the school during lunch break and after classes finish.

FREE **Royal Fine Arts Museum**   MUSEUM
(150 Đ Nguyen Hue; ⊙6.30am-5.30pm summer, 7am-5pm winter) This museum is located in the Baroque-influenced An Dinh Palace, commissioned by Emperor Khai Dinh in 1918 and full of elaborate murals, floral motifs and trompe lœil details. Emperor Bao Dai lived here with his family after abdicating in 1945. Inside you'll find some outstanding ceramics, paintings, furniture and royal clothing.

FREE **General Museum Complex**   MUSEUMS
(Đ 23 Thang 8; ⊙7.30-11am & 1.30-5pm Tue-Sun) Formerly a school for princes and the sons of high-ranking mandarins, this slightly rundown complex has a pagoda devoted to archaeology, a small Natural History Museum and a building with exhibitions about anticolonial resistance. Out front are war relics from the 1975 battle when Hue fell to the North.

FREE **Bao Quoc Pagoda**   PAGODA
(Ham Long Hill) Founded in 1670, this hilltop pagoda is on the southern bank of the Perfume River and has a striking triple-gated entrance reached via a wide staircase. On the right is a centre for training monks, which has been functioning since 1940. To the left is a cemetery for monks.

To get here, head south from Đ Le Loi on Đ Dien Bien Phu and take the first right after crossing the railway tracks.

Ho Chi Minh Museum   MUSEUM
(7 Đ Le Loi; admission 10,000d; ⊙7.30-11am & 1.30-4.30pm Tue-Sun) Every town's got one, but this Ho museum is better than most. The father of the modern Vietnamese nation spent 10 years in Hue, and you'll find some intriguing photographs with English captions.

Tang Tau Lake   LAKE
(Đ Dien Tien Hoang) An island on Tang Tau Lake, which is northeast of Tinh Tam Lake, was once the site of a royal library. It is now occupied by the small **Ngoc Huong Pagoda**.

🛏 Sleeping

Hue has an excellent choice of accommodation in all price categories. The main tourist enclave is centred on the lanes between Đ Le Loi and Đ Vo Thi Sau.

TOP CHOICE **Pilgrimage Village**   RESORT HOTEL $$$
(☎388 5461; www.pilgrimagevillage.com; 130 Đ Minh Mang; r/bungalows from US$121/172; ☀❄@☎⚡) A wonderful hideaway, this chic lodge has been designed around a verdant

valley that harbours a 40m pool, lotus ponds and a state-of-the-art spa and yoga space. It feels more like a Zen ecoretreat than a hotel. Rooms are all supremely comfortable, but for the ultimate experience book one of the bungalows with private plunge pool. There's a fine restaurant, lovely breakfast room and bar. Pilgrimage Village is about 3km from the centre of Hue, and connected by a complimentary shuttle bus.

TOP CHOICE Mercure
HOTEL $$

(☎393 6688; www.mercure.com; 38 Đ Le Loi; r from US$58; ❄️✳️@🛜🏊) Soaring above the Perfume River, this elegant new hotel offers exceptional value for money, a prime location and great service. A bold imposing lobby, replete with Vietnamese design influences, is a fitting introduction, while the stunning rooms, complete with polished wood furnishings, hip bathrooms, balconies and all mod cons, are beautifully finished. There's also a restaurant with French and Vietnamese cuisine and the Sky Bar; the kidney-shaped pool is smallish, though. Book via the web for a deal.

Google Hotel
HOTEL $

(☎383 7468; www.googlehotel-hue.com; 26 Đ Tran Cao Van; d/tr US$15/18; ✳️@🛜) Yes, the name's a bit cheeky, but as this excellent new place offers flashpacker chic at backpacker prices, the owners are definitely onto a winner. The light, spacious rooms have luxurious beds, huge flat-screen TVs and en suite bathrooms, while downstairs the large bar-restaurant (with decent local and Western grub and cold beer) is a good place to socialise.

La Residence
HOTEL $$$

(☎383 7475; www.la-residence-hue.com; 5 Đ Le Loi; r from US$151; ❄️✳️@🛜🏊) Once the French governor's residence, this wonderful hotel is the result of a sympathetic conversion, and is now one of the city's principal luxury addresses. On the banks of the Perfume River, its art deco design evokes memories of Indochine. Rooms are sumptuously appointed, the pool is sublime and the restaurants are excellent – the buffet breakfast spread is truly a sight to behold.

Orchid Hotel
HOTEL $$

(☎383 1177; www.orchidhotel.com.vn; 30A Đ Chu Van An; r US$35-60; ✳️@🛜) This is a very well-run modern hotel offering warm, efficient service and gorgeous accommodation, complete with laminate flooring, bright scatter cushions and DVD player. The pricier rooms have a desktop computer and some even have a jacuzzi with city views. Your complimentary breakfast is good (eggs are cooked to order) and children are well looked after.

Huenino
GUESTHOUSE $

(☎625 2171; www.hueninohotel.com; 14 Đ Nguyen Cong Tru; r US$14-22; ✳️@🛜) The family owners at Huenino go the extra mile to look after their guests (offering homemade snacks and drinks) and the rooms are very attractively presented with artwork, minibar, cable TV and good-quality beds. A generous breakfast is included. Book ahead.

Hue Backpackers
HOSTEL $

(☎382 6567; www.hanoibackpackershostel.com /hue; 10 Đ Pham Ngu Lao; dm US$6, r US$20; ✳️@🛜) With a prime site just off the Perfume River, eager-to-please staff, good info and a fearsome happy hour, it's easy to see why this is a backpacker mecca. Dorms (separate sex or mixed, and with four or eight beds) are well designed and have quality mattresses, fans, air-con and lockers; the private room is only fair value though.

Hue Thuong
HOTEL $

(☎388 3793; 11 Đ Chu Van An; r 250,000d; ✳️@🛜) A great little minihotel, where the newly renovated rooms, though smallish, have a real sparkle and are immaculately clean – all come with purple and white linen and attractive furniture.

Guesthouse Nhat Thanh
GUESTHOUSE $

(☎393 5589; nhatthanhguesthouse@gmail.com; 17 Đ Chu Van An; r US$13-15; ✳️🛜) A good choice in the heart of Hue, this place is run by a friendly family that makes sure the premises are kept spick and span. Rooms are light and spacious, with good beds, minibar and TV, and most have a little desk.

Hotel Saigon Morin
HOTEL $$$

(☎382 3526; www.morinhotel.com.vn; 30 Đ Le Loi; r/ste from US$112/222; ❄️✳️@🛜🏊) Built in 1901, this was the first hotel in central Vietnam and once the hub of French colonial life in Hue. The building is very classy, with accommodation set around two inner courtyards and a small pool. Rooms are grand and beautifully presented, with plush carpets and period detail that evokes a real 'wow' factor. Breakfast is included.

Halo
HOTEL $

(☎382 9371; huehalo@yahoo.com; 10a/66 Đ Le Loi; r US$8-15; ✳️@🛜) A well-run budget stronghold with tidy attractive rooms, many with balcony and a bath-tub, right in the heart of backpacker alley. Staff are accommodating.

Thai Binh Hotel 2   HOTEL $$
(✆382 7561; www.thaibinhhotel-hue.com; 2 Đ Luong The Vinh; r US$18-35; ✳@✨) One street away from the tourist thoroughfare, this powder-blue hotel is near to the action, yet quiet. Views from the higher floors are excellent, staff are pretty efficient and there's a restaurant (meals from US$3).

Hung Vuong Inn   HOTEL $
(✆382 1068; truongdung2000@yahoo.com; 20 Đ Hung Vuong; r US$11-17; ✳@✨) Nine spacious rooms with cable TV and attractive bathrooms, and the location is convenient, although it's on a busy road. There's a restaurant that's very popular with travellers here too.

Binh Minh Sunrise 1   HOTEL $
(✆382 5526; www.binhminhhue.com; 36 Đ Nguyen Tri Phuong; r US$10-30; ✳@✨) A six-storey hotel that offers a central location, pleasant staff and clean, fair-sized rooms, some with balcony. Budget options do not have air-con (and exclude breakfast).

Bamboo Hotel   HOTEL $
(✆832 8888; huuthuan@dng.vnn.vi; 61 Đ Hung Vuong; r US$11-16; ✳@✨) There's a vague bamboo theme running through the rooms of this decent, if unexceptional budget hotel. A simple breakfast is included.

Century Riverside Hotel   HOTEL $$
(✆382 3390; www.centuryriversidehue.com; 49 Đ Le Loi; s/d from US$60/70; ✳@✨☀) Large hotel that offers a wonderful riverside location and leafy grounds. Rooms are spacious though a little dated.

✖ Eating

We have the famed fussy eater Emperor Tu Duc to thank for the culinary variety of Hue (see p482) and an imperial cuisine banquet is usually a memorable experience.

Royal rice cakes, the most common of which are *banh khoai*, are worth seeking out. You'll find these along with other variations *(banh beo, banh loc, banh it* and *banh nam)* in street stalls and restaurants at **Dong Ba Market** (Đ Tran Hung Dao; dishes 5000-10,000d) and around town.

Vegetarian food has a long tradition in Hue. Stalls in Dong Ba Market serve lots of options on the first and 15th days of the lunar month. Vegie options, some using soybean mock meat, are quite common.

TOP CHOICE Take   JAPANESE $
(34 Đ Tran Cao Van; meals 50,000-120,000d; ⊙11.30am-9.30pm) Offering incredible value and a delightful dining experience, this fine Japanese restaurant has appropriate furnishings (including lanterns, calligraphy wall hangings and even cherry blossom) and a highly authentic menu. Sample some sushi (around 24,000d for two pieces), enjoy a yakitori dish (45,000d) and wash it all down with some sake (30,000d a cup).

TOP CHOICE Anh Binh   VIETNAMESE $$
(✆382 5305; 65 Đ Vo Thi Sau; dishes 40,000-155,000d; ⊙11.30am-9.30pm) A veritable foodie heaven, this elegant upmarket Vietnamese restaurant has a refined ambience and thoughtful service. It serves delicious Hue cuisine including fresh crab, rice patties with shrimp, and grilled chicken with chilli and ginger.

TOP CHOICE Lien Hoa   VEGETARIAN $
(3 Đ Le Quy Don; meals 30,000-50,000d; ⊙11am-9.30pm; ✍) Superb, highly authentic Viet vegie restaurant renowned for providing top-drawer food at rock-bottom rates. Eat like an emperor on fresh *banh beo* (steamed rice pancakes), noodle dishes and steam pots on a peasant's pay packet. The menu has photos and (rough) English translations to help you order (staff speak little or no English). It's about 800m southeast of Trang Tien bridge.

🖉 Restaurant Bloom   INTERNATIONAL, CAFE $
(14 Đ Nguyen Cong Tru; snacks from 15,000d; ✨) Ideal for a sandwich, baguette, croissant or homemade cake (baked on the premises), this likeable little cafe employs disadvantaged youths and graduates of the ACWP (Aid to Children Without Parents) training program.

Mandarin Café   VIETNAMESE $
(24 Đ Tran Cao Van; mains from 26,000d) Your host at this fine family restaurant is photographer Mr Cu, whose inspirational pictures adorn the walls. You'll find lots of vegetarian and breakfast choices on the varied East-meets-West menu, and copious copies of *National Geographic* to browse. Also operates as a tour agency.

Tropical Garden Restaurant VIETNAMESE $$
(☏384 7143; 27 Đ Chu Van An; dishes 25,000-140,000d) This place has tables set under thatched shelters in a pretty, fecund tropical garden. The cuisine is good, featuring many central Vietnamese specialities, though prepare yourself for the live band (7pm to 9pm nightly) and its popularity with tour groups.

Japanese Restaurant JAPANESE $
(12 Đ Chu Van An; dishes US$1.50-9; ☺6-9pm) A far more humble affair than its rival, this simple little place offers all your usual Japanese faves (including teriyaki, soba noodles and sushi). It's a little lacking in terms of ambience, but does employ former street children and supports a home for them.

Stop & Go Café INTERNATIONAL $
(3 Đ Hung Vuong; meals 20,000-60,000d; ☎) Casual little chalet-style place with tasty Vietnamese and backpacker fare, including good rice cakes, tacos, pizza and pasta, and filling Western breakfasts. Doubles as a tour operator, and they rent bikes too.

La Carambole FRENCH $$
(☏381 0491; www.lacarambole.com; 19 Đ Pham Ngu Lao; mains 32,000-155,000d) This long-running bistro is run by a Frenchman and his Vietnamese wife. Reliable Gallic and local cuisine, including imperial-style Hue specialities are offered, and the wine list is impressive. It's very popular with French tour groups, so book ahead and note that you may be seated outdoors in a terrace-cum-car park.

Little Italy ITALIAN $$
(www.littleitalyhue.com; 2A Đ Vo Thi Sau; mains 45,000-115,000d) Large trattoria with a decent line-up of Italian favourites (pasta, calzone, pizzas and seafood), a wide choice of beers and a palatable Sicilian house wine.

Hung Vuong Inn INTERNATIONAL $
(20 Đ Hung Vuong; meals 30,000-60,000d) Stick to the Western grub – like pasta, salads or burgers – at this bright, hip-looking little place. The Vietnamese food is on the bland side.

Caphé Bao Bao VIETNAMESE $
(38 Đ Le Thanh Ton; meals 15,000-25,000d) A simple courtyard place serving delicious and very cheap barbecued pork kebabs, served with noodles and vegetables.

Ngo Co Nhan SEAFOOD $$
(47 Đ Nguyen Dieu; dishes 30,000-100,000d) A huge, pretty formal restaurant with two floors of seating in a residential area of the Citadel. Renowned for steamed and grilled seafood.

Vegetarian Restaurant Bo De VEGETARIAN $
(11 Đ Le Loi; dishes 12,000-55,000d; ☑) Offers a tranquil riverside setting and tasty Vietnamese vegetarian fare, though service can be a tad brusque.

Omar Khayyam's Indian Restaurant INDIAN $
(34 Đ Nguyen Tri Phuong; mains 35,000-95,000d; ☺noon-10pm) Don't expect much in terms of ambience or decor, but if you're dreaming of a spice fix, this place makes a pretty decent stab at Indian curries, samosas and vegie dishes.

Drinking

Hue Backpackers BAR
(10 Đ Pham Ngu Lao; ☎) Party central for young travellers, this open-sided bar packs 'em in with its infused vodkas and (unashamedly tacky) cocktail list – those of a frigid nature beware the 'Passionfruit Leg-Opener'. A good bet for the footy, or big sporting events. Happy Hour is from 8pm to 9pm. Hic.

Café on Thu Wheels BAR
(10/2 Đ Nguyen Tri Phuong; ☎) Hole-in-the-wall backpackers' bar par excellence. Graffiti-splattered walls, a sociable vibe and good info from the feisty owner, Thu, and her family. They also offer good tours.

DMZ Bar BAR
(www.dmz-bar.com; 60 Đ Le Loi; ☎) The most lively joint in town, the DMZ has river views, a free pool table and a raucous buzz most nights. It serves food till midnight, including the entire menu from Little Italy.

Bar Why Not? BAR
(www.whynotbarhue.com; 21 Đ Vo Thi Sau) Number two with travellers, this place has a more relaxed vibe than Hue Backpackers, a sensational list of cocktails and a great street terrace.

New Sky BAR
(34 Đ Vo Thi Sau) For more of a local flavour, this club-bar is wildly popular with Hue's bright young things and showcases upcoming DJ talent.

Shopping

Hue produces the finest conical hats in Vietnam. The city's speciality is 'poem hats', which, when held up to the light, reveal shadowy scenes of daily life. It's also known for its rice paper and silk paintings.

CRAFTSMANSHIP FIT FOR A KING

Building the imperial monuments of Hue took the work of thousands of craftsmen and labourers, not only to erect the structures but also to fill them with the requisite appurtenances and objets d'art. Though the days of imperial patronage are long over, descendants of some craftsmen still make a living from these skills today.

At **Duc Thanh** (☑352 7707; 82 Đ Phan Dang Luu) in the Citadel, proprietor Mr Kinh Van Le is passing down the tradition of silk embroidery art. His father was a third-generation embroidery artisan who worked for Emperors Khai Dinh and Bao Dai, and Mr Kinh learned the way all apprentices do: from observing his father and relatives. When he was eight he embarked on his first solo project (still framed and displayed in his shop), but by the time he was an adult the days of the Nguyen dynasty were numbered.

Mr Kinh kept up his skills and later established a cooperative for embroidery artisans. He had to stop practising when his eyesight worsened with age, but now he runs classes that teach advanced embroidery techniques, such as how to make images appear more fanciful and lively, or to create an illusion of changing colours if one looks at the artwork from different angles. He also gives free classes to some children with disabilities. He'll tell you with pride that all the embroidery art in his shop is painstakingly hand-stitched, which is why he gets orders all the way from Japan.

Also toiling away at the family métier is septuagenarian Mr De Van Nguyen, who runs a small **foundry** (☑383 2151; 324/7 Đ Bui Thi Xuan) by the Perfume River southwest of the city. This is where he casts bells, statues and cauldrons, some for temples in Hue and neighbouring provinces.

Mr De's family has been in Hue since the early 19th century and their work for the royal family included some of the Citadel's cannons. His own particular skill is in the making of *kham tam khi* – a type of bronzework that uses a blend of bronze, silver and gold. He has 10 workers in his foundry, including his son; even then it takes them two months to complete a larger-than-life Buddha statue.

Mr Kinh and Mr De are happy to train new blood, but the hard part is finding young people who are interested. It takes years to hone one's skill, not to mention a lot of sweat and intense concentration – yet the earning power, even of a master artisan, can't compare with that of a modern job. These crafts aren't quite dying out yet, but former imperial prestige will only go so far.

🖉 Spiral Foundation Healing the Wounded Heart Center   HANDICRAFTS
(www.hwhshop.com; 23 Đ Vo Thi Sau) Generating cash from trash, this store stocks gorgeous, eco-friendly handicrafts – such as picture frames from recycled beer cans and hand-woven bags – made by artists with disabilities. Profits aid heart surgery for children in need.

Dong Ba Market   MARKET
(Đ Tran Hung Dao; ⊙6.30am-8pm) Just north of Trang Tien Bridge, this is Hue's largest market, selling anything and everything.

Trang Tien Plaza   MALL
(6 Đ Tran Hung Dao; ⊙8am-10pm) A small shopping centre between Trang Tien Bridge and Dong Ba Market with a Coopmart supermarket.

ℹ Information

Internet Access
There are lots of internet cafes on the tourist strips of Đ Hung Vuong and Đ Le Loi.

Medical Services
Hue Central Hospital (Benh Vien Trung Uong Hue; ☑382 2325; 16 Đ Le Loi)

Money
Vietcombank (30 Đ Le Loi; ⊙closed Sun)
Vietin Bank (12 Đ Hung Vuong) Has an ATM and exchange services.

Post
Post office (8 Đ Hoang Hoa Tram) Offers postal, internet and telephone services.

Travel Agencies
Cafe on Thu Wheels (☑383 2241; minhthuhue@yahoo.com; 10/2 Đ Nguyen Tri Phuong) Inexpensive cycle, motorcycle (from US$10 per person) and car tours (DMZ for US$40 per person) around Hue and beyond, run by Minh and his mates. Gets consistently good feedback.
Mandarin Café (☑382 1281; www.mrcumandarin.com; 24 Đ Tran Cao Van) Watched over by the eagle eyes of photographer Mr Cu (who speaks English and French), this place is great for information, transport and tours.

Sinh Tourist (☑382 3309; www.thesinhtourist .vn; 7 Đ Nguyen Tri Phuong) Books open-tour buses and buses to Laos.

Stop & Go Café (☑382 7051; www.stopand go-hue.com; 3 Đ Hung Vuong) Personalised motorbike and car tours. A full-day DMZ car tour guided by a Vietnamese vet costs US$42 per person.

❶ Getting There & Away

AIR The main office of **Vietnam Airlines** (☑382 4709; 23 Đ Nguyen Van Cu; ⊘closed Sun) handles reservations. Three flights a day connect Hue to both Hanoi and HCMC. **Jetstar** (☑395 5955; Đ 176 Hung Vuong; ⊘closed Sun) also connects Hue with HCMC daily. The office is about 1.5km southeast of the Trang Tien bridge.

BUS The main bus station, 4km southeast, has connections to Danang and south to HCMC. **An Hoa bus station** (Hwy 1), northwest of the Citadel, serves northern destinations, including Dong Ha (35,000d, two hours, every half hour).

Hue is a regular stop on open-tour bus routes. Most drop off and pick up passengers at central Hue hotels. Expect some hassle from persistent hotel touts when you arrive.

Mandarin, Sinh and Stop & Go Café can arrange bookings for buses to Savannakhet, Laos.

Hue Backpackers can book you on a minibus (150,000d, 7½ hours, 1pm) that runs daily to Phong Nha Farmstay (p153).

TRAIN The **Hue train station** (2 Đ Phan Chu Trinh) is at the southwestern end of Đ Le Loi.

❶ Getting Around

Hue's Phu Bai Airport is 14km south of the city. Metered taxis meet all flights and cost about 175,000d to the centre, or use the minibus service for 40,000d. Vietnam Airlines also runs an airport shuttle, which can collect you from your hotel (tickets 55,000d).

Pedal power is a fun way to tour Hue and the nearby Royal Tombs. Many hotels rent out bicycles for US$1 to US$2 per day. Self-drive motorbikes are available from US$4 to US$10. A car with driver costs around US$40 per day.

While Hue is an easy city to walk around, a typical street scene is a foreigner walking down the street with two *cyclos* (pedicabs or bicycle rickshaws) and a motorbike in hot pursuit – the drivers yelling, 'hello *cyclo*' and 'hello motorbike' and the foreigner yelling, 'no, thank you, no!' Both types of drivers will quote outrageous prices, but a fair rate is 12,000d per kilometre.

For a taxi, try the reliable **Mai Linh** (☑389 8989).

Around Hue

ROYAL TOMBS

(⊘6.30am-5.30pm summer, 7am-5pm winter) The tombs of the rulers of the Nguyen dynasty (1802–1945) are extravagant mausoleums, spread out along the banks of the Perfume River between 2km and 16km south of Hue. Almost all were planned by the emperors during their lifetimes, and some were even used as residences while they were still alive.

Most of the mausoleums consist of five essential elements. The first is a stele pavilion dedicated to the accomplishments, exploits and virtues of the emperor. Next is a temple for the worship of the emperor and empress. The third is an enclosed sepulchre, and fourth an honour courtyard with stone elephants, horses, and civil and military

HUE TRANSPORT CONNECTIONS

DESTINATION	AIR	BUS	CAR/ MOTORBIKE	TRAIN
Hanoi	from US$30, 1hr, 3 daily	US$18-27, 13-16hr, 8 daily	16hr	US$20-41, 12-16½hr, 5 daily
HCMC	from US$32, 1¼hr, 4 daily	US$23-37, 19-24hr, 8 daily	22hr	US$27-54, 19½-22hr, 4 daily
Ninh Binh	n/a	US$13-22, 10½-12hr, 7 daily	11hr	US$17-35, 10-13hr, 5 daily
Danang	n/a	US$3, 3hr, every 20min	2½-4hr	US$3-6, 2½-4hr, 8 daily
Dong Hoi	n/a	US$4-7, 3½hr, 12 daily	3½hr	US$5-10, 3-5½hr, 8 daily
Vinh	n/a	US$9-16, 7½-9hr, 7 daily	7hr	US$21-38, 6½-10hr, 5 daily

mandarins. Finally, there's a lotus pond surrounded by frangipani and pine trees.

While many of the tombs can be reached by boat, you'll have more time to enjoy them by renting your own bicycle or motorbike. Alternatively hire a *xe om* (motorbike taxi) or car and driver for the day.

Tomb of Tu Duc   TOMB

(admission 55,000d) This tomb, constructed between 1864 and 1867, is the most popular, and certainly one of the most impressive of the royal mausoleums. Emperor Tu Duc designed it himself, for use both before and after his death. The enormous expense of the tomb and the forced labour used in its construction spawned a coup plot that was discovered and suppressed in 1866.

Tu Duc lived a life of imperial luxury and carnal excess (he had 104 wives and countless concubines), though no offspring. All members of his harem were checked for weapons before being allowed into his bedroom.

From the entrance a path leads to the shore of **Luu Khiem Lake**. The tiny island to the right, **Tinh Khiem**, is where Tu Duc used to hunt small game. Across the water to the left is **Xung Khiem Pavilion**, where he would sit with his concubines, composing or reciting poetry.

Hoa Khiem Temple is where Tu Duc and his wife, Empress Hoang Le Thien Anh, were worshipped – today it just houses a jumble of dusty, unlabelled royal artefacts. The larger throne was for the empress; Tu Duc was only 153cm tall.

Minh Khiem Chamber, to the right behind Hoa Khiem Temple, was originally meant to be a theatre. Cheesy dress-up photo ops and cultural performances are available here today. Directly behind Hoa Khiem Temple is the quieter **Luong Khiem Temple** dedicated to Tu Duc's mother, Tu Du.

Just around the lakeshore is the **Honour Courtyard**. You pass between a guard of elephants, horses and diminutive mandarins (they were made even shorter than the emperor) before reaching the **Stele Pavilion**, which shelters a 20-tonne stone tablet. Tu Duc drafted the inscriptions himself. He freely admitted that he had made mistakes and chose to name his tomb Khiem ('modest').

The **tomb**, enclosed by a wall, is on the far side of a tiny lagoon. It's a drab grey monument and the emperor was never interred here – the site where his remains were buried (along with great treasure) is not known.

Around Hue

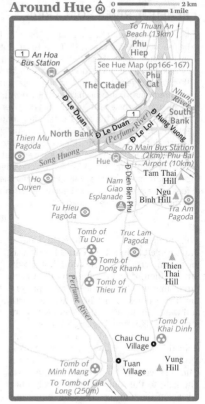

To keep it a secret from grave robbers, all of the 200 servants who buried the king were beheaded.

Tu Duc's tomb is about 5km south of Hue on Van Nien Hill in Duong Xuan Thuong village.

Tomb of Minh Mang   TOMB

(admission 55,000d) This majestic tomb is renowned for its architecture and sublime natural setting, surrounded by a forest. The tomb was planned during Minh Mang's reign (1820–1840) but built by his successor, Thieu Tri.

The **Honour Courtyard** is reached via three gates on the eastern side of the wall. Three granite staircases lead from the courtyard to the square **Stele Pavilion** (Dinh Vuong).

Sung An Temple, which is dedicated to Minh Mang and his empress, is reached via three terraces and the rebuilt Hien Duc Gate. On the other side of the temple, three

PERFUME RIVER BOAT TRIPS

Many sights around Hue, including Thien Mu Pagoda and several of the Royal Tombs, can be reached by boat via the Perfume River. Rates for chartering a boat are around US$10 for an hour's sightseeing on the river; a half-day charter costs from US$20.

Ask directly at the moorings on the south side of the river; it's cheaper than going through an agency and you can negotiate your own route. However, be clear on your requirements, preferably having them in writing. Don't get scammed into paying more for lunch or motorbike fees (to get from the river to the tombs).

Most hotels and travellers' cafes offer shared tours hitting the main sights from as little as US$3 per person. These tours usually run from 8am to 4pm. Given the time constraints, you'll need to ride a motorbike to get from the moorings to the first tomb. The second tomb is less than a 1km walk, but guides will try to get you on a bike for that too. The third tomb is 1.5km inland, a considerable hike, especially since it's usually one of the later stops on the cruise and during the intense heat of the day. Once the various fees and sweaty walks have been factored in, many travellers wish they had cycled or arranged a motorbike instead.

stone bridges span **Trung Minh Ho** (Lake of Impeccable Clarity). The central bridge was for the emperor's use only. **Minh Lau Pavilion** (Pavilion of Light) stands on the top of three superimposed terraces that represent the 'three powers': the heavens, the earth and water. To the left is the **Fresh Air Pavilion**, to the right, the **Angling Pavilion**.

From a stone bridge across crescent-shaped **Tan Nguyet Lake** (Lake of the New Moon), a monumental staircase with dragon banisters leads to Minh Mang's **sepulchre**. The gate to the tomb is opened only once a year on the anniversary of the emperor's death.

The tomb of Minh Mang is in An Bang village, on the west bank of the Perfume River, about 12km from Hue.

Tomb of Khai Dinh   TOMB

(admission 55,000d) This hillside monument is a synthesis of Vietnamese and European elements. Most of the tomb's grandiose exterior is covered in blackened concrete, creating an unexpectedly Gothic air, while the interiors resemble an explosion of colourful mosaic.

Khai Dinh was the penultimate emperor of Vietnam, from 1916 to 1925, and widely seen as a puppet of the French. The construction of his flamboyant tomb took 11 years.

Steps lead to the **Honour Courtyard** where mandarin honour guards have a mixture of Vietnamese and European features. Up three more flights of stairs is the stupendous main building, **Thien Dinh**. The walls and ceiling are decorated with murals of the Four Seasons, Eight Precious Objects and Eight Fairies. Under a graceless, gold-speckled concrete canopy is a gilt bronze statue of Khai Dinh. His remains are interred 18m below the statue.

The tomb of Khai Dinh is 10km from Hue in Chau Chu village.

Tomb of Gia Long   TOMB

(admission free) Emperor Gia Long founded the Nguyen dynasty in 1802 and ruled until 1819. According to royal annals, the emperor himself chose the site after scouting the area on the back of an elephant. Both the emperor and his queen are buried here. The rarely visited tomb is presently in a state of ruin. It is around 14km south of Hue and 3km from the west bank of the Perfume River.

Tomb of Thieu Tri   TOMB

(admission 55,000d) The only royal tomb not enclosed by a wall, the recently restored tomb of Thieu Tri (built 1848) has a similar floor plan to his father Minh Mang's tomb but is substantially smaller.

The tomb is about 7km from Hue. There's a pretty 2km cross-country track that leads here from the tomb of Dong Khanh.

Tomb of Dong Khanh   TOMB

Dong Khanh's modest mausoleum was built in 1889. He was placed on the throne by the French in 1885, and, predictably, was docile till his death three years later.

This tomb is the subject of a lengthy restoration project and was closed at the time of research. It's 500m behind the Tomb of Tu Duc.

THIEN MU PAGODA

(Linh Mu) Built on a hill overlooking the Perfume River, 4km southwest of the Citadel, this pagoda is an icon of Vietnam and as potent a symbol of Hue as the Citadel. The 21m-high octagonal tower, **Thap Phuoc Duyen**, was constructed under the reign of Emperor Thieu Tri in 1844. Each of its seven storeys is dedicated to a *manushi-buddha* (a Buddha that appeared in human form).

Thien Mu Pagoda was originally founded in 1601 by Nguyen Hoang, governor of Thuan Hoa province. Over the centuries its buildings have been destroyed and rebuilt several times. Since the 1960s it has been a flashpoint of political demonstrations (see the boxed text, below).

To the right of the tower is a pavilion containing a stele dating from 1715. It's set on the back of a massive marble turtle, a symbol of longevity. To the left of the tower is another six-sided pavilion, this one sheltering an enormous bell (1710), which weighs 2052kg and is said to be audible 10km away.

The temple itself is a humble building in the inner courtyard, past the triple-gated entrance where three statues of Buddhist guardians stand at the alert. In the main sanctuary behind the bronze laughing Buddha are three statues: A Di Da, the Buddha of the Past; Thich Ca, the historical Buddha (Sakyamuni); and Di Lac Buddha, the Buddha of the Future.

The best time to visit is early in the morning, before the tour groups show up. For a scenic bicycle ride, head southwest (parallel to the Perfume River) on riverside Đ Tran Hung Dao, which turns into Đ Le Duan after Phu Xuan Bridge. Cross the railway tracks and keep going on Đ Kim Long. Thien Mu Pagoda can also be reached by boat.

TU HIEU PAGODA

Nestled in a pine forest, this popular pagoda was built in 1843 and later co-opted by eunuchs from the Citadel (who have their own cemetery on the left-hand side). Tu Hieu is associated with Zen master Thich Nhat Hanh, who studied at the monastery here in the 1940s, but lived in exile for more than 40 years, and was only permitted to return to Vietnam in 2005. Today 70 monks reside at Tu Hieu; they welcome visitors to the twin temples (one dedicated to Cong Duc, the other to Buddha). You can listen to their chanting (daily at 4.30am, 10am, noon, 4pm and 7pm). Tu Hieu Pagoda is about 5km from the centre of Hue, on the way to the tomb of Tu Duc.

THUAN AN TO VINH HIEN

Thuan An Beach, 15km northeast of Hue, is on the splendid Tam Giang–Cau Hai Lagoon near the mouth of the Perfume River, at the tip of a long thin island. It's quite undeveloped except for a few kiosks, but between September and April the water's often too rough for swimming. Beyond the beach a 50km road stretches the length of the island from Thuan An to Vinh Hien. This makes a

A FIERY PROTEST

Behind the main sanctuary of the Thien Mu Pagoda is the Austin motorcar that transported the monk Thich Quang Duc to the site of his 1963 self-immolation. He publicly burned himself to death in Saigon to protest the policies of South Vietnamese President Ngo Dinh Diem. A famous photograph of this act was printed on the front pages of newspapers around the world, and his death inspired a number of other self-immolations.

The response of the president's notorious sister-in-law, Tran Le Xuan (Madame Nhu), was to crassly proclaim the self-immolations a 'barbecue party', saying 'Let them burn and we shall clap our hands'. Her statements greatly aggravated the already substantial public disgust with Diem's regime. In November both President Diem and his brother Ngo Dinh Nhu (Madame Nhu's husband) were assassinated by Diem's military. Madame Nhu was overseas at the time.

Another self-immolation sparked fresh protest in 1993. A man arrived at the pagoda and, after leaving offerings, set himself alight chanting the word 'Buddha'. Although his motivation remains a mystery, this set off a chain of events whereby the pagoda's leading monks were arrested and linked with the independent United Buddhist Church of Vietnam, the banned alternative to the state-sanctioned Vietnam Buddhist Church. This led to an official complaint to the UN by the International Federation of Human Rights accusing the Vietnamese government of violating its own constitution, which protects freedom of religion.

great day trip by motorbike or car from Hue. Coming from Thuan An, the road winds past villages alternating with shrimp lagoons and vegetable gardens. Look out for the colourful and opulent graves and family temples lining the road. From Vinh Hien, Tu Hien Bridge connects the island to the mainland, where the road hugs the southeastern shore of the lagoon all the way to Hwy 1.

HO QUYEN

(Tiger Arena; admission free) Wildly overgrown but still evocative, Ho Quyen was built in 1830 for the royal pastime of watching elephants and tigers face off in combat. The tigers (and leopards) were usually relieved of their claws and teeth so that the elephants – a symbol of the emperor's power – triumphed every time. You can climb up grassy ramparts and look down on the old arena and imagine the scene – the last fight was held here in 1904. The south-facing section was reserved for the royal family, while diametrically opposite are the tiger cages. Ho Quyen is about 3km outside Hue in Truong Da village. Follow Đ Bui Thi Xuan west from the train station, then look out for the blue sign near the market that indicates the turnoff on the left. Follow this lane for about 200m to a fork in the road and go right.

NAM GIAO ESPLANADE

This three-tiered esplanade was once the most important religious site in Vietnam, the place where the Nguyen emperors made animal sacrifices and elaborate offerings to the deity Thuong De. Ceremonies (the last was held in 1946) involved a lavish procession and a three-day fast by the emperor at the nearby **Fasting Palace**. Since 2006 the ceremony has been re-enacted as part of the Festival of Hue. The Fasting Palace, located at the furthest end of the park, has an informative display of photographs and English captions. Nam Giao Esplanade is at the southern end of Đ Dien Bien Phu, about 2km from the railway tracks.

THANH TOAN BRIDGE

A classic covered Japanese footbridge in picturesque countryside and without a souvenir shop in sight, this makes a lovely diversion from Hue. The bridge is in sleepy Thuy Thanh village, 7km east of Hue. Finding it is a bit tricky. Head north for a few hundred metres on Đ Ba Trieu until you see a sign to the Citadel Hotel. Turn right and follow the bumpy dirt road for another 6km past villages, rice paddies and several pagodas.

Bach Ma National Park

📷 054 / ELEV 1450M

A French-era hill station, this **national park** (Vuon Quoc Gia Bach Ma; 📷 387 1330; www.bachma .vnn.vn; adult/child/child under 6 20,000/10,000d/ free) reaches a peak of 1450m at Bach Ma mountain, only 18km from the coast. The cool climate attracted the French, who built over a hundred villas here. Not surprisingly the Viet Minh tried hard to spoil the holiday – the area saw some heavy fighting in the early 1950s and again during the American War.

There's currently a lot of construction going on inside Bach Ma to upgrade the road to the summit; at the time of research only the lower reaches were open. Work is scheduled to finish sometime in 2013.

The national park, extended in 2008, stretches from the coast to the Annamite mountain range at the Lao border. More than 1400 species of plants, including many rare ferns and orchids, have been discovered here, representing a fifth of the flora of Vietnam. There are 132 mammals found in Bach Ma, three of which were only discovered in the 1990s: the antelope-like saola, Truong Son muntjac and the giant muntjac. Nine species of primates are also present, including small numbers of the rare red-shanked Douc langur. It's hoped wild elephants will return from the Lao side of the border.

As most of the park's resident mammals are nocturnal, sightings demand a great deal of effort and patience. Bird-watching is fantastic but you need to be up at dawn for the best chance of glimpsing some of the 358 species logged here, including the fabulous crested argus pheasant.

The **visitor centre** at the park entrance has a small exhibition on the park's flora and fauna, and hiking trail booklets. You can book village and bird-watching tours and English- or French-speaking guides (200,000d per day). Unexploded ordnance is still in the area, so stick to the trails. Cars and motorbikes are not permitted inside the national park.

Bach Ma is the wettest place in Vietnam, with the heaviest of the rain falling in October and November (and bringing out the leeches). It's not out of the question to visit then, but check road conditions first. The best time to visit Bach Ma is from February to September, particularly between March and June.

🛏 Sleeping & Eating

National Park GUESTHOUSES **$**

(🛈387 1330; bachmaeco@gmail.com; camp sites per person 10,000d, r with fan/air-con 180,000/270,000d) The park authority has a small camping ground and two functional guesthouses near the entrance, with basic twin-bed rooms that have en-suite bathrooms. Note that karaoke can be a part of the nocturnal park life.

There are also has four guesthouses and a hotel near the summit, but these are closed until 2013; one should reopen with a dorm. Give at least four hours' notice for meal requirements, as fresh food is brought up to the park on demand.

ℹ Getting There & Around

Bach Ma is 28km west of Lang Co and 40km southeast of Hue. The turn-off is signposted in the town of Cau Hai on Hwy 1. You can also enter from the town of Phu Loc.

From the visitor centre – when the road reopens – it's a steep, serpentine 16km up to the summit. Private transport is available from the visitor centre. Walking down from the summit takes about three to four hours; you'll need water and sunscreen.

Buses from Danang (38,000d, two hours) and Hue (22,000d, one hour) stop at Cau Hai, where *xe om* drivers can ferry you to the entrance. Cau Hai has a **train station** (Loc Dien village), but it's only served twice daily.

Suoi Voi (Elephant Springs)

About 15km north of Lang Co Beach, **Suoi Voi** (admission per person 10,000d, motorbike/car 3000/10,000d) is a secluded recreation area of crystal-clear waters and lush forest that's a good pit stop for those with their own wheels.

The main pool is ringed by huge boulders, one vaguely in the shape of an elephant's head and cosmetically enhanced to look more like it. Further exploration will lead to less-populated swimming holes.

Foreign visitors here are scarce and on weekdays you may have the whole place to yourself. Weekends and holidays are jam-packed with locals.

The turn-off to the springs from Hwy 1 is well signposted near the road markers reading 'Danang 52km' (if coming from the north) or 'Phu Bai 44km' (from the south). You'll see the 19th-century Thua Luu Church

just ahead of you. Keep the church on your left and follow the dirt road for 5km to the entry gate. Buy a ticket here and keep it in case you have to show it again. From here it's a bumpy 1.5km to the parking area.

There are some food stalls at the springs, but they're only open when the park is busy. It's better to bring a picnic.

Lang Co Beach

🛈054

Lang Co is an attractive island-like stretch of palm-shaded white sand, with a crystal-clear, turquoise lagoon on one side and 10km of beachfront on the other. Many open-tour buses make a lunch stop here and if the weather's nice, it's a fine place to hop off for a night or two. Swimming is best away from the central section where the sands could do with a clean-up.

The beach is best enjoyed between April and July. From late August till November rains are frequent, and from December to March it can get chilly.

🛏 Sleeping

Most of the accommodation is north of the town along the highway.

Vedana Lagoon RESORT HOTEL **$$$**

(🛈381 9397; www.vedanalagoon.com; Phu Loc; bungalows/villas from US$300/450; 🐾❄@🛜🏊) Combining contemporary chic with natural materials, this new commodious spa hotel has gorgeous villas and bungalows that boast thatched roofs, modish furnishings and outdoor bathrooms. Some have private pools, others jut out into the lagoon to maximise the views. The whole complex has been beautifully designed, and includes a wonderful wellness centre where you could spend many a happy day taking advantage of the massages and other treatments on offer after a morning of t'ai chi or yoga. Vedana is about 15km north of Lang Co near the town of Phu Loc. Check the website for special deals.

Lang Co Beach Resort RESORT HOTEL **$$**

(🛈387 3555; www.langcobeachresort.com.vn; s/d US$35/40, villas from US$100; ❄@🛜🏊) Yes, it's a large government-owned resort complex, but the accommodation is well-maintained, if a little unexciting, and the grounds are lovely. Beach-facing villas have large balconies and sea views, while the budget rooms are very cheap (from US$15) in winter.

Chi Na Guesthouse GUESTHOUSE **$**
(☑387 4597; s/d 140,000/160,000d; ☀) One of
several clean, basic guesthouses north of the
centre, but here the family speaks a little
English. Rooms are ageing but serviceable.

ℹ Getting There & Away

Lang Co is on the north side of the Hai Van Tunnel and Danang. Tourist buses pass through daily. However, those on two wheels will still need to take the 35km scenic route over the Hai Van Pass.

Lang Co's **train station** (☑387 4423) is 3km from the beach, in the direction of the lagoon. Getting a *xe om* to get you to the beach shouldn't be difficult. The train journey from here to Danang (24,000d, 1½ to two hours, four daily) is one of the most spectacular in Vietnam. Services also connect to Hue (41,000d, 1½ to two hours, three daily).

Hai Van Pass & Tunnel

The **Hai Van (Sea Cloud) Pass** crosses over a spur of the Truong Son mountain range that juts into the sea. About 30km north of Danang, the road climbs to an elevation of 496m, passing south of the Ai Van Son peak (1172m). It's an incredibly mountainous stretch of highway – you may have seen the spectacular views on BBC TV's *Top Gear* Vietnam special. The railway track, with its many tunnels, goes around the peninsula, following the beautiful and deserted shoreline.

In the 15th century this pass formed the boundary between Vietnam and the kingdom of Champa. Until the American War it was heavily forested. At the summit is a bullet-scarred French fort, later used as a bunker by the South Vietnamese and US armies.

If you cross in winter, the pass serves as something of a visible dividing line between the climates of the north and south, protecting Danang from the fierce 'Chinese winds' that sweep in from the northeast. From about November to March the exposed Lang Co side of the pass can be wet and chilly, while just to the south it's often warm and dry.

The top of the pass is the only place you can pull over for a while. The view is well worth it, but you'll have to fight off a rather large crowd of very insistent vendors and dodgy money changers.

In 2005 the 6280m-long **Hai Van Tunnel** opened, bypassing the pass and shaving an hour off the journey between Danang and Hue. Motorbikes and bicycles are not permitted in the tunnel but most cars and buses now take this route. Sure it saves time, but on a nice day it really is a shame to miss the views from the pass.

Despite the odd hair-raising encounter, the pass road is safer than it used to be. If you can take your eyes off the highway, keep them peeled for the small altars on the roadside – sobering reminders of those who have died in accidents on this winding route.

Ba Na Hill Station

☑0511 / ELEV 1485M

A hill resort inherited from the French, lush **Ba Na** (admission per person 10,000d, per motorbike/car 5000/10,000d) has refreshingly cool weather and gorgeous countryside views. Established in 1919, the resort area once held 200-odd villas, but only a few ruins remain.

Until WWII the French were carried up the last 20km of rough mountain road by sedan chair, but now a 5km (the world's longest) **cable car** system has really opened up access. The ride involves a vertical rise of almost 1300m, a truly spectacular trip over dense jungle. However, be warned that a tourism boom has resulted in a lot of ugly construction (and a serious garbage problem) once you get to the hill top.

Take an extra layer or two whatever time of year you visit – when it's 36°C on the coast, it could be 15°C on the mountain. Cloud and mist also cling to the hill top, so if you can, try to visit on a clear day.

Mountain tracks lead to **waterfalls** and viewing points. Near the top is the **Linh Ung Pagoda** (2004) and a colossal 24m-high white **seated Buddha** that's visible for miles around.

There's an ATM at Ga Suoi Mo, the (lowest) cable-car station. Up on the hill you can change money at the hotels.

🛏 Sleeping

All three hotels at the hill station are poor value for money despite recent renovations. It's best to see Ba Na on a day trip.

Indochine Hotel HOTEL **$$**
(☑379 1504; www.banahills.com.vn; r/villas 930,000/1,100,000d; ☀@☎) Formerly the Le Nim, this hotel combines a bizarre mix of French colonial and Champa architectural styles. Its rooms have been renovated but remain very average and overpriced. At least the views from its terraces and restaurant are sublime.

❶ Getting There & Away

Ba Na is 42km west of Danang. By far the best way to get to the hill station is via the new cable-car link (return 220,000d, 20 minutes), which is in two sections. There's a cafe at the central station. Note that the cable car can be suspended during heavy wind. Otherwise you can access Ba Na via a beautiful, very steep winding road that is tough unless you have a powerful motorbike. Locals offer rides for 80,000d.

Danang

📞 0511 / POP 901,000

Right about now Danang is Vietnam's most happening city. For decades it had a reputation as a slightly mundane provincial backwater, but big changes are afoot. Stroll along the Han riverfront and gleaming new modernist hotels, apartments and restaurants are emerging. Head up north and you'll find the landmark new D-City rising from the flatlands. Venture south and the entire China Beach strip has been set aside for five-star hotel developments. Oh, and for good measure, a revamped international airport should open in 2012.

That said, the city itself still has few conventional sightseeing spots, except for a very decent museum. So for most travellers, a few days off the tourist trail enjoying the city's restaurants and nightlife is probably enough. Danang also makes a great base for day trips. Perched on the western bank of the Han River, the city is part of a long thin peninsula, at the northern tip of which is Nui Son Tra (called Monkey Mountain by US soldiers). China Beach and the five Marble Mountains lie southwest of the city.

History

Known during French colonial rule as Tourane, Danang succeeded Hoi An as the most important port in central Vietnam during the 19th century, a position it retains to this day.

As American involvement in Vietnam escalated, Danang became the recipient of the first American combat troops in South Vietnam – 3500 Marines in March 1965. Memorably they stormed Nam O Beach in full battle gear, only to be greeted by a bevy of *ao dai*-wearing Vietnamese girls bearing cheerful flower garlands. A decade later, with the Americans and South Vietnamese in full retreat, the scene could not have been more different as desperate civilians fled the city. On 29 March 1975 two truckloads of communist guerrillas, more than half of them women, declared Danang liberated without firing a shot.

Today Danang has one of the most progressive local governments and most vibrant economies in Vietnam.

◎ Sights & Activities

Museum of Cham Sculpture   MUSEUM
(Map p182; 1 Đ Trung Nu Vuong; admission 30,000d; ⏰7am-5pm) This one's for the history buffs: a museum with the world's largest collection of Cham artefacts, housed in buildings that marry French-colonial architecture with Cham elements. Founded in 1915 by the École Française d'Extrême Orient, it has more than 300 pieces on display including altars, lingas, garudas, apsaras, Ganeshas and images of Shiva, Brahma and Vishnu – all dating from the 5th to 15th centuries.

The treasures come from Dong Duong (Indrapura), Khuong My, My Son, Tra Kieu and other sites. Note that the museum's organisation and English captions could be better so it's worth hiring a well-informed guide (or pick up one of the English-language guidebooks at the museum shop).

There are also exhibits focusing on Cham culture today, with a handful of contemporary artefacts and photos of the Kate Festival (the Cham New Year).

Cao Dai Temple   TEMPLE
(Map p182; 63 Đ Hai Phong) After Tay Ninh, this temple is the largest such structure in Vietnam, serving about 50,000 followers in central Vietnam. As with all Cao Dai temples, prayers are held four times a day, at 5.30am, 11.30am, 5.30pm and 11.30pm.

The left-hand gate to the complex is for women; the right-hand gate for men. The doors to the sanctuary are similarly segregated, although priests of either gender use the central door. Behind the main altar sits an enormous globe with the Cao Dai 'divine eye' symbol on it.

A sign reading *van giao nhat ly* (all religions have the same reason) hangs from the ceiling in front of the altar. Behind the gilded letters is a picture of the founders of five of the world's great religions. From left to right are Mohammed, Laotse (wearing Eastern Orthodox-style robes), Jesus, a Southeast Asian-looking Buddha and Confucius (looking as Chinese as could be).

FREE **Ho Chi Minh Museum**   MUSEUM
(Map p188; 3 Đ Nguyen Van Troi; ⏰7-11am & 1.30-4.30pm) Despite its huge grounds, this

Danang

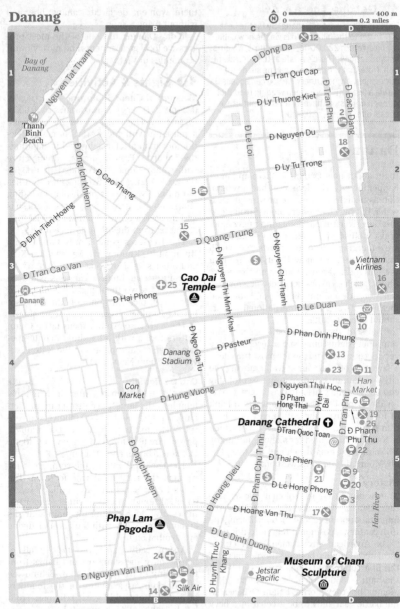

Bay of Danang

Thanh Binh Beach

Nguyen Tat Thanh

Đ Ong Ich Khiem
Đ Cao Thang
Đ Dinh Tien Hoang
Đ Tran Cao Van
Danang
Đ Hai Phong
Đ Dong Da
Đ Tran Qui Cap
Đ Ly Thuong Kiet
Đ Nguyen Du
Đ Le Loi
Đ Ly Tu Trong
Đ Tran Phu
Đ Bach Dang
Vietnam Airlines
Đ Quang Trung
Đ Nguyen Thi Minh Khai
Đ Nguyen Chi Thanh

Cao Dai Temple

Đ Le Duan
Đ Phan Dinh Phung
Đ Ngo Gia Tu
Đ Pasteur
Danang Stadium
Con Market
Đ Hung Vuong
Đ Nguyen Thai Hoc
Han Market
Đ Pham Hong Thai
Đ Yen Bai

Danang Cathedral

Đ Tran Quoc Toan
Đ Pham Phu Thu
Đ Ong Ich Khiem
Đ Hoang Dieu
Đ Phan Chu Trinh
Đ Thai Phien
Đ Le Hong Phong
Đ Hoang Van Thu

Phap Lam Pagoda

Đ Le Dinh Duong
Đ Huynh Thuc Khang
Jetstar Pacific

Museum of Cham Sculpture

Đ Nguyen Van Linh
Silk Air
Han River

museum is typically unenlightening for a site venerating Ho Chi Minh. At the front is a display of the usual US, Soviet and Chinese weaponry. Hidden behind the Party buildings are a replica of Ho Chi Minh's house in Hanoi and a museum about him.

The complex is not often visited by tourists, so you may be escorted by one of the staff.

Danang Cathedral　　　　CHURCH
(Map p182; Đ Tran Phu) Known to locals as Con Ga Church (Rooster Church) because

Danang

of the weathercock on top of the steeple, the candy-pink Danang Cathedral was built for the city's French residents in 1923. Today it serves a Catholic community of over 4000 – it's standing room only if you arrive late.

Mass is usually held from Monday to Saturday at 5.30am and 5.30pm, and on Sunday at 5.30am, 6.30am, 7.30am, 3.30pm and 5pm.

Phap Lam Pagoda PAGODA
(Map p182; 574 Đ Ong Ich Khiem; ⊙5-11.30am & 1-9.30pm) Recently rebuilt, this pagoda has three giant Buddha statues in the courtyard, and an equally imposing large gold one in the temple.

⌂ Sleeping

An excellent selection of new minihotels has opened along the riverside in central Danang, though good budget hotels aren't as easy to find. Hilton and Novotel hotels are under construction just north of Song Han bridge. For information on accommodation just across the river, see My Khe Beach.

TOP CHOICE New Moon Hotel HOTEL $$
(Map p182; ☑382 8488; info@newmoonhotel.vn; 126 Đ Bach Dang; r 300,000-800,000d; ❀@⌂) New in 2011, this small hotel offers unrivalled value for money, with a selection of beautifully finished rooms in different price

categories, all with flat-screen TV, minibar, wi-fi and inviting en-suite marble bathrooms. The river-view rooms are positioned right over the Han and have breathtaking vistas across fishing boats to the hills of Nui Son Tra. There's a lift and the helpful staff speak some English.

TOP CHOICE Rainbow Hotel HOTEL $$
(Map p182; ☑382 2216; www.rainbowhotel.com.vn; 220 Đ Bach Dang; r 450,000-600,000d; ❀@⌂) A spanking new minihotel with a prime riverfront location, the Rainbow is a hip hotel with a budget price tag. There's a lift and an inviting lobby, and you'll love the rooms, which have contemporary decor and flooring, artwork, modern furniture and all mod cons. Floor-to-ceiling plate-glass windows make the most of the inspirational vistas in the river-view rooms.

Winn Hotel HOTEL $
(Map p182; ☑388 8571; ngockhanh_nk@yahoo .com; 36 Hung Vuong; r US$17-20; ❀@⌂) Another new place, this excellent little hotel has 15 modern rooms, painted white and pale pink, all with a good TV and in-room wi-fi. The cheaper options don't have windows, but are still pretty light and airy thanks to their high ceilings.

HAGL Plaza Hotel Da Nang HOTEL $$$
(Map p182; ☑222 3344; 1 Đ Nguyen Vanh Linh; r US$95-140, ste US$365; ⊖❀@⌂⊠) This tower

hotel has quickly established itself as the city's number one choice for business (and luxury-leisure) travellers thanks to the efficient, welcoming service and facilities. The sleek modern rooms are huge and very well appointed, the restaurants and top-floor bar are great, and there's a complimentary airport shuttle-bus service.

Sun River Hotel
HOTEL $$
(Map p182; ☎384 9188; www.sunriverhoteldn.com.vn; 132-134 Đ Bach Dang; r 850,000-1,400,000d; ❄@🛜) A tempting option, this riverfront hotel offers immaculate modish rooms with really sleek bathrooms (though the standard -class options do not have windows and only the VIPs have a river view). Check out the top-floor restaurant for a commanding perspective of the city and Han river.

Green Plaza Hotel
HOTEL $$$
(Map p182; ☎322 3399; www.greenplazahotel.vn; 238 Đ Bach Dang; s US$83, d US$90-183, ste US$246; ❄@🛜❄) This landmark riverside hotel offers a prestigious address in the heart of town, a good gym and a 12m pool with city views. Rooms, most with balcony, have attractive rattan furniture, huge beds and contemporary bathrooms.

Bao Ngoc Hotel
HOTEL $
(Map p182; ☎381 7711; baongochotel@dng.vnn.vn; 48 Đ Phan Chu Trinh; r US$18-22; ❄@🛜) Incredibly spacious, carpeted and comfortable rooms full of solid, dark-wood furniture and some with sofas. The ageing five-storey building also retains a glint of colonial character, with its chocolate-brown French-style shutters.

Prince Hotel
HOTEL $$
(Map p182; ☎381 7929; princehotel2009@yahoo.com; 60 Đ Tran Phu; r 350,000-550,000d; ❄@🛜) All but the cheapest rooms are very spacious and well-appointed at this good-value downtown Danang minihotel. Those at the rear of the building have tiny windows.

Elegant Hotel
HOTEL $$
(Map p182; ☎389 2893; elegant@dng.vnn.vn; 22a Đ Bach Dang; r US$32-70, ste US$70-80; ❄@🛜) A long-running place at the north end of the riverfront near the port. The carpeted rooms here are well maintained, though a little perfunctory. The 6th-floor restaurant's panoramic perspective makes it a fab location for your complimentary breakfast.

Stargazer Hotel
HOTEL $$
(Map p182; ☎381 5599; www.stargazer.net; 77 Đ Tran Phu; r 350,000-600,000d; ❄@🛜) The

lobby is a little underwhelming but the very neat, if smallish rooms here are in excellent shape, with attractive wood furniture, large TVs and comfy beds with duvets. Number 301 has a balcony and river view. The owner is very helpful and speaks fluent English.

Hai Van Hotel
HOTEL $
(Map p182; ☎382 3750; kshaivan.dng@vnn.vn; 2 Đ Nguyen Thi Minh Khai; s/d US$12/19; ❄) It's never going to win a design award, but this old-fashioned place has functional spacious rooms that represent a reasonable deal.

Phu An Hotel
HOTEL $
(Map p182; ☎382 5708; phuanhoteldng@gmail.com; 29 Đ Nguyen Van Linh; s 240,000d, d 275,000-300,000d; ❄@🛜) Big rooms with modern bathrooms, but those at the front suffer traffic noise.

🍴 Eating

Danang has a very lively street-food scene, and it's hard to find a street in town that doesn't have a resident *bun cha* (barbecued pork), *com* (rice) or *mi quang* (noodle soup) stall. There are also some vegetarian eateries. The dining scene is flourishing, with a number of good restaurants popping up across town.

🏆 Waterfront
TOP CHOICE
INTERNATIONAL $$
(Map p182; ☎384 3373; www.waterfrontdanang.com; 150-152 Đ Bach Dang; meals 90,000-300,000d; ⏱10am-11pm) This outstanding new riverfront lounge-cum-restaurant has really helped put Danang on the map. The building itself is astonishing, a faultlessly styled concrete shell complete with hip seating, a sweeping bar and small garden terrace. Upstairs you'll find a superb restaurant – book the terrace deck for a stunning river vista. Gourmet sandwiches are immense, light snacks like salt 'n' pepper calamari are delicious – or get stuck into the à la carte menu. It's not so hip that it's pretentious, and operates both as a casual bar, where you can read a copy of the *Economist* or *CNN Traveller* and sink a few cold beers, and destination restaurant for a special meal.

Red Sky
INTERNATIONAL $$
(Map p182; Đ 248 Tran Phu; meals 80,000-200,000d; ⏱11.30am-10.30pm) This casual bar-restaurant scores highly for Western grub, including good-value steaks, pork chops, generous salads, chicken wings and Italian food; the Vietnamese dishes are also reliable. The beer is cheap (Larue is just 15,000d)

and happy hour (5pm to 8pm) is very popular. You'll find the well-trained staff are attentive and welcoming.

Vietnamese Home VIETNAMESE, INTERNATIONAL $$
(Map p182; 34 Đ Bach Dang; meals 50,000-250,000đ) Something of an institution, this rustic-style restaurant has a huge open courtyard and adjoining dining rooms. The menu takes in lots of seafood (including steamboats), meat (try the pork with chilli and citronella), noodles and soup. There's an extensive wine list and it's also a good bet for a filling Western breakfast.

Phi Lu Chinese Restaurant CHINESE $$
(Map p188; ☎361 1888; 1-3 Đ 2/9; dishes 42,000-430,000đ) This large formal place is decked out in Chinese style including red lanterns at night. It's excellent for seafood and there are two other branches in town.

Memory Lounge INTERNATIONAL, VIETNAMESE $$$
(Map p182; www.loungememory.com; 7 Đ Bach Dang; meals 120,000-400,000đ; ⊘closed Sun) This landmark new bar-restaurant juts into the river, right by the Song Han bridge. The ambitious East-meets-West menu has healthy snack (dishes around 60,000đ), dinner and VIP options (poached salmon fillet with chunky prawn sauce, black-olive potato, baked artichoke and spinach foam is 250,000đ). It also boasts a decadent cocktail list and a great terrace to sip them from.

Bread of Life INTERNATIONAL $
(Map p182; www.breadoflifedanang.com; 4 Đ Dong Da; meals 40,000-100,000đ; ⊘closed Sun) Although in a new location, this American-style diner-cum-bakery's menu of pancakes, burgers, sandwiches, pizza and other comfort foods remains as familiar and popular as ever. Run by deaf staff, proceeds go towards training activities for the deaf in Danang (see the boxed text, p200).

Le Bambino INTERNATIONAL $$
(Map p182; ☎389 6386; www.lebambino.com; 122/11 Đ Quang Trung; meals 120,000-300,000đ) A delightful European oasis run by a couple (French husband, Vietnamese wife) who have crafted a great menu that takes in French classics, pub food, barbecued meat (try the ribs) and Vietnamese favourites. There are well-appointed rooms (US$30) upstairs too.

Com Nieu VIETNAMESE $
(Map p182; 25 Đ Yen Bai; dishes 14,000-120,000đ) A contemporary restaurant that offers a wide choice of tasty Vietnamese fare, including succulent seafood and the clay pot rice signature dish.

Com Tay Cam Cung Dinh VIETNAMESE $
(Map p182; K254/2 Đ Hoang Dieu; most dishes 15,000-40,000đ) This simple place is good for local dishes including *hoanh thanh* – a wonton-like combination of minced pork and shrimp. It's down a little alley.

🍸 Drinking

For a lounge-bar-style drink with a view, also check out Waterfront and Memory Lounge.

Le Funk BAR
(Map p182; 166 Đ Bach Dang) This lively hole-in-the-wall is a great bet early in the evening when Danang's young hipsters gather here. The genial French owner is a DJ, so expect pumping house and dance tunes.

Tulip Brewery BAR
(Map p188; 174 Đ 2/9) Huge Czech-style brewery pub (with vats proudly on display) that draws the locals in their hundreds. Lager-style and dark beer on tap, plus a menu of Western and Vietnamese dishes.

Tam's Pub & Surf Shop BAR
(Map p188; 38 An Thuong 5) A stone's throw from China Beach, this is a friendly, popular bar-restaurant with inexpensive grub. As the name suggests you can rent boards (US$5 per day) and get advice here.

Chillout Cafe BAR
(Map p182; 36 Đ Thai Phien) This hospitable Vietnamese-Western-owned place has a relaxed atmosphere, filling food, quiz nights, book exchange and great local information.

Bamboo 2 Bar BAR
(Map p182; 230 Đ Bach Dang) Your standard-issue expat bar with a regular clientele and a busy pool table. It's slightly staid, though fine for a low-key drink.

ℹ️ Information

Internet Access

Danang has hundreds of internet cafes. For 24-hour access, try **Skynet** (Map p182; 172 Đ Tran Phu; per hr 7000đ).

Medical Services

Danang Family Medical Practice (Map p182; ☎358 2700; www.vietnammedicalpractice.com; 50-52 Đ Nguyen Van Linh) Set up like a minihospital with in-patient facilities, this is an excellent practice run by an Australian doctor.

CENTRAL VIETNAM DANANG

Hospital C (Map p182; Benh Vien C; ☑382 1483; 122 Đ Hai Phong) The most advanced of the four hospitals in town.

Money

Agribank (Map p182; 202 Đ Nguyen Chi Thanh) ATM and exchange service.

Vietcombank (Map p182; 140 Đ Le Loi) The only bank that changes travellers cheques.

Post

Main post office (Map p182; 64 Đ Bach Dang)

Travel Agencies

Dana Tours (Map p182; ☑382 5653; 76 Đ Hung Vuong; ☺closed Sun) Offers competitive rates for car rentals, boat trips, visa extensions and day trips.

Sinh Tourist (Map p182; ☑384 3258; www.the sinhtourist.vn; 154 Đ Bach Dang) Books open-tour buses and tours and offers currency exchange.

Trong's Real Easy Riders (☑0903 597 971; www.easyridersvietnam.wordpress.com) A motorbike collective that operates out of Danang. Day trips (from US$20) or tours to Hoi An and the central highlands are offered.

Websites

Check out www.indanang.com for up-to-date reviews and information about the city.

❶ Getting There & Away

AIR Danang's only scheduled international connection at the time of research was **Silk Air** (☑356 2708; www.silkair.com; HAGL Plaza Hotel, 1 Đ Nguyen Van Linh) flights (four per week) to Singapore, but expect more routes to open when the new airport terminal opens in 2012. For domestic connections, **Jetstar Pacific** (Map p182; ☑358 3538; www.jetstar.com; 307 Đ Phan Chu Trinh) has daily flights from Danang to HCMC and Hanoi, while **Vietnam Airlines** (Map p182; ☑382 1130; www.vietnamairlines.com; 35 Đ Tran Phu) operates direct flights to Hanoi, HCMC, Haiphong, Buon Ma Thuot and Nha Trang.

BUS Danang's newish **intercity bus station** (Map p188; Đ Dien Bien Phu) is 3km west of the city centre. A metered taxi to the riverside will cost around 60,000d.

Buses leave for all major centres, including Quy Nhon (72,000d to 125,000d, six hours, four daily).

For Laos, there are three weekly services to Savannakhet at 8pm (130,000d, 14 hours), crossing the border at Lao Bao. There's also a daily service to Pakse at 6.30am (190,000d, 14 hours). Buses to the Lao Bao border alone are 95,000d (six hours); you may have to change buses at Dong Ha.

Yellow public buses to Hoi An (18,000d, one hour, hourly) travel along Đ Tran Phu in the heart of town; overcharging is common on this route.

With a booking, the Sinh Tourist open-tour buses will pick up from the company office twice daily en route to Hue (70,000d, 2½ hours), Hoi An (60,000d, one hour) and Hanoi (300,000d, 14 hours).

CAR & MOTORCYCLE A car to Hoi An costs around 330,000d via your hotel or a local travel agency, while *xe om* will do it for around 120,000d. Bargain hard if you want to stop at the Marble Mountains or China Beach en route.

TRAIN Danang's **train station** (Map p182; 202 Đ Hai Phong) has services to all destinations on the north–south main line.

The train ride to Hue is one of the best in the country – it's worth taking as an excursion in itself.

❶ Getting Around

TO/FROM THE AIRPORT Danang's airport is 2km west of the city centre, close enough to reach by *xe om* in 10 minutes (40,000d). A metered taxi costs about 55,000d.

DANANG TRANSPORT CONNECTIONS

DESTINATION	AIR	BUS	CAR/MOTORBIKE	TRAIN
HCMC	from US$35, 1hr, 4 daily	US$20-34, 19-25hr, 7 daily	18hr	US$25-49, 17-23hr, 5 daily
Nha Trang	from US$28, 30min, 1 daily	US$16-23, 10-13hr, 7 daily	13hr	US$15-28, 9-12hr, 5 daily
Hue	n/a	US$3, 3hr, every 20min	2½-4hr	US$3-6, 2½-4hr, 8 daily
Dong Hoi	n/a	US$7-12, 6½hr, 5 daily	6-7hr	US$8-16, 5½-8½hr, 6 daily
Hanoi	from US$38, 1hr, 3 daily	US$22-31, 16-19hr, 7 daily	19hr	US$22-43, 15½-21hr, 6 daily

CYCLO & XE OM Danang has plenty of motor-bike taxis and *cyclo* drivers; as usual, be prepared to bargain. Trips around town shouldn't cost more than 10,000d to 15,000d. Be careful of *xe om* drivers at night offering to take you to bars/girls – you may find yourself heavied into parting with hundreds of dollars.

TAXI If you need a metered taxi use **Mai Linh** (☏356 5656).

Around Danang
☏0511

NUI SON TRA (MONKEY MOUNTAIN)
ELEV 850M

Jutting out into the sea like a giant pair of Mickey Mouse ears, the Son Tra peninsula is crowned by the mountain that the American soldiers called Monkey. Grandly overlooking Danang to the south and the Hai Van Pass to the north, it was a prized radar and communications base during the war. Until recently it was a closed military area (and virtually untouched except for the port Cang Tien Sa), but new roads and beach resorts are slowly opening.

The highlight of visiting Monkey Mountain is the view from the **summit**, which is stupendous on a clear day. What remains of the American military presence are a couple of radar domes (still used by the Vietnamese military and a no-go for tourists) next to a helicopter pad, now a lookout point. The steep road to the summit is pretty deserted and road conditions can be iffy. If you're going on a motorbike, you'll need a powerful one to make it to the top. The turn-off to this road is about 3km before Tien Sa Port and marked by a blue sign that reads 'Son Tra Eco-Tourism'.

Most Vietnamese who come here head to one of the beach resorts along the peninsula's southwestern coast. The other big attraction on the peninsula is **Linh Ung**, a colossal new Buddha statue positioned on a lotus-shaped platform that looks south to Danang city; there's a monastery here too. Eventually you should be able to complete a loop of the peninsula; when completed, the road will make an incredibly scenic drive.

On the other side of Nui Son Tra, next to the port, is sheltered **Tien Sa Beach**. A memorial near the port commemorates an unfortunate episode of colonial history. Spanish-led Filipino and French troops attacked Danang in August 1858, ostensibly to end Emperor Tu Duc's mistreatment of Catholics. The city quickly fell, but the invaders were hit by cholera, dysentery, scurvy, typhus and mysterious fevers. By the summer of 1859, the number of invaders who had died of illness was 20 times the number who had been killed in combat.

Many of the **tombs of Spanish and French soldiers** are below a chapel that's located behind Tien Sa Port.

🛏 Sleeping & Eating
There's not much choice at the moment, but new places are under construction, including a five-star resort.

Bien Dong Resort RESORT $$
(☏392 4464; www.biendongresortdanang.com; Son Tra; US$34-39; ❄@❅) Nestled in an attractive cove beach that's sheltered from cool northerly winds, this well-maintained resort has a cluster of spacious bungalows with wooden decor, two swimming pools and a restaurant.

Bay Ban SEAFOOD $$
(☏221 4237; Son Tra; meals 80,000-250,000d) Large, highly authentic seafood restaurant that's very popular with Vietnamese families on weekends and during holiday season, but usually quiet the rest of the time. Eat right over the water in one of the thatched shelters in the bay. There are all kinds of delicious fresh fish, spider crab, eel and shrimp dishes.

NAM O BEACH
Nam O Beach, 15km northwest of the city, was where the first US combat troops landed in South Vietnam in 1965. Today it's reverted to a more humble form. There are a few hotels here, but the beach is not as attractive as those south of Danang.

Nam O village used to support itself by producing firecrackers until the government imposed a ban on them in 1995. Now the villagers make *nuoc mam* (fish sauce) and *goi ca*. The latter is a kind of Vietnamese sushi: fresh, raw fish fillets marinated in a special sauce and coated in a spicy powder. It's served with fresh vegetables on rice-paper rolls. You'll find it for sale on the beach in summer or look for it in the village.

MARBLE MOUNTAINS
Just off the China Beach coastal road, the **Marble Mountains** (Ngu Hanh Son) consist of five craggy marble outcrops topped with pagodas. Each mountain is named for the natural element it's said to represent: Thuy Son (Water), Moc Son (Wood), Hoa Son (Fire), Kim Son (Metal or Gold) and Tho

Around Danang

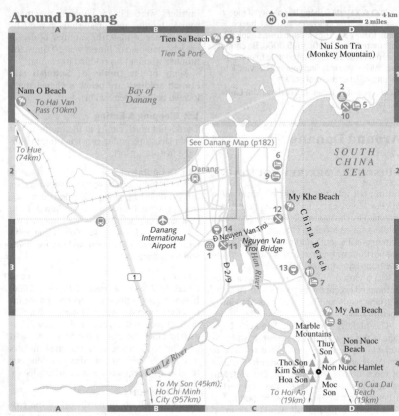

Tien Sa Beach 🚻 ♨ 3

Tien Sa Port

Nui Son Tra
(Monkey Mountain)

Nam O Beach
🚻 To Hai Van
Pass (10km)

Bay of
Danang

2
⛽🏨 5
10

To Hue
(74km)

See Danang Map (p182)

Danang
🚉

6

9 🏨

SOUTH
CHINA
SEA

My Khe Beach

12 🍴

Danang
International
Airport

14
Đ Nguyen Van Troi
11

Nguyen Van
Troi Bridge

1

China Beach

1

Đ 2/9

13 🏨

4
🏨
7

My An Beach

8

Marble
Mountains

Thuy
Son

Non Nuoc
Beach

Tho Son
Kim Son
Hoa Son

Non Nuoc Hamlet

Moc
Son

To My Son (45km);
Ho Chi Minh
City (957km)

To Hoi An
(19km)

To Cua Dai
Beach
(19km)

Cam Le River

Han River

Son (Earth). The villages that have sprung up at the base of the mountains specialise in marble sculpture, though they now astutely use marble from China rather than hacking away at the mountains that bring the visitors (and buyers) in.

Thuy Son (admission 15,000d; ⏱7am-5pm) is the largest and most famous of the five mountains, with a number of natural caves in which first Hindu and later Buddhist sanctuaries have been created. Of the two paths heading up the mountain, the one closer to the beach (at the end of the village) makes for a better circuit.

At the top of the staircase is a gate, **Ong Chon**, which is pockmarked with bullet holes. Behind it, a path heads through two tunnels to caverns that contain several Buddhas and Cham carvings. A flight of steps also leads up to another cave, partially open to the sky, with two seated Buddhas in it.

Immediately to the left as you enter Ong Chon Gate is the main path to the rest of Thuy Son, beginning with **Xa Loi Pagoda**, a beautiful stone tower that overlooks the coast. Stairs off the main pathway lead to **Vong Hai Da**, a viewing point that would yield a brilliant panorama of China Beach if it weren't so untended. The stone-paved path continues to the right and into a minigorge. On the left is **Van Thong Cave**, opposite which is a cement Buddha.

Exit the gorge through a battle-scarred masonry gate. There's a rocky path to the right leading to **Linh Nham**, a tall chimney-shaped cave with a small altar inside. Nearby, another path leads to **Hoa Nghiem**, a shallow cave with a Buddha. Left of here is cathedral-like **Huyen Khong Cave**, lit by an opening to the sky. The entrance to this spectacular chamber is guarded by two administrative mandarins (to the left of the doorway) and two military mandarins (to the right).

Around Danang

Scattered about the cave are Buddhist and Confucian shrines; note the inscriptions carved into the stone walls. On the right a door leads to a chamber with two stalactites – during the American War this was used as a VC field hospital. Inside is a plaque dedicated to the Women's Artillery Group, which destroyed 19 US aircraft from a base below the mountains in 1972.

Back on the main path, just to the left of the masonry gate, is **Tam Thai Tu Pagoda**. A path heading obliquely to the right goes to the monks' residence, or take the stairs on the left to **Vong Giang Dai**, which offers a fantastic view of the other Marble Mountains.

A torch (flashlight) is handy but not essential for exploring the caves. The gradient of the walk is quite comfortable, but whichever end you start at, the ascent up the mountain begins with a fairly strenuous climb.

Local buses between Danang and Hoi An (tickets 18,000d) can drop you at Marble Mountains, 10km south of Danang.

CHINA BEACH

Thanks to the eponymous TV series, China Beach will forever be associated with pretty young military nurses complaining about their love lives to the accompaniment of the Rolling Stones' *Paint It Black*. During the war the Americans used the name to refer to the beautiful 30km swoop of fine white sand that starts at Monkey Mountain and ends near Hoi An. The part they were most familiar with was the area close to Danang where soldiers stationed all over the country would be sent for some R&R. For some, a picnic on the beach was their last meal before returning to combat.

The Vietnamese call sections of the beach by different names, including My Khe, My An, Non Nuoc, An Bang and Cua Dai. The northernmost stretch, My Khe, is now basically a suburb of Danang, while in the far south Cua Dai is widely considered Hoi An's beach. The area in between has been carved up among the likes of the Raffles, Hyatt and other five-star brands, with swanky beach resorts under construction and leaving only a pitiful stretch of beach open to the public. Of course, how they'll fill all those ritzy rooms is another matter.

The best time for swimming at China Beach is from May to July, when the sea is at its calmest. At other times the water can get rough. Be warned that lifeguards only patrol some sections of the beach.

The surf can be very good from around mid-September to December, particularly in the morning when wind conditions are right.

⊙ Sights & Activities

My Khe BEACH
Just across the Song Han Bridge (10,000d by *xe om*), My Khe is fast becoming Danang's easternmost suburb. In the early morning and evening the beach fills up with city folk doing t'ai chi. Tourists emerge during peak sun-tanning hours, while locals start showing up in the evening. Despite its popularity, the beach is still blessedly free of roaming vendors and the only thing you might be coaxed to purchase is time on a lounger (15,000d).

The water has a dangerous undertow, especially in winter. However, it's protected by the bulk of Nui Son Tra and is safer than the rest of China Beach.

My An & Non Nuoc BEACHES
Much of the central section of China Beach has been blocked off for new resort developments, but there are a few existing hotels that are good for avoiding the weekend rush at My Khe Beach. **Da Boys Surf Shop** (www .daboyssurf.com; Furama Resort, 68 Đ Ho Xuong Huong, My An) sells quality surfboards, boogie

boards and paddle boards and offers surf instruction.

🛏 Sleeping & Eating

There's no beachfront accommodation here, but all of these places are just a short stroll from the sea. Locals head here for seafood and sea breezes (ocean winds, that is, not cocktails).

TOP CHOICE Eena Hotel   HOTEL $

(222 5123; www.geocities.jp/eenahotel; Khu An Cu 3, My Khe; s/d/tw US$14/19/24; ❋@🛜) Eena offers astonishing value. This Japanese-owned minihotel has immaculately clean, light, spacious, white rooms, some with sea or mountain views, all with firm beds. There's a lift, fast wi-fi, friendly English-speaking staff and a good complimentary breakfast (Japanese, Vietnamese or Western).

Jimmy Hotel   HOTEL $$

(394 5888; www.jimmyhoteldanang.com.vn; Lot F 18, An Cu No 3, My Khe; s US$22, d US$30-40; ❋@🛜) Step past the chintzy foyer at Jimmy Hotel and you'll find 30 decent, if unexceptional rooms with flat-screen TV and minibar, and en suites with either a fancy shower unit or bath-tub.

Fusion Maia   HOTEL $$$

(3967999; www.fusionmaiadanang.com; Đ Truong Sa, Khue My Beach; ste/villas from US$305/520; ⊕❋@🛜🏊) An intriguing new contemporary hotel right on the beach with an outstanding spa, where all guests get access to unlimited treatments. And what a spa it is, one of Asia's most impressive: a magnificent wellness zone with 16 treatment rooms, saunas and steam rooms set around a courtyard-style garden that even has an artificial waterfall. Suites and villas don't disappoint either: all boast minimalist decor, private pool, music-loaded iPods and even an espresso machine. Thoughtful touches (you can have breakfast any time of day you like) complete the experience.

Hoa's Place   GUESTHOUSE $

(396 9216; hoasplace@hotmail.com; 215/14 Đ Huyen Tran Cong Chua, My An Beach; r U$8) A very hospitable owner, who cooks great meals, and a sociable vibe are the plus points at Hoa's Place, a humble guesthouse just off the beach. List bare-bones rooms with wafer-thin mattresses in the minus column. You'll find a few beat-up surfboards for rent. Get in touch before you turn up, as resort development plans may close this place in the next year or two.

Van Xuan   SEAFOOD $

(233a Đ Nguyen Van Thoai, My Khe; dishes 25,000-125,000d; ☺lunch & dinner) Offers a pleasant garden setting for tasty seafood (and crocodile) dishes, and it also serves its own Czech-style microbrew, Five Mountains Beer.

ℹ Getting There & Around

The My Khe section of China Beach is just 3km or so east of central Danang and costs around 20,000/35,000d by *xe om*/taxi.

Hoi An

📞0510 / POP 131,000

Graceful historic Hoi An is Vietnam's most atmospheric and delightful town. Once a major port, it boasts the grand architecture and beguiling riverside setting that befits its heritage, but the 21st-century curses of traffic and pollution are almost entirely absent. Whether you've as little as a day or as long as a month in the town, it'll be time well spent.

Hoi An owes its easygoing provincial demeanour and remarkably harmonious old-town character more to luck than planning. Had the Thu Bon River not silted up in the late 19th century – so ships could no longer access the town's docks – Hoi An would doubtless be very different today. For a century, the city's allure and importance dwindled until an abrupt rise in fortunes in the 1990s, when a tourism boom transformed the local economy. Today Hoi An is once again a cosmopolitan melting pot, one of the nation's most wealthy towns, a culinary mecca and one of Vietnam's most important tourism centres.

This revival of fortunes has preserved the face of the Old Town and its incredible legacy of tottering Japanese merchant houses, Chinese temples and ancient tea warehouses – though, of course, residents and rice fields have been gradually replaced by tourist businesses. Lounge bars, boutique hotels, travel agents and a glut of tailor shops are very much part of the scene here. And yet, down by the market and over on neighbouring An Hoi Peninsula and Cam Nam Island you'll find life has changed little. Travel a few kilometres further – you'll find some superb bicycle, motorbike and boat trips – and some of central Vietnam's most enticing, bucolic scenery and beaches are within easy reach.

History

The earliest evidence of human habitation here dates back 2200 years: excavated

WATERWORLD

Hoi An's riverside location makes it particularly vulnerable to flooding during the rainy season (October and November). It's common for the waterfront to be hit by sporadic floods of about 1m and a typhoon can bring levels of 2m or more. In late 2006 and 2007 the town experienced some of the worst flooding in recent history.

ceramic fragments are thought to belong to the late Iron Age Sa Huynh civilisation, which is related to the Dong Son culture of northern Vietnam. From the 2nd to the 10th centuries, this was a busy seaport of the Champa kingdom, and archaeologists have found the foundations of numerous Cham towers around Hoi An.

In 1307 the Cham king presented Quang Nam province as a gift when he married a Vietnamese princess. When his successor refused to recognise the deal, fighting broke out and for the next century chaos reigned. By the 15th century peace was restored, allowing commerce to resume. During the next four centuries Hoi An – also known as Faifoo to Western traders – held sway as one of Southeast Asia's major international ports. Chinese, Japanese, Dutch, Portuguese, Spanish, Indian, Filipino, Indonesian, Thai, French, British and American ships came to call, and the town's warehouses teemed with the treasures of the Orient: high-grade silk (for which the area is famous), fabrics, paper, porcelain, tea, sugar, molasses, areca nuts, pepper, Chinese medicines, elephant tusks, beeswax, mother-of-pearl, lacquer, sulphur and lead.

Chinese and Japanese traders in particular left their mark on Hoi An. Both groups came in the spring, driven south by monsoon winds. They would stay in Hoi An until the summer, when southerly winds would blow them home. During their four-month sojourn in Hoi An, they rented waterfront houses for use as warehouses and living quarters. Some began leaving full-time agents in Hoi An to take care of their off-season business affairs.

The Japanese ceased coming to Hoi An after 1637 (when the Japanese government forbade contact with the outside world), but the Chinese lingered. The town's Chinese assembly halls still play a special role for southern Vietnam's ethnic Chinese, some of whom come from all over the region to participate in congregation-wide celebrations.

This was also the first place in Vietnam to be exposed to Christianity. Among the 17th-century missionary visitors was Alexandre de Rhodes, who devised the Latin-based *quoc ngu* script for the Vietnamese language.

Although Hoi An was almost completely destroyed during the Tay Son Rebellion, it was rebuilt and continued to be an important port until the late 19th century, when the Thu Bon River silted up. Danang (Tourane) took over as the region's main port.

Under French rule Hoi An served as an administrative centre. It was virtually untouched in the American War, thanks to the cooperation of both sides. The town was declared a Unesco World Heritage site in 1999 and today there are very strict rules in place to safeguard the Old Town's unique heritage.

◉ Sights

By Unesco decree more than 800 historical buildings in Hoi An have been preserved, so much of the **Old Town** (www.hoianworldheritage.org.vn; tickets 90,000d) looks as it did several centuries ago.

The Chinese who settled in Hoi An, like their counterparts in other parts of Asia, identified themselves according to their province of origin. Each community built its own assembly hall, known as *hoi quan* in Vietnamese, for social gatherings, meetings and celebrations.

All the old houses except Diep Dong Nguyen and Quan Thang now offer short guided tours. Efficient but sometimes coming across as perfunctory, you'll be whisked to a heavy wooden chair while your guide recites a carefully scripted introduction to the house, and given a souvenir soft sell. You're free to wander around the house after the tour.

One downside to putting these old houses on show is that what were once living spaces now seem dead and museum-like, the family having sequestered itself away from visitors' eyes. Huge tour groups can completely spoil the intimacy of the experience too, as they jostle for photo opportunities. They don't hang around for long though, so it's worth returning a little later when you can enjoy the building in peace.

Hoi An

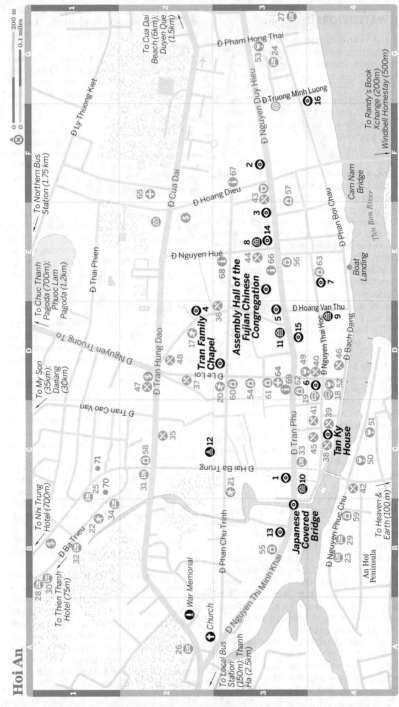

200 m
0.1 miles

To Cua Dai Beach (6km); Duyen Que (1.5km)

Đ Pham Hong Thai

Đ Nguyen Duy Hieu

Đ Truong Minh Luong

To Randy's Book Xchange (200m); Windbell Homestay (500m)

To Northern Bus Station (1.75km)

Đ Ly Thuong Kiet

Đ Cua Dai

Đ Hoang Dieu

Đ Nguyen Hue

Thu Bon River

Cam Nam Bridge

Boat Landing

Đ Phan Boi Chau

Đ Thai Phien

To Chuc Thanh Pagoda (700m); Phuoc Lam Pagoda (1.2km)

Assembly Hall of the Fujian Chinese Congregation

Đ Hoang Van Thu

To My Son (35km); Danang (30km)

Đ Nguyen Truong To

Tran Family Chapel

Đ Tran Hung Dao

Đ Le Loi

Đ Nguyen Thai Hoc

Đ Bach Dang

To Nhi Trung Hotel (700m)

Đ Tran Cao Van

Đ Hai Ba Trung

Đ Tran Phu

Tan Ky House

To Thien Thanh Hotel (75m)

Đ Phan Chu Trinh

Japanese Covered Bridge

Đ Ba Trieu

Đ Nguyen Thi Minh Khai

War Memorial

Đ Nguyen Phuc Chu

To Heaven & Earth (100 m)

An Hoi Peninsula

To Local Bus Station (150m); Thanh Ha (2.5km)

Church

Hoi An

All four museums are small. Displays are pretty basic and the information provided minimal.

Eighteen of these buildings are open to visitors and require an Old Town ticket for admission; the fee goes towards funding conservation work. Buying a ticket at any of the Old Town booths is easy enough; planning your visit around the byzantine admission options is another matter. Each ticket allows you to visit five different heritage attractions: museums, assembly halls, ancient houses and a traditional music show at the Handicraft Workshop. Tickets are valid for three days.

Most buildings are scrupulous about collecting ticket stubs, and one hopes that the fees go towards restoration and preservation. At lunchtime many houses and halls are closed, though the museums stay open.

Despite the number of tourists who flood into Hoi An, it is still a conservative town. Visitors should dress modestly, especially since some of the old houses are still private homes.

FREE **Japanese Covered Bridge**   BRIDGE
(Cau Nhat Ban) This beautiful little bridge has become a modern-day icon of Hoi An. A bridge was first constructed on this site in the 1590s by the Japanese community in order to link them with the Chinese quarters across the stream.

The bridge is very solidly constructed because the original builders were concerned about the threat of earthquakes. Over the centuries the ornamentation has remained relatively faithful to the original understated Japanese design. The French flattened out the roadway for their motor vehicles, but the original arched shape was restored in 1986.

The entrances to the bridge are guarded by weathered statues: a pair of monkeys on one side, a pair of dogs on the other. According to one story, many of Japan's emperors were born in the years of the dog and monkey. Another tale says that construction of the bridge started in the year of the monkey and was finished in the year of the dog. The stelae, listing all Vietnamese and Chinese contributors to a subsequent restoration of the bridge, are written in *chu nho* (Chinese characters) – the *nom* script had not yet become popular.

While access to the Japanese Bridge is free, you have to surrender a ticket to see a small, not very impressive **temple** (Chua Cau; admission by Hoi An Old Town ticket) built into the bridge's northern side. According to legend, there once lived an enormous monster called Cu that had its head in India, its tail in Japan and its body in Vietnam. Whenever the monster moved, terrible disasters befell Vietnam. The bridge was built on the monster's weakest point and killed it, but the people of Hoi An took pity and built this temple to pray for its soul. The writing over the temple door is the name given to the bridge in 1719: Lai Vien Kieu (Bridge for Passers-by from Afar). However it never quite caught on.

Assembly Hall of the Fujian Chinese Congregation   TEMPLE
(Phuc Kien Hoi Quan; opposite 35 Đ Tran Phu; admission by Old Town ticket; ⊘7am-5.30pm) What began as a traditional assembly hall was later transformed into a temple for the worship of Thien Hau, a deity from Fujian province. The gaudy, green-tiled triple gateway was built in 1975.

The mural on the right-hand wall – if you can see it behind the prayer coils – depicts Thien Hau, her way lit by lantern light as she crosses a stormy sea to rescue a foundering ship. On the wall opposite is a mural of the heads of the six Fujian families who fled from China to Hoi An in the 17th century, following the overthrow of the Ming dynasty.

The penultimate chamber contains a statue of Thien Hau. To either side of the entrance stand red-skinned Thuan Phong Nhi and green-skinned Thien Ly Nhan, deities who alert Thien Hau when sailors are in distress.

The central altar in the last chamber contains seated figures of the heads of the six Fujian families. The smaller figures below them represent their successors as clan leaders. Behind the altar on the right are three fairies and smaller figures representing the 12 *ba mu* (midwives), each of whom teaches newborns a different skill necessary for the first year of life: smiling, sucking and so forth. Childless couples often come here to pray for offspring and leave fresh fruit as offerings.

Tan Ky House   HISTORIC HOUSE
(101 Đ Nguyen Thai Hoc; admission by Old Town ticket; ⊘8am-noon & 2-4.30pm) Built two centuries ago as the home of a well-to-do ethnic-Vietnamese merchant, Tan Ky House has been lovingly preserved through seven

generations of the same family. Don't be spooked by the portrait of a stern-looking matriarch over the entry hall; this gem of a house is worth lingering in.

Look out for signs of Japanese and Chinese influences on the architecture. Japanese elements include the ceiling (in the sitting area), which is supported by three progressively shorter beams, one on top of the other. There are similar beams in the salon. Under the crab-shell ceiling are carvings of crossed sabres wrapped in silk ribbon. The sabres symbolise force, the silk represents flexibility.

The interior is brightened by a beautiful detail: Chinese poems written in inlaid mother-of-pearl hang from some of the columns that hold up the roof. The Chinese characters on these 150-year-old panels are formed entirely of birds gracefully portrayed in various positions of flight.

The courtyard has several functions: to let in light, provide ventilation, bring a glimpse of nature into the home, and collect rainwater and provide drainage. The carved wooden balcony supports around the courtyard are decorated with grape leaves, which are a European import and further evidence of the unique blending of cultures in Hoi An.

The back of the house faces the river and was rented out to foreign merchants. Marks on one wall record recent flood heights, including the 1964 record when the water covered almost the entire ground level, and a 2m-high mark in 2007. There are two pulleys attached to a beam in the loft – in the past they were used for moving goods into storage, and today for raising furniture for safekeeping from the floods.

The exterior of the roof is made of tiles; inside, the ceiling consists of wood. This design keeps the house cool in summer and warm in winter.

Tran Family Chapel
HISTORIC HOUSE

(21 Đ Le Loi; admission by Old Town ticket; ⊗7.30am-noon & 2-5.30pm) This chapel was built for worshipping the family ancestors in 1802. It was built by Tran Tu, one of the clan who ascended to the rank of mandarin and served as an ambassador to China. His picture is to the right of the chapel.

The architecture of the building reflects the influence of Chinese (the 'turtle' style roof), Japanese (triple beam) and vernacular (look out for the bow-and-arrow detailing) styles. The central door is reserved for the dead – it's opened at Tet and on 11 November, the death anniversary of the main ancestor. Traditionally, women entered from the left and men from the right, although these distinctions are no longer observed.

The wooden boxes on the altar contain the Tran ancestors' stone tablets, with chiselled Chinese characters setting out the dates of birth and death, along with some small personal effects. On the anniversary of each family member's death, their box is opened, incense is burned and food is offered.

The small garden behind is where the placentas of newborn family members were buried. The practice was meant to prevent fighting between the children, but it hasn't been observed in more than 20 years, now that all babies are born in hospital.

After a short tour you'll be shown to the 'antique' room, where there are lots of coins for sale, and a side room full of souvenirs.

Quan Cong Temple
TEMPLE

(Chua Ong; 24 Đ Tran Phu; admission by Old Town ticket) Founded in 1653, this small temple is dedicated to Quan Cong, an esteemed Chinese general who is worshipped as a symbol of loyalty, sincerity, integrity and justice. His partially gilded statue, made of papier-mâché on a wooden frame, is on the central altar at the back of the sanctuary. When someone makes an offering to the portly looking Quan Cong, the caretaker solemnly strikes a bronze bowl that makes a bell-like sound.

On the left of Quan Cong is a statue of General Chau Xuong, one of his guardians, striking a tough-guy pose. On the right is the rather plump administrative mandarin Quan Binh. The life-sized white horse recalls a mount ridden by Quan Cong.

Check out the carp-shaped rain spouts on the roof surrounding the courtyard. The carp is a symbol of patience in Chinese mythology and is popular in Hoi An.

Shoes should be removed when mounting the platform in front of the statue of Quan Cong.

Phuoc Lam Pagoda
PAGODA

(Thon 2a, Cam Ha; ⊗8am-5pm) This pagoda was founded in the mid-17th century. The head monk at the end of that century was An Thiem, a Vietnamese prodigy who became a monk at the age of eight. When he was 18, the king drafted An Thiem's brothers into his army to put down a rebellion. An Thiem volunteered to take the places of the other men in his family and eventually rose to the rank of general. After the war he returned

HOI AN HOUSES: A CLOSER LOOK

The historical buildings of Hoi An not only survived the 20th century's wars, they also retain features of traditional architecture rarely seen today. As they have been for centuries, some shopfronts are shuttered at night with horizontal planks inserted into grooves that cut into the columns that support the roof.

Some roofs are made up of thousands of brick-coloured *am* and *duong* (yin and yang) roof tiles – so called because of the way the alternating rows of concave and convex tiles fit snugly together. During the rainy season the lichens and moss that live on the tiles spring to life, turning entire rooftops bright green.

A number of Hoi An's houses have round pieces of wood with an *am-duong* symbol in the middle surrounded by a spiral design over the doorway. These *mat cua* (door eyes) are supposed to protect the residents from harm.

It's not just individual buildings that have survived – it's whole streetscapes. This is particularly true around Đ Tran Phu and waterside promenade Đ Bach Dang. In the former French quarter to the east of Cam Nam Bridge there's a whole block of colonnaded houses, painted in the mustard yellow typical of French colonial buildings.

Hoi An's historic structures are being gradually, sincerely restored. Old houses must be licensed for (tasteful) restoration work, which keeps most modernisation attempts within reason. Strict rules govern the colour houses can be painted and the signs that can be used.

to monkhood, but felt guilty about the many people he had slain. To atone for his sins, he volunteered to clean the Hoi An market for 20 years, then joined this pagoda as its head monk.

To reach the pagoda, continue past Chuc Thanh Pagoda for 500m. The path passes an obelisk that was erected over the tomb of 13 ethnic Chinese who were decapitated by the Japanese during WWII for resistance activities.

Museum of Trading Ceramics   MUSEUM
(80 Đ Tran Phu; admission by Old Town ticket; ☺7am-5.30pm) Occupies a simply restored wooden house and contains artefacts from all over Asia, with oddities from as far afield as Egypt. While this reveals that Hoi An had some rather impressive trading links, frankly it would take an expert eye to appreciate the display. However the small exhibition on the restoration of Hoi An's old houses provides a useful crash course in Old Town architecture.

FREE Chinese All-Community
Assembly Hall   HISTORIC BUILDING
(Chua Ba; 64 Đ Tran Phu; ☺8am-5pm) Founded in 1773, this assembly hall was used by Fujian, Cantonese, Hainan, Chaozhou and Hakka congregations in Hoi An. To the right of the entrance are portraits of Chinese resistance heroes in Vietnam who died during WWII. The well-restored main temple is a total assault on the senses with great smoking

incense spirals, demonic-looking deities, dragons and lashings of red lacquer – it's dedicated to Thien Hau.

Assembly Hall of the Chaozhou Chinese Congregation   HISTORIC BUILDING
(Trieu Chau Hoi Quan; opposite 157 Đ Nguyen Duy Hieu; admission by Old Town ticket; ☺8am-5pm) Built in 1752, the highlight in this congregational hall is the gleaming woodcarvings on the beams, walls and altar – absolutely stunning in their intricacy. You could stand here for hours to unravel the stories, but if you're just popping by quickly, look for the carvings on the doors in front of the altar of two Chinese women wearing their hair in an unexpectedly Japanese style.

Chuc Thanh Pagoda   PAGODA
(Khu Vuc 7, Tan An; ☺8am-6pm) Founded in 1454 by a Buddhist monk from China, this is the oldest pagoda in Hoi An. Among the antique ritual objects still in use are several bells, a stone gong that is two centuries old and a carp-shaped wooden gong said to be even more venerable.

To get to Chuc Thanh Pagoda, go north all the way to the end of Đ Nguyen Truong To and turn left. Follow the lane for 500m.

Handicraft Workshop   CRAFTS
(9 Đ Nguyen Thai Hoc; admission by Old Town ticket) Housed in the 200-year-old Chinese trading house, the Handicraft Workshop has artisans making silk lanterns and practising

traditional embroidery in the back. In the front is your typical tourist-oriented cultural show (10.15am and 3.15pm) with traditional singers, dancers and musicians. It makes a sufficiently diverting break from sightseeing.

Tran Duong House HISTORIC HOUSE
(25 Ð Phan Boi Chau; admission 20,000d; ☺9am-6pm) There's a whole block of colonnaded French-colonial buildings on Ð Phan Boi Chau between Nos 22 and 73, among them the 19th-century Tran Duong House. It's mainly a showcase of antique French and Chinese furniture, including a sideboard buffet and a sitting room set with elaborate mother-of-pearl inlay. By contrast, the large plain wooden table in the front room is the family bed.

**Hoi An Museum of
History & Culture** MUSEUM
(7 Ð Nguyen Hue; admission by Old Town ticket; ☺7am-5.30pm) Housed in the Quan Am Pagoda, this museum provides a sampling of pre-Cham, Cham and port-era artefacts, with some huge bells, historic photos, old scales and weights alongside plenty of ceramics.

Quan Thang House HISTORIC HOUSE
(77 Ð Tran Phu; admission by Old Town ticket; ☺7am-5pm) This house is three centuries old and was built by an ancestor who was a Chinese captain. As usual, the architecture includes Japanese and Chinese elements. There are some especially fine carvings of peacocks and flowers on the teak walls of the rooms around the courtyard, on the roof beams and under the crab-shell roof (in the salon beside the courtyard).

**Assembly Hall of the Cantonese
Chinese Congregation** HISTORIC BUILDING
(Quang Trieu Hoi Quan; 176 Ð Tran Phu; admission by Old Town ticket; ☺8am-5pm) Founded in 1786, this assembly hall has a tall, airy entrance hall that opens onto a splendidly over-the-top mosaic statue of a dragon and a carp. The main altar is dedicated to Quan Cong. The garden behind has an even more incredible dragon statue.

FREE **Assembly Hall of the Hainan
Chinese Congregation** HISTORIC BUILDING
(Hai Nam Hoi Quan; 10 Ð Tran Phu; ☺8am-5pm) Built in 1851, this assembly hall is a memorial to 108 merchants from Hainan Island who were mistaken for pirates and killed in Quang Nam province in 1851. The elaborate dais contains plaques to their memory.

In front of the central altar is a fine gilded woodcarving of Chinese court life.

Phung Hung Old House HISTORIC HOUSE
(4 Ð Nguyen Thi Minh Khai; admission by Old Town ticket; ☺8am-7pm) Just a few steps down from the Japanese Covered Bridge, this old house has a wide, welcoming entrance hall decorated with exquisite lanterns, wall hangings and embroidery. There's also an impressive suspended altar.

FREE **Diep Dong Nguyen
House** HISTORIC HOUSE
(58 Ð Nguyen Thai Hoc; ☺8am-noon & 2-4.30pm) Built for a wealthy Chinese merchant in the late 19th century, this old house looks like an apothecary from another era. The front room was once a dispensary for *thuoc bac* (Chinese medicine); the medicines were stored in the glass-enclosed cases lining the walls.

Museum of Folklore in Hoi An MUSEUM
(33 Ð Nguyen Thai Hoc/62 Ð Bach Dang; admission by Old Town ticket; ☺7am-5.30pm) Located in a 150-year-old Chinese trading house. The exhibits give some idea of local customs and culture, though it's awfully dusty and de-contextualised for a folk-history museum. The view of the river from upstairs is very picturesque.

Phac Hat Pagoda PAGODA
(673 Ð Hai Ba Trung) Phac Hat Pagoda has a colourful facade of ceramics and murals and an elaborate roof with snake-like dragons. There's a huge central courtyard containing hundreds of potted plants and bonsai trees.

**Museum of Sa Huynh Culture &
Museum of the Revolution** MUSEUM
(149 Ð Tran Phu; admission by Old Town ticket; ☺7am-5.30pm) This building contains two odd bedfellows (though the upper-level Museum of the Revolution was closed at the time of research). On the lower floor you'll find stone, bronze, gold, glass and agate jewellery, assorted ceramic fragments and burial jars dating from the early Dong Son civilisation of Sa Huynh.

Ba Le Well LANDMARK
This square well's claim to fame is that it's the source of water for making authentic *cao lau,* a Hoi An speciality. The well is said to date from Cham times and elderly people make their daily pilgrimage to fill pails here. To find it, turn down the alley opposite 35 Ð

Phan Chu Trinh and take the second laneway to the right.

🏃 Activities

Diving & Snorkelling

Two reputable dive schools, both run by British instructors, offer trips to the Cu Lao Cham Marine Park. Both charge exactly the same rates: a PADI Discover Scuba dive costs US$65, two fun dives are US$75, while Open Water courses are US$370. The diving is not world class, but can be intriguing, with good macro life – and the trip to the Cham islands is a superb day out. Snorkelling costs US$30 to US$40, depending on the trip, including gear. It's usually only possible to dive or snorkel between February and September; the best conditions and visibility are in June, July and August.

Cham Island Diving Center   DIVING
(☎391 0782; www.chamislanddiving.com; 88 Đ Nguyen Thai Hoc) This business has been operating since 2002. It has a large boat and also a speedboat for zippy transfers.

Blue Coral Diving   DIVING
(☎627 9297; www.divehoian.com; 77 Đ Nguyen Thai Hoc) This new professional outfit has an 18m dive boat, additional speedboat and highly experienced team.

Massage & Spa

There are scores of massage and treatment centres in Hoi An. Most are of a very average quality indeed, run by locals with little

or no experience and minimal training. At these places a basic massage costs around US$12 an hour – there's a strip of them on Đ Ba Trieu. At the other end of the scale you'll find some seriously indulgent places that offer a wonderful spa experience (with prices to match); these are mostly based in the luxury hotels.

TOP CHOICE Palmarosa   SPA
(☎393 3999; www.palmarosaspa.vn; 90 Đ Ba Trieu; 1hr massage from US$19) Highly professional and enjoyable spa that offers a full range of treatments (a 40-minute scrub is US$16), facials, hand and foot care (manicures from US$5) and other beauty services. Massages are wonderful and excellent value; options include Asian blend, Indian head massage, Thai and Swedish.

Duyen Que   SPA
(☎350 1584; 512 Đ Cua Dai; 1hr massage from US$15) On the road to the beach, 2km east of the town centre, this treatment centre is owned by the ex-manager of the Victoria Hotel spa. Staff are well trained and know their stuff. Try the foot beauty ritual (US$15) or a botanical wrap (US$17).

Life Spa   SPA
(☎391 4555, ext 525; www.life-resorts.com; Life Heritage Resort, 1 Đ Pham Hong Thai; 1hr massage from US$58) This luxury hotel's spa is a lovely place to unwind, and has the full gamut of treatments and massages, including anti-

---

MARK WYNDHAM: DIRECTOR, HOI AN MOTORBIKE ADVENTURES

An Australian from the Queensland highlands, Mark worked as a tour leader for Intrepid Travel before settling in Hoi An.

What drew you to Hoi An in the first place? Great weather, good food, beaches, mountains close by and an international feel due to modern-day tourism and the old trading days. I came to Hoi An as a lifestyle choice to get out of big Asian cities.

What makes the town special? Its unique 'lost in time' feel with the Old Town's architecture, its laid-back lifestyle and easygoing locals. It's a small town with big-city services.

Best place for local food in Hoi An? Fresh seafood at Mr Ca's restaurant. Go to An Bang Beach, turn left and it's the last local restaurant.

What about Western food? Alfresco's (p204), or Jasper's Beach Club at An Bang Beach.

What's your favourite ride around Hoi An? It has to be our two-day Hill Tribe Village Adventure Loop, staying at Ba Hon village. It gives you rice paddies in the delta, ethnic minority villages, abseiling, trekking and amazing scenery.

Can you share an insiders' tip or secret? Resist the temptation to spend all your time shopping. The hinterland is beautiful; get out and explore.

oxidant facials (US$52), sea-salt scrubs (US$26) and hot-stone therapies (US$57).

Ba Le Beauty Salon SPA
(☎0905 226 974; www.balewellbeautysalon.com; 45-11 Đ Tran Hung Dao; ⓧclosed Sun) Up a little lane off Tran Hung Dao, Ba Le is run by a fluent English speaker, who has trained in the UK, and offers inexpensive threading, waxing and facials.

Courses

Hoi An is an ideal place not only to sample some of the nation's most delectable and complex cuisine, but to learn how to create it too. There are many local specialities unique to the region, but most are fiendishly tricky to prepare – all the more reason to seek out some expert help. Almost every restaurant offers cooking classes, from no-fuss introductory lessons to more in-depth affairs for the dedicated chef. Best of all, at the end of it you get to eat what you cook.

Informal classes can be found at Phone Café (US$12) and Lighthouse Café and Restaurant (US$21 with market tour and boat trip to the restaurant).

Morning Glory Cooking School COOKING
(☎224 1555; www.restaurant-hoian.com; 106 Đ Nguyen Thai Hoc) Based at the eponymous restaurant, this is the best-known course. It's directed by the acclaimed Trinh Diem Vy, born and bred in Hoi An and owner of several restaurants in town, or Lu, her protégé. The day starts with a visit to the market to learn about the key Vietnamese ingredients. Classes then concentrate on local recipes including *cao lau* (doughy flat noodles combined with croutons, crispy rice paper, bean sprouts and greens and topped off with pork slices), *banh khoai* and 'white rose' (steamed minced-shrimp dumplings served with dipping sauce), plus a dish or two from north and south Vietnam. You'll learn to cook in a very professionally organised, school-room-style environment with your own gas burner, ingredients and kitchen gear. However, note that classes can have up to 30 people.

Red Bridge Cooking School COOKING
(☎393 3222; www.visithoian.com/redbridge) At this school, going to class first involves a relaxing 4km cruise down the river. There are half-day (US$27) and full-day (US$43) courses, both of which include market visits. The half-day class focuses on local spe-

cialities, with rice-paper making and food decoration tips thrown in for good measure. The full-day class, which has a maximum of eight people, takes on a more ambitious menu. You'll learn how to cook *cha ca* (clay-pot fish with dill), and visit the Tra Que organic herb gardens. Or for a taster, go for the US$16 evening class. As an added sweetener, there's a 20m swimming pool at the school! Bookings are made through the Hai Cafe.

Conkhi Cocktail Classes COCKTAILS
(Dive Bar, 88 Đ Nguyen Thai Hoc; courses US$20-30) This is a fun way to learn all about the art of mixology. Courses (either 'virgin' or alcoholic) include a market visit, drinks, bar snacks and a recipe book. The Viet Espresso Martini is something else.

Festivals

Hoi An is a delightful place to be on the 14th day of each lunar month, when the town celebrates a **Full Moon Festival** (ⓧ5-11pm). Motorised vehicles are banned from the Old Town, street markets selling handicrafts, souvenirs and food open up, and all the lanterns come out! Traditional plays and musical events are also performed.

Sleeping

Hoi An has an excellent selection of good-value accommodation in all price categories. The best places book up fast, so plan as far ahead as you can and confirm the booking shortly before you arrive – reservations are mysteriously lost at many hotels. This is particularly important during peak periods.

Savvy hoteliers are very tuned in to travellers' needs here. Even budget places can have swimming pools, and free in-room wi-fi is pretty much standard everywhere.

Although there are a couple of hotels in the Old Town, most budget and midrange accommodation is spread out to the northwest around Đ Hai Ba Trung and Đ Ba Trieu, or to the east along Đ Cua Dai. There are also some great new places opening on An Hoi Peninsula.

Many luxury hotels are a few kilometres from town, on the beach, but all offer shuttle-bus transfers. At the time of research there were no hostels in Hoi An, and there might not be any in the future as the city government is bent on pushing upmarket tourism.

ENABLING THE DISABLED

For the nine million or so Vietnamese who have disabilities, chances are they won't have the opportunity to go to school or pick up skills that will let them earn a living as independent adults. Most schools aren't equipped to receive students with disabilities, and most employers don't look at people with disabilities favourably. Many are cooped up at home, entirely dependent on their families or the government for support.

It's a dismal prospect, but one that individual Vietnamese and expats are working hard to change through businesses that train, employ and empower people with disabilities.

In Hoi An, Mr Binh Nguyen Le has been running the fair-trade shop **Reaching Out** (p205) since 2001. Wheelchair-bound due to botched medical treatment when he was 16, he understands the frustrations faced by young people with disabilities. At Reaching Out, he hires workers with disabilities who first receive training and then start work in a comfortable workshop behind the shop (open to visitors). Besides giving people an employable skill, Mr Binh runs his business on fair-trade policies, contracts workers with disabilities all over Vietnam, and reinvests profits into expanding the business.

Another organisation helping children with disabilities is the **Kianh Foundation** (www.kianh.org.uk), a UK charity that has been providing special education, physiotherapy and speech therapy programs in Hoi An since 2001. It is now working in an impoverished district called Dien Ban, 15 minutes outside Hoi An, that was heavily bombed during the American War and has the highest proportion of disabilities in the province. There are over 900 children with disabilities who do not have access to essential education and therapy services; the Foundation is building a day centre to assist some of these children. If travellers wish to assist, the foundation accepts donations, and volunteers with special skills are also sought.

Based in Dong Ha, **Tam's Cafe** (www.tamscafe.co.nr; 81 Ð Tran Hung Dao) is a charitable business supported by the Global Community Service Foundation that employs and supports deaf people. Hearing-impaired young people are given hospitality and sign-language training with the aim of helping them find employment.

Tam's Cafe has links to the bakery-restaurant **Bread of Life** (www.breadoflifedanang. com; 4 Ð Dong Da) in Danang. Run by Americans Kathleen and Bob Huff, it finances sign-language and vocational training for the hearing impaired. The principles are similar to Tam's: giving the deaf an employable skill so that they can be financially independent. In this case the skills learnt are baking and cooking everything from pizzas to Southern-style biscuits to sloppy Joes (ground beef with tomato in a bun). All profits go to support sign-language training for deaf children (which is not taught in schools).

TOP CHOICE Ha An Hotel HISTORIC HOTEL **$$**
(☎386 3126; www.haanhotel.com; 6-8 Ð Phan Boi Chau; r US$58-115; ✳@🛜) This wonderful French Quarter hotel, set around a gorgeous central garden studded with palm and bamboo, feels more like a colonial mansion than a hotel. All rooms have nice individual touches – perhaps a tribal textile wall hanging or painting. The helpful, well-trained staff make staying here a very special experience and there's a little cafe for good measure. It's about a 10-minute walk from the heart of the Old Town.

TOP CHOICE Long Life Riverside HOTEL **$$**
(☎391 1696; www.longlifehotels.com; 61 Nguyen Phuc Chu; r US$45-90; ✳@🛜🏊) Impressive new hotel that enjoys a terrific location just over the bridge from the heart of the Old Town on the peaceful An Hoi Peninsula. Rooms are incredibly spacious and finished to a very high standard, all boasting tasteful modern furnishings, a computer and state-of-the-art bathrooms complete with jacuzzi-style bath-tubs. Breakfast is served in a dining room that overlooks the river. The only drawback is that the pool area, in the centre of the hotel, is cramped – you may want to hit the beach instead on one of the free guest bikes.

TOP CHOICE Thien Nga Hotel HOTEL **$$**
(☎391 6330; thienngahotel@gmail.com; 52 Ð Ba Trieu; r US$30-35; ✳@🛜🏊) Offering amazing value, this place has lovely, spacious, light and airy rooms, all with balcony and a contemporary feel (though the bathrooms are more prosaic). Book one at the rear if you

can for garden views. Staff are smiley and accommodating, and the sleek lobby has magazines to browse and a restaurant. The pool is covered by a roof.

Hoang Trinh Hotel
HOTEL $

(✆391 6579; www.hoianhoangtrinhhotel.com; 45 Đ Le Quy Don; r US$20-28; ✴@) Don't let the garish green facade put you off: this is a well-run place with really helpful, friendly staff that represents good value. Rooms are a little cluttered but spacious and clean, with high ceilings, cable TV and a double bed or twin beds. Guests also get a good complimentary breakfast with plenty of choice, including smoothies, pancakes and omelettes.

Hoa Binh Hotel
HOTEL $

(✆391 6838; www.hoianbinhhotel.com; 696 Đ Hai Ba Trung; r US$12-18; ✴@🕸) With a good selection of simple, modern comfortable rooms, all with wi-fi, minibar, cable TV and air-con, this is getting close to budget chic. Annoyingly, staff change rates from day to day, according to demand. Note also that the pool's layout is more than a little bizarre (it's virtually in the lobby and covered by a low roof).

Life Heritage Resort
HOTEL $$$

(✆391 4555; www.life-resorts.com; 1 Đ Pham Hong Thai; r US$141, ste from US$216; ❂✴@🕸) Large colonial-style resort with beautifully furnished rooms that have a real hip-hotel look, thanks to the contemporary furniture and fixtures and sleek bathrooms. The expansive grounds are immaculately maintained and there's a classy bar, fine restaurant, cafe, spa and sublime riverside pool area. Guests get free use of bikes.

Windbell Homestay
HOMESTAY $$

(✆393 0888; www.windbellhomestay.com.vn; Chau Trung, Cam Nam Island; r US$55, villas US$80-110; ❂✴@🕸) For a Vietnamese family-run experience with all the creature comforts, this fine new luxury homestay is hard to beat. All the lovely spacious rooms and villas have either a pool or garden view, writing desks and a huge flat-screen TV with cable. The host family is a delight and the Cam Nam location, a 10-minute walk from the Old Town, is very tranquil. To get here, cross the bridge to Cam Nam Island, continue south for 300m, bear left, and Windbell is on the left.

Vinh Huy
HOTEL $

(✆391 6559; www.vinhhuyhotel.com; 203 Đ Ly Thuong Kiet; r US$10-12; ✴@🕸) All the very cheap, clean, well-appointed rooms here represent a great deal and have minibars, fan and cable TV; some also have large bathrooms with tubs. It's run by friendly people who are used to putting up Western travellers. Drawbacks include the location, a 15-minute walk north of the Old Town (head up Đ Nguyen Truong To, turn left onto Đ Ly Thuong Kiet), and the tiny pool.

Vinh Hung 1 Hotel
HISTORIC HOTEL $$$

(✆386 1621; www.vinhhunghotels.com.vn; 143 Đ Tran Phu; r US$80-100; ❂✴🕸) For a unique Hoi An experience, this hotel (occupying a 200-year-old town house) is unmatched. The whole timber structure simply oozes history and mystique – you can almost hear echoes of the house's ancestors as they negotiate spice deals with visiting traders from Japan and Manchuria. Rooms at the rear are a little dark – if you can, book 208 (featured in Michael Caine's version of *The Quiet American*), which has a wonderful street-facing wooden balcony.

Vinh Hung Resort
RESORT HOTEL $$$

(✆391 0393; www.vinhhungresort.com; 111 Ngo Quyen, An Hoi Peninsula; r US$70-100, ste US$125; ✴@🕸) This large resort hotel makes a tranquil base, and its coconut-tree-shaded gardens that border the river estuary are a delight. Guests get the run of a spa, gym and 30m pool, and the breakfast buffet spread is quite something. All rooms are spacious, but the best look directly over the water. It's a five-minute walk from the Old Town over on the An Hoi Peninsula – cross the bridge, take the third turning on the left and look for the sign.

Thien Thanh Hotel
HOTEL $$

(Blue Sky Hotel; ✆391 6545; www.hoianthienthanh hotel.com; 16 Đ Ba Trieu; r US$40-60; ✴@🕸) Cross the koi pond to this hotel's spacious, inviting and well-equipped rooms that have Vietnamese decorative flourishes, DVD players and bath-tubs. The 8m pool is an indoor-outdoor affair, and there's a small spa and an oasis-like rear deck where your breakfast is served.

Vinh Hung 3 Hotel
HOTEL $$

(✆391 6277; www.hoianvinhhung3hotel.com; 96 Đ Ba Trieu; r US$35-40; ✴@🕸) Recently upgraded, this smart four-storey minihotel has elegant modish rooms with good attention to detail, huge beds, dark-wood furniture, writing desks and satellite TV; some rooms also have balconies. All bathrooms are sleek and inviting, and breakfast is included.

Long Life Hotel HOTEL $$
(☎391 6696; www.longlifehotels.com; 30 Đ Ba Trieu; r US$45-55; ❄@☎☀) This good mid-ranger's trump card is its exquisite secret garden and pool area, complete with a little thatched bar-restaurant, accessed via a bamboo bridge. Rooms are in fine shape too, all with fancy bath-tubs – the more expensive options are well worth the extra cost as they're lighter, more airy and have a balcony.

Orchid Garden Hotel HOTEL $$
(☎386 3720; www.hoian-homestay-orchidgarden .com; 382 Đ Cua Dai; r US$39-60; ❄@☎☀) Halfway between the town and the beach, this lovely little set-up has spacious accommodation with hardwood and marble flooring. The inviting bungalows with kitchen are ideal for self-catering. It's a well-maintained and managed place, and guests get free bike use and breakfast.

Phuong Dong Hotel HOTEL $
(☎391 6477; www.hoianphuongdonghotel.com; 42 Đ Ba Trieu; s/d/tr US$10/12/15; ❄@☎) The rooms here are quite plain but good value, with comfortable mattresses, reading lights, fan and air-con, and in-room wi-fi – some have bathrooms with tubs too.

Nhi Trung Hotel HOTEL $
(☎386 3436; 700 Đ Hai Ba Trung; r US$16-25; ❄@☎) An attractive well-run place with spacious, light rooms with balconies that represent great value; cheaper options are on the lower floor. Staff are switched on, there are computers for guests in reception, and a free breakfast is chucked in too. It's 1.5km north of the Old Town.

An Hoi Hotel HOTEL $$
(☎391 1888; www.anhoihotel.com.vn; 69 Đ Nguyen Phuc Chu; r US$20-35; ❄@☎☀) The location of this hotel – peaceful, yet a stone's throw from the Old Town – is excellent and rooms are a good size, clean and modern (though some on the lower floor lack natural light). Make sure you get your room rate (highly flexible) written down before you check in.

Thanh Van Hotel HOTEL $
(☎391 6916; www.thanhvanhotel.com; 78 Đ Tran Hung Dao; r US$15-20; ❄@☀) One of the best-value places in town, Thanh Van Hotel has comfortable rooms in a good location near the livelier section of the Old Town. Prices include breakfast, served beside the pool, and the staff are forthcoming with information and suggestions.

✗ Eating

Dining out in Hoi An is a delight. Central Vietnamese cuisine is arguably the nation's most complex and flavoursome, combining judicious use of fresh herbs (which are sourced from organic gardens close by) with extraneous influence due to centuries of links with China, Japan and Europe.

While you're here, be sure to try Hoi An specialities like the incredibly delicate and subtle *banh bao* or 'white rose'. *Cao lau* is another unique dish. Other local specialities are fried *hoanh thanh* (wonton) and *banh xeo* (crispy savoury pancakes rolled with herbs in fresh rice paper). Most restaurants serve these items, but quality varies widely.

The beauty of Hoi An is that you can snag a spectacular (and spectacularly cheap) meal at the central market and in casual eateries – or you can splash out on a serious fine-dining experience. The town is home to some incredibly talented local and foreign chefs creating a taste of the new Vietnam at prices that are still very affordable for most travellers.

Being such a cosmopolitan place, Hoi An is also blessed with myriad Western dining choices, including Parisian-style bakeries, delis, and Italian, Mediterranean, Japanese, Indian and tapas restaurants.

TOP CHOICE Morning Glory Street Food Restaurant VIETNAMESE $$
(☎224 1555; www.restaurant-hoian.com; 106 Đ Nguyen Thai Hoc; dishes 42,000-120,000đ; ☎) This simply outstanding restaurant concentrates on street food and traditionally prepared Vietnamese dishes (primarily from central Vietnam, but there are also some key dishes from the north and south). Frankly, you could eat here every day for a month and not experience an average meal, but some highlights include the shrimp mousse on sugarcane skewers and caramelised pork with young bamboo. There's an excellent vegetarian selection, including many wonderful salads and dishes like smoky eggplant in clay pot. The historic premises are huge, and there's an open kitchen downstairs.

TOP CHOICE Cargo Club INTERNATIONAL, VIETNAMESE $$
(☎391 0489; www.restaurant-hoian.com; 107 Đ Nguyen Thai Hoc; dishes 35,000-105,000đ; ☎) First things first: the Western breakfasts here are the best in town, possibly in the nation, offering simply outstanding value. Second up, you'll find the freshly baked pa-

tisserie and *boulangerie* selections are to die for, with perfect croissants pumped out daily and a chocolate-truffle cake that's so rich it can't be legal. Cargo Club works equally well for fine-dining too, either Vietnamese or Western, with the grilled sea bass and lamb shank rating very highly indeed. Head for the upper terrace for stunning river views.

Casa Verde
TOP CHOICE
EUROPEAN **$$$**

(☑391 1594; www.casaverde-hoian.com; 99 Đ Bach Dang; mains 85,000-190,000d; ☺noon-10pm) The Austrian chef-patron here sets very high standards and consistently hits them – his ethos is to seek out the finest ingredients (chocolate from Belgium, beef from Australia) and combine them with the freshest market produce. Casa Verde's riverside premises are relatively modest but the cooking – Mediterranean classics, thin-crust pizzas and authentic Asian dishes – is not. Be sure to leave room for ice cream, which is unquestionably the best in town and homemade on the premises.

Shree Ganesh Indian Restaurant
TOP CHOICE
INDIAN **$$**

(☑386 4538; www.ganeshindianrestaurant.com; 24 Đ Tran Hung Dao; meals 60,000-120,000d; ☺noon-10.30pm) There are some very disappointing Indian restaurants in Vietnam but the highly authentic Shree Ganesh certainly doesn't fall into that category. The thalis are tantalising, the nans are baked in a tandoor oven, and the fiery curries don't pull any punches. Prices are reasonable and portions are generous.

Mango Mango
FUSION **$$$**

(☑391 0839; www.mangorooms.com; 111 Đ Nguyen Thai Hoc; meals US$30; ☎) This is celebrity chef Duc Tran's third and most beautiful Hoi An restaurant. Situated in a prime spot just over the bridge in An Hoi, it has Old Town views to die for and gorgeous shabby-chic decor utilising zany colours to the max. The restaurant puts a global spin on Vietnamese cuisine, with fresh unexpected combinations such as seasoned yellowfin tuna with mango-avocado sauce. Perhaps at times the flavour matches are just a little too out there, but you have to admire the ambition. The two other Mango restaurants have very similar menus.

Mermaid Restaurant
VIETNAMESE **$**

(☑386 1527; www.restaurant-hoian.com; 2 Đ Tran Phu; most dishes 35,000-90,000d) The first res-

taurant in Hoi An (since 1992), this modest-looking place is still going strong with its menu of Hoi An specialities and family recipes. Local legend Vy, the owner, originally chose the location because it was close to the market, ensuring the freshest produce was directly at hand, and this principle is still wonderfully apparent in the flavours and authenticity of the cooking here. Try the mackerel in banana leaf or papaya salad and book ahead.

Bale Well
VIETNAMESE **$**

(45-51 Đ Tran Cao Van; meals 40,000-75,000d; ☺11.30am-10pm) Down a little alley near the famous well, this local place is renowned for one dish – barbecued pork, served up satay-style, which you then combine with fresh greens and herbs to create your own fresh spring roll. Nontouristy, and has plenty of atmosphere in the evenings.

White Sail
SEAFOOD **$$**

(47/6 Trang Hung Dao; dishes 45,000-140,000d; ☺11.45am-10pm) Want to really chow down with the locals? Head to this no-frills sea-food place in someone's front yard, where no one cares about the decor (there isn't any) because it's all about the freshness of the seafood. Little English is spoken, so take your phrasebook to help you work your way through the menu, which takes in fragrant steamboats, crispy turmeric-smeared fish, crab and giant prawns.

Hai Cafe
INTERNATIONAL **$$**

(www.visithoian.com; 98 Đ Nguyen Thai Hoc; mains 60,000-105,000d; ☎) Making the most of a wonderful Old Town trading house, the effortlessly hip and inviting Hai Cafe has a front porch for people-watching, a rear courtyard garden and an atmospheric dining room. On the menu are good sandwiches, Western breakfasts, Vietnamese dishes, European mains and vegie specials. There's also a popular barbecue – try the smoked pork ribs – and plenty of wine by the glass, or bottle.

Lighthouse Café & Restaurant
VIETNAMESE, INTERNATIONAL **$$**

(☑393 6235; www.lighthousecafehoian.com; To 5 Khoi Xuyen Trung, Cam Nam Island; dishes 24,000-110,000d; ☺closed Tue; ☎) Run by a Dutch-Vietnamese couple, this restaurant on Cam Nam Island has sweeping views of the river from its upper floors and a tranquil location. Vietnamese favourites include the stuffed squid and claypot dishes, plus there's a mean Dutch apple cake for dessert. Walk over Cam Nam Bridge and take the first lane on the left to get here, or catch the free boat (marked 'Hai Dang') from the waterfront on Đ Bach Dang. Reservations are required after 7pm.

Dingo Deli   WESTERN **$$**
(www.dingodeli.com; 229 Đ Cua Dai; snacks & meals 50,000-105,000d; ❋ ⧈) Midway between town and coast on the beach road, this smart deli-restaurant has excellent sandwiches, salads, breakfasts, pasta and filling Western grub – even Aussie pies – as well as all the espresso coffee combos you could want. Inside it's a smart air-con space with leather sofas for lounging and Macs for surfing, while the rear garden has kids' climbing frames.

Gourmet Garden   INTERNATIONAL **$$**
(55 Đ Le Loi; tapas 40,000-60,000d, mains 80,000-110,000d; ⧈) This restaurant occupies a beautifully restored town house and Mediterranean-style rear patio, and has an eclectic menu of Asian and Western dishes, including lots of Spanish tapas. Try the pumpkin, parmesan and sage crêpes or crispy calamari with sweet chilli sauce.

Miss Ly Cafeteria 22   VIETNAMESE **$$**
(☑386 1603; 22 Đ Nguyen Hue; dishes 28,000-110,000d) A very civilised, enjoyable restaurant run by a Vietnamese-North American team with mellow music and antique wall prints. Dishes include tasty *cao lau* and other Vietnamese favourites. Presentation is superb, service excellent and the wine selection is very decent too.

Bobo Café   VIETNAMESE **$**
(18 Đ Le Loi; dishes 16,000-55,000d) This simple, reliable family operation has courtyard seating.

Phone Café   VIETNAMESE **$**
(80b Đ Bach Dang; dishes 22,000-62,000d) This humble-looking place serves up the usual faves, plus some good claypot specialities.

Alfresco's   INTERNATIONAL **$$**
(www.alfrescosgroup.com; 83 Đ Tran Hung Dao; dishes 60,000-130,000d) Yes it's a chain, but the pasta, pizza, steaks, ribs and Western comfort grub all hit the spot.

🍷 **Drinking**

Hoi An is not a huge party town as the local authorities keep a fairly strict lid on late-night revelry. That said, there's plenty of action if you want it, with everything from upmarket wine bars to grungy dive bars. Options are quite limited in the Old Town itself, with more and more lively places opening up just across the river in An Hoi. Happy hours keep costs down considerably.

Most bars close by 1am in Hoi An, though Why Not? usually stays open till the wee hours. If you've the stamina for more action, catch one of the free minibus shuttles that leave Before & Now to the Zero SeaMile club on Cua Dai Beach.

Beware of *xe om* drivers offering to take you to out-of-the-way venues at night; some demand extortionate prices for the return trip.

TOP CHOICE Dive Bar   BAR
(88 Đ Nguyen Thai Hoc; ⧈) The switched-on British team behind this bar has created a great vibe through welcoming service, contemporary electronic tunes and a party atmosphere. Check out the gorgeous cocktail garden and bar at the rear, and learn the trade by taking one of their mixology classes. Also home to the Cham Island Diving Center.

Why Not?   DIVE BAR
(10B Đ Pham Hong Thai; @) Great late-night hang-out run by a friendly local character who's been in the bar game for decades. There's a popular pool table, an upper terrace and often a convivial atmosphere. Check out the DIY jukebox: choose a tune from YouTube and it'll be beamed over the sound system. It's about 1km east of the centre.

Q Bar   LOUNGE BAR
(94 Đ Nguyen Thai Hoc; ⧈) The hippest bar in town, Q Bar offers stunning lighting, lounge music and electronica, and the best cocktails in town. It always draws a cool crowd. Not cheap, but very classy and it's also gay-friendly.

White Marble   WINE BAR
(www.visithoian.com; 99 Đ Le Loi; ⧈) Gorgeous new wine-bar-cum-restaurant with a great corner plot in the heart of the Old Town. The historic premises have been very carefully renovated and you'll find a fine selection of wines (12 are available by the glass, from US$4).

Before & Now   BAR
(www.beforennow.com; 51 Đ Le Loi; ⧈) Your standard-issue travellers' bar, complete with pool table and (slightly clichéd) pictures

of icons like Che, Marilyn and er...Charles Manson. Hmmm. It's always busy, though the music policy is very mainstream pop and rock. Happy hour is from 6pm to 9pm.

River Lounge
LOUNGE BAR

(www.lounge-collection.com; 35 Đ Nguyen Phuc Chu; ☏) Gorgeous-looking minimalist bar-restaurant with a prime riverfront location. The terrace is a wonderful setting for a cocktail, especially during the 2-4-1 happy hour (6pm to 9pm), or a coffee and croissant. The food is mediocre though.

Sleepy Gecko
BAR

(To 5 Khoi Xuyen Trung, Cam Nam Island) This relaxed spot on Cam Nam is a popular expat hang-out and has comfort grub, views of Hoi An and ice-cold beer. Take the first lane on the left after the bridge and follow the road around.

Sun Bar
BAR

(44 Đ Ngo Quyen, An Hoi) Over on An Hoi, this scruffy bar is a key backpackers' hang-out with its booming sound system (choose a tune from the studenty playlist), dance floor and happy hour (8pm to 11pm).

🛍 Shopping

Hoi An has a history of flogging goods to international visitors, and today's residents haven't lost their commercial edge. It's common for travellers not planning to buy anything to leave Hoi An laden down with extra bags – which, by the way, you can buy here too.

Clothes are the biggest lure. Hoi An has long been known for fabric production, and the voracity of tourist demand has swiftly shoehorned enough tailor shops for a small province into the tiny Old Town. Pop into the **Hoi An Cloth Market** (Đ Tran Phu) for a selection of local fabrics.

Coming in a close second in popularity are shoes, also copied from Western designs – trainers (sneakers), boots, high heels and more. Prices are very low, but quality is very variable.

Hoi An has over a dozen art galleries too, concentrating on everything from predictable Vietnamese scenery to breathtaking contemporary pieces. Check the streets near the Japanese Covered Bridge, along Đ Nguyen Thi Minh Khai, Đ Tran Phu and Đ Nguyen Thai Hoc.

Woodcarvings are another local speciality. Cross to Cam Nam Village to watch the carvers at work, or hop on a ferry to Cam Kim Island, where many woodcarving workshops are clustered near the jetty.

🏆 Reaching Out
TOP CHOICE   SOUVENIRS, CLOTHING

(www.reachingoutvietnam.com; 103 Đ Nguyen Thai Hoc) A very worthwhile fair-trade gift shop started by a Vietnamese couple, one of whom has a disability. It stocks good-quality silk scarfs, clothes, jewellery, hand-painted Vietnamese hats, and very cute handmade toys and teddy bears. The shop employs artisans with disabilities, and proceeds are ploughed back into the business to aid those with disabilities across the nation; see the boxed text on p200 for more background.

Lotus Jewellery
ACCESSORIES

(www.lotusjewellery-hoian.com; 100 Đ Nguyen Thai Hoc) If you're interested in jewellery beyond the bits and bobs sold in souvenir shops, this place has very affordable and attractive hand-crafted pieces loosely modelled on butterflies, dragonflies, Vietnamese sampans, conical hats and Chinese symbols.

Mosaique Decoration
HANDICRAFTS

(www.mosaiquedecoration.com; 6 Đ Ly Quoc) Well worth a browse for its very stylish modern lighting, silk, linen and hemp clothing, bamboo matting, hand-embroidered cushion covers, gifts and furniture.

Avana
CLOTHING

(www.hoiandesign.com; 57 Đ Le Loi) Stylish boutique run by a European fashion designer that stocks fab off-the-peg dresses, blouses, shoes and accessories (including great hats and bags).

Tuoi Ngoc
HANDICRAFTS

(103 Đ Tran Phu) This family-owned business has been making Chinese-style lanterns for generations and has a great selection for sale.

Randy's Book Xchange
BOOKS

(www.randysbookxchange.com; To 5 Khoi Xuyen Trung) Head to Cam Nam Island and take the first right to get to this genuine bookshop. Set up like a personal library, it has more than 5000 used books for sale or exchange.

ℹ Information

Dangers & Annoyances

Hoi An is one of the safer towns in Vietnam, but there are occasional stories of late-night bag-snatching or assaults on women. If you are a lone female, try to make sure you walk home with somebody.

GETTING CLOTHES THAT MEASURE UP

Let's face it: the tailor scene in Hoi An is out of control. The estimated number of tailors working here ranges anywhere from 300 to 500. Hotels and tour guides all have their preferred partners – 'We give you good price' they promise before shuttling you off to their aunt/cousin/in-law/neighbour (from whom they'll probably earn a nice commission).

In such a demanding environment, what's an aspiring fashionista, or someone who just wants a new suit or dress to do? The first rule of thumb is that while you should always bargain and be comfortable with the price, you also get what you pay for. A tailor who quotes you a price that is drastically lower than a competitor's is probably cutting corners (pun intended) without telling you. Better tailors and better fabrics cost more, as do tighter deadlines. If a shop promises to deliver you a new wardrobe within 24 hours, think about it: either they're working an army of sweatshop apprentices to the bone, or you're probably going to get some dodgy items (or both).

Hoi An's tailors are renowned as master copiers – show them a picture ripped out of a magazine, and they'll whip out a near-identical outfit in a day or two. If you don't know what you want, the helpful shop assistants will heave out tomes of catalogues for you to leaf through. They don't just do *ao dai* (the national dress of Vietnam) or summer dresses; winter coats, wedding dresses and full two- or three-piece suits are perfectly within their repertoire.

It helps if you know your fabrics and preferences, right down to details like thread colour, linings and buttons. When buying silk, make sure you're paying for the real thing. The only real test is with a cigarette or match (synthetic fibres melt, silk burns). Similarly, don't accept on face value that a fabric is 100% cotton or wool without giving it a good feel for the quality. Prices currently hover around US$12 to US$15 for a men's shirt, and about US$22 for skirts and trousers. If a suit costs less than US$100, make sure the fabric and workmanship is up to scratch.

Although many travellers try to squeeze in a clothing order within a 48-hour sojourn, that doesn't leave much time for fittings and alterations, which are more important than most people anticipate. Remember to check the seams of the finished garment: a single set of stitching along the inside edges will soon cause fraying and, eventually, gaping holes. Well-tailored garments have a second set of stitches (known in the trade as blanket stitching), which binds the edge, oversewing the fabric so fraying is impossible.

If you have a big order in mind, it might make sense to try out a few different shops on small items first. Shops can pack and ship orders to your home country. Although there are occasional reports of packages going astray or the wrong order arriving, the local post office's hit rate is better than most.

In such a crowded field, it's tough to sort the wheat from the chaff, particularly since all the shops outsource their orders to a growing legion of anonymous workers. It may be worth your while to scour the Old Town for a small operation that isn't tainted by being too popular. If you're pressed for time, places that we regularly hear good things about are (in alphabetical order): **A Dong Silk** (☑386 3170; www.adongsilk.com; 40 Đ Le Loi); **B'lan** (☑386 1866; www.hoianblan.com; 23 Đ Tran Phu); **Kimmy** (☑386 2063; www.kimmy tailor.com; 70 Đ Tran Hung Dao); **Long Life Silk** (☑391 1955; www.longlifesilk.com; 47 Đ Nguyen Phuc Chu); **Thu Thuy** (☑386 1699; www.thuthuysilk.com; 60 Đ Le Loi) and **Yaly** (☑391 0474; www.yalycouture.com; 47 Đ Nguyen Thai Hoc).

Don't be fooled into thinking that the kids who sell trinkets, postcards and newspapers get to keep the money.

Hoi An has more than its share of small-time hustlers trying to peddle tours, boat trips, motorbikes, souvenirs and the like, so prepare yourself for plenty of attention.

Emergency
Hoi An Police Station (☑386 1204; 84 Đ Hoang Dieu)

Internet Access
Min's Computer (2 Truong Minh Luong; per hr 5000d) Lots of terminals and you can also print, scan, burn and Skype here.

Medical Services

Dr Ho Huu Phuoc Practice (☑386 1419; 74 Đ Le Loi; ☉11am-12.30pm & 5-9.30pm) A local doctor who speaks English.

Hoi An Hospital (☑386 1364; 4 Đ Tran Hung Dao) If it's anything serious, make for Danang.

Money

Agribank (Đ Cua Dai), **Vietcombank** (642 Đ Hai Ba Trung) and **Vietin Bank** (4 Đ Hoang Dieu) all change cash and travellers cheques, and have ATMs.

Post

Main post office (☑386 1480; 6 Đ Tran Hung Dao)

Tourist Information

There are no official tourist information centres in Hoi An – try one of the travel agencies or tour operators. Four **Hoi An Old Town Booths** (☉7am-5pm) sell Old Town tickets: these are located at 30 Đ Tran Phu, 10 Đ Nguyen Hue, 5 Đ Hoang Dieu and 78 Đ Le Loi.

Travel Agencies

Competition is pretty fierce, so it's worth checking out a few options and negotiating.

Rose Travel Service (☑391 7567; www.rose travelservice.com; 111 Đ Ba Trieu) Offers tours all over Vietnam, car rental, bus bookings, and boat, jeep and motorbike trips.

Sinh Tourist (☑386 3948; www.thesinhtourist .vn; 587 Đ Hai Ba Trung) Books reputable open-tour buses.

Websites

Have a look at www.livehoianmagazine.com, which also publishes a monthly magazine with cultural content, features and reviews.

ⓘ Getting There & Away

AIR The closest airport is 45 minutes away in Danang.

BUS Most north–south bus services do not stop at Hoi An, as Hwy 1 passes 10km west of the town, but you can head for the town of Vinh Dien and flag down a bus there.

It's easier to travel by open-tour bus. You'll find very regular connections to and from Hue (US$5, four hours) and Nha Trang (seated/sleeping US$10/17, 11 to 12 hours).

The **main bus station** (96 Đ Hung Vuong), 1km west of the town centre, mainly covers local routes. Foreigners are routinely overcharged here. Buses run to Danang (18,000d, one hour), Quang Ngai and other points. More frequent services to Danang leave from the **northern bus station** (Đ Le Hong Phong).

CAR & MOTORCYCLE To get to Danang (30km), you can either head north out of town

and join up with Hwy 1, or head east to Cua Dai Beach and follow the China Beach coastal road. The going rate for a motorbike taxi between Danang and Hoi An is around 120,000d. A taxi costs approximately 330,000d.

A trip in a car to Hue starts from US$70 (depending on how many stops you plan to make along the way), while a half-day trip around the surrounding area, including My Son, is around US$35.

ⓘ Getting Around

Hoi An is best explored on foot; the Old Town is compact and highly walkable. To go further afield, rent a bicycle (20,000d per day). The route east to Cua Dai Beach is quite scenic, passing rice paddies and a river estuary.

A motorbike without/with a driver will cost around US$5/12 per day. Reckon on about 50,000d for a taxi to the beach.

BOAT Boat trips on the Thu Bon River can be a fascinating experience. A simple rowboat (which comes complete with rower) should cost about 60,000d per hour, and one hour is probably long enough. Some My Son tours include a return journey by boat, so you can cruise into central Hoi An in style.

Motorboats for small groups can be hired to visit handicraft and fishing villages in the area; expect to pay 120,000d to 170,000d per hour. Lots of captains will try to entice you aboard their craft; they wait on the riverbank between the Cam Nam and An Hoi bridges in central Hoi An.

TAXI For a metered cab, try **Hoi An Taxi** (☑391 9919) or **Mai Linh** (☑392 5925).

Around Hoi An

THANH HA

This small village of about 70 families has long been known for its pottery industry, but demand has been declining and most villagers have gradually switched from making bricks and tiles to making pots and souvenirs for the tourist trade. The artisans employed in this hot, sweaty and painstaking work don't mind if you come for a gander and a chat, though they're happier if you buy something.

Thanh Ha is 3km west of Hoi An and can be easily reached on bicycle, or on the way back from My Son.

CAM KIM ISLAND

The master woodcarvers, who in previous centuries produced the intricate detail that graced the homes of Hoi An's merchants and the town's public buildings, came from

TOURS AROUND HOI AN

The evergreen, quintessentially Vietnamese countryside and rural lanes around Hoi An beg to be explored, and you'll find several excellent tour operators offering trips in the region.

Motorbike and bicycle trips are wildly popular and there's no better way to appreciate the countryside than on two wheels. **Hoi An Motorbike Adventures** (☑391 1930; www .motorbiketours-hoian.com; 54a Đ Phan Chu Trinh; tours US$35-910) specialises in tours on cult Minsk motorbikes. These guides really know the terrain and their trips make use of beautiful back roads and riverside tracks.

The cycling tours run by **Heaven & Earth** (☑386 4362; www.vietnam-bicycle.com; 57 Đ Ngo Quyen, An Hoi; tours US$15-19) are well thought out and not too strenuous; they explore the Song Thu river delta area using ferries and floating bridges. The office is 250m south of the bridge in Hoi An.

Love of Life (☑393 9399; www.hoian-bicycle.com; 95 Đ Phan Chu Trinh; tours US$19) also has good bicycle tours along quiet country lanes past vegetable gardens, shrimp ponds and fishing villages.

Operating near Cua Dai Beach, **Hoi An Eco Tour** (☑392 8900; www.hoianecotour.com .vn; Phuoc Hai village; tours US$35-70) runs trips along the river, where you can see traditional village life and try your hand at fishing or paddling a basket boat. Bike tours and sunrise and sunset cruises are also organised. Phuoc Hai is about 5km west of Hoi An.

Heading up into the hills of central Vietnam, **Active Adventures** (☑391 1930; www .homestay-vietnam.com; 54a Đ Phan Chu Trinh; tours US$90-250) offers tours in original US jeeps to a Co Tu tribal village, where you stay in a stilt-house homestay. There are hot springs and great hikes in the region. The company also plans to offer kayak trips in the future.

The idyllic Cham Islands make another perfect day-trip destination during the March to September season. Both Hoi An dive schools run tours.

Kim Bong village on Cam Kim Island. Most of the woodcarvings on sale in Hoi An are produced here.

Boats to the island leave from the boat landing at Đ Bach Dang in Hoi An (15,000d, 30 minutes). The village and island, quite rural in character, are also fun to explore by bicycle.

CUA DAI BEACH

Heading east of Hoi An, you cruise through paddy fields and follow the meandering riverbank for 5km or so before hitting glorious golden sandy beaches. This palm-fringed coastline heads north all the way up to Danang, and, if you choose your spot carefully, there are still some wonderful undeveloped stretches.

The nearest beach to Hoi An, **Cua Dai** is subject to intense development and is probably best avoided. This is also where gangs of hard-selling beach vendors target tourists – even with an iPod and an eye mask, their attentions are impossible to block out. There are some seafood restaurants here (and the Zero SeaMile club), but better places lurk close by. The 5km of coastline south to Cua Dai port (where boats leave for the Cham Islands) is being totally transformed, as a strip of five-star resorts emerges from the sand dunes. Coastal erosion is a huge problem, and several of these hotels have seen opening ceremonies postponed for years due to vanishing beaches and resulting construction woes.

The shore-side club **Zero SeaMile** (www .zeroseamile.com; ☎☒) really looks the part, with a large covered dance floor that catches the sea breeze, stylish decor and even a pool. However, don't expect anything too interesting sonically – a predictable flow of party and chart anthems is usually served up. It's also open in the day for drinks and meals. Free hourly buses leave from (and return to) the Before & Now bar in Hoi An from midnight between April and September.

🛏 Sleeping

Victoria Hoi An Resort   BEACH RESORT $$$
(☑392 7040; www.victoriahotels.asia; r/ste from US$170/260; ❂❄@☎☒) Combining French colonial and Hoi An architectural styles, this well-established beachside hotel offers refined taste and comfort. Rooms are very

swish, modern and immaculately presented, some with teak floors and jacuzzis. Other perks include the blissful 30m ocean-side pool and a couple of tennis courts.

Hoi An Riverside Resort   HOTEL $$$
(☑386 4800; www.hoianriverresort.com; 175 Đ Cua Dai; r from US$115; ☺✷@☎☎) Classy rooms with hardwood floors and nicely designed decor make this hotel fine value for money. Many of the rooms have balconies right over the river. It's a well-run establishment, about a kilometre from the beach and has a good restaurant, and massage and fitness facilities.

AN BANG BEACH

Just 3km north of Cua Dai, **An Bang** is fast emerging as one of Vietnam's most happening and enjoyable beaches. The approach track is scruffy, but after you've parked up and hit the shore it's easy to see what all the fuss is about – you're greeted with a wonderful stretch of fine sand, a huge empty ocean and an enormous horizon, with only the distant Cham Islands interrupting the seaside symmetry.

More and more cool little beachfront bar-restaurants are opening here, and the scene looks set to take off. At the time of research visitors were not being hassled by beach vendors, but as An Bang's star rises, this situation will probably change. Luckily the coastline immediately to the north – a glorious broad beach lined with casuarina and pandan trees and dotted with the curious coracles of local fishermen – remains pristine.

🛏 Sleeping

A Novotel and several other luxury hotels are under construction on the beachfront, though coastal erosion has delayed many projects.

STAY SAFE

Note that the ocean can get very rough along the stretch of coast east of Hoi An, particularly between the months of October and March. Many local people get into trouble in heavy seas here, resulting in regular fatalities. In May 2011 four lifeguards were hired and a watchtower constructed, but it still pays to be cautious.

Nam Hai   HOTEL $$$
(☑394 0000; www.thenamhai.com; Dien Duong village; villas/pool villas from US$525/845; ☺✷@☎☎) About 8km north of An Bang and 15km from Hoi An, this beachfront temple of indulgence has it all: three pools (one is heated), butler service, vast villas kitted out with contemporary gadgets and private plunge pools, excellent fitness facilities and a world-class spa (try the four-hand Jade massage). Of course all this comes at an astonishing cost, but at least service standards are both thoughtful and excellent.

🍴 Eating & Drinking

New places are opening each month in happening An Bang, so expect plenty more choices during the lifetime of this guidebook. The area is much quieter in the winter months.

TOP CHOICE Soul Kitchen   INTERNATIONAL $$
(☑0906 440 320; www.soulkitchen.sitew.com; meals 70,000-160,000d; ⊘closed Mon evening; ☎) This wonderful beach restaurant has a prime setting above the waves and a menu that changes daily. Specials are chalked up on a blackboard and might include anchovies carpaccio, chicken with mashed potato and green-pepper sauce, or seafood salad. You'll find good wines, cocktails and mocktails too. Soul Kitchen is a key hangout for expats, and has a grassy garden and thatched dining area.

La Plage   INTERNATIONAL $
(☑392 8244; www.laplagehoian.com; snacks/meals 60,000/100,000d; ☎) Simple-looking French-Vietnamese-owned bamboo-and-thatch beachfront place that makes a very relaxed base for a day by the sea. Delicious snacks include *croque monsieur/madame* (fancy toasted ham-and-cheese sandwiches, the female version of which comes with a fried or poached egg on top), *tartine du pêcheur* (open-sided sandwich with fish topping) and Arab-style *merguez* (spicy sausages) with *frites*. There's always a fresh fish of the day, and also full English breakfasts, cocktails, pastis and French wine.

Luna D'Autunno   ITALIAN $$
(meals US$10-15; ☎) This fine new Italian restaurant has an authentic menu of pasta, salads, meat dishes and the best pizza, from a wood-fired oven, in central Vietnam. It's set just back from the shore and is worth the splurge.

CHAM ISLANDS

☎ 0510 / POP 2700

A breathtaking cluster of granite islands, around 15km directly offshore from Hoi An, the serene **Cham Islands** are blissfully undeveloped – though this will change in the next few years, so get here quick. Until very recently they were closed to visitors and under close military supervision, but it's now possible to visit as a day trip, dive or snorkel the reefs, or stay overnight. These delightful islets, set in aquamarine seas, are only accessible for about seven months of the year (March to September), as the ocean is usually too rough at other times.

Only the main island, **Hon Lao**, is inhabited – the other seven Chams are tiny, rocky specks, covered in dense bush. Dip beneath the ocean and you'll find a rich underwater environment, with 135 species of soft and hard coral and varied macrolife. The islands are now protected as a marine park. Fishing and the collection of bird's nests (for soup) are the two key industries here.

Bai Lang, Hon Lao's little port, is the only real settlement (aside from two remote hamlets). A pretty, very relaxed, overgrown village, its leeward location has long offered protection for mariners from the rough waters of the South China Sea. You'll find its lanes are a delight to explore – the laid-back ambience and slow pace of life here are a real tonic for road-weary travellers. This is where all (three) guesthouses are located.

◎ Sights & Activities

Ong Ngu   TEMPLE

The only real sight in Bai Lang is a tiny, but very curious temple, Ong Ngu, whose modest appearance belies a fascinating history – for it's dedicated to the whales (and whale sharks) that were once abundant around the Chams. Locals worshipped whales as oceanic deities who would offer them protection at sea. When a carcass washed ashore, they'd clean the bones and perform an elaborate ceremony at the temple before giving the bones a burial. Similar rituals are performed in Mui Ne, Vung Tau and other coastal locations in Vietnam. Sadly, whales are very seldom seen around the Chams today.

Beach   SWIMMING

A dirt track heads southwest from Bai Lang for 2km past a couple of glorious little coves to a fine, sheltered beach, where there's great swimming in azure waters, powdery sand, hammocks and thatched parasols that

belong to the excellent Cham Restaurant. Trails also sneak up into the forested hills behind Bai Lang.

Dive Trips   DIVING

Unsurprisingly divers and snorkellers are some of the main visitors. While the diving isn't world class (visibility can be poor and overfishing is a problem) it is intriguing: five species of lobster, 84 species of mollusc and some 202 species of fish are endemic to the Chams. Dive trips and overnight stays can be arranged through dive centres in Hoi An, such as **Cham Island Diving Center** (☎ 391 0782; www.chamislanddiving.com; 88 Đ Nguyen Thai Hoc, Hoi An), whose tours are highly recommended; a full-day trip that includes snorkelling, a short hike, lunch and beach time is US$40.

🛏 Sleeping & Eating

Work has already begun on a huge new Four Seasons resort towards the southwest tip of the island, though it probably won't be completed until 2013 or 2014.

Luu Ly   GUESTHOUSE $

(☎ 393 0240; r with shared bathroom 200,000d) Luu Ly is an excellent new place with neat little rooms that have mozzie nets, TV, fan and wardrobe. Three meals a day can be cooked for you for around 200,000d. There's also a back-up generator here.

Thu Trang   GUESTHOUSE $

(☎ 393 0007; r with shared bathroom 200,000d) Second choice is Thu Trang, right by the whale temple. It's tidy and clean, though rooms get hot (power cuts are common). As with Luu Ly, meals are available (around 200,000d for three).

Cham Restaurant   RESTAURANT $

(☎ 224 1108; meals 50,000-90,000d) About 2km south of town, Cham Restaurant sits pretty on a stunning sandy beach and serves wonderful Vietnamese dishes, including lots of seafood. Call ahead to book your meal so they can get sufficient supplies.

ⓘ Getting There & Away

Public boats to Cham Island dock at Bai Lang village. There's a scheduled daily connection from Đ Bach Dang in Hoi An (20,000d, two hours, 7.30am daily); foreigners are routinely charged more – as much as 100,000d. Note that boats do not sail during heavy seas. Bring a copy of your passport and visa, as the boat captain needs to prepare a permit.

Tour agencies charge US$25 to US$40 for island tours.

THE KINGDOM OF CHAMPA

The kingdom of Champa flourished between the 2nd and 15th centuries. It first appeared around present-day Danang and later spread south to what is now Nha Trang and Phan Rang. Champa became Indianised through commercial ties: adopting Hinduism, using Sanskrit as a sacred language and borrowing from Indian art.

The Chams, who lacked enough land for agriculture, were semipiratical and conducted attacks on passing ships. As a result they were in a constant state of war with the Vietnamese to the north and the Khmers to the southwest. The Chams successfully threw off Khmer rule in the 12th century, but were entirely absorbed by Vietnam in the 17th century.

They are best known for the many brick sanctuaries (Cham towers) they constructed throughout the south. The greatest collection of Cham art is in the Museum of Cham Sculpture in Danang. The major Cham site is at My Son, and other Cham ruins can be found in Quy Nhon and its surrounds, Tuy Hoa, Nha Trang, Thap Cham and the Po Shanu towers at Mui Ne.

Numbering around 140,000 people, the Cham remain a substantial ethnic minority in Vietnam, particularly around Phan Rang. Elements of Cham civilisation can still be seen in techniques for pottery, fishing, sugar production, rice farming, irrigation, silk production and construction throughout the coast. There are both Muslim and Hindu Cham living in Vietnam today, and the latter's towers in the south are still active places of worship.

My Son

The site of Vietnam's most extensive Cham remains, **My Son** (admission 60,000d; ⊙6.30am-4pm) enjoys an enchanting setting in a lush jungle valley, overlooked by Cat's Tooth Mountain (Hon Quap). The temples are in poor shape – only about 20 structures survive where at least 68 once stood – but the intimate nature of the site, surrounded by gurgling streams, is still enthralling.

My Son was once the most important intellectual and religious centre of the kingdom of Champa and may also have served as a burial place for Cham monarchs. It was rediscovered in the late 19th century by the French, who restored parts of the complex, but American bombing later devastated the temples. Today it is a Unesco World Heritage site.

The ruins get very busy, so go early or late if you can. By departing from Hoi An at 5am or 6am, you will arrive to wake up the gods (and the guards) for sunrise and could be leaving just as the tour groups hit the area.

The large **Exhibition Buildings** contain Sanskrit-inscribed stones and historical information (including the hairstyles of Cham women and a large map).

Archaeologists have divided My Son's monuments into 10 main groups, uninspiringly named A, A', B, C, D, E, F, G, H and K. Each structure within that group is given a number.

Note that only a handful of the monuments are properly labelled and there are virtually no information panels on site.

History

My Son (pronounced 'me sun') became a religious centre under King Bhadravarman in the late 4th century and was continuously occupied until the 13th century – the longest period of development of any monument in Southeast Asia. Most of the temples were dedicated to Cham kings associated with divinities, particularly Shiva, who was regarded as the founder and protector of Champa's dynasties.

Because some of the ornamentation work at My Son was never finished, archaeologists know that the Chams first built their structures and only then carved decorations into the brickwork.

During one period in their history, the summits of some of the towers were completely covered with a layer of gold. After the area fell into decline, many of the temples were stripped of their glory. The French moved some of the remaining sculptures and artefacts to the Museum of Cham Sculpture in Danang – fortuitously so, because the VC used My Son as a base during the American War and American bombing destroyed many of the most important monuments.

GROUP C

The 8th-century **C1** was used to worship Shiva, portrayed in human form. Inside is an altar where a statue of Shiva, now in the Museum of Cham Sculpture in Danang, used to stand. Note the motifs, characteristic of the

My Son

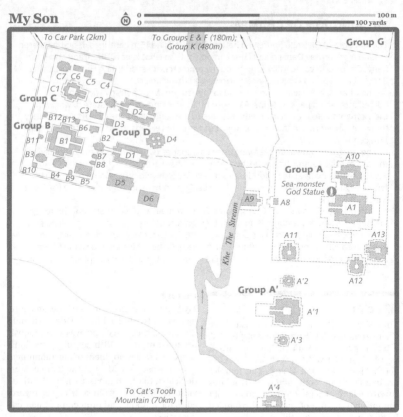

To Car Park (2km)

To Groups E & F (180m); Group K (480m)

Group G

C7 C6 C5 C4
C1
Group C
C2
C3
D2
Group B B12 B13 B6 D3
B11 B1 B2 **Group D** D4
B3 B7 D1
B10 B8
B4 B9 B5 D5
D6

Khe The Stream

Group A
Sea-monster God Statue
A10
A9 A8
A1
A11 A13
A12
A'2

Group A'
A'1
A'3

To Cat's Tooth Mountain (70km)

A'4

8th century, carved into the brickwork of the exterior walls. With the massive bomb crater in front of this group, it's amazing that anything's still standing.

GROUP B

The main *kalan* (sanctuary), **B1**, was dedicated to Bhadresvara, which is a contraction of the name of King Bhadravarman, who built the first temple at My Son, combined with '-esvara', which means Shiva. The first building on this site was erected in the 4th century, destroyed in the 6th century and rebuilt in the 7th century. Only the 11th-century base, made of large sandstone blocks, remains. The niches in the wall were used to hold lamps (Cham sanctuaries had no windows). The linga inside was discovered during excavations in 1985, 1m below its current position.

B5, built in the 10th century, was used for storing sacred books and objects used in ceremonies performed in B1. The boat-shaped

roof (the 'bow' and 'stern' have fallen off) demonstrates the Malay-Polynesian architectural influence. Unlike the sanctuaries, this building has windows and the Cham masonry inside is original. Over the window on the outside wall facing B4 is a brick bas-relief of two elephants under a tree with two birds in it.

The ornamentation on the exterior walls of **B4** is an excellent example of a Cham decorative style, typical of the 9th century and said to resemble worms. The style is unlike anything found in other Southeast Asian cultures.

B3 has an Indian-influenced pyramidal roof typical of Cham towers. Inside **B6** is a bath-shaped basin for keeping sacred water that was poured over the linga in B1; this is the only known example of a Cham basin. **B2** is a gate.

Around the perimeter of Group B are small temples, **B7** to **B13**, dedicated to the gods of the directions of the compass (*dikpalaka*).

GROUP D

Buildings **D1** and **D2** were once meditation halls and now house small displays of Cham sculpture.

GROUP A

Group A was almost completely destroyed by US bombs. According to locals, the massive **A1**, considered the most important monument at My Son, remained impervious to aerial bombing and was intentionally finished off by a helicopter-borne sapper team. All that remains today is a pile of collapsed brick walls. After the destruction of A1, Philippe Stern, an expert on Cham art, wrote a letter of protest to US president Nixon, who ordered US forces to stop damaging Cham monuments.

A1 was the only Cham sanctuary with two doors. One faced east, in the direction of the Hindu gods; the other faced west towards Groups B, C and D and the spirits of the ancestor kings reputedly buried there. Inside A1 is a stone altar. Among the ruins, some of the brilliant brickwork (typical 10th-century style) is still visible. At the base of A1 on the side facing A10 (decorated in 9th-century style) is a carving of a small worshipping figure flanked by round columns, with a Javanese sea-monster god (*kala-makara*) above.

OTHER GROUPS

Dating from the 8th century, **Group A'** is at present overgrown and inaccessible. Preservation work is ongoing at **Group G**, where scaffolding and roofs have been erected over the 12th-century temples. **Group E** was built between the 8th and 11th centuries, while **Group F** dates from the 8th century; both were badly bombed. If you follow the path towards **K**, a stand-alone small tower, you can loop back towards the car park.

ℹ️ Getting There & Away

BUS & MINIBUS Almost every hotel in Hoi An can arrange a day trip for you to My Son (US$4 to US$7). Minibuses depart at 8am and return between 1pm and 2pm. If you go for the boat-ride option on the return leg, add an extra hour to the trip.

CAR My Son is about 55km from Hoi An. A hired car with driver costs around US$35.

MOTORCYCLE The site is adequately signposted so it's easy to find if you've got your own wheels. The starting price of a *xe om* from Hoi An is 150,000d (including waiting time).

Tra Kieu (Simhapura)

Formerly called Simhapura (Lion Citadel), Tra Kieu was the first capital of Champa and remained so from the 4th century to the 8th century. Today nothing remains of the ancient city except the rectangular ramparts. A large number of artefacts, including some of the finest carvings in the Museum of Cham Sculpture in Danang, were found here.

Atop Buu Chau Hill is the modern **Mountain Church** (Nha Tho Nui), built in 1970 to replace an earlier structure destroyed by an American bomb. It offers wonderful views. The church is about 200m from the morning **market** (Cho Tra Kieu).

The 19th-century **Tra Kieu Church** (Dia So Tra Kieu) is home to a **museum** (Van Hoa Cham) of Cham artefacts, collected by local people and then amassed by a priest. The artefacts are kept in a locked, dusty room on the 2nd floor of the building to the right of the church. According to local belief this church was the site of a miracle in 1885. Catholic villagers, under attack by anti-French forces, saw a vision of a lady in white, believed to be Mary, who they credit with protecting them from intense shelling. To get here, follow the signs from the Mountain Church.

Tra Kieu is 6.5km from Hwy 1 and 19.5km from My Son. Some day trips to My Son from Hoi An include a stop-off at Tra Kieu.

Chien Dan

The elegant Cham towers at **Chien Dan** (Chien Dan Cham; Hwy 1; admission 12,000d; ⊙8-11.30am & 1-5.30pm Mon-Fri) are located just outside the town of Tam Ky on a wide open field; the only other building nearby is a small museum. Dating from the 11th or 12th century, each *kalan* faces east. Many of the decorative friezes remain on the outside walls.

The middle tower was dedicated to Shiva; at the front left-hand edge of its base there are carvings of dancing girls and a fight scene. Look for the grinning faces high up between this and the left tower (honouring Brahma) and the two elephants at the rear. The right-hand tower is dedicated to Vishnu.

Although the towers escaped the bombing that ravaged My Son, scars from the American War are evident – witness the numerous bullet holes in the walls.

This rarely visited site is to the right of the road on your approach to Tam Ky, 47km south of Hoi An.

South-Central Coast

Best Places to Eat

» Veranda (p239)

» Lanterns (p239)

» Sandals Restaurant
at the Sailing Club (p239)

» La Taverna (p254)

» Lam Tong (p253)

Best Places
to Stay

» Full Moon Resort (p250)

» Cham Villas (p250)

» Violet Hotel (p236)

» Jungle Beach (p226)

» Six Senses Con Dao (p268)

Why Go?

Vietnam has an incredibly curvaceous coastline and it is in this region that it is at its most alluring. The country is staking its claim as one of the new coastal meccas in Asia, offering vast tracts of unexplored coastline with towering cliffs and concealed bays. Many of the voluptuous beaches along this stretch are yet to be discovered and developed. Not for long.

Nha Trang, Mui Ne and Con Dao attract the headlines here, but the beach breaks come thick and fast in this part of Vietnam. If your idea of paradise is reclining in front of turquoise waters, weighing up the merits of a massage or a mojito, then you have come to the right place. On hand to complement the sedentary delights are activities to set the pulse racing, including scuba diving, snorkelling, surfing, windsurfing and kitesurfing. Action or inaction, these places bubble with opportunities.

When to Go
Quang Ngai

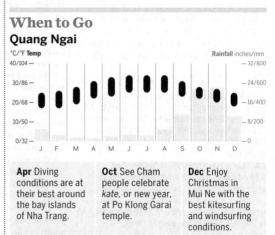

Apr Diving conditions are at their best around the bay islands of Nha Trang.

Oct See Cham people celebrate *kate*, or new year, at Po Klong Garai temple.

Dec Enjoy Christmas in Mui Ne with the best kitesurfing and windsurfing conditions.

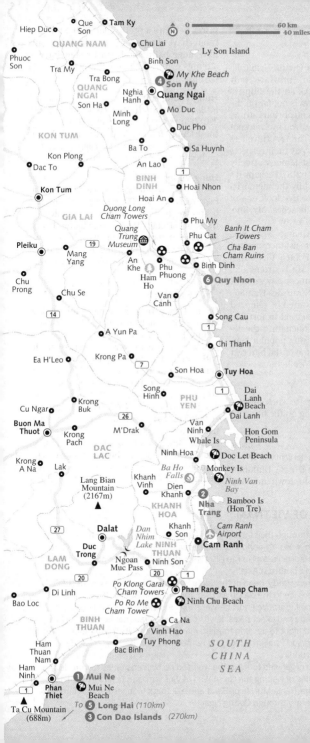

South-Central Coast Highlights

1 Surfing on sand or sea or kitesurfing above the waves at the adrenalin capital of **Mui Ne** (p247)

2 Crawling your way around the bars of **Nha Trang** (p240) after a day of exploring offshore islands by boat

3 Combing the beautiful beaches, snorkelling coral reefs and motorbiking the empty coastal roads around the **Con Dao Islands** (p263)

4 Coming face-to-face with the horrors of war at the poignant **Son My Memorial** (p217)

5 Taking a road trip up the coast to explore the endless sands of **Long Hai** (p258), **Ho Tram** (p257) and **Ho Coc** (p257)

6 Sampling fresh seafood or sunning yourself on empty beaches in the friendly local town of **Quy Nhon** (p219)

Quang Ngai

☑055 / POP 145,000

The eponymous capital of Quang Ngai (aka Quang Nhia or Quangai) province only earned city status in 2005, so the impression of a large country town is not far off the mark. The city itself offers no obvious attractions, so most visitors only drop by for a spot of grazing at lunchtime. The few travellers that venture here come to pay their respects to the victims of the most famous atrocity of the American War (see p218). Perhaps it's the sombre mood induced by the memorial that has caused tourists to overlook one of Vietnam's less celebrated beaches, My Khe, just a couple of kilometres away.

Even before WWII, Quang Ngai was an important centre of resistance against the French. During the Franco–Viet Minh War, the area was a Viet Minh stronghold. In 1962 the South Vietnamese government introduced its ill-fated Strategic Hamlets Program. Villagers were forcibly removed from their homes and resettled in fortified hamlets, infuriating and alienating the local population and increasing popular support for the Viet Cong. Some of the bitterest fighting of the war took place here.

🛏 Sleeping

If you really feel the urge to stick around for a night, consider staying on the beach at nearby My Khe (p217).

Central Hotel　　　　　　　HOTEL $$
(☑382 9999; www.centralhotel.com.vn; 784 Đ Quang Trung; r US$40-80; ❋@🖥🌊) Undoubtedly the smartest hotel in town and the prices here are a pretty good deal. Standard rooms have shower only, but the VIP rooms have huge bathtubs. Extra touches include a tennis court and a pool that is verging on Olympic sized.

Hung Vuong Hotel　　　　　　HOTEL $
(☑381 8828; 33 Đ Hung Vuong; r 180,000-250,000d; ❋🖥) One of the cheapies in town, the friendly family speak little English, but offer good-value rooms at a fair price. The higher-priced rooms are almost quads.

Hung Vuong Hotel　　　　　　HOTEL $$
(☑371 0477; www.hungvuong-hotel.com.vn; 45 Đ Hung Vuong; r US$30-50; ❋@🖥) Déjà vu? Yes, it's pretty confusing, there are two hotels on the same street with the same name. This is the more glamorous of the two, although we are talking Quang Ngai glamour here. It has 64 spacious rooms with plenty of creature comforts.

🍴 Eating

Quang Ngai province is famous for *com ga*, although it actually originates further north at Tam Ky. It consists of boiled chicken over yellow rice (steamed with chicken broth) with mint, egg soup and pickled vegetables. You'll find *com ga* restaurants all over town. Locals tend to eat it with a spoon, so don't stress about struggling with the chopsticks. Try it at **Nhung 1** (474 Đ Quang Trung; meals 20,000-35,000d), a bustling eatery on the main drag.

Bac Son (23 Đ Hung Vuong; mains 25,000-75,000d) has been in business since 1943, and has good Vietnamese food, an English menu and a friendly owner. Next door and

---

THE GREAT WALL OF VIETNAM

Stretching some 127km through the hinterlands of Quang Ngai and Binh Dinh provinces, the 'Long Wall of Vietnam' was only announced to the world in early 2011. Less the Great Wall of China and more Hadrian's Wall in the UK, this historic structure is now considered the longest monument in Southeast Asia.

Back in 2005, Dr Andrew Hardy, head of the École Française d'Extrême Orient (EFEO) in Hanoi, discovered reference to the wall in an 1885 manuscript. Built in 1819, it was believed to have been a collaborative effort between lowland Viet people and highland Tre people to regulate trade and exact taxes. It was declared a National Heritage Site in March 2011 and plans are afoot to develop tourism along the route, in consultation with English Heritage. Plans include walking trails and homestays, but this may take a few years before it is up and running.

There are currently no organised tours to the wall and no trained guides to introduce its history. The best chance of visiting the Great Wall of Vietnam is to talk to experienced Easy Riders in Hoi An, Nha Trang, Mui Ne or Dalat and ask them to incorporate it into an off-the-beaten-track itinerary through Quang Ngai.

in a similar vein is **Mimosa** (21 Đ Hung Vuong; mains 25,000-70,000d).

ℹ Information

Deluxe Taxis (☑383 8383)

Main post office (80 Đ Phan Dinh Phung) Internet access available.

Vietcombank (45 Đ Hung Vuong) Branch in the Hung Vuong Hotel with an ATM.

ℹ Getting There & Away

AIR Tam Ky airport (VCL) lies 36km north of Quang Ngai. **Vasco** (www.vasco.com.vn) has flights from here to Hanoi from around 1,200,000d, and to HCMC from around 1,050,000d. A metered taxi to Tam Ky airport will cost about 350,000d.

BUS Quang Ngai bus station (Đ Le Thanh Ton) is situated to the south of the centre, 50m east of Đ Quang Trung. Regular buses head to all the major stops on Hwy 1, including Danang (from 35,000d, two hours) and Quy Nhon (from 60,000d, 3½ hours). Open-tour buses can drop off here, but pick-ups are harder to arrange.

CAR & MOTORBIKE By road from Quang Ngai, it's 100km to Hoi An, 174km to Quy Nhon and 412km to Nha Trang.

TRAIN Trains stop at **Quang Ngai Train Station** (Ga Quang Nghia; ☑382 0280; 204 Đ Nguyen Chi Thanh), 1.5km west of the town centre. Destinations include Danang (70,000d, three hours), Quy Nhon (82,000d, five hours) and Nha Trang (225,000d, seven hours).

Around Quang Ngai

SON MY (MY LAI)

It's hard to believe that this tranquil rural spot was the setting for one of the most horrific crimes of the American War. On the morning of 16 March 1968, US troops swept through four hamlets in the Son My subdistrict, killing 504 villagers, many of them elderly and children. The largest mass killing took place in Xom Lang (Thuan Yen) subhamlet, where the **Son My Memorial** (admission 10,000d; ⊘8-11.30am & 1-4.30pm Mon-Fri) now stands. However, it was one of the other hamlets that lent the name the world remembers: the My Lai massacre.

The memorial is centred on a dramatic stone sculpture of an elderly woman holding up her fist in defiance, a dead child in her arms, surrounded by the injured and dying at her feet. The scene has been recreated to reflect the aftermath of that fateful day. Burnt-out shells of homes stand in their original locations, each marked with a plaque listing the names and ages of the family that once resided there. The concrete connecting the ruins is coloured to represent a dirt path, and indented with the heavy bootprints of American soldiers and the bare footprints of fleeing villagers. However, the overall effect is rather kitsch, making it feel more like a film set than a memorial for some international visitors.

The massacre was painstakingly documented by a US military photographer and these graphic images are now the showcase of a small **museum** on the site. While a distressing experience, the display ends on a hopeful note, chronicling the efforts of the local people to rebuild their lives afterwards. A prominent section honours the GIs who tried to stop the carnage, shielding a group of villagers from certain death, and those responsible for blowing the whistle.

The road to Son My passes through particularly beautiful countryside: rice paddies, cassava patches and vegetable gardens shaded by casuarinas and eucalyptus trees. However, if you look closely you can still make out the odd bomb crater, and the bare hilltops are testimony to the continuing environmental devastation caused by Agent Orange.

The best way to get to Son My is by motorbike (around 100,000d including wait time) or regular taxi (about 350,000d including wait time). From Quang Ngai head north on Đ Quang Trung (Hwy 1) and cross the long bridge over the Tra Khuc River. Take the first right (eastward, parallel to the river) where a triangular concrete stela indicates the way and follow the road for 12km.

MY KHE BEACH

A world away from the sombre atmosphere of the Son My Memorial, but only a couple of kilometres down the road, My Khe (not to be confused with the other My Khe Beach near Danang) is a superb beach, with fine white sand and clear water. It stretches for kilometres along a thin, casuarina-lined spit of sand, separated from the mainland by Song Kinh Giang, a body of water just inland from the beach. If you want a pretty beach largely to yourself, this is one place to come, as most travellers are hotfooting it between Hoi An and Nha Trang. The only downside is the presence of litter which rather detracts from the picture-postcard setting.

Accommodation offerings are thin on the ground here, as the anticipated boom in visitors simply never happened.

MY LAI MASSACRE

At about 7.30am on 16 March 1968, the US Army's Charlie Company landed by helicopter in the west of Son My, regarded as a Viet Cong stronghold. The area had been bombarded with artillery, and the landing zone raked with rocket and machine-gun fire from helicopter gunships. They encountered no resistance during the 'combat-assault', nor did they come under fire at any time during the operation; but as soon as their sweep eastward began, so did the atrocities.

As the soldiers of the 1st Platoon moved through Xom Lang, they shot and bayoneted fleeing villagers, threw hand grenades into houses and bomb shelters, slaughtered livestock and burned dwellings. Somewhere between 75 and 150 unarmed villagers were rounded up and herded to a ditch, where they were executed by machine-gun fire.

In the next few hours, as command helicopters circled overhead and American Navy boats patrolled offshore, the 2nd Platoon, the 3rd Platoon and the company headquarters group also became involved in the attacks. At least half a dozen groups of civilians, including women and children, were assembled and executed. Villagers fleeing towards Quang Ngai were shot. As these massacres were taking place, at least four girls and women were raped or gang-raped by groups of soldiers.

According to the memorial here, a total of 504 Vietnamese were killed during the massacre; US Army sources determined the total number of dead at 347.

Troops who participated were ordered to keep their mouths shut, but several disobeyed orders and went public with the story after returning to the USA, including helicopter pilot Hugh Thompson Jr who managed to rescue several women and children that fateful day. When it broke in the newspapers it had a devastating effect on the military's morale and fuelled further public protests against the war. It did little to persuade the world that the US Army was fighting on behalf of the Vietnamese people. Unlike WWII veterans, who returned home to parades and glory, soldiers coming home from Vietnam often found themselves ostracised and branded 'baby killers'.

A cover-up of the atrocities was undertaken at all levels of the US army command, eventually leading to several investigations. Lieutenant William Calley, leader of the 1st Platoon, was court-martialled and found guilty of the murders of 22 unarmed civilians. He was sentenced to life imprisonment in 1971 and spent three years under house arrest at Fort Benning, Georgia, while appealing his conviction. Calley was paroled in 1974 after the US Supreme Court refused to hear his case. Calley's case still causes controversy – many claim that he was made a scapegoat because of his low rank, and that officers much higher up ordered the massacres. What is certain is that he didn't act alone.

For the full story of this event and its aftermath, pick up a copy of *Four Hours in My Lai* by Michael Bilton and Kevin Sim, a stunning piece of journalism.

My Khe Resort (☎368 6111; ks_mytra@dng.vnn.vn; Tinh Khe; r from US$20; ❉☎) has a somewhat abandoned feel to it. Staff are often hard to find and service is slow. Rooms have satellite TV and bathtubs. Breakfast is theoretically included at the beachfront restaurant across the road.

A better option may well be the **My Khe Hotel** (☎384 3316; My Khe), under construction at the time of writing, but with an attractive pavilion restaurant out front.

There are dozens of ramshackle stalls spread along the beach here, although they can be a bit hard-sell. Relatively deserted during the week, they fill up with escaping urbanites at the weekend. The seafood is fresh and delicious, but settle on prices in advance.

Sa Huynh
☎055

Sa Huynh is a popular lunchstop for truckers and transport heading north or south on Hwy 1. There are lots of *com ga* places lining the highway, many of which offer decent seafood. Expect to pay around 50,000d a main dish.

Approaching the bay, there is a beautiful semicircular beach, but sadly it doesn't look quite so exotic at close quarters due to a surfeit of litter. The little town is also known for its salt marshes and salt-evaporation ponds, as well as a pungent *nuoc mam* (fish sauce) industry. Archaeologists have unearthed remains from the Dong Son civilisation dating from the 1st century AD in the vicinity of Sa Huynh.

Sa Huynh is on Hwy 1, about 60km south of Quang Ngai (25,000d; 1½ hours by bus) and 114km north of Quy Nhon (40,000d; two hours by bus).

Quy Nhon

📞 056 / POP 275,000

Flanked by blissful beaches and the surrounding countryside dotted with ancient Cham temples, Quy Nhon (Qui Nhon; pronounced 'hwee ngon') remains largely untouristed compared with Nha Trang and Hoi An. This can be in part explained by the sprawling city, which is not one of the most alluring in the country, but the lack of visitors can be an attraction in itself. The trickle of foreigners who venture here find friendly locals and far fewer hassles than in the better-known beach towns to the south. The capital of Binh Dinh province and one of Vietnam's more active second-string seaports, this is a good spot to sample some fresh seafood. In short, it's one way to avoid the herd on their 'Open Tour'.

During the American War there was considerable South Vietnamese, US, VC and South Korean military activity in the area. The mayor of Quy Nhon, hoping to cash in on the presence of US troops, turned his official residence into a large massage parlour.

◉ Sights

Municipal Beach   BEACH
The long sweep of Quy Nhon's beachfront extends from the port in the northeast to the hills in the south. It's a beautiful stretch of sand and has been given a major facelift in recent years, making it almost as nice as Nha Trang, but with a fraction of the visitors.

At the top end, the nicest section is near the Saigon Quy Nhon Hotel, where a grove of coconut trees lines the road. At dawn and in the evenings this area is packed with locals practising t'ai chi. In the distance you can see a giant **statue of Tran Hung Dao** giving the Chinese the finger on the far headland (see 'Playing for High Stakes' boxed text, p89). It is possible to climb the statue if the door is open and peek up through the eyes. Heading south, a striking socialist-realist **war memorial** dominates a small square.

From here, the waterfront opens up to a parklike promenade, punctuated by large hotels, stretching to the south end of the bay. Here the beach gets more beautiful and secluded, away from the bustle of town. At night the bright lights of the squid boats give the illusion of a floating village far out to sea.

FREE **Binh Dinh Museum**   MUSEUM
(28 Đ Nguyen Hue; ⊗7-11am & 2-5pm Apr-Sep, 7.30-11am & 1.30-4.30pm Oct-Mar) This small museum features exhibits on regional history. The entry hall focuses on local communism, including an interesting silk print (by Zuy Nhat, 1959) showing a fat French colonist sitting aloft mandarins, in turn supported by bureaucrats, and cruel bosses, with the struggling masses supporting the whole ensemble. The room to the left has a small Natural History section and some Cham statues, while the rear room has the bulk of the impressive Cham collection. The room to the right of the entrance is devoted to the American War, with local relics such as the 'Spittoon of Heroic Vietnamese Mother Huynh Thi Bon'.

Thap Doi Cham Towers   HISTORIC TEMPLE
(admission 5000d; ⊗8-11am & 1-6pm) This ancient pair of Cham towers sits within the city limits in a pretty little park. Steep steps lead up to the former temples, which are open to the sky. Atypically for Cham architecture, they have curved pyramidal roofs rather than the usual terracing. The larger tower (20m tall) retains some of its ornate brickwork and remnants of the granite statuary that once graced its summit. The dismembered torsos of garuda (half human, half bird) can be seen at the corners of the roofs.

Take Đ Tran Hung Dao west away from the centre and look out for the towers on the right.

Long Khanh Pagoda   TEMPLE
It's hard to miss the 17m-high Buddha (built in 1972) heralding Quy Nhon's main pagoda, set back from the road next to 143 Đ Tran Cao Van. The pagoda was founded in 1715 by a Chinese merchant, and the monks who reside here preside over the religious affairs of the city's active Buddhist community.

The pagoda was repaired in 1957 after being damaged during the Franco–Viet Minh War. Mosaic dragons with manes of broken glass lead up to the main building, flanked by towers sheltering a giant drum (on the left) and an enormous bell. Inside, in front of the large copper Thich Ca Buddha (with its multicoloured neon halo) is a drawing of

Quy Nhon

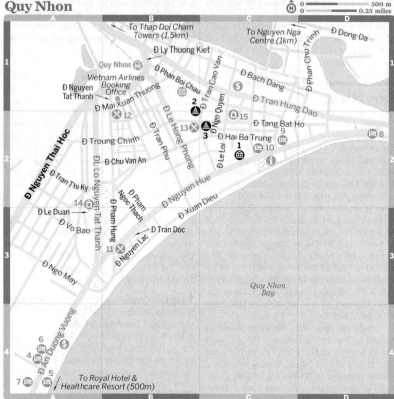

multi-armed and multi-eyed Chuan De (the Goddess of Mercy); the numerous arms and eyes symbolise her ability to touch and see all.

Tam An Pagoda
TEMPLE
(58B Đ Ngo Quyen) Quy Nhon's second most active pagoda, Tam An is a charming little place that attracts mostly female worshippers, although it's open to all.

Queen's & Quy Hoa Beaches
BEACHES
The clarity of the water at the beaches improves considerably once you round Ganh Rang Hill to the south of the town. Several beaches are easily accessible by bicycle.

Queen's Beach
Popular with locals, this stony little beach at the foot of Ganh Rang was once a favourite holiday spot of Queen Nam Phuong. There's a cafe and great views back over Quy Nhon. To get here, take Đ An Duong Vuong to the

far south end of Quy Nhon's beachfront and continue as the road starts to climb. After it crosses a small bridge, turn to the left and head through the gates and pay the entrance fee (5000d). Follow the path up the hill, keeping to the left where it forks. Queen's Beach is signposted to the left.

Quy Hoa Beach & Leper Hospital
Leprosy may not conjure up images of fun in the sun, but this really is a lovely spot. As leper hospitals go, this one is highly unusual. Rather than being a depressing place, it's a sort of model village near the seafront, where treated patients live together with their families in small, well-kept houses. Depending on their abilities, the patients work in the rice fields, in fishing, and in repair-oriented businesses or small craft shops – one supported by Handicap International produces prosthetic limbs.

The **hospital grounds** (☎364 6343; admission 5000d; ☺7am-7pm) are so well maintained

Quy Nhon

that it looks a bit like a resort, complete with a guitar-shaped pavilion and numerous busts of distinguished and historically important doctors, both Vietnamese and foreign. Fronting the village is **Quy Hoa Beach**, one of the nicer stretches of sand around Quy Nhon and a popular weekend hang-out for the city's small expat community. Just up from the beach, there's a dirt path to the hillside **tomb of Han Mac Tu**, a mystical poet who died in 1940.

If travelling by foot or bicycle, continue along the road past Queen's Beach until it descends to the hospital's entrance gates, about 1.5km south of Quy Nhon. It's also accessible from the road to Song Cau by taking a left turn once the water comes back into view after crossing the hills south of town.

🛏 Sleeping

Quy Nhon offers great value for money, so it is one destination where you might consider spending a little extra for a lot more comfort.

Hotel Au Co – Ben Bo Bien   HOTEL $
(☎374 7699; hotel_auco@yahoo.com; 8 & 24 Đ An Duong Vuong; r 180,000-300,000d; ❄) Under the same ownership, these two hotels share the same name, one of them confusingly sharing the same street address as the Anh Vy Hotel

(below). Number 8 is the slightly more atmospheric of the two, looking like the Vietnamese take on a San Francisco townhouse. Narrow stairs with carved wooden dragons on the balustrades lead to clean rooms with small bathrooms but genuine sea views and balconies. Number 24 is even more kitsch, with fake trees predominating in the lobby. The friendly management speak good English. Bicycles are available for 30,000d per day, motorbikes for 120,000d per day.

Hoang Yen Hotel   HOTEL $$
(☎374 6900; www.hoangyenhotel.com.vn; 5 Đ An Duong Vuong; r 400,000-950,000d; ❄@🛜🏊) The smart rooms at this 10-storey pad overlooking the beach in the south of town remain a very good deal. The trim includes satellite TV and minibar, as well as some heavy wooden furnishings. Secure a sea view, as the rates aren't much higher and include breakfast.

Life Resort   BOUTIQUE HOTEL $$$
(☎384 0132; www.life-resorts.com; Bai Dai Beach; r US$106-120, ste US$147; ❄@🛜🏊) This gorgeous resort, set on a private beach about 18km south of town, is the most luxurious place in Binh Dinh. A subtle Cham influence pervades the architecture and interior design. The spacious rooms are striking, with stunning open-plan bathrooms. You can indulge in a spa treatment, enjoy t'ai chi on the beach or go snorkelling. The wonderful staff offer friendly service and speak excellent English. The restaurant's food and wine selection is impressive.

Anh Vy Hotel   HOTEL $
(☎384 7763; 8 Đ An Duong Vuong; r 130,000-220,000d; ❄) Sharing its address with the aforementioned Hotel Au Co, this family-run enterprise has clean rooms with satellite TV and hot-water showers. Some of the upper rooms also include a sea view for anyone willing to tackle the stairs and triples are available.

Quy Nhon Hotel   HOTEL $$
(☎389 2401; www.quynhonhotel.com.vn; 8 Đ Nguyen Hue; r from 400,000d; ❄@🛜) The impressive colonial facade belies an old school government hotel behind, but the rates are some of the best value in town for the size and trim of the rooms.

Lan Anh Hotel   HOTEL $
(☎389 3109; 102 Đ Xuan Dieu; r 200,000-300,000d; ❄@🛜) Located next door to Barbara's, Quy

Nhon's answer to a backpacker cafe, the rooms here include TV, fridge and hot-water bathrooms. There is a good strip of local restaurants just north of here.

Saigon–Quy Nhon Hotel
HOTEL $$

(☑382 0100; www.saigonquynhonhotel.com.vn; 24 Đ Nguyen Hue; s US$40-50, d US$50-60, ste from US$120; ❄@🎧🌊) Run by Saigon Tourist, the smart, modern rooms include deep-pile carpets and bathrobes. Other facilities include in-room safety boxes, free wi-fi, a small swimming pool and a rooftop bar with serious sea views.

Royal Hotel & Healthcare Resort
RESORT HOTEL $$

(☑374 7100; www.royalquynhon.com; 1 Đ Han Mac Tu; r US$55-65, ste US$110; ❄@🎧🌊) Last time around we recommended this place due to its plummeting rates. Now they have skyrocketed again, perhaps in honour of its new royal pedigree, so it's not such good value as it was. It's a huge place with 133 rooms; other facilities include an immense pool, a fitness centre, tennis courts and the inevitable massage.

Eating & Drinking

Quy Nhon also has lots of delicious street food all around the town centre.

Barbara's: The Kiwi Connection
BACKPACKER CAFE $

(102 Đ Xuan Dieu; mains 25,000-75,000đ) A popular place for comfort food from home, this place draws a mix of backpackers and expats each night. Popular mains include a reliable fish and chips, plus there are healthy smoothies and international breakfasts. Cheap beers include some local brews.

2000
SEAFOOD $

(1 Đ Tran Doc; dishes 40,000-250,000đ) No need to worry about how fresh the seafood is here, as there are tubs and tanks downstairs full of live crabs, shrimp and fish. There is also an upstairs dining area with a balcony. The seafood hotpots are legend.

Que Huong
SEAFOOD $

(125 Đ Tang Bat Ho; dishes 30,000-190,000đ) Follow the local crowd to this place, which serves everything from seafood to snake. The staff are friendly to the few foreigners who pass through.

Tinh Tam
VEGETARIAN $

(141 Đ Tran Cao Van; mains 10,000-20,000đ; ☑) Located next to Long Khanh Pagoda, this hole-in-the-wall serves vegetarian meals in basic surrounds. The mixed plate is filling and hearty.

Khanh My
CAFE $

(100 Đ Pham Hung; mains 30,000-90,000đ) With the demise of the Vespa Cafe, this is now one of the most popular cafes in this part of town. Caffeine fixes are popular, but the menu does include a range of popular Vietnamese fishes. Free wi-fi.

🛍 Shopping

Lon Market
MARKET

(Cho Lon, Đ Tang Bat Ho) The famous Lon Market burnt to the ground in December 2006 and it has been rebuilt as a less interesting shopping-centre-style market. However, street sellers spill over into the surrounding roads making for some good photo opportunities.

Co-op Mart
SUPERMARKET

(☑382 1321; 7 Đ Le Duan) This huge shopping complex is officially a supermarket but, like a traditional market, sells a little bit of everything. It's a great place to stock up on treats for a day trip to nearby Cham towers or a long bus ride.

Nguyen Nga Centre
HANDICRAFTS

(☑381 8272; www.nguyennga.org; 91 Đ Dong Da) This shop sells lovely homemade weavings, handicrafts, clothing and jewellery, with the money going towards running a centre for disabled students.

ℹ Information

Barbara's: The Kiwi Connection (☑389 2921; nzbarb@yahoo.com; 102 Đ Xuan Dieu) Free tourist information, bike and motorbike hire, local maps and connections with English-speaking drivers.

Binh Dinh Tourist (☑389 2524; 10 Đ Nguyen Hue) Government-run tourist office.

Main post office (197 Đ Phan Boi Chau; ⊙6.30am-10pm) Plus cheap internet.

Vietcombank (148 Đ Le Loi) On the corner of Đ Tran Hung Dao; has a 24-hour ATM

ℹ Getting There & Away

Air

Vietnam Airlines (☑382 5313; 1 Đ Nguyen Tat Thanh) flights link Quy Nhon with Ho Chi Minh City (HCMC; 983,000đ) daily. There are flights to Danang (983,000đ), continuing on to Hanoi (2,033,000đ) four times a week.

Vietnam Airlines offers a minibus transfer (40,000đ) for airline passengers between the office and Phu Cat airport, 36km north of the city.

Bus

Quy Nhon bus station (Đ Tay Son) is on the south side of town. The next major stop north is Quang Ngai (60,000d, 3½ hours), with frequent buses heading on to Danang (75,000d, six hours) and the odd one to Hue (120,000d, nine hours). Heading south, there are regular services to Nha Trang (80,000d, five hours).

Quy Nhon is a great access point for the central highlands. There are frequent buses to Pleiku (70,000d, four hours), several of which continue to Kon Tum (80,000d, five hours) and some services to Buon Ma Thuot (120,000d, seven hours).

It is now possible to get a bus all the way to Pakse (from 250,000d, 20 hours, four per week) in Laos, crossing the border at Bo Y. See the boxed text, p296.

Car & Motorbike

By road from Quy Nhon, it's 238km to Nha Trang, 186km to Pleiku, 198km to Kon Tum, 174km to Quang Ngai and 303km to Danang.

Train

The nearest mainline station to Quy Nhon is Dieu Tri, 10km west of the city. **Quy Nhon train station** (Đ Le Hong Phong) is at the end of a 10km spur off the main north–south track. Only very slow local trains stop here and they are not worth bothering with. It's better to get to/from Dieu Tri by taxi (150,000d) or *xe om* (motorbike taxi) for around 80,000d.

Destinations include: Quang Ngai (82,000d, five hours), Danang (178,000d, seven hours) and Nha Trang (132,000d, four hours).

Cha Ban Cham Area

The former Cham capital of Cha Ban (also known as Vijay and Quy Nhon) was located 26km north of Quy Nhon and 5km from Binh Dinh. While of archaeological importance, there's very little to see for the casual visitor. However, there are several interesting Cham structures dotted around the area.

BANH IT CHAM TOWERS

The most impressive of the area's Cham sites, this group of four towers sitting atop a hill 20km to the north of Quy Nhon is clearly visible from Hwy 1. The architecture of each tower is distinctly different, although all were built around the turn of the 12th century. The smaller, barrel-roofed tower has the most intricate carvings, although there's still a wonderfully toothy face looking down on it from the wall of the largest tower. A large Buddhist pagoda sits on the side of the hill under the lowest of the towers. There are great views of the surrounding countryside from the top of the hill.

The **towers** (Phuoc Hiep, Tuy Phuoc district; admission free; ☉7-11am & 1.30-4.30pm) are easily reached by taking Đ Tran Hung Dao out

---

THE LOST CITY OF CHAMPA

Cha Ban, which served as the capital of Champa from the year 1000 (after the loss of Indrapura/Dong Duong) until 1471, was attacked and plundered repeatedly by the Vietnamese, Khmers and Chinese.

In 1044 the Vietnamese prince Phat Ma occupied the city and carried off a great deal of booty along with the Cham king's wives, harem, female dancers, musicians and singers. Cha Ban was under the control of Jayavarman VII and the Khmer empire from 1190 to 1220. In 1377 the Vietnamese were defeated and their king was killed in an attempt to capture Cha Ban. The Vietnamese emperor Le Thanh Ton breached the eastern gate of the city in 1471 and captured the Cham king and 50 members of the royal family. During this, the last great battle fought by the Cham, 60,000 Cham were killed and 30,000 more were taken prisoner by the Vietnamese.

During the Tay Son Rebellion, Cha Ban served as the capital of central Vietnam, and was ruled by the eldest of the three Tay Son brothers. It was attacked in 1793 by the forces of Nguyen Anh (later Emperor Gia Long), but the assault failed. In 1799 they laid siege to the city again, under the command of General Vu Tinh, capturing it at last.

The Tay Son rebels soon reoccupied the port of Thi Nai (modern-day Quy Nhon) and then laid siege to Cha Ban themselves. The siege continued for over a year, and by June 1801, Vu Tinh's provisions were gone. Food was in short supply; all the horses and elephants had long since been eaten. Refusing to consider the ignominy of surrender, Vu Tinh had an octagonal wooden tower constructed. He filled it with gunpowder and, arrayed in his ceremonial robes, went inside and blew himself up. Upon hearing the news of the death of his dedicated general, Nguyen Anh wept.

of Quy Nhon for about 30 minutes, when you'll see the towers in the distance to the right of the road. After the traffic lights joining the main highway, cross the bridge and turn right. Take the left turn heading up the hill to reach the entrance.

DUONG LONG CHAM TOWERS

These towers (Binh Hoa, Tay Son district; admission free; ⊙7-11am & 1.30-4.30pm) are harder to find, sitting in the countryside about 50km northwest of Quy Nhon. Dating from the late 12th century, the largest of the three brick towers (24m high) is embellished with granite ornamentation representing *naga* (a mythical serpent being with divine powers) and elephants (Duong Long means 'Towers of Ivory'). Over the doors are bas-reliefs of women, dancers, monsters and various animals. The corners of the structure are formed by enormous dragon heads.

It is best to visit the towers with a driver or a tour, as the site is reached by a succession of pretty country lanes through rice paddies and over rickety bridges.

Quang Trung Museum

Nguyen Hue, the second-oldest of the three brothers who led the Tay Son Rebellion, crowned himself Emperor Quang Trung in 1788. In 1789, Quang Trung led the campaign that overwhelmingly defeated a Chinese invasion of 200,000 troops near Hanoi. This epic battle is still celebrated as one of the greatest triumphs in Vietnamese history.

During his reign, Quang Trung was something of a social reformer. He encouraged land reform, revised the system of taxation, improved the army and emphasised education, opening many schools and encouraging the development of Vietnamese poetry and literature. He died in 1792 at the age of 40. Communist literature portrays him as the leader of a peasant revolution whose progressive policies were crushed by the reactionary Nguyen dynasty, which came to power in 1802 and was overthrown by Ho Chi Minh in 1945.

The Quang Trung Museum (Phu Phong; admission 10,000d; ⊙8-11.30am & 1-4.30pm Mon-Fri) is built on the site of the brothers' house and encloses the original well and a more-than-200-year-old tamarind tree said to have been planted by the brothers. Displays include various statues, costumes, documents and artefacts from the 18th century, most of them labelled in English. Especially

notable are the elephant-skin battle drums and gongs from the Bahnar tribe. The museum is also known for its demonstrations of *vo binh dinh,* a traditional martial art that is performed with a bamboo stick.

The museum is about 50km from Quy Nhon. Take Hwy 19 west for 40km towards Pleiku. The museum is about 5km north of the highway (the turn-off is signposted) in Phu Phong, Tay Son district.

Ham Ho Nature Reserve

A beautiful nature reserve 55km from Quy Nhon, Ham Ho (☑388 0860; Tay Phu; admission 12,000d; ⊙7-11.30am & 1-4.30pm) can easily be combined with a trip to the Quang Trung Museum. Taking up a jungle-lined 3km stretch of clean, fish-filled river, the park is best enjoyed by kayak (60,000d). The further up river you travel, the better the swimming spots. Accommodation is available via the reserve at 220,000d for a twin room.

The road to Ham Ho is signposted to the south of Hwy 19 at Tay Son.

Song Cau

☑057

The village of Song Cau is an obscure place that you could easily drive past without ever noticing, but nearby is an immense beautiful bay. It makes a good rest stop for overland travellers doing the Nha Trang–Hoi An run.

WORTH A TRIP

BAI BAU BEACH

While the nearby Life Resort charges nonguests US$10 to lounge on their beach (whether they've dined at the restaurant or not), those in the know will head 2km south for an even better beach at a fraction of the price. Bai Bau (admission 10,000d) is a beautiful white-sand crescent no more than 150m wide, sheltered by rocky headlands, with mountains for a backdrop. It can get busy on the weekend and during Vietnamese holidays, but midweek you'll likely have the place to yourself.

Bai Bau is well signed, just off the road to Song Cau, about 20km south of Quy Nhon. Approach by motorbike or taxi from Quy Nhon.

Song Cau is 170km north of Nha Trang and 50km south of Quy Nhon. Highway buses can drop off and pick up here (with luck). If travelling with your own wheels, take the stunning coastal road north of Song Cau that winds its way to Quy Nhon, as there are several isolated beaches en route.

Tuy Hoa

☎057 / POP 165,000

The capital of Phu Yen province, Tuy Hoa (pronounced 'twee hwa') is a sprawling if friendly town with a wide, empty beach with coarse golden sand. It's a possible overnight stop to break up a longer journey, especially for cyclists brave enough to tackle Hwy 1, but most visitors are just passing through.

The few sights the town has are all on hilltops visible from the main highway. There's a huge **seated Buddha** that greets you if you're approaching from the north. To the south of town the **Nhan Cham Tower** is an impressive sight, particularly when illuminated at night. The climb to the tower takes you through a small **botanic garden** and is rewarded with great views. On the same hill is a massive white **war memorial**, designed with sails that are vaguely reminiscent of the Sydney Opera House.

🛏 Sleeping & Eating

There are plenty more nondescript mini-hotels in addition to the following, and a glut of humble restaurants and street vendors along the main highway and Đ Tran Hung Dao, but it's not the nicest part of town due to the constant rumble of traffic.

The best dining is to be had on the beach, where a stretch of seafood shacks and *bia hoi* (draught beer) joints serve fresh seafood. Many charge by the kilogram, so be sure to agree on prices to avoid an expensive surprise.

Cong Doan Hotel   HOTEL $
(☎382 3187; 53 Đ Doc Lap; r 200,000d; ❄@🛜) The Trade Union Hotel has a prime beachfront location, but sometimes feels as deserted as The Overlook Hotel in *The Shining*. Sizeable rooms are good value for just US$10, including satellite TV and hot water. Request a sea view.

Cendeluxe Hotel   HOTEL $$
(☎381 8818; cendeluxe.com; Đ Hai Duong; r from US$65; ❄@🛜🏊) It's easy to spot this skyscraper long before arriving in the town centre, as it's a 14-storey landmark. It claims

5-star status, and internet specials include all meals plus use of the hotel's beachside pool.

ⓘ Information

Incombank ATM (239 Đ Tran Hung Dao) Opposite the market.

Main post office (cnr Đ Tran Hung Dao & Nguyen Thai) Plus internet access.

ⓘ Getting There & Away

AIR Vietnam Airlines (☎382 6508; 353 Đ Tran Hung Dao) is in the centre of town and the airport is 8km to the south. There are several flights weekly between Tuy Hoa and HCMC (780,000d), operated by Vasco.

BUS From Tuy Hoa, there are regular buses to Quy Nhon (40,000d, two hours, 110km) and Nha Trang (60,000d, three hours, 123km).

TRAIN Tuy Hoa Train Station (Đ Le Trung Kien) is on the road parallel to the highway, north of the main street. Destinations include Danang (eight hours) and Nha Trang (2½ hours).

Tuy Hoa to Nha Trang

☎058

The coastal drive between Tuy Hoa and Nha Trang on Hwy 1 provides tantalising glimpses of a number of remote and beautiful spots, while others are hidden away in the jungle along promontories or on secluded islands. Leave behind the guidebook for a day or two and go exploring. Money-changing facilities and ATMs are thin on the ground here, so plan ahead in Nha Trang, Tuy Hoa or Quy Nhon.

DAI LANH BEACH

Crescent-shaped Dai Lanh Beach has a split personality: a scruffy fishing village occupies the northern end, but yields to an attractive beach shaded by casuarina trees. About 1km south is a vast sand-dune causeway worth exploring. It connects the mainland to Hon Gom, a mountainous peninsula almost 30km in length. Boats for Whale Island leave from Hom Gom's main village, **Dam Mon**, set on a sheltered bay.

It's possible to stay overnight under the trees right on Dai Lanh Beach, but the accommodation options around Doc Let are much better. **Thuy Ta Restaurant** (☎384 2117; r 300,000d) has some basic bungalows at the back of beach including air-con and attached bathroom. Fresh seafood features prominently on the menu with mains from 50,000d to 150,000d.

EAST BY SOUTHEAST: VUNG RO BAY

Celebrated as Vietnam's most easterly point on the mainland, Vung Ro Bay is also famed for its beautiful and isolated bays which hide some unspoilt beaches. It is also one of the deepest water ports in this part of Vietnam and hit the headlines back in February 1965 when a US helicopter detected the movement of a North Vietnamese supply ship in the area. Vung Ro was part of the alternative Ho Chi Minh Sea Trail and was being used to smuggle arms into South Vietnam for Viet Cong forces. The discovery of a sea supply route from north to south confirmed US suspicions and was used as justification to ramp up US involvement in the war. The small town of Vung Ro lies about 33km southeast of Tuy Hoa and can be reached by motorbike or car.

Dai Lanh is situated 40km south of Tuy Hoa and 83km north of Nha Trang on Hwy 1.

WHALE ISLAND

Whale Island is a tiny speck on the map and home to the romantic and secluded **Whale Island Resort** (☎384 0501; www.whaleisland resort.com; s/d from US$29/41), just a 15-minute boat ride from Dam Mon. The bungalows are atmospheric, finished in designer-rustic style with bamboo and rattan furnishings. However, it's all about location, location, location. Compulsory but hearty meals are an extra US$24 per person per day. Transfers are available daily – a bus-boat combination from Nha Trang costs US$19 per person or US$56 for a minibus.

Rainbow Divers has a permanent base on the island, and the Nha Trang office (see p234) can make resort bookings and help with transfers. Scuba-diving season ends in mid-October, starting up again in mid-January. Whale sharks pass this way for a krill feed between April and July.

DOC LET BEACH

This lovely stretch of beachfront is brochure material, with chalk-white sand and shallow waters. Doc Let (pronounced 'yop lek') is easily accessible from Nha Trang and worth considering as a day trip (beach entrance fee 10,000d) or overnight stop. Unfortunately

the main strip around the government-run Doc Let Resort has been well and truly overrun by domestic tourists on whistlestop coastal tours, so it pays to explore the area at your own pace on a rented motorbike. Although there's a small town nearby, the resorts on the beach are fairly isolated, so when staying here, be prepared to do nothing but lounge around.

🛏 Sleeping

Jungle Beach   GUESTHOUSE **$**
(☎366 2384; syl@dng.vnn.vn; r 450,000d) Just when we thought that Vietnam was too conservative to deliver the hippy-trippy vibe of Thailand or Goa, along comes Jungle Beach. It's hard to find, but some say harder to leave, despite the very basic accommodation, which involves camping in the garden or opting for a beachfront lean-to with only rattan blinds for privacy. There are also some more solid rooms in a longhouse. All meals are included in the price, adding to the atmosphere of a commune where it is all about relaxing. Given the obscure location, it makes sense to come with a *xe om* driver.

Paradise Resort   HOTEL **$$**
(☎367 0480; www.vngold.com/doclet/paradise; bungalows s US$25, d US$40-50, apt US$70; ✳@🛜) This chilled-out retreat is popular with travellers seeking to escape the 24-hour party people of Nha Trang. Set in the quiet village of Dom Hai where the beach is less developed, this French-run place offers accommodation in basic beach-view huts or more upmarket (and air-conditioned) apartments. Incredibly, the prices include three delicious meals a day and free water, tea, coffee and fruits. Follow the blue signs past the turn-off for Doc Let Resort for 2km, turning right at a petrol station and then right again halfway through the village.

White Sand Doclet
Resort & Spa   RESORT HOTEL **$$$**
(☎367 0670; www.whitesandresort.com.vn; r US$77-85, villas US$92-123; ✳@🛜🏊) This is a swanky place, offering tastefully decorated rooms complete with everything from bathrobes to a safety box. All rooms front the beach, but the villas include a widescreen TV and DVD player.

Ki-em Art House   BOUTIQUE HOTEL **$$$**
(☎367 0952; www.ki-em.com; bungalows US$160-190; ✳@🛜🏊) Set in the grounds of a stunning Vietnamese-German artist's retreat, this is as boutique as it gets. The elegant

bungalows are lovingly decorated with works of art and feature four-poster beds, all set amid a gorgeous garden that faces a lovely tropical beach. Other features include an antique museum and art gallery, with works of art produced by the owner. The website announces 'This is not a hotel...' and they are right, it's so much better than that.

ⓘ **Getting There & Away**

Head 35km north of Nha Trang on Hwy 1, turning right (east) about 4km past Ninh Hoa where there is a big sign for the Hyundai Port. Continue 10km past photogenic salt fields, looking out for the signs to the resorts (except Jungle Beach). Make a left turn through Doc Let village and then a right to the beach. Most of the hotels and resorts also offer some sort of transfer service for a fee.

NINH VAN BAY

Welcome to an alternate reality populated by European royalty, film stars and the otherwise rich and secretive. Sadly for the average punter, this place doesn't really exist. Occupying a secluded beach at the end of a dense jungle-covered peninsula, there are no roads to the unique home of **Six Senses Ninh Van Bay** (☏ 372 8222; www.sixsenses.com; villas US$734-2401; ❄@✱❄). The resort is so sophisticated, it even has its own time zone – setting the clocks an hour ahead in an effort to encourage guests to enjoy the sunrise. The traditionally inspired architecture and the winding paths between buildings give the illusion of a jungle village – albeit one where every dwelling is an elegant two-storey villa, each with its own swimming pool and round-the-clock butler service. As you would expect for the price, the detail is superb and the setting is simply magical. Facilities include several restaurants and bars, including Dining on the Rocks above the resort, and a signature Six Senses Spa.

Nha Trang

☏ 058 / POP 375,000

Welcome to the beach capital of Vietnam. It may not be a charmer like Mui Ne or a historic jewel like Hoi An, but there is a certain something about Nha Trang that just keeps them coming back for more. For most it is the beautiful beach, the best municipal stretch of sand in the country, while the offshore islands add to the appeal, offering decadent boat trips on the water and some of Vietnam's best diving under it.

The setting is stunning, with towering mountains looming up behind the city and the sweeping beach stretching into the distance, the turquoise waters dotted with little islands. The beachfront has been given a huge makeover in recent years, with parks and sculpture gardens spread along the shorefront, although by night it still reverts to a bit of a circus with motorbike drivers doubling as pimps and dealers, and kamikaze hookers hoping to relieve drunken tourists of their remaining dong.

Nha Trang is a study in contrasts, as the main city is still a bustling Vietnamese entity, buzzing along oblivious to the tourist crowds lining the shore. Hugging the coast for a few blocks is a fully fledged international resort, complete with high-rise hotels, souvenir shops, stylish restaurants and sophisticated bars. This part of town could be anywhere in the world, but the steady soundtrack of *xe om* drivers will soon bring you back to the Vietnamese reality.

It is not only the blissful beaches and glorious coastline that define Nha Trang. It also offers some of the best dining beyond Hanoi and Saigon, with a bounty from the sea and an array of international flavours. As the restaurants wind down, the nightlife cranks up – Nha Trang is a party town at heart, like any self-respecting resort should be. Forget the curfews of the capital; people play late in this town.

If cocktails and shooters aren't your flavour, there are some more sedate activities on offer beyond the waters. Try an old-school spa treatment with a visit to a mudbath or explore centuries-old Cham towers still standing in the centre of town. Or throw culture to the wind and experience Vinpearl Land, Nha Trang's attempt at Disneyworld. Nha Trang has something for everyone.

This part of the country has its very own microclimate and the rains tend to come from October until December, a time best avoided if you are into lazing on the beach or diving in crystal-clear waters.

◉ **Sights**

Nha Trang Beach   BEACH
The clear turquoise waters of Nha Trang's 6km beach are best enjoyed during the dry season, from June to early October. During heavy rains, run-off from the rivers at each end of the beach flows into the bay, gradually turning it a murky brown. Most of the year, however, the sea is just like it appears in the

SOUTH-CENTRAL COAST NHA TRANG

Nha Trang

further south past the Evason Ana Mandara Resort and it's still possible to find a stretch of sand to yourself.

Po Nagar Cham Towers   TEMPLE
(Thap Ba; Lady of the City; Map p228; admission 16,000d; ⊘6am-6pm) The Cham towers of Po Nagar were built between the 7th and 12th centuries, although the site was first used for worship as early as the 2nd century AD. To this day Cham, ethnic Chinese and Vietnamese Buddhists come to Po Nagar to pray and make offerings, according to their respective traditions. This site has a continuing religious significance, so be sure to remove your shoes before entering.

The towers serve as the Holy See, honouring Yang Ino Po Nagar, the goddess of the Dua (Liu) clan, which ruled over the southern part of the Cham kingdom covering Kauthara and Pan Duranga (present-day Khanh Hoa and Thuan Hai provinces). The original wooden structure was razed to the ground by attacking Javanese in AD 774 but was replaced by a stone-and-brick temple (the first of its kind) in 784. There are inscribed stone slabs scattered throughout the complex, most of which relate to history and religion and provide insight into the spiritual life and social structure of the Cham.

Originally the complex covered an area of 500 sq metres and there were seven or eight towers; four towers remain. All of the temples face east, as did the original entrance to the complex, which is to the right as you ascend the hillock. In centuries past, a per-

brochures. Even in the wettest months, rain usually falls only at night or in the morning. The best beach weather is generally before 1pm, as the afternoon sea breezes can whip up the sand.

Beach chairs are available for rent where you can sit and enjoy the drinks, light food or massages that the beach vendors offer. About the only time you'll need to move is to use the toilet or when the tide comes up. The two most popular lounging spots are the Sailing Club and Louisiane Brewhouse. The Four Seasons Cafe opposite Nha Trang Lodge has more of a local vibe. Head a bit

son coming to pray passed through the pillared meditation hall, 10 pillars of which can still be seen, before proceeding up the steep staircase to the towers.

The 28m-high North Tower (Thap Chinh), with its terraced pyramidal roof, vaulted interior masonry and vestibule, is a superb example of Cham architecture. One of the tallest Cham towers, it was built in 817 after the original temples here were sacked and burned. The raiders also carried off a *linga* (stylised phallus venerated by Hindus) made of precious metal. In 918, King Indravarman III placed a gold *mukha-linga* (carved phallus with a human face painted on it) in the North Tower, but it too was taken, this time by the Khmers. This pattern of statues being destroyed or stolen and then replaced continued until 965, when King Jaya Indravarman IV replaced the gold *mukha-linga* with the stone figure, Uma (*shakti*, or female consort of Shiva), which remains to this day.

Above the entrance to the North Tower, two musicians, one of whose feet is on the head of the bull Nandin, flank a dancing four-armed Shiva. The sandstone doorposts are covered with inscriptions, as are parts of the walls of the vestibule. A gong and a drum stand under the pyramid-shaped ceiling of the antechamber. In the 28m-high pyramidal main chamber, there is a blackstone statue of the goddess Uma with 10 arms, two of which are hidden under her vest; she is seated and leaning back against a monstrous beast.

The Central Tower (Thap Nam) was built partly of recycled bricks in the 12th century on the site of a structure dating from the 7th century. It is less finely constructed than the other towers and has little ornamentation; the pyramidal roof lacks terracing or pilasters, although the interior altars were once covered with silver. There is a *linga* inside the main chamber.

The South Tower (Mieu Dong Nam), at one time dedicated to Sandhaka (Shiva), still shelters a *linga,* while the richly ornamented Northwest Tower (Thap Tay Bac) was originally dedicated to Ganesh. To the rear of the complex is a less impressive museum with a few examples of Cham stonework.

The towers of Po Nagar stand on a granite knoll 2km north of central Nha Trang on the banks of the Cai River. To get here from central Nha Trang, take Ð Quang Trung (which becomes Ð 2 Thang 4) north across the Ha Ra and Xom Bong Bridges. Po Nagar can also be reached via the Tran Phu Bridge along the beachfront road.

Long Son Pagoda
PAGODA

(Map p228; ☯7.30-11.30am & 1.30-5.30pm) This striking pagoda was founded in the late 19th century and has been rebuilt several times over the years. The entrance and roofs are decorated with mosaic dragons constructed of glass and bits of ceramic tile. The main sanctuary is a hall adorned with modern interpretations of traditional motifs. Note the ferocious nose hairs on the colourful dragons wrapped around the pillars on either side of the main altar.

At the top of the hill, behind the pagoda, is a huge white Buddha (Map p228; Kim Than Phat To) seated on a lotus blossom and visible from all over the city. Around the statue's base are fire-ringed relief busts of Thich Quang Duc and six other Buddhist monks who died in self-immolations in 1963 (see p177). The platform around the 14m-high figure has great views of Nha Trang and nearby rural areas. As you approach the pagoda from the street, the 152 stone steps up the hill to the Buddha begin to the right of the structure. Take some time to explore off to the left, where there's an entrance to another hall of the pagoda.

Beggars congregate within the complex, as do a number of scam-artists. There's a persistent scam here, where visitors are approached by children (and occasionally older people) with pre-printed name badges claiming to work for the monks. After showing you around the pagoda, whether invited to or not, they will then demand money 'for the monks' or, if that fails, insist that you buy postcards for 100,000d. The best course of action is to firmly let them know you don't require their services when they first appear. If they persist, tell them that you know they don't work for the monks and you're not about to give them any money – this should ensure a quick disappearance. If you want to give money towards the monks and the upkeep of the complex, leave it in the donation boxes as you would in any other pagoda.

The pagoda is located about 400m west of the train station, just off Ð 23 Thang 10.

Nha Trang Cathedral
CHURCH

(Map p232; cnr Ð Nguyen Trai & Ð Thai Nguyen) Built between 1928 and 1933 in French Gothic style, complete with stained-glass windows, Nha Trang Cathedral stands on a

VINPEARL LAND

Nha Trang's answer to Disneyland (well, sort of), the island resort of **Vinpearl Land** (☑359 0111; www.vinpearlland.com; Hon Tre Island; adult/child 320,000/230,000d; ☺8am-10pm) has funfair rides, a water park, arcade games and plenty of other attractions to keep the kiddies amused. There is also an Underwater World aquarium here featuring some of the sealife you won't get to see if you're not a diver. It's not yet a world-class adventure park, but it does have some thrills like a rollercoaster called Evolution. It will keep children amused for a full day, including the world's longest over-the-sea cable car (oooh!) and the biggest wave pool in Southeast Asia (ahhh!). The leading attraction is undoubtedly the water park, with more than 20 serious slides for adrenalin-seekers.

Most visitors arrive by cable car or fast boat, both included in the ticket price. Both depart from the coast just south of Cau Da dock area.

small hill overlooking the train station. It's a surprisingly elegant building given that it was constructed of simple cement blocks. Some particularly colourful Vietnamese touches include the red neon outlining the crucifix, the pink back-lighting on the tabernacle and the blue neon arch and white neon halo over the statue of St Mary. In 1988 a Catholic cemetery not far from the church was disinterred to make room for a new railway building. The remains were brought to the cathedral and reburied in the cavities behind the wall of plaques that line the ramp up the hill.

National Oceanographic Museum   MUSEUM
(Map p228; ☑359 0037; haiduong@dng.vnn.vn; 1 Cau Da; adult/child 15,000/7000d; ☺6am-6pm) Housed in a grand French-colonial building in the port district of Cau Da at the far south end of Nha Trang is the National Oceanographic Museum. It's attached to the Oceanographic Institute founded in 1923, and signs direct you around the tanks of colourful live marine life and the 60,000 jars of pickled specimens that make up the collection. There are also stuffed birds and sea mammals and displays of local boats and fishing artefacts. Most of the signs have English translations, so a guide is unnecessary.

Alexandre Yersin Museum   MUSEUM
(Map p232; 10 Đ Tran Phu; admission 26,000d; ☺7.30-11am & 2-4.30pm Mon-Fri, 8-11am Sat) Dr Alexandre Yersin (1863–1943) founded Nha Trang's Pasteur Institute in 1895. He was the foreigner most loved by the Vietnamese. Born in Switzerland, he came to Vietnam in 1889 after working under Louis Pasteur in Paris. He learned to speak Vietnamese fluently, and spent the next few years travelling throughout the central highlands and recording his observations. During this period he came upon the site of what is now Dalat and recommended to the government that a hill station be established there. Yersin also introduced rubber and quinine-producing trees to Vietnam. In 1894, while in Hong Kong, he discovered the rat-borne microbe that causes bubonic plague. At his request, Dr Yersin was buried near Nha Trang.

Today, the Pasteur Institute in Nha Trang coordinates vaccination and hygiene programs for the country's southern coastal region. The institute produces vaccines and carries out medical research and testing to European standards. Physicians at the clinic here offer medical advice to around 70 patients a day. Vietnam's two other Pasteur Institutes are in HCMC and Dalat.

Yersin's library and office are now an interesting museum. Items on display include laboratory equipment (such as astronomical instruments), books from Yersin's library, a fascinating 3-D photo viewer and some of the thousand or so letters written to his mother. The model boat was given to him by local fishermen with whom he spent a great deal of his time. Tours of the museum are guided in French, English and Vietnamese, and a short film on Yersin's life is also shown.

It's a small museum and will mostly be of interest to European visitors or those who follow the history or practice of medicine.

Photographic Galleries   ART GALLERY
There are several superb black-and-white photographic galleries in Nha Trang. **Long Thanh Gallery** (Map p232; ☑382 4875; www.longthanhart.com; 126 Đ Hoang Van Thu; ☺9am-7pm Mon-Fri) showcases the work of Vietnam's most prominent photographer. Long Thanh developed his first photo in 1964 and continues to shoot extraordinary black-and-white images of everyday Vietnamese moments. The powerful images capture the

heart and soul of Vietnam. Among his most compelling works, *Under the Rain* is a perfectly timed shot of two young girls caught in a sudden downpour, with a mysterious beam of sunlight streaming down on them. Look out for *Sulkiness,* a stunning portrait of children and their petty squabbles. His

work has been honoured at photographic competitions around the world.

Do Dien Khanh Gallery (Map p232; ☑351 2202; www.ddk-gallery.com; 126B Đ Hong Bat; ◷8am-6pm Mon-Fri) is another private gallery with contemporary lighting. Photographer Do Dien Khanh is a welcoming host and his

---

DON'T MISS

TRIPPING THE BAY BY BOAT

The 71 offshore islands around Nha Trang are renowned for the remarkably clear water surrounding them. A trip to these islands is one of Nha Trang's main draws and virtually every hotel and travel company in town books island-hopping boat tours. Or you can pay more for a less-crowded and more-luxurious boat that takes you to more islands. Indeed, you'll have to do this if you want to get in much snorkelling.

The most popular boat trips are the hedonistic party tours originally pioneered by Mama Hanh back in the 1990s. Mama Hanh was formally retired by local party officials: perhaps they deemed her floating bar and free marijuana joints too counter-revolutionary for their tastes. However, Mama Linh, Funky Monkey and others have since continued the party tradition in one form or the other, albeit without the ganja.

The typical schedule includes the Tri Nguyen Aquarium (50,000d entry) on Hon Mieu, a spot of snorkelling off Hon Mun and then lunch around Hon Mot. The cultural element complete, the party kicks off in the afternoon with DJs on the deck and a floating bar in the water. Remember sunscreen and drinking water in between the fun; a lot of people forget and end up half-baked in the afternoon sun. The trips usually finish by swinging past Hon Mieu and the chance to spend some beach time (20,000d entry including deck chair). The boat trip over, the mayhem often rumbles on to various bars, helping cement Nha Trang's reputation as a party town.

It's definitely the backpacker answer to Club 18–30 and might not be the best environment for families with children (or for recovering alcoholics). If the cultural fanfare of the party-boat experience does not sound up your alley, there are other more orthodox boat tours around.

Some of the more popular boat tours include:

Booze Cruise (Map p232; ☑016-8844 7233; Đ Nguyen Thien Thuat; cruise 350,000d) For those who prefer their booze cruise by night, this boat-trip kicks off from 4.30pm and includes all the cocktails and shooters you can slam, plus a dinner buffet.

Con Se Tre (Map p228; ☑381 1163; www.consetre.com.vn; 100/16 Đ Tran Phu; ◷8am-6pm) Offers more sedate tours to Hon Tam, including snorkelling and lunch (from US$13 per person), and snorkelling trips to Hon Mun (from $US18 per person).

Funky Monkey (Map p232; ☑352 2426; www.funkymonkeytour.com.vn; 75A Đ Hung Vuong; cruise incl pick-up 100,000d) One of the hottest new party boats, this trip includes live entertainment from the Funky Monkey boy band, as well as the usual stops.

Mama Linh's Boat Tours (Map p232; ☑352 2844; mamalinhvn@yahoo.com; 23C Đ Biet Thu) One of the longest-running boat trips on the bay and still a popular party option, although there are plenty of copycats these days.

Khanh Hoa Tourist Information (Map p232; ☑352 8000; khtourism@dng.vnn.vn; Đ Tran Phu; cruise incl lunch 349,000d) For something a little different, consider a far-flung boat trip to beautiful Van Phong Bay. The two-hour drive puts many off, but this trip takes in remote and secluded beaches and bays far from the tourist crowd. Contact the tourist office for details and bookings.

The cheapest way to get out on the water is to take the regular local ferry to Vinpearl Land on Hon Tre (adult/child 45,000/20,000d each way), leaving from Phu Quy harbour just past Cau Da dock. There is also the massive Vinpearl Land cable car, which is strung out across the bay and takes 10 minutes. Most people use this in conjunction with their entry ticket to Vinpearl Land.

Central Nha Trang

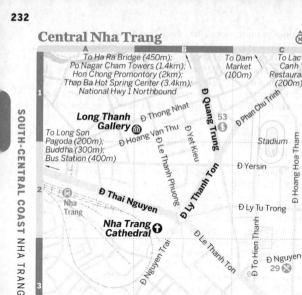

portraits of surrounding Cham communities are hauntingly beautiful.

Hon Chong Promontory LANDMARK

The narrow granite promontory of Hon Chong (Map p228; entry 11,000d) offers views of the mountainous coastline north of Nha Trang and the nearby islands. The beach here has a more local flavour than Nha Trang Beach, but the accompanying refuse makes it a less attractive option for swimming or sunbathing. There is a reconstruct-

Central Nha Trang

ed Ruong residence here known as House of the Bay. While it makes for a good photo opportunity, the interior is more about tourist tat than tradition.

There's a gargantuan handprint on the massive boulder balanced at the tip of the promontory. According to legend, a drunken giant male fairy made it when he fell while spying on a female fairy bathing nude at Bai Tien (Fairy Beach), the point of land closest to Hon Rua (Tortoise Island). They fell in love but the gods intervened, sending the male fairy away. The lovesick female fairy waited patiently for him to return, but after a very long time she lay down in sorrow and turned into **Nui Co Tien** (Fairy Mountain). Looking to the northeast from Hon Chong Promontory, the peak on the right is supposed to be her face, gazing up towards the sky; the middle peak is her breasts; and the summit on the left (the highest) forms her crossed legs.

About 300m south of Hon Chong (towards Nha Trang) and a few dozen metres from the beach is tiny **Hon Do** (Red Island), which has a Buddhist temple on top. To the northeast is **Hon Rua** (Tortoise Island), which really does resemble a tortoise. The two islands of **Hon Yen** (Bird's-Nest Island) are off in the distance to the east.

🏃 Activities

Nha Trang has emerged as an adrenaline centre over the past decade or so. Choose from diving, surfing, wake-boarding, parascending, whitewater rafting, mountain biking and more, as well as the ever popular boat trips around the bay.

Islands

Island tours are a big part of the Nha Trang experience. For details on boat tours and charters see p231.

Hon Tre (Bamboo Island)　　THEME PARK
The beauty of Nha Trang's largest and closest offshore island is now marred by a huge Hollywood-style sign advertising Vinpearl Land amusement park (p230). You can access this island by cable car or boat.

Hon Mieu　　ISLAND TOURS
All the tourist literature touts Hon Mieu (also called Tri Nguyen Island) as the site of an outdoor **aquarium** (Ho Ca Tri Nguyen; entry 50,000d). In fact, the aquarium is an important fish-breeding farm, where over 40 species of fish, crustacean and other marine creatures are raised in three separate areas. There is also a cafe built on stilts over the water.

Most visitors will take some sort of boat tour booked through a hotel or cafe. DIY travellers might catch one of the regular ferries that go to Tri Nguyen village from Cau Da dock.

Hon Mun (Ebony Island)　　SNORKELLING
Hon Mun is situated just southeast of Bamboo Island and is well known for its snorkelling.

Hon Mot　　SNORKELLING
Sandwiched neatly between Ebony Island and Hon Tam or Silkworm Island, is tiny Hon Mot, another popular place for snorkelling.

Hon Yen (Bird's-Nest Island)　　ISLAND TOURS
Also known as Salangane Island, this is the two lump-shaped islands visible from Nha Trang Beach. These and other islands off Khanh Hoa province are the source of Vietnam's finest *salangane* (swiftlet) nests (see the boxed text, p239). There is a small, secluded beach here. The 17km trip out to the islands takes three to four hours by small boat from Nha Trang.

Hon Lao (Monkey Island)　　ISLAND TOURS
The island is named after its large contingent of resident monkeys and has become a big hit with domestic Vietnamese tourists. Most of the monkeys have grown quite accustomed to receiving food handouts, providing ample photo opportunities. However, these are wild animals and should be treated as such, particularly by those travelling with children. Bear in mind that monkey bites are a possible source of rabies.

Aside from being unwilling to participate in a cuddle, the monkeys are materialistic. They'll grab the sunglasses off your face or snatch a pen from your shirt pocket and run off. So far, we haven't heard of monkeys slitting open travellers' handbags with a razor blade, but keep a close eye (and hand) on your possessions.

A word of warning: there's also a bear-and-monkey show that you may want to avoid. Travellers have reported seeing the animals beaten by their trainers during performances. Read between the lines; we don't really recommend this experience.

Long Phu Tourist (☑383 9436; www.long phutourist.com; Vinh Luong) runs trips here including a visit to Orchid Island and snorkelling from 230,000d. Optional extras include elephant and ostrich rides. Hmmm.

Diving

Nha Trang is Vietnam's most popular scuba-diving centre, although not necessarily its best. Visibility averages 15m but can be as much as 30m, depending on the season. February to September is considered the best time to dive, while October to December is the worst time of year.

There are around 25 dive sites in the area, both shallow and deep. There are no wrecks to visit, but some sites have good drop-offs and there are a few small underwater caves to explore. The waters support a good variety of soft and hard corals, and a reasonable number of small reef fish.

A full-day outing including boat transport, two dives and lunch typically costs between US$40 and US$70. Most dive operators also offer a range of dive courses, including a 'discover diving' program for uncertified first-time divers to experience the underwater world with the supervision of a qualified dive master. SSI courses are usually about US$50 cheaper than PADI courses so have really taken off around Nha Trang.

There are a dozen or so dive operators with offices in the tourist centre of Nha Trang. The places listed below are all long-running operators with responsible diving practices.

Angel Dive   DIVING
(Map p232; ☎352 2461; www.angeldivevietnam .info; 1/33 Đ Tran Quang Khai) Reliable operator with English, French and German instruction, plus the choice of PADI or SSI certification.

Rainbow Divers   DIVING
(Map p232; ☎352 4351; www.divevietnam.com; 90A Đ Hung Vuong) One of the longest-running dive companies in Vietnam, operating centres nationwide. Here at HQ, there is also a popular restaurant and bar.

Sailing Club Divers   DIVING
(Map p232; ☎352 2788; www.sailingclubdivers .com; 72-74 Đ Tran Phu) Also known as Octopus Diving, this is the underwater arm of the famous Sailing Club.

More Watery Fun

Phu Dong Water Park   SWIMMING
(Map p228; Đ Tran Phu; adult/child 40,000/ 20,000d; ⊙9am-5pm) Right on the beachfront, Phu Dong Water Park has hydroslides, shallow pools and fountains. If salt water is not your thing, this is the place for you.

CONSIDERATIONS FOR RESPONSIBLE DIVING

The popularity of diving is placing immense pressure on many sites. Please consider the following tips when diving and help preserve the ecology and beauty of Vietnam's reefs.

» Do not anchor on the reef, and take care not to ground boats on coral. Encourage dive operators and regulatory bodies to establish permanent moorings at popular dive sites.

» Avoid touching living marine organisms with your body or dragging equipment across the reef. Polyps can be damaged by even the gentlest contact. Never stand on corals, even if they look solid and robust. If you must hold on to the reef, touch only exposed rock or dead coral.

» Be conscious of your fins. Even without contact, the surge from heavy fin strokes near the reef can damage delicate organisms. When treading water in shallow reef areas, take care not to kick up clouds of sand. Settling sand can easily smother the delicate organisms of the reef.

» Practise and maintain proper buoyancy control. Major damage can be done by divers descending too fast and colliding with the reef. Make sure you are correctly weighted and that your weight belt is positioned so that you stay horizontal. If you have not dived for a while, have a practice dive in a pool before taking to the reef. Be aware that buoyancy can change over the period of an extended trip: initially you may breathe harder and need more weight; a few days later you may breathe more easily and need less weight.

» Resist the temptation to collect or buy coral or shells. Aside from the ecological damage, taking home marine souvenirs depletes the beauty of a site and spoils the enjoyment of others. The same goes for marine archaeological sites (mainly shipwrecks). Respect their integrity; some sites are protected from looting by law.

» Ensure that you take home all your rubbish and any litter you may find as well. Plastics in particular are a serious threat to marine life. Turtles can mistake plastic for jellyfish and eat it.

» Resist the temptation to feed fish. You may disturb their normal eating habits, encourage aggressive behaviour or feed them food that is detrimental to their health.

» Minimise your disturbance of marine animals.

Waves Watersports · WATERSPORTS

(Map p232; ☎090-544 7393; www.waveswater sports.com; Louisiane Brewhouse, 29 Đ Tran Phu) If salt water is your thing, check out Waves Watersports. Offering windsurfing, sea kayaking, wakeboarding, water-skiing and sailing lessons, Waves uses state-of-the-art equipment and has access to some great surfing spots along Bai Dai near Cam Ranh Bay.

Shamrock Adventures · RAFTING

(Map p232; ☎090-515 0978; www.shamrockadven tures.vn; Đ Tran Quang Khai; from US$35 per person inc lunch) Back to freshwater, this is pretty gentle whitewater rafting by international standards, so don't expect the Zambezi or the Nile. However, it makes for a fun escape from the city and can be combined with mountain biking. Located close to Angel Dive on Đ Tran Quang Khai.

Thap Ba Hot Spring Center · THERMAL BATHS

(Map p228; ☎383 4939; www.thapbahotspring .com.vn; 25 Ngoc Son; ⊙7am-7.30pm) The only way to get really clean in Nha Trang is to get deep down and dirty. Thap Ba Hot Spring Center is one of the most memorable experiences in the Nha Trang area. For 220,000/400,000d you can sit in a single/ double wooden bathtub full of hot thermal mud. For 100,000d per person you can go communal and slop around with a group of friends in a larger pool. The centre also has hot and cold mineral swimming pools (50,000d), complete with thermal waterfalls. More expensive treatments are available such as the Tien Sa Mineral Bath and the VIP Spa. To get here, follow the signpost on the second road to the left past the Po Nagar Cham Towers and follow the winding road for 2.5km. Transfers are available for 40,000d return.

Spas

There is a burgeoning spa industry in Nha Trang. Some of the best places include the following:

Crazy Kim Spa & Gym · SPA, GYM

(Map p232; ☎352 7837; 1Đ Đ Biet Thu) Helping to fund the 'Hands off the Kids!' campaign run by Kimmy Le of Crazy Kim Bar fame (see p241), this is indulgence for a good cause. A workout is 60,000d, nails are just 30,000d and a body massage starts from 160,000d.

Su Spa · SPA

(Map p232; ☎352 3242; www.suspa.vn; 93 Đ Nguyen Thien Thuat) A designer spa with a range

of scrubs, rubs and tubs. Facials from US$27 and body massages from US$21.

🛏 Sleeping

There is no shortage of hotels in Nha Trang, with hundreds of places to choose from and counting. They range from dives to the divine and there are new places sprouting up all the time, including a number of chain hotels under construction at the time of writing, such as the immense Crowne Plaza. It makes sense to stay near the beach, given this is the big attraction. There are many midrange and top-end options lining Đ Tran Phu, the waterfront boulevard. However, there are also several budget options just a stroll away from the beachfront action. Most budget places don't include breakfast, but there are no 'plus plus' (++ or $$) charges for tax and service as there are at some of the midrange and top-end pads.

There is a cluster of mini-hotels in an alleyway at 64 Đ Tran Phu, within striking distance of the beach. All offer similar air-conditioned rooms for around US$10 or so, cheaper if you go with the flow of a fan. Another good hunting ground for budget digs is around the Chanh Quang Pagoda, either side of Đ Hung Vuong, which has a real local neighbourhood feel.

For more beachfront options to the north of Nha Trang, see p225.

🏆 TOP CHOICE Ha Van Hotel · HOTEL $$

(Map p232; ☎352 5454; www.in2vietnam.com; 3/2 Đ Tran Quang Khai; r US$22-32; ✴@🛜) Under French management, this hotel strives to offer a higher standard of service than local competition. The rooms are well-appointed and include a bit more decorative flair than the neighbours. New additions include an inviting rooftop restaurant-bar and a Fanny ice-cream counter in reception. The hotel is in a small street just off Đ Tran Quang Khai.

🏆 TOP CHOICE Violet Hotel · HOTEL $$

(Map p232; ☎352 2314; www.violethotelnha trang.com; 12 Đ Biet Thu; r 450,000-800,000d; ✴@🛜▨) It's hard to beat this new hotel for location and value for money. Rooms are tastefully finished and facilities include a small courtyard swimming pool. Breakfast is also included.

🏆 TOP CHOICE Evason Ana Mandara Resort & Spa · RESORT HOTEL $$$

(Map p228; ☎352 2522; www.evasonresorts.com; Đ Tran Phu; villa US$279-537; ✴@🛜▨) Nha

Trang's most desirable address, the Ana Mandara is a charming cluster of beach villas on an exclusive strip of sand. There is more than a hint of Bali about the place with classic furnishings and four-poster beds. Facilities include two swimming pools and an indulgent Six Senses Spa. Personal touches every week include guest appearances by local cooks for a slice of street food and a hosted cocktail evening on the beach.

Mai Huy Hotel HOTEL $

(Map p232; ☑ 352 7553; maihuyhotel.vn@gmail. com; 7H Quan Tran, Đ Hung Vuong; r US$7-15; ❇@🖱) The family here really make their guests feel at home. The rooms are great value, meticulously clean and include cheaper fan options for those counting the dong.

AP Hotel HOTEL $

(Map p232; ☑352 7545; 34 Đ Nguyen Thien Thuat; r 290,000-450,000d; ❇@🖱) The official one-star rating seems a bit stingy given the excellent facilities at this mini-hotel, where rooms have flatscreen TV, minibar and bathtub. The cheaper rooms have no windows, which isn't ideal, but the VIP rooms with balcony just about afford a sea view.

Axar Hotel HOTEL $

(Map p232; ☑352 1655; axarhotel@vnn.vn; 148/10 Đ Hung Vuong; r US$12; ❇@🖱) A new hotel tucked away down a side alley, rooms are spacious and light, which is not always the case at this price. The trim is a cut above the competition, making it excellent value.

Perfume Grass Inn HOTEL $$

(Map p232; ☑352 4286; www.perfume-grass.com; 4A Đ Biet Thu; r US$12-30; ❇@🖱) Consistently popular, this welcoming inn has rooms with a touch of character, particularly the pricier options with wood panelling. Cheaper fan rooms include satellite TV and hot shower. Add to the mix a free breakfast and a cosy lobby downstairs, and it remains a good deal.

La Suisse Hotel HOTEL $$

(Map p232; ☑352 4353; www.lasuissehotel.com; 3/4 Đ Tran Quang Khai; r US$22-45; ❇@🖱) Switzerland is famous for its hoteliers and there is a touch of la Suisse about the efficient service here. All rooms have smart furnishings and the family suites include a jacuzzi-style tub and a huge balcony with sun loungers.

King Town Hotel HOTEL $$

(Map p232; ☑352 5818; www.kingtownhotel. vn; 92 Đ Hung Vuong; r US$20-40; ❇@🖱🏊) A smart new hotel on the popular Hung Vuong strip, King Town has a good range of rooms with silk trim and stylish bathrooms. Tucked away on the top floor is a rooftop swimming pool with city views.

Golden Rain Hotel HOTEL $$

(Map p232; ☑352 7799; www.goldenrainhotel.com; 142 Đ Hung Vuong; r US$26-55; ❇@🖱🏊) New in 2010, this is another smart new offering on Đ Hung Vuong. Rooms are elegant enough and some include large windows. The rooftop pool and gym round things off nicely.

Hotel An Hoa HOTEL $

(Map p232; ☑352 4029; www.anhoahotel.com .vn; 64B/6 Đ Tran Phu; r US$8-14; ❇@🖱) A reliable option in the heart of the budget alley, this friendly hostelry has small rooms with no windows or air-con, or bigger and better rooms with larger bathrooms and a smarter trim, including $14 'VIP' rooms.

Phong Lan Hotel HOTEL $

(Map p232; ☑352 2647; orchid hotel2000@yahoo .com; 24/44 Đ Hung Vuong; r US$6-12; ❇@🖱) Located in a small alley off Hung Vuong, the Orchid Hotel, as it translates, is a friendly, family-run place. The clean rooms include TV and fridge. The owners speak both English and French.

Sao Mai Hotel HOTEL $

(Map p232; ☑352 6412; saomai2hotel@yahoo .com; 99 Đ Nguyen Thien Thuat; dm US$4, r US$6-12; ❇@🖱) This budget crash-pad has been around for years, but still offers no-nonsense value for money for those on a budget. The rooms are simple yet clean, plus there is a nice rooftop terrace to escape the bustle below. Receptionist Mr Mao Loc has some classic black-and-white photographs for sale and can help arrange customised photographic tours.

Rainbow Hotel HOTEL $

(Map p232; ☑352 5480; rainbowhotel@dng.vnn.vn; 10A Đ Biet Thu; r US$15-25; ❇@🖱) It is not affiliated with the nearby Rainbow Divers, but it's still a popular place thanks to 50 rooms at tempting prices. Solar-heated water earns brownie points, as does the top-floor restaurant with views over town.

Rosy Hotel HOTEL $

(Map p232; ☑352 2661; 20 Quan Tran, Đ Hung Vuong; r 250,000-300,000d; ❇@🖱) One of the tall, skinny hotels so popular in urban Vietnam, this new hotel in a little alley off Đ Hung

Vuong is clean and comfortable. Rosy offers tasteful decor and the chance of a breezy balcony out front for an extra 50,000d.

Backpacker's House
HOSTEL $

(Map p232; ☎352 3884; www.backpackershouse .net; 54G Đ Nguyen Thien Thuat; dm US$7-8, r US$12-24; ❄@) This flashpacker pad is popular with the party set, as it is only a stumble from the nearby Red Apple Club. The dorms are mixed and have four to six beds. The rooms are a smarter choice, including DVD player and ensuite, but don't check in here if you need a deep sleep, as it can be noisy.

Novotel Nha Trang
HOTEL $$$

(Map p232; ☎625 6900; www.novotel.com/6033; 50 Đ Tran Phu; r US$116-162, ste US$231; ❄@✿➳) One of a generation of stylish new Novotels in Vietnam, this is very contemporary, featuring split-level rooms with sunken bathtubs. Invest in a sea view on the upper floor to see Nha Trang in all its glory.

Sheraton Nha Trang Hotel & Spa
HOTEL $$$

(Map p232; ☎388 0000; sheraton.com/nhatrang; 26-28 Đ Tran Phu; r from US$176, ste from US$287; ❄@✿➳) One of the tallest buildings in Nha Trang, the Sheraton is everything you would expect from this 5-star chain. Rooms are spacious and modern with open-plan bathrooms. Suites include access to the Club Lounge.

Phu Quy 2 Hotel
HOTEL $$

(Map p232; ☎352 5050; www.phuquyhotel.com .vn; 1 Đ Tue Tinh; r US$33-53, ste US$86; ❄@✿➳) This towering hotel includes a rooftop pool with views to the beach. Rooms are squeaky clean and well appointed, although it is worth investing a few more bucks for a spacious sea-view. Breakfast included.

Bao Dai's Villas
HOTEL $$

(Map p228; ☎359 0148; www.vngold.com/nt/bao dai; Cau Da village; r US$25-80; ❄@✿) Originally reserved for royalty, Emperor Bao Dai's villas are now open to the masses. Built in the 1920s, this was a beachside retreat for the last emperor, but it is not particularly opulent these days. Aside from the historical-pull factor and its lush grounds, the rooms themselves are very average for the price. Entry to the complex is 10,000d for nonguests, but the small beach is pretty scruffy with the port as a backdrop.

Summer Hotel
HOTEL $$

(Map p232; ☎352 2186; www.thesummerhotel .com.vn; 34C Đ Nguyen Thien Thuat; r US$25-90;

❄@✿➳) A smart new 3-star hotel with affordable prices, standard rooms are being upgraded to include a window and there is a rooftop pool.

Green Peace E Hotel
HOTEL $$

(Map p232; ☎352 2835; www.greenpeacehotel .com.vn; 102 Đ Nguyen Thien Thuat; r US$20-30; ❄@✿) Just two-weeks old when we visited, rooms are smart and contemporary with flat-screen TVs and rain showers. Take a front room with a big window.

62 Tran Phu Hotel
HOTEL $

(Map p232; ☎352 5095; 62 Đ Tran Phu; r US$10-15; ❄@✿) The old reception is in desperate need of some TLC, but continue to the back where there is a new block offering good-value rooms.

Ha Tram Hotel
HOTEL $

(Map p232; ☎352 1819; 64B/5 Đ Tran Phu; r US$10-15; ❄@✿) One of the smarter hotels on budget alley, rooms here are light and bright and include smart bathrooms. Plus there's a lift.

Quang Vinh Hotel
HOTEL $

(Map p232; ☎352 4258; 84A Đ Tran Phu; r US$15-20; ❄@✿) In a more Vietnamese strip of beachfront hotels, this place offers unfettered sea views for just US$20, making for an enticing deal.

Nha Trang Lodge Hotel
HOTEL $$

(Map p232; ☎352 1500; www.nhatranglodge.com; 42 Đ Tran Phu; r US$65-140; ❄) High-rise but low on atmosphere, this is a business-style place with splendid views. Almost top end, this place offers midrange online deals.

T78 Guesthouse
HOTEL $$

(Map p232; ☎352 3445; 44 Đ Tran Phu; r 220,000-1,400,000d; ❄) This beautiful old French-colonial building is begging to be a boutique hotel, but it remains a rundown state entity for now, with a certain raffish charm.

✖ Eating

Nha Trang is a diner's delight, with a diverse mix of international flavours. Vietnamese, French, Italian, Indian – anything and everything is available. Đ Tran Quang Khai and Đ Biet Thu are popular hunting grounds, but more authentic Vietnamese is found further afield. Seafood-lovers are in for a treat with fresh fish, crab, shrimp and an assortment of exotic shells.

For a more traditional local experience, try **Dam Market** (Map p232; Đ Trang Nu Vuong;

breakfast & lunch), which has a colourful collection of stalls, including *com chay* (vegetarian) options, in the 'food court'.

TOP CHOICE Lanterns   VIETNAMESE **$$**

(Map p232; 72 Đ Nguyen Thien Thuat; dishes 35,000-178,000d; ☺lunch & dinner) The flavours are predominantly Vietnamese, such as braised pork in claypot or fried tofu with lemongrass, but there are a few international offerings for anyone who is riced out. The restaurant supports a local orphanage and invites the children and their carers to dine each month. Cooking classes are available from 9am on Tues, Thurs, Sat and Sun, costing US$18.

TOP CHOICE Lac Canh Restaurant   VIETNAMESE **$$**

(Map p232; 44 Đ Nguyen Binh Khiem; dishes 30,000-150,000d; ☺lunch & dinner) Locals flock here in numbers to fire up the tabletop barbecues and grill their own meats, squid, prawns, lobsters and more. There are plenty of accompaniments on the menu, making this a definitive stop in Nha Trang.

TOP CHOICE Veranda   INTERNATIONAL **$**

(Map p232; 66 Đ Tran Phu; mains 40,000-120,000d; ☺lunch & dinner) This stylish little restaurant offers a small menu of food with flair, blending Vietnamese ingredients with an international outlook to create some original flavours. There is a huge variety of three-course set menus on offer from just US$5, including a drink.

TOP CHOICE Sandals Restaurant
at the Sailing Club   INTERNATIONAL **$$**

(Map p232; 72-74 Đ Tran Phu; mains 50,000-250,000d; @) This Nha Trang institution offers not one, but three dining options, including Vietnamese, Italian and Indian, not forgetting a smattering of international dishes. The beachfront terrace is the nicest of the dining areas with people-watching by day and brisk breezes by night. It is possible to order from any of the menus, so don't feel duty bound to sit in the streetside garden if you are hankering for Italian or Indian.

Le Petit Bistro   FRENCH **$$**

(Map p232; ☏352 7201; 26Đ Đ Tran Quang Khai; mains 50,000-250,000d; ☺lunch & dinner; ✱) Arguably the most popular of the French restaurants with the French crowd (always a good sign), this is the place for the *fromage* you have been pining for, some select cold

BIRD-SPIT SOUP

The nests of the *salangane* (swiftlet) are used in bird's-nest soup as well as in traditional medicine, and are considered an aphrodisiac. It is said that the extraordinary virility of Emperor Minh Mang, who ruled Vietnam from 1820 to 1840, was derived from the consumption of swiftlet nests.

The nests, which are built out of silk-like salivary secretions, are 5cm to 8cm in diameter. They are usually harvested twice a year. Red nests are the most highly prized. Annual production in Khanh Hoa and Phu Yen provinces is about 1000kg. At present, swiftlet spit fetches up to US$2000 per kilogram in the international marketplace.

cuts or duck specialities. The wine list is professional for those who like to quaff.

La Mancha   SPANISH **$$**

(Map p232; 78 Đ Nguyen Thien Thuat; mains 45,000-210,000d; ☺10am-midnight) This Spanish restaurant-bar is an delightful surprise for Nha Trang, with an extensive tapas menu and larger plates like paella. Try *gambas con ajillo* or Serrano ham, all washed down with some Spanish wine.

Louisiane Brewhouse   INTERNATIONAL **$$**

(Map p232; 29 Đ Tran Phu; www.louisianebrew house.com.vn; mains 50,000-350,000d; ☺7am-1am; @☀) It's not only the beer that draws a crowd here, as there is an eclectic menu offering international classics, some fiery Thai dishes, Vietnamese favourites and Japanese. The beachside pool is a beautiful place to while away some time digesting the meal, and there are some great cakes and pastries for inveterate snackers.

Nha Trang Xua   VIETNAMESE **$$**

(Thai Thong, Vinh Thai; dishes 50,000-180,000d; ☺8am-10pm) Causing a stir among Nha Trang residents, this is a classic Vietnamese restaurant set in a beautiful old house in the countryside outside Nha Trang, around 5km west of town. Think Hue or Hoi An style with a refined menu, beautiful presentation and atmospheric surrounds.

Truc Linh 2   VIETNAMESE **$$**

(Map p232; www.truclinhrest.vn; 21Đ Biet Thu; dishes 40,000-190,000d; ☺lunch & dinner) The Truc

Linh empire includes several eateries in the heart of backpackersville. Number 2 has a pretty garden setting and serves authentic dishes at affordable prices.

Omar's Tandoori Cafe
INDIAN $

(Map p232; 89B Đ Nguyen Thien Thuat; dishes 40,000-120,000đ) For an authentic slither of the subcontinent, look no further than Omar's. There is a wide selection of curries available, plus a lot of tandoori specialities. It's the venue of choice with curry-craving expats in town.

Grill House
INTERNATIONAL $$$

(Map p232; 1/18 Đ Tran Quang Khai; www.grill -house.org; mains 50,000-450,000đ; ☉lunch & dinner) This fashionable new grill restaurant offers meat lovers the chance to sate their appetite for flesh. Half-pounder burgers and 600g T-bones dominate the menu, although seafood is also on offer.

Artful Ca Phe
CAFE $

(Map p232; 20A Đ Nguyen Thien Thuat; mains 20,000-100,000đ) Part photography gallery and part cafe, this intimate place is a relaxing stop for a coffee, juice or light bite. Upstairs is a small terrace for those seeking a romantic retreat.

Café des Amis
CAFE $

(Map p232; 2D Đ Biet Thu; dishes 25,000-100,000đ) Long a backpacker favourite thanks to cheap eats and plentiful beer, this place has a strong selection of Vietnamese dishes, inexpensive seafood and a pick-and-mix of international dishes. Look out for local artworks adorning the walls.

Lang Nuong Phu Dong Hai San
SEAFOOD $

(Map p228; Đ Tran Phu; dishes 30,000-150,000đ; ☉2pm-3am) It may be plastic-chair fantastic and nothing like as fancy as neighbouring Ngoc Suong, but the seafood is fresh and delicious. Choose from scallops, crab, prawns and lobster, all at market prices, as the owner exports seafood to HCMC.

Something Fishy
SEAFOOD $

(Map p232; 12A Đ Biet Thu; mains 50,000-80,000đ; ☉lunch & dinner) This cosy little cafe-restaurant serves a great range of inexpensive fish and seafood, including a hearty fish and chips.

Da Fernando
ITALIAN $$

(Map p232; 96 Đ Nguyen Thien Thuat; mains 50,000-180,000đ; ☉lunch & dinner) Reliable Italian restaurant with freshly made pastas and wines from the homeland.

Kirin Restaurant
VIETNAMESE $

(Map p232; 1E Đ Biet Thu; dishes 20,000-120,000đ) Set in an old colonial-era property, the upstairs terrace and inner courtyard are atmospheric places to sample affordable and authentic Vietnamese cuisine.

Thanh Thanh Cafe
CAFE $

(Map p232; 10 Đ Nguyen Thien Thuat; meals 25,000-105,000đ) A popular backpacker cafe that used to be in the heart of the action, it remains a reliable stop for tasty Vietnamese food and surprisingly good pizzas.

Romy's
ITALIAN $

(Map p232; 1C Đ Biet Thu; 25,000đ per scoop; ☉7am-10pm) An Italian cafe serving homestyle gelato in a wide range of flavours. Plus pastries, cakes and good coffee.

Au Lac
VEGETARIAN $

(Map p232; 28C Đ Hoang Hoa Tham; meals from 12,000đ, ✐) This is a long-running I-can't-believe-it's-not-meat restaurant near the corner of Đ Nguyen Chanh. A mixed vegetarian plate is just about the best value meal you can find in Nha Trang.

🍷 Drinking

Oasis
BAR

(Map p232; 3 Đ Tran Quang Khai) This is a very popular spot for drinking cocktails and buckets or smoking shishas. Happy hours run right through from 4pm to midnight and the garden terrace is a lively place to catch a big sporting event. Stays open until dawn if you dare.

Sailing Club
BAR

(Map p232; 72-74 Đ Tran Phu; @) Despite its evident gentrification, Sailing Club remains the definitive Nha Trang night spot. Drinks are more expensive than around town, so it tends to fill up as the night wears on. Full moon beach parties are memorable, but busy nights attract a cover charge. In line with its sophisticated image, drunkards will be unceremoniously ejected from the bar.

Louisiane Brewhouse
BREWERY

(Map p232; ☎352 1948; 29 Đ Tran Phu; @☀) Homebrew, Nha Trang-style. Self-respecting beer drinkers will want to stop by here to sample the wares of this elegant micro-brewery. Beyond the shiny copper vats lie an inviting swimming pool and a private strip of sand.

Guava
LOUNGE BAR

(Map p232; www.clubnhatrang.com; 17 Đ Biet Thu; @) A hip lounge bar, Guava is the place to

DRINK SPIKING

There have been a number of reports of laced cocktail buckets doing the rounds in popular night spots. This might mean staff using home-made moonshine instead of legal spirits or could mean the addition of drugs of some sort by other punters. While buckets are fun and communal, take care in Nha Trang and try and keep an eye on what goes into the bucket. You don't want your night to end in paranoia or robbery.

come if you are seeking some style while you drink. Choose from sunken sofas inside or a leafy garden patio outside. Regular drink promotions include two-for-one surprises most days, such as Bloody Marys to accompany the Sunday 'hangover breakfast'. On that subject, great food is served here.

Red Apple Club BAR
(Map p232; 54H Đ Nguyen Thien Thuat; @) One of the places where backpackers wind down after a boat trip or wind up before the next one. Cheap beer, flowing shots, regular promotions and indie anthems ensure this place is crammed every night. Watch out for the beer funnel, as things can get very messy. The pool table is a popular institution.

Crazy Kim Bar BAR
(Map p232; www.crazykimbar.com; 19 Đ Biet Thu; @) This busy bar is home to the commendable 'Hands off the Kids!' campaign, which works to prevent paedophilia. There is now a permanent classroom for vulnerable street kids on the premises. Part of the proceeds from the food, booze and T-shirt sales go towards the cause. Sign up at the bar if you're interested in volunteering to teach English. Crazy Kim's has regular themed party nights, great music, devilish cocktail buckets and free wi-fi.

Altitude BAR
(Map p232; 26-28 Đ Tran Phu) Located on the 28th Floor of the Sheraton Nha Trang, this comes with panoramic views of the coast. Expect 5-star prices for the 5-star vista.

Nghia Bia Hoi BAR
(Map p232; 7G/3 Đ Hung Vuong) Probably the cheapest beer in Nha Trang, including a light lager and a darker brown beer, this place draws a backpacker crowd.

🛍 Shopping

Nha Trang has emerged as a popular place to look for local arts and crafts. A number of shops can be found in the blocks surrounding the corner of Đ Tran Quang Khai and Đ Hung Vuong.

Saga du Mekong CLOTHING
(Map p232; 1/21 Đ Nguyen Dinh Chieu) This stylish fashion boutique specialises in linen and cotton clothing, perfect for the tropical climes.

Bambou CLOTHING
(Map p232; 15 Đ Biet Thu) Part of the Bambou empire, this shop specialises in casual clothing with Vietnamese motifs, including beach wear.

A Mart FOOD
(Map p232; 17A Đ Biet Thu) A Mart is a centrally located minimart that offers a good selection of imported items, including sunscreen and beauty products.

XQ HANDICRAFTS
(Map p232; www.xqhandembroidery.com; 64 Đ Tran Phu; ⊙8am-8pm) At this place, designed to look like a traditional rural village, you are invited to enjoy a complimentary glass of green tea as you wander around. You can watch the artisans at work in the embroidery workshop and gallery.

ℹ Information

Dangers & Annoyances

In Nha Trang there are many ways for you and your money to part company. We've heard reports of thefts on the beach (pickpockets, and jewellery disappearing during an embrace), during massages (a third person sneaks into the room and removes money from clothes) and from hotel rooms (none of those included in this book, but you should still be cautious). Don't carry too much on you, and consider leaving surplus cash at the hotel reception. That way the hotel is responsible if it goes missing, although even this may not protect you from unscrupulous operators. Drive-by bag snatching is on the rise, which can be highly dangerous if you fall victim while on the back of a *xe om*. There are also some stories of gangs of youths using tasers around the beachfront at night to stun people before robbing them.

Some female tourists have reported being photographed by young Vietnamese males when emerging from the water or just lying on the beach. These guys are quite blatant about it and are rather persistent.

At tourist sites unobservant foreigners may be overcharged – check the price on pre-printed tickets, check your change and don't get stung for bicycle or motorbike parking.

Internet Access

Most hotels and travellers cafes offer an online fix. Most restaurants and bars also offer wi-fi: search for a network on Đ Trang Quang Khai or Đ Biet Thu and you'll be overwhelmed with options.

Medical Services

Pasteur Institute (Map p232; ☑382 2355; 10 Đ Tran Phu) Offers medical consultations and vaccinations. Located inside the Alexandre Yersin Museum (see 230).

Money

There are ATMs all over Nha Trang.

Vietcombank (Map p232; 17 Đ Quang Trung; ⊘Mon-Fri) Changes travellers cheques and offers cash advances.

Post

Main post office (Map p232; 4 Đ Le Loi; ⊘6.30am-10pm)

Travel Agencies

Highland Tours (Map p232; ☑352 4477; www .highlandtourstravel.com; 54G Đ Nguyen Thien Thuat) An extensive program of affordable tours in the central highlands.

Khanh Hoa Tourist Information (Map p232; ☑352 8000; khtourism@dng.vnn.vn; Đ Tran Phu) Government-run tourism office on the seafront with various tour programs, including boat trips.

Sinh Tourist (Map p232; ☑352 2982; www .thesinhtourist.vn; 2A Đ Biet Thu) Offers cheap local tours as well as open-tour buses.

ⓘ Getting There & Away

Air

Vietnam Airlines (Map p232; ☑352 6768; 91 Đ Nguyen Thien Thuat) connects Nha Trang with HCMC (from 680,000d), Hanoi (from 1,700,000d) and Danang (from 980,000d) daily. **Jetstar** (www.jetstar.com) offer cheaper connections with Hanoi starting at 775,000d.

Bus

Phia Nam Nha Trang bus station (Đ 23 Thang 10) is Nha Trang's main intercity bus terminal, 500m west of the train station. Regular daily buses head north to Quy Nhon (100,000d, five hours), with a few continuing to Danang (170,000d, 12 hours). Regular buses head south to Phan Rang (40,000d, two hours), plus there are regular services to HCMC (180,000d, 11 hours), including sleeper buses from 7pm. Buses also head into the highlands to Dalat (100,000d, five hours) and Buon Ma Thuot (85,000d, four hours).

Nha Trang is a major stopping point on all of the tourist open-tour buses. These are the best option for accessing Mui Ne, which is not served by local buses. These buses usually depart between 7am and 8am, reaching Mui Ne at lunchtime, before continuing on to HCMC. There are also regular open-tour buses to Dalat (five hours) and Hoi An (11 hours).

Car & Motorbike

By road from Nha Trang it's 235km to Quy Nhon, 523km to Danang, 104km to Phan Rang, 250km to Mui Ne, 448km to HCMC, 205km to Dalat and 205km to Buon Ma Thuot.

There are quite a number of Easy Riders based in Nha Trang. While some backpackers travel with the Easy Riders through the Central Highlands, one of the best trips to experience by motorbike is the new mountain pass from Nha Trang to Dalat, as seen on the BBC's iconic *Top Gear* special. Throw the mountain road back down from Dalat to Mui Ne into the mix and you have some of the best rides in the south available as a bite-sized chunk. See boxed text 'Easy Does It' (p282) for more on the Easy Riders.

Train

The **Nha Trang train station** (Map p232; Đ Thai Nguyen; ⊘ticket office 7-11.30am, 1.30-6pm & 7-9pm) is west of the cathedral. Destinations include Quy Nhon (132,000d, four hours), Danang (285,000d soft seat/475,000d soft sleeper, 10 hours) and HCMC (247,000d soft seat/420,000d soft sleeper, nine hours).

ⓘ Getting Around

To/From the Airport

Nha Trang is now served by Cam Ranh Airport, about 28km south of the city. A beautiful coastal road links Nha Trang with Cam Ranh. A shuttle bus runs the route (40,000d), leaving from the site of the old airport (near 86 Đ Tran Phu) two hours before scheduled departure times, taking about 40 minutes. Departing town, a taxi might be a more convenient option to avoid waiting around at the airport. **Nha Trang Taxi** (☑382 6000), the official maroon-coloured cabs, cost 320,000d from the airport to downtown. Conversely, it is only 190,000d from town out to the airport. Other taxi companies charge by the meter, meaning at least 300,000d.

Bicycle

It's easy to get around all of the sights, including Thap Ba, by bicycle. Most hotels have rentals from 30,000d per day. Watch out for the one-way system around the train station, and the chaotic roundabouts.

Taxi, Cyclo & Xe Om

Nha Trang has an excessive number of all three. The *xe om* drivers are the most persistently annoying, although like taxis all over the world

NHA TRANG TRANSPORT CONNECTIONS

DESTINATION	AIR	BUS	CAR/MOTORBIKE	TRAIN
HCMC	from US$34, 1 hr, 3 daily	US$9-12, 11 hr, frequent	10 hr	US$8-23, 9-12 hr, frequent
Mui Ne	N/A	US$5-7, 6 hr, regular	5 hr	N/A
Dalat	N/A	US$3.50-6, 5 hr, regular	4 hr	N/A
Quy Nhon	N/A	US$5-7, 5 hr, frequent	4 hr	US$3-7, 4-6 hr, frequent
Danang	from US$49, 1 hr, 1 daily	US$9-12, 12 hr, regular	11 hr	US$9-24, 12-15 hr, frequent

they seem to disappear when you actually want one. A motorcycle ride anywhere in the centre shouldn't cost more than 20,000d. Be careful at night, when some less reputable drivers moonlight as pimps and drug dealers. It is generally safer to take a metered taxi with a reputable company such as Mai Linh.

Around Nha Trang

THANH CITADEL

This citadel dates from the 17th-century Trinh dynasty. It was rebuilt by Prince Nguyen Anh (later Emperor Gia Long) in 1793 during his successful offensive against the Tay Son Rebels. Only a few sections of the walls and gates remain. Thanh Citadel is 11km west of Nha Trang near Dien Khanh town.

BA HO FALLS

The three waterfalls and pools at **Ba Ho Falls** (Suoi Ba Ho) are in a forested area about 20km north of Nha Trang and about 2km west of Phu Huu village. Turn off Hwy 1 just north of Quyen Restaurant. It is quite fun clambering upstream through the pools and it sees far fewer tourists than other natural sites in the area.

SUOI TIEN (FAIRY SPRING)

This enchanting little spring seems to pop out of nowhere. Like a small oasis, the **Fairy Spring** (10,000d) is decorated with its own natural garden of tropical vegetation and smooth boulders. It has been earmarked as the next big ecotourism site, and the entrance area is rapidly being enveloped in concrete, but it is still peaceful if you hike upstream. Vietnamese like to picnic here, so

there can be a surfeit of litter, but this dries up as you follow the spring.

You'll need to rent a motorbike or car to reach the spring. From Nha Trang, drive south on Hwy 1 for 27km to Suoi Cat, turning right (west) at the blue and white 'Ho chua nuoc Suoi Dau' sign. After 5km you'll see a sign directing you to the spring.

CAM RANH HARBOUR

The gorgeous natural harbour of **Cam Ranh Bay** starts 25km south of Nha Trang and 56km north of Phan Rang. With the opening of the stunning airport road, beautiful **Bai Dai** (Long Beach), forming the northern head of the harbour, has become much more accessible. Largely unspoilt, the government has been encouraging development and as if to confirm its international arrival, a Miss Universe contest was held at the Diamond Bay Resort in August 2008. What would Ho Chi Minh make of it all?

The military still controls access to much of this area but is starting to work with tourist operators. Nha Trang's Waves Watersports (see p236) has negotiated access to some of the best surf breaks in Vietnam. **Shack Vietnam** (www.shackvietnam.com) also offers board rental and instruction in Bai Dai.

Most of the beach is very undeveloped by Nha Trang standards, so it is a good place to escape the crowds for the day. There are several beach shacks offering fresh seafood in the area.

To get here you can take the airport shuttle bus (see p242), although you'll need to time your visit around flight times. A one-way journey in a taxi will cost around 250,000d, but a *xe om* is cheaper. Aim for 150,000d or so including wait time.

GOODBYE SAILOR

Cam Ranh Harbour has long been considered one of Asia's prime deep-water anchorages. The Russian fleet of Admiral Rodjestvenski used it in 1905 at the end of the Russo-Japanese War, as did the Japanese during WWII. At this time the surrounding area was still considered an excellent place for tiger hunting. In the mid-1960s the Americans constructed a vast base here, including an extensive port, ship-repair facilities and an airstrip.

After reunification the Russians and their fleet came back, enjoying far better facilities than they had left seven decades before. For a while this became the largest Soviet naval installation outside the USSR. With the collapse of the Soviet Union in 1991 and the end of the Cold War, economic problems forced the Russians to cut back vastly on their overseas military facilities. Although the initial contract on Cam Ranh Bay was due to expire in 2004, the Russians vacated their position by the end of 2002, the last hurrah for the Russian navy in Asia.

Phan Rang & Thap Cham

♩068 / POP 170,000

This really is a tale of two cities: Phan Rang hugging the shoulders of Hwy 1 and Thap Cham straddling Hwy 20 as it starts its long climb to Dalat. Anyone travelling Vietnam from north to south will notice a big change in the vegetation when approaching the joint capitals of Ninh Thuan province. The familiar lush green rice paddies are replaced with sandy soil supporting only scrubby plants. Local flora includes poinciana trees and prickly-pear cacti with vicious thorns. The area is famous for its production of table grapes, and many of the houses on the outskirts of town are decorated with vines on trellises.

The area's best-known sight is the group of Cham towers known as Po Klong Garai, from which Thap Cham (Cham Tower) derives its name. However, with the advent of a new mountain highway between Dalat and Nha Trang, this temple sees far fewer visitors than in the past. There are many more towers dotted about the countryside in this area and the province is home to tens of thousands of Cham people. The Cham, like other ethnic minorities in Vietnam, have suffered from discrimination and are usually poorer than their ethnic-Vietnamese neighbours. There are also several thousand Chinese in the area, many of whom come to worship at the 135-year old Quang Cong Pagoda (Đ Thong Nhat), a colourful Chinese temple in the town centre.

With two major highways (1A and 20) intersecting in the town, this is a good pit-stop on the coastal run. Nearby Ninh Chu Beach (p246) is another, quieter alternative to the celebrity beaches along this coast. Hwy 1 becomes Đ Thong Nhat as it passes through the centre of town. From the main roundabout, Đ 16 Thang 4 heads east to Ninh Chu Beach.

◉ Sights

Po Klong Garai Cham Towers   TEMPLE
(Thap Cham; admission 10,000d; ⊘7.30am-6pm) The four brick towers of Po Klong Garai were constructed at the end of the 13th and beginning of the 14th century. Built as Hindu temples, they stand on a brick platform at the top of Cho'k Hala, a crumbly granite hill covered with some of the most ornery cacti this side of the Rio Grande.

A large modern building in a vaguely Cham style sitting at the base of the hill is dedicated to Cham culture, with separate galleries of photographs, paintings and traditional pottery. It's a good reminder that while the Cham kingdom is long gone, the Cham people are an important minority in this region (see p211).

Over the entrance to the largest tower (the *kalan*, or sanctuary) is a beautiful carving of a dancing Shiva with six arms. Note the inscriptions in the ancient Cham language on the doorposts. These tell of past restoration efforts and offerings of sacrifices and slaves. If you want to look inside, you'll need to remove your shoes as this is still an active place of worship. Inside the vestibule is a statue of the bull Nandin, vehicle of the Hindu god Shiva. Nandin is also a symbol of the agricultural productivity of the countryside. To ensure a good crop, farmers would place an offering of fresh greens, herbs and areca nuts in front of Nandin's muzzle. Under the main tower is a *mukha-linga* sitting under a wooden pyramid.

Inside the smaller tower opposite the entrance to the sanctuary, you can get a good look at some of the Cham's sophisticated building technology; the wooden columns that support the lightweight roof are visible. The structure attached to it was originally the main entrance to the complex.

Po Klong Garai is just north of Hwy 20, at a point 6km west of Phan Rang towards Dalat. The towers are on the opposite side of the tracks to Thap Cham train station. Some of the open-tour buses running the coastal route make a requisite pit stop here.

Po Ro Me Cham Tower   TEMPLE

(admission free, donation welcome) Po Ro Me is one of the most atmospheric of Vietnam's Cham towers thanks in part to its isolated setting on top of a craggy hill with sweeping views over the cactus-strewn landscape. The temple honours the last ruler of an independent Champa, King Po Ro Me (r 1629–51), who died as a prisoner of the Vietnamese. His image and those of his family are found on the external decorations. Note the flame motif repeated around the arches, a symbol of purity, cleansing visitors of any residual bad karma.

The temple is still in active use, with ceremonies taking place twice a year. The rest of the time it's locked up, but the caretakers, who are based at the foot of the hill, will open the sanctuary for you. Consider leaving a small donation with them and don't forget to remove your shoes.

The occupants of the temple aren't used to having their rest disturbed, and it can be a little creepy when the bats start chattering and swooping overhead in the confined dark space. Through the gloom you'll be able to make out a blood-red and black centrepiece – a bas-relief representing the deified king in the form of Shiva. Behind the main deity and to the left is one of his queens, Thanh Chanh. Look out for the inscriptions on the doorposts and a stone statue of the bull Nandin.

The best way to reach the site is with your own motorbike or a *xe om*. The trip is worthwhile, as long as getting lost is a part of your agenda. Take Hwy 1 south from Phan Rang for 9km. Turn right at the turn-off to Ho Tan Giang, a narrow sealed road just after the petrol station, and continue for a further 6km. Turn left in the middle of a dusty village at a paddock that doubles as a football field and follow the road as it meanders to the right until the tower comes into sight. A sign points the way cross-country for the last 500m.

Bau Truc Village   NEIGHBOURHOOD

This Cham village is known for its pottery and you'll see several family shops in front of the mud and bamboo houses. On the way to Po Ro Me turn right off Hwy 1 near the war memorial, into the commune with the banner 'Lang Nghe Gom Bau Truc'. Inside the village take the first left for some of the better pottery stores.

🛏 Sleeping

There are lots more luxurious accommodation options out at Ninh Chu Beach (p246).

Ho Phong Hotel   HOTEL $

(✆392 0333; www.hophong.co.net; 363 Đ Ngo Gia Tu; r 230,000-450,000d; ❈@🛜) Located near the main bridge, this grandiose building is the best all-rounder in town, and is highly visible by night when it is lit up like a Christmas tree. All rooms are well-furnished with some nice touches, including power showers and toilets with gold trim.

Viet Thang Hotel   HOTEL $

(✆383 5899; 430 Đ Ngo Gia Tu; s/d/q 160,000/ 180,000/300,000d; ❈🛜) Just off the main

---

CHAM NEW YEAR

The Cham New Year (*kate*) is celebrated at Po Klong Garai in the seventh month of the Cham calendar (around October). The festival commemorates ancestors, Cham national heroes and deities such as the farmers' goddess Po Ino Nagar.

On the eve of the festival, a procession guarded by the mountain people of Tay Nguyen carries King Po Klong Garai's clothing, to the accompaniment of traditional music. The procession lasts until midnight. The following morning the garments are carried to the tower, once again accompanied by music, along with banners, flags, singing and dancing. Notables, dignitaries and village elders follow behind. This colourful ceremony continues into the afternoon.

The celebrations then carry on for the rest of the month, as the Cham attend parties and visit friends and relatives. They also use this time to pray for good fortune.

road on Đ Ngo Gia Tu, this place looks a bit weather-worn from the outside, but the rooms are a fair deal and the owners are very friendly, although they don't speak English.

✖ Eating

One of the local delicacies here is roasted or baked *ky nhong* (gecko), served with fresh green mango; see p247. If you prefer self-catering and have quick reflexes, most hotel rooms in Vietnam have a ready supply.

More palatable is another local speciality, *com ga* (chicken with rice). The local chickens seem to have more meat on them than Vietnam's usual spindly specimens, and Vietnamese travellers make a point of buying chickens (or at least stopping for a snack) as they pass through. There are a few *com ga* restaurants on Đ Tran Quang Dieu. The best is **Phuoc Thanh** (3 Đ Tran Quang Dieu; mains 20,000-50,000d), located just north of D 16 Thang 4, the road to Ninh Chu Beach.

Phan Rang is the table-grape capital of Vietnam. Stalls in the market sell fresh grapes, grape juice and dried grapes (too juicy to be called raisins). Also worth sampling is the green *thanh long* (dragon fruit). Its mild, kiwifruit-like taste is especially refreshing when chilled.

ⓘ Information

Agriculture Bank (540-544 Đ Thong Nhat) Near the market, exchanges currency.

Main post office (217A Đ Thong Nhat) Near the bus station, this post office also offers internet access.

ⓘ Getting There & Away

BUS Phan Rang bus station (opposite 64 Đ Thong Nhat) is on the northern outskirts of town. Regular buses head north to Nha Trang (42,000d, 2½ hours), northwest to Dalat (55,000d, four hours), and south to Ca Na (15,000d, one hour) and beyond.

CAR & MOTORBIKE Phan Rang is 344km from HCMC, 147km from Phan Thiet, 104km from Nha Trang and 108km from Dalat.

TRAIN The **Thap Cham train station** (7 Đ Phan Dinh Phung) is about 6km west of Hwy 1, within sight of Po Klong Garai Cham towers, but only slower trains stop here. Destinations include Nha Trang (around two hours) and HCMC (around eight hours).

Ninh Chu Beach

☑068

Southeast of Phan Rang, Ninh Chu Beach is increasingly popular with Vietnamese tourists. Apart from the occasional blight of litter, the 10km-long beach is attractive and relatively empty on a weekday. It makes a quieter alternative to Phan Rang as a base for visiting the Cham ruins.

A bizarre local attraction is the **Hoan Cau Resort** (☑389 0077; www.hoancautourist.com .vn; waterpark adult/child 20,000/10,000d), where Disneyland meets Vietnamese folklore. Hilarious plaster statues adorn the grounds and rooms are shaped like tree stumps. A brief visit is definitely more enjoyable than staying in the kitsch, fake treehouse style bungalows. Basically, it looks like the local party hacks enjoyed a visit to Dalat's Crazy House (p272) so much that they brought the blueprint back with them and built a resort.

🛏 Sleeping & Eating

TOP CHOICE Den Gion Resort   BOUTIQUE HOTEL $$
(☑387 4223; www.dengion-resort.com; r US$40-60; ✳@🛜🏊) This resort has been beautifully upgraded in recent years and is an atmospheric place to stay. There are a range of bungalows set in a lush garden by the beach, all offering the same trim which includes smart showers and elegant furnishings. Breakfast is included, taken at the open-air **restaurant** (mains 50,000d to 125,000d).

Con Ga Vang Resort   RESORT HOTEL $$
(☑387 4899; www.congavangresort.com; r 700,000-1,500,000d; ✳@🛜🏊) One of many new resorts popping up along Ninh Chu Beach, the prices here are pretty enticing when you factor in smart, spacious rooms and facilities such as a swimming pool and tennis courts. The hotel's beachfront **Huong Dua Restaurant** (mains 40,000-100,000d) is one of the best in Ninh Chu, with great value seafood such as a plate of oysters baked with garlic for less than US$5. Some English spoken.

Anh Duong Hotel   HOTEL $
(☑389 0009; www.anhduonghotel.com.vn; r 200,000-400,000d; ✳🛜) Away from the beach, lots of modern hotels have sprung up along the roadside offering cheaper rooms. One of the newer pads, the Anh Duong has a smart trim and it's a short walk to the beach.

ⓘ Getting There & Away

Turn left (southeast) into Đ Ngo Gia Tu, the street immediately before the Cai River bridge in Phan Rang, and continue on, following the signs for 7km. Unless you're driving yourself, it's easiest to take a *xe om* (around 30,000d) or a metered taxi (80,000d).

Ca Na

♪ 068

During the 16th century, princes of the Cham royal family would fish and hunt tigers, elephants and rhinoceros here. Today Ca Na (pronounced 'kah nah' – not like the site of the biblical booze-up) is better known for its white-sand beaches, which are dotted with huge granite boulders. The best of the beach is just off Hwy 1, a kilometre north of the fishing village. It's a beautiful spot, but it's tough to ignore the constant honking and rumble of trucks.

The terrain is studded with magnificent prickly-pear cacti. Bright yellow **Lac Son**, a small pagoda on the hillside, makes for an interesting but steep climb.

If you stay here, be aware that there are no banks or ATMs and absolutely no-one accepts credit cards or travellers cheques.

Ca Na Hotel (☑376 0922; www.canahotel .com.vn; r 180,000-250,000d; ❀@☎) is a small hotel with eight bungalows and a further 12 rooms in the 'motel' building. There is a slightly forlorn feel about the place due to a lack of regular guests.

❶ Getting There & Away

Ca Na is 114km north of Phan Thiet and 32km south of Phan Rang. Many long-haul buses cruising Hwy 1 offer drop offs, but pick-ups are a harder proposition. Local buses from Phan Rang (15,000d, one hour) head to Ca Na fishing village – ask to be let out on the highway and catch a *xe om* for the last kilometre.

Mui Ne

♪ 062 / POP 15,000

Once upon a time, Mui Ne was an isolated stretch of sand, but it was too beautiful to be ignored. Times have changed and it is now a string of resorts, expanding in number every year. However, the beach retains much of its charm and the resorts are, for the most part, mercifully low-rise, set amid pretty gardens by the sea. The original fishing village is still here, but tourists outnumber locals these days. Mui Ne is definitely moving upmarket, as more exclusive resorts open their doors, complemented by swish restaurants and swanky shops, but there is still a surfer vibe to the town.

Mui Ne is the adrenalin capital of southern Vietnam. There's no scuba diving or snorkelling to speak of, but when Nha Trang and Hoi An get the rains, Mui Ne gets the waves. Surf's up from August to December. For windsurfers, the gales blow as well, especially from late October to late April, when swells stir thanks to the Philippine typhoons. Kitesurfing has really taken off and the infinite horizon is often obscured by dozens of kites flapping in the wind. If this all sounds too much like hard work you can simply lounge around on the beach, watching others take the strain.

Mui Ne sees only about half the rainfall of nearby Phan Thiet. The sand dunes help protect its unique microclimate, and even during the wet season (from June to September) rains tend to be fairly light and sporadic.

One major problem the area faces is the steady creep of coastal erosion. Many resorts north of Km 12 have almost completely lost their beaches and rely on sandbagging to keep the little they have left. On the plus side, it's almost impossible to get lost in Mui Ne, as everything is spread out along a 10km stretch of highway. Most accommodation lines the beach side, while restaurants and shops flank the other.

SOUTH-CENTRAL COAST NINH CHU BEACH

LIZARD FISHING

When most people think of fishing in the mountains they conjure up images of hooking river trout or lake bass. But in the arid foothills of the south-central coast (notably around places like Ca Na, Phan Rang, Phan Thiet and Mui Ne) there is a whole other kind of angling, and a walk in these hills can yield one of the strangest sights in Vietnam – lizard fishing.

These lizards, called *than lan nui*, are members of the gecko family and good for eating – some say they taste like chicken. The traditional way of catching the lizards is by setting a hook on a long bamboo fishing pole and dangling bait from the top of a boulder until the spunky little reptiles strike.

Lizards are served grilled, roasted or fried, and are often made up into a pâté (complete with finely chopped bones) and used as a dip for rice-paper crackers.

Mui Ne Beach

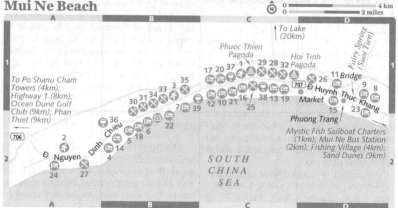

Ironically Mui Ne is not the destination most people stay in during their time here. Mui Ne is a fishing village located at the eastern end of Route 706. The main village near all the tourist action actually goes by the name of Ham Tien. So welcome to Ham Tien.

◎ Sights

Sand Dunes
BEACH

Mui Ne is famous for its enormous red and white sand dunes. These have been a favourite subject for many a Vietnamese photographer, including some who sit like camels on the blazing hot sand for hours, waiting for the winds to sculpt the dunes into that perfect Kodak moment. If you visit, be sure to try the sand-sledding.

You'll need a jeep to explore these properly, but be careful to agree on an itinerary for the tour, preferably in writing. We've heard complaints, particularly about 'sunset tours' that cut short with the sun high in the sky and the drivers getting aggressive when challenged. Also bear in mind the white dunes have been massively commercialised in recent times, with quad bikes and dune buggies destroying the peace of the place.

Also of interest is the **Fairy Spring** (Suoi Tien), which is really a stream that flows through a patch of dunes with interesting sand and rock formations. It's a beautiful trek wading up the stream from the sea to its source, though it might be wise to hire a local guide. You can do the trek barefoot, but if you're heading out into the big sand dunes, you'll need leather soles on your feet; sandals are even questionable during the midday sun. Bizarrely, ostrich riding

(40,000d) is now offered as an activity here, but we don't recommend it.

Po Shanu Cham Towers
TEMPLE

(Km5; admission 5000d; ⊗7.30-11.30am & 1.30-4.30pm) To the west, Po Shanu Cham Towers occupies a hill near Phan Thiet, with sweeping views of the town and a cemetery filled with candylike tombstones. Dating from the 9th century, this complex consists of the ruins of three towers, none of which are in very good shape. There's a small pagoda on the site, as well as a gallery and shop.

🏃 Activities

Courses

Taste of Vietnam
COOKING

(☎091-665 5241; atasteofvietnam@gmail.com; Sunshine Beach Resort, 82 Đ Nguyen Dinh Chieu; ⊗9am-12.30pm & 1.30-4pm) Learn the secrets of Vietnamese cuisine with a cooking class by the beach. Morning classes (US$25) include a market visit; afternoon classes are a little cheaper (US$20). Impress friends back home with *banh xeo,* spring rolls and *pho bo.*

Golf

Tropical Minigolf Mui Ne
MINI GOLF

(97 Đ Nguyen Dinh Chieu; ⊗10am-10.30pm; 100,000d) Head here for a round of mini golf. The attractive garden course is dotted with craggy rock formations to challenge your putting skills. Rates include one drink or pay 120,000d by night, including a mojito or tequila sunrise.

Sealinks Golf & Country Club
GOLF

(☎374 1777; www.sealinksvietnam.com; Km 8, Mui Ne; from 1,945,000d for 18 holes) This new ocean-view course is considered one of the most

Mui Ne Beach

challenging in Vietnam. Play a discounted twilight round from 2.30pm. The complex includes a resort hotel and residential villas.

Ocean Dunes Golf Club GOLF
(382 3366; www.oceandunesgolf.vn; 1 Đ Ton Duc Thang; per round from US$77, plus caddy & cart) Located out of town, near the beachfront in Phan Thiet, this is a top-notch 18-hole, par 72 course designed by Nick Faldo. Very reasonably priced golf package tours, including accommodation at the nearby Novotel Ocean Dunes, are available if you book through the website.

Spas

Many of the upmarket hotels have their own spa, offering a range of rubs, scrubs and tubs.

Nina Spa SPA
(384 7577; 165 Đ Nguyen Dinh Chieu; 9am-10pm) Set in a beautiful traditional house complete with its own swimming pool, this is the most alluring spa in Mui Ne. Massages start from US$21 or spoil yourself rotten with a two-hour treatment for US$65.

Watersports

It is worth investing in a short kitesurfing lesson before opting for a multi-day course, as some people find it harder than others. Bear in mind it is an extreme sport and most places will not offer a refund on an immersion course for anyone who drops out.

Jibes KITESURFING
(☎384 7405; www.windsurf-vietnam.com; 90 Đ
Nguyen Dinh Chieu; ☺7.30am-6pm) The original
kitesurfing school, Jibes is watersports heaven, offering lessons and renting state-of-the-art gear, including windsurfs, surfboards,
kitesurfs and kayaks. Insurance costs extra.

Sankara Kitesurfing Academy KITESURFING
(☎91-491 0607; www.kiteschoolmuine.com; 78 Đ
Nguyen Dinh Chieu) Based at ultra-hip Sankara
(see p254), this place is run by experienced
kitesurfers and offers kitesurfing lessons
and equipment rentals.

Vietnam Kitesurfing Tours KITESURFING
(☎090-946 9803; www.vietnamkitesurfingtours
.com) Based out of Mellow guesthouse, this
company takes you to parts others cannot
reach. Day trips cost US$80 and two-day
trips start at US$180.

Mystic Fish Charters SAILING
(☎012-7287 8801; www.mysticfishcharters.com;
108 Đ Huynh Thuc Khang) Hello sailor! Experience a sailing trip aboard a Corsair Marine
Sprint catamaran. It costs US$295, but this
can be split between up to seven punters.

Surf Vietnam SURFING
(www.surf-vietnam.com) Offers lessons from
(US$50) on several different waves around
Mui Ne. Shortboards (US$18 half-day) available for rent.

🛏 Sleeping

The accommodation scene is booming in
Mui Ne, offering a great range of places to
stay to suit all budgets. Mui Ne was traditionally the escape of choice for expats working in HCMC and affluent Vietnamese seeking to escape the big-city smoke, meaning
that the smarter accommodation was often
full during weekends and holidays. However, this is changing with the horrendous
traffic on Highway 1A, as nobody wants to
spend six hours each way crawling their way
to the coast, so it is not always necessary to
book ahead. However, if you are fixed on a
particular place, it is probably wise to make
a reservation.

Most of the places at the top end usually
charge an extra 10% tax and 5% service.

TOP CHOICE Mui Ne Backpackers GUESTHOUSE $
(☎384 7047; www.muinebackpackers.com; 88
Đ Nguyen Dinh Chieu; dm US$6-10; r US$20-60;
✸@⊕≋) One of the most popular places to
stay in Mui Ne thanks to the friendly, hospitable Aussie management and the wide
range of rooms. Choose from smart four-bed
dorms with access to hot showers or private
rooms that have been fully renovated. Best
of the lot are the beachfront bungalows with
an unrestricted view of the sea. They arrange a nightly session on the town, including dinner and a selection of the best bars.
Great for the social set and keeps the resort
nicely quiet by night.

TOP CHOICE Full Moon Resort BOUTIQUE HOTEL $$
(☎384 7008; www.windsurf-vietnam.com; 84 Đ
Nguyen Dinh Chieu; r US$48-165; ✸@⊕≋) One
of the pioneering resorts in Mui Ne, the
committed owners have consistently upgraded this place to keep up with the competition. Beachfront bungalows are very atmospheric with wall hangings and jacuzzi-like bathtubs. Family rooms are available
that include a sofa bed for the kiddies.

TOP CHOICE Cham Villas BOUTIQUE HOTEL $$$
(☎374 1234; www.chamvillas.com; 32 Đ Nguyen
Dinh Chieu; r US$150-185; ✸@⊕≋) Arguably
the most boutique of many 'boutique' resorts in Mui Ne, there are just 20 stylish villas available here, so it does tend to book up
during peak periods. Verdant gardens surround the large pool and there is 60m-strip
of private beach.

Indochina Dreams BOUTIQUE HOTEL $$
(☎384 7271; www.indochinadream.com; 74 Đ
Nguyen Dinh Chieu; r US$40-55; ✸@⊕≋) Now
expanded to include 12 rooms, the new
bungalows are finished in local stone and
are dotted about the extensive gardens. The
swimming pool is a great place to unwind,
but the odds are that more bungalows will
be built at some stage.

Mia Resort BOUTIQUE HOTEL $$$
(☎384 7440; www.sailingclubvietnam.com; 24 Đ
Nguyen Dinh Chieu; r US$66, bungalows US$85-170;
✸@⊕≋) The Sailing Club is rebranding its
resorts as Mia, but the recipe remains the
same: a sophisticated and stylish resort offering sensibly priced rooms with designer
furnishings, wooden trim and private balconies. The beachside pool includes the excellent Sandals Restaurant overlooking the sea,
which is open to all-comers for a meal or a
drink. Cooking classes are also available.

Shades APARTMENTS $$$
(☎374 3236; www.shadesmuine.com; 98A Đ Nguyen Dinh Chieu; r US$74-380; ✸@⊕≋) Small in

size, but big in personality, Shades offers luxurious studio apartments with sleek contemporary lines. Open plan kitchens are a feature of the larger studios, but all include a flat screen TV, electric beds, a wholesome breakfast and laundry.

Sunsea Resort BOUTIQUE HOTEL **$$$**
(✆384 7711; www.sunsearesort-muine.com; 50 Đ Nguyen Dinh Chieu; r US$75-150; ❄@🖥≋) Following a major facelift, this resort is now one of the most attractive on the beach. Smarter rooms are set in beautiful bandastyle buildings with views over the pool and sea. There is a second shady pool fronted by the cheaper rooms with garden view. The Sukothai Restaurant is super-stylish and well-regarded for Thai cuisine.

Coco Beach Resort BOUTIQUE HOTEL **$$$**
(✆384 7111; www.cocobeach.net; 58 Đ Nguyen Dinh Chieu; r US$110-270; ❄@🖥≋) The resort where it all began, Coco Beach opened its doors in 1995 with not a restaurant, spa or bar in sight. It has matured with the destination and remains one of the prettiest of the resorts around Mui Ne, with spacious bungalows set in a lush garden.

Victoria Phan Thiet Beach Resort RESORT HOTEL **$$$**
(✆381 3000; www.victoriahotels-asia.com; Km 9; r US$170-460; ❄@🖥≋) The original luxury resort in Mui Ne, the Victoria is still a good place to stay. The open-plan bungalows feature huge bathrooms with deep tubs and Balinese-style outdoor showers. There is a lengthy strip of beach and two pools.

Paris Mui Ne Plage HOTEL **$$**
(✆090-278 8020; www.parismuineplage.com.vn; 94 Đ Nguyen Dinh Chieu; r US$20-75; ❄@🖥≋) A tale of two hotels, the beachside pad is the more upmarket of the two with rooms starting from US$55. Opt for roadside and there are cracking deals available and both properties include a separate swimming pool.

Bien Dua Resort GUESTHOUSE **$**
(Coconut Beach; ✆384 7241; www.bienduaresort.com; 136 Đ Nguyen Dinh Chieu; r US$10-20; ❄@🖥) At this intimate and friendly Frenchrun place, the bungalow-style rooms remain enticing value for the prime beachfront location. Cheaper rooms have fan, but all rooms have hot water and TV.

Rang Garden Bungalow HOTEL **$**
(✆374 3638; 233A Đ Nguyen Dinh Chieu; r US$10-30; ❄@🖥≋) Newly opened in 2011, this is

THE CHANGING FACE OF THE STRIP

Until the explosion of resorts in Mui Ne, addresses were designated by their distance in kilometres from Hwy 1 in Phan Thiet (to the west). Properties now follow a new numbering system, with Route 706 renamed Đ Nguyen Dinh Chieu on the west half of the beach and Đ Huynh Thuc Khang beyond Ham Tien.

From Phan Thiet, development is sporadic until the Km 8 mark and the rather splendid looking University of Phan Thiet. After this, there are several resorts, restaurants and a golf course, as the development unfolds. From Km 10 to Km 12, Mui Ne has quite a Russian feel, with souvenir shops and spas galore emblazoned with Cyrillic script. Km 12 to Km 14 is where many of the popular midrange resorts and restaurants are found. From here there is a break in the resorts, with a strip of seafood stalls and some late-night beach clubs before another cluster of backpacker accommodation and restaurant-bars around the Km 16 strip. This is where the village of Ham Tien starts before giving way to more backpacker accommodation around Km 18. Look out for superb views over the Mui Ne fishing fleet around Km 20 and you've arrived at the end of the strip.

seriously smart for the money. Rooms are set in attractive villas around the generously proportioned swimming pool. The higher standard rooms are positively on the 3-star side and there is a small restaurant out front.

Paradise Huts HOTEL **$$**
(✆384 7177; www.chezninaresort.com; 86 Đ Nguyen Dinh Chieu; r US$35-50; ❄@🖥) Also known as Chez Nina, in case you were wondering about the website, these pretty bungalows are housed in a leafy garden in the middle of Mui Ne. There is no pool here, but the beachfront is on your doorstep.

Thai Hoa Mui Ne Resort HOTEL **$$**
(✆384 7320; www.thaihoaresort.com; 56 Đ Huynh Thuc Khang; r US$20-50; ❄@🖥) This place has slowly gentrified over the years, but remains popular thanks to attractive bungalows fronting a spacious garden. Pay a premium to get up close and personal with the beach.

Lu Hoang Guesthouse
HOTEL $

(☑350 0060; 106 Đ Nguyen Dinh Chieu; r US$15-20; ✳@☎) Staying here is like coming to a charming bed-and-breakfast thanks to the warm and welcoming hosts. The house has been lovingly decorated and several rooms include a sea view and breezy balconies, plus all have spotless bathrooms.

Salina Resort
HOTEL $$

(☑374 3666; www.salinaresort.net; 130D Đ Nguyen Dinh Chieu; r 600,000-700,000d; ✳@☀) A new family-run place around the Km16 mark, Salina offers the atmosphere of a boutique homestay. Rooms are large and those at the front include a sea-view balcony.

Hai Yen Guesthouse
GUESTHOUSE $

(☑384 7243; www.haiyenguesthouse.com; 132 Đ Nguyen Dinh Chieu; r US$15-25; ✳@☎☀) The friendly Hai Yen has a great selection of rooms set behind the seafront swimming pool, all now including air-con. Spend US$25 and enjoy a sea view plus a fridge. There is beachfront access, plus a small restaurant.

Sea Winds Resort
GUESTHOUSE $

(☑384 7018; 139 Đ Nguyen Dinh Chieu; r US$7-18; ✳@☎) The road frontage is tiny, but like Dr Who's Tardis, it opens up – to reveal a lovely little garden surrounded by some crackingly good-value rooms. Fan rooms are very spacious for this sort of money.

Hotel 1 & 10
GUESTHOUSE $

(☑384 7815; 261A Đ Nguyen Dinh Chieu; dm US$3, r US$5-15; ✳@☎) Where else in Mui Ne can you stay in a minority house for just US$3 per night? This is the Mai Chau experience with mattresses on the floor, with about 25 berths in the old wooden house. If you crave more sophistication, rooms are available at the back. The restaurant-bar dabbles in cheap shishas at just US$4 a pop.

Duy An Guesthouse
GUESTHOUSE $

(☑384 7799; 87 Đ Huynh Thuc Khang; r US$7-20; ✳@☎) Located on the far side of Ham Tien where there are several budget guesthouses, the Duy An stands out thanks to friendly owners who speak good English. Rooms include quads for US$20, and most can accommodate an extra mattress on the floor. Bikes for hire at 30,000d.

Little Mui Ne Cottages
HOTEL $$$

(☑384 7550; www.littlemuine.com; 10B Huynh Thuc Khang; r US$55-176; ✳@☎☀) Set amid extensive gardens, this is a little oasis that promotes its personal service. The cottages are generously spread out so it doesn't feel too crowded and the huge pool is big enough for laps.

Mui Ne Resort
HOTEL $$

(☑384 7542; www.thesinhtourist.vn; 114 Đ Nguyen Dinh Chieu; r US$30-60; ✳@☎☀) Under the stewardship of the Sinh Tourist, this is more flashpacker than backpacker. The rooms are spotless and the staff friendly, plus there is an attractive pool surrounded by lush foliage.

Bao Quynh Bungalow
HOTEL $$

(☑374 1007; www.baoquynh.com; 26 Đ Nguyen Dinh Chieu; r US$36-115; ✳@☎☀) Choose from cheaper rooms or spacious bungalows at this attractively designed resort. Includes a decent stretch of beach.

Mellow
GUESTHOUSE $

(☑374 3086; 117C Đ Nguyen Dinh Chieu; r US$6-15; ✳@☎) Just as the name suggests, this is a chilled place to stay for those wanting a good value place to rest their head. The cheapest rooms involve a shared bathroom.

Mui Ne Lodge
GUESTHOUSE $

(☑384 7327; www.muinelodge.com; 150 Đ Nguyen Dinh Chieu; r US$12-25; ✳@☎) A small and atmospheric backpackers, the lodge offers 12 rooms with thatched roofs. The bar area includes a pool table.

Hiep Hoa Beachside Bungalow
HOTEL $$

(☑384 7262; www.muinebeach.net/hiephoa; 80 Đ Nguyen Dinh Chieu; r US$20-30; ✳@☎☀) A small, family-run hotel that offers a good deal for those wanting a little more than the cheap guesthouses can offer.

Hoang Kim Golden
HOTEL $$

(☑384 7689; www.hoangkim-golden.com; 140 Đ Nguyen Dinh Chieu; r US$15-40; ✳@☎☀) Fully renovated in the past few years, this old-timer offers bungalow-style rooms set around the small swimming pool and beachfront.

Golden Sunlight Guesthouse
GUESTHOUSE $

(☑374 3124; 19B Đ Nguyen Dinh Chieu; r US$8-12; ✳@☎) One of the first cheapies to open on the Km 18 budget strip, it remains a good choice. It's a friendly place with clean, airy rooms with fan and attached bathroom.

Duyen Vu Guesthouse
GUESTHOUSE $

(☑374 3404; 77A Đ Huynh Thuc Khang; r US$10; ✳@☎) Fronted by a large restaurant, there

INSIDER TIPS FROM MUI NE

Travel writer Adam Bray has contributed to more than 20 guidebooks and numerous travel magazines about Vietnam. Adam lives in Mui Ne and is fluent in both Vietnamese and Cham. Follow his adventures at www.muinebeach.net and www.fisheggtree.com.

If friends are coming to town, where do you usually recommend they stay? I usually send friends to Mia Resort. It's a cosy, boutique resort with beautiful landscaping and one of the prettiest beachside pool bars on the strip.

Where is the best place to get authentic Vietnamese seafood in Mui Ne? The seafood stands in the middle of Mui Ne. The most popular is Bo Ke, so in typical Vietnamese fashion all the others call themselves Bo Ke. Head to the largest one on the east end for awesome grilled scallops.

What is your favourite international restaurant in town? It's a toss-up between Shree Ganesh, our original Indian restaurant, and Joe's Café (p255), with their great burgers, sandwiches, pasta and coffee.

Mui Ne nightlife is really taking off; do you have any favourite spots? I like the chilled-out atmosphere at the new beach bar, Fun Key, which also has great food and cheap cocktails.

Your grandfather is the renowned archaeologist Dr David Livingston; have you made any recent interesting discoveries yourself? In the last two years I've discovered the ruins of three ancient Cham temples. Last year I was the first journalist to visit the Long Wall of Quang Ngai (p216), reporting on it for the BBC.

are only a small number of bungalow-style rooms overlooking a sandy, shady garden. But come on down, the price is right.

Beach Resort RESORT HOTEL $$
(☑384 7626; www.thebeachresort.com.vn; 18 Đ Nguyen Dinh Chieu; r from 1,300,000d; ✳@🛜🏊) A popular 3-star resort in the heart of the action; plans are afoot to upgrade it further.

Allez Boo Resort RESORT HOTEL $$$
(☑374 1081; www.allezboo.com; 8 Đ Nguyen Dinh Chieu; r US$80-410; ✳@🛜🏊) It's hard to believe this place is related to the original backpacker bar of Pham Ngo Lao, thanks to the colonial-style decor in the rooms, huge pool and bubbling jacuzzi.

L'Anmien Resort LUXURY RESORT $$$
(☑374 1888; www.lanmienresort.com; 12A Đ Nguyen Dinh Chieu; r US$250-980; ✳@🛜🏊) Billing itself a lifestyle resort, this is the smartest place in Mui Ne, a member of Small Luxury Hotels of the World.

Princess d'Annam LUXURY RESORT $$$
(☑368 2222; www.princessannam.com; r US$350-1370; ✳@🛜🏊) Promoting itself as Vietnam's first all-villa resort, this is unashamed luxury, located on Ke Ga beach, about 30km south of Mui Ne.

🍴 Eating

Venture beyond the Km 14 mark and there are a host of seafront shacks that serve affordable seafood from sundown. Opt for one with the most Vietnamese dining or try **Bo Ke** (Đ Nguyen Dinh Chieu; mains 30,000-80,000d), which local residents recommend, although you'll be hard-pressed to work out which is which given most have now copied the name! **Bo De** (Đ Nguyen Dinh Chieu; mains 30,000-80,000d) has also been recommended.

For another popular local experience, try the goat restaurants in Ham Tien around the Km 18 mark. Choose from barbecued goat or goat hotpot, herbs and all.

TOP CHOICE **Lam Tong** VIETNAMESE $
(92 Đ Nguyen Dinh Chieu; dishes 25,000-75,000d) It doesn't look like much, sandwiched in between the fancy-pants resorts of Mui Ne, but this family-run beachfront restaurant serves some of the best value food in town. Fresh seafood is popular and cheap, so the place is always busy with a mix of travellers and locals.

TOP CHOICE **Phat Hamburgers** INTERNATIONAL $
(☑374 3502; 253 Đ Nguyen Dinh Chieu; burgers 50,000-75,000d; ⏱lunch & dinner; 🛜) Vietnam's finest burgers are available here in a variety of shapes and sizes. Try Baby Phat if you

are only snacking or experiment with the Phatarella, including cashew nut pesto and mozzarella cheese. Phat dogs also available, but these are the American variety and not your friendly neighbourhood pooch.

TOP CHOICE La Taverna ITALIAN $$
(☎374 3272; 229C Đ Nguyen Dinh Chieu; mains 50,000-150,000d; ⏱10am-11pm; 📶) A new Italian restaurant in Mui Ne around the Km 16 mark, La Taverna is already popular thanks to its thin-crust pizzas and homemade pastas. The extensive menu also includes Vietnamese faves, fresh seafood and Italian vino.

Info Café INTERNATIONAL $
(241 Đ Nguyen Dinh Chieu; drinks 20,000-50,000d; ⏱7am-10pm; 📶) Travellers are wild about the coffee here, which comes in a veritable cocktail list of styles and flavours. This is also a reliable spot for travel info on Mui Ne.

Hoa Vien Brauhaus INTERNATIONAL $$
(www.hoavien.vn; 2A Đ Nguyen Dinh Chieu; mains 50,000-150,000d; ⏱lunch & dinner; 📶) Freshly brewed draft Pilsner Urquell is the big draw here, although it feels a bit surreal to be sipping it overlooking the South China Sea. The huge restaurant offers some Czech and international dishes, as well as a dizzying array of live seafood (thankfully not served live, in most cases).

Peaceful Family Restaurant VIETNAMESE $
(Yen Gia Quan; 53 Đ Nguyen Dinh Chieu; dishes 30,000-70,000d; ⏱lunch & dinner) A long-running local restaurant, the family here serve up traditional Vietnamese cuisine under a breezy thatched roof. Prices are still pretty reasonable and the service is always efficient and friendly.

Hoang Vu VIETNAMESE $$
(121 Đ Nguyen Dinh Chieu; dishes 40,000-90,000d; ⏱lunch & dinner) Like many successful businesses in Vietnam, this one has cloned itself into two restaurants, but this branch gets our vote. The menu is predominantly Asian, with Vietnamese, Chinese and Thai tastes on offer. The setting is atmospheric and the service attentive.

Rung Forest VIETNAMESE $$
(65A Đ Nguyen Dinh Chieu; dishes 49,000-179,000d; ⏱lunch & dinner) As the name aptly suggests, there is something of the forest about this place, with hanging vines, jungle motifs and ethnic handicrafts featuring prominently. The seafood is good, but steer clear of turtle and snake.

Le Chasseur Blanc FRENCH $$
(www.chasseurblanc.com; 97 Đ Nguyen Dinh Chieu; mains 80,000-200,000d; ⏱lunch & dinner; 📶) Ostensibly the leading French restaurant in Mui Ne, but as well as serving succulent steaks and duck, it also offers some unexpected meats such as crocodile, kangaroo and ostrich. There is also free wi-fi, plus a pool table.

Luna d'Autunno ITALIAN $$
(51A Đ Nguyen Dinh Chieu; mains 80,000-200,000d; ⏱lunch & dinner; 📶) For sophisticated Italian, Luna is a small chain with about five branches that's well represented in the region from Hanoi to Phnom Penh. Prices are higher than some places in Mui Ne, but the pizzas and pastas are authentic and the seafood specials have an Italian twist.

Snow FUSION $$
(109 Đ Nguyen Dinh Chieu; mains 50,000-250,000d; ⏱lunch & dinner; ❄📶) One of the few air-conditioned restaurants in Mui Ne, it's aptly named Snow. Choose from decent Japanese sushi and sashimi or sample Russian, international and Vietnamese cuisine. Rumbles on as a cocktail bar later in the evening.

Other good eateries:

Shree Ganesh INDIAN $$
(57 Đ Nguyen Dinh Chieu; mains 50,000-150,000d; ⏱lunch & dinner; 📶) A stylish Indian-run restaurant offering authentic flavours from the homeland. Local expats rave about the place.

Guava INTERNATIONAL $$
(57 Đ Nguyen Dinh Chieu; mains 40,000-160,000d; ⏱lunch & dinner; 📶) A southern relative of the trendy Nha Trang spot, Guava Mui Ne is more restaurant than bar, offering fresh seafood, fusion flavours and cocktails.

Mui Ne Health Bar VEGETARIAN $
(101 Đ Nguyen Dinh Chieu; mains 40,000-80,000d; ⏱lunch & dinner; 🖉📶) A new vegetarian health bar, this is also the place to come for a yoga session or gym workout.

Drinking

It wouldn't be a surf centre without a legion of beachside bars, and Mui Ne delivers.

Sankara BAR, CLUB
(www.sankaravietnam.com; 78 Đ Nguyen Dinh Chieu; 📶) Wow! This place is quite unexpected in Mui Ne and signals a new sophis-

ticated direction for nightlife. Think Ku De Ta in Bali, a sleek beach bar, including chill-out pavilions and day beds, a swimming pool and a globalista menu. However, prices reflect the chic.

DJ Station   BAR, CLUB
(120C Đ Nguyen Dinh Chieu; ☎) Also known as El Vagabundo, this is the most popular late-night spot in Mui Ne with a resident DJ and dastardly drink promotions. It doesn't really get going until after 10pm, but can rock on 'til sunrise.

Fun Key   BAR
(124 Đ Nguyen Dinh Chieu; ☎) New in 2011, this is another 'in' spot with the backpacker crowd looking for the Ko Pha Ngan experience in Mui Ne. Drink promotions pack this place out as the evening warms up.

Wax   BAR
(68 Đ Nguyen Dinh Chieu; ☎) One of the longer-running beach bars in town, Wax has happy hours until midnight when they light up the beach bonfire. Drunken bopping and beach-side flopping draw the crowds.

Joe's Café   BAR, RESTAURANT
(139B Đ Nguyen Dinh Chieu; ☎) The only 24-hour restaurant-bar in town, Joe's draws a more sedate crowd with live music nightly from 8pm. They also show movies in the 'loft' and film garden. If the midnight munchies strike after a beach bar session, this is the place.

Other places worth the time include:

Deja Vu   BAR, RESTAURANT
(21 Đ Nguyen Dinh Chieu; ☎) This is a hip lounge-bar at the Phan Thiet end of the strip, offering shishas, cocktails and an international menu.

Pogo   BAR
(138 Đ Nguyen Dinh Chieu; ☎) It is worth hopping along to Pogo for the chilled atmosphere, crazy cocktail specials, free pool and big beanbags.

ⓘ Information

A great resource for information on Mui Ne is www.muinebeach.net, packed with information on things to see and do in the area.

Internet and wi-fi is available at pretty much all hotels and resorts, as well as at many restaurants and bars. There are several ATMs along the main Mui Ne strip.

Main post office (348 Đ Huynh Thuc Khang) In Mui Ne village.

ⓘ DRUNK AND DISORDERLY

Perhaps in some part due to the insane drink promotions on offer in Mui Ne nightspots, the odd fight breaks out each month. Keep your distance from trouble, especially if it involves local Vietnamese, as you don't know who they are, how many friends they have or what they might be carrying in their pockets.

Post office branch (44 Đ Nguyen Dinh Chieu) A more convenient location at Swiss Village.

Sinh Tourist (144 Đ Nguyen Dinh Chieu) Operates out of Mui Ne Resort, booking open-tour buses and offering credit-card cash advances.

ⓘ Getting There & Away

Mui Ne offers both north and south links to Hwy 1. The newer northern link is a scenic stretch, passing deserted beaches and a beautiful lake ringed with water lilies, which allows the open-tour buses to pass through Mui Ne without backtracking, reducing journey times. Parallel to the beach strip, there is also a major road running through the dunes to Mui Ne village, which should eventually ease the traffic along the narrow beach road.

BUS Open-tour buses are the most convenient option for Mui Ne, as most public buses serve Phan Thiet. Several companies have daily services to/from HCMC (90,000d, six hours), Nha Trang (90,000d, five hours) and Dalat (100,000d, five hours). There are also night buses to HCMC (160,000d), Nha Trang (160,000d) and Hoi An (200,000d). **Phuong Trang** (97 Đ Nguyen Dinh Chieu) has four buses a day running in either direction between Mui Ne and HCMC (90,000d). A local bus makes trips between Phan Thiet bus station and Mui Ne, departing from the Coopmart, on the corner of Đ Nguyen Tat Thanh and Đ Tran Hung Dao, every 15 minutes.

MOTORBIKE There are some Easy Riders in Mui Ne, although not as many as in Dalat or Nha Trang. One of the best trips to experience by motorbike is actually the triangle between these three destinations, as the mountain roads from Mui Ne to Dalat and on to Nha Trang are some of the most dramatic in the south. See Easy Does It (p282) for more on the Easy Riders. A xe om ride from Phan Thiet to Mui Ne will cost around 60,000d.

ⓘ Getting Around

CAR & MOTORBIKE Given that the area isn't highly populated and it's not on the main highway, this is not a bad place to hire a bicycle or motorbike through your hotel or one of the travel agencies. However, take care, as traffic is moving pretty fast and accidents involving tourists have been known to happen.

TAXI Mui Ne is so spread out that it's difficult to wander about on foot if it is very hot. There are plenty of *xe om* drivers to take you up and down the strip; no trip should cost more than 20,000d to 40,000d, depending on how far you want to go. For something more comfortable, **Mai Linh** (☑389 8989) operates meter taxis, although call ahead to book later in the evening or ask the restaurant or bar to assist.

Phan Thiet

☑062 / POP 175,000

Before the discovery of Mui Ne, Phan Thiet was an emerging resort town in its own right, but it has been eclipsed by the new kid on the block. Phan Thiet is traditionally known for its *nuoc mam* (fish sauce), producing 16 to 17 million litres of the stinky stuff per annum. The population includes descendants of the Cham, who controlled this area until 1692. During the colonial period the Europeans lived in their own segregated ghetto stretching along the northern bank of the Phan Thiet River, while the Vietnamese, Cham, Southern Chinese, Malays and Indonesians lived along the southern bank.

The river flowing through the centre of town creates a small **fishing harbour**, which is always chock-a-block with boats, making for a photo opportunity. To get to Phan Thiet's **beachfront**, turn off Đ Tran Hung Dao (Hwy 1) into Đ Nguyen Tat Thanh – the road opposite the **Victory Monument**, an arrow-shaped concrete tower with a cluster of victorious patriots around the base.

Binh Thuan Tourist (www.binhthuantourist .com; 82 Đ Trung Trac; ☺7-11am & 1.30-5pm Mon-Fri, 8-10.30am Sat & Sun) is the place to go for tourist maps and information.

ℹ Getting There & Away

Phan Thiet bus station (Đ Tu Van Tu) is on the northern outskirts of town. Phan Thiet is on Hwy 1, 198km east of HCMC, 250km from Nha Trang and 247km from Dalat. The nearest train station to Phan Thiet is 12km west of town in dusty little Muong Man.

Ta Cu Mountain

☑062

The highlight here is the **white reclining Buddha** (Tuong Phat Nam). At 49m long, it's the largest in Vietnam. The pagoda was constructed in 1861, but the Buddha

was only added in 1972. It has become an important pilgrimage centre for Buddhists, who stay overnight in the pagoda's dormitory. Foreigners can't do this without police permission, but **Thien Thay Hotel** (☑386 7484; r 250,000d; ✳) offers basic rooms atop the mountain.

The mountain is just off Hwy 1, 28km south from Phan Thiet, from which the Buddha is a beautiful two-hour trek (15,000d), or a 10-minute cable-car ride (75,000d return) and a short, but steep, hike.

Binh Chau Hot Springs

☑064

About 150km from HCMC, and 60km northeast of Long Hai, is **Binh Chau Hot Springs** (Suoi Khoang Nong Binh Chau; admission 30,000d), home to the **Binh Chau Hot Springs Resort** (☑387 1131; www.saigonbinhchauecoresort .com; r 800,000-3,000,000d, villas 2,200,000d-4,500,000d; ✳@🛜🏊). While prices look pretty high, they offer some multi-activity specials on their website that work out much cheaper than the official rates.

Chief among the attractions on this 35-hectare site is an outdoor hot-spring-fed swimming pool (admission 150,000d), although visitors wanting the full experience might opt for a soak in a mudbath (400,000d). The pool temperature is around 37°C, and the minerals in the water are said to be beneficial to bones, muscles and skin, and are able to improve blood circulation and mental disorders. There's also a spa, with massages available. On-site are a golf practice range, tennis court, restaurant and playground.

The rooms at the resort are airy and clean, with trim furnishings, but the cheaper options are on the small side. Bungalows provide roomier quarters for families. Rates include free entry, plus fancier rooms include bonuses such as a free mudbath or free eggs. Whoopee!

Until about just over a decade ago there was wildlife in the area, but it seems humans have driven the animals out. In 1994 six elephants were captured near the springs, but after a few months of keeping them as pets their captors turned them over to the zoo in HCMC. Nowadays the only wildlife you are likely to spot are ceramic lions, cheetahs and panthers, which decorate the marshes around the springs.

The hottest spring reaches 82°C, which is hot enough to boil an egg in 10 to 15 minutes. Vietnamese visitors boil eggs in the bamboo baskets set aside for this purpose. There are a couple of giant chicken statues decorating the springs where you too can boil up a snack for yourself, with raw eggs on sale. Kitsch indeed, but a nice jungle setting all the same.

ℹ Getting There & Away

The resort is in a compound 6km north of the village of Binh Chau. There's no public transport, so arrange a motorbike or car; if you choose the latter, try to find some travellers to share the expense.

Phan Thiet to Long Hai

♪064

A beautiful road winds along the coast between Binh Chau and Long Hai, passing the up-and-coming beaches of Ho Coc, Ho Tram and Loc An, crossing through the towns of La Gi and Phuoc Hai, and eventually connecting Mui Ne with Vung Tau, making it perfect for DIY motorbikers with a bit of experience. This also makes for a great day trip on a motorbike from Vung Tau or Long Hai. The new road is in fantastic shape, and it's a beautiful ride past towering sand dunes and wide ocean views, particularly between Ho Coc and Ho Tram.

Travelling by private car is not quite as exhilarating, but it is arguably a nicer way to travel than tackling the nightmarish Hwy 1. Schedule a lunch stop and a couple of beach breaks along the route and you have the makings of a memorable road trip. Public transport is a bit more challenging. There are daily buses between Phan Thiet and Vung Tau that can drop you off along the way, but continuing the journey is not easy. There are also local buses between Long Hai and La Gi that include these blissful beaches. In short, a motorbike is the way to go.

HO COC BEACH

The coastal road just keeps on snaking its way along the coast and about 12km or so from Ho Tram you'll arrive at the remote and beautiful Ho Coc Beach. Golden sands, rolling dunes and clear waters, along with the lack of development, make it a real draw, particularly on weekdays when you'll have the beach largely to yourself. As elsewhere along the coast, weekends bring crowds of Vietnamese tourists and it can kill the atmosphere.

🛏 Sleeping

Hotel Ven Ven HOTEL $$

(☏379 1121; http://venvenhotel.com; r 350,000-800,000d; ❄@🕾) Although it lacks a beachfront location, this is a pretty place to stay with lush gardens. The rooms are smart and include quads (rooms not bikes) for 600,000d, as well as some more expensive bungalows.

Saigon-Ho Coc Beach Resort RESORT HOTEL $$$

(☏387 8175; r 800,000-3,500,000d; ❄@🕾☷) A sprawling resort, this place includes three accommodation areas known as Prosperity Sea Village Resort, Viet Village Resort and South East Wind Seaside Resort. Golf buggies cart guests around and it fills up to capacity with Vietnamese tourists at weekends. Pleasant enough, but more aimed at the local market.

HO TRAM BEACH

Ho Tram is one of the most beautiful stretches of sand along this coast, home to towering dunes and windswept brochuresque beaches. It remains relatively undeveloped for the time being, but nearby is a huge investment project billed the Ho Tram Strip, which will see the construction of a massive MGM Grand Resort and Casino complex, plus restaurants and shops. Change is coming.

🛏 Sleeping & Eating

Ho Tram Beach Resort & Spa BOUTIQUE HOTEL $$$

(☏378 1525; www.hotramresort.com; bungalow 2,781,000-6,336,000d; ❄@🕾☷) Also known as the Ho Tram Osaka, this beautifully landscaped complex is dotted with attractive bungalows in the Hoi An style. Each has high ceilings and unique furnishings and design. There's also a spa, a beach bar and an open-plan restaurant that's open to nonguests for a memorable lunchstop.

Sanctuary BOUTIQUE RESORT $$$

(☏378 1631; www.sanctuary.com.vn; villas US$420-780; ❄@🕾☷) Home to state-of-the-art contemporary villas, Sanctuary is the ultimate getaway for Saigonese wanting to indulge. Three-bedroom villas include open-plan kitchens, private pools and flat-screen TVs. No detail is missed and the prices aren't quite so scary if you have three couples or families. This is a statement: Ho Tram is going places.

Long Hai

☑064

If Vung Tau is all a bit bling for you, then consider Long Hai, a less-commercialised seaside retreat within a few hours' drive of HCMC. The fishing village of Long Hai, now only 15km northeast of Vung Tau thanks to a major bridge, has a pretty white-sand beach and the area benefits from a microclimate that brings less rain than other parts of the south. This is why Bao Dai, the last emperor of Vietnam, built a private residence here (now the Anoasis Beach Resort).

Long Hai can be a peaceful place to visit during the week, but it loses its local character on the weekends when Vietnamese tourists pack the sands. While there are a couple of low-key resorts in the Long Hai vicinity, Western travellers have yet to arrive in numbers, so if you're looking for a lively spot with dining and nightlife action, Mui Ne (p247) is the better choice.

◉ Sights & Activities

The western end of Long Hai's beach is where fishing boats moor and is not so clean. However, the eastern end is pretty, with white sand and swaying palms. For an even prettier beach, keep heading east.

After the Tet holiday, Long Hai hosts an annual major **fishermen's pilgrimage festival**, where hundreds of boats come from afar to worship at **Mo Co Temple**.

🛏 Sleeping

Thuy Lan Guesthouse   GUESTHOUSE $
(☑366 3567; Rte 19; r 250,000-450,000d; ❋@🕾)
One of a cluster of small, family-run places behind the Military Guesthouse 298, this guesthouse is cleaner and newer than the government option. Rooms are well-tended and the bathrooms surprisingly swish. Some English is spoken here.

**Tropicana Beach
Resort & Spa**   RESORT HOTEL $$$
(☑367 8888; r US$100-160; ❋@🕾🏊) Overlooking a windswept beach and the Long Hai Hills, this is a great resort for a weekday visit when you might well have the place to yourself. Rooms are finished in contemporary Vietnamese style and include sea views. Chalets are a good option for families and facilities include a tennis court.

Anoasis Beach Resort   BOUTIQUE RESORT $$$
(☑386 8227; www.anoasisresort.com.vn; Provincial Rd 44; bungalows US$189-1500; ❋@🕾🏊) Em-

peror Bao Dai's former residence is one of the most charming beachside retreats on the south coast, the bungalows and cottages set in immaculate gardens fronting the beautiful private beach. Diversions include cycling, fishing, tennis and a plush spa. Extensions and renovations mean the resort now includes ultra-luxurious villas with private pools.

Thuy Duong Tourist Resort   HOTEL $$
(☑388 6215; www.thuyduongresort.com.vn; r 700,000-2,200,000d; ❋@🕾🏊) This huge place sprawls across the coastal road and is located about 4km south of Long Hai. Rooms here come in every shape and size, including suites and villas. The beach here is particularly beautiful, with large boulders for kids to clamber around. Day entry is 60,000/70,000d weekday/weekend.

✖ Eating

There's a rustic cluster of thatch-roof beachside restaurants called **Can Tin 1, 2, 3** and **4** (mains around 30,000-100,000d; ⊘7am-9pm) near Military Guesthouse 298. These serve reliable Vietnamese cuisine, including fresh seafood dishes. Dine, relax in a deckchair and then take a dip.

ⓘ Getting There & Away

Long Hai is 124km from HCMC and takes about three hours to reach by road. It is more relaxing to arrive by a combination of hydrofoil and road via Vung Tau (p262). The 15km road between Vung Tau and Long Hai will cost about 100,000d by *xe om* or about 200,000d by meter taxi.

From Mui Ne, follow the road less-travelled along coastal Rte 55. It is very scenic, passing a series of stunning beaches and traffic is mercifully light for Vietnam.

Vung Tau

☑064 / POP 270,000

A popular escape from the city for expats and locals alike, Vung Tau has long been overlooked by travellers from HCMC as they rush up the coast to Mui Ne or Nha Trang. Perhaps not for much longer thanks to the beautiful new coastal road connecting Vung Tau to Phan Thiet and Mui Ne via idyllic and empty beaches. Vung Tau rocks at weekends when HCMC exiles descend in numbers, but it is relatively quiet during the week. Vung Tau's beaches have been a favourite of the Saigonese since French colonists first began coming here around 1890. It's changed a bit since then and is now big and brash, with a somewhat seedy underbelly, as the infamous case of UK glam rocker Gary Glitter highlighted during 2005–06. Lots of retired Anzac servicemen have washed up here over the years, ensuring this is almost Vietnam's answer to Pattaya.

Known under the French as Cap St Jacques, Vung Tau is on a peninsula jutting into the South China Sea, about 128km southeast of HCMC. The beaches here aren't Vietnam's best, but Vung Tau is a convenient beach fix from HCMC via the memorable hydrofoil ride. Oil is big business here, so the horizon is regularly dotted with oil tankers, and the industry has attracted a surprisingly large population of Russians to the city, who also make up a significant percentage of the tourists.

◉ Sights & Activities

Welcome to Rio di Vietnam, where a **giant Jesus** (admission free, parking 2000d; ☺7.30-11.30am & 1.30-5pm) stands atop Small Mountain with arms outstretched to embrace the South China Sea. The Vietnamese claim this is the highest Jesus statue in the world at 32m, a good 6m taller than His illustrious Brazilian cousin. It is possible to ascend to the arms for a panoramic view of Vung Tau. At His foot are a couple of major field guns from the French period. Some 900-odd stairs wind their way up the mountain, a Vietnamese version of stairway to heaven, but it is possible to take a short-cut by motorbike up a bumpy mountain road if you can find a local who knows the way. It starts from Hem 220, off Ð Phan Chu Trinh.

ⓘ BACK TO FRONT BEACHES

Vung Tau's peninsula is punctuated by Small Mountain (Nui Nho) to the south and Big Mountain (Nui Lon) in the north. Popular Back Beach (Bai Sau) stretches for kilometres, with a wide, sandy beach and a long strip of guesthouses and hotels. The downtown action is at Front Beach (Bai Truoc), which has been redeveloped into a series of attractive parks with marble pavements, but there's not much in the way of sand. For a quiet, but pebbly beach, head for tranquil Mulberry Beach (Bai Dau), up the northwest coast.

WORTH A TRIP

THE WORLDWIDE ARMS MUSEUM

Another white villa above Front Beach plays home to the **Worldwide Arms Museum** (14 Ð Hai Dong; admission by donation), an unexpected treasure trove hiding in the backstreets of Vung Tau. It was yet to officially open during our visit, but conceals a stunning collection of military uniforms, decorative weaponry and ornate pistols from all over the world. There may well be a fixed entry fee once it is officially open.

Located at the rear of the museum is a private primate rescue centre with spacious enclosures for gibbons and monkeys rescued from traffickers. It is not a zoo, but the private passion of the museum owner who takes such good care of the mammals that he even funded a pioneering cataract operation to restore the sight of one female gibbon.

A kilometre or so northwest, the 1910 **lighthouse** (admission free, parking 2000d; ☺7am-5pm) boasts a spectacular 360-degree view of Vung Tau. From Cau Da Pier on Ð Ha Long, take a sharp right on the alley north of the Hai Au Hotel, then roll on up the hill. Although Jesus and the lighthouse look temptingly close, it is not possible to walk or drive directly between them, as there is a military base in the hills here.

The **White Villa** (Bach Dinh or Villa Blanche; Ð Tran Phu; admission 15,000d) was the weekend retreat of French governor Paul Doumer (later French President) and is a gorgeous, grand colonial-era residence that smacks of boutique hotel for the future. It is possible to wander the extensive gardens and spot art-nouveau features on the ageing exterior. Inside is some Ming pottery retrieved from shipwrecks off the coast. The villa sits about 30m above the road, up a winding lane.

Further along Tran Phu beyond Mulberry Beach, a pretty road winds up the hillside to some old **French Field Guns** (admission free). There are six of these massive cannons, all with support trenches, demonstrating how strategically important Cap St Jacques was to the French colonial authorities as it guarded the waterways to Saigon. Look out for Hem 444 in the fishing village, about

Vung Tau

0   1 km
0   0.5 miles

Đ Thu Khoa Huan
Đ Trieu Au
Đ Ba Cu
To Long Hai (15km)
ĐL Le Hong Phong
Đ Tran Phu
Đ Ngoc Han
Đ Hoang Dieu
Đ Le Quy Don
Đ Truong Cong Dinh
Đ Le Loi
Đ Ly Tu Trong
To Cable Car (200m); White Villa (300m); Binh An Village (1.3km); Ganh Dao (1.6km); Mulberry Beach (2km); Cay Bang (3km); Huong Sen Hotel (3.5km); Nathalie's (4.5km); Vung Tau Port (15km)
Đ Quang Trung
Đ Tran Hung Dao
Đ Thong Nhat
Đ Nam Ky Khoi Nghia
To Vungtau Interco Resort (900m)
Khu Bau Sen
Đ Nguyuyen Du
Đ Truong Cong Dinh
Đ Vo Thi Sau
Đ Thuy Van
Đ Nguyen Trai
Tran Hung Dao Statue & Park
Đ Hoang Hoa Tham
Cau Da Pier
⊙ Worldwide Arms Museum
⊙ 1
Đ Ha Long
South China Sea
Đ Thuy Van
Đ Phan Chu Trinh
Roches Noires Beach (Bai Dua)
Small Mountain (Nui Nho)
▲ ① Giant Jesus

Vung Tau

8km from Vung Tau, and turn right on a small track.

Pagodas dot the length of Đ Ha Long, but pretty **Hon Ba pagoda** sits offshore on an islet – *the* place to be if low tide coincides with sunrise.

If you have had enough of the salty sea, there are a couple of swimming pools: **Seagull** and **Dolphin** (Đ Thuy Ban, Back Beach). The pools are almost opposite the Imperial Plaza and both charge 50,000d for the day.

Surf Station (www.vungtausurf.com; 8 Đ Thuy Ban), based at the Vung Tau Beach Club, is in the same area of Back Beach and offers kite-surfing and surfing classes if the wind is up.

And now for something completely different: greyhound racing. Believe it or not, it really exists in Vietnam and **Lam Son Stadium** (☑380 7309; 15 Đ Le Loi; admission 30,000d stands/60,000d VIP; ☉7-10.30pm Sat) is the place.

🛏 Sleeping

During weekends and holidays, Vung Tau's hundred or more hotels can be heavily booked, so it is sensible to make a reservation. Most foreigners prefer to stay on Front Beach where the restaurants and bars are found, while the majority of Vietnamese visitors head for Back Beach.

BACK BEACH

Lua Hong Motel   HOTEL $

(☑381 8992; 137 Đ Thuy Van; r 250,000-350,000d; ❄@☎) For a more Vietnamese take on Vung Tau, this area is littered with hotels and guesthouses. This 'motel' has a touch (but only a touch, mind you) more decorative flair than in some of the neighbouring places, plus sea views.

Vungtau Intourco Resort   RESORT HOTEL $$

(☑385 3481; www.intourcoresort.com; 1A Đ Thuy Van; r from 850,000d, bungalows from 1,250,000d; ❄@☎☀) One of the only places located directly on the beach in this strip, this resort has extensive gardens and a free-form pool. Rooms are sophisticated enough and the bungalows make a good investment for families.

FRONT BEACH

Lan Rung Resort & Spa   HOTEL $$

(☑352 6010; www.lanrungresort.com; 3-6 Đ Ha Long; s/d from US$60/80; ❄@☎☀) One of the smartest hotels in town, the Lan Rung is also one of the few places with a beachside setting, albeit a rocky one. The rooms

are pristine and include heavy wooden furniture, plus all the usual extras. The pool overlooks the sea, plus there are seafood and Italian restaurants.

Son Ha Hotel   HOTEL $

(☑385 2356; 17A Đ Thu Khoa Huan; r US$18; ❄@☎) One of the few budget options near Front Beach, this family-run mini hotel offers a homely welcome. Rooms are in good shape, including satellite TV and a fridge.

Grand Hotel   HOTEL $$

(☑385 6888; www.grand.oscvn.com; 2 Đ Nguyen Du; s/d from US$75/90; ❄@☎☀) It is indeed one of the grandest in town, offering smart rooms with safety-deposit box and bathrobes. The pool is particularly appealing, shaded by a huge banyan tree.

MULBERRY BEACH

Binh An Village   BOUTIQUE HOTEL $$$

(☑351 0016; www.binhanvillage.com; 1 Đ Tran Phu; r & ste US$85-250; ❄@☀) *The* desirable address in Vung Tau, the oasis that is Binh An Village feels like it has been transported straight from Bali. The bungalows are beautifully decorated with Asian antiques and set amid serene oceanfront scenery. There are two swimming pools, one ocean-fed and one freshwater, both near the sea's edge. There's also a good open-air restaurant here, with live jazz most weekend nights and à la carte cuisine.

Huong Sen Hotel   HOTEL $$

(☑355 1711; 182 Đ Tran Phu; r US$29-49; ❄@☎) Right at the end of Mulberry Beach, this is affiliated with the long-running Huong Sen in HCMC. Rates are very reasonable for the standards and it's a nice escape if you want to get away from the honky tonk part of town.

🍴 Eating

Vung Tau offers a good range of dining for the visitor, including traditional Vietnamese seafood restaurants and a range of international flavours from Indian to Italian.

FRONT BEACH

Tommy's 3   INTERNATIONAL $$

(3 Đ Ba Cu; mains 50,000-300,000d; ☎) Also known as Someplace Else, this restaurant offers a large patio for dining that draws a mixed crowd of locals, expats and tourists. The menu is predominantly international, including imported Aussie meats and regular barbecues, but also some authentic

Vietnamese dishes. It was on the move as we go to print to a new location near International SOS. The original **Tommy's** is located at 94 Đ Halong and is a quieter place to watch the ocean action unfold.

Nine
FRENCH **$$**

(9 Đ Truong Vinh Ky; mains 50,000-150,000đ) Formerly known as Plein Sud, Nine is the leading French restaurant in town. The patio is a good place for authentic coffee, pastries and ice creams throughout the day. The menu includes fresh seafood with a Gallic twist, plus pizzas and homemade desserts such as profiteroles.

David Italian Restaurant
ITALIAN **$$**

(130 Đ Halong; mains 50,000-200,000đ) Located on a prime strip overlooking the hydrofoil dock, this is an authentic Italian-run restaurant. The pasta is freshly prepared and the pizzas are the best in town.

Ali Baba
INDIAN **$$**

(☑ 351 0685; 7 Đ Nguyen Trai; mains around 50,000-120,000đ) A popular Indian restaurant located on one of the late-night bar strips in town. The tandoori kebab platter is great for sharing or take advantage of the coastal setting with one of the excellent seafood curries. Delivery available.

BACK BEACH

Imperial Plaza
VIETNAMESE **$**

(159 Đ Thuy Van; ✲) This shiny new shopping centre offers a selection of dining options. Downstairs is a branch of the popular Highlands Coffee, with great frappes and shakes. Upstairs, the small food court is perfect (and air-conditioned) for those overheating with indecisiveness: choose from pizza through to *pho*.

MULBERRY BEACH

Ganh Hao
SEAFOOD **$$**

(3 Đ Tran Phu; mains 40,000-180,000đ; ☺lunch & dinner) Set above the bay on the road to Mulberry Beach, this restaurant is regularly packed out with locals. It offers the full monty, including lobster or king crab, and prices are very reasonable.

Cay Bang
SEAFOOD **$$**

(69 Đ Tran Phu; mains 30,000-200,000đ; ☺11am-10pm) Another seafood institution with a great location on the water, Cay Bang is set under the shadow of the Virgin Mary and Baby Jesus. At weekends, it draws a huge crowd of the Vung Tau faithful for the shellfish.

Nathalie's
THAI **$$**

(220 Đ Tran Phu; mains 50,000-220,000đ; ☺lunch & dinner) The first Thai restaurant to open in Vung Tau, the location is quite dramatic, set in a large house overlooking the ocean. Choose from the Thai favourites, including a good seafood selection.

🍷 Drinking

Vung Tau nightlife is a little raucous by Vietnamese standards with lots of hostess bars and the occasional floor show.

Another Bar
BAR

(3 Đ Ba Cu) An Aussie sports bar in the same compound as Someplace Else, this offers a sane retreat from the more in-yer-face bars of Đ Nguyen Trai. Ice-cold beer and plenty of friendly banter.

Vitamin C
BAR

(27 Đ Ba Cu) While there are a lot of hostesses here, it also functions as a restaurant. The decor makes it a cut above the competition and there is a popular pool table.

Red Parrot
BAR

(6 Đ Le Quy Don) One of the late-night spots that picks up as the evening wears on, this is Vung Tau at its most decadent, complete with war veterans, oil workers, alcoholics and working girls.

ℹ️ Information

Check out www.vungtau-city.com for relatively up-to-date information on the city of Vung Tau.

International SOS (☑ 385 8776; 1 Đ Le Ngoc Han; ☺24hr) An international clinic with international standards and international prices.

Le Loi Hospital (☑ 383 2667; 22 Đ Le Loi) Main hospital, but HCMC offers better standards.

Main post office (8 Đ Hoang Dieu) Located at the ground level of the Petrovietnam Towers building.

OSC Vietnam Travel (☑ 385 2008; www .oscvietnamtravel.com.vn; 2 Đ Le Loi) Vung Tau's government-run travel agency offers a host of local trips.

Vietcombank (27-29 Đ Tran Hung Dao) Exchanges cash, travellers cheques and offers credit-card advances.

ℹ️ Getting There & Away

BUS From Mien Dong bus station in HCMC, air-con minibuses (40,000đ, three hours, 128km) leave for Vung Tau throughout the day until around 4.30pm. From Vung Tau's **bus station** (192A Đ Nam Ky Khoi Nghia) to Mulberry

ANZAC SITES AROUND VUNG TAU

Nearly 60,000 Australian soldiers were involved in the American War throughout the 1960s and 1970s. The Long Tan Memorial Cross commemorates a particularly fierce battle that took place on 18 August 1966 between Australian troops and Viet Cong fighters. Originally erected by Australian survivors of the battle, the current cross is a replica installed by the Vietnamese in 2002. It is located about 18km from Ba Ria town or 55km from Vung Tau, near the town of Nui Dat. It is no longer necessary to arrange a permit to visit and can be combined with the seldom visited Lon Phuoc tunnels, an underground network that is a much smaller version of the more famous Cu Chi.

At Minh Dam, 5km from Long Hai, there are **caves** with historical connections to the Franco–Viet Minh and American Wars. Although the caves are little more than spaces between the boulders covering the cliff-face, VC soldiers bunked here off and on between 1948 and 1975; you can still see bullet holes in the rocks from the skirmishes that took place. Steps hewn into the rock-face lead up to the caves, with spectacular views over the coastal plains at the top.

Nearby there is a **mountain-top temple** with more great panoramic views of the coastline.

Tommy's (☑351 5181; 3 Đ Ba Cu; www.tommysvietnam.com) operate tours for returning vets that include Long Tan, Long Phuoc and Minh Dam. The cost including transport and guide is US$120 for two people or US$40 per person for more than three.

Otherwise hook up with a *xe om* driver and expect to pay US$10 to US$15 for a tour around these sights.

Beach or Back Beach, a *xe om* will cost around 40,000d.

BOAT It's much more enjoyable to catch a hydrofoil. **Greenlines** (HCMC ☑08-3821 5609; Vung Tau ☑351 0720), **Petro Express** (HCMC ☑08-3821 0650; Vung Tau ☑351 5151) and **Vina Express** (HCMC ☑08-3825 3333; Vung Tau ☑385 6530) all run regular services to HCMC (adult/child 200,000/100,000d, 75 minutes). There are services every half hour until about 4.30pm and additional boats at weekends, when it pays to book ahead. In Vung Tau the boat leaves from Cau Da pier, opposite the Hai Au Hotel.

There are two ferries connecting Con Son Island with Vung Tau, with sailings approximately every second day. For more details, see p269. Tickets can be purchased from the office at 1007/36 Đ 30/4 which reads **BQL Cang Ben Dam Huyen Con Dao** (☉7.30-11.30am & 1.30-4.30pm Mon-Fri). The ferry departs at 5pm from Vung Tau port, which lies about 15km west of the city.

❶ Getting Around

Vung Tau is easily traversed on two wheels or four. Guesthouses and restaurants can arrange bicycle hire (per day US$2) and motorbikes (from US$7 to US$10 per day). Metered taxis will likely work out cheaper than trying to negotiate with ruthless *cyclo* or *xe om* drivers. Mai Linh is a reliable operator and has plenty of cabs cruising the streets.

Con Dao Islands

☑064 / POP 5500

Isolated from the mainland, the Con Dao Islands are one of the star attractions in Vietnam. Long the Devil's Island of Indochina, the preserve of political prisoners and undesirables, this place is now turning heads thanks to its striking natural beauty. Con Son, the largest of this chain of 15 islands and islets, is ringed with lovely beaches, coral reefs and scenic bays, and remains partially covered in thick forests. In addition to hiking, diving and exploring empty coastal roads and deserted beaches, there are some excellent wildlife-watching opportunities.

Con Son Island (with a total land area of 20 sq km) is also known by its Europeanised Malay name, Ile Poulo Condore (Pulau Kundur), which means 'Island of the Squashes'. Although it seems something of an island paradise, Con Son was once hell on earth for the thousands of prisoners who languished in confinement during the French- and American-backed regimes.

Roughly 80% of the land area in the island chain is part of Con Dao National Park, which protects Vietnam's most important **sea turtle nesting grounds**. For the last decade the World Wildlife Foundation (WWF) has been working with local park rangers on a long-term monitoring program.

During nesting season (May to November) the park sets up ranger stations to rescue threatened nests and move them to the safe haven of hatcheries.

Other interesting sea life around Con Dao includes the **dugong**, a rare and seldom-seen marine mammal in the same family as the manatee. Dugongs live as far north as Japan, and as far south as the subtropical coasts of Australia. Their numbers have been on a steady decline, and increasingly efforts are being made to protect these gentle creatures. Major threats include coastal road development, which causes the destruction of shallow-water beds of seagrass, the dugong's staple diet.

Con Dao is one of those rare places in Vietnam where there are very few structures over two storeys, and where the visitor experience is almost hassle-free. Owing to the relatively high cost and the inaccessibility of the islands, mass tourism has thankfully been kept at bay.

Even today, most visitors to Con Son are package-tour groups of former VC soldiers who were imprisoned on the island. The Vietnamese government generously subsidises these jaunts as a show of gratitude for their sacrifice. However, travellers are discovering the islands and numbers are on the rise, so it is only a matter of time before these little islands become a big attraction.

The driest time to visit Con Dao is from November to February, although the seas are calmest from March to July. The rainy season lasts from June to September, but there are also northeast and southwest monsoons from September to November that can bring heavy winds. In November 1997 typhoon Linda unleashed her fury here: 300 fishing boats were lost, reefs were wiped out and the forests flattened. September and October are the hottest months, though even then the cool island breezes make Con Dao relatively comfortable when compared with HCMC or Vung Tau.

Change has been almost glacial compared with the mainland resorts of Nha Trang and Mui Ne, but things are really starting to move. The arrival of the super-luxurious Six Senses is a sign of the times and puts Con Dao on the map for the international jet-set. Watch this space.

History

Occupied at various times by the Khmer, Malays and Vietnamese, Con Son Island also served as an early base for European commercial ventures in the region. The first recorded European arrival was a ship of Portuguese mariners in 1560. The British East India Company maintained a fortified trading post here from 1702 to 1705 – an experiment that ended when the English on the island were massacred in a revolt by the Makassar soldiers they had recruited on the Indonesian island of Sulawesi.

Con Son Island has a strong political and cultural history, and an all-star line-up of Vietnamese revolutionary heroes were incarcerated here. (Many streets are named after them.) Under the French, Con Son was used as a major prison for opponents of French colonialism, earning a reputation for the routine mistreatment and torture of prisoners. In 1954 the island was taken over by the South Vietnamese government, which continued to utilise its remoteness to hold opponents of the government (including students) in horrendous conditions. During the American War the South Vietnamese were joined here by US forces.

⊙ Sights

Con Son town is a sleepy seafront settlement that would make a perfect location for a period film. The main seafront drag of Đ Ton Duc Thang includes a strip of forlorn single-storey French villas that are abandoned or in disrepair, but much of this area is slated for ambitious redevelopment. Nearby is the local **market**, which is busiest between 7am and 8am.

Historic Prisons   HISTORIC BUILDINGS
The main sights on Con Son Island include a museum, several French and American-era prisons and a sombre cemetery. The only place that advertises entrance tickets is **Phu Hai Prison** (20,000d; ⊙7-11.30am & 1-5pm Mon-Sat) but this should cover all other sights according to the theory.

The **Revolutionary Museum** (⊙7-11am & 1.30-5pm Mon-Sat) is next to Saigon Con Dao Hotel and has exhibits on Vietnamese resistance to the French, communist opposition to the Republic of Vietnam, and the treatment of political prisoners (including some gruesome photos of torture). There is also a mock-up of the islands and some curiously embalmed animals, including a monkey smoking a pipe. An impressive-looking new **Con Dao Museum** is located at the eastern end of Đ Nguyen Hue and exhibits from the Revolutionary Museum will be moved here once it opens its doors.

THE RETURN OF THE GREEN SEA TURTLE

Two decades ago the fate of the Green Sea Turtle (*Chelonia mydas*) in Con Dao was in jeopardy. They were prized for their meat, and their shells had value as souvenirs. To make matters worse, the turtles' numbers were decimated by destructive fishing practices. And yet, today, following a decade of local and foreign initiatives, the turtle has made a remarkable comeback. One of Vietnam's most important sea-turtle nesting sites lies scattered around the shores of the Con Dao archipelago. The World Wildlife Foundation (WWF) has given substantial help, as have other international organisations, by setting up conservation stations on the islands of Bay Canh, Tre Lon, Tai and Cau. According to the WWF, since 1995 more than 800,000 hatchlings have been released into the sea. Up to 85% of sea-turtle eggs hatch successfully, which is the highest percentage in Vietnam. WWF has also launched a satellite tracking program (the first of its kind in Vietnam) to give conservation workers a better understanding of migration patterns, as well as key habitats used by the turtles for feeding and mating. Though the population is on the rise, many turtles still die after nesting, often by getting ensnared in fishing nets.

Visitors wishing to see the turtles in their natural habitat can arrange a trip to Bay Canh Island and spend the night at the conversation site. (Turtles only lay their eggs at night, each one producing one to 10 nests with an average of 90 eggs.) The best time to see them is during the nesting season, which is from May to November. For information on trips, inquire at Con Dao National Park headquarters (p268). Tours prices vary depending on numbers, but you need to budget around 5,000,000d to rent the national park boat, 400,000d for a guide, 40,000d for overnight park fees and 150,000d for basic accommodation. Dive! Dive! Dive! also offers boat trips to see the turtles, including an afternoon dive and a night dive, plus meals and overnight camping. Non-divers and snorkellers can join these trips for a reasonable price.

Phu Hai Prison, a short walk from the museum, is the largest of the 11 prisons on the island. Built in 1862, the prison houses several enormous detention buildings, one with about 100 shackled and emaciated mannequins that are all too lifelike. Equally eerie are the empty solitary cells with ankle shackles (the decree on the walls in Vietnamese means 'no killing fleas', as prisoners were not allowed to dirty the walls). Nearby is the equally disturbing **Phu Son Prison.**

The notorious **Tiger Cages** were built by the French in the 1940s. From 1957 to 1961 nearly 2000 political prisoners were confined in these tiny cells. Here there are 120 chambers with ceiling bars, where guards could watch down on the prisoners like tigers in a zoo, and another 60 solariums with no roof at all.

Over the course of four decades of war, some 20,000 people were killed on Con Son and 1994 of their graves can be seen at the peaceful **Hang Duong Cemetery**, located at the eastern edge of town. Sadly, only 700 of these graves bear the name of the victims. Vietnam's most famous heroine, Vo Thi Sau (1933–52), was the first woman executed by a firing squad on Con Son, on 23 January 1952. Today's pilgrims come to burn incense at her tomb, and make offerings of mirrors and combs, symbolic because she died so young. In the distance behind the cemetery you'll see a huge **monument** symbolising three giant sticks of incense.

Phu Binh Camp is also part of the main prison circuit, though it's on the edge of town. Built in 1971 by the Americans, this one has 384 chambers and was known as Camp 7 until 1973, when it closed following evidence of torture. After the Paris Agreements in 1973, the name was changed to Phu Binh Camp. Watch out for bats nesting among the silent cells.

Con Son Beaches & Other Islands BEACHES
On Con Son there are several good beaches worth seeking out. Inquire at the hotels about snorkelling-gear rental for about 100,000d per day or rent new gear through Dive! Dive! Dive! for US$10 per day. **Bai Dat Doc** is a beautiful beach with a long stretch of sand, although most of this is now part of the new Six Senses Con Dao. Keep an eye out for dugongs frolicking in the water off the nearby cape.

Bai Nhat is small and very nice, though it's exposed only during low tide. **Bai An Hai** looks appealing, but there are a good

Con Dao Islands

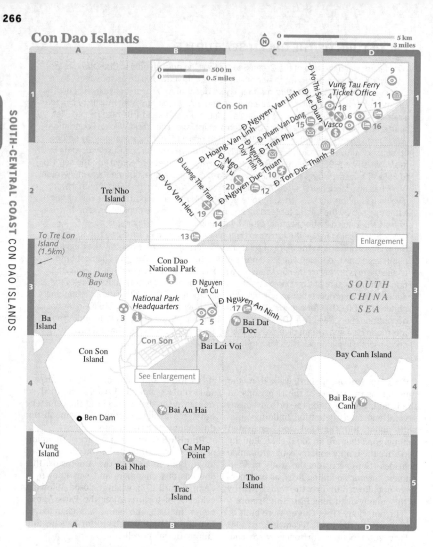

number of fishing boats moored nearby, and a few too many sandflies. **Bai Loi Voi** is another option, but there can be a fair bit of rubbish and lots of sea shells. **Bai Dam Trau** is arguably the best all-rounder, a secluded cove on the southern end of the island.

Some of the more pristine beaches are on the smaller islands, such as the beautiful white-sand beach on **Tre Lon**, to the west of Con Son Island. Perhaps the best all-round island to visit is **Bay Canh**, to the east, which has lovely beaches, old-growth forest, mangroves, coral reefs (good snorkelling at low tide) and sea turtles (seasonal). There is a fantastic two-hour walk to a functioning

French-era **lighthouse** on Bay Canh's eastern tip, although it involves a steep climb of 325m. Once at the summit, the panoramic views are breathtaking.

Activities

For more information on treks and boat trips around the Con Dao Islands, visit www.condaopark.com.vn, the official website for Con Dao National Park. It costs 20,000d to enter the park by day or 40,000d by night.

Diving & Snorkelling

Experienced divers who know the waters of Vietnam have long talked up Con Dao as

Con Dao Islands

the most pristine marine environment in the country. As many of the waters around the islands are protected, there is abundant coral and a variety of larger fish such as rays and sharks. Diving is possible year round, but for ideal conditions and good visibility, March to September is considered the best time. Diving is generally a bit more expensive than at more developed mainland destinations such as Nha Trang. Some wrecks have been discovered in the waters around Con Dao, offering huge potential for more experienced divers.

There are now two dive operators exploring the waters around Con Dao:

Dive! Dive! Dive!   DIVING
(☑383 0701; www.dive-condao.com; 36 Đ Ton Duc Thang) A new American-run operation, resident instructor Larry has years of experience diving the waters of Vietnam. Daily dive and snorkelling tours are available, plus SSI courses for beginners. The seafront dive shop is a great source of general information on the island.

Rainbow Divers   DIVING
(☑090-557 7671; www.divevietnam.com; Six Senses Con Dao) One of Vietnam's most established dive operators has an island base at the Six Senses Con Dao. However, they also offer diving to nonguests and can meet to discuss the various programmes at Con Dao Seatravel from 5pm daily.

Trekking

There are lots of treks around Con Son Island, as much of the interior remains heavily forested. It is necessary to take a national park guide when venturing into the forest.

Rates range from 150,000d to 250,000d depending on the duration of the trek.

One of the more beautiful walks leads through thick forest and mangroves, past a hilltop stream to **Bamboo Lagoon** (Dam Tre). This spot is stunning and there's good snorkelling in the bay. This leisurely two-hour trek starts from near the airport runway, but you'll definitely need a local guide to do this.

A hike that you can do yourself is a 1km walk (about 25 minutes each way) through rainforest to **Ong Dung Bay**. The trail begins a few kilometres north of town. On the road to the trailhead, you'll also pass the ruins of the **Ma Thien Lanh Bridge**, which was built by prisoners under the French occupation. The bay itself has only a rocky beach, although there is a good coral reef about 300m off shore.

It is also possible to trek to the old fruit plantations of **So Ray**, which are now being used to feed and rejuvenate the resident wildlife population in the hills of Con Dao. There are sweeping views over the main town and the islands beyond.

🛏 Sleeping

There are now a dozen or more hotels and resorts on Con Son, but some of the minihotels (and the National Park Guesthouse) are permanently occupied with staff from the Six Senses Con Dao, so there are no rooms at the inn.

Con Dao Camping   HOTEL $$
(☑383 1555; condaocamping.com; Đ Nguyen Duc Thuan; r 600,000d; ❋@🐾) The curious triangular bungalows may look more holiday

camp than heavenly retreat, but they are great value for the beachfront location. Frills (if not thrills) include satellite TV, minibar and showers with a view of the night sky.

Six Senses Con Dao
BOUTIQUE HOTEL $$$

(📞383 1222; www.sixsenses.com; Dat Doc Beach; villas from US$685; ❄@🛜🏊) Six Senses properties are something to be savoured and the new Con Dao retreat is no exception. Rustic luxury, this is the designer castaway experience complete with stunning seafront villas, each with its own pool, Bose stereo and wine cellar. The food is in a league of its own for a remote location such as Con Dao.

Hai Nga Mini Hotel
HOTEL $

(📞363 0308; 7 Đ Tran Phu; r 200,000-550,000đ; ❄@🛜) Tucked away in the heart of town, this small hotel is run by a friendly family who can speak English, French and German. Rooms are basic but good value, including air-con, TV and hot water showers. More expensive rooms sleep four to five people.

Con Dao Seatravel
HOTEL $$

(📞363 0768; www.condaoseatravel.com; 6 Đ Nguyen Duc Thuan; r US$70; ❄@🛜) A small resort with attractive bungalows dotted about the garden, the rooms here are spacious and bright, including pine furnishings and smart bathrooms with rain shower. The restaurant -bar here is arguably the most popular in town and draws a crowd from sunset.

ATC Con Dao Resort & Spa
HOTEL $$

(📞383 0111; www.atcvietnam.com; 8 Đ Ton Duc Thang; s US$55-80, d US$65-90; ❄@🛜🏊) Formerly the 'A' resort, this hotel has been rebranded and offers smart villa-style accommodation set around an inviting swimming pool. There are also two spacious thatch-roof stilt houses relocated here from Hoa Binh which were being renovated during our visit, all set in lovely gardens.

Saigon Con Dao Resort
HOTEL $$$

(📞383 0155; www.saigoncondao.com; 18 Đ Ton Duc Thang; s US$75-145, d US$80-150; ❄@🛜🏊) Originally set in a cluster of old French buildings on the waterfront, a new wing was recently added with a swimming pool which is where most foreign visitors are hosted. The old wing is reserved for visiting veterans and party loyalists on tours of the Con Dao prisons.

Con Dao Resort
HOTEL $$

(📞383 0939; www.condaoresort.com.vn; 8 Đ Nguyen Duc Thuan; r US$58-94; ❄@🛜🏊) One of the biggest resorts on Con Dao, it has an inviting stretch of beach and a large swimming pool. However, the rooms are slightly showing their age these days, especially the bathrooms, and it may be time for a gentle facelift.

🍴 Eating & Drinking

The dining scene is fast improving in Con Son. Much of the seafood is shipped off to the mainland for consumption or export, but local fishermen are now selling their catch in town. Among the hotels, **Con Dao Seatravel** has the best atmosphere for a meal or a drink. **Six Senses Con Dao** is the place for a sumptuous treat with a virtuoso menu.

Thu Tam
VIETNAMESE $

(Đ Nguyen Hue; mains 20,000-100,000đ; ⊙lunch & dinner) Formerly located at Ben Dam port, the owner has relocated to the Con Son strip and offers fresh seafood from bubbling tanks. Shells in many shapes and sizes, plus huge fish to feed a family.

Tri Ky
VIETNAMESE $$

(7 Đ Nguyen Duc Thuan; mains 40,000-200,000đ; ⊙lunch & dinner) Another place that is popular with island residents for its fresh seafood. Try the squid grilled in five spices or go the full monty with a seafood hotpot.

Phuong Hanh
VIETNAMESE $

(38 Đ Nguyen Hue; mains 40,000-120,000đ; ⊙lunch & dinner) A long-running local restaurant behind Phu Hai Prison, choose from yet more seafood or a selection of Vietnamese staples from the mainland.

ℹ Information

The **national park headquarters** (📞383 0669; eco-tourism@condaopark.com.vn; www.condao park.com.vn; 29 Đ Vo Thi Sau; ⊙7-11.30am & 1.30-5pm daily) is a good place to get information. Since the military controls access to parts of the national park, stop here first to learn more about possible island excursions and hikes, plus pick-up a useful free handout on walks around the island. Some hiking trails have interpretive signage in English and Vietnamese. The headquarters also has an exhibition hall with displays on the diversity of local forest and marine life, threats to the local environment, and local conservation activities.

There is now a branch of **Vietin Bank** (Đ Le Duan) with two ATMs. However, these are notorious for running out of dong and the bank does not change foreign currency, so come prepared.

Internet access is available at hotels in town, including free wi-fi for guests, plus terminals in the lobby for wired access.

Getting There & Away

AIR There are now several flights daily between Con Son and HCMC. **Vasco** (☑383 1831; www .vasco.com.vn; 44 Đ Nguyen Hue) offers three flights daily at 863,000d one way, although they often have special fares on the website. **Air Mekong** (☑08-3514 6666; www.airmekong .info) is planning to introduce daily flights as Con Dao takes off.

The tiny airport is about 15km from the town centre. All of the hotels on the island provide free transport both to and from the airport. Although it's advisable to book a hotel in advance, it is possible to show up and grab a seat on one of the hotel shuttle vans that meet the planes, costing about 60,000d.

BOAT There are two ferries connecting Con Son Island with Vung Tau, with sailings approximately every second day. The ferries depart from Ben Dam port at 5pm, taking about 12 hours. Seats cost 125,000d but it is better to invest in a sleeper berth for 200,000d, with six bunks to a room. Facilities are pretty basic and the crossing can be rough at certain times of years, leading to frequent cancellations, but you'll be one of the only foreigners on the boat.

Tickets can be purchased from a small office near the market in town. Look out for the sign at the kiosk on Đ Vo Thi Sau which reads **BQL Cang Ben Dam Huyen Con Dao** (◎8-11.30am & 1-5pm). A *xe om* to Ben Dam will cost about 80,000d if you can find one.

PENNILESS IN PARADISE

Make sure you have sufficient funds before travelling to the Con Dao Islands. There is one bank in town, but it is risky to rely on the temperamental ATMs here. Most midrange hotels accept credit cards, but if you need to arrange cash on the spot, exchange rates are notoriously poor in this remote location.

Getting Around

BOAT Exploring the islands by boat can be arranged through the national park office. A 12-person boat costs around 2,000,000d to 5,000,000d per day depending on the destinations.

MOTORBIKE & BICYCLE Some of the main sites on Con Son, such as the Revolution Museum and Phu Hai Prison, are within walking distance of town, but to get further afield a motorbike is ideal. Most hotels rent motorbikes for about US$7 to US$10 per day. Bicycles cost around US$2 per day. There are good coastal cycling routes, such as from town to Bai Nhat and onto the tiny settlement of Ben Dam. The ups and downs are pretty gentle and, thankfully, there is little motorised traffic. If motorbiking or cycling to Ben Dam, be very careful of the high winds around Mui Ca Map. Locals have been blown off their bikes during gales.

Central Highlands

Best Places to Eat

» V Cafe (p279)

» Nam Phan (p280)

» Black & White Restaurant (p286)

» Dakbla Restaurant (p295)

Best Places to Stay

» Dalat Hotel du Parc (p278)

» Dreams Hotel (p278)

» Forest Floor Lodge (p284)

» Ana Mandara Villas Dalat (p278)

Why Go?

The undulating landscape that once sheltered Viet Cong (VC) soldiers down the Ho Chi Minh Trail offers an off-the-beaten-track destination for travellers. There's a rugged charm to its villages, valleys, waterfalls and winding roads. Most people come here to visit the hill-tribe villages, as the roads less travelled offer a more unspoiled existence than the touristed areas of the northwest.

Two notable national parks are found here. One of the region's big hitters is Cat Tien National Park, a Unesco-rated biosphere boasting an impressive variety of flora and fauna. Yok Don is Vietnam's largest protected area and is home to monkeys and deer. Both parks give visitors the opportunity to explore Vietnam's all-too-rare wild side.

Despite its fraught history, the central highlands are safe and easy to travel around. Dalat is perfect for a weekend's respite from the heat, the rest of the highlands for a week-long immersion in a life far from the madding crowd.

When to Go
Dalat

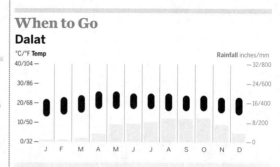

Mar Great for the annual Coffee Festival in Buon Ma Thuot or elephant races in nearby Don.

Oct Autumn climes come to Dalat, the perfect time for exploring or adrenaline activities.

Dec Trek or cycle through Cat Tien National Park in cooler times, visiting the wild gibbons.

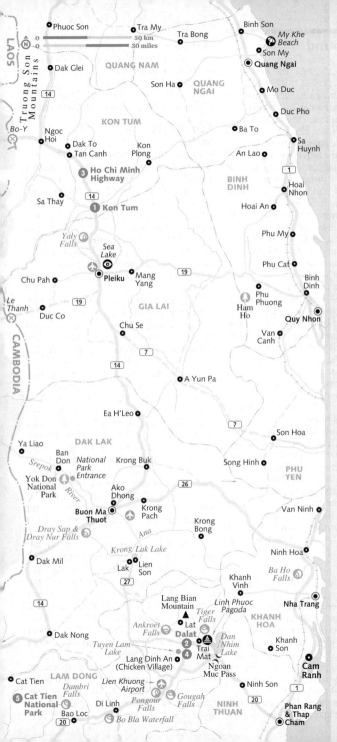

Central Highlands Highlights

1 Discover the hill-tribe way of life in remote village homestays around **Kon Tum** (p293)

2 Experience the fresh air and French flair of **Dalat** (p272), Vietnam's mountain resort

3 Jump on a motorbike and wind along the twists and turns of the **Ho Chi Minh Highway** (p291)

4 Crank up the adrenaline rate with an adventure in the hills **around Dalat** (p277)

5 Hike, bike or track down wild gibbons in the lush forests of **Cat Tien National Park** (p283)

Dalat & Around

🎵 063 / POP 250,000 / ELEV 1475M

Dalat is Vietnam's alter ego: the weather is spring-like cool instead of tropical hot, the town is dotted with elegant French-colonial villas rather than stark socialist architecture, and the farms around are thick with strawberries and flowers, not rice. As a highland resort it's been welcoming tourists for a century and it has all the attractions to prove it.

The French came first, fleeing the heat of Saigon. They left behind not only their holiday homes but also the vibe of a European town and the local bohemian artists' predilection for swanning around in berets. The Vietnamese couldn't resist adding little touches to, shall we say, enhance Dalat's natural beauty. Whether it's the Eiffel Tower–shaped radio tower, the horse-drawn carriages or the zealously colourful heart-shaped cut-outs at the Valley of Love, this is a town that takes romance very seriously, although it teeters on the brink of kitsch.

But don't let the Disneyfied feel stop you from enjoying the pretty scenery and charming town. This used to be hunting territory too, described in the 1950s as 'abounding in deer, roe, peacocks, pheasants, wild boar, black bear, panthers, tigers, gaurs and elephants'. Unfortunately hunters were so efficient that only taxidermied specimens remain, in the local museum.

Dalat is a big draw for domestic tourists. It's Le Petit Paris, the honeymoon capital and the City of Eternal Spring (daily temperatures hover between 15°C and 24°C) all rolled into one. Vietnamese visitors arrive in summer, but the dry season (December to March) is the better time to visit. The wet season takes over for the rest of the year, but even then mornings normally remain dry, allowing time for sightseeing before the downpours begin.

History

Home to hill tribes for centuries, 'Da Lat' means 'river of the Lat tribe' in their language. The first European to 'discover' the area was Dr Alexandre Yersin in 1893. The city was established in 1912 and quickly became fashionable with Europeans. At one point during the French-colonial period, some 20% of Dalat's population was foreign, as is evidenced by the 2500-odd chateau-style villas scattered around the city.

During the American War, Dalat was spared by the tacit agreement of all parties concerned. Indeed, it seems that while South Vietnamese soldiers were being trained at the city's military academy and affluent officials of the Saigon regime were relaxing in their villas, VC cadres were doing the same thing not far away (also in villas). On 3 April 1975 Dalat fell to the North without a fight.

⊙ Sights

DALAT

Hang Nga Crazy House   NOTABLE BUILDING
(3 Đ Huynh Thuc Khang; admission 30,000d) A free-wheeling architectural exploration of surrealism, Hang Nga Crazy House defies easy definition. Architecture buffs will marvel at the echoes of Antoni Gaudi, shutter-happy tourists will pose in the strangely decorated rooms (some with ceiling mirrors, many with creepy animal statues with glowing red eyes) and children will simply enjoy getting lost in the maze of tunnels, walkways and ladders.

There are 10 rooms, each named after an unlikely animal or plant, all built into an organic-looking structure that resembles an enormous tree unfurling itself. You can wander around as you please; clearly, getting lost is part of the experience. Rooms at the top offer a splendid view of Dalat, if you can tear your eyes away long enough to appreciate it.

The brainchild of owner Mrs Dang Viet Nga, the Crazy House has been an imaginative work-in-progress since 1990. Hang Nga, as she's known locally, has a PhD in architecture from Moscow and has designed a number of other buildings around Dalat, including the Children's Cultural Palace and the Catholic church in Lien Khuong. One of her earlier masterpieces, the 'House with 100 Roofs', was torn down as a fire hazard because the People's Committee thought it looked antisocialist.

Hang Nga started the Crazy House project to entice people back to nature and though it's becoming more outlandish every year, she's not likely to have any more trouble with the authorities. Her father, Truong Chinh, was Ho Chi Minh's successor, serving as Vietnam's second president from 1981 until his death in 1988. There's a display about him in one of the ground-floor spaces (part living room, part limestone cave).

If an hour or so spent in the embrace of this kitschy extravaganza isn't enough for you, stay overnight (double rooms from US$35) and see what waking up in Alice's Wonderland feels like.

Crémaillère Railway Station
HISTORIC BUILDING

(Ga Da Lat; 1 Đ Quang Trung; admission free; ☉6.30am-5pm) Dalat's pretty train station is now largely decorative. The cog-railway linked Dalat and Thap Cham from 1928 to 1964, but was closed due to VC attacks. A short section of the track to Trai Mat village has been running since 1997 and the government has pledged to restore the rest of the line. If completed this would provide a great tourist link to the main north–south lines.

There are old locomotives on display, including a Japanese steam train. Five scheduled trains run to Trai Mat (return ticket 100,000d, 30 minutes, 8km) every day between 7.45am and 4.05pm. In reality tickets must be booked half an hour ahead and they won't leave without at least two passengers.

Xuan Huong Lake
LAKE

Created by a dam in 1919, this banana-shaped lake was named after a 17th-century Vietnamese poet known for her daring attacks on the hypocrisy of social conventions and the foibles of scholars, monks, mandarins and kings. The lake can be circumnavigated along a 7km sealed path that leads past several of Dalat's main sights, including the flower gardens, golf club and the Dalat Palace Hotel. Swan paddle boats are available for rent, a very popular pastime for visiting Vietnamese.

Dalat Flower Gardens
GARDENS

(Vuon Hoa Thanh Pho; Đ Tran Nhan Tong; admission 10,000d; ☉7.30am-4pm) An unusual sight in Vietnam, these gardens were established in 1966. Flowers include hydrangeas, fuchsias and orchids, the latter in shaded buildings to the left of the entrance. It's a good place to see a cross-section of Dalat foliage.

Like any good Dalat park, the gardens have also been embellished with kitschy topiary. To amuse the kids (or the couples), there are horse-drawn carriage rides and heroic statues of hill-tribe people.

Bao Dai's Summer Palace
HISTORIC BUILDING

(off Đ Trieu Viet Vuong; admission 10,000d; ☉7am-5pm) This art deco–influenced villa was constructed in 1933 and was one of three palaces Bao Dai kept in Dalat. The decor has not changed in decades, making a visit here akin to wandering on to a film set.

In Bao Dai's office, the life-sized white bust above the bookcase is of the man himself (he died in 1997); the smaller gold and brown busts are of his father, Emperor Khai Dinh. Note the heavy brass royal seal (on the right) and military seal (on the left). The photographs over the fireplace are of Bao Dai, his eldest son Bao Long (in uniform), and his wife Empress Nam Phuong.

Upstairs are the living quarters. The huge semicircular couch was used by the emperor and empress for family meetings, with their three daughters seated in the yellow chairs and their two sons in the pink chairs.

The rooms at the rear have been converted into a fancy-dress parlour, popular with visiting Vietnamese. For just 15,000d they don 'royal' costumes and take a photograph on a fake throne.

Bao Dai's Summer Palace is set in a pine grove, 2km southwest of the city centre. Cloth coverings or 'shoe condoms' must be placed over your shoes before entering.

Lam Dong Museum
MUSEUM

(4 Đ Hung Vuong; admission 10,000d; ☉7.30-11.30am & 1.30-4.30pm Mon-Sat) Housed in a modern pink building, this hillside museum displays ancient artefacts and pottery, as well as costumes and musical instruments of local ethnic minorities and propaganda about the government support for their mountain neighbours. There are informative exhibits

---

THE NEW BATTLE FOR THE CENTRAL HIGHLANDS

In 2001 and 2004 protests erupted in Buon Ma Thuot, Pleiku and other parts of the highlands, objecting to the government's resettlement and land policies and alleged discrimination against hill tribes. While things are generally quiet now, recent problems in the Dien Bien Phu area could spread southwards and reignite lingering discontent. International human-rights groups continue to report instances of ill treatment of ethnic minorities.

As for the natural landscape of the highlands, it's beautiful but in some places marred, first by Agent Orange in the American War, then by slash-and-burn agriculture, now by expanding farms and dams. If it's jaw-dropping scenery you crave, then travel further north up the Ho Chi Minh Hwy or head to the far north of the country.

Central Dalat

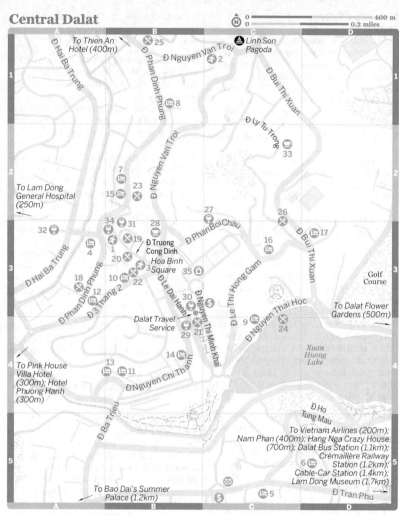

about Alexandre Yersin and the history of Dalat on the upper level.

Du Sinh Church
CHURCH

(Đ Huyen Tran Cong Chua; admission free) This church resembles a temple more than a traditional church and was built in 1955 by Catholic refugees from the north. The four-post, Sino-Vietnamese steeple was constructed at the insistence of a Hue-born priest of royal lineage. Look up as you pass under the entryway arch to see a statue in classical Greek style flanked by two fiercely golden Chinese dragons.

The church is on a hilltop with panoramic views in all directions. To get here, follow Đ Tran Phu out of the centre until it becomes Đ Hoang Van Thu, turn left onto Đ Huyen Tran Cong Chua towards the former **Couvent des Oiseaux**, now a teachers' training college, and the church is 500m southwest up the road.

AROUND DALAT

Valley of Love
PARK

(Thung Lung Tinh Yeu; Đ Phu Dong Thien Vuong; adult/child 10,000/5000d; ⊙7am-5pm) When even the locals find the place tacky, you

Central Dalat

know it's reached new depths of kitsch. This park surrounding a lake in a valley is attractive in its own right but burdened with the responsibilities of its name (proffered by Dalat University students in 1972). Romantically themed props and statues are scattered across its landscaped gardens, and the lake can get woefully noisy with the splashing of paddle boats, canoes and motorboats.

Adding to the surreal atmosphere are the 'Dalat cowboys'. Yee-haa! These are good old Vietnamese boys dressed as American cowboys. They rent horses for a guided tour around the lake.

The Valley of Love is 5km north of Xuan Huong Lake. It's a popular stop for tour buses.

Cuong Hoan Traditional Silk Centre
GALLERY

(⊙7.30am-5pm) This is a small family-run factory where you can inspect the entire process of silk production, from the sorting of locally grown cocoons, to boiling them and unravelling the thread, then dyeing the threads and weaving them into shimmering new fabric. You can even sample the cooked grub, which has a nutty flavour. There are some beautiful garments and lengths of cloth for sale.

The centre is in Nam Ban Village, 30km west of Dalat, near Elephant Falls. Many Easy Riders stop here.

Waterfalls
LANDMARKS

There are a number of waterfalls around Dalat. None are royally spectacular and quite a few have dwindled in size as more dams are built in the region. The two most popular falls are Datanla Falls and Elephant Falls because they're convenient to Dalat. Other waterfalls in the area are more useful as waypoints if you're exploring the countryside on your own wheels; popular ones include **Ankroët Falls**, **Gougah Falls** and **Pongour Falls**, all with a 5000d admission charge.

Datanla Falls

(admission 5000d) This is the closest waterfall to Dalat, which dooms it to popularity even though the cascade is quite modest. Follow the paved path down to the falls. There's also a **bobsled ride** (adult one-way/return 30,000/40,000d) for those who'd rather steer themselves down a winding elevated track. With the loud music and weekend crowds, this once-peaceful spot has become quite a circus. The waterfalls are about 7km south of Dalat. Take Hwy 20 and turn right about

NATIONAL HIGHWAY 20: ROADSIDE ATTRACTIONS

Open tour buses and private cars tackle the twists and turns from Ho Chi Minh City to Dalat and there are several possible stops along the way.

Langa Lake

The HCMC–Dalat road (Hwy 20) spans this reservoir, which is traversed by a bridge. Lots of floating houses, where families harvest the fish underneath, can be seen here. It's a very scenic spot for photography, and most tourist vehicles on the HCMC–Dalat road make a short pit stop here.

Volcanic Craters

Near Dinh Quan on Hwy 20 there are three volcanoes, now extinct, but nonetheless very impressive. The craters date from the late Jurassic period, about 150 million years ago. You'll have to do a little walking to see the craters. One is on the left-hand side of the road, about 2km south of Dinh Quan, and another on the right-hand side about 8km beyond Dinh Quan, towards Dalat.

Underground Lava Tubes

A bit beyond the volcanic craters, towards Dalat, are underground lava tubes. These rare caves were formed as the surface lava cooled and solidified, while the hotter underground lava continued to flow, leaving a hollow space. Lava tubes differ sharply in appearance from limestone caves (the latter are formed by underground springs). While limestone caves have abundant stalactites and stalagmites, the walls of lava caves are smooth.

The easiest way to find the lava tubes is to first find the teak forest on Hwy 20 between the Km120 and Km124 markers. The children who live around the forest can point you to the entrance of the lava tubes. However, you are strongly advised not to go into the tubes alone; as with caving there is the risk of becoming lost or stuck. Local kids hang out on the roadside and will sometimes act as guides for a small fee of 40,000d or so. Take a torch (flashlight).

200m past the turn-off to Tuyen Lam Lake. It's well signposted.

Elephant Falls
(admission free) A popular stop on the Easy Rider trail, these imposing curved falls are best seen from below. An uneven and sometimes hazardous path heads down to the base of the waterfall. It's also possible to inch behind the falls, but watch your footing carefully and expect to get wet. Nearby, the Linh An Pagoda (2004) has been built to take advantage of the good feng shui of having water in front and a mountain behind. Inside, the three large Buddhas are flanked by two multi-armed Buddhas. More statues lurk in the garden out the back, including a particularly Happy Buddha with neon halos and a room built into his ample belly. The falls are situated near Nam Ban village, 30km west of Dalat. Combine this with a visit to Cuong Hoan Traditional Silk Centre.

Tuyen Lam Lake & Truc Lam Pagoda LAKE
(Ho Tuyen Lam; admission free) Also known as Quang Trung Reservoir, this artificial lake was created by a dam in 1980. The hill to the right of the lake is crowned by Truc Lam Pagoda. Despite its popularity, the sprawling grounds and temple don't feel crowded, and the views of the lake are wonderful. If you'd like a little spiritual recharge, enquire about the sessions at the meditation centre (6am-5pm). Hiking and canoeing are possible in the area; ask the adventure companies in Dalat. Tuyen Lam Lake is about 7km outside Dalat. Take Hwy 20, turn right at the signpost 5km from town and continue for 2km. The fun way to get here is by cable car (adult one-way/return 50,000/70,000d, child 30,000/40,000d), though it's not for the faint-hearted. From the cable-car station (Cap Treo; off Đ 3 Thang 4, Dalat; 7-11.30am & 1.30-5pm), it runs along a 2.3km wire over majestic pine forests to the hill where Truc Lam Pagoda stands.

Lang Bian Mountain NATURE RESERVE
(admission 10,000d) Also called Lam Vien Mountain, this spot has five volcanic peaks ranging in altitude from 2100m to 2400m.

Of the two highest peaks, the eastern one is known by the woman's name K'Lang, while the western one bears a man's name, K'Biang. Only the upper reaches of the mountain remain forested, whereas just half a century ago the foothills had lush foliage that sheltered many wild animals. The hike up to the top's spectacular views takes three to four hours from the ticket booth. Lang Bian Mountain is about 13km north of Dalat. Follow Đ Xo Viet Nghe Tinh until you reach Tung Lam Hamlet. Continue straight on (northwest) rather than to the left. On bicycle it takes about 45 minutes. Adventure activities on offer here include paragliding.

Lat & Lang Dinh An Villages VILLAGES

There are two minority villages a short drive from Dalat, both unremarkable despite their popularity. If you're interested in hill-tribe life, you're better off heading to Kon Tum or the far north of the country. Less than 1km from the base of Lang Bian Mountain is Lat Village (pronounced 'lak'), a community of about 6000 people spread across nine hamlets. Only five of the hamlets are actually Lat; residents of the other four are members of the Chill, Ma and Koho tribes. It's a sleepy little place with a few handicraft shops. Sometimes it hosts wine-drinking sessions or gong performances for tour groups.

Lang Dinh An (Chicken Village) has the distinction of having a giant concrete chicken caught mid-strut in the village centre. The statue is part of a long-dysfunctional water system, and used to crow as water was pumped. It's home to about 600 of the Koho people, now largely Vietnamised, and offers the same woven objects and 'cultural' activities as Lat Village. The village is on Hwy 20, 17km from Dalat.

🏃 Activities

Dalat's cool climate and mountainous surrounds mean this is a great area for all kinds of outdoor activities. There are many adventure outfits clustered along Đ Truong Cong Dinh, offering trekking, mountain biking, kayaking, canyoning, abseiling and rock climbing, as well as trips to the central highlands. It doesn't hurt to compare prices, but make sure that you're comfortable with all the equipment and safety procedures.

Phat Tire Ventures ADVENTURE TOURS

(☑382 9422; www.ptv-vietnam.com; 109 Đ Nguyen Van Troi) This is the most experienced operator around Dalat, with trekking programs

from US$26, as well as kayaking from US$37 and canyoning from US$40. It also offers one-day (US$77) or two-day (US$169) bike rides to Mui Ne and Nha Trang. Shorter day rides, like the aptly named Skid Marks, start from US$42.

Groovy Gecko Adventure Tours ADVENTURE TOURS

(☑383 6521; www.groovygeckotours.net; 65 Đ Truong Cong Dinh) One of the more popular and experienced agencies. Prices start at around US$25 for canyoning or mountain biking. Longer bike trips to Mui Ne or Nha Trang are also available, including mountain-bike descents.

Youth Action ADVENTURE TOURS

(☑351 0357; www.youthactiontour.com; 45 Đ Truong Cong Dinh) Similar offerings to Groovy Gecko and Phat Tire (trekking from US$20, mountain biking from US$24, rock climbing from US$30), as well as horse riding (US$34 per half day) and paragliding (US$80) around Long Bian Mountain.

Dalat Palace Golf Club GOLF

(☑382 1202; www.dalatpalacegolf.vn; Đ Tran Nhan Tong) Visitors can play 18-hole rounds on this attractive course near the lake – once used by Emperor Bao Dai himself – for

WORTH A TRIP

MADAGUI FOREST RESORT

Yes, this is a major tourist attraction for the Vietnamese, but they just might be on to something. **Madagui Forest Resort** (☑061-394 6999; www.madagui .com.vn; Km152, Hwy 20; adult/child 30,000/20,000d) is a one-stop shop for adventures en route to or from Dalat. **Paintballing** (47,000d, plus per shot 1500d) is a major draw here, although it is a fairly surreal experience. And no, Rambo or Viet Cong costumes are not available. Other activities on offer include white-water rafting, kayaking, mountain biking, horse riding and fishing. Madagui's translated-to-English website also proudly offers 'drug-out canoes', which sound like a trip though we're sure they're actually just good, wholesome fun. Accommodation is available from 1,300,000d a night, but it's probably better experienced as a pit stop between Dalat and HCMC.

US$95 and up. Ask about Twilight Specials from US$45. Clubs, caddies and carts are all extra. To get here, follow D Ba Huyen Thanh Quan north along Xuan Huong Lake and turn left on to D Tran Nhan Tong. The clubhouse is about 300m on the left.

🛏 Sleeping

Dalat is one of the few places in Vietnam where you won't need to worry about air-conditioning. The town's enduring popularity with local tourists means that there's a wealth of budget and midrange options, including some of the best-value accommodation in the highlands.

The quiet lane off Đ Hai Thuong opposite the Lam Dong General Hospital is home to a cluster of decent budget hotels. The only downside is that you have to walk up a steep hill to get home. Choices include the following.

TOP CHOICE Dreams Hotel HOTEL $
(☑383 3748; dreams@hcm.vnn.vn; 151 Đ Phan Dinh Phung; r US$20-25; @🛜) Quite simply the friendliest and most comfortable place to stay in Dalat. The buffet breakfast spread is legendary – Vegemite, Marmite and peanut butter are available – and well worth the price of the room. There's no hassling over tours, as the hotel doesn't sell them. Dreams includes a sauna, steam room and hot tub, free for guests from 4pm to 7pm. There is a second Dreams just down the road at 164b offering the same tasty recipe.

TOP CHOICE Dalat Hotel du Parc HOTEL $$
(☑382 5777; www.hotelduparc.vn; 7 Đ Tran Phu; r US$55-85, ste US$105; ✳@🛜) A class apart for those seeking the Dalat of old, this respectfully refurbished 1932 building offers colonial-era chic at enticing prices. The old lobby lift sets the tone and rooms include wooden furnishings, historic photos and modern touches such as flat-screen TVs.

Thi Thao Hotel HOTEL $$
(☑383 3333; www.thithaogardenia.com/en; 29 Đ Phan Boi Chau; r from US$25; ✳@🛜) Somewhat confusingly, this place is also known as the Gardenia Hotel, but don't be dissuaded as it offers the best-value style in town. Rooms are new and spacious, with flat-screen TVs and superb bathrooms. All very tasteful.

Ana Mandara Villas Dalat BOUTIQUE HOTEL $$$
(☑355 5888; www.anamandara-resort.com; Đ Le Lai; r US$142-259, ste US$372-435; ✳@🛜) One of the most striking places to stay in all of Vietnam, this property consists of 70 rooms and suites spread across 17 lovingly restored French colonial–era villas. Rooms are finished in period furnishings and each villa group has a lounge and fireplace and the option of private dining. The sophisticated spa was originally designed by Six Senses. Tucked away in the suburbs, this spa is well signposted; follow signs from the city centre.

Hotel Chau Au – Europa HOTEL $
(☑382 2870; europa@hcm.vnn.vn; 76 Đ Nguyen Chi Thanh; r US$10-20; ✳@🛜) A likeable hotel run by a delightful owner who speaks English and French. This place really feels homely; choose a room at the front with a balcony for views over Dalat Cathedral and the 'Eiffel Tower'.

Trung Cang Hotel HOTEL $
(☑382 2663; www.thesinhtourist.vn; 4a Đ Bui Thi Xuan; r US$15-25; @🛜) Prices have been dropping at this smart Sinh Tourist establishment. Rooms are tastefully decorated, including local silks, and there is no shortage of tour and transport information available from the attached travel desk.

Le Phuong Hotel HOTEL $
(☑382 3743; lephuonghotel@gmail.com; 80 Đ Nguyen Chi Thanh; r 250,000-330,000d; ✳@🛜) A new family-run hotel in a busy accommodation strip, this place stands out from the pack thanks to the large rooms, oversized beds and tasteful bathrooms.

Empress Hotel HOTEL $$
(☑383 3888; www.empresshotelvn.com; 5 Đ Nguyen Thai Hoc; r from US$60; ✳@🛜) In a prime location overlooking the Xuan Huong Lake, this is an intimate and atmospheric place to stay. The 20 rooms are spacious and tasteful, and many face onto the peaceful courtyard garden. Discounts of 30% are common.

Dalat Palace COLONIAL HOTEL $$$
(☑382 5444; www.dalatpalace.vn; 12 Đ Tran Phu; s US$246-306, d US$260-320, ste US$446-510; ✳@🛜) The grande dame of Dalat hotels (1922) has unimpeded views of Xuan Huong Lake. Inside, the opulence of French-colonial life has been splendidly preserved, from claw-foot tubs and working fireplaces to sumptuous chandeliers and paintings. It may no longer have its Sofitel branding, but it hasn't lost any of its lustre.

Hoan Hy Hotel HOTEL $
(☑351 1288; hoanhyhotel@yahoo.com; 16 Đ 3 Thang 2; r US$15; @🛜) A new hotel near the

epicentre of town, the rooms here are serious value for money with midrange touches such as flat-screen TVs. It is located above a popular bakery, so you can enjoy fresh bread each morning.

Thien An Hotel HOTEL **$**
(☎352 0607; thienanhotel@vnn.vn; 272a Đ Phan Dinh Phung; r US$18-25; @🖥) Continuing the winning family formula, this hotel (run by Mr Anh, brother of the owner of Dreams) provides spacious rooms, glorious breakfasts and warm hospitality. It's a little further out for those who want to avoid the town's neon lights, but free bicycles are provided.

Cam Do Hotel HOTEL **$$**
(☎382 2732; 81 Đ Phan Dinh Phung; r US$30-60; @🖥) A smart midranger in the centre of Dalat, the Cam Do offers three-star rooms with all the trimmings, including complimentary in-room tea service. If that doesn't excite you, perhaps the karaoke and massage will.

Ngoc Lan Hotel BOUTIQUE HOTEL **$$**
(☎382 2136; www.ngoclanhotel.vn; 42 Đ Nguyen Chi Thanh; r from US$65; ✳@🖥) The first of a new breed of boutique-ish hotels to open in Dalat, this is all clean white lines with stylish purple accents. There's a dash of colonial character with the wooden floors and French windows, but everything else is impeccably modern.

River Prince Hotel HOTEL **$$**
(☎356 5888; 135 Đ Phan Dinh Phung; r from US$60; ✳@🖥) A new hotel in the heart of town, the 104 rooms include parquet flooring, ultra-modern bathrooms and cinema-sized TVs if you are missing the movies.

Hotel Phuong Hanh HOTEL **$**
(☎383 8839; phuonghanhhotel@gmail.com; 80-82 Đ 3 Thang 2; r US$10-20; @🖥) Travellers enjoy staying here thanks to the effusive staff (although they can be over-enthusiastic at times) and the good-value rooms. Shop around before choosing a room, as a couple of dollars more buys a larger or quieter room.

Hotel Phuong Hanh HOTEL **$**
(☎356 0528; 7/1 Đ Hai Thuong; r US$6-10; @🖥) The predecessor to its sister property along Đ 3 Thang 2, this is in a well-maintained place with plenty of character and cheap rooms.

Pink House Villa Hotel HOTEL **$**
(☎381 5667; ahomeawayfromhome_dalat@yahoo.com; 7 Đ Hai Thuong; s/d/tr US$10/15/20; @🖥) Super friendly, well-run and good value, this is a great little place to stay. Overseen by the affable Mr Rot, he can also arrange traditional countryside tours away from the tourist trail.

✖ Eating

Dalat has an appealing selection of smart restaurants that make the most of the local produce. For cheap eats in the day, head to the upper level of the **Central Market** (Cho Da Lat). At night, **food stalls** (Đ Nguyen Thi Minh Khai) congregate outside the market.

V Cafe INTERNATIONAL **$$**
(☎352 0215; 1/1 Đ Bui Thi Xuan; dishes 25,000-79,000d; ⊙lunch & dinner) A travellers' favourite, this friendly bistro is decorated with Chinese lanterns and serves a mix of Asian and Western mains, most with sides of mash and fresh vegetables. Owned by an American muso, there is a live duet performing here most nights.

Chocolate Café INTERNATIONAL **$**
(40a Đ Truong Cong Dinh; dishes 20,000-70,000d; ⊙lunch & dinner) A newer restaurant in the busy backpacker strip, this has become very

---

DELECTABLE DALAT

It's a vegetable lover's heaven: Dalat's climate is conducive to growing peas, carrots, radishes, tomatoes, cucumbers, avocados, capsicums, lettuce, beets, green beans, potatoes, garlic, spinach, squash and yams. Translation: you can get meals here that are unavailable elsewhere in the country.

The Dalat area is justly famous for strawberry jam, dried blackcurrants and candied plums, persimmons and peaches. Apricots are popular, often served in a heavily salted hot drink. Other local delicacies include avocado ice cream, sweet beans (*mut dao*) and strawberry, blackberry and artichoke extracts (for making drinks). Artichoke tea, another local speciality, is said to lower blood pressure and benefit the liver and kidneys.

Dalat wine is served all over Vietnam. The reds are pleasantly light, while the whites tend to be heavy on the oak.

popular thanks to affordable pizzas and pastas and well-presented Vietnamese dishes. The decor is stylish and the coffee menu includes macchiato and espresso.

Art Café VIETNAMESE $$
(70 Đ Truong Cong Dinh; dishes 25,000-75,000d; ⊙lunch & dinner) Owned by an artist whose work adorns the walls, this elegant eatery has intimate tables and soft lighting. The menu features Vietnamese dishes with a twist, including plenty of vegetarian options. Linger over a glass of wine to admire the artwork.

Da Quy VIETNAMESE $
(Wild Sunflower; 49 Đ Truong Cong Dinh; dishes 25,000-65,000d; ⊙lunch & dinner) With a sophisticated ambience but unsophisticated prices, this place earns consistently good reviews from travellers of all taste buds. Try the traditional clay-pot dishes with fish or shrimp.

Nam Phan VIETNAMESE $$$
(☑381 3816; 7 Đ Tran Hung Dao; dishes 55,000-1,500,000d; ⊙lunch & dinner) A mountain relation of the famous Nam Phan in HCMC, this stunning Vietnamese restaurant is set in a beautifully restored colonial-era mansion with manicured gardens and sweeping views. Set dinners run from US$20 to US$90 and include superb seafood and artfully presented classics.

Cafe de la Poste FRENCH $$$
(☑382 5777; Đ Tran Phu; dishes US$6-58) Set in a gorgeous old French-era building, this stylish French restaurant is owned by Dalat Hotel du Parc. The menu is ambitious indeed, but the best-value meals are salads, sandwiches, pastas and fresh bakery products.

Thanh Thuy Blue Water Restaurant INTERNATIONAL $$
(2 Đ Nguyen Thai Hoc; dishes 30,000-105,000d) With an unbeatable location right on the lake, this restaurant serves an eclectic menu of Cantonese fare, with some Vietnamese and Western dishes for good measure. The view is the real draw here.

Le Rabelais FRENCH $$$
(☑382 5444; 12 Đ Tran Phu; mains US$10-47) For fine French dining, the signature restaurant at the Dalat Palace is the destination. The impressive dining room oozes gentility at every turn. While away the night like the French might have, with a *digestif* and live piano

music. Gourmands may like to attempt the seven-course degustation menu at US$85.

An Lac VEGETARIAN $
(71 Đ Phan Dinh Phung; meals from 10,000d) There's an English menu here, and options range from noodle soups to *banh bao* (steamed dumplings) or steamed rice-flour dumplings stuffed with a savoury filling. There is a second branch at 26 Đ Bui Thi Xuan.

Trong Dong VIETNAMESE $
(220 Đ Phan Dinh Phung; mains 25,000-80,000d; ⊙lunch & dinner) A friendly and unpretentious eatery designed in French bistro style, this place is decorated with mirrors, making it feel bigger than it actually is. It's popular for its rabbit specialities and eel dishes.

Long Hoa INTERNATIONAL $$
(6 Đ 3 Thang 2; dishes 25,000-100,000d; ⊙lunch & dinner) A cosy bistro run by a Francophile owner who has decked it out with images of France. Westerners come here for the Vietnamese food; Vietnamese come here to try the steaks. Top off your meal with a glass of Dalat wine.

Nhat Ly VIETNAMESE $$
(88 Đ Phan Dinh Phung; dishes 30,000-120,000d; ⊙lunch & dinner) A very local place that serves hearty meals, including a sumptuous hot pot that really hits the spot. There's also rabbit and frog on the menu if you are feeling adventurous.

🍷 Drinking

While Dalat has a lively night-market scene, sadly the same cannot be said for its night scene. The best thing is to go where the locals go: to the lively strip of **cafe-bars** (Đ Le Dai Hanh). The music isn't great but it's perfect for people watching while knocking back a few beers.

The Hangout DIVE BAR
(71 Đ Truong Cong Dinh) It does just what it says on the tin and acts as a popular hang-out for some of Dalat's Easy Riders, as well as visiting backpackers. Cheap beers and a pool table complete the picture.

Saigon Nite DIVE BAR
(11a Đ Hai Ba Trung) Proudly boasting to be the oldest bar in town and it's really starting to show. That said, the friendly owner runs a classic dive where people come for the beer and pool, not the decor.

100 Roofs Café CAFE, BAR
(57 Đ Phan Boi Chau) Designed by a student of the Crazy House school of architecture, this is a surreal drinking experience. They claim Gandalf and his hobbit friends have drunk here, and the place does look rather like a location from Middle Earth.

Peace Cafe BAR
(64 Đ Truong Cong Dinh) Attached to the Peace Hotel, this noisy cafe is always packed, thanks to the enthusiastic owners rounding up every passing traveller. It's a good place to meet other backpackers by night or Easy Riders by day.

Envy Lounge Bar LOUNGE BAR
(Đ Le Dai Hanh) This is so much more Saigon than Dalat. Located on the popular local bar strip, this is lounge in the extreme, with velour sofas and a live band that can pull off Lady Gaga covers. Expensive drinks.

Cafe Tung CAFE
(6 Hoa Binh Sq) There are also some Bohemian cafes in Dalat, including Cafe Tung, a famous hang-out for Saigonese intellectuals in the 1950s. It remains exactly as it was then, serving only tea, coffee, hot cocoa, lemon soda and orange soda to the sound of mellow French music.

Stop & Go Cafe CAFE
(2a Đ Ly Tu Trong) Run by a welcoming bearded poet, this Bohemian cafe is more a home than a business. Female guests are given a flower, while males get to listen to poetry recitals in several languages.

🛍 Shopping

If you are not continuing to Buon Ma Thuot, then it might be worth picking up some Vietnamese coffee in Dalat. The shops in and around the **Central Market** (⊙6am-6pm) are a good place to browse and bargain.

XQ Historical Village HANDICRAFTS
(http://tranhtheuxq.com; 258 Đ Mai Anh Dao, Ward 8) Less a historical village and more a historic shopping gallery, this compound includes 'museums' on various handicrafts, with plenty of opportunities to purchase anything from silk paintings to embroidered linen. It's best to get here by taxi, as it's quite far from town and difficult to find on your own.

ℹ Information

Medical Services
Lam Dong General Hospital (☑382 1369; 4 Đ Pham Ngoc Thach)

Money
Vietcombank (6 Đ Nguyen Thi Minh Khai) Changes travellers cheques and foreign currencies.
Vietin Bank (1 Đ Le Dai Hanh) Changes travellers cheques and foreign currencies.

Post
Main post office (14 Đ Tran Phu) Has international telephone and fax.

Travel Agencies
For guided motorbike tours, see the boxed text, p282. For adventure tours around Dalat, like mountain biking, rock climbing and trekking, see Activities, p277.
Dalat Travel Service (☑382 2125; dalattravel service@vnn.vn; Đ Nguyen Thi Minh Khai) Tours and vehicle rentals.
The Sinh Tourist (☑382 2663; www.thesinh tourist.vn; 4a Đ Bui Thi Xuan) Tours and open-tour bus bookings located within Trung Cang Hotel (p278).

ℹ Getting There & Away

AIR Vietnam Airlines (☑383 3499; 2 Đ Ho Tung Mau) has daily services to HCMC (680,000d), Danang (980,000d) and Hanoi (1,700,000d). Lien Khuong Airport is 30km south of the city.
BUS Dalat's **long-distance bus station** (Đ 3 Thang 4) is 1km south of Xuan Huong Lake, although many private services can make pick-ups and drop-offs at your hotel. Services are available to most of the country, including several to HCMC (110,000d, six to seven hours), Phan Rang

DALAT TRANSPORT CONNECTIONS

DESTINATION	BUS	AIR	CAR/MOTORBIKE
HCMC	US$7-10, 11hr, frequent	from US$34, 1hr, 4 daily	9hr
Mui Ne	n/a	n/a	5hr
Nha Trang	US$3.50-6, 5hr, frequent	n/a	4hr
Buon Ma Thuot	US$4-6, 5hr, frequent	n/a	4hr
Danang	n/a	from US$49, 1hr, 1 daily	15hr

(45,000d, 4½ hours), Nha Trang (70,000d to 100,000d, new road four hours, old road seven hours) and Buon Ma Thuot (from 85,000d, four hours). **Phuong Trang** (✆358 5858) operates a sleeper bus to HCMC (160,000d), departing hourly between 10pm and 1am.

Dalat is a major stop for open-tour buses. The Sinh Tourist (p281) has a daily bus to Mui Ne (100,000d, four hours) and Nha Trang (100,000d, five hours).

CAR & MOTORCYCLE From HCMC, taking the inland (Hwy 20) route to Dalat is faster than taking the coastal route (Hwy 1A). From Nha Trang, a new road shaves almost 70km off the old-road distance, and offers spectacular views to boot – a dream for motorbikers and cyclists. Besides wending across forested hills for much of the way, the road hits a height of 1700m at Hon Giao mountain, where it follows a breathtaking 33km pass. The roads linking Dalat to both Mui Ne and Nha Trang are two of the most beautiful in the south, so those with some motorbike experience might consider a triangular circuit.

The following are road distances from Dalat: Nha Trang (140km), Phan Rang (108km), Phan Thiet (247km) and HCMC (308km). Hwy 27 runs along a scenic route to Buon Ma Thuot (200km).

🛈 Getting Around

TO/FROM THE AIRPORT The Vietnam Airlines shuttle bus between Lien Khuong Airport and Dalat (35,000d, 30 minutes) is timed around flights, leaving from the door of the terminal and, in Dalat, from in front of 40 Đ Ho Tung Mau two hours before each departure.

Private taxis can be hired to make the trip for around 300,000d, while a motorbike taxi should cost about 200,000d.

BICYCLE Pedal power is a great way of seeing Dalat, but the hilly terrain and long distances between the sights make it hard work. Several hotels rent out bicycles and some provide them free to guests. It's also worth looking into cycling tours.

CAR Daily rentals (with driver) start at US$40; ask your hotel or try Dalat Travel Service (p281).

EASY DOES IT

For many travellers, the highlight of their trip to the central highlands is an off-the-beaten -track motorcycle tour with an Easy Rider. Besides the romance of cruising down endless highways, the Easy Riders' stock-in-trade is good company and insider knowledge, providing a brief but intimate window into highland life.

The flip side to the popularity of the Easy Riders is that now everyone claims to be one. In central Dalat, you can't walk down the street without being invited (sometimes harassed) for a tour. Some Easy Riders have banded together to protect 'their' brand, donning blue jackets and charging membership fees. Similarly, in Danang (said by some to be where they started out before they gained guidebook-endorsed eminence), Hoi An and Nha Trang, the Easy Rider moniker applies to other packs of motorcycle guides, with jackets of different colours.

Whether you're speaking to a jacket-wearing chap or an indie-spirited upstart, it's prudent to find out just what they can show you that you can't see on your own. Easy Riders don't come cheap. The going rate now is US$20 or more. Extended trips starting at US$50 per day run across the central highlands, across the south, even all the way north to Hanoi. It's also good to gauge the rider's command of English.

Not every jacketed Easy Rider is a good guide and many freelance riders are perfectly talented guides (perhaps because they don't have a 'brand' behind them). In the convoluted politics of the motorcycle-guide world, some freelancers now disdain the term Easy Rider and call themselves Free Riders or just plain motorcycle guides.

Before you commit to a long-haul trip, it's a good idea to test a rider out with a day trip. Is he a safe driver? Can you spend the next 48 hours or more with him? Are your bags safely strapped on the bike? Is the seat padded and the helmet comfortable (and clean)? Most riders can produce a logbook of glowing testimonials from past clients; also, check internet forums for recommendations.

One more important element to consider is the route. The most beautiful roads in southern Vietnam are actually the new coastal highways that link Dalat to Mui Ne and Nha Trang, plus the old road to the coast via Phan Rang, although this is currently in poor condition. The main roads through the Central Highlands, particularly the Buon Ma Thuot to Pleiku run, are not particularly scenic, so it may be wise to discuss a back-roads option. If breathtaking scenery is the order of the day, consider motorbiking the far north of Vietnam around the Northwest Loop, Sapa, Ha Giang and Cao Bang, or take a look at the area between the DMZ and Phong Nha-Ke Bang National Park.

MOTORCYCLE Dalat is too hilly for *cyclos*, but a motorbike is a good way of getting around. For short trips around town (10,000d to 20,000d), *xe om* drivers can be flagged down around the Central Market area. Self-drive motorbikes are 150,000d to 200,000d per day.

TAXI Taxis are easy to find; if you need to call for one, try **Mai Linh** (☑352 1111) or **Dalat Taxi** (☑355 6655).

Bao Loc

POP 145,000

The heartbeats of Bao Loc are tea, silk and the cultivation of mulberry leaves that make up the silkworms' diet. Roadside rest stops offer free samples of the local tea. There are also a few guesthouses here, making it a practical place to break the journey between HCMC (180km) and Dalat (118km); Easy Riders often stop here.

Nearby **Dambri Falls** (admission 10,000d) is one of the highest (90m), most magnificent and easily accessible waterfalls in Vietnam. To reach the falls, turn off the main highway north of Bao Loc and follow the road for 18km through tea and mulberry plantations. The high peak to your right is May Bay Mountain.

Ngoan Muc Pass

ELEV 980M

Known to the French as Bellevue Pass, Ngoan Muc Pass is 43km from Dalat, 64km from Phan Rang and 5km from Dan Nhim Lake (altitude 1042m). On a clear day you can see the ocean, 55km away. As the highway winds down the mountain it passes under two gargantuan water pipes that link the lake with the hydroelectric power station at the base of the pass.

South of the road (to the right as you face the ocean) you can see the steep tracks of the crémaillère (cog railway) linking Thap Cham with Dalat. At the top of the pass there's a **waterfall** next to the highway, pine forests and the old Bellevue train station.

Cat Tien National Park

☑061 / ELEV 700M

Cat Tien (☑366 9228; www.cattiennation alpark.vn; adult/child 50,000d/20,000d; ⊘7am-10pm) comprises an amazingly biodiverse area of lowland tropical rainforest. The 72,000-hectare park is one of the outstanding natural treasures in Vietnam, and the hiking, mountain biking and bird-watching here are the best in southern Vietnam. Always call ahead for reservations as the park can accommodate only a limited number of visitors. However, a word of caution: visitors rarely see any of the larger mammals resident in the park, so don't come expecting to encounter tigers and elephants.

In the 2nd century AD, the Cat Tien area was a religious centre of the Funan empire, and ancient Oc-Eo cultural relics have been discovered in the park. Cat Tien was hit hard by defoliants during the American War, but the large old-growth trees survived and the smaller plants have recovered. Just as importantly, the wildlife has made a comeback and in 2001 Unesco added Cat Tien National Park to its list of biosphere reserves. Since then, infrastructure has improved markedly with decent overnight options. It's worth spending at least two full days here, if possible.

Fauna in the park includes 326 bird species, 100 types of mammal, 79 types of reptile, 41 amphibian species, plus an incredible array of insects, including 400 or so species of butterfly. In the early 1990s, a rare group of Javan rhinoceros was discovered in the park, but conservationists now believe their number may have plummeted to an unsustainable level of just one or two ageing adults. Leopards are also believed to roam here. Rare birds in the park include the orange-necked partridge, green peafowl and Siamese fireback. There is also a healthy population of monkeys. Leeches are a less desirable member of the local fauna so come prepared, especially during the wet season.

◉ Sights & Activities

Cat Tien National Park can be explored on foot, by mountain bike, by 4WD and also by boat along the Dong Nai River. There are many well-established hiking trails in the park, but these require the services of a guide (from 250,000d), as well as transportation to and from the start of the trail.

The park also offers a **night safari** (300,000d), although deer are the only animals usually seen. Wherever you decide to go, be sure to book a guide in advance and take plenty of insect repellent.

Crocodile Swamp   LAKE

(Bau Sau; admission 100,000d, guide fee 300,000d, boat trip 300,000d) A visit to the Crocodile Swamp is popular. It involves a 9km drive from the park headquarters and a 4km trek to the swamp; the walk takes about three hours return. It may be possible for smaller groups (four or less) to spend the night at the ranger's post here. It's a good place to view the wildlife that comes to drink in the swamp.

Dao Tien Endangered
Primate Species Centre   NATURE RESERVE

(www.go-east.org; adult/child including boat ride 150,000/50,000d; ☺8am & 2pm) This centre, located on an island in the Dong Nai River near the park entrance, is a wonderful addition to the park. Linked to Monkey World in the UK, it's a rehabilitation centre hosting gibbons, langurs and loris that have been confiscated as pets or from traffickers. The eventual goal is to release the primates back into the wild. As well as viewing gibbons in a semiwild environment, you have the chance to hear their incredible calls when they are animated. The centre includes some fantastic fund-raising merchandise, like cuddly gibbons, bags and T-shirts.

☞ Tours

Although many travel agencies in HCMC operate tours to the park, we've received mixed reviews about the budget agencies. For a reputable customised birding, biking or hiking tour, contact **Sinhbalo Adventures** (☎3837 6766; www.sinhbalo.com; 283/20 Đ Pham Ngu Lao; ☺7.30am-noon & 1.30-5.30pm Mon-Fri, 7.30am-noon Sat) in HCMC.

🛏 Sleeping & Eating

The national park offers several accommodation options and there is a lovely privately run lodge. It might be wise to avoid weekends and holidays if possible, as this is when the Vietnamese descend in numbers.

TOP CHOICE Forest Floor Lodge   ECOLODGE

(☎366 9890; www.vietnamforesthotel.com; luxury tents from US$100, traditional houses from US$100; ❄@) This new ecolodge sets the standard for atmospheric accommodation in Vietnam's national parks. There are several lovely safari tents overlooking the Dong Nai River, and a range of rooms set in reclaimed, traditional wooden houses, including family-friendly suites with an extra bed.

The **Hornbill Bar-Restaurant** (meals from 75,000d) serves a good range of Vietnamese and international food and has a reassuring selection of wines and spirits. The lodge and restaurant are located across from Dao Tien Primate Centre, so it is often possible to see and hear gibbons on the island. The lodge can also arrange transfers to and from the park, as well as a range of activities within the park.

Cat Tien National Park   GUESTHOUSE

(☎366 9228; small tents/big tents 200,000/300,000d, bungalows from 500,000d; ❄) The park offers bungalow rooms and tented accommodation close to the park headquarters. The rooms are fairly basic, but include a bathroom. The large tents (sleeping up to 12...if you happen to be small Vietnamese students) operate on a communal basis, so these could be fun if you travel in a group.

Park Restaurants   CAFE, RESTAURANT

(☺7am-9pm) There are two small restaurants near the park entrance, including a simple thatch-roof canteen (mains 25,000d to 75,000d) and a fully-blown restaurant (mains 25,000d to 220,000d) serving a wider range of dishes just down the path. For 220,000d you'll get a full hot pot, which is quite the Vietnamese experience.

ℹ Getting There & Around

BICYCLE Bicycle hire is available in the park, starting from just 20,000d per day.

ELEPHANTS VERSUS THE PEOPLE

Elephants are found in Cat Tien National Park, but their presence has caused some controversy. In the early 1990s a herd of 10 hungry elephants fell into a bomb crater just outside Cat Tien. Local villagers took pity on the elephants and dug out a ramp to rescue them. Tragically, since then a number of villagers have been killed by rampaging elephants. In the longer term such conflicts are likely to continue because of the increasing competition between Vietnam's wildlife and its growing population for the same living space. Several elephants have been poisoned by villagers in recent years, according to national park staff, and their numbers are dwindling to dangerously low levels.

DON'T MISS

WILD GIBBON TREK

Trekking to see mountain gorillas, chimpanzees and golden monkeys is big business in the mountains of East Africa and now it is possible to trek with gibbons right here in Vietnam. A family of gibbons in Cat Tien has been habituated and this experience offers a rare insight into the lives of these primates. The trek (US$60 per person, maximum four people) runs daily and involves a 4am start to get out to the gibbons in time for their dawn chorus. Relax in a hammock as the forest slowly comes alive with their songs before watching the family go about their everyday business.

In the afternoon the trip includes a fully guided tour of the Dao Tien Primate Centre. All proceeds are ploughed back into the national park and assisting the rangers in their protection efforts. To avoid disappointment, book in advance through ecotourism@cat tiennationalpark.vn or call ahead (☏366 9228). Check out www.go-east.org for more on what to wear and rules of engagement. Thoroughly recommended.

BOAT One approach to Cat Tien National Park is to take a boat across Langa Lake and then go by foot from there. **Phat Tire Ventures** (☏063-382 9422; www.ptv-vietnam.com) is a reputable ecotour operator in Dalat and a good place to enquire about this.

BUS Take any Dalat-bound service (around 50,000d, four hours) and ask to be let off at Vuon Quoc Gia Cat Tien. From this junction, you can hire a motorbike (around 150,000d, but negotiate very hard) to cover the remaining 24km to the park. Or contact Forest Floor Lodge to arrange a car transfer from the main road.

Whichever way you come, you'll be dropped off at the park office, 100m before the boat that crosses the Dong Nai River to park headquarters. Buy your entrance ticket here, which includes the price of the boat crossing.

CAR & MOTORCYCLE The most common approach to the park is from Hwy 20, which connects HCMC with Dalat. To reach the park, follow the narrow 24km road, which branches west from Hwy 20 at Tan Phu, 125km north of HCMC and 175km south of Dalat. The road to the park is signposted at the junction, and with your own wheels getting there shouldn't be a hassle.

Buon Ma Thuot

☏0500 / POP 312,000 / ELEV 451M

The Ede name translates as 'Thuot's father's village', but Buon Ma Thuot has outgrown its rustic origins without acquiring any real charm. An affluent modern town, pronounced 'boon me tote' and also spelled as Ban Me Thuot, it is inundated by traffic from three highways and powdered with orange-brown dust. Its only saving grace is coffee: the region grows some of the best in Vietnam, plenty of which is sold and drunk in town. Buon Ma Thuot plays host to an annual Coffee Festival in March that sees gallons of the black nectar drunk and elephant races held in nearby Don village.

Most travellers stop in Buon Ma Thuot en route to the attractions around it: Yok Don National Park, a couple of striking waterfalls and heaps of minority villages. The province is home to 44 ethnic groups, including some who have migrated here from the north. Among indigenous hill tribes, the dominant groups are the Ede, Jarai, M'nong and Lao. However the government's policy of assimilation has been effective: nearly all of these groups now speak Vietnamese fluently.

Before WWII, this was a centre for big-game hunting, attracting Emperor Bao Dai, but the animals have all but disappeared. Towards the end of the American War, Buon Ma Thuot was a strategic but poorly defended South Vietnamese base. It fell to the North in a one-day surprise attack in March 1975, pushing the South into a retreat from which it never recovered.

The rainy season around Buon Ma Thuot lasts from May to October, though downpours are usually short. Because of its lower elevation, Buon Ma Thuot is warmer and more humid than Dalat. It is also very windy.

◉ Sights

Victory Monument MONUMENT
Smack in the centre of town, this monument commemorates the events of 10 March 1975 when VC and North Vietnamese troops liberated the city. It's an interesting piece of socialist realist sculpture, consisting of a column supporting a central group of figures holding a flag, with a modernist arch forming a rainbow over a concrete replica tank.

Ako Dhong Village NEIGHBOURHOOD
At the northern end of Buon Ma Thuot is this Ede village, a neat little community of stilt-house suburbia. Strolling around the village makes for a pleasant break from the down-town din, and you may be able to find some locals at work weaving traditional fabrics.

The village is about 1.5km from the centre of town and is an easy walk. Take Đ Phan Chu Trinh north and hang a left on Đ Tran Nhat Duat. The village is about 500m down the road, bordered to the east by Yang Sing Hotel and to the west by a cemetery.

Dak Lak Museum MUSEUM
(4 Đ Nguyen Du; admission 10,000d; ☉7.30-11am & 2-5pm) This musty, little-visited museum has a small display of cultural artefacts and photographs about indigenous minority groups. The Ho Chi Minh quotation, posted boldly over a golden bust of him in the main hall, blithely declares that all ethnic minori-ties are 'the children of Vietnam' and 'blood brothers' to the Vietnamese.

The museum is housed in the Bao Dai Villa, a grand French-colonial building that was one of the emperor's many residences.

Dak Lak Water Park SWIMMING POOL
(Đ Nguyen Chi Thanh; adult/child 35,000/25,000d; ☉8am-5.30pm) Strictly in the 'if you have time to kill' category, the waterslides at Dak Lak Water Park are a passable diversion on a hot afternoon. It's about 4km from town, just before the bus station.

🛏 Sleeping

Damsan Hotel HOTEL $$
(☎385 1234; www.damsanhotel.com.vn; 212-214 Đ Nguyen Cong Tru; r US$25-50; ✹@☎☂) The best all-rounder in town, this hotel comes with such unexpected extras as a swimming pool and tennis court, both set amid a care-fully manicured garden. Rooms are spacious and comfortable, some with views over nearby lush coffee plantations. The restau-rant is also well regarded by BMT standards.

Thanh Cong Hotel HOTEL $
(☎385 8243; daklaktour@dng.vnn.vn; 51 Đ Ly Thuong Kiet; r 220,000-400,000d; ✹@☎) Run by Dak Lak Tourist, this is one of the nicer places on Ly Thuong Kiet. Rooms with a bath-tub start from 280,000d, and all rates include breakfast.

Thanh Binh Hotel HOTEL $
(☎385 3812; 24 Đ Ly Thuong Kiet; r 200,000-240,000d; ✹@☎) Conveniently located in the middle of the guesthouse strip, this hotel has good-value rooms, although it is worth trying to secure one with a window.

Dakruco Hotel HOTEL $$$
(☎397 0888; www.dakrucohotels.com; 30 Đ Nguyen Chi Thanh; r US$65-200; ✹@☎☂) This new-comer is the most fancy place in town, as-piring to four-star status and with prices to match. Near the bus station, it is the place of choice for coffee traders and tour groups. Head out of town on D Nguyen Tat Thanh and you can't miss it when you hit the big roundabout near the bus station.

🍴 Eating & Drinking
It is fair to say that Buon Ma Thuot is not particularly famous for its cuisine.

Black & White Restaurant VIETNAMESE $$
(171 Đ Nguyen Cong Tru; mains 30,000-200,000d; ☉lunch & dinner) The most stylish restaurant in town by some distance, this wouldn't feel out of place in Hanoi or HCMC. Set over two floors, the menu includes delicious seafood, as well as sparrow and pigeon.

Thanh Loan VIETNAMESE $
(22 Đ Ly Thuong Kiet; mains 25,000d; ☉lunch & dinner) There's only one thing on the menu here: roll-your-own rice-paper rolls, with salad and herbs, fried pork, crunchy rice pa-per and raw garlic. Dip the rolls in either a meaty broth or a mixture of fish sauce and chilli. It's a light meal, full of fresh flavours.

Cafe Hoa Da Quy CAFE $
(173 Đ Nguyen Cong Tru) This stylish yet cosy three-storey bar-cafe is a popular night-time spot next door to the Black & White Restaurant. The rooftop seating is pleasant and cool, a good spot to sip a cold beer or a strong local coffee.

Hanoi Bakery BAKERY $
(123-125 Đ Le Hong Phong) Part bakery, part general store, this popular neighbourhood joint is known for its pastries and breads, as well as stocks of cheese and chocolate.

🛍 Shopping
Stock up on coffee here, as the price is lower and the quality higher than in HCMC or Ha-noi. Browse the coffee shop strip on Đ Ly Thuong Kiet before you buy.

ℹ Information
Medical Services
Dak Lak General Hospital (☎385 2665; 2 Đ Mai Hac De)

Buon Ma Thuot

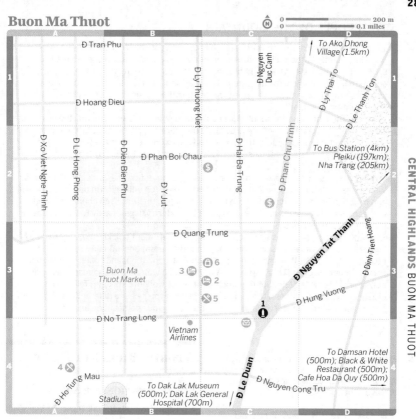

Money

Agribank (37 Đ Phan Boi Chau) Changes currency and travellers cheques.

Dong A Bank (9 Đ Phan Chu Trinh) Foreign-currency exchange and an ATM.

Post & Internet Access

Main post office (1 Đ No Trang Long) Also has internet access.

Travel Agencies

For tours of villages, waterfalls, Lak Lake and Yok Don National Park.

DakLak Tourist (☑ 385 8243; www.daklak tourist.com.vn; 51 Đ Ly Thuong Kiet) On the ground floor of Thanh Cong Hotel.

Damsan Tours (☑ 385 2505; damsantour@ dng.vnn.vn; 212-214 Đ Nguyen Cong Tru) Attached to the Damsan Hotel.

Vietnam Highland Travel (☑ 385 5009; high landco@dng.vnn.vn; Thanh Binh Hotel 24 Đ Ly Thuong Kiet) Experienced guides, homestays and off-the-beaten-track trekking trips.

Buon Ma Thuot

◉ Sights
1	Victory Monument	C3

🛏 Sleeping
2	Thanh Binh Hotel	C3
3	Thanh Cong Hotel	B3

🍴 Eating
4	Hanoi Bakery	A4
5	Thanh Loan	C3

🛍 Shopping
6	Coffee Shop Strip	C3

ℹ Information
	DakLak Tourist	(see 3)
	Vietnam Highland Travel	(see 2)

THE PEOPLE OF THE MOUNTAIN

The uneasy relationship in the central highlands between the hill tribes and the Vietnamese majority dates back centuries, when Vietnamese expansion pushed the tribes up into the mountains. While French-colonial rule recognised the tribes as a separate community, South Vietnam later attempted to assimilate them through such means as abolishing tribal schools and courts, prohibiting the construction of stilt houses and appropriating their land.

In response the minority people formed nationalist guerrilla movements, the best-known of which was the Front Unifié de Lutte des Races Opprimées (FULRO) or the United Front for the Struggle of the Oppressed Races. In the 1960s the hill tribes were courted by the US as allies against North Vietnam, and were trained by the CIA and US Special Forces.

They paid dearly for this after the war, when government policies brought more ethnic Vietnamese into the highlands, along with clampdowns on education in native languages and religious freedom (many hill-tribe people belong to unauthorised churches). Many of these minority people have been relocated to modern villages, partly to discourage slash-and-burn agriculture. It also speeds up assimilation.

In 2001 and 2004 protests erupted, which the government quickly and, according to human-rights organisations, violently suppressed. International human-rights groups point to more deaths than the government admits to, and thousands of hill-tribe people fled to Cambodia or the US afterwards. Ask the ethnic Vietnamese and many will probably repeat the state's line that the protests were the work of outsiders. Talk to any organisation that works with the minority people and you'll hear a different story: one of continuing government surveillance, harassment, religious persecution and abuse.

Travel Permits

Permits are required to visit minority villages in the area, except for Ako Dhong and Ban Don. Any of the local travel agencies can make the arrangements.

ℹ Getting There & Around

AIR There are daily **Vietnam Airlines** (⟁395 4442; 17-19 Đ No Trang Long) flights serving HCMC (from 983,000d) and Hanoi (from 2,044,000d), and services four times a week to Danang (from 983,000d). The airport is 8km east of town. A taxi should cost about 120,000d.

BUS Buon Ma Thuot's **bus station** (71 Đ Nguyen Chi Thanh) is about 4km from the centre, with plenty of services to Dalat (80,000d, four hours), Nha Trang (85,000d, five hours), Pleiku (85,000d, four hours) and Kon Tum (90,000d, five hours).

CAR & MOTORCYCLE Highway 26 links the coast with Buon Ma Thuot, intersecting Hwy 1A at Ninh Hoa (157km), 34km north of Nha Trang. The road is surfaced and in good condition, although fairly steep in places. Highway 14 to Pleiku (199km) is in very good shape, while Hwy 27 is a scenic sealed road connecting Buon Ma Thuot with Dalat (200km, via Lak Lake). Though the latter is full of twists and turns, it's in reasonable shape.

TAXI For reliable metered fares, use **Mai Linh** (⟁381 9819).

Around Buon Ma Thuot
⟁0500

YOK DON NATIONAL PARK

🖉 **Yok Don National Park** (⟁378 3049; www.yokdonnationalpark.vn; admission free as part of package), the largest of Vietnam's nature reserves, has been gradually expanded and today encompasses 115,545 hectares of mainly dry deciduous forest. The park runs all the way up to the border with Cambodia, with the beautiful Srepok River flowing through it.

Yok Don is home to 67 mammal species, 38 of which are listed as endangered in Indochina and 17 of those endangered worldwide. The park habitat accommodates elephants, tigers, leopards and rare red wolves, as well as nearly 250 different species of bird – including a pair of critically endangered giant ibis (Thaumatibis gigantea). More common wildlife includes muntjac, monkeys and snakes.

Within the park's boundaries are four minority villages, predominantly M'nong but also with Ede and Lao people. Three villages are accessible while the fourth is deep inside the park. The M'nong are a matrilineal tribe known for their skills in capturing wild elephants.

The delicate balance between ecological conservation and the preservation of local cultures is a challenge, considering the poverty of the region's people and their traditional means of survival, such as hunting. However, the Vietnamese government is working with international agencies such as the United Nations to manage this balance, aiming towards education and community participation in conservation practices.

To explore the national park, you'll have to either engage your own guide from Buon Ma Thuot or pick one up at the park entrance. Guides (150,000d for basic sightseeing or 250,000d per half day for trekking) are available and can lead overnight treks (1,000,000d including overnight at one of the ranger stations); there's also a 100,000d boat fee to cross the Srepok River. It's possible to arrange a night visit to see the park's nocturnal inhabitants.

Elephant rides and treks can also be arranged. A direct booking at the park costs 200,000d per hour per person or from 4,000,000d for a full-day trek.

◉ Sights & Activities

Most of the tourist action centres on the village of **Ban Don** in Ea Sup district, 45km northwest of Buon Ma Thuot. The village is 5km beyond the turn-off into the national park and often gets overrun with busloads of visitors, particularly at the **Ban Don Tourist Centre** (☑378 3020; ttdl.buon don@gmail.com). Traditional activities such

---

AN ELEPHANT'S LIFE

Behind the apparently glorious status of the elephant in Vietnam is a tortured history spanning centuries. Prized by kings, these gentle and intelligent creatures were trapped around present-day Yok Don National Park by M'nong hunters. The animals were then tamed through savage beatings before being presented as royal gifts or put to work by the tribe.

And what work it was – elephants were (and still are) used as combination bulldozers, fork-lifts and semitrailers. Now they're more often seen in the lucrative tourist industry, lugging people through the forests or as part of minority festivals.

It's not necessarily a better life. Many elephants were trapped as babies so that they would be easier to train – neglecting the fact that they need their mother's milk up to the age of four in order to develop healthily. It's also easy to overestimate what adult elephants can tolerate. Elephant skin appears to be rough and impermeable, but it's as sensitive as human skin, vulnerable to sunburn, dirt and infections.

Another misconception is that elephants are strong, even indefatigable, but their spines were not designed to carry heavy burdens for extended periods of time. Above all, they need 250kg of food a day – an expensive undertaking, even for the most successful owner.

Before you decide on an elephant ride, take a closer look at the animal and its work environment:

» The elephant should have a shaded area to rest, with clean water and food. There should be enough slack in the chain so that it can move around. Given enough space, elephants don't defecate where they eat (who would want to?).

» The seat placed on the elephant should be made of light bamboo, not heavy wood, and there should be about seven layers of padding between the seat and the skin. There should be rubber hoses to line the binding ropes, or they will abrade the skin horribly.

» The elephant should work for only four or five hours a day, bearing up to only two adults at a time.

» The elephant caretaker should not have to use the bullhook or whip on the elephant with every command.

Though elephant trapping was banned in 1990, it was not strictly enforced. Vietnam's native elephant species has been listed as endangered since 1976 and it's estimated that only a few hundred elephants remain in the highlands. Without elephant sanctuaries or alternative employment, their fate seems grim: a lifetime of tourist rides, illicit employment in logging and construction, or, if the money runs out, abandonment or death.

Compiled with assistance from Jin Pyn Lee

as gong performances and drinking wine from a communal jug (everybody drinks at the same time through very long straws) are held for the edification of foreigners. Near the Tourist Centre a 200m-long bamboo **suspension bridge** (admission 20,000d) crosses the Srepok River – a pretty, shaded walk but there's nothing 'ethnic' about it.

🛏 Sleeping & Eating

At the park entrance, 5km southeast of Ban Don, **Yok Don Guesthouse** (☎378 3049; r US$19; ❄) has rooms with hot water. You can also overnight at one of three **forest stations** (per person US$5) located 7km, 17km and 25km into the park. These are simple huts used by park rangers.

In Ban Don, contact Ban Don Tourist Centre about staying in minority **stilt houses** (per person 150,000d) or **bungalows** (per person 300,000d). The bungalows are either beside the lake or out on nearby Aino Island, reached via a rickety series of bamboo suspension bridges. There is a restaurant in Ban Don, which sometimes hosts performances of gong music and dancing for groups.

ℹ Getting There & Around

BUS Local buses head from Buon Ma Thuot bus station to Yok Don National Park (20,000d, 40km, hourly).

XE OM Motorbike taxis in Buon Ma Thuot can take you to the park for around 200,000/300,000d one way/return.

DRAY SAP & DRAY NUR FALLS

Located on the Krong Ana River, these stunning **waterfalls** (admission 20,000d) offer good riverside trekking opportunities. From the car park, the first one is the 100m-wide **Dray Sap** ('smoky falls' in Ede). For a better view, head down the path beside the river to a suspension bridge that crosses the river.

Across the bridge, follow the path through cornfields for another 250m. It leads to another bridge overlooking the 30m-wide **Dray Nur** waterfall. At the end of this bridge is a dirt path that brings you closer to Dray Nur.

However, bear in mind that due to the many dams located on the Srepok River, these falls have no water during the dry season.

To reach the falls, follow Đ Le Duan out of Buon Ma Thuot until it becomes Đ Nguyen Thi Dinh and eventually Hwy 14 heading south. After 12km look left for the sign for the turn-off to the waterfalls. Drive for another 11km through a small industrial zone, then farmland, before you arrive at the entrance to the falls.

LAK LAKE

The largest natural body of water in the central highlands, Lak Lake (Ho Lak) covers 700 hectares in the rainy season, shrinking in the dry season to 400 hectares surrounded by rice paddies. While there are pockets of tourist development, it's nowhere near as orchestrated as Ban Don Village near Yok Don National Park.

The scenery around the lake is a postcard portrait of rural life, which sufficiently impressed Emperor Bao Dai enough to build yet another of his palaces overlooking the lake. There are two minority villages around the lake that often receive visitors. On the south shores near the town of Lien Son lies **Jun village**, a fairly traditional M'nong settlement filled with rattan and wooden stilt houses. The villagers are surprisingly nonplussed about visitors, even though DakLak Tourist has a small set-up and runs elephant rides (US$30 per hour). The second village of **M'lieng** is on the southwestern shore and can be reached by elephant or boat; enquire at DakLak Tourist.

🛏 Sleeping & Eating

If you're interested in staying overnight in one of the minority villages, Mr Duc at **Cafe Duc Mai** (☎358 6280; 268 Đ Nguyen Tat Thanh; per person US$5) can organise a mattress in one of several traditional stilt longhouses, along with activities such as gong concerts, elephant rides, and kayaking or walking tours.

🌿 **Lak Resort**   HOTEL **$$**
(☎358 6164; bungalows US$27, shared longhouses US$10; ❄@☎☎) In a pretty lakeside setting, this resort has spacious bungalows set around a reasonably clean swimming pool. Cheaper dorms are available in traditional minority longhouses, although US$10 seems a little optimistic for a threadbare mattress. The lakeside restaurant offers Vietnamese meals from about 30,000d to 100,000d. More impressively, the resort is committed to employing at least 51% M'nong staff.

Bao Dai Villa   COLONIAL HOTEL **$$**
(☎358 6164; r US$30-50) Pretend to live like a king at this former royal residence on a hilltop overlooking the lake. It is actually not particularly palatial, but there are six enormous rooms, dressed up with photographs of the emperor and empress. The small cafe

HO CHI MINH TRAIL

This legendary route was not one but many paths that formed the major supply link for the North Vietnamese and VC during the American War. Supplies and troops leaving from the port of Vinh headed inland along mountainous jungle paths, crossing in and out of Laos, and eventually arrived near Saigon. With all the secrecy, propaganda and confusion regarding the trail, it's hard to say how long it was in full; estimates range from over 5500km (said the US military) to more than 13,000km (boasted the North Vietnamese).

While elephants were initially used to cross the Truong Son Mountains into Laos, eventually it was sheer human power that shouldered supplies down the trail, sometimes supplemented by ponies, bicycles or trucks. Travelling from the 17th Parallel to the vicinity of Saigon took about six months in the mid-1960s; years later, with a more complex network of paths, the journey took only six weeks but it was still hard going.

Each person started out with a 36kg pack of supplies, as well as a few personal items (eg a tent, spare uniform and snake antivenom). What lay ahead was a rugged and mountainous route, plagued by flooding, disease and the constant threat of American bombing. At their peak, more than 500 American air strikes hit the trail every day and more ordnance was dropped on it than was used in all the theatres of war in WWII.

Despite these shock-and-awe tactics and the elaborate electronic sensors along the McNamara Line, the trail was never blocked. Most of it has returned to the jungle, but you can still follow sections of the trail today. Note that this is usually the more developed trail from the early 1970s, as the older trail was over the border in Laos. The Ho Chi Minh Hwy is the easiest way to get a fix; it's an incredible mountain road running along the spine of the country. Starting near Hanoi, it passes through some popular tourist destinations and former battlefields, including the Phong Nha Cave, Khe Sanh, Aluoi, Kon Tum and Buon Ma Thuot on its way to Saigon. The most spectacular sections include the roller-coaster ride through the Phong Nha-Ke Bang National Park, where looming karsts are cloaked in jungle, and pretty karsts north of the Phong Nha Cave that are punctuated with traditional villages.

Travel this route by car (or 4WD), motorbike or even bicycle if you are training for the King of the Mountains jersey; or arrange a tour through the Easy Riders in Dalat (see boxed text, p282) or one of the leading motorbike touring companies in Hanoi (see p520). **Explore Indochina** (www.exploreindochina.com) specialise in trail tours. **Hoi An Motorbike Adventures** (www.motorbiketours-hoian.com) offer shorter rides along sections between Hoi An and Phong Nha.

here only serves drinks; for meals, head down to Lak Resort.

🛈 Getting There & Away

BUS Public buses to Lak Lake leave regularly from the Buon Ma Thuot bus station (20,000d).

MOTORBIKE Lak Lake is located on the mountainous road between Dalat (154km southeast) and Buon Ma Thuot (50km north). It's regularly visited on the Easy Rider trail. A day trip on the back of a motorbike from Buon Ma Thuot should cost around 200,000d, including waiting time. All the tour agencies in Buon Ma Thuot offer tours.

Pleiku

♪ 059 / POP 250,000 / ELEV 785M

The rather forgettable capital of Gia Lai province, Pleiku (or Playcu) is better known as a strategic American and South Vietnamese base during the American War than for any postwar accomplishments. It makes an adequate pit stop, but there's little to detain a traveller for more than a few hours. Torched by departing South Vietnamese soldiers in 1975, the city was rebuilt in the 1980s with help from the Soviet Union, which thoroughly explains its lack of appeal today.

In 2001 and 2004 Pleiku was the scene of hill-tribe protests against the government (see the boxed text, p288); the latter promptly responded by prohibiting foreigners from visiting the area. While these rules have gradually been relaxed and the province is safe for travel, you'll need a permit to visit the minority villages around here. Venturing out without one is not recommended, unless you enjoy being questioned by the police.

When US troops departed in 1973 the South Vietnamese kept Pleiku as their main combat base in the area. They fled the advancing VC in 1975, and the civilian population of Pleiku and nearby Kon Tum fled with them. The stampede to the coastline along the only road, Hwy 7, became known as the 'Convoy of Tears' as they were relentlessly attacked by North Vietnamese forces en route; it's estimated that only a quarter or a third of the 100,000 people survived.

◉ Sights

Ho Chi Minh Museum   MUSEUM
(1 Phan Dinh Phuong; admission free; ◷8-11am & 1-4.30pm Mon-Fri) The Ho Chi Minh Museum offers the usual paeans to Uncle Ho, with an emphasis on his affinity for hill-tribe people and their love for him. There are also displays about Bahnar hero Anh Hung Nup (1914–98), who led the hill tribes against the French and Americans. There's a **statue** (cnr Đ Le Loi & Đ Tran Hung Dao) of him nearby.

🛏 Sleeping & Eating

Duc Long Gia Lai Hotel   HOTEL $
(🖀387 6303; thienhc@diglgroup.com; 95-97 Đ Hai Ba Trung; r 180,000-300,000d; ✴@🛜) The smart spotless rooms in this hotel are the best value in town. The more expensive rooms have balconies and corner tubs. There is little English spoken, but good coffee is available in the adjacent cafe.

Dien Hong Lake Tourist Village   HOTEL $
(🖀371 6450; Đ Ho Dien Hong; s/d 300,000/ 360,000d; ✴) For peace and quiet away from the busy centre, opt for this neat row of bungalows on the shore of an artificial lake. Rooms are still in good shape and come with all the mod cons.

My Tam   VIETNAMESE $
(3 Đ Quang Trung; meals from 30,000d; ◷lunch & dinner) A hole-in-the-wall joint where the house speciality is roasted chicken, crisped to perfection and served with rice cooked with tomato and garlic.

Hoang Ha Cafe   CAFE
(26 Đ Nguyen Van Troi) A pair of solemn arowana fish greets you at the entrance to this three-storey cafe. The decor is as modern as it gets in Pleiku, and there's a good range of cocktails.

ℹ Information

A permit (US$10) and guide (US$20) are compulsory to visit villages in Gia Lai province. This puts many travellers off, who usually skip Pleiku and head north to Kon Tum. Gia Lai Tourist can arrange the permit and guide as part of one of its packages.

BIDV (1 Đ Nguyen Van Troi) Foreign exchange and credit-card advances.

Gia Lai Tourist (🖀387 4571; www.gialaitourist .com; 215 Đ Hung Vuong) English- and French-speaking guides who lead a variety of tours.

Main post office (69 Đ Hung Vuong)

Vietin Bank (1 Đ Tran Hung Dao) Foreign exchange and credit-card advances.

ℹ Getting There & Around

AIR Vietnam Airlines (🖀382 4680; 18 Đ Le Lai) has daily flights to Hanoi (from 1,500,000d), HCMC (from 900,000d) and Danang (from 900,000d). **Air Mekong** (🖀08-3514 6666; www.airmekong.info) also offers regular flights and shares the Vietnam Airlines office. The airport is about 5km from the town and accessible by taxi (80,000d) or xe om (around 40,000d).

BUS Pleiku's **bus station** (45 Đ Ly Nam De) is located about 2.5km southeast of town. Regular buses head to Buon Ma Thuot (85,000d, four

---

TO DIE JARAI

The Jarai minority of the Pleiku area honour their dead in graveyards set up like miniature villages. These graveyards are located to the west of the village, where the sun sets.

Each grave is marked with a shelter or bamboo stakes. Carved wooden figures are placed along the edge, often pictured in a squatting position with their hands over their faces in an expression of mourning. A jar is placed on the grave that represents the deceased person, and objects that the deceased might need in the next world are buried with them.

For seven years after the death, relatives bring food to the grave and pass death anniversaries at the gravesite, mourning and celebrating the deceased by feasting and drinking rice wine. After the seventh year, the spirit is believed to have moved on from the village and the grave is abandoned.

BORDER CROSSING: LE THANH–O YADAW

Remote and rarely used by foreigners, this border crossing lies 90km from Pleiku and 64km from Ban Lung, Cambodia. Travelling from Vietnam, visas are available on arrival in Cambodia, but not the reverse. If travelling from Cambodia, you must obtain your Vietnam visa in advance.

The road has been improved on the Cambodian side of the border and there are now daily minibuses connecting Ban Lung and the border, but currently no international services.

From Pleiku there is a local bus leaving several times a day for Moc Den (30,000d, two hours, 80km), where another bus (20,000d, 15km) heads to the border. After entering Cambodia at O Yadaw, you'll have to ask around for a seat on a minibus (30,000r or US$7.50) or motorbike (US$15) to Ban Lung. Departing early should make it easier to arrange affordable transport on the Cambodian side.

Heading from Ban Lung to Pleiku, take a morning minibus to the border, then wait for a bus heading to Moc Den or Duc Co (20,000d); from either town you can connect to Pleiku. There are *xe om* waiting on the Vietnamese side, who will swear that there are no bus services to Pleiku in order to drive a hard bargain.

hours), Kon Tum (15,000d, one hour) and Quy Nhon (85,000d, four hours). It's also possible to catch buses towards Cambodia (see the boxed text, 'Border Crossing: Le Thanh–O Yadaw') or through to Laos (see the boxed text, p296).

Pleiku sits at the intersection of Hwys 14 and 19, linking it to Buon Ma Thuot (199km), Quy Nhon (186km) and Kon Tum (47km).

Kon Tum

📞 060 / POP 145,000 / ELEV 525M

There is not a whole lot of action in Kon Tum, but it makes a good base to explore the surrounding countryside. Most foreigners who pass here are on their way to see hill-tribe villages (there are 700 dotting the area), to pick up the Ho Chi Minh Hwy or to cross the remote border to Laos. Besides a couple of Bahnar villages on the edge of town, there's little in the way of conventional sightseeing spots.

Kon Tum saw its share of combat during the American War. A major battle between the South and North Vietnamese took place in and around Kon Tum in the spring of 1972, when the area was devastated by hundreds of American B-52 raids. In March 1975 the South withdrew from the province after Buon Ma Thuot fell to the North and many civilians joined them in the 'Convoy of Tears'.

More recently, in the 2004 protests against government policies in the highlands, hill tribes in Kon Tum province clashed with police and soldiers. On the surface things have cooled off, but relations between the hill tribes and the authorities remain fraught.

⊙ Sights

Minority Villages NEIGHBOURHOODS

There are several clusters of Bahnar villages on the periphery of Kon Tum, where cows, pigs, chickens and children ramble nonchalantly through the dirt lanes. These neighbourhoods look (and are) significantly poorer than the town itself. Village life centres on the traditional *rong* house (*nha rong*), a tall thatched-roof community house built on stilts. The stilts were originally for protection from elephants, tigers and other animals. *Rong* houses are usually locked, unless they're hosting community meetings, weddings, festivals or prayer sessions.

The three closest village clusters lie to the east, south and west of town. To the east is the original Kon Tum village that the modern town grew out of. It's made up of two villages: **Kon Tum Konam** (Lower Kon Tum) and **Kon Tum Kopong** (Upper Kon Tum), each with its own *rong* house. To the south of town is the village **Kon Harachot**, in the middle of which lies the Vinh Son 2 orphanage (see the boxed text, p295). The cluster to the west is near the hospital and comprises about five villages.

Generally the local people welcome tourists and it's fine to wander around the village. But ask permission before pointing a camera into people's faces or homes. Some of the older people might be conversant in French but not English. You also probably won't see people in traditional garb unless they're on their way to Mass in the Bahnar

Kon Tum

Kon Tum

⊙ Sights
1	Immaculate Conception Cathedral.............................C3
2	Kon Harachot...................................B3
3	Kon Tum Konam................................D3
4	Kon Tum Kopong..............................D2
5	Seminary & Hill-Tribe Museum......................................C2
6	Vinh Son 1 Orphanage.....................C3
7	Vinh Son 2 Orphanage.....................B3

⊜ Sleeping
8	Dakbla Hotel....................................A3
9	Family Hotel.....................................B2
10	Indochine Hotel.............................A3
11	Viet Nga Hotel................................A3

✕ Eating
12	Dakbla Restaurant.........................A3
13	Quan 58...C1

⊙ Drinking
14	Eva Café..D1

ⓘ Information
	Highland Eco Tours....................(see 11)
15	Kon Tum General Hospital................A1
	Kon Tum Tourist..........................(see 8)

language, held on Sunday nights at the Immaculate Conception Cathedral.

If you have time to spend several days here, Kon Tum Tourist can arrange village homestays. Because the guides here are careful not to intrude too frequently on any one village, visitors are always welcomed and traditions remain intact. Day trips are also available from about US$25 for a guide and an additional US$2 to US$12 per person, depending on the places visited. Permits are no longer required, but be on the

safe side by checking in with Kon Tum Tourist before venturing off.

Immaculate Conception Cathedral CHURCH
(Đ Nguyen Hue) This is a beautiful French wooden cathedral with a dark front, sky-blue trim and wide terraces. Inside it's light, airy and elegant. The heart of the 160-year-old Kon Tum diocese, it primarily serves the ethnic minority community and the altar is bedecked in traditional woven fabrics.

Seminary & Hill-Tribe Museum
MUSEUM
(Đ Tran Hung Dao; admission free; ⏰8-11am & 2-4pm Mon-Sat) This lovely old Catholic seminary wouldn't look out of place in a provincial French town. Built in 1934, it has a chapel with beautiful wood carvings and a 'Traditional Room' upstairs that functions as an unofficial museum of hill-tribe life and the Kon Tum diocese. You may have to ask one of the seminary residents to unlock the museum for you.

🛏 Sleeping

Family Hotel
HOTEL $
(☎386 2448; phongminhkt@yahoo.com; 55 & 61 Đ Tran Hung Dao; r US$15-25; ✳@🛜) The allure of this place is not immediately apparent from the street, but wander through to the back of the property and there is a lovely garden courtyard with bungalow rooms. The friendly family has a small restaurant here and there's live music some nights.

Dakbla Hotel
HOTEL $
(☎386 3333; 2 Đ Phan Dinh Phung; r US$10; ✳@🛜) An old government-run monolith. Don't be put off by the exterior as the rooms have been recently renovated and are great value with pucker new bathrooms.

Viet Nga Hotel
HOTEL $
(☎224 0247; 160 Đ Nguyen Hue; r US$8-15; ✳@🛜) Rooms at this simple family-run minihotel are spacious and light. Amenities include satellite TV, a mini fridge and hot-water showers.

Indochine Hotel
HOTEL $$
(☎386 3335; www.indochinehotel.vn; 30 Đ Bach Dang; r US$25-33; ✳@🛜) The smartest hotel in town. Room rates have dropped in the past few years, making it better value than before. Opt for a spacious river-view room to really take advantage of the location.

🍴 Eating & Drinking

Dakbla Restaurant
VIETNAMESE $
(168 Đ Nguyen Hue; dishes 20,000-120,000d; ⏰8am-10pm) One of Kon Tum's few genuine restaurants, Dakbla has a good Vietnamese menu spiced up with meats like wild boar and frog. The ethnic decor is tastefully done with tribal artefacts adorning the walls.

Quan 58
VIETNAMESE $
(58 Đ Phan Chu Trinh; hot pot 90,000d; ⏰lunch & dinner) All goat, all the time. This modest operation will serve you goat just about any way you might want to eat it: steamed (de hap),

---

SUFFER THE LITTLE CHILDREN

A popular 'sightseeing' stop for tourists passing through Kon Tum are the **Vinh Son 1 and 2 orphanages**, run by the Sisters of the Miraculous Medal. Each orphanage is home to about 200 mostly hill-tribe children. Not all are orphans – some have been placed here by families who are unable to support them.

Although both orphanages welcome visitors and foreign support, having large groups of tourists suddenly descend upon them can be disruptive to the children's lessons and other learning activities. Like children anywhere in the world, the kids are happy to be distracted, particularly by foreigners keen to fawn upon and cuddle them. They enjoy these feel-good moments, but you have to wonder about the emotional impact if this becomes their typical interaction with foreigners.

If you plan to visit, their minders ask that you avoid giving the children sweets or candy; their dentists will thank you for it. If you'd like to bring a gift, consider some fruit or nutritious fresh food instead. Other possible gifts are clothing, toys and school supplies, though it's hard to precisely anticipate what's needed.

Monetary contributions are of course appreciated, but standards of transparency and accountability are not what Westerners are used to. Another way is to use an intermediary, such as California-based **Friends of Vinh Son Montagnard Orphanage** (www .friendsofvso.org), Pennsylvania-based **Friends of Central Highlands, Vietnam** (www .fochvn.org) or American NGO **East Meets West Foundation** (www.eastmeetswest.org); the latter runs a dental program for the orphanages and other education projects in the highlands. There are many orphanages and projects in Kon Tum (and all over Vietnam) that need help.

Vinh Son 1 is just behind the Immaculate Conception Cathedral on Đ Nguyen Hue. Vinh Son 2 is in Kon Harachot, a small village at the southern edge of town; it's at the end of the second dirt track on the right after the small paddock.

BORDER CROSSING: BO Y–PHOU KEAU

The Bo Y–Phou Keau border crossing lies 86km northwest of Kon Tum and 119km north-east of Attapeu (Laos). Although it opened to tourists in 2006, some locals will swear it isn't open. Vietnamese visas aren't available at this border, but Lao visas can be arranged.

Coming from Vietnam, buses leave Pleiku at 8am daily for Attapeu (240,000d, eight hours, 250km), continuing to Pakse (320,000d, 12 hours, 440km). Kon Tum Tourist can arrange for you to join the bus when it passes through Kon Tum at 9.30am. In the opposite direction, buses leave Pakse and pass through Attapeu en route to Kon Tum and Pleiku. **Mai Linh Express** (☎391 3888; www.mailinh.vn) also runs daily buses on this route.

There are also buses from Quy Nhon several times a week, passing through Pleiku and Kon Tum en route to Attapeu and Pakse. The schedule fluctuates and it's best to inquire at the bus station for the latest details. Prices range from 250,000d to US$16 depending on the bus company.

Crossing the border independently can be a challenge. On the Vietnam side, the near-est major town is Ngoc Hoi, which can be reached by bus from Kon Tum (30,000d, 1½ hours, 60km). You'll have to catch a minibus or *xe om* from Ngoc Hoi to cover the 14km to the border. On the Laos side, things are even quieter and you'll be at the mercy of passing traffic to hitch a ride onwards. It's best to take a through bus from Kon Tum or Pleiku, as local transport invites rip offs.

grilled *(de nuong)*, sautéed *(de xao lan)*, cur-ried *(de cari)* and the ever-popular hot pot *(lau de)*.

Eva Cafe CAFE $
(1 Đ Phan Chu Trinh) A cosy neighbourhood cafe with plenty of quirk, from the tree house-like setting to the solemn tribal masks overhead. A nice place to unwind with a beer or coffee, as local couples have established.

ⓘ Information

BIDV (1 Đ Tran Phu) Has an ATM, exchanges US dollars and gives cash advances on major credit cards.

Highlands Eco Tours (☎391 2788; www .vietnamhighlands.com; 41 Đ Ho Tung Mau) Another independently run travel company specialising in village visits and homestays in off-the-beaten-track communities.

Kon Tum General Hospital (☎386 2565; 224a Đ Ba Trieu)

Kon Tum Tourist (☎386 1626; ktourist@dng .vnn.vn; 2 Đ Phan Dinh Phung) Located in the Dakbla Hotel, this agency has English-speaking staff who can arrange tours to Bahnar and Jarai villages, including homestays.

Main post office (205 Đ Le Hong Phong)

Vietcombank (108 Đ Le Hong Phong)

ⓘ Getting There & Around

AIR Vietnam Airlines (☎386 2282; 131 Đ Ba Trieu) offers flights with Vietnam Airlines and Air Mekong; the nearest airport is in Pleiku.

BUS Kon Tum's **bus station** (279 Đ Phan Dinh Phung) has plenty of services to Pleiku (20,000d, one hour) and Danang (107,000d, four hours). From Kon Tum, Hwy 14 runs to Pleiku (49km south) and Danang (300km north).

XE OM Kon Tum is easy to traverse on foot, but *xe om* are in ready supply. It shouldn't cost more than 20,000d to get anywhere on the back of a bike.

TAXI If you need a taxi, try **Mai Linh** (☎395 5555).

Ho Chi Minh City

♪08 / POP: 7.4 MILLION

Best Places to Eat

» Cuc Gach Quan (p329)
» Nha Hang Ngon (p325)
» Lion City (p329)
» Pho Hoa (p329)
» Temple Club (p325)

Best Places to Stay

» Giang & Son (p322)
» Hong Han (p323)
» Ma Maison (p324)
» Park Hyatt (p321)
» Ngoc Son (p324)

Why Go?

Ho Chi Minh City (HCMC) is Vietnam at its most dizzying: a high-octane city of commerce and culture that has driven the whole country forward with its limitless energy. It is a living organism that breathes life and vitality into all who settle here, and visitors cannot help but be hauled along for the ride.

From the finest of hotels to the cheapest of guesthouses, the classiest of restaurants to the tastiest of street stalls, the choicest of boutiques to the scrum of the markets, HCMC has it all. Wander through timeless alleys to ancient pagodas before fast-forwarding into the future in designer malls beneath sleek skyscrapers. The ghosts of the past live on in buildings that one generation ago witnessed a city in turmoil, but the real beauty of the former Saigon's urban collage is that these two worlds blend so seamlessly into one thrilling, seething mass. Put simply, there's nowhere else quite like it.

When to Go
Ho Chi Minh City

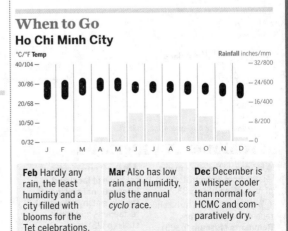

Feb Hardly any rain, the least humidity and a city filled with blooms for the Tet celebrations.

Mar Also has low rain and humidity, plus the annual *cyclo* race.

Dec December is a whisper cooler than normal for HCMC and comparatively dry.

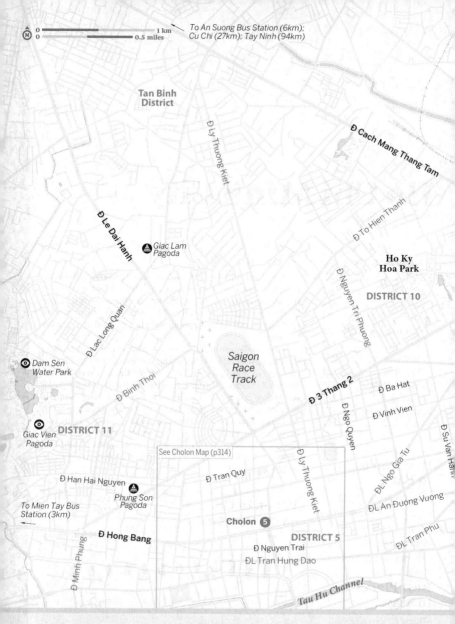

To An Suong Bus Station (6km);
Cu Chi (27km); Tay Ninh (94km)

0   1 km
0   0.5 miles

**Tan Binh
District**

Đ Cach Mang Thang Tam

Đ Ly Thuong Kiet

Đ Le Dai Hanh

Đ To Hien Thanh

Giac Lam
Pagoda

**Ho Ky
Hoa Park**

Đ Nguyen Tri Phuong

DISTRICT 10

Đ Lac Long Quan

Dam Sen
Water Park

Đ Binh Thoi

*Saigon
Race
Track*

Đ 3 Thang 2

Đ Ba Hat

Đ Ngo Quyen

Đ Vinh Vien

Giac Vien
Pagoda

DISTRICT 11

ĐL Ngo Gia Tu

Đ Su Van Hanh

See Cholon Map (p314)

Đ Ly Thuong Kiet

Đ Tran Quy

ĐL An Duong Vuong

Đ Han Hai Nguyen

Phung Son
Pagoda

Cholon 5

ĐL Tran Phu

To Mien Tay Bus
Station (3km)

DISTRICT 5

Đ Nguyen Trai

Đ Minh Phung

Đ Hong Bang

ĐL Tran Hung Dao

Tau Hu Channel

Ho Chi Minh City Highlights

1 Soak up the city's manic energy from a perch atop one of its **rooftop bars** (p333)

2 Retreat into the turbulent recent past at the **War Remnants Museum** (p305)

3 Feast on a diverse selection of **local and international cuisine** at the city's many wonderful restaurants and street stalls (p325)

4 Pass through the clouds of incense and enter the mystical world of the **Jade Emperor Pagoda** (p304)

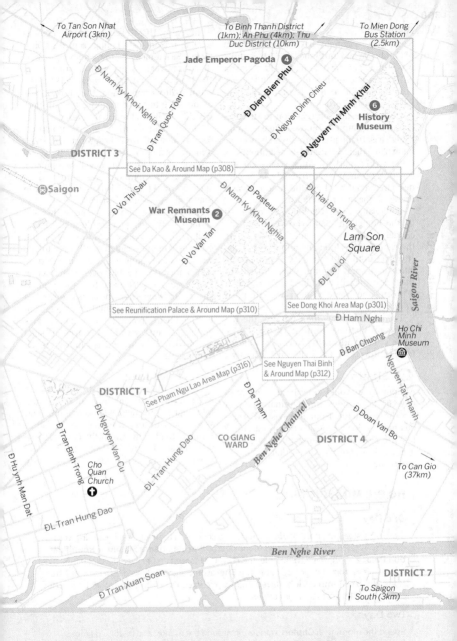

To Tan Son Nhat
Airport (3km)

To Binh Thanh District
(1km); An Phu (4km); Thu
Duc District (10km)

To Mien Dong
Bus Station
(2.5km)

Jade Emperor Pagoda ④

Đ Nam Ky Khoi Nghia

Đ Tran Quoc Toan

Đ Dien Bien Phu

Đ Nguyen Dinh Chieu

Đ Nguyen Thi Minh Khai

**History
Museum** ⑥

DISTRICT 3

See Da Kao & Around Map (p308)

Đ Vo Thi Sau

Đ Nam Ky Khoi Nghia

Đ Pasteur

ĐL Hai Ba Trung

**War Remnants
Museum** ②

Đ Vo Van Tan

*Lam Son
Square*

ĐL Le Loi

See Reunification Palace & Around Map (p310)

See Dong Khoi Area Map (p301)

Đ Ham Nghi

*Ho Chi
Minh
Museum*

Saigon River

See Pham Ngu Lao Area Map (p316)

See Nguyen Thai Binh
& Around Map (p312)

Đ Ban Chuong

Nguyen Tat Thanh

DISTRICT 1

Đ De Tham

**CO GIANG
WARD**

ĐL Nguyen Van Cu

Đ Tran Binh Trong

Đ Huynh Man Dat

*Cho
Quan
Church*

ĐL Tran Hung Dao

Ben Nghe Channel

Đ Doan Van Bo

DISTRICT 4

To Can Gio
(37km)

ĐL Tran Hung Dao

Ben Nghe River

DISTRICT 7

Đ Tran Xuan Soan

To Saigon
South (3km)

⑤ Experience the Chinese
pagodas of colourful **Cholon**
(p311)

⑥ Step back to ancient times
amid the archaeological relics
of the **History Museum** (p305)

⑦ Enter the surreal,
subterranean world of the Viet
Cong in the claustrophobic **Cu
Chi Tunnels** (p343).

⑧ Attend a religious service
at Tay Ninh's fantastic (in all
senses of the word) **Cao Dai
Great Temple** (p346)

History

Saigon was originally part of the kingdom of Cambodia and, until the late 17th century, was a small port town known as Prey Nokor. As Vietnamese settlers moved south it was absorbed by Vietnam and became the base for the Nguyen Lords.

During the Tay Son rebellion in the 18th century, a group of Chinese refugees established a settlement nearby, which became known by their Vietnamese neighbours as Cholon (big market). After seeing off the rebels, Nguyen Anh constructed a large citadel here (roughly where the American and French embassies now stand).

Both Saigon and Cholon were captured by the French in 1859 (who destroyed the citadel in the process) and Saigon became the capital of Cochinchina a few years later. It wasn't until 1931, after the neighbouring cities had sprawled into each other, that they were officially combined to form Saigon-Cholon (the name Cholon was dropped in 1956).

The city served as the capital of the Republic of Vietnam from 1956 until 1975, when it fell to advancing North Vietnamese forces and was renamed Ho Chi Minh City.

◉ Sights

Although few would describe it as a pretty city, HCMC provides some fascinating sights for the wanderer, from little-visited pagodas hidden down quiet lanes, to museums, historic sites and teeming markets all set against the chaotic pastiche that is the urban scene.

In reality, HCMC is not so much a city as a small province stretching from the South China Sea almost to the Cambodian border. Rural regions make up about 90% of the land area and hold around 25% of the municipality's population; the other 75% is crammed into the remaining 10% of land, which constitutes the urban centre.

HCMC is divided into 19 urban districts (*quan,* derived from the French *quartier*) and five rural districts *(huyen)*. It is city growing fast, with many new developments underway in upmarket residential areas such as An Phu in District 2 and Saigon South, also known as District 7.

The majority of places and sights described in this chapter are located in District 1, the district still known as Saigon (although many residents still refer to the whole city as Saigon, just to confuse things), which includes the backpacker district of Pham Ngu Lao (PNL) and the more upmarket area of Dong Khoi. The city's neoclassical and international-style buildings, along with its tree-lined streets set with shops, cafes and restaurants, give neighbourhoods such as District 3 an attractive, almost French atmosphere.

DONG KHOI AREA

This area, immediately west of the Saigon River, incorporates the heart of old Saigon into a glitzy precinct of designer stores and skyscrapers. Cutting from the river to Notre Dame Cathedral by way of the Opera House (Municipal Theatre), Đ Dong Khoi is the main shopping strip and surreptitiously

---

HO CHI MINH CITY IN...

One Day

Slurp up a steaming bowl of *pho* (rice-noodle soup) and then follow our **walking tour** itinerary. After lunch at **Shri**, head to the nearby **War Remnants Museum**, **Reunification Palace** and, if there's still time, the **HCMC Museum**. In the evening, catch the sunset views from the rooftop bar of the **Sheraton Saigon**, followed by a meal at **Nha Hang Ngon** or **Temple Club**. Have a nightcap at **Vasco's** or one of the other bars in the courtyard of the former opium refinery.

Two Days

Spend the morning in **Cholon**, wandering around the market and historic pagodas. Catch a taxi up to District 3 for a cheap traditional lunch at **Pho Hoa** or **Banh Xeo 46A** and then walk through Da Kao ward to the **Jade Emperor Pagoda** and **History Museum**. It's your last night in HCMC, so make the most of it. Start your evening at another of the city's superb restaurants – perhaps **Cuc Gach Quan**, **Camargue** or **Lion City** – and then catch a band at **Acoustic** or **Yoko**. If you're ready for the evening to descend into a very Saigon state of messiness, continue on to **Apocalypse Now** and **Go2**.

lends its name to the encircling civic centre and central business district. Yet it's the wide, tree-lined boulevards of Le Loi and Nguyen Hue, perpetually swarming with motorbikes, that leave more of an impression – not least if you've survived crossing them on foot. It's in these grand thoroughfares that French colonial aspirations collide head-on with the thrilling modern city.

HCMC Museum   MUSEUM
(Bao Tang Thanh Pho Ho Chi Minh; Map p301; www .hcmc-museum.edu.vn; 65 Đ Ly Tu Trong; admission 15,000d; ⊙8am-4pm) A grand, neoclassical structure built in 1885 and once known as

Gia Long Palace (and later the Revolutionary Museum), HCMC's city museum is a singularly beautiful and impressive building.

It tells the story of the city through archaeological artefacts, ceramics, old city maps and displays on the marriage traditions of its various ethnicities. Of course, the struggle for independence is extensively covered, with most of the upper floor devoted to it.

Deep beneath the building is a network of reinforced concrete bunkers and fortified corridors. The system, branches of which stretch all the way to Reunification Palace, included living areas, a kitchen and a large meeting hall. In 1963 President Diem and

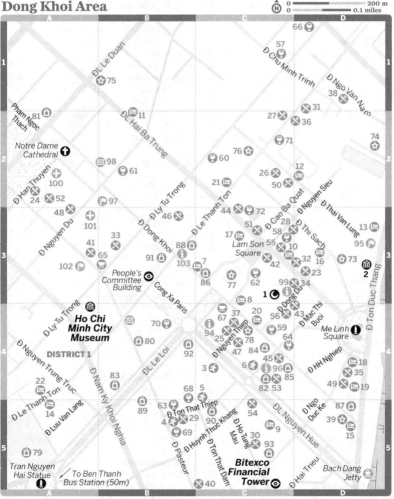

Dong Khoi Area

Dong Khoi Area

HO CHI MINH CITY SIGHTS

his brother hid here before fleeing to Cha Tam Church. The network is not open to the public because most of the tunnels are flooded.

In the gardens around the museum are various items of military hardware, including the American-built F-5E jet used by a renegade South Vietnamese pilot to bomb the Presidential Palace (now Reunification Palace) on 8 April 1975.

Bitexco Financial Tower NOTABLE BUILDING
(Map p301; 36 Đ Ho Tung Mau; entry 200,000d; ◎1-9pm Mon-Fri, 10am-10pm Sat & Sun) Opened in late 2010, this magnificent, 68-storey, 262m-high, Carlos Zapata-designed skyscraper dwarfs all around it. It's meant to be shaped like a lotus bulb, but we can't help thinking it looks a little like a CD rack with a tambourine shoved into it. That tambourine is actually the **Saigon Skydeck**, on the 48th floor, with a helipad on its roof. The views are, of course, extraordinary but there's not a lot else up here.

FREE **Ton Duc Thang Museum** MUSEUM
(Bao Tang Ton Duc Thang; Map p301; 5 Đ Ton Duc Thang; ◎7.30-11.30am & 1.30-5pm Tue-Sun) This small, seldom-visited museum is dedicated to Ton Duc Thang, Ho Chi Minh's successor as president of Vietnam. Born in 1888 in Long Xuyen in the Mekong Delta region, he died in office in 1980. Photos and exhibits illustrate his role in the Vietnamese Revolution, including some fascinating displays on French colonial brutality. Upstairs there's an intriguing oddball collection of mosaic portraits of Uncle Ton made from telephone wires, sesame seeds, rice, stamps and buttons.

Saigon Central Mosque MOSQUE
(Map p301; 66 Đ Dong Du) Built by South Indian Muslims in 1935 on the site of an earlier mosque, Saigon Central is an immaculately clean and well-kept island of calm in the middle of the bustling Dong Khoi area. In front of the sparkling white and blue structure, with its four non-functional minarets, is a pool for the ritual ablutions required by Islamic law before prayers.

The simplicity of the mosque is in marked contrast to the exuberance of Chinese temple decoration and the rows of figures and elaborate ritual objects in Buddhist pagodas. Islamic law strictly forbids using human or animal figures for decoration. Take off your shoes before entering the building.

Clustered around this mosque are several Malaysian and Indian restaurants serving halal food, including an excellent but humble eatery directly behind the mosque. There are 12 other mosques in HCMC serving the city's 6000 or so Muslims.

DA KAO & AROUND
This old District 1 ward, directly north of the city centre, is home to most of the consulates

RENAMING THE PAST

One of the main battlegrounds for the hearts of the people during the last four decades has been the naming of Vietnam's provinces, districts, cities, towns, streets and institutions. Some places have borne three or more names since WWII and, often, more than one name is still used.

When French control of Vietnam ended in 1954, almost all French names were replaced in both the North and the South. Saigon's Rue Catinat, a familiar name to anyone who has read Graham Greene's *A Quiet American,* was renamed Đ Tu Do (Freedom). Since reunification it has been known as Đ Dong Khoi (General Uprising). In 1956, the US-backed government changed the names of some provinces and towns in the South in an effort to erase from popular memory the Viet Minh's anti-French exploits, which were often known by the places in which they occurred. The village-based southern communists, who by this time had gone underground, continued to use the old designations and boundaries in running their regional and local organisations. The peasants – now faced with two masters – quickly adapted to this situation, using one set of place names when talking to South Vietnamese officials and a different set of names when dealing with the communists.

After reunification, the first task of Saigon's provisional government was to rename the southern capital Ho Chi Minh City, a decision confirmed in Hanoi a year later. The new government began changing street names considered inappropriate, dropping English and French names in favour of Vietnamese ones. The only French names still in use are those of Albert Calmette (1893–1934), developer of a tuberculosis vaccine; Marie Curie (1867–1934), who won the Nobel Prize for her research into radioactivity; Louis Pasteur (1822–95), chemist and bacteriologist; and Alexandre Yersin (1863–1943), discoverer of the plague bacillus.

Although the new street names have caught on, many people still refer to the city by its old name, Saigon.

and some beautiful buildings dating from the French colonial period. Hidden within its historic streets (and those bordering it in the eastern corner of District 3) are some of HCMC's hippest new restaurants and bars, along with some of the city's best traditional eateries.

Jade Emperor Pagoda   PAGODA
(Phuoc Hai Tu or Chua Ngoc Hoang; Map p308; 73 Đ Mai Thi Luu) Built in 1909 by the Cantonese (Quang Dong) Congregation in honour of the supreme Taoist god (the Jade Emperor or King of Heaven, Ngoc Hoang), this is one of the most spectacularly atmospheric pagodas in HCMC, filled with statues of phantasmal divinities and grotesque heroes. The pungent smoke of burning joss sticks fills the air, obscuring the exquisite woodcarvings decorated with gilded Chinese characters. The roof is covered with elaborate tile work, while the statues, which represent characters from both the Buddhist and Taoist traditions, are made of reinforced papier mâché.

Inside the main building are two especially fierce and menacing figures. On the right (as you face the altar) is a 4m-high statue of the general who defeated the Green Dragon (depicted underfoot). On the left is the general who defeated the White Tiger, which is also being stepped on.

The Jade Emperor, draped in luxurious robes, presides over the main sanctuary. He is flanked by his guardians, the Four Big Diamonds (Tu Dai Kim Cuong), so named because they are said to be as hard as diamonds.

Out the door on the left-hand side of the Jade Emperor's chamber is another room. The semi-enclosed area to the right (as you enter) is presided over by Thanh Hoang, the Chief of Hell; to the left is his red horse. Other figures here represent the gods who dispense punishments for evil acts and rewards for good deeds. The room also contains the famous **Hall of the Ten Hells** – carved wooden panels illustrating the varied torments awaiting evil people in each of the Ten Regions of Hell.

On the other side of the wall is a fascinating little room in which the **ceramic figures** of 12 women, overrun with children and wearing colourful clothes, sit in two rows of six. Each of the women exemplifies a human characteristic, either good or bad (as in the case of the woman drinking alcohol from a jug). Each figure represents a year in the 12-year Chinese astrological calendar. Presiding over the room is Kim Hoa Thanh Mau, the Chief of All Women.

History Museum   MUSEUM
(Bao Tang Lich Su; Map p308; Đ Nguyen Binh Khiem; admission 15,000d; ☺8-11am & 1.30-5pm Tue-Sun) It's worth a visit just to view the impressive Sino-French architecture of the History Museum, built in 1929 by the Société des Études Indochinoises. It houses an excellent collection of artefacts that illustrate the evolution of the cultures of Vietnam, from the Bronze Age Dong Son civilisation (which emerged in 2000 BC) and the Funan civilisation (1st to 6th centuries AD), to the Cham, Khmer and Vietnamese. Highlights include valuable relics taken from Cambodia's Angkor Wat.

The museum is located just inside the main gate to the city's botanic gardens and zoo, although we don't recommend that any animal lovers visit this thoroughly depressing place. Note: while the zoo ticket office is in front of the museum, you don't need to buy a ticket until you reach the museum's entrance.

Temple of King Hung Vuong   TEMPLE
(Map p308; Đ Nguyen Binh Khiem) Directly opposite the History Museum, this elaborate, high-ceilinged temple honours the first of the legendary Hung kings. They're said to have been the first rulers of the Vietnamese nation, having established their rule in the Red River region before it was invaded by the Chinese. Hung Vuong is both a semi-mythical figure (the son of the dragon lord and a mountain fairy) and the name taken by many of the early kings.

FREE Military Museum   MUSEUM
(Bao Tang Quan Doi; Map p308; ☎3822 9387; 2 ĐL Le Duan; ☺7.30-11am & 1.30-4.30pm Tue-Sat) Just a short distance from the history museum, this small collection is devoted to Ho Chi Minh's campaign to liberate the south. The exhibits inside are of minor interest but some US, Chinese and Soviet war material is on display outdoors, including a South Vietnamese Air Force Cessna A-37 and a US-built F-5E Tiger with the 20mm nose gun still loaded. The tank on display is one of the tanks that broke into the grounds of Reunification Palace on 30 April 1975.

Pho Binh   HISTORIC SITE
(Map p308; 7 Đ Ly Chinh Thang, District 3; noodle soup 30,000d) It might seem strange to introduce a humble noodle-soup restaurant as a sight, but there is more to Pho Binh than meets the eye. It was the secret headquarters of the VC in Saigon and it was from here that they planned their attacks on the US embassy and other places in Saigon during the Tet Offensive of 1968. One has to wonder how many US soldiers ate here, completely unaware. By the way, the *pho* makes it a worthwhile stop for lunch or breakfast.

Tran Hung Dao Temple   TEMPLE
(Den Tho Tran Hung Dao; Map p308; 36 Đ Vo Thi Sau; ☺6-11am & 2-6pm Mon-Fri) This popular little temple is dedicated to Tran Hung Dao, a national hero who in 1287 vanquished Mongol emperor Kublai Khan's invasion force, said to have numbered 300,000 men.

REUNIFICATION PALACE & AROUND
Straddling District 1 and District 3, this grid of busy streets encloses the open spaces of Tao Dan Park and the grounds of the Reunification Palace. It's here that you'll find some of HCMC's most popular sights and a smattering of terrific restaurants.

War Remnants Museum   MUSEUM
(Bao Tang Chung Tich Chien Tranh; Map p310; 28 Đ Vo Van Tan; admission 15,000d; ☺7.30am-noon & 1.30-5pm) Despite being once known as the Museum of Chinese and American War Crimes, the War Remnants Museum is consistently the most popular museum in HCMC with Western tourists. Many of the atrocities documented here were well publicised but rarely do Westerners have the opportunity to hear the victims of US military action tell their own stories. While the displays are one-sided and could be considered a touch propagandist, it's worth noting that many of the most disturbing photographs illustrating US atrocities are from US sources, including those of the infamous My Lai Massacre (p218).

US armoured vehicles, artillery pieces, bombs and infantry weapons are on display outside. One corner of the grounds is devoted to the notorious French and South Vietnamese prisons on Phu Quoc and Con Son Islands. Artefacts include that most iconic of French punishment devices, the guillotine, and the notoriously inhumane 'tiger cages' used to house Viet Cong (VC) prisoners.

The ground floor of the museum is devoted to a collection of posters and photographs

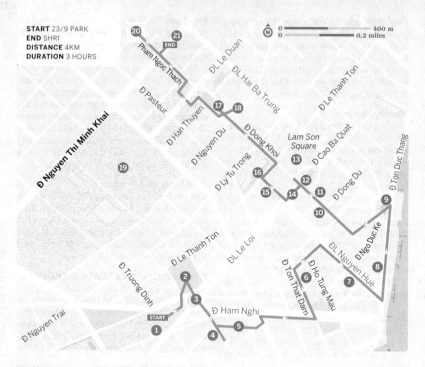

START 23/9 PARK
END SHRI
DISTANCE 4KM
DURATION 3 HOURS

Walking Tour
Old Saigon

❯ HCMC may be hurtling into the future at a thrilling rate but ghosts of the past still linger in the heart of District 1. This walking tour aims to strip back the layers of modern lacquer to get at the historic city beneath.

Start at ❶ **23/9 Park**, which borders Đ Pham Ngu Lao and the city's unofficial backpacker district. The park owes its long, thin shape to a former tenure as the city's main railway terminus. Wander through the park to ❷ **Ben Thanh Market**, which is at its bustling best in the morning. Known to the French as Les Halles Centrales, it was built in 1914 from reinforced concrete. The main entrance, with its belfry and clock, has become a symbol of HCMC.

After exploring the market, cross to the massive roundabout (very carefully!) where you'll see an equestrian ❸ **statue of Tran Nguyen Han**, a trusted general of 15th century leader Le Loi. On a pillar at its base is a small white bust of Quach Thi Trang, a 15-year-old girl who was killed near here during antigovernment protests in 1963.

Muster up the courage and cross the road again, this time to the bus station and beyond. On Đ Pho Duc Chinh you'll see the lovely Sino-French ❹ **Fine Arts Museum**. Built as a private home by a wealthy merchant, it holds the distinction of having Saigon's first elevator. Turn onto Đ Le Cong Kieu, a short street lined with ❺ **antique shops**. At the end turn (in quick succession) left, left again, then right onto Đ Ham Nghi. Before 1870 this wide boulevard was a canal with roads on either side of it.

Turn left onto Đ Ton That Dam and stroll through the colourful outdoor ❻ **street market**. Turn right onto Đ Huynh Thuc Khang and follow it to ĐL Nguyen Hue, another former canal that's now a grand boulevard. Turn right and head past the ❼ **Bitexco Financial Tower**, a glitzy modern skyscraper rising behind a colonial façade.

Turn left onto Đ Ton Duc Thang, the busy riverside road. At the corner of Đ Dong Khoi is the grand ❽ **Majestic Hotel**. During WWII the Japanese requisitioned this elegant 1925 building for use as their military barracks.

Continue along the river to the giant **9** **statue of Tran Hung Dao**, defeater of the Mongols, lording it over a semi-circular plaza with roads radiating out from it. Take the second one, Đ Ho Huan Nghiep, and at the end turn right onto Dong Khoi, the former Rue Catinat and still the city's most famous street. At number 151 is the former **10** **Brodard Café**, immortalised in Graham Greene's *The Quiet American*. It's still a cafe but it's now a branch of the Australian Gloria Jean's chain.

Further up Dong Khoi is the **11** **Caravelle Hotel**. The curved corner section was the original 1959 hotel which, during the American War, housed foreign news bureaux, the Australian and New Zealand embassies, and members of the press corps. In August 1964 a bomb exploded on the 5th floor. No-one was killed but the hotel spent the rest of the war with its corner windows taped up in case of further bombings.

Across the road is what is officially called the **12** **Municipal Theatre**, although most people still refer to it by its more romantic former name, the Opera House. Built in 1897, this grand colonial building, accessed via a sweeping staircase, captures the flamboyance of France's *belle époque* (beautiful era). During the 1950s and 1960s it housed the National Assembly of South Vietnam.

On the next corner is perhaps HCMC's most famous hotel, the **13** **Continental**. Built in 1880, it was a favourite of the press corps during the French War. Graham Greene regularly stayed in room 214 and the hotel featured prominently in *The Quiet American*. Key scenes were set at the cafe known as the Continental Shelf, which once occupied the 1st floor balcony.

Facing the Municipal Theatre, **14** **Lam Son Park** often has interesting propaganda displays. Walk through it and turn right, where you'll see another little park featuring a prominent **15** **statue of Ho Chi Minh** in front of the **16** **People's Committee Building**. One of the city's most prominent land-marks, the former Hôtel de Ville (city hall) is notable for its ornate renaissance-inspired façade and elegant interior lit with crystal chandeliers. Built between 1901 and 1908, it's a fine companion piece to the opera house and one of the most photographed buildings in Vietnam. At night, the exterior is usually covered with thousands of geckos feasting on insects. You'll have to content yourself with admiring the exterior only. The building is not open to the public and requests by tourists to visit the interior are aggressively dismissed.

Turn right and then left again, back onto Dong Khoi. Directly ahead, looking like it's been beamed in directly from Normandy, is **17** **Notre Dame Cathedral**. It sits behind a large white statue of St. Mary holding an orb – not a bowling ball as first impressions might suggest. The Cathedral was built between 1877 and 1883 from materials shipped in from France. Romanesque arches and twin 40m-high towers create an imposing façade but the church itself is relatively unadorned and, by European standards, not all that interesting. Its original stained-glass windows were damaged in WWII and never replaced.

To the right of the cathedral is the impressive French-style **18** **Central Post Office**, designed by Gustave Eiffel and built between 1886 and 1891. Painted on the walls of its grand concourse are fascinating historic maps of South Vietnam, Saigon and Cholon – while a mosaic of Ho Chi Minh takes pride of place on the far wall.

Cross the square in front of the Cathedral, turn right and head into 30/4 Park – a lovely formal space providing a grand approach to the **19** **Reunification Palace**. Stop to explore the palace if you have time, otherwise continue north along Pham Ngoc Thach to the large roundabout known as **20** **Turtle Lake** (Ho Con Rua), with its concrete walkways and unusual flower-like sculpture.

Backtrack a block and turn left onto Đ Nguyen Thi Minh Khai where you can finish your tour with a drink at **21** **Shri** on the 23rd floor of the Centec Tower, enjoying views stretching to your starting point and far beyond.

Da Kao & Around

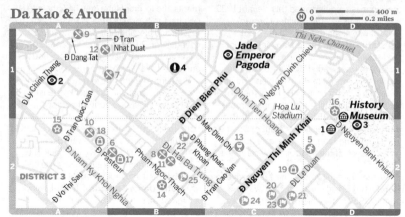

showing support for the antiwar movement internationally. This somewhat upbeat display provides some respite from the horrors upstairs.

There are few museums in the world that drive home so well the point that war is horribly brutal and that many of its victims are civilians. Even those who supported the war are likely to be horrified by the photos of children affected by US bombing and napalming. You'll also have the rare chance to see some of the experimental weapons used in the war, which were at one time military secrets, such as the *fléchette,* an artillery shell filled with thousands of tiny darts. There are also pictures of deformed babies and jars of pickled foetuses, their defects attributed to the USA's widespread use of chemical herbicides.

Upstairs, look out for the **Requiem Exhibition**. Compiled by legendary war photographer Tim Page, this striking collection documents the work of photographers killed during the course of the conflict, on both sides, and includes works by Larry Burrows and Robert Capa.

The War Remnants Museum is in the former US Information Service building, at the intersection with Đ Le Quy Don. Captions are in Vietnamese and English.

Reunification Palace   HISTORIC BUILDING
(Dinh Thong Nhat; Map p310; Đ Nam Ky Khoi Nghia; adult/child 30,000/3000d; ⏱7.30-11am & 1-4pm) The striking modern architecture and the eerie feeling you get as you walk through the deserted halls make this government building one of the most fascinating sights in HCMC. The first communist tanks to ar-

rive in Saigon rumbled here on the morning of 30 April 1975 and it's as if time has stood still since then.

After crashing through the wrought-iron gates – in a dramatic scene recorded by photojournalists and shown around the world – a soldier ran into the building and up the stairs to unfurl a VC flag from the balcony. In an ornate reception chamber, General Minh, who had become head of the South Vietnamese state only 43 hours before, waited with his improvised cabinet. 'I have been waiting since early this morning to transfer power to you', Minh said to the VC officer who entered the room. 'There is no question of your transferring power', replied the officer. 'You cannot give up what you do not have.'

In 1868 a residence was built on this site for the French governor-general of Cochinchina and gradually it expanded to become Norodom Palace. When the French departed, the palace became home to the South Vietnamese President Ngo Dinh Diem. So unpopular was Diem that his own air force bombed the palace in 1962 in an unsuccessful attempt to kill him. The president ordered a new residence to be built on the same site, this time with a sizeable bomb shelter in the basement. Work was completed in 1966, but Diem did not get to see his dream house as he was killed by his own troops in 1963.

The new building was named Independence Palace and was home to the successive South Vietnamese President, Nguyen Van Thieu, until his hasty departure in 1975. Designed by Paris-trained Vietnamese architect Ngo Viet Thu, it is an outstanding

Da Kao & Around

example of 1960s architecture, with an airy and open atmosphere.

The ground floor has various meeting rooms, while upstairs are a grand set of reception rooms, used for meeting foreign and national dignitaries. In the back of the structure are the president's living quarters; check out the model boats, horse tails and severed elephants' feet. The second floor has a shagadelic card-playing room, complete with a round leather banquette, a barrel-shaped bar, hubcap light fixtures and groovy three-legged chairs set around a flared-legged card table. There's also a cinema and a rooftop nightclub, complete with helipad: James Bond/Austin Powers – eat your heart out.

Perhaps most interesting of all is the basement with its telecommunications centre, war room and network of tunnels, with the best map of Vietnam you'll ever see pasted on the wall. Towards the end are rooms where you can watch a video about the palace and its history in a variety of languages. The national anthem is played at the end of the tape and you are expected to stand up – it would be rude not to.

Reunification Palace is open to visitors as long as official receptions or meetings aren't taking place. English- and French-speaking guides are on duty during opening hours (prices are 'up to you').

Mariamman Hindu Temple　　TEMPLE
(Chua Ba Mariamman; Map p310; 45 Đ Truong Dinh; ⊙7.30am-7.30pm) Though there are only a small number of Hindus in HCMC, this colourful piece of southern India is also considered sacred by many ethnic Vietnamese and Chinese. Indeed, it is reputed to have miraculous powers. The temple was built at the end of the 19th century and dedicated to the Hindu goddess Mariamman.

The lion to the left of the entrance used to be carried around the city in a street procession every autumn. In the shrine in the middle of the temple is Mariamman, flanked by her guardians Maduraiveeran (to her left) and Pechiamman (to her right). In front of the Mariamman figure are two *linga* (stylised phalluses that represent the Hindu god Shiva). Favourite offerings placed nearby include joss sticks, jasmine, lilies and gladioli.

After reunification, the government took over the temple and turned part of it into a factory for joss sticks. Another section was occupied by a company producing seafood for export, which was dried on the roof in the sun.

Mariamman Hindu Temple is three blocks west of Ben Thanh Market. Remove your shoes before stepping onto the slightly raised platform.

HO CHI MINH CITY SIGHTS

Reunification Palace & Around

Tao Dan Park

PARK

(Map p310; Đ Nguyen Thi Minh Khai) A city of this size needs its breathing spaces and one of the biggest and most popular of them is 10-hectare Tao Dan Park, its bench-lined walks shaded with avenues of enormous tropical trees.

It's a particularly interesting place to visit in the early morning and late afternoon when thousands of locals take advantage of the relative cool to exercise. The communal activities are especially entertaining to watch, ranging from the languid grace of t'ai chi to the unabashed uncoordination of an alfresco dance session. Equally unusual is the daily gathering of the city's bird lovers (mainly elderly gentlemen), who arrive, cages in hand, at what is universally known as the bird cafe.

The park is split down the middle by Đ Truong Dinh. To the southwest of this street are formal gardens with topiary dragons and small-scale reconstructions of Vietnamese architectural landmarks, including Nha Trang's Cham towers. In the lead-up to the Tet Festival, this section is filled with colourful floral displays.

To the north of Đ Truong Dinh are a small contemporary **sculpture garden** and the old Cercle Sportif, which was an elite sporting club during the French-colonial period and is now the thoroughly egalitarian **Workers' Club.** It has 11 tennis courts, a colonnaded Art Deco swimming pool (see p318) and a clubhouse, all of which have a faded colonial feel about them.

Xa Loi Pagoda

PAGODA

(Chua Xa Loi; Map p310; 89 Đ Ba Huyen Thanh Quan; ⊙7-11am & 2-5pm) Famed as the repository of a sacred relic of the Buddha, this large 1956 building is perhaps most interesting for its dramatic history. In August 1963 truckloads of armed men under the command of President Ngo Dinh Diem's brother, Ngo Dinh Nhu, attacked Xa Loi Pagoda, which had become a centre of opposition towards the Diem government. The pagoda was ransacked and 400 monks and nuns, including the country's 80-year-old Buddhist patriarch, were arrested. This raid and others elsewhere helped solidify opposition among Buddhists to the regime, a crucial factor in the US decision to support the coup against Diem. The pagoda was also the site of several self-immolations by monks protesting against the Diem regime and the American War.

Women enter the main hall of Xa Loi Pagoda, housing a giant golden Buddha, by the staircase on the right as you come in the gate, and men use the stairs on the left.

Reunification Palace & Around

The walls of the sanctuary are adorned with paintings depicting the Buddha's life.

A monk preaches here every Sunday from 8am to 10am. On days of the full moon and new moon, special prayers are held from 7am to 9am and 7pm to 8pm.

NGUYEN THAI BINH & AROUND
This District 1 ward is a busy workaday neighbourhood nestled between the central city, Ben Thanh Market, the Pham Ngu Lao backpacker strip and Ben Nghe channel.

Fine Arts Museum   ART GALLERY
(Bao Tang My Thuat; Map p312; www.baotang mythuatphcm.vn; 97A Đ Pho Duc Chinh; admission 10,000d; ◷9am-5pm Tue-Sun) A classic yellow-and-white colonial-era building with a modest Chinese influence, the Fine Arts Museum houses one of the more interesting collections in Vietnam, ranging from lacquer- and enamelware to contemporary oil paintings by Vietnamese and foreign artists. If that doesn't sound enticing, just come to see the huge hall with its beautiful tiled floors.

As well as contemporary art, much of it (unsurprisingly) inspired by the wars, the museum displays historical pieces dating back to the 4th century. These include elegant Funan-era sculptures of Vishnu, the Buddha and other revered figures (carved in both wood and stone), and Cham art dating from the 7th to 14th century. One room is devoted to a collection of totem-like funeral sculptures from the Hill Tribes of the Central Highlands.

More statuary is scattered around the grounds and in the central courtyard (accessed from the rear of the building). A cluster of commercial galleries at the back of the property are worth checking out, whether you're considering a purchase or not.

CHOLON
A treasure trove of interesting temples and pagodas awaits in Cholon (District 5). HCMC's Chinatown is decidedly less Chinese than it used to be, largely due to the anticapitalist and anti-Chinese campaign from 1978 to 1979, when many ethnic Chinese fled the country – taking with them their money and entrepreneurial skills. A lot of those refugees have since returned (with foreign passports) to explore investment possibilities.

Cholon means 'big market' and during the American War it was home to a thriving black market. Like much of HCMC, Cholon's historic shopfronts are swiftly disappearing under advertising hoardings or succumbing to developers' bulldozers, but there is still an atmospheric strip of **traditional herb shops** (Map p314; Đ Hai Thuong Lan Ong) between Đ Luong Nhu Hoc and Đ Trieu Quang Phuc, providing both a visual and an olfactory reminder of the old Chinese city.

Binh Tay Market
MARKET

(Cho Binh Tay; Map p314; www.chobinhtay.gov.vn; 57A ĐL Thap Muoi) Cholon's main market is a Chinese-style architectural masterpiece with a great clock tower and a central courtyard with gardens. Much of the business here is wholesale but it's also very popular with tour groups, so a lot of foreigners pass through.

Thien Hau Pagoda
PAGODA

(Ba Mieu, Pho Mieu or Chua Ba Thien Hau; Map p314; 710 Đ Nguyen Trai) Built by the Cantonese Congregation in the early 19th century, this gorgeous pagoda is dedicated to the deity Thien Hau and always has a mix of worshippers and visitors, who mingle beneath the large coils of incense suspended overhead.

It is believed that Thien Hau can travel over the oceans on a mat and ride the clouds to wherever she pleases. Her mobility allows her to save people in trouble on the high seas. The Goddess is very popular in Hong Kong and Taiwan, which might explain why this pagoda is included on so many tour-group itineraries.

Though there are guardians to each side of the entrance, it is said that the real protectors of the pagoda are the two land turtles that live here. There are intricate ceramic friezes above the roof line of the interior courtyard. Near the large braziers are two miniature wooden structures in which a small figure of Thien Hau is paraded around the nearby streets on the 23rd day of the third lunar month.

On the main dais are three figures of Thien Hau, one behind the other, all flanked by two servants or guardians. To the right is a scale-model boat and on the far right is the Goddess Long Mau, Protector of Mothers and Newborns. To the left of the dais is Thien Hau's bed.

Khanh Van Nam Vien Pagoda
PAGODA

(Map p314; 269/2 Đ Nguyen Thi Nho) Built between 1939 and 1942 by the Cantonese Congregation, this pagoda is said to be the only pure Taoist pagoda in Vietnam and is unique for its colourful statues of Taoist disciples. The number of true Taoists in HCMC is estimated at no more than 5000, though most Chinese practise a mixture of Taoism and Buddhism.

Features to seek out include the unique 150cm-high statue of Laotse located upstairs. His surreal, mirror-edged halo is one of the more intriguing uses of fluorescent lighting. Off to the left of Laotse are two stone plaques with instructions for inhalation and exhalation exercises. A schematic drawing represents the human organs as a scene from rural China. The diaphragm, agent of inhalation, is at the bottom; the stomach is represented by a peasant ploughing with a water buffalo. The kidney is marked by four yin and yang symbols, the liver is shown as a grove of trees and the heart is represented by a circle with a peasant standing in it, above which is a constellation. The tall pagoda represents the throat and the broken rainbow is the mouth. At the top are mountains and a seated figure that represent the brain and imagination, respectively.

Nguyen Thai Binh & Around

Nguyen Thai Binh & Around

The pagoda operates a home for several dozen elderly people who have no family. Each of the old folk, most of whom are women, have their own wood stove (made of brick) on which to cook. Next door is a free medical clinic, which is also run by the pagoda and offers Chinese herbal medicines and acupuncture treatments to the community. If you would like to support this venture you can leave a donation with the monks.

Quan Am Pagoda   PAGODA

(Chua Quan Am; Map p314; 12 Đ Lao Tu) One of Cholon's most active and colourful pagodas, Quan Am was founded by the Fujian Congregation in the early 19th century and displays obvious Chinese influences. It's named for the Goddess of Mercy, Quan The Am Bo Tat whose statue lies hidden behind a remarkably ornate exterior.

Fantastic ceramic scenes decorate the roof and depict figures from traditional Chinese plays and stories. The tableaux include ships, village houses and several ferocious dragons. Other unique features of this pagoda are the gold-and-lacquer panels of the entrance doors. Just inside the walls of the porch are murals, in relief, of scenes of China from around the time of Quan Cong, a deified 3rd century general. There are elaborate woodcarvings above the porch.

Phuoc An Hoi Quan Pagoda   PAGODA

(Map p314; 184 Đ Hong Bang) Built in 1902 by the Fujian Congregation, this is one of the most beautifully ornamented pagodas in HCMC, although the effect is marred by some utilitarian brickwork, bad formica tiles and neon halos. Of special interest are the elaborate brass ritual objects and the fine woodcarvings on the altars, walls, columns and hanging lanterns. From the exterior, look out for the ceramic scenes, each containing innumerable small figurines, which decorate the roof.

To the left of the entrance is a life-size figure of the sacred horse of Quan Cong. Before leaving on a journey, people make offerings to the horse, then stroke its mane and ring the bell around its neck. Behind the main altar, with its stone and brass incense braziers, is a statue of Quan Cong, to whom the pagoda is dedicated.

Tam Son Hoi Quan Pagoda   PAGODA

(Chua Ba; Map p314; 118 Đ Trieu Quang Phuc) Built by the Fujian Congregation in the 19th century, this pagoda is dedicated to Me Sanh, the Goddess of Fertility, and is particularly popular with local women who come here to pray for children.

It retains much of its original rich ornamentation. Among the striking figures is Quan Cong with his long black beard. He's found to the right of the covered courtyard. Flanking him are two guardians, the Military Mandarin Chau Xuong on the left and the Administrative Mandarin Quan Binh on the right. Next to Chau Xuong is Quan Cong's sacred red horse.

Across the courtyard from Quan Cong is a small room containing ossuary jars and memorials in which the dead are represented by their photographs. Next to this chamber is a small room containing the papier mâché head of a dragon of the type used by the Fujian Congregation for dragon dancing.

Ong Bon Pagoda   PAGODA

(Chua Ong Bon or Nhi Phu Hoi Quan; Map p314; 264 ĐL Hai Thuong Lan Ong) Built by the Fujian Congregation, this is yet another atmospheric pagoda full of gilded carvings, burning incense and the constant hubbub of kids from the large school next door. It's dedicated to Ong Bon, the guardian who presides over happiness and wealth. In the hope of securing good fortune from the deity, believers burn fake paper money in the pagoda's furnace, located across the courtyard from the pagoda entrance.

Another feature of the pagoda is the intricately carved and gilded wooden altar, which faces Ong Bon. Along the walls of the chamber are murals of five tigers (to the left) and two dragons (to the right).

Nghia An Hoi Quan Pagoda   PAGODA

(Map p314; 678 Đ Nguyen Trai) Built by the Chaozhou Chinese Congregation, this pagoda is noteworthy for its gilded woodwork. A large carved wooden boat hangs over the entrance and inside, to the left of the doorway, is an enormous representation of Quan Cong's red horse with its groom. The great general Quan Cong himself occupies a position in a glass case behind the main altar, with his assistants flanking him on both sides. Nghia An Hoi Quan lets its hair down on the 14th day of the first lunar month when various dances are staged in front of the pagoda, with offerings made to the spirits.

Ha Chuong Hoi Quan Pagoda   PAGODA

(Map p314; 802 Đ Nguyen Trai) This typical Fujian pagoda is dedicated to Thien Hau, who was born in Fujian. The four carved stone pillars, wrapped in painted dragons, were

Cholon

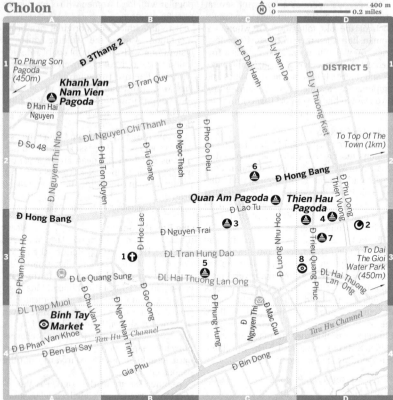

Cholon

⊙ Top Sights

Binh Tay Market	A4
Khanh Van Nam Vien Pagoda	A1
Quan Am Pagoda	C2
Thien Hau Pagoda	D3

⊙ Sights

1	Cha Tam Church	B3
2	Cholon Jamail Mosque	D3
3	Ha Chuong Hoi Quan Pagoda	C3
4	Nghia An Hoi Quan Pagoda	D3
5	Ong Bon Pagoda	C3
6	Phuoc An Hoi Quan Pagoda	C2
7	Tam Son Hoi Quan Pagoda	D3
8	Traditional Herb Shops	D3

made in China and brought to Vietnam by boat. There are interesting murals to each side of the main altar and impressive ceramic relief scenes on the roof.

The pagoda becomes extremely active during the **Lantern Festival**, a Chinese holiday held on the 15th day of the first lunar month (the first full moon of the new lunar year).

Cha Tam Church　　　　　　　CHURCH
(Map p314; 25 Đ Hoc Lac) Built around the turn of the 19th century, this decaying church has a sleepy, tropical feel to it, a far cry from its role during one of the city's more harrowing epochs.

President Ngo Dinh Diem and his brother Ngo Dinh Nhu took refuge here on 2 November 1963, after fleeing the Presidential Palace. When their efforts to contact loyal military officers (of whom there were almost none) failed, Diem and Nhu agreed to surrender unconditionally and revealed where they were hiding. The coup leaders sent an M-113 armoured personnel carrier to the church and the two were taken into custody. However, before the vehicle reached central

Saigon the soldiers had killed Diem and Nhu by shooting them at point-blank range and then repeatedly stabbing their bodies.

When news of the deaths was broadcast on radio, Saigon exploded with rejoicing. Portraits of the two were torn up and political prisoners, many of whom had been tortured, were set free. The city's nightclubs, which had closed because of the Ngos' conservative Catholic beliefs, were reopened. Three weeks later the US president, John F Kennedy, was assassinated. As his administration had supported the coup against Diem, some conspiracy theorists speculated that Diem's family orchestrated Kennedy's death in retaliation.

The statue in the tower is of François Xavier Tam Assou (1855–1934), a Chinese-born vicar apostolic (delegate of the pope) of Saigon. Today, the church has a very active congregation of 3000 ethnic Vietnamese and 2000 ethnic Chinese. Masses are held daily.

Cholon Jamail Mosque   MOSQUE
(Map p314; 641 Đ Nguyen Trai) The clean lines and minimal ornamentation of this mosque contrast starkly with nearby Chinese and Vietnamese Buddhist pagodas. Note the pool for ritual ablutions in the courtyard and the tiled niche (*mihrab*) in the wall of the prayer hall, indicating the direction of Mecca. This mosque was built by Tamil Muslims in 1935 but since 1975 it has served the Malaysian and Indonesian Muslim communities.

Cho Quan Church   CHURCH
(Map p298; 133 Đ Tran Binh Trong; ⊙4-7am & 3-6pm Mon-Sat, 4-9am & 1.30-6pm Sun) Built by the French, this is one of the largest churches in HCMC. Jesus on the altar has a neon halo, though the main reason to come here is for the view from the belfry (a steep climb). The church is on the eastern fringe of District 5 between ĐL Tran Hung Dao and Đ Nguyen Trai.

DISTRICT 11

Immediately west of Cholon, District 11's 5 sq km is home to 312,000 people. The main enticements to visit are a couple of interesting old pagodas, a popular water park and the Saigon Race Track. A taxi from Pham Ngu Lao should cost around 100,000d.

Giac Vien Pagoda   PAGODA
(Map p298; Đ Lac Long Quan, District 11; ⊙7-11.30am & 1.30-7pm) In a land where so many ancient pagodas have been 'restored' in concrete and neon, it's a pleasure to come across one that looks its age. The pagoda was founded by Hai Tinh Giac Vien in the late 1700s and it is said that Emperor Gia Long, who died in 1819, used to worship here. Architecturally similar to Giac Lam (p316), it shares its atmosphere of scholarly serenity, although Giac Vien is less visited and in a more secluded setting, down an alley near Dam Sen Lake.

Hidden behind a warren of winding lanes, the approach to the pagoda has several impressive **tombs** on the right – a popular playground for local kids. The pagoda itself boasts some 100 lavish carvings of various divinities. Funeral tablets line the first chamber of the entry room, while the second chamber is dominated by a statue of Hai Tinh Giac Vien holding a horse-tail switch. Nearby portraits depict his disciples and successors.

The **main sanctuary** is on the other side of the wall behind the Hai Tinh Giac Vien statue. The dais is set behind a fantastic brass incense basin with fierce dragon heads emerging from each side. On the altar to the left of the dais is Dai The Chi Bo Tat (Mahasthamaprapta), a bodhisattva who represents wisdom and strength; on the altar to the right is Quan The Am Bo Tat. In between the two, a statue of the Jade Emperor sits in front of the main Buddha figure. The Guardian of the Pagoda is against the wall opposite the dais. Nearby is a prayer tree similar to the one in Giac Lam Pagoda. Lining the side walls are the Judges of the 10 Regions of Hell (holding scrolls) and 18 other bodhisattvas.

Phung Son Pagoda   PAGODA
(Phung Son Tu or Chua Go; Map p298; 1408 ĐL 3 Thang 2, District 11) This Vietnamese Buddhist pagoda was built between 1802 and 1820 on the site of structures from the Funan period, dating back at least to the early centuries of Christianity. The pagoda is extremely rich in gilded, painted and beautifully carved statuary made of bronze, wood, ceramic and beaten copper. The **main dais**, with its many levels, is dominated by a large gilded A Di Da Buddha (the Buddha of Infinite Light).

Once upon a time, it was decided that Phung Son Pagoda should be moved to a different site. The pagoda's ritual objects – bells, drums, statues – were loaded onto the back of a white elephant, but the elephant slipped because of the great weight and all the precious objects fell into a nearby pond.

This event was interpreted as an omen that the pagoda should remain in its original location. All the articles were retrieved except for the bell, which locals say was heard ringing, until about a century ago, whenever there was a full or new moon.

Prayers are held three times a day, from 4am to 5am, 4pm to 5pm and 6pm to 7pm. The main entrances are locked most of the time, but the side entrance (to the right as you approach the building) is open during prayer times.

OTHER NEIGHBOURHOODS

Giac Lam Pagoda
PAGODA

(Chua Giac Lam; Map p298; 118 Đ Lac Long Quan, Tan Binh District; ⏰6am-noon & 2-8.30pm) Believed to be the oldest pagoda in HCMC (1744), Giac Lam is a fantastically atmospheric place set in peaceful, garden-like grounds. The looming Bodhi tree in the front garden was the gift of a monk from Sri Lanka in 1953. Next to the tree is a gleaming white statue of Quan The Am Bo Tat standing on a lotus blossom, a symbol of purity.

Like many Vietnamese Buddhist pagodas it also incorporates aspects of Taoism and Confucianism. For the sick and elderly, the pagoda is a minor pilgrimage sight, as it contains a bronze bell that, when rung, is believed to answer the prayers posted by petitioners.

Inside the reception area of the **main building** is the 18-armed Chuan De, another form of the Goddess of Mercy. Carved hardwood columns bear gilded Vietnamese inscriptions, with the portraits of great monks from previous generations looking down on proceedings.

The main **sanctuary** lies in the next room, filled with countless gilded figures. On the dais in the centre of the back row sits the A Di Da Buddha (Amitabha), easily spotted by his colourful halo. The fat laughing fellow, seated with five children climbing all over him, is Ameda, the Buddha of enlightenment, compassion and wisdom. On the altars along the side walls of the sanctuary are various Bodhisattvas (enlightened beings).

The red-and-gold Christmas tree-shaped object is a wooden altar bearing 49 lamps and 49 miniature Bodhisattva statues. People pray for sick relatives or ask for happiness by contributing kerosene for use in the lamps. Petitioners' names and those of ill family members are written on slips of paper, which are attached to the branches of the 'tree'.

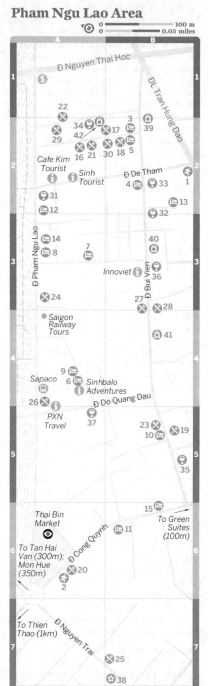

Pham Ngu Lao Area

Pham Ngu Lao Area

HO CHI MINH CITY SIGHTS

Prayers are held daily from 4am to 5am, 11am to noon, 4pm to 5pm and 7pm to 9pm. They consist of chanting to the accompaniment of drums, bells and gongs, following a traditional rite which is seldom performed these days.

Giac Lam Pagoda is about 3km from Cholon in Tan Binh district, and is best reached by taxi (about 100,000d from Pham Ngu Lao) or *xe om*.

Le Van Duyet Temple TEMPLE
(Đ Dinh Tien Hoang, Binh Thanh District) Dedicated to Marshal Le Van Duyet (1763–1831), this shrine is also his burial place, alongside that of his wife. The marshal was a South Vietnamese general and viceroy who helped put down the Tay Son Rebellion and reunify Vietnam. When the Nguyen dynasty came to power in 1802, he was elevated by Emperor Gia Long to the rank of marshal. He fell out of favour with Gia Long's successor, Minh Mang, who tried him posthumously and desecrated his grave. Emperor Thieu Tri, who succeeded Minh Mang, restored the tomb, thus fulfilling a prophecy of its destruction and restoration. Le Van Duyet was considered a national hero in the South before 1975 but is disliked by the communists because of his involvement in the expansion of French influence.

Among the items on display are a portrait of Le Van Duyet, some of his personal effects (including European-style crystal goblets), two wonderful life-size horse statues and a stuffed and mounted tiger.

During celebrations of Tet and on the 30th day of the seventh lunar month (the anniversary of Le Van Duyet's death), the tomb is thronged with pilgrims. The caged birds for sale in and around the grounds are bought by pilgrims and freed to earn merit. The unfortunate creatures are often recaptured (and liberated again). Vietnamese used to come here to take oaths of good faith if they could not afford the services of a court of justice.

The temple is reached by heading north from Da Kao on Đ Dinh Tien Hoang.

Ho Chi Minh Museum
MUSEUM

(Bao Tang Ho Chi Minh; Map p298; 1 Đ Nguyen Tat Thanh, District 4; admission 10,000d; ☺7.30-11.30am & 1.30-5pm Tue-Sun) Nicknamed the 'Dragon House' (Nha Rong), this former customs house was built by the French authorities in 1863. The link between Ho Chi Minh and the museum building is tenuous: 21-year-old Ho, having signed on as a stoker and galley boy on a French freighter, left Vietnam from here in 1911 and thus began 30 years of exile in France, the Soviet Union, China and elsewhere.

The museum houses many of Ho's personal effects, including some of his clothing (he was a man of informal dress), his sandals and his spectacles. Otherwise, it covers the story of the man born Nguyen Tat Than – from his childhood, to his political awakening to his role in booting out the French and leading North Vietnam, to his death in 1969 – mainly through photographs (captioned in Vietnamese and English).

The museum is on the waterfront, just across Ben Nghe Channel from District 1. It's easily reached on foot from the central city by heading south along the river on Đ Ton Duc Thang and crossing the bridge.

Saigon South
NEIGHBOURHOOD

(off Map p298) Just as the movie *District 9* depicted an extraterrestrial enclave on the outskirts of Johannesburg, so Saigon's District 7 is an utterly alien environment within HCMC's fringes – a sleek and fashionable retreat for the rich. Businesspeople, both expats and the local nouveau riche, have embraced this planned neighbourhood of wide streets, fancy shops and manicured parks. A centrepiece is the **Crescent** (Ho Ban Nguyet), a glitzy promenade along a scooped-out section of canal.

It's well worth visiting Saigon South for a stroll and a look around. If you're a fitness freak, it's one of the less petrol-fumed places for a jog. Plenty of big-name city restaurants and chains have rushed to colonise the area, so you won't go hungry. The Crescent is 7km south of Pham Ngu Lao; it should only take 15 minutes by cab, outside of peak times.

🏃 Activities

River Cruises

There's always someone hanging around the vicinity of **Bach Dang jetty** (Map p301; Đ Ton Duc Thang) looking to charter a boat to tour the Saigon River. The price should be around US$10 per hour for a small boat or US$15 to US$30 for a larger, faster craft. Since you hire boats by the hour, some will go slowly because they know the meter is running. It's better to set an itinerary and a time limit at the start. Ask them to bring the boat to you, rather than you going to the boat.

The government has been clearing the worst of the shanties from the sides of the inner-city canals and gradually converting them into parks and promenades. So far, this has done little to improve the water quality, which is still a forbidding inky black colour and quite whiffy.

Bonsai River Cruise
DINNER CRUISE

(✆3910 5095; www.bonsaicruise.com.vn; tickets US$36) Set onboard a striking wooden boat painted like a dragon, the Bonsai's dinner cruises feature live music. The price includes a welcome drink, canapés, buffet dinner, soft drink and, incongruously, a head and shoulder massage.

Tau Sai Gon
DINNER CRUISE

(✆3823 0393; www.tausaigon.com) Saigon Tourist's large floating restaurant takes to the waters every evening, offering both an Asian and European menu. There's a fixed charge for the Sunday buffet lunch (per adult/child 150,000/100,000d; departing 11.30am, returning 1.30pm).

Indochina Junk
DINNER CRUISE

(✆3824 8299; www.indochinajunk.com.vn) Another dinner cruise, this one with set menus (US$15–35) in an atmospheric wooden junk.

Swimming Pools & Water Parks

When the weather gets sticky, the city's pools can provide a welcome respite. Several inner-city hotels also offer access to their pools to nonguests for a fee, including the Legend (p321), Park Hyatt (p321), Majestic (p321), Renaissance Riverside (p322) and Rex (p333).

Dam Sen Water Park
WATER PARK

(Map p298; ✆3858 8418; www.damsenwaterpark.com.vn; 3 Đ Hoa Binh, District 11; adult/child 80,000/50,000d; ☺9am-6pm) Water slides, rivers with rapids (or slow currents) and rope swings.

Workers' Club
POOL

(Map p310; rear, 55B Đ Nguyen Thi Minh Khai, District 3; admission 14,000d) The swimming pool of the old Cercle Sportif still has its colonnades and some Art Deco charm.

Dai The Gioi Water Park
WATER PARK

(off Map p314; Đ Ham Tu, Cholon; admission 35,000-65,000d; ☺8am-9pm Mon-Fri, 10am-9pm Sat & Sun) Large pool and slides.

Massage & Spa

HCMC offers some truly fantastic hideaways for pampering, the perfect antidote to a frenetic day spent dodging motorbikes. While many hotels have massage services, some are more legitimate than others. For male travellers, even 'a traditional foot massage' can end up in somewhat higher bodily regions if you're not careful. Unfortunately, it can be very hard to tell the reputable massage establishments from the more dubious ones. To the best of our knowledge, the places reviewed here are all strictly legit. Check out www.spasvietnam.com for extensive reviews and online bookings.

L'Apothiquaire
SPA

(www.lapothiquaire.com) La Maison de L'Apothiquaire (Map p310; ☎3932 5181; 64A Đ Truong Dinh, District 3; ☺9am-9pm; ☎); Artisan Beauté (Map p301; ☎3822 2158; 100 Đ Mac Thi Buoi, District 1; Saigon South (☎5413 6638; 103 Đ Ton Dat Thien, District 7) Long considered the city's most elegant spa, L'Apothiquaire is housed in a beautiful white mansion tucked down a quiet alley, with a pool and sauna. Guests enjoy body wraps, massages, facials, foot treatments and herbal baths, and L'Apothiquaire makes its own line of lotions and cosmetics. The offshoot branches are smaller and concentrate on beauty treatments.

Aqua Day Spa
SPA

(Map p301; ☎3827 2828; www.aquadayspasaigon.com; Sheraton Saigon, 88 Đ Dong Khoi; 1hr massage 1,350,000d; ☺10am-11pm) One of HCMC's fanciest hotel spas, this beautiful space offers a range of treatments, including warm-stone massage, foot pampering and facials.

Vietnamese Traditional Massage Institute
MASSAGE

(Map p316; ☎3839 6697; 185 Đ Cong Quynh, District 1; per hr in fan/air-con room 50,000/60,000d; ☺9am-8pm) Sure, it's not the classiest act in town, but it does offer inexpensive, no-nonsense massages performed by well-trained blind masseurs from the HCMC Association for the Blind.

Just Men
SPA

(Map p301; ☎3914 1407; 40 Đ Ton That Thiep, District 1; ☺9am-8pm) In a city where establishments catering exclusively to men prioritise stimulation over relaxation, Just Men is the exception. This perfectly legit establishment offers the discerning gentleman haircuts, shaves and excellent facials, or the opportunity to get a manicure and pedicure while nattering with all the other blokes.

Jasmine
SPA

(Map p301; ☎3827 2737; 45 Đ Ton That Thiep, District 1; ☺9am-8pm) Just Men's unisex sister.

Glow
SPA

(Map p301; ☎3823 8368; www.glowsaigon.com; 129A Đ Nguyen Hue, District 1, 1hr massage US$32; ☺11am-9pm) Offers an array of aromatherapy facials, hair treatments and therapeutic massage.

Other Activities

Diamond Superbowl
BOWLING

(Map p301; ☎3825 7778; 4th fl, Diamond Department Store, 34 ĐL Le Duan; bowling 35,000-60,000d; ☺10am-1am; ☎) Who won the war again? This central bowling alley, surrounded by American junk food chains, may have you wondering. It's very popular with locals thanks to fluorescent bowling balls and state-of-the-art scoring. Attached is a large amusement centre with billiards and video games.

Vietnam Golf & Country Club
GOLF

(Cau Lac Bo Golf Quoc Te Viet Nam; ☎6280 0101; www.vietnamgolfcc.com; Long Thanh My Village, District 9; 18 holes weekday/weekend US$109/143) Playing golf has become a mark of status in Vietnam and this club, about 20km east of central HCMC, caters to the city's would-be high flyers. As well as 36 holes of golf, other facilities include tennis courts and a swimming pool.

X-Rock Climbing
CLIMBING

(Map p310; ☎6278 5794; www.xrockclimbing.com; 75 ĐL Nguyen Dinh Chieu, District 3; trial package/day-pass 80,000/180,000d) Get in some practice for Cat Ba or Halong Bay by scaling the 16m climbing wall here.

☚ Courses

Saigon Cooking Class
COOKING

(Map p301; ☎3825 8485; www.saigoncookingclass.com; 74/7 ĐL Hai Ba Trung, District 1; per adult/child (over 14) US$39/25; ☺10am & 2pm Tue-Sun) Watch and learn from the chefs at Hoa Tuc as they prepare three mains (including *pho bo* and some of their signature dishes) and one dessert. A market visit is optional (per adult/child over 14 US$44/25, including three-hour class).

Vietnam Cookery Centre COOKING
(☑3512 7246; www.vietnamcookery.com; 362/8 Đ Ung Van Khiem, Binh Thanh District) Offers introductory classes, market visits and VIP premium classes.

University of Social Sciences & Humanities LANGUAGE
(Dai Hoc Khoa Hoc Xa Hoi Va Nhan Van; Map p308; ☑3822 5009; www.vns.edu.vn; 12 Đ Dinh Tien Hoang) If you're planning a longer stay in HCMC, the university's group classes are a reasonably priced way to learn the language.

☞ Tours

There are dozens of travel agencies offering tours of the city, day trips to surrounding areas and lengthier itineraries taking in sights throughout the country (see p339 for recommended agencies). The best-value tours are available from agencies in the Pham Ngu Lao area, although cheap rates often mean large groups, less flexibility and, if you're staying overnight, rudimentary accommodation. Usually you can upgrade the accommodation for an additional fee.

City tours generally include Notre Dame Cathedral, the old post office, the Reunification Palace, the War Remnants Museum and Cholon's Thien Hau Pagoda. Other stops might include the Jade Emperor Pagoda, Binh Tay Market or a lacquer workshop. Prices range from US$7 to US$9 for a group tour, to US$80 for a personalised one-on-one tour.

The most popular day trip is to the Cu Chi Tunnels, either as a half-day tour (US$4 to US$7) or combined with a visit to the Cao Dai Great Temple in Tay Ninh (US$7 to US$9). Day trips to the Mekong Delta invariably include a boat ride and either head to My Tho and Ben Tre (US$8 to US$28) or to Vinh Long and Cai Be Floating Market

(US$13 to US$33). Another day trip option is Can Gio mangrove forest (US$25).

Hiring a *cyclo* for a half day or full day of sightseeing is an interesting option, but be sure to agree on the price before setting out (most drivers charge around US$2 per hour).

Vietnam Vespa Adventure
(Map p316; ☑0122 565 6264; www.vietnamvespaadventure .com; 169A Đ De Tham), which operates out of Cafe Zoom, offers guided city tours on classic scooters (from US$48) as well as multiday trips around southern Vietnam.

✵ Festivals & Events

Tet NATIONAL HOLIDAY
(First day of first lunar month) The whole city parties and then empties out for family breaks. Đ Nguyen Hue is closed off for a huge flower exhibition, blooms fill Tao Dan Park and everyone exchanges lucky money.

Saigon Cyclo Race CHARITY RACE
(mid-March) Professional and amateur *cyclo* drivers find out who's fastest; money raised is donated to local charities.

🛏 Sleeping

District 1 is the obvious choice for lodging in HCMC given its proximity to almost everything of interest, its relative closeness to the airport and its vast array of establishments at every price level. Within District 1, you can either head east towards Đ Dong Khoi for fancy digs close to the city's best restaurants and bars, west towards Đ Pham Ngu Lao for budget guesthouses and cheap tours, or somewhere in between – geographically and price-wise.

At the lower end, a few dollars can be the difference between a dank, dirty, windowless shoebox and a pleasant, clean, well-appointed room with free wi-fi and air-conditioning. Needless to say, there are cheaper places than those listed below but you get what you pay for. If finding a rock-bottom price is your only consideration, a quick door-to-door around Pham Ngu Lao will turn up dives for US$10 or even less.

Upgrading to a midrange property can seem a little pointless when there are excellent, comfortable, moderately hip rooms with all the bells and whistles available for US$20 around Pham Ngu Lao. More discerning budget travellers can book ahead for similar places at slightly lower rates in the surrounding wards, such as the Co Giang and Nguyen Thai Binh wards.

HCMC FOR CHILDREN

At first glance, the frenzied streets of Ho Chi Minh City might not look that kiddie-friendly but there are water parks (p318), plenty of leafy gardens and lots of cafes and ice-cream shops that are family-friendly. There are also plenty of activities for older children to enjoy such as ten-pin bowling (p319) and rock-climbing (p319). Beyond the city is Dai Nam Theme Park (p350), the closest thing to Disneyland in Vietnam.

At the top end, many of the city's best hotels occupy historic, character-filled buildings and offer swimming pools and luxurious spas. The standards are international, as are the prices.

If you book ahead, many hotels will fetch you at the airport for between US$5 and US$10.

DONG KHOI AREA

The Dong Khoi area is home to most of HCMC's top-notch hotels but there are also some excellent midrange options.

TOP CHOICE **Park Hyatt Saigon** HOTEL $$$

(Map p301; ✈3824 1234; www.saigon.park.hyatt.com; 2 Lam Son Sq; r around US$350; ❄@🔊≋) Setting the standard as the smartest hotel in Saigon, the Park Hyatt has a prime location opposite the Opera House. This neoclassical structure is as easy on the eye as its lavishly appointed rooms. There's an inviting pool, the acclaimed Xuan Spa, and a highly regarded (yet affordable) Italian restaurant, Opera.

Intercontinental Asiana Saigon HOTEL $$$

(Map p301; ✈3520 9999; www.intercontinental.com; cnr ĐL Hai Ba Trung & ĐL Le Duan; r from US$189; ❄@🔊≋) Modern and tasteful without falling into generic blandness, the Intercontinental is a welcome recent addition to Saigon's ever-expanding range of luxury establishments. Rooms have separate shower cubicles and free-standing baths, and many have wonderful views. A neighbouring tower of apartment-style residences caters to longer stayers.

Caravelle Hotel HOTEL $$$

(Map p301; ✈3823 4999; www.caravellehotel.com; 19 Lam Son Sq; r from US$218; ❄@🔊≋) One of the first luxury hotels to re-open its doors in post-war Saigon, the Caravelle still sets a high standard. Rooms are quietly elegant, well equipped and spread between 16 new floors and the historic 'signature' wing. The rooftop Saigon Saigon Bar is a spectacular spot for a cocktail.

Legend Hotel Saigon HOTEL $$$

(Map p301; ✈3823 3333; www.legendsaigon.com; 2A-4A Ð Ton Duc Thang; s US$160-390, d US$175-415; ❄@🔊≋) An exercise in Asian glam, the lobby of this large hotel is an explosion of marble, stained glass, Roman-style chairs, golden storks standing on golden turtles, fountains, palm trees with fairy lights, and

two immense bronze horses. Visible from the lobby is Saigon's most beautiful resort-style pool. The rooms feel slightly dated but are extremely comfortable, with luxurious linen.

Spring Hotel HOTEL $$

(Map p301; ✈3829 7362; www.springhotelvietnam.com; 44-46 Ð Le Thanh Ton; s US$35-55, d US$40-60, ste US$72-97; ❄@🔊) An old favourite, this welcoming hotel is handy to dozens of restaurants and bars on the popular Le Thanh Ton and Hai Ba Trung strips. The rooms are a little dated but bas reliefs and moulded cornices give it a touch of class.

Liberty Central HOTEL $$$

(Map p301; ✈3823 9269; www.libertycentralhotel.com; 177 Ð Le Thanh Ton; s US$100-140, d US$110-150; ❄@🔊≋) Acres of creamy marble and a giant sepia-toned painting of old Saigon set the scene at this chic new hotel. Upstairs, the rooms are furnished to a high standard and a rooftop pool offers thrilling city views. Given its busy location near Ben Thanh Market, street noise is unavoidable.

Northern Hotel HOTEL $$$

(Map p301; ✈3825 1751; www.northernhotel.com.vn; 11A Ð Thi Sach; s US$70-110, d US$80-120; ❄@🔊⊝) Asian glam on a budget, the Northern's rooms are some of the smartest in town for this kind of money. The bathrooms are a cut above the average, plus there's a rooftop bar and gym.

Majestic Hotel HOTEL $$$

(Map p301; ✈3829 5517; www.majesticsaigon.com.vn; 1 Ð Dong Khoi; s/d from US$148/158; ❄@🔊≋) Dollar for dollar it may not have the best rooms in town, but the colonial atmosphere of this venerable 1925 riverside hotel makes it a romantic option. Take a dip in the courtyard pool on a hot afternoon or sip a cocktail on the rooftop bar on a breezy evening. Breakfast and fruit basket included.

King Star Hotel HOTEL $$

(Map p301; ✈3822 6424; www.kingstarhotel.com; 8A ĐL Thai Van Lung; r US$40-70; ❄@🔊) Completely refurbished in 2008, this hotel is now verging on the boutique-business look. The decoration is very contemporary and all rooms have flat-screen TVs and snazzy showers.

Duxton Hotel HOTEL $$$

(Map p301; ✈3822 2999; www.duxtonhotels.com; 63 Ð Nguyen Hue; r from US$110; ❄🔊≋) A grand entry (complete with an oversized birdbath of a fountain) welcomes guests to this smart business hotel. It's well located for city explorations on foot.

Sheraton Saigon
HOTEL $$$

(Map p301; ☑3827 2828; www.sheraton.com/sai gon; 88 Đ Dong Khoi; r from US$225; ☞❄@☀) The Sheraton lives up to expectations with luxurious rooms, an excellent spa and an elegant pool.

Riverside Hotel
HOTEL $$$

(Map p301; ☑3822 4038; www.riversidehotelsg .com; 18 Đ Ton Duc Thang; s $US59-150, d US$69-169; ❄@☀) Its grand 1920s bones might hark to better days gone by, but the Riverside still delivers excellent value for money for a prime location.

Renaissance Riverside Saigon
HOTEL $$$

(Map p301; ☑3822 0033; www.renaissance-saigon .com; 8-15 Đ Ton Duc Thang; r from US$162; ❄@☀❄) A towering riverside skyscraper with smart rooms and slick service. The cinematic river views are worth the extra dollars.

Indochine Hotel
HOTEL $$

(Map p301; ☑3822 0082; www.indochinehotel .com; 40-42 ĐL Hai Ba Trung; r US$30-50, ste US$65-100; ❄@☀) The location's excellent for this solid midrange hotel. The cheapest rooms don't have windows, so it's worth paying US$10 extra for a superior.

Asian Hotel
HOTEL $$

(Map p301; ☑3829 6979; asianhotel@hcm.fpt.vn; 150 Đ Dong Khoi; s/d US$43/48; ❄@☀) A central hotel with clean and comfortable rooms albeit devoid of any noticeable design flair.

Thien Xuan
HOTEL $$

(Map p301; ☑3824 5680; www.thienxuanhotel .com.vn; 108 Đ Le Thanh Ton; r US$39-51; ❄@☀) Mere metres away from Ben Thanh Market, this is another friendly mid-tier option. Windowless rooms are cheaper and quieter.

REUNIFICATION PALACE & AROUND

Sherwood Residence
APARTMENTS $$$

(Map p310; ☑3823 2288; www.sherwoodresidence .com; 127 Đ Pasteur; apt US$128-143; ❄☀❄) The epaulettes on the uniformed doormen provide a hint of what's to come in the grand (bordering on camp) lobby, with its painted and gilded ceiling inset, giant chandelier and lush circular carpet. The two- to three-bedroom apartments are much more restrained – and available for monthly rental (c US$2000). In the complex you'll find a

gym, sauna, kid's play area, small supermarket and wonderful indoor pool.

Lavender Hotel
HOTEL $$$

(Map p310; ☑2222 8888; www.lavenderhotel.com .vn; 208 Đ Le Thanh Ton; r US$70-110, ste US$140; ❄☀) Eschewing the nana-ish connotations of its name, Lavender drapes itself stylishly in creamy marble and muted tones. The location, right by Ben Thanh Market, is excellent if potentially noisy.

Saigon Star Hotel
HOTEL $$

(Map p310; ☑3930 6290; www.saigonstarhotel .com.vn; 204 Đ Nguyen Thi Minh Khai; s US$50-75, d US$60-85; ❄☀) Although it is starting to show its age (a fact taken account of in the rates) this business hotel warrants a mention for families due to its location opposite Tao Dan Park.

PHAM NGU LAO AREA

Most budget travellers head to Pham Ngu Lao, as it is an easy place to hunt for a hotel or guesthouse on foot. Four streets (Đ Pham Ngu Lao, Đ De Tham, Đ Bui Vien and Đ Do Quang Dau) along with a warren of intersecting alleys form the heart of this backpacker ghetto, with more than 100 places in which to stay. But don't let that backpacker tag put you off. If you consider yourself more of a midrange traveller, you'll find some excellent deals here, often at budget prices. Breakfasts are usually included but they tend to be fairly basic and lacking in variety.

Among the options are countless family-run guesthouses (US$10 to US$35) and mini-hotels (US$25 to US$55), and even the odd dorm. We have highlighted some of the better places but there are dozens more, with new places opening all the time. It's a sad fact that poor building practices and a lack of maintenance can mean that sparkling new guesthouses can quickly turn mouldy and smelly – so it pays to check your room first.

TOP CHOICE Giang & Son
GUESTHOUSE $

(Map p316; ☑3837 7548; www.giangson.netfirms .com; 283/14 Đ Pham Ngu Lao; r US$16-25; ❄@☀) It's hard to justify staying anywhere more expensive when there are guesthouses as clean, comfortable and friendly as this one, located on our favourite, surprisingly quiet, PNL alley. Tall and thin, with three rooms on each floor, Giang & Son's only downer is that there's no lift – which makes a trip up to the rooftop terrace quite unappealing. It's worth upgrading to a US$20 room for a window.

TOP CHOICE **Hong Han Hotel**   GUESTHOUSE **$**

(Map p316; ☎3836 1927; www.honghan.netfirms .com; 238 Đ Bui Vien; r US$20-25; ❋@🛜) Another corker guesthouse in the tall and skinny mode (seven floors and no lift), Hong Han has upped the ante in terms of style. The front rooms have thrilling views down Đ Bui Vien to the Bitexco Tower but the smaller rear rooms are quieter and cheaper. Free breakfast is served on a 1st floor terrace overlooking the street.

Bich Duyen Hotel   GUESTHOUSE **$**

(Map p316; ☎3837 4588; bichduyenhotel@yahoo .com; 283/4 Đ Pham Ngu Lao; r US$17-25; ❋@🛜) On the same lovely lane as Giang & Son, this welcoming place follows a similar template. The US$25 rooms are worth the extra money for the luxury of a window. There are excellent shower stalls but, unusually, no soap is provided.

Diep Anh   GUESTHOUSE **$**

(Map p316; ☎3836 7920; dieptheanh@hcm.vnn.vn; 241/31 Đ Pham Ngu Lao; r US$20; ❋@🛜) A step above most PNL guesthouses, figuratively and literally (there are endless stairs), Diep Anh's tall and narrow shape makes for light and airy upper rooms. The gracious staff ensure they're kept in good nick.

An An Hotel   HOTEL **$$**

(Map p316; ☎3837 8087; www.anan.vn; 40 Đ Bui Vien; r US$40-50; ❋@🛜) Unassuming, unpretentious and affable, this skinny but smart, midrange mini-hotel has well-proportioned, businesslike rooms with showers fitted over bathtubs. Unexpected extras include safety deposit boxes and in-room computers.

Elios Hotel   HOTEL **$$**

(Map p316; ☎3838 5584; www.elioshotel.vn; 233 Đ Pham Ngu Lao; s US$48-102, d US$53-107; ❋@🛜) The swish entrance to this hotel is proof of the ongoing gentrification of the PNL area. The rooms don't quite live up to the lobby's promise but they're clean and modern, with safes and writing desks. For huge views, head to the rooftop Blue Sky Restaurant.

Beautiful Saigon 2   HOTEL **$$**

(Map p316; ☎3920 8929; www.beautifulsaigon2ho tel.com; 40/19 Đ Bui Vien; s US$26-37, d $US29-42; ❋@🛜) Unlike its Beautiful sister which sits around the corner on busy Bui Vien, this new mini-hotel lurks down a back lane. The ground floor is taken up by a restaurant, giving it more of a guesthouse feel. Deluxe rooms have balconies.

ⓘ **FINDING YOUR ALLEY**

Ho Chi Minh might seem like a modern city but it's one that's grown higgledy-piggledy over many years. Every scrap of land is precious and many (if not most) people live in the fine lacework of alleys that connect the main streets.

These alleys don't have names but rather take the street number of the main street that they are closest to, i.e. 175 Đ Pham Ngu Lao is the name of the alley running off Đ Pham Ngu Lao at number 175. Within the alley the buildings are numbered consecutively, with the number placed in the address after a slash: Le Pub's address is 175/22 Đ Pham Ngu Lao, for instance. In particularly crowded alleys a confusing array of sub-numbers and letters can sometimes be added after a second slash.

If the alley runs between two main streets, the two ends often take different names. Hence properties at the southern end of 175 Đ Pham Ngu Lao have the address 28 Đ Bui Vien. Confused?

Beautiful Saigon   HOTEL **$$**

(Map p316; ☎3836 4852; www.beautifulsaigonho tel.com; 62 Đ Bui Vien; s US$26-45, d $US29-55; ❋@🛜) Another tall and skinny mini-hotel, this one has a modern reception staffed by staff wearing red *ao dai* (traditional dresses). A glass-and-marble lift ascends to the tidy rooms, the cheaper of which are small and windowless.

Green Suites   HOTEL **$$**

(off Map p316; ☎3836 5400; www.greensuiteshotel .com; 102/1 Đ Cong Quynh; s US$22-40, d $US26-50; ❋@🛜) Treat 'em to green to keep 'em keen seems to be the motto of this relatively large hotel, slunk down a quiet alley off Đ Cong Quynh, immediately south of Đ Bui Vien. Behind the pastel green façade you can rest on a pea-green couch until the staff in forest green suits show you to your room. The tiled rooms are clean and, obstinately, not very green at all.

Mai Phai Hotel   HOTEL **$**

(Map p316; ☎3836 5868; maiphaihotel@saigonnet .vn; 209 Đ Pham Ngu Lao; r US$18-25; ❋@🛜) The service is friendly and the rooms are well furnished in this mini-hotel right on the main strip. Bonus features include a lift and curious sculpted paintings in the corridors.

Nhat Thao
GUESTHOUSE $

(Map p316; ☑3836 8117; Nhatthaohotel@yahoo
.com; 35/4 Đ Bui Vien; r US$20-22; ✹🛜) Small
but clean rooms are offered in this family-
run place, set behind a small courtyard. It's
worth paying the extra US$2 for a window.

Madame Cuc's 127
GUESTHOUSE $

(Map p316; ☑3836 8761; www.madamcuchotels
.com; s US$16-20, d US$25-30; 127 Đ Cong Quynh;
✹@🛜) The original and by far the best of
three hotels run by the welcoming Madame
Cuc and her friendly staff. Rooms are clean
and spacious.

Spring House Hotel
HOTEL $

(Map p316; ☑3837 8312; www.springhousehotel.com
.vn; 221 Đ Pham Ngu Lao; r US$18-40; ✹@🛜) Fur-
nished in bamboo and rattan, this is a cosy
hotel in the middle of the Pham Ngu Lao
strip. Rooms come in many shapes and sizes.

Xuan Mai Hotel
GUESTHOUSE $

(Map p316; ☑3838 6418; xuan_mai_hotel@yahoo
.com; 140 Đ Cong Quynh; s/d US$22/24; ✹@🛜)
Don't be put off by the shabby reception, the
rooms here are fine.

NGUYEN THAI BINH & AROUND

Blue River Hotel 2
GUESTHOUSE $

(Map p312; ☑3915 2852; www.blueriverhotel
.com; 54/13 Đ Ky Con; r US$17-25; ✹@🛜) Close
to both Dong Khoi and Pham Ngu Lao but
far enough away to feel like you've escaped
the tourist enclave, this friendly, family-run
guesthouse is an excellent option. It's located down a quiet lane, offering a window into
local urban life. Its PNL sister property isn't
bad either.

Quynh Kim
GUESTHOUSE $

(Map p312; ☑3821 0533; 28 Đ Trinh Van Can; r
US$17-25; ✹) A line of plastic flowers and
mushrooms edge the stairs up to reception,
where you're greeted by a friendly family
and their array of household gods. Rooms
are sizeable and clean.

CO GIANG

For a quieter and slightly cheaper alternative to Pham Ngu Lao, there's a string of
excellent guesthouses in Co Giang ward
(District 1) in a quiet alley connecting Đ Co
Giang and Đ Co Bac. To reach the alley, head
southwest on ĐL Tran Hung Dao, turn left
at Đ Nguyen Kac Nhu and then first right
onto Đ Co Bac. The guesthouses are down
the first alley to the left.

Given the homely, workaday nature of the
neighbourhood, all of the guesthouses down

this lane are popular with long-timers (expat
English teachers and the like), so you'll need
to book well ahead to nab a place. Preference is given to longer-term bookings.

Ngoc Son
TOP CHOICE
GUESTHOUSE $

(☑3836 4717; ngocsonguesthouse@yahoo.com;
178/32 Đ Co Giang; s/d US$12/17; ✹🛜) Fresh as
a daisy, this small guesthouse has a family
lounge with feature wallpaper downstairs
and good value rooms above. The art and
books in the bedrooms are a nice touch.

California
GUESTHOUSE $

(☑3837 8885; guesthousecaliforniasaigon@yahoo.
com; 171A Đ Co Bac; r US$15-18; ✹@🛜) 'Such a
lovely place...' or so the Eagles might have
said. Intimate, friendly and clean, the Cali-
fornia has a guest kitchen (a rarity), stocked
with coffee and cake (unheard of), and free
laundry (an absolute miracle).

Miss Loi's
GUESTHOUSE $

(☑3837 9589; missloi@hcm.fpt.vn; 178/20 Đ Co
Giang; r US$12-25; ✹@🛜) The original Co
Giang guesthouse, with a homely atmosphere and helpful staff. Miss Loi is an attentive host and the rates include a light
breakfast.

Dan Le Hotel
GUESTHOUSE $

(☑3836 9651; danle_hotel@yahoo.com.vn; 171/10
Đ Co Bac; s/d US$12/16; ✹) Down the end of a
dead-end arm of the alley, this smart place
has tidy rooms, potted palms everywhere
and koi in tanks. There's also a little roof
terrace.

OTHER NEIGHBOURHOODS

Ma Maison Boutique Hotel
TOP CHOICE
HOTEL $$

(☑3846 0263; www.mamaison.vn; 656/52 Cach
Mang Thang Tam, District 3; s US$65-90, d US$75-95;
✹🛜) Down a peaceful lane off a busy arterial
route, friendly Ma Maison is located halfway
between the airport and the city centre (about
80,000d by cab) – and, decor-wise, partly in
the French countryside. Wooden shutters sof-
ten the exterior of the modern, medium-rise
block, while in the rooms, painted French
provincial–style furniture and first-rate bath-
rooms add a touch of panache.

Thien Thao
HOTEL $$

(off Map p316; ☑3929 1440; www.thienthaohotel
.com; 89 Đ Cao Thang, District 3; r US$32-60;
✹@🛜) All you'd want from a midrange hotel, Thien Thao has affable staff and clean,
comfortable, smallish rooms kitted out with
bathrobes, safes and proper shower stalls.

Deluxe rooms are quieter but otherwise not very different from the standards. From the Pham Ngu Lao area, take Đ Bui Thi Xuan, which becomes Đ Cao Thang.

✗ Eating

Although Hanoi might think of itself as more cultured, HCMC is the culinary heavyweight of Vietnam. Restaurants here range from dirt-cheap sidewalk stalls to atmospheric villas, each adding a unique twist to traditional Vietnamese flavours.

As well as delicious regional fare, the city offers a welcoming dose of world cuisine, with Indian, Japanese, Thai, Italian and East-West fusions well represented. Unsurprisingly, given its heritage, HCMC has a fine selection of French restaurants, from the casual bistro to haute cuisine. English-language menus are common in most restaurants these days.

Good foodie neighbourhoods include the Dong Khoi area, with a high concentration of top-quality restaurants, as well as the bordering sections of District 3. Pham Ngu Lao's eateries, attempting to satisfy every possible culinary whim, are generally less impressive but good value. Chinese fare rules Cholon, although restaurants here can seem sparser than pagodas on a casual stroll through the area. There are also a few escapes further afield for those willing to explore.

Markets always have a good selection of stalls whipping up tasty treats. Ben Thanh's night market is particularly good. Most of these stalls, like the vendors at the street, specialise in only one dish. Pick one that's busy with locals and you're unlikely to be disappointed.

Banh mi – sandwiches with a French look and a very Vietnamese taste – are sold by street vendors. Fresh baguettes are stuffed with something resembling pâté (don't ask), pickled gherkins and various other fillings. A sandwich costs between 15,000d and 25,000d, depending on what you choose.

The largest concentration of vegetarian restaurants is around the Pham Ngu Lao area and you'll usually find one in the vicinity of a Buddhist pagoda. On the first and 15th days of the lunar month (Vietnamese Buddhism's compulsory vegetarian days), food stalls around the city, especially in the markets, serve vegetarian versions of meaty Vietnamese dishes. While these stalls are quick to serve, they're usually swamped on these special days. Be patient, as it's worth the wait.

DONG KHOI AREA

TOP **CHOICE** **Nha Hang Ngon** VIETNAMESE $
(Map p301; ☑3827 7131; 160 Đ Pasteur; mains 35,000-205,000d; ☺7am-10pm; ⊖☎) Always heaving with locals and foreigners alike, this is one of the most popular places in town, offering the opportunity to sample a large range of the very best street food in stylish surroundings. Set in a leafy garden ringed by food stalls, each cook serves up a specialised traditional dish, ensuring an authentic taste. Follow your nose and browse the stalls.

TOP **CHOICE** **Temple Club** VIETNAMESE $
(Map p301; ☑3829 9244; 29 Đ Ton That Thiep; mains 59,000-98,000d; ☺11.30am-10.30pm; ⊖☎✐) This classy establishment is housed

FAST PHO

Proving that fast food doesn't need to be bland, generic or unhealthy, HCMC's chain restaurants serve up tasty, traditional treats that won't leave you covered in grease.

Pho 24 VIETNAMESE
(www.pho24.com.vn; mains 45,000-68,000d; ☺7am-late; ☎); 71-73 Đ Dong Khoi (Map p301); 5 Đ Nguyen Thiep (Map p301); 82 Đ Nguyen Du (Map p301); Diamond Department Store (Map p301; 34 Đ Le Duan); Parkson Plaza (Map p301; Le Thanh Ton); Vincom Centre (Map p301; 72 Le Thanh Ton); 271 Đ Pham Ngu Lao (Map p316) It may be the leading noodle-soup chain in the country, but this is no McPho. Choose your cuts of meat and enjoy a steaming bowl accompanied by a veritable jungle of herbs.

Wrap & Roll FAST FOOD
(Map p301; www.wrap-roll.com; mains 38,000-98,000d; ☺10.30am-10.30pm; ✐); 62 Đ Hai Ba Trung; 115 ĐL Nguyen Hue); Vincom Centre (basement, 72 Le Thanh Ton); Diamond Department Store (34 Đ Le Duan); Parkson Plaza (Le Thanh Ton) Stylish-looking restaurants offering a big selection of pre-rolled or roll-your-own dishes from all around the country. Perfect for those who love to play with their food.

on the 2nd floor of a beautiful colonial-era villa, decked out in spiritual motifs. There's a massive selection of delectable Vietnamese dishes on offer, including a range of vegetarian specialities, and the spirited cocktails are a good way to prepare for the experience.

Huong Lai
VIETNAMESE $

(Map p301; ☑3822 6814; 38 Đ Ly Tu Trong; mains 40,000-120,000d) Set in the airy loft of an old French-era shop house, this is dining with a difference. All of the staff are from disadvantaged families or are former street children and receive on-the-job training, education and a place to stay. Many have gone on to secure jobs at top hotels and restaurants. A must for beautifully presented, traditional Vietnamese food.

Xu
VIETNAMESE $$

(Map p301; ☑3824 8468; www.xusaigon.com; 1st fl, 75 ĐL Hai Ba Trung; lunch 50,000-165,000d, dinner 175,000-340,000d; ⊘11am-midnight; 🛜) This super-stylish restaurant-lounge serves up a menu of Vietnamese-inspired fusion dishes. The name means coin and it is expensive, but well worth the flutter. Top service, a classy wine list and the happening lounge-bar round things off nicely. For a gastronomic adventure, try the tasting menu (850,000d).

Flow
EUROPEAN $$

(Map p301; ☑3915 3691; www.flowsaigon.com; 88 Đ Ho Tung Mau; mains 130,000-365,000d; ⊘10am-midnight Mon-Fri, 10am-midnight Sat, 10am-3.30pm Sun; ⊜🛜) Going with the Flow has a lot to recommend it. Firstly, there's the elegant rock star–chic ambience of the dining room (black studded chairs, crimson banquettes, edgy art) and then there's the wonderfully creative cuisine. Add to that the cocktail conjurers in the downstairs bar, an appealing terrace and occasional after-hours performances, and you've got one of HCMC's hippest establishments.

Warda
MIDDLE EASTERN $$

(Map p301; ☑3823 3822; 71/7 Đ Mac Thi Buoi; 140,000-258,000d; ⊘8am-midnight; ⊜🛜) Suitably located in a medina-like alley off Mac Thi Buoi, this is a chic place with sensuous flavours covering the distance from Morocco to Persia. Lamb and prune tagine, sizzling kebabs, mezze – it's all here, including the inevitable shishas for an after-dinner puff.

El Gaucho
ARGENTINEAN $$$

(Map p301; ☑3825 1879; www.elgaucho.com.vn; 5 Đ Nguyen Sieu; 250,000-690,000d; ⊘4-11pm) Nirvana for the serious meat-lover, El Gaucho dishes up hearty serves of fall-apart lamb shanks, tender skewers and juicy steaks in a fine dining environment. They even make their own chorizo and salchicha (spicy sausage).

Cepage
INTERNATIONAL $$

(Map p301; ☑3823 8733; www.cepage.biz; Lancaster Bldg, 22 Đ Le Thanh Ton; mains 200,000-350,000d; ⊘7.30am-midnight Mon-Sat, 5pm-midnight Sun; ⊜🛜) An impressive mainstay of the international dining scene, Cepage is a trendy wine bar with a lounge downstairs and a serious foodie palace upstairs. Try the 'black box' – a mystery three-course set lunch for 135,000d.

Golden Elephant
THAI $

(Map p301; ☑3822 8544; 34 ĐL Hai Ba Trung; mains 75,000-250,000d; ⊘11am-10pm; ⊜) The ever-present Thai royals gaze approvingly from the walls as steaming plates of their country's favourite dishes (along with a few Cambodian add-ons) are delivered to the linen-dressed tables. The upmarket ambience is enhanced with live music.

Augustin
FRENCH $$

(Map p301; ☑3829 2941; 10 Đ Nguyen Thiep; mains 140,000-380,000d; ⊘Mon-Sat) It may look unassuming but this little bistro serves delectable French food accompanied with wines from the old country. Some dishes (such as the caramelised duck breast with ginger and spices) tip their hat to indigenous flavours, while others (like the grand marnier soufflé) practically march to the table singing La Marseillaise.

Hoa Tuc
VIETNAMESE $

(Map p301; ☑3825 1676; 74/7 ĐL Hai Ba Trung; mains 50,000-190,000d; ⊘10.30am-10.30pm; ⊜🛜) Waving the flag for Vietnamese cuisine in the trendy courtyard of the former opium refinery, Hoa Tuc offers atmosphere and style to match the excellence of its food. Signature dishes include mustard leaves rolled with crispy vegetables and shrimp, and spicy beef salad with kumquat, baby white eggplant and lemongrass. Home chefs can pick up tricks at an in-house cooking class (p319).

Pacharan
SPANISH $$

(Map p301; ☑8825 6024; www.pacharan.com .vn; 97 Đ Hai Ba Trung; tapas 80,000-120,000d, mains 260,000-340,000d; ⊘9am-midnight; ⊜🛜) Spread over three floors in one of the most desirable locations in town, Pacharan's bites include succulent chorizo, marinated anchovies and chilli *gambas* (prawns), plus some more substantial mains like an authentic paella for two. The rooftop terrace is a great place to sample some Spanish wine and there's a cosy bar downstairs.

Au Parc   CAFE $
(Map p301; 23 Đ Han Thuyen; mains 95,000-165,000đ; ⏰7.30am-10.30pm Mon-Sat, 8am-5pm Sun; 🍴🍹) Expats flock to this little cafe for a Mediterranean-inflected selection of salads, quiches, baguettes, focaccia, pasta, mezze and light grills. The smoothies and juices are sublime, the coffee not so much.

Bernie's Bar & Grill   INTERNATIONAL $$
(Map p301; 19 Đ Thai Van Lung; mains 85,000-660,000đ; ⏰7.30am-11pm; 🍹) Dishing up high-quality comfort food and cold beer to homesick expats, Bernie's is the kind of bar that could easily become your local. The menu ranges from Aussie steaks and burgers (with beetroot, naturally) to pizza, pasta, sandwiches, salads and excellent MSG-free Vietnamese dishes.

Elbow Room   AMERICAN $$
(Map p301; www.elbowroom.com.vn; 52 Đ Pasteur; mains 100,000-350,000đ; ⏰8am-10pm Mon-Sat, 8am-5pm Sun; 🍹) If you're a lumberjack, you'll be ok at this upmarket American-style cafe-bistro where there's a big breakfast with your name on it (pancakes, bacon, eggs, ham, fries, toast). Otherwise there's a hefty menu of burgers, burritos, hot dogs, pizza, pasta, sandwiches and, in a concession to the coronary-adverse, wraps.

Ty Coz   FRENCH $$
(Map p301; ☎3822 2457; 178/4 Đ Pasteur; mains 190,000-300,000đ; ⏰Tue-Sun; 🍴🍹) The brothers who run this homely establishment are enthusiasm personified – eager to talk through the classic French dishes on their ever-changing blackboard menu. It's a peculiar set-up: you enter through their home to get to the old-fashioned dining room on the upper floor. When the weather's fine, the rooftop tables facing the cathedral book up quickly.

Skewers   MEDITERRANEAN $$
(Map p301; ☎3822 4798; www.skewers-restaurant.com; 9A Đ Thai Van Lung; mains 250,000-400,000đ; ⏰lunch Mon-Sat, dinner daily; 🍴🍹) The Mediterranean menu here takes in all stops from the Maghreb to Marseilles, with the accent on... skewers. It's an atmospheric place with an open-plan kitchen and usually draws a crowd.

Tandoor   INDIAN $
(Map p301; ☎3930 4839; www.tandoorvietnam.com; 74/6 Đ Hai Ba Trung; mains 55,000-120,000đ; 🍴🍹🍽) Always full of Indian diners (a good sign), this shiny, long-running restaurant sprawls up over several floors. The lengthy menu has vegetarian and South Indian sections, but the focus here is mainly on authentic North Indian dishes.

Fanny   ICE CREAM $
(Map p301; 29-31 Đ Ton That Thiep; per scoop 26,000-30,000đ; 🍹) Set in the lavish French villa that houses Temple Club, Fanny creates excellent Franco-Vietnamese ice cream in a healthy range of home-grown flavours, including durian (an acquired taste), star anise and green tea.

Le Jardin   FRENCH $$
(Map p301; ☎3825 8465; 31 Đ Thai Van Lung; mains 100,000-160,000đ; ⏰Mon-Sat; 🍹) This place is consistently popular with French expats seeking an escape from the busier boulevards. It has a wholesome bistro-style menu with a shaded terrace cafe in the outdoor garden of the French cultural centre, Idecaf.

3T Quan Nuong   VIETNAMESE $
(Map p301; ☎3821 1631; 29 Đ Ton That Thiep; mains 75,000-130,000đ; ⏰5-11pm) Does the address look familiar? That's because this breezy barbecue restaurant is set on the rooftop above Temple Club and Fanny. Choose from a range of meat, fish, seafood and vegies and fire it up right there on the table.

Mandarine   VIETNAMESE $$$
(Map p301; ☎3822 9783; www.orientalsaigon.com.vn; 11A Đ Ngo Van Nam; set menu per person US$38-120) Make no mistake: Mandarine is aimed firmly at wealthy tourists. Traditional architecture and nightly musical performances create a magical setting, while the set menus offer a tempting array of dishes from all regions of the country.

Maxim's Nam An   VIETNAMESE $$
(Map p301; ☎3829 6676; 15 Đ Dong Khoi; mains 160,000-350,000đ) Something of a Saigon legend, this supper club is distinguished more for its over-the-top jazz club ambience and live music than for the food, which is fine if not jaw-dropping. If you're after a memorable experience, you could do a lot worse.

Lemon Grass   VIETNAMESE $
(Map p301; ☎3822 0496; 4 Đ Nguyen Thiep; mains 69,000-119,000đ) This long-running restaurant sprawls over three floors. It can be a bit

LOCAL KNOWLEDGE

NICK ROSS: CHIEF EDITOR, *THE WORD HCMC*

We asked the man behind the city's expat bible to list some of his favourite local hotspots.

Where would you take guests that you want to impress? I'd probably choose Camargue (p329). It's classic with a contemporary twist; good quality white-tablecloth cuisine done well.

Favourite gourmet Vietnamese? Hoa Tuc (p326), Cuc Gach Quan (p329), Temple Club (p325), Tib (p329) and, for modern Vietnamese, Xu (p326).

Other Southeast Asian? Lion City (p329), Golden Elephant (p326), Coriander (p330)

Favourite Indian? Ganesh (p328), Mumtaz (p330), Tandoor (p327)

Favourite cheap eats? Two Hainanese places on Đ Le Thi Hong Gam: Tien Com Ga Hai Nam (p331) and Anh Ky (p331).

Favourite French? Ty Coz (p327) and Refinery (p332)

Favourite international? Au Parc (p327), Bernies (p327), Elbow Room (p327), Warda (p326), Pasha (p328), Skewers (p327), Flow (p326), Au Lac do Brazil (p329), El Gaucho (p326), Shri (p329), The Deck (p331)

Best resto-bars? Zan Z Bar (p328), Ala Mezon (p332), Long Phi (p334), Pacharan (p326)

Best cocktails? Cepage (p326); they also do the best Japanese-influenced, contemporary European cuisine.

Best sports bar? Phatty's (p333)

Best wine bar? Qing (p332)

Most stylish bar? 2 Lam Son (p332)

---

touristy but many locals still rate the place. Reservations essential.

Ganesh
INDIAN $

(Map p301; www.ganeshindianrestaurant.com; 15B4 Đ Le Thanh Ton; mains 52,000-99,000d; ✐) Offers an authentic range of North and South Indian meals, including tandoori dishes, thali plates and plentiful vegetarian selections, in pleasant surrounds.

Zan Z Bar
INTERNATIONAL $$

(Map p301; ✐3822 7375; www.zanzbar.com; 41 Đ Dong Du; meals US$8-25; ✐7am-1am; ✐) An ultra-hip resto-bar on Dong Du, Zan Z Bar has generated a buzz thanks to its Pacific-Rim fusion cuisine.

La Hostaria
ITALIAN $$

(Map p301; ✐3823 1080; www.lahostaria.com; 17B Đ Le Thanh Ton; mains 140,000-670,000d; ✐) A homely trattoria-style restaurant, this is a pleasant place to immerse yourself in Italian cuisine.

Java Coffee Bar
CAFE $

(Map p301; 38-42 Đ Dong Du; mains 65,000-195,000; ✐7.30am-midnight; ✐) This stylish corner cafe has Western breakfasts and

silken smoothies, not forgetting some of the comfiest lounge chairs around.

Pasha
TURKISH $$

(Map p301; ✐6291 3677; www.pasha.com.vn; 25 Đ Dong Du; mains 140,000-360,000d; ✐10am-2am; ✐✐) Exuberant Ottoman-inspired decor matches the food, which includes tasty mezze, kofte and, that old favourite, lamb shish kebabs.

La Fourchette
FRENCH $$

(Map p301; ✐3829 8143; 9 Đ Ngo Duc Ke; mains 160,000-180,000d; ✐✐) Much-loved little restaurant in a central location serving, in proper French style, only a handful of choices each night.

Mogambo
AMERICAN $$

(Map p301; ✐3825 1311; 50 Đ Pasteur; mains 120,000-200,000d; ✐9am-11pm; ✐) Some residents swear this place has the best burgers in town. A good menu of Tex-Mex and Americana.

Restaurant 13
VIETNAMESE $

(Map p301; ✐3823 9314; 15 Đ Ngo Duc Ke; mains 42,000-240,000d) Popular with a generation of adventure-tour leaders, this is one of a handful of numbered eateries in this area that serve tasty, no-nonsense Vietnamese favourites.

Annam Gourmet Shop
MINI-MARKET **$$**

(Map p301; 16 Đ Hai Ba Trung; ⊙9am-8pm) A small but high-class shop stocking imported cheeses, wines, chocolates and all the other delicacies you won't find elsewhere.

Pat a Chou
BAKERY **$**

(Map p301; 74B Đ Hai Ba Trung; filled baguettes 29,000-37,000d) French-style bakery treats.

DA KAO & AROUND

TOP CHOICE Cuc Gach Quan
VIETNAMESE **$**

(Map p308; ☑3848 0144; http://en.cucgachquan .com; 10 Đ Dang Tat; mains 50,000-200,000d; ⊙9am-midnight) It will come as no surprise that the owner is an architect when you step into this cleverly renovated old villa. The decor is rustic and elegant at the same time, which is also true of the food. Despite its tucked-away location in the northernmost reaches of District 1, this is no secret hideaway; book ahead.

TOP CHOICE Pho Hoa
VIETNAMESE **$**

(Map p308; 260C Đ Pasteur; mains 45,000-50,000d; ⊙6am-midnight) A contender for the title of HCMC's best *pho* restaurant, this long-running establishment is more up-market than most but is definitely the real deal – as evidenced by its popularity with regular Saigonese patrons. Tables come pre-laden with herbs, chilli and lime, as well as *gio chao quay* (fried Chinese bread), *banh xu xe* (glutinous coconut cakes with mung bean paste) and *cha lua* (pork paste sausages wrapped in banana leaves).

Banh Xeo 46A
VIETNAMESE **$**

(Map p308; 46A Đ Dinh Cong Trang; mains 25,000-50,000d; ⊙10am-9pm) Locals will always hit the restaurants that specialise in a single dish and this renowned spot serves some of the best *banh xeo* in town. These Vietnamese rice-flour pancakes stuffed with bean sprouts, prawns and pork (vegetarian versions available) are the stuff of legend.

Camargue
FRENCH **$$$**

(Map p308; ☑3520 4888; www.vascosgroup.com; 191 Đ Hai Ba Trung; mains 370,000d; ⊙6-10.30pm; ⊕🎅) Long one of the grand dames of Mediterranean dining in Saigon, Camargue occupies the romantic 1st-floor terrace of an old French villa. The menu includes rustic dishes such as duck breast and rabbit.

Au Lac do Brazil
BRAZILIAN **$$$**

(Map p308; ☑3820 7157; www.aulacdobrazil.com; 238 Đ Pasteur; mains 450,000-530,000d; ⊙5-10.30pm; ⊕🎅) For a taste (and then some) of Brazil, head to Au Lac. Decked out with Carnival-themed paintings, this *churrascaria* (barbecue restaurant) serves all-you-can-eat steak (and 11 other cuts of meat), just like back in Rio.

Tib
VIETNAMESE **$**

(www.tibrestaurant.com.vn); Hai Ba Trung (Map p308; ☑3829 7242; 187 Đ Hai Ba Trung; mains 60,000-240,000d; 🎅); Express (Map p310; 162 Đ Nguyen Dinh Chieu; mains 28,000-50,000; 🍴); Vegetarian (Map p308; 11 Đ Tran Nhat Duat; mains 30,000-40,000; 🍴) Visiting presidents and prime ministers have slunk down this lantern- and fairy light-festooned alley and into this atmospheric old house to sample Tib's Imperial Hue cuisine. While you could probably find similar food for less money elsewhere, the setting is wonderful. Tib Express and Tib Vegetarian offer a cheaper, more relaxed take on the same.

REUNIFICATION PALACE & AROUND

TOP CHOICE Lion City
SINGAPOREAN **$**

(Map p310; www.lioncityrestaurant.com; 45 Đ Le Anh Xuan; mains 65,000-200,000d; ⊙7am-3pm; ⊕) Representing the cuisine of a city-state famously obsessed with food is a big challenge, but Lion City more than rises to the occasion. The restaurant is justifiably acclaimed for its frog porridge and chilli crab but we also adore the Malaysian-style curry and sambal dishes.

Shri
JAPANESE FUSION **$$**

(Map p310; ☑3827 9631; 23rd fl, Centec Tower, 72-74 Đ Nguyen Thi Minh Khai; mains 200,000-400,000d; ⊙11am-midnight; ⊕🎅) Perched up a tower block, classy Shri has the best views in town bar none. Book ahead for a terrace table or settle for the overly dark, industrial-chic dining room. Two menus run side-by-side: a selection of Japanese-influenced Western mains and a more traditional (and considerably cheaper) Japanese section featuring sushi, sashimi, udon and ramen.

Marina
VIETNAMESE, SEAFOOD **$$**

(Map p310; ☑3930 2379; www.ngocsuong.com.vn; 172 Đ Nguyen Dinh Chieu; mains 50,000-500,000d) Ask a sample of well-to-do Saigonese where to go for seafood and the chances are they will recommend this place or its sister restaurant **Ngoc Suong** (Map p310; 17 Đ Le Quy

Don), just around the corner. They're both geared to local tastes (bright lights, TVs playing sports and bad piped music) but the food is delicious, particularly the soft-shell crabs.

Au Manoir de Khai   FRENCH $$$
(Map p310; ☑3930 3394; www.khaisilkcorp.com; 251 Đ Dien Bien Phu; mains 370,000-520,000d; ✆6-11pm; ✉☎) The most glamorously appointed restaurant in Ho Chi Minh City, this five-star classical French eatery is set in and around a grand colonial villa surrounded by ponds and chequerboard tiles. What else would you expect from the city's leading silk merchants? It's a touch pretentious, but there's no doubting the pedigree.

Beefsteak Nam Son   VIETNAMESE $
(Map p310; 88 Đ Nam Ky Khoi Nghia; mains 35,000-75,000d; ✆6am-10pm; ☎) If you are craving a steak and can't afford the fancier places, this is a real bargain. Local steak, other beef dishes (such as the spicy beef soup *bun bo Hue*), imported Canadian fillets and even cholesterol-friendly ostrich feature on the menu.

Pho 2000   VIETNAMESE $
(Map p310; 1-3 Đ Phan Chu Trinh; mains 42,000-58,000d; ✆6am-2am) Near Ben Thanh Market, Pho 2000 is where former US president Bill Clinton stopped by for a bowl.

PHAM NGU LAO AREA
Mumtaz   INDIAN $
(Map p316; ☑3837 1767; www.mumtazrest.com; 226 Đ Bui Vien; mains 45,000-90,000d; ✆11am-11pm; ☑) Excellent service, pleasant surrounds and succulent food are the hallmarks of this popular restaurant. The wide-ranging menu includes vegetarian options, tandoori dishes and the greatest hits of both North and South Indian cuisine. At 110,000d, the lunch buffet and thali plates are great value for big appetites.

Coriander   THAI $
(Map p316; 185 Đ Bui Vien; mains 40,000-140,000d; ✆9.30am-11.30pm) It is one of the smaller Thai restaurants in the city, but Coriander punches above its weight with authentic Siamese delights. The *pad Thai* is excellent and the green curry is particularly zesty.

Dinh Y   VEGETARIAN $
(Map p316; 171B Đ Cong Quynh; mains 12,000-40,000d; ☑) Run by a friendly Cao Dai family, this humble eatery is in a very 'local' part of PNL near Thai Binh Market. The food is

delicious and cheap, plus there's an English menu.

Margherita &
An Lac Chay   INTERNATIONAL, VEGETARIAN $
(Map p316; 175/1 Đ Pham Ngu Lao; mains 22,000-77,000d; ✆8am-10pm; ☑) Another golden oldie, humble Margherita turns out Vietnamese, Italian and Mexican food at a steal. Head up the stairs at the rear of the dining room and you're in An Lac Chay, a purely vegetarian restaurant offering the same eclectic mix of cuisines. Purists will be pleased to know that An Lac Chay has a completely separate kitchen, untainted by karma-depleting meat products.

Mon Hue   VIETNAMESE $
(off Map p316; 98 Đ Nguyen Trai; mains 29,000-150,000d; ✆6am-11pm) Once the preserve of emperors, Hue's famous cuisine is now accessible to HCMC's discerning proletariat through this chain of eight restaurants. This handy branch offers a good introduction for travellers who don't make it to the old capital.

Sozo   CAFE $
(Map p316; www.sozocentre.com; 176 Đ Bui Vien; bagels 40,000d; ✆7am-10.30pm Mon-Sat; ☎) A classy little cafe at the budget end of town, Sozo's attractions include excellent smoothies, doughy cinnamon rolls, home-made cookies and other sweet treats. Best of all, the cafe trains and employs disadvantaged Vietnamese. Use the free wi-fi to spread the word.

Pho Quynh   VIETNAMESE $
(Map p316; 323 Đ Pham Ngu Lao; pho 40,000d) Occupying a bustling corner on Pham Ngu Lao, this place always seems to be packed with a mixture of backpackers and Vietnamese locals. As well as regular *pho* (noodle soup), it specialises in *pho bo kho,* a stew-like broth.

Asian Kitchen   PAN-ASIAN $
(Map p316; ☑3836 7397; 185/22 Đ Pham Ngu Lao; mains 15,000-60,000d; ✆7am-midnight; ☎☑) A reliable PNL cheapie, the menu here includes Japanese, Vietnamese, Chinese and Indian.

Pho Hung   VIETNAMESE $
(Map p316; 241 Đ Nguyen Trai; mains 40,000-50,000d; ✆6am-3am) Popular *pho* place near backpackersville which is open into the early hours.

Tan Hai Van   CHINESE $
(off Map p316; 162 Đ Nguyen Trai; mains 52,000-260,000d; ✆24hr) The Chinese place to come

to if you have an attack of the midnight munchies; it never closes.

Vietnamese Aroma   VIETNAMESE, INTERNATIONAL $
(Map p316; 175/10 Đ Pham Ngu Lao; mains 45,000-89,000d; ✍) Fragrant Vietnamese staples plus a smattering of Italian and Mexican dishes.

Stella   ITALIAN, CAFE $
(Map p316; ✍3836 9220; www.stellacaffe.com; 119 Đ Bui Vien; mains 25,000-119,000d; ☉7am-11.30pm; ✆) A class above some of the budget places here, this predominantly Italian cafe has salads, pasta, gnocchi and pizzas. The coffee is also pretty good.

Bread & Butter   INTERNATIONAL, CAFE $
(Map p316; 40/24 Đ Bui Vien; mains 75,000-110,000d; ☉Tue-Sun; ✆) A tiny place on 'hotel alley' that is popular with resident English teachers, serving comfort food such as burgers and Sunday roasts.

Zen   VEGETARIAN $
(Map p316; 185/30 Đ Pham Ngu Lao; mains 90,000-120,000d; ✍) The food at this long-running place is consistently good and cheap. From braised mushrooms in claypot to fried tofu with chilli and lemongrass, the menu is packed with taste and goodness.

Chi's Cafe   INTERNATIONAL, CAFE $
(Map p316; 40/27 Đ Bui Vien; mains 30,000-80,000d; ☉7am-11pm; ✆✍) One of the better budget cafes in the area with big breakfasts, Western favourites and some local dishes.

Hong Hoa Mini-Market   MINI-MARKET $
(Map p316; Hong Hoa Hotel, 185/28 Đ Pham Ngu Lao; ☉9am-8pm) Small but packed with toiletries, alcohol and Western junk food, such as chocolate bars.

NGUYEN THAI BINH & AROUND

Tiem Com Ga Hai Nam   CHINESE $
(Map p312; http://comgahainam.vn; 67 Đ Le Thi Hong Gam; mains 27,000-80,000d) Boiled chicken and Peking duck hang from the window of this humble eatery where the food is prepared out the front and most punters choose to eat on the street. Hainanese chicken with rice is the speciality – a tasty, cheap, filling treat.

Anh Ky   CHINESE $
(Map p312; 80 Đ Le Thi Hong Gam; mains 30,000d; ☉6.30am-midnight) Delicious wonton noodle soup is the go at this lowly roadside eatery.

Tin Nghia   VEGETARIAN $
(Map p312; 9 ĐL Tran Hung Dao; mains 22,000-35,000d; ☉7am-8.30pm) The setting is simple, but the Buddhist owners turn out delicious traditional treats without resorting to fake meat.

AN PHU (DISTRICT 2)

The An Phu neighbourhood of District 2, east of the Saigon River, is very popular with resident expats and there are plenty of eateries catering to this affluent crowd. You'll need to catch a taxi (130,000d to 150,000d from Pham Ngu Lao); make sure your driver knows where he's going before you set off.

Deck   FUSION $$
(✍3744 6632; www.thedecksaigon.com; 33 Đ Nguyen U Di; mains 105,000-425,000d; ☉8am-midnight; ✆) Housed in an architecturally impressive pavilion set between an elegant garden and the river, this is the kind of place where you could happily linger all afternoon, knocking off a few bottles of wine and several dim sum plates along the way. Mains combine European cooking styles with the flavours of Asia.

Mekong Merchant   CAFE, BISTRO $$
(✍3744 6788; 23 Đ Thao Dien; breakfast 40,000-200,000d, mains 95,000-170,000d; ☉8am-10pm; ✆✆) Thatched-roof buildings clustered around a courtyard provide an atmospheric setting for this informal but upmarket cafe/bistro/bar. It's worth the trip for the best eggs Benedict and pizza in HCMC, although the speciality is Phu Quoc seafood – delivered directly and chalked up on the blackboard menu daily.

🍷 Drinking

Wartime Saigon was known for its riotous nightlife. Liberation in 1975 put a real dampener on the fun and games, but the pubs and clubs are well and truly back in business. However, periodic 'crack-down, clean-up' campaigns – officially to control drugs, prostitution and excessive noise – continue to keep the city's nightlife on the early side for a city of this size.

Happening HCMC is concentrated around the Dong Khoi area, with everything from dives to designer bars. However, places in this area generally close around 1am as they are under the watchful gaze of the local authorities. Pham Ngu Lao rumbles on into the wee hours.

DONG KHOI AREA

Many of Dong Khoi's coolest bars double as restaurants (see Flow, Cepage, Pacharan, Bernie's Bar & Grill and Zan Z Bar) or hover at the top of hotels (see Drinks With A View boxed text).

TOP CHOICE Vasco's
BAR, NIGHTCLUB
(Map p301; www.vascosgroup.com; 74/7D ĐL Hai Ba Trung; ⊙4pm-late; 🖶🛜) The tallest poppy in the courtyard of the former opium refinery, Vasco's is one of the hippest hangouts in town. Downstairs is a breezy spot for cocktails and pizza, while upstairs a nightclub-like space regularly plays host to DJs and live bands.

Ala Mezon
BAR
(Map p301; 10 Đ Chu Minh Trinh; ⊙11.30am-1am; 🛜) As chic as only a French-managed and Japanese-themed bar could be, Ala Mezon serves up inventive cocktails and Japanese tapas in several cosy spaces. You can play board games, Wii or Xbox in a frilly pink room done up like a Harajuku girl's bedroom or head up to the roof terrace for an altogether more elegant tipple.

2 Lam Son
COCKTAIL BAR
(Map p301; www.saigon.park.hyatt.com; 2 Lam Son Sq, enter ĐL Hai Ba Trung; ⊙4pm-2am; 🖶) The last word in opium den elegance (appropriately situated directly opposite the old opium refinery), the Park Hyatt's cocktail bar is the city's most stylish watering hole – and also one of its most expensive.

Alibi
COCKTAIL BAR
(Map p301; www.alibi.vn; 5A Đ Nguyen Sieu; ⊙10am-late; 🖶🛜) A happening New York–looking bar, with black-and-white photographs on the wall and a long central table, Alibi turns out creative cocktails and, upstairs, excellent fusion food.

Q Bar
BAR
(Map p301; www.qbarsaigon.com; 7 Lam Son Sq; ⊙5pm-late) The mother of all trendy nightspots in HCMC, Q Bar seems to have been around almost as long as the opera house it inhabits. An enduring and endearing spot, it pulls the beautiful people thanks to hip music and sophisticated decor.

Lush
BAR, NIGHTCLUB
(Map p301; www.lush.vn; 2 Đ Ly Tu Trong; ⊙7.30pm-late) Once you're done chatting in the garden bars, move to the central bar for serious people-watching and ass-shaking. The decor is very manga, with cool graphics plastering the walls. DJs spin most nights, with Fridays devoted to hip-hop.

La Fenetre Soleil
CAFE, BAR
(Map p301; 1st fl, 44 Đ Ly Tu Trong; ⊙10am-midnight; 🛜) Making the most of the bones of a French colonial building, this slick hangout has exposed brickwork and beams, chandeliers and frilly mirrors. It's great for a quiet drink, along with a bite from the Japanese-Vietnamese menu.

L'Usine
CAFE
(Map p301; www.lusinespace.com; 151/1 Đ Dong Khoi; ⊙9am-10pm; 🖶🛜) A very cool, tucked-away cafe in an interesting colonial building, with a designer gift/clothing store attached; head through the Art Arcade, turn right along the enclosed lane between the buildings and head upstairs.

Refinery
BISTRO
(Map p301; 74/7C ĐL Hai Ba Trung; ⊙11am-10.30pm; 🖶🛜) The venue that sparked the hipster takeover of the French opium refinery, this is a bistro bar with excellent cocktails (try the pomegranate martini) and appetising snacks.

Vino
WINE BAR
(Map p301; www.vinovietnam.com; 74/17 ĐL Hai Ba Trung; ⊙10am-10pm; 🛜) Opening onto the opium refinery courtyard, Vino is an inviting shop window for a leading wine importer so it always has an array of tipples to choose between.

Centro Caffe
CAFE
(Map p301; 11-13 Lam Son Sq; 🖶🛜) Just about as central as it gets, this place has excellent Italian coffee in every shape and size. There's also a menu of Italian food.

Amber Room
COCKTAIL BAR
(Map p301; www.theamberoom.com; 1st fl, 59 Đ Dong Du; ⊙3pm-midnight; 🛜) A nondescript entrance leads upstairs to this chic cocktail bar, suffused in an amber glow. The little terrace spies on the comings and goings at the Sheraton.

Qing
WINE BAR
(Map p301; 110 Đ Pasteur; 🛜) A cosy place with an upmarket feel and a large selection of wines.

Casbah
BAR
(Map p301; 57 Đ Nguyen Du; 🛜) Hidden away down an alley near the main post office, this

DRINKS WITH A VIEW

There's something madly exciting about gazing over the neon city at night, preferably with a cocktail in hand. From above, the multitudinous motorbikes look like schools of phosphorescent fish, breaking and regrouping around taxis and other obstructions. It's well worth the extra dong to enjoy the frenetic pace of life on the streets from the lofty vantage point of a rooftop bar. Among our favourite spots are:

Rooftop Garden Bar (Map p301; www.rexhotelvietnam.com; 141 ĐL Nguyen Hue; ⊘24h) The Rex Hotel's relatively diminutive height actually works to this bar's advantage, leaving you close enough to soak up the energy of the street. The decor is several shades of camp: life-size elephants, birdcage lanterns, topiary draped in fairy lights and, to cap it all off, a giant, rotating, golden crown. There's also live music most nights.

Sheraton Saigon (Map p301; www.sheraton.com/saigon; 88 Đ Dong Khoi; ⊘4pm-midnight) The highest of the downtown bars, this is a great place to see the sheer size of HCMC and the streams of traffic heading down ĐL Le Loi. Last stop 23rd floor, with live music and food.

Shri (Map p310; ☑3827 9631; 23rd fl, Centec Tower, 72-74 Đ Nguyen Thi Minh Khai) On the 23rd floor, Shri's stylish terrace has a separate area for non-diners reached by stepping stones over a tiny stream.

Saigon Saigon (Map p301; www.caravellehotel.com; 19 Lam Son Sq; ⊘11am-2am; 🛜) One of the first high-rise bars to open, the Caravelle Hotel's rooftop has live music, pricey drinks, great views and some alfresco tables.

M Bar (Map p301; www.majesticsaigon.com.vn; 1 Đ Dong Khoi; ⊘4pm-1am) On the 8th floor of the Majestic Hotel, this is a great spot for a sundowner, with panoramic views of the river and a certain colonial-era cachet.

Top Of The Town (www.windsorplazahotel.com; 18 Đ An Duong Vuong, District 5; ⊘5pm-midnight) For a reverse angle, try the 25th floor of Cholon's Windsor Plaza Hotel, where the 360-degree views put downtown in perspective.

is an exotic Arabic-style setting for a coffee or a cocktail.

Phatty's SPORTS BAR
(Map p301; www.phattysbar.com; 46-48 Đ Ton That Thiep; ⊘9am-midnight; 🛜) The after-work expat crowd heads here for a convivial atmosphere, good grub and sports on the big screens.

Juice JUICE BAR
(Map p301; 49 Đ Mac Thi Buoi; ⊜🛜) Tardis-like, this small shopfront is set over four floors with fresh juices and smoothies plus healthy snacks.

Drunken Duck SPORTS BAR
(Map p301; 58 Đ Ton That Thiep; ⊘4pm-late; 🛜) The lethal shooters served here probably got the duck in that state in the first place.

Sheridan's Irish House PUB
(Map p301; www.sheridansbarvn.com; 17/13 Đ Le Thanh Ton; ⊘8am-midnight; ⊜🛜) Of course there's an Irish bar in Saigon. It's pretty

authentic, serving a dangerous selection of Irish whiskies plus good pub grub.

Blue Gecko SPORTS BAR
(Map p301; www.bluegeckosaigon.com; 31 Đ Ly Tu Trong; ⊘5pm-midnight; 🛜) Aussie bar with seriously cold beer, regular music, pool tables and plenty of screens for sport.

DA KAO & AROUND
Hoa Vien MICROBREWERY
(Map p308; www.hoavien.vn; 28 Đ Mac Dinh Chi; ⊘8am-midnight; ⊜🛜) An unexpected find in the backstreets of HCMC, this Czech restaurant brews up fresh pilsner daily.

REUNIFICATION PALACE & AROUND
Serenata CAFE
(Map p310; ☑3930 7436; 6D Đ Ngo Thoi Nhiem; ⊘7.30am-10.30pm; 🛜) Down the same lively alley as the happening Acoustic (p335), this grand house is the perfect setting for a coffee. The garden is scattered with tables around a pond-filled courtyard, making it a romantic retreat. It hosts live music every

evening from 8.30pm and a tinkling piano on weekend mornings.

Cloud 9 BAR
(Map p310; 6th fl, 2 bis Cong Truong Quoc Te; ☺5.30pm-midnight) Fashionable young things flock to the rooftop bar, while dance music pounds in the room below. It's located above Gloria Jean's cafe where Đ Tran Cao Van meets the roundabout.

PHAM NGU LAO AREA
Le Pub PUB
(Map p316; www.lepub.org; 175/22 Đ Pham Ngu Lao; ☺7am-late; ☎) The name sums it up perfectly – British pub meets French cafe-bar – and the result is popular with expats and travellers alike. An extensive beer list, nightly promotions, cocktail jugs and pub grub draw them in.

Go2 BAR
(Map p316; 187 Đ De Tham; ☎) There's no better street theatre than watching the crazy goings-on from the outside seats of this all-night venue. The music's usually excellent and there's a club upstairs if you feel the need to boogie, and a rooftop bar if you want to cool off. Food's served into the wee hours or you can suck on a shisha pipe until you're sleepy.

Allez Boo BAR
(Map p316; 195 Đ Pham Ngu Lao; ☺7am-late) Hard to miss, Allez Boo proudly displays its tropical kookiness on a prominent street corner: think bamboo-lined walls and a rattan-shaded bar. A merry-go-round of backpackers and the late-night action upstairs ensures its popularity.

Spotted Cow SPORTS BAR
(Map p316; 111 Đ Bui Vien; ☺11am-midnight) Aussie-run sports bar with lots of drink specials and a cow-print fetish.

Street Pub PUB
(Map p316; 43-45 Đ Do Quang Dau) A Le Pub clone spread over two levels, with a pool table and small terrace upstairs.

Long Phi BAR
(Map p316; 207 Đ Bui Vien; ☺Tue-Sun) One of the PNL originals, this French-run bar stays open extremely late and sometimes hosts live bands.

Bobby Brewers CAFE
(Map p316; www.bobbybrewers.com; 45 Đ Bui Vien; ☺☎) Part of a local chain, this contemporary cafe is set over three floors, offering juices, sandwiches, pastas and salads, plus movies upstairs.

OTHER NEIGHBOURHOODS
Himiko Visual Cafe CAFE, GALLERY
(off Map p310; www.himikokoro.com; 1st fl, 324B Đ Dien Bien Phu, District 10; ☺10am-11pm; ☺☎) Run by a Vietnamese artist who trained in Japan, this place occasionally falls foul of the artistically staid authorities. A cafe-bar and gallery combined, these are intriguing surroundings for a drink.

☆ Entertainment

Pick up *The Word HCMC, Asialife HCMC* or *The Guide* to find out what's on during your stay in HCMC, or log onto www.anyarena.com or www.thewordhcmc.com. Monthly listings include club nights, live music, art shows and theatre performances.

Nightclubs
HCMC's hippest club night is the semiregular **Everyone's a DJ** (www.everyonesadjvietnam.wordpress.com) loft party, held at **La Fenetre Soleil** (p332). Other purveyors of fine events worth looking out for include **dOSe** and **The Beats Saigon** (www.thebeats-saigon.com).

Most of the following dance clubs don't really warm up until after 10pm; ask around popular bars about the latest greatest places. Not quite a club but more than a bar, **Lush** (p332) is a reliable option. Once everything else shuts down you can keep the buzz going at **Go2** (p334).

Apocalypse Now NIGHTCLUB
(Map p301; 2C Đ Thi Sach; ☺7pm-2am) Others have come and gone, but 'Apo' has been around since the early days and remains one of the must-visit clubs. A sprawling place with a big dance floor and an outdoor courtyard for cooling off, it's quite a circus with a cast comprising travellers, expats, Vietnamese movers and shakers, plus the odd hooker (some odder than others). The music is thumping and it's apocalyptically rowdy. The 150,000d charged on weekends includes a free drink.

Gossip NIGHTCLUB
(Map p312; 79 ĐL Tran Hung Dao; admission 120,000d; ☺9.30pm-2.30am) Housed in the Dai Nam Hotel, this long-running club heats up at the weekend when dressed-up expats and locals come out to play to a hard techno soundtrack.

GAY & LESBIAN HO CHI MINH CITY

Though there are few openly gay venues in town, most of HCMC's popular bars and clubs are generally gay-friendly. **Villa** (Map p301; 131 Đ Dong Khoi), above the Brodard Café (now Gloria Jean's), is a tiny club that fills up with well-groomed young Vietnamese men on weekends. **Apocalypse Now** (p334) sometimes attracts a small gay contingent among an otherwise straight crowd, as does **Q Bar** (p332) and the **Amber Room** (p332). The most happening night out is the monthly **Bitch Party** (www.bitchpartysaigon.com; admission incl 1st drink 100,000d), which swaps venues but is often held at the **Factory** (Map p301; Đ 102 Mac Thi Buoi).

A word of warning: masseurs travel by bicycle through the streets of the Pham Ngu Lao area, rattling a small bell to announce their services. They often offer cheap massages along with other services, but some of them try to extort money afterwards. As things can sometimes get nasty, it's best to avoid them altogether.

Fuse NIGHTCLUB
(Map p301; 3A Đ Ton Duc Thang; ⊙7pm-late) Small club, loud techno.

Barocco NIGHTCLUB
(Map p308; 254B Đ Nam Ky Khoi Nghia) Go-go dancers strut their stuff while red and green lasers slice up the dancefloor.

Live Music

The pre-war appetite for live rock music has been rekindled in modern HCMC, with all styles of bands hitting the city's stages. **Bernie's Bar & Grill** (p327) has live bands every weekend, **Pacharan** (p326) on Wednesday and Friday nights, and **Sheridan's** nightly (p333). Most nights you'll find a Cuban band turning up the heat at **Saigon Saigon** (p333) while **Vasco's** (p332) regularly hosts international artists.

Acoustic LIVE MUSIC
(Map p310; 6E1 Đ Ngo Thoi Nhiem; ⊙7pm-midnight; ☎) Don't be misled by the name: most of the musicians are fully plugged and dangerous when they take to the intimate stage of the city's leading live-music venue. And judging by the numbers that turn up nightly, the crowd just can't get enough.

Yoko BAR
(Map p310; 22A Đ Nguyen Thi Dieu; ⊙8am-late; ☎) The blend here could be anything from funk-rock to metal, and kicks off around 9pm nightly. A small stage, comfy chairs and revolving artworks keep it cool.

Hard Rock Cafe BAR
(Map p301; www.hardrock.com; 39 Đ Le Duan; ⊙11am-midnight; ☎☎) Live bands or DJs every Friday and Saturday night.

Municipal Theatre CONCERT HALL
(Nha Hat Thanh Pho Ho Chi Minh; Map p301; ☎3829 9976; Lam Son Sq) The French-era opera house is home to the HCMC Ballet, Symphony Orchestra & Opera (www.hbso.org.vn) and hosts performances by visiting artists.

Conservatory of Music CONCERT HALL
(Nhac Vien Thanh Pho Ho Chi Minh; Map p310; ☎3824 3774; 112 Đ Nguyen Du) Performances of both traditional Vietnamese and Western classical music are held here.

MZ Bar NIGHTCLUB
(Map p310; 56 Đ Bui Thi Xuan) A live cover band blasts out danceable classics.

Bar Bui BAR
(Map p308; 39/2 Đ Pham Ngoc Thach; ⊙10am-midnight) Flamenco and country music from 8.30pm nightly.

Metallic BAR
(Map p310; www.metallicbar.com; 41 Đ Ba Huyen Thanh Quan; ⊙9pm-1am; ☎☎) Metal's so big here that it's even spawned its own venue. Go figure.

Water Puppets

Although it originates in the north, the art of water puppetry has migrated to HCMC in the last decade – in part because of its popularity with tourists.

Golden Dragon Water Puppet Theatre WATER PUPPETS
(Map p310; ☎3930 2196; www.goldendragon waterpuppet.com; 55B Đ Nguyen Thi Minh Khai) The main water puppet venue, with shows starting at 5pm and 6.30pm and lasting about 50 minutes.

Saigon Water Puppet Theatre WATER PUPPETS
(Map p308; History Museum, Đ Nguyen Binh Khiem; entry 40,000d) Within the History Museum, this small theatre has performances at 9am, 10am, 11am, 2pm, 3pm and 4pm, lasting about 20 minutes.

Cinemas

There are plenty of international-standard cinemas *(rap)* in the city centre, several of which show English-language blockbusters. Tickets are around 60,000d to 70,000d.

Lotte Cinema Diamond CINEMA
(Map p301; 13th fl, Diamond Department Store, 34 Đ Le Duan) Three screens with films in their original languages with Vietnamese subtitles.

Galaxy CINEMA
(www.galaxycine.vn; tickets 60,000-160,000d) 116 Đ Nguyen Du (Map p310) 230 Đ Nguyen Trai (Map p316) Hollywood blockbusters and local hits.

Idecaf FRENCH CINEMA
(Map p301; ✆3829 5451; www.idecaf.gov.vn; 31 Đ Thai Van Lung) The *Institut d'Échanges Culturels avec la France* screens French-language films and occasional theatre.

Horseracing

Saigon Racing Club HORSERACING
(Cau Lac Bo The Thao Phu To; Map p298; ✆3855 1205; www.vietnamracing.net; 2 Đ Le Dai Hanh, District 11; ☺noon-5pm Sat & Sun) When South Vietnam was liberated in 1975, one of the Hanoi government's policies was to ban debauched, capitalistic pastimes such as gambling. Racetracks – mostly found in the Saigon area – were shut down. However, the government's need for hard cash caused a rethink and the Saigon Race Track re-opened in 1989.

Like the state lottery, the track has proven extremely lucrative. The overwhelming majority of gamblers are Vietnamese, as this is one of the few legal forms of gambling. There is no rule prohibiting foreigners from joining in the fun of risking their dong. The minimum legal bet is 10,000d and, for the high rollers hoping to become a dong billionaire, the sky's the limit. Form guides are available for those who are serious about their bets.

A taxi from downtown will cost about 100,000d.

🔒 Shopping

While there's much junk being peddled to the tourist masses on the city's teeming streets, there are also plenty of great discoveries just waiting to be unearthed. The hunting grounds include sprawling markets, antique stores, silk boutiques and speciality stores selling ceramics, ethnic fabrics, lacquered bamboo and custom-made clothing. And although the art scene is better up north, HCMC has a growing number of galleries selling everything from lavish oil paintings to photographs and vintage propaganda posters.

There are also the quirkier gems like miniature *cyclos,* and helicopters made from beer and soda cans – one place to browse for these is at the War Remnants Museum gift shop (p305).

There are plenty of places where you can shop for chic apparel or opt for a custom-made *ao dai,* the couture symbol of Vietnam. This quite flattering outfit of silk tunic and trousers is tailored at shops in and around Ben Thanh Market and at the top end of Đ Pasteur. There are also male *ao dai* available, which are a looser fit and come with a silk-covered head wrap to match.

One thing worth remembering is that Vietnam manufactures a lot of rucksacks, suitcases and other expensive forms of luggage, all of which are available in HCMC very cheaply. There are shops all over District 1 stocking North Face, Samsonite and more, mostly original and way cheaper than back home. So don't worry about too much shopping – just buy another bag.

DONG KHOI AREA

The best place to begin any shopping journey is gallery- and boutique-lined Đ Dong Khoi and the streets that intersect with it. This is also the place to look for high-quality handicrafts. If you're pressed for time, several shopping centres are reliable one-stop destinations.

Ben Thanh Market MARKET
(Map p301; Cho Ben Thanh; ĐL Le Loi, ĐL Ham Nghi, ĐL Tran Hung Dao & Đ Le Lai) The most central of all the markets, Ben Thanh and its surrounding streets comprise one of the city's liveliest areas. Everything that's commonly eaten, worn or used by the Saigonese is available here: vegetables, meats, spices, sweets, tobacco, clothing, hardware and so forth. There's also a healthy selection of souvenir items. However, you will need to bargain efficiently here, as prices are usually higher than elsewhere.

Vietnam Quilts   HANDICRAFTS
(Map p301; www.mekong-quilts.org; 64 Đ Ngo Duc Ke) This is the place to buy beautiful hand-made silk quilts, sewn by the rural poor in support of a sustainable income.

Dogma   SOUVENIRS
(Map p301; www.dogmavietnam.com; 1st fl, 43 Đ Ton That Thiep; 9am-10pm) This knowingly kitsch store stocks reproduction propaganda posters and has emblazoned them on coffee mugs, coasters, jigsaws and T-shirts. Who said the authorities don't have a sense of humour?

Mai's   CLOTHING
(Map p301; www.mailam.com.vn; 132-134 Đ Dong Khoi) Looking more like an avant garde gallery than the insanely hip designer boutique that it is, Mai's carries beautiful but pricy hand-stitched men's and women's clothing and accessories.

Nguyen Freres   ANTIQUES, HANDICRAFTS
(Map p301; 2 Đ Dong Khoi) Stocks a lovely assortment of new and antique furnishings and textiles, pillowcases, silks, pottery and lamps.

Khai Silk   CLOTHING
(Map p301; www.khaisilkcorp.com; 107 Đ Dong Khoi) This is one of several branches in HCMC of the nationwide silk empire. Expensive but high quality.

Song   CLOTHING
(Map p301; 76D Đ Le Thanh Ton) A central boutique that specialises in sophisticated linens and cottons for men and women.

Sapa   HANDICRAFTS, ACCESSORIES
(Map p301; 7 Đ Ton That Thiep) Small store incorporating ethnic fabrics and designs with modern styling; also sells gifts and jewellery.

Art Arcade   ARTWORK
(Map p301; 151 Đ Dong Khoi) A passageway leading off Dong Khoi, lined with art vendors.

Fahasa Bookshop   BOOKSTORE
(Map p301; 8am-10pm) ĐL Nguyen Hue (40 ĐL Nguyen Hue) ĐL Le Loi (60-62 ĐL Le Loi) Government-run bookshops with dictionaries, maps and general books in English and French.

Lucky Plaza   SHOPPING CENTRE
(Map p301; 69 Đ Dong Khoi) A great place to buy cheap luggage, this low-rent, single-level shopping plaza also has stalls selling the

THIS COFFEE TASTES LIKE...

Vietnamese coffee is exported all over the world. The best grades are from Buon Ma Thuot and the beans are roasted in butter. Lovers of weasels and strange things should get their hands on *ca phe chon* ('weasel coffee', No 8 of the signature Trung Nguyen brand). These coffee beans are fed to weasels first, then harvested from their droppings before being sold to you. Brew and enjoy. Look for it in the city's major markets.

usual selection of lacquerware and bamboo bowls.

Tax Trade Centre   SHOPPING CENTRE
(Map p301; Thuong Xa Tax; cnr Đ Nguyen Hue & Đ Le Loi; 9am-9.30pm) Mainly small stallholders, with lots of handicrafts on the top floor.

Diamond Department Store   DEPARTMENT STORE
(Map p301; 34 Đ Le Duan) Four floors of sleek, Western-style shopping topped by a very American level of ten-pin bowling, arcade games and junk food.

Saigon Centre   SHOPPING CENTRE
(Map p301; 65 ĐL Le Loi) A tower block with flashy international stores and cafes on its lower floors.

Parkson Plaza   DEPARTMENT STORE
(Map p301; 41-45 Đ Le Thanh Ton) Clothing and cosmetics.

Chi Chi   CLOTHING
(Map p301; 138 Đ Pasteur) Offers custom tailoring.

DA KAO & AROUND

Thu Quan Sinh Vien   BOOKSTORE
(Map p308; 2A ĐL Le Duan; 8am-10pm;) Full of university students making the most of the free wi-fi in the appealing cafe, this upmarket store stocks imported books and magazines in English, French and Chinese.

Adidas Puma Factory Shop   SHOES, CLOTHING
(Map p308; 232 Đ Pasteur) Authentic sneakers at a fifth of the price you'll pay back home.

Orange   CLOTHING, ACCESSORIES
(Map p308; 238B Đ Pasteur) Funky T-shirts and bags.

Cham Khanh
CLOTHING, TAILOR

(Map p308; 256 Đ Pasteur) One of several *ao dai* shops on this stretch of Đ Pasteur, it sells blinged-up versions of the traditional tunic dress and is a reliable place for getting one made.

REUNIFICATION PALACE & AROUND

Gaya
HOMEWARES, CLOTHING

(off Map p310; www.gayavietnam.com; 1 Đ Nguyen Van Trang) Designer homeware and clothing boutique that includes the collection of leading Cambodian-French designer Romyda Keth. The store is directly across the park from Pham Ngu Lao.

Vinh Loi Gallery
ART

(Map p310; www.galerievinhloi.com; 41 Đ Ba Huyen Thanh Quan; ⊙9am-6pm) Fine art gallery.

PHAM NGU LAO AREA

For cheap reproductions of famous paintings, visit the art shops along Đ Bui Vien.

🖉 Mekong Creations
HANDICRAFTS

(Map p316; www.mekong-creations.org; 141 Đ Bui Vien) Profits from the sale of this shop's bamboo bowls and serving platters are pumped back into remote Mekong villages.

Hanoi Gallery
PROPAGANDA POSTERS

(Map p316; 79 Đ Bui Vien; ⊙9am-10pm) Fans of Socialist Realism should visit this very cool little store selling both original (or so we're told) propaganda posters (US$600) and A3 prints (US$8).

SahaBook
BOOKSTORE

(Map p316; www.sahabook.com; 175/24 Đ Pham Ngu Lao) Specialises in guidebooks and travel literature; those Lonely Planet guides lining the walls are authentic copies with readable maps – unlike the knockoffs you'll see on the street.

Blue Dragon
HANDICRAFTS

(Map p316; 1B Đ Bui Vien) Popular souvenir store which stocks objets d'art made from recycled motorbike parts, among other things.

NGUYEN THAI BINH & AROUND

If you're in the market for art, there are some excellent commercial galleries at the rear of the Fine Arts Museum, including **Blue Space** (Map p312; www.bluespacearts.com; 1A Đ Le Thi Hong Gam) and **Lacquer & Oil** (Map p312; 97A Đ Pho Duc Chinh). Antique-hunters should head to Đ Le Cong Kieu, directly across the road from the museum. Of course, there's no guarantee that the objects for sale are actually old, so purchase with care.

Dan Sinh Market
MARKET

(Map p312; 104 Đ Yersin) Also known as the War Surplus Market, this is the place to shop for authentic combat boots or rusty (perhaps less authentic) dog tags. Stall after stall sells everything from handy gas masks and field stretchers to rain gear and mosquito nets. You can also find canteens, duffel bags, ponchos and boots. Anyone planning on spending time in a combat zone should consider picking up a secondhand flak jacket, as prices are reasonable.

OTHER NEIGHBOURHOODS

🖉 Mai Handicrafts
HANDICRAFTS

(📞3844 0988; www.maihandicrafts.com; 298 Đ Nguyen Trong Tuyen, Tan Binh District; ⊙10am-7pm Mon-Sat) A fair-trade shop dealing in ceramics, ethnic fabrics and other gift items which, in turn, support disadvantaged families and street children. To get here, head northwest on ĐL Hai Ba Trung, which becomes Đ Phan Dinh Phung and turn left on Đ Nguyen Trong Tuyen.

ℹ️ Information

Dangers & Annoyances

Be careful in the Dong Khoi area and along the Saigon riverfront, where motorbike 'cowboys' operate and specialise in bag- and camera-snatching. See the boxed text on p342 for common taxi and *xe om* scams.

Media

Hotels, bars and restaurants around HCMC carry free city-centric magazines, such as excellent monthly magazine **The Word HCMC** (www.wordhcmc.com), **Asialife HCMC** (www.asialife hcmc.com) and *The Guide,* a monthly magazine published by the *Vietnam Economic Times* (VET).

There is also an eclectic selection of foreign newspapers and magazines for sale in bookstores and smarter hotels. Street vendors wander the popular Dong Khoi and Pham Ngu Lao areas touting magazines, but check the cover date and bargain over price.

Medical Services

FV Hospital (Franco-Vietnamese Hospital; 📞5411 3333; www.fvhospital.com; 6 Đ Nguyen Luong Bang, District 7; ⊙24hr) French-, Vietnamese- and English-speaking physicians; superb care and equipment.

HCMC Family Medical Practice (Map p301; 24hr emergency 📞3822 7848; www.vietnam medicalpractice.com; rear, Diamond Department Store, 34 ĐL Le Duan; ☺24hr) Well-run practice with branches in Hanoi and Danang.

International Medical Centre (Map p301; ✆3827 2366, 24hr emergency ✆3865 4025; www.cmi-vietnam.com; 1 Đ Han Thuyen; ☺24hr) A nonprofit organisation with English-speaking French doctors.

International SOS (Map p301; ✆8382 8424, 24hr emergency ✆3829 8520; www.interna tionalsos.com; 65 Đ Nguyen Du; ☺24hr) Has an international team of doctors who speak English, French, Japanese and Vietnamese.

Money

There are several exchange counters in the arrivals hall at Tan Son Nhat Airport just after clearing customs and most offer the official rates. Turn right after leaving the terminal for ATMs.

There are plenty of ATMs scattered around the city, although most will only dispense a maximum of 2,000,000d per day. Some ANZ ATMs in the inner city will allow withdrawals up to 4,000,000d but the largest withdrawal limit we found was at **Citibank** (Map p301; 115 Đ Nguyen Hue) in the foyer of the Sun Wah Tower, which will dispense 8,000,000d. Visa or MasterCard cash advances for larger amounts of dong, as well as US dollars, can be handled at bank counters during banking hours.

Post

Central Post Office (Map p301; 2 Cong Xa Paris; ☺7am-9.30pm) HCMC's grandiose French-style post office is right next to Notre Dame Cathedral. Countless other branches are scattered around the city.

Federal Express (Map p301; ✆3829 0995; www.fedex.com; 146 Đ Pasteur; ☺8am-6pm Mon-Fri, 8am-2pm Sat)

Travel Agencies

HCMC's official government-run travel agency is **Saigon Tourist** (Map p301; ✆3824 4554; www .saigontourist.net; 45 Đ Le Thanh Ton; ☺8-11.30am & 1-5.30pm). The agency owns, or is a joint-venture partner in, more than 70 hotels, numerous restaurants, a car-rental agency, golf clubs and assorted tourist traps.

There's a plethora of other travel agencies in town, virtually all of them joint ventures between government agencies and private companies. These places can provide cars, book air tickets and extend visas. Competition is keen and you can often undercut Saigon Tourist's tariffs by a reasonable margin if you shop around. Many agencies have multilingual guides.

Most tour guides and drivers are not paid that well, so if you're happy with their service, tipping is common. Many travellers on bus tours to Cu Chi or the Mekong Delta, for example, collect a kitty (say US$1 or US$2 per person) and give it to the guide and driver at the end of the trip.

We suggest visiting several tour operators to see what's being offered to suit your taste and budget. Plenty of cheap tours – of varying quality – are sold around Pham Ngu Lao. One worthwhile strategy is to grill other travellers who've just returned from a tour.

Another appealing option is to arrange a customised private tour with your own car, driver and guide. Travelling this way provides maximum flexibility and, split between a few people, it can be surprisingly affordable.

Sinhbalo Adventures (Map p316; ✆3837 6766; www.sinhbalo.com; 283/20 Đ Pham Ngu Lao; ☺7.30am-noon & 1.30-5.30pm Mon-Fri, 7.30am-noon Sat) For customised tours, this is one of the best agencies in Vietnam. Sinhbalo specialises in cycling trips, but also arranges innovative special-interest journeys to the Mekong Delta, Central Highlands and further afield. Their most popular package trips are a two-day Mekong tour and three-day Mekong cycling tour.

Handspan Adventure Travel (✆3925 7605; www.handspan.com; 7th fl, Titan Bldg, 18A Đ Nam Quoc Cang, District 1) The branch office of a Hanoi-based agency, known for their quality tours.

Exotissimo (Map p301; ✆3827 2911; www .exotissimo.com; 64 Đ Dong Du; ☺9am-6pm Mon-Sat)

Sinh Tourist (Map p316; ✆3838 9593; www .thesinhtourist.vn; 246 Đ De Tham; ☺6.30am-10.30pm)

Buffalo Tours (Map p301; ✆3827 9170; www .buffalotours.com; 81 Đ Mac Thi Buoi)

Innoviet (Map p316; ✆6291 5406; www.inno viet.com; 158 Đ Bui Vien)

Cafe Kim Tourist (Map p316; ✆3836 5489; www.thekimtourist.com; 270 Đ De Tham)

PXN Travel (Map p316; ✆6271 9208; www .pxntravel.com; 38 Đ Do Quang Dau)

Asiana Travel Mate (Map p301; ✆3525 0615; www.asianatravelmate.com; 92-96 Đ Nguyen Hue)

Getting There & Away
Air

Tan Son Nhat International Airport (SGN; www.tsnairport.hochiminhcity.gov.vn; Tan Binh District) This was one of the three busiest airports in the world in the late 1960s. Even today, the runways are still lined with lichen-covered, mortar-proof, aircraft-retaining walls, hangars and other military structures.

For more details on international air travel see p511. The following airlines all fly domestically from HCMC:

Vietnam Airlines (✆3832 0320; www.vietnam airlines.com) Flies to/from Hanoi, Hai Phong, Vinh, Dong Hoi, Hue, Danang, Quy Nhon, Nha

Trang, Dalat, Buon Ma Thuot, Pleiku, Rach Gia and Phu Quoc Island.

Air Mekong (☑3846 3666; www.airmekong .com.vn) Flies to/from Hanoi, Quy Nhon, Dalat, Buon Ma Thuot, Pleiku, Con Dao Islands and Phu Quoc Island.

Jetstar Pacific Airlines (☑1900 1550; www .jetstar.com) Flies to/from Hanoi, Hai Phong, Vinh, Hue and Danang.

Vietnam Air Service Company (VASCO; www .vasco.com.vn) Flies to/from Tuy Hoa, Chu Lai, Con Dao Islands and Ca Mau.

Boat

Hydrofoils (adult/child 200,000/100,000d, 1¼ hours) depart for Vung Tau almost hourly from **Bach Dang jetty** (Map p301; Đ Ton Duc Thang). The main companies are:

Greenlines (☑3821 5609; www.greenlines .com.vn)

Petro Express (☑3821 0650)

Vina Express (☑3825 3333; www.vinaexpress .com.vn)

Bus

Intercity buses operate from three large stations on the outskirts of HCMC, which are themselves all well served by local bus services from Ben Thanh Market. HCMC is one place where the open-tour buses really come into their own, as they depart and arrive in the very convenient Pham Ngu Lao area, saving the extra local bus journey or taxi fare. Destinations include Mui Ne (US$5 to US$10), Nha Trang (US$7 to US$20), Dalat (US$8 to US$15), Hoi An (US$15 to US$37) and Hanoi (US$31 to US$49).

Mien Tay bus station (Ben Xe Mien Tay; Đ Kinh Duong Vuong) serves all areas south of HCMC, which basically means the Mekong Delta. This huge station is about 10km west of HCMC in An Lac, a part of Binh Chanh district (Huyen Binh Chanh). A taxi here from Pham Ngu Lao costs around 150,000d. Buses and minibuses from Mien Tay serve most towns in the Mekong Delta using air-conditioned express buses and premium minibuses. For a smattering of prices, see the relevant destination in the Mekong Delta chapter.

Buses to locations north of HCMC leave from the immensely huge and busy **Mien Dong bus station** (Ben Xe Mien Dong) in Binh Thanh district, about 5km from central HCMC on Hwy 13 (Quoc Lo 13; the continuation of Đ Xo Viet Nghe Tinh). The station is just under 2km north of the intersection of Đ Xo Viet Nghe Tinh and Đ Dien Bien Phu. Note that express buses depart from the east side, and local buses connect with the west side of the complex.

Buses to Tay Ninh, Cu Chi and points northwest of HCMC depart from the newer **An Suong bus station** (Ben Xe An Suong) in District 12. To get here, head all the way out on Đ Cach Mang Thang Tam and Đ Truong Chinh. The station is close to the flyover for Quoc Lo 1 (Hwy 1). Note that it's not really worth using local buses to visit the Cu Chi tunnels as they are off the main highway, making it a nightmare to navigate. Plus, the tourist buses are extremely competitively priced and leave from District 1.

INTERNATIONAL BUS There are plenty of international bus services connecting HCMC and Cambodia, most with departures from the Pham Ngu Lao area. **Sapaco** (Map p316; ☑3920 3623; 309 Pham Ngu Lao) has nine direct daily services to Phnom Penh (departing between 6am and 3pm; US$10), as well as one to Siem Reap (US$20).

Car & Motorbike

Enquire at almost any hotel, tourist cafe or travel agency to arrange car rental. Just remember that your rental will include a driver as it's illegal for foreigners to drive in Vietnam without a Vietnamese licence. The agencies in the Pham Ngu Lao area generally offer the lowest prices. **Budget Car Rental** (☑3930 1118; www.budget .com.vn) offers new cars with English-speaking drivers at reasonable rates.

Motorbikes are available in the Pham Ngu Lao area for around US$10 per day, although this is one city where it helps to have experience. Check the quality of the helmet provided as it may be worth investing in a better one for a long trip.

Train

Trains from **Saigon train station** (Ga Sai Gon; Map p298; ☑3823 0105; 1 Đ Nguyen Thong, District

HCMC TRANSPORT CONNECTIONS

DESTINATION	AIR	BUS	TRAIN
Dalat	50 min/from $39	7 hr/$8-15	n/a
Nha Trang	55 min/from $44	13 hr/$7-20	6½ hr/$13-27
Hue	80 min/from $37	29 hr/$26-37	18 hr/$32-54
Hanoi	2 hr/from $70	41 hr/$31-49	30 hr/$50-79

3; ☺ticket office 7.15-11am & 1-3pm) head north to destinations including:

Nha Trang (272,000d to 550,000d; 6½ to nine hours, eight daily)

Danang (616,000d to 1,019,000d, 15½ to 20¾ hours, six daily)

Hue (655,000d to 1,100,000d, 18 to 24½ hours, six daily)

Dong Hoi (759,000d to 1,199,000d, 21 to 26 hours, five daily)

Hanoi (1,036,000d to 1,622,000d, 30 to 41 hours, four daily)

In Pham Ngu Lao, purchase tickets from **Saigon Railway Tours** (Map p316; ☎3836 7640; www.railtour.com.vn; 275C Đ Pham Ngu Lao; ☺7.30am-8pm) or from most travel agents for a small fee.

ⓘ Getting Around

To/From the Airport

Tan Son Nhat Airport is 7km northwest of central HCMC. At the time of writing, a company called **Saigon Airport Taxis** had the monopoly over the rank in front of the international terminal, while **Sasco Taxi** had the concession for the domestic terminal. English-speaking controllers will shuffle you into a waiting cab and tell the drivers your destination. Check with the driver, preferably in front of the controller, as to whether the trip will be metered or a set fee (which can be as high as US$10 to the city centre).

Metered cabs should only cost around 100,000d, so if you're travelling light and prepared to waste time for the chance of saving a few dollars, head upstairs to the arrivals area or into the carpark of the domestic terminal and try to catch a rival cab after it has dropped someone off. However, make sure you use a reputable company; see p342.

Be aware that taxi drivers will probably recommend a 'good and cheap' hotel, and deliver you there so that they can earn a commission. Problems may arise, however, when you ask a taxi driver to take you to a place that doesn't pay commission. The driver may tell you the hotel is closed, burned down, is dirty and dangerous, or anything else they can think of to steer you somewhere else.

To get to the airport from town, ask your hotel to call a trustworthy taxi for you. Some cafes in the Pham Ngu Lao area offer runs to the airport – some have sign-up sheets where you can book share-taxis for around US$4 per person.

Most economical is the air-conditioned bus (route 152; 4000d, plus a variable fee for luggage) going to and from the airport. Buses leave approximately every 15 minutes and make regular stops along Đ De Tham (Pham Ngu Lao area) and international hotels along Đ Dong Khoi, such as the Caravelle and the Majestic. Buses are labelled in English, but you might also look for the words 'Xe Buyt San Bay'. This service only operates between 6am and 6pm.

Consider a motorbike taxi only if you're travelling light, as the traffic is even more manic if you are trying to balance baggage. Drivers can't access the airport, so you will need to walk outside and negotiate: 60,000d to the city centre is the going rate.

Bicycle

For pedal power devotees, a bicycle can be a useful (if sometimes scary) way to get around the city. Bikes can be rented from a number of places, including hotels, cafes and travel agencies.

Bicycle parking lots are usually just roped-off sections of pavement. For about 2000d you can safely leave your bicycle, bearing in mind that theft is a big problem. Your bicycle will have a number written on the seat in chalk or stapled to the handlebars and you'll be given a reclaim chit. Don't lose it. If you come back and your bicycle is gone, the parking lot is supposedly required to replace it.

Bus

Local buses are cheap and plentiful, serving more than 130 routes around greater HCMC. There is a useful, free *Ho Chi Minh Bus Route Diagram* (map to you and me) available at the **Ben Thanh bus station** (off Map p301; ĐL Tran Hung Dao).

Some useful numbers from Ben Thanh include the 152 to Tan Son Nhat Airport, 149 to Saigon train station, 1 to Binh Tay Market in Cholon, 102 to Mien Tay bus station and 26 to Mien Dong bus station. All buses have air-con and the average ticket price is just 3000d. Buy your ticket on board from the attendant.

Car & Motorbike

Travel agencies, hotels and tourist cafes all rent cars (with drivers) and motorbikes. Many expats swear that motorbike rental is the fastest and easiest way to get around the city – or to the hospital, if you don't know what you're doing. Even if you're an experienced biker, make sure you've spent some time observing traffic patterns before venturing forth. A 100cc motorbike can be rented for US$7 to US$10 per day, including some sort of helmet, and your passport may be kept as collateral. Before renting one, make sure it's in good working order.

Saigon Scooter Centre (☎3848 7816; www.saigonscootercentre.com; 25/7 Đ Cuu Long, Tan Binh district; ☺noon-5pm Tue-Fri, 10am-4pm Sat) is a reliable source for restored classic Vespa scooters and new trail bikes. Daily rates start from US$20 (US$100 per week), with a minimum rental period of four days. For an extra fee it is possible to arrange a one-way service, with a pick-up of the bikes anywhere between HCMC and Hanoi.

XE OM OR TAXI?

You'd expect to pay extra for the relative comfort and safety of an air-conditioned taxi as opposed to a white-knuckle motorbike ride, and in theory that's the case. However, rampant overcharging by *xe om* drivers in the tourist areas can make any difference negligible. Until you're familiar with the distances and fares involved, catching a metered taxi can be a good way of avoiding any am-I-getting-ripped-off angst. Plus, if there's more than one of you, taxis are likely to be cheaper. However, weaving through the traffic on the back of a motorbike will often get you to your destination quicker, especially in rush hour.

Just as there are unscrupulous *xe om* drivers, so too are there dodgy taxis with meters that spin around faster than Kylie in her gold hotpants. Whenever possible, only catch cabs from reputable companies, such as Vinasun and Mai Linh. But beware: both companies have spawned a raft of impersonators using similar logos, slightly altered names (Vinasum, Vina, Vinamet, Ma Lin, M.Group) and badly tampered meters.

If you're catching a *xe om*, agree on a price in advance. A trip from Pham Ngu Lao to Dong Khoi shouldn't cost more than 20,000d. One common trick is for drivers to offer to take you for 15,000d but then insist that they really said 50,000d.

Cyclo

No longer the icon that it once was, the *cyclo* still makes its appearance along certain streets, particularly along Đ Pham Ngu Lao and around Đ Dong Khoi. Although some Vietnamese still enjoy them, use has declined significantly in the day of the motorbike and taxi, and tourists are largely the consumers of this poorly paid trade. In HCMC, a few of the older riders are former South Vietnamese army soldiers and quite a few know at least basic English, while others are quite fluent. Some drivers have stories of war, 're-education', persecution and poverty to tell (and will often gladly regale you with tales over a bowl of *pho* or a beer at the end of the day).

In an effort to control HCMC's traffic problems, there are dozens of streets on which *cyclos* are prohibited. As a result, your driver must often take a circuitous route to avoid these trouble spots (and possible fines levied by the police) and may not be able to drop you at the exact address. Try to have some sympathy as it is not the driver's fault.

Overcharging tourists is the norm, so negotiate a price beforehand and have the exact change ready. If more than one person is travelling make sure you're negotiating the price for both and not a per-passenger fee. It sometimes pays to sketch out numbers and pictures with pen and paper so all parties agree. Unfortunately, 'misunderstandings' do happen. Unless the *cyclo* driver has pedalled you to all the districts of HCMC, US$25 is not the going rate. That said, don't just assume the driver is trying to cheat you.

Short hops around the city centre will cost around 15,000d to 25,000d; District 1 to central Cholon costs about 40,000d. You can rent a *cyclo* for around 40,000d per hour, a fine idea if you will be doing a lot of touring; most *cyclo* drivers around the Pham Ngu Lao area can produce a sample tour program.

You should enjoy *cyclos* while you can, as the municipal government plans to phase them out, and it won't be too long before the *cyclo* disappears entirely from the city's streets.

Motorbike Taxi

Far more prevalent and much faster than the *cyclo* taxis is the *xe om* (sometimes called a *Honda om*), or motorbike taxi. *Xe om* drivers usually hang out on their parked bikes on street corners, touting for passengers. When looking for one, it's highly unlikely that you'll have to walk more than 10 steps before being offered a ride. The accepted rate is 20,000d for short rides (Pham Ngu Lao to Dong Khoi area for instance) or you can charter one for around US$3 per hour or US$15 per day.

Taxi

Metered taxis cruise the streets, but it is worth calling ahead if you are off the beaten path. The flagfall is around 15,000d for the first kilometre. Most rides in the city centre cost just a couple of bucks. Be wary of dodgy taxi meters that are rigged to jump quickly (see *Xe Om* or *Taxi?* boxed text).

The following are HCMC's most highly regarded taxi companies:

Mai Linh Taxi (☏ 3838 3838)
Vinasun Taxi (☏ 3827 2727)

AROUND HO CHI MINH CITY

As HCMC continues its insatiable expansion in every direction, swallowing up rural communities and country backwaters, finding a respite from urban life has become more of a challenge. Thankfully, there are still some rewarding escapes, such as wilderness areas and fascinating historical and cultural sights, just a short journey from town.

Cu Chi

If the tenacious spirit of the Vietnamese can be symbolised by a place, then few candidates could make a stronger case than Cu Chi. This district of greater HCMC now has a population of about 350,000 but during the American War it had about 80,000 residents. At first glance there is little evidence here to indicate the intense fighting, bombing and destruction that occurred in Cu Chi during the war. To see what went on, you have to dig deeper – underground.

The tunnel network of Cu Chi became legendary during the 1960s for its role in facilitating VC control of a large rural area only 30km to 40km from HCMC. At its peak the tunnel system stretched from the South Vietnamese capital to the Cambodian border; in the district of Cu Chi alone there were more than 250km of tunnels. The network, parts of which were several storeys deep, included innumerable trapdoors, constructed living areas, storage facilities, weapons factories, field hospitals, command centres and kitchens.

The tunnels facilitated communication and coordination between the VC-controlled enclaves, isolated from each other by South Vietnamese and American land and air operations. They also allowed the VC to mount surprise attacks wherever the tunnels went – even within the perimeters of the US military base at Dong Du – and to disappear suddenly into hidden trapdoors without a trace. After ground operations against the tunnels claimed large numbers of US casualties and proved ineffective, the Americans resorted to massive firepower, eventually turning Cu Chi's 420 sq km into what the authors of *The Tunnels of Cu Chi* have called 'the most bombed, shelled, gassed, defoliated and generally devastated area in the history of warfare'.

Cu Chi has become a place of pilgrimage for Vietnamese school children and Communist Party cadres.

History

The tunnels of Cu Chi were built over a period of 25 years that began sometime in the late 1940s. They were the improvised response of a poorly equipped peasant army to its enemy's high-tech ordnance, helicopters, artillery, bombers and chemical weapons.

The Viet Minh built the first tunnels in the hard red earth of Cu Chi during the war against the French. The excavations were used mostly for communication between villages and to evade French army sweeps of the area.

When the VC's National Liberation Front (NLF) insurgency began in earnest in around 1960, the old Viet Minh tunnels were repaired and new extensions were excavated. Within a few years the tunnel system assumed enormous strategic importance, and most of Cu Chi district and the nearby area came under VC control. In addition Cu Chi was used as a base for infiltrating intelligence agents and sabotage teams into Saigon. The audacious attacks in the South Vietnamese capital during the 1968 Tet Offensive were planned and launched from Cu Chi.

In early 1963 the Diem government implemented the Strategic Hamlets Program, under which fortified encampments, surrounded by many rows of sharp bamboo spikes, were built to house people who had been 'relocated' from Communist-controlled areas. The first strategic hamlet was in Ben Cat district, next to Cu Chi. However, the VC were able to tunnel into the hamlets and control them from within, so that by the end of 1963 the first showpiece hamlet had been overrun.

Over the years the VC developed simple but effective techniques to make their tunnels difficult to detect or disable. Wooden trapdoors were camouflaged with earth and branches; some were booby-trapped. Hidden underwater entrances from rivers were constructed. To cook they used 'Dien Bien Phu kitchens', which exhausted the smoke through vents many metres away from the cooking site. Trapdoors were installed throughout the network to prevent tear gas, smoke or water from moving from one part of the system to another. Some sections were even equipped with electric lighting.

The series of setbacks and defeats suffered by the South Vietnamese forces in the Cu Chi area rendered a complete VC victory by the end of 1965 a distinct possibility. In the early months of that year, the guerrillas boldly held a victory parade in the middle of Cu Chi town. VC strength in and around Cu Chi was one of the reasons the Johnson

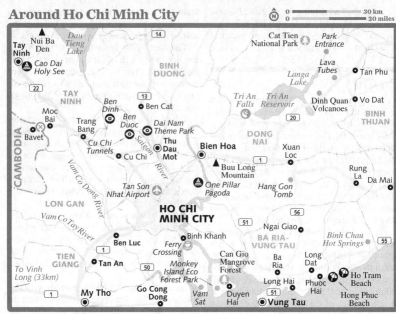

administration decided to involve US troops in the war.

To deal with the threat posed by VC control of an area so near the South Vietnamese capital, one of the USA's first actions was to establish a large base camp in Cu Chi district. Unknowingly, they built it right on top of an existing tunnel network. It took months for the 25th Division to figure out why they kept getting shot at in their tents at night.

The US and Australian troops tried a variety of methods to 'pacify' the area around Cu Chi, which came to be known as the Iron Triangle. They launched large-scale ground operations involving tens of thousands of troops but failed to locate the tunnels. To deny the VC cover and supplies, rice paddies were defoliated, huge swathes of jungle bulldozed, and villages evacuated and razed. The Americans also sprayed chemical defoliants on the area aerially and a few months later ignited the tinder-dry vegetation with gasoline and napalm. But the intense heat interacted with the wet tropical air in such a way as to create cloudbursts that extinguished the fires. The VC remained safe in their tunnels.

Unable to win this battle with chemicals, the US army began sending men down into the tunnels. These 'tunnel rats', who were often involved in underground fire fights, sustained appallingly high casualty rates.

When the Americans began using German shepherd dogs, trained to use their keen sense of smell to locate trapdoors and guerrillas, the VC began washing with American soap, which gave off a scent the canines identified as friendly. Captured US uniforms were put out to confuse the dogs further. Most importantly, the dogs were not able to spot booby traps. So many dogs were killed or maimed that their horrified handlers then refused to send them into the tunnels.

The USA declared Cu Chi a free-strike zone: little authorisation was needed to shoot at anything in the area, random artillery was fired into the area at night and pilots were told to drop unused bombs and napalm there before returning to base. But the VC stayed put. Finally, in the late 1960s, American B-52s carpet-bombed the whole area, destroying most of the tunnels along with everything else around. The gesture was almost symbolic by then because the USA was already on its way out of the war. The tunnels had served their purpose.

The VC guerrillas serving in the tunnels lived in extremely difficult conditions and suffered serious casualties. Only about 6000 of the 16,000 cadres who fought in the tunnels survived the war. Thousands of civilians in the area were also killed. Their tenacity was extraordinary considering the bombings, the claustrophobia of living underground for weeks or months at a time and the deaths of countless friends and comrades.

The villages of Cu Chi have since been presented with numerous honorific awards, decorations and citations by the government and many have been declared 'heroic villages'. Since 1975 new hamlets have been established and the population of the area has exploded; however, chemical defoliants remain in the soil and water, and crop yields are still poor.

The Tunnels of Cu Chi, by Tom Mangold and John Penycate, is a powerful book documenting the story of the tunnels and the people involved on both sides.

◉ Sights

Cu Chi Tunnels HISTORIC SITES
(www.cuchitunnel.org.vn; adult/child 80,000/20,000d) Two sections of this remarkable tunnel network (which are enlarged and upgraded versions of the real thing) are open to the public. One is near the village of Ben Dinh and the other is 15km beyond at Ben Duoc. Most tourists visiting the tunnels end up at Ben Dinh, as it's easier for tour buses to reach.

Visits to both sites usually start with an extremely dated propaganda video before guides in army greens lead small groups through some short sections of tunnel. Even if you wimp out and stay above ground, it's still an interesting experience.

Both sites have gun ranges attached where you shell out a small fortune to shell up and fire genuine AK47s and machine guns. You pay per bullet so be warned: if you're firing an automatic weapon, they come out pretty fast.

Ben Dinh
The most visited of the tunnel sites, this small, renovated section is near the village of Ben Dinh, about 50km from HCMC. In one of the classrooms at the visitors centre a large map shows the extent of the network while another shows cross-section diagrams of the tunnels.

The section of the tunnel system presently open to visitors is a few hundred metres south of the visitors centre. It snakes up

and down through various chambers along its 50m length. The tunnels are about 1.2m high and 80cm across, and are unlit. Some travellers find them too claustrophobic for comfort. A knocked-out M-41 tank and a bomb crater are near the exit, which is in a reforested eucalyptus grove.

Be warned that this site tends to get crowded and you can feel like you're on a tourist conveyor belt most days.

Ben Duoc
Like Ben Dinh, the tunnels here have been enlarged to accommodate tourists, although they're still a tight squeeze. Inside the underground chambers are bunkers, a hospital and a command centre that played a role in the 1968 Tet Offensive. The set pieces include tables, chairs, beds, lights, and dummies outfitted in guerrilla gear.

What Ben Duoc has that Ben Dinh doesn't is the massive **Ben Duoc temple**, built in 1993 in memory of the Vietnamese killed at Cu Chi. It's flanked by a nine-storey tower with a flower garden in front. You'll only be permitted to enter if you're dressed appropriately – although temple wear (long trousers etc) may not be conducive to clambering through earthen tunnels.

FREE **Cu Chi War History Museum** MUSEUM
(Nha Truyen Thong Huyen Cu Chi) The small Cu Chi War History Museum is not actually at the tunnel sites but just off the main highway in the central part of Cu Chi town. Like most such museums its displays consist mainly of photographs (some quite graphic) and some large items of military hardware rusting away outside. It's a moderately interesting place to visit, but the subject is covered much more comprehensively in the War Remnants Museum in HCMC. You'll see many of the same photos at the tunnels themselves.

Cu Chi Wildlife Rescue Station WILDLIFE
(www.wildlifeatrisk.org; adult/child US$5/free; ☉7.30-11.30am & 1-4.30pm) Just a few kilometres down the road from the tunnels of Ben Dinh, this rescue centre is a welcome addition to the sites around Cu Chi. It's a small centre dedicated to the protection of wildlife that has been confiscated from owners or illegal traders. Animals here include bears, otters and gibbons. The centre is expanding its enclosures to create more comfortable habitats and there is an informative display on the rather depressing state of wildlife in

Vietnam, including the 'room of death' featuring a host of traps and baits. It's tough to navigate these back roads on your own, so talk to a travel agent about incorporating it into a Cu Chi Tunnels trip.

ⓘ Getting There & Around

Cu Chi district covers a large area, parts of which are as close as 30km to central HCMC. The Cu Chi War History Museum is closest to the city, while the Ben Dinh and Ben Duoc tunnels are about 50km and 65km, respectively, from central HCMC.

CAR To visit the rescue centre as well as the tunnels, you should consider hiring a car and driver. This can be done relatively cheaply if the cost is shared between a few people. It is hard to find, so make sure your driver knows where he's going.

PUBLIC TRANSPORT It is very difficult to visit by public transport, as it involves several changes of bus. Tay Ninh buses pass though Cu Chi, but getting from the town of Cu Chi to the tunnels by public transport is tough.

TOURS By far the easiest way to get to the tunnels is by guided tour (see p320) and, as the competition is stiff, prices are exceptionally reasonable. For something a little different, try the half-day boating trip (US$12) to the tunnels organised by **Delta Adventure Tours** (Map p316; ☑3920 2112; www.deltaadventure tours.com; 267 Đ De Tham; tour 378,000d) or the cycling trip offered by **Exotissimo** (Map p301; ☑3827 2911; www.exotissimo.com; 64 Đ Dong Du; per 1/2/3/4 people 3,110,000/ 3,900,000/4,600,000/6,200,000d; ☺9am-6pm Mon-Sat).

BORDER CROSSING: MOC BAI–BAVET

This busy border crossing is the fastest way to get between HCMC and Phnom Penh. Numerous traveller cafes in the Pham Ngu Lao area sell bus tickets. Allow about six hours for the trip, including time spent on border formalities. Cambodian visas (US$20) are issued at the border, although you'll need a passport-sized photo. Moc Bai has become a major duty-free shopping zone for the Vietnamese, with a handful of hypermarkets. Across the border, Bavet is a mini Macau complete with half-a-dozen or more casinos.

Tay Ninh

POP 127,000

Tay Ninh town, the capital of Tay Ninh province, serves as the headquarters of one of Vietnam's most intriguing indigenous religions, Cao Daism. The Cao Dai Great Temple at the sect's Holy See is one of the most unusual structures in all of Asia. Built between 1933 and 1955, the temple is a rococo extravaganza combining the conflicting architectural idiosyncrasies of a French church, a Chinese pagoda and Hong Kong's Tiger Balm Gardens.

Tay Ninh province, northwest of HCMC, is bordered by Cambodia on three sides. The area's dominant geographic feature is Nui Ba Den (Black Lady Mountain), which towers above the surrounding plains. Tay Ninh province's eastern border is formed by the Saigon River. The Vam Co River flows from Cambodia through the western part of the province.

Because of the once-vaunted political and military power of the Cao Dai, this region was the scene of prolonged and heavy fighting during the Franco–Viet Minh War. Tay Ninh province served as a major terminus of the Ho Chi Minh Trail during the American War, and in 1969 the Viet Cong captured Tay Ninh town and held it for several days.

During the period of conflict between Cambodia and Vietnam in the late 1970s, the Khmer Rouge launched a number of cross-border raids into Tay Ninh province and committed atrocities against civilians. Several cemeteries around Tay Ninh are stark reminders of these events.

⊙ Sights

Cao Dai Holy See　　　　　　TEMPLE
Home to the **Cao Dai Great Temple** (Thanh That Cao Dai), the Cao Dai Holy See, founded in 1926, is 4km east of Tay Ninh, in the village of Long Hoa. As well as the Great Temple, the complex houses administrative offices, residences for officials and adepts, and a hospital of traditional Vietnamese herbal medicine which attracts people from all over the south for its treatments. After reunification the government took parts of the complex for its own use (and perhaps to keep an eye on the sect).

Prayers are conducted four times daily in the Great Temple (suspended during Tet). It's worth visiting during prayer sessions (the one at noon is most popular with tour groups from HCMC) but don't disturb the worshippers. Only a few hundred adherents, dressed in special garments, participate in weekday prayers but during festivals several thousand may attend.

The Cao Dai clergy have no objection to visitors photographing temple objects, but do not photograph people without their permission, which is seldom granted. However, it is possible to photograph the prayer sessions from the upstairs balcony, an apparent concession to the troops of tourists who come here every day.

It's important that guests wear modest and respectful attire inside the temple, which means no shorts or sleeveless T-shirts.

Set above the front portico of the Great Temple is the **divine eye**. Lay women enter the Great Temple through a door at the base of the tower on the left. Once inside they walk around the outside of the colonnaded hall in a clockwise direction. Men enter on the right and walk around the hall in an anticlockwise direction. Hats must be removed upon entering the building. The area in the centre of the sanctuary is reserved for Cao Dai priests.

A **mural** in the front entry hall depicts the three signatories of the 'Third Alliance between God and Man': the Chinese statesman and revolutionary leader Dr Sun Yat-sen (1866–1925) holds an ink stone, while the Vietnamese poet Nguyen Binh Khiem (1492–1587) and French poet and author Victor Hugo (1802–85) write 'God and Humanity' and 'Love and Justice' in Chinese and French (Nguyen Binh Khiem writes with a brush; Victor Hugo uses a quill pen). Nearby signs in English, French and German each give a slightly different version of the fundamentals of Cao Daism.

The main hall is divided into nine sections by shallow steps, representing the nine steps to heaven, with each level marked by a pair of columns. Worshippers attain each new level depending on their years as Cao Dao adherents. At the far end of the sanctuary, eight plaster columns entwined with multicoloured dragons support a dome representing the heavens. Under the dome is a giant star-speckled blue globe with the 'divine eye' on it.

The largest of the seven chairs in front of the globe is reserved for the Cao Dai pope, a position that has remained vacant since 1933. The next three chairs are for the three men responsible for the religion's law books.

The remaining chairs are for the leaders of the three branches of Cao Daism, represented by the colours yellow, blue and red.

On both sides of the area between the columns are two pulpits similar in design to the *minbar* in mosques. During festivals the pulpits are used by officials to address the assembled worshippers. The upstairs balconies are used if the crowd overflows.

Up near the altar are barely discernible portraits of six figures important to Cao Daism: Sakyamuni (Siddhartha Gautama, the founder of Buddhism), Ly Thai Bach (Li Taibai, a fairy from Chinese mythology), Khuong Tu Nha (Jiang Taigong, a Chinese saint), Laozi (the founder of Taoism), Quan Cong (Guangong, Chinese God of War) and Quan Am (Guanyin, the Goddess of Mercy).

Nui Ba Den
TEMPLES, MOUNTAIN

(Black Lady Mountain; adult/child 10,000/5000d) Fifteen kilometres northeast of Tay Ninh, Nui Ba Den rises 850m above the rice paddies, corn, cassava (manioc) and rubber plantations of the surrounding countryside. Over the centuries it has served as a shrine for various peoples of the area, including the Khmer, Cham, Vietnamese and Chinese, and there are several interesting **cave temples** here. The summits of Nui Ba Den are much cooler than the rest of Tay Ninh province, most of which is only a few dozen metres above sea level.

Nui Ba Den was used as a staging area by both the Viet Minh and the VC, and was the scene of fierce fighting during the French and American Wars when it was defoliated and heavily bombed by US aircraft.

There are several stories surrounding the name Black Lady Mountain. One is derived from the legend of Huong, a young woman who married her true love despite the advances of a wealthy Mandarin. While her husband was away doing military service, she would visit a magical statue of Buddha at the mountain's summit. One day Huong was attacked by kidnappers but, preferring death to dishonour, she threw herself off a cliff. She then reappeared in the visions of a monk who lived on the mountain, and he told her story.

The hike from the base of the mountain to the main temple complex and back takes about 1½ hours. Although steep in parts, it's not a difficult walk – plenty of older pilgrims in sandals make the journey to worship at the temple. Around the temple complex are a few stands selling snacks and drinks.

CAO DAISM

A fascinating fusion of East and West, Cao Daism *(Dai Dao Tam Ky Pho Do)* is a syncretic religion born in 20th-century Vietnam that contains elements of Buddhism, Confucianism, Taoism, native Vietnamese spiritualism, Christianity and Islam – as well as a dash of secular enlightenment thrown in for good measure. The term Cao Dai (meaning high tower or palace) is a euphemism for God. There are an estimated two to three million followers of Cao Daism worldwide.

History

Cao Daism was founded by the mystic Ngo Minh Chieu (also known as Ngo Van Chieu; born 1878), a civil servant who once served as district chief of Phu Quoc Island. He was widely read in Eastern and Western religious works and became active in séances. In 1919 he began receiving revelations in which the tenets of Cao Dai were set forth.

Cao Daism was officially founded as a religion in 1926 and over the next few decades attracted thousands of followers, with the Cao Dai running Tay Ninh province as an almost independent feudal state. By 1956 the Cao Dai were a serious political force with a 25,000-strong army. Having refused to support the VC during the American War, the sect feared the worst after reunification. And for good reason: all Cao Dai lands were nationalised by the new government and four members of the sect were executed in 1979. Only in 1985, when the Cao Dai had been thoroughly pacified, were the Holy See and some 400 temples returned to their control.

Philosophy

Much of Cao Dai doctrine is drawn from Mahayana Buddhism, mixed with Taoist and Confucian elements (Vietnam's 'Triple Religion'). Cao Dai ethics are based on the Buddhist ideal of 'the good person' but incorporate traditional Vietnamese beliefs as well. The ultimate goal of the Cao Dai disciple is to escape the cycle of reincarnation. This can only be achieved by refraining from killing, lying, luxurious living, sensuality and stealing.

The main tenets of Cao Daism are the existence of the soul, the use of mediums to communicate with the spiritual world and belief in one god – although it also incorporates the duality of the Chinese yin and yang. In addition to séances, Cao Dai practices include priestly celibacy, vegetarianism and meditative self-cultivation.

According to Cao Daism, history is divided into three major periods of divine revelation. During the first period, God's truth was revealed to humanity through Laotse (Laozi) and figures associated with Buddhism, Confucianism and Taoism. The human agents of revelation during the second period were Buddha (Sakyamuni), Mohammed, Confucius, Jesus and Moses. The third and final revelation is the product of the 'Third Alliance between God and Man', which is where séances play a part. Disciples believe that Cao Daism avoids the failures of the first two periods because spirits of the dead guide the living. Among the contacted spirits who lived as Westerners are Joan of Arc, William Shakespeare, Vladimir Ilyich Lenin and Victor Hugo, who was posthumously named the chief spirit of foreign missionary works owing to his frequent appearance.

All Cao Dai temples observe four daily ceremonies, held at 6am, noon, 6pm and midnight. These rituals, during which dignitaries wear ceremonial dress, include offerings of incense, tea, alcohol, fruit and flowers. All Cao Dai altars have the 'divine eye' above them, which became the religion's official symbol after Ngo Minh Chieu saw it in a vision.

Read more on the official Cao Dai site: www.caodai.org.

If you need more exercise, a walk to the summit and back takes about six hours. The fastest, easiest way is via the **chair lift** (one way/return adult 50,000/90,000d, child 30,000/50,000d) that shuttles the pilgrims up and down the hill. For a more exhilarating descent, try the 'slideway', a sort of winding track that drops 1700m around the mountain and is the closest thing to the luge in Vietnam.

At the base of the mountain there are lakes and manicured gardens and (as with many such sacred sites in Asia) a mix of religious and tacky amusement park–style attractions: paddle boats for hire and a train to save the weary a bit of walking.

Very few foreign tourists visit the mountain, but it's a popular place for Vietnamese people. Because of the crowds, visiting on Sunday or during a holiday or festival is a bad idea.

Nui Ba Den appears prominently in a memoir published by a former American soldier, *Black Virgin Mountain: A Return to Vietnam* by Larry Heinemann.

ℹ Getting There & Away

Tay Ninh is on Hwy 22 (Quoc Lo 22), 96km from HCMC. The road passes through **Trang Bang**, the place where the famous photograph of a severely burnt young girl, Kim Phuc, screaming and running, was taken during a napalm attack. Read more about her story in *The Girl in the Picture* (1999) by Denise Chong.

BUS & TOURS There are buses from HCMC to Tay Ninh that leave from the An Suong bus station (minibus 50,000d), but by far the easiest way to get here is by one of the Tay Ninh/Cu Chi tours leaving from District 1. You could consider leaving one of the cheaper tours (US$7) at the Holy See. A taxi from here to Nui Ba Dem costs around 100,000d, while a *xe om* should only be around 40,000d. It would then cost a similar amount to return to the bus station in Tay Ninh town.

One Pillar Pagoda

Officially known as Nam Thien Nhat Tru, most people call this Buddhist site the **One Pillar Pagoda of Thu Duc** (Chua Mot Cot Thu Duc; ☏3896 0780; 1/91 Đ Nguyen Du, Thu Duc district). Modelled on Hanoi's One Pillar Pagoda, the structure is similar but not identical, consisting of a small, one-room pagoda rising on a pillar above a pond, containing a multiarmed image of the Goddess of Mercy. Other shrines surround it, including a large new one that was being built at the time of research. At the rear of the compound are tombs holding urns containing bones of monks and other Buddhist faithful.

Hanoi's original pagoda was built in the 11th century but rebuilt after being destroyed by the French in 1954. When Vietnam was partitioned during the same year, many Buddhist monks and Catholic priests fled south to avoid possible persecution. One monk from Hanoi, Thich Tri Dung, petitioned the South Vietnamese government

for permission to construct a replica of Hanoi's famous One Pillar Pagoda. However, it was denied by President Ngo Dinh Diem, a Catholic with little tolerance for Buddhist clergy. Nevertheless, Thich and his supporters raised the funds and built the pagoda in 1958, in defiance of the president's orders.

At one point the Diem government ordered the monks to tear down the temple but they refused even though they were threatened with imprisonment for not complying. Faced with significant opposition, the government's dispute with the monks reached a standoff. However, the president's attempts to harass and intimidate the monks in a country that was 90% Buddhist did not go down well and ultimately contributed to Diem's assassination by his own troops in 1963.

The pagoda is 15km northeast of central HCMC. Traveller cafes and travel agencies in HCMC should be able to put together a customised tour to the pagoda or to arrange a car and driver for you.

Can Gio

Notable for its extensive mangrove forest, which some say acts as nature's check on the growing pollution of the city, Can Gio is a low palm-fringed island sitting at the mouth of the Saigon River, some 25km southeast of HCMC. It was formed from silt washing downstream from the river, so don't expect any white-sand beaches. Nevertheless, a few hopeful resorts have sprung up along the murky 10km shoreline and more are planned – although it's hard to imagine them appealing to international visitors.

Of more interest is the forest. This listed UNESCO Biosphere Reserve contains a high degree of biodiversity, with more than 200 species of fauna and 150 species of flora. If you're looking for a relatively traffic-free route to explore by motorbike, Can Gio makes a great day trip.

◉ Sights

Monkey Island
Eco Forest Park NATURE RESERVE
(www.cangioresort.com.vn; admission 30,000d) As with many 'ecotourism' activities in Vietnam, Saigon Tourist has got in on the act and turned the experience into a bit of an event. While this is the most interesting and accessible part of the forest to visit, it's hard to stomach the cruel conditions in which the

WORTH A TRIP

DAI NAM THEME PARK

Equal parts Disneyland, Buddhist fantasia, historical homage and national propaganda piece, **Dai Nam Theme Park** (Lac Canh Dai Nam Van Hien; www.laccanhdainamvanhien.vn; adult/child 50,000/25,000d; ◷8am-6pm) is a fantastically cheesy experience. Located about 30km from HCMC on Hwy 13, this ambitious enterprise is split into four constituent parts sheltered behind giant walls (guarded by life-size model soldiers) which owe more to the Great Wall of China than anything we've seen in Vietnam.

The **amusement park** (◷8am-6pm) has a serious rollercoaster with corkscrews and loops, a log flume, an indoor snow world and plenty of rides for smaller kids. Most hilarious is the Ngu Lan (Five Unicorns) Palace, a Buddhist take on Disney's 'It's A Small World', where inflatable boats glide through tableaux representing life, death, reincarnation, a descent into hell (a splatterfest of body parts, torture and sadistic demons) and an eventual arrival in nirvana; it's definitely not suitable for small children. Its counterpart, the Ngu Phung (Five Phoenixes) Palace 'makes tourists feel like being lost in the heaven'. Each ride is charged separately (20,000d to 50,000d).

Dai Nam's 12.5-hectare **zoo** (adult/child 40,000/20,000d) is the only one in the greater HCMC area where the animals have a modicum of space and certainly the only one we'd recommend visiting. The bigger critters include tigers, lions, white rhinos and bears. The neighbouring **beach** (adult/child 50,000/20,000d) has large fresh and saltwater pools and is a good place for cooling off the kids if they're starting to get frazzled.

Best of all, for Disneyland kitsch on a monumental scale, is the **temple complex**. Set behind a vast plaza, there are artificial lakes, mountains, walking paths, towers and pagodas. In the mammoth temple every god, goddess and personage of importance in Vietnamese history gets a look in, with Ho Chi Minh taking pride of place, naturally.

Local bus 18 runs from Ben Thanh bus station to Dai Nam daily. There's plenty of car parking on site.

If you're interested in buying lacquerware, it's well worth stopping off at **Tuong Binh Hiep** en route. This village has been known for producing quality lacquered goods since the early 18th century and you'll pick up items here for a fraction of the price that you'll spend in HCMC. Tuong Binh Hiep is 5km south of the theme park; if you're coming from HCMC, turn left immediately after the second set of toll booths onto Đ Le Chi Dan. Various workshops are scattered along this road.

stars of their animal circus (including bears and monkeys) are kept.

The island is also home to a monkey sanctuary, which houses at least a hundred wild but unafraid simians. Take care: like monkeys everywhere, the line between cheeky charmer, thieving pest and dangerous beast is very fine. Keep a firm hold on your possessions.

The motorboat ride (about 150,000d) through the waterways to the VC's **Rung Sac base** is the highlight of a visit. At the reconstructed base, dummies portray VC cadres sawing open unexploded American bombs in order to salvage the explosives and wrestling with crocodiles, which were once common here but are now confined to crocodile farms like the one by the entrance. A small **museum** has wildlife displays, along with exhibits relating to local war history and archaeological finds.

Coming from HCMC, Monkey Island is to the right of the main road, about 34km past the ferry.

Vam Sat NATURE RESERVE
This section of the forest is noted for crab-angling, a crocodile farm and **Dam Doi** (Bat Swamp), an area where fruit bats nest. Boats to Vam Sat (around 150,000d) depart from under the Dan Xay Bridge, which is on the main road, 22km south of the ferry and 12km north of Monkey Island.

Duyen Hai TOWN
Facing Vung Tau at the southeastern tip of Can Gio district, this small town has a **Cao Dai temple** and a large **market**, which is made very conspicuous by some rather powerful odours. Seafood and salt are the local specialities; the vegetables, rice and fruit are all imported by boat from around

HCMC. Adjacent to the local shrimp hatchery is a vast **cemetery** and **war memorial** (Nghia Trang Liet Si Rung Sac), 2km from Can Gio Market.

ℹ️ Getting There & Away

CAR & MOTORBIKE Can Gio is about 60km southeast of central HCMC, and the fastest way to make the journey is by car or motorbike (about two hours). There's a ferry crossing (motorbike/car 2000/10,000d) 15km from HCMC at Binh Khanh (Cat Lai), a former US naval base. Once you get past the ferry, there is little traffic and the sides of the road are lined with mangrove forests. The motorbike ride is an excellent day out in itself.

TOURS There are day trips from HCMC offered by Cafe Kim Tourist (US$25) and Saigon Tourist (from US$56); see p339.

Mekong Delta

Best Places to Eat

» Dinh Cao Night Market (p389)

» Bassac Restaurant (p399)

» Tan Phat (p396)

» Noi Ben Tre (p360)

Best Places to Stay

» Kim Tho Hotel (p369)

» La Veranda (p387)

» Victoria Can Tho Resort (p369)

» Bamboo Cottages (p388)

Why Go?

The 'rice bowl' of Vietnam, the Mekong Delta is a landscape carpeted in a dizzying variety of greens. It's also a water world where boats, houses, restaurants and even markets float upon the innumerable rivers, canals and streams that flow through the region like arteries.

Although the area is primarily rural, it is one of the most densely populated regions in Vietnam and nearly every hectare is intensively farmed. Visitors can experience southern charm in riverside cities where few tourists venture, sample fruits traded in the colourful floating markets, or dine on home-cooked delicacies before overnighting as a homestay guest. There are also bird sanctuaries, impressive Khmer pagodas and, inevitably, war remnants.

Those seeking a tropical hideaway will find it on Phu Quoc, an island lined with white-sand beaches and crisscrossed with empty dirt roads, ideal for motorbike explorations.

When to Go
My Tho

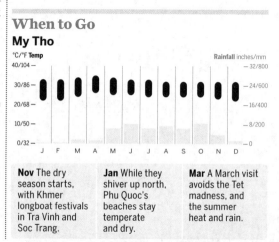

Nov The dry season starts, with Khmer longboat festivals in Tra Vinh and Soc Trang.

Jan While they shiver up north, Phu Quoc's beaches stay temperate and dry.

Mar A March visit avoids the Tet madness, and the summer heat and rain.

History

The Mekong Delta was once part of the Khmer kingdom, and was the last region of modern-day Vietnam to be annexed and settled by the Vietnamese. Cambodians, mindful that they controlled the area until the 18th century, still call the delta Kampuchea Krom, or 'Lower Cambodia'.

The Khmer Rouge attempted to reclaim the area by raiding Vietnamese villages and killing their inhabitants. This provoked the Vietnamese army to invade Cambodia on 25 December 1978 and oust the Khmer Rouge from power.

Most of the current inhabitants of the Mekong Delta are ethnic Vietnamese, but there are also significant populations of ethnic Chinese and Khmer, as well as a smaller Cham community. For more information on the story of the Khmer people

MEKONG DELTA

Mekong Delta Highlights

1 Witnessing the bustling commerce of the floating markets on a boat trip from **Can Tho** (p366)

2 Meandering along the **canals** (p356) between My Tho and Ben Tre, then stepping ashore a lush river island to feast on fresh fish

3 Kicking up red dirt during a motorbike ride to the isolated corners of **Phu Quoc Island** (p381)

4 Washing off said dirt at any of Phu Quoc Island's white-sand **beaches** (p381)

5 Experiencing river life up close and personal at

one of the many **homestays** (p367) around Vinh Long

6 Seeking out striking Khmer pagodas in **Tra Vinh** (p360)

7 Feeling like a minor celebrity in remote foreigner-free cities such as **Ca Mau** (p376)

and their place in the Mekong Delta region, see p364.

When the government introduced collective farming to the delta in 1975, production fell significantly and there were food shortages in Saigon, although farmers in the delta easily grew enough to feed themselves. The Saigonese would head down to the delta to buy sacks of black-market rice, but to prevent profiteering the police set up checkpoints and confiscated rice from anyone carrying more than 10kg. All this ended in 1986 and farmers in this region have since propelled Vietnam to become one of the world's largest rice exporters.

ℹ Getting There & Around

Most travellers head to the Mekong Delta on an organised tour – a cheap and easy way to get a taste of things. Those travelling on their own will have greater access to areas off the beaten track, with many little-visited places to discover.

With the opening of several border crossings between Vietnam and Cambodia, including the river border at Vinh Xuong (near Chau Doc) and the land border at Xa Xia (near Ha Tien), many travellers are choosing these delta routes ahead of the original land crossing at Moc Bai–Bavet. Cambodian visas are available on arrival at all border crossings.

AIR Flights head from Hanoi to Can Tho and from HCMC to Rach Gia and Ca Mau. Phu Quoc Island welcomes flights from Hanoi, HCMC, Can Tho and Rach Gia.

BOAT Some delta towns have ferry connections between them – which is a fascinating way to travel. The trip between Ca Mau and Rach Gia is particularly scenic. Boats to Phu Quoc Island leave from Rach Gia and Ha Tien.

BUS It's surprisingly easy to navigate your own way around the delta using public transport. Bus connections are excellent, due to there being so many major population centres. Each urban centre has a bus station used by both buses and minibuses – although it's usually located on the edge of town and necessitates a short *xe om* (motorbike taxi) or taxi ride to wherever you're staying. Minibuses tend to be faster, moderately more comfortable and not much more expensive.

If you're coming from HCMC, delta buses leave from Mien Tay bus station, 10km west of the centre. To avoid the slight inconvenience of getting to Mien Tay, you might want to consider booking one of the cheap day tours to My Tho departing from Đ Pham Ngu Lao and abandoning the tour after the boat trip.

CAR, MOTORCYCLE & BICYCLE The most flexible way to see the delta is by private car, bicycle or rented motorbike. Two-wheeling

around the delta is good fun, especially getting lost among the maze of country roads. Wherever you travel in the delta, be prepared for toll roads and ferry crossings – although gradually these are being replaced with new bridges. Fruit, soft drinks and sticky rice-based snacks are sold in the waiting areas and ferries are cheap and frequent.

☞ Tours

There are literally dozens of tours heading from Ho Chi Minh City (HCMC) to the Mekong Delta, either as day trips or longer jaunts. These can be a great option if you're short on time but it does mean abdicating control over your itinerary and choice of hotels.

The cheapest tours are sold around the Pham Ngu Lao area. Shop around before you book, but remember that you usually get what you pay for. This is not to say pricey tours are necessarily better, but sometimes 'rock-bottom' means that all you will get is a brief glance at the region from a packed bus full of other tourists. The cost largely depends on how far from HCMC the tour goes. The standard of accommodation, transport, food and the size of the group will be other determining factors.

My Tho

♪073 / POP 180,000

Gateway to the Mekong Delta, My Tho is the capital of Tien Giang province and an important market town – although for the famous floating markets, you'll need to continue on to Can Tho.

Its proximity to Ho Chi Minh City (HCMC) means that My Tho is a popular day-trip destination for those who want a taste of river life – a flotilla of boats tours the local islands and their cottage industries daily.

My Tho was founded in the 1680s by Chinese refugees fleeing Taiwan after the fall of the Southern Ming dynasty. The economy is based on tourism, fishing and the cultivation of rice, coconuts, bananas, mangoes, longans and citrus fruit. The riverfront makes for a pleasant stroll and the town is easily explored on foot.

◉ Sights

Vinh Trang Pagoda   PAGODA
(60A Đ Nguyen Trung Truc; admission free; ⊗9-11.30am & 1.30-5pm) Giant Buddha statues tower over the beautiful grounds of this peaceful pagoda, where the monks maintain an ornate sanctuary, decorated with carved and gilded wood.

THE RIVER OF NINE DRAGONS

The Mekong River is one of the world's great rivers and its delta is one of the world's largest. The Mekong originates high in the Tibetan plateau, flowing 4500km through China, between Myanmar (Burma) and Laos, through Laos, along the Laos–Thailand border, and through Cambodia and Vietnam on its way to the South China Sea. At Phnom Penh (Cambodia), the Mekong River splits into two main branches: the Hau Giang (Lower River, also called the Bassac River), which flows via Chau Doc, Long Xuyen and Can Tho to the sea; and the Tien Giang (Upper River), which splits into several branches at Vinh Long and empties into the sea at five points. The numerous branches of the river explain the Vietnamese name for the Mekong: Song Cuu Long (River of Nine Dragons).

The Mekong's flow begins to rise around the end of May and reaches its highest point in September; it ranges from 1900 to 38,000 cubic metres per second depending on the season. A tributary of the river that empties into the Mekong at Phnom Penh drains Cambodia's Tonlé Sap Lake. When the Mekong is at flood stage, this tributary reverses its direction and flows into Tonle Sap, acting as one of the world's largest natural flood barriers. Unfortunately, deforestation in Cambodia is disturbing this delicate balancing act, resulting in more flooding in Vietnam's portion of the Mekong River basin.

In recent years seasonal flooding has claimed the lives of hundreds and forced tens of thousands of residents to evacuate from their homes. In some areas inhabitants are not able to return to their homes until the waters fully recede several months later. Floods cause millions of dollars' worth of damage and have a catastrophic effect on regional rice and coffee crops.

Living on a flood plain presents some technical challenges. Lacking any high ground to escape flooding, many delta residents build their houses behind the houses on bamboo stilts to avoid the rising waters. Many roads are submerged or turn to muck during floods; all-weather roads have to be built on raised embankments, but this is expensive. The traditional solution has been to build canals and travel by boat. There are thousands of canals in the Mekong Delta – keeping them properly dredged and navigable is a constant but essential chore.

A further challenge is keeping the canals clean. The normal practice of dumping all garbage and sewage directly into the waterways that line them is taking its toll. Many of the more populated areas in the Mekong Delta are showing signs of unpleasant waste build-up. The World Wildlife Foundation (WWF) is one organisation that's working with local and provincial governments to improve conservation techniques and sponsoring environmental education and awareness programs.

In 2011 controversy was swirling once again in the murky Mekong waters, with Laos planning to build the first downstream dam on the river. Dams on the Chinese stretch have already been blamed for reduced water levels and the 263 environmental groups who have petitioned the Laos government to put the plans on hold are concerned that it will disrupt the breeding cycles of dozens of fish species. There are also fears that the reduced flows will cause more salt water to enter the Vietnamese section, which could have a catastrophic effect on rice production.

Life in the waters of the Mekong includes copious catfish, one of the rarest being the giant Mekong catfish, the largest freshwater fish in the world, which can reach 3m in length. Further north in Cambodia and Laos, the freshwater Irrawaddy dolphin is still present in small pockets. As well as bountiful fish, there are also many varieties of water snakes, turtles and aquatic insects. To learn more, visit **WWF Greater Mekong Programme** (www.worldwildlife.org).

They also provide a home for orphans, disabled and other needy children; donations are always welcome.

The pagoda is about 1km from the city centre. To get here, head north on Le Loi, turn right onto Nguyen Trai and take the bridge across the river. After 400m turn left onto Nguyen Trung Truc. The entrance to the sanctuary is about 200m from the turn-off, on the right-hand side of the building as you approach it from the ornate gate.

My Tho

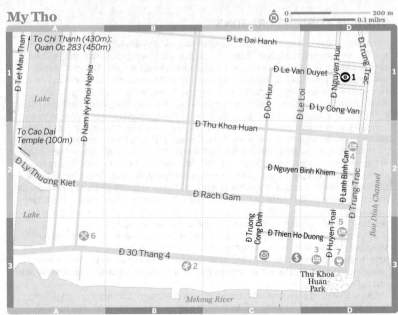

My Tho

◉ Sights
  1 My Tho Market.....................................D1

✦ Activities, Courses & Tours
  2 My Tho Tourist Boat Station B3

◉ Sleeping
  3 Minh Quan Hotel.................................D3
  4 Song Tien D2
  5 Song Tien Annex.................................D3

✖ Eating
  6 Hu Tieu 44..A3
    Hu Tieu Chay 24 .... (see 6)

◉ Drinking
  7 Lac Hong D3

My Tho Market   MARKET
(Cho My Tho; Đ Trung Trac) Spilling out onto the street facing Bao Dinh Channel, this market has the usual array of dried fish, exotic fruits, doomed animals and strange smells.

Cao Dai Temple   TEMPLE
(85 Đ Ly Thuong Kiet) A colourful little temple that's worth a quick look.

👉 Tours

In a prominent building on the riverfront, the **My Tho Tourist Boat Station** (8 Đ 30 Thang 4) is home to several tour companies offering cruises to the neighbouring islands and through the maze of small canals. Depending on what you book, destinations usually include a coconut-candy workshop, a honey farm (try the banana wine) and an orchid garden. A two-and-a-half-hour boat tour costs around 350,000d for one person or 450,000d for two. If you're a day-tripper it's easiest to book your package (including connecting transport) through an HCMC-based tour operator. Prices are significantly better if you can join a group, although you may be able to negotiate a more flexible itinerary if you go it alone. Boat Station–based operators include:

Tien Giang Tourist (☑387 3184; www.tien giangtourist.com)

Vietnamese Japanese Tourist (☑397 5559; www.dulichvietnhat.com).

🛏 Sleeping

With the big city so close, you're unlikely to be tempted to stay the night – although there are some excellent options if you do.

Song Tien Annex
HOTEL $$

(☎387 7883; www.tiengiangtourist.com; 33 Đ Thien Ho Duong; r US$30-40; ❄☎) The phrases 'boutique hotel' and 'state tourist company' rarely go together, but in this case, they've pulled it off. Rooms have polished wooden floors, natty extras such as bathrobes and hair dryers, and some of the nicest bathrooms you'll find at this price, complete with freestanding claw-footed bathtubs. Rooms are accessed from a narrow wraparound terrace which diminishes the river views – but the rooftop restaurant compensates for that.

Song Tien
HOTEL $

(☎387 2009; www.tiengiangtourist.com; 101 Đ Trung Trac; r from 400,000d; ❄☎) At this reliable seven-storey hotel (don't worry, there's a lift) the rooms include satellite TV, minibars and hot water while the 'suites' have fancier furniture. Some of the cheaper ones are windowless but there's little sign of the dampness that so often plagues internal rooms.

Minh Quan
HOTEL $

(☎397 9979; minhquanhotel@gmail.com; 69 Đ 30 Thang 4; r 400,000-750,000d; ❄@☎) Despite the luridly coloured pilasters in the corridors, the rooms here are smart and tasteful, if a little on the small side. The rooftop cafe can be noisy, but it's usually all over by 11pm.

✗ Eating & Drinking

My Tho is known for a special vermicelli soup, *hu tieu My Tho,* which is richly garnished with fresh and dried seafood, pork, chicken, offal and fresh herbs. It is served either with broth or dry and can also be made vegetarian.

Although *hu tieu* can be found at almost any eatery in town, there is a handful of specialty restaurants. Carnivores should try Hu Tieu 44 (46 Đ Nam Ky Khoi Nghia; soups 20,000d), while vegetarians can indulge at Hu Tieu Chay 24 (24 Đ Nam Ky Khoi Nghia; mains 10,000-14,000d).

Ngoc Gia Trang
VIETNAMESE $

(196 Đ Ap Bac; mains 45,000-150,000d) Popular with bus tour groups, this friendly spot is down a lane off the main road into My Tho from HCMC. Tables are set alongside ponds amidst lots of greenery and the lengthy menu is translated into English and French. The seafood is excellent and beautifully presented.

Quan Oc 283
VIETNAMESE, SEAFOOD $

(283 Đ Tet Mau Than; mains 15,000-100,000d) This is the place to come for a bargain seafood barbecue. Point at the platters out the front, piled high with clams, scallops, mussels and snails, or venture behind to the tanks of live fish, crab and shrimp. Quan Oc 283 is opposite the war monument. To get here, take Đ Ly Thuong Kiet and turn right immediately after the lake.

Chi Thanh
CHINESE, VIETNAMESE $

(279 Đ Tet Mau Than; mains 35,000-80,000d) This small but extremely popular restaurant does a steady trade in tasty Chinese and Vietnamese fare (beef, chicken, pork, crab, squid, crab, noodles, hot pots), with a menu in English. It's near Quan Oc 283.

Lac Hong
BAR, CAFE

(3 Đ Trung Trac; ☎) Set in a gorgeous old colonial-era trading house on the riverfront, this stylish place wouldn't be out of place in downtown HCMC. Downstairs are lounge chairs and free wi-fi; upstairs, breezes and river views. Live music on Thursdays.

ⓘ Getting There & Around

New bridges and freeways have considerably shortened travel distances to My Tho. It now takes only about an hour to 90 minutes (traffic depending) from central HCMC (70km), while Ben Tre town is a mere 17km away via the new bridge.

The **My Tho bus station** (Ben Xe Tien Giang; 42 Đ Ap Bac) is 3km west of the town centre on Đ Ap Bac, the main road to HCMC. Buses head to HCMC's Mien Tay bus station (30,000d), Can Tho (50,000d), Cao Lanh (25,000d), Chau Doc (51,000d) and Ca Mau (100,000d).

Around My Tho

PHOENIX ISLAND

Until his imprisonment for antigovernment activities and the consequent dispersion of his flock, the Coconut Monk (Dao Dua) led a small community on Phoenix Island (Con Phung), a few kilometres from My Tho. In its heyday the island was dominated by a somewhat trippy open-air sanctuary (admission 5000d; ⏲8-11.30am & 1.30-6pm). The dragon-emblazoned columns and the quirky tower, with its huge metal globe, must have once been brightly painted but these days the whole place has become faded, rickety and silent. Nevertheless, it is seriously kitsch, with a model of the Apollo rocket set among the Buddhist statues. With some imagination you can almost picture how it all must have appeared as the Coconut Monk presided over his congregation, flanked by enormous elephant tusks and seated on a richly ornamented throne. Private boat operators can include the island as part of an organised tour.

If you really wish to be at one with the island, it is possible to spend the night at the simple **Con Phung Hotel** (☏075-382 2198; www.conphungtourist.com; r 200,000d; ✴). The VIP quarters have river views, but all rooms include TV, fridge and hot water. The restaurant serves a range of delta-flavour dishes (mains 40,000d to 220,000d).

OTHER ISLANDS

Famed for its longan orchards, **Dragon Island** (Con Tan Long) makes for a pleasant stop and stroll, just a five-minute boat trip from My Tho. Some of the residents of the island are shipwrights and the lush, palm-fringed shores are lined with wooden fishing boats. The island has some small restaurants and cafes.

Tortoise Island (Con Qui) and **Unicorn Island** (Thoi Son) are popular stops for the coconut candy and banana wine workshops.

TAN TACH VILLAGE

Across the river in Ben Tre Province, this former ferry stop has faded into obscurity with the opening of the new bridge. The only reasons to visit are to chill out in its rustic guesthouse or to visit its riverside restaurant – a popular stop on the river tours.

Sleeping & Eating

Thao Nhi Guesthouse GUESTHOUSE **$**
(☏075-386 0009; thaonhitours@yahoo.com; Hamlet 1, Tan Thach village; r $US6-15; ✴) For some-

thing a little different, this friendly rural guesthouse offers a traditional homestay-type experience amid abundant greenery. Rooms are quite basic although some have air-conditioning and TVs. Cheaper rooms are in bungalows with fans. Hearty meals include excellent elephant-ear fish, and there's free bike rental. The owner's son speaks excellent English and offers tours around Ben Tre and neighbouring provinces.

Hao Ai VIETNAMESE **$**
(Hamlet 2, Tan Thach village; mains 50,000-80,000d) Set in lush landscaped gardens complete with chickens and buffalos, this attractive island restaurant does a roaring trade with tour groups exploring the delta by boat. There are enough pavilions for independent travellers to hide away and generous set menus are available for two or more. Lunch only.

ℹ Getting There & Away

Tan Tach is part of Chau Thanh District. It's 6km north of the Ben Tre bus station (30,000d by *xe om*); take Hwy 60 back towards My Tho, veer right at the big intersection marked Chau Thanh and follow it to the end. The guesthouse and restaurant are both down the last narrow road to the right; Thao Nhi is signposted to the right after 300m, where it's a further 50m down a small lane.

Ben Tre

☏075 / POP 120,000

As tourism took off in the Mekong Delta, the picturesque little province of Ben Tre was always one ferry beyond the tourist traffic of My Tho and consequently has developed at

THE COCONUT MONK

The Coconut Monk was so named because he once ate only coconuts for three years; others claim he only drank coconut juice and ate fresh young corn. Whatever the story, he was born Nguyen Thanh Nam in 1909, in what is now Ben Tre province. He studied chemistry and physics in France at Lyon, Caen and Rouen from 1928 until 1935, when he returned to Vietnam, got married and had a daughter.

In 1945 the Coconut Monk left his family in order to pursue a monastic life. For three years he sat on a stone slab under a flagpole and meditated day and night. He was repeatedly imprisoned by successive South Vietnamese governments, which were infuriated by his philosophy of achieving reunification through peaceful means. He died in 1990.

Plaques on the 3.5m-high porcelain jar (created in 1972) on Phoenix Island tell all about the Coconut Monk. He founded a religion, Tinh Do Cu Si, which was a mixture of Buddhism and Christianity. Representations of Jesus and the Buddha appeared together, as did the Virgin Mary and eminent Buddhist women, together with the cross and Buddhist symbols. Today only the symbols remain, as the Tinh Do Cu Si community has dissolved from the island.

Ben Tre

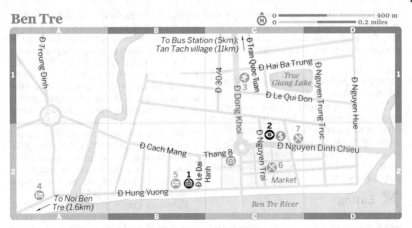

a more languid pace. The opening of a new bridge has (thus far) done little to change that. The town's sleepy waterfront, lined with ageing villas, is easy to explore on foot, as is the rustic settlement across the bridge to the south of the centre. This is also a good place to arrange boat trips in the area, particularly for those wanting to escape the tour buses.

Ben Tre is particularly famous for its *keo dua* (coconut candy). Many local women work in small factories making these sweets, spending their days boiling cauldrons of the sticky coconut mixture before rolling it out and cutting sections off into squares, and finally wrapping them into paper for sale.

👁 Sights

FREE **Ben Tre Museum**   MUSEUM
(Bao Tang Ben Tre; Đ Hung Vuong; ⊗8-11am & 1-5pm) The Ben Tre Museum is set in an ageing but atmospheric old yellow villa. It has the usual assortment of rusty weapons and American War photos, most captioned in English. The rear room has some artefacts from archaeological digs, sadly with no English translations.

Vien Minh Pagoda   PAGODA
(Đ Nguyen Trai; ⊗7-11am & 1-9pm) You won't miss this central pagoda, fronted as it is with large white statues of the Buddha and Quan The Am Bo Tat (the Goddess of Mercy). An earlier wooden shrine (thought to be 19th century) was demolished to make way for the current 1950s building, which is adorned with Chinese calligraphy painted by one of the earlier monks.

Ben Tre

👁 Sights
1 Ben Tre Museum B2
2 Vien Minh Pagoda C2

🚩 Activities, Courses & Tours
3 Ben Tre Tourist C1

🛏 Sleeping
4 Ham Luong Hotel A2
5 Hung Vuong Hotel B2

🍴 Eating
6 Food Stalls C2
7 Nam Son C2

👉 Tours

Ben Tre Tourist   CYCLING, BOAT TOURS
(✆382 9618; www.bentretourist.vn; 65 Đ Dong Khoi; ⊗7-11am & 1-5pm) Rents out bikes (per hour/day US$1/4), motor boats (per hour US$10) and speed boats (per hour $100), and arranges excursions, including a motorcart/canal boat trip to the honey farm and coconut candy workshop (per one/two/three/four people $25/30/42/52) and an 'ecological tour' by bike to coconut, guava and grapefruit groves.

🛏 Sleeping

Ham Luong   HOTEL $
(✆356 0560; www.hamluongtourist.com.vn; 200 Đ Hung Vuong; s US$18-23, d US$23-29; ✳@✵) A large modern hotel on the riverfront, Ham Luong is clearly betting on the bridge to bring it success. Corridors are huge and starkly decorated but the rooms are nicely

furnished and there's even a swimming pool and a fitness room, unheard of in little old Ben Tre. Free cable internet makes up for the lack of a wireless connection.

Hung Vuong HOTEL $

(☑382 2408; 166 Đ Hung Vuong; d/tw/ste 350,000/370,000/530,000đ; ❄⊛) Hung Vuong has an attractive riverfront location and large, clean rooms with tiled floors and polished wooden furnishings. All have modern bathrooms, although some are older than others. It's good value, if a little characterless – aside from the mermaid perched in the goldfish pond in reception.

✕ Eating

For ultra-cheap eats, head to the market, which has plenty of food stalls (dishes around 15,000d). The best place for a drink or an ice cream is Ham Luong's rooftop cafe.

Noi Ben Tre VIETNAMESE $

(Đ Hung Vuong; mains 20,000-60,000d) A multistorey barge moored in the river, this place doesn't cruise but it does draw a healthy breeze by night. The menu (with English translations) includes piquant prawn salads, delicious frog in lemongrass, egg soups, and mudfish, chicken and pork dishes.

Nam Son VIETNAMESE $

(40 Đ Phan Ngoc Tong; mains 20,000-60,000d) Centrally located, this place attracts a lively local crowd thanks to its popular grilled chicken, best washed down with draught beer.

ℹ Getting There & Away

Buses stop at the big new **bus station** (Ben Xe Ben Tre; Hwy 60), 5km northeast of the town centre (30,000d by *xe om*). Destinations include HCMC (67,000d), Can Tho (55,000d), Ca Mau (103,000d) and Ha Tien (134,000d). The last buses to HCMC depart between 4pm and 5pm.

ℹ Getting Around

Slow boats can be rented at the public pier near the market. Here you can figure on about 70,000d to 90,000d per hour, with a minimum of two hours cruising the local canals.

Tra Vinh

☑074 / POP 131,000

The boulevards of Tra Vinh, one of the prettiest towns in the Mekong Delta, are still lined with shady trees, harking back to an earlier era. Boasting more than 140 Khmer pagodas scattered about the province, Tra Vinh is a quiet place for exploring the Mekong's little-touted Cambodian connection. The town itself sees minimal tourist traffic, owing to its somewhat isolated location on a peninsula.

About 300,000 ethnic Khmer live in Tra Vinh province. At first glance they might seem to be an invisible minority since they all speak fluent Vietnamese and there's nothing outwardly distinguishing about their clothing or lifestyle. However, digging a little deeper quickly reveals that Khmer culture is alive and well in this part of Vietnam. Many of its numerous pagodas have schools to teach the Khmer language and many Tra Vinh locals can read and write Khmer at least as well as Vietnamese.

Vietnam's Khmer minority are almost all followers of Theravada Buddhism. If you've visited monasteries in Cambodia, you may have observed that Khmer monks are not involved in growing food and rely on donations from the local community. Here in Tra Vinh, Vietnamese guides will proudly point out the monks' rice harvest as one of the accomplishments of liberation. To the Vietnamese government, nonworking monks were seen as parasites. The Khmer don't necessarily see it the same way and continue to donate funds to the monasteries surreptitiously.

Between the ages of 15 and 20, most boys set aside a few months to live as monks (they decide themselves on the length of service). Khmer monks are allowed to eat meat, but they cannot kill animals.

There is also a small but active Chinese community in Tra Vinh, one of the few such communities that remain in the Mekong Delta region.

◉ Sights

Ba Om Pond & Ang Pagoda PAGODA, MUSEUM

Known as Ao Ba Om (Square Lake), this large, square pond is surrounded by tall trees and is a pleasing place for a stroll. It's a spiritual site for the Khmers and a picnic and drinking spot for local Vietnamese. It would have once served as a bathing pond for the 10th-century Angkor-era temple that was situated here.

Built on the temple ruins, Ang Pagoda (Chua Ang in Vietnamese; Angkor Rek Borei in Khmer) is a beautiful and venerable Khmer-style pagoda, fusing classic Khmer architecture with French colonial influences. The interior features brightly painted scenes from the Buddha's life.

Opposite the pagoda entrance is the nicely presented Khmer Minority People's

LE VAN SINH: TOURISM TRAILBLAZER & CYCLING ENTHUSIAST

Few people have had more of an impact on Vietnam tourism than Le Van Sinh, owner of Sinhbalo Adventures and mentor to generations of Lonely Planet authors.

What makes the Mekong Delta special? I have always been interested in waterways, as it is such a great way to relax – in a hammock, cruising along the river. The system of canals and floating markets here is incredible and so different that all tourists should see it.

Why cycle? Bicycles are the best way to enjoy the scenery and get off the beaten track. Cycling in the far north or even the Central Highlands requires some experience and endurance, but for the pancake-flat Mekong, everyone can manage a few days exploring on two wheels. It doesn't matter whether you're a serious cyclist or a city slicker, there are so many routes in the Mekong to enjoy and explore.

Best routes? My favourite backroads include the small trail under the shade of coconut palms that runs from Ben Tre through Mo Cay and the pretty town of Tra Vinh to Can Tho. Most tourists only experience Hwy 1A on the way to Can Tho, but this is another world.

Museum (Bao Tang Van Hoa Dan Tac; admission free; ⊙7-11am & 1-5pm Fri-Wed), which displays photos, costumes and other artefacts of traditional Khmer culture. The building itself is interesting, grafting distinctly Khmer roof flourishes onto a modern structure built around a pond.

Ba Om Pond is 5km southwest of Tra Vinh, along the highway towards Vinh Long.

Ong Pagoda   PAGODA
(Chua Ong & Chua Tau; 44 Dien Bien Phu) The very ornate, brightly painted Ong Pagoda is a fully fledged Chinese pagoda and a very active place of worship. The red-faced god on the altar is deified general Quan Cong. He is believed to offer protection against war and is based on a historical figure, a soldier of the 3rd century. You can read more about him in the Chinese classic *The Romance of the Three Kingdoms*.

The Ong Pagoda was founded in 1556 by the Fujian Chinese Congregation, but has been rebuilt a number of times. Recent visitors from Taiwan and Hong Kong have contributed money for the pagoda's restoration, which explains why it is in such fine shape.

President Ho Chi Minh Temple   TEMPLE
(Den Tho Chu Tich Ho Chi Minh; parking car/bike 5000/2000d; ⊙7-11am & 1-5pm) This highly unusual temple is dedicated to the late president Ho Chi Minh and contains a shrine to Uncle Ho as well as a small museum displaying photos of his life. The little rattan-roofed shrine (now enclosed in a round concrete building) was built in 1971, while the war was still raging – testimony to Communist support in large swathes of the Mekong. There's a US helicopter, jeep and 105mm gun in the park-like grounds, along with some giant pythons in cages. The temple is in Long Duc commune, 5km north of Tra Vinh town.

Hang Pagoda   PAGODA
(Chua Hang; Kampongnigrodha; Đ Dien Bien Phu) This modern Khmer pagoda is also known as the stork pagoda owing to the great white birds that nest in the tall trees here. It's a beautiful, peaceful complex and the birds are an interesting sight in themselves. You're more likely to see them around dusk during the rainy season, although we spotted plenty in the early afternoon during the dry season. Chua Hang is located 6km south of town, about 300m past the bus station.

Ong Met Pagoda   PAGODA
(Chua Ong Met, Chua Bodhisalaraja-Kompong; Đ Ngo Quyen) The chief reason for visiting this large Khmer pagoda is its accessibility as it's located right in the centre of town. This complex has some giant new buildings.

☞ Tours

Tra Vinh Tourist   TOURS
(☎385 8556; tvtourist@yahoo.com; 64 Đ Le Loi; ⊙7.30-11am & 1.30-5pm) arranges trips to various sites around the province, including a boat cruise to local islands (500,000d).

Tra Vinh

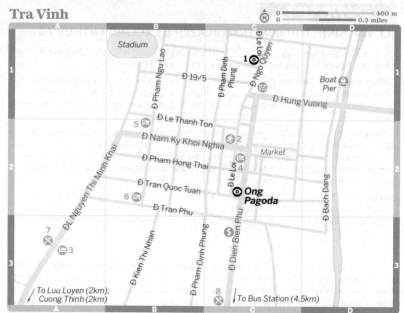

Tra Vinh

◎ Top Sights
Ong Pagoda...C2

◎ Sights
1 Ong Met Pagoda C1

◎ Activities, Courses & Tours
2 Tra Vinh Tourist....................................C2

◎ Sleeping
3 Hoan My A3
4 Tan Hang...C2
5 Tra Vinh Palace.....................................B2
6 Tra Vinh Palace 2..................................B2

◎ Eating
7 Cuu Long Restaurant A3
8 Vi Huong...C3

🛏 Sleeping

Tra Vinh Palace 2　　　　　　　HOTEL $
(📞386 3999; 48 Đ Pham Ngu Lao; d/tw/tr
180,000/220,000/250,000đ; 🌬@📶) Pretty
in pink, this friendly new mini-hotel has
sparkling, modern rooms with tiled floors
and either a bathtub or a shub (shower
tub). The double rooms are internal and
windowless, so you might want to consider

upgrading to a triple. Don't be afraid to aim
high – there is a lift.

Hoan My　　　　　　　　　　　HOTEL $
(📞386 2211; 105A ĐL Nguyen Thi Minh Khai; r
200,000-360,000đ; 🌬📶) There's a bit of design flair to this mini-hotel – with some natty
exposed brickwork, polished wooden floors,
dark wooden furniture and a lift. The pricier
rooms are a real treat with wide-screen TV,
DVD player, oodles of space and a balcony.
It's still relatively new, although sadly it's already starting to look a little scuffed and we
did spot a few cobwebs.

Luu Luyen　　　　　　　　　　HOTEL $
(📞384 2306; 16 ĐL Nguyen Thi Minh Khai; r with fan
90,000-120,000đ, with air-con 190,000-550,000đ;
🌬) A little out of the way on the road to Vinh
Long, Luu Luyen's rooms are smart and stylish, with large floral images on the walls –
although the worn carpets detract from the
effect. The main block is set behind a little
courtyard garden.

Tra Vinh Palace　　　　　　　HOTEL $
(📞386 4999; www.travinh.lofteight.com; 3 Đ Le
Thanh Ton; r 250,000-350,000đ; 🌬📶) Domi-
nating the corner of a sleepy backstreet,
this four-storey hotel conveys its palatial
aspirations with pink columns, decorative
plasterwork, terracotta tiling and balco-

nies. The spacious rooms have high ceilings and ornate mother-of-pearl-inlaid wooden furniture.

Tan Hang   HOTEL $
(☑626 6999; 14 Dien Bien Phu; r 200,000-500,000d; ✳❋) Slap bang in the centre of town, this tall, skinny mini-hotel is still new enough to have the edge on its older, poorly maintained neighbours. The pale brick and inlaid wooden furniture downstairs makes a good first impression. For 200,000d you'll get a small internal room with a good shower stall and no sign of mildew (yet). Upgrade for a window.

✗ Eating

Cuu Long Restaurant   VIETNAMESE $
(☑386 2615; 999 ĐL Nguyen Thi Minh Khai; mains 60,000-190,000d) Hiding behind the stolid facade of the government-run Cuu Long Hotel, this restaurant has a pleasant setting under a huge thatched roof. The English-language menu lists an extensive range of dishes, including delicious salads and viscous soups, and, for the more adventurous, snake and snails. Bands play (loudly) some evenings.

Cuong Thinh   VIETNAMESE $
(18A ĐL Nguyen Thi Minh Khai; mains 25,000-180,000d) A huge open-plan restaurant, Cuong Thinh is popular for its traditional mains and palm-lined ambience. The menu (in Vietnamese only) offers a large selection of local favourites and popular imports such as Singapore noodles. It's 2km south of town on the road to Vinh Long.

Vi Huong   VIETNAMESE $
(37A Đ Dien Bien Phu; mains 15,000-40,000d) A cheap and cheerful local hole-in-wall, Vi Huong sticks with wholesome traditional dishes like sour soup, fish in clay pot and pork with rice.

❶ Getting There & Away

Tra Vinh is 65km from Vinh Long and 185km from HCMC. From Ben Tre it's easily reached by yet another new bridge and then a car ferry across the Co Chien River (per car 35,000d); work has already commenced on a bridge to replace this ferry.

The bus station (Ben Xe Khach Tra Vinh) is about 5km south of the town centre on Hwy 54 which is the continuation of the main street, Đ Dien Bien Phu. Buses head to HCMC (85,000d), Cao Lanh (45,000d) and Ha Tien (116,000).

Around Tra Vinh

CHUA CO
A Khmer monastery, Chua Co is interesting because the grounds form a **bird sanctuary**. Several types of stork and ibis arrive here in large numbers before sunset to spend the night. There are many nests here, so take care not to disturb the birds when visiting.

Chua Co is 43km from Tra Vinh. Travel 36km to Tra Cu then follow the sandy road for 7km to the monastery.

BA DONG BEACH
The dirty shoreline, murky water, caged monkeys and run-down accommodation will not appeal to many Westerners, but if you fancy an off-the-beaten-path target, Ba Dong at least offers nice sunsets. It can get busy on the weekends with regional visitors but otherwise it's very quiet.

The big event here – well worth attending if you happen to be in the area – is the **Khmer Oc Bom Boc Festival**, featuring colourful boat races. It's held on a weekend in late October or November – ask for details at Tra Vinh Tourist.

To get here from Tra Vinh, head 50km along the paved road to Duyen Hai and follow the bumpy dirt road for 12km until you reach the beach. About five buses a day make the trip from Tra Vinh to Duyen Hai, from where you can hire a *xe om* (about 50,000d) to take you to the beach.

Vinh Long

☑070 / POP 130,000
It may not be the largest town in the Mekong but as a major transit hub it can be noisy and chaotic nonetheless. Escape the mayhem by heading to the riverfront, where there are plenty of cafes and restaurants. Despite a lack of in-town attractions, Vinh Long is the gateway to island life and some worthwhile sites, including Cai Be floating market, abundant orchards and rural homestays, which can be a highlight of a Mekong journey. Vinh Long is the capital of Vinh Long province and situated about midway between My Tho and Can Tho.

◉ Sights

Mekong River Islands   ISLANDS
What makes a trip to Vinh Long worthwhile is not the town but the beautiful islands dotting the river. The islands are dedicated to

KAMPUCHEA KROM

Visitors to some Mekong provinces may be surprised to find Khmer towns whose inhabitants speak a different language, follow a different brand of Buddhism and have a vastly different history and culture to their Vietnamese neighbours. Though the Khmer are a minority in the Mekong, they were the first inhabitants here, with an ancestry dating back more than 2000 years.

Kampuchea Krom (meaning 'Lower Cambodia') is the unofficial Khmer name for the Mekong Delta region, whose indigenous inhabitants are the Khmer Krom, an ethnic minority living in southern Vietnam. The Khmer Krom trace their origins back to the 1st century AD, to the founding of Funan, a maritime empire that stretched from the Malay peninsula to the Mekong. Archaeologists believe Funan was a sophisticated society that built canals, traded in precious metals and had a high level of political organisation as well as agricultural know-how. Following the Funan came the Chenla empire (630–802 AD) and then the Khmer empire, the mightiest in Southeast Asia, which saw the creation of Angkor Wat among other great achievements. By the 17th century, however, the empire was in ruins, under pressure from the expansionist Thais and Vietnamese. This was a time of rising power for the Vietnamese empire which began expanding south, conquering first the Cham empire before setting their sights on Khmer lands in the Mekong Delta.

According to some historians, there were around 40,000 Khmer families living around Prey Nokor when the Vietnamese arrived in the 1600s, following the granting of settlement rights by King Chey Chettha in 1623. Prey Nokor was an important port for the Cambodian kingdom and was renamed Saigon in 1698. Waves of Vietnamese settlers populated the city as other colonists continued south. Prior to their arrival there were 700 Khmer temples scattered around south Vietnam. Over the next century the Khmer Krom fought and won some minor victories in the region, expelling the intruders, only to lose their gains in new rounds of attacks.

When the French subjugated Indochina in the 19th century, the hope of an independent Kampuchea Krom would be forever destroyed. Although the ethnic Khmer were a majority in southern Vietnam at that time, the French didn't incorporate the colony with Cambodia but made it a separate protectorate called Cochinchina. On 4 June 1949, the French formally annexed Kampuchea Krom, a day of sorrow for many Cambodians, although the writing had been on the wall centuries earlier as the area was colonised.

Since independence in 1954, the Vietnamese government has adopted a policy of integration and forced assimilation (the Khmer Krom must take Vietnamese family names and learn the Vietnamese language, among other things). According to the Khmer Kampuchea-Krom Federation (KKF; www.khmerkrom.org), the Khmer Krom continue to suffer persecution. They report difficult access to Vietnamese health services, religious discrimination (Khmer Krom are Theravada Buddhists, unlike Vietnam's Mahayana Buddhists) and racial discrimination. Several monks have been defrocked for nonviolent protest and the Cambodian government has even assisted in deporting some agitators according to Human Rights Watch (www.hrw.org).

The Khmer are the poorest segment of the population. Even their numbers remain a contentious topic. Vietnam reports one million Khmer Krom, who are called 'Nguoi Viet Goc mien' (Vietnamese of Khmer origin) by Vietnamese officials, while KKF claims there are seven million Khmer living in southern Vietnam.

agriculture, especially the growing of tropical fruits, which are shipped to markets in HCMC. This low-lying region is as much water as land and houses are generally built on stilts.

Some of the more popular islands to visit include Binh Hoa Phuoc and An Binh, but there are many others. You can take the public ferry (per person/motorbike 500/1000d) to one of the islands and then walk or cycle around on your own. However, this isn't as interesting as a boat tour, since you won't cruise the narrow canals. You should be able to arrange a two- to three-hour cruise with one of the operators along the wharf for less than 300,000d.

Cai Be Floating Market   FLOATING MARKET
(☺5am-5pm) This bustling river market is worth including on a boat tour from Vinh Long, but it is best to arrive early in the morning. Wholesalers on big boats moor here, each specialising in just a few types of fruit or vegetable. Customers cruise the market in smaller boats and can easily find what they're looking for as the larger boats hang samples of their goods from tall wooden poles. One interesting thing you won't see at other floating markets is the huge Catholic cathedral on the riverside – a popular and memorable backdrop for photographs.

It takes about an hour to reach the market from Vinh Long, but most people make detours on the way there or back to see the canals or visit orchards. For those travelling on an organised tour of the delta, it is customary to board a boat here, explore the islands and moor in Vinh Long before continuing to Can Tho.

Van Thanh Mieu Temple   TEMPLE
(Phan Thanh Gian Temple; Đ Tran Phu; ☺5-11am & 1-7pm) One surprise in Vinh Long is the Van Thanh Mieu Temple, sitting in pleasant grounds across from the river. Confucian temples such as this are rare in southern Vietnam. The front hall honours local hero Phan Thanh Gian, who led an uprising against the French colonists in 1930. When it became obvious that his revolt was doomed, Phan killed himself rather than be captured by the colonial army.

The rear hall, built in 1866, has a portrait of Confucius above the altar. The building was designed in the Confucian style and looks like it was lifted straight out of China.

Van Thanh Mieu Temple is southeast of town. Don't confuse it with the smaller Quoc Cong Pagoda, which you'll pass on the way.

☞ Tours

Cuu Long Tourist   BOAT TOURS
(☑382 3616; www.cuulongtourist.com; 2 Phan Boi Chau; ☺7am-5pm) Offers a variety of boat tours ranging from three hours to three days. Destinations include small canals, fruit orchards, brick kilns, a conical palm hat workshop and the Cai Be Floating Market. We don't necessarily recommend you use them for other travel arrangements.

🛏 Sleeping
You'll find much better accommodation in Ben Tre, Tra Vinh and Can Tho, and much more atmospheric accommodation in one of the local homestays (see boxed text, p367). If you really must stay in Vinh Long town, the following are the best options.

Cuu Long Hotel   HOTEL $$
(☑382 3656; www.cuulongtourist.com; 2 Phan Boi Chau; s 440,000-580,000d; d 560,000-700,000d; ❀☎) This government-run hotel is clean but characterless. Most midrange tour groups stay here, as the boats leave from directly across the road. The rooms are spacious and have baths and either balconies or river views.

Van Tram Guesthouse   GUESTHOUSE $
(☑382 3820; 4 Đ 1 Thang 5; r 250,000-300,000d; ❀) A small place with just five rooms, the real bonus here is the location, near the riverfront and lively market. The rooms are a good size but the bathrooms are tiny.

🍴 Eating & Drinking

Dong Khanh   VIETNAMESE $
(49 Đ 2 Thang 9; mains 30,000-50,000d) Popular Dong Khanh offers a varied menu, including lots of hotpots and rice dishes. It has an English-language menu and the tablecloths add a touch of class.

Vinh Long Market   MARKET $
(Đ 3 Thang 2) A good spot for a range of local fruit and inexpensive street snacks.

Com 36   VIETNAMESE $
(36 Đ Hoang Thai Hieu; mains 20,000-40,000d) This is the real Vietnamese deal, with barebones furnishing, no decor and no English menu, but the authentic food is displayed behind a glass counter so just point and eat.

Phuong Thuy   VIETNAMESE $
(Đ Phan Boi Chau; mains 25,000-80,000d) Great location on the riverside, but it can fill up with tour groups, detracting from the atmosphere.

Hoa Nang Cafe   CAFE, BAR
(Đ 1 Thang 5) Perched on the riverbank, this is a good place to enjoy an iced coffee or scented tea in the morning or to quaff your first beer back on dry land after a river trip.

❶ Getting There & Away
BOAT Cargo boats sometimes take passengers from Vinh Long all the way to Chau Doc (near the Cambodian border); enquire locally, near the ferry landing.

Vinh Long

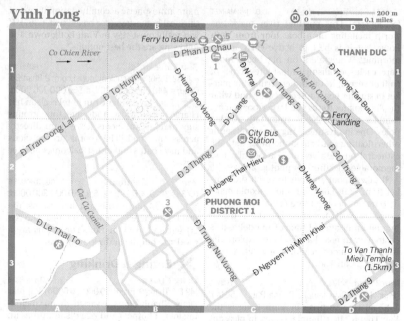

Vinh Long

Activities, Courses & Tours
Cuu Long Tourist ....(see 1)

Sleeping
1 Cuu Long Hotel C1
2 Van Tram Guesthouse C1

Eating
3 Com 36 .... B2
4 Dong Khanh D3
5 Phuong Thuy C1
6 Vinh Long Market C1

Drinking
7 Hoa Nang Cafe C1

BUS Vinh Long's **city bus station** (Ben Xe Thanh Pho Vinh Long; Ð 3 Thang 2), conveniently located in the middle of town, has buses to HCMC (70,000d) and Sa Dec (9,000d). For other services you're best to go to the **provincial bus station** (Ben Xe Khach Vinh Long; Hwy 1A), 3km south of town on the way to Can Tho. Buses to Can Tho (34,000d), Cao Lanh (17,000d) and other destinations leave from here.

CAR & MOTORBIKE Vinh Long is just off Hwy 1A, 33km from Can Tho, 66km from My Tho and 136km from HCMC.

Can Tho

071 / POP 1.1 MILLION

The epicentre of the Mekong Delta, Can Tho is the largest city in the region and feels like a veritable metropolis after a few days exploring the backwaters. As the political, economic, cultural and transportation centre of the Mekong Delta, it's a buzzing town with a lively waterfront lined with sculpted gardens and an appealing blend of narrow backstreets and wide boulevards that make for some rewarding exploration. It is also the perfect base for nearby floating markets, the major draw for tourists who come here to boat along the many canals and rivers leading out of town.

Sights

Ong Temple   TEMPLE

In a fantastic location facing the Can Tho River, this temple is set inside the **Guangzhou Assembly Hall** (Ð Hai Ba Trung) and is the most interesting religious site in town. It was originally built in the late 19th century to worship Kuang Kung, a deity symbolising loyalty, justice, reason, intelligence, honour and courage, among other merits. It is designed to symbolise the Chinese character for nation, with rows of enclosed sections laid out symmetrically. Approaching the engraved screen, the right side is dedicated to the Goddess of Fortune and the left side is reserved for the worship of General Ma Tien. In the centre of the temple is Kuang Kung flanked by the God of Earth and the God of Finance.

Can Tho once had a large ethnic-Chinese population, but most of them fled after the anti-Chinese persecutions (1978-79).

FREE **Can Tho Museum** MUSEUM
(1 ĐL Hoa Binh; 8-11am & 2-5pm Tue-Thu, 8-11am & 6.30-9pm Sat & Sun) The large, well-presented Can Tho Museum brings local history to life with manikins and life-size reproductions of buildings, including a Chinese pagoda and the interior of a house. Displays (with ample English translations) focus on the Khmer and Chinese communities, plant and fish specimens, rice production and, inevitably, the war, with the usual gruesome photos and an actual skeleton.

FREE **Military Museum** MUSEUM
(6 ĐL Hoa Binh; 8-11am & 2-4.30pm Tue, Thu & Fri, 8-11am & 7-9pm Sat) Devoted to all things militaristic, this museum has the usual assortment of American War weaponry and photos. Missiles and a US A37 Bomber sit on

'HOMESTAYS' AROUND VINH LONG

For many travellers, the chance to experience river life and to share a home-cooked meal with a local family is a highlight of a Mekong visit. The homestay concept has taken off on the islands around Vinh Long, although perhaps 'homestay' is the wrong word. In most cases you won't actually be staying in the family home but in specially constructed accommodation which is more akin to a rudimentary hostel.

Some homestays have large communal rooms with bunks while others offer basic bungalows with shared facilities and some even have rooms with en suites. Dinner and breakfast is usually included. In some places you'll share a meal with the family, while in bigger places the experience is more like a restaurant. The only constant that you can be guaranteed is a verdant, rustic setting and a taste of rural life.

Although many tourists book through group tours in HCMC, there's no reason you can't do it yourself – just take the ferry from Vinh Long and then a *xe om* to your preferred choice. Note that hosts are unlikely to speak much English but welcome foreign guests just the same. Most of the places listed below are perched on the banks of a river or canal.

Bay Thoi (385 9019; Binh Thuan 2 hamlet, Hoa Ninh village; per person US$13-15) One of the smartest and friendliest options, Bay Thoi is set around an attractive wooden family home. A newer block out the back has tiled floors and some en suites – it's worth the extra $2. Free bikes are provided.

Song Tien (385 8487; An Thanh hamlet, An Binh village; per person US$10) Across the Co Chien River from Vinh Long, this friendly place offers beds in small bungalows with stop-and-drop toilets. The surroundings here are particularly lush and the owners are known to bust out the mandolin from time to time for a bit of traditional singing for their guests. It's one of the smaller operations and one with a real family feel.

Tam Ho (385 9859; info@caygiong.com; Binh Thuan 1 hamlet, Hoa Ninh village; per person dm/r US$11/15) About 1.5km from Vinh Long, Tam Ho is a working orchard run by a friendly, welcoming family. Three private rooms are available but the canal can be noisy.

Ngoc Sang (385 8694; 95/8 Binh Luong, An Binh village; per person US$15) Readers love this friendly, canal-facing homestay. Free bikes are available and you can even help out in the family's orchard, if you feel so inclined.

Mai Quoc Nam 1 (385 9912; maiquocnam@yahoo.com; Phuan 1 hamlet, Binh Hoa Phuoc village; per person 250,000-300,000d) A short hop by boat from Vinh Long, Mai Quoc Nam has a modern concrete building in front with a large dormitory upstairs. More attractive are the wooden bungalows hidden away in the gardens behind. The owners can help arrange boat trips around the canals. This is one of the larger operations with less of an intimate feel.

Mai Quoc Nam 2 (385 9912; maiquocnam@yahoo.com; Binh Hoa 2 hamlet, Binh Hoa Phuoc village; per person 300,000d) Built on stilts over the wide Co Chien River, this offshoot of Mai Quoc Nam offers absolute river views and plenty of atmosphere but it's not really a homestay. Dorms are in well-ventilated rattan-roofed buildings and meals are served in a central stilt building.

MEKONG DELTA CAN THO

Can Tho

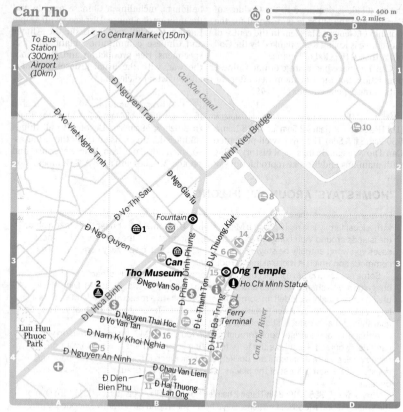

MEKONG DELTA CAN THO

the front lawn, while the central courtyard has a re-creation of a jungle camp.

In a separate building within the same complex is the **Ho Chi Minh Museum**, containing yet more photos (no English captions) and objects of cultural worth such as the great man's plastic soap holder and chopsticks.

Munirensay Pagoda   PAGODA
(36 ĐL Hoa Binh) A flurry of construction was underway when we last visited this pagoda, originally built in 1946 to serve Can Tho's Khmer community. The ornamentation is typical of Khmer Theravada Buddhist pagodas: it doesn't have any of the multiple Bodhisattvas and Taoist spirits common in Vietnamese Mahayana pagodas.

🏃 Activities

Van Tho   MASSAGE
(56/68 Tran Quan Khai; massage 40,000d; ⊘9am-10pm) Van Tho is an employment agency for the blind that hires professional therapists trained at Ho Chi Minh University in Vietnamese and Japanese massage techniques. The massages are an absolute bargain, very legit compared to what is on offer in some places and a good way to put some money into a worthy project.

It's near the market; take Đ Nguyen Trai and turn right at the third street after the bridge.

Can Tho Water Park   WATER PARK
(Đ Le Loi; water park/pool only 40,000/25,000d; ⊘9am-6pm) For a cooling dip and glorious chlorinated fun, head straight for the wave pool and water slides of this large complex. Children under a metre tall are admitted free.

Cross the Ninh Kien Bridge and you'll see the slides directly in front of you, behind the giant roundabout.

Can Tho

☞ **Tours**

The undisputed highlight of any visit to Can Tho is taking a boat ride through the canals to a floating market. The cost is around US$5 per hour for a small boat, which can carry two or three passengers. For boat operators (mostly women), just wander along the riverside near the giant statue of Ho Chi Minh. You can also book through Can Tho Tourist, but this leaves little room for negotiation.

Larger motorboats can go further afield and it's worth hiring one to make a tour of the Mekong River itself. Check the going rates at Can Tho Tourist then see what's on offer at the pier by the Ninh Kieu Hotel. Prices range from 200,000d for a three-hour tour to 350,000d for a five-hour tour. Negotiation is the name of the game.

🛏 **Sleeping**

Can Tho boasts the best range of accommodation in the Mekong Delta, so lie back and enjoy.

TOP CHOICE Kim Tho Hotel   HOTEL **$$**

(☑381 7517; www.kimtho.com; 1A Đ Ngo Gia Tu; r US$40-120; ❄️🛜) A smart hotel, verging on the boutique, Kim Tho sets a new standard for midrange properties in the Mekong. The rooms are stylish throughout and include designer bathrooms. The US$50 river-view rooms are a great deal. There is also a rooftop coffee bar.

TOP CHOICE Victoria Can Tho Resort   RESORT **$$$**

(☑381 0111; www.victoriahotels.asia; Cai Khe Ward; r US$91-230, ste US$277-310; ❄️@🛜🏊) This hotel defines style and sophistication in the Mekong Delta. Designed with a French colonial look, the rooms are set around an inviting pool that looks out over the river. Facilities include an excellent restaurant, an open-air bar and a riverside spa. There are plenty of activities on offer, including cycling tours, cooking classes and cruises on the Lady Hau, a converted rice barge.

Kim Lan Hotel   HOTEL **$**

(☑381 7049; www.kimlancantho.com.vn; 138A Đ Nguyen An Ninh; r US$18-50; ❄️@🛜) Just another skinny mini-hotel from the outside, there is more to Kim Lan than meets the eye. The chic rooms include contemporary furnishings in bamboo and wood, plus artworks on the wall. Even the small, windowless standard rooms are perfectly adequate, and excellent for the price. Solar-powered water (thumbs up) and free wi-fi complete the picture.

Xuan Mai Minihotel   HOTEL **$**

(☑382 3578; tcdac@yahoo.com; 17 Đ Dien Bien Phu; r US$12; ❄️🛜) Don't be put off by the spartan reception. This place has a real local feel, as it is located down a small lane which doubles as An Lac Market by day. It's popular with budget tour groups thanks to spacious, clean and surprisingly quiet rooms with TVs, fridges and hot showers.

Hello 2
HOTEL $

(☑381 0666; 31 Đ Chau Van Liem; r 200,000-260,000d; ❋🛜) Having a lift already places it above most of Can Tho's cheapies, but this chirpily monikered mini-hotel goes further. For 260,000d you'll get a nice, very-nearly-stylish room with large windows, interesting wallpaper and a corner tub crammed into the bathroom. The cheaper rooms are windowless but perfectly adequate.

Phuong Nam
HOTEL $

(☑376 3959; 118/9/39 Đ Tran Van Kheo; r US$20; ❋@🛜) If you want to escape your fellow tourists, this smart, not-so-mini hotel (seven storeys, with a lift) is closer to the bus station in a bustling part of the central city. Rooms have big bathrooms and wi-fi. It's on the same road as the Central Market.

Tay Do Hotel
HOTEL $$

(☑382 7009; www.taydohotel.com.vn; 61 Đ Chau Van Liem; r US$28-35; ❋@🛜) So three stars is pushing it a bit, but this is a smart hotel with a full range of amenities. All rooms include satellite TV and most have bathtubs and balconies. Breakfast is included.

Saigon Cantho
HOTEL $$

(☑382 5831; www.saigoncantho.com; 55 Đ Phan Dinh Phung; s US$35-65, d US$40-70; ❋@) This well-kept hotel has a good range of rooms and prices have remained static for a while now, making it good value. Deluxe rooms are like suites and come with flat-screen TVs and fruit baskets. All rooms have safety deposit boxes and guests enjoy free internet access, including wi-fi.

Ninh Kieu 2
HOTEL $$

(☑625 2377; www.ninhkieuhotel.com; 3 ĐL Hoa Binh; r US$35-70, ste US$110; ❋🛜) It's owned by the army and the staff can be a little officious, but this large new hotel near the museums has clean, comfortable rooms finished to a good standard. The lobby is a study in Vietnamese glam, with big chandeliers, marble tiles and a neon sign over reception.

Ninh Kieu Hotel
HOTEL $$

(☑382 1171; 2 Đ Hai Ba Trung; r old wing US$41-46, new wing US$48-99; ❋@🛜) Although it belongs to the army, this hotel is a world away from boot camp. It has an enviable location on the riverfront and occupies several creamy coloured colonial buildings. The new wing is considerably smarter than the dated old wing.

✗ Eating & Drinking

For tasty cheap eats, try the **central market food stalls** (Đ Tran Quang Khai). They're in their own covered area, two scant blocks north of the main market building.

Hop Pho
VIETNAMESE, CAFE $

(6 Đ Ngo Gia Tu; mains 30,000-130,000d; 🛜) For discount designer dining, look no further than this stylish cafe-restaurant offering Vietnamese favourites at fair prices. While its location and look would suggest it's aimed at tourists, it's a testament to its quality and affordability that locals are usually in the majority. It's a great spot for a coffee or a cocktail, either in air-conditioned comfort inside or outside in the lush garden.

Sao Hom
VIETNAMESE, INTERNATIONAL $

(☑381 5616; 50 Đ Hai Ba Trung; mains 35,000-150,000d; ◷8am-midnight) Set in the (now upmarket) former market, Sao Hom has an atmospheric riverside setting. The menu includes Vietnamese, international and some fusion dishes, including crispy spring rolls and some tandoori dishes. It is very popular at lunch and remains one of Can Tho's most alluring spots.

Mekong
VIETNAMESE, PIZZA $

(☑382 1646; 38 Đ Hai Ba Trung; mains 25,000-105,000d; ◷8am-2pm & 4-10pm) Right opposite the Ho Chi Minh statue, this has long been a travellers' favourite thanks to a good blend of local and international food at very reasonable prices. It's the closest thing to a riverfront bar by night with a few tables spilling onto the street.

La Ca
VIETNAMESE $

(118/15A Đ Tran Van Kheo; mains 45,000-180,000d; ◷8am-10pm) This stylish barbecue restaurant is fun, unless you happen to be a suckling pig, the house speciality (you can order a whole one for 360,000d). The menu is typically huge, with a few Western and Korean dishes to even it out. Staff are on rollerskates to speed up the service. It's east of the central market, on the same main street.

Cafe Dong Tau
ITALIAN $

(☑346 1981; Đ Hai Ba Trung; mains 35,000-90,000d) This Italian restaurant may not look that stylish but looks can be deceiving, as the menu features some delicious dishes at absurdly affordable prices. Pastas, risottos and pizzas sit alongside steaks, goulash and Mexican and Vietnamese dishes.

Quan Com 16   VIETNAMESE $
(45 Đ Vo Van Tan; mains 20,000-50,000đ) This long-running place is a bit of a Can Tho institution and very popular with the locals. The name signals rice (*com*) laden with piles of freshly cooked fish, meat and vegetable dishes. Service is swift.

Phuong Nam   VIETNAMESE $
(48 Đ Hai Ba Trung; mains 50,000-110,000đ) Next door to the Mekong, this place has the advantage of an upstairs terrace for people-watching, although downstairs is slightly more upmarket. Snake is the specialty but there's a huge selection of other options on the menu.

Du Thuyen   VIETNAMESE $
(☑381 0841; Đ Hai Ba Trung; mains 45,000-130,000đ) A floating restaurant set over three floors, it's all aboard from 8pm.

Xe Loi   BAR, NIGHTCLUB
(Hau Riverside Park; ⏱5pm-late) Or Cyclo Club to you and me, this is the most happening nightspot in Can Tho, although it doesn't usually crank up until late in the evening. There are tables in the large garden and even a fake beach on the riverside. Inside, the Wild West-ish saloon is a full-on nightclub with DJs and regular live music. Free entry unless there is an event, but drinks are pricey.

🛍 Shopping

Old Market   MARKET
(50 Đ Hai Ba Trung) Roofed with terracotta tiles edged with ceramic decorations, this atmospheric French-era market building is the centrepiece of the city's attractive riverfront tourist district. The blood, guts and chaos of the original market have moved north to the Central Market (and, to a lesser degree, some of the neighbouring streets), leaving in its wake upmarket tourist-orientated stalls selling lacquerware, clothes, pillowslips and the like.

Central Market   MARKET
(Đ Tran Van Kheo) Can Tho's local market sprawls over four buildings and several blocks abutting the Cai Khe Canal, which many local farmers and wholesalers still use to transport their goods. The main market building focuses on produce: a colourful, smelly mess of meat, fish, fruit and vegetables. Across the road is the cloth market. Food stalls take up the following block and behind that is another large building full of bags, belts and jewellery.

To get here take Đ Nguyen Trai and turn right after crossing the bridge.

ℹ Information

Can Tho Tourist (☑382 1852; www.cantho tourist.com.vn; 50 Đ Hai Ba Trung) Staff at this provincial tourism authority are very helpful and speak both English and French. Decent city maps are available here, as well as general information on attractions in the area. There is also a booking desk for Vietnam Airlines and Jetstar.

Hospital (Benh Vien; ☑382 0071; 4 Đ Chau Van Liem)

Main post office (2 ĐL Hoa Binh) Postal services and internet access.

ℹ Getting There & Away

AIR Can Tho opened a new international airport in early 2011, but at the time of writing the only services were **Vietnam Airlines** (www.vietnam airlines.com) flights to Phu Quoc Island (from 500,000đ, daily), the Con Dao islands (from 400,000đ, four per week) and Hanoi (from 1,700,000đ, daily). The airport is 10km northwest of the city centre, accessed from Đ Le Hong Phong, the continuation of Đ Nguyen Trai.

BUS Can Tho's **bus station** (Ben Xe Khach Can Tho; cnr Đ Nguyen Trai & Đ Hung Vuong) is centrally located on the northern edge of the city centre. There are regular buses to HCMC's Mien Tay bus station (75,000đ, five hours). Express minibuses (90,000đ) save almost an hour. Other services include Cao Lanh (30,000đ), My Tho (50,000đ), Tra Vinh (55,000đ), Vinh Long (34,000đ), Soc Trang (50,000đ), Ca Mau (65,000đ) and Ha Tien (83,000đ).

BOAT There are several boat services to other cities in the Mekong Delta, including hydrofoils to Ca Mau (150,000đ, three to four hours), passing through Phung Hiep.

ℹ Getting Around

The *xe loi* is the main form of transport around Can Tho; these makeshift vehicles are unique to the Mekong Delta. Essentially a two-wheeled wagon attached to the rear of a motorbike, they resemble a motorised *cyclo*, but with four wheels touching the ground rather than two. Fares around town should be about 10,000đ per person (they can carry two, or sometimes more).

Around Can Tho

Arguably the biggest drawcard of the delta is its colourful **floating markets**, which hug the banks of wide stretches of river. Most market folk set out early to avoid the daytime heat, so try to visit between 6am

A NIGHT ON THE MEKONG

As well as homestays, guesthouses, hotels and resorts, it's possible to spend the night onboard a boat on the Mekong River. This is a good way to explore more of the waterways that make up this incredible region and helps bring you closer to life on the river. The more interesting options include the following:

Bassac (📞0710-382 9540; www.transmekong.com; overnight US$232) Offers a range of beautiful wooden boats for small groups. The standard itinerary is an overnight between Cai Be and Can Tho, but custom routes are possible.

Exotissimo (📞08-3827 2911; www.exotissimo.com; overnight 4,123,000-12,659,000d) Up-market tour operator Exotissimo offers a variety of single or multi-day tours of the delta by boat.

Le Cochinchine (📞08-3993 4552; www.lecochinchine.com; price on application) Offers cruises on a luxurious converted rice barge and a traditional sampan that are akin to floating hotels. The main routes are Cai Be to Can Tho (overnight) or Cai Be to Sa Dec, Ving Long and Can Tho (two nights). Private trips are available.

Mekong Eyes (📞0710-246 0786; www.mekongeyes.com; price on application) A stunningly converted traditional rice barge, the name plays on the ever-present eyes painted on fishing boats throughout Vietnam. This stylish boat travels between Can Tho and Cai Be, but is also available for charter.

As well as these options, there are various companies offering luxury cruises between My Tho (including transfers from Ho Chi Minh City) and Siem Reap. **Pandaw Cruises** (www.pandaw.com; 7 nights US$1132-2713) is favoured by high-end tour companies. **Compagnie Fluviale du Mekong** (www.cf-mekong.com; 5 nights from US$2415) is smaller and is well regarded for its personal service and excellent food. Taking the competition to a new level of lush are **AmaWaterways** (www.amawaterways.com; 6 nights US$1599-2599) and **Heritage Line** (www.heritage-line.com; 7 nights US$3384-8129). The longer cruises mean a lot of time looking at very similar scenery, so it's arguably better just to opt for a shorter sector such as My Tho to Phnom Penh.

and 8am and beat the tourist tide. The real tides, however, are also a factor as bigger boats must often wait until the water is high enough for them to navigate.

Some of the smaller, rural floating markets are disappearing, largely because of improved roads and access to private and public transport. Many of the larger markets near urban areas, however, are still going strong.

Rural areas of Can Tho province, renowned for their durian, mangosteen and orange orchards, can be easily reached from Can Tho by boat or bicycle.

◎ Sights

Cai Rang Floating Market   FLOATING MARKET
Just 6km from Can Tho in the direction of Soc Trang is Cai Rang, the biggest floating market in the Mekong Delta. There is a bridge here that serves as a great vantage point for photography. The market is best before 9am, although some vendors hang out until noon. It is quite an experience to see this in full swing, but it is well worth getting up extra early to beat the tour group crowds or you may end up seeing almost as many foreigners as market traders.

Cai Rang can be seen from the road, but getting here is far more interesting by boat. From the market area in Can Tho it takes about an hour by river, or you can drive to the Cau Dau Sau boat landing (by the Dau Sau Bridge), from where it takes only about 10 minutes to reach the market.

Phong Dien Floating Market   FLOATING MARKET
Perhaps the best floating market in the Mekong Delta, Phong Dien has fewer motorised craft and more stand-up rowing boats. It's less crowded than Cai Rang and there are far fewer tourists. The market is at its bustling best between 6am and 8am. It is 20km southwest of Can Tho and most get here by road.

It is theoretically possible to do a whirlwind boat trip here, visiting the small canals on the way and finishing back at the Cai Rang floating market. This journey should take approximately five hours return from Can Tho.

Vuon Co
BIRD-WATCHING

(admission 20,000d; ☺5am-6pm) On the road between Can Tho and Long Xuyen, Vuon Co is a 1.3-hectare bird sanctuary, popular with group tours coming to view the thousands of resident storks. There is a tall wooden viewing platform to see the storks chattering away in their nests; the best times of day are around dawn and dusk.

Vuon Co is in the Thot Not district, about 15km southeast of Long Xuyen. Look for a sign in the hamlet of Thoi An saying 'Ap Von Hoa'. Coming from Can Tho the sign is on the west side of the road, immediately after a small bridge. It is a couple of kilometres off the main highway – reachable on foot within 30 minutes, or hire a motorbike taxi for about 20,000d.

Soc Trang
📞079 / POP 174,000

Soc Trang isn't the most charming of Mekong towns, but it is an important centre for the Khmer people who make up 28% of the province's population. It's a useful base for exploring some impressive Khmer temples in the area, although you can probably pass on these if Cambodia is on your radar. There is a colourful annual festival (usually in November) and, if you're in the vicinity at the right time, it's worth checking it out.

◉ Sights

Bat Pagoda
PAGODA

The Bat Pagoda (Chua Doi) is a large, peaceful, Khmer monastery compound that has become a favourite stop-off for both foreign and domestic tourists due to its resident colony of fruit bats. There are literally hundreds of these creatures hanging from the trees. The largest bats weigh about 1kg and have a wingspan of about 1.5m.

Fruit bats are not toilet trained, so watch out when standing under a tree, or bring an umbrella. The best times for visiting are early morning and at least an hour before sunset, when the bats are most active. Around dusk hundreds of bats swoop out of the trees to go foraging in orchards all over the Mekong Delta, much to the consternation of farmers, who are known to trap the bats and eat them. Inside the compound the creatures are protected and the bats seem to know this and stick around.

The monks don't ask for money, although it doesn't hurt to leave a donation. The pagoda is decorated with gilt Buddhas and murals paid for by overseas Vietnamese contributors. In one room there's a life-size statue of the monk who was the former head of the complex.

The Bat Pagoda is 2km south of Soc Trang. You can catch a *xe om* (20,000d) or easily walk here. Head south on Đ Le Hong Phong and after about a kilometre veer right onto Đ Van Ngoc Chinh.

Clay Pagoda
PAGODA

(163 Đ Ton Duc Thang) Buu Son Tu (Precious Mountain Temple) was founded over 200 years ago by a Chinese family named Ngo. Today the temple is better known as Chua Dat Set, or Clay Pagoda.

Unassuming from the outside, this pagoda is highly unusual in that nearly every object inside is made entirely of clay. The hundreds of statues and sculptures that adorn the interior today were hand-sculpted by the monk Ngo Kim Tong. From the age of 20 until his death at 62, this ingenious artisan dedicated his life to decorating the pagoda. Though the decor borders on kitsch, the pagoda is an active place of worship, and totally different from the Khmer and Vietnamese pagodas elsewhere in Soc Trang.

Entering the pagoda, visitors are greeted by one of Ngo's largest creations – a six-tusked clay elephant, which is said to have appeared in a dream of Buddha's mother. Behind this is the central altar, which was fashioned from more than five tonnes of clay. In the altar are a thousand Buddhas seated on lotus petals. Other highlights include a 13-storey Chinese-style tower over 4m tall. The tower features 208 cubby holes, each with a mini-Buddha figure inside, and is decorated with 156 dragons.

Needless to say, the clay objects in the pagoda are fragile, so explore with care. Donations are welcome.

Kh'leang Pagoda
PAGODA

(Chua Kh'leang; 68 Đ Ton Duc Thang) Except for the rather garish paint job, this pagoda could have been transported straight from Cambodia. Originally built from bamboo in 1533, it had a complete rebuild in 1905 (this time using concrete). There are seven religious festivals held here every year, drawing people from outlying areas of the province.

Several monks reside in the pagoda, which also serves as a base for over 150 novices who come from around the Mekong Delta to study at Soc Trang's College of Buddhist Education across the street.

FREE **Khmer Museum** MUSEUM
(23 Đ Nguyen Chi Thanh; ⏰7.30-11am & 1.30-5pm Mon-Fri) Dedicated to the history and culture of Vietnam's Khmer minority, this small museum doubles as a sort of cultural centre. Traditional dance and music shows are periodically staged here for larger groups. Displays are limited to photos and a few traditional costumes and other artefacts.

The Khmer Museum is opposite Kh'leang Pagoda and often appears closed; you may have to rouse someone to let you in.

FREE **Soc Trang Museum** MUSEUM
(Bao Tang Tinh Soc Trang; So 4 Đ Hung Vuong) The most interesting display in this grand building is the life-size interior of a traditional wood-panelled house. Otherwise it's mainly photos (no English captions) along with some bronze and ceramic artefacts, models of Khmer buildings and ethnic costumes. Unsurprisingly, there's a US tank and anti-aircraft gun littering the forecourt.

Hung Vuong roundabout MONUMENT
If you're a fan of Socialist Realist sculpture, the monument welcoming people into town at the end of Đ Hung Vuong is a doozy. It consists of three giants, arms aloft, in front of a colossal obelisk. Two provide a perch for a dove while another brandishes an atom.

✯✦ Festivals

Once a year, the Khmer community turns out for the **Oc Bom Boc Festival** (known as Bon Om Touk or the Water Festival in Cambodia), with longboat races on the Soc Trang River. This event attracts visitors from all over Vietnam and even Cambodia. First prize is more than US$1000, so it's not difficult to see why competition is so fierce. The races are held according to the lunar calendar on the 15th day of the 10th moon, which roughly means November. The races start at noon, but things get jumping in Soc Trang the evening before. Hotel space is at a premium during the festival.

🛏 Sleeping & Eating

Soc Trang has several hotels but it's hard to be particularly enthusiastic about any of them. You're better off continuing on to Can Tho. New hotels have been springing up along the

highway outside of town. If you've got your own wheels, take a cruise past and pick the newest looking of them – that way you might beat the black mould and dank smells that seem to plague most places after about a year.

Few restaurants in Soc Trang have English menus and prices are often omitted from the Vietnamese ones.

Que Huong Hotel HOTEL $
(☎361 6122; khachsanquehuong@yahoo.com; 128 Đ Nguyen Trung Truc; r 270,000d, ste 450,000-600,000d; ✳🔌) The best of a mediocre bunch is run by the local People's Committee. The rooms here are in better shape than the no-nonsense exterior might first suggest. The suites include a sunken bath and a full-size bar, although drinks are not included. Wireless extends only to the lobby.

Quan Hung VIETNAMESE $
(24/5 Đ Hung Vuong; mains 40,000-120,000d) Located down a lane off the main road into town, this large, open-sided restaurant is perpetually popular – serving up delicious grilled meat and fish. If there are a few of you, try a hotpot.

Hang Ky VIETNAMESE $
(67 Đ Hung Vuong; mains around 70,000d) Not to be sniffed at, Hang Ky is a reliable stop, offering a large selection of traditional dishes including goat curry and hotpots. The view of motorbikes racing around the main roundabout distracts from the brightly lit, atmosphere-deficient dining room.

ℹ Getting There & Away

Buses run between Soc Trang and most Mekong cities. The bus station is on Hwy 1A, near the corner of Đ Hung Vuong, the main road into town. The 90-minute ride to Can Tho costs 50,000d; to Cao Lanh, 55,000d; to Bac Lieu, 65,000d; and to Ha Tien, 105,000d.

Bac Lieu

☎0781 / POP 136,000
Few people stop in Bac Lieu but birdwatchers may find themselves passing through en route to the excellent sanctuary near town. The town has a few elegant but forlorn French colonial buildings lining the waterfront, but little else of interest.

Of these, the grandest is **Cong Tu Hotel** (☎395 3304; 13 Đ Dien Bien Phu; r 300,000-500,000d; ✳), built in 1919 as a private mansion with materials imported from France. The family's oldest son was a notorious playboy (*cong tu*) whose fabled exploits included burning money to boil an egg in an effort to impress a woman. After squandering the family fortune, the house was sold and converted into a hotel. You can still stay here but it's in need of a renovation. Alternatively, there are inexpensive guesthouses lining the road into town from Soc Trang (rooms cost around US$10).

Farming is a difficult occupation in this region because of saltwater intrusion, and the province is better known for its healthy longan orchards. The enterprising locals also eke out a living from fishing, oyster collection and shrimp farming, as well as salt production, obtained by evaporating saltwater ponds that form immense salt flats.

✗ Eating & Drinking

The local specialty is *bun nuoc leo Soc Trang,* a noodle soup made with fish, shrimp and roast pork. A great place to try it is a stall set up during the day outside a pretty pale blue house at 179 Đ Tran Phu (soup 20,000d).

Pho Ngheu Thanh Huong   VIETNAMESE $
(43 Tran Quynh; mains 25,000-47,000d) While you could probably buy similar *pho* (noodle soups) and *banh mi* (filled baguettes) from a street stall, this smart eatery offers a fairly-lit rooftop from which to watch the traffic zoom by. A range of *pho* is served, including a delicious mushroom variety.

Sai Gon 3   VIETNAMESE $
(38 Ba Trieu; soup 19,000d) During the morning rush the floor of this extremely popular *pho bo* joint is covered in picked-over herbs and abandoned serviettes. It's a friendly place and there's only one dish served, so sit down and join in the fragrant, belly-filling chaos.

Kitty   CAFE, BAR
(cnr Đ Tran Phu & Ba Trieu) Surprisingly upmarket for a provincial city, this 1st-floor cafe overlooks one of the many busy roundabouts on Đ Tran Phu. This playful Kitty is black and white and chrome all over, with chic chairs and a wall of TV screens. It's a good spot for Vietnamese coffee and cake, or something a little harder.

ℹ Information

Bac Lieu Tourist (✆382 4273; www.baclieu tourist.com; 2 Đ Hoang Van Thu; ⏱7-11am & 1-5pm) Extremely helpful tourist office with basic town maps and information about trips to the bird sanctuary.
Post Office (20 Đ Tran Phu)

WORTH A TRIP

XA LON PAGODA

Originally built in wood in the 18th century, this magnificent Khmer pagoda was completely rebuilt in 1923 but proved to be too small. From 1969 to 1985, the present-day large pagoda was slowly built as funds trickled in from donations. The ceramic tiles on the exterior of the pagoda are particularly impressive.

As at other pagodas, the monks lead an austere life. They eat breakfast at 6am and seek alms until 11am, when they hold an hour of worship. They eat again just before noon and study in the afternoon – they do not eat dinner. The pagoda also operates a school for the study of Buddhism and Sanskrit.

It's located 12km from Soc Trang, towards Bac Lieu, on Hwy 1A.

ℹ Getting There & Around

The **bus station** (Ben Xe Tinh Bac Lieu) is on the main road into town, 1km north of the centre. From here you can catch regular buses to Ho Chi Minh City (130,000d), Soc Trang (65,000d), Ha Tien (89,000d), Ca Mau (30,000d), Can Tho (65,000d) and Cao Lanh (65,000d).

Around Bac Lieu

BAC LIEU BIRD SANCTUARY

(Vuon Chim Bac Lieu; ✆383 5991; admission 10,000d; ⏱7.30am-5pm) One of the more interesting sights in this sleepy corner of the Mekong Delta, Bac Lieu Bird Sanctuary is notable for its 50-odd species of bird, including a large population of graceful white herons. It's surprisingly popular with Vietnamese tourists, but foreign visitors are rare, probably because Bac Lieu is so out of the way.

Whether or not you see any birds depends on what time of year you visit. Bird populations are at their peak in the rainy season – approximately May to October. The birds hang around to nest until about January, then fly off in search of greener pastures. There are basically no birds here from February until the rainy season begins again.

The drive is only 5km but the road is in poor shape. The rest of the trek is through dense (and often muddy) jungle. Bring plenty of repellent, good shoes, water and binoculars.

Pay the admission fee when you reach the entrance of the bird sanctuary. You can (and should) hire a guide here, as you may get lost without one. The guides aren't supposed to receive money, so tip them discreetly; most guides do not speak English. Transport and guides can also be arranged through the Bac Lieu Tourist office (at a mark-up).

MOI HOA BINH PAGODA

This Khmer pagoda (Chua Moi Hoa Binh or Se Rey Vongsa) is in the village of Hoa Binh, 13km west of Bac Lieu along Hwy 1A. The pagoda is uniquely designed and chances are good that the monastery's enormous tower will catch your eye even if you're not looking for it. The complex was built in 1952, with the tower added in 1990 to store the bones of the dead. There is a large, impressive meeting hall in front of the tower.

Most Khmer people in the area head for monastery schools in Soc Trang to receive a Khmer education. Apart from the small contingent of student monks, very few study here.

Ca Mau

☎ 0780 / POP 205,000

Built on the swampy shores of the Ganh Hao River, Ca Mau is the capital and the only city in Ca Mau province, which covers the southern tip of the Mekong Delta. It's a remote and inhospitable area that wasn't cultivated until the late 17th century. Owing to the boggy terrain, the province has the lowest population density in southern Vietnam. It incorporates the country's largest swamp and is known for its voracious mosquitoes.

Given that, it's perhaps surprising that Ca Mau city is such a pleasant place. The overall impression is of wide boulevards, parks, busy shopping streets and (if you don't look too closely at the river and the shacks lining it) cleanliness. Ca Mau has developed rapidly in recent years but the city doesn't have many actual sights. Consequently it doesn't get a lot of tourists – so you might well feel like a celebrity due to the stares and greetings you'll garner, especially from the local kids.

The main attractions here are the nearby swamps and forests, which can be explored by boat. Bird-watchers and aspiring botanists get excited about stork-sighting opportunities and swamp ecology.

◉ Sights

Ca Mau Market   MARKET

(Đ Le Loi) Traditionally Ca Mau life was lived facing the water, and while the floating market has disappeared in recent years, the main market still sprawls along the streets to the west of Phung Hiep Canal, south of Đ Phan Ngoc Hien.

Cao Dai Temple   TEMPLE

(Đ Phan Ngoc Hien) Like all Cao Dai places of worship, this temple (built 1966) is a riot of colour and ornamentation, complete with dragons, storks standing on turtles and clouds on the ceiling.

🛏 Sleeping

Quoc Te Hotel   HOTEL $

(International Hotel; ☎366 6666; www.hotelquocte .com; 179 Đ Phan Ngoc Hien; r 280,000-480,000d; ❀🛜🛁) Breakfast and airport pick-ups are included in the prices at this hotel, which is clearly targeting the business market. Facilities include a swimming pool, massage service and a lift. While it falls short of international business standards, the rooms are smart enough and have bathtubs, satellite TV and minibars.

Anh Nguyet Hotel   HOTEL $$

(☎356 7666; www.anhnguyethotel.com; 207 Đ Phan Ngoc Hien; r US$29-59; ❀🛜) Romantically translating as the Moonlight Hotel, this hotel's attempts to be glitzy have left it looking a little like a child's toy. The rooms are perfectly fine, if not as flash as they think they are, although the walls are as thin as the carpets are cheap.

Thanh Son Hotel   GUESTHOUSE $

(☎355 0992; 23 Đ Phan Ngoc Hien; r 80,000-230,000d; ❀) A typical mini-hotel, this five-storey block has clean rooms with tiled floors and plenty of light. Extras include TV and hot water, plus bathtubs in the more expensive rooms. Little English is spoken.

🍴 Eating

Ca Mau's speciality is shrimp, which are raised in ponds and mangrove forests. The best food is to be found at the cluster of small, cheap roadside restaurants and *banh mi* stalls in the streets around the market, particularly at the end of Đ Nguyen Huu Le. In the evening, the eastern end of Đ Pham Ngoc Hien becomes a big outdoor cafe.

Pho Xua   VIETNAMESE, SEAFOOD $

(126 Đ Phan Ngoc Hien; mains 50,000-290,000d) The menu here is heavy on shrimp, seafood and fish dishes – although you can try goat's scrotum if you're so inclined. It's an atmospheric place, set amid landscaped gardens draped in fairy lights.

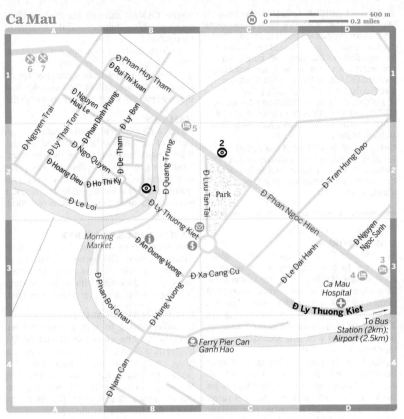

Ca Mau

Thanh Truc VIETNAMESE $
(126 Đ Phan Ngoc Hien; mains 30,000-80,000d)
Right next door to Pho Xua, this is the place
to sample a bubbling hotpot or the popular
grilled meat dishes.

ℹ Information

Ca Mau Hospital (Benh Vien Ca Mau; ☏ 383
1015; Đ Ly Thuong Kiet)

Ca Mau Tourist (☏ 381 7057; www.camau
travel.vn; 1B Đ An Duong Vuong) Runs boat
trips to Dat Mui (Cape Ca Mau) and the Da Bac
Islands.

ℹ Getting There & Around

AIR Vietnam Air Service Company (VASCO;
www.vasco.com.vn), a subsidiary of Vietnam
Airlines, has two daily flights to and from HCMC
(399,000–863,000d). The airport is 3km east
of the centre, on Hwy 1A.

BOAT At least three hydrofoils a day travel
between Ca Mau and Rach Gia (110,000d, three

Ca Mau

◉ Sights
| 1 Ca Mau Market | B2 |
| 2 Cao Dai Temple | C2 |

🛏 Sleeping
3 Anh Nguyet Hotel	D3
4 Quoc Te Hotel	D3
5 Than Son Hotel	B2

🍴 Eating
| 6 Pho Xua | A1 |
| 7 Thanh Truc | A1 |

hours) from Ferry Pier Can Ganh Hao. This pier
is also where you can catch a speedboat south
to Nam Can (60,000d, one hour). Boats to Can
Tho (150,000d, three to four hours), with a stop
in Phung Hiep, depart from Cong Ca Mau pier
(Đ Quang Trung), 3km east of town.

BUS Buses from HCMC to Ca Mau leave from Mien Tay bus station. The trip takes around eight to nine hours by express bus (130,000d). There are several daily express buses to HCMC leaving between 5am and 10.30am. Daily buses also connect to other towns in the region, including Rach Gia (50,000d), Ha Tien (89,000d), Bac Lieu (50,000d), Can Tho (65,000), Cao Lanh (83,000d), My Tho (100,000d) and Ben Tre (103,000d). The Ca Mau bus station is around 2.5km from the centre of town; head along Hwy 1A towards Bac Lieu.

CAR & MOTORBIKE Hwy 1A now continues to Nam Can (50km), the southernmost town in Vietnam. Ca Mau is 176km from Can Tho (around three hours) and 329km from HCMC (approximately seven hours).

Around Ca Mau

U-MINH FOREST

The town of Ca Mau borders the U-Minh Forest, a huge mangrove forest covering 1000 sq km of Ca Mau and Kien Giang provinces. Local people use certain species of mangrove as a source of timber, charcoal, thatch and tannin. When the mangroves flower, bees feed on the blossoms, providing both honey and wax. The area is an important habitat for waterfowl.

The U-Minh Forest, which is the largest mangrove forest in the world beyond the Amazon basin, was a favourite hideout for the VC during the American War. US patrol boats were frequently ambushed here and the VC regularly planted mines in the canals. The Americans responded with chemical defoliation, which made their enemy more visible while doing enormous damage to the forests. Replanting efforts at first failed because the soil was so toxic, but gradually the heavy rainfall has washed the dioxin out to sea and the forest is returning. Many eucalyptus trees have also been planted here because they have proved to be relatively resistant to dioxin.

Unfortunately the mangrove forests are being further damaged by clearing for shrimp-farming ponds, charcoal production and woodchipping. The government has tried to limit these activities, but the conflict between nature and humans continues. The conflict will probably get worse before it gets better, because Vietnam's population is still growing rapidly. In 2002 an area of 80 sq km was preserved as U Minh Thuong (Upper U-Minh) National Park.

The forest is known for its birdlife, but these creatures have also taken a beating. Nevertheless, twitchers will enjoy a boat trip around Ca Mau, although the flocks of birds aren't nearly as ubiquitous as the swarms of mosquitoes.

Ca Mau Tourist can arrange a boat tour. Once you have established a price with these guys (around US$140, but seemingly negotiable), you can also talk to the locals down at the ferry piers to see if there are better deals.

NAM CAN

Except for a minuscule fishing hamlet (Tran De) and an offshore island (Hon Khoai), Nam Can stakes its claim as the southernmost town in Vietnam. Few tourists come to this isolated community, which survives mainly from the shrimp industry. Regular ferries head here from Ca Mau (60,000d, one hour).

CA MAU NATURE RESERVE

Sometimes referred to as Ngoc Hien Bird Sanctuary, these 130 hectares form one of the least developed and most protected parts of the Mekong Delta region. Shrimp farming is prohibited here. Access is by boat.

DAT MUI (CAPE CA MAU)

If you're looking to visit another remote spot, you can hire a boat (about 70,000d, 1½ hours) from Nam Can to take you to Dat Mui (Cape Ca Mau), the southwestern tip of Vietnam. Motorbikes can whisk you from Dat Mui to the stone marking Vietnam's southern tip, about 2km beyond. However, few people find this worthwhile.

Rach Gia

077 / POP 206,000

Rach Gia is something of a southern boom town, flush with funds from the thriving port on the Gulf of Thailand but also benefiting from a serious injection of Viet Kieu money, as former boat people ride the wave of development. The population includes significant numbers of both ethnic Chinese and ethnic Khmers. Most travellers give the busy centre short shrift, heading straight to the port for boats to Phu Quoc Island. Those who linger can explore the lively waterfront and bustling backstreets, where there are some inexpensive seafood restaurants.

With its easy access to the sea and the proximity of Cambodia and Thailand, fishing, agriculture and smuggling are profitable trades in this province. The area was once famous for supplying the large feathers used to make ceremonial fans for the Imperial Court.

Like Ha Tien, there are big plans for the expansion of Rach Gia. New suburbs have been carved out along the coastline to the south of the centre, complete with new hotels and cafes.

Sights

Nguyen Trung Truc Temple TEMPLE
(18 Đ Nguyen Cong Tru) This temple is dedicated to Nguyen Trung Truc, a leader of the resistance campaign of the 1860s against the newly arrived French. Among other exploits, he led the raid that resulted in the burning of the French warship *Esperance*. Despite repeated attempts to capture him, Nguyen Trung Truc continued to fight until 1868, when the French took his mother and a number of civilians hostage and threatened to kill them if he did not surrender. Nguyen Trung Truc turned himself in and was executed by the French in the marketplace of Rach Gia on 27 October 1868.

The first temple structure was a simple building with a thatched roof; over the years it has been enlarged and rebuilt several times. In the centre of the main hall is a portrait of Nguyen Trung Truc on an altar.

Phat Lon Pagoda PAGODA
(Chua Phat Lon; 151 Đ Quang Trung) This large Cambodian Theravada Buddhist pagoda, whose name means Big Buddha, was founded in the 19th century. Though all of the monks who live here are ethnic Khmers, ethnic Vietnamese also frequent the pagoda.

Inside the sanctuary *(vihara)*, figures of the Thich Ca Buddha (Sakyamuni, the Historical Buddha) wear pointed hats. Around the exterior of the main hall are eight small altars. The two towers near the main entrance are used to cremate the bodies of deceased monks. Near the pagoda are the tombs of about two dozen monks. Prayers are held here daily from 4am to 6am and 5pm to 7pm.

Tam Bao Pagoda PAGODA
(3 Đ Su Thien An; ⌚prayers 4.30-5.30am & 5.30-6.30pm) Chua Sac Tu Tam Bao (Three Jewels Pagoda) was built in 1803 by Emperor Gia Long to honour a local woman who aided him after the Tay Son Rebellion. It was extensively remodelled in 1917. The garden contains numerous trees sculpted as dragons, deer and other animals. The pagoda played a part in the anti-colonial revolutionary movement; several monks were imprisoned after homemade weapons were found here during a French raid.

FREE **Kien Giang Museum** MUSEUM
(21 Đ Nguyen Van Troi; ⌚7.30-11am Mon-Fri & 1.30-5pm Mon-Wed) Housed in an ornate gem of a French colonial-era building, once a private house, the collection includes lots of war photos and some Oc-Eo artefacts and pottery.

Cao Dai Temple TEMPLE
(189 Đ Nguyen Trung Truc) This small Cao Dai Temple was constructed in 1969 and is well worth a peek.

Sleeping

There are clusters of hotels near the bus station on Đ Le Thanh Ton and near the boat pier on Đ Tu Do.

Linda HOTEL $
(☎391 8818; cnr Đ 3 Thang 2 & Nguyen An Ninh; r 180,000-400,000d; ❄📶) One of the first hotels to open its doors in the new seafront suburb, Linda has some of the smartest rooms in Rach Gia. The priciest rooms are corner suites with two balconies and a massage bath, but the cheapest are a tight squeeze. To get here, head south on Nguyen Trung Truc and turn right on Nguyen An Ninh.

Kim Co Hotel HOTEL $
(☎387 9610; www.kimcohotel.com; 141 Đ Nguyen Hung Son; r 300,000d; ❄📶) The most centrally located of the hotels, Kim Co is a masterclass in pastel shades. The rooms are in good shape, some including decadent bathtubs, making it tempting value. Most face the corridor, so you'll need to pull the shades to get some privacy.

Hong Yen HOTEL $
(☎387 9095; 259 Đ Mac Cuu; r 150,000-250,000d; ❄@📶) Stretching over four pink floors, Hong Yen is a likeable mini-hotel with sizable, clean rooms and friendly owners. There's a lift and some of the rooms have balconies.

Phuong Hong Hotel GUESTHOUSE $
(☎387 8777; phuonghonghotel@ymail.com; 5 Đ Tu Do; r fan/air-con US$10/15; ❄@📶) A friendly little spot that is conveniently close to the boat pier. Rooms are small but clean and some include hot water and air-con.

Thanh Nhan Hotel GUESTHOUSE $
(☎394 6694; 21 Đ Tu Do; r US$10-13; ❄@📶) Another welcoming little guesthouse within walking distance of the boat pier.

Rach Gia

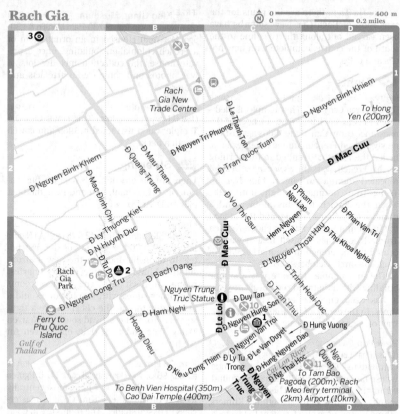

Rach Gia

◎ Sights

🛏 Sleeping

⊗ Eating

Hoang Gia 2 Hotel   HOTEL **$**
(Royal Hotel; ☎392 0980; www.hoanggiahotels
.com.vn; 31 Đ Le Than Thon; s 250,000; d 350,000-
400,000d; ✳🛜) A cut above the competition

near the bus station, this hotel has rooms
that are both very pink and very tidy.

🍴 Eating

Rach Gia is known for its seafood, dried cut-
tlefish, dried fish slices *(ca thieu),* fish sauce
and black pepper.

Than Binh   VIETNAMESE **$**
(2 Đ Nguyen Thai Hoc; mains 18,000-35,000d) The
throng of local diners stopping by to slurp
up a fish noodle soup for breakfast attests
to the quality and the reasonableness of the
prices at this humble street-side restaurant.
There's no menu, so try the point and gesture 'I'll have what she's having' approach.

Hai Au   VIETNAMESE, INTERNATIONAL **$$**
(2 Đ Nguyen Trung Truc; mains 25,000-200,000d;
🛜) A fancy restaurant by local standards, it
is worth the investment for the great loca-
tion at the side of the Cai Lon River. Choose
from an air-con interior or the livelier ter-

race. Seafood is popular, including crayfish and crab. Western-style dishes include bread and eggs for breakfast and spaghetti bolognaise.

Quan F28 VIETNAMESE, SEAFOOD $
(28 Đ Le Than Thon; mains 25,000-60,000d) Convenient for the bus station hotels, this is lively by night and does inexpensive molluscs – shrimp, snails, blood cockles and the like.

Song Binh Bakery BAKERY $
(9 Đ Ly Tu Trong; buns 8000d) Offers a finger-licking selection of savoury and sweet sticky buns.

❶ Information

Benh Vien Hospital (☑394 9494; 80 Đ Nguyen Trung Truc) One of the better medical facilities in the Mekong Delta; privately operated.

Kien Giang Tourist (Du Lich Lu Hanh Kien Giang; ☑386 2081; ctycpdulichkg@vnn.vn; 5 Đ Le Loi; ⏰7am-5pm) Provincial tourism authority.

Main post office (☑387 3008; 2 Đ Mau Than) Has the usual attached internet services.

❶ Getting There & Away

AIR Vietnam Airlines has daily flights to and from HCMC (from 500,000d) and Phu Quoc Island (from 500,000d). The airport is 10km southeast of the centre, along Hwy 80 in the direction of Long Xuyen.

BOAT Boats to Phu Quoc Island leave from the centrally located ferry terminal at the western end of Đ Nguyen Cong Tru. See the Phu Quoc section for details of those services. Approximately three hydrofoils leave daily for Ca Mau (110,000d, three hours) from the **Rach Meo ferry terminal** (Đ Ngo Quyen), about 2km south of town.

BUS There are regular services to Ca Mau (50,000d, three hours), Ha Tien (38,000d, two hours) and other cities in the region from the **central bus station** (Đ Nguyen Binh Khiem).

CAR & MOTORBIKE Rach Gia is 90km from Ha Tien, 120km from Can Tho and 270km from HCMC.

Phu Quoc Island
☑077 / POP 85,000

Fringed with white-sand beaches and with large tracts still covered in dense, tropical jungle, Phu Quoc has been quickly morphing from a sleepy backwater to a favoured beach escape of Western expats and sun-seeking tourists. Beyond the chain of resorts lining

---

❶ TRAVEL BY HYDROFOIL

If you're tossing up between taking a hydrofoil or a bus, take the hydrofoil every time. As well as being less crowded and generally more comfortable, the journey is a lot more interesting. The boats are low and long, meaning your views are from just above the waterline. From this vantage point you'll see river life in all its bustle and squalor. The trip between Ca Mau and Rach Gia is particularly good, as it switches from a green, undeveloped section dotted with rattan houses near Ca Mau to a heavily built-up and industrial stretch approaching Rach Gia.

Long Beach, it's still largely undeveloped – and unlike Phuket, to which it aspires, you won't find a lot to do here after dark. Opt instead for daytime adventures by diving the reefs, kayaking in the bays or exploring the backroads on a motorbike – or live the life of a lotus eater by lounging on the beach, indulging in a massage and dining on fresh seafood.

The tear-shaped island lies in the Gulf of Thailand, 45km west of Ha Tien and 15km south of the coast of Cambodia. At 48km long (with an area of 1320 sq km), Phu Quoc is Vietnam's largest island and one of its most politically contentious: Phu Quoc is claimed by Cambodia who call it Koh Tral and this explains why the Vietnamese have built a substantial military base covering much of the northern end of the island. It was only granted to Vietnam by the French in 1949, as part of the formal annexation of the Mekong Delta.

Phu Quoc is not really part of the Mekong Delta and doesn't share the delta's extraordinary ability to produce rice. The most valuable crop is black pepper, but the islanders here have traditionally earned their living from the sea. Phu Quoc is also famous in Vietnam for its production of high-quality fish sauce (*nuoc mam*).

The island has some unusual hunting dogs, which have ridgebacks, curly tails and blue tongues and are said to be able to pick up their masters' scent from over one kilometre away (the *nuoc mam* their masters eat probably helps). Unfortunately, the dogs have decimated much of the island's wildlife.

Phu Quoc Island

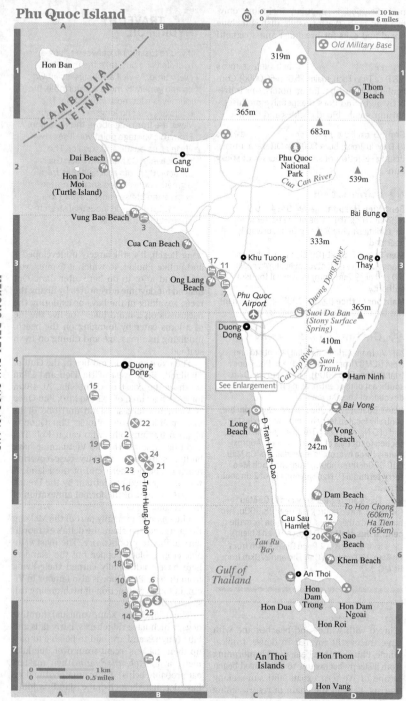

Old Military Base

0 — 10 km
0 — 6 miles

Hon Ban

CAMBODIA
VIETNAM

319m

Thom Beach

365m

683m

Dai Beach

Gang Dau

Phu Quoc National Park

Cua Can River

539m

Hon Doi Moi (Turtle Island)

Vung Bao Beach

3

Bai Bung

Cua Can Beach

17   11

Khu Tuong

333m

Ong Thay

Ong Lang Beach

7

Phu Quoc Airport

Duong Dong River

365m

Suoi Da Ban (Stony Surface Spring)

Duong Dong

410m

Cai Lop River

Suoi Tranh

See Enlargement

Ham Ninh

1

Bai Vong

Long Beach

Đ Tran Hung Dao

Vong Beach

242m

Dam Beach

To Hon Chong (60km); Ha Tien (65km)

Cau Sau Hamlet

12

Duong Dong

20   Sao Beach

15

Tau Ru Bay

Khem Beach

22

Gulf of Thailand

An Thoi

2

19   24

13   21

23

Hon Dam Trong

Hon Dam Ngoai

16

Hon Dua

Đ Tran Hung Dao

Hon Roi

5

18

An Thoi Islands

Hon Thom

10   6

8

9   25

14

4

0 — 1 km
0 — 0.5 miles

Hon Vang

MEKONG DELTA PHU QUOC ISLAND

Phu Quoc Island

⊙ Sights

Despite impending development (a new international airport, a golf course and a casino), much of this island is still protected since becoming a national park in 2001. Phu Quoc National Park covers close to 70% of the island, an area of 31,422 hectares.

Phu Quoc's rainy season is from July to November. The peak season for tourism is midwinter, when the sky is blue and the sea is calm, but it can get pretty damn hot around April and May.

At the time of research, several major road projects seemed to be stalled – leaving a confusing hodgepodge of incomplete roads and diversions crisscrossing the island. Until such time as they're completed, our maps (and everyone else's) will be slightly off. Expect a bit of confusion while you're scooting around the island – but rest assured you're unlikely to get lost for long. It's a relatively small island, after all.

History
Phu Quoc Island served as a base for the French missionary Pigneau de Behaine during the 1760s and 1780s. Prince Nguyen Anh, who later became Emperor Gia Long, was sheltered here by Behaine when he was being hunted by the Tay Son rebels.

Being a relatively remote and forested island (and an economically marginal area of Vietnam), Phu Quoc was useful to the French colonial administration as a prison.

The prison's harsh conditions are well remembered in HCMC's War Remnants Museum, with displays and re-creations.

The Americans took over where the French left off and housed about 40,000 VC prisoners here. The island's main penal colony, which is still in use today, was known as the Coconut Tree Prison (Nha Lao Cay Dua) and is near An Thoi town. Though it's considered an historic site, plans to open a museum here have stalled.

⊙ Sights

Duong Dong   TOWN
The island's main town and chief fishing port on the central west coast is also home to the small airport. To the south of here is Long Beach, the most developed area of the island, where most of the hotels and resorts are located.

The town itself is not that exciting, though the filthy, bustling market is interesting. In contrast, the excellent night market is scrupulously clean and filled with its delicious food stalls. The old bridge in town is a good vantage point to photograph the island's fishing fleet crammed into the narrow channel.

Cau Castle
(Dinh Cau; Đ Bach Dang) Less of a castle, more of a combination temple and lighthouse, Dinh Cau was built in 1937 to honour Thien

Duong Dong

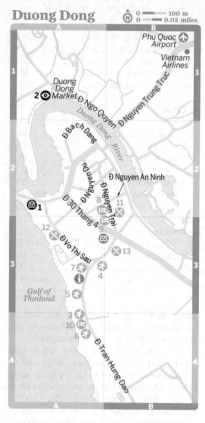

0 ____ 100 m
0 ____ 0.05 miles

Phu Quoc Airport

Vietnam Airlines

Duong Dong Market

Đ Ngo Quyen

Duong Dong River

Đ Nguyen Trung Truc

Đ Bach Dang

Đ Nguyen Trai

Đ Nguyen An Ninh

Đ 30 Thang 4

Đ Vo Thi Sau

Gulf of Thailand

Đ Tran Hung Dao

The factory is a short walk from the market in Duong Dong. There is no admission charge to visit, although you'd be best off taking a guide along unless you speak Vietnamese. Keep in mind that although *nuoc mam* makes a wonderful gift for your distant relatives, you may not be able to take it out of the country. Vietnam Airlines, among other carriers, has banned it from its planes.

Long Beach BEACH
(Bai Truong) The aptly named Long Beach stretches from Duong Dong southward along the west coast, almost to An Thoi port. Development has all been concentrated in the northern section near Duong Dong, where most of the sand is taken up with the recliners and rattan umbrellas of the various resorts. Like all beaches in Vietnam, these are the only stretches that are kept clean. There should be no problem for beachcombers to stretch out their towels on the sand, but you'll get moved on quickly if you get too close to the paying guests.

Long Beach is easily accessible from Duong Dong on foot, but a motorbike or bicycle is necessary to reach some of the remote stretches towards the southern end of the island. There are several small lanes heading from the main Đ Tran Hung Dao drag down to Long Beach that shelter some of the nicest places to stay and eat. There are a few bamboo huts where you can buy drinks, but bring water if planning a long

Hau, the Goddess of the Sea, who provides protection for sailors and fishermen. The 'castle' is worth a quick look and gives you a good view of the harbour entrance. Around sunset, locals stroll along the promenade leading from the castle to Đ Tran Hung Dao.

Fish Sauce Factory
(admission free; ⊙8-11am & 1-5pm) OK, so it's not your average sightseeing attraction, but more than a few have enjoyed a visit to the distillery of Nuoc Mam Hung Thanh, the largest of Phu Quoc's fish-sauce makers. At first glance, the giant wooden vats may make you think you've arrived for a wine tasting, but one sniff of the festering *nuoc mam* essence brings you right back to reality. It's actually not so bad after a few minutes.

Most of the sauce produced is exported to the mainland for domestic consumption, though an impressive amount finds its way abroad to kitchens in Japan, North America and Europe.

hike along the beach. Beachside massages are popular, but be clear what you're paying for; a neck rub can quickly turn into a foot massage, a manicure and a leg hair threading – often all simultaneously.

Phu Quoc Pearls

(www.treasuresfromthedeep.com; ⊘8am-5pm) On an isolated stretch of Long Beach, Phu Quoc Pearls is a requisite stop if you're in the market for pearls. A small shop sells pearl necklaces and earrings, and wall panels describe (in English) how the oysters yield their bounty. There's also a display of 16th century pottery retrieved from wrecks in the area and a small cafe on site. Avid pearl hunters can find cheaper wares at kiosks in the village of Ham Ninh, but at least you have a guarantee of authenticity here.

Sao, Dam & Vong Beaches   BEACHES
(Bai Sao; Bai Dam & Bai Vong) Sao and Dam are two beautiful white-sand beaches, just a few kilometres from An Thoi, the main shipping port at the southern tip of the island. There are a couple of beachfront restaurants at Sao Beach, where you can settle into a deckchair or partake in water sports.

North of here is Vong Beach, where the fast boats from the mainland dock. It's also home to Mui Duong Watersports, which offers jetskiing, waterskiing and other aquatic fun. The water around the pier was thick with jellyfish last time we visited, so check before heading into the water.

South of these beaches is undeveloped Khem Beach, one of the most beautiful beaches on the island but one of the few remaining areas that is under military control and closed to the public.

Cua Can & Ong Lan Beaches   BEACHES
(Bai Cua Can & Bai Ong Lan) The most accessible of the northern beaches, Cua Can is about 11km from Duong Dong. It remains mercifully quiet during the week, but can get busy at weekends. Just south of here is Ong Lan, with a series of sandy bays sheltered by rocky headlands. There are several midrange resorts in this area which are popular with those wanting to get away from it all.

A ride through the villages around Cua Can is interesting, with the road crossing the river several times on rickety wooden bridges.

Vung Bau, Dai & Thom Beaches   BEACHES
(Bai Vung Bau, Bai Dai & Bai Thom) Still retaining their isolated, tropical charm, these northern beaches are rarely peopled, let alone crowded. A newer road follows the coast along Vung and Dai Beaches, cutting down on motorbike time and red dust in your face. The road from Dai to Thom via Ganh Dau is very beautiful, passing through dense forest with tantalising glimpses of the coast below.

Phu Quoc National Park   NATURE RESERVE
Phu Quoc's poor soil and lack of surface water have disappointed farmers for generations, although their grief has been the island's environmental salvation. About 90% of the island is forested and the trees and adjoining marine environment now enjoy official protection. Indeed, this is the last large stand of forest in the south. In July 2010, the park was declared an Unesco Biosphere Reserve.

The forest is most dense in the northern half of the island. The area is a forest reserve (Khu Rung Nguyen Sinh). You'll need a motorbike or mountain bike to get through the reserve. There are a few primitive dirt roads, but no real hiking trails.

Suoi Tranh & Suoi Da Ban   WATERFALLS
(admission 3000d, motorbike 1000d) Compared with the waterlogged Mekong Delta, Phu Quoc has very little surface moisture, but there are several springs originating in the hills. The most accessible of these is Suoi Tranh; look for the entrance sign and concrete tree from the Duong Dong-Vong Beach road. From the ticket counter it's a 10-minute walk through the forest to the falls.

Suoi Da Ban (Stony Surface Spring) is a white-water creek tumbling across some attractive large granite boulders. There are deep pools and it's nice enough for a dip. Bring plenty of mosquito repellent.

For both of these falls, the best months to visit are between May and September – by the end of the dry season there's little more than a trickle.

An Thoi Islands   ISLANDS
(Quan Dao An Thoi) Just off the southern tip of Phu Quoc, these 15 islands and islets can be visited by chartered boat. It's a fine area for sightseeing, fishing, swimming and snorkelling. Hon Thom (Pineapple Island) is about 3km in length and is the largest island in the group. Other islands here include Hon Dua (Coconut Island), Hon Roi (Lamp Island), Hon Vang (Echo Island), Hon May Rut (Cold Cloud Island), the Hon Dams (Shadow Islands), Chan Qui (Yellow Tortoise) and Hon Mong Tay (Short Gun Island). As yet, there is

no real development on the islands, but expect some movement in the next few years.

Most boats depart from An Thoi on Phu Quoc, but you can make arrangements through hotels and resorts on Long Beach. You can also inquire at the dive operators, as they have boats heading down there regularly for diving. Boat trips are seasonal and generally do not run during the rainy season.

✖ Activities

Diving & Snorkelling

Although Nha Trang is arguably the best all-round dive destination in Vietnam, there is also plenty of underwater action around Phu Quoc, but only during the dry months (from November to May). Two fun dives cost from US$40 to US$80 depending on the location and operator; four-day PADI Open Water courses hover between US$320 and US$360; snorkelling trips are US$20 to US$30.

Rainbow Divers   DIVING, SNORKELLING
(Map p384; ☑0913-400 964; www.divevietnam
.com; 17A Đ Tran Hung Dao; ☺9am-6pm) This reputable PADI outfit was the first to set up shop on the island and offers a wide range of diving and snorkelling trips. As well as their walk-in office, they are well represented at resorts on Long Beach.

Coco Dive Center   DIVING, SNORKELLING
(Map p384; ☑398 2100; www.cocodivecenter.com; 58 Đ Tran Hung Dao) Long running and popular operator with its HQ in Nha Trang.

Searama   DIVING, SNORKELLING
(Map p384; ☑629 1679; www.searama.com; 50 Đ Tran Hung Dao) French- and English-speaking operators, with new equipment. It tends to be a bit cheaper than the competition.

Vietnam Explorer   DIVING
(Map p384; ☑384 6372; 36 Đ Tran Hung Dao) Well-known outfit that also operates out of Nha Trang.

X Dive   DIVING, SNORKELLING
(Map p384; ☑399 4877; www.phuquocdiving.com
.vn; 12 Đ Tran Hung Dao) Another Duong Dong-based operator.

Kayaking

There are several places to rent kayaks along Sao Beach, and its protected, fairly calm waters make for a smooth ride. In addition to locals who hire out boats, you can ask at the beachside restaurants. The going rate is about 60,000d per hour.

☞ Tours

Your best bet for booking tours is through your hotel or resort, as there's no government-run tourist office in Duong Dong. Most travellers get around the island by rental motorbike. There are a handful of English-speaking motorbike guides on the island.

Other specialised companies offering boat excursions and fishing trips include:

Anh Tu's Tours   BOAT TRIPS
(☑399 6009; anhtupq@yahoo.com) Snorkelling, squid fishing, island tours, plus motorbike rental.

John's Tours   BOAT TRIPS
(☑091-910 7086; www.johnsislandtours.com; 4 Đ Tran Hung Dao) Well represented at hotels and resorts, these cruises include snorkelling, island-hopping and fishing trips.

🛏 Sleeping

Accommodation prices on Phu Quoc yo-yo up and down depending on the season and the number of visitors in town. The variations are more extreme than anywhere else in Vietnam, but tend to affect budget and midrange places more than the high-end resorts. Some places will treble their prices for the peak season of December and January. Bookings are essential at this time. Across all of the budget categories you'll get less for your money than you'd expect for the price.

DUONG DONG

Most travellers prefer to stay at the beach, but Duong Dong has some guesthouses if the beach is bursting at the seams. Prices are more reasonable here.

Sea Breeze   HOTEL $
(Gio Bien; ☑399 4920; www.seabreezephuquoc
.com; 62A Đ Tran Hung Dao; r fan $US15, air-con US$25-40; ❄@) As fresh and tropical as its namesake cocktail, this curvaceous new hotel offers smart, contemporary rooms and a breezy rooftop terrace. The location is handy for the night markets, at the beginning of the beach road.

Hiep Phong Hotel   GUESTHOUSE $
(☑384 6057; nguyet_1305@yahoo.com; 17 Đ Nguyen Trai; r 280,000d; ❄@) A very friendly, family-run mini-hotel in the middle of town. The rooms include satellite TV, fridge and hot water, something you won't find on the beach at this price.

My Linh Hotel
GUESTHOUSE **$**

(☎384 8674; 9 Đ Nguyen Trai; r 300,000d; ❄) Just a few doors down from Hiep Phong, this mini-hotel offers a similar sort of deal with solid wooden beds and some balconies. English-speaking staff.

LONG BEACH

There are now several dozen resorts stretched in a continuous line along the sands of Long Beach. Some hotels provide free transport to and from the airport; enquire when making a booking. Most can be accessed off Đ Tran Hung Dao.

TOP CHOICE La Veranda
RESORT HOTEL **$$$**

(☎398 2988; www.laverandaresort.com; 118/9 Đ Tran Hung Dao; r US$275-375; ❄@☒) Still the most stylish place to stay on Phu Quoc, La Veranda is designed in colonial style and is small enough to remain intimate, with just 44 rooms. There is a pool with a kiddies' area, a stylish spa and all rooms feature large beds and designer bathrooms. The beach is very pretty and for food you can choose between a cafe on the lawn and the Peppertree Restaurant upstairs.

Sea Star Resort
RESORT HOTEL **$$**

(☎398 2161; www.seastarresort.com; r US$40, bungalow US$50-75; ❄@☎) A fun and friendly place to stay, the management have a quirky sense of humour but definitely know how to look after their guests. The extensive compound includes 37 rooms and bungalows, many fronting on to a manicured stretch of sand with sea-view balconies. Prices drop by about 20% in the low season.

Beach Club
RESORT HOTEL **$**

(☎398 0998; www.beachclubvietnam.com; r US$25-35; ☎) This chilled retreat, run by an English-Vietnamese couple, is a great place to escape the bustle of the main drag. The tightly grouped bungalows are well kept and spacious if simple. The owner is a great source of local info if he's around, plus there is a breezy beachside restaurant for stunning sunsets.

Cassia Cottage
RESORT HOTEL **$$$**

(☎384 8395; www.cassiacottage.com; 100C Đ Tran Hung Dao; r US$120-190; ❄☎☒) A boutique-style resort on Long Beach, the rooms have handsome furnishings and are set amid a flourishing garden. Some include a pool view or sea view, plus there is a pretty garden restaurant with beachside tables.

Mai House
RESORT HOTEL **$$**

(☎384 7003; maihouseresort@yahoo.com; 118 Đ Tran Hung Dao; r fan/air-con US$75/85; ❄@☎) Mai House offers one of the nicest settings on Long Beach, nailing the whole tropical paradise vibe with its well-tended gardens, open-sided restaurant and loungers shaded by rattan umbrellas. Scattered on the lawns, the bungalows have plenty of character, although the back ones are much more tightly spaced than the front couple of rows. The food here is excellent.

Thanh Kieu Beach Resort
RESORT HOTEL **$$**

(☎384 8394; www.thanhkieuresort.com; 100C/14 Đ Tran Hung Dao; r US$39-49; @☎) On a lovely beachfront, the attractive brick bungalows are set in a leafy garden dotted with swaying palms and clumps of bamboo. Rooms are well furnished and the popular Rainbow Bar is located here on the beach.

Saigon-Phu Quoc Resort
RESORT HOTEL **$$$**

(☎384 6999; www.sgphuquocresort.com; 1 Đ Tran Hung Dao; r US$159-480; ❄@☎☒) This smart resort features 98 rooms in villas or bungalows, most with views over the beach. The sprawling complex includes a disco, karaoke rooms, spa, minigolf, tennis courts and petanque courts. Check the website for seasonal deals.

Thien Hai Son Resort
RESORT HOTEL **$$$**

(☎398 3044; www.phuquocthienhaison.com; 68 Đ Tran Hung Dao; r US$90-99, bungalow US$132-161; ❄☎☒) There's a mixture of hotel blocks and bungalows in this sprawling, lemon-and-lime beachfront complex. The wide concrete paths and occasional concrete tree suggest that it's targeted mainly to locals.

Lien Hiep Thanh Hotel
RESORT HOTEL **$**

(☎384 7583; lienhiepthanh2007@yahoo.com.vn; 118/12 Tran Hung Dao; r fan US$15, air-con US$20-45; ❄☎) Also known as the Family Hotel, this complex includes 21 simple rooms and bungalows. Beachfront rooms include air-con and hot water. There's a small restaurant on the beach.

A74 Hotel
HOTEL **$**

(☎398 2772; www.a74hotel.com; 74 Đ Tran Hung Dao; r US$10-25; ❄) On the main drag near Long Beach, this is a reliable overspill option when the beach is heaving. Rooms are reasonably basic but some have sea views.

Paris Beach
HOTEL **$**

(☎399 4548; www.phuquocparisbeach.com; r fan/air-con US$25/30; ❄@☎) Simple rooms are

MEKONG DELTA PHU QUOC ISLAND

offered in this mini-hotel, facing the beach over a large tiled terrace. It's located next to Beach Club, south of the main stretch of resorts.

Moon Resort RESORT HOTEL $
(☏399 4520; www.moonresort.vn; 82 Tran Hung Dao; bungalows fan $15, air-con US$30-35; ✻@🛜) These rustic, woven rattan bungalows, set in a scrappy garden, are excellent value and right on the beach. The beachside bar is a lively hang-out.

Charm HOTEL $$
(☏399 4606; www.phuquoccharm.com; 118/1 Đ Tran Hung Dao; r US$40-75; ✻@🛜) The charm of this traditionally styled place, set back from the beach, would be more pronounced if the rooms were better maintained and if the staff had more of it.

Nhat Lan GUESTHOUSE $
(☏384 7663; nhanghinhatlan@yahoo.com; 118/13 Đ Tran Hung Dao; bungalow fan/air-con US$20/40) The last in a string of affordable beachfront guesthouses, this place has bungalows in a shady garden, including two with a sea view.

SAO BEACH

Mango Garden B&B $$
(☏629 1339; mangogarden.inn@gmail.com; r US$35; ◷Sep-Apr; ✻@🛜) Best suited to those with their own (two) wheels, this isolated B&B is reached by a bumpy dirt road (turn left just before Sao Beach and follow the signs). Run by a Vietnamese-Canadian, this Western-style B&B sits surrounded by gorgeous flower and mango gardens, enclosed by a high fence. The handful of rooms open on to a central water feature decorated with hanging baskets of orchids. Book well ahead.

ONG LANG BEACH

Although it is rockier than Long Beach, Ong Lang, 7km north of Duong Dong, has the advantage of being substantially less crowded and hence feeling much more like a tropical island escape. Because of its relative isolation, expect to spend most of your time in and around your resort – although most places can arrange bike or motorbike hire to get you out and about. Definitely book ahead if planning to stay around here.

TOP CHOICE **Chen Sea Resort & Spa** RESORT HOTEL $$$
(☏399 5895; www.chenla-resort.com; bungalows US$234-473; ✻@🛜⊠) Competing for the title of the most upmarket resort on the island,

Chen Sea has attractive villas with deep verandas, designed to resemble ancient terracotta-roofed houses. A large pool faces the resort's beautiful sandy beach. The isolation is mitigated by plenty of activities on hand: borrow a bike, kayak or catamaran – or settle into the spa or the open-sided restaurant.

Mango Bay RESORT HOTEL $$
(☏3981693; www.mangobayphuquoc.com; r US$75-80; @🛜) Set around a small cove accessed from a dusty road through a mango orchard, this ecofriendly resort uses solar panels and organic and recycled building materials. The bungalows all include a private terrace. All in all it's a romantic, if simple, getaway for those who want some privacy.

Freedomland HOMESTAY $$
(☏399 4891; www.freedomlandphuquoc.com; r US$30-40; @) More like a little hippy commune than a resort, Freedomland has eleven basic bungalows (with mosquito nets and fans; no hot water) scattered around a shady plot. Guests who can't be bothered with the five minute walk to the beach slump into the hammocks strung between the trees. The friendly, communal nature and the shared meals make it a popular place, particularly with solo budget travellers.

Bo Resort RESORT HOTEL $$
(☏398 6142; www.boresort.com; bungalows with cold/hot water US$50/80; @) With bungalows scattered higgledy-piggledy over a jungle-clad hill stretching down to a rocky beach, this French-run resort offers intimacy and seclusion, plus excellent food.

Thang Loi RESORT HOTEL $$
(☏398 5002; www.phu-quoc.de; bungalows US$29-47; 🛜) Next to Bo Resort, Thang Loi has a similar hilly setting, with bungalows under the shade of cashew nut, palm and mango trees. No hot water.

VUNG BAU BEACH

TOP CHOICE **Bamboo Cottages & Restaurant** RESORT HOTEL $$
(☏281 0345; www.bamboophuquoc.com; r US$50-85; ✻@) Run by a friendly family with a coterie of cheeky dogs, Bamboo Cottages has Vung Bau Beach largely to itself. The focal point is a big, open-sided restaurant and bar, with the beach at its doorstep. Set around the lawns, the 14 attractive, lemon-coloured villas have private, open-roofed bathrooms

THE FRUITS OF VIETNAM

One of the great rewards of travelling through the Mekong is sampling the extraordinary array of fruits available at markets, orchards and street stalls all over the region. Fruits worth sampling include the following:

Buoi (pomelo) This gargantuan grapefruit has thick skin and sweeter, less acidic fruit than ordinary grapefruit.

Chom chom (rambutan) A tiny fiery-red fruit with hairy skin and tender sweet white flesh; most prevalent during the rainy season (May to October).

Du du (papaya) Vietnam boasts 45 species of papaya; it's great in juices or raw when ripe (orange to red flesh), and used in tangy salads when green.

Dua (pineapple) Another common Mekong fruit, some aren't so sweet; locals sometimes doctor them up with salt and chilli powder.

Khe (starfruit) A five-pointed, shiny skinned fruit that is intensely juicy.

Mang cau (custard apple) Inside this fruit's bumpy green skin lie black pips surrounded by white flesh, which does indeed taste very much like custard.

Mang cut (mangosteen) A violet, tennis-ball-sized fruit; break it open to reveal delectable white flesh inside.

Mit (jackfruit) Giant and blimp-shaped, this fruit contains chewy yellow segments; it's loaded with vitamins.

Nhan (longan) This tiny fruit has light-brown skin, a translucent juicy white pulp and is used for many purposes in the Mekong (it's even dried and used for kindling).

Oi (guava) With green, edible skin and pink flesh, the guava is loaded with vitamins and is great raw or in juice.

Sau rieng (durian) This huge spiky fruit has a memorable odour and its creamy rich interior has a taste somewhat resembling custard; you'll either love it or hate it.

Thanh long (dragon fruit) Unusual in appearance, dragon fruit is a red fruit with spiky fronds tipped with green. It has a mild, crisp flesh with numerous edible seeds.

Trai vai (lychee) Very common, this small, round red spiky fruit has a white fleshy inside, which is particularly sweet.

Xoai (mango) Mangoes come in several varieties; the sweetest are large round ones with bright yellow skin. The best mango season is April and May when the heat ripens them to perfection.

Vu sua (star apple) A round, smooth fruit that produces a sweet, milky juice (its name means 'milk from the breast').

MEKONG DELTA PHU QUOC ISLAND

with solar-powered hot water. The family support an education scholarship for needy local kids.

 Eating

Many of the recommended resorts have excellent restaurants, often with a beachside location or a sunset view. Guests staying at more remote resorts such as those at Ong Lang Beach tend to eat in, as it is a long way into town.

Some of the standouts include **Bo Resort** (mains around US$14), **Mai House** (mains US$4-18) and **Peppertree Restaurant** (La Veranda; mains US$6-20), each of which offer a combination of Vietnamese and French fare. **Charm** (mains 70,000-160,000d) has a restaurant set in a traditional Vietnamese-style compound that feels more Hoi An than Phu Quoc.

For something a bit more local, try the seafood restaurants in the fishing village of Ham Ninh. There are several along the pier at the end of the main road, including **Kim Cuong I** (mains 30,000-300,000d).

DUONG DONG

Dinh Cao Night Market   MARKET $

(Đ Vo Thi Sau) Hands down the most atmospheric, affordable and excellent place to dine on the island, Duong Dong's night market has around a dozen stalls serving a delicious range of Vietnamese seafood, grills and vegetarian options. Look for a local crowd, as they are a discerning bunch, or try the excellent **Thanh Xuan** (45,000-100,000d), which offers freshly barbecued fish and seafood.

Buddy Ice Cream
ICE CREAM $

(www.visitphuquoc.info; 26 Đ Nguyen Trai; mains 25,000-130,000d; @ 🛜) This ice-cream shop is a good stop for budget travellers looking for a side of free internet and tourist information with their New Zealand ice cream (per scoop 25,000d). Plus there are toasted sandwiches, fish and chips, and more.

Le Giang
VIETNAMESE $

(289 Đ Tran Hung Dao; mains 40,000-80,000d) A wide range of Vietnamese favourites is served in this large, local-style place, including flavoursome caramelised fish claypots. An English menu is available and upstairs there's a breeze-catching terrace.

Tuoi Tham
VIETNAMESE $

(289 Đ Tran Hung Dao; mains 35,000-100,000d) Another popular local place with good food and a welcoming atmosphere.

LONG BEACH

Mondo
TAPAS $

(82 Đ Tran Hung Dao; tapas 50,000-90,000d) Serving a mixture of traditional Spanish tapas (grilled haloumi, chorizo, spicy meatballs, garlic prawns) and other more region-specific treats (fragrant Thai-style chicken wrapped in banana leaf), chic little Mondo is a welcome addition to the Long Beach scene. It also serves Western-style breakfasts all day long.

Ganesh
INDIAN $$

(www.ganeshindianrestaurant.com; 97 Đ Tran Hung Dao; mains 52,000-99,000d; ⊙11am-10pm; 🖉) A sampling of authentic North and South Indian cuisine is served in this attractive, airy restaurant, including tandoori dishes and ample vegetarian selections. If you're dining alone, the multi-dish *thali* plates are an excellent option (vegetarian 110,000d, meat or seafood 160,000d).

Hop Inn
VIETNAMESE $

(Đ Tran Hung Dao; mains 50,000-130,000d) Despite the incongruous kangaroo logo, Hop Inn offers the best Vietnamese food on the Tran Hung Dao strip. The wide-ranging menu includes plenty of seafood, as well as sandwiches if you fancy more familiar

fare. Hanging lanterns add some night-time charm.

Pepper's Pizza & Grill
ITALIAN, GERMAN $

(🖉384 8773; 89 Đ Tran Hung Dao; mains 65,000-190,000d) Pepper's is home to the best pizzas on the island, according to long-term residents, and they'll even deliver to your resort. The rest of the menu is a mixture of Italian, German and Asian dishes, including steaks, ribs and the like.

Restaurant Chez Carole
VIETNAMESE, FRENCH $

(88 Đ Tran Hung Dao; mains 50,000-200,000d) This place is French in accent, but the menu includes a whole lot of fresh Vietnamese seafood, such as the signature shrimps in cognac or pastis.

SAO BEACH

To get to these places, follow the paved road a few kilometres north of An Thoi and look for the 'My Lan' sign on the right, which leads down a dirt road to the beach.

My Lan
VIETNAMESE, SEAFOOD $

(mains 55,000-110,000d) Located on the white sands of Sao beach, this place has succulent barbecued seafood and fish in claypots. Tables are a few metres from the lapping waves.

An Xi
VIETNAMESE, SEAFOOD $

(mains 50,000-100,000d). About 400m north of My Lan, An Xi offers similarly good seafood and the same beachside allure.

🍺 Drinking & Entertainment

Given its popularity in the dry season, it's strange that Phu Quoc is so lacking in the nightlife department. Even when the resorts are packed with tourists there never seems to be more than a handful of punters at any of the island's nightspots. The following are all on Long Beach.

Oasis
BAR

(118/5 Đ Tran Hung Dao; 🛜) Located on the lane leading to La Veranda and Mai House, Oasis is noted for its excellent Brit Pop soundtrack and a wall of bizarre canvas collages, featuring the likes of Muhammad Ali, Shane Warne, Jonny Wilkinson and the Gallagher brothers. There's a pool table out the back and terrace dining at the front.

Amigo's
BAR, NIGHTCLUB

(www.amigosphuquoc.com; 118/10 Đ Tran Hung Dao; 🛜) If any place deserves to be filled with booty-shaking holidaymakers it's this large venue, with red and green laser lights, a decent dancefloor and an appealing beach bar. Unfortunately too few people obey the writing on the wall: 'You feel like dancing from 10pm everynight till late'. Take it on yourself to get the party started – the lethal cocktails should help. You'll find it directly next to La Veranda.

Rainbow Bar BAR
(Thanh Kieu Beach Resort, 100C/14 Đ Tran Hung Dao) Beachside bar with a pool table serving tropical shakes and cocktails. Rainbow Divers hold court here from 6pm to 9pm nightly.

Luna Bar BAR
(Moon Resort, 82 Tran Hung Dao) Another sandy bar with a pool table.

🛍 Shopping

Your best bets for souvenirs are the night markets in Duong Dong and the pearl farm near the centre of Long Beach.

ℹ Information

There are ATMs in Duong Dong and in many resorts on Long Beach. A handy one is positioned at the top of the lane at 118 Đ Tran Hung Dao, opposite Charm.

Post Office (Map p384; D 30 Thang 4)

ℹ Getting There & Away

AIR Demand can be high in peak season, so book ahead. A new international airport is due to open at the end of 2012; check the latest details online if you're planning to fly after this time.

Air Mekong (☑04-3718 8199; www.airmekong .com.vn) Flies to/from HCMC (from 450,000d, four daily) and Hanoi (from 2,230,000, two daily).

Vietnam Airlines (Map p384; ☑399 6677; www.vietnamairlines.com; 122 Đ Nguyen Trung Truc) Flies to/from Rach Gia (from 500,000d, daily), Can Tho (from 500,000d, daily) and HCMC (from 450,000d, 10 daily).

BOAT Fast boats connect Phu Quoc to both Ha Tien (1½ hours) and Rach Gia (2½ hours). Phu Quoc travel agents, such as **Green Cruise** (☑397 8111; www.greencruise.com.vn; 14 Đ Tran Hung Dao, Duong Dong), have the most up-to-date schedules and can book tickets.

From Ha Tien there are two small boats (departing 8am, 180,000d; and departing 1pm, 230,000d) and a massive 200-passenger car ferry (departing 9.30am from Ha Tien and 2.30pm from Phu Quoc; per passenger/motorbike/car 145,000d/100,000d/US$50) departing every day.

Rach Gia has two reputable operators servicing the route:

Savanna Express (☑369 2888; www.savanna express.com; adult/child 295,000/200,000d) Departs Rach Gia at 8.05am and Phu Quoc at 1.05pm; 2½ hours.

Superdong (☑Rach Gia 077-387 7742; Phu Quoc 077-398 0111; www.superdong.com.vn; adult/child 225,000/295,000d) Departs Rach Gia at 8am, 1pm and 1.30pm and Phu Quoc at 8am, 8.30am and 1pm; 2½ hours.

Ferries depart from the pier at Vong Beach (Bai Vong). Buses, timed to meet the ferries, pick up on Đ Tran Hung Dao and Đ 30 Thang 4 (20,000d).

ℹ Getting Around

TO/FROM THE AIRPORT Phu Quoc's airport is currently in central Duong Dong, but if you're travelling from late 2012 onwards, a new international airport may have opened 10km out of town (check when you make your booking). The motorbike drivers at the current airport will charge you about US$1 to US$2 to most places on Long Beach, but are notorious for trying to cart people off to where they can collect a commission. If you know where you want to go, tell them you've already got a reservation.

A metered taxi costs around 90,000d to Long Beach and 250,000d to Ong Lang Beach.

BICYCLE If you can ride a bicycle in the tropical heat over these dusty, bumpy roads, all power to you. Bicycle rentals are available through most hotels from US$3 per day.

BUS There is a skeletal bus service between An Thoi and Duong Dong. Buses run perhaps once every hour or two. A bus (20,000d) waits for the ferry at Bai Vong to take passengers to Duong Dong. Several hotels operate shuttles or will offer free transfers for guests.

MOTORBIKE You won't have to look for the motorbike taxis – they'll find you. Some polite bargaining may be necessary. For short runs, 20,000d should be sufficient. Otherwise, figure on around 50,000d for about 5km. From Duong Dong to Bai Vong will cost you about 70,000d or so.

Motorbikes can be hired from most hotels and bungalows for around US$7 (semi-automatic) to US$10 (automatic) per day. The cheaper bikes tend to be pretty old and in poor condition, so inspect them thoroughly before setting out. Most places prefer not to rent out overnight, so make sure you are clear on the arrangements before taking the bike.

TAXI There are several metered taxi companies operating on the island. **Mai Linh** (☑397 9797) is reliable and drivers always use the meter. It costs about 250,000d from Duong Dong to the dock at Vong Beach.

Ha Tien

☑077 / POP 93,000

Ha Tien may be part of the Mekong Delta but lying on the Gulf of Thailand it feels a world away from the rice fields and rivers that typify the region. There are dramatic limestone formations peppering the area, which are home to a network of caves, some of which have been turned into temples. Plantations of pepper trees cling to the hillsides. On a clear day, Phu Quoc Island is easily visible to the west.

The town itself has a languid charm, with crumbling colonial villas and a colourful riverside market. Visitor numbers have recently soared thanks to the opening of the nearby border with Cambodia at Xa Xia–Prek Chak and the creation of a special economic zone – allowing visa-free travel in the town and its immediate surrounds.

Oh yes, Ha Tien is on the map. And it's occupying a bigger portion of it thanks to major expansion plans that will see the city spread southwest along the coast. Already a precinct of markets and hotels has sprung up on land reclaimed from the river between the end of Phuong Thanh and the still-quite-new bridge (which superseded Ha Tien's atmospheric old pontoon bridge). With development concentrated in this neighbourhood, the charming colonial shopfronts around the old market have thankfully been left to decay in peace.

History

Ha Tien was a province of Cambodia until 1708. In the face of attacks by the Thai, the Khmer-appointed governor, a Chinese immigrant named Mac Cuu, turned to the Vietnamese for protection and assistance. Mac Cuu thereafter governed this area as a fiefdom under the protection of the Nguyen Lords. He was succeeded as ruler by his son, Mac Thien Tu. During the 18th century the area was invaded and pillaged several times by the Thai. Rach Gia and the southern tip of the Mekong Delta came under direct Nguyen rule in 1798.

During the Khmer Rouge regime, Cambodian forces repeatedly attacked Vietnamese territory and massacred thousands of civilians here. The entire populations of Ha Tien and nearby villages (in fact, tens of thousands of people) fled their homes. Also during this period, areas north of Ha Tien along the Cambodian border were sown with mines and booby traps, some of which have yet to be cleared.

◉ Sights

Mac Cuu Family Tombs   TOMBS
(Lang Mac Cuu, Nui Binh San; Đ Mac Cuu) Not far from town are the Mac Cuu Family Tombs, known locally as Nui Lang, the Hill of the Tombs. Several dozen relatives of Mac Cuu are buried here in traditional Chinese tombs decorated with figures of dragons, phoenixes, lions and guardians.

At the bottom of the complex is an ornate shrine dedicated to the Mac family. Heading up the hill, the largest tomb is that of Mac Cuu himself; it was constructed in 1809 on the orders of Emperor Gia Long and is decorated with carved figures of Thanh Long (Green Dragon) and Bach Ho (White Tiger). The tomb of Mac Cuu's first wife is flanked by dragons and phoenixes.

Tam Bao Pagoda   PAGODA
(Sac Tu Tam Bao Tu; 328 Đ Phuong Thanh; ☺prayers 8-9am & 2-3pm) Founded by Mac Cuu in 1730, Tam Bao Pagoda is home to a community of Buddhist nuns. In front of the pagoda is a statue of Quan The Am Bo Tat (the Goddess of Mercy) standing on a lotus blossom. Inside the sanctuary, the largest statue on the dais is of A Di Da (the Buddha of the Past), made of painted brass. Outside in the tranquil grounds are the tombs of 16 monks.

Near Tam Bao Pagoda is a section of the city wall dating from the early 18th century.

Phu Dung Pagoda   PAGODA
(Phu Cu Am Tu; Đ Phu Dung; ☺prayers 4-5am & 7-8pm) This pagoda was founded in the mid-18th century by Mac Thien Tich's wife, Nguyen Thi Xuan. Her tomb and that of one of her female servants are on the hillside behind the pagoda. Nearby are the tombs of four monks.

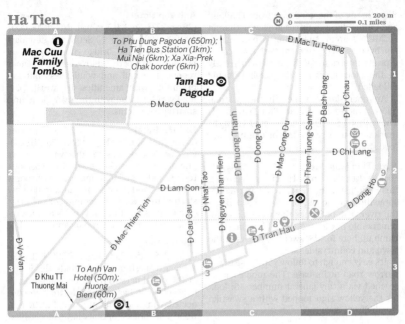

Ha Tien

Inside the main hall of the pagoda, the most interesting statue on the central dais is a bronze Thich Ca Buddha from China. Behind this hall is a small temple, Dien Ngoc Hoang, which is dedicated to the Taoist Jade Emperor. Head up the steep blue stairs to the shrine. The figures inside are of Ngoc Hoang (the Jade Emperor) flanked by Nam Tao, the Taoist God of the Southern Polar Star and the God of Happiness (on the right); and Bac Dao, the Taoist God of the Northern Polar Star and the God of Longevity (on the left). The statues are made of papier mâché which has been moulded over bamboo frames.

To get here, continue north past the Mac Cuu Tombs and take the first right onto Đ Phu Dung.

Thach Dong Cave Pagoda   PAGODA
Also known as Chua Thanh Van, this is a subterranean Buddhist temple 4km northeast of town. To the left of the entrance is the Stele of Hatred (Bia Cam Thu), shaped like a raised fist, which commemorates the Khmer Rouge massacre of 130 people here on 14 March 1978.

Several of the chambers contain funerary tablets and altars to Ngoc Hoang, Quan The Am Bo Tat and the two Buddhist monks who founded the temples of this pagoda.

The wind here creates extraordinary sounds as it blows through the grotto's passageways. Openings in several branches of the cave afford views of nearby Cambodia.

Markets   MARKETS
Ha Tien has a series of markets in large pavilions east of the bridge along the To Chau

River. Many of the goods are from Thailand and Cambodia, and prices are lower than in HCMC. Cigarette smuggling is particularly big business. The **fish market** (*cho ca*) is a pretty interesting sight, particularly early in the morning when the catch is being unloaded.

An open-sided market in the colonial quarter (between Đ Tuan Phu Dat and Đ Tham Tuong Sanh) opens at 3pm as a **night market**, with a scattering of clothing and food stalls.

Ngoc Tien Monastery
MONASTERY

(Tinh Xa Ngoc Tien) From Ha Tien's riverfront, this Buddhist monastery is a striking sight – sprawling up the hill on the other side of the river. The buildings themselves are unremarkable but it's worth making the steep climb up here for the sweeping views of the town and countryside.

It's easy enough to follow your nose to the narrow road at its base. The monastery is reached via a tiny lane at number 48; look for the yellow sign topped with a swastika (symbolising eternity).

Dong Ho
INLET

The name translates as East Lake, but Dong Ho is not a lake but an inlet of the sea. The 'lake' is just east of Ha Tien, and is bounded to the east by a chain of granite hills known as the Ngu Ho (Five Tigers) and to the west by the To Chan hills. Dong Ho is said to be most beautiful on nights when there is a full or almost-full moon. According to legend, on such nights fairies dance here.

🛏 Sleeping

While there are a lot of mini-hotels in town, the standard isn't particularly high – but then neither are the prices. Being local-style establishments, you're unlikely to get a top sheet or duvet cover on your bed. At the time of research a flash, architecturally interesting hotel (rumoured to be five-star) was being constructed on the waterfront.

Hai Phuong
HOTEL $

(📞385 2240; So 52, Đ Dong Thuy Tram; r 200,000-700,000d; ❄🖧) Friendly and family-run, this smart, six-level hotel was the newest kid on the block when we visited and hence in the best nick of them all. Some rooms have excellent river views from their balconies – although it's likely that these will be built out before long with the rampant development in this neighbourhood.

Anh Van Hotel
HOTEL $

(📞395 9222; So 2, Đ Tran Hau; d/tw/f 200,000/400,000/500,000d; ❄🖧) Set in the new part of town near the bridge, this large hotel is one of the better all-rounders. Cheaper rooms are small and windowless but are brimming with amenities. It's worth paying extra for those with the river views and smarter bathrooms.

Ha Tien Hotel
HOTEL $$

(📞395 2093; 36 Đ Tran Hau; s US$30-50, d US$40-60; ❄🖧) Not too long ago this was Ha Tien's grandest hotel, as evidenced by its spacious rooms, wide corridors, marbled bathrooms (with tubs) and in-house restaurant. It's now starting to look a little scrappy for the price (the carpets are thin and the beds uncomfortable) but it's clean, roomy and central.

Hai Yen Hotel
HOTEL $

(📞385 1580; 15 Đ To Chau; r 250,000-400,000d; ❄) Like a guesthouse on steroids, this is one of the old timers by Ha Tien standards. A huge place, it has expanded into two connected wings. Rooms are well finished in wood and pricier options have nicely tiled bathrooms and river views.

Du Hung Hotel
HOTEL $

(📞395 1555; duhung@hcm.vnn.vn; 27A Đ Tran Hau; r 250,000d; ❄) Right in the middle of the main drag, this mini-hotel offers good-value rooms and a lift. Opt for one of the corner ones, with panoramic views of the river and coast. It also hires bikes (per day 80,000d) and motorbikes (per day 200,000d).

🍴 Eating & Drinking

Ha Tien's speciality is an unusual variety of coconut that can only be found in Cambodia and this part of Vietnam. These coconuts contain no milk, but the delicate flesh is delicious. Restaurants all around the Ha Tien area serve the coconut flesh in a glass with ice and sugar.

There are excellent food stalls both in the new markets and the night market.

Xuan Thanh
VIETNAMESE $

(20 Đ Tran Hau; mains 30,000-60,000d) You know you have hit the coast when shrimp is the cheapest dish on the menu. This local eatery has an English menu boasting a range of seafood and grills, plus cheap breakfasts.

Huong Bien
VIETNAMESE $

(Đ Khu Trung Tam Thuong Mai; mains 25,000-70,000d) This old favourite has relocated to the new part of town near the bridge. The

MEKONG DELTA AROUND HA TIEN

menu remains blissfully simple with fewer than 20 dishes, but it draws a local crowd.

Oasis BAR
(www.oasisbarhatien.com; 42 Tuan Phu Dat; ☺9am-9pm; @) Run by Ha Tien's only resident Western expat and his Vietnamese wife, this friendly little bar is not just a great spot for a cold beer or plunger coffee, it's also a great source of impartial travel information. When we visited, plans were afoot to start a limited bar menu, including English breakfasts, sandwiches and salads.

Thuy Tien CAFE
(☑385 1828; Đ Dong Ho) Overlooking Dong Ho, this floating cafe is a nice spot for an iced coffee or sundowner beer.

❶ Information

Ha Tien Tourism (☑395 9598; 1 Đ Phuong Thanh) Handles transport bookings, including boats to Phu Quoc and buses to Cambodia. Also arranges Cambodian visas (US$25).
Post Office (☑385 2190; 3 Đ To Chau; ☺7am-10pm; @)

❶ Getting There & Away

BOAT Ferries stop across the river from the town. See the Phu Quoc transport section for details of the daily island services.

BUS Ha Tien bus station (Ben Xe Ha Tien; Hwy 80) is on the main road to Mui Nai Beach and the Cambodian border, about one kilometre north from the centre. Buses from here head to Chau Doc (52,000d), Long Xuyen (67,000d), Rach Gia (38,000d), Ca Mau (89,000d), Soc Trang (105,000d), Can Tho (83,000d), Tra Vinh (116,000d), Ben Tre (134,000d) and Ho Chi Minh City (132,0000d, about 10 hours).

For buses to Cambodia, see the boxed text on p396.

CAR & MOTORBIKE Ha Tien is 90km from Rach Gia, 95km from Chau Doc, 206km from Can Tho and 338km from HCMC. The Ha Tien–Chau Doc road is narrow and bumpy but interesting, following a canal along the border. As you approach Ha Tien, the land turns into a mangrove forest that is infertile and almost uninhabited. The drive takes about three hours, and it's possible to visit Ba Chuc and Tuc Dup en route. If you don't plan to drive yourself, xe om drivers typically charge about US$20 to US$30 for this route, or arrange a car through travel agencies or hotels in town.

Around Ha Tien

MUI NAI

The beaches in this part of Vietnam face the Gulf of Thailand. The water is incredibly warm and calm here; good for bathing and diving but hopeless for surfing. The best of them, **Mui Nai** (Stag's Head Peninsula; admission person/car 2500/10,000d) is 8km west of Ha Tien; it supposedly resembles the head of a stag with its mouth pointing upward. On top is a lighthouse and there are beaches on both sides of the peninsula, lined with simple restaurants and guesthouses.

There's no public transport to the beach. A xe om here should set you back around 40,000d.

HON GIANG & NGHE ISLANDS

There are many islands along this coast and some locals make a living gathering swiftlet nests (the most important ingredient of that famous Chinese delicacy, bird's-nest soup) from their rocky cliffs. About 15km from Ha Tien and accessible by small boat, **Hon Giang Island** has a lovely, secluded beach.

Nghe Island, near Hon Chong, is a favourite pilgrimage spot for Buddhists. The island contains a **cave pagoda** (Chua Hang) next to a large statue of Quan The Am Bo Tat, which faces out to sea. Boats moored near Hon Chong's cave pagoda will transport you here for around US$150.

HON CHONG

Home to photogenic stone grottoes and the nicest stretch of sand on the delta's mainland, Hon Chong once showed great potential as a beach resort. Now its litter-strewn shoreline sits under a permanent cloud of discharge from a cement factory – and with a giant coal-fired power station on the way, it seems destined to languish in obscurity for some time. Apart from the beach, the main reason to visit is an atmospheric Buddhist cave shrine.

After passing through the scrappy, polluted village, the road rounds a headland and follows **Duong Beach** (Bai Duong) for 3km. An entrance fee is charged only at the far end of the beach (per person/car 5000/10,000d), where there are food stalls, karaoke bars and pigs and chickens wandering around. From the beach you can see remnants of **Father and Son Isle** (Hon Phu Tu) several hundred metres offshore. It was said to be shaped like a father embracing his son, but the father was washed away in 2006. Boats can be hired at the shore to row out for a closer look

You need to walk through the market to reach the **cave pagoda** (Chua Hang), which is set against the base of a stony headland.

BORDER CROSSING: XA XIA–PREK CHAK

The Xa Xia–Prek Chak crossing connects Ha Tien with Kep and Kampot on Cambodia's south coast, making a trip to Phu Quoc that much easier for visitors coming from Cambodia. Direct buses cross the border twice a day, terminating in Sihanoukville or Phnom Penh. Casinos and a massive hotel (the ominously named Ha Tien Vegas; www.hatien vegas.com) have sprung up in the no-man's-land between the two border posts. While there are casinos in both countries, locals aren't allowed to gamble in them – making this limbo zone a popular destination in its own right.

Direct buses leave Ha Tien for Cambodia at midday and 4pm daily, heading to Kep (US$12, one hour, 47km), Kampot (US$15, 1½ hours, 75km), Sihanoukville (US$20, four hours, 150km) and Phnom Penh (US$18, four hours, 180km). Bookings are through Ha Tien Tourism, who can also arrange the Cambodian visa.

The entry to the cave containing **Hai Son Tu** (Sea Mountain Temple) is inside the pagoda. Visitors light incense and offer prayers here before entering the grotto itself, whose entrance is located behind the altar. Inside are statues of the Buddha and Quan The Am Bo Tat. The pagoda is swamped with pilgrims 15 days before and one month after Tet. Another worship deluge occurs in March and April.

🛏 Sleeping & Eating

Hontrem Resort　　　RESORT HOTEL **$$**
(☎385 4331; ctycpdulichkg@vnn.vn; r US$60; ❄️🛜) The smartest place in Hon Chong by some stretch, Hontrem is draped over a hillock towards the end of the main strip. The hexagonal bungalows are attractively set overlooking the sea and include a large bed with light linen and generous baths. They even feature safes for valuables. The gardens are well kept and there is a reputable restaurant overlooking the beach. Breakfast included.

Green Hill Guesthouse　　GUESTHOUSE **$**
(☎385 4369; r 500,000d; ❄️) Set in an imposing villa on the northern headland of Duong Beach, this is a friendly, family-run place with a range of spacious rooms. The communal balcony on the 2nd floor is a breezy place, while the room of choice is on the top floor if available.

Tan Phat　　　　　　RESTAURANT **$**
(mains 60,000-90,000d; ❄️) Located on Hon Chong's main road, a kilometre or so before Duong Beach, this seafood restaurant looks like a tumbledown shack from the outside, but it serves excellent food on pavilions over the water with good views of the local fishing fleet. An English menu is available; try the sweet and sour squid.

ℹ Getting There & Away

Hon Chong is 32km from Ha Tien towards Rach Gia. The access road branches off the Rach Gia–Ha Tien highway at the small town of Ba Hon. Buses can drop you off at Ba Hon, from where you can hire a motorbike to continue the journey on to Hon Chong (around 60,000d).

TUC DUP HILL

Because of its network of connecting caves, Tuc Dup Hill (216m) served as a strategic base of operations during the American War. *Tuc dup* is Khmer for 'water runs at night' and it is also known locally as 'Two Million Dollar Hill', in reference to the amount of money the Americans sank into securing it.

This is a place of historical interest but there isn't much to see. You'll pass near it if you're taking the back road through Ba Chuc to Chau Doc.

BA CHUC

Ba Chuc's **Bone Pagoda** stands as a grisly reminder of the horrors perpetrated by the Khmer Rouge. Between 1975 and 1978 Khmer Rouge soldiers regularly crossed the border into Vietnam and slaughtered innocent civilians. Over the border, things were even worse, where nearly two million Cambodians were killed during the period of Pol Pot's Democratic Kampuchea regime.

Between 12 April and 30 April 1978, the Khmer Rouge killed 3157 people at Ba Chuc. Only two people are known to have survived. Many of the victims were tortured to death. The Vietnamese government might have had other motives for invading Cambodia at the end of 1978, but certainly outrage at the Ba Chuc massacre was a major justification.

The Bone Pagoda has a common tomb housing the skulls and bones of more than 1100 victims. This resembles Cambodia's

Choeung Ek killing fields, where thousands of skulls of Khmer Rouge victims are on display. Near the skull collection is a building displaying photos taken shortly after the massacre – which even by the standards of Vietnamese museums are graphic and gruesome. Be warned: once seen they're difficult images to erase from the memory banks.

Ba Chuc is located close to the Cambodian border; to reach it, follow the road that runs along the canal from Ha Tien to Chau Doc. Turn off this main road onto Hwy 3T and follow it for 4km.

Chau Doc

☑ 076 / POP 112,000

Draped along the banks of the Hau Giang River (Bassac River), Chau Doc sees plenty of travellers passing through on the river route between Cambodia and Vietnam. It is a likeable little town with significant Chinese, Cham and Khmer communities. Its cultural diversity – apparent in the mosques, temples, churches and nearby pilgrimage sites – makes it a fascinating place to explore even if you aren't continuing to Cambodia. Taking a boat trip to the Cham communities across the river is another highlight, while the bustling market and interesting waterfront provide fine backdrops to a few days of relaxing before heading out.

◉ Sights

30 Thang 4 Park   PARK

(Đ Le Loi) Stretching from the market to the Victoria Chau Doc Hotel, this formal park is the city's main promenading place and a great spot for river gazing. Between its manicured lawns and paths are interesting sculptures and a fountain. If you're interested in getting out on the river, you're likely to be approached by women here offering rides in small boats (see p400).

Chau Phu Temple   TEMPLE

(Dinh Than Chau Phu; cnr Đ Nguyen Van Thoai & Đ Gia Long) In 1926 this temple was built to worship the Nguyen dynasty official Thoai Ngoc Hau, who is buried at Sam Mountain (p400). The structure is decorated with both Vietnamese and Chinese motifs. Inside are funeral tablets bearing the names of the deceased and some biographical information about them. There's also a shrine to Ho Chi Minh.

Mosques   MOSQUES

Domed and arched **Chau Giang Mosque**, in the hamlet of Chau Giang, serves the local Cham Muslims. To get there, take the car ferry from Chau Giang ferry landing across the Hau Giang River. From the ferry landing, walk inland from the river for 30m, turn left and walk 50m.

The **Mubarak Mosque** (Thanh Duong Hoi Giao), where children study the Quran in Arabic script, is also on the river bank opposite Chau Doc (about 800m east of Chau Giang Mosque). Visitors are permitted, but you should avoid entering during the calls to prayer (five times daily) unless you are a Muslim.

There are other small mosques in the Chau Doc area. They are accessible by boat but you'll need a local guide to find them all.

Floating Houses   FLOATING HOUSES

These houses, whose floats consist of empty metal drums, are both a place to live and a livelihood for their residents. Under each house, fish are raised in suspended metal nets: the fish flourish in their natural river habitat; the family can feed them whatever scraps are handy; and catching the fish requires less exertion than from fishing. You can find these houses floating around Chau Doc and get a close-up look by hiring a boat (but please be respectful of their privacy).

MEKONG DELTA CHAU DOC

BORDER CROSSING: TINH BIEN–PHNOM DEN

This border crossing is less convenient for Phnom Penh–bound travellers, but may be of interest for those who savour the challenge of obscure border crossings. It has been rather eclipsed by the newer crossing of Xa Xia near Ha Tien, which offers a more convenient link between Phu Quoc Island and the colonial era towns of Kep and Kampot in Cambodia. Cambodian visas can be obtained here, although it's not uncommon to be charged US$25, a few dollars more than the official rate.

Buses from Chau Doc to Phnom Penh depart at 7.30am and can be booked through Mekong Tours in Chau Doc (US$15-21, five hours). The roads leading to the border are terrible.

Chau Doc

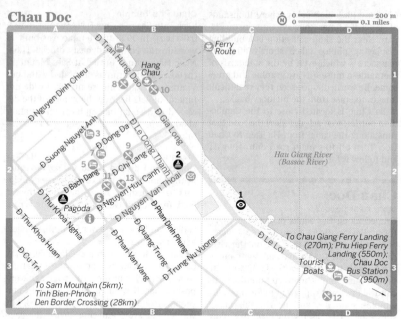

🛏 Sleeping

As well as these places in Chau Doc, there are more accommodation options out near Sam Mountain.

TOP CHOICE Victoria Chau Doc Hotel   HOTEL **$$$**
(☑386 5010; www.victoriahotels-asia.com; 32 Đ Le Loi; r US$162-210, ste US$220-275; ❋@☎☒) Seriously stylish for Chau Doc, the Victoria is built in classic colonial style. With a striking location on the riverfront, the grand rooms here have timber floors, inviting bathtubs and classy drapes. The swimming pool overlooks the busy river action and there is a small spa upstairs. A range of tours is available to guests, including a two-hour border cruise (US$25) or a Sam Mountain trip (US$32).

TOP CHOICE Trung Nguyen Hotel   HOTEL **$**
(☑386 6158; trunghotel@yahoo.com; 86 Đ Bach Dang; r US$13-15; ❋@☎) Following a facelift, this is definitely the best of the budget places, with a trim and panache that is decidedly more midrange. Rooms feature more decorative verve than the competition and have balconies overlooking the market. It's a busy corner site, so pack earplugs.

Hai Chau   HOTEL **$**
(☑626 0026; www.haichauhotel.com; 61 Đ Suong Nguyet Anh; r 360,000-560,000d; ❋☎) Another excellent, central choice, Hai Chau has sixteen rooms spread over four floors above a restaurant – and, unlike Trung Nguyen, there's a lift. The well-kept rooms are smartly fitted out with dark wooden furniture and good shower capsules.

Thuan Loi Hotel   HOTEL **$**
(☑386 6134; ksthuanloi@yahoo.com; 275 Đ Tran Hung Dao; r fan/air-con 200,000/230,000; ❋) This is the only cheap hotel with a riverside location and it uses it to its best advantage with a floating restaurant set under a thatched roof. The rooms are not so atmospheric but are good value. Fan rooms have cold water only, so it's worth investing in a bigger air-con room.

Vinh Phuoc Hotel   HOTEL **$**
(☑3866242;www.hotels-chaudoc.com/Vinh_Phuoc _hotel; 12 Đ Quang Trung; r fan US$7-10, air-con US$10-12; ❋@) The friendly staff at this popular budget hotel have a good knowledge of the delta region. Rooms range from cheapies with only a fan to smarter air-con options with hot water. The restaurant is good value and there are usually some beer drinkers lurking around.

Chau Doc

🍴 Eating

The **Chau Doc Covered Market** (Đ Bach Dang) has delicious Vietnamese food (10,000d to 20,000d). At night, you can also try a variety of cool *che* (dessert soups) at *che* stalls on Đ Bach Dang, next to the pagoda. There are also lots of other inexpensive stalls with large whiteboard menus displaying their wares.

Bassac Restaurant   FRENCH, VIETNAMESE **$$**
(☎386 5010; 32 Đ Le Loi; mains US$9-18) The most sophisticated dining experience in Chau Doc is to be found here at the Victoria Chau Doc Hotel. The menu includes some beautifully presented Vietnamese food, as well as a wonderful selection of inventive French dishes to make the mouth water.

Bay Bong   VIETNAMESE **$**
(22 Đ Suong Nguyet Anh; mains 40,000-90,000d) It doesn't look like much, but the food here is really something. Bay Bong specialises in hotpots and soups, as well as fresh fish dishes. Try the *ca kho to* (stewed fish in a clay pot) or *canh chua* (sweet-and-sour soup).

Mekong   VIETNAMESE **$**
(41 Đ Le Loi; mains 35,000-70,000d) Located directly opposite the Victoria Chau Doc Hotel, this restaurant has a large covered section or an outdoor area in front of the gracefully decaying old villa. A good spot for Vietnamese greatest hits at affordable prices.

Chau Giang Floating Restaurant   VIETNAMESE **$**
(Đ Tran Hung Dao; mains 40,000-90,000d) Fish and seafood dishes are served on the upper deck of this permanently moored boat. It's a good place to try Mekong favourite *hu tieu* – the noodle soup coming in beef, seafood or chicken versions.

Lam Hung Ky   CHINESE **$**
(71 Đ Chi Lang; mains 50,000-120,000d) Busy Lam Hung Ky is part of a strip of Chinese restaurants on Chi Lang. The window is hung with the usual cooked ducks and chickens, and an English language menu is available.

Thanh Tinh   VIETNAMESE **$**
(42 Đ Quang Trung; mains 30,000-80,000d; ✎) This place translates as 'to calm the body down' and it will do just that for vegetarians looking for a reliable menu.

🍷 Drinking

It may be best to leave the disco clothes in the bag, as Chau Doc is a pretty sleepy place. For a stylish tipple, try the poolside **Bamboo Bar** or **Tan Chau Salon Bar** at the Victoria Chau Doc Hotel. Another atmospheric but considerably cheaper spot for a casual drink is **Chau Giang Floating Restaurant**.

ℹ Information

Mekong Tours (☎386 8222; www.mekongvietnam.com; 14 Đ Nguyen Huu Canh) Local travel agency where you can book boat or bus transport to Phnom Penh, boat trips on the Mekong, and cars with drivers.
Post Office (☎386 9200; 2 Đ Le Loi; @)

ℹ Getting There & Away

BOAT For information on boats to Cambodia see the boxed text on p401.

BUS The buses from HCMC to Chau Doc leave from the Mien Tay bus station. Express buses can make the run in six hours and costs around 120,000d. **Chau Doc bus station** (Ben Xe Chau Doc) is on the eastern edge of town, where Đ Le Loi becomes Hwy 91. Other destinations include Ha Tien (52,000d) and My Tho (51,000d).

CAR & MOTORBIKE By road, Chau Doc is approximately 95km from Ha Tien, 117km from Can Tho, 181km from My Tho and 245km from HCMC. See p404 for details on the road to Ha Tien.

FISH FARMING & BIOFUEL

Fish farming constitutes around 20% of Vietnam's total seafood output and is widely practised in An Giang province, in the region near the Cambodian border. The highest concentration of 'floating houses' with fish cages can be observed on the banks of the Hau Giang River (Bassac River) in Chau Doc. It is interesting to note that even with two tides a day here, there is no salt water in the river.

The fish farmed are two members of the Asian catfish family, basa (*Pangasius bocourti*) and tra (*Pangasius hypophthalmus*). About 1.1 million tonnes are produced by this method annually and much of it is exported, primarily to European and American markets (as well as Australia and Japan), in the form of frozen white fish fillets.

The two-step production cycle starts with capturing fish eggs from the wild, usually sourced in the Tonle Sap Lake in Cambodia, followed by raising the fish to a marketable size – usually about 1kg. Fish are fed on a kind of dough made by the farmers from cereal, vegetables and fish scraps. The largest cage measures 2000 cubic metres and can produce up to 400 tonnes of raw fish in each 10-month production cycle.

One of the more interesting developments affecting fish farming is the move to convert fish fat, a by-product of processing, into biofuel. One kilogram of fish fat can yield 1L of bio-diesel fuel, according to specialists. It is claimed that the biofuel will be more efficient than diesel, is nontoxic and will generate far fewer fumes. Those who've gotten a whiff of *nuoc mam* (fish sauce) and thought, 'you can power a dump truck on this stuff' aren't far off the mark.

Due to concerns about detrimental environmental effects from fish farming (particularly related to waste management and the use of antibiotics and other chemicals), the World Wildlife Fund (WWF) placed farmed Vietnamese *pangasius* on a red list for environmentally conscious European consumers to avoid. It was subsequently removed in 2011 and the WWF has devised a set of standards and an accreditation agency to certify sustainable Vietnamese producers.

ⓘ Getting Around

Boats to Chau Giang district (across the Hau Giang River) leave from two docks: vehicle ferries depart from **Chau Giang ferry landing** (Ben Pha Chau Giang), opposite 419 Đ Le Loi; smaller, more frequent boats leave from **Phu Hiep ferry landing** (Ben Pha FB Phu Hiep), a little further southeast.

Private boats (80,000d for a couple of hours), which are rowed standing up, can be hired from either of these spots or from 30 Thang 4 Park, and are highly recommended for seeing the floating houses and visiting nearby Cham minority villages and mosques. Motorboats (100,000d per hour) can be hired in the same area.

Around Chau Doc

SAM MOUNTAIN

A holy place for Buddhists, Sam Mountain (Nui Sam, 284m) and its surrounds are crammed with dozens of pagodas and temples. A strong Chinese influence makes it particularly popular with ethnic Chinese but Buddhists of all ethnicities visit here. The views from the top are excellent (weather permitting), stretching deep into Cambodia. There's a military outpost on the summit, a legacy of the days when the Khmer Rouge made cross-border raids and massacred Vietnamese civilians.

Along with the shrines and tombs, the steep path to the top is lined with the unholy clamour of commerce. There are plenty of cafes and stalls in which to stop for a drink or a meal, shelter from the sun or buy incense, sunglasses or a hat. Walking down is easier than walking up, so if you want to cheat, have a motorbike take you to the summit (about 20,000d). The road to the top is a pretty ride on the east side of the mountain. Veer left at the base of the mountain and turn right after about 1km where the road begins its climb.

◉ Sights

Tay An Pagoda   PAGODA
(Chua Tay An) Although it was founded in 1847 on the site of an earlier bamboo shrine, Tay An's current structure dates from 1958. Aspects of its unusual architecture, particularly its domed tower, reflect Hindu and Islamic influences

The main gate is of traditional Vietnamese design. On its roofline are figures of lions and two dragons fighting for possession of pearls, chrysanthemums, apricot trees and lotus blossoms. Nearby is a statue of Quan Am Thi Kinh, the Guardian Spirit of Mother and Child.

The pagoda itself is guarded by statues of a black elephant with two tusks and a white elephant with six tusks. Inside are the complex's main claims to fame – fine carving of hundreds of religious figures, most of which are made of wood and some of which have been blinged up with psychedelic disco-light halos.

If you're coming from Chau Doc on Hwy 91, Tay An Pagoda is located straight ahead at the foot of the mountain.

Temple of Lady Xu   TEMPLE

(Mieu Ba Chua Xu) Founded in the 1820s to house a statue that's become the subject of a popular cult, this large compound faces Sam Mountain, on the same road as Tay An Pagoda. Originally made of bamboo and leaves, the pagoda has been remade many times. The last reconstruction took place between 1972 and 1976, combining mid-20th century design with Vietnamese Buddhist decorative motifs. The statue itself is possibly a relic of the Oc-Eo culture, dating from the 6th century, and is also possibly that of a man – but don't suggest that around one of the faithful.

According to one of several legends, the statue of Lady Xu used to stand at the summit of Sam Mountain. In the early 19th century Siamese troops invaded the area and, impressed with the statue, decided to take it back to Thailand. But as they carried the statue down the hill, it became heavier and heavier, and they were forced to abandon it by the side of the path.

One day some villagers who were cutting wood came upon the statue and decided to bring it back to their village in order to build a temple for it; but it weighed too much for them to budge. Suddenly, there appeared a girl who, possessed by a spirit, declared herself to be Lady Xu. She announced to them that nine virgins were to be brought and that they would be able to transport the statue down the mountainside. The virgins were then summoned and carried the statue down the slope, but when they reached the plain, it became too heavy and they had to set it down. The people concluded that the site where the virgins halted had been selected by Lady Xu for the temple construction and it's here that the Temple of Lady Xu stands to this day.

Offerings of roast whole pigs are frequently made here, providing an interesting photo opportunity. The temple's most important festival is held from the 23rd to the 26th day of the fourth lunar month, usually late May or early June. During this time, pilgrims flock here, sleeping on mats in the large rooms of the two-storey resthouse next to the temple.

Tomb of Thoai Ngoc Hau   TOMB

(Lang Thoai Ngoc Hau) A high-ranking official, Thoai Ngoc Hau (1761–1829) served the Nguyen Lords and, later, the Nguyen dynasty. In early 1829, Thoai Ngoc Hau ordered that a tomb be constructed for himself at the foot of Sam Mountain. The site he chose is nearly opposite the Temple of Lady Xu.

The steps are made of red 'beehive' stone (da ong) brought from the southeastern part

MEKONG DELTA AROUND CHAU DOC

BORDER CROSSING: VINH XUONG–KAAM SAMNOR

One of the most enjoyable ways to enter Cambodia is via this crossing located just northwest of Chau Doc along the Mekong River. If coming from Cambodia, arrange a visa in advance; if you're leaving Vietnam, Cambodian visas are available at the crossing but minor overcharging is common (plan on paying around US$23).

Several companies in Chau Doc sell boat journeys from Chau Doc to Phnom Penh via the Vinh Xuong border. **Hang Chau** (Chau Doc ☏076-356 2771; Phnom Penh ☏855-12-883 542; www.hangchautourist.com.vn) has boats departing Chau Doc at 7.30am from a pier at 18 Đ Tran Hung Dao, arriving at 12.30am (US$24). From Phnom Penh they depart at noon.

The more upmarket **Blue Cruiser** (www.bluecruiser.com; HCMC ☏08-3926 0253; Phnom Penh ☏855-236-333 666) pulls out at 7am, costing US$55. It takes about 4½ hours, including the border check, and leaves from the pier at the Victoria Hotel. Also departing from this pier at 7am (and from Phnom Penh at 1.30pm) are the **Victoria Speedboats** (www.victoriahotels-asia.com). They are exclusive to Victoria Hotel guests, take five hours and cost a hefty US$97 per person.

of Vietnam. In the middle of the platform is the tomb of Thoai Ngoc Hau and those of his wives, Chau Thi Te and Truong Thi Miet. There's a shrine at the rear and several dozen other tombs in the vicinity where his officials are buried.

Cavern Pagoda
PAGODA

(Chua Hang) Also known as Phuoc Dien Tu, this pagoda is halfway up the western (far) side of Sam Mountain. The lower part of the pagoda includes monks' quarters and two hexagonal tombs in which the founder of the pagoda, a female tailor named Le Thi Tho, and a former head monk, Thich Hue Thien, are buried.

The upper section has two parts: the main sanctuary, in which there are statues of A Di Da (the Buddha of the Past) and Thich Ca Buddha (Sakyamuni, the Historical Buddha); and the cavern. At the back of the cave behind the sanctuary building is a shrine dedicated to Quan The Am Bo Tat.

According to legend, Le Thi Tho came from Tay An Pagoda to this site half a century ago to lead a quiet, meditative life. When she arrived, she found two enormous snakes, one white and the other dark green. Le Thi Tho soon converted the snakes, which thereafter led pious lives. Upon her death, the snakes disappeared.

🛏 Sleeping & Eating

There is now quite a bustling community at the base of Sam Mountain, with hotels, guesthouses and restaurants lining the street.

Long Chau
RESORT HOTEL $

(☑386 1249; www.vamcotravel.com; Hwy 91; r US$10-20; ❇🛜) This pretty compound of rattan-roofed bungalows is set around a lily pond amid the rice paddies about 4km outside Chau Doc on the way to Sam Mountain. There are great views to the holy mountain and the rooms are good value with air-con options starting at just US$15. The attractive restaurant is worth a visit, even if you're not staying here.

Ben Da Nui Sam
RESORT HOTEL $

(☑386 1745; www.angiangtourimex.com.vn; Hwy 91; r 300,000-720,000d; ❇🛜) The rooms at this immense government hotel are smart enough and some overlook the extensive gardens. As well as satellite TV and minibar, breakfast is included.

Long Bo
VIETNAMESE $

(Hwy 91; mains 40,000-90,000d) This is a bit of a legend among Chau Doc locals, a grilled meat restaurant offering such delights as *bo lui xa* (beef wrapped around lemongrass). Cook it yourself on the hot coals brought to your table. It's 1km west of the Temple of Lady Xu.

ℹ Getting There & Away

Most people get here by rented motorbike or on the back of a *xe om* (about 40,000d one-way). There are also local buses heading this way from Chau Doc (5000d).

PHU CHAU (TAN CHAU) DISTRICT

Traditional silk-making has made Phu Chau (Tan Chau) district famous throughout southern Vietnam. The **market** in Phu Chau has a selection of competitively priced Thai and Cambodian goods.

To get to Phu Chau district from Chau Doc, take a boat across the Hau Giang River from the Phu Hiep ferry landing, then catch a ride on the back of a *xe om* (about 60,000d) for the 18km trip to Phu Chau district.

Long Xuyen

☑076 / POP 300,000

Aside from a few minor sights and a lively market, the capital of An Giang province offers little to detain travellers. It's a relatively affluent city, making its money from agriculture (particularly cashew nuts) and fish processing.

Long Xuyen was once a stronghold of the Hoa Hao sect. Founded in 1939, the sect emphasises simplicity in worship and does not believe in temples or intermediaries between humans and the Supreme Being. Until 1956 the Hoa Hao had an army and constituted a major military force in this region.

The town's other claim to fame is being the birthplace of Vietnam's second president, Ton Duc Thang. There is a museum in town dedicated to Bac Ton (Uncle Ton) as well as a large statue bearing his likeness.

History

During the 1st to 6th centuries AD, when southern Vietnam and southern Cambodia were under the rule of the Indian-influenced Cambodian kingdom of Funan, Oc-Eo (the scant remains of which lie 37km southwest of Long Xuyen) was a major trading city. Much of what is known about the Funan empire, which reached its height during the 5th century AD, comes from contemporary Chinese sources and the excavations at Oc-Eo and Angkor Borei in neighbouring Cam-

Long Xuyen

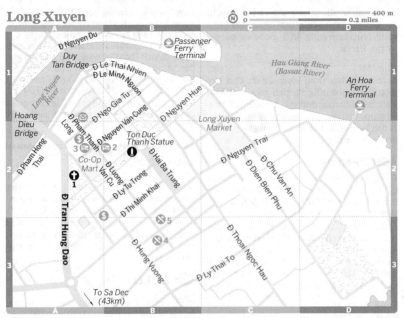

bodia. The excavations have uncovered evidence of contact between Oc-Eo and what is now Thailand, Malaysia and Indonesia, as well as Persia and the Roman Empire.

An elaborate system of canals around Oc-Eo was once used for both irrigation and transportation, prompting Chinese travellers of the time to write about 'sailing across Funan' on their way to the Malay peninsula. Most of the buildings of Oc-Eo were built on piles and pieces of these structures indicate the high degree of refinement achieved by Funanese civilisation. Artefacts found at Oc-Eo are on display at the History Museum and Fine Arts Museum in HCMC and at the History Museum in Hanoi.

◉ Sights

FREE Blue Sky Crocodile Land   CROCODILE FARM
(Ca Sau Long Xuyen; 44/1A Đ Tran Hung Dao; ☺7am-6pm) For a close-up view of the reptile that once ruled the Mekong, head to this farm which is home to thousands of crocodiles ranging in size from 10cm to 4m; we feel sorry for the peacocks in the neighbouring pen having to put up with those beady-eyed stares all day long. The meat and skin of these animals is largely exported, though

Long Xuyen

◉ Sights

🛏 Sleeping

🍴 Eating

some Vietnamese drop in to buy fresh or frozen crocodile meat or to eat at the onsite restaurant. A little shop sells crocodile-skin wallets and bags. The farm lies 8km south of town on the road to Can Tho.

Long Xuyen Catholic Church   CHURCH
(Đ Tran Hung Dao) One of the largest churches in the Mekong Delta, this impressive modern structure boasts a 50m-high bell tower and can (and often does) seat 1000 worshippers. It was constructed between 1966 and 1973 – and you can tell. The interior is cavernous and well-ventilated (in Vietnam only some of the newer Protestant churches are air-conditioned; the Catholics and

Buddhists are dismissive of such lightweight comforts), with a sculptural centrepiece of a giant crucifix resting on a globe supported by two hands.

Cho Moi
DISTRICT

Across the river from Long Xuyen, Cho Moi district is known for its rich groves of fruit such as bananas, durians, guava, jackfruit, longans, mangoes, mangosteens and plums. It can be reached by boat from the passenger ferry terminal.

🛏 Sleeping

Dong Xuyen Hotel
HOTEL $

(☑394 2260; www.angiangtourimex.com.vn; Đ 9A Luong Van Cu; r 400,000-770,000d; ste 800,000d; ❄⊛⊚) Already the smartest place in town, Dong Xuyen isn't resting on its laurels; renovations were taking place when we last visited. The rooms are nicely furnished in wood and include the usual suspects like a minibar. The staff are friendly and helpful and speak good English.

Long Xuyen Hotel
HOTEL $

(☑384 1927; www.angiangtourimex.com.vn; 19 Đ Nguyen Van Cung; r 300,000-420,000d; ⊛⊚) Dong's older brother Long is directly across the road and also state-owned. It could certainly do with an overhaul, but prices remain reasonable in the meantime. The rooms have some charm and include satellite TV, hot water and shared balconies.

🍴 Eating

Hong Phat
VIETNAMESE $

(242/4 Đ Luong Van Cu; mains 30,000-80,000d) This restaurant features air-conditioning, a bonus on a hot day. English menus, grilled meats, plenty of seafood and friendly staff make it a reliable choice.

Hai Thue
VIETNAMESE $

(245/3 Đ Luong Van Cu; mains 15,000-40,000d) A good stop for cheap, authentic Vietnamese food.

Buu Loc
VIETNAMESE $

(246/3 Đ Luong Van Cu; mains 20,000-40,000d) Another popular local place for filling meals, but no English menu.

ℹ Getting There & Away

BOAT To get to the Long Xuyen ferry dock from Đ Pham Hong Thai, you'll need to cross Duy Tan Bridge and turn right. Passenger ferries leave from here to Sa Dec and other Delta destinations.

BUS The buses heading from HCMC to Long Xuyen leave from the Mien Tay bus station (from 85,000d). **Long Xuyen bus station** (Ben Xe Khach Long Xuyen) is a roadside terminus about 1.5km down Đ Phan Cu Luong, off Đ Tran Hung Dao, at the southern end of town. Buses from Long Xuyen head to Can Tho (62km), Chau Doc (55km), Ha Tien (130km) and Rach Gia (75km).

CAR & MOTORCYCLE To get to Cao Lanh or Sa Dec you'll need to take the car ferry from An Hoa ferry terminal.

Cao Lanh
☑067 / POP 150,000

A newish town carved from the jungles and swamps of the Mekong Delta region, Cao Lanh is big for business, but it doesn't draw a lot of tourists. Its main appeal is as a base to explore Rung Tram (Tram Forest) and Tran Nong National Park, both reachable by boat.

◉ Sights

FREE Dong Thap Museum
MUSEUM

(226 Đ Nguyen Thai Hoc; ⊙7-11.30am & 1.30-5pm) The impressive-looking Dong Thap Museum is among the best museums in the Mekong. The ground floor displays an anthropological history of Dong Thap province, with exhibits of tools, sculpture, models of traditional houses and a few stuffed animals and pickled fish. Upstairs is devoted to war history and, of course, to Ho Chi Minh. All interpretive signs are in Vietnamese.

War Martyrs Monument
MEMORIAL

Situated on the eastern edge of town off Hwy 30, the War Memorial (Dai Liet Si) is Cao Lanh's most prominent landmark. This Socialist Realist–style sculpture features a large white concrete statue of a decorated soldier holding flowers in front of a stylised star. The rear of this statue is decorated with storks, a symbol of the Mekong. Behind a lotus pond the memorial shrine looms, decorated with bas-reliefs depicting the struggle. Within the grounds are the graves of 3112 VC who died while fighting in the American War.

Tomb of Nguyen Sinh Sac
PARK

(Lang Cu Nguyen Sinh Sac; off Đ Pham Huu Lau; car parking 6000d) Another significant tomb in Cao Lanh is that of Ho Chi Minh's father, Nguyen Sinh Sac (1862–1929). His tomb is the centrepiece of a pretty 9.6-hectare park and model heritage village of wooden

RICE PRODUCTION

The ancient Indian word for rice, *dhanya* ('sustainer of the human race'), is apt when describing the importance of this 'white gold' to the Vietnamese.

A Vietnamese fable tells of a time when rice did not need to be harvested. Instead, it would be summoned through prayer and arrive in each home from the heavens in the form of a large ball. One day a man ordered his wife to sweep the floor in preparation for the coming of the rice, but she was still sweeping when the huge ball arrived and struck it by accident, causing it to shatter into many pieces. Since then, the Vietnamese have had to toil to produce rice by hand.

While some remote parts of Vietnam today are similar to how they would have been centuries ago – women in *non bai tho* (conical hats) irrigating fields by hand, farmers stooping to plant the flooded paddies and water buffalo ploughing seedbeds with harrows – things are steadily becoming more mechanised as Vietnam ramps up its production.

Rice is the single most important crop in Vietnam and involves up to 50% of the working population. While always playing an important role in the Vietnamese economy, its production intensified considerably as a result of economic reforms, known as *doi moi* ('renovation'), in 1986. The reforms helped transform Vietnam from a rice importer to exporter in 1989. Today rice is a substantial part of the country's earnings and the country is the second largest exporter after Thailand. In 2010 Vietnam exported 6.5 million tonnes.

The importance of rice in the diet of the Vietnamese is evident in the many rice dishes available, including *banh xeo* (crispy rice pancake), *chao* (rice porridge) and extremely potent *ruou gao* (rice wine), to name a few. Vietnam's ubiquitous *com pho* (rice-noodle soup) restaurants serve white rice *(com)* with a variety of cooked meat and vegetables, as well as *pho*.

Rice plants take three to six months to grow, depending on the type and environment. In Vietnam the three major cropping seasons are winter–spring, summer–autumn and the wet season. When ready to harvest, the plants are thigh-high and in about 30cm of water. The grains grow in drooping fronds and are cut by hand, then transported by wheelbarrows to threshing machines that separate the husk from the plant. Other machines are used to 'dehusk' the rice (for brown rice) or 'polish' it (for white rice). At this stage, brown carpets of rice spread along roads to dry before milling are a familiar sight.

In 2006, Vietnam, along with Thailand, announced a ban on growing genetically engineered varieties of rice, citing health concerns. The announcement came in the wake of scandals caused by the US and China contaminating the global rice supply with unapproved and illegal genetically engineered rice varieties.

houses peopled by manikins depicting traditional pursuits (grinding rice, processing tobacco, playing music).

The tomb itself is located under a curious shell-shaped shrine set behind a star-shaped lotus pond. Although various plaques (in Vietnamese) and tourist pamphlets extol Nguyen Sinh Sac as a great revolutionary, there is little evidence confirming that he was involved in the anticolonial struggle against the French, but his son more than made up for it. Next to the shrine is a small museum devoted to Ho Chi Minh consisting mainly of photographs with Vietnamese captions. Check out the creepy portrait in room two with a beard made of real hair (who knew Uncle Ho was ginger?).

The complex is located at the southwest approach to town; turn right after Hoa Long Pagoda and follow the fence around until you get to the entrance.

🛏 Sleeping

Hoa Anh   HOTEL **$**
(☎224 567; hoaanhhotel@yahoo.com.vn; 40 Đ Ly Tu Trung; r 170,000-350,000d; ❇️🛜) Decked out in hues of lemon and burnt orange, Hoa Anh is a burst of citrusy freshness on the Cao Lanh hotel scene. For 200,000d you'll get a tidy, smallish double with marble tiles and a small bathroom. The 250,000d rooms are larger, with two beds, while the 350,000d rooms would fit a family.

Cao Lanh

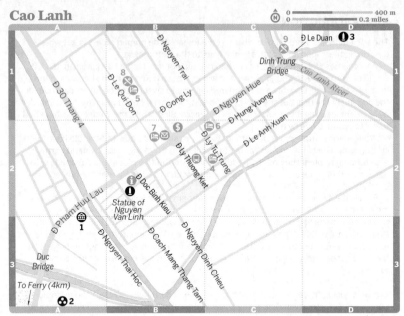

Cao Lanh

⊙ Sights
1	Dong Thap Museum	A3
2	Tomb of Nguyen Sinh Sac	A3
3	War Martyrs Monument	D1

🛏 Sleeping
4	Hoa Anh	C2
5	Nha Khach Dong Thap	B1
6	Song Tra Hotel	C2
7	Xuan Mai Hotel	B2

🍽 Eating
8	A Chau	B1
9	Tan Nghia	C1

Xuan Mai Hotel　　　　　　　　HOTEL **$**
(☎385 2852; 33 Ð Le Qui Don; r 200,000-300,000d;
🅰🛜) A long-time favourite and still great
value, this mini-hotel has neat and tidy
rooms, all finished with bathtubs and hot
water. It is located just behind the post office
and rates include breakfast.

Nha Khach Dong Thap　　　　　HOTEL **$**
(☎387 2670; 48 Ð Ly Thuong Kiet; r 260,000-
800,000d; 🅰🛜) Another Communist Party
special; the boys in red are obviously doing all right as their hotels are quite smart

these days. This place has large airy rooms
with polished floors, a reception dripping in
marble and corridors wide enough to drive
a jeep down. Suites, while pricey, are enormous and large enough to accommodate a
family or politburo chief.

Song Tra Hotel　　　　　　　　HOTEL **$**
(☎385 2624; www.dongthaptourist.com; 178 Ð
Nguyen Hue; r US$19-35, ste US$50; 🅰) The exterior is a bit clunky but the rooms are in
reasonable shape and include big windows,
satellite TV, a minibar and hot water. The
staff are friendlier than you'll find in most
other state-run places.

🍽 Eating

Cao Lanh is famous for *chuot dong* (rice-
field rats) so come with room in your stomach to sample the local delicacy. At the very
least, it'll make a great story when you get
back home.

A Chau　　　　　　　　　　VIETNAMESE **$**
(42 Ð Ly Thuong Kiet; mains 20,000-70,000d)
Head here for the tasty *banh xeo* (fried
pancakes), a house speciality that you roll
up and dip in fish sauce. The *lau de* (goat
hotpot) is also a winner. Or go for the rat,
we dare you.

Tan Nghia VIETNAMESE $
(331 Đ Le Duan; mains 30,000-110,000d) Over-looking the river, Tan Nghia pulls a regular crowd, eager to chow down on the wide range of meats and seafood dishes on offer. If you don't fancy beef or chicken there's always those popular fallbacks, rat and frog.

ℹ️ Information

Dong Thap Tourist (☑385 5637; www.dong thaptourist.com; 2 Đ Doc Binh Kieu) A particularly friendly, helpful outfit that can arrange boat and other tours of the surrounding area. It also has a **branch office** (☑391 8487) at My Hiep village.
Post Office (85 Đ Nguyen Hue; @)

ℹ️ Getting There & Around

Cao Lanh Bus Station (Ben Xe Cao Lanh; 71/1 Đ Ly Thuong Kiet) is conveniently located right in the centre of town. There are services to HCMC (85,000d), Sa Dec (15,000d), Vinh Long (17,000d), My Tho (25,000d), Tra Vinh (45,000d), Can Tho (30,000d), Soc Trang (55,000d), Bac Lieu (65,000d), and Ca Mau (83,000d).

The sights around Cao Lanh are best visited by river. Although you could possibly arrange something privately with boat owners, you'll find it easier – though slightly more expensive – to deal with Dong Thap Tourist. Plan on spending about US$30 for a half-day boat tour.

Around Cao Lanh

RUNG TRAM

(Xeo Quyt, Xeo Quit; admission 5,000d; ⏲7am-5pm) Southeast of Cao Lanh and accessible by boat tour is the 52-hectare Rung Tram near My Hiep village. The area is one vast swamp with a beautiful thick canopy of tall trees and vines. It's one of the last natural forests left in the Mekong Delta and by now probably would have been turned into a rice paddy were it not for its historical significance.

During the American War the VC had a base here called Xeo Quyt, where top-brass VC lived in underground bunkers. But don't mistake this for another Cu Chi Tunnels – it's very different. Only about 10 VC were here at any given time. They were all generals who directed the war from here, just two kilometres from a US military base. The Americans never realised that the VC generals were living right under their noses. Naturally, they were suspicious about that patch of forest and periodically dropped some bombs on it to reassure themselves, but the VC remained safe in their underground bunkers.

During the rainy season a 20-minute **canoe tour** (10,000d) takes you past old bunkers and former minefields along narrow canals filled with ever-present dragonflies and water hyacinths. During the dry season you can explore this area on foot.

From My Hiep, you can hire a boat (about US$15 to US$20, seating up to 10 persons) that takes around 40 minutes to make the two-kilometre journey to Rung Tram. Dong Thap Tourist includes a guided trip in several of its tour programmes.

TRAM CHIM NATIONAL PARK

FREE **Tram Chim National Park** is due north of Cao Lanh in Tam Nong district (Dong Thap province) and notable for its eastern sarus cranes (*Grus antigone sharpii*). More than 220 species of bird have been identified within the reserve, but ornithologists will be most interested in these rare red-headed cranes, which grow to an impressive 1.5m high. Seeing these birds, however, requires a considerable commitment (time, effort and money), so it's really for bird enthusiasts only.

The birds nest here from about December to May; from June to November they migrate to northwest Cambodia, so schedule your visit to coordinate with the birds' travel itinerary if you want to see them. The birds are early risers, though you might get a glimpse when they return home in the evening. During the day, the birds are engaged in the important business of eating.

Tam Nong is a sleepy town 45km from Cao Lanh. The one-way drive takes an hour by car. From Tam Nong it takes another hour by small boat (around 1,800,000d) to reach the area where the cranes live and another hour to return. Add to this whatever time you spend (perhaps an hour) staring at your feathered friends through binoculars (bring your own), and then the requisite two hours to return to Cao Lanh, depending on your mode of transport. There are a few rudimentary guesthouses in Tam Nong if you decide to stay late or hit the park early. Tam Nong shuts down early so if you want to eat dinner here, make arrangements before 5pm.

Sa Dec

☑067 / POP 108,000
The drowsy former capital of Dong Thap province, Sa Dec is a comparatively peaceful city of tree-lined streets and fading colonial

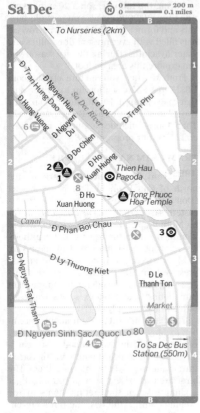

Sa Dec

ing but basic rooms here (US$22); shared bathrooms are located at the rear of the property.

Huong Pagoda PAGODA
(Chua Huong; Đ Hung Vuong) Chua Huong, the Perfume Pagoda, was built in a classic Chinese style in 1838. Marguerite Duras fans should seek out the shrine of Huynh Thuy Le, the real-life inspiration for the lover in her book – although you may find it hard to tell from the photos of the septuagenarian and his wife.

A bright white statue of Quan The Am Bo Tat stands on a pedestal between this and the adjacent **Buu Quang Pagoda**, which is somewhat less glamorous.

Nurseries NURSERIES
(Vuon hoa; ⊙8-11am & 1-5pm) The nurseries operate year-round, though they are practically stripped bare of their flowers just before the Tet festival. Domestic tourists from HCMC arrive in droves on Sundays and the nurseries are a major sightseeing attraction around the Tet holiday. There are many small operators lining the river and canals here, each with a different speciality. It's interesting to swing by in the morning and watch the plants being loaded on to boats.

🛏 **Sleeping & Eating**
Not many foreigners overnight in Sa Dec, but there are some hotels if you get stuck. There are a few good **noodle-soup shops** (soups around 15,000d) on Đ Hung Vuong.

Phuong Nam HOTEL $
(☑386 7867; hotelphuongnam@yahoo.com; 384A Đ Nguyen Sinh Sac; r 180,000-300,000d; 🟦🖧) For a mini-hotel this well-tended establishment on the highway is verging on stylish. Rooms

villas, ringed with orchards and flower markets. It has a minor claim to fame as the setting for *The Lover,* a semi-autobiographical novel by Marguerite Duras, made into a film by Jean-Jacques Annaud.

Groups doing a whirlwind tour of the Mekong Delta often make a lunch stop here and drop in on the nurseries.

⊙ **Sights**

Huynh Thuy Le Old House HISTORIC BUILDING
(Nha Co Huynh Thuy Le; ☑093-953 3523; 225A Đ Nguyen Hue; entry 10,000d) This wonderfully atmospheric 1895 house on the riverfront was once the residence of Huynh Thuy Le, the 27-year-old son of a rich Chinese family who Marguerite Duras had an affair with in 1929 when she was only 15 – immortalising the romance in *The Lover.* The house is a Sino-French design with intricate interior woodwork and original tiled floors. It's possible to stay overnight in one of two charm-

range from small cheapies with a tiny bathroom and a balcony, to large rooms with wooden floors.

Bong Hong Hotel   HOTEL $

(☑386 8288; bonghonghotel@yahoo.com.vn; 251A Đ Nguyen Sinh Sac; r with fan US$10, with air-con US$16-22, ste US$32; ✳@☎) The upper rooms with balconies are the most appealing at this large, cheerless hotel. Breakfast is included and there are tennis courts next door.

Sa Dec Hotel   HOTEL $

(☑386 1430; sadechotel@yahoo.com.vn; 108/5A Đ Hung Vuong; r with fan US$9, with air-con US$14-16, ste US$25; ✳@☎) A perfectly adequate government-owned pad with a slightly groovalicious 1970s feel to architecture. Rooms are by no means flash and bathrooms are basic, but some have bathtubs and balconies.

Quan Com Thuy   VIETNAMESE $

(☑386 1644; 439 Đ Hung Vuong; mains 15,000-30,000đ) One of the few restaurants in town, this reputable meat-and-rice joint feels a little like a family lounge room, with a votive shrine and a TV in the corner.

❶ Getting There & Away

Sa Dec is midway between Vinh Long, Chau Doc and Long Xuyen – although getting to the latter two requires a ferry crossing. **Sa Dec Bus Station** (Ben Xe Sa Dec) is on Hwy 80, immediately southeast of the centre. Services head to Vinh Long (9000đ) and Cao Lanh (15,000đ).

Siem Reap & the Temples of Angkor

Cambodia Fast Facts

» **Area** 181,035 sq km

» **Border Crossings with Vietnam** eight

» **Capital** Phnom Penh

» **Country Code** ☑855

» **Head of State** King Sihamoni

» **Population** 15 million

» **Money** US$1 = 4000r (riel)

» **National Holiday** *Chaul Chnam* or Khmer New Year, mid-April

» **Phrases** *sua s'dei* (hello), *lia suhn hao-y* (goodbye), *aw kohn* (thank you)

Why Go?

Where to begin with Angkor? There is no greater concentration of architectural riches anywhere on earth. Choose from the world's largest religious building, Angkor Wat, one of the world's weirdest, Bayon or the riotous jungle of Ta Prohm. All are global icons and have helped put Cambodia on the map as the temple capital of Asia. Today, the monuments are a point of pilgrimage for all Khmers, and no traveller to the region will want to miss their extravagant beauty. Many visitors to Vietnam continue their trip into Cambodia to visit these fabled temples.

Despite the headlining act that is Angkor and the contemporary chic of Siem Reap, Cambodia's greatest treasure is its people. The Khmers have been to hell and back, but they have prevailed with a smile and no visitor comes away from this enigmatic kingdom without a measure of admiration and affection for its inhabitants.

When to Go
Siem Reap

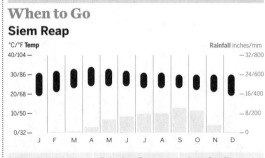

Dec–Jan Humidity is low, there's little rain and cool breezes. Peak season for visitors.

Feb–Jun Temperatures rise and in May or June the monsoon brings rain and humidity.

Jun–Oct The wet season: Angkor is surrounded by lush foliage and the moats are full of water.

SIEM REAP

♪063 / POP 119,500

Life-support system for the temples of Angkor, Siem Reap (see-em ree-ep) is the epicentre of the new Cambodia, a pulsating place that's one of the most popular destinations on the planet right now. At heart though, Siem Reap – whose name rather undiplomatically means 'Siamese Defeated' – is still a little charmer, with old French shophouses, shady tree-lined boulevards and a slow-flow river.

⊙ Sights

Angkor National Museum   MUSEUM
(www.angkornationalmuseum.com; 968 Charles de Gaulle Blvd; adult US$12, child under 1.2m US$6, audio guide US$3; ⊙8.30am-6pm) A worthwhile introduction to the glories of the Khmer empire, this state-of-the-art museum helps define Angkor's historic, religious and cultural significance. Displays include 1400 exquisite stone carvings and artefacts.

Les Chantiers Écoles   CULTURAL CENTRE
(Puok Village; ⊙7am-5pm Mon-Fri, 7am-noon Sat) Tucked down a side road, this silk farm teaches traditional Khmer artisanship, including lacquer making and wood- and stone-carving, to impoverished youngsters; tours of the workshops are possible when school is in session. On the premises is an exquisite shop, Artisans d'Angkor. To see the entire silk-making process, from mulberry trees to silk worms and spinning to weaving, visit Les Chantiers Écoles' **silk farm** (⊙7.30am-5.30pm), 16km west of town. Shuttle buses leave the school at 9.30am and 1.30pm daily for a three-hour tour.

Cambodian Cultural Village CULTURAL CENTRE
(Map p419; www.cambodianculturalvillage.com; NH6; foreigner/Khmer US$11/4, child under 12 US$2; ⊙8am-7pm Mon-Thu, to 8.30pm Fri-Sun) This place aims to represent all of Cambodia in a whirlwind tour of recreated houses and villages. It may be kitsch, but it's very popular with Cambodians, and the dance and music performances will delight the kiddies.

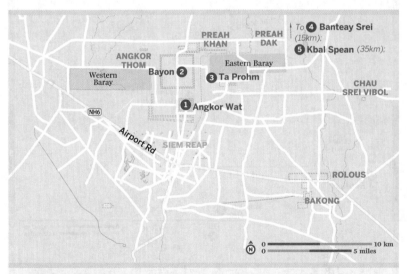

Angkor Highlights

❶ See the sun rise over one of the world's most iconic buildings, the one and only **Angkor Wat** (p418)

❷ Contemplate the serenity and splendour of the **Bayon** (p419), its 216 enigmatic faces staring out into the jungle

❸ Witness nature running riot at the mysterious ruin of **Ta Prohm** (p423), the *Tomb Raider* temple

❹ Stare in wonder at the delicate carvings adorning **Banteay Srei** (p424), the finest seen at Angkor

❺ Trek deep into the jungle to discover the River of a Thousand Lingas at **Kbal Spean** (p424)

Siem Reap

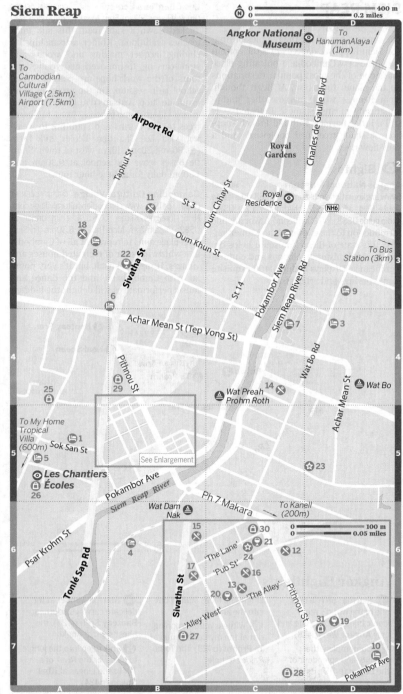

Angkor National Museum

To HanumanAlaya (1km)

To Cambodian Cultural Village (2.5km); Airport (7.5km)

Airport Rd

Taphul St

St 3

Oum Chhay St

Royal Gardens

Charles de Gaulle Blvd

Royal Residence

NH6

11

18

8

22

Sivatha St

Oum Khun St

St 14

2

To Bus Station (3km)

9

6

Achar Mean St (Tep Vong St)

Pokambor Ave

Siem Reap River Rd

7

3

Wat Bo Rd

Pithnou St

29

14

Wat Preah Prohm Roth

Achar Mean St

Wat Bo

25

To My Home Tropical Villa (600m)

Sok San St

1

5

23

Les Chantiers Écoles

26

Pokambor Ave

Siem Reap River

Ph. 7 Makara

To Kanell (200m)

Wat Dam Nak

Psar Krohm St

Tonlé Sap Rd

4

15

30

0   100 m
0   0.05 miles

Sivatha St

17

21

'The Lane'

24

12

'Pub St'

16

13

20

'The Alley'

Pithnou St

'Alley West'

31

19

27

10

28

Pokambor Ave

Siem Reap

🛏 Sleeping

Siem Reap offers everything from US$3 shacks with shared toilets to five-star luxury palaces. For more recommended guesthouses and hotels in Siem Reap, visit www.hotels .lonelyplanet.com.

TOP CHOICE La Résidence d'Angkor BOUTIQUE HOTEL **$$$**
(📞963390; www.residencedangkor.com; Siem Reap River Rd; r from US$225; ❄@🛜🏊) The wood-appointed rooms, among the most tasteful and inviting in town, come with verandahs and huge jacuzzi-sized tubs. The new wing includes superb suites and the striking Kong Kea Spa.

TOP CHOICE My Home Tropical Garden Villa GUESTHOUSE **$**
(📞760035; www.myhomecambodia.com; Psar Khrom; r US$12-26; ❄@🛜🏊) With hotel standards at guesthouse prices, this is a fine place to rest your head. The decor includes subtle silks and the furnishings are tasteful.

Seven Candles Guesthouse GUESTHOUSE **$**
(📞963380; www.sevencandlesguesthouse.com; 307 Wat Bo Rd; r US$10-20; ❄@🛜) An original guesthouse with rooms that include hot water, TV and fridge. Profits help the Ponheary Ly Foundation, which seeks to promote education in rural communities.

Frangipani Villa Hotel BOUTIQUE HOTEL **$$**
(📞963030; www.frangipanihotel.com; Wat Bo Rd; r US$30-60; ❄@🛜🏊) One of the better-value budget boutique hotels in Siem Reap. The contemporary rooms have clean lines and bright spaces, plus there's a courtyard pool.

Hotel de la Paix HOTEL **$$$**
(📞966000; www.hoteldelapaixangkor.com; Sivatha St; r from US$205; ❄@🛜🏊) This place is all about funky contemporary design, trendy interiors and minimalist style. Rooms include open-plan bathrooms and iPods.

HanumanAlaya BOUTIQUE HOTEL **$$$**
(📞760582; www.hanumanalaya.com; off Charles De Gaulle Blvd; r US$60-100; ❄@🛜🏊) Billing itself as 'Angkor's boutique residence', this traditional Khmer-style resort is a home away from home thanks to its friendly staff.

Shadow of Angkor Guesthouse GUESTHOUSE **$**
(📞964774; www.shadowofangkor.com; 353 Pokambor Ave; r US$15-25; ❄@🛜) In a grand old French-era building overlooking the river, this friendly 15-room place offers affordable air-con and free internet.

Golden Banana BOUTIQUE HOTEL $$
(☎012-885366; www.goldenbanana.info; Wat Dam-nak area; r US$48-98; ❄@🖥🛋) A mellow place with two incarnations: a 10-room boutique hotel and a 16-room boutique resort, both gay-friendly and very popular.

Encore Angkor Guesthouse GUESTHOUSE $$
(☎969400; www.encoreangkor.com; 456 Sok San St; r US$20-50; ❄@🖥🛋) The stylish lobby

sets the tone for a budget boutique experience. Rooms include all the usual touches, plus oversized beds and in-room safes.

Golden Temple Villa HOTEL $
(☎012-943459; www.goldentemplevilla.com; off Sivatha St; r US$13-23; ❄@🖥) Readers love this place thanks to its funky colourful decor and fun outlook. It's surrounded by a lush garden, and there's also a small bar-restaurant.

VIETNAM–CAMBODIA RELATIONS

Entering Cambodia from Vietnam is a leap from a powerhouse economy into one of Southeast Asia's poorest nations. Though chaotic, Saigon and Hanoi feel downright urban and orderly compared to less-developed Siem Reap.

As any proud Cambodian might tell you, Vietnam wasn't always economically superior. Cambodia's Khmer empire once controlled much of mainland Southeast Asia, including the ports of Saigon. By the 1800s however, Vietnam's political dominance was established and Cambodia came under its power.

The French later occupied both countries but favoured Vietnamese workers and bureaucrats. Though the colonialists were driven out in 1954, the 20th century's latter half brought more war – this time proxy conflicts fed by China, the US and the Soviet Union. During the American War – in a period when Cambodia was backed by the US – American planes heavily bombed its countryside to wipe out communist guerrillas. This didn't work. A sect of hardline China-backed communists, the Khmer Rogue, overran the weak US-allied government in 1975 to found a Communist regime that went on to become one of the most notorious dictatorships of the 20th century.

By 1975 both Vietnam and Cambodia had birthed communist independence movements. But despite their ideological kinship, the ancient feud didn't die, and in the late 1970s Cambodia's Khmer Rouge under Pol Pot attempted to retake land lost to Vietnam centuries before, beginning with Phu Quoc Island and later mounting a series of short-lived invasions in Vietnam's Dong Thap Province.

The Vietnamese responded by invading and occupying Cambodia for 10 years and installing supplicant Cambodian leaders. Many of the same individuals remain in power there today.

Leaders in both countries now speak of brotherhood between the nations, but you may hear regular Cambodians on the street speaking of Vietnam as the bully next door, and Vietnamese colloquially speaking of Cambodia as a 'little brother'. Despite this sibling rivalry, Cambodia and Vietnam share plenty of cultural common ground. Gesturing with feet, for example, is taboo. Elders are revered. Both cultures prefer to tiptoe around social confrontation and angry outbursts are regarded as a lapse into insanity.

Differences in the home, however, are more pronounced. Swayed by Confucianism, many Vietnamese worship long-dead ancestors. Cambodians usually honour only their immediate family. Vietnam's 'two-child' laws have also kept families smaller than those in Cambodia, where more children mean more hands to support the family.

In contrast to the go-getter vibe in Saigon and Hanoi, Siem Reap still oozes laid-back warmth, but Cambodia is slowly becoming more like its rival. Visitors expecting a crumbling backwater will be taken aback by Siem Reap's deluxe new resorts and chic lounges. Though you'll still hear roosters crowing, you might also find a KFC up the block.

On the street, the ever-growing tourism wave is exposing all walks of Cambodian life to outsiders. Though Cambodians openly grumble about Vietnam, the kingdom is following in its footsteps: shaking off a tragic past, welcoming global trade and sprouting office towers from a sea of tin-roof shacks. Vietnam may think of Cambodia as a 'little brother', but it must concede its sibling is growing by the day.

By Patrick Winn – Southeast Asia Correspondent, Global Post

✗ Eating

Worthy restaurants are sprinkled all around town but Siem Reap's culinary heart is the Psar Chaa area, whose focal point, the Alley, is literally lined with mellow eateries offering great atmosphere. Cheap eats can be found at the nearby local food stalls (Pub St; mains 4000-8000r; ⊘4pm-3am), around Pub St's western end.

For self-caterers, markets have fruit and vegies. Angkor Market (Sivatha St; ⊘7.30am-10pm) can supply international treats such as olives and cheeses.

TOP CHOICE Blue Pumpkin INTERNATIONAL $
(Pithnou St; mains US$2-6; ⊘6am-10pm; ❅☎) Downstairs it looks like any old cafe, albeit with a delightful selection of cakes, breads and homemade ice cream. Upstairs is another world of white minimalism, with beds to lounge on and free wi-fi.

Le Tigre de Papier INTERNATIONAL $
(Pub St; Khmer mains US$3-6.50; ⊘24hr; ☎) This established spot has a wood-fired oven and a great menu of Italian, French and Khmer food. There's also affordable cooking classes.

Sugar Palm CAMBODIAN $$
(Taphul St; mains US$5-8; ⊘11.30am-3pm & 5.30-10pm) Set in a beautiful wooden house, this is an excellent place to sample traditional flavours infused with herbs and spices.

Sala Bai INTERNATIONAL $$
(☏963329; www.salabai.com; Taphul St; set lunches US$8; ⊘noon-2pm Mon-Fri) This school trains young Khmers in the art of hospitality and serves an affordable menu of Western and Cambodian cuisine.

Le Café INTERNATIONAL $
(Wat Bo area; mains US$3.75-5; ⊘7.30am-8pm; ☎) Brings five-star, Sofitel-inspired sandwiches, salads and shakes to the French Cultural Centre.

Cambodian BBQ CAMBODIAN $$
(The Alley; mains US$5.50-8.75; ⊘11am-11pm; ☎) Crocodile, snake, ostrich and kangaroo meat add an exotic twist to the traditional *phnom pleung* ('hill of fire') grills.

Chamcar VEGETARIAN $
(The Alley; mains US$3-5; ⊘11am-11pm, closed Sun lunch; ☎) The name translates as 'farm' and the supplies must be coming from a pretty impressive organic vegetable supplier, given the creative Asian dishes on the menu here.

Le Malraux FRENCH $$
(155 Sivatha St; mains US$5-15; ⊘7am-1am; ☎) A good spot for gastronomes, this classy art deco cafe-restaurant offers fine French food and some local Cambodian specialities.

Kanell INTERNATIONAL $$
(www.kanellrestaurant.com; 7 Makara St; mains US$5-15; ⊘11am-midnight; ☎✺) Set in a handsome Khmer villa on the edge of town, Kanell offers extensive gardens and a swimming pool for those seeking to dine and unwind.

🍷 Drinking

Siem Reap is now firmly on Southeast Asia's nightlife map, with many of the most interesting places situated in the vicinity of Psar Chaa, on or near Pub St or the Alley.

Warehouse BAR
(Pithnou St; ⊘10.30am-3am; ☎) At this popular bar opposite Psar Chaa, enjoy indie anthems, table football, a pool table and devilish drinks.

Laundry Bar LOUNGE BAR
(off Pithnou St, Psar Chaa area; ⊘1pm-3am) One of the most alluring bars in town thanks to discerning decor, low lighting and a laid-back soundtrack. Happy hour is 5.30pm to 9pm.

Linga Bar LOUNGE BAR
(www.lingabar.com; The Alley; ⊘10am-about 1am; ☎) This chic gay bar, colourful, cool and contemporary, has a relaxed atmosphere and a cracking cocktail list.

Miss Wong LOUNGE BAR
(The Lane; ⊘6pm-late) Miss Wong carries you back to the chic of 1920s Shanghai and is famous for its sophisticated cocktails.

Nest BAR
(Sivatha St; ⊘4pm-late; ☎) A memorable bar thanks to its sweeping sail-like shelters and stylish seating. This place has one of the hippest cocktail lists in town.

☆ Entertainment

Classical dance shows take place all over town, but only a few are worth considering.

Apsara Theatre CLASSICAL DANCE
(www.angkorvillage.com; off Wat Bo Rd; show incl dinner US$22) Nightly performances in a *wat*-style wooden pavilion opposite Angkor Village.

La Résidence d'Angkor CLASSICAL DANCE
(Siem Reap River Rd; admission free, mains US$12-25; ⊘8pm Tue, Thu & Sat) Try the Dining Room

at La Résidence for fine food and authentic dance performances, with shadow puppetry on alternate nights.

Temple Club CLASSICAL DANCE
(Pub St; dance show incl buffet US$5) A very popular bar-restaurant that offers the best value classical dance show in town. Performances upstairs.

🛍 Shopping

Siem Reap has an excellent selection of Cambodian-made handicrafts. Psar Chaa is well stocked with anything you may want to buy in Cambodia, and lots you don't. There are bargains to be had if you haggle patiently and humorously. **Angkor Night Market** (www.angkornightmarket.com; near Sivatha St; ☉4pm-midnight) is packed with silks, handicrafts and souvenirs. Up-and-coming Alley West is also a great strip to browse.

A number of shops support Cambodia's disabled and disenfranchised.

Artisans d'Angkor HANDICRAFTS
(www.artisansdangkor.com; off Sivatha St; ☉7.30am-7.30pm) One of the best places in Cambodia for quality souvenirs and gifts – everything from silk clothing and accessories to elegant reproductions of Angkorian-era statuary.

Keo Kjay CLOTHING
(www.keokjay.org; Alley West; ☉11am-10pm) Translating as 'fresh' in Khmer, this hip little boutique is a fair-trade fashion enterprise that aims to provide HIV-positive women with a sustainable income.

Rajana HANDICRAFTS
(www.rajanacrafts.org; Sivatha St; ☉8am-10pm Mon-Sat, 2-10pm Sun) Sells fair-trade silk, silver jewellery and handmade cards.

Samatoa CLOTHING
(Pithnou St; ☉8am-11pm) Fair-trade fashion: select designer clothes finished in silk, with the option of a tailored fit in 48 hours.

Senteurs d'Angkor BEAUTY
(www.senteursdangkor.com; Pithnou St; ☉7am-10pm) Cambodia's answer to the Body Shop, this place offers natural beauty products, massage oils, spices, coffees and teas.

ℹ Information

Pick up the free *Siem Reap Angkor Visitors Guide* (www.canbypublications.com) or the two handy booklets produced by *Pocket Guide Cambodia* (www.cambodiapocketguide.com), or look them up online.

There are ATMs at the airport and in banks and minimarts all over central Siem Reap, especially along Sivatha Blvd. The greatest concentration of internet shops is along Sivatha Blvd and around Psar Chaa.

Royal Angkor International Hospital (☎761888; www.royalangkorhospital.com; NH6) A modern, international-standard facility affiliated with the Bangkok Hospital.

Tourist police (☎097-778 0013) At the main Angkor ticket checkpoint.

ℹ Getting There & Away

There are two main options for travelling between Vietnam and Cambodia. Air travel is more convenient and there are daily flight connections between both Ho Chi Minh City (HCMC)and Hanoi and Siem Reap. Road travel is a more daunting prospect as it takes an entire day to travel direct between HCMC and Siem Reap, including a change of bus in Phnom Penh. However, it is easy enough to break the journey in the lively Cambodian capital for a night or two.

Air

Siem Reap International Airport (www.cambodia-airports.com) is verging on the boutique and is a very stylish facility in which to arrive. It is 7km west of the centre. Vietnam Airlines offers regular daily connections between Siem Reap and HCMC (one-way from US$135, five daily) or Hanoi (from US$195, four daily). Silk Air also offers two flights a week connecting Siem Reap and Danang (from US$243). For details of Vietnam Airlines offices in Vietnamese cities, see the relevant sections in this book.

VISAS FOR CAMBODIA

For most nationalities, one-month tourist visas (US$20) are available on arrival at Siem Reap and Phnom Penh airports and all land border crossings. One passport-sized photo is required. One-month tourist e-visas (US$20 plus a US$5 processing fee), which take three business days to issue and are valid for entry to Cambodia at the airports and the Bavet–Moc Bai border crossing with Vietnam, are available at www.mfaic.gov.kh.

Anyone planning a side trip to the temples of Angkor and then returning to Vietnam will need a multiple-entry Vietnam visa or will need to arrange another visa while in Cambodia. Re-entry visas are no longer available in Vietnam.

Airlines servicing Siem Reap for onward travel from Cambodia include the following:

Air Asia (www.airasia.com) To Bangkok and Kuala Lumpur.

Bangkok Airways (www.bangkokair.com) To Bangkok.

Cambodia Angkor Air (www.cambodiaangkor air.com) To Saigon; code shares with Vietnam Airlines.

Dragonair (www.dragonair.com) To Hong Kong.

Jetstar Asia (www.jetstarasia.com) To Singapore.

Lao Airlines (www.laos-airlines.com) To Luang Prabang and Pakse.

Silk Air (www.silkair.com) To Singapore and Danang.

Vietnam Airlines (www.vietnamairlines.com) To Hanoi, Ho Chi Minh City and Luang Prabang.

Bus

Most travellers use international buses between HCMC and Phnom Penh, crossing at the Moc Bai (Vietnam)–Bavet (Cambodia) border. Buses take about six hours or so, including border crossing formalities. Tickets usually cost US$10 to US$12. There are regular services throughout the day between 6am and about 2pm in both directions. Buses leave from the Pham Ngu Lao area of Ho Chi Minh City. In Phnom Penh, they arrive and depart from various bus offices around the city, including the following popular operators:

Capitol Tour (☎217627; 14 St 182)

Mai Linh (☎211888; 391 Sihanouk Blvd)

Mekong Express (☎427518; 87 Sisowath Quay)

Sapaco (☎210300; 307 Sihanouk Blvd)

In theory it is possible to connect the same day with a change of bus in Phnom Penh, but this is easier travelling from Ho Chi Minh City to Siem Reap as opposed to the other direction, as Phnom Penh to Siem Reap services operate later in the afternoon.

Tickets between Siem Reap and Phnom Penh (six hours) cost US$5 to US$11, depending on the level of service (air-con, leg room, a toilet, a host).

There is also a night bus between Phnom Penh and Siem Reap operated by **Virak Buntham** (☎016-786270; St 106). This service starts in Sihanoukville and usually passes through Phnom Penh around 11.30pm.

In Siem Reap, all buses depart from the bus station, which is 3km east of town and about 200m south of NH6. Tickets are available at guesthouses, hotels, bus offices, travel agencies and ticket kiosks. Some bus companies send a minibus around to pick up passengers at their place of lodging. Upon your arrival in Siem Reap, be prepared for a rugby scrum of eager *moto* (motorbike taxi) drivers when you get off the bus.

🛈 Getting Around

From the airport, an official *moto*/taxi/van costs US$2/7/8; *remork-motos* (tuk-tuk; US$4 or US$5) are available outside the terminal. From the bus station, a *moto/remork* to the city centre should cost about US$1/2.

Short *moto* trips around the centre of town cost 2000r or 3000r (US$1 at night). A *remork* should be about double that, more with lots of people.

For information on getting to and from the temples, see Exploring the Temples on p422.

AROUND SIEM REAP

Cambodia Landmine Museum

The nonprofit **Cambodia Landmine museum** (www.cambodialandminemuseum.org; Banteay Srei District; admission US$1; ⊙7am-6pm) is popular with travellers thanks to its informative displays on Cambodia's enemy within. It has a mock minefield where visitors can search for deactivated mines. Situated about 25km from Siem Reap and 6km south of Banteay Srei temple.

Chong Kneas

The floating village commune of Chong Kneas is now so popular with visitors that it's become something of a floating scam, at least insofar as hiring a boat (US$13 or more per person for 1½ hours) is concerned. The small, floating **Gecko Environment Centre** (www.tsbr-ed.org; admission free; ⊙7am-4pm) has displays on the Tonlé Sap's remarkable annual cycle. By moto, the 11km trip to Chong Kneas costs US$3.

Kompong Pluk

For a floating village more memorable than Chong Kneas, but also harder to reach, head for the friendly village of Kompong Pluk, an other-worldly place built on soaring stilts. In the wet season you can explore the nearby flooded forest by canoe. To get here, either catch a boat (about US$55 return) at Chong Kneas or come via the small town of Roluos by a two-hour combination of road (about US$7 return by *moto*) and boat (US$20 for eight people).

THE HEARTBEAT OF CAMBODIA

The largest freshwater lake in Southeast Asia, the Tonlé Sap is an incredible natural phenomenon that provides fish and irrigation water for half of Cambodia's population.

The lake is linked to the Mekong at Phnom Penh by a 100km-long channel, the Tonlé Sap River. From mid-May to early October (the wet season), rains raise the level of the Mekong, backing up the Tonlé Sap River and causing it to flow northwest into the Tonlé Sap Lake. During this period, the lake swells from 2500 sq km to 13,000 sq km or more, its maximum depth increasing from about 2.2m to more than 10m. Around the start of October, as the water level of the Mekong begins to fall, the Tonlé Sap River reverses its flow, draining the waters of the lake back into the Mekong.

This extraordinary process makes the Tonlé Sap one of the world's richest sources of freshwater fish and an ideal habitat for water birds.

TEMPLES OF ANGKOR

Angkor is, quite literally, heaven on earth. It is the earthly representation of Mt Meru, the Mt Olympus of the Hindu faith and the abode of ancient gods. Angkor is the perfect fusion of creative ambition and spiritual devotion. The Cambodian 'god-kings' of old each strove to better their ancestors in size, scale and symmetry, culminating in the world's largest religious building, Angkor Wat.

The hundreds of temples surviving today are but the sacred skeleton of the vast political, religious and social centre of the ancient Khmer empire. Angkor was a city that, at its zenith, boasted a population of one million when London was an insignificant town of 50,000. The houses, public buildings and palaces of Angkor were constructed of wood – now long decayed – because the right to dwell in structures of brick or stone was reserved for the gods.

Angkor is one of the most impressive ancient sites on earth, the eighth wonder of the world, with the epic proportions of the Great Wall of China, the detail and intricacy of the Taj Mahal, and the symbolism and symmetry of the pyramids, all rolled into one.

Angkor Wat

The traveller's first glimpse of Angkor Wat, the ultimate expression of Khmer genius, is simply staggering and is matched by only a few select spots on earth such as Machu Picchu or Petra.

Soaring skyward and surrounded by a moat that would make its European castle counterparts blush, Angkor Wat is one of the most inspired and spectacular monuments ever conceived by the human mind. It is a sumptuous blend of form and function, a spellbinding shrine to Vishnu, its captivating image replicated in the reflective pools below, a feast for unbelieving eyes.

Like the other temple-mountains of Angkor, Angkor Wat replicates the spatial universe in miniature. The central tower is Mt Meru, with its surrounding smaller peaks, bounded in turn by continents (the lower courtyards) and the oceans (the moat). The seven-headed *naga* (mythical serpent) serves as a symbolic rainbow bridge for humans to reach the abode of the gods.

Angkor Wat is surrounded by a moat, 190m wide, which forms a giant rectangle measuring 1.5km by 1.3km. Stretching around the outside of the central temple complex is an 800m-long series of astonishing bas-reliefs, designed to be viewed in an anticlockwise direction. Rising 31m above the third level (and 55m above the ground) is the central tower, which gives the whole ensemble its sublime unity.

Angkor Wat was built by Suryavarman II (r 1112–52), who unified Cambodia and extended Khmer influence across much of mainland Southeast Asia. He also set himself apart religiously from earlier kings by his devotion to the Hindu deity Vishnu, to whom he consecrated the temple – built, coincidentally, around the same time as European Gothic cathedrals such as Notre-Dame and Chartres.

The upper level of Angkor Wat is once again open to modern pilgrims, but visits are strictly timed to 20 minutes.

Angkor Thom

It is hard to imagine any building bigger or more beautiful than Angkor Wat, but at

Angkor Thom the sum of the parts add up to a greater whole. It is the gates that grab you first, flanked by a monumental representation of the Churning of the Ocean of Milk, 54 demons and 54 gods engaged in an epic tug of war on the causeway. Each of the gates – **North**, **South**, **East**, **West** and **Victory** – towers above the visitor, the magnanimous faces of the Bodhisattva Avalokiteshvara staring out over the kingdom. Can you imagine being a peasant in the 13th century approaching the forbidding capital for the first time? It would have been an awe-inspiring yet unsettling experience to enter such a gateway and come face to face with the divine power of the god kings.

The last great capital of the Khmer empire, Angkor Thom took monumental to a whole new level, set over 10 sq km. Built in part as a reaction to the surprise sacking of Angkor by the Chams, Jayavarman VII (r 1181–1219) decided that his empire would never again be vulnerable at home. Beyond the formidable walls is a massive moat that would have stopped all but the hardiest invaders in their tracks.

◉ Sights

Bayon TEMPLE
Right at the heart of Angkor Thom is the Bayon, the mesmerising if slightly mindbending state temple of Jayavarman VII, epitomising the creative genius and inflated

The Temples of Angkor

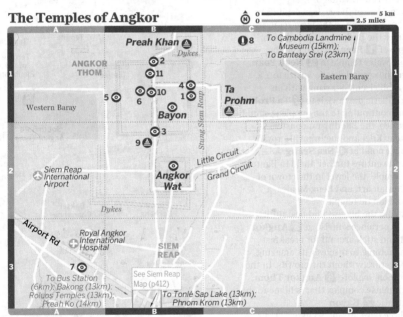

The Temples of Angkor

Temples of Angkor

THREE-DAY EXPLORATION

The temple complex at Angkor is simply enormous and the superlatives don't do it justice. This is the site of the world's largest religious building, a multitude of temples and a vast, long-abandoned walled city that was arguably Southeast Asia's first metropolis, long before Bangkok and Singapore got in on the action.

Starting at the Roluos group of temples, one of the earliest capitals of Angkor, move on to the big circuit, which includes the Buddhist-Hindu fusion temple of **1 Preah Khan** and the ornate water temple of **2 Neak Poan**.

On the second day downsize to the small circuit, starting with an atmospheric dawn visit to **3 Ta Prohm**, before continuing to the temple pyramid of Ta Keo, the Buddhist monastery of Banteay Kdei and the immense royal bathing pond of **4 Sra Srang**.

Next venture further afield to Banteay Srei temple, the jewel in the crown of Angkorian art, and Beng Mealea, a remote jungle temple.

Saving the biggest and best until last, experience sunrise at **5 Angkor Wat** and stick around for breakfast in the temple to discover its amazing architecture without the crowds. In the afternoon, explore **6 Angkor Thom**, an immense complex that is home to the enigmatic **7 Bayon**.

Three days around Angkor? That's just for starters.

TOP TIPS

» **Dodging the Crowds** Early morning at Ta Prohm, post sunrise at Angkor Wat and lunchtime at Banteay Srei does the trick.

» **Extended Explorations** Three-day passes can now be used on non-consecutive days over the period of a week but be sure to request this.

Bayon
The surreal state temple of legendary king Jayavarman VII, where 216 faces bear down on pilgrims, asserting religious and regal authority.

Terrace of the Leper King

Preah Palilay

Phimeanakas Temple

Tep Pranar

West Gate Angkor Thom

Baphuon Temple

Terrace of the Elephants

South Gate Angkor Thom

Phnom Bakheng

Baksei Chamrong

Beng Mealea

Angkor Wat
The world's largest religious building. Experience sunrise at the holiest of holies, then explore the beautiful bas-reliefs – devotion etched in stone.

Angkor Thom
The last great capital of the Khmer empire conceals a wealth of temples and its epic proportions would have inspired and terrified in equal measure.

Preah Khan
A fusion temple dedicated to Buddha, Brahma, Shiva and Vishnu; the immense corridors are like an unending hall of mirrors.

Neak Poan
If Vegas ever adopts the Angkor theme, this will be the swimming pool, a petite tower set in a lake, surrounded by four smaller ponds.

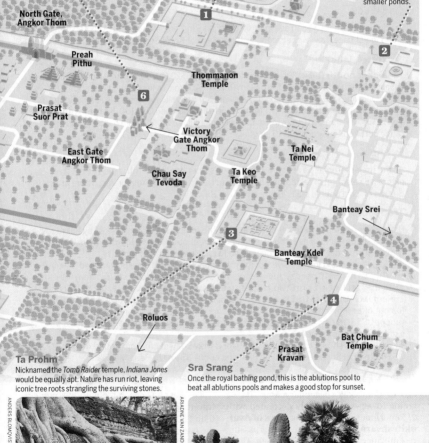

North Gate, Angkor Thom

Preah Pithu

Prasat Suor Prat

Thommanon Temple

East Gate Angkor Thom

← **Victory Gate Angkor Thom**

Chau Say Tevoda

Ta Keo Temple

Ta Nei Temple

Banteay Srei →

Banteay Kdei Temple

↙ **Roluos**

Prasat Kravan

Bat Chum Temple

Ta Prohm
Nicknamed the *Tomb Raider* temple, *Indiana Jones* would be equally apt. Nature has run riot, leaving iconic tree roots strangling the surviving stones.

Sra Srang
Once the royal bathing pond, this is the ablutions pool to beat all ablutions pools and makes a good stop for sunset.

EXPLORING THE TEMPLES

One Day

Hit Angkor Wat for sunrise, after which you can explore the mighty temple while it's still quiet. From there continue to Ta Prohm before breaking for lunch. In the afternoon, explore the temples within the walled city of Angkor Thom and the beauty of the Bayon in the late afternoon light.

Three Days

After the first action-packed day, beat the tourists to beautiful Banteay Srei, with a quick stop at Preah Khan along the way. Then make your way to the River of a Thousand Lingas at Kbal Spean. On the third day, head out to the Roluos area and then back to Angkor Wat and Angkor Thom for another look.

One Week

In addition to what you can see in three days, take in Beng Mealea and even Koh Ker. For a change of pace, take a boat to the watery village of Kompong Pluk (p417).

Tickets & Guides

The **ticket booth** (1-day/3-day/1-week tourist pass US$20/40/60, children under 12 free; ⊘5am-5.30pm) is on the road from Siem Reap to Angkor. Tickets issued after 5pm (for sunset viewing) are valid the next day. Tickets are not valid for Phnom Kulen or Beng Mealea. Get caught ticketless in a temple and you'll be fined US$100. **Khmer Angkor Tour Guide Association** (www.khmerangkortourguide.com; ⊘7-11am & 2-5pm) can arrange certified tour guides in 10 languages (US$25 to US$50 a day).

Eating

All the major temples have some sort of nourishment near the entrance. The most extensive selection of restaurants is opposite the entrance to Angkor Wat. There are dozens of local noodle stalls just north of the Bayon.

Transport

Bicycles are a great way to get to and around the temples, which are linked by flat roads in good shape. Various guesthouses and hotels rent out **White Bicycles** (www.thewhite bicycles.org; per day US$2) and proceeds go to local development projects.

Motos, zippy and inexpensive, are the most popular form of transport around the temples (US$8 to US$10 per day, more for distant sites). Drivers accost visitors from the moment they set foot in Siem Reap, but they often end up being knowledgeable and friendly.

Remorks (US$12 to US$15 a day, more for distant sites) take a little longer than *motos* but offer protection from the rain and sun. Even more protection is offered by cars (about US$30 a day, more for distant sites), though these tend to isolate you from the sights, sounds and smells.

Hiring a car should cost about US$30 for a whole day of cruising around Angkor, US$45 to Kbal Spean and Banteay Srei, and about US$70 to Beng Mealea.

ego of Cambodia's legendary king. Its 54 gothic towers are famously decorated with 216 enormous, coldly smiling **faces of Avalokiteshvara** that bear more than a passing resemblance to the great king himself. These huge visages glare down from every angle, exuding power and control with a hint of humanity – precisely the blend required to hold sway over such a vast empire, ensuring that disparate and far-flung populations yielded to the monarch's magnanimous will.

The Bayon is decorated with 1.2km of extraordinary **bas-reliefs** incorporating more than 11,000 figures. The famous carvings on the outer wall of the first level vividly depict everyday life in 12th-century Cambodia.

Baphuon
TEMPLE

About 200m northwest of Bayon, the Baphuon is a pyramidal representation of mythical Mt Meru that marked the centre of the city that existed before the construction of Angkor

Thom. Restoration efforts were disrupted by the Cambodian civil war and all records were destroyed during the Khmer Rouge years, leaving French experts with the world's largest jigsaw puzzle. On the western side, the retaining wall of the second level was fashioned – apparently in the 15th or 16th century – into a reclining Buddha 60m in length.

Terrace of Elephants HISTORIC BUILDING
The 350m-long Terrace of Elephants – decorated with parading elephants towards both ends – was used as a giant viewing stand for public ceremonies and served as a base for the king's grand audience hall. As you stand here, try to imagine the pomp and grandeur of the Khmer empire at its height, with infantry, cavalry, horse-drawn chariots and, of course, elephants parading across the Central Square in a colourful procession, pennants and standards aloft.

Terrace of the Leper King HISTORIC BUILDING
The Terrace of the Leper King, just north of the Terrace of Elephants, is a 7m-high platform. On top of the platform stands a nude, though sexless, statue, another of Angkor's mysteries. Legend has it that at least two of the Angkor kings had leprosy. More likely it is Yama, the god of death, and that the Terrace of the Leper King housed the royal crematorium.

Around Angkor Thom
TA PROHM
The ultimate *Indiana Jones* fantasy, Ta Prohm is cloaked in dappled shadow, its crumbling towers and walls locked in the slow muscular embrace of vast root systems. If Angkor Wat, the Bayon and other temples are testimony to the genius of the ancient Khmers, Ta Prohm reminds us equally of the awesome fecundity and power of the jungle. There is a poetic cycle to this venerable ruin, with humanity first conquering nature to rapidly create, and nature once again conquering humanity to slowly destroy.

Built from 1186 and originally known as Rajavihara (Monastery of the King), Ta Prohm was a Buddhist temple dedicated to the mother of Jayavarman VII. Ta Prohm is a temple of towers, close courtyards and narrow corridors. Ancient trees tower overhead, their leaves filtering the sunlight and casting a greenish pall over the whole scene. It is the closest most of us will get to feeling the magic of the explorers of old.

PHNOM BAKHENG
Around 400m south of Angkor Thom, this hill's main draw is the sunset view of Angkor Wat, though this has turned into something of a circus, with hundreds of visitors jockeying for space. The temple, built by Yasovarman I (r 889–910), has five tiers, with seven levels.

PREAH KHAN
The temple of Preah Khan (Sacred Sword) is one of the largest complexes at Angkor, a maze of vaulted corridors, fine carvings and lichen-clad stonework. Constructed by Jayavarman VII, it covers a very large area, but the temple itself is within a rectangular wall of around 700m by 800m. Preah Khan is a genuine fusion temple, the eastern entrance dedicated to Mahayana Buddhism with equal-sized doors, and the other cardinal directions dedicated to Shiva, Vishnu and Brahma with successively smaller doors, emphasising the unequal nature of Hinduism.

NEAK POAN
Another late-12th-century work of – no surprises here – Jayavarman VII, this petite

---

ON LOCATION WITH TOMB RAIDER

Several sequences for *Tomb Raider* (2001), starring Angelina Jolie as Lara Croft, were shot around the temples of Angkor. The Cambodia shoot opened at Phnom Bakheng with Lara looking through binoculars for the mysterious temple. The baddies were already trying to break in through the East Gate of Angkor Thom, by pulling down a giant polystyrene apsara statue. Reunited with her custom Landrover, Lara made a few laps around the Bayon before discovering a back way into the temple from Ta Prohm, where she plucked a sprig of jasmine and fell through into...Pinewood Studios. After battling a living statue and dodging Daniel Craig (aka 007) by diving off the waterfall at Phnom Kulen, she emerged in a floating market in front of Angkor Wat, as you do. She came ashore here before borrowing a mobile phone from a local monk and venturing into the temple, where she was healed by the abbot.

Nick Ray worked as Location Manager for Tomb Raider in Cambodia

temple just east of Preah Khan has a large square pool surrounded by four smaller square pools, with a circular 'island' in the middle. Water once flowed from the central pond into the four peripheral pools via four ornamental spouts, in the form of an elephant's head, a horse's head, a lion's head and a human head.

ROLUOS GROUP
The monuments of Roluos, which served as Indravarman I's (r 877–89) capital, are among the earliest large permanent temples built by the Khmers and mark the dawn of Khmer classical art. **Preah Ko**, dedicated to Shiva, has elaborate inscriptions in Sanskrit on the doorposts of each tower and some of the best surviving examples of Angkorian plasterwork. The city's central temple, **Bakong**, with its five-tier central pyramid of sandstone, is a representation of Mt Meru. Roluos is 13km east of Siem Reap along NH6.

BANTEAY SREI
Considered by many to be the jewel in the crown of Angkorian art, Banteay Srei – a Hindu temple dedicated to Shiva – is cut from stone of a pinkish hue and includes some of the finest stone carving anywhere on earth. Begun in AD 967, it is one of the few temples around Angkor not to be commissioned by a king, but by a Brahman, perhaps a tutor to Jayavarman V.

Banteay Srei, 21km northeast of Bayon and about 32km from Siem Reap, can be visited along with Kbal Spean and the Cambodia Landmine Museum.

KBAL SPEAN
Kbal Spean is a spectacularly carved riverbed, set deep in the jungle about 50km northeast of Angkor. More commonly referred to in English as the 'River of a Thousand Lingas', it's a 2km uphill walk to the carvings. From there you can work your way back down to the waterfall to cool off. Carry plenty of water.

At the nearby **Angkor Centre for Conservation of Biodiversity** (ACCB; www.accb -cambodia.org), trafficked animals are nursed back to health. Free tours generally begin at 1pm daily except Sunday.

PHNOM KULEN
The most sacred mountain in Cambodia, Phnom Kulen (487m) is where Jayavarman II proclaimed himself a *devaraja* (god-king) in AD 802, giving birth to Cambodia. A popular place of pilgrimage during weekends and festivals, the views it affords are absolutely tremendous.

Phnom Kulen is 50km from Siem Reap and 15km from Banteay Srei. The road toll is US$20 per foreign visitor; none of this goes towards preserving the site.

BENG MEALEA
Built by Suryavarman II to the same floor plan as Angkor Wat, Beng Mealea (admission US$5) is the Titanic of temples, utterly subsumed by jungle. Nature has well and truly run riot here. Jumbled stones lie like forgotten jewels swathed in lichen, and the galleries are strangled by ivy and vines.

Beng Mealea is about 65km northeast of Siem Reap on a sealed toll road.

KOH KER
Abandoned to the forests of the north, Koh Ker (admission US$10), capital of the Angkorian empire from AD 928 to AD 944, is now within day-trip distance of Siem Reap. Most visitors start at **Prasat Krahom**, where impressive stone carvings grace lintels, doorposts and slender window columns. The principal monument is Mayan-looking **Prasat Thom**, a 55m-wide, 40m-high sandstone-faced pyramid whose seven tiers offer spectacular views across the forest. However, access to Prasat Thom is currently prohibited for safety reasons.

Koh Ker is 127km northeast of Siem Reap (car hire around US$80, 2½ hours).

Understand
Vietnam

population per sq km

VIETNAM   UK   USA

= 80 people

Vietnam Today

Few places on earth have changed as much as Vietnam in the past few decades. One of the poorest, war-wounded corners of the globe has transformed itself into a stable, prospering nation through industriousness, ingenuity and ambition. The overall standard of living has risen incredibly, and education and healthcare have greatly improved. Blue-chip finance has flooded into a red-flag Communist society. Comrades have become entrepreneurs. It's been a breathtaking, and largely successful transformation.

And yet, take a peek beneath those headline-grabbing growth figures and there are concerns. Double-digit growth has faltered as the economy has cooled. Corruption remains systemic. Vietnamese people have to pay backhanders for everything from getting an internet connection to securing a hospital appointment. At the highest level, corrupt politicians have been caught demanding millions of dollars to facilitate infrastructure projects.

» Population: 90.5 million

» Life expectancy: 69 for men, 75 for women

» Infant mortality: 21 per 1000 births

» GDP: US$104.6 billion

» Adult literacy rate: 94%

The Political Landscape

Vietnam's political system could not be simpler: the Communist Party is the sole source of power. Officially, according to the Vietnamese constitution, the National Assembly (or parliament) is the country's supreme authority, but in practice it's a tool of the Party and carefully controlled elections ensure 90% of delegates are Communist Party members.

Officially, communism is still king, but there can be few party hacks who really believe Vietnam is a Marxist utopia. Market-oriented socialism is the new mantra. Capitalism thrives like never before, the dynamic private sector driving the economy. On the street, everyone seems to be out to make a fast buck.

The reality is that the state still controls a vast swathe of the economy. More than 100 of the 200 biggest companies in Vietnam are state-owned

Top Books

» **The Quiet American** (Graham Greene) Classic novel set in the 1950s.

» **The Sorrow of War** (Bao Ninh) The North Vietnamese perspective.

» **Vietnam: Rising Dragon** (Bill Hayton) A candid assessment of the nation today.

» **Catfish & Mandala** (Andrew X Pham) Biographical tale of a Vietnamese-American.

Best Films

» **Apocalypse Now** (1979) Director: Francis Ford Coppola

» **Cyclo** (*Xich Lo*; 1995) Director: Anh Hung Tran

» **The Deer Hunter** (1978) Director: Michael Cimino

belief systems
(% of population)

if Vietnam were 100 people

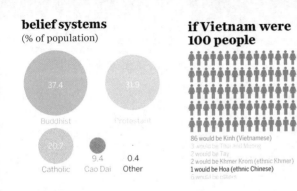

86 would be Kinh (Vietnamese)
3 would be Thai and Muong
2 would be Tay
2 would be Khmer Krom (ethnic Khmer)
1 would be Hoa (ethnic Chinese)
6 would be others

37.4 Buddhist

31.9 Protestant

20.7 Catholic

9.4 Cao Dai

0.4 Other

and the key sectors of oil production, shipbuilding, cement, coal and rubber are government controlled.

There's no sign that Party hegemony is slipping in other areas. Political dissent is a complete no-no and the entire nation's internet operates behind a firewall that blocks anything – including Facebook – that might potentially lead to trouble. In 2007, democracy movement members Nguyen Van Dai and Le Thi Cong Nhan were sent to prison for spreading 'anti-state propaganda'.

North & South
The Vietnamese economy has been buoyant for 20 years, but some areas are more buoyant than others. In 2011, the Ho Chi Minh City (HCMC) economy was growing at double the national rate (10.3% compared to 5.5%). It's the south that's benefited most from inward investment as Viet Kieu (overseas Vietnamese, the vast majority of whom are southerners) have returned and invested in the region.

The government is aware of these divisions and tries to balance the offices of state so if the prime minister is from the south, the head of the Communist Party is from the north.

When it comes to the older generation, the south has never forgiven the north for bulldozing their war cemeteries, imposing communism and blackballing whole families. The north has never forgiven the south for siding with the Americans against their own people. Luckily for Vietnam, the new generation seems to have less interest in the country's harrowing history.

Vietnam's Place in the World
In 2000 Bill Clinton became the first US president to visit northern Vietnam. George W Bush followed suit in 2006. Today relations with the

» Annual rice production: 36 million tonnes

» Bombs dropped on Vietnam in the American War: 8 million tonnes

» Number of mobile phones: 98 million+

» Annual *nuoc mam* (fish sauce) production: 200 million litres

Best Fruit

» **Platoon** (1986) Director: Oliver Stone
» **The Lover** (*L'amant*; 1992) Director: Jean-Jacques Annaud

» **Mangosteen** (*mang cut*) Subtle, fragrant and delicately flavoured.
» **Rambutan** (*chom chom*) Looks like a sore testicle, inside it's sweet and juicy.

» **Papaya** (*du du*) Delicious unripe in salads, or refreshing when ripe.
» **Longan** (*nhan*) Light-brown skin and a lychee-like flavour.

USA are politically cordial and economically vibrant (bilateral trade was worth more than US$18 billion in 2010). US and Vietnamese militaries hold annual Defense Policy Dialogue talks. Vietnam's suppression of political dissent and issues of freedom of speech and religion remain areas of contention. For the Vietnamese, the legacy of Agent Orange and dioxin poisoning remains unresolved – the USA has never paid compensation to the estimated three million victims of dioxin poisoning resulting from aerial bombing during the American War.

Relations with Vietnam's historic enemy China have improved significantly. Trade is booming, borders are hyper-busy and joint cooperation in everything from steel manufacturing to naval patrols continues. Chinese is the second most popular foreign language studied in Vietnam. The Spratly Islands, rich in oil deposits, remain a potential flashpoint however, with both nations claiming sovereignty. Escalating tensions resulted in protests against the Chinese occupation of the islands in Hanoi and HCMC in June 2011.

Vietnam counterbalances its power politics with China and the USA with active membership of ASEAN, and by fostering important links with India, Russia and former Soviet block countries (from which it buys most of its military hardware).

Principal Agricultural Exports:

- » Rice
- » Coffee
- » Rubber
- » Cotton
- » Tea
- » Pepper
- » Soybeans
- » Cashews
- » Sugar cane
- » Peanuts
- » Bananas

State of the Nation

Most Vietnamese have accepted their status quo, for now. They're living in an age of rising prosperity. Times are pretty good for most, though inflation (running at 22% in July 2011) is a huge concern. The country is stable. Tourism is booming, empowering a new generation of young Viets to a better life. Of course if things turn sour the tide may turn, but for now the outlook looks decent as long as opportunities remain and the economy prospers.

Must Experience

- » Learn the art of crossing the street.
- » Saddle-up and see the nation on two wheels.
- » Squat down and get stuck into street food.
- » Meet the minorities in a mountain village.
- » Play *tram phan tram* (100%) or bottoms-up in a backstreet bar.

History

To get an idea of Vietnam's turbulent history all you have to do is stroll through any town in the country and take at look at the street names. Then try it again somewhere else. You'll soon get déjà vu. The same names occur again and again, reflecting the national heroes who, over the last 2000 years, have repelled a succession of foreign invaders. If the street borders a river it'll be called Bach Dang (after the battles of 938 and 1288); a principal boulevard will be Le Loi (the emperor who defeated the Chinese in 1428).

For millennia the Vietnamese, in the backyard of a giant neighbour, have first and foremost had to deal with China. They've been resisting Chinese domination from as far back as the 2nd Century BC and had to endure a 1000-year occupation. The struggle to nationhood has been immense.

Sure, the American War in Vietnam captured the attention of the West, but for the Vietnamese the Americans were simply the last in a long line of visitors who had come and gone. As far as Ho Chi Minh was concerned, no matter what was required or how long it took, they too would be vanquished.

In centuries past the Khmers, the Mongols and Chams were all defeated. There was a humbling period of colonialism under the French. As recently as 1979, just after the cataclysmic horrors of the American War, with the country on its knees, they took on an invading Chinese army – and sent them home in a matter of weeks.

Inevitably all these invaders have left their mark. The Chinese brought Buddhism, Taoism and the principals of Confucianism: community above individual, a respect for education and family. The French introduced railways, and bequeathed some grand architecture and fabulous cuisine. And though the Americans left a devastated nation, at least Vietnamese pride remained intact.

In recent years progress has been remarkable, as Vietnam has become a key member of Asean and its economy has boomed – though systemic

TIMELINE	2789 BC	2000 BC	300BC
	The Van Lang kingdom, considered the first independent Vietnamese state, is founded by the Hung Vuong kings. It's referred to by both the Chin and Tang Chinese dynasties.	The Bronze Age Dong Son culture emerges in the Red River Delta around Hanoi, renowned for its rice cultivation and the production of bronzeware, including drums and gongs.	Vietnamese people of the northern region were culturally divided between Au Viet (highland Vietnamese) and Lac Viet (Vietnamese of the plains) who settled the Red River basin.

corruption, creaking infrastructure and an anti-democratic ruling party remain. But the country is united and prospering, its borders secure, and the Vietnamese people can look forward to a lasting period of stability and progress.

The Early Days

Humans first inhabited northern Vietnam about 500,000 years ago, though it took until 7000 BC for these hunter gatherers to practise rudimentary agriculture. The sophisticated Dong Son culture, famous for its bronze moko drums, emerged sometime around the 3rd century BC. The Dong Son period also saw huge advances in rice cultivation and the emergence of the Red River Delta as a major agricultural centre.

From the 1st to 6th centuries AD, southern Vietnam was part of the Indianised Cambodian kingdom of Funan – famous for its refined art and architecture. Based around the walled city of Angkor Borei it was probably a grouping of feudal states rather than a unified empire. The people of Funan constructed an elaborate system of canals both for transportation and the irrigation of rice. Funan's principal port city was Oc-Eo in the Mekong Delta and archaeological excavations here suggest there was contact with China, Indonesia, Persia and even the Mediterranean. Later on the Chenla empire replaced the Funan kingdom, spreading along the Mekong River.

The Hindu kingdom of Champa emerged around present-day Danang in the late 2nd century AD (see p211). Like Funan, it adopted Sanskrit as a sacred language and borrowed heavily from Indian art and culture. By the 8th century Champa had expanded southward to include what is now Nha Trang and Phan Rang. The Cham were a feisty bunch who conducted raids along the entire coast of Indochina, and thus found themselves in a perpetual state of war: with the Vietnamese to the north and the Khmers to the south. Ultimately this cost them their kingdom, as they found themselves squeezed between these two great powers. Check out some exquisite sculptures in the Museum of Cham Sculpture in Danang (p181).

1000 Years of Chinese Occupation

The Chinese conquered the Red River Delta in the 2nd century BC. Over the following centuries, large numbers of Chinese settlers, officials and scholars moved south seeking to impress a centralised state system on the Vietnamese.

In the most famous act of resistance, in AD 40, the Trung Sisters (Hai Ba Trung) rallied the people, raised an army and led a revolt against the Chinese. The Chinese counter-attacked, but, rather than surrender, the Trung Sisters threw themselves into the Hat Giang River. There were

Archaeologists conducting excavations at Oc-Eo discovered a Roman medallion dating from AD 152, bearing the likeness of Antoninus Pius.

The people of the Bronze Age Dong Son period were major traders in the region and bronze drums from northern Vietnam have been found as far afield as the island of Alor, in eastern Indonesia.

250 BC	225–248BC	111 BC	AD 40
Van Lang is conquered by a Chinese warlord and a new kingdom known as Au Lac is established at Co Loa, close to the modern-day capital of Hanoi.	Female warrior, Trieu Thi Trinh, described as a giant who rode war elephants to battle, confronts the Chinese for decades until defeat and her suicide in 248.	The Han emperors of China annex the Red River Delta region of Vietnam, heralding 1000 years of Chinese rule. Confucianism prevails as the governing philosophy.	The Trung Sisters (Hai Ba Trung) led a rebellion against the Chinese occupiers, raising an army that sends the Chinese governor fleeing. They proclaim themselves queens of an independent Vietnam.

IN THE BEGINNING...

Every country has a creation myth and Vietnam is no exception. The Vietnamese are supposed to be descended from a union of Dragon Lord Lac Long Quan and the fairy Au Co. Their relationship was fruitful, producing 100 sons, 50 migrating with their mother to the mountains and the other half travelling with their father to the sea. These sons founded the first Vietnamese dynasty, the Hung, who ruled over the kingdom of Van Lang, whose people were the first to be known as the Lac Viet.

numerous small-scale rebellions against Chinese rule – which was characterised by tyranny, forced labour and insatiable demands for tribute – from the 3rd to 6th centuries, but all were defeated.

However, the early Viets learned much from the Chinese, including the advancement of dykes and irrigation works – reinforcing the role of rice as the 'staff of life.' As food became more plentiful the population expanded, forcing the Vietnamese to seek new lands. The Truong Son Mountains prevented westward expansion, as the climate was harsh and terrain unsuited to rice cultivation, so instead the Vietnamese moved south along the coast.

During this era, Vietnam was a key port of call on the sea route between China and India. The Chinese introduced Confucianism, Taoism and Mahayana Buddhism to Vietnam, while the Indian influence brought Theravada Buddhism and Hinduism (to Champa and Funan). Monks carried with them the scientific and medical knowledge of these two great civilisations and Vietnam was soon producing its own doctors, botanists and scholars.

Liberation from China

In the early 10th century the Tang dynasty collapsed, provoking the Vietnamese to launched a revolt against Chinese rule. In AD 938 popular patriot Ngo Quyen defeated Chinese forces by luring the Chinese fleet up the Bach Dang river in a feigned retreat, only to counter-attack and impale their ships on sharpened stakes hidden beneath the waters. This ended 1000 years of Chinese rule (though it was not to be the last time the Vietnamese would tussle with their mighty northern neighbour).

From the 11th to 13th centuries, Vietnamese independence was consolidated under the emperors of the Ly dynasty, founded by Ly Thai To. This was a period of progress that saw the introduction of an elaborate dyke system for flood control and cultivation, and the establishment of the country's first university. During the Ly dynasty the Chinese, the Khmer and the Cham launched attacks on Vietnam, but all were repelled.

446	602	938	1010
Relations between the kingdom of Champa and the Chinese deteriorate. China invades Champa, sacks the capital of Simhapura and plunders a 50-tonne golden Buddha statue.	Rebellions by leaders including Ly Bon and Trieu Quang Phuc against Chinese rule ultimately fail as the Sui Dynasty reconquers Vietnam, with its capital Dai La Thanh (Hanoi).	The Chinese are kicked out of Vietnam after a thousand years of occupation, as Ngo Quyen leads his people to victory in the battle of the Bach Dang River.	Thanh Long (City of the Soaring Dragon), known today as Hanoi, is founded by Emperor Ly Thai To and becomes the new capital of Vietnam.

Meanwhile, the Vietnamese continued their expansion southwards and slowly but surely began to consolidate control of the Cham kingdom.

Bach Dang Again

Mongol warrior Kublai Khan completed his conquest of China in the mid-13th century. For his next trick, he planned to attack Champa and demanded the right to cross Vietnamese territory. The Vietnamese refused, but the Mongol hordes – all 500,000 of them – pushed ahead. They met their match in the revered general Tran Hung Dao. He defeated them at Bach Dang River, utilising acute military acumen by repeating the same tactics (and location) as Ngo Quyen in one of the most celebrated scalps in Vietnamese history (see p89 for more on this battle).

China Bites Back

The Chinese took control of Vietnam again in the early 15th century, taking the national archives and some of the country's intellectuals back to Nanjing – a loss that was to have a lasting impact on Vietnamese civilisation. Heavy taxation and slave labour were also typical of the era. The poet Nguyen Trai (1380–1442) wrote of this period:

> Were the water of the Eastern Sea to be exhausted, the stain of their ignominy could not be washed away; all the bamboo of the Southern Mountains would not suffice to provide the paper for recording all their crimes.

Enter Le Loi

In 1418 wealthy philanthropist Le Loi sparked the Lam Son Uprising by refusing to serve as an official for the Chinese Ming dynasty. By 1428, local rebellions had erupted in several regions and Le Loi travelled the countryside to rally the people against the Chinese.

Following Le Loi's victory over the Chinese, poet Nguyen Trai, Le Loi's companion in arms, wrote his infamous Great Proclamation (Binh Ngo Dai Cao). Still guaranteed to fan the flames of Vietnamese nationalism almost six centuries later, it articulated the country's fierce spirit of independence:

> Our people long ago established Vietnam as an independent nation with its own civilisation. We have our own mountains and our own rivers, our own customs and traditions, and these are different from those of the foreign country to the north...We have sometimes been weak and sometimes powerful, but at no time have we suffered from a lack of heroes.

Le Loi and his successors launched a campaign to take over Cham lands to the south, which culminated in the occupation of its capital

For a closer look at China's 1000-year occupation of Vietnam, which was instrumental in shaping the country's outlook and attitude today, try *The Birth of Vietnam* by Keith Weller Taylor.

1010–1225	1076	1288	14th century
Under the 200-year Ly dynasty Vietnam maintains many institutions and traditions of the Chinese era including Confucianism and its civil service structure. Wet rice cultivation remains vital.	The Vietnamese military, led by General Ly Thuong, attack the Sung Chinese and win a decisive battle near the present-day city of Nanning, and later defeat Cham forces.	The Mongols invade Dai Viet but General Tran Hung Dao repeats history by spearing the Mongol fleet on sharpened stakes on the Bach Dang River.	Cham forces led by king Che Bong Nga kill Viet Emperor Tran Due Tong and lay siege to his capital Thang Long in 1377 and 1383.

Vijaya, near present-day Quy Nhon in 1471. This was the end of Champa as a military power and the Cham people began to migrate southwards as Vietnamese settlers moved in to their territory.

The Coming of the Europeans

The first Portuguese sailors came ashore at Danang in 1516 and were soon followed by a party of Dominican missionaries. During the following decades the Portuguese began to trade with Vietnam, setting up a commercial colony alongside those of the Japanese and Chinese at Faifo (present-day Hoi An). With the exception of the Philippines, which was ruled by the Spanish for 400 years, the Catholic Church has had a greater impact on Vietnam than on any country in Asia.

Lording It Over the People

In a dress rehearsal for the tumultuous events of the 20th century, Vietnam found itself divided in two throughout much of the 17th and 18th centuries. The powerful Trinh Lords were later Le kings who ruled the North. To the South were the Nguyen Lords. The Trinh failed in their persistent efforts to subdue the Nguyen, in part because their Dutch weaponry was matched by the Portuguese armaments supplied to the Nguyen. By this time, several European nations were interested in Vietnam's potential and were jockeying for influence. For their part, the Nguyen expanded southwards again, absorbing territories in the Mekong Delta.

Tay Son Rebellion

In 1765 a rebellion erupted in the town of Tay Son near Qui Nhon, ostensibly against the punitive taxes of the Nguyen family. The Tay Son Rebels, as they were known, were led by the brothers Nguyen, who espoused the sort of Robin Hood–like philosophy of take from the rich and redistribute to the poor. It was clearly popular and in less than a decade they controlled the whole of central Vietnam. In 1783 they captured Saigon and the South, killing the reigning prince and his family. Nguyen Lu became king of the South, while Nguyen Nhac was crowned king of central Vietnam.

Continuing their conquests, the Tay Son Rebels overthrew the Trinh Lords in the North, while the Chinese moved in to take advantage of the power vacuum. In response, the third brother, Nguyen Hue, proclaimed himself Emperor Quang Trung. In 1789 Nguyen Hue's armed forces overwhelmingly defeated the Chinese army at Dong Da in another of the greatest hits of Vietnamese history.

In the South, Nguyen Anh, a rare survivor from the original Nguyen Lords – yes, know your Nguyens if you hope to understand Vietnamese history! – gradually overcame the rebels. In 1802 Nguyen Anh proclaimed himself Emperor Gia Long, thus beginning the Nguyen dynasty.

Ho Chi Minh City (HCMC) began life as humble Prey Nokor in the 16th century, a backwater of a Khmer village in what was then the eastern edge of Cambodia.

One of the most prominent early missionaries was French Jesuit Alexandre de Rhodes (1591–1660), widely lauded for his work in devising *quoc ngu*, the Latin-based phonetic alphabet in which Vietnamese is written to this day.

1428	1471	1516	1524
Le Loi triumphs over the Chinese, declaring himself emperor, the first in the long line of the Le dynasty. He is revered as one of the nation's greatest heroes.	The Vietnamese inflict a humbling defeat on the kingdom of Champa, killing more than 60,000 Cham soldiers and capturing 36,000, including the king and most of the royal family.	Portuguese traders land at Danang, sparking the start of European interest in Vietnam. They set up a trading post in Faifo (present-day Hoi An) and introduce Catholicism.	A period of instability and warfare ensues as feudal conflicts rage between the Trinh from the north (Thang Long) and the Nguyen from the South (based around Hue).

When he captured Hanoi, his work was complete and, for the first time in two centuries, Vietnam was united, with Hue as its new capital city.

The Traditionalists Prevail

Emperor Gia Long returned to Confucian values in an effort to consolidate his precarious position, a calculated move to win over conservative elements of the elite.

Gia Long's son, Emperor Minh Mang, worked to strengthen the state. He was profoundly hostile to Catholicism, which he saw as a threat to Confucian traditions, and extended this antipathy to all Western influences.

The early Nguyen emperors continued the expansionist policies of the preceding dynasties, pushing into Cambodia and Lao territory. Clashes with Thailand broke out in an attempt to pick apart the skeleton of the fractured Khmer empire.

The return to traditional values may have earned support among the elite at home, but the isolationism and hostility to the West ultimately cost the Nguyen emperors as they failed to modernise the country quickly enough to compete with the well-armed Europeans.

The French Takeover

France's military activity in Vietnam began in 1847, when the French Navy attacked Danang harbour in response to Emperor Thieu Tri's imprisonment of Catholic missionaries. Saigon was seized in early 1859 and, in 1862, Emperor Tu Duc signed a treaty that gave the French three eastern provinces of Cochinchina (the southern part of Vietnam during the French-colonial era). However, over the next four decades the French colonial venture in Indochina faltered repeatedly and, at times, only the reckless adventures of a few mavericks kept it going.

In 1872 Jean Dupuis, a merchant seeking to supply salt and weapons via the Red River, seized the Hanoi Citadel. Captain Francis Garnier, ostensibly dispatched to rein in Dupuis, instead took over where Dupuis left off and began a conquest of the North.

A few weeks after the death of Tu Duc in 1883, the French attacked Hue and the Treaty of Protectorate was imposed on the imperial court. A tragi-comic struggle then began for royal succession that was notable for its palace coups, the death of emperors in suspicious circumstances and heavy-handed French diplomacy.

The French colonial authorities carried out ambitious public works, such as the construction of the Saigon–Hanoi railway and draining of the Mekong Delta swamps. These projects were funded by heavy government taxes which had a devastating impact on the rural economy. Such operations became notorious for the abysmal wages paid by the French and the appalling treatment of Vietnamese workers.

1651

The first *quoc ngu* (Romanised Vietnamese) dictionary, the Dictionarium Annamiticum Lusitanum et Latinum, is produced, following years of work by Father Alexandre de Rhodes.

17th century

Ethnic Vietnamese settlers arrive in the Mekong Delta and Saigon region, taking advantage of Khmer weaknesses, who are torn apart by internal strife and Siamese invasions.

OLIVER CIRENDINI / LONELY PLANET IMAGES ©

» The Mekong Delta today in Vinh Long

Independence Aspirations

Throughout the colonial period, the desire of many Vietnamese for independence simmered under the surface. Nationalist aspirations often erupted into open defiance of the French. This ranged from the publishing of patriotic periodicals to a dramatic attempt to poison the French garrison in Hanoi.

The imperial court in Hue, although allegedly quite corrupt, was a centre of nationalist sentiment and the French orchestrated a game of musical thrones, as one emperor after another turned against their patronage. This culminated in the accession of Emperor Bao Dai in 1925, who was just 12 years old at the time and studying in France.

Leading patriots soon realised that modernisation was the key to an independent Vietnam. Phan Boi Chau launched the Dong Du (Go East) movement which planned to send Vietnamese intellectuals to Japan for study with a view to fomenting a successful uprising in the future. Phan Tru Chinh favoured the education of the masses, the modernisation of the economy and working with the French towards independence. It was at this time that the Roman script of *quoc ngu* came to prominence, as educators realised this would be a far easier tool with which to educate the masses than the elaborate Chinese-style script of nom.

Rise of the Communists

However, the most successful of the anti-colonialists were the communists, who were able to tune into the frustrations and aspirations of the population – especially the peasants – and effectively channel their demands for fairer land distribution.

The story of Vietnamese communism, which in many ways is also the political biography of Ho Chi Minh (see p436), is convoluted. The first Marxist grouping in Indochina was the Vietnam Revolutionary Youth League, founded by Ho Chi Minh in Canton, China, in 1925. This was succeeded in February 1930 by the Vietnamese Communist Party. In 1941 Ho formed the Viet Minh, which resisted the Vichy French government, as well as Japanese forces, and carried out extensive political activities during WWII. Despite its nationalist platform, the Viet Minh was, from its inception, dominated by Ho's communists. However, as well as a communist, Ho appeared pragmatic, patriotic and populist and understood the need for national unity.

WWII & Famine

When France fell to Nazi Germany in 1940, the Indochinese government of Vichy France–collaborators acquiesced to the presence of Japanese troops in Vietnam. The Japanese left the French administration in charge of the day-to-day running of the country and, for a time, Vietnam was

Buddhism flourished during the 17th and 18th centuries and many pagodas were erected across the country. However, it was not pure Buddhism, but a peculiarly Vietnamese blend mixed with ancestor worship, animism and Taoism.

Between 1944 and 1945, the Viet Minh received funding and arms from the US Office of Strategic Services (OSS; today the CIA). When Ho Chi Minh declared independence in 1945, he had OSS agents at his side and borrowed liberally from the American Declaration of Independence.

1765	1802	1862	1883
The Tay Son Rebellion erupts near Quy Nhon, led by the brothers Nguyen, and they take control of the whole country over the next 25 years.	Emperor Gia Long takes the throne and the Nguyen dynasty is born, ruling over Vietnam until 1945. The country is reunited for the first time in more than 200 years.	Following French attacks on both Danang and Saigon, Emperor Tu Duc signs a treaty ceding control of the Mekong Delta provinces to France, renaming them Cochinchina (Cochinchine).	The French impose the Treaty of Protectorate on the Vietnamese, marking the start of 70 years of colonial control, although active resistance continues throughout this period.

spared the ravages of Japanese occupation. However, as WWII drew to a close, Japanese rice requisitions, combined with floods and breaches in the dykes, caused a horrific famine in which perhaps two million North Vietnamese people starved to death. The only force opposed to both the French and Japanese presence in Vietnam was the Viet Minh, and Ho Chi Minh received assistance from the US government during this period. As events unfolded in mainland Europe, the French and Japanese fell out and the Viet Minh saw its opportunity to strike.

A False Dawn

By the spring of 1945 the Viet Minh controlled large swathes of the country, particularly in the north. In mid-August, Ho Chi Minh called for a

UNCLE OF THE PEOPLE

Father of the nation, Ho Chi Minh (Bringer of Light) was the son of a fiercely nationalistic scholar-official. Born Nguyen Tat Thanh near Vinh in 1890, he was educated in Hue and adopted many pseudonyms during his momentous life. Many Vietnamese affectionately refer him as Bac Ho ('Uncle Ho') today.

In 1911 he signed up as a cook's apprentice on a French ship, sailing to North America, Africa and Europe. While odd-jobbing in England and France as a gardener, snow sweeper, waiter, photo retoucher and stoker, his political consciousness began to develop.

Ho Chi Minh moved to Paris, where he mastered a number of languages (including English, French, German and Mandarin) and began to promote the issue of Indochinese independence. He was a founding member of the French Communist Party in 1920 and later travelled to Guangzhou in China, where he founded the Revolutionary Youth League of Vietnam.

During the early 1930s the English rulers of Hong Kong obliged the French government by imprisoning Ho for his revolutionary activities. After his release he travelled to the USSR and China. In 1941 he returned to Vietnam for the first time in 30 years, and founded the Viet Minh, the goal of which was the independence of Vietnam. As Japan prepared to surrender in August 1945, Ho Chi Minh led the August Revolution, and his forces then established control throughout much of Vietnam.

The return of the French compelled the Viet Minh to conduct a guerrilla war, which ultimately led to victory against the colonists at Dien Bien Phu in 1954. Ho then led North Vietnam until his death in September 1969 – he never lived to see the North's victory over the South.

The party has worked hard to preserve the reputation of Bac Ho. His image dominates contemporary Vietnam – no town is complete without a Ho statue, and most cities have a museum in his name. This cult of personality is in stark contrast to the simplicity with which Ho lived his life. For more Ho, check out *Ho Chi Minh,* the excellent biography by William J Duiker.

late 19th century	1925	1930s	1940
The Romanised *quoc ngu* alphabet for Vietnamese grows in popularity as a means of eradicating illiteracy and promoting education. Traditional Chinese-style scripts are phased out.	Ho Chi Minh moves towards organised political agitation, establishing the Revolutionary Youth League of Vietnam in southern China, an early incarnation of the Vietnamese Communist Party.	Marxism gains in popularity with the formation of three Communist parties, which later unite to form the Vietnamese Communist Party with Tran Phu as the first Secretary General.	The Japanese occupation of Vietnam begins, as the pro–Vichy France colonial government offers the use of military facilities in return for the continued control over administration.

general uprising, later known as the August Revolution. Meanwhile in central Vietnam, Bao Dai abdicated in favour of the new government, and in the South the Viet Minh soon held power in a shaky coalition with non-communist groups. On 2 September 1945, Ho Chi Minh declared independence at a rally in Hanoi. Throughout this period, Ho wrote eight letters to US president Harry Truman and the US State Department asking for US aid, but received no replies.

A footnote on the agenda of the Potsdam Conference of 1945 was the disarming of Japanese occupation forces in Vietnam: Chinese Kuomintang would accept the Japanese surrender north of the 16th Parallel and the British would do so in the south.

When the British arrived in Saigon anarchy ruled with private militia, the remaining Japanese forces, the French, and Viet Minh competing for hegemony. When armed French paratroopers reacted to Ho's declaration of independence by attacking civilians, the Viet Minh began a guerrilla campaign. On 24 September French general Jacques Philippe Leclerc arrived in Saigon, declaring 'we have come to reclaim our inheritance'.

In the north, Chinese Kuomintang troops were fleeing the Chinese communists and making their way southward towards Hanoi. Ho tried to placate them, but as the months of Chinese occupation dragged on, he decided to accept a temporary return of the French, deeming them less of a long-term threat than the Chinese. The French were to stay for five years in return for recognising Vietnam as a free state within the French Union.

War With the French

The French had managed to regain control of Vietnam, at least in name. However, following the French shelling of Haiphong in November 1946, which killed hundreds of civilians, the détente with the Viet Minh began to unravel. Fighting soon broke out in Hanoi, and Ho Chi Minh and his forces fled to the mountains to regroup, where they would remain for the next eight years.

In the face of determined Vietnamese nationalism, the French proved unable to reassert their control. Despite massive US aid to halt communism throughout Asia, for the French it was ultimately an unwinnable war. As Ho said to the French at the outset: 'You can kill 10 of my men for every one I kill of yours, but even at those odds you will lose and I will win.'

After eight years of fighting, the Viet Minh controlled much of Vietnam and neighbouring Laos. On 7 May 1954, after a 57-day siege, more than 10,000 starving French troops surrendered to the Viet Minh at Dien Bien Phu (p121). This defeat brought an end to the French colonial adventure in Indochina. The following day, the Geneva Conference opened

In May 1954 the Viet Minh dug a tunnel network under French defences on Hill A1 at Dien Bien Phu and rigged it with explosives. Comrade Sapper Nguyen Van Bach volunteered himself as a human fuse in case the detonator failed. Luckily for him it didn't and he is today honoured as a national hero.

In Hanoi and the North, Ho Chi Minh created a very effective police state. The regime was characterised by ruthless police power, denunciations by a huge network of secret informers, and the blacklisting of dissidents, their children and their children's children.

1941	mid-1940s	1945	1946
Ho Chi Minh forms the Viet Minh (short for the League for the Independence of Vietnam), a liberation movement seeking independence from France and fighting the Japanese occupation.	The combination of Japanese rice requisitions and widespread flooding leads to a disastrous famine in which 10% of North Vietnam's population dies, around two million people.	Ho Chi Minh proclaims Vietnamese independence on 2 September in Ba Dinh Square in central Hanoi, but the French aim to reassert their authority and impose colonial rule once more.	Strained relations between the Viet Minh forces and the French colonialists erupt into open fighting in Hanoi and Haiphong, marking the start of the eight-year Franco–Viet Minh War.

to negotiate an end to the conflict, but the French had no cards left to bring to the table. Resolutions included an exchange of prisoners; the 'temporary' division of Vietnam into two zones at the Ben Hai River (near the 17th Parallel) until nationwide elections could be held; the free passage of people across the 17th Parallel for a period of 300 days; and the holding of nationwide elections on 20 July 1956. In the course of the Franco–Viet Minh War, more than 35,000 French fighters had been killed and 48,000 wounded; there are no exact numbers for Vietnamese casualties, but they were certainly higher.

A Separate South Vietnam

After the Geneva Accords were signed and sealed, the South was ruled by a government led by Ngo Dinh Diem, a fiercely anti-communist Catholic. His power base was significantly strengthened by 900,000 refugees, many of them Catholics, who had fled the communist North during the 300-day free-passage period.

Nationwide elections were never held, as the Americans rightly feared that Ho Chi Minh would win with a massive majority. During the first few years of his rule, Diem consolidated power fairly effectively, defeating the Binh Xuyen crime syndicate and the private armies of the Hoa Hao and Cao Dai religious sects. During Diem's 1957 official visit to the USA, President Eisenhower called him the 'miracle man' of Asia. As time went on Diem became increasingly tyrannical, closing Buddhist monasteries, imprisoning monks and banning opposition parties. He also doled out power to family members (including his sister-in-law Madame Nhu, who effectively became First Lady).

In the early 1960s the South was rocked by anti-Diem unrest led by university students and Buddhist clergy, which included several highly publicised self-immolations by monks that shocked the world (see p177). The US began to see Diem as a liability and threw its support behind a military coup. A group of young generals led the operation in November 1963. Diem was to go into exile, but the generals executed both Diem and his brother. Diem was succeeded by a string of military rulers who continued his policies.

A New North Vietnam

The Geneva Accords allowed the leadership of the Democratic Republic of Vietnam to return to Hanoi and assert control of all territory north of the 17th Parallel. The new government immediately set out to eliminate those elements of the population that threatened its power. Tens of thousands of landlords, some with only tiny holdings, were denounced to security committees by their neighbours and arrested. Hasty trials resulted in between 10,000 and 15,000 executions and the imprisonment of

---

The 2002 remake of *The Quiet American*, starring Michael Caine, is a must-see. Beautifully shot, it is a classic introduction to Vietnam in the 1950s, as the French disengaged and the Americans moved in to take their place.

The USA closed its consulate in Hanoi on 12 December 1955 and would not officially re-open an embassy in the Vietnamese capital for more than 40 years.

Viet Cong and VC are both abbreviations for Viet Nam Cong San, which means Vietnamese communist. American soldiers nicknamed the VC 'Charlie', as in 'Victor Charlie'.

---

late-1940s	1954	1955	1960
While the Viet Minh retreat to the mountains to regroup, the French attempt to forge a Vietnamese government under Emperor Bao Dai, last ruler of the Nguyen dynasty.	French forces surrender to Viet Minh fighters as the siege of Dien Bien Phu comes to a dramatic close on 7 May, marking the end of colonial rule in Indochina.	Vietnam is 'temporarily' divided at the 17th Parallel into North Vietnam and South Vietnam and people are given 300 days to relocate to either side of the border.	The National Liberation Front (better known as the Viet Cong) launch a guerrilla war against the Diem government in the South, sparking the 'American War'.

thousands more. In 1956, the party, faced with widespread rural unrest, recognised that things had got out of control and began a Campaign for the Rectification of Errors.

The North–South War

The Communists' campaign to liberate the South began in 1959. The Ho Chi Minh Trail reopened for business, universal military conscription was implemented and the National Liberation Front (NLF), later known as the Viet Cong (VC) was formed.

As the NLF launched its campaign, the Diem government quickly lost control of the countryside. To stem the tide, peasants were moved into fortified 'strategic hamlets' in order to deny the VC potential support.

And for the South it was no longer just a battle with the VC. In 1964 Hanoi began sending regular North Vietnamese Army (NVA) units down the Ho Chi Minh Trail. By early 1965 the Saigon government was on its last legs. Desertions from the Army of the Republic of Vietnam (ARVN) had reached 2000 per month. The South was losing a district capital each week, yet in 10 years only one senior South Vietnamese army officer had been wounded. The army was getting ready to evacuate Hue and Danang, and the central highlands seemed about to fall.

Enter the Cavalry

The Americans saw France's war in Indochina as an important element in the worldwide struggle against communist expansion. Vietnam was the next domino and could not topple. In 1950 US advisers rolled into Vietnam, ostensibly to train local troops – but American soldiers would remain on Vietnamese soil for the next 25 years. As early as 1954, US military aid to the French topped US$2 billion.

A decisive turning point in US strategy came with the August 1964 Gulf of Tonkin Incident. Two US destroyers claimed to have come under unprovoked attack off the North Vietnamese coast. Subsequent research suggests that there was a certain degree of provocation: one ship was assisting a secret South Vietnamese commando raid, and according to an official National Security Agency report in 2005, the second one never happened.

However, on US president Lyndon Johnson's orders, 64 sorties unleashed bombs on the North – the first of thousands of such missions that would hit every single road and rail bridge in the country, as well as 4000 of North Vietnam's 5788 villages. A few days later, the US Congress overwhelmingly passed the Tonkin Gulf Resolution which gave the president the power to take any action in Vietnam without congressional control.

As the military situation of the Saigon government reached a new nadir, the first US combat troops splashed ashore at Danang in March 1965.

The Tet Offensive was a long-term success, but in the short-term it fundamentally weakened the VC's military capacity and ensured that North Vietnamese soldiers would play a decisive role in the future of the war.

The American War in Vietnam claimed the lives of countless journalists. For a look at the finest photographic work from the battlefront, *Requiem* is an anthology of work from fallen correspondents on all sides of the conflict and a fitting tribute to their trade.

HISTORY THE NORTH–SOUTH WAR

1962	1963	1964	1965
Cuc Phuong National Park, just west of the city of Ninh Binh is declared Vietnam's first national park as Ho Chi Minh declares 'forest is gold.'	South Vietnam's president Ngo Dinh Diem is overthrown and killed in a coup backed by the USA, which brings a new group of young military commanders into power.	Although the US is not officially at war, it launches Operation Pierce Arrow and bombs North Vietnam for the first time in retaliation for the Gulf of Tonkin incident.	To prevent the total collapse of the Saigon regime, US President Lyndon Johnson intensifies bombing of North Vietnam and approves the dispatch of American combat troops to the South.

By December 1965 there were 184,300 US military personnel in Vietnam and 636 Americans had died. By December 1967 the figures had risen to 485,600 US soldiers in the country and 16,021 dead. There were 1.3 million soldiers fighting for the Saigon government, including the South Vietnamese and other allies.

The War in Numbers

» 3689 US fixed-wing aircraft lost

» 4857 US helicopters downed

» 15 million tonnes of US ammunition expended

» 4 million Vietnamese killed or injured

US Strategies

By 1966 the buzz words in Washington were 'pacification', 'search and destroy' and 'free-fire zones'. Pacification involved developing a pro-government civilian infrastructure in each village, and providing the soldiers to guard it. To protect the villages from VC raids, mobile search-and-destroy units of soldiers moved around the country hunting VC guerrillas. In some cases, villagers were evacuated so the Americans could use heavy weaponry such as napalm and tanks in areas that were declared free-fire zones.

These strategies were only partially successful: US forces could control the countryside by day, while the VC usually controlled it by night. Even without heavy weapons, VC guerrillas continued to inflict heavy casualties in ambushes and through extensive use of mines and booby traps. Although free-fire zones were supposed to prevent civilian casualties, plenty of villagers were nevertheless shelled, bombed, strafed or napalmed. These attacks turned out to be a fairly efficient recruiting tool for the VC.

The Turning Point

For a human perspective on the North Vietnamese experience during the war, read *The Sorrow of War* by Bao Ninh, a poignant tale of love and loss that suggests the soldiers from the North had the same fears and desires as most American GIs.

In January 1968 North Vietnamese troops launched a major attack on the US base at Khe Sanh (p161) in the Demilitarised Zone (DMZ). This battle, the single largest of the war, was in part a massive diversion from the Tet Offensive.

The Tet Offensive marked a decisive turning point in the war. On the evening of 31 January, as the country celebrated the Lunar New Year, the VC broke an unofficial holiday ceasefire with a series of coordinated strikes in more than 100 cities and towns. As the TV cameras rolled, a VC commando team took over the courtyard of the US embassy in central Saigon. However, the communists miscalculated the mood of the population, as the popular uprising they had hoped to provoke never materialised. In cities such as Hue, the VC were not welcomed as liberators and this contributed to a communist backlash against the civilian population.

Although the US were utterly surprised – a major failure of military intelligence – they immediately counter-attacked with massive firepower, bombing and shelling heavily populated cities. The counter-attack devastated the VC, but also traumatised the civilian population. In Hue,

1967	1968	1969	1970
By the end of the year, there are 1.3 million soldiers fighting for the South – nearly half a million of these are from the US.	The Viet Cong launches the Tet Offensive, a surprise attack on towns and cities throughout the South. Hundreds of Vietnamese civilians are killed in the My Lai Massacre.	After a lifetime dedicated to revolution, Ho Chi Minh dies in Hanoi in September 1969, of heart failure. He's succeeded by a 'collective leadership,' headed by Le Duan.	Nixon's national security advisor, Henry Kissinger, and Le Duc Tho, for the Hanoi government, start talks in Paris as the US begins a reduction in troop numbers.

TRACKING THE AMERICAN WAR

The American War in Vietnam was the story for a generation. Follow in the footsteps of soldiers, journalists and politicians on all sides with a visit to the sites where the story unfolded.

» **China Beach** (p189) The strip of sand near Danang where US soldiers dropped in for some rest and relaxation.

» **Cu Chi Tunnels** (p345) The Vietnamese dug an incredible and elaborate tunnel network to evade American forces, just 30km from Saigon and right under the noses of a US base.

» **Demilitarised Zone** (DMZ; p158) The no-man's land at the 17th Parallel, dividing North and South Vietnam. After 1954 it became one of the most heavily militarised zones in the world.

» **Ho Chi Minh Trail** (p291) The supply route for the South; the North Vietnamese moved soldiers and munitions down this incredible trail through the Truong Son Mountains in an almost unparalleled logistical feat.

» **Hue Citadel** (p164) The ancient Citadel was razed to the ground during street-to-street fighting in early 1968 when the Americans retook the city from the communists after a three-week occupation.

» **Khe Sanh** (p161) This was the biggest smokescreen of the war, as the North Vietnamese massed forces around this US base in 1968 to draw attention away from the coming Tet Offensive.

» **Long Tan Memorial** (p263) The Australian contingent who fought in Vietnam, mostly based near Vung Tau in the south, is remembered here with the Long Tan Memorial Cross.

» **My Lai** (p218) The village of My Lai is infamous as the site of one of the worst atrocities in the war, when American GIs massacred hundreds of villagers in March 1968.

» **Vinh Moc Tunnels** (p158) The real deal: these tunnels haven't been surgically enlarged for tourists and they mark yet another feat of infrastructural ingenuity.

a US officer bitterly remarked that they 'had to destroy the town in order to save it'.

The Tet Offensive killed about 1000 US soldiers and 2000 ARVN troops, but VC losses were more than 10 times higher.

The VC may have lost the battle, but were on the road to winning the war. The US military had long been boasting that victory was just a matter of time. Watching the killing and chaos in Saigon beamed into their living rooms, many Americans stopped swallowing the official line. While US generals were proclaiming a great victory, public tolerance of the war and its casualties reached breaking point.

1971	**1972**	**1973**	**1975**
The ARVN's Operation Lam Son, aimed at cutting the Ho Chi Minh trail in Laos, ends in calamitous defeat as half its invading troops are either captured or killed.	The North Vietnamese cross the Demilitarized Zone (DMZ) at the 17th parallel to attack South Vietnam and US forces in what became known as the Easter Offensive.	All sides put pen to paper to sign the Paris Peace Accords on 27 January 1973, stipulating an end to hostilities, but the conflict rumbles on.	On 30 April 1975 Saigon falls to the North Vietnamese, as the last Americans scramble to leave the city.

Simultaneously, stories began leaking out of Vietnam about atrocities and massacres carried out against unarmed Vietnamese civilians, including the infamous My Lai Massacre (see p218). This helped turn the tide and a coalition of the concerned emerged. Anti-war demonstrations rocked American university campuses and spilled onto the streets.

Nixon & His Doctrine

Once elected president, Richard Nixon released a doctrine which called on Asian nations to be more 'self-reliant' in matters of defence. Nixon's strategy advocated 'Vietnamisation' – making the South Vietnamese fight the war without the support of US troops.

Meanwhile the first half of 1969 saw the conflict escalate further as the number of US soldiers in Vietnam reached an all-time high of 543,400. While the fighting raged, Nixon's chief negotiator, Henry Kissinger, pursued peace talks in Paris with his North Vietnamese counterpart Le Duc Tho.

In 1969 the Americans began secretly bombing Cambodia in an attempt to flush out Vietnamese communist sanctuaries. In 1970, US ground forces were sent into Cambodia and the North Vietnamese moved deeper into Cambodian territory. By summer 1970 they (together with their Khmer Rouge allies) controlled half of Cambodia, including Angkor Wat.

This new escalation provoked violent anti-war protests in the US and elsewhere. A peace demonstration at Kent State University in Ohio resulted in four protesters being shot dead. The rise of organisations such as Vietnam Veterans Against the War demonstrated that it wasn't just those fearing military conscription who wanted the USA out of Vietnam. It was clear that the war was tearing America apart.

In the spring of 1972 the North Vietnamese launched an offensive across the 17th Parallel; the USA responded with increased bombing of the North and by laying mines in North Vietnam's harbours. The 'Christmas bombing' of Haiphong and Hanoi at the end of 1972 was calculated to wrest concessions from North Vietnam at the negotiating table. Eventually, the Paris Peace Accords were signed by the USA, North Vietnam, South Vietnam and the VC on 27 January 1973, which provided for a ceasefire, the total withdrawal of US combat forces and the release of 590 American POWs. The agreement failed to mention the 200,000 North Vietnamese troops still in South Vietnam.

US teams continue to search Vietnam, Laos and Cambodia for the remains of their fallen comrades. In more recent years, the Vietnamese have been searching for their own MIAs in Cambodia and Laos.

Other Foreign Involvement

Australia, New Zealand, South Korea, the Philippines and Thailand also sent military personnel to South Vietnam as part of what the Americans

Author and documentary film-maker John Pilger was ripping into the establishment long before Michael Moore rode into town. Get to grips with his hard-hitting views on the American War at www.johnpilger.com.

Oliver Stone, never one to shy away from political point-scoring, earns a maximum ten in *Platoon*, the first of his famous trilogy about Vietnam. It is a brutal and cynical look at the conflict through the eyes of rookie Charlie Sheen, with great performances from Tom Berenger and Willem Dafoe.

1976

The Socialist Republic of Vietnam is proclaimed as Saigon is re-named Ho Chi Minh City. Hundreds of thousands flee abroad, including many boat people.

1978

Vietnamese forces invade Cambodia on Christmas Day 1978, sweeping through the shattered country and later overthrowing the Khmer Rouge government on 7 January 1979.

» Ho Chi Minh portrait in the central post office, HCMC

THE COST OF WAR

In total, 3.14 million Americans (including 7200 women) served in Vietnam. Officially, 58,183 Americans were killed in action or are listed as missing in action (MIA). The direct cost of the war was officially put at US$165 billion, though its real cost to the economy was likely to have been considerably more.

By the end of 1973, 223,748 South Vietnamese soldiers had been killed in action; North Vietnamese and VC fatalities have been estimated at one million. Approximately four million civilians (or 10% of the Vietnamese population) were injured or killed during the war. At least 300,000 Vietnamese and 2200 Americans are still listed as MIA.

called the 'Free World Military Forces', whose purpose was to help internationalise the American war effort in order to give it more legitimacy.

Australia's participation in the conflict constituted the most significant commitment of its military forces since WWII. Of the 46,852 Australian military personnel who served in the war, casualties totalled 496, with 2398 soldiers wounded.

Most of New Zealand's contingent, which numbered 548 at its highest point in 1968, operated as an integral part of the Australian Task Force, which was stationed near Baria, just north of Vung Tau.

The Fall of the South

Most US military personnel departed Vietnam in 1973, leaving behind a small contingent of technicians, advisors and CIA agents. The bombing of North Vietnam ceased and the US POWs were released. Still the war rumbled on, only now the South Vietnamese were fighting alone.

In January 1975 the North Vietnamese launched a massive ground attack across the 17th Parallel using tanks and heavy artillery. The invasion provoked panic in the South Vietnamese army, which had always depended on US support. In March, the NVA occupied a strategic section of the central highlands at Buon Ma Thuot. South Vietnam's president, Nguyen Van Thieu, decided on a strategy of tactical withdrawal to more defensible positions. This was to prove a spectacular military blunder.

Whole brigades of ARVN soldiers disintegrated and fled southward, joining hundreds of thousands of civilians clogging Hwy 1. City after city – Hue, Danang, Quy Nhon, Nha Trang – were simply abandoned with hardly a shot fired. The ARVN troops were fleeing so quickly that the North Vietnamese army could barely keep up.

Nguyen Van Thieu, in power since 1967, resigned on 21 April 1975 and fled the country, allegedly carting off millions of dollars in ill-gotten wealth. The North Vietnamese pushed on to Saigon and on the morning

Neil Sheehan's account of the life of Colonel John Paul Vann, *Bright Shining Lie*, won the Pulitzer Prize and is the portrayal of one man's disenchantment with the war, mirroring America's realisation it could not be won.

1979	1980s	1986	1989
China invades northern Vietnam in February in a retaliatory attack against Vietnam's overthrow of the Khmer Rouge, but the Vietnamese emerge relatively unscathed. Thousands of ethnic Chinese flee Vietnam.	During the decade Vietnam receives nearly $3 billion a year in economic and military aid from the Soviet Union and trades mostly with the USSR and eastern block nations.	*Doi moi* (economic reform), Vietnam's answer to *perestroika* and the first step towards re-engaging with the West, is launched with a rash of economic reforms.	Vietnamese forces pull out of Cambodia in September as the Soviet Union scales back its commitment to its communist partners. Vietnam is at peace for the first time in decades.

of 30 April 1975 their tanks smashed through the gates of Saigon's Independence Palace (now called Reunification Palace). General Duong Van Minh, president for just 42 hours, formally surrendered, marking the end of the war.

Just a few hours before the surrender, the last Americans were evacuated by helicopter from the US embassy roof to ships stationed just offshore. Harrowing images of US Marines booting Vietnamese people off their helicopters were beamed around the world. And so more than a quarter of a century of American military involvement came to a close. Throughout the entire conflict, the USA never actually declared war on North Vietnam.

The Americans weren't the only ones who left. As the South collapsed, 135,000 Vietnamese also fled the country; over the next five years, at least half a million of their compatriots would do the same. Those who left by sea would become known to the world as 'boat people'. These refugees risked everything to undertake perilous journeys on the South China Sea, but eventually some of these hardy souls found a new life in places as diverse as Australia and France.

The Paris Peace Accords of 1973 included a provision for US reparations to Vietnam totalling US$3.5 billion and this became the main stumbling block to normalising relations in 1978. No money has ever been paid to Vietnam.

Reunification of Vietnam

On the first day of their victory, the communists changed Saigon's name to Ho Chi Minh City (HCMC). This was just for starters.

The sudden success of the 1975 North Vietnamese offensive surprised the North almost as much as it did the South. Consequently, Hanoi had no detailed plans to deal with the reintegration of the North and South, which had totally different social and economic systems.

The party faced the legacy of a cruel and protracted war that had literally fractured the country. There was bitterness on both sides, and a daunting series of challenges. Damage from the fighting was extensive, including anything from unmarked minefields to war-focused, dysfunctional economies; from a chemically poisoned countryside to a population who were physically or mentally scarred. Peace may have arrived, but the struggle was far from over.

'WE WERE WRONG'

Commentators and historians have since observed that if Washington had allowed Vietnam's long history of successfully repelling invaders to deter it, the tragedy of this war might have been averted, and likewise the resulting social disruption in America, as people sought to come to terms with what had happened in Vietnam. An entire generation of Americans had to assess its conduct. Years later, one of the architects of the war, former Defense Secretary Robert NcNamara, stated in his memoir, 'we were wrong, terribly wrong. We owe it to future generations to explain why.'

1991	1992	1994	1995
Vietnam, a hard currency–starved nation, opens its doors to tourism in a bid to boost its finances. The first backpackers arrive, though tough restrictions apply to travel.	A new constitution is drawn up which allows selective economic reforms and freedoms. However the Communist Party remains the leading force in Vietnamese society and politics.	The US trade embargo on Vietnam, in place in the North since 1964 and extended to the reunified nation since 1975, is revoked as relations begin to normalise.	Vietnam joins the Association of South-East Asian Nations (ASEAN), an organisation originally founded as a bulwark against the expansion of communism in the region.

Until the formal reunification of Vietnam in July 1976, the South was ruled by the Provisional Revolutionary Government. The Communist Party did not trust the Southern urban intelligentsia, so large numbers of Northern cadres were sent southward to manage the transition. This fuelled resentment among Southerners who had worked against the Thieu government and then, after its overthrow, found themselves frozen out.

The party opted for a rapid transition to socialism in the South, but it proved disastrous for the economy. Reunification was accompanied by widespread political repression. Despite repeated assurances to the contrary, hundreds of thousands of people who had ties to the previous regime had their property confiscated and were rounded up and imprisoned without trial in forced-labour camps, euphemistically known as re-education camps. Tens of thousands of businesspeople, intellectuals, artists, journalists, writers, union leaders and religious leaders – some of whom had opposed both the Southern government and the war – were held in terrible conditions.

Contrary to its economic policy, Vietnam sought a rapprochement with the USA and by 1978 Washington was close to establishing relations with Hanoi. But the China card was ultimately played: Vietnam was sacrificed for the prize of US relations with Beijing and Hanoi moved into the orbit of the Soviet Union, on whom it was to rely for the next decade.

China & the Khmer Rouge

Relations with China to the north and its Khmer Rouge allies to the west were rapidly deteriorating. War-weary Vietnam felt encircled by enemies. An anti-capitalist campaign was launched in March 1978, seizing private property and businesses. Most of the victims were ethnic Chinese – hundreds of thousands soon became refugees or 'boat people', and relations with China soured further.

Meanwhile, repeated attacks on Vietnamese border villages by the Khmer Rouge forced Vietnam to respond. Vietnamese forces entered Cambodia on Christmas Day 1978. They succeeded in driving the Khmer Rouge from power on 7 January 1979 and set up a pro-Hanoi regime in Phnom Penh. China viewed the attack on the Khmer Rouge as a serious provocation. In February 1979 Chinese forces invaded Vietnam and fought a brief, 17-day war before withdrawing (see the boxed text, p112).

Liberation of Cambodia from the Khmer Rouge soon turned to occupation and a long civil war, which exacted a heavy toll on Vietnam. The command economy was strangling the commercial instincts of Vietnamese rice farmers. Today one of the world's leading rice exporters, back in the early 1980s Vietnam was a rice importer. War and revolution

The majority of Vietnamese 'boat people' who fled the country in the late 1970s were ethnic Chinese whose wealth and business acumen, to say nothing of their ethnicity, made them an obvious target for the revolution.

2000
Bill Clinton becomes the first American president to set foot in Hanoi, cementing a new chapter in Vietnamese-US relations. It was the last scheduled foreign visit of his presidency.

2003
Crime figure Nam Can is sentenced to death for corruption, embezzlement, kidnap and murder, the case implicates dozens of police and politicians, rocking the reputation of the government.

2004
The first US commercial flight since the end of the Vietnam War touches down in Ho Chi Minh City, as US-Vietnamese business and tourism links mushroom.

2006
Vietnam plays host to the glitzy APEC summit, welcomes US president George W Bush, and prepares to join the WTO.

had brought the country to its knees and a radical change in direction was required.

Opening the Door

In 1985 President Mikhael Gorbachev came to power in the Soviet Union. *Glasnost* (openness) and *perestroika* (restructuring) were in, radical revolutionaries were out. Vietnam followed suit in 1986 by choosing reform-minded Nguyen Van Linh to lead the Vietnamese Communist Party. *Doi moi* (economic reform) was experimented with in Cambodia and introduced to Vietnam. As the USSR scaled back its commitments to the communist world, the far-flung outposts were the first to feel the pinch. The Vietnamese decided to unilaterally withdraw from Cambodia in September 1989, as they could no longer afford the occupation. The party in Vietnam was on its own and needed to reform to survive.

However, dramatic changes in Eastern Europe in 1989 and the collapse of the Soviet Union in 1991 were not viewed with favour in Hanoi. The party denounced the participation of non-communists in Eastern bloc governments, calling the democratic revolutions 'a counter-attack from imperialist circles' against socialism. Politically, things were moving at a glacial pace, but economically the Vietnamese decided to embrace the market. Capitalism has since taken root and it is unlikely that Ho Chi Minh would recognise the dynamic Vietnam of today.

Relations with Vietnam's old nemesis, the USA, have also vastly improved. In early 1994 the USA lifted its economic embargo, which had been in place against the North since the 1960s. Full diplomatic relations were restored and presidents Clinton and George W Bush have subsequently visited Hanoi.

During the occupation of Cambodia in the 1980s, the Vietnamese laid the world's longest minefield belt, K-5, as a defence against Khmer Rouge guerrilla attacks from Thailand. It stretched from the Mekong River to the Gulf of Thailand and remains one of the most heavily mined areas in the world.

2008	2009	2010	June 2011
Rampant inflation grips the country, as commodity prices soar; the local stock market bubble bursts and house prices spiral downwards leaving many saddled with high debts.	Pro-democracy activists are jailed for 'spreading propaganda against the government' by actions including hanging pro-democracy banners on a road bridge and publishing articles on the internet.	Hanoi celebrates its 1000th birthday in October with exhibitions and wild celebrations grip the capital; its imperial Citadel is declared a Unesco World Heritage site.	Tourist arrivals for the first six months of 2011 are almost 3 million, representing an 18% growth over 2010. Chinese, Korean, Japanese, American and Taiwanese are the top five arrivals.

People & Culture

The National Psyche

Industrious, proud, stubborn and yet mischievous, quick to laugh and fond of a joke, the Vietnamese are a complicated bunch. For Westerners the national character can be difficult to fathom: direct questions are frequently met with evasive answers. A Vietnamese person would never tell a relative stranger their life story or profound personal thoughts the way people sometimes share feelings in the West. The national mentality is to work as a team, in harmony rather than in conflict – unless you're on the highway, when it's everyone for themselves. Their deep respect for tradition, family and the state reflect core Confucian principles.

My Generation

In many ways Vietnam is still a traditional, conservative society, particularly for the older generation, who remember the long, hard years and every inch of the territory for which they fought. Brought up on restraint and moderation, many remain unmoved by 21st-century consumer culture. For the new generation, Vietnam is very different: a place to succeed and to ignore the staid structures set by the Communists. And yes, to show off that gleaming new motorbike, sharp haircut or iPhone.

North–South Divide

The north–south divide lingers on. It's said that Southerners think, then do; while Northerners think, then think some more. Southerners typically reckon Northerners have 'hard faces', that they take themselves too seriously and don't know how to have fun. Northerners are just as likely to think of Southerners as superficial, frivolous and business-obsessed. Caricatures these may be, but they shed light on the real differences between north and south that reach beyond the (very different) regional dialects.

Climate plays its part too. Life is easier in the south, where the fertile Mekong Delta allows three rice harvests a year. The north endures a long winter of grey skies, drizzle, mist and cool winds. Think of the differences between northern and southern Europe (or Maine and Alabama) and

Shadows and Wind (1999) by journalist Robert Templer is a snappily written exploration of contemporary Vietnam, from Ho Chi Minh personality cults to Vietnam's rock-and-roll youth.

FACE

Face is all important in Asia, and in Vietnam it is above all. Having 'big face' is synonymous with prestige, and prestige is particularly important in Vietnam. All families, even poor ones, are expected to have big wedding parties and throw their money around like it's water in order to gain face. This is often ruinously expensive, but far less distressing than 'losing face'. And it is for this reason that foreigners should never lose their tempers with the Vietnamese; this will bring unacceptable 'loss of face' to the individual involved and end any chance of a sensible solution to the dispute.

you have a snapshot of how one people can become two. Don't forget that the north has also lived with communism for more than half a century, while the south had more than two decades of free-wheelin' free-for-all with the Americans.

For more on this, see p427.

Lifestyle

Traditionally, Vietnamese life has revolved around family, fields and faith, with the rhythm of rural existence continuing for centuries at the same pace. All this has been disrupted by war, the impact of communism and globalisation. Whilst it's true that several generations may still share the same roof, the same rice and the same religion, lifestyles have changed immeasurably.

Vietnam is experiencing its very own '60s swing, which is creating feisty friction as sons and daughters dress as they like, date who they want and hit the town until all hours. But few live on their own and they still come home to Mum and Dad at the end of the day, where arguments might arise, particularly when it comes to marriage and settling down.

Some things never change. Most Vietnamese despise idleness and are early risers. You'll see parks full of t'ai chi devotees as dawn breaks, and offices are fully staffed by 7am. Indeed the whole nation seems supercharged with energy and vitality, no matter how hot and humid it is.

> Failing businesses often call in a geomancer (feng shui expert). Sometimes the solution is to move a door or a window. If this doesn't do the trick, it might be necessary to move an ancestor's grave.

Family

In Vietnam the status of your family is more important than your salary. A family's reputation commands respect and opens doors.

Extended family is important to the Vietnamese and that includes second or third cousins, the sort of family that many Westerners may not even realise they have. The extended family comes together during times of trouble and times of joy, celebrating festivals and successes, mourning deaths or disappointments. This is a source of strength for many of the older generation.

With so many family members traditionally under one roof, the Vietnamese generally don't share Western concepts of privacy and personal space. Don't be surprised if people walk into your hotel room without knocking: you may be sitting starkers when the maid unlocks the door and walks in unannounced.

BUSINESS, VIETNAMESE STYLE

Western visitors regularly complain about the business practices of many Vietnamese they encounter, which can range from mild price hiking to outright scamming. For many foreigners it's the most off-putting aspect of their time in the nation. At times it seems impossible to get the local price for anything. A little background is important.

Most of these rapacious individuals work in tourism; chronic overcharging is rare once you're off the main gringo trail. The mentality is that Westerners do not bother to learn the real price, don't learn any Vietnamese and are only in country for a week or two. For years, many Vietnamese have only thought about the short term – about making a fast buck. As they've become more experienced in tourism, the concept has grown that good service will bring repeat business (and bad service will be all over internet forums immediately).

It's not an excuse, but Vietnam is a unique country. Famine killed 2 million in the 1940s, and the country was among the poorest of the poor following the American War. Vietnam's tourism industry is still very young and the Vietnamese state actually helped forge this overcharging mentality – until relatively recently the government set separate local and foreign rates (which were four to 10 times more) for everything from train fares to hotel rooms.

Population

Vietnam's population reached 90.5 million in 2011, ranking it the 13th most populous country in the world. Birth rates have steadily decreased from an average of 3.6 children per woman in 1991 to 1.91 per woman in 2011.

Traditionally a rural agrarian society, the race is on for the move to the cities. Vietnam is experiencing a tremendous shift in the balance of population, as increasing numbers of young people desert the fields in search of those mythical streets paved with gold in Hanoi and Ho Chi Minh City (HCMC). By 2011, 30% of Vietnamese lived in urban areas. The population of HCMC and its suburbs is already more than seven million, the Hanoi conurbation over six million. Danang, Haiphong and Can Tho are all millionaires.

The People of Vietnam

Vietnamese culture and civilisation have been profoundly influenced by the Chinese, who occupied the country for 1000 years (see p429) and whose culture deeply permeates Vietnamese society.

History has of course influenced the mix of Vietnamese minorities. The steady expansion southwards in search of cultivable lands absorbed first the Kingdom of Champa and later the eastern extent of the Khmer Empire, and both the Chams and the Khmers are sizeable minorities today.

Traffic was not only one-way. Many of the 50 or more minority groups that inhabit the far northwest only migrated to these areas from Yunnan (China) and Tibet in the past few centuries. They moved into the mountains that the lowland Vietnamese considered uncultivable, and help make up the most colourful part of the ethnic mosaic that is Vietnam today. For more on Vietnam's minority hill-tribe groups, see p457.

The largest minority group in Vietnam has always been the ethnic-Chinese community, which makes up much of the commercial class in the cities. While the government has traditionally viewed them with suspicion, and drove many of them out of the country as 'boat people' in the late 1970s, many are now comfortably resettled and play a major part in driving economic development.

Religion

Many Vietnamese are not very religious and some surveys indicate that only 20% of the population consider themselves to have a faith. That said, over the centuries, Confucianism, Taoism and Buddhism have fused with popular Chinese beliefs and ancient Vietnamese animism to create the Tam Giao (Triple Religion) that many Vietnamese identify with. When discussing religion, Vietnamese people are likely to say that they are Buddhist, but when it comes to family or civic duties they are likely to follow the moral and social code of Confucianism, and turn to Taoist concepts to understand the nature of the cosmos.

Although the majority of the population has only a vague notion of Buddhist doctrines, they invite monks to participate in life-cycle ceremonies, such as funerals. Buddhist pagodas are seen by many Vietnamese as a physical and spiritual refuge from an uncertain world.

Christianity, present in Vietnam for 500 years, and Cao Daism (unique to the region) are other important religions.

Buddhism

Buddhism, like other great religions, has been through a somewhat messy divorce and arrived in Vietnam in two forms: Mahayana Buddhism (the Northern school) proceeded north into Nepal, Tibet, China,

Young Western travellers, depending on their dress, are often greeted with *tay balo!* (literally, 'Westerner backpack'), an unflattering term for scruffy-looking foreigners.

PEOPLE & CULTURE POPULATION

Vietnamese who have emigrated are called Viet Kieu. They have traditionally been maligned by locals as cowardly, arrogant and privileged. In the 1990s, returning Viet Kieu were often followed by police but now official policy is to welcome them, and their money, back to the motherland.

As in many Southeast Asian countries, substantial numbers of Vietnamese women (estimated at up to 2 million) end up in prostitution of some sort or another, working in massage parlours, karaoke clubs or dubious bars.

WHEN IN NAM... DO AS THE VIETS

Take your time to learn a little about the local culture in Vietnam. Not only will this ensure you don't inadvertently cause offence or, worse, spark an international incident, but it will also endear you to your hosts. Here are a few tips to help you go native.

Dress Code

Respect local dress standards: shorts to the knees, women's tops covering the shoulder, particularly at religious sites. Always remove your shoes before entering a temple. Nude sunbathing is considered totally inappropriate, even on beaches.

Meet & Greet

The traditional Vietnamese form of greeting is to press your hands together in front of your body and bow slightly. These days, the Western custom of shaking hands has almost completely taken over.

It's on the Cards

Exchanging business cards is an important part of even the smallest transaction or business contact. Get some printed before you arrive in Vietnam and hand them out like confetti.

Deadly Chopsticks

Leaving a pair of chopsticks sitting vertically in a rice bowl looks very much like the incense sticks that are burned for the dead. This is a powerful sign and is not appreciated anywhere in Asia.

Mean Feet

Like the Chinese and Japanese, Vietnamese strictly maintain clean floors and it's usual to remove shoes when entering somebody's home. It's rude to point the bottom of your feet towards other people. Never, ever point your feet towards anything sacred, such as a Buddha image.

Hats Off to Them

As a form of respect to elderly or other esteemed people, such as monks, take off your hat and bow your head politely when addressing them. In Asia, the head is the symbolic highest point – never pat or touch an adult on the head.

Korea, Mongolia and Japan, while Theravada Buddhism (the Southern school) took the southerly route through India, Sri Lanka, Myanmar and Cambodia.

The predominant school of Buddhism, and indeed religion, in Vietnam is Mahayana Buddhism (Dai Thua, or Bac Tong, meaning 'From the North'). The largest Mahayana sect in the country is Zen (Dhyana, or Thien), also known as the school of meditation. Dao Trang (the Pure Land school), another important sect, is practised mainly in the south.

Theravada Buddhism (Tieu Thua, or Nam Tong) is found mainly in the Mekong Delta region, and is mostly practised by ethnic Khmers.

Mahayana Buddhists believe in Boddhisatvas (Quan Am in Vietnam) or Buddhas that attain nirvana but postpone their enlightenment to stay on earth to save their fellow beings.

Taoism

Taoism (Lao Giao, or Dao Giao) originated in China and is based on the philosophy of Laotse (Old One), who lived in the 6th century BC. Little is known about Laotse and there is some debate as to whether or not he actually existed. He is believed to have been the custodian of the imperial archives for the Chinese government, and Confucius is supposed to have consulted him.

Understanding Taoism is not easy. The philosophy emphasises contemplation and simplicity. Its ideal is returning to the Tao (The Way, or the essence of which all things are made), and it emphasises *am* and *duong,* the Vietnamese equivalents of yin and yang. Much of Taoist ritualism has been absorbed into Chinese and Vietnamese Buddhism, including most commonly, the use of dragons and demons to decorate temple rooftops.

Confucianism

More a philosophy than an organised religion, Confucianism (Nho Giao, or Khong Giao) has been an important force in shaping Vietnam's social system and the lives and beliefs of its people.

Confucius (Khong Tu) was born in China around 550 BC. He saw people as social beings formed by society yet also capable of shaping their society. He believed that the individual exists in and for society and drew up a code of ethics to guide the individual in social interaction. This code laid down a person's obligations to family, society and the state, which remain the pillars of the Vietnamese nation today.

Cao Daism

Cao Daism is a Vietnamese sect that seeks to create the ideal religion by fusing the secular and religious philosophies of both East and West. It was founded in the early 1920s based on messages revealed in seances to Ngo Minh Chieu, the group's founder. For more on Cao Daism, see boxed text p348.

There are thought to be between two and three million followers of Cao Daism in Vietnam. The sect's colourful headquarters is in Tay Ninh, 96km northwest of HCMC.

To learn about Vietnamese Buddhism, check out www.quang duc.com, the website of Quang Duc Monastery in Melbourne, Australia. Also worth a look are leading Buddhist magazine and website Shamb-hala Sun (www.shambhalasun.com), and the informative UK-based Buddhist Society (www.thebuddhist society.org).

PEOPLE & CULTURE RELIGION

TET: THE BIG ONE

Tet is Christmas, New Year and birthdays all rolled into one. Tet Nguyen Dan (Festival of the First Day) ushers in the Lunar New Year and is the most significant date in the Vietnamese calendar. It's a time when families reunite in the hope of good fortune for the coming year, and ancestral spirits are welcomed back into the family home. And the whole of Vietnam celebrates a birthday; everyone becomes one year older.

The festival falls between 19 January and 20 February, the same dates as Chinese New Year. The first three days after Tet are the official holidays but many people take the whole week off.

Tet rites begin seven days before New Year's Day. Altars, laden with offerings, are prepared to ensure good luck in the coming year. Cemeteries are visited and the spirits of dead relatives invited home for the celebrations. Absent family members return home. It's important that the new year is started with a clean slate; debts are paid and cleaning becomes the national sport. A New Year's tree *(cay neu)* – kumquat, peach or apricot blossom – is displayed to ward off evil spirits.

At the stroke of midnight on New Year's Eve, all problems are left behind and mayhem ensues. The goal is to make as much noise as possible: drums and percussion fill the night air.

The events of New Year's Day are crucial as it's believed they affect the year ahead. People take extra care not to be rude or show anger. Other activities that are believed to attract bad spirits include sewing, sweeping, swearing and breaking things.

It's crucial that the first visitor of the year to each household is suitable – a wealthy married man with several children is ideal – foreigners may not be considered auspicious!

Apart from New Year's Eve itself, Tet is a quiet family affair – *banh chung* (sticky rice with pork and egg) is eaten at home. Shops are closed, and virtually all transport ceases to run. It's a troublesome time to travel in Vietnam. However, it is a special time of year and you're sure to be invited to join in the celebrations, just remember this phrase: *chuc mung nam moi* – Happy New Year!

Hoa Hao Buddhism

The Hoa Hao Buddhist sect (Phat Giao Hoa Hao) was founded in the Mekong Delta in 1939 by Huynh Phu So. After he was miraculously cured of an illness, So began preaching a reformed Buddhism that was based on the common people and embodied in personal faith rather than elaborate rituals. His Buddhist philosophies involve simplicity in worship and no intermediaries between humans and the Supreme Being. Hoa Hao Buddhists are thought to number approximately 1.5 million.

Cao Daism is a cocktail of the world's faiths and philosophies. Its prophets include Buddha, Confucius, Jesus Christ, Moses and Mohammed, and some wacky choices, such as Joan of Arc, William Shakespeare and Victor Hugo.

Christianity

Catholicism was introduced in the 16th century by missionaries. Today Vietnam has the second-highest concentration of Catholics (8% to 10% of the population) in Asia after the Philippines. Under the Communist government, Catholics faced severe restrictions on their religious activities. In Vietnam churches were viewed as a rival centre of power linked to capitalism that could subvert the government. Since 1990, the government has taken a more liberal line and Catholicism is making a comeback.

Protestantism was introduced to Vietnam in 1911 and most of the 200,000 or so followers today are hill-tribe people in the central highlands.

In recent years vast new Buddhist temples have been constructed, including Chua Bai Dinh, while giant new Buddha statues now define the coastline of Danang and Vung Tao.

Islam

Around 70,000 Muslims, mostly ethnic Chams, live in Vietnam, mainly in the south of the country. Many Cham Muslims follow a localised adaptation of Islamic theology and law, praying only on Fridays and celebrating Ramadan for only three days. Traditionally their Islamic-based religious rituals co-existed with animism and the worship of Hindu deities. Today more orthodox Muslim practises have been adopted by many, as Chams have gained greater contact with the wider Islamic world and more mosques are under construction.

Hinduism

Champa was profoundly influenced by Hinduism, and many of the Cham towers, built as Hindu sanctuaries, contain *lingas* (phallic fertility symbols that represent Shiva) that are still worshipped by ethnic Vietnamese and ethnic Chinese alike. After the fall of Champa in the 15th century, many Chams who remained in Vietnam became Muslims but continued to practise various Hindu rituals and customs. Hundreds of thousands more migrated southwest to Cambodia, where they make up an important minority today.

There are around 60,000 Cham living in Vietnam who identify themselves as Hindus. They predominantly live in the same region as Cham Muslims, concentrated around Phan Rang on the south-central coast.

PAGODA OR TEMPLE?

Travelling around Vietnam, there are a lot of pagodas and temples, but how does the average person know which is which? The Vietnamese regard a *chua* (pagoda) as a place of worship where they make offerings or pray. A Vietnamese *den* (temple) is not really a place of worship, but rather a structure built to honour a great historical figure (Confucius, Tran Hung Dao, and even Ho Chi Minh).

The Cao Dai Temple seems to somehow fall between the cracks. Given the mixture of ideas that is part and parcel of Cao Daism, it's arguably a blend of temple, pagoda, church and mosque.

ANCESTOR WORSHIP

Vietnamese ancestor worship dates from before the arrival of Confucianism or Buddhism. Ancestor worship is based on the belief that the soul lives on after death and becomes the protector of its descendants. Because of the influence that the spirits of one's ancestors exert on the living, it is considered not only shameful for the spirits to be upset or restless, but downright dangerous.

Traditionally, the Vietnamese worship and honour the spirits of their ancestors regularly, especially on the anniversary of a particular ancestor's death. To request help for success in business or on behalf of a sick child, sacrifices and prayers are given to the ancestral spirits. Important worship elements are the family altar and a plot of land, the income of which is set aside for the support of the ancestors.

Women in Vietnam

As in many parts of Asia, Vietnamese women take a lot of pain for little gain, with plenty of hard work to do but little authority at the decision-making level. Vietnamese women were highly successful as guerrillas in the American War and brought plenty of grief to US soldiers. After the war, their contributions were given much fanfare, but most of the government posts were given to men. In the countryside, you'll see women doing backbreaking jobs, such as crushing rocks at construction sites and carrying heavy baskets.

The country's two-children-per-family policy is once again being strictly enforced, at least in urban areas, and is boosting the independence of Vietnamese women, with more delaying marriage to get an education. Around 50% of university students are female, but they're not always given the same opportunity as males to shine after graduation.

Arts

Traditional Music

Vietnam's traditional music is original, though heavily influenced by Chinese and also Indianised Khmer and Cham music. Written music and the five note (pentatonic) scale may be of Chinese origin, but Vietnamese choral music is unique, as the melody and the tones move as one; the melody cannot rise during a verse that has a falling tone.

Vietnamese folk music is usually sung without any instrumental accompaniment and was adapted by the Communist Party for many a patriotic marching song.

Classical, or 'learned music', is rather formal and frigid. It was performed at the imperial court for the entertainment of the mandarin elite. There are two main types of classical chamber music: *hat a dao* from the north and *ca Hue* from central Vietnam.

Traditional music is played on a wide array of indigenous instruments, dating back to ancient *dong son* (bronze drums). Key instruments are the *dan bau,* a single-stringed zither that generates an astounding array of tones, *dan tranh,* a 16-string zither with a haunting melody, and the *trung,* a large bamboo xylophone.

Each of Vietnam's minorities has its own musical traditions that often include distinctive costumes and instruments, such as reed flutes, lithophones (similar to xylophones), bamboo whistles, gongs and stringed instruments made from gourds.

Vietnamese traditional music is performed at restaurants and museums in Hanoi, HCMC and Hue.

For a look at the impact of *doi moi* (economic reform) on some Vietnamese women, Vu Xuan Hung's film *Misfortune's End* (Giai Han; 1997) tells the tale of a silk weaver deserted by her husband for an upwardly mobile businesswoman.

Tieng Hat Que Huong, which was founded in 1981, has a mission to preserve, develop and promote Vietnamese traditional music, building a bridge between artists, old and new. Visit it at www .tienghatque huong.com and look up details of forthcoming performances in HCMC.

A WHITER SHADE OF PALE

The Vietnamese consider pale skin to be beautiful. On sunny days Vietnamese women can often be seen strolling under the shade of an umbrella in order to keep from tanning. Women who work in the fields will go to great lengths to preserve their pale skin by wrapping their faces in towels and wearing long-sleeved shirts, elbow-length silk gloves and conical hats. To tell a Vietnamese woman that she has white skin is a great compliment; telling her that she has a 'lovely suntan' is a grave insult.

Contemporary Music

Vietnam's music scene is pretty middle of the road. There are small hip hop (Hanoi's Lenin Park is a key meeting point for breakdancers), rock and punk (check out Hanoi's Rock City) and DJ scenes but little rebellion in evidence. Hip hoppers tend to be well behaved and preoccupied with dance moves rather than searing broadsides against authority.

The most celebrated artist is Khanh Ly (www.khanhly.com), who left Vietnam in 1975 for the USA. She is massive both in Vietnam and abroad. Her music is widely available in Vietnam, but the government frowns on her recently composed lyrics that recall the trials of her life as a refugee.

Vietnam's number one domestic heart-throb is Hue-born Quang Linh, who is adored by Vietnamese of all ages for his love songs.

Another celebrated local pop singer is sex symbol Phuong Thanh, who has spoken out on issues including homosexuality and prostitution. Hot bands include rock band Microwave, metal merchants Black Infinity, the punk band Giao Chi and also alt-roots band 6789.

Trinh Cong Son, who died in 2001 was a prolific writer-composer of anti-war and reconciliation songs; he was once called the Bob Dylan of Vietnam by folksinger Joan Baez.

For an in-depth insight into the culture of Vietnam, including fashion, film and music, check out www.thingsasian.com.

Dance

Traditionally reserved for ceremonies and festivals, Vietnamese folk dance is again mainstream thanks to tourism. The Conical Hat Dance is one of the most visually stunning dances. A group of women wearing *ao dai* (the national dress of Vietnam) shake their stuff and spin around, whirling their classic conical hats.

Vietnam's ethnic minorities have their own distinct dance traditions.

Theatre & Puppetry

Vietnamese theatre fuses music, singing, recitation, dance and mime into an artistic whole. These days, the various forms of Vietnamese theatre are performed by dozens of state-funded troupes and companies around the country.

Classical theatre is known as *hat tuong* in the north and *hat boi* in the south and is based on Chinese opera. It's very formal, employing fixed gestures and scenery and has an accompanying orchestra (dominated by the drum) and a limited cast of characters.

Popular theatre *(hat cheo)* expresses social protest through satire. The singing and verse are in everyday language and include many proverbs and sayings, accompanied by folk melodies.

Modern theatre *(cai luong)* originated in the south in the early 20th century and shows strong Western influences. Spoken drama *(kich noi* or *kich),* with its Western roots, appeared in the 1920s and is popular among students and intellectuals.

Conventional puppetry *(roi can)* and the uniquely Vietnamese art form of water puppetry *(roi nuoc),* draw their plots from the same legendary and historical sources as other forms of traditional theatre.

Dancing Girl, directed by Le Hoang, caused a major splash with its release in 2003. It tells the story of two HIV-positive prostitutes, and Hoa (played by My Duyen) is seen mainlining heroin.

There are water-puppet theatres in both Hanoi and HCMC. To learn more about this 'Punch and Judy in a pool' art form, see p75.

Cinema

One of Vietnam's earliest cinematographic efforts was a newsreel of Ho Chi Minh's 1945 Proclamation of Independence. Later, parts of the battle of Dien Bien Phu (p123) were restaged for the benefit of movie cameras.

Prior to reunification, the South Vietnamese movie industry produced a string of sensational, low-budget flicks. Conversely, North Vietnamese film-making efforts were very propagandist.

Contemporary films span a wide range of themes, from warfare to modern romance.

In Nguyen Khac's *The Retired General* (1988), the central character copes with adjusting from his life as a soldier during the American War to life as a civilian family man.

Dang Nhat Minh is perhaps Vietnam's most prolific film-maker. In *The Return* (1993), he hones in on the complexities of modern relationships, while *The Girl on the River* (1987) tells the stirring tale of a female journalist who joins an ex-prostitute in search of her former lover, a Viet Cong soldier.

Young overseas-Vietnamese film directors are steadily carving a niche for themselves in the international film industry and snapping up awards.

Tran Anh Hung's touching *The Scent of Green Papaya* (1992) celebrates the coming of age of a young servant girl in Saigon. *Cyclo* (1995), his visually stunning masterpiece, cuts to the core of HCMC's gritty underworld and its violent existence.

Vietnamese-American Tony Bui made a splash in 1999 with his exquisite feature debut *Three Seasons* (1999) set in HCMC, which featured Harvey Keitel.

Literature

There are three veins of Vietnamese literature. Traditional oral literature *(truyen khau)* began long before recorded history and includes legends, folk songs and proverbs. Sino-Vietnamese literature was written in Chinese characters *(chu nho)*. Dominated by Confucian and Buddhist texts, it was governed by strict rules of metre and verse. Modern Vietnamese literature *(quoc am)* includes anything recorded in *nom* characters. The earliest text written in *nom* was the late–13th century *Van Te Ca Sau* (Ode to an Alligator).

One of Vietnam's literary masterpieces, *Kim Van Kieu* (The Tale of Kieu) was written during the first half of the 19th century by Nguyen Du (1765–1820), a poet, scholar, mandarin and diplomat.

Architecture

Historically the Vietnamese were not prolific builders like their Khmer neighbours, or the Chams, whose towers and temples you'll see in southern Vietnam. For more on architecture see p467.

Painting & Sculpture

Painting on frame-mounted silk dates from the 13th century and was at one time the preserve of scholar-calligraphers, who painted grand scenes from nature. Realistic portraits for use in ancestor worship were also produced.

During the past century, Vietnamese painting has been influenced by Western trends. Much recent work has had political rather than aesthetic or artistic motives – some of this propaganda art is now highly collectable.

Paradise of the Blind, by Duong Thu Huong, was the first Vietnamese novel to be published in the USA. It is set in a northern village and a Hanoi slum, and recalls the lives of three women and the hardships they faced over some 40 years.

The Sacred Willow (2000), by Duong Van Mai Elliot, spans four tumultuous generations of an upper-class Vietnamese family. This enlightening historical memoir traces French colonisation, WWII and the wars with France and America.

PEOPLE & CULTURE ARTS

INSIDE LACQUER

Lacquer *(son mai)* is made from resin extracted from the rhus tree. It is creamy white in raw form, but is darkened with pigments in an iron container for 40 hours. After the object has been treated with glue, the requisite 10 coats of lacquer are applied. Each coat must be dried for a week and then thoroughly sanded with pumice and cuttlebone before the next layer can be applied. A specially refined lacquer is used for the 11th and final coat, which is sanded with a fine coal powder and lime wash before the object is decorated. Designs include engraving in low relief, or inlaying mother-of-pearl, eggshell or precious metals.

The art of making lacquerware was brought to Vietnam from China in the mid–15th century. During the 1930s, the Fine Arts School in Hanoi had several Japanese teachers who introduced new styles and production methods.

Many young artists now concentrate on producing commercial paintings. Some have gone back to the traditional-style silk or lacquer paintings, while others experiment with contemporary subjects. Hanoi and Hoi An have some great galleries.

The Chams produced spectacular carved sandstone figures for their Hindu and Buddhist sanctuaries. Cham sculpture was profoundly influenced by Indian art. The largest single collection of Cham sculpture in the world is found at the Museum of Cham Sculpture (p181) in Danang. For the lowdown on Cham architecture, see p244.

Sport

Football (soccer) is Vietnam's number-one spectator sport and the country is mad for it. During the World Cup, the Champions League or other major clashes, half the country stays up all night to watch live games. The national team is one of the stronger teams in Southeast Asia, having won the Asean Championships in 2008, though they remain minnows on the international stage and have not yet qualified for a Word Cup.

Tennis has considerable appeal these days and trendy Vietnamese like to both watch and play. Similarly, golf has taken off and courses are dotted all over the country, although membership fees ensure it remains a game for the elite.

The Vietnamese are a nation of badminton players and every street is a potential court. Other favourite sports include volleyball and table tennis.

Hill Tribes of Vietnam

Hanhi ethnic minority girls carrying rice stalks in Lai Chau Province

A mosaic of ethnic minorities inhabits the mountainous regions of Vietnam. Exploring their highland homelands, hiking remote trails and experiencing a hill-tribe market are unforgettable experiences.

The French called these ethnic minorities Montagnards while ethnic Vietnamese traditionally referred to them as *moi*, a derogatory term meaning savages. The current government prefers the term *nguoi thuong* 'highland people'.

The most colourful of these minorities live in the far north of Vietnam, carving an existence out of the lush mountain landscapes along the Chinese and Lao borders. Here most hill-tribe people wear incredible hand-woven costumes – some so elaborate that it's easy to believe the girls learn to embroider before they can walk. In the central highlands, attachment to traditional dress is rare and minorities can be difficult to distinguish, at least visually, from other Vietnamese.

Some hill-tribe groups have lived in Vietnam for thousands of years, while others like the H'mong migrated south from China in the past few centuries. The areas inhabited by each group are often delineated by altitude, with more recent arrivals settling higher up. First come, first served even applies to the remote mountains.

Each hill tribe has its own language, customs, mode of dress and spiritual beliefs. Language and culture constitute the borders of their world. Some groups are caught between the medieval and the modern, while others have assimilated into modern life.

Most groups share a rural, agricultural lifestyle with similar village architecture and rituals. The majority are semi-nomadic, and cultivate their crops using slash-and-burn methods. The government has been trying to encourage the hill tribes to adopt standard agriculture at lower altitudes, with incentives such as subsidised irrigation, education and health care. However the hill tribes' long history of independence and distrust of the ethnic-Vietnamese majority keep many away from the lowlands.

As in other parts of Asia, the traditional culture of the ethnic minorities is gradually giving way to outside influences. Many no

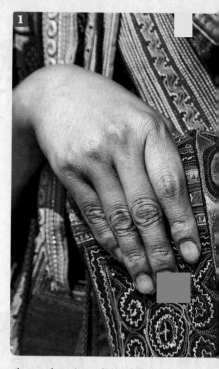

longer dress in traditional clothing, and those who do are often found only in the remote villages of the far north. Often it is the women of the community who keep the costume alive, wearing tribal clothes and passing their weaving knowledge on to their daughters.

THE LEGACY OF WAR

During the American War, many of the minorities in the central highlands were enrolled in the Civilian Irregular Defense Program (CIDG), part of the US Army Special Forces. US special forces considered the tribes the hardiest and most loyal forces on the South Vietnamese side.

Following the end of the war in 1975, some of these experienced fighters continued to resist the new communist government based in Hanoi. The United Front for the Liberation of Oppressed Races (FULRO) conducted small-scale attacks on government forces right through the 1980s.

Clockwise from top left
1. Black H'mong embroidery at Sapa market **2.** White H'mong girl, Sinho **3.** Flower H'mong children, Cao Son

Minorities Today

Tourism is effecting change in some hill-tribe regions. With growing numbers of people travelling to the highlands there's increased exposure to business-savvy lowlanders, Western wealth and commerce. Agriculture is often abandoned when there are easier pickings available. Some children, particularly in Sapa, expect handouts of money or sweets. Others dodge school to peddle trinkets to tourists. Worse, domestic tourism has created a market for karaoke, massage and sex, and some minority women have been lured into this trade. However there are now H'mong-owned tour agencies (p126) which are supporting educational and development work in the highlands. Vietnam's hill-tribe minorities have some autonomy and, though the official national language is Vietnamese, children can still learn their local languages, (see p528 for useful phrases), although this has been a sensitive issue in parts of the central highlands, where tensions remain high.

Prejudices against hill-tribe people endure. Attitudes are changing slowly but the Vietnamese media can still present them as primitive and exotic. It's not uncommon for Vietnamese people to still see minorities as subversive (some sided with the USA during the American War).

The reality is that minorities remain at the bottom of the educational and economic ladder. Despite improvements in rural schooling and regional healthcare, many hill-tribe people marry young, have large families and die early. They remain the poorest section of Vietnamese society: according to 2006 World Bank figures 52% live in poverty, compared to 10% of ethnic Vietnamese.

Clockwise from top left

1. Elderly Flower H'mong woman in traditional dress
2. Cong minority woman on bamboo raft, Muong Tei
3. Portrait of Red Dzao woman in traditional headdress

PROTEST

Many highlanders feel excluded from mainstream society, and religious tensions (many are Christian) and land ownership issues (ethnic Vietnamese have colonised large areas of their homeland) have simmered for decades.

Protests have erupted several times in recent years. Minorities in the central highlands demonstrated against discrimination and religious persecution in 2001 and 2004 resulting in arrests, reports of up to eight deaths and 1000 people fleeing the country.

Reports from Dien Bien Phu province in May 2011 suggest up to 7000 H'mong highlanders gathered to call for greater autonomy and religious freedom, prompting a crackdown by the Vietnamese military and news blackout. There were unconfirmed reports of 28 deaths, according to the US-based pro-H'mong Center for Public Policy Analysis. The Vietnamese government accused 'bad elements' of provoking crowds to call for an independent H'mong homeland and said "the situation in Muong Nhe is still being resolved by all levels of party and government so that the lives of the compatriots there can return to stability".

The Ethnic Mosaic

Vietnam has 53 recognised minority groups, accounting for 14% of the population. Some groups are comprised of just a few hundred people, others more than a million. Together they number nearly 11 million.

Bahnar

The Bahnar (pop 175,000) are believed to have migrated long ago to the central highlands from the coast. They are animists and worship trees, such as the banyan and ficus. They keep a traditional calendar that calls for 10 months of cultivation, with the remaining two months set aside for social and personal duties, such as marriage, weaving and festivals. Traditionally when babies reached one month old, an ear-piercing ceremony was held to make them a member of the village. The Bahnar are skilled woodcarvers and wear similar dress to the Jarai.

Dzao

The Dzao (or Zao/Dao) are one of the largest (pop 650,000) of Vietnam's ethnic groups and live in the northwestern provinces. The Dzao practise ancestor worship or *ban ho* and hold elaborate rituals with animal sacrifices. The group's proximity to China explains the common use of traditional medicine and the similarity of the *nom dao* script to Chinese characters. The Dzao are famous for their elaborate dress. Women's clothing features intricate weaving and silver-coloured beads and coins. Their long hair, shaved above the forehead, is tied up into a large red or embroidered turban.

Ede

The polytheistic Ede (pop 270,000) live communally in beamless boat-shaped longhouses on stilts. About a third of these homes are for communal use, with the rest

Clockwise from top left
1. Hill-tribe girl in a small village, Coc Ly 2. Black Dzao woman with child, Tien Binh 3. Hanhi people, Muong Te

partitioned into sections to give privacy to married couples. In Ede courtship, girls propose to men. After marriage, the couple resides with the wife's family and bears the mother's name. Inheritance is also the preserve of women. Ede women generally wear colourful embroidered vests with copper and silver jewellery. Many live around Kon Tum and Dac Lac.

H'mong

Since migrating from China in the 19th century, the H'mong have become one of Vietnam's largest ethnic groups (pop 900,000). They are spread across the far north, but most visitors will meet them in Sapa or Bac Ha. Most are animists, and worship spirits. The H'mong live at high altitudes, cultivate dry rice and medicinal plants (including opium, though this is being phased out due to government pressure) and raise animals. There are several groups of H'mong, including Black, White, Red, Green and Flower, each with its own subtle dress code. Black H'mong wear indigo-dyed linen clothing, with

women wearing skirts, aprons, leggings and cylindrical hats. The Flower H'mong women wear outfits with bright rainbow banding. Many H'mong women don large silver necklaces, earrings and silver bracelets. H'mong also live in neighbouring Laos and Thailand, and many have fled to Western countries as refugees.

Jarai

The Jarai are the most populous minority in the central highlands (pop 340,000); many live around Pleiku. Villages are often named after a nearby river or tribal chief, and a *nha-rong* (communal house) is usually at the centre. Jarai women typically propose marriage to men through a matchmaker. Animistic beliefs and rituals abound, and the Jarai pay respect to their ancestors and nature through a host or *yang* (genie). They construct elaborate cemeteries with totem-style effigies of the deceased. They're also renowned for musical instruments, from bamboo tubes (used as wind flutes and percussion), to bronze gongs.

464

Muong

Mainly concentrated around Hoa Binh, the male-dominated Muong (pop 1.4 million) live in small stilt-house hamlets and their culture is similar to the Thai. They are known for producing literature, poems and songs. Muong music is performed with instruments such as the gong, drums, pan pipes and two-stringed violin.

Nung

The Nung (pop 750,000) inhabit the far northeastern provinces. Concentrated into small villages, Nung homes are typically divided into two areas: one for living, the other for work and worship. From ancestral worship to festivities, the Nung are spiritually and socially similar to the Tay. Nung brides traditionally command high dowries from prospective grooms. Most Nung villages still have shamans, and the tribe is renowned for its handicrafts, including basketwork.

Sedang

Native to the central highlands, the Sedang (pop 140,000) have been adversely affected by centuries of war and invaders (Cham and Khmer). They do not carry family names, and there's said to be complete equality between the sexes. The children of one's siblings are also given the same treatment as one's own, creating a strong familial tradition. The Sedang practise unique customs, such as grave abandonment, sharing of property with the deceased and giving birth at the forest's edge.

Tay

The Tay (pop 1.5 million) are the largest hill-tribe group and live at low elevations in the north. They adhere to Vietnamese beliefs in Buddhism, Confucianism and Taoism, but also worship genies and spirits. Since developing their own script in the 16th century, Tay literature and arts have become famous. Nong Duc Manh, General Secretary of the Vietnamese Communist Party for 10 years until January 2011, is from the Tay minority.

Clockwise from top left
1. Red Dzao girl, Ta Phin 2. Muong people fishing for shellfish, Lai Chau 3. Flower H'mong children, Coc Ly

Thai

The Thai (pop 1.4 million) originated in southern China before settling along the riverbanks of the northwest from Hoa Binh to Muong Lay. Villages consist of 40 or 50 thatched stilt houses. The Thai are usually categorised by colour, such as Red, Black and White Thai. Black Thai women wear vibrant blouses and headgear, while White Thai tend to dress in contemporary clothing. Using a script developed in the 5th century, the Thai have produced literature ranging from poetry and love songs to folk tales.

ETHNIC MINORITY ETIQUETTE 101

Though you'll meet hill-tribe girls with mobile phones, the culture of Sapa's ethnic minorities remains strong. Interaction with travellers threatens this, but visitors can minimise their impact. The following is adapted from a sign in Ta Van, a Giay village.

» Avoid white headbands or bandanas; white is often worn at funerals.
» Avoid public displays of affection and don't wear revealing clothing
» Don't enter homes that have leaves, bones or feathers hanging from the entrance or roof.
» When entering a home, take your backpack off and carry it in your hands.
» If staying overnight, respect the villagers as they go to bed early.
» Avoid photographing or touching the head of a newborn child.
» Don't take photographs of people without asking permission.
» Set a good example by not using drugs or asking where you can purchase them.
» Show respect for religious symbols and rituals.
» Avoid cultivating begging. Rather than offering money for photography or handing out gifts to children, better ways to assist include employing a local guide, investigating charities in the area, or asking your guide if you can donate to a local school.

2

Where to Visit the Hill Tribes

The best introduction to highland culture is Hanoi's outstanding and highly informative Museum of Ethnology (p53) which has replica stilt houses and superb tribal art.

Vietnam's minorities are spread throughout the northern and central highlands. Sapa is the most popular place to encounter the hill tribes, including Black H'mong and Red Dzao. Close by are the colourful Flower H'mong markets around Bac Ha.

Homestays are a rewarding experience and Mai Chau is famous for the warm welcome of the White Thai people. Other important minority centres in the northwest include Ha Giang and Lai Chau.

Further east, the province of Cao Bang is a less-travelled region with several minorities, including H'mong, Nung and Tay. Lang Son also provides a home to these minority groups, but sees fewer tourists still.

Down in the central highlands, Buon Ma Thuot, Dalat, Kon Tum and Pleiku are useful bases to meet Bahnar, Jarai and Sedang people. However, most families here have forsaken their traditional costumes, so meet-the-minorities tourism has less pulling power than in the north.

MEET THE MINORITIES

Sapa (p125) Dzao and H'mong people inhabit the dramatic valleys around this hill station.

Bac Ha (p133) Famous for its market, which draws Flower H'mong from far and wide.

Mai Chau (p118) Beautiful valley home of the White Thai with many homestays.

Cao Bang (p112) Rugged mountains with a diverse range of minority groups.

Kon Tum (p293) A base for minorities in the Central Highlands.

Below
Elderly Red Dzao woman at Sapa market

Architecture in Vietnam

Vietnamese Architecture »
Colonial Buildings »
Pagodas & Temples »
Soviet Influences »

City Hall building, Ho Chi Minh City

PETER STUCKINGS / LONELY PLANET IMAGES ©

Vietnamese Design

Traditional Vietnamese architecture is unusual, as most important buildings are single-storey structures with heavy tiled roofs based on a substantial wooden framework (to withstand typhoons).

In rural parts houses are chiefly constructed from timber and built in stilted style, so that the home is above seasonal floods (and away from snakes and wild animals). Bamboo and palm leaves (for roofing) are also well suited to the tropical monsoon climate. Homes are usually divided into sections for sleeping, cooking and storage while livestock live below the house.

Quirky Vietnamese styles include the narrow tube houses of Hanoi's Old Quarter – the government collected tax according to the width of the commercial space, so the slimmer the cheaper. The Nung minority people's homes are also unusual, sometimes built with mud walls and with only one part elevated on stilts.

Consider the Vietnamese saying 'land is gold' as you survey a typical townscape today. Skinny concrete blocks of dubious architectural merit, many up to seven storeys high, soar above empty lots or loom above paddy fields. Planning laws (or the virtual lack of them) allow land owners to construct whatever they like, so cement constructions painted lime green or pink kitted out with mirror windows, built with vaguely French-inspired ornate balconies or Chinese details, are the flavour of the day in many places – the seafront in Cat Ba Town is one such example.

SKY HIGH

» **Bitexco Financial Tower** (HCMC; 269m) Completed in 2010. Ascend to its Skydeck for stupendous Saigon views.

» **Keangnam Hanoi Landmark Tower** (Hanoi; 345m) Topped out in 2011, this glass block is Vietnam's highest building.

» **PVN Tower** (Hanoi) Petrovietnam's proposed capital tower, if built, will reach around 400m.

Clockwise from top left
1. Floating houses, Chau Doc 2. M'nong hill-tribe house near Dalat 3. Bahnar thatch house in Kon Tum village

Colonial Buildings

Vietnam's French legacy is pronounced in the nation's architecture. Stately neoclassical buildings reinforced notions of European hegemony in the colonial era, and many still line grand city boulevards.

After the 1950s, most of these were left to rot as they symbolised an era many wished to forget. However recent renovation programs have led to structures, such as the former Hôtel de Ville (People's Committee Building) in Ho Chi Minh City (HCMC) and the Sofitel Metropole Hotel in Hanoi, being restored to their former glory. If you have a postcard to send in HCMC, stop to admire the spectacular halls and vaulted ceiling of the central post office – designed by Gustave Eiffel. Haiphong is another city with wonderful French designs.

In Hanoi's French Quarter many grand villas have fallen on hard times and are today worth a fortune to developers. Down in Dalat, French villas have been converted into hotels (including the spectacular Ana Mandara Villas) and restaurants.

Colonial churches were built in a range of architectural styles. In Hanoi the sombre neo-Gothic form of St Joseph is enhanced by dark grey stone, whereas all the bricks used to construct Ho Chi Minh City's cathedral were imported from France.

Art deco curiosities built under French rule include Dalat's wonderful train station, with its multi-coloured windows and the sleek La Residence Hotel in Hue.

COLONIAL STYLE

» **Balconies** Elegant colonnaded balconies grace important municipal buildings.
» **Louvered windows** Usually green or brown, these allow air to circulate.
» **Stucco features** A decorative flourish.
» **Colour** Classy ochre or pale mustard.
» **Terracotta roof tiles** Evoke memories of the Mediterranean.

Clockwise from top left
1. The balconies of Hanoi Opera House 2. Ho Chi Minh City Museum's classical interior 3. Hanoi's now-restored Sofitel Metropole Hotel

Pagodas & Temples

Unlike other many Asian nations, Vietnamese religious structures do not follow a specific national prototype. Pagoda styles echo the unique religious make-up of the nation, with strong Chinese content (including Confucian, Tao and Mahayana Buddhist elements) while southern Cham temples reflect influences from India, Hindu culture and the Khmer empire.

Pagodas

Pagodas *(chua)* incorporate Chinese ornamentation and motifs and follow a similar design, with buildings grouped around garden courtyards and adorned with plenty of statues and stelae. Most have single or double roofs with elevated hip rafters, though there are some with multi-tiered towers *(thap)* like Hue's Thien Mu Pagoda.

Vietnamese pagodas are designed according to feng shui (locally called *dia ly*) to achieve harmony of surroundings. They're primarily Buddhist places of worship, even though they may be dedicated to a local deity. Most are single-storey structures, with three wooden doors at the front. Inside are a number of chambers, usually filled with statues of Buddhas, Bodhisattvas and assorted heroes and deities (Thien Hau, Goddess of the Sea, is popular in coastal towns). Flashing fairy lights, giant smoking incense spirals, gongs and huge bells add to the atmosphere. Garden courtyards, many with sculptures and some with a sacred pond (perhaps filled with turtles), connect to other temple structures and there's often accommodation for monks at the rear.

Check out Hanoi's Temple of Literature for a superb example of a traditional Vietnamese temple or the wonderful pagodas in Hue's Imperial City.

Clockwise from top left
1. The altar within Jade Emperor Pagoda, HCMC
2. Bich Dong Pagoda, Ninh Binh Province **3.** Ha Chuong Hoi Quan Pagoda entrance, HCMC

CHAM TEMPLES

The Cham primarily practised the Hindu religion, worshipping the trinity of Shiva, Brahma and Vishnu, though some elements of Buddhism were also introduced. Temple-building commenced as early as the 4th century. Important Cham sights with surviving structures include My Son (near Hoi An), Po Nagar (near Nha Trang), Po Klong Garai (near Phan Rang), and Po Shanu (Phu Hai) near Phan Thiet, but all these sights have been ravaged by time and some devastated by war.

Most Cham temples were built from brick, with decorative carvings and detailing probably added later, cut into the brick sides of the monuments. The main features of a Cham complex include the *kalan* (tower, the home of the deity), saddle-roofed *kosagrha* temples (which housed valuables belonging to the gods) and the *gopura* gateway. Dotting the temple sites are stone statues of deities such as Yan Po Nagar (goddess of the country) and numerous stelae (My Son has 32) with inscriptions listing important events.

PAGODA FEATURES

» **Bodhisattvas** Enlightened earthly figures usually depicted as royals.

» **Cheung Huang Yeh** Greatly feared God of the City akin to the grim reaper.

» **Quan Am** Goddess of Mercy – a pale figure or statue with multiple arms.

» **Swastika** Ancient Asian sacred symbol that signifies the heart of the Buddha.

» **Thien Hau** Goddess who provides protection at sea.

Clockwise from top left

1. Po Klong Garai Cham Towers near Phan Rang
2. Dancing Shiva depicted at Po Nagar Cham Towers, Nha Trang 3. Cham sculptures at My Son

Soviet Influences

Across Vietnam a Soviet influence is deeply evident in many concrete municipal buildings, marketplaces and apartment blocks. Most Soviet architecture was in the prefabricated style of the mid-1950s, using inexpensive concrete and archetypal Modernist lines. Even in small towns you can stumble across reminders of Vietnam's past in the Soviet orbit: an austere concrete cinema facade in Hoi An or an ageing town hall.

Soviet architects and planners, such as Garold Isakovich, spent extended periods in the North Vietnamese capital, designing both Ho Chi Minh's Mausoleum and the bust of Lenin in Lenin Park, Hanoi. Other prominent Soviet examples in Hanoi include the State Bank, a blend of Soviet and Asian styles; the brutalist-style People's Committee building; and the National Assembly, which shows a Le Corbusier influence.

Meanwhile, in HCMC, there's less Soviet style about (unsurprisingly given the city's history). The one building that stands out is Reunification Palace. Completed in 1966, it's a concrete masterpiece designed by Ngo Viet Thu.

To see the results of communist planning, head to Vinh in North-Central Vietnam. Decades of incessant bombing reduced the city to rubble (only two buildings were left standing in 1972). East German architects and planners reinvented the city in the mould of their homeland, with cheap, hastily-erected concrete apartment buildings that have aged poorly, suffering from a lack of maintenance. The buildings have a quirky appeal, though remain unpopular with residents.

Right
1. A Reception Room at the Reunification Palace, HCMC
2. Ho Chi Minh's Mausoleum at dusk, Hanoi

Regional Specialities

Crab rice-paper rolls, served with fresh dipping sauce

By Andrea Nguyen. Andrea is the acclaimed author of *Into the Vietnamese Kitchen* and *Asian Tofu*. She also publishes Vietworldkitchen.com.

Vietnam's cuisine is as multifaceted as its lengthy coastline. Travelling north to south is a journey that, geographically and gastronomically, begins in China and ends in Southeast Asia. Despite being a small country, there are differences in the regional dishes of Vietnam – differences with roots in history, culture and geography. This has resulted in a fascinating spectrum of techniques, ingredients and tastes, all linked by the Vietnamese love for vibrant flavours, fresh herbs, noodles and seafood.

The dishes of Vietnam's north tend to be mild, somewhat rustic and have a significant Chinese influence. Soy is used as frequently as fish sauce, vinegar is more likely to add sourness than lime juice or tamarind, chillies give way to black pepper, and long cooking is used to coax maximum flavour from unpretentious ingredients.

Everything seems smaller in central Vietnam; baguettes and herbs are miniature versions of their southern selves, while Hue's imperial cuisine is a procession of dainty, delicate dishes. Emperor Tu Duc was a demanding diner, but his legacy is some of the best food in Vietnam. Imperial-style banquets, including up to 15 dishes, can be booked at a few high-end hotels, but one edible legacy of the royal court is easily found on the street: *banh beo*, delicate steamed cakes made from rice flour.

The central Vietnamese also like gutsy and spicy flavours, and briny shrimp sauce and spritely lemongrass add to the cornucopia of flavours.

In southern Vietnam the food reflects the region's natural abundance and year-round growing season. Dishes are bigger, colourful and attractive. Coconut milk is the base for mild curries and also lends richness to sweets. The southern love of fresh herbs, fruit and vegetables comes to the fore in refreshing *goi* (salads), of green papaya, grapefruit-like pomelo, or lotus stems.

Clockwise from top left

1. Market produce in HCMC 2. Street sellers preparing food, HCMC 3. Dining at a street stall, Hanoi Old Quarter

North

Northern Vietnamese food most clearly bears the imprint of the centuries of Chinese occupation. Comforting noodle dishes, generally mild flavours and rustic elegance are all hallmarks of the region's cuisine.

Banh Cuon

1 These rolls are made from rice-flour batter that's poured onto a piece of muslin cloth stretched over a steamer; once firm, the noodle sheet is scattered with chopped pork, mushrooms and dried shrimp, then rolled up, sprinkled with crispy shallots, and served alongside a tangle of bean sprouts, slivered cucumber and chopped fresh herbs, with a saucer of *nuoc cham* (dipping sauce) for drizzling.

Bun Cha

2 This street favourite features barbecued sliced pork or pork patties served with thin rice vermicelli, a heap of fresh herbs and green vegetables, and a bowl of lightly sweetened *nuoc mam* (fish sauce) with floating slices of pickled vegetables. The Hanoi version combines sliced pork belly and pork patties formed from chopped pork shoulder.

Pho Bo

3 A culinary highlight of the north is *pho bo* (beef noodle soup). A good *pho* hinges on the broth, which is made from beef bones boiled for hours in water with shallot, ginger, fish sauce, black cardamom, star anise and cassia. Hardcore northern pho lovers frown upon adding lime, basil, and bean sprouts to their bowls.

Clockwise from top left
1. Making *banh cuon* 2. Bowl of *bun cha* 3. A Vietnamese classic, *pho bo* (beef-noodle soup) from a street cart

Centre

Positioned between culinary extremes, the food of central Vietnam seems to be the product of moderation and balance – except where it concerns the locals' love of chilli. People cook from the land, turning their modest resources into fare fit for an emperor.

Banh Khoai

1 These hearty, dessert-plate-sized crepes are made with rice-flour batter and cooked with copious amounts of oil in special long-handled pans. They feature a spare filling of shrimp, pork, egg and bean sprouts, are encased with fresh herbs in lettuce, and then dunked in a sauce based on earthy fermented soybeans.

Bun Bo Hue

2 This punchy rice-noodle soup with beef and pork exemplifies the central Vietnamese proclivity for spicy food. Tinged yellow-orange by chillies and annatto, the broth is laden with lemongrass notes and anchored by savoury shrimp sauce (*mam tom*). Like most Vietnamese noodle soups, it's accompanied by a riot of herbs and leafy greens.

Com Hen

3 Room temperature rice is served with the flesh of tiny clams, their cooking broth, and myriad garnishes that include roasted rice crackers, crisp pork crackling, peanuts, sesame seeds, fresh herbs and vegetables. Add the broth and sauce to the other ingredients in your bowl; the liquid components moisten, season and harmonise.

Clockwise from top left
1. *Banh khoai* (folded rice crepe with savoury filling)
2. *Com hen*, made with tiny clams **3.** Spicy *bun bo Hue*

REBECCA SKINNER / LONELY PLANET IMAGES ©

ROBERTLAMPHOTO / SHUTTERSTOCK ©

South

Southern cuisine plays up the region's abundance and tends to be on the sweet side. No matter the season, vendors at southern markets display heaps of lush, big-leafed herbs, fruits in every colour and the freshest fish possible.

Canh Chua Ca

1 This soup is the Mekong Delta in a bowl: plentiful fish, usually snakehead or catfish; fruits like tomato and pineapple; and vegetables including bean sprouts, okra and *bac ha* (taro stem), all in a broth that's tart with tamarind and salty with *nuoc mam*. Topped with vivid green herbs and golden fried garlic, it's as lovely to look at as it is to taste.

Banh Mi

2 This sandwich is a legacy of French and Chinese colonialism, but it's 100% Vietnamese. The baguette merely encases the filling, which might be a smearing of pâté or a few slices of silky sausage and a sprinkling of pepper. Mayonnaise moistens the bread and a sprinkling of soy sauce imparts *umami* (savoury) goodness.

Banh Xeo

3 This giant crispy, chewy rice crepe is made in 12- or 14-inch skillets or woks and amply filled with pork, shrimp, mung beans and bean sprouts. Take a portion and encase it in lettuce or mustard leaf, add some fresh herbs, then dunk in the *nuoc cham*.

Hu Tieu

4 This noodle soup is a Chinese original that the Vietnamese deliciously appropriated. The noodles can be chewy clear tapioca noodles, opaque white rice noodles like you'd use for pho noodle soup, or thin Chinese egg noodles. The toppings also vary and may include boneless pork, pork ribs, pork offal, shrimp, squid, Chinese celery, fried garlic, fried shallot, and/or garlic chives.

Right
1. Hot and sour fish soup, *canh chua ca* 2. Crisp *banh mi*

Food & Drink

If you're the sort of traveller who believes that eating locally is one of the best ways to immerse yourself in a culture, prepare to be amazed by Vietnam. From traditional street stalls to contemporary big-city temples of upscale dining, the country serves up an endless banquet of exquisite eating.

Diverse landscapes – fertile highlands, waterlogged rice paddies, forest-cloaked mountains and sandy coasts – lend the cuisine variety, while a long history of contact with outsiders brings complexity. Over the centuries locals have absorbed and adapted Chinese, Indian, French and even Japanese techniques and specialities to their own kitchens and palates, and expatriates and Vietnamese chefs who have spent time overseas are breathing new life into the white-tablecloth dining scenes in Hanoi and Ho Chi Minh City (HCMC). In Vietnam, to 'eat local' can mean anything from supping on rice-flour vermicelli flavoured with fish sauce, to feasting on beef stew accompanied by a crispy baguette.

The country's vast range of excellent edibles invites experimentation. Though Vietnam's well-known classics – *pho,* spring rolls, and shrimp paste grilled on sugar cane – are all well and tasty, it pays to venture into the unknown. Every bustling wet market, every bicycle-riding vendor and every open-air eatery is a potential trove of delights that rarely make it beyond the country's borders. Keep your eyes open, follow your nose, and you'll depart with mouth-watering memories that will have you saying *Hen gap lai* (see you again).

Flavours

Vietnamese palates vary from north to south, but no matter where they are, local cooks work to balance hot, sour, salty and sweet flavours in each dish. Sugar's centrality to the cuisine is best illustrated by the ever popular *kho:* a sweet-savoury dishes of fish or meat simmered in a clay pot with fish sauce and another oft-used seasoning, bitter caramel sauce made from cane sugar. Vietnamese cooks also use sugar to sweeten dipping sauces, desserts and, of course, coffee.

Sweetness is countered with fruity tartness, derived from the lime wedges mounded in bowls on restaurant tables (to squeeze into noodle soups and dipping sauces) and from *kalamansi* (a small green-skinned, orange-fleshed citrus fruit that tastes like a cross between a lime and a mandarin), the juice of which is combined with salt and black pepper as a dip for seafood, meats and omelettes. In the south, the tart pulp of the tamarind pod is mixed with water and strained, then added as a souring agent to a fish and vegetable soup called *canh chua* and a delectable dish of whole prawns coated with sticky sweet-and-sour sauce. Northern cooks who seek sourness are more likely to turn to vinegar. A clear, yellowish vinegar mixed with chopped ginger is often served alongside snail specialities such as *bun oc* (rice noodle and snail soup).

Vietnamese cooking uses less hot chilli than Thai cuisine, though central Vietnamese cooks do use more of them than their fellow nationals.

Local chillies vary from the mild-flavoured, long, red, fleshy variety that appears in many southern dishes and is served chopped to accompany noodles, to the smallish pale-chartreuse specimen served as an accompaniment in restaurants specialising in Hue cuisine. Beware – the latter really pack a punch. Dried ground chillies and spicy chilli sauces are tabletop condiments in many a central Vietnamese eatery.

Vietnam is a huge peppercorn exporter (though it's said that much pepper labelled 'Vietnamese' originates in southern Cambodia), and ground black and white peppercorns season everything from *chao* (rice porridge) to beef stew. Wonderfully pungent, Vietnamese black peppercorns put what's sold in supermarkets back home to shame; if your country will allow it in, a half-kilogram bag purchased at a Vietnamese wet market for 50,000d makes a fine edible souvenir.

Vietnamese food's saltiness comes from, well, salt – the coastal area around Nha Trang is the site of numerous salt flats – but also from the fermented seafood sauces that grace the shelves of every Vietnamese pantry. The most common is *nuoc mam* (fish sauce), which is so elemental to the cuisine that, sprinkled over a bowl of rice, it's considered a meal. *Nuoc mam* is made from small fish (most often anchovies) that are layered with salt in large earthenware, concrete or wooden containers, weighted to keep the fish submerged in their own liquid, and left in a hot place for up to a year. As they ferment the fish release a fragrant (some might say stinky) liquid that is drawn off through a spigot near the container's bottom. The first extraction, called *nuoc mam cot,* is dark brown and richly flavoured – essentially an 'extra virgin' fish sauce reserved for table use. The second extraction, obtained by adding salted water to the already fermented fish and leaving them for a few more months, is used for cooking. Phu Quoc Island (p381) is famous for its *nuoc mam,* though some cooks prefer the milder version made around coastal Phan Thiet (p256).

When it comes to fermented fish products, *nuoc mam* is only the tip of the iceberg. At some point most travellers come face-to-face with *mam tom,* a violet paste of salted, fermented shrimp. At the table, it's added to noodle soups, smeared onto rice-paper rolls, and even serves as a dip for sour fruits like green mango. It's also used extensively in cooking, lending a pungent salty backbone to specialities like *bun mam* (a southern fish-and-vegetable noodle soup). *Mam tom* has close cousins in every Southeast Asian cuisine, as well as many versions in Vietnam, including ones made from crabs, shrimp of all sizes (*mam tep,* a southern speciality, is made from especially small shrimp), and various types of fish. Try to get past the odour and sample a range of dishes made with it: the flavour it lends to food is much more subtle than its stench might imply!

Fish flavours also come from dried seafood. Vietnamese cooks are quite choosy about dried shrimp, with market stalls displaying up to 15 grades. You'll also find all sorts and sizes of dried fish, both whole and in fillets, and dried squid. The latter is often barbecued and sold from roving stalls.

Beyond *nuoc mam* and *mam,* Vietnamese cooks use quite a few sauces, such as soy, oyster and fermented soybean – culinary souvenirs of China's almost 1000-year rule over the country's north. Warm spices like star anise and cinnamon are essential to a good *pho.* Curries were introduced to Vietnam by Indian traders, probably through the once-important port of Hoi An; now they're cooked up using packets of locally made curry powder and small jars of curry paste packed in oil. Vietnamese curries, such as *ca ri ga* (chicken curry cooked with coconut milk and lemongrass) and *lau de* (curried goat hotpot), tend to be more aromatic than fiery.

Kim Fay's *Communion – A Culinary Journey Through Vietnam* offers a real insight into Vietnam's wonderful food scene as the author travels the nation, shifting from street food stalls to exquisite seafood restaurants. Engaging text is accompanied by recipes and photographs.

Vietnamese food is often described as 'fresh' and 'light' owing to the plates heaped with gorgeous fresh herbs that seem to accompany every meal. Coriander, mint and anise-flavoured Thai basil will be familiar to anyone who's travelled elsewhere in the region. Look also for green-and-garnet *perilla* leaves; small and pointy, pleasantly peppery astringent *rau ram* leaves; and *rau om* (rice-paddy herb), which has delicate leaves that hint of lemon and cumin. *Rau om* invariably shows up atop bowls of *canh chua*. Shallots, thinly sliced and slowly fried in oil until caramelised, add a bit of sweetness when sprinkled on salad and noodle dishes.

Staples

Rice

Rice, or *com,* is the very bedrock of Vietnamese cuisine. In imperial Hue, rice with salt was served to distinguished guests by royal mandarins; these days locals eat at least one rice-based meal every day and offer a bowl of rice to departed ancestors. If a Vietnamese says '*An com*' (literally 'let's eat rice'), it's an invitation to lunch or dinner, and you can also get your fill of the stuff, accompanied by a variety of stir-fried meat, fish and vegetable dishes, at specialised eateries called *quan com binh dan,* informal restaurants serving cheap dishes prepared ahead of time. Cooked to a soupy state with chicken, fish, eel or duck, rice becomes *chao* (rice porridge); fried in a hot wok with egg, vegetables and other ingredients, it's *com rang;* and 'broken' into short grains, steamed, topped with barbecued pork, an egg, and sliced cucumber, and accompanied by *nuoc cham* (a dipping sauce of sweetened fish sauce), it's *com tam.* Tiny clams called *hen* are sautéed with peppery Vietnamese coriander and ladled over rice to make *com hen.* Sticky or glutinous rice (white, red and black) is mixed with pulses or rehydrated dried corn, peanuts and sesame seeds for a filling breakfast treat called *xoi* (*ngo* in central Vietnam). It can also be mixed with sugar and coconut milk then moulded into sweet treats, or layered with pork and steamed in bamboo or banana leaves for *banh chung,* a Tet speciality. Soaked and ground into flour, rice becomes the base for everything from noodles and sweets to crackers and the dry round, translucent 'papers' that Vietnamese moisten before using to wrap salad rolls and other specialities.

Noodles

Noodles are an anytime-of-day Vietnamese meal or snack. *Pho* is made with *banh pho* (flat rice noodles) and though this northern dish gets all the culinary press, the truth is that truly fine versions, featuring a rich, carefully made broth are hard to come by. Other northern-style noodle dishes worth seeking out include *bun cha,* barbecued sliced pork or pork patties served with thin rice vermicelli, and *banh cuon,* stuffed noodle sheets that recall Hong Kong-style noodle rolls.

If you're a noodle lover, do yourself a favour and look for dishes featuring *bun,* the round rice noodles that are a central element in *bun bo Hue,* a spicy, beef speciality from central Vietnam. Other characteristically central Vietnamese noodle dishes include *my quang,* a dish of rice noodles tinted yellow with annatto seeds or pale pink (if made from red rice flour) topped with pork, shrimp, slivered banana blossoms, herbs and chopped peanuts, and doused with just enough broth to moisten. It's eaten with rice crackers (crumbled over to add crunch) and sweet hot chilli jam. *Cao lau,* a noodle dish specific to the ancient port town of Hoi An, features thick, rough-textured noodles that are said to have origins in the soba noodles brought by Japanese traders. Like *my quang, cao lau* is moistened with just a smidge of richly flavoured broth; it is topped with slices of stewed pork, blanched bean sprouts, fresh greens

MENU DECODER

Turn to p530 for a list of Vietnamese words and phrases that may come in handy at meal times.

and herbs, and crispy square 'croutons' made from the same dough as the noodles. Authentic *cao lau* is made with water from a particular well in Hoi An's Old Town, though few believe that every bowl served today carries that pedigree.

Southerners lay claim to a number of noodle specialities as well, such as the cool salad noodle *bun thit nuong* and *bun mam,* a strong fish-flavoured rice-noodle broth that includes tomatoes, pineapple and *bac ha.* (An identically named but significantly more challenging dish of cool rice noodles, bean sprouts and herbs dressed with straight *mam* is found in central Vietnam.)

Across Vietnam, keep an eye open also for *banh hoi,* very thin rice-flour noodles that are formed into delicate nests and eaten rolled with grilled meat in leafy greens. Chinese-style egg noodles (*mi*) are thrown into soups or fried and topped with a stir-fried mixture of seafood, meats and vegetables in gravy for a dish called *mi xao. Mien* (bean-thread noodles) made from mung-bean starch are stir-fried with *mien cua* (crab meat) and eaten with steamed fish.

Rice-Paper Rolls

Vietnamese will wrap almost anything in crackly rice paper. Steamed fish and grilled meats are often rolled at the table with herbs, lettuce and slices of sour star fruit and green banana, and dipped in *nuoc cham.* Fat *goi cuon,* a southern speciality popularly known as 'salad' or 'summer' rolls, contain shrimp, pork, rice noodles and herbs and are meant to be dipped in bean paste or hoisin sauce. *Bo pia,* thin rice-paper cigars filled with slices of Chinese sausage, dried shrimp, cooked jicama (a crisp root vegetable), lettuce and chilli paste, are usually knocked up to order by street vendors with mobile carts. Hue has its own version of the spring roll: soft, fresh *nem cuon Hue,* filled with sweet potato, pork, crunchy pickled prawns, water spinach and herbs. And then there's *nem ran ha noi,* northern-style crispy deep-fried spring rolls.

Fish, Meat & Fowl

Thanks to Vietnam's long coastline and plentiful river deltas, seafood is a major source of protein. From the ocean comes fish such as tuna, pomfret, red snapper and sea bass, as well as prawns, crabs and clams. Flooded rice paddies yield minuscule crabs and golf ball-sized snails called *oc.* In northern Vietnam the former go into *bun rieu cua,* thin rice noodles in a crimson-hued broth made from tomatoes and pulverised crab shells; on top floats a heavenly layer of crab fat sautéed with shallots. Snails can be found in *bun oc,* or chopped with lemongrass and herbs, stuffed into the snail shells and steamed, for *oc nhoi hap la xa* (a sort of Vietnamese escargot). A length of lemongrass leaf protrudes from each snail shell – give it a tug to pull out the meat.

Other favourite freshwater eats include the well-loved *ca loc* (snake-head fish), catfish, and along the central coast, *hen* (small clams). The latter are eaten with rice in *hen com,* in broth with noodles, or scooped up with rice crackers (*banh da*).

Chicken and pork are widely eaten. In the mornings the tantalising aroma of barbecuing *nuoc mam*-marinated pork, intended to fill breakfast baguette sandwiches and top broken rice, scents the air of many a city street. Beef is less frequently seen but does show up in bowls of *pho,* in *kho bo* (beef stew with tomato), in *thit bo bit tet* (Vietnamese pan-seared beefsteak), and wrapped in *la lot* (wild pepper leaves) and grilled. Other sources of protein include goat (eaten in hotpot with a curried broth), frogs, insect larvae and – yes, in the Mekong Delta – rat, although you're unlikely to encounter the latter in most restaurants.

A legacy of the French, *banh mi* refers to the crackly crusted rice and wheat-flour baguettes sold everywhere (eaten plain or dipped in beef stew and soups) and the sandwiches made with them, stuffed with meats, vegies and pickles. If you haven't tried stuffed *banh mi,* you haven't eaten in Vietnam.

Vegetables & Fruit

Vegetables range from the mundane – tomatoes, potatoes, eggplants (delicious grilled and topped with ground pork and *nuoc mam*), cucumbers, asparagus – to the exotic. Banana blossoms and lotus-flower stems are made into *goi* (salads), a thick, spongy plant stem called *bac ha* is added to soups, and *thien ly*, a wild plant with tender leaves and fragrant blossoms, is eaten stir-fried with garlic. Bunches of sunshine-yellow squash blossoms are a common sight in southern markets; locals like them simply stir-fried with garlic. All sorts of delicious wild mushrooms sprout on forest floors during the rainy season, and if you're off the beaten track then you might also be treated to tender fern tips which, like the more common *rau muong* (water spinach), get the stir-fry treatment. Especially loved are leafy greens such as lettuce, watercress, and mustard, which Vietnamese use to wrap *banh xeo* (crispy pork and shrimp pancakes) into bite-sized parcels suitable for dipping in *nuoc mam*.

If you're a fruit lover you've come to the right place. Depending on when you're travelling you'll be able to gorge on mangoes, crispy and sour green or soft and tartly floral pink guavas, juicy lychees and longans, and exotic mangosteen, passionfruit and jackfruit. Hue cooks treat young jackfruit as a vegetable, boiling the flesh (which tastes like a cross between artichoke and asparagus), shredding it, dressing it with fish sauce, scattering the lot with sesame seeds, and serving the dish (called *nom mit non*) with rice crackers. Tamarind is a typically southern ingredient; it also sauces shelled or unshelled prawns in *tom rang me* – a messy but rewarding sweet-tart dish.

Sweets

Do ngot (Vietnamese sweets) and *do trang mieng* (desserts) are popular everywhere, and are especially prevalent during festivals, when sweet varieties of *banh* (traditional cakes) come in a wide assortment of shapes and flavours. Rice flour is the base for many desserts, sweetened with sugar and coconut milk and enriched with lotus seeds, sesame seeds and peanuts. Yellow mung beans turn up in many desserts, while the French influence is evident in crème caramel. Cold sweets, like *kem* (ice cream), *thach,* lovely layered agar-agar jellies in flavours like pandan and coffee-and-coconut, and locally made sweetened yoghurt sold in small glass pots, hit the spot on steamy days.

Che are sweet 'soups' that combine ingredients like lotus seeds or tapioca pearls and coconut milk; they're also a scrumptious shaved-ice treat, for which a mound of ice crystals with your choice of toddy palm seeds, bits of agar-agar jelly, white or red beans, corn, and other bits is doused with coconut milk, condensed milk, sugar syrup or all three. The combination of beans, corn and sweet liquid might sound strange, but in addition to being delicious, *che* is surprisingly refreshing.

Drinks

You're unlikely to go thirsty in Vietnam where, thanks to a healthy drinking culture, there exists all manner of beverages to slake your thirst. Sooner or later every traveller succumbs to *bia hoi* ('fresh' or draught beer) – local brands are served straight from the keg by the glass for a pittance in restaurants, eateries and specialist shops on seemingly every street corner. If you're looking to pay a little more for a beer of better quality, Saigon Beer isn't horrible, and La Rue, brewed on the central coast and more often available bottled than draught, is quite good. While imported liquor can be expensive, Vietnam brews a number of its own spirits, including a drinkable, dirt-cheap vodka called Ha Noi. Distilled sticky-rice wine called *ruou* (which means, literally, 'alcohol') is often flavoured with

Keep an eye out for *sinh to* stalls stocked with a variety of fruits (including avocado, which Vietnamese treat as a fruit rather than a vegetable) and a blender, where you can treat yourself to a refreshing blended-to-order iced fruit smoothie. It doesn't get much fresher than that.

Northerners favour hot green tea, while in the south the same is often served over big chunks of ice. Chrysanthemum and jasmine infusions are also popular; particularly delicious is a fragrant non-caffeinated tea made from lotus seeds.

herbs, spices, fruits and even animals. Travel to the northern highlands and you may be offered *ruou can,* sherry-like rice wine drunk through long bamboo straws from a communal vessel. And you'll undoubtedly encounter *ruou ran* (snake wine), supposedly a cure-all elixir. Cobras and many other snakes in Vietnam are officially listed as endangered, a fact that producers rarely heed.

In Vietnam the preparation, serving and drinking of tea (*tra* in the south and *che* in the north) has a social importance seldom appreciated by Western visitors. Serving tea in the home or office is more than a gesture of hospitality, it is a ritual.

Vietnam is also a major **coffee** producer; when the country flooded the world market with robusta beans (arabica's cheaper, less aromatic cousin) nearly 10 years ago, the bottom dropped out of the wholesale coffee market. Whiling away a morning or an afternoon over endless glasses of iced coffee, with or without milk (*ca phe sua da* or *ca phe da*) is something of a ritual for Vietnam's male population, and cafes (either a proper shop with tables and chairs or a one-vendor stall that serves customers seated on tiny plastic stools) are as ubiquitous as *bia hoi* joints. Vietnamese coffee is thick and strong – coffee jockeys measure it out with small cups that resemble shot glasses – and is mixed with sweetened condensed milk to become almost chocolatey. Other liquid options in Vietnam include *mia da,* a freshly squeezed sugar-cane juice that is especially refreshing served over ice with a squeeze of *kalamansi; sinh to* (fresh fruit smoothies blended to order); and soy milk.

MEAL TIMES

There are often no set dining hours, but as a general rule cafes are open most of the day and into the night. Street stalls are open from very early in the morning until late at night. Restaurants usually open for lunch between 11am and 3pm, and for dinner between 5pm or 6pm and 10pm or 11pm.

Where to Eat & Drink

Whatever your likes and dislikes, one eatery or another in Vietnam is almost certain to cater to them, be it the humble peddler with his yoke, a roadside stall, a simple *pho* shop or a fancy restaurant. If you're new to the cuisine and not squeamish about **street food**, wet-market food courts, with vendors serving everything from coffee and fruit juices to noodles and steamed rice with side dishes, are the perfect place to graze.

Don't neglect French and Chinese restaurants. Though not as common as they used to be (except in HCMC's Cholon, or Chinese district), they serve up an important part of Vietnam's culinary and cultural legacy. And in recent years a flood of expatriates to Ho Chi Minh City and Hanoi have precipitated an explosion of truly international eateries serving Turkish and Thai, Malaysian and Moroccan, Indian and Italian.

Vegetarians & Vegans

The good news is that there is now more choice than ever before when it comes to vegetarian dining. The bad news is that you have not landed in Veg Heaven, for the Vietnamese are voracious omnivores. While they dearly love vegies, they also adore much of what crawls on the ground, swims in the sea or flies in the air. In keeping with Buddhist precepts, many vendors and eateries go vegetarian on the 1st and 15th days of each lunar month; this is a great time to scour the markets and sample dishes that would otherwise be off-limits. Otherwise, be wary. Any dish of vegetables may well have been cooked with fish sauce or shrimp paste. If you're vegan, you're facing a bigger challenge still. 'Mock meat' restaurants are something to seek out for those who want to remain true to their vegetarian principles but secretly miss their bacon butties. Found throughout Vietnam, these places use tofu and gluten to create meat-like entities that even hardened carnivores enjoy.

Habits & Customs

Enter the Vietnamese kitchen and you will be convinced that good food comes from simplicity. Essentials consist of a strong flame, basic cutting

TABLE ETIQUETTE

Sit at the table with your bowl on a small plate, chopsticks and a soup spoon at the ready. Each place will include a small bowl at the top right-hand side for the *nuoc mam* or other dipping sauces. When serving yourself from the central bowls, use the communal serving spoon so as not to dip your chopsticks into it. Pick up the bowl with the left hand, bring it close to your mouth and use the chopsticks to manoeuvre the food. If you're eating noodles, lower your head till it hangs over the bowl and slurp away. It is polite for the host to offer more food than the guests can eat, and it is polite for the guests not to eat everything.

Also, remember not to leave chopsticks standing in a V-shape in your bowl – this is a symbol of death.

utensils, a mortar and pestle, and a well-blackened pot or two. The kitchen is so sacred that it is inhabited by its own deity, Ong Tao (Kitchen God). The spiritual guardian of the hearth must have its due and the most important object in the kitchen is its altar.

Vietnamese generally eat three meals a day and snack in between. Breakfast is simple and may be noodles or *chao*. Baguettes are available at any time of day or night, and go well with coffee or tea. Lunch starts early, around 11am. In earlier years workers went home to eat with their families, but most now eat at nearby street cafes. Dinner is a time for family bonding. The dishes are arranged around a central rice bowl and diners each have a small eating bowl. When ordering from a restaurant menu don't worry about the succession of courses. All dishes are placed in the centre of the table as soon as they are ready and diners serve themselves. If it's a special occasion, the host may drop a morsel or two into your rice bowl.

Cooking Courses

The best way to tackle Vietnamese cuisine head-on is to sign up for a cooking course during your stay. For those who fall in love with the food, there is no better experience than re-creating the real recipes back home. It's also a great way to introduce your Vietnam experience to friends; they may not want to hear the stories or see the photos, but offer them a mouth-watering meal and they'll come running. Cooking courses have really taken off in the past few years as more travellers combine the twin passions of eating and exploring. Courses range from budget classes in the local specialities of Hoi An to gastronomic gallops through the country's classic cuisine at five-star hotels in Hanoi and HCMC.

If you are set on serious studies in Vietnamese cooking, try a short course in Hoi An and negotiate for something longer once you've had a taste of the experience.

Environment

The Landscape

As the Vietnamese are quick to point out, their nation resembles a *don ganh,* the ubiquitous bamboo pole with a basket of rice slung from each end. The baskets represent the main rice-growing regions of the Red River Delta in the north and the Mekong Delta in the south. The country bulges in the north and south and has a very slim waistline – at one point it's only 50km wide. Mountain ranges define most of Vietnam's western and northern borders.

Many interesting environmental articles are published in the online edition of *Thanh Nien,* where you can keep up with current issues (www.thanhnien news.com).

Coast & Islands

Vietnam's extraordinary 3451km-long coastline is one the nation's biggest draws and it doesn't disappoint, with sweeping sandy beaches, towering cliffs, undulating dunes and countless uninhabited offshore islands. The largest of these islands is Phu Quoc in the Gulf of Thailand, others include Cat Ba and Van Don, the 2000 or so islets of Halong Bay, a spattering of dots off Nha Trang and the fabled Con Dao Islands way out in the South China Sea.

River Deltas

The Red River and Mekong River Deltas are both pancake-flat and prone to flooding. Silt carried by the Red River and its tributaries, confined to

DOING YOUR BIT

» Vietnam has a low level of environmental awareness and responsibility, and many people remain unaware of the implications of littering. Try to raise awareness of these issues by example and dispose of your litter as responsibly as possible.

» Vietnam's fauna populations are under considerable threat from domestic consumption of 'bush meat' and the illegal international trade in animal products. Though it may be 'exotic' to drink snake wine, or eat wild meat such as muntjac, bat, deer, sea horse, shark fin and so on – or to buy products made from endangered plants and animals – doing so will indicate your support or acceptance of such practices and add to the demand for them.

» When snorkelling or diving, or simply boating around coral reefs, be careful not to touch live coral or anchor boats on it, as this hinders the coral's growth. Boat operators should use buoys, or anchor in sandy areas – indicate your willingness to swim to the coral. Be aware that buying coral souvenirs supports the destruction of the very reefs you've come to see.

» When visiting limestone caves, be aware that touching the formations hinders growth and turns the limestone black.

» Do not remove or buy 'souvenirs' that have been taken from historical sites and natural areas; it may be illegal and is certainly unethical.

» Refill plastic water bottles when possible.

VINH VU: FOUNDER, HANDSPAN TRAVEL

In a nation of clone-like tour operators, few stand out. Handspan is one company that does, with its highly-innovative trips. We grilled Handspan founder Vinh Vu for his tips.

Where's Vietnam's most spectacular scenery? The Ha Giang rock plateau of Dong Van and Meo Vac, and Phong Nha-Ke Bang National Park.

Where do you like to escape the crowds? In the northern mountains, especially where road conditions are not great. Also I love island beaches such as Co To, Quan Lan, Con Dao and Con Co.

Which regions are emerging? Improved roads have opened up Ngoc Son Ngo Luong in Hoa Binh Province, which is a Muong tribal area with great countryside, rice paddies and innocent people. The Moc Chau plateau, which has a cool climate, tea plantations and H'mong and Thai culture, is another.

Your tips for travellers to get more out of Vietnam? Try to balance between must-see and off-the-beaten track places for better impact on the country and to diversify your experience. Must-see places are already popular so you won't feel that special. Off-the-beaten-track destinations require more study, organising and costs but your experiences are unique and these places are changing too, so be quick.

their paths by 3000km of dykes, has raised the level of the river beds above the surrounding plains so that breaches in the dykes result in disastrous flooding. The Mekong Delta has no such protection and when *cuu long* 'the nine dragons' (the nine channels of the Mekong in the delta) burst their banks it creates havoc for communities and crops.

Highlands

Three-quarters of the country consists of rolling hills (mostly in the south) and mighty mountains (mainly in the north), the highest of which is 3143m Fansipan, close to Sapa. The Truong Son Mountains, which form the central highlands, run almost the full length of Vietnam along its borders with Laos and Cambodia. The coastal ranges near Nha Trang and those at Hai Van Pass (Danang) are composed of granite, and the giant boulders littering the hillsides are a surreal sight. The western part of the central highlands is well known for its fertile, red volcanic soil. However Northern Vietnam's incredible karst formations are probably the nation's most iconic physical features.

Wildlife

Despite some disastrous bouts of deforestation, Vietnam's flora and fauna are as exotic and varied as in any tropical country. Intensive surveys by the World Wildlife Fund along the Mekong River (including in Vietnam) found a total of 1068 new species from 1997 to 2007, placing this area on Conservation International's list of the top five biodiversity hot spots in the world. Numerous areas inside Vietnam remain unsurveyed or poorly known and many more species are likely to be found.

Animals

On paper, Vietnam has plenty to offer those who are wild about wildlife, but in reality many animals live in remote forested areas and encountering them is extremely unlikely. Most of the wildlife in readily accessible areas is disappearing rapidly thanks to a growing resource-hungry human population and the destruction of habitats. Hunting, poaching and pollution are taking their toll too.

With a wide range of habitats – from equatorial lowlands to high, temperate plateaus and even alpine peaks – the wildlife of Vietnam is

Tram Chim in the Mekong Delta is one of Vietnam's most important wetland reserves, and home to the giant sarus crane, which can measure up to 1.8m in height.

Flora and Fauna International produce an excellent Nature Tourism Map of Vietnam, which includes detailed coverage of all the national parks in Vietnam (www.fauna -flora.org). All proceeds from sales of the map go towards supporting primate conservation in Vietnam.

enormously diverse. One recent tally listed 275 species of mammals, more than 800 birds, 180 reptiles, 80 amphibians, hundreds of fish and tens of thousands of invertebrates, but new species are being discovered at such a rapid rate that this list is constantly being revised upward.

More than any location in the world, Vietnam is revealing new creatures that elude scientific classification. Since Vietnam reopened for business around 1990, biologists have discovered several previously unknown species of large mammal in Vietnam, including finding three new hoofed animals within a span of four years. Most significant among these was a large antelope-like wild ox named the saola. Scientists have yet to even see a saola in the wild – one was captured by villagers in Laos in 2010 but died in captivity before it could be released.

Rare and little-known birds previously thought to be extinct have been spotted and no doubt there are more in the extensive forests along the Lao border. Edwards's pheasant, previously believed to be extinct, was found on a scientific expedition, and other excursions have yielded the white-winged wood duck and white-shouldered ibis.

Even casual visitors will spot a few bird species: swallows and swifts flying over fields and along watercourses; flocks of finches at roadsides and in paddies; and bulbuls and mynas in gardens and patches of forest. Vietnam is on the east-Asian flyway and is an important stopover for migratory waders en route from Siberian breeding grounds to their Australian winter quarters.

Vietnam: A Natural History, a collaboration between American and Vietnamese experts, is the best book for those wanting to learn about Vietnam's extraordinary flora and fauna.

Endangered Species

Tragically, Vietnam's wildlife has been in significant decline as forest habitats are destroyed and waterways polluted. Widespread illegal and subsistence hunting has decimated local animal populations, in some cases wiping out entire species. Continued deforestation and poaching means that many endangered species are on a one-way ticket to extinction. Captive-breeding programs may be the only hope for some, but rarely are the money and resources available for such expensive efforts.

Officially, the government has recognised 54 species of mammal and 60 species of bird as endangered. Larger animals at the forefront of the country's conservation efforts include elephant, tiger, leopard, black bear, honey bear, snub-nosed monkey, flying squirrel, crocodile and turtle. In the early 1990s a small population of Javan rhinoceroses, the world's rarest rhino, was discovered in Cat Tien National Park (p283). Less than a dozen are thought to remain in the entire country and their two main blocks of habitat are separated by heavily used agricultural areas so it's unlikely there are enough to build a self-sustaining population.

Cat Tien is also the site of a remarkable wildlife recovery story involving the Siamese crocodile, which was extinct in the wild due to excessive

If you see endangered animals for sale, or listed on a restaurant menu, call the toll-free hotline 1800 1522 run by ENV (Education for Nature Vietnam; www .envietnam.org).

KARST YOUR EYES

Karsts are eroded limestone hills, the result of millennia of monsoon rains that have shaped towering tooth-like outcrops pierced by fissures, sinkholes, caves and underground rivers. Northern Vietnam contains some of the world's most impressive karst mountains, with stunning landscapes at Halong Bay (p94), Bai Tu Long Bay (p108), around Ninh Binh (p143) and in the Phong Nha region (p151). At Halong and Bai Tu Long Bays, an enormous limestone plateau has dramatically eroded so that old mountain tops stick out of the sea like bony vertical fingers pointing towards the sky. Phong Nha's cave systems are on an astonishing scale, stretching for tens of kilometres deep into the limestone land mass.

NATIONAL PARKS: THE TOP 10

PARK (HECTARES)	FEATURES	ACTIVITIES	BEST TIME TO VISIT	PAGE
Ba Be (9022)	lakes, rainforest, waterfalls, towering peaks, caves, bears, langurs	hiking, boating, bird-watching	Apr-Nov	p89
Bai Tu Long (15,600)	karst peaks, tropical evergreen forest, caves, hidden beaches	swimming, surfing, boating, kayaking, hiking	Apr-Nov	p108
Bach Ma (37,500)	waterfalls, tigers, primates	hiking, bird-watching	Feb-Sep	p178
Cat Ba (15,331)	jungle, caves, trails, langurs, boars, deer, waterfowl	hiking, swimming, bird-watching	Apr-Aug	p101
Cat Tien (71,457)	primates, elephants, birdlife, rhinoceroses, tigers	jungle exploration, hiking	Nov-Jun	p283
Con Dao (19,991)	dugongs, turtles, beaches	bird-watching, snorkelling, diving	Nov-Jun	p263
Cuc Phuong (22,406)	jungle, grottoes, primates, bird-watching centre, caves	endangered-primate viewing, hiking	Nov-Feb	p147
Hoang Lien (28,500)	mountains, birdlife, minority communities	hiking, cycling, bird-watching, mountain climbing	Sep-Nov, Apr-May	p126
Phong Nha-Ke Bang (125,362)	caves, karsts	boat trips, caving, kayaking, hiking	Apr-Sep	p152
Yok Don (112,102)	stilt houses, minority communities	elephant rides, hiking	Nov-Feb	p288

hunting and cross-breeding with introduced Cuban crocodiles. It took a lot of detective work, but scientists tested the DNA of individual crocodiles in captivity until they found a handful of pure Siamese crocodiles that were then reintroduced to an isolated lake in the park where they are now thriving.

Another positive sign is that some wildlife populations are re-establishing themselves in reforested areas. Birds, fish and crustaceans have reappeared in replanted mangrove forests. Areas in which large animals were thought to have been wiped out by war are now hot spots of biodiversity and abundance. The extensive forests of the central highlands and far north remain a home to some of nature's most spectacular creatures, including tigers, elephants, clouded leopards and sun bears. Their chances of survival rest in the balance, as Vietnam's population continues to expand, eating up more and more of the remaining wilderness areas.

Twitchers with a serious interest in the birdlife of Vietnam should carry a copy of *Birds of Southeast Asia* (2005) by Craig Robson, which includes thorough coverage of Vietnam.

National Parks

Vietnam has 31 national parks, from Hoang Lien in the far north to Mui Ca Mau on the very southern tip of Vietnam, plus dozens of nature reserves. Levels of infrastructure and enforcement vary widely but every park has a ranger station. You can hire a ranger to guide you in most parks.

The management of national parks is a continuing source of conflict because Vietnam is still figuring out how to balance conservation with the needs of the adjoining rural populations (many of them minority people). Rangers are often vastly outnumbered by villagers who rely on forests for food and income. Some parks now use high-tech mapping software to track poaching and logging activity.

If you can, try to visit the more popular parks during the week. For many locals a trip to a park is all about having a good time, and noise and littering can be all part of the weekend scene.

Many parks have accommodation and a restaurant; you should always call ahead and order food though.

Ho Chi Minh, taking time off from the war in 1963 to dedicate Cuc Phuong National Park, said: 'Forest is gold. If we know how to conserve it well, it will be very precious. Destruction of the forest will lead to serious effects on both life and productivity.'

Environmental Issues

Vietnam's environment is not yet teetering on the brink but it's reaching crisis level on several fronts. Vietnam is a poor, densely populated country and the government's main priorities are job creation and economic growth. There's little to no monitoring of pollution and dirty industries, while loggers and animal traffickers are all too often able to escape trouble through bribery and official inaction. Quite simply, the environment is a low priority despite the government signing up to key conservation treaties.

Deforestation

Deforestation is a key issue. While 44% of the nation was forested in 1943, by 1983 only 24% was left and in 1995 it was down to 20%. In a positive turnaround, recent reforestation projects by the Forest Ministry, including the banning of unprocessed timber exports in 1992, have produced a rise in the amount of forest cover. However this has been bad news for the neighbours, because it simply means Vietnam buys its timber from Laos and Cambodia, where environmental enforcement is lax. Also much of this reforestation consists of homogenous plantations of trees (like acacia for furniture) in straight rows that have little ecological merit.

The Vietnam Association for Conservation of Nature and Environment acts as a bit of a clearing house for stories and projects related to Vietnam's environment; www .vacne.org.vn.

Hunting

Wildlife poaching has decimated forests of animals; snares capture and kill indiscriminately, whether animals are common or critically endangered. Figures are very difficult to ascertain, but a 2007 survey by wildlife trade monitoring organisation Traffic estimated that a million animals were illegally traded each year in Vietnam.

Some hunting is done by minority people simply looking to put food on the table, but there's a far bigger market (fuelled by domestic and Chinese traders) for *dac san* (bush meat) and traditional medicine. For many locals, a trip to the country involves dining on wild game, the more exotic the better, and there are bush meat restaurants on the fringes of

LENDING A HAND

Vietnam has a growing number of very effective local NGOs, plus many international organisations are active in the country, creating a tremendous number of fascinating opportunities to volunteer on environmental and community projects.

The Vietnam Volunteer Network (www.vietnamvolunteernetwork.com) runs orphanages in Ho Chi Minh City, Haiphong, Hanoi and Nha Trang and are always looking for volunteers. Project Vietnam Foundation (www.pvnf.org) provides free healthcare to remote rural communities, and welcomes volunteers with medical expertise.

PanNature is a Vietnamese NGO promoting nature-friendly solutions to environmental problems and sustainable development issues. It occasionally offers volunteer opportunities; www.nature.org.vn. And you can find many other volunteer projects through www.idealist.org.

PARADISE IN PERIL

Unesco World Heritage site Halong Bay is one of Vietnam's crown jewels. A dazzling collection of jagged limestone karst islands emerging from a cobalt sea, its beauty is breathtaking.

This beauty has proved a blessing for the tourist industry, yet cursed Halong with an environmental headache. In 2009, 1.5 million people cruised the karsts. In order to accommodate everyone, the authorities have ripped up mangroves to build coastal roads and new docks. Inadequate toilet waste facilities and diesel spills from cruise boats contaminate once-pristine seas.

Even more alarming are the gargantuan Cam Pha coal mines and cement factory, just 20km east of Halong City, from which tonnes of coal dust and waste leak into the bay. A new deep-water port in Hon Gai draws hundreds of container ships a year through an international shipping channel that cuts through the heart of Halong.

The resulting silt and dust has cloaked the sea grasses and shallow sea bottom, making it a struggle for sea life to survive, and putting the entire marine ecosystem in peril.

---

many national parks. A 2010 survey by the Wildlife Conservation Society found that 57 out of 68 restaurants in Dalat were offering wild game (including civet, porcupine and wild pig).

Attempts to curtail this trade at local and national level are thwarted by bribery, corruption and understaffing of the Forest Protection Department. Education for Nature Vietnam is a local NGO combating the illegal wildlife trade by lobbying politicians and educational programs in schools. It maintains files on restaurants offering bush meat and campaigns against the bear bile trade.

Industry & Pollution

Unsurprisingly for a developing nation, Vietnam has serious pollution issues. Air quality in Ho Chi Minh City (HCMC) and Hanoi is punishing, with respiratory ailments on the rise. Motorbikes are the main culprits – these cities have an average of one bike per two citizens – all running on low-quality fuel that has choking levels of benzene, sulphur and microscopic dust (PM10).

Water pollution affects many regions, particularly the cities and coastal areas (where groundwater has become saline due to overexploitation). Manufacturers have flooded into Vietnam to build clothing, footwear and food processing plants but most industrial parks have no waste water treatment plants. The result is that discharge has caused biological death for rivers like the Thi Van near Vung Tau. Nationwide only 14% of all city waste water is treated.

Vietnam is the world's second largest coffee producer. It's a vital cash crop in the central highlands where it's known as 'brown gold'. Around 97% of Vietnamese coffee is the cheaper, caffeine-packed robusta bean.

Global Warming

Vietnam is ranked as one of the most vulnerable countries in the world in the face of climate change, because rising tides, flooding and hurricanes will likely inundate low-lying areas. A 2008 conference determined that a sea-level rise of only 1m would flood more than 6% of the country and affect up to 10 million people. HCMC already experiences serious flooding every month, and the Saigon river only has to rise 1.35m for its dyke defences to be breached. If monsoons worsen, similar flooding will create havoc in the vast deltas of the Red River and Mekong River.

The Vietnam Green Building Council posts articles about current environmental and global warming issues on its website, www.vgbc.org.vn.

Ecocide: The Impact of War

The American War witnessed the most intensive attempt to destroy a country's natural environment the world has ever seen. Forty years later Vietnam is still in recovery mode, such was the devastation caused. American forces sprayed 72 million litres of defoliants (including Agent Orange, loaded with dioxin) over 16% of South Vietnam to destroy the Viet Cong's natural cover.

Enormous bulldozers called 'Rome ploughs' ripped up the jungle floor, removing vegetation and topsoil. Flammable melaleuca forests were ignited with napalm. In mountain areas, landslides were deliberately created by bombing and spraying acid on limestone hillsides. Elephants, useful for transport, were attacked from the air with bombs and napalm. By the war's end, extensive areas had been taken over by tough weeds (known locally as 'American grass'). The government estimates that 20,000 sq km of forest and farmland were lost as a direct result of the American War.

13 million tonnes of bombs – equivalent to 450 times the energy of the Hiroshima atomic bomb – were dropped on Indochina during the American War. This equates to 265kg for every man, woman and child in Vietnam, Cambodia and Laos.

Scientists have yet to conclusively prove a link between the dioxin residues of chemicals used by the USA and spontaneous abortions, stillbirths, birth defects and other human health problems. Links between dioxin and other diseases including several types of cancer are well established.

Chemical manufacturers that supplied herbicides to the US military paid US$180 million to US war veterans, without admitting liability. However the estimated four million Vietnamese victims of dioxin poisoning in Vietnam have never received compensation. Court cases brought by the pressure group Vietnamese Association of Victims of Agent Orange (VAVA) have so far been rejected in the USA.

Many journalists and other commentators have concluded that the Vietnamese government has been reluctant to pursue compensation claims for Agent Orange poisoning through the international courts because it has placed a higher priority on normalising relations with the USA.

Survival Guide

Directory A–Z

Accommodation

In general, accommodation in Vietnam offers superb value for money and excellent facilities. In big cities and main tourism centres you'll find everything from hostel dorm beds to luxe hotels. If you're travelling in the countryside and visiting provincial towns there's less choice; you'll usually be deciding between guesthouses and basic-but-decent hotels.

Cleanliness standards are generally good and there are very few real dumps – even in remote rural areas there are some excellent budget places. Communication can be an issue at times (particularly off-the-beaten-path where few staff speak English), but it's usually possible to get an understanding. Perhaps because of this, service standards in Vietnam can be a little haphazard.

Prices are quoted in dong or US dollars throughout this book based on the preferred currency of the particular property. Most rooms fall into a budget price category and dorm bed prices are given individually. The price ranges used are:

Budget ($) Less than US$25 (525,000d) a night

Midrange ($$) Between US$25 (525,000d) and US$75 (1,575,000d)

Top End ($$$) Over US$75 (1,575,000d)

These reflect high-season prices for rooms with attached bathroom, unless stated otherwise. Discounts are often available at quiet times of year.

Passports are almost always requested on arrival at a hotel. It is not absolutely essential to hand over your actual passport, but at the very least you need to provide a photocopy of the passport details, visa and departure card.

Guesthouses & Hotels

Hotels are called *khach san* and guesthouses *nha khach* or *nha nghi*. Many hotels have a wide variety of rooms (a spread of between US$15 and US$60 is not unusual). Often the cheapest rooms are at the end of several flights of stairs, or lack a window.

» **Budget hotels** Guesthouses (usually family-run) vary enormously depending on the standards of the owner, often the newest places are in best condition. The good news is that most rooms in this category are very well equipped, with US$12–15 often bagging you in-room wi-fi, air-con, hot water and a TV. Some places even throw in a free breakfast too. Towards the upper end of this category, minihotels – small, smart private hotels – usually represent excellent value for money. Few budget places have lifts (elevators) however.

» **Midrange hotels** At the lower end of this bracket, many of the hotels are similar to budget hotels but with bigger rooms or balconies. Flash a bit more cash and the luxury factor rises exponentially with contemporary design

---

HOTELS FROM HELL

There are a lot of hotel scams in Vietnam, mostly, but not exclusively, happening in the budget sector in Hanoi. A hotel will get a good reputation and recommendation in a guidebook and before you know it a copycat place with exactly the same name opens down the road. Dodgy taxi drivers work in tandem with these copycat hotels, ferrying unsuspecting visitors to the fake place. Check out your room before you check in if you have any concerns. Some Hanoi hotels also harass you to book tours with them. That said, most guesthouse and hotel operators are decent and honest folk. For more on horror hotels in Hanoi and how to avoid them, see p61.

touches and a swimming pool and massage or spa facilities becoming the norm.

» **Top-end hotels** Expect everything from faceless business hotels, colonial places resonating with history and chic boutique hotels where you can live it up *Wallpaper**-style in this bracket. Resort hotels are dotted along the coastline. Top beach spots such as China Beach, Nha Trang and Mui Ne all have a range of sumptuous places. Villa-hotels (where your accommodation has a private pool) are becoming popular, while others even have private butler service or complimentary spa facilities. You'll find ecolodges in the mountains of the north and in the far-flung corners of Bai Tu Long Bay, and a new privately run jungle lodge in Cat Tien National Park.

Homestays

Homestays are a popular option in parts of Vietnam, but it's highly advisable not to just drop into a random tribal village and hope things work out; there are strict rules about registering foreigners who stay overnight.

Areas that are well set up include the Mekong Delta (p367), the White Thai villages of Mai Chau (p119) and Ba Be (p90).

Some specialist tour companies (p519) and motorbike touring companies (p520) have developed excellent relations with remote villages and offer homestays as part of their trips.

Taxes

Most hotels at the top end levy a tax of 10% and a service charge of 5%, displayed as ++ ('plus plus') on the bill. Some midrange (and even the odd budget place) also try to levy a 10% tax, though this can often be waived.

Business Hours

Vietnamese people rise early and consider sleeping in to

BOOK YOUR STAY ONLINE

For more accommodation reviews by Lonely Planet authors, check out hotels.lonelyplanet.com/Vietnam. You'll find independent reviews, as well as recommendations on the best places to stay. Best of all, you can book online.

be a sure indication of illness. Lunch is taken very seriously and virtually everything shuts down between noon and 1.30pm. Government workers tend to take longer breaks, so figure on getting nothing done between 11.30am and 2pm. Many government offices are open to noon Saturday, but closed Sunday. In this book, opening hours are only included when they differ from these standard hours.

Post offices 6.30am to 9pm
Banks 8am to 11.30am and 1pm to 4pm weekdays, 8am to 11.30am Saturday
Offices, museums and shops 7am or 8am to 5pm or 6pm. Museums generally close on Monday
Temples and pagodas 5am to 9pm
Small shops, restaurants and street stalls Open late, seven days a week

Children

Children get to have a good time in Vietnam, mainly because of the overwhelming amount of attention they attract and the fact that almost everybody wants to play with them. However, this attention can sometimes be overwhelming, particularly for blond-haired, blue-eyed babes. Cheek pinching, or worse still (if rare), groin grabbing for boys, are distinct possibilities, so keep them close. For the full picture check out Lonely Planet's *Travel with Children*.

Big cities have plenty to keep kids interested, though in most smaller towns and rural areas boredom may set in from time to time. There are some great beaches, but

pay close attention to any playtime in the sea, as there are some big riptides along the main coastline. Some popular beaches have warning flags and lifeguards, but at quieter beaches parents should test the current first. Seas around Phu Quoc Island (p381) are more sheltered.

Kids generally enjoy local cuisine, which is rarely too spicy: the range of fruit is staggering and spring rolls usually go down very well. Comfort food from home (pizzas, pasta, burgers and ice cream) is available in most places too.

Pack plenty of high-factor sunscreen before you go as it's not that widely available in Vietnam (and costs more than in many Western countries).

Babies & Infants

Baby supplies are available in the major cities, but dry up quickly in the countryside. You'll find cots in most mid-range and top-end hotels, but not elsewhere. There are no safety seats in rented cars or taxis, but some restaurants can find a highchair.

Breastfeeding in public is quite common in Vietnam, but there are few facilities for changing babies other than using toilets and bathrooms. For kids who are too young to handle chopsticks, most restaurants also have cutlery.

The main worry throughout Vietnam is keeping an eye on what strange things infants are putting in their mouths. Their natural curiosity can be a lot more costly in a country where dysentery, typhoid and hepatitis are commonplace. Keep their hydration levels up and slap on the sunscreen.

HIGHLIGHTS FOR CHILDREN

ATTRACTION	DETAILS	PAGE
Ho Chi Minh City's water parks	Cool off with a big grin on your face. Not bad for grown-ups either	(p318)
Hanoi's water puppets	The theatrics, music and performance always go down well	(p74)
Cuc Phuong Primate Rescue Center	Monkey business (and conservation education) galore	(p147)
Halong Bay	Sleeping on a boat is an adventure, plus caves and islands to explore	(p94)

Customs Regulations

Enter Vietnam by air and the procedure usually takes a few minutes. If entering by land, expect to attract a bit more interest, particularly at remote borders. Duty limits:

» 200 cigarettes

» 1.5 litres of spirit

» Unlimited foreign currency, large sums (US$7000 and greater) must be declared

Electricity

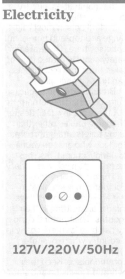

127V/220V/50Hz

The usual voltage is 220V, 50 cycles, but sometimes you'll encounter 110V, also at 50 cycles, just to confuse things. Electrical sockets are usually (round) two-pin.

Embassies & Consulates

It's important to realise what your country's embassy can and can't do to help if you get into trouble. Generally speaking, it won't be much help if the trouble you're in is remotely your own fault. Your embassy won't be sympathetic if you end up in jail after committing a crime, even if such actions are legal in your own country.

In genuine emergencies you might get some assistance, but only if other channels have been exhausted. If you have your passport stolen, it can take some time to replace as some embassies in Vietnam do not issue new passports, which have to be sent from a regional embassy.

Australia (www.vietnam.em bassy.gov.au) Hanoi (☑3774 0100; 8 Ð Dao Tan, Ba Dinh District); HCMC (☑3521 8100; 5th fl, 5B Ð Ton Duc Thang)

Cambodia Hanoi (☑3942 4788; cambocg@hcm.vnn.vn; 71A P Tran Hung Dao); HCMC (☑3829 2751; 41 Ð Phung Khac Khoan)

Canada (www.canadainter national.gc.ca/vietnam) Hanoi (☑3734 5000; 31 Ð Hung Vuong); HCMC (☑3827 9899; 10th fl, 235 Ð Dong Khoi)

China (http://vn.china -embassy.org/chn) Hanoi (☑8845 3736; 46 P Hoang Dieu); HCMC (☑3829 2457; 39 Ð Nguyen Thi Minh Khai)

France (www.ambafrance-vn .org) Hanoi (☑3944 5700; P Tran Hung Dao); HCMC (☑3520 6800; 27 Ð Nguyen Thi Minh Khai)

Germany (www.hanoi.diplo .de) Hanoi (☑3845 3836; 29 Ð Tran Phu); HCMC (☑3829 1967; 126 Ð Nguyen Dinh Chieu)

Japan (www.vn.emb-japan.go .jp) Hanoi (☑3846 3000; 27 P Lieu Giai, Ba Dinh District); HCMC (☑3822 5341; 13-17 ÐL Nguyen Hue)

Laos (www.embalaohanoi .gov.la) Danang (12 Ð Tran Qui Cap); Hanoi (☑3942 4576; 22 P Tran Binh Trong); HCMC (☑3829 7667; 93 Ð Pasteur)

Netherlands (www.nether lands-embassy.org.vn) Hanoi (☑3831 5650; 6th fl, Daeha Office Tower, 360 Kim Ma St, Ba Dinh); HCMC (☑3823 5932; Saigon Tower, 29 ÐL Le Duan)

New Zealand (www.nzem bassy.com/viet-nam) Hanoi (☑3824 1481; Level 5, 63 P Ly Thai To); HCMC (☑3827 2745; 8th fl, The Metropolitan, 235 Ð Dong Khoi)

Philippines Hanoi (☑3943 7948; hanoi.pe@dfa.gov.ph; 27B P Tran Hung Dao)

Singapore (www.mfa.gov.sg /hanoi) Hanoi (☑3848 9168; 41-43 Ð Tran Phu)

Sweden (www.swedenabroad .com) Hanoi (☑3726 0400; 2 Ð Nui Truc)

Thailand (www.thaiembassy .org) Hanoi (☑3823 5092; 63-65 P Hoang Dieu); HCMC (☑3932 7637; 77 Ð Tran Quoc Thao)

UK (http://ukinvietnam.fco .gov.uk) Hanoi (☑3936 0500; Central Bldg, 31 P Hai Ba Trung); HCMC (☑3829 8433; 25 ÐL Le Duan)

USA (http://vietnam.us embassy.gov) Hanoi (☑3850

5000; 7 P Lang Ha, Ba Dinh District); HCMC (☑3822 9433; 4 ĐL Le Duan)

Food

Eating out in Vietnam is generally very inexpensive and a real highlight of travelling in the nation; for the full picture see p485. For this guidebook we've used the following price categories to indicate the typical cost of a meal, excluding drinks:

Budget Up to US$5
Midrange US$5 to US$15
Top-end Above US$15

Gay & Lesbian Travellers

Vietnam is a relatively hassle-free place for homosexuals. There are no official laws on same-sex relationships in Vietnam, nor much in the way of individual harassment. Indeed the Vietnamese authorities authorised an exhibition of photographs about gay culture to tour universities in 2010 called 'Open mind, Open life.'

That said, the government is notorious for clamping down on gay venues and most keep a very low profile. There are, however, healthy gay scenes in Hanoi (p74) and Ho Chi Minh City (p335). Homosexuality is still far from accepted in the wider community, though the lack of any laws keeps things fairly safe. Most gay Vietnamese have to hide their sexuality from their families and friends and a lot of stigma remains.

Gay travellers shouldn't expect any problems in Vietnam. Checking into hotels as a same sex couple is perfectly acceptable though it's prudent not to flaunt your sexuality. As with heterosexual couples, passionate public displays of affection are considered a basic no-no.

Utopia (www.utopia-asia .com) has gay travel informa-

tion and contacts, including detailed sections on the legality of homosexuality in Vietnam and some local gay terminology.

Insurance

Insurance is a must for Vietnam, as the cost of major medical treatment is prohibitive. Although you may have medical insurance in your own country, it is probably not valid while you are in Vietnam. A travel insurance policy to cover theft, loss and medical problems is the best bet.

Some insurance policies specifically exclude such 'dangerous activities' as riding motorbikes, diving and even trekking. Check that your policy covers an emergency evacuation in the event of serious injury.

Worldwide travel insurance is available at www .lonelyplanet.com/travel _services. You can buy, extend or claim anytime – even if you're already on the road.

Internet Access

Internet and wi-fi is widely available throughout towns and cities in Vietnam. However beware that the government regularly blocks access to social networking sites, including Facebook. For more see p19.

The cost of internet access generally ranges from 3000d to 10,000d per hour in cybercafes; hotels rarely charge for access (except some five-star places).

Remember that the power-supply voltage might vary from that at home so laptop users should bring a universal AC adapter.

Language Courses

There are Vietnamese-language courses offered in Ho Chi Minh City (HCMC), Hanoi and elsewhere. Note that the northern and southern dialects are quite different. For details, see the Language Courses sections

---

PRACTICALITIES

» **Laundry** Most guesthouses and hotels have cheap laundry services, but check there is a dryer if the weather is bad. There are also dry-cleaning outlets in every town.

» **Newspapers & magazines** *Vietnam News* and the *Saigon Times* are propagandist English-language dailies. Popular listings mags include the *Guide,* which covers the whole country, plus *AsiaLife* and *The Word* in Ho Chi Minh City.

» **Radio & TV** *Voice of Vietnam* hogs the airwaves all day and is pumped through loudspeakers in many rural towns (and Hanoi). There are several TV channels and a steady diet of satellite stuff.

» **Smoking** Vietnam is a smoker's paradise (and a non-smoker's nightmare). People spark up everywhere, though there's an official ban against smoking in public places and on public transportation. It's not socially acceptable to smoke on air-conditioned transport – so those long bus journeys are usually smoke-free.

» **Weights & measures** The Vietnamese use the metric system for everything except precious metals and gems, where they follow the Chinese system.

in the Hanoi (p57) and HCMC (p319) chapters.

Legal Matters

Civil Law

On paper it looks good, but in practice the rule of law in Vietnam is a fickle beast. Local officials interpret the law any way it suits them, often against the wishes of Hanoi. There is no independent judiciary. Not surprisingly, most legal disputes are settled out of court.

Drugs

The drug trade has made a comeback in Vietnam, with plentiful supplies making it overland along the porous Lao border. The country has a very serious problem with heroin these days and the authorities are clamping down hard. Life sentences or the death penalty are liberally handed out.

Marijuana and, in the northwest, opium are readily available but giving in to temptation is a risk. There are many plain-clothes police in Vietnam and if you're arrested, the result might be a large fine and/or a long prison term.

Police

Few foreigners experience much hassle from police and demands for bribes are very rare. That said, police corruption is an everyday reality for locals and it has been acknowledged in official newspapers. If something does go wrong, or if something is stolen, the police can't do much more than prepare an insurance report for a negotiable fee – take an English-speaking Vietnamese with you to translate.

Maps

The *Viet Nam Administrative Atlas,* published by Ban Do, is perfect for cyclists or motorcyclists looking for roads less travelled and costs less than US$10 in hardback. Ban Do also publishes reasonable tourist maps of HCMC, Hanoi, Danang, Hue and a few other cities.

Vietnamese street names are preceded with the words Pho, Duong and Dai Lo – on the maps and in the text in this book, they appear respectively as P, Đ and ĐL.

It's also worth picking up a copy of the highly informative *Xin Chao Map of Hanoi,* which has tips and recommendations.

Money

The Vietnamese currency is the dong (abbreviated to 'd'). Banknotes come in denominations of 500d, 1000d, 2000d, 5000d, 10,000d, 20,000d, 50,000d, 100,000d, 200,000d and 500,000d. Coins include 500d, 1000d and 5000d. US dollars are also widely used, though less so in rural areas.

The dong has experienced its ups and downs and has depreciated significantly in recent years to around 22,000d to the US dollar.

Where prices on the ground are quoted in dong, we quote them in dong in this book. Likewise, when prices are quoted in dollars, we follow suit.

Consult p18 for exchange rates.

ATMs

ATMs are now very widespread in Vietnam and are present in virtually every town in the country. You shouldn't have any problems getting cash with a regular Maestro/Cirrus debit card, or with a Visa or MasterCard debit or credit card. Watch out for stiff withdrawal fees however (typically 20,000d to 30,000d), and withdrawal limits – most are around 3,000,000d but Agribank allows up to 6,000,000d.

Bargaining

Some bargaining is essential in most tourist transactions. Remember that in Asia 'saving face' is important, so bargaining should be good-natured. Smile and don't get angry or argue. In some cases you will be able to get a 50% discount or more, at other times this may only be 10%. And once the money is accepted, the deal is done.

Black Market

There's a small black market in Vietnam but it's hardly worth bothering with as it's technically illegal, rates are only fractionally better than the banks (and sometimes worse!) and the chances of rip-offs exist.

Cash

The US dollar remains king of foreign currencies and can be exchanged and used pretty much everywhere. Other major currencies can be exchanged at leading banks including Vietcombank and HSBC.

Check that any big dollar bills you take do not look too tatty, as no-one will accept them in Vietnam.

You cannot legally take dong out of Vietnam but you can reconvert reasonable amounts of it into US dollars on departure.

Most land border crossings now have some sort of official currency exchange, offering the best rates available in these remote parts of the country.

Credit Cards

Visa, MasterCard and JCB cards are accepted in major cities and many tourist centres, however don't expect budget guesthouses or noodle bars to take plastic. Commission charges (around 3%) are sometimes asked for. Some merchants also accept Amex, but the surcharge is typically 4%.

If you wish to obtain a cash advance, this is possible at Vietcombank branches in most cities, as well as foreign banks in HCMC and Hanoi. Banks generally charge a 3% commission for this service.

Tipping

Tipping is not expected in Vietnam, but it is enormously appreciated. For a person who earns US$100 per month, a US$1 tip is significant. Upmarket hotels and some restaurants may levy a 5% service charge, but this may not make it to the staff.

You should consider tipping drivers and guides – after all, the time they spend on the road with you means time away from home and family. Typically, travellers on minibus tours will pool together to collect a communal tip to be split between the guide and driver.

It is considered proper to make a small donation at the end of a visit to a pagoda, especially if a monk has shown you around; most pagodas have contribution boxes for this purpose.

Travellers Cheques

Travellers cheques can only be exchanged at authorised foreign exchange banks, but these aren't found throughout Vietnam.

Banks charge 0.5% to 2% commission to cheques to cash. Vietcombank charges no commission for exchanging Amex travellers cheques; a reasonable 0.5% for other types.

Travellers cheques in currencies other than US dollars can be next to useless beyond the major cities.

Photography

Memory cards are pretty cheap in Vietnam, which is fortunate given the visual feast awaiting even the amateur photographer. Most internet cafes can also burn photos on to a CD or DVD to free up storage space. It's worthwhile bringing the attachment for viewing your files on the big screen, as many hotels come equipped with televisions.

Colour print film is widely available and prices are pretty reasonable at about US$2.50 for a roll of 36 print film. Slide film can be bought in Hanoi and HCMC, but don't count on it elsewhere. Supplies of black-and-white film are rapidly disappearing, so bring your own.

Photo-processing shops are located all over Vietnam and developing costs are about US$4 per roll depending on the print size selected. The quality is generally very good. Printing digital shots is fairly cheap and works out at between 1000d and 2000d a photo.

Cameras are reasonably priced in Vietnam but the selection is limited. All other camera supplies are readily available in major towns, but soon dry up in remote areas.

For plenty of tips on better travel photography, pick up a copy of Lonely Planet's *Travel Photography*.

Sensitive Subjects

The Vietnamese police usually don't care what you photograph, but on occasion they get pernickety. Avoid snapping airports, military bases and border checkpoints. Don't even think of trying to get a snapshot of Ho Chi Minh in his glass sarcophagus!

Photographing anyone, particularly hill-tribe people, demands patience and the utmost respect for local customs. Photograph with discretion and manners. It's always polite to ask first and if the person says no, don't take the photo. If you promise to send a copy of the photo, make sure you do.

Post

Every city, town, village and rural subdistrict in Vietnam has some sort of post office (*buu dien*). Post offices all over the country keep long hours, from about 6.30am to 9pm including weekends and public holidays (even Tet).

Vietnam has a quite reliable post service, a postcard to most destinations will cost around 10,000d. For anything important, express-mail service (EMS), available in the larger cities, is twice as fast as regular airmail and everything is registered.

Private couriers such as FedEx, DHL and UPS are reliable for transporting small parcels or documents.

Poste restante works well in post offices in Hanoi and HCMC. Even receiving a small package from abroad can cause a headache while large ones will produce a migraine, involving a lengthy inspection process.

Public Holidays

Politics affects everything in Vietnam, including many public holidays. If a public holiday falls on a weekend, it is observed on the Monday.

» **New Year's Day (Tet Duong Lich)** 1 January
» **Vietnamese New Year (Tet)** A three-day national holiday; January or February
» **Founding of the Vietnamese Communist Party (Thanh Lap Dang CSVN)** 3 February – the date the party was founded in 1930

PLANET OF THE FAKES

You'll probably notice a lot of cut-price Lonely Planet *Vietnam* titles available as you travel around the country. Don't be deceived. These are pirate copies, churned out on local photocopiers. Sometimes the copies are OK, sometimes they're awful. The only certain way to tell is price. If it's cheap, it's a copy. Look at the print in this copy...if it is faded and the photos are washed out, then this book will self-destruct in five seconds.

» **Hung Kings Commemorations (Hung Vuong)** 10th day of the 3rd lunar month – March or April

» **Liberation Day (Saigon Giai Phong)** 30 April – the date of Saigon's 1975 surrender is commemorated nationwide

» **International Workers' Day (Quoc Te Lao Dong)** 1 May

» **Ho Chi Minh's Birthday (Sinh Nhat Bac Ho)** 19 May

» **Buddha's Birthday (Phat Dan)** Eighth day of the fourth moon (usually June)

» **National Day (Quoc Khanh)** 2 September – commemorates the Declaration of Independence by Ho Chi Minh in 1945

Safe Travel

All in all, Vietnam is an extremely safe country to travel in. The police keep a pretty tight grip on social order and we very rarely receive reports about muggings, armed robberies and sexual assaults. Sure there are scams and hassles in some cities, particularly in Hanoi and Nha Trang, which we've dealt with in relevant sections of the book. But perhaps the most important thing you can do is to be extra careful if you're travelling on two wheels on Vietnam's anarchic roads – traffic accident rates are woeful and driving standards are pretty appalling.

Sea Creatures

If you plan to spend your time swimming, snorkelling and scuba diving, familiarise yourself with the various hazards. The list of dangerous creatures that are found in seas off Vietnam is extensive and includes sharks, jellyfish, stonefish, scorpion fish, sea snakes and stingrays. However, there is little cause for alarm as most of these creatures avoid humans, or humans avoid them, so the number of people injured or killed is very small.

Jellyfish tend to travel in groups, so as long as you look before you leap into the sea, avoiding them should not be too hard. Stonefish, scorpion fish and stingrays tend to hang out in shallow water along the ocean floor and can be very difficult to see. One way to protect against these nasties is to wear plastic shoes in the sea.

For more advice on creatures that bite, see p527.

Undetonated Explosives

For more than three decades, four armies expended untold energy and resources mining, booby-trapping, rocketing, strafing, mortaring and bombarding wide areas of Vietnam. When the fighting stopped, most of this ordnance remained exactly where it had landed or been laid; American estimates at the end of the war placed the quantity of unexploded ordnance (UXO) at 150,000 tonnes.

Since 1975 more than 40,000 Vietnamese have been maimed or killed by this leftover ordnance. While cities, cultivated areas and well-travelled rural roads and paths are safe for travel, straying from these areas could land you in the middle of danger.

Never touch any rockets, artillery shells, mortars, mines or other relics of war you may come across. Such objects can remain lethal for decades. And don't climb inside bomb craters – you never know what undetonated explosive device is at the bottom.

You can learn more about the issue of landmines from the Nobel Peace Prize–winning **International Campaign to Ban Landmines** (ICBL; www .icbl.org), or visit the **Halo Trust** (www.halotrust.org) or **Mines Advisory Group** (MAG; www.maginternational .org) websites, both British organisations specialising in clearing landmines and UXO around the world. Cluster munitions were outlawed in a 2008 treaty signed by more than 100 countries, the usual suspects declining to sign: visit www.stopcluster munitions.org.

Telephone

For all-important numbers like emergency services and the international access code, check out p18.

Every city has a **general information service** (☏1080) that provides everything from phone numbers and train and air timetables to exchange rates and the latest football scores. It even provides marriage counselling or bedtime lullabies for your child – no kidding! You can usually be connected to an operator who speaks English or French.

GOVERNMENT TRAVEL ADVICE

The following government websites offer travel advisories and information on current hot spots:

Australian Department of Foreign Affairs (☏1300 139 281; www.smartraveller.gov.au)

British Foreign Office (☏0845-850-2829; www.fco.gov.uk/en/travel-and-living-abroad)

Canadian Department of Foreign Affairs (☏800-267 6788; www.dfait-maeci.gc.ca)

New Zealand Ministry of Foreign Affairs & Trade (04-439 8000; www.safetravel.govt.nz)

US Bureau of Consular Affairs (☏888-407 4747; http://travel.state.gov)

International Calls

Charges for international calls from Vietnam have dropped significantly in the past few years. It's usually cheapest to use a mobile phone to make international phone calls; rates can be as little as US$0.10 a minute.

Otherwise you can web-call from any phone in the country, just dial ☑17100, the country code and your number – most countries cost a flat rate of just US$0.50 per minute. Many budget hotels now operate even cheaper web-call services, as do post offices.

Of course, using services such as Skype cost next to nothing; many budget and midrange hotels now have Skype and webcams set up for their guests.

Reverse charges or collect calls are possible to most, but not all, Western countries including Australia, Canada, France, Japan, New Zealand, the UK and the USA.

Local Calls

Phone numbers in Hanoi, HCMC and Haiphong have eight digits. Elsewhere around the country phone numbers have seven digits. Telephone area codes are assigned according to the province.

Local calls can usually be made from any hotel or restaurant phone and are often free. Confirm this with the hotel so you don't receive any unpleasant surprises when you check out. Domestic long-distance calls are reasonably priced and cheaper if you dial direct. Save up to 20% by calling between 10pm and 5am.

Mobile (Cellular) Phones

Vietnam has an excellent, comprehensive cellular network. The nation uses GSM 900/1800, which is compatible with most of Asia, Europe and Australia but not with North America.

» **Viet Sim cards** It's well worth getting a local SIM card if you're planning to spend any time in Vietnam. A local number will enable you to send texts (SMS) anywhere in the world for around 2500d per message. If you don't want to bring your flash handset from home, you can buy a cheap phone in Vietnam for as little as US$20, often with US$10 of credit included. Get the shop owner (or someone at your hotel) to set up your phone in English, or your native language. There are three main mobile phone companies (Viettel, Vinaphone and Mobifone) battling it out in the local market. All these companies have offices and branches nationwide.

» **Roaming** If your phone has roaming, it is easy enough, although can be outrageously expensive, to use your handset in Vietnam – particularly if you use the internet.

Time

Vietnam is seven hours ahead of Greenwich Mean Time/Universal Time Coordinated (GMT/UTC). Because of its proximity to the equator, Vietnam does not have daylight-saving or summer time. When it's noon in Vietnam, it is 9pm the previous day in Vancouver, midnight in New York, 5am in London, and 3pm in Sydney.

Toilets

The issue of toilets and what to do with used toilet paper causes some confusion. In general, if there's a waste-paper basket next to the toilet, that is where the toilet paper goes, as many sewage systems cannot handle toilet paper. If there's no basket flush paper down the toilet.

Toilet paper is usually provided, except in bus and train stations, though it's wise to keep a stash of your own while on the move.

There are still some squat toilets around in public places and out in the countryside.

The scarcity of public toilets is more of a problem for women than for men. Vietnamese men often urinate in public. Women might find roadside toilet stops easier if wearing a sarong. You usually have to pay a few dong to an attendant to access a public toilet.

Tourist Information

Tourist offices in Vietnam have a different philosophy from the majority of tourist offices worldwide. These government-owned enterprises are really travel agencies whose primary interests are booking tours and turning a profit. Don't come here hoping for freebies.

Vietnam Tourism and Saigon Tourist are old examples of this genre, but nowadays every province has at least one such organisation. Travel agents, backpacker cafes and your fellow travellers are a much better source of information than any of the so-called 'tourist offices'.

There are privately operated, fairly helpful, tourist offices in Hanoi and Ho Chi Minh City.

Travellers with Disabilities

Vietnam is not the easiest of places for travellers with disabilities, despite the fact that many Vietnamese are disabled as a result of war injuries. Tactical problems include the chaotic traffic, a lack of lifts in smaller hotels and pavements that are routinely blocked by parked motorbikes and food stalls.

That said, with some careful planning it is possible to enjoy a trip to Vietnam. Find a reliable company to make the travel arrangements and don't be afraid to double-check things with hotels and restaurants yourself. In the major cities many hotels have lifts, and disabled

ON THE ROAD

Deaf travellers might like to drop by Tam's Café if they're in Dong Ha (p162) and Bread of Life while in Danang (p185), which both support and employ deaf people.

Take a look at the boxed text on p200 for more about organisations supporting the disabled in central Vietnam.

access is improving. Bus and train travel is not really geared for disabled travellers, but rent a private vehicle with a driver and almost anywhere becomes instantly accessible. As long as you are not too proud about how you get in and out of a boat or up some stairs, anything is possible, as the Vietnamese are always willing to help.

The hazards for blind travellers in Vietnam are pretty acute, with traffic coming at you from all directions. Just getting across the road in cities like Hanoi and HCMC is tough enough for those with 20:20 vision, so you'll definitely need a sighted companion!

The Travellers With Disabilities forum on Lonely Planet's **Thorn Tree** (www .lonelyplanet.com/thorntree) is a good place to seek the advice of other disabled travellers.

You might try contacting the following organisations:
Accessible Journeys (☑610-521 0339; www.disabili tytravel.com)
Mobility International USA (☑54-1343 1284; www .miusa.org)
Royal Association for Disability Rights (Radar; ☑020-7250 3222; www.radar .org.uk)
Society for Accessible Travel & Hospitality (SATH; ☑212-447 7284; www.sath.org)

Visas

Most nationalities have to endure the hassle of pre-arranging a visa (or approval letter) in order to enter Vietnam. Entry and exit points include Hanoi, HCMC and Danang airports or any of its plentiful land borders, shared with Cambodia, China and Laos.

Certain favoured nationalities (see Visa On Arrival table) qualify for an automatic visa on arrival. Everyone else has to sort out a visa in advance. Arranging the paperwork has become fairly straightforward, but it remains expensive and unnecessarily time consuming. Processing a tourist visa application typically takes four or five working days in Western countries.

Tourist visas are valid for a 30-day or 90-day stay (and can be single or multiple entry).

In Asia the best place to pick up a Vietnamese visa is Cambodia, where it costs around US$45 and can be arranged the same day. Bangkok is also a popular place, as many agents offer cheap packages with an air ticket and visa thrown in.

If you plan to spend more than a month in Vietnam, or if you plan to exit Vietnam and enter again from Cambodia or Laos, arrange a

90-day multiple-entry visa. These cost around US$95 in Cambodia, but are not available from all Vietnamese embassies.

In our experience, personal appearance influences the reception you'll receive from airport immigration – if you wear shorts or scruffy clothing, or look dirty or unshaven, you can expect problems. Try your best to look 'respectable'.

Business Visas

Business visas are usually valid for 90 days (180-day visas were once easily obtained but seem to only be available now in Cambodia) and allow both single and multiple entries as you wish. (Work permits are required in order to work legally in Vietnam.) Getting a business visa has now become cheap and easy, although more expensive than a tourist visa. Obtain these at Vietnamese embassies or online. Immigration policies change with the wind and could offer six-month visas again in the future.

Multiple-entry Visas

It's possible to enter Cambodia or Laos from Vietnam and then re-enter without having to apply for another visa. However, you must apply for a multiple-entry visa before you leave Vietnam.

VISA ON ARRIVAL

Citizens of the following countries do not need to apply in advance for a Vietnamese visa if arriving by air. Always double check visa requirements before you travel as policies regularly change.

COUNTRY	DAYS
Kyrgyzstan	90
Thailand, Malaysia, Singapore, Indonesia, Laos, Cambodia	30
Philippines	21
Japan, Korea, Russia, Norway, Denmark, Sweden, Finland, Brunei	15

Multiple-entry visas are easiest to arrange in Hanoi or HCMC, but you will almost certainly have to ask a travel agent to do the paperwork for you. Travel agents charge about US$45, and the procedure takes up to seven days.

Visa Extensions

If you've got the dollars, they've got the rubber stamp. Tourist-visa extensions officially cost as little as US$10, but it is easier to pay more and sort this out through a travel agency. Getting the stamp yourself can be a bureaucratic nightmare. The procedure can take seven days and you can only extend them for 30 or 90 days depending on the visa that you hold.

In theory, you should be able to extend your visa in any provincial capital. In practice, it works most smoothly in major cities, such as HCMC, Hanoi, Danang and Hue, which cater to regular visitors.

Volunteering

There are fewer opportunities for volunteering than one might imagine in a country such as Vietnam. This is partly due to the sheer number of professional development workers based here.

For information on volunteer-work opportunities, chase up the full list of non-government organisations (NGOs) at the **NGO Resource Centre** (☑04-3832 8570; www.ngocentre.org .vn; Hotel La Thanh, 218 P Doi Can, Hanoi), which keeps a database of all of the NGOs assisting Vietnam. Service Civil International (www.sciint .org) has links to options in Vietnam, including the SOS Village in Viet Tri, north of Hanoi, and the **Friendship Village** (www.vietnamfriend ship.org), established by veterans from both sides to help victims of Agent Orange. Or try contacting the following

VIETNAM VISA AGENTS

If you're arriving by air at Ho Chi Minh City, Hanoi or Danang it's now usually easiest and cheapest to get your visa approved in advance through a visa-service company or travel agent. This system does not operate at land border crossings.

They will need passport details, and will email you an approval document two to three days later (one day for rush service), which you need to print and bring with you to the airport. On arrival, present the approval document and passport picture, then pay a stamping fee (US$25 for single-entry, US$50 for multiple-entry visas). Many travellers prefer this method since they don't have to deal with Vietnamese bureaucratic hassles or give up their passport for any amount of time, and it also works out to be cheaper than using an embassy in the West.

Recommended companies include **Vietnam Visa Center** (www.vietnamvisacenter.org) and **Visa Vietnam** (www.visatovietnam.org).

organisations if you want to help in some way:

15 May School Schools in HCMC and Vinh for disadvantaged children, which provide free education and vocational training.

KOTO (www.koto.com.au) Here, you can donate your skills, time or money to help give street children career opportunities. Street Voices' primary project is KOTO Restaurant in Hanoi.

Volunteers for Peace (www.vpv.vn) Always looking for volunteers to help in an orphanage on the outskirts of Hanoi.

Another avenue is professional volunteering through an organisation back home that offers one- or two-year placements in Vietnam. One of the largest is **Voluntary Service Overseas** (VSO; www.vso.org.uk) in the UK, but other countries have their own organisations, including **Australian Volunteers International** (AVI; www.aus tralianvolunteers.com) and **Volunteer Service Abroad** (VSA; www.vsa.org.nz). The UN also operates its own volunteer program; details are available at www.unv.org. Other general volunteer sites

with links all over the place include www.volunteer abroad.com, www.idealist .org and www.globalvolunteer network.org.

Women Travellers

Like most other Southeast Asian countries, Vietnam is relatively free of serious hassles for Western women. There are issues to consider of course, but thousands of women travel alone through the country each year and love the experience. Most Vietnamese women enjoy relatively free, fulfilled lives and a career, the sexes mix freely and society does not expect women to behave in a subordinate manner. That said, Vietnamese women take their appearance very seriously and femininity is still defined by beauty, slimness and grace.

East Asian women travelling in Vietnam, especially if they look Vietnamese, may want to dress quite conservatively. Things have improved as more Vietnamese people are exposed to foreign visitors but very occasionally some ill-educated locals may think an Asian woman accompanying a Western male could be a Vietnamese prostitute.

Many Vietnamese women dress modestly and expose as little body flesh as possible (partly to avoid the sun). Be aware that exposing your upper arms (by wearing a vest top) will attract plenty of attention. However, there's no need to be overly paranoid.

For information about women's health, see p527.

Work

As Vietnam has taken its place on the global stage, all sorts of work opportunities for Westerners have opened up. Generally speaking, the best-paid Westerners living in Vietnam are those working for international organisations or foreign companies, but many of these jobs are secured before arrival in the country.

There's some casual work available in Western-owned bars and restaurants throughout the country of the cash-in-hand variety where you'll be working without paperwork. Dive schools and adventure sports specialists will always need instructors, but for most travellers the main work opportunities are teaching a foreign language.

Looking for employment is a matter of asking around – jobs are rarely advertised. The longer you stay, the easier it is to find work. Check out the website www .livinginvietnam.com for job opportunities.

Teaching

English is by far the most popular foreign language with Vietnamese students, but some students also want to learn French. There is also a limited demand for teachers of Chinese, Japanese, German, Spanish and Korean.

Government-run universities in Vietnam hire some foreign teachers. Pay is generally around US$5 to US$10 per hour, but benefits such as free housing and unlimited visa renewals are usually thrown in.

There is also a budding free market in private language centres and home tutoring; this is where most newly arrived foreigners seek work. Pay in the private sector is slightly better, at about US$8 to US$15 per hour, but these private schools won't offer the same extras as a government-run school. Private tutoring usually pays even better, at around US$12 to US$25 per hour.

Finding teaching jobs is quite easy in HCMC and Hanoi, and is sometimes possible in towns that have universities. Pay in the smaller towns tends to be lower and the work opportunities fewer.

Transport

GETTING THERE & AWAY

Most travellers enter Vietnam by plane or bus, but there are also train links from China and boat connections from Cambodia via the Mekong River.

Entering Vietnam

Formalities at Vietnam's international airports are generally smoother than at land borders, as the volume of traffic is greater. That said, crossing overland from Cambodia and China is now relatively stress free. Crossing the border between Vietnam and Laos can be slow.

Passport

Your passport must be valid for six months upon arrival in Vietnam. Most nationalities need to arrange a visa in advance (see p508).

Overseas Vietnamese may be given a harder time by immigration and customs than non-Vietnamese visitors.

Air

Airlines

Vietnam Airlines (www.vietnamairlines.com.vn) Hanoi (☑3832 0320); HCMC (☑3832 0320) The state-owned flag carrier has flights to 28 international destinations, mainly in east Asia, but new routes were announced to the UK and Australia in 2011.

The airline has a modern fleet of Airbuses and Boeings, and has a good recent safety record.

Airports

There are three established international airports in Vietnam. A fourth major international airport, in Phu Quoc, should become fully operational in 2012.

Danang (DAD; ☑1383 0339) Only has a handful of international flights, but its new terminal should result in additional routes.

Ho Chi Minh City (HCMC) (SGN; ☑3845 6654; www.tsnairport.com) Tan Son Nhat Airport is Vietnam's busiest international air hub.

Hanoi (HAN; ☑3827 1513; www.hanoiairportonline.com) Noi Bai Airport serves the capital.

Several other airports are classified as 'international', including those at Hue and Haiphong, but currently only have domestic flights. Nha Trang's Cam Ranh Airport does have one seasonal link to Russia and more connections may emerge.

Tickets

From Europe or North America it's usually more expensive to fly to Vietnam than other Southeast Asian countries. Consider buying a discounted ticket to Bangkok, Singapore or Hong Kong and picking up a flight from there: Air Asia and other low-cost airlines fly to Vietnam.

It's hard to get reservations for flights to and from Vietnam during holidays, especially Tet (see p451), which falls between late January and mid-February.

Land

Vietnam shares land borders with Cambodia, China and Laos and there are plenty of border crossings open to foreigners with each neighbour: a big improvement on a decade ago. The downside is that it is still not possible to get a Vietnamese visa on arrival at any of these borders.

Border Crossings

Exact border crossing details are dealt with in individual chapters. Border opening hours may vary slightly, but standard times that foreigners are allowed to cross are usually 7am to 5pm daily.

There are now legal money-changing facilities on the Vietnamese side of these border crossings, which can deal with US dollars and some other key currencies, including Chinese renminbi, Lao kip and Cambodian riel. Avoid black marketeers, as they have a well-deserved reputation for short-changing and outright theft.

Flights, tours, rail tickets and other travel services can be booked online at www.lonelyplanet.com/travel_services.

Air Routes

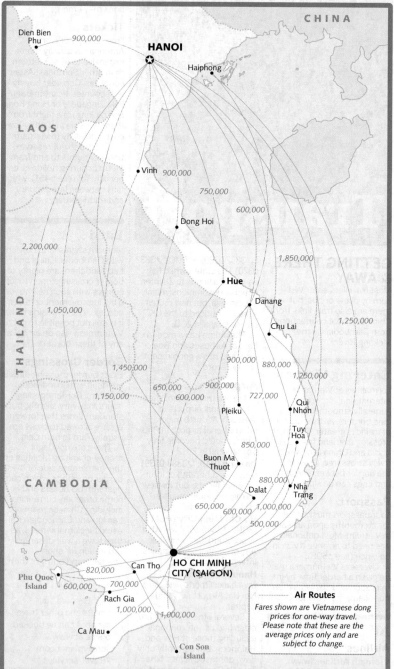

CHINA

Dien Bien Phu

900,000

★ HANOI

Haiphong

LAOS

• Vinh

900,000

750,000

Dong Hoi

600,000

• Hue

Danang

2,200,000

1,850,000

THAILAND

1,050,000

Chu Lai

1,250,000

1,450,000

900,000

880,000

1,250,000

650,000

900,000

Qui Nhon

1,150,000

600,000

727,000

Pleiku

Tuy Hoa

850,000

CAMBODIA

Buon Ma Thuot

880,000

Dalat

Nha Trang

650,000

600,000

1,000,000

500,000

Can Tho

HO CHI MINH CITY (SAIGON)

Phu Quoc Island

820,000

600,000

700,000

Rach Gia

1,000,000

1,000,000

Ca Mau •

Con Son Island

Air Routes

Fares shown are Vietnamese dong prices for one-way travel. Please note that these are the average prices only and are subject to change.

Travellers at border crossings are occasionally asked for an 'immigration fee' of a dollar or two.

CAMBODIA
Cambodia and Vietnam share a long frontier with seven (and counting) border crossings. One-month Cambodian visas are issued on arrival at all border crossings for US$20, but overcharging is common at all borders except Bavet.

Cambodian border crossings are officially open daily between 8am and 8pm. Here are some of the most popular:
» **Le Thanh–O Yadaw** Vietnam's central highlands to Cambodia's northeast, see p293.
» **Moc Bai–Bavet** Links HCMC to Phnom Penh, see p354.
» **Vinh Xuong–Kaam Samnor** Leisurely river crossing in Mekong Delta, see p401.
» **Xa Xia–Prek Chak** Connects the Delta and Phu Quoc with Cambodian coast, see p396.

CHINA
There are currently three border checkpoints where foreigners are permitted to cross between Vietnam and China: Huu Nghi Quan (the Friendship Pass), Lao Cai and Mong Cai. It is necessary to arrange a Chinese visa in advance.

China time is one hour ahead.
» **Lao Cai–Hekou** Connects northern Vietnam with Kunming; trains do not currently run on the Chinese side, p132.
» **Mong Cai–Dongxing** Halong Bay to Hainan Island, but little used by travellers, p110.
» **Youyi Guan–Huu Nghi Quan** Links Hanoi with Nanning, and ultimately Hong Kong; Vietnam–China trains use this route, see p113.

LAOS
There are seven (and counting) overland crossings between Vietnam and Laos. Thirty-day Lao visas are now available at all borders.

Try to use direct city-to-city bus connections between the countries as you'll already have a ticket and potential hassle will be greatly reduced – immigration and local transport scams are very common on the Vietnamese side. Lies about journey times are common. Worse are the devious drivers who stop buses in the middle of nowhere and renegotiate the price.

Transport links on both sides of the border can be hit and miss, so don't use the more remote borders unless you have plenty of time, and patience, to spare.

Here are links to the most popular crossings:
» **Bo Y–Pho Keau** Worth considering for trips between Hoi An or Quy Nhon and the Pakse part of Laos, see p296.
» **Cau Treo–Nam Phao** Connects Vinh with Tha Khaek, and used by buses on the rough overland trip between Hanoi and Vientiane, see p152.
» **Lao Bao–Dansavanh** The most popular and hassle-free crossing, links Dong Ha with Savannakhet, see p163.
» **Nam Can–Nong Haet** Links Vinh with Plain of Jars region of Laos, see p150.
» **Tay Trang–Sop Hun** Connects Dien Bien Phu with northern Laos, see p124.

Bus
It is possible to cross into Vietnam by bus from Cambodia, Laos and China. The most popular way to or from Cambodia are the international buses via the Moc Bai–Bavet border crossing. When it comes to Laos, many travellers take the nightmare bus between Vientiane and Hanoi via the Cau Treo crossing, or the easier route from Savannakhet in southern Laos to Hue in central Vietnam via the Lao Bao border crossing. Twice-daily buses also link Hanoi with Nanning in China.

Car & Motorbike
It is theoretically possible to travel in and out of Vietnam by car or motorbike, but only through borders shared with Cambodia and Laos. In reality, the bureaucracy makes this a real headache. It is generally easy enough to take a Vietnamese motorbike into Cambodia or Laos, but very difficult in the other direction (and the permits are costly). It's currently not possible to take any vehicle into China.

Consult the forums on www.gt-rider.com for the latest cross-border biking information.

Paperwork
Drivers of cars and riders of motorbikes will need the vehicle's registration papers, liability insurance and an International Driving Permit, in addition to a domestic licence. Most important is a *carnet de passage en douane*, which is effectively a passport for the vehicle and acts as a temporary waiver of import duty.

Train
Several international trains link China and Vietnam. A daily train connects Hanoi with Nanning (and on to Beijing!). The most scenic stretch of railway is between Hanoi and Kunming via Lao Cai; trains are currently not operating on the Chinese side. There are no railway lines linking Vietnam with Cambodia or Laos.

River
There's a river border crossing between Cambodia and Vietnam on the banks of the Mekong. Regular fast boats ply the route between Phnom Penh in Cambodia and Chau Doc in Vietnam via the Vinh Xuong–Kaam Samnor border. There are also several luxury river boats with cabins running all the way to the

Border Crossings

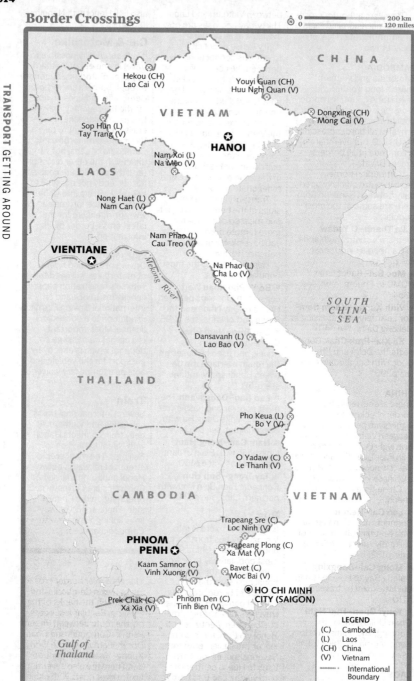

0   200 km
0   120 miles

CHINA

VIETNAM

Hekou (CH)
Lao Cai (V)

Youyi Guan (CH)
Huu Nghi Quan (V)

Dongxing (CH)
Mong Cai (V)

Sop Hun (L)
Tay Trang (V)

★ HANOI

Nam Xoi (L)
Na Meo (V)

LAOS

Nong Haet (L)
Nam Can (V)

Nam Phao (L)
Cau Treo (V)

VIENTIANE ★

Na Phao (L)
Cha Lo (V)

Mekong River

SOUTH
CHINA
SEA

Dansavanh (L)
Lao Bao (V)

THAILAND

Pho Keua (L)
Bo Y (V)

O Yadaw (C)
Le Thanh (V)

CAMBODIA

VIETNAM

Trapeang Sre (C)
Loc Ninh (V)

PHNOM
PENH ★

Trapeang Plong (C)
Xa Mat (V)

Kaam Samnor (C)
Vinh Xuong (V)

Bavet (C)
Moc Bai (V)

Prek Chak (C)
Xa Xia (V)

Phnom Den (C)
Tinh Bien (V)

● HO CHI MINH
CITY (SAIGON)

*Gulf of
Thailand*

LEGEND
(C)   Cambodia
(L)   Laos
(CH)   China
(V)   Vietnam
- · - · - International
     Boundary

CHINA GUIDEBOOKS CONFISCATED

Travellers entering China by road or rail from Vietnam report that Lonely Planet *China* guidebooks have been confiscated by border officials. The guidebook's maps show Taiwan as a separate country, and this is a sensitive issue. If you are carrying a copy of Lonely Planet's *China* guide, consider putting a cover on the book to make it less recognisable and, just to be safe, copy down any crucial details you might need while in China.

temples of Angkor at Siem Reap in Cambodia.

GETTING AROUND

Air

Vietnam now has good domestic flight connections, and very affordable prices (if you book early). Airlines accept bookings on international credit or debit cards. However note that cancellations are not unknown. It's safest not to rely on a flight from a regional airport to make an international connection the same day – travel a day early if you can.

Air Mekong (www.airmekong .com.vn) Covers destinations in southern Vietnam and Hanoi.

Jetstar Pacific Airlines (www.jetstar.com) This budget airline has very affordable fares, though serves far fewer destinations.

Vasco (www.vasco.com.vn) Connects HCMC with Con Dao and the Mekong Delta.

Vietnam Airlines (www.viet namairlines.com.vn) The leading local carrier with the most comprehensive network and best reliability.

Bicycle

Bikes are a great way to get around Vietnam, particularly when you get off the main highways. In the countryside, Westerners on bicycles are often greeted enthusiastically by locals who don't see many foreigners pedalling around.

Long-distance cycling is popular in Vietnam. Much of the country is flat or only moderately hilly, and the major roads are in good shape. Safety, however, is a considerable concern. Bicycles can be transported around the country on the top of buses or in train baggage compartments if you run out of puff.

Bike Types

Decent bikes can be bought at a few speciality shops in Hanoi and HCMC, but it's better to bring your own if you plan on cycling long distances. Mountain bikes are preferable, as large potholes or unsealed roads are rough on the rims, but a touring bike is fine for coastal routes or the Mekong Delta. Basic cycling safety equipment and authentic spare parts are also in short supply, so bring all this from home. A bell or horn is mandatory – the louder the better.

Rentals

Hotels and some travel agencies rent bicycles for US$1 to US$3 per day, better quality models cost US$8 or more. Cycling is the perfect way to explore smaller cities like Hoi An, Hue or Nha Trang (unless it's the rainy season!). There are innumerable bicycle repair stands along the side of the roads to get punctures fixed and the like.

Tours

Groups of foreign cyclists touring Vietnam are a common sight these days, and there are several tour companies that specialise in bicycle trips (see p519).

Boat

Vietnam has an enormous number of rivers that are at least partly navigable, but the most important by far is the Mekong River and its tributaries. Scenic day trips by boat are possible on rivers in Hoi An, Danang, Hue, Tam Coc and even HCMC, but only in the Mekong Delta are boats used as a practical means of transport.

Boat trips are also possible on the sea. Cruising the islands of Halong Bay is a must for all visitors to northern Vietnam. In central Vietnam you shouldn't miss the lovely Cham Islands (accessed from Hoi An), while in the south, trips to the islands off Nha Trang are popular.

In some parts of Vietnam, particularly the Mekong Delta, there are frequent ferry crossings. Don't stand between parked vehicles on the ferry as they can roll and you could wind up as the meat in the sandwich.

Bus

Vietnam has an extensive network of buses that reach the far-flung corners of the country. Most are painfully slow and seriously uncomfortable local services, but modern buses are increasingly available on the main routes.

Whichever class of bus you're on, bus travel in Vietnam is never speedy – reckon on just 50kph on major routes (including Hwy 1) due to the sheer number of motorbikes, trucks and pedestrians competing for space. That said, the sublime scenery usually makes the journey pass quickly.

Bus Stations

Many cities have several bus stations, and responsibilities

FARE'S FAIR?

For most visitors one of the most frustrating aspects of travelling in Vietnam is the perception that they are being ripped off. Here are some guidelines to help you navigate the maze.

» **Airfares** Dependent on when you book and what dates you want to travel. No price difference between Vietnamese and foreigners.

» **Boat fares** Ferries and hydrofoils have fixed prices, but expect to pay more for the privilege of being a foreigner on smaller local boats around the Mekong Delta and to places like the Cham Islands.

» **Bus fares** More complicated. If you buy a ticket from the point of departure (ie the bus station), then the price is fixed and very reasonable. However, should you board a bus along the way, there's a good chance the driver or conductor will overcharge. In remote areas drivers may ask for four, or even 10, times what the locals pay. Local bus prices are fixed and displayed by the door.

» **Rail fares** Fixed, although naturally there are different prices for different classes.

» **Taxis** Mostly metered and very cheap, but very occasionally some taxis have dodgy meters that run fast.

» **Xe om and cyclos** Fares are definitely not fixed and you need to bargain. Hard.

While this is all very frustrating, in many ways it's a legacy of the early days of tourism in Vietnam, when all hotels were government-owned and charged foreigners five times the local rate. A similar fare structure existed for rail travel until quite recently too.

are divided according to the location of the destination (whether it is north or south of the city) and the type of service (local or long distance, express or nonexpress).

Bus stations can look chaotic but many now have ticket offices with official prices and departure times clearly displayed.

When arriving by bus, it is generally better to try to arrange a metered taxi on to your hotel or guesthouse of choice, as *xe oms* and *cyclos* can demand ridiculous prices.

Deluxe Buses

On most popular routes, modern air-conditioned Korean and Chinese buses are becoming highly popular.

These buses make a beeline from place to place. This is the deluxe class and you can usually be certain of there being enough space.

Some offer comfortable reclining seats, others have padded flat beds for really long trips. These sleeper buses can be a good alternative to trains, and costs are comparable.

Deluxe buses are non-smoking. On the flipside, most of them are equipped with TVs and some with dreaded karaoke machines. You can ignore the crazy kung fu videos by closing your eyes, but you'd need to be deaf to sleep through the karaoke sessions – ear plugs and eye patches are recommended.

Private companies offering smart minibuses with

pre-allocated seats on short and medium-distance routes, such as **Mai Linh Express** (www.mailinh.vn), are also an excellent way to get about.

Local Buses

Short-distance buses – some are French, American and Russian models from the '50s, '60s and '70s – depart when full (jam-packed with people and luggage). They often operate throughout the day, but don't count on many leaving after about 4pm.

These buses and minibuses drop off and pick up as many passengers as possible along the route, so the frequent stops make for a slow journey.

Conductors tend to routinely overcharge foreigners on these local services so they're not popular with travellers.

Be aware that luggage is easily pilfered at toilet stops unless someone is looking after it. No matter how honest your fellow passengers might seem, never accept drinks from them, as there is a chance you may be drugged and robbed.

Open Tours

In backpacker haunts throughout Vietnam, you'll see lots of signs advertising 'Open Tour', 'Open Date Ticket' or 'Open Ticket'. These are bus services catering mostly to foreign budget travellers, but increasing numbers of Vietnamese are using the services due to convenient central departure points. The air-conditioned buses run between HCMC and Hanoi and passengers can hop on and hop off the bus at any major city along the route.

Prices are reasonable. A through ticket from Ho Chi Minh City to Hanoi costs US$45, depending on the exact route. Sample prices are given in the Open Tour Prices table.

The downside to the open tour concept is that operators depend on kickbacks from sister hotels and restaurants along the way, making the whole experience feel like being part of the herd. On the plus side, the buses depart from central places, avoiding an extra journey to the bus station.

Buying shorter point-to-point tickets on the open-tour buses costs a bit more but you achieve more flexibility, including the chance to take a train, rent a motorbike or simply change your plans.

Nevertheless, cheap open-tour tickets are a temptation and many people go for them. A couple of shorter routes to try are HCMC–Dalat and HCMC–Mui Ne Beach, two places not serviced by train.

If you're set on open-tour tickets, look for them at budget cafes in HCMC and Hanoi. **The Sinh Tourist** (www.the sinhtourist.com) started the concept and has a good reputation, but there are now lots of other companies.

Reservations & Costs

Reservations aren't required for most of the frequent, popular services between towns and cities, but it doesn't hurt to purchase the ticket the day before. Always buy a ticket from the office, as bus drivers are notorious for overcharging.

On rural runs foreigners are typically charged anywhere from twice to 10 times the going rate. If you have to battle it out with the bus driver, it is helpful to determine the cost of the ticket

for locals before starting negotiations. As a benchmark, a typical 100km ride is between US$2 and US$3.

Car & Motorbike

Having your own set of wheels gives you maximum flexibility to visit remote regions and stop when and where you please. Car hire always includes a driver. Motorbike hire is good value and this can be self-drive or with a driver.

Driving Licence

In order to drive a car in Vietnam, you need a Vietnamese licence and an International Driving Permit, usually issued by your automobile association back home. This effectively means it is easy enough for expatriates to arrange, but pretty complicated for visitors. When it comes to renting motorbikes, it's a case of no licence required.

Fuel

Fuel prices rose sharply in Vietnam during 2011 to around 21,000d per litre of unleaded gasoline.

Even the most isolated communities usually have someone selling petrol by the roadside. Some sellers mix this fuel with kerosene to make a quick profit – try to fill up from a proper petrol station.

Hire

The major considerations are safety, the mechanical condi-

tion of the vehicle, the reliability of the rental agency, and your budget.

Car & Minibus

Self-drive rental cars have yet to make their debut in Vietnam, which is a blessing given traffic conditions, but cars with drivers are popular and plentiful. Renting a vehicle with a driver-cum-guide is a realistic option even for budget travellers, providing there are enough people to share the cost.

Hanoi and HCMC have an especially wide selection of travel agencies that rent vehicles with drivers for sightseeing trips. For the rough roads of northwestern Vietnam you'll definitely need a 4WD.

Approximate costs per day:
» **Standard model car** US$40 to US$60
» **4WD** US$80 to US$115

Motorbike

Motorbikes can be rented from virtually anywhere, including cafes, hotels and travel agencies. Some places will ask to keep your passport until you return the bike. Try to sign some sort of agreement clearly stating what you are renting, how much it costs, the extent of compensation and so on.

To tackle the mountains of the north, it is best to get a slightly more powerful model like a Minsk or trail bike. There are also plenty of local drivers willing to act as a chauffeur and guide for around US$7 to US$12 per day.

The approximate costs per day:
» **Moped (semi-auto)** US$4 to US$6
» **Moped (fully auto)** US$8 to US$10
» **Minsk** from US$15
» **Trail and road bikes** from US$20

Insurance

If you're travelling in a tourist vehicle with a driver, then it is almost guaranteed to

OPEN TOUR PRICES

ROUTE	PRICE
Ho Chi Minh City–Dalat	US$9
Ho Chi Minh City–Mui Ne	US$9
Ho Chi Minh City–Nha Trang	US$12
Nha Trang–Hoi An	US$12
Hoi An–Hue	US$9
Hoi An–Nha Trang	US$16
Hue–Hanoi	US$20

HELMET LAW

It is compulsory to wear a helmet when riding a motorbike in Vietnam, even when travelling as a passenger. Consider investing in a decent imported helmet if you are planning extensive rides on busy highways or winding mountain roads, as the local eggshells don't offer much protection. Better quality helmets are available in major cities from US$25.

be insured. When it comes to motorbikes, many rental bikes are not insured and you will have to sign a contract agreeing to a valuation for the bike if it is stolen. Make sure you have a strong lock and always leave it in guarded parking where available.

Do not even consider renting a motorbike if you are daft enough to be travelling in Vietnam without insurance. The cost of treating serious injuries can be bankrupting for budget travellers.

Road Conditions & Hazards

Road safety is definitely not one of Vietnam's strong points. The intercity road network of two-lane highways is becoming more and more dangerous. High-speed, head-on collisions are a sickeningly familiar sight on main roads.

In general, the major highways are hard surfaced and reasonably well maintained, but seasonal flooding can be a problem. A big typhoon can create potholes the size of bomb craters. In some remote areas, roads are not surfaced and transform themselves into a sea of mud when the weather turns

bad – such roads are best tackled with a 4WD vehicle or motorbike. Mountain roads are particularly dangerous: landslides, falling rocks and runaway vehicles can add an unwelcome edge to your journey.

Emergencies

Vietnam does not have an efficient emergency-rescue system, so if something happens on the road, it could be some time before help arrives and a long way to even the most basic of medical facilities. Locals might help in extreme circumstances, but in most cases it will be up to you or your guide to get you to the hospital or clinic.

Precautions

For motorcyclists, serious sunburn is a major risk and well worth preventing. The cooling breeze prevents you from realising how badly you are burning until it's too late.

A rainsuit or poncho is essential, especially during the monsoon season.

Road Rules

Basically, there aren't many; arguably any. Size matters and the biggest vehicle wins by default. Be particularly careful about children on the road. It's common to find kids playing hopscotch in the middle of a major highway. Livestock on the road is also a menace; hit a cow on a motorbike and you'll both be hamburger.

Although the police frequently stop drivers and fine

them for all sorts of real and imagined offences, speeding is the flavour of the month. New speed limits are surprisingly slow. In cities, there is a rule that you cannot turn right on a red light. It's easy to run foul of this law in Vietnam and the police might fine you for this offence.

Honking at all pedestrians and bicycles (to warn them of your approach) is not road rage, but considered an essential element of safe driving – larger trucks and buses might as well have a dynamo-driven horn. There is no national seatbelt law.

Legally a motorbike can carry only two people, but we've seen up to six on one vehicle...plus luggage! This law is enforced in major cities, but wildly ignored in rural areas.

Spare Parts

Vietnam is awash with Japanese (and increasingly Chinese) motorbikes, so it is easy to get spare parts for most bikes. But if you are driving something obscure, bring substantial spares.

Local Transport

Bus

Few travellers deal with local buses due to communication issues and the cheapness of taxis, cyclos and xe om. That said, the bus systems in Hanoi and HCMC are not impossible to negotiate – get your hands on a bus map.

ROAD DISTANCES (KM)

	Dalat	Hoi An	Sapa	Hue	Halong City	Hanoi
Hoi An	716					
Sapa	1868	1117				
Hue	830	138	1038			
Halong City	1653	911	545	823		
Hanoi	1488	793	380	658	165	
HCMC	310	942	2104	1097	1889	1724

Note: Distances are approximate

Cyclo

The *cyclo* is a bicycle rickshaw. This cheap, environmentally friendly mode of transport is steadily dying out, but is still found in Vietnam's main cities.

Groups of *cyclo* drivers always hang out near major hotels and markets, and many speak at least broken English. To make sure the driver understands where you want to go, it's useful to bring a city map. Bargaining is imperative. Settle on a fare before going anywhere or you're likely to get stiffed.

Some approximate fares:

» **Short ride** 10,000d
» **Over 2km or night ride** 20,000d
» **Per hour** 40,000d

Travellers have reported being mugged by *cyclo* drivers in HCMC so, as a general rule, it's safe to hire *cyclos* only during the day. When leaving a bar late at night, take a metered taxi.

Taxi

Western-style taxis with meters, found in most major cities, are very cheap by international standards and a safe way to travel around at night. Average tariffs are about 10,000d to 15,000d per kilometre. However, there are many dodgy taxis roaming the streets of Hanoi and HCMC, with meters clocked to run at two or three times the normal pace. Only travel with reputable or recommended companies.

One nationwide company with an excellent reputation is **Mai Linh** (www.mailinh.vn).

Xe Om

The *xe om* (*zay*-ohm) is a motorbike taxi. *Xe* means motorbike, and *om* means hug (or hold), so you get the picture. Getting around by *xe om* is easy, as long as you don't have a lot of luggage.

Fares are comparable with those for a *cyclo*, but negotiate the price beforehand. There are plenty of *xe om* drivers hanging around

HIRING A VEHICLE & DRIVER

Renting a car with a driver and guide gives you the chance to design a tailor-made tour. Seeing the country this way is almost like independent travel, except that it's more comfortable, less time-consuming and allows for stops anywhere, or everywhere, along the way.

Most travel agencies and tour operators can hook you up with a vehicle and driver. A good guide can be your translator and travelling companion and can offer all kinds of cultural knowledge and open up the door to some unique experiences. A bad guide can ruin your trip. Consider the following:

» Try to meet your driver-guide before starting out and make sure that this is someone you can travel with.
» How much English (French or other language) does he or she speak?
» The driver usually pays for his own costs including accommodation and meals, you pay for the petrol. Check this is the case.
» Settle on an itinerary and get a copy from the travel agency. If you find your guide is making it up as he goes along, use it as leverage.
» Make it clear you want to avoid tourist-trap restaurants and shops.
» Tip if you've had a good experience.

street corners, markets, hotels and bus stations. They will find you before you find them...

Tours

The quality of bottom-end budget tours being peddled in HCMC and Hanoi is often terrible. You tend to get what you pay for.

These are some of the most popular tour destinations in Vietnam:

» **Halong Bay** p97
» **DMZ** p158
» **Hue** p176
» **Mekong Delta** p354
» **Mui Ne** p248
» **My Son** p211
» **Nha Trang** p231
» **Phong Nha** p151
» **Sapa** p125

Recommended tour operators include:

Buffalo Tours (☎3828 0702; www.buffalotours.com; 94 P Ma May, Hanoi) Popular travel company offering diverse trips, from hiking Fansipan to a nine-day Gourmet Vietnam tour.

Destination Asia (☎3844 8071; www.destination-asia .com; 143 Đ Nguyen Van Troi, Phu Nhuan, HCMC) High-end travel company for the discerning visitor.

Exotissimo (☎3995 9898; www.exotissimo.com; 80-82 Đ Phan Xich Long, Phu Nhuan District, HCMC) Leading regional player with a good range of tours, including cycling, trekking and golfing. The five-day Ha Giang tour takes in Dong Van and custom-made trips can be set up.

Handspan (☎3926 2828; www.handspan.com; 78 P Ma May, Hanoi) Innovative tour operator with a great selection of interesting options: community-based trips, seakayaking, jeep tours, mountain biking and trekking.

Ocean Tours (☎3926 0463; www.oceantours.com.vn; 22 P

Hang Bac, Hanoi) Well-structured trips to Halong Bay, national parks, and northern mountains, as well as 4WD road trips.

Sinhbalo Adventures (☑8337 6766; www.sinhbalo .com; 283/20 Đ Pham Ngu Lao, District 1, HCMC) The leading cycling specialist with tours to the Mekong Delta, central highlands and the northern mountains.

Sisters Tours (☑3562 2733; www.sisterstoursvietnam.com; 37 Đ Thai Thinh, Hanoi) Locally owned high-end company with an eclectic range of themed tours, from photography to family.

Motorbike Tours

Specialised motorbike tours through Vietnam are growing in popularity. They are a great way to get off the trail and explore the mountainous regions of the north and centre – two-wheels can reach the parts that four-wheels sometimes can't, by traversing small trails and traffic-free back roads. A little experience helps, but many leading companies also offer tuition for first-timers. Mounting a bike to take on the peaks of the north is one of Vietnam's defining moments and should not be missed.

Foreign guides charge considerably more than local guides. Based on a group of four people, you can expect to pay from US$100 per person per day for an all-inclusive tour that provides motorbike rental, petrol, guide, food and accommodation. Some of the best companies running trips include the following:

Explore Indochina (☑0913 093 159; www.exploreindochina.com) Long-established motorbike tour operator offering excellent tours along the Ho Chi Minh Highway and in the far north on vintage 650 Urals or modified Minsks; US$150–200 per day.

Free Wheelin' Tours (☑3926 2743; www.freewheelin-tours.com) Run by Fredo (Binh in Vietnamese), who speaks French, English and Vietnamese, this company has its own homestays in the northeast and offers some excellent trips as well as custom-made tours. Prices start from US$100 per day for a group of four.

Hoi An Motorbike Adventure (☑391 1930; www.motorbiketours-hoian.com) Specialises in short trips (from US$35) along beautiful backroads in the Hoi An region on well-maintained Minsk bikes. Longer tours up to the DMZ and Hue are also offered.

Offroad Vietnam (☑3926 3433; www.offroadvietnam.com) Professional, well-organised tours on Honda road and dirt bikes. Trips across large swathes of northern Vietnam including Ha Giang and Dong Van. Also offers competitive bike hire (from US$20 per day) and rents riding gear including saddle bags.

Voyage Vietnam (☑3926 2373; www.voyagevietnam.net) A locally run outfit with a good reputation for its trips in the north, Mekong and HCMC highway. Prices start from around US$85 per day. For more on Easy Riders, operating out of Dalat, see p282. There are a host of other motorbike and bicycle day trips covered under individual towns throughout this book.

Train

The Vietnamese railway system, operated by **Vietnam Railways** (Duong Sat Viet Nam; ☑3747 0308; www.vr.com.vn) is an ageing but pretty dependable service, and offers a relaxing way to get around the nation. Travelling in an air-con sleeping berth sure beats a hairy overnight bus journey along Hwy 1. And of course there's some spectacular scenery to lap up too.

Classes

Trains classified as SE are the smartest and fastest, while those referred to as TN are slower and older.

There are four main ticket classes: hard seat, soft seat, hard sleeper and soft sleeper. These are also split into air-con and non air-con options. Presently, air-con is only available on the faster express trains. Hard-seat class is usually packed, and is tolerable for day travel, but expect plenty of cigarette smoke.

Private Carriages
Comfortable, even luxurious private carriages tagged onto the back of trains offer a classy way of travelling between Lao Cai and Hanoi: those offered by Victoria Hotels are renowned, but there are others; most tickets are US$40 to US$95. There is also a luxury service running between Hanoi and Danang (US$65), operated by **Livitrans** (www.livitrans.com) and another connects Nha Trang and HCMC.

Sleepers
A hard sleeper has three tiers of beds (six beds per compartment), with the upper berth cheapest and the lower berth most expensive. Soft sleeper has two tiers (four beds per compartment) and all bunks are priced the same. Fastidious travellers will probably want to bring a sleep sheet, sleeping bag and/or pillow case with them, although linen is provided.

Costs

Ticket prices vary depending on the train; the fastest trains are more expensive. See the Fares from Hanoi table for some sample fares. For all the details on trains from Hanoi to Haiphong see p94; Hanoi to Lao Cai see p133; and Hanoi to Lang Son see p112.

Eating

The food supplied by the railway company, included in the ticket price on some long journeys, isn't Michelin-starred, but it fills the void. Food vendors also board trains. It's a good idea to stock up on your favourite munchies before taking a long trip.

Freight

Bicycles and motorbikes must travel in freight carriages. Sometimes it's not possible to travel on the same train as your bike.

Reservations

The supply of train seats is frequently insufficient to meet demand. Reservations for all trips should be made at least one day in advance. For sleeping berths, it's wise to book several days before the date of departure.

Many travel agencies, hotels and cafes sell train tickets for a small commission, and this can save considerable time and trouble. It's a good idea to make reservations for onward travel as soon as you arrive in a city.

Routes

Aside from the main HCMC–Hanoi run, three rail-spur lines link Hanoi with the other parts of northern Vietnam. One runs east to the port city of Haiphong. A second heads northeast to Lang Son and continues across the border to Nanning, China. A third runs northwest to Lao Cai and on to Kunming, China.

The train journey between Hanoi and HCMC takes from 30 to 41 hours, depending on the train. There are also local trains that only cover short routes, but these can crawl along at 15km/h.

Safety

Petty crime can be a problem on Vietnamese trains. Thieves occasionally try to grab stuff as trains pull out of stations. Always keep your bag nearby and lock or tie it

THE REUNIFICATION EXPRESS

Construction of the 1726km-long Hanoi–Saigon railway, the Transindochinois, began in 1899 and was completed in 1936. In the late 1930s, the trip from Hanoi to Saigon took 40 hours and 20 minutes at an average speed of 43km/h.

During WWII the Japanese made extensive use of the rail system, resulting in Viet Minh sabotage on the ground and US bombing from the air. After WWII, efforts were made to repair the Transindochinois, major parts of which were either damaged or had become overgrown.

During the Franco–Viet Minh War, the Viet Minh again engaged in sabotage against the rail system. At night the Viet Minh made off with rails to create a 300km network of tracks (between Ninh Hoa and Danang) in an area wholly under their control – the French quickly responded with their own sabotage.

In the late 1950s the South, with US funding, reconstructed the track between Saigon and Hue, a distance of 1041km. But between 1961 and 1964 alone, 795 Viet Cong (VC) attacks were launched on the rail system, forcing the abandonment of large sections of track (including the Dalat spur).

By 1960 North Vietnam had repaired 1000km of track, mostly between Hanoi and China. During the US air war against the North, the northern rail network was repeatedly bombed. Even now, clusters of bomb craters can be seen around virtually every rail bridge and train station in the north.

Following reunification in 1975, the government immediately set about re-establishing the Hanoi–Ho Chi Minh City rail link as a symbol of Vietnamese unity. By the time the *Reunification Express* trains were inaugurated on 31 December 1976, 1334 bridges, 27 tunnels, 158 stations and 1370 shunts (switches) had been repaired.

Today the *Reunification Express* chugs along only slightly faster than the trains did in the 1930s, at an average speed of 50km/h.

Plans for a massive overhaul of the rail system to a high-speed network have now been shelved.

FARES FROM HANOI

DESTIN-ATION	SOFT SEAT A/C	HARD SLEEPER A/C (UPPER, 6 BERTH)	SOFT SLEEPER A/C (LOWER, 4 BERTH)
Hue	508,000d	785,000d	833,000d
Danang	570,000d	853,000d	915,000d
Nha Trang	1,030,000d	1,340,000d	1,510,000d
HCMC	1,175,000d	1,590,000d	1,690,000d

to something, especially at night.

Schedules

Several *Reunification Express* trains depart from Hanoi and HCMC every day. The train schedules change frequently so check departure times on the Vietnam Railway website (if working), at stations, or with travel agents. Another excellent resource is www.seat61 .com, the international train website.

The train schedule is 'bare bones' during the Tet festival when most trains are suspended for nine days, beginning four days before Tet and continuing for four days afterwards.

Health

Health issues (and the quality of medical facilities) vary enormously depending on where you are in Vietnam. The major cities are generally not high risk and have good facilities, though rural areas are another matter.

Travellers tend to worry about contracting infectious diseases in Vietnam, but serious illnesses are rare. Accidental injury (especially traffic accidents) account for most life-threatening problems. That said, a bout of sickness is a relatively common thing. The following advice is a general guide only.

BEFORE YOU GO

» Pack any medications in clearly labelled containers.

» Bring a letter from your doctor describing your medical conditions and medications.

» If carrying syringes or needles, have a physician's letter documenting their medical necessity.

» If you have a heart condition, bring a copy of a recent ECG.

» Bring extra supplies of any regular medication (in case of loss or theft).

Insurance

Even if you are fit and healthy, don't travel without health insurance – accidents do happen. If your health insurance doesn't cover you for medical expenses abroad, get extra insurance – check our website (www .lonelyplanet.com) for more information. Emergency evacuation is expensive – bills of US$100,000 are not unknown – so make sure your policy covers this.

Recommended Vaccinations

The only vaccination required by international regulations is yellow fever. Proof of vaccination will only be required if you have visited a country in the yellow-fever zone within the six days prior to entering Vietnam.

Most vaccines don't produce immunity until at least two weeks after they're given, so visit a doctor four to eight weeks before departure. See the Required & Recommended Vaccinations box for more information.

Medical Checklist

Recommended, but not exhaustive items for a personal medical kit:

» antibacterial cream, eg mupirocin

» antihistamines for allergies, eg cetirizine for daytime and promethazine for night

» antiseptic for cuts and scrapes, eg iodine solution such as Betadine

» DEET-based insect repellent

» diarrhoea 'stopper', eg loperamide

» first-aid items, such as scissors, plasters (such as Band Aids), bandages, gauze, safety pins and tweezers

» paracetamol for pain

» steroid cream for allergic/itchy rashes, eg 1% hydrocortisone

» sunscreen and hat

» antifungal treatments for thrush and tinea, eg clotrimazole or fluconazole

Websites

There's a wealth of travel-health advice on the internet.

World Health Organization (WHO; www.who.int/ith) Publishes a superb book called *International Travel & Health,* which is revised annually and is available free online.

MD Travel Health (www .mdtravelhealth.com) Provides complete travel health recommendations.

Centers for Disease Control and Prevention (CDC; www.cdc.gov) Good general information.

Further Reading

Lonely Planet's *Asia & India: Healthy Travel Guide* – is packed with useful information including pre-trip planning, emergency first aid, immunisation and disease information, and what to do if you get sick on the road.

IN VIETNAM

Availability & Cost of Health Care

The significant improvement in Vietnam's economy has brought with it some major advances in public health. However in remote parts, local clinics will only have basic supplies – if you become seriously ill in rural Vietnam, get to HCMC, Danang or Hanoi as quickly as you can. For surgery or other extensive treatment, don't hesitate to fly to Bangkok, Singapore or Hong Kong.

Private Clinics

These should be your first port of call. They are familiar with local resources and can organise evacuations if necessary. The best medical facilities – in Hanoi, HCMC and Danang – have health facility standards that come close to those in developed countries.

State Hospitals

Most are overcrowded and basic. In order to treat foreigners, a facility needs to obtain a special license and so far only a few have been provided.

Self-Treatment

If your problem is minor (eg travellers' diarrhoea) this is an option. If you think you may have a serious disease, especially malaria, do not waste time – travel to the nearest quality facility to receive attention.

Buying medication over the counter is not recommended, as fake medications and poorly stored or out-of-date drugs are common. Check expiry dates on all medicines.

Infectious Diseases

Bird Flu

The HN-51 rears its head from time to time in Vietnam. It occurs in clusters, usually amongst poultry workers. Recently it has been extremely rare (two humans were infected in Vietnam during 2010). When outbreaks do occur, eggs and poultry are banished from the menu in many hotels and restaurants.

Dengue

This mosquito-borne disease is becoming increasingly problematic in Southeast Asia. Several hundred thousand people are hospitalised with dengue haemorrhagic fever in Vietnam every year, but the fatality rate is less than 0.3 per cent. As there is no vaccine available, it can only be prevented by avoiding mosquito bites. The mosquito that carries dengue bites throughout the day and night, so use insect-avoidance measures at all times. Symptoms include a high fever, a severe headache and body aches (dengue was once known as 'breakbone fever'). Some people develop a rash and experience diarrhoea. There is no specific treatment, just rest and paracetamol – do not take aspirin as it increases the likelihood of haemorrhaging. See a doctor to be diagnosed and monitored.

Hepatitis A

A problem throughout the region, this food- and water-

REQUIRED & RECOMMENDED VACCINATIONS

The World Health Organization (WHO) recommends the following vaccinations for travellers to Southeast Asia:

» **Adult diphtheria and tetanus** – single booster recommended if you've had none in the previous 10 years.

» **Hepatitis A** – provides almost 100% protection for up to a year; a booster after 12 months provides at least another 20 years' protection.

» **Hepatitis B** – now considered routine for most travellers. Given as three shots over six months. A rapid schedule is also available, as is a combined vaccination with Hepatitis A. Lifetime protection occurs in 95% of people.

» **Measles, mumps and rubella** – two doses of MMR are required unless you have had the diseases. Many young adults require a booster.

» **Typhoid** – recommended unless your trip is less than a week and only to developed cities. The vaccine offers around 70% protection and lasts for two or three years.

» **Varicella** – if you haven't had chickenpox, discuss this vaccination with your doctor.

Long-term Travellers

These vaccinations are recommended for people travelling for more than one month, or those at special risk:

» **Japanese B Encephalitis** – three injections in all. A booster is recommended after two years. A sore arm and headache are the most common side effects reported.

» **Meningitis** – single injection.

» **Rabies** – three injections in all. A booster after one year will provide 10 years of protection.

» **Tuberculosis** – adults should have a TB skin test before and after travel, rather than the vaccination.

borne virus infects the liver, causing jaundice (yellow skin and eyes), nausea and lethargy. There is no specific treatment for hepatitis A, you just need to allow time for the liver to heal. All travellers to Vietnam should be vaccinated against hepatitis A.

Hepatitis B

The only serious sexually transmitted disease that can be prevented by vaccination, hepatitis B is spread by body fluids, including sexual contact. In some parts of Southeast Asia up to 20% of the population are carriers of hepatitis B, and usually are unaware of this. The long-term consequences can include liver cancer and cirrhosis.

HIV

The official figures on the number of people with HIV/AIDS in Vietnam are vague, but they are on the rise. Health-education messages relating to HIV/AIDS are visible all over the countryside, but the official line is that infection is largely limited to sex workers and drug users. Condoms are widely available throughout Vietnam.

Japanese B Encephalitis

This viral disease is transmitted by mosquitoes. It's very rarely caught by travellers but vaccination is recommended for those spending extended time in rural areas. There is no treatment, and a third of infected people will die while another third will suffer permanent brain damage.

Malaria

For such a serious and potentially deadly disease, there is an enormous amount of misinformation concerning malaria. You must get expert advice as to whether your trip actually puts you at risk. Many parts of Vietnam, particularly city and resort areas, have minimal to no risk of malaria. For most rural areas, however, the risk of contracting the disease far outweighs the risk of any tablet side effects. Travellers to isolated areas in high-risk regions such as Ca Mau and Bac Lieu provinces, and the rural south, may like to carry a treatment dose of medication for use if symptoms occur. Remember that malaria can be fatal. Before you travel, seek medical advice on the right medication and dosage for you.

Malaria is caused by a parasite transmitted by the bite of an infected mosquito. The most important symptom of malaria is fever, but general symptoms such as headache, diarrhoea, cough or chills may also occur. Diagnosis can only be made by taking a blood sample.

Two strategies should be combined to prevent malaria – mosquito avoidance, and antimalarial medications.

MALARIA PREVENTION

» Choose accommodation with screens and fans (if not air-conditioned).

» Impregnate clothing with permethrin in high-risk areas.

» Sleep under a mosquito net.

» Spray your room with insect repellent before going out for your evening meal.

» Use a DEET-containing insect repellent on all exposed skin, particularly the ankle area. Natural repellents such as citronella can be effective but must be applied frequently.

» Use mosquito coils.

» Wear long sleeves and trousers in light colours.

MALARIA MEDICATION

There are various medications available.

» **Chloroquine & Paludrine** The effectiveness of this combination is now limited in Vietnam. Generally not recommended.

» **Doxycycline** A broad-spectrum antibiotic that has the added benefit of helping to prevent a variety of tropical diseases, including leptospirosis, tick-borne disease, typhus and melioidosis. Potential side effects include a tendency to sunburn, thrush in women, indigestion and interference with the contraceptive pill. It must be taken for four weeks after leaving the risk area.

» **Lariam (Mefloquine)** Receives a lot of bad press, some of it justified, some not. This weekly tablet suits many people. Serious side effects are rare but include depression, anxiety, psychosis and seizures. It's around 90% effective in Vietnam.

» **Malarone** Side effects are uncommon and mild, most commonly nausea and headaches. It is the best tablet for scuba divers and for those on short trips to high-risk areas.

» A final option is to take no preventive medication but to have a supply of emergency medication (Malarone is usually recommended: four tablets once daily for three days) should you develop the symptoms of malaria. This is less than ideal, and you'll still need to get to a good medical facility within 24 hours of developing a fever.

Measles

Measles remains a problem in Vietnam, including the Hanoi area. Many people born before 1966 are immune as they had the disease in childhood. Measles starts with a high fever and rash but can be complicated by pneumonia and brain disease. There is no specific treatment.

Rabies

This uniformly fatal disease is spread by the bite or lick of an infected animal – most commonly a dog or monkey. Seek medical advice immediately after any animal bite and commence post-exposure treatment. Having a pre-travel vaccination means the post-bite treatment is greatly simplified. If an animal bites you, gently wash the wound with soap and water, and apply an iodine-based antiseptic. If you are not vaccinated you will need to receive rabies immunoglobulin as soon as possible.

Schistosomiasis

Schistosomiasis (also called bilharzia) is a tiny parasite that enters your skin after you've been swimming in contaminated water. If you are concerned, you can be tested three months after exposure. Symptoms are coughing and fever. Schistosomiasis is easily treated with medications.

STDs

Condoms, widely available throughout Vietnam, are effective in preventing the spread of most sexually transmitted diseases. However they may not guard against genital warts or herpes. If after a sexual encounter you develop any rash, lumps, discharge or pain when passing urine, seek immediate medical attention.

Tuberculosis

Tuberculosis (TB) is very rare in short-term travellers. Medical and aid workers, and long-term travellers who have significant contact with the local population should take precautions. Vaccination is usually only given to children under the age of five, but it is recommended that at-risk adults have pre- and post-travel TB testing. The main symptoms are fever, cough, weight loss, night sweats and tiredness.

Typhoid

This serious bacterial infection is spread via food and water. It gives a high, slowly progressive fever and headache. Vaccination is recommended for all travellers spending more than a week in Vietnam, or travelling outside of the major cities. Be aware that vaccination is not 100% effective so you must still be careful with what you eat and drink.

Typhus

Murine typhus is spread by the bite of a flea whereas scrub typhus is spread via a mite. These diseases are rare in travellers. Symptoms include fever, muscle pains and a rash. You can avoid these diseases by following general insect-avoidance measures. Doxycycline will also help prevent them.

Travellers' Diarrhoea

Travellers' diarrhoea is by far the most common problem affecting travellers – between 30% and 50% of people will suffer from it within two weeks of starting their trip. In over 80% of cases, travellers' diarrhoea is caused by a bacteria, and therefore responds promptly to treatment with antibiotics. It can also be provoked by a change of diet, and your stomach may settle down again after a few days.

Treatment consists of staying hydrated, or you could take rehydration solutions.

Loperamide is just a 'stopper' and doesn't get to the cause of the problem. It is helpful if you have to go on a long bus ride, but don't take loperamide if you have a fever or blood in your stools.

Amoebic Dysentery

Amoebic dysentery is very rare in travellers. Symptoms are similar to bacterial diarrhoea (eg fever, bloody diarrhoea and generally feeling unwell). You should always seek medical care if you have blood in your diarrhoea. Treatment involves two drugs: tinidazole or metronidazole to kill the parasite in your gut and then a second drug to kill the cysts.

Giardiasis

Giardia lamblia is a parasite that is relatively common in travellers. Symptoms include nausea, bloating, excess gas, fatigue and intermittent diarrhoea. 'Eggy' burps are often attributed solely to giardiasis, but they are not specific to this infection. The treatment of choice is tinidazole.

Environmental Hazards

Air Pollution

Air pollution, particularly vehicle pollution, is severe in Vietnam's major cities. If you have severe respiratory problems consult your doctor before travelling.

Food

Eating in restaurants is the biggest risk factor for contracting travellers' diarrhoea. Ways to avoid it include eating only freshly-cooked food, and avoiding shellfish and buffets. Peel all fruit and try to stick to cooked vegetables. Eat in busy restaurants with a high turnover of customers.

Heat

Many parts of Vietnam are hot and humid throughout the year. Take it easy when you first arrive. Swelling of the feet and ankles is common, as are muscle cramps caused by excessive sweating. Prevent these by avoiding dehydration and excessive activity in the heat. Drink rehydration solution and eat salty food.

» **Heat exhaustion** Symptoms include feeling weak, headache, irritability, nausea or vomiting, sweaty skin and a fast, weak pulse. Cooling treatment involves getting out of the heat and/or sun and into a room with powerful fan or air-conditioning and rehydrating with water containing a quarter of a teaspoon of salt per litre.

» **Heatstroke** is a serious medical emergency. Symptoms come on suddenly and include weakness, nausea, a temperature of over 41°C, dizziness, confusion and eventually collapse and loss of consciousness. Seek

DRINKING WATER

Be very careful of what you drink. Tap water is heavily chlorinated in urban areas, but you should still avoid it. Stick to bottled water, which is available everywhere. Ice is generally safe in the cities and resorts, and is often added to drinks and coffee.

medical help and commence cooling by following cooling treatment (see above).

» **Prickly heat** is a common skin rash in the tropics. Treat by moving out of the heat and into an air-conditioned area for a few hours and by having cool showers.

Bites & Stings

» **Bedbugs** These don't carry disease but their bites are very itchy. Move hotel, and treat the itch with an antihistamine. Silk sleeping bag liners offer some protection.

» **Jellyfish** In Vietnamese waters most are not dangerous, just irritating. Pour vinegar (or urine) onto the affected area. Take painkillers, and seek medical advice if you feel ill in any way. Take local advice if there are dangerous jellyfish around and keep out of the water.

» **Leeches** Found in humid forest areas. They do not transmit any disease but their bites can be intensely itchy. Apply an iodine-based antiseptic to any leech bite to help prevent infection.

» **Snakes** Poisonous and harmless snakes are common in Vietnam, though very few travellers are ever bothered by them. Wear boots and avoid poking around dead logs and wood when hiking. First aid in the event of a snakebite involves pressure immobilisation via an elastic bandage firmly wrapped around the affected limb, starting at the bite site and working up towards the chest. The bandage should not be so tight that the circulation is cut off, and the fingers or toes should be kept free so the circulation can be checked. Immobilise the limb with a splint and carry the victim to medical attention. Do not use tourniquets or try to suck the venom out. Antivenom is available only in major cities.

» **Ticks** Contracted during walks in rural areas. If you have had a tick bite and experience symptoms such as a rash (at the site of the bite or elsewhere), fever or muscle aches you should see a doctor. Doxycycline prevents tick-borne diseases.

Skin Problems

» **Fungal rashes** Common in humid climates. Moist areas that get less air, such as the groin, armpits and between the toes, are often affected. It starts as a red patch that slowly spreads and is usually itchy. Treatment involves using an antifungal cream such as clotrimazole. Consult a doctor.

» **Cuts & scratches** Minor cuts and scratches can become infected easily in humid climates and may fail to heal because of the humidity. Take meticulous care of any wounds: immediately wash in clean water and apply antiseptic.

Sunburn

» Even on a cloudy day sunburn can occur rapidly:

» Always use a strong sunscreen (at least factor 30).

» Reapply after swimming.

» Wear a hat.

» Avoid the sun between 10am and 2pm.

Women's Health

Supplies of sanitary products are readily available in urban areas. Birth control options may be limited, so bring adequate stocks.

Pregnant women should receive specialised advice before travelling. The ideal time to travel is in the second trimester (between 16 and 28 weeks), during which the risk of pregnancy-related problems is at its lowest. Some advice:

» **Rural Areas** Avoid remote areas with poor transportation and medical facilities.

» **Travel Insurance** Ensure you're covered for pregnancy-related possibilities, including premature labour.

» **Malaria** None of the more effective antimalarial drugs are completely safe in pregnancy.

» **Travellers' Diarrhoea** Many diarrhoea treatments are not recommended during pregnancy. Azithromycin is considered safe.

Language

WANT MORE?

For in-depth language information and handy phrases, check out Lonely Planet's *Vietnamese Phrasebook* and *Hill Tribes Phrasebook*. You'll find it at **shop. lonelyplanet.com**, or you can buy Lonely Planet's iPhone phrasebooks at the Apple App Store.

Vietnamese, or *tiếng Việt* dee·úhng vee·ụht, is the official language of Vietnam and spoken by about 85 million people worldwide, both in Vietnam and among migrant communities around the world. It belongs to the Mon-Khmer language family and has Muong (a hill-tribe language) as its closest relative.

More than two thirds of Vietnamese words are derived from Chinese sources – this vocabulary is termed *Hán Việt* haán vee·ụht (Sino-Vietnamese) and is the result of centuries of Chinese rule. Some French vocabulary also entered the Vietnamese language after the French added the country to Indochina by taking control of Saigon in 1859.

Until the early 20th century Vietnamese was written in adapted Chinese characters, but in 1910 the Latin-based *quốc ngữ* gwáwk ngũhr script was declared the official written form. It's a 29-letter phonetic alphabet, invented in the 17th century by Alexandre de Rhodes, a French Jesuit missionary.

Vietnamese pronunciation is not as hard as it may seem at first as most Vietnamese sounds also exist in English. With a bit of practice and reading our coloured pronunciation guides as if they were English, you shouldn't have much trouble being understood. Note that the vowel a is pronounced as in 'at', aa as in 'father', aw as in 'law', er as in 'her', oh as in 'doh!', ow as in 'cow', u as in 'book', uh as in 'but' and uhr as in 'fur' (without the 'r'). Vowel sounds can also be combined in various ways within a word – we've used dots (eg dee·úhng) to separate the different vowel sounds to keep pronunciation straightforward. As for the consonants, note that the ng sound, which is also found in English (eg in 'sing') can also appear at the start of a word in Vietnamese. Also note that d is pronounced as in 'stop', đ as in 'dog' and ğ as in 'skill'.

You'll notice that some vowels are pronounced with a high or low pitch while others swoop or glide in an almost musical manner. This is because Vietnamese uses a system of tones. There are six tones in Vietnamese, indicated in the written language (and in our pronunciation guides) by accent marks above or below the vowel: mid (ma), low falling (mà), low rising (má), high broken (mã), high rising (má) and low broken (mạ). Note that the mid tone is flat. In the south, the low rising and the high broken tones are both pronounced as the low rising tone. Vietnamese words are considered to have one syllable, so word stress is not an issue.

The variation in vocabulary between the Vietnamese of the north and that of the south is indicated in this chapter by (N) and (S) respectively.

At the end of this chapter, we have also included some phrases in a few of the many regional languages spoken in Vietnam, particularly in the central highlands and in the far north of the country.

BASICS

Hello.	*Xin chào.*	sin jòw
Goodbye.	*Tạm biệt.*	daạm bee·ụht
Yes.	*Vâng.* (N)	vuhng
	Dạ. (S)	yạ
No.	*Không.*	kawm
Please.	*Làm ơn.*	laàm ern
Thank you (very much).	*Cảm ơn (rất nhiều).*	ğaảm ern (zúht nyee·oò)
You're welcome.	*Không có chi.*	kawm ğó jee
Excuse me./ Sorry.	*Xin lỗi.*	sin lõy

How are you?
Có khỏe không?   ğáw kwả kawm

Fine, thank you. And you?
Khỏe, cám ơn.   kwả ğaảm ern
Còn bạn thì sao?   kwả ğòn baạn teè sow

What's your name?
Tên là gì?   den laà zeè

My name is ...
Tên tôi là ...   den doy laà ...

Do you speak English?
Bạn có nói được   baạn ğó nóy đuhr·ẹrk
tiếng Anh không?   díng aang kawm

I (don't) understand.
Tôi (không) hiểu.   doy (kawm) heẻ·oo

ACCOMMODATION

Where is a (cheap) ...?	*Đâu có ... (rẻ tiền)?*	doh ğó ... (zả dee·ùhn)
campsite	*nơi cắm trại*	ner·ee ğúhm chại
hotel	*khách sạn*	kaák saạn
guesthouse	*nhà khách*	nyaà kaák

I'd like (a) ...	*Tôi muốn ...*	doy moo·úhn ...
single room	*phòng đơn*	fòm dern
double room (big bed)	*phòng giường đôi*	fòm zuhr·èrng đoy
twin room	*phòng gồm hai giường ngủ*	fòm gàwm hai zuhr·èrng ngoỏ
room with a bathroom	*phòng có phòng tắm*	fòm ğó fòm dúhm
to share a dorm	*ở chung phòng nội trú*	ẻr jum fòm nọy choó

How much is it per night/person?
Giá bao nhiêu một đêm/người?   zaá bow nyee·oo mạwt đem/nguhr·eè

May I see it?
Tôi có thể xem phòng được không?   doy ğó tẻ sam fòm đuhr·ẹrk kawm

air-con	*máy lạnh*	máy laạng
bathroom	*phòng tắm*	fòm dúhm
fan	*quạt máy*	gwaạt máy
hot water	*nước nóng*	nuhr·érk nóm
mosquito net	*màng*	maàng
sheet	*ra trải giường*	zaa chải zuhr·èrng
toilet	*nhà vệ sinh*	nyaà vẹ sing
toilet paper	*giấy vệ sinh*	záy vẹ sing
towel	*khăn tắm*	kúhn dúhm

To get by in Vietnamese, mix and match these simple patterns with words of your choice:

When's (the next bus)?
Khi nào là (chuyến xe buýt tối)?   kee nòw laà (jwee·úhn sa bweét der·eé)

Where's (the station)?
(Nhà ga) ở đâu?   (nyaà gaa) ẻr đoh

Where can I (buy a ticket)?
Tôi có thể (mua vé) ở đâu?   doy ğó tẻ (moo·uh vá) ẻr đoh

I'm looking for (a hotel).
Tôi tìm (khách sạn).   doy dìm (kaát saạn)

Do you have (a map)?
Bạn có (bản đồ) không?   baạn ğó (baản đàw) kawm

Is there (a toilet)?
Có (vệ sinh) không?   ğó (vẹ sing) kawm

I'd like (the menu).
Xin cho tôi (thực đơn).   sin jo doy (tụhrk đern)

I'd like to (hire a car).
Tôi muốn (xe hơi).   doy moo·úhn (sa her·ee)

Could you please (help me)?
Làm ơn (giúp đỡ)?   laàm ern (zúp đẻr)

I have (a visa).
Tôi có (visa).   doy ğó (vee·saa)

DIRECTIONS

Where is ...?
... ở đâu?   ... ẻr đoh

What is the address?
Địa chỉ là gì?   dee·ụh cheé laà zeè

Could you write it down, please?
Xin viết ra giùm tôi.   sin vee·úht zaa zùm doy

Can you show me (on the map)?
Xin chỉ giùm (trên bản đồ này).   sin jeé zùm (chen baản đàw này)

Go straight ahead.
Thẳng tới trước.   tủhng der·eé chuhr·érk

at the corner	*ở góc đường*	ẻr góp đuhr·èrng
at the traffic lights	*tại đèn giao thông*	dại đèn zow tawm
behind	*đằng sau*	đùhng sow
in front of	*đằng trước*	đùhng chuhr·érk
far	*xa*	saa
near (to)	*gần*	gùhn
opposite	*đối diện*	dóy zee·ụhn
Turn left.	*Sang trái.*	saang chái
Turn right.	*Sang phải.*	saang fai

EATING & DRINKING

I'd like a table for ...	Tôi muốn đặt bàn cho ...	doy moo·úhn đụht baàn jo ...
(two) people	(hai) người	(hai) nguhr·eè
(eight) o'clock	vào lúc (tám) giờ	vòw lúp (dúhm) zèr

Do you have a menu in English?
Bạn có thực đơn bằng tiếng Anh không? — baạn káw tụhrk đern bùhng díng aang kawm

What's the speciality here?
Ở đây có món gì đặc biệt? — ér đay kó món zeè dụhk bee·ụht

I'd like ...
Xin cho tôi ... — sin jo doy ...

Not too spicy, please.
Xin đừng cho cay quá. — sin dùrng jo ğay gwaá

I'm a vegetarian.
Tôi ăn chay. — doy uhn jay

I'm allergic to (peanuts).
Tôi bị dị ứng với (hạt lạc). — doy beẹ zeẹ úhrng ver·eé (haạt laạk)

Can you please bring me ...?
Xin mang cho tôi...? — sin maang jo doy ...

Can I have a (beer), please?
Xin cho tôi (chai bia)? — sin jo doy (jai bee·uh)

Cheers!
Chúc sức khoẻ! — júp súhrk kwả

Thank you, that was delicious.
Cám ơn, ngon lắm. — ğaám ern ngon lúhm

The bill, please.
Xin tính tiền. — sin díng dee·ùhn

Key Words

bottle	chai	jai
bowl	bát/ chén (N/S)	baát/ jén
breakfast	ăn sáng	uhn saáng
chopsticks	đôi đũa	đoy·ee đoõ·uh
cold	lạnh	laạng
dessert	món tráng	món chaáng
dinner	ăn tối	uhn dóy
fork	cái dĩa/ nĩa (N/S)	ğaí deẽ·uh/ neẽ·uh
glass	cốc/ly (N/S)	káwp/lee
hot (warm)	nóng	nóm
knife	con dao	ğon zow
lunch	ăn trưa	uhn chuhr·uh
plate	đĩa	đeẽ·uh
restaurant	nhà hàng	nyaà haàng
snack	ăn nhẹ	uhn nyạ

Signs

Lối Vào	Entrance
Lối Ra	Exit
Mở	Open
Đóng	Closed
Hướng Dẫn	Information
Cấm	Prohibited
Cảnh Sát/Công An	Police
Nhà Vệ Sinh	Toilets
Đàn Ông	Men
Phụ Nữ	Women

spicy	cay	ğay
spoon	cái thìa	ğaí tee·ùh
with	với	ver·eé
without	không có	kawm ğó

Meat & Fish

beef	thịt bò	tịt bò
chicken	thịt gà	tịt gaà
crab	cua	ğoo·uh
eel	lươn	luhr·ern
fish	cá	kaá
frog	ếch	ék
goat	thịt dê	tịt ze
offal	thịt lòng	tịt lòm
pork	thịt lợn/ heo (N/S)	tịt lẹrn/ hay·o
prawns/ shrimp	tôm	dawm
snail	ốc	áwp
squid	mực	mụhrk

Fruit & Vegetables

apple	táo/bơm (N/S)	dów/berm
banana	chuối	joo·eé
cabbage	bắp cải	búhp ğaï
carrot	cà rốt	ğaà záwt
coconut	dừa	zuhr·ùh
corn	ngô/bắp (N/S)	ngow/búp
cucumber	dưa leo	zuhr·uh lay·o
eggplant	cà tím	ğaà dím
grapes	nho	nyo
green beans	đậu xanh	đọh saang
green pepper	ớt xanh	ért saang
lemon	chanh	chaang

lettuce	*rau diếp*	zoh zee·úhp
lychee	*vải*	vaí
mandarin	*quýt*	gweét
mango	*xoài*	swaì
mushrooms	*nấm*	núhm
orange	*cam*	ğaam
papaya	*đu đủ*	doo đỏo
peas	*đậu bi*	đọh bee
pineapple	*dứa*	zuhr·úh
potato	*khoai tây*	kwai day
pumpkin	*bí ngô*	beé ngaw
strawberry	*dâu*	zoh
sweet potato	*khoai lang*	kwai laang
tomato	*cà chua*	ğaà joo·uh
watermelon	*dưa hấu*	zuhr·uh hóh

Other

chilli sauce	*tương ớt*	duhr·erng ért
eggs	*trứng*	chúhrng
fish sauce	*nước mắm*	nuhr·érk múhm
flat rice noodles	*phở*	fẻr
fried rice	*cơm rang thập cẩm* (N)	ğerm zaang tụhp ğủhm
	cơm chiên (S)	ğerm jee·uhn
honey	*mật ong*	mụht om
rice	*cơm*	ğerm
salad	*sa lát*	saa laát
soup	*canh*	ğaang
steamed rice	*cơm trắng*	ğerm chaáng
ice	*đá*	đaá
pepper	*hạt tiêu*	hạat dee·oo
salt	*muối*	moo·eé
sugar	*đường*	dur·èrng
thin rice noodles	*bún*	bún
yellow egg noodles	*mì*	meè

Question Words

How?	*Làm sao?*	laàm sow
Who?	*Ái?*	aí
What?	*Cái gì?*	ğaí zeè
When?	*Khi nào?*	kee nòw
Where?	*Ở đâu?*	ẻr đoh
Which?	*Cái nào?*	ğaí nòw
Why?	*Tại sao?*	tại sow

Drinks

beer	*bia*	bi·a
coffee	*cà phê*	ğaà fe
fruit shake	*sinh tố*	sing dáw
hot black coffee	*cà phê đen nóng*	ğaà fe đen nóm
hot black tea	*trà nóng*	chaà nóm
hot milk black tea	*trà sữa nóng*	chaà sũhr·uh nóm
hot milk coffee	*nâu nóng* (N) *cà phê sữa nóng* (S)	noh nóm ğaà fe sũhr·uh nóm
iced black coffee	*cà phê đá*	ğaà fe đaá
iced lemon juice	*chanh đá*	jaang đaá
iced milk coffee	*nâu đá* (N) *cà phê sữa đá* (S)	noh đaá ğaà fe sũhr·uh đaá
milk	*sữa*	sũhr·uh
mineral water	*nước khoáng* (N) *nước suối* (S)	nuhr·érk kwaáng nuhr·érk soo·eé
orange juice	*cam vắt*	ğaam vúht
red wine	*rượu vang đỏ*	zee·oọ vaang đỏ
soy milk	*sữa đậu nành*	sũhr·uh đọh naàng
sparkling wine	*rượu vang có ga*	zee·oọ vaang ğó gaa
tea	*chè/trà* (N/S)	jà/chaà
white wine	*rượu vang trắng*	zee·oọ vaang chaáng

EMERGENCIES

Help!
Cứu tôi!   ğuhr·oó doy

There's been an accident!
Có tai nạn!   ğó dai nạan

Leave me alone!
Thôi!   toy

I'm lost.
Tôi bị lạc đường.   doi beẹ lạak đuhr·èrng

Where is the toilet?
Nhà vệ sinh ở đâu?   nyaà veẹ sing ẻr đoh

Please call the police.
Làm ơn gọi công an.   laàm ern gọy ğawm aan

Please call a doctor.
Làm ơn gọi bác sĩ.   laàm ern gọy baák seẽ

I'm sick.
Tôi bị đau.   doy beẹ đoh

It hurts here.
Chỗ bị đau ở đây.   jãw beẹ đoh ẻr đay

I'm allergic to (antibiotics).
Tôi bị dị ứng với — doy beẹ zeẹ úhrng ver·eé
(thuốc kháng sinh). — (too·úhk kaáng sing)

SHOPPING & SERVICES

I'd like to buy ...
Tôi muốn mua ... — doy moo·úhn moo·uh ...

Can I look at it?
Tôi có thể xem — doy ğó tẻ sam
được không? — đuhr·erk kawm

I'm just looking.
Tôi chỉ ngắm xem. — doy jeé ngúhm sam

I don't like it.
Tôi không thích nó. — doy kawm tík nó

How much is this?
Cái này giá bao nhiêu? — ğaí này zaá bow nyee·oo

It's too expensive.
Cái này quá mắc. — ğaí này gwaá múhk

Do you accept credit cards?
Bạn có nhận thẻ — baạn kó nyụhn tả
tín dụng không? — dín zụm kawm

There's a mistake in the bill.
Có sự nhầm lẫn — ğó sụhr nyùhm lũhn
trên hoá đơn. — chen hwaá đern

more	*nhiều hơn*	nyee·oò hern
less	*ít hơn*	ít hern
smaller	*nhỏ hơn*	nyỏ hern
bigger	*lớn hơn*	lérn hern

I'm looking for a/the ...	*Tôi tìm ...*	doy đìm ...
bank	*ngân hàng*	nguhn haàng
market	*chợ*	jẹr
post office	*bưu điện*	buhr·oo dee·ụhn
public phone	*phòng điện thoại*	fòm dee·ụhn twại
tourist office	*văn phòng hướng dẫn du lịch*	vuhn fòm huhr·érng zũhn zoo lịk

TIME & DATES

What time is it?
Mấy giờ rồi? — máy zèr zòy

It's (eight) o'clock.
Bây giờ là (tám) giờ. — bay zèr laà (dúhm) zèr

morning	*buổi sáng*	boỏ·ee saáng
afternoon	*buổi chiều*	boỏ·ee jee·oò
evening	*buổi tối*	boỏ·ee dóy
yesterday	*hôm qua*	hawm ğwaa
today	*hôm nay*	hawm nay
tomorrow	*ngày mai*	ngày mai

Numbers

1	*một*	mạwt
2	*hai*	hai
3	*ba*	baa
4	*bốn*	báwn
5	*năm*	nuhm
6	*sáu*	sóh
7	*bảy*	bảy
8	*tám*	dúhm
9	*chín*	jín
10	*mười*	muhr·eè
20	*hai mươi*	hai muhr·ee
30	*ba mươi*	ba muhr·ee
40	*bốn mươi*	báwn muhr·ee
50	*năm mươi*	nuhm muhr·ee
60	*sáu mươi*	sów muhr·ee
70	*bảy mươi*	bảy muhr·ee
80	*tám mươi*	daám muhr·ee
90	*chín mươi*	jín muhr·ee
100	*một trăm*	mạwt chuhm
1000	*một nghìn* (N)	mạwt ngyìn
	một ngàn (S)	mọt ngaàn

Monday	*thứ hai*	túhr hai
Tuesday	*thứ ba*	túhr baa
Wednesday	*thứ tư*	túhr duhr
Thursday	*thứ năm*	túhr nuhm
Friday	*thứ sáu*	túhr sóh
Saturday	*thứ bảy*	túhr bảy
Sunday	*chủ nhật*	jỏo nhụht

January	*tháng giêng*	taáng zee·uhng
February	*tháng hai*	taáng hai
March	*tháng ba*	taáng baa
April	*tháng tư*	taáng tuhr
May	*tháng năm*	taáng nuhm
June	*tháng sáu*	taáng sóh
July	*tháng bảy*	taáng bảy
August	*tháng tám*	taáng dúhm
September	*tháng chín*	taáng jín
October	*tháng mười*	taáng muhr·eè
November	*tháng mười một*	taáng muhr·eè mạwt
December	*tháng mười hai*	taáng muhr·eè hai

TRANSPORT

Public Transport

When does the (first)... leave/arrive?	Chuyến ... (sớm nhất) chạy lúc mấy giờ?	jwee·úhn (sérm nyúht) jay lúp máy zèr
boat	tàu/ thuyền	dòw/ twee·ùhn
bus	xe buýt	sa beét
plane	máy bay	máy bay
train	xe lửa	sa lúhr·uh

I'd like a ... ticket.	Tôi muốn vé ...	doy moo·úhn vá ...
1st class	hạng nhất	haạng nyúht
2nd class	hạng nhì	haạng nyeè
one way	đi một chiều	đee mạt jee·oò
return	khứ hồi	kúhr haw·eè

I want to go to ...
Tôi muốn đi ...   doy moo·úhn đee ...

How long does the trip take?
Chuyến đi sẽ   jwee·úhn đee sã
mất bao lâu?   múht bow loh

What time does it arrive?
Mấy giờ đến?   máy zèr đén

How long will it be delayed?
Nó sẽ bị đình   nó sã beẹ đìng
hoãn bao lâu?   hwaãn bow loh

bus station	bến xe	bén sa
railway station	ga xe lửa	gaa sa lúhr·uh
sleeping berth	giường ngủ	zùhr·erng ngoỏ
the first	đầu tiên	dòw dee·uhn
the last	cuối cùng	ğoo·eé ğùm
the next	kế tiếp	ğé dee·úhp
ticket office	phòng bán vé	fòm baán vá
timetable	thời biểu	ter·eè beé·oo

Driving & Cycling

I'd like to hire a ...	Tôi muốn thuê ... (N) Tôi muốn muốn ... (S)	doy moo·úhn twe ... doy moo·úhn muhr·érn ...
car	xe hơi	sa her·ee
bicycle	xe đạp	sa đạp
motorbike	xe moto	sa mo·to
pedicab	xe xích lô	sa sík law

Is this the road to ...?
Con đường nầy   ğon đuhr·èrng này
có dẫn đến ...?   ğó zũhn đén ...

How many kilometres to ...?
... cách đây bao   ... ğaák đay bow
nhiêu ki-lô-mét?   nyee·oo kee·law·mét

Where's a service station?
Trạm xăng ở đâu?   chaạm suhng ér doh

Please fill it up.
Làm ơn đổ đầy bình.   laàm ern đỏ đày bìng

I'd like ... litres.
Tôi muốn ... lít.   doy moo·úhn ... léet

diesel	dầu diesel	zòh dee·sel
highway	xa lộ	saa lạw
leaded petrol	dầu xăng có chì	zòh suhng ğó jeè
map	bản đồ	baản đàw
unleaded petrol	dầu xăng	zòh suhng

(How long) Can I park here?
Chúng tôi có thể đậu   júm doy ğó tẻ dọh
xe được (bao lâu)?   sa đuhr·erk (bow loh)

I need a mechanic.
Chúng tôi cần thợ   júm doy ğùhn tẹr
sửa xe.   sủhr·uh sa

The car/motorbike has broken down (at ...)
Xe bị hư (tại ...).   sa beẹ huhr (dại ...)

The car/motorbike won't start.
(Xe hơi/Xe moto)   (sa her·ee/sa mo·to)
không để được.   kawm đè đuhr·ẹrk

I have a flat tyre.
Bánh xe tôi bị xì.   baáng sa doy beẹ seè

I've run out of petrol.
Tôi bị hết dầu/xăng.   doy beẹ hét zòh/suhng

I've had an accident.
Tôi bị tai nạn.   doy beẹ dai naạn

Road Signs

Cấm Đậu Xe	No parking
Cấm Vượt Qua	No overtaking
Chạy Chậm Lại	Slow down
Dừng Lại	Stop
Điện Cao Thế	High voltage
Đường Đang Sửa Chữa	Roadworks
Đường Sắt	Railway
Giao Thông Một Chiều	One-way
Lối Ra	Exit
Lối Vào	Entrance
Nguy Hiểm	Danger
Thu Thuế	Toll

LANGUAGE HILL-TRIBE LANGUAGES

HILL-TRIBE LANGUAGES

Ethnologists typically classify the hill tribes by linguistic distinction and commonly refer to three main groups. The Austro-Asiatic family includes the Viet-Muong, Mon-Khmer (of which Vietnamese is also a member), Tày-Tai and Meo/H'mong-Dzao language groups; the Austronesian family includes Malayo-Polynesian languages; and the Sino-Tibetan family encompasses the Chinese and Tibeto-Burmese language groups. In addition, within a single spoken language there are often myriad dialectical variations.

The following phrases should prove useful if you are visiting members of the larger Vietnamese hill tribes.

H'Mong

The H'mong are also known as Meo, Mieu, Mong Do (White H'mong), Mong Du (Black H'mong), Mong Lenh (Flower H'mong) and Mong Si (Red H'mong). They belong to the H'mong-Dzao language group.

Hello.	Ti nấu./Caó cu.
Goodbye.	Caó mun'g chè.
Yes.	Có mua.
No.	Chúi muá.
Thank you.	Ô chờ.
What's your name?	Caó be hua chan'g?
Where are you from?	Caó nhao từ tuả?
How much is this?	Pổ chố chá?

Tày

Also known as the Ngan, Pa Di, Phen, Thu Lao and Tho, the Tày belong to the Tày-Tai language group.

Hello.	Pá prama.
Goodbye.	Pá paynó.

Yes.	Mi.
No.	Boomi.
Thank you.	Đay fon.
What's your name?	Ten múng le xăng ma?
Where are you from?	Mu'ng du' te là ma?
How much is this?	Ău ni ki lai tiên?

Dzao

Also known as Coc Mun, Coc Ngang, Dai Ban, Diu Mien, Dong, Kim Mien, Ian Ten, Lu Gang, Tieu Ban, Trai and Xa. They belong to the H'mong-Dzao language group.

Hello./Goodbye.	Puang tọi.
Yes.	Mái.
No.	Mái mái.
Thank you.	Tờ dun.
What's your name?	Mang nhi búa chiên nay?
Where are you from?	May hải đo?
How much is this?	Pchiả nhăng?

GLOSSARY

For food and drink terms, see p530.

A Di Da – Buddha of the Past

Agent Orange – toxic, carcinogenic chemical herbicide used extensively during the American War

am duong – Vietnamese equivalent of Yin and Yang

American War – Vietnamese name for what is also known as the Vietnam War

Annam – old Chinese name for Vietnam, meaning 'Pacified South'

ao dai – Vietnamese national dress worn by women

apsaras – heavenly maidens

ARVN – Army of the Republic of Vietnam (former South Vietnamese army)

ba mu – midwife. There are 12 'midwives', each of whom teaches newborns a different skill necessary for the first year of life: smiling, sucking, lying on their stomachs, and so forth

ban – mountainous village

bang – congregation (in the Chinese community)

bar om – literally 'holding' bars associated with the sex industry. Also known as 'karaoke om'.

buu dien – post office

cai luong – Vietnamese modern theatre

Cao Daism – indigenous Vietnamese religion

Cham – ethnic minority descended from the people of Champa

Champa – Hindu kingdom dating from the late 2nd century AD

Charlie – nickname for the Viet Cong, used by US soldiers

chua – pagoda

chu nho – standard Chinese characters (script)

Cochinchina – the southern part of Vietnam during the French-colonial era

com pho – rice and rice-noodle soup

crémaillère – cog railway

cyclo – pedicab or bicycle rickshaw

Dai The Chi Bo Tat – an assistant of *A Di Da*

dan bau – single-stringed zither that generates an astounding magnitude of tones

dan tranh – 16-stringed zither

den – temple

Di Lac Buddha – Buddha of the Future

dikpalaka – gods of the directions of the compass

dinh – communal meeting hall

DMZ – Demilitarised Zone, a strip of land that once separated North and South Vietnam

doi moi – economic restructuring or reform, which commenced in Vietnam in 1986

dong – natural caves. Also Vietnamese currency.

dong son – drums

ecocide – term used to describe the devastating effects of the herbicides sprayed over Vietnam during the American War

fléchette – experimental US weapon. An artillery shell containing thousands of darts.

Funan – see *Oc-Eo*

garuda – half human-half bird

gom – ceramics

hai dang – lighthouse

hat boi – classical theatre in the south

hat cheo – Vietnamese popular theatre

hat tuong – classical theatre in the north

ho ca – aquarium

Ho Chi Minh Trail – route used by the North Vietnamese Army and Viet Cong to move supplies to the south

Hoa – ethnic Chinese, one of the largest single minority groups in Vietnam

hoi quan – Chinese congregational assembly halls

huong – perfume

huyen – rural district

Indochina – Vietnam, Cambodia and Laos. The name derives from Indian and Chinese influences.

kala-makara – sea-monster god

kalan – a religious sanctuary

khach san – hotel

Khmer – ethnic Cambodians

Khong Tu – Confucius

kich noi – spoken drama

Kinh – Vietnamese language

Kuomintang – Chinese Nationalist Party, also known as KMT. The KMT controlled China between 1925 and 1949 until defeated by the communists.

li xi – lucky money distributed during the Vietnamese Lunar New Year

liberation – 1975 takeover of the South by the North. Most foreigners call this 'reunification'.

Lien Xo – literally, Soviet Union. Used to call attention to a foreigner

linga – stylised phallus which represents the Hindu god Shiva

manushi-buddha – Buddha who appeared in human form

moi – derogatory word meaning 'savages', mostly used by ethnic Vietnamese to describe hill-tribe people

Montagnards – term meaning highlanders or mountain people, sometimes used to refer to the ethnic minorities who inhabit remote areas of Vietnam

muong – large village unit made up of *quel* (small stilt-houses)

naga – Sanskrit term for a mythical serpent being with divine powers; often depicted forming a kind of shelter over the Buddha

nam phai – for men

napalm – jellied petrol (gasoline) dropped and lit from aircraft; used by US forces with devastating repercussions during the American War

nguoi thuong – the current government's preferred term for highland people

nha hang – restaurant

nha khach – hotel or guesthouse

nha nghi – guesthouse

nha rong – large stilt house, used by hill tribes as a kind of community centre

nha tro – dormitory

NLF – National Liberation Front, the official name for the VC

nom – Vietnamese script, used between the 10th and early 20th centuries

nu phai – for women

nui – mountain

nuoc mam – fish sauce, added to almost every main dish in Vietnam

NVA – North Vietnamese Army

Oc-Eo – Indianised Khmer kingdom (also called Funan) in southern Vietnam between the 1st and 6th centuries

Ong Bon – Guardian Spirit of Happiness and Virtue

OSS – US Office of Strategic Services. The predecessor of the CIA.

pagoda – traditionally an eight-sided Buddhist tower, but in Vietnam the word is commonly used to denote a temple

phong thuy – literally, 'wind and water'. Used to describe geomancy. Also known by its Chinese name, feng shui.

PRG – Provisional Revolutionary Government, the temporary Communist government set up by the VC in the South. It existed from 1969 to 1976.

quan – urban district

Quan Cong – Chinese God of War

Quan The Am Bo Tat – Goddess of Mercy

quoc am – modern Vietnamese literature

quoc ngu – Latin-based phonetic alphabet in which Vietnamese is written

rap – cinema

Revolutionary Youth League – first Marxist group in Vietnam and predecessor of the Communist Party

roi can – conventional puppetry

roi nuoc – water puppetry

ruou (pronounced xeo) – rice wine

RVN – Republic of Vietnam (the old South Vietnam)

salangane – swiftlet

sao – wooden flute

saola – antelope-like creature

shakti – feminine manifestation of Shiva

song – river

SRV – Socialist Republic of Vietnam (Vietnam's official name)

Strategic Hamlets Program – program (by South Vietnam and the USA) of forcibly moving peasants into fortified villages to deny the VC bases of support

sung – fig tree

Tam Giao – literally, 'triple religion'. Confucianism, Taoism and Buddhism fused over time with popular Chinese beliefs and ancient Vietnamese animism.

Tao – the Way. The essence of which all things are made.

Tay ba lo – backpacker

Tet – Vietnamese Lunar New Year

thai cuc quyen – Vietnamese for t'ai chi

Thich Ca Buddha – the historical Buddha Sakyamuni, whose real name was Siddhartha Gautama

thong nhat – reunification. Also a common term for the Reunification Express train.

thuoc bac – Chinese medicine

toc hanh – express bus

Tonkin – the northern part of Vietnam during the French-colonial era. Also the name of a body of water in the north (Tonkin Gulf).

truyen khau – traditional oral literature

UNHCR – UN High Commissioner for Refugees

VC – Viet Cong or Vietnamese Communists

Viet Kieu – overseas Vietnamese

Viet Minh – League for the Independence of Vietnam, a nationalistic movement that fought the Japanese and French but later became communist dominated

VNQDD – Viet Nam Quoc Dan Dang. Largely middle-class nationalist party.

xang – petrol

xe Honda loi – wagon pulled by a motorbike

xe lam – tiny three-wheeled trucks used for short-haul passenger and freight transport

xe loi – wagon pulled by a motorbike in the Mekong Delta region

xe om – motorbike taxi, also called *Honda om*

xich lo – *cyclo*, from the French *cyclo-pousse*

behind the scenes

SEND US YOUR FEEDBACK

We love to hear from travellers – your comments keep us on our toes and help make our books better. Our well-travelled team reads every word on what you loved or loathed about this book. Although we cannot reply individually to postal submissions, we always guarantee that your feedback goes straight to the appropriate authors, in time for the next edition. Each person who sends us information is thanked in the next edition – and the most useful submissions are rewarded with a free book.

Visit **lonelyplanet.com/contact** to submit your updates and suggestions or to ask for help. Our award-winning website also features inspirational travel stories, news and discussions.

Note: We may edit, reproduce and incorporate your comments in Lonely Planet products such as guidebooks, websites and digital products, so let us know if you don't want your comments reproduced or your name acknowledged. For a copy of our privacy policy visit lonelyplanet.com/privacy.

OUR READERS

Many thanks to the travellers who used the last edition and wrote to us with helpful hints, useful advice and interesting anecdotes:

A Simon Abbott, Claudia Aebi, Adam Ain, Bernice Ang, Tracy Ang, Sarah Attwell **B** Reinier Bakels, Amy Barber, Jessica Barker, Wendy Barker, Mark Baxter, R Beck, Evelyn Bienefelt, Yvonne Bierings, Rhys Bithell, Caroline Jeanne Blanchet, Harrie Boin, Janet Booth, Jim Bradbury, Zoe Buck, Dermot Byrne, Vicki Byrne **C** Annalena Caffa, Christian Cantos, Agostino Carli, Henrik Carstensen, Jo-anne Chadwick, Chantereau Chantal, Samuel Chik, Charlotte Clements, Robert Constabile, Jules Cooper, Nicolas Corino, Margaret Crisp, Cheri Cross, Leonie Culpin **D** Ariane De Dominicis, Berthus De Boer, Sylvie De Leeuw, Hans Dewaele, Ruth Dillen, Tim Diltz, Henry Domzalski, John Doyle, Megan Dredge **E** Annie Eagle, Christine Ebdy, Albrecht Eisen, Pieter Eisenga, Avi Elazat, Jeffrey Eng **F** Hylke Faber, Sergey Filin, Emma Findlay, Nicola Frame, Stephen Frampton, Marc Freeman, Astrid Freier, Andrea Fuernkranz **G** Nagy Gabriella, Rubén García-Benito, Duncan Gardner, Stuart Geddes, Alyce Geenen-Hager, Roy Gillette, Annick Gilliot, Marianne Göldlin, David Gordon, Daniel Gregg, Sandra Greven, Chris Grey, W Gröhling, Denise Grohs, Bertille Guilbert

H Eva Hagman, Emma Hanid, Jennifer Hashley, Mike Hedlund, Celine Heinbecker, Nicola Hewitt, Adrian Ho, Benjamin Hodgetts, Richard T Howard, Keegan Hughes, Jakobien Huisman, Kim Huynh, Nick Hyde **J** Chris Jackson, Ralpha Jacobson, Therese Jarrett, Karin Joelsson, Sigurd Joergensen, Roel Jongbloed, Linards Jonins **K** Jane Kelly, Marianna Kettlewell, Huynh Kim, Damien Kingsbury, Chelsea Kinsey, James Kruger, Martin Kuipers, Chris Kuschel **L** Danielle Lafferre, Steve Lee, Cindy-Marie Leicester, Caroline Lemoine, Philippe Lesage, Stewart Linda, David Lindsay, Diego Lizardez-Ruiz, James Locke, Alex Long, Andrew Long, Jack Lowrey, Harald Luckerbauer **M** Nguyen Thi Man, Desmond Macmahon, Philippe Magerle, Justyn Makarewycz, Martin Mallin, Barbara Martinus, Philippe May, Craig Mayo, Peter McKallen, Tim McGivern, Sasha McHardy, Dick McKenzie, Lucinda McRobbie, Tamar Meijers, Phil Mellifont, Els Mellink, Jane Metlikovec, Konrad Mohrmann, Krishnendu Mondal **N** Chelsey Naka, Harry Newton, Truong Ngoc, Long Nguyen, Luu Nguyen, Joseph Nicholson, Paul Nunn, Philip Nygren **O** Monica O'Brien, Magnus Olsson, Paul O'Neill, Leonhard Orgler, Maria Ougaard **P** Andy Parsons, Rick Passaro, Natalie Patterson, Colin Payne, Dr Pehr Granqvist, Paola Penaherrera, Alexia Pepicelli, Daniell Pérez, Daniela Perkins, Andrew Pettit,

David R Phillips, Ben Pike, Igor Polakovic, Arianna Ponzini, Jeremy Presser, Helen Putland **Q** Philip Quinn **R** Edmund Raczkowski, Frances Rein, Carol Resch, Frank Richard, Doug Roberts, Barbara Robinson, Walter Roedenbeck, Rick Ruffin, Thomas Russo **S** Rolf Schaefer, Mike Schellenberg, Stefanie Schick, Almut Schindler, Valerie & Mario Schnee, Isabel Schünemann, Tobias Schwarzmueller, Helen Scott, Breck Scott-Young, Pietro Scòzzari, Patricia Selley, Erin Sharaf, Larissa Spacinsky, Hayden Spencer, Frants Staugaard, Margie Symons, Kathy Szybist **T** Ivica Tanaskovic, Vera Tang, Will Thai, Christian Thaller, Mary Ann Thomas, Scott Thomson, Lam Trang, Catharina Treber, Peter Trojok, Bill Tsocanos, Yves Tychon, Andrew Tzembelicos **U** Natalie Uglow, Zeynep Uraz, Mari Nythun Utheim **V** Adria Galian Valldeneu, Charlene Vallory, Bo Van Nieuwenhuizen, Bob Van Deusen, Jaap Van Helmond, Stefaan Van Rosendaal, Stephen Van Riet, Ray Varnbuhler, Tyson Verse, Henrique Villena, Jeff Vize, Alexandra Von Muralt, Ronny Vorbeck, Erwin Vos **W** Valentin Waldman, Lex & Yvonne Warners-Evers, Sue Wise, Art Wright, Jsue Wright, Siye Wu, Line Wulff-Jensen **Y** Courtney Yates, Margrette Young **Z** Marianne Zahnd, Peter Zimmermann.

AUTHOR THANKS

Iain Stewart

What a trip! Many thanks to Ilaria and the Melbourne team for inviting me aboard another Southeast Asia title and to my co-pilots in Vietnam: Nick, Peter and Brett. I was greatly aided by kings of the highway Vinh Vu and Mark Wyndham, Ben and Bich in Phong Nha, Tam in Dong Ha, and a great crew in Hoi An including the Dive Bar boys, Ludo, Neil and Caroline, and Dzung the tennis ace.

Nick Ray

First thanks to my wonderful wife Kulikar Sotho who has joined me on many a trip to Vietnam. Travel has been considerably enlivened by our two children, Julian and Belle, although they only get to do the gentle bits for now.

Many people in Vietnam were very helpful along the way. In no particular order, many thanks to Vinh, Dave, Mark, Karl and Greg for company on the long ride through the highlands, although we should try not to get arrested next time. A big thanks also to Sinh, Linh, Truong, Nick, Glenn, Fred, Phuong, Larry, John, Jamie, Rofail, Susan, Larry, Ross and many more.

Thanks to my co-authors, Iain, Peter and Brett, for all their work in other parts of Vietnam. And a big thanks to the in-house team at Lonely Planet who carry this from conception to reality.

Peter Dragicevich

Generations of Lonely Planet Vietnam writers, this one included, have benefited from the companionship and generosity of Le Van Sinh. Thanks too to Nick Ross, an invaluable source of Saigon knowledge. Working on this book was an absolute pleasure, due in large

THIS BOOK

This 11th edition of *Vietnam* was coordinated by Vietnam aficionado Iain Stewart, who wrote the Plan Your Trip, Understand and Survival Guide chapters, as well as updating the North-Central Vietnam and Central Vietnam chapters. Iain was assisted by some of Lonely Planet's finest: veteran 'Nam author Nick Ray (Central Highlands, South-Central Coast and Siem Reap & the Temples of Angkor chapters); and talented Kiwi boys Brett Atkinson (Hanoi, Northeast Vietnam and Northwest Vietnam) and Peter Dragicevich (Ho Chi Minh City and Mekong Delta). They worked with the text from *Vietnam* 10, which was written by Nick Ray, Iain Stewart and Yu-Mei Balasingamchow. The Food & Drink chapter for this edition was written by Robyn Eckhardt and revised by Southeast Asian food guru Austin Bush. The Regional Specialities section was written by celebrated food writer Andrea Nguyen, with a little editorial help from the aforementioned Mr Bush. David Lukas wrote the Environment chapter, which was revised by Iain Stewart. Rebecca Skinner did an incredible job on the images, going to amazing lengths to make sure this book had accurate images of the mouth-watering Vietnamese dishes we mention. This guidebook was commissioned in Lonely Planet's Melbourne office, and produced by the following:

Commissioning Editor
Ilaria Walker
Coordinating Editor
Catherine Naghten
Coordinating Cartographer Julie Dodkins
Coordinating Layout Designer Wibowo Rusli
Managing Editor
Bruce Evans
Managing Cartographers
Shahara Ahmed, David Connolly
Managing Layout Designer Jane Hart
Assisting Editors
Holly Alexander, Judith Bamber, Michelle Bennett, Paul Harding, Alan Murphy
Cover Research
Naomi Parker
Internal Image Research Rebecca Skinner
Illustrator Javier Zarracina
Language Content
Branislava Vladisavljevic, Annelies Mertens

Thanks to Wayne Murphy, Ryan Evans, Trent Paton, Ross Macaw, Averil Robertson, Gerard Walker

part to David Holmes (cheers Tim Benzie),
Tran Thi Kim Hue, Kyla Ellis, Robert Cotgrove,
Devon Morrissey, Andrew "Chronic" Poole,
Jason Donovan, Mark Zazula, Nick Ray, Iain
Stewart and, back home, Brett Atkinson.

Brett Atkinson

The biggest thanks of all must go to Mr Kien
and driver extraordinaire, 'Ladykiller'. Who
knew that 'Bee Wine' could taste so interesting? Next time we should maybe order the
horse as well. Thanks also to everyone in
Hanoi, Sapa, Bac Ha, Ha Giang, Cat Ba Island
and Bai Tu Long for unswerving assistance
and information on the road. At home in
Auckland, thanks to Carol. I promise to cook
you some Hanoi street food very soon.

ACKNOWLEDGMENTS

Climate map data adapted from Peel MC,
Finlayson BL & McMahon TA (2007) 'Updated
World Map of the Köppen-Geiger Climate
Classification', *Hydrology and Earth System
Sciences*, 11, 163344.

Cover photograph: Workers carrying salt
across shallow evaporation ponds at
Hon Khoi salt factory near Doc Let Beach.
Karen Kasmauski / Getty Images ©

Many of the images in this guide are available
for licensing from Lonely Planet Images:
www.lonelyplanetimages.com.

index

000 Map pages
000 Photo pages

how to use this book

These symbols will help you find the listings you want:

- ⊙ Sights
- 🏖 Beaches
- 🏃 Activities
- 🎣 Courses
- ☞ Tours
- 🎉 Festivals & Events
- 🛏 Sleeping
- 🍴 Eating
- 🍷 Drinking
- ☆ Entertainment
- 🛍 Shopping
- ℹ Information/Transport

Look out for these icons:

- TOP CHOICE — Our author's recommendation
- FREE — No payment required
- 🌿 — A green or sustainable option

Our authors have nominated these places as demonstrating a strong commitment to sustainability – for example by supporting local communities and producers, operating in an environmentally friendly way, or supporting conservation projects.

These symbols give you the vital information for each listing:

- ☑ Telephone Numbers
- ⊙ Opening Hours
- ℗ Parking
- ⊝ Nonsmoking
- ✳ Air-Conditioning
- @ Internet Access
- 🛜 Wi-Fi Access
- 🏊 Swimming Pool
- 🥗 Vegetarian Selection
- 📖 English-Language Menu
- 👪 Family-Friendly
- 🐾 Pet-Friendly
- 🚌 Bus
- ⛴ Ferry
- Ⓜ Metro
- Ⓢ Subway
- ⊖ London Tube
- 🚊 Tram
- 🚆 Train

Reviews are organised by author preference.

Map Legend

Sights
- Beach
- Buddhist
- Castle
- Christian
- Hindu
- Islamic
- Jewish
- Monument
- Museum/Gallery
- Ruin
- Winery/Vineyard
- Zoo
- Other Sight

Activities, Courses & Tours
- Diving/Snorkelling
- Canoeing/Kayaking
- Skiing
- Surfing
- Swimming/Pool
- Walking
- Windsurfing
- Other Activity/Course/Tour

Sleeping
- Sleeping
- Camping

Eating
- Eating

Drinking
- Drinking
- Cafe

Entertainment
- Entertainment

Shopping
- Shopping

Information
- Bank
- Embassy/Consulate
- Hospital/Medical
- Internet
- Police
- Post Office
- Telephone
- Toilet
- Tourist Information
- Other Information

Transport
- Airport
- Border Crossing
- Bus
- Cable Car/Funicular
- Cycling
- Ferry
- Metro
- Monorail
- Parking
- Petrol Station
- Taxi
- Train/Railway
- Tram
- Other Transport

Routes
- Tollway
- Freeway
- Primary
- Secondary
- Tertiary
- Lane
- Unsealed Road
- Plaza/Mall
- Steps
- Tunnel
- Pedestrian Overpass
- Walking Tour
- Walking Tour Detour
- Path

Geographic
- Hut/Shelter
- Lighthouse
- Lookout
- Mountain/Volcano
- Oasis
- Park
- Pass
- Picnic Area
- Waterfall

Population
- Capital (National)
- Capital (State/Province)
- City/Large Town
- Town/Village

Boundaries
- International
- State/Province
- Disputed
- Regional/Suburb
- Marine Park
- Cliff
- Wall

Hydrography
- River, Creek
- Intermittent River
- Swamp/Mangrove
- Reef
- Canal
- Water
- Dry/Salt/Intermittent Lake
- Glacier

Areas
- Beach/Desert
- Cemetery (Christian)
- Cemetery (Other)
- Park/Forest
- Sportsground
- Sight (Building)
- Top Sight (Building)

OUR STORY

A beat-up old car, a few dollars in the pocket and a sense of adventure. In 1972 that's all Tony and Maureen Wheeler needed for the trip of a lifetime – across Europe and Asia overland to Australia. It took several months, and at the end – broke but inspired – they sat at their kitchen table writing and stapling together their first travel guide, *Across Asia on the Cheap*. Within a week they'd sold 1500 copies. Lonely Planet was born.

Today, Lonely Planet has offices in Melbourne, London and Oakland, with more than 600 staff and writers. We share Tony's belief that 'a great guidebook should do three things: inform, educate and amuse'.

OUR WRITERS

Iain Stewart

Coordinating Author, North-Central Vietnam, Central Vietnam Iain Stewart first visited and was captivated by Vietnam as a traveller in 1991 (armed with a trusty Lonely Planet). He's now a Brighton-based writer, specialising in hot countries a long way from his English seaside abode. Iain has written over 30 guidebooks for destinations including Guatemala, Ibiza and Indonesia, for many publishers. This trip was quite a blast – motorbiking the Ho Chi Minh Highway, sailing to the Chams, partying in Saigon, exploring the heart of Phong Nha and eating the best food in the world.

Read more about Iain at:
lonelyplanet.com/members/iainstewart

Brett Atkinson

Hanoi, Northeast Vietnam, Northwest Vietnam Brett Atkinson first visited Vietnam in late 1993, a few months before the United States lifted their trade embargo. For this trip he dived headfirst into Hanoi's brilliant street food scene, returned to Halong Bay, and explored northern Vietnam's emerging destinations for intrepid travellers: Ha Giang province and Bai Tu Long. When he's not home in Auckland, Brett's exploring the planet as a food and travel writer. See www.brett-atkinson.net for what he's been eating, and where he's headed next.

Peter Dragicevich

Ho Chi Minh City, Mekong Delta Being a self-declared big-city junkie, Peter was thrilled to return to Vietnam to write about Ho Chi Minh City after a four-year hiatus. Things change quickly in Vietnam, but despite a few new skyscrapers and a fresh crop of international bars and restaurants, he was pleased to find Saigon just as crazy, chaotic and thrilling as ever. This is the 21st Lonely Planet guidebook that he's contributed to, including a previous edition of this book. When he's not slurping up noodle soup on motorcycle-clogged streets he's based in his hometown of Auckland, New Zealand.

Read more about Peter at:
lonelyplanet.com/members/peterdragicevich

Nick Ray

Central Highlands, South-Central Coast, Siem Reap & the Temples of Angkor A Londoner of sorts, Nick comes from Watford, the sort of town that makes you want to travel. As he lives in Phnom Penh, Vietnam is Nick's backyard. He has co-authored *Cycling Vietnam*, *Laos & Cambodia*, as well as the *Cambodia* book for Lonely Planet. Nick has been to almost every province from Ha Giang in the north to Ca Mau in the south. He was exploring in-between this time around and enjoyed motorbiking the Central Highlands and hanging out on Con Dao.

Published by Lonely Planet Publications Pty Ltd
ABN 36 005 607 983
11th edition – Feb 2012
ISBN 978 1 74179 715 2
© Lonely Planet 2012   Photographs © as indicated 2012
10 9 8 7 6 5 4 3 2 1
Printed in China